1 MONTH OF
FREE
READING

at

www.ForgottenBooks.com

By purchasing this book you are eligible for one month membership to ForgottenBooks.com, giving you unlimited access to our entire collection of over 1,000,000 titles via our web site and mobile apps.

To claim your free month visit:
www.forgottenbooks.com/free928193

ISBN 978-0-260-10376-5
PIBN 10928193

AMERICAN STATE REPORTS,

CONTAINING THE

CASES OF GENERAL VALUE AND AUTHORITY,

SUBSEQUENT TO THOSE CONTAINED IN THE "AMERICAN
DECISIONS" AND THE "AMERICAN REPORTS,"

DECIDED IN THE

COURTS OF LAST RESORT

OF THE SEVERAL STATES.

SELECTED, REPORTED, AND ANNOTATED

By A. C. FREEMAN,

AND THE ASSOCIATE EDITORS OF THE "AMERICAN DECISIONS."

VOL. XVI.

SAN FRANCISCO:
BANCROFT–WHITNEY COMPANY,
LAW PUBLISHERS AND LAW BOOKSELLERS.
1891.

THE FILMER-ROLLINS ELECTROTYPE COMPANY,
TYPOGRAPHERS AND STEREOTYPERS.

AMERICAN STATE REPORTS.

VOL. XVI

SCHEDULE

showing the original volumes of reports in which the cases herein selected and re-reported may be found, and the pages of this volume devoted to each state.

SCHEDULE

SHOWING IN WHAT VOLUMES OF THIS SERIES THE CASES
REPORTED IN THE SEVERAL VOLUMES OF OFFICIAL
REPORTS MAY BE FOUND.

State reports are in parentheses, and the numbers of this series in bold-faced figures.

ALABAMA. — (83) **3**; (84) **5**; (85) **7**; (86) **11**; (87) **13**; (88) **16**.

ARKANSAS. — (48) **3**; (49) **4**; (50) **7**; (51) **14**.

CALIFORNIA. — (72) **1**; (73) **2**; (74) **5**; (75) **7**; (76) **9**; (77) **11**; (78, 79) **12**; (80) **13**; (81) **15**; (82) **16**.

COLORADO. — (10) **3**; (11) **7**; (12) **13**; (13) **16**.

CONNECTICUT. — (54) **1**; (55) **3**; (56) **7**; (57) **14**.

DELAWARE. — (5 Houst.) **1**.

FLORIDA. — (22) **1**; (23) **11**; (24) **12**.

GEORGIA. — (76) **2**; (77) **4**; (78) **6**; (79) **11**; (80, 81) **12**; (82) **14**.

ILLINOIS. — (121) **2**; (122) **3**; (123) **5**; (124) **7**; (125) **8**; (126) **9**; (127) **11**; (128) **15**; (129) **16**.

INDIANA. — (112) **2**; (113) **3**; (114) **5**; (115) **7**; (116) **9**; (117, 118) **10**; (119) **12**; (120, 121) **16**.

IOWA. — (72) **2**; (73) **5**; (74) **7**; (75) **9**; (76, 77) **14**; (78) **16**.

KANSAS. — (37) **1**; (38) **5**; (39) **7**; (40) **10**; (41) **13**; (42) **16**.

KENTUCKY. — (83, 84) **4**; (85) **7**; (86) **9**; (87) **12**.

LOUISIANA. — (39 La. Ann.) **4**; (40 La. Ann.) **8**.

MAINE. — (79) **1**; (80) **6**; (81) **10**.

MARYLAND. — (67) **1**; (68) **6**; (69) **9**; (70) **14**.

MASSACHUSETTS. — (145) **1**; (146) **4**; (147) **9**; (148) **12**; (149) **14**; (150) **15**.

MICHIGAN. — (60, 61) **1**; (62) **4**; (63) **6**; (64, 65) **8**; (66, 67) **11**; (68, 69, 75) **13**; (70) **14**; (71, 76) **15**; (72, 73, 74) **16**.

MINNESOTA. — (36) **1**; (37) **5**; (38) **8**; (39, 40) **12**; (41) **16**.

MISSISSIPPI. — (65) **7**; (66) **14**.

MISSOURI. — (92) **1**; (93) **3**; (94) **4**; (95) **6**; (96) **9**; (97) **10**; (98) **14**.

NEBRASKA. — (22) **3**; (23, 24) **8**; (25) **13**.

NEVADA. — (19) **3**.

NEW HAMPSHIRE. — (64) **10**; (62) **13**.

NEW JERSEY. — (43 N. J. Eq.) **3**; (44 N. J. Eq.) **6**; (50 N. J. L.) **7**; (51 N. J. L.; 45 N. J. Eq.) **14**.

NEW YORK. — (107) **1**; (108) **2**; (109) **4**; (110) **6**; (111) **7**; (112) **8**; (113) **10**; (114) **11**; (115) **12**; (116, 117) **15**; (118, 119) **16**.

NORTH CAROLINA. — (97, 98) **2**; (99, 100) **6**; (101) **9**; (102) **11**; (103) **14**.

OHIO. — (45 Ohio St.) **4**; (46 Ohio St.) **15**.

OREGON. — (15) **3**; (16) **8**; (17) **11**.

PENNSYLVANIA. — (115, 116, 117 Pa. St.) **2**; (118, 119 Pa. St.) **4**; (120, 121 Pa. St.) **6**; (122 Pa. St.) **9**; (123, 124 Pa. St.) **10**; (125 Pa. St.) **11**; (126 Pa. St.) **12**; (127 Pa. St.) **14**; (128, 129 Pa. St.) **15**.

RHODE ISLAND. — (15) **2.**
SOUTH CAROLINA. — (26) **4;** (27, 28, 29) **13;** (30) **14.**
TENNESSEE. — (85) **4;** (86) **6;** (87) **10.**
TEXAS. — (68) **2;** (69; 24 Tex. App.) **5;** (70; 25, 26 Tex. App.) **8;** (71) **10;**
(27 Tex. App.) **11;** (72) **13;** (73, 74) **15;** (75) **16.**
VERMONT — (60) **6;** (61) **15.**
VIRGINIA. — (82) **3;** (83) **5;** (84) **10.**
WEST VIRGINIA — (29) **6;** (30) **8;** (31) **13.**
WISCONSIN. — (69) **2;** (70, 71) **5;** (72) **7;** (73) **9.**

AMERICAN STATE REPORTS.

VOL. XVI.

CASES REPORTED.

(ii)

AMERICAN STATE REPORTS.

VOL. XVI.

CASES

SUPREME COURT

OF

ALABAMA.

HOLMES *v.* STATE.

[88 ALABAMA, 26.]

CRIMINAL LAW — EVIDENCE — PROOF OF CHARACTER. — A witness who testifies on direct examination that he has never heard anything against defendant may be asked on cross-examination if he has not heard that defendant "wore stripes" while working on the streets.

CRIMINAL LAW — PROOF OF CHARACTER. — WITNESS IS INCOMPETENT TO TESTIFY, either affirmatively or negatively, as to character, who knows nothing of the reputation borne by defendant in the neighborhood in which he lived, or where he was known, and who was not in such position, as to defendant's residence or acquaintances, that the fact of his not hearing anything against him would have any tendency to show that nothing had been said, and that therefore his character was good.

CRIMINAL LAW — MURDER. — The killing of one who intercedes to prevent the accused from unlawfully shooting at another is murder, and not manslaughter, though the fatal shot was fired accidentally.

CRIMINAL LAW — MURDER — MANSLAUGHTER. — Sudden provocation, acted on in the heat of passion produced thereby, may reduce a homicide to manslaughter; but if the provocation is not of such character as would, in the mind of a reasonable man, stir resentment to violence endangering life, the killing is murder.

INDICTMENT and conviction for murder in the first degree. The defendant, Holmes, and one Woods, both freedmen, quarreled, after which defendant went away, but soon returned with a pistol in his hands. The deceased told him that he did not want any trouble on the premises, at the same time catching him by the arm or shoulder. In a struggle which ensued between them, the pistol was discharged, killing the deceased. The other facts are stated in the opinion.

William L. Martin, attorney-general, for the state.

AM. ST. REP., VOL. XVI. — 2   17

McClellan, J. It was clearly competent to ask the witness Farley, on cross-examination, if he had not heard that the defendant "wore stripes" while working on the streets of Montgomery; the witness having testified, on his examination in chief, that he had never heard anything against the defendant. To say of one that he "wore stripes," the appellation commonly applied to the garb of a convict, necessarily implies a conviction of some infraction of the law, and is therefore derogatory to the person so referred to. In this instance, the testimony tended directly to contradict and weaken the negative evidence of good character given by the witness, and its admission was free from error.

The witness McHugh was incompetent to testify, either affirmatively or negatively, as to character. He knew nothing of the reputation borne by the prisoner in the neighborhood in which he lived, or where he was known; and he failed to show that he was in such a position with reference to the defendant's residence or circle of acquaintances as that the fact of his not hearing anything against him would have any tendency to show that nothing had been said, and that therefore his character was good. This witness swore that "he thought the character of prisoner for peace and quiet was good"; but he further testified that this was his personal opinion merely, based on what he himself knew from a personal acquaintance which had existed for about two years, during which time he had seen him frequently, "but their relations were not intimate, and he did not know where the defendant lived." Very clearly this witness neither knew the reputation of the defendant affirmatively, nor was he in a position to have heard what was said in derogation of good character, in such sort that his having heard nothing against the defendant could have shed any light on the inquiry. His evidence was properly excluded: *Cheritree* v. *Roggen*, 67 Barb. 124; *Dave* v. *State*, 22 Ala. 23; *Mose* v. *State*, 36 Ala. 211; *Martin* v. *Martin*, 25 Ala. 201; *Sorrelle* v. *Craig*, 9 Ala. 334; *Hadjo* v. *Gooden*, 13 Ala. 718.

It appeared on the trial that the defendant, while seeking a difficulty with one King Woods, and endeavoring to get to him, was intercepted by the deceased, solely for the purpose of preventing a consummation of defendant's design against Woods, and that in the scuffle incident to this interference, the fatal shot was fired. The charge given at the instance of the state, and the first, second, and third charges asked by the defendant and refused, related to the passion assumed to have been aroused by the interference, and the sufficiency of passion thus excited to reduce the homicide below the grade of murder. The principle laid down in *Field* v. *State*, 52 Ala. 348, and elaborated in the later cases of *Judge* v. *State*, 58 Ala. 406, 29 Am. Rep. 757, and *Mitchell* v. *State*, 60 Ala. 26, that "an affray may occur, or sudden provocation be given, which, if acted on in the heat of passion produced thereby, might mitigate homicide to manslaughter, yet if the provocation, though sudden, be not of that character which would, in the mind of a just and reasonable man, stir resentment to violence endangering life, the killing would be murder," applies here. The provocation shown by the evidence, and hypothesized in the charges referred to, was not sufficient to arouse passion the existence of which would have reduced the homicide to manslaughter; and hence the action of the court, as well in giving the charge requested by the state, as in refusing those referred to above asked by the defendant, was free from error.

On the facts supposed in the defendant's fourth charge, he could not have been guiltless. If, as there hypothesized, he was returning to Robinson's store for the purpose of killing Woods, if it became necessary, thus endeavoring to put himself under a necessity which it was his duty and within his power to avoid, he was engaged in an unlawful act; and if the deceased interfered to arrest this unlawful act, and in the scuffle incident to that interference he was accidentally shot by the defendant and killed, — manifestly this killing, while, abstractly considered, it was misadventure, yet when referred to the intent of the defendant towards Woods, and treated as a resultant of an effort to thwart that intent, was a crime; and on this ground the refusal of this charge may be justified. The charge was bad, moreover, because it was involved and argumentative, and naturally tended to mislead and confuse the jury.

The fifth charge requested by the defendant is unsupported in several of the facts upon which it proceeds, and was properly refused on this ground: *Jordan* v. *State*, 81 Ala. 20.

The judgment of the city court is affirmed.

HOMICIDE. — Murder, statutory degrees of: Note to *Whiteford* v. *Commonwealth*, 18 Am. Dec. 774–787; *State* v. *Turner*, 29 S. C. 34; 13 Am. St. Rep. 706; *Green* v. *State*, 27 Tex. App. 244; *Moody* v. *State*, 27 Id. 287; *People* v. *Lanagan*, 81 Cal. 142; *State* v. *Woods*, 97 Mo. 31. One who kills another is not guilty of murder in the first degree, unless there existed in his mind before the act of killing a specific intent to take the life of the deceased: *Green* v. *State*, 51 Ark. 189. Under the laws of Louisiana, "in all trials for murder the jury may find a verdict of manslaughter": *State* v. *Brown*, 40 La. Ann. 725. An instruction that "deliberately" means "in a cool state of blood, that is, not in a heat of passion caused by some just cause or provocation to passion," is not erroneous, where the only provocation was the application of opprobrious words, provided in other instructions such words are declared capable of being deemed just provocation, and that murder with the element of deliberation left out is merely murder in the second degree: *State* v. *Stephens*, 96 Mo. 637. Compare note to *State* v. *Scheele*, 14 Am. St. Rep. 121; *State* v. *Alexander*, 30 S. C. 74; 14 Am. St. Rep. 879, and note 882; *High* v. *State*, 26 Tex. App. 545; 8 Am. St. Rep. 488, and note. Where there was a quarrel between defendant and the father of the deceased boy, followed by a fight, in which defendant, after having retreated to his cabin, used a gun, which was discharged, and the boy was unintentionally killed, the court should not refuse an instruction as to voluntary manslaughter: *Crawford* v. *People*, 12 Col. 290. For one who, in attempting to kill one person, by mistake kills another, is guilty of murder or manslaughter: *Butler* v. *People*, 125 Ill. 641; 8 Am. St. Rep. 423, and note. And under the New York Penal Code, the killing of any human being by one engaged in the commission of a felony is murder in the first degree: *People* v. *Greenwall*, 115 N. Y. 520. Compare *Barcus* v. *State*, 49 Miss. 17; 19 Am. Rep. 1, and note 2, 3.

An information for murder in the first degree will always sustain a conviction of murder in the second degree: *Giskie* v. *State*, 71 Wis. 612.

The verdict of the jury in murder cases must always specify the degree: *People* v. *O'Neil*, 78 Cal. 388; *Kearney* v. *People*, 11 Col. 258; *Zwicker* v. *State*, 27 Tex. App. 539.

CRIMINAL LAW. — Cross-examination of witnesses in criminal cases must be confined to matters stated by them in their direct examination, or matters closely connected therewith: *State* v. *Wright*, 40 La. Ann. 589; or matters showing hostility of the witness under examination to defendant: *Selph* v. *State*, 22 Fla. 537.

WITNESSES, IMPEACHMENT OF, AS TO GENERAL CHARACTER: See *Griffin* v. *State*, 26 Tex. App. 157; 8 Am. St. Rep. 460, and note. The character of a person in the neighborhood in which he lives consists in the opinion and estimation of his neighbors in regard to the traits of his moral character: *State* v. *Parker*, 96 Mo. 382. Evidence of character goes to general reputation only, and cannot be extended to particular acts of conduct: *Hussey* v. *State*, 87 Ala. 122; *Davenport* v. *State*, 85 Id. 336. The defendant in a criminal case testifying in his own behalf is to be treated in the same manner as other witnesses; so that his character for truth and veracity, as well as his general moral character, may be put in issue by the commonwealth: *Lockland* v. *Commonwealth*, 87 Ky. 201; *State* v. *Parker*, 96 Mo. 382; *Peck* v. *State*, 86 Tenn. 259.

In criminal cases, evidence of the good character of defendant is evidence of a substantive fact, like any other fact tending to establish defendant's innocence: *Hanney* v. *Commonwealth*, 116 Pa. St. 322; and where an accused introduces witnesses to establish his good character, the prosecution may introduce witnesses in rebuttal: *State* v. *Huckins*, 23 Neb. 309.

A witness may be impeached by showing that he made statements out of court contradictory to his evidence as a witness; but evidence that he made statements out of court in harmony with his evidence cannot be admitted in rebuttal: *State* v. *Porter*, 74 Iowa, 623.

MOSES *v.* STATE.

[88 ALABAMA, 78.]

CRIMINAL LAW — EVIDENCE — RES GESTÆ. — Unsworn statements of the person robbed, made to a third person from one to four hours after the robbery, as to who committed it, are mere hearsay evidence, and inadmissible as part of the *res gestæ.*

EVIDENCE OF WITNESS WHO TESTIFIES THAT DEFENDANT CHARGED WITH ROBBERY had made contradictory statements to him as to how certain articles came into his possession, but who cannot recollect and testify wherein such statements differed, should be ruled out as incompetent, and merely an expression of opinion.

William L. Martin, attorney-general, for the state.

SOMERVILLE, J. The defendant was convicted of the crime of robbery, and was sentenced to death by hanging: Crim. Code 1886, sec. 3742. The bill of exceptions taken in the case raises no question for our consideration, except the rulings of the court on the evidence.

The person robbed was a female, and was not introduced as a witness on the trial, possibly for some good reason not shown by the record. But the state was allowed to prove certain unsworn statements which she was heard to make, some time after the alleged robbery, purporting to be explanatory of the transaction.

It appeared, from the evidence, that she was seen on the day of the robbery in company with the defendant, and between twelve and one o'clock they entered the woods together. A witness for the state was allowed to testify that, "about one o'clock, while walking in the woods, he saw the Egyptian woman [the victim of the robbery] coming towards him out of the woods, all bruised, wounded, and bleeding, and her clothes badly torn; that she was gesticulating, and trying to talk, but he did not understand, and did not suffer her to come near him, but went off, and a short time afterwards, with others to whom he had reported the incident, he returned, and found the woman badly cut and beaten, and they asked her who had cut her, and she replied and gesticulated, 'the woman that went with her.'" This was objected to, as the mere statement of the person robbed. A similar statement made by the woman robbed to another witness, about four o'clock, P. M., of the same day, or about three hours after the robbery, was allowed to go to the jury, against the objection of the defendant.

The court clearly erred in admitting these unsworn statements of the person robbed, which were mere hearsay, and not competent evidence of the facts stated. Even dying declarations are inadmissible in prosecutions for robbery. So in rape cases, the complaint of the prosecutrix, unless it constitutes a part of the *res gestæ*, is not admissible, on her direct examination by the state, to identify the perpetrator of the crime: *Barnett* v. *State*, 83 Ala. 40.

The time elapsing between the alleged act of robbery and the declarations made by the person robbed, in explanation of it, is not sufficiently brief, nor are the two transactions otherwise so clearly connected as to bring the declarations within the principle of *res gestæ*. The statement is rather a narrative of a by-gone transaction, past and completed: *Kennedy* v. *State*, 85 Ala. 326; *Alabama etc. R. R. Co.* v. *Hawk*, 72 Ala. 112; 47 Am. Rep. 403; *Dismukes* v. *State*, 83 Ala. 287; *Burns* v. *State*, 49 Ala. 370.

The objection taken to the witness Wright's testimony should, in our opinion, have been sustained. He asserted that the defendant had made three several statements to him as to where she had obtained the articles of jewelry discovered in her possession. The first was, that she had gotten them from her husband. The other two statements he did not remember, "except that they were different from each other and from the first statement." Wherein they differed, or in what respect their alleged contradiction consisted, the witness did not pretend to recollect. If the statements had been before the jury, they might have come to another conclusion than that reached by the witness. His assertion savored rather of an opinion than a fact, and should have been excluded.

For the errors above pointed out, the judgment is reversed, and the cause remanded for a new trial. The prisoner, in the mean while, will be retained in custody until discharged by due process of law.

Reversed and remanded.

EVIDENCE — HEARSAY. — The existence of a fact cannot be proved by hearsay testimony: *Woods* v. *Montevallo etc. Tr. Co.*, 84 Ala. 560; 5 Am. St. Rep. 393. Hearsay testimony should be rejected by the court: *Forman* v. *Commonwealth*, 86 Ky. 605; *Craig* v. *Scudder*, 98 Mo. 664; *Sharpe* v. *Williams*, 41 Kan. 57; *Bluitt* v. *State*, 12 Tex. App. 39; 41 Am. Rep. 666; note to *Wormsdorf* v. *Detroit etc. R'y Co.*, 13 Am. St. Rep. 457.

RES GESTÆ. — As to what is admissible as part of the *res gestæ: Dundas* v. *City of Lansing*, 75 Mich. 499; 13 Am. St. Rep. 457, and note. Where the defense to a criminal accusation is, that another committed the offense, the confession of such other person, made after the commission of the crime, is

not part of the *res gestæ*, and is inadmissible: *Peck* v. *State*, 86 Tenn 259.
Nor are exculpatory statements of a defendant, made after the commission of
an offense, part of the *res gestæ*, and admissible in his favor: *Kennedy* v. *State*,
85 Ala. 326. In the case of *Beck* v. *State*, 76 Ga. 452, where defendant was
accused of killing two men, and was upon trial for the homicide of one of
them, it was held to be improper to admit the statement of the other deceased
man, made to a third party a short time after the shooting, in which he stated
that defendant did the shooting, but "would not have done so if he had been
in his right mind"; for such statement was not part of the *res gestæ*, but the
mere expression of an opinion. But in a murder trial, evidence of acts of an
alleged co-conspirator, done before the commission of the crime, tending to
show an understanding between him and the defendant with reference to its
perpetration, is part of the *res gestæ*, and admissible to prove conspiracy:
People v. *Bentley*, 75 Cal. 407. So the clothing worn by a murdered man at
the time of his death is admissible as part of the *res gestæ:* *People* v. *O'Brien*,
78 Id. 41. Dying declarations should be restricted to transactions immediately attending the killing and forming a part of the *res gestæ: State* v. *Parker*, 96 Mo. 382. In the case of *State* v. *Deuble*, 74 Iowa, 509, where a woman
had been shot, but had had the wound dressed, and was lying upon a sofa,
statements made by her in response to a question as to how she became
wounded, with reference to circumstances occurring and conversations had
between herself and defendant before the wound was inflicted, in which she
said defendant was drunk, and purposely shot her, are not part of the *res gestæ*, and inadmissible. So the offer of defendant to lift up the deceased, made
a few minutes after the shooting, is not part of the *res gestæ*, and is inadmissible: *Goley* v. *State*, 87 Ala. 58.

ALDRIDGE *v.* STATE.

[88 ALABAMA, 113.]

CRIMINAL LAW — BURGLARY. — INDICTMENT for burglary upon premises belonging to a corporation, and occupied by an agent or servant thereof,
must, in order to support conviction, allege the ownership of the premises to be in the corporation, and not in the agent, and the corporate
-name and character of the owner must be averred.

William L. Martin, attorney-general, for the state.

SOMERVILLE, J. The defendant was convicted of the burglary of a storehouse, in which goods and merchandise were
stored: Crim. Code 1886, sec. 3786. The objection urged is
an alleged variance between the averment of ownership in
the indictment and the proof of such ownership. The indictment lays the ownership in one "Wilburn M. Bass, business
manager of Beulah co-operation store of the Beulah Alliance."
The evidence tends to show that Bass was the salaried agent
of the Beulah Alliance, which was a body corporate, and that
he had charge of the store as the servant of the corporation.

It also tends to show that he used the store as a post-office, — a business with which the alliance had no connection. Whether this occupancy was by mere license, or otherwise, does not affirmatively appear from the evidence.

Where premises belonging to a corporation are occupied by a naked agent or servant of the corporation, the rule is, that the ownership must be averred to be in the corporation, and not in the agent; and the corporate name and character of the owner must be stated: Clark's Manual of Criminal Law, sec. 872; *Emmonds* v. *State,* 87 Ala. 12; 2 Pomeroy's Archbold's Pl. & Pr. 1093–1101; 2 Am. & Eng. Ency. of Law, 682, 683; 2 Bishop's Crim. Law, 3d ed., secs. 137, 138.

The use of the storeroom for receiving and distributing the United States mails does not appear to rise to the dignity of a tenancy, estate, or other ownership in the premises. And this collateral business being carried on in the mode known to be customary in this country, there is no presumption that there was a letting of the premises to Bass for this purpose, but rather a license; and this fact would not disturb the ownership of the corporation, or its constructive possession through Bass as their agent: 2 Pomeroy's Archbold's Crim. Pl. & Pr. 1098, note; 2 East P. C., c. 15, sec. 14, pp. 501–502. The allegation of the indictment, moreover, is, that his occupancy was in the capacity of an agent of the Beulah Alliance, — not of the federal government, — and this negatives the idea of a tenancy or ownership in himself personally. The alleged breaking, in other words, is into a storehouse as such, not into a post-office.

The court erred in refusing to give the two charges requested by the defendants.

Reversed and remanded.

BURGLARY — OWNERSHIP OF PROPERTY ENTERED. — Indictment for burglary, in breaking and entering the storehouse of Perry Mason Shoe Company, must either allege that such company is a corporation, or if it is a partnership, allege such fact, and name the individual partners, showing that defendant is not one of them: *Emmonds* v. *State,* 87 Ala. 12. An indictment for burglary was held sufficient, which described the building entered as "the property of the estate of L.," who was a person deceased before the offense was committed: *Anderson* v. *State,* 48 Id. 665; 17 Am. Rep. 36. An indictment for burglary to the chamber of a guest at a hotel must allege ownership of the dwelling-house in the hotel-keeper, not in the guest: *Rodgers* v. *People,* 86 N. Y. 360; 40 Am. Rep. 548. An indictment properly laid ownership of the house in the wife, where the house was occupied by a husband and wife, but was leased by the wife, who had a separate estate, and owned the goods in the house: *State* v. *Trapp,* 17 S. C. 467; 43 Am. Rep. 614. Indictment for house-breaking need only describe the house with such precision as to necessarily inform the accused of the actual offense charged against him, and to bar a second conviction therefor: *Johnson* v. *Commonwealth,* 87 Ky. 189. Information for burglary, in the language of the statute, is sufficient: *People* v. *Rogers,* 81 Cal. 209.

<hr>

McGuff v. State.

[88 Alabama, 147.]

CRIMINAL LAW. — INDICTMENT FOR CRIMINAL ASSAULT following the statute (Ala. Crim. Code, sec. 3739), and charging that the accused "did carnally know, or abuse in the attempt to carnally know, a girl [naming her] under the age of ten years," is sufficient.

CRIMINAL LAW. — INDICTMENT CHARGING DISJUNCTIVELY OFFENSES OF THE SAME CHARACTER, and subject to the same punishment, will support a general verdict of guilty.

CRIMINAL LAW — PLACE OF IMPRISONMENT. — When, upon conviction, the jury fixes the penalty at "imprisonment for life," without specifying the place of imprisonment, the defendant may properly be sentenced to imprisonment in the state penitentiary for and during his natural life.

WITNESS — EXCLUSION OF — DISCRETION OF COURT. — Refusal of the court to put a witness under the rule, and compel his withdrawal from the court-room during the examination of another witness, is a matter within the discretion of the court, and not subject to review on appeal.

WITNESS — AGE AT WHICH CHILD MAY TESTIFY TO AN ALLEGED RAPE. — There is no fixed age as to the time within which infants are excluded from giving evidence; this depends upon the sense and reason they entertain of the danger and impiety of falsehood, which is to be collected from their answers to questions propounded to them by the court. Under this rule, a girl of intelligent moral comprehension between seven and eight years of age is competent to testify as to the particulars of a rape or an attempted rape upon her.

CRIMINAL LAW — PERSONAL EXAMINATION IN PROSECUTIONS FOR RAPE. — In a prosecution for rape of an infant under ten years of age, the prosecutrix cannot be compelled, as matter of right, to submit to a personal medical examination. If such right exists, it is a matter of discretion with the trial court, to be exercised only in cases of extreme necessity, and not subject to review on appeal.

CRIMINAL LAW — CONFESSIONS — WEIGHT OF, FOR JURY. — It is within the exclusive province of the jury to determine the weight of voluntary confessions admitted in evidence without objection.

Matthews and Daniel, for the appellant.

William L. Martin, attorney-general, for the state.

SOMERVILLE, J. The indictment is found under section 3739 of the Criminal Code, which provides that "any person who has carnal knowledge of any female under ten years of age, or abuses such female in the attempt to have carnal knowledge of her, must, on conviction, be punished, at the discretion of the jury, either by death or by imprisonment in the penitentiary for life": Crim Code 1886, sec. 3739. The indictment charges, in proper form, that the defendant "did carnally know, or abuse in the attempt to carnally know, Cora Bishop, a girl under the age of ten years." It follows the form prescribed by the code by literal compliance, and is therefore sufficient: *Myers* v. *State*, 84 Ala. 11.

It is objected that the verdict of the jury should have specified which of the disjunctive offenses charged in the indictment the defendant was convicted of, and that a general verdict of guilty is erroneous, and proper ground for reversal of the judgment. The offenses, thus charged disjunctively, are of the same character, and subject to precisely the same punishment. They could therefore be charged in the same count in the alternative: Crim. Code 1886, sec. 4385; *Horton* v. *State*, 53 Ala. 488. Where this form of indictment is authorized, we have uniformly held that a general verdict of guilty is not ground of error, or for motion in arrest of judgment: *Johnson* v. *State*, 50 Ala. 456; *Cawley* v. *State*, 37 Ala. 152.

The jury had the discretion, under the statute, to fix the punishment, either by death or by imprisonment in the penitentiary for life. They adopted the latter alternative, fixing the penalty at "imprisonment for life," without specifying the place of imprisonment. The court properly sentenced the defendant to imprisonment in the state penitentiary for and during his natural life. The statute fixed the place, and it could not have been elsewhere: Crim. Code 1886, secs. 3739, 4492; *Gunter* v. *State*, 83 Ala. 96.

The refusal of the court to put the witness Bishop, the father of the injured girl, under the rule, by compelling his withdrawal from the court-room during the child's examination, was a matter within the sound discretion of the trial court, and is not subject to our review on appeal: *Ryan* v. *Couch*, 66 Ala. 244; 1 Greenl. Ev., 14th ed., sec. 431.

It is objected that the witness Cora Bishop, upon whose person the alleged abuse was practiced, was incompetent, on account of her tender years and her inability to comprehend the nature and binding obligation of an oath. She is shown to have been between seven and eight years old at the time she was examined. There is no particular age at which a witness may, in all cases, be pronounced legally competent or incompetent to testify. This would be unwise, not only because children differ greatly in powers of observation and memory, but because such a rule would practically "proclaim immunity to certain offenses of a serious nature against the persons of children, which it is next to impossible to establish without receiving their account of what has taken place," as the one here under consideration: 1 Best on Evidence, Morgan's ed., sec. 151. This·is especially true in view of the frequency of rapes upon very young children, to which writers on medical jurisprudence have often taken occasion to call attention; which has been accounted for, not alone by the comparatively less danger of exposure and conviction attributable to the mental and moral deficiency of such children as witnesses, but "by the comparative ease with which a child's resistance may be overcome, and by its entire ignorance of the nature and consequence of the sexual act": 3 Wharton and Stillé's Medical Jurisprudence, sec. 217. These facts are eminently proper to be considered by courts in the formulation of a correct rule of evidence on this subject. This court has accordingly followed, in substance, the rule laid down in *Brasier's Case*, 1 Leach, 199, 1 East P. C. 443, where it was held that there was "no precise or fixed rule as to the time within which infants are excluded from giving evidence, but their admissibility depends upon the sense and reason they entertain of the danger and impiety of falsehood, which is to be collected from their answers to questions propounded to them by the court": *Kelly* v. *State*, 75 Ala. 21; 51 Am. Rep. 422; *State* v. *Morea*, 2 Ala. 275; *Wade* v. *State*, 50 Ala. 164; *Carter* v. *State*, 63 Ala. 52; 35 Am. Rep. 4; *Beason* v. *State*, 72 Ala. 191; Rapalje's Crim. Pr., sec. 298. If the promise to tell the truth, in other words, is made under an immediate sense of the witness's responsibility to God, and with a conscientious sense of the wickedness and danger of falsehood, this would seem to be all that is requisite for the accomplishment of justice: 1 Greenl. Ev., 14th ed., secs. 328, 368.

The examination of the witness by the circuit judge disclosed on her part a very intelligent comprehension of the belief that falsehood was not only morally wrong, but would be severely punished in the future. She was clearly competent to testify, showing, as she did, neither intellectual nor moral deficiency which would disqualify her, and there was no error in receiving her testimony.

We do not doubt the correctness of the court's ruling in refusing to compel the infant to submit to an examination of her person by medical experts, on motion of the defendant made at the trial. Such a practice has never prevailed in this state, and if adopted as matter of right in all cases of prosecution for rape, the temptation to its abuse would be so great that it might be perverted into an engine of oppression to deter many modest and virtuous females from testifying in open court against the perpetration of one of the most barbarous and detestable of all crimes. We have repeatedly held that a conviction for rape may be sustained on the uncorroborated testimony of a prosecutrix, which excludes the idea of any necessity for corroboration by an examination of her person, either by medical experts or others. In *Barnett* v. *State*, 83 Ala. 40, we accordingly held there was no error in the trial court's refusal to advise the jury not to convict, unless the testimony was corroborated by an examination of her person by medical or other experts, and that her refusal to submit to such examination would subject her evidence to discredit. "However forcible," we observed, "such a suggestion may be, under some circumstances, as an argument to a jury, the law does not require it."

It is true that, in divorce cases, the courts of this country and of England, as also of Scotland and France, have exerted their jurisdiction to compel the parties to suits to submit to a surgical examination or inspection of the person in order to ascertain the fact of incurable impotence, when made the ground upon which the dissolution of the bonds of marriage is sought. This is limited to the necessity of the particular case, and is permitted only to prevent the miscarriage of justice: 2 Bishop on Marriage and Divorce, 6th ed., secs. 590, 599; *Anonymous*, 35 Ala. 226; *Devanbagh* v. *Devanbagh*, 5 Paige, 554; 28 Am. Dec. 443, and note 450. So in a recent case, cited by appellant's counsel, in an action of damages for permanent injury to the plaintiff's eyes, no medical expert having testified, it was held error in the trial court to refuse to make an order, on defendant's request, to compel the plaintiff to submit to an examination by a medical expert who had been called as a witness, and was then present in court ready to testify: *Atchison etc. R. R. Co.* v. *Thul*, 29 Kan. 466; 44 Am. Rep. 659. There are many similar decisions, made in modern civil actions for physical injuries, where the courts in proper cases have compelled the plaintiff or injured person to

submit his person to the inspection of experts, in order to
ascertain the nature and extent of such injuries: 1 Thompson
on Trials, sec. 859; *Schroeder* v. *Chicago etc. R. R. Co.*, 47
Iowa, 379; *Sibley* v. *Smith*, 46 Ark. 275; *White* v. *Milwaukee
City R'y Co.*, 61 Wis. 536; 50 Am. Rep. 154; *Hatfield* v. *St.
Paul R. R. Co.*, 33 Minn. 130; *Richmond etc. R. R. Co.* v. *Chil-
dress*, 82 Ga. 719; 14 Am. St. Rep. 189; Rogers on Expert
Testimony, sec. 75.

The authority and soundness of these cases need not be challenged, although some courts in this country have declined to
follow them.   They are cases where the court had jurisdiction
of the parties to a litigated case pending before it, who were
invoking the assistance of its arm in aid of their civil rights.
In this case, the witness is no party to any civil suit, but has
been summoned at the instance of the state to testify in a
criminal prosecution against an alleged violator of the law.
It may be well doubted, in cases of rape and cognate offenses,
whether the court has the power to make an order compelling
the inspection of the private person of a prosecutrix, in the
event of her refusal to submit to such examination.   If such
right exists at all, we should hold it to be a matter of judicial
discretion with the trial court, to be exercised only in cases of
extreme necessity, and not a subject of review on appeal to
this court.   There being other corroboration of the local marks
of violence in this case, made soon after the injuries, no such
necessity is made to appear.   The proposed examination by
medical experts, moreover, not having been suggested until
more than a month after the occurrence, could not be expected
to afford any very useful results: 3 Wharton and Stillé's Medical Jurisprudence, sec. 212.   The refusal of the court to grant
this motion was free from error.

The confessions of the defendant appear to have been made
voluntarily, and they were allowed to go the jury as evidence,
without objection.   It was for the court to determine their admissibility, and this action could not have been reviewed by
the jury, although it was within the exclusive province of the
jury to determine the weight to which they were entitled as
evidence.   The charges requested by the defendant in effect
denied to the jury any right to consider these confessions as
competent evidence in forming their verdict.   Their admissibility, as voluntary or involuntary, could not be raised in this
way, and the court properly refused to give these charges:

Long v. State, 86 Ala. 36; Nolen v. State, 46 Am. Rep. 255, note; Redd v. State, 69 Ala. 256.

We discover no error in the record, and the judgment is affirmed.

INDICTMENT — TWO OFFENSES CHARGED. — If the charges in the different counts of an indictment are of the same general character, and are manifestly inserted in good faith for the purpose of meeting the various aspects of the case, the court will neither quash the indictment nor compel the prosecution to elect upon which count it will try the defendant: State v. Shores, 31 W. Va. 491; 13 Am. St. Rep. 875, and note; compare People v. Aikin, 66 Mich. 460; 11 Am. St. Rep. 512. An indictment may charge the same offense in two different counts: State v. Doyle, 15 R. I. 527; and in the case of misdemeanors, several distinct offenses of the same kind may be joined in the same indictment: Burrell v. State, 25 Neb. 581. The making up a fraudulent poll-book is a single offense, whether consisting of one or more votes, or of votes for one or more candidates for office, and different counts charging this offense is not a misjoinder of offenses because it is but one offense: Commonwealth v. Duff, 87 Ky. 586; to the same effect is Commonwealth v. Selby, 87 Id. 595. An indictment attempting to charge two offenses is not therefore bad for duplicity, when one offense is not sufficiently charged: State v. Henn, 39 Minn. 464.

INDICTMENT — SUFFICIENCY OF. — An indictment following the language of the statute is generally sufficient: People v. King, 110 N. Y. 418; 6 Am. St. Rep. 389, and note; State v. Light, 17 Or. 358; State v. Sparks, 30 W. Va. 101; State v. Watkins, 101 N. C. 702; State v. Lee, 17 Or. 488; People v. McKenna, 81 Cal. 158; People v. Rozelle, 78 Id. 84; Meyers v. State, 84 Ala. 11.

ASSAULT UPON OR RAPE OF CHILD UNDER THE AGE OF CONSENT: See note to Smith v. State, 80 Am. Dec. 363, 364, 373, 374. Taking indecent liberties with a female child under the age of consent is an assault, notwithstanding the fact that she consented: State v. West, 39 Minn. 321. And carnally knowing a female child under the statutory age of consent, with or without her consent, is rape: Coates v. State, 50 Ark. 330.

The indictment in such cases need not aver that the child was forcibly ravished against her will: Murphy v. State, 120 Ind. 115. If a child under the statutory age of consent has been forcibly ravished, her age need not be averred in the indictment; but where she consented, her age must be alleged: State v. Johnson, 100 N. C. 494. And to obviate proving want of consent, it is merely necessary to aver and prove that the child was at the commission of the crime under the statutory age of consent: Bonner v. State, 65 Miss. 293; and it is not necessary to prove that the woman has not reached the age of physical puberty, when it is shown that she was under the age of consent as fixed by statute: State v. Wright, 25 Neb. 38.

Upon the trial of one for carnally knowing and abusing a female child under the age of consent, even with her actual consent, declarations made by her several days after the crime are inadmissible, without good reasons shown why she delayed in making such statements: Dunn v. State, 45 Ohio St. 249; such as fear induced by threats made by the accused: People v. Gage, 62 Mich. 271; 4 Am. St. Rep. 854.

Under an indictment for rape of a child under the age of consent, defendant may be convicted for assault with intent to rape, without proving that the child resisted or could resist: Murphy v. State, 120 Ind. 116.

PHYSICAL EXAMINATION OF PERSONS WHO HAVE SUSTAINED INJURIES.— It rests within the discretion of the court whether or not to order a compulsory examination of the person of one who has been injured in body, in order to ascertain the nature and extent of the injuries: *Richmond etc. R. R. Co.* v. *Childress*, 82 Ga. 719; 14 Am. St. Rep. 189, and note.

WITNESSES — CHILDREN. — A child of any age may be a witness, if capable of distinguishing between good and evil: *State* v. *Whittier*, 21 Me. 341; 38 Am. Dec. 272. A child of seven years is not competent as a witness when she does not understand the nature of an oath, nor the consequences of perjury: *Holst* v. *State*, 23 Tex. App. 1; 59 Am. Rep. 770. A boy of twelve years, who habitually repeated the Lord's prayer, and had heard that the bad man caught liars, but never heard of a God, or the Devil, or of heaven or hell, or of the Bible, and had no idea what became of the good or bad people after death, is not a competent witness: *State* v. *Belton*, 24 S. C. 185; 58 Am. Rep. 245; see also *Taylor* v. *State*, 22 Tex. App. 529; 58 Am. Rep. 656, and note 658, 659; *Carter* v. *State*, 63 Ala. 52; 35 Am. Rep. 4; *Kelly* v. *State*, 75 Ala. 21; 51 Am. Rep. 422; *State* v. *Lyon*, 81 N. C. 600; 31 Am. Rep. 518; *McGuire* v. *People*, 44 Mich. 286; 38 Am. Rep. 265. A boy ten years old is a competent witness, if he understands the nature of an oath: *Moore* v. *State*, 79 Ga. 498. A boy of twelve years, with the ordinary intelligence of boys of his age, understanding the obligations of an oath, is not rendered incompetent because he could not speak English: *State* v. *Severson*, 78 Iowa, 653. There is no precise age under which a child is deemed incompetent as a witness, but, under fourteen years of age, competency is within the discretion of the trial court, and is to be determined by an examination of the child: *Hawkins* v. *State*, 27 Tex. App. 273; *Hughes* v. *Detroit etc. R'y Co.*, 65 Mich. 11. One may be competent as a witness at a second trial, though upon the first trial of the same case she was decided incompetent by reason of her tender years: *Johnson* v. *State*, 76 Ga. 76.

BOYD *v.* STATE.

[88 ALABAMA, 169.]

COMMON SCHOOLS — TEACHER'S RIGHT TO PUNISH, AND CRIMINAL LIABILITY THEREFOR. — A schoolmaster is, within reasonable bounds, a substitute for the parent, exercising his delegated authority. He is vested with the power and discretion to administer moderate correction, with a proper instrument, in cases of misconduct, always having reference to the character of the offense, and age, sex, size, and physical strength of the pupil, and, within the circumscribed sphere of his authority, he is not liable; but he is liable criminally, if in punishing a pupil he exceeds the exercise of reasonable judgment and discretion, and acts with legal malice, or from wickedness of motive.

COMMON SCHOOLS. — SCHOOLMASTERS EXCEED THE LIMIT OF THEIR AUTHORITY to punish pupils when they inflict lasting injury; they act within the limits of it when they inflict temporary pain.

COMMON SCHOOLS — LIABILITY OF TEACHER FOR PUNISHMENT INFLICTED ON PUPIL. — In determining whether the teacher in correcting a pupil has acted with reasonable judgment, or from malice and wickedness of motive, the nature of the instrument used for correction has a strong bearing and influence on the question of motive or intention.

JURY — WAIVER OF — JUDGMENT ON FACTS WITHOUT JURY CONCLUSIVE. — When a jury is waived, a decision of the court upon the facts is, in legal effect, equivalent to a verdict of the jury, and in the absence of statutory power will not be reviewed on appeal, except in cases where such verdict cannot, as matter of law, be supported by any reasonable inferences from the evidence.

COMMON SCHOOLS — TEACHER'S CRIMINAL LIABILITY FOR IMPROPER CHASTISEMENT OF PUPIL. — A schoolmaster is not justified in using a "limb or stick," nor his "clenched fist applied in bruising the pupil's eye," in further correcting a pupil eighteen years of age, after he has been severely chastised, and has apologized. Such implements are not proper instruments of correction to be used on such occasion, and from their use there is ample room to imply legal malice in connection with unreasonable and immoderate correction, which will support a conviction of assault and battery.

William L. Parks, for the appellant.

William L. Martin, attorney-general, for the state.

SOMERVILLE, J. The defendant, a schoolmaster, being indicted, was convicted of an assault and battery on one Lee Crowder, a pupil in his school, who is shown to have been about eighteen years of age. The defense is, that the alleged battery was a reasonable chastisement inflicted by the master in just maintenance of discipline, and in punishment of conduct on the part of the pupil which tended to the subversion of good order in the school.

The case involves a consideration of the proper rule of law prescribing the extent of the schoolmaster's authority to administer corporal correction to a pupil.

The principle is commonly stated to be, that the schoolmaster, like the parent, and others *in foro domestico*, has the authority to moderately chastise pupils under his care, or as stated by Chancellor Kent, "the right of inflicting moderate correction, under the exercise of a sound discretion": 2 Kent's Com. *203–206. In other words, he may administer reasonable correction, which must not "exceed the bounds of due moderation, either in the measure of it, or in the instrument made use of for the purpose." If he go beyond this extent, he becomes criminally liable, and if death ensues from the brutal injuries inflicted, he may be liable not only for assault and battery, but to the penalties of manslaughter, or even murder, according to the circumstances of the case: 1 Archbold's Crim. Pr. *218; 1 Bishop's Crim. Law, 7th ed., secs. 881, 882.

This power of correction, vested by law in parents, is founded on their duty to maintain and educate their offspring. In support of that authority, they must have " a right to the exercise of such discipline as may be requisite for the discharge of their sacred trust": 2 Kent's Com. *203. And this power, allowed by law to the parent over the person of the child, "may be delegated to a tutor or instructor, the better to accomplish the purpose of education": 2 Kent's Com. *205; 1 Bla. Com. *507.

The better doctrine of the adjudged cases, therefore, is, that the teacher is, within reasonable bounds, the substitute for the parent, exercising his delegated authority. He is vested with the power to administer moderate correction, with a proper instrument, in cases of misconduct, which ought to have some reference to the character of the offense, the sex, age, size, and physical strength of the pupil. When the teacher keeps within the circumscribed sphere of his authority, the degree of correction must be left to his discretion, as it is to that of the parent, under like circumstances. Within this limit, he has the authority to determine the gravity or heinousness of the offense, and to mete out to the offender the punishment which he thinks his conduct justly merits; and hence the parent or teacher is often said, *pro hac vice*, to exercise "judicial functions."

All of the authorities agree that he will not be permitted to deal brutally with his victim, so as to endanger life, limb, or health. He will not be permitted to inflict "cruel and merciless punishment": Schouler on Domestic Relations, 4th ed., sec. 244. He cannot lawfully disfigure him, or perpetrate on his person any other permanent injury. As said by Gaston, J., in *State* v. *Pendergrass*, 2 Dev. & B. 365, 31 Am. Dec. 416, a case generally approved by the weight of American authority: "It may be laid down as a general rule that teachers exceed the limit of their authority when they cause lasting mischief; but act within the limits of it when they inflict temporary pain."

There are some well-considered authorities which hold teachers and parents alike liable criminally, if, in the infliction of chastisement, they act clearly without the exercise of reasonable judgment and discretion. The test which seems to be fixed by these cases is, the general judgment of reasonable men: *Patterson* v. *Nutter*, 78 Me. 509; 57 Am. Rep. 818. The more correct view, however, and the one better sustained by authority, seems to be, that when, in the judgment of reasonable men, the punishment inflicted is immoderate or excessive, and a jury would be authorized, from the facts of the

case, to infer that it was induced by legal malice, or wickedness of motive, the limit of lawful authority may be adjudged
to be passed. In determining this question, the nature of the
instrument of correction used may have a strong bearing on
the inquiry as to motive or intention. The latter view is indorsed by Mr. Freeman in his note to the case of *State* v.
Pendergrass, 31 Am. Dec. 419, as the more correct. "The
qualification," he observes, "that the schoolmaster shall not
act from malice will protect his pupils from outbursts of brutality, whilst, on the other hand, he is protected from liability
for mere errors of judgment": *Lander* v. *Seaver*, 32 Vt. 114; 76
Am. Dec. 156, and note 164–167; *State* v. *Alford*, 68 N. C.
322; *State* v. *Harris*, 63 N. C. 1.

Judge Reeves, in his work on domestic relations, indorses
the same view, asserting that the parent and schoolmaster, in
imposing chastisement for cause, must be considered as acting
in a judicial capacity, and are not to be held legally responsible for errors of judgment, although the punishment may appear to the trial court or jury to be unreasonably severe, and
not proportioned to the offense, provided they act "conscien-
tiously, and from motives of duty." "But," he says further,
"when the punishment is, in their opinion, thus unreasonable,
and it appears that the parent acted *malo animo*,—from wicked
motives,—under the influence of an unsocial heart, he ought
to be liable to damages. For error of opinion, he ought to be
excused; but for malice of heart, he must not be shielded from
the just claims of the child. Whether there was malice may
be collected from the circumstances attending the punishment": Reeves on Domestic Relations, 4th ed., 357, 358.

Dr. Wharton, in his work on criminal law, thus states the
principle: "The law confides to schoolmasters and teachers a
discretionary power in the infliction of punishment upon their
pupils, and will not hold them responsible, unless the punishment be such as to occasion permanent injury to the child, or
be inflicted merely to gratify their own evil passions. The
teacher must be governed, when chastisement is proper, as to
the mode and severity of the punishment, by the nature of the
offense, the age, size, and apparent powers of endurance of the
pupil. It is for the jury to decide whether the punishment is
excessive": 1 Wharton's Crim. Law, 9th ed., sec. 632.

Mr. Bishop adds, pertinent to the same subject: "The law
has provided no means whereby a parent, meditating chastisement, can first obtain a judicial opinion as to its necessity,

the proper instruments, and its due extent. In reason, therefore, if he acts in good faith, prompted by pure parental love,
without passion, and inflicts no permanent injury on the child,
he should not be punished merely because a jury, reviewing
the case, do not deem that it was wise to proceed so far": i
Bishop's Crim. Law, 7th ed., sec. 882; see also Schouler on
Domestic Relations, 4th ed., sec. 244; 1 Bla. Com. *556; 1
Greenl. Ev., sec. 97; 2 Addison on Torts, Wood's ed., sec.
840; *Danenhoffer* v. *State*, 69 Ind. 295; 35 Am. Rep. 216; *Commonwealth* v. *Randall*, 4 Gray, 36; *State* v. *Burton*, 45 Wis. 150;
35 Am. Rep. 706.

To the foregoing authorities I may add, as a matter of
literary curiosity, rather than legal authority, the following
views expressed on this subject by Dr. Samuel Johnson, to
his biographer, Boswell, as far back as 1772. Boswell was of
counsel for a schoolmaster in Scotland, who had been somewhat severe in his chastisement of one of his pupils, and the
case was pending on appeal from the court of sessions before
the English house of lords, on a proceeding to remove him
from his office. The opinion of this most learned of literary
philosophers having been solicited, he discoursed as follows:
" The government of the schoolmaster is somewhat of the
nature of a military government; that is to say, it must be
arbitrary; it must be exercised by the will of one man, according to particular circumstances. A schoolmaster has a
prescriptive right to beat, and an action of assault and battery
cannot be admitted against him, unless there be some great
excess, some barbarity. In our schools in England many
boys have been maimed, yet I never heard of an action against
a schoolmaster on that account. Puffendorf, I think, maintains the right of a schoolmaster to beat his scholars ": 2 Boswell's Life of Johnson, 89, 96.

While, on the one hand, we should recognize that every
child has rights which ought to be protected against the
brutality of a cruel teacher or barbarous parent, on the other,
it is equally important not to paralyze that power of correction and discipline by the rod, given, as Blackstone asserts,
"for the benefit of education," which has for ages been deemed
necessary alike on the part of parents to prevent their children from becoming "the victims of bad habits, and thereby
proving a nuisance to the community," and on the part of
teachers to preserve that discipline of the schools, without
which all efforts to promote the education of the present and

future generations will prove a lamentable failure: Reeves on
Domestic Relations, 367. No regulation of the school-room,
any more than a law of the state, can be successfully enforced
without the aid of coercive penalties. A law without a penalty
is in practice a dead letter. Moderate chastisement is established by immemorial usage as the only available terror to
vicious and incorrigible evil-doers, both in the homestead and
the school-room; at least in cases where the more humane
law of kindness and moral suasion has proved ineffectual.
"Foolishness," said Solomon, "is bound up in the heart of a
child, but the rod of correction shall drive it far from him."
"The rod and reproof give wisdom, but a child left to himself
causeth shame to his mother." And again: "Train up a
child in the way he should go, and even when he is old, he
will not depart from it." These words are as true now as
they were a hundred generations ago, when they were uttered
by the wise man. This right of discipline with the rod, administered without malice or immoderation, has been well
characterized as a part of the common law of the school-room.
The more thoroughly the right is established, as experience
in all discipline shows, the less frequent will be the necessity
of resorting to its exercise to enforce obedience to the lawful
mandates of the parent or of the schoolmaster.

We have said this much in order that we may not be misunderstood in the conclusion reached by us, not to disturb the
judgment of conviction in this case. We cannot say, under
the principles above stated, that the judge of the criminal
court reached an erroneous conclusion in adjudging that the
defendant exceeded his lawful authority so as to render himself liable for an assault and battery.

The statute organizing the criminal court of Pike County
confers upon convicted parties the right of appeal to this
court. But where a jury is waived, and the judge tries the
facts, the decision of the court upon the facts is, in legal effect,
equivalent to the verdict of a jury, and in the absence of statutory power, will not be reviewed by this court on appeal:
Bell v. *State,* 75 Ala. 25; *Calloway* v. *State,* 75 Ala. 37;
Knowles v. *State,* 80 Ala. 9; *Wynn* v. *State,* 87 Ala. 137. The
statute under consideration confers no such jurisdiction on
this court: Acts 1888–89, pp. 631–634, sec. 15.

It is only where, upon the undisputed facts of the case, with
all proper inferences deducible from such facts, a jury would
not have been lawfully authorized to find the defendant guilty

of the crime charged that we will review and reverse the
judgment of the lower court; in other words, where the whole
question raised is reduced to one of law, and the verdict cannot, as matter of law, be supported by any reasonable inferences from the evidence. This was the case of *Skinner* v.
State, 87 Ala. 105.

There was evidence in this case from which the inference of
malice could have been deduced as influencing the conduct of
the defendant in his chastisement of young Crowder, both as
to his outbursts of temper, and in the use of improper instruments of correction. Taking, as we must, every reasonable
inference which the judge, acting as a jury, could have drawn
from the evidence, we take as true, among others, the following
facts: That after the severe chastisement administered in the
school-room, the defendant followed Crowder into the school-
yard, and struck him with "a limb or stick," and then "put
his hands in his pocket, as if to draw a knife"; that although
Crowder did not strike back, but only protested against and
resisted castigation, and after apologizing for the objectionable
language imputed to him, asked permission to withdraw from
the school, the defendant, after promising not to strike him,
"afterwards struck him in the face three licks with his fist,
and hit him several licks over the head with the butt-end of
the switch." From these blows, the eye of the young man
was "considerably swollen," and was "closed for several days."
The attending physician testified that there were "marks on
his head, made by a stick, in his opinion." One witness asserts that the defendant declared he "would conquer him
[Crowder] or kill him." All the witnesses for the state say
that the defendant was apparently very angry all the time,
and was very much excited, and after he got through whip-
ping Crowder he remarked, in an excited, angry voice, in the
presence of the school, and others, that he "could whip any
man in China Grove beat!" From this unseemly conduct
on the part of one whose duty it was to set a good example of
self-restraint and gentlemanly deportment to his pupils, there
was ample room for the inference of legal malice, in connection with unreasonable and immoderate correction. Nor was
the limb of a tree, of the size indicated by the evidence, nor a
clenched fist applied in bruising the pupil's eye, after the
manner of a prize-fighter, a proper instrument of correction to
be used on such an occasion.

The conviction must accordingly be sustained, without assuming any jurisdiction to review the correctness of the judge's finding on the facts.

Affirmed.   ____

SCHOOL-TEACHER — RIGHT TO PUNISH PUPILS. — As to the powers and liabilities of teachers concerning punishment of pupils: *Vanvactor v. State*, 113 Ind. 276; 3 Am. St. Rep. 645, and note. Where school boards have made no regulations for the government of the school, a teacher stands *in loco parentis:* *State v. Burton*, 45 Wis. 150; 30 Am. Rep. 706. Teacher must not chastise a pupil wantonly and without cause, and the chastisement must be proportionate to the offense and within the bounds of moderation, or the teacher will be guilty of assault and battery: *Anderson v. State*, 3 Head, 455; 75 Am. Dec. 774. Authority and powers of schoolmasters, generally: Extended note to *Lander v. Seaver*, 76 Id. 164–167. Teacher cannot require a pupil to pay for wanton distruction of school property, nor enforce such a requirement by chastisement: *State v. Vanderbilt*, 116 Ind. 11; 9 Am. St. Rep. 820.

____

YELLOW-STONE KIT *v.* STATE.

[88 ALABAMA, 196.]

LOTTERY, WHAT IS. — A lottery the carrying on of which is intended to be prohibited as criminal by statute embraces only schemes in which a valuable consideration of some kind is paid, directly or indirectly, for a chance to draw a prize. The gratuitous distribution of property by lot or chance is not a lottery.

LOTTERY, WHAT IS NOT. — A vendor of medicine does not maintain a lottery who distributes prizes by lot to parties to whom he has given tickets at various exhibitions which entitle them to a chance in the prizes, but for which they have paid no valuable consideration, directly or indirectly, and this though he may have charged an admission fee of ten cents on the evening when the prizes were drawn, and the same fee of those occupying seats at other times, if this was done regardless of whether the party from whom the fee was collected was a holder of such ticket or must be present at the drawing.

McCarron and Lewis, and B. M. Allen, for the appellant.

William L. Martin, attorney-general, and Leslie B. Sheldon, for the state.

SOMERVILLE, J. The defendant was convicted of the offense of carrying on a lottery in this state.

The case turns largely on what is to be taken as a proper definition of the word "lottery," within the meaning of the statute and the constitution of Alabama: Code 1886, secs. 4068, 4069; Const. 1875, art. 4, sec. 26.

The word cannot be regarded as having any technical or legal signification different from the popular one.

It is defined by Webster as "a distribution of prizes by lot or chance." This definition is substantially adopted by Bouvier and Rapalje, in their law dictionaries.

Worcester defines it as "a distribution of prizes and blanks by chance; a game of hazard, in which small sums are ventured for the chance of obtaining a larger value." So the American Cyclopædia thus defines a lottery: "A sort of gaming contract, by which, for a valuable consideration, one may by favor of the lot obtain a prize of a value superior to the amount or value of that which he risks."

In *Buckalew* v. *State*, 62 Ala. 334, it was said, after citing Webster's definition, that "whenever chances are sold, and the distribution of prizes determined by lot, this, it would seem, is a lottery. This, we think, is the popular acceptation of the term."

In Bishop on Statutory Crimes, sec. 952, it is said: "A lottery may be defined to be any scheme whereby one, on paying money or other valuable thing to another, becomes entitled to receive from him such a return in value, or nothing, as some formula of chance may determine."

In *Hull* v. *Ruggles*, 56 N. Y. 424, the New York court of appeals adopts the following as the result of the accepted definitions: "Where a pecuniary consideration is paid, and it is determined by lot or chance, according to some scheme held out to the public, what and how much he who pays the money is to have for it, that is a lottery." This definition is approved in *Wilkinson* v. *Gill*, 74 N. Y. 63, 30 Am. Rep. 264, as the popular meaning of the word, and one proper to be adopted with a view of remedying the mischief intended to be prevented by the statutes prohibiting lotteries; and it is said: "Every lottery has the characteristics of a wager or bet, although every bet is not a lottery."

It may be safely asserted, as the result of the adjudged cases, that the species of lottery the carrying on of which is intended to be prohibited as criminal by the various laws of this country embraces only schemes in which a valuable consideration of some kind is paid, directly or indirectly, for the chance to draw a prize: *United States* v. *Olney*, 1 Deady, 461; 1 Abb. 275; *Governor* v. *American Art Union*, 7 N. Y. 228; *Ehrgott* v. *Mayor*, 96 N. Y. 264; 48 Am. Rep. 622; *Bell* v. *State*, 5 Sneed, 507; *Commonwealth* v. *Thacher*, 97 Mass. 583; 93 Am. Dec. 125.

There is no law which prohibits the gratuitous distribution

of one's property by lot or chance. If the distribution is a
pure gift or bounty, and not in name or pretense merely,
which is designed to evade the law,—if it be entirely unsupported by any valuable consideration moving from the taker,
—there is nothing in this mode of conferring it which is vio-
lative of the policy of our statutes condemning lotteries or
gaming. We may go further, and say, that there would seem
to be nothing contrary to public policy, or *per se* morally
wrong, in the determination of rights by lot. A member of
the college of Christian Apostles, as sacred history informs us,
was once chosen by lot. And under the law of this state, a
tie vote on a contested election of any state officer is required
to be settled in the same mode. So our statutes authorize a
distribution of property owned by joint tenants to be made by
lot, under the direction of the judge of probate.

These are not the evils against which the law is directed.
The gratuitous distribution of money or property by lot has
never prevailed to such extent as to require police regulation
at the hands of the state, nor, so long as human nature remains
as it now is, and has been for so many thousand years, is it
likely ever to be otherwise. The history of lotteries for the
past three centuries in England, and for nearly a hundred
years in America, shows that they have been schemes for the
distribution of money or property by lot, in which chances
were sold for money, either directly or through some cunning
device. The evil following from them has been the cultivation
of the gambling spirit,—the hazarding of money with the
hope, by chance, of obtaining a larger sum, often stimulating
an inordinate love of gain, arousing the most violent passions
of one's baser nature, sometimes tempting the gambler to risk
all he possesses on the turn of a single card or cast of a single
die, and "tending, as centuries of human experience now fully
attest, to mendicancy and idleness on the one hand, and moral
profligacy and debauchery on the other": *Johnson* v. *State*, 83
Ala. 65. It is in the light of these facts, and the mischief
thus intended to be remedied, that we must construe our statutory and constitutional prohibitions against lotteries, and devices in the nature of lotteries: *Ehrgott* v. *Mayor*, 48 Am. Rep.
622.

The cases on this subject are very numerous, and while the
courts have shown a general disposition to bring within the
term "lottery" every species of gaming involving a distribution of prizes by lot or chance, and which comes within the

mischief to be remedied,—regarding always the substance and not the semblance of things, so as to prevent evasions of the law,—we find no decision in which the element of a valuable consideration parted with, directly or indirectly, by the purchaser of a chance, does not enter into the transaction: *Buckalew* v. *State*, 62 Ala. 334; *State* v. *Bryant*, 74 N. C. 207; *Commonwealth* v. *Wright*, 137 Mass. 250; 50 Am. Rep. 306; *State* v. *Clarke*, 33 N. H. 329; 66 Am. Dec. 723; *State* v. *Shorts*, 32 N. J. L. 398; 90 Am. Dec. 668; *Wilkinson* v. *Gill*, 74 N. Y. 63; 30 Am. Rep. 264; *Governor* v. *American Art Union*, 7 N. Y. 228; *State* v. *Mumford*, 73 Mo. 647; 39 Am. Rep. 532; *Hull* v. *Ruggles*, 56 N. Y. 424; *Thomas* v. *People*, 59 Ind. 160; *Dunn* v. *People*, 40 Ill. 465; *Seidenbender* v. *Charles*, 4 Serg. & R. 151; 8 Am. Dec. 682; *United States* v. *Olney*, 1 Deady, 461; *Bell* v. *State*, 5 Sneed, 507; Bishop on Statutory Crimes, 2d ed., sec. 952; 2 Wharton's Crim. Law, 9th ed., sec. 1491.

In this case, it is not denied that the defendant has distributed presents or prizes to the holders of tickets given to the public,—eight prizes among some eight thousand ticket holders. It is also uncontroverted that this distribution has been made by lot or chance. This was done by two children chosen from the audience, who selected, by lot, eight tickets from a large number of duplicates, which were thrown by the defendant at random on the stage or platform. These tickets were numbered, and the persons holding the corresponding numbers were entitled to these prizes, or presents, according to their number.

But we can see nothing in the evidence from which it can be inferred that any one, present or absent, paid any valuable consideration, directly or indirectly, for these tickets, or for the chance of getting a prize. It is true that, on the day of the drawing, the defendant has held one of his customary performances, consisting of acrobatic· contortions, exhibitions of magic-lantern, and of music, dancing, and song, and the like, and between the acts he always sold his medicines, for which he claimed great curative virtues. These exhibitions were in a tent which would seat between nine hundred and one thousand people, and would furnish standing-room for about two thousand five hundred persons. For tickets of admission to see this performance,—the closing one of the season, advertised as a "jubilee performance,"—a charge of ten cents was made. But these tickets had no connection whatever with those entitling the holders to a chance for the eight prizes. For these latter tickets, or chances, nothing was charged. They had been distributed free, to any and all persons present at his previous performances, and for admission to these exhibitions no charge was made. The only fee charged was for the occupancy of a seat; there was none for entrance. Nor was it necessary that a holder of a successful ticket should be present to get his prize, in case he drew one. It would be delivered as well at the defendant's private house. This fact was advertised in a Mobile paper, and one of the prizes was actually delivered there. The suspicion, even though well founded, that these presents may have been given away in order to induce a large crowd to assemble at the defendant's performances, with the expectation that they would buy medicines, or pay a fee for occupying a seat in the tent, would be too remote to constitute a legal consideration for the tickets. So with the expectation that it would increase the attendance at the so-called "jubilee" performance. The holders of thousands of these tickets, given away as gratuitous, were not present, and yet stood an equal chance in the distribution as those who were. And the doors were thrown open for free admission when the distribution took place, this event occurring just after the close of the exhibition, or performance proper.

The element of gaming, which is wanting to constitute this transaction a lottery, is the fact that no money was paid, directly or indirectly, for the chance of receiving a prize, or of participating in the distribution by lot. Nor would a jury be authorized to make a contrary inference reasonably from any evidence contained in the bill of exceptions.

Many rulings of the court are directly opposed to these views. It follows from what we have said that the city court erred in not giving the general affirmative charge requested by the defendant.

The judgment of conviction is reversed, and a judgment will be rendered in this court discharging the defendant from further prosecution under the present indictment.

Reversed and rendered.

———

LOTTERY, WHAT IS. — The generally accepted definition of a lottery is, that it is a scheme for the distribution of prizes, and for the obtaining of money or goods by chance: *People* v. *Noelke*, 94 N. Y. 137; 46 Am. Rep. 128; *Randle* v. *State*, 42 Tex. 580; *Rolfe* v. *Dalmar*, 7 Robt. 80; *Commonwealth* v. *Sheriff*, 10 Phila. 203. It has otherwise been defined to be a game of hazard, in which small sums are ventured for the chance of obtaining greater. Payment of prizes in money is not essential: *Fleming* v. *Bills*, 3 Or. 286; *Bell* v. *State*, 5 Sneed, 507. In the late case of *People* v. *Elliott*, 74 Mich. 264, *post*, this vol., it is said that "a lottery is a scheme by which a result is reached by some action or means taken, and in which result man's choice or will has no part, nor can human reason, foresight, sagacity, or design enable him to know or determine such result until the same has been accomplished. . . . . It is not the drawing of the lots, but the disposing and selling the chances, that brings the case within the statute. It is promoting the lottery for money by paying the money for the chance of receiving more. It is of little consequence where the drawing takes place." A game in which a price is paid for the chance of a prize, and in which it purports to be determined by chance whether the one who has paid the money should have the prize or nothing, is a lottery: *Commonwealth* v. *Sullivan*, 146 Mass. 142. Lottery, in its popular acceptation, is a distribution of prizes by lot or chance; and when chances are sold, and the distribution of prizes determined by lot, this constitutes a lottery: *Buckalew* v. *State*, 62 Ala. 334; *Solomon* v. *State*, 28 Id. 83. Any scheme whereby one, on paying money or other valuable things to another, becomes entitled to receive from him such a return in value, or nothing, as some formula of chance may determine, is a lottery: *State* v. *Kaub*, 15 Mo. App. 433–436. The authorities are generally agreed that, in order to constitute the scheme a lottery, a valuable consideration must be paid for the chance of obtaining a prize.

In discussing this question in *State* v. *Overton*, 16 Nev. 136, Hawley, J., said: "What is a lottery? Every scheme for the distribution of prizes by chance is a lottery: *Governors* v. *American Art Union*, 7 N. Y. 239; *Dunn* v. *People*, 40 Ill. 467; *State* v. *Shorts*, 32 N. J. L. 401; 90 Am. Dec. 668; *Randle* v. *State*, 42 Tex. 585; *Chavannah* v. *State*, 49 Ala. 396; *Commonwealth* v. *Mannerfield*, 8 Phila. 459; *United States* v. *Olney*, 1 Abb. 279. A lottery is a game of hazard in which small sums are ventured for the chance of obtaining greater: *Bell* v. *State*, 5 Sneed, 507. 'A contrivance for the distribution of prizes by chance; a reliance upon the result of hazard; a decision of the adventurer's investment of the favors of a fortune,'—is a lottery: *Wooden* v. *Shotwell*, 23 N. J. L. 465; 24 Id. 789. 'Where a pecuniary consideration is paid, and it is determined by lot or chance, according to some scheme held out to the public what the party who pays the money is to have for it, or whether he is to have anything, it is a lottery': *State* v. *Clarke*, 33 N. H. 335; 66 Am. Dec. 723; *Hull* v. *Ruggles*, 56 N. Y. 424, 427. If a tract of land is divided into lots of unequal value, and the lots sold to different purchasers at a uniform price, and are distributed amongst those purchasers by drawing or lot, this transaction is a lottery: *Seidenbender* v. *Charles*, 4 Serg. & R. 160; 8 Am. Dec. 682; *Ridgeway* v. *Wood*, 4 Wash. C. C. 133; *Wooden* v. *Shotwell*, 23 N. J. L. 465; 24 Id. 789; *United States* v. *Olney*, 1 Abb. 278. Where the payment of five dollars by a member of the American Art Union entitled him to a chance of drawing a painting by means of names and numbers drawn from a box, this was held to be a lottery: *Governors* v. *American Art Union*, 7 N. Y. 239, affirming same case, 13 Barb. 577; *People* v. *American Art Union*, 7 N. Y. 240; *Bennett* v. *American Art Union*, 5 Sand. 614. A gift sale of books according to a scheme by which the books are offered for sale at prices above their real value, and by which each purchaser of a book is entitled in addition to a gift or prize, is a lottery: *State* v. *Clarke*, 33 N. H. 335; 66 Am. Dec. 723. In *Dunn* v. *People*, 40 Ill. 467, the defendant was conducting a 'gift-sale' establishment. He kept upon his desk at his place of business a box filled with envelopes. Each of the envelopes had printed upon its back an advertisement, purporting that the envelope contained some valuable receipts and popular songs, and also a card descriptive of some article 'in an immense stock of over two hundred and fifty thousand pianos, watches, sewing-machines, engravings, sets of jewelry, books, etc., worth one million five hundred thousand dollars, all to be sold for one dollar each, without regard to value, and not to be paid for until you know what you are to receive.' The sale of one of these envelopes was held to be a sale of a lottery ticket. A ticket which purports to entitle the holder to whatever prize may be drawn by its corresponding number, in a scheme called a prize-concert, is a lottery ticket: *Commonwealth* v. *Thacher*, 97 Mass. 583; 93 Am. Dec. 125. A ticket in a 'grand gift concert,' for the benefit of the 'Foundling Asylum of the Sisters of Charity, in the city of New York, and the Soldiers' and Sailors' Orphans' Home of Washington, District Columbia,' stating that the bearer was 'entitled to admission to a grand concert, and to whatever gift may be awarded to its number,' is a lottery ticket: *Negley* v. *Devlin*, 12 Abb. Pr., N. S., 210.

"It makes no difference what name is given to the scheme.

> "'A rose by any other name would smell as sweet';
> A thorn by any other name would prick as deep.

"When the element of chance enters into the distribution of prizes, it is a lottery, without reference to the name by which it is called. 'He may choose to call his business a gift sale,' said the court in *Dunn* v. *People*, *supra;* 'but it is none the less a lottery, and we cannot permit him to evade the penalties of the law by so transparent a device as a mere change of name. If it differs from ordinary lotteries, the difference lies chiefly in the fact that it is more artfully contrived to impose upon the ignorant and credulous, and is therefore more thoroughly dishonest and injurious to society. . . . . The name given to the process and form of machinery used to accomplish the object is not material, provided the substance of the transaction is a distribution and disposition of property by lot': *State* v. *Clarke*, *supra.* 'Courts will not inquire into the name, but will determine the character of the scheme by the nature of the transaction, or business in which the parties are engaged': *Randle* v. *State*, *supra.* 'The character of the scheme is in no wise changed by the charitable purposes expressed in its title, nor by calling the drawings entertainments or gift-concerts': *Ex parte Blanchard*, 9 Nev. 101. 'The fact that no plan of distribution has been determined upon does not relieve the scheme of its character as a lottery': *Thomas* v. *People*, 59 Ill. 163. 'Nor is it material,' said the court of appeals in *Governors* v. *American Art Union*, *supra*, 'to the question in hand that the prizes were not known and designated when the tickets and chances were subscribed and paid for. The scheme in this respect is more objectionable than a scheme in which the prizes are previously fixed, because it affords less security to the subscribers that the chance purchased is worth the-money paid for it.' In *Wooden* v. *Shotwell*, *supra*, the court said: 'The prizes were distributed by lot. The fact that the scheme contained no blanks, but that every adventurer was to receive something for his money, only rendered the device the more successful, and its results consequently the more injurious, without altering its essential character.' In *Dunn* v. *People*, *supra*, the court said: 'Neither would the character of the transaction be changed by assuming that the ticket in every envelope really represents some article of merchandise intrinsically worth the dollar which the holder will be obliged to pay. If every ticket in an ordinary lottery represented a prize of som. val ·, yet if these prizes were of unequal values, the scheme of distribution wo..ld still remain a lottery.'"

The basis of the above discussion in *State* v. *Overton, supra*, was an "act to aid the Nevada Benevolent Association in aiding and providing means for the care and maintenance of the insane of Nevada, and for other charitable purposes," and providing that "it shall be lawful for the Nevada Benevolent Association of the state of Nevada to give not exceeding five public entertainments or concerts, to sell tickets of admission to the same, to distribute among the holders of such tickets personal property, real estate, things in action, demands, or other valuables, and to regulate the distribution of all such property or gifts by raffle or other schemes of like character"; and the court unhesitatingly declared the contrivance a lottery, and the act unconstitutional and void. A scheme for the disposal of town lots, by the terms of which a number of lots are sold and others are reserved to be distributed by lot among the purchasers of the first portion, so that the chance of obtaining one of the reserved or prize lots forms a part of the inducement or consideration for which each purchaser pays the price agreed upon for the lot sold to him, is a lottery: *United States* v. *Olney*, 1 Abb. 275. So where a tract of land is divided into lots of unequal value, and these are sold to purchasers at a uniform price, and are distributed among them by drawings or lot, and a deed given to each purchaser for the lot drawn by him, the scheme is a lottery, and the deed is void and conveys no title: *Wooden* v. *Shotwell*, 23 N. J. L. 465; 24 Id. 789; *Swain* v. *Bussell*, 10 Ind. 438; *Seidenbender* v. *Charles*, 4 Serg. & R. 150; 8 Am. Dec. 682; *Allebach* v. *Godshalk*, 116 Pa. St. 329. In speaking of such a scheme in *Randle* v. *State*, 42 Tex. 580–587, Devine, J., said that "whether the pretext be to dispose of books, money, jewelry, land, or 'lots,' or any species of property, be it real or personal, that the giving of something certain, whether it be a postal-card worth one cent, or a watch worth one hundred dollars, cannot relieve it of the illegal character; neither will the object or pretense that it is in aid of a church, a school, an orphans' home, or any other religious, educational, or charitable object improve its legal *status*. It makes not the slightest difference whether it be styled a 'gift enterprise,' 'book sale,' 'land distribution,' or 'art association,' each and all are lotteries when the element of chance is connected with or enters into the distribution of its prizes."

Where packages of candy are sold, in some of which coupons are placed which are cashed at a counter upon presentation, the drawing of such prize being announced by the sounding of a gong, the scheme is a lottery, and placing the words "No lottery" over the door is immaterial: *Commonwealth* v. *Sheriff*, 10 Phila. 203. A sale of candy in boxes represented to contain, besides the candy, a prize of money or jewelry, each purchaser selecting his box without knowing its contents, is a lottery, and punishable as such: *Holman* v. *State*, 2 Tex. App. 610. The sale of packages of candies at more than value, and known as "prize packages," in some of which are tickets with the name of a piece of silverware upon them entitling the purchaser of a package containing such ticket to the article of silverware named, in addition to the package, is a lottery: *Hull* v. *Ruggles*, 56 N. Y. 424. A sale of small boxes of candy, of trifling value to customers, for the chance of designating one of certain pictures, behind some of which are small sums of money, and behind others a card on which is the letter "C," the purchaser getting either the money or the card, according to his selection, but getting another box of candy if he selected a card, is a lottery: *State* v. *Lumsden*, 89 N. C. 572. This case defines a lottery to be "a scheme, device, or game of hazard, whereby, for a smaller sum of money, or other thing of value, the person dealing therein, by chance or hazard or contingency, may or may not get money or other thing of value, of greater or less value, or in some cases of no value at all, from the owners or managers of such lottery." Where a merchant, in order to increase the sale of his goods, gives to each purchaser a ticket which entitles him to a chance to draw one of several prizes mentioned in an advertised distribution of prizes to be made by the merchant, the scheme is a lottery, whether the prize distribution is ever made or not: *Montana* v. *Harris*, 8 Mont. 140. A sale of slips of paper having characters which represent the purchaser's title to a prize which may fall to such characters then intended to be drawn is a lottery, and it is not necessary to the completion of the offense that the lottery be "regular," or that any lottery be actually drawn, as there is no such thing as a "regular" lottery of which judicial cognizance must be taken: *State* v. *Hindman*,   4 Mo. App. 582. Where ten cents are charged for the privilege of designating three numbers among a large number of other numbers, and the person paying the fee is entitled to forty-six cents if two of the numbers designated are drawn, or nothing if two of them are not drawn, the scheme is a lottery: *Trout* v. *State*, 111 Ind. 499; *Watson* v. *State*, 111 Id. 599. So the sale of a slip of paper having certain numbers which represent the purchaser's title to a prize which may be drawn by such numbers in a game of chance is a lottery: *Wilkinson* v. *Gill*, 74 N. Y. 63; 30 Am. Rep. 264; *Smith* v. *State*, 68 Md. 168; *State* v. *Rothschild*, 19 Mo. App. 137; *State* v. *Russell*, 17 Id. 16; *State* v. *Sellner*, 17 Id. 39; *State* v. *Bruner*, 17 Id. 274. Where tickets headed "Horse combination," and indorsed, "Decided to be legal by the highest tribunal in the state of Maryland," the purchaser paying nine cents for a chance of winning three dollars and sixty cents, the scheme is a lottery. In this case, it was insisted that the contrivance was betting on a horse-race, and not a lottery, but the court said: "If the heading and indorsement was stricken from these tickets, they would represent lottery tickets, or, what is the same thing, policy tickets. The real and only question presented to us is, whether the appellant can legalize an illegal act by calling it by another name, and that all the courts of justice in the land are bound to regard the act itself what he may choose to call it. If such be the law, the courts of criminal jurisdiction may as well be closed": *Boyland* v. *State*, 69 Md. 511. Where one chooses a number and pays a certain sum, and the seller draws an envelope from a box full containing a slip with many numbers upon it, and if the number chosen is on the slip, the buyer receives a multiple of the sum paid, greater or less according to agreement, and if not, he loses what he has paid, the contrivance is a lottery: *Commonwealth* v. *Wright*, 137 Mass. 250; 50 Am. Rep. 306; *Commonwealth* v. *Sullivan*, 146 Mass. 142.

A scheme is none the less a lottery because it promises a prize to each ticket holder, the prizes to be drawn being of different values, nor because the prizes are called presents in the prospectus, nor because the tickets consist of receipts for subscriptions to a newspaper, but numbered to compare with the numbers upon the articles to be distributed. The court said: "It is denied that the paper indicates a game of chance. It is contended that the word 'chance' in the paper means opportunity. We do not concur in this interpretation. It is conceded that the careless reader might see in the advertisement a game of chance; but that would be so only because the meaning would be there to be seen. In such case the reader gets the author's real meaning, which must be the same for all persons. However disguised by indirect or deceptive expression, the paper, as a whole, discloses a lottery. If it were not, readers would not become buyers. It informs its patrons that every subscriber is sure to get a present, and the presents are of various values. Assurance is given that the presents will be 'awarded fairly.' How can presents of unequal value be awarded fairly, unless by some lot or chance? A purchaser or subscriber receives for his money a 'numbered receipt.' What can be the purpose of numbers if all numbers are favored alike? Each number will take a 'prize,' and has a 'chance to win' a very valuable one. Of course all cannot win the highest prize or present. It is not an opportunity to win so much as it is an opportunity of a chance to win. It is not an easy thing for a notice to have the effect of advertising vice to one and virtue to another ": *State* v. *Willis*, 78 Me. 70. So where the proprietors of a newspaper offer as an inducement to subscription and gratuitously give away to every new subscriber a ticket entitling him to participate in a distribution of prizes to be made by lot, the scheme is a lottery. The subscription price of the paper, "when paid by the subscriber, entitled him to a copy of the paper, and also to a ticket, which might draw a prize (as, for instance, a piano) worth a hundred-fold more than the subscription price to the paper. The drawing of such a prize under the scheme was within the range of probabilities, and doubtless many subscriptions for the paper were made and induced solely by the consideration that the person subscribing would be entitled to a ticket which might bring him some one of the many valuable prizes to be disposed of in the drawing. The fact that the subscription price of the Times was not increased does not alter the character of the scheme, inasmuch as the price paid entitled the subscriber to a ticket in the lottery as well as to a copy of the paper. The facts agreed upon, we think, brings the case clearly within the statute upon which the indictment is framed, and make the defendant amenable to the penalty therein prescribed ": *State* v. *Mumford*, 73 Mo. 647; 39 Am. Rep. 532.

A scheme called a "gift enterprise," and so licensed, where small cards are sold with certain numbers on them, and there is also a box kept containing a certain number of envelopes, each containing a card with a number upon it, the party buying a card being permitted to draw from the box and envelope, and if the number on the card therein corresponds with the numbers on the card purchased, the purchaser to get ten times the amount of his investment, is a lottery: *State* v. *Bryant*, 74 N. C. 207. Where the proprietors of a public exhibition advertised to give away, at their performance, a large number of valuable presents to the spectators, the proprietor to appear upon the stage and call out numbers at random, and the person who held the ticket which corresponded with it to be given any of the prizes which the proprietor might select, is a lottery, and it makes no difference that the proprietor reserved the right to refuse to make any distribution at all, or to refuse to give a prize to any one whose personal appearance did not suit him: *State* v. *Shorts*, 32 N. J. L. 398; 90 Am. Dec. 668.

The fact that no plan of distribution in such a scheme had been determined upon at the time of the sale of the ticket does not relieve it of its character of a lottery, when it is apparent that some of the purchasers of tickets would fail to get a prize, though the entertainment may have been worth the price of a ticket: *Thomas* v. *People*, 59 Ill. 160.

A scheme adopted and put in force by an incorporated association, by which the holder of a certificate therein may have a fair chance to have awarded to him, by the casting of lots or by chance, in such way as the by-laws of the association may direct, any of the articles subject to distribution according to his certificate, provided such award or allotment be fairly made in public, after advertisement, as required by the charter, of the articles subject to distribution, by casting lots, by chance, or other mode mentioned, with the value of each article in money annexed, is a lottery: *Boyd* v. *State*, 61 Ala. 177; *Tuscaloosa etc. Art Ass'n* v. *State*, 58 Id. 55. "Auction pools," "French pools," and "combination pools" upon horse-races are lotteries: *State* v. *Lovell*, 39 N. J. L. 458. The publication of an offer of a gold watch to the person buying goods at a store to a certain amount, and guessing nearest the number of beans in a glass globe, is an advertisement of a lottery: *Huddleson* v. *State*, 94 Ind. 426; 48 Am. Rep. 171.

In an early case in South Carolina, the court declared that a raffle of watches or other articles was not a lottery: *State* v. *Pinchback*, 2 Mill Const. 128. And where a government, in order to obtain a loan, issues bonds for principal and interest, and a prize or premium, which the holder of a bond may become entitled to under a drawing to be had as provided in the bond, to the effect that certain of the bonds shall become payable each year, to ascertain which are so payable a drawing shall be had, and that the bonds bearing the numbers drawn shall become due and payable, and that the holders of the bonds corresponding with the first forty numbers drawn are entitled to premiums of larger or smaller amounts, the scheme is not a lottery: *Ex parte Shobert*, 70 Cal. 632; *Kohn* v. *Koehler*, 96 N. Y. 362; 48 Am. Rep. 628. When money is put upon a round board in equal amounts by several persons, each in turn whirling a hand made fast in the center, the one so whirling who makes the hand register the greatest number on the rim of the board taking all the money thereon, the owner of the board sometimes putting up money, and at other times charging a sum, to be paid by the winner, for the use of the board, the contrivance and operation of the scheme is not a lottery: *Buckalew* v. *State*, 62 Ala. 334.

BARNES *v.* STATE.

[88 ALABAMA, 204.]

CRIMINAL LAW — RAPE — EVIDENCE. — In a prosecution for rape, declarations made by the accused three months before the commission of the crime, tending to show his desire to have carnal knowledge of the prosecutrix, as well as his belief that she would not yield to his wishes, are relevant, as affording the jury a basis for inferring that he had gratified his passion in the manner charged in the indictment.

CRIMINAL LAW — RAPE — EVIDENCE. — Defendant in rape is entitled to prove prior acts of undue intimacy between himself and the prosecutrix to raise the presumption of consent; but he cannot prove jealousy on the part of the husband of the prosecutrix against her and the accused as an incentive for the prosecution.

CRIMINAL LAW — RAPE — EVIDENCE. — In a prosecution for rape, a witness cannot testify to the effect that the place, which he supposed or had been informed was the scene of the alleged offense, showed nothing to indicate a struggle, when the place described by him was in no way identified as that at which the crime had been committed.

WITNESS. — EXCLUSION OF WITNESSES, or of any particular witness, from the court-room during the trial is within the discretion of the trial court, and cannot be reviewed on appeal.

CRIMINAL LAW — RAPE — EVIDENCE. — In prosecutions for rape, the evidence of the husband of the prosecutrix of complaint made by his wife to him regarding the offense, and to the circumstances under which such complaint was made, is admissible.

INDICTMENT and conviction of rape, committed on August 23, 1888. One Adams testified that in the May preceding the crime, the accused said to him that "Adeline Ballard was a nice-looking woman, and he guessed she had a good ——, but he did not suppose there was any chance for him to get any of it." The other facts are stated in the opinion.

NeSmith and Sanford, for the appellant.

William L. Martin, attorney-general, for the state.

McCLELLAN, J. The testimony of the witness Sid Adams was properly admitted. It tended to show the desire of the defendant to have carnal knowledge of the prosecutrix, as well as his belief that she would not yield to his wishes; and it was relevant as affording the jury a basis for the inference that he had gratified his passion in the manner charged in the indictment. Such evidence, of itself, is entitled to little weight, especially when the declarations deposed to were made a great length of time before the alleged offense; but the mere lapse of time will not render them incompetent. Thus on a trial for murder it was held to be proper to prove that the defendant, two or three years before the homicide, had said of the deceased: "There is a man I cannot get along with": *Evans v. State,* 62 Ala. 6; 2 Taylor on Evidence, sec. 1209. Evidence of the defendant's carnal passion for the prosecutrix, on a charge of rape, is strictly analogous to unfriendliness and hostility in a prosecution for murder. In the latter case, declarations of hostility, not amounting to threats, made at any time prior to the offense, are clearly admissible: *Hudson v. State,* 61 Ala. 333; *Johnson v. State,* 87 Ala. 39.

The defendant was, of course, entitled to prove prior acts of undue intimacy between himself and the prosecutrix, as furnishing a predicate for the presumption of consent on the occasion of the alleged crime; and we do not understand that the court below denied him this right in any degree. Evidence that the husband of the prosecutrix "was jealous of her," or "jealous of her and the defendant," and objected to her being with the defendant, or with the witness Stewart, in its strongest aspect for the defense, could only show that he suspected her of improper conduct or undue intimacy with those parties; and we are unable to conceive a case which would authorize the proof or disproof of a material fact by evidence of the mere conjecture or suspicion of its existence.

There was no error in excluding the testimony of the witness McCarver, to the effect that the place which he supposed or had been informed was the scene of the alleged offense disclosed nothing to indicate a struggle. The locality described by him was in no way identified as that at which the crime had been committed.

It is the settled doctrine of this court that the discretion of the presiding judge as to the exclusion of witnesses, or any particular witness, from the court-room during the progress of the trial, is not revisable: *McGuff* v. *State*, 88 Ala. 147; *ante,* p. 25, and cases cited.

The evidence of the husband of the prosecutrix, as to the fact that his wife made complaint to him in regard to the alleged offense, and as to the circumstances under which the complaint was made, was clearly competent: *Leoni* v. *State*, 44 Ala. 110; *Lacy* v. *State*, 45 Ala. 80; *Griffin* v. *State,* 76 Ala. 29; *Barnett* v. *State*, 83 Ala. 40.

We discover no error in the record, and the judgment of the circuit court must be affirmed.

TRIAL — EXCLUSION OF WITNESSES — DISCRETION OF TRIAL COURT. — The refusal of the court to put a witness under the rule is a matter of discretion, not reviewable in the appellate court: *McGuff* v. *State*, 88 Ala. 147; *ante,* p. 25.

RAPE — ADMISSIBILITY OF STATEMENTS OF PROSECUTRIX: See note to *Smith* v. *State*, 80 Am. Dec. 371, 372. That the party injured made complaint while the injury was recent may be proved, but the details of the perpetration of the crime cannot be shown by her statements: *Parker* v. *State*, 69 Md. 329; 1 Am. St. Rep. 387, and cases cited in note 389. As to the effect of a delay, on the part of the ravished woman, in making complaint: *People* v. *Gage*, 62 Mich. 271; 4 Am. St. Rep. 854. But nothing is better settled than the rule that in prosecutions for rape, the fact that prosecutrix made complaint soon after the perpetration of the crime is admissible in corroboration of her testimony: *State* v. *Reid*, 39 Minn. 277; *People* v. *Snyder*, 75 Cal. 323; *Barnett* v. *State*, 83 Ala. 40; *Bean* v. *People*, 124 Ill. 576. In the case of *Allen* v. *State*, 87 Ala. 107, where the mother of the prosecutrix testified that her daughter had complained to her immediately after the commission of the offense, it was decided that defendant might elicit the particulars of such complaint.

HALL *v.* STATE.

[88 ALABAMA, 236.]

PLEADING AND PRACTICE — CHARGE DIRECTING VERDICT. — A charge assuming a fact as proved, when the evidence only tends to establish it, invades the province of the jury, and is erroneous. Thus to direct the jury that "the fact that a married man makes frequent visits in the daytime, and sometimes at night, to the house of a woman of known bad reputation for virtue, without any legitimate business, is a fact tending to show an adulterous connection between them," is error, when the evidence on this point is negative only, and does not exclude a contrary inference.

CRIMINAL LAW. — INSTRUCTIONS AS TO LIVING IN ADULTERY, that if the jurors believe, beyond a reasonable doubt, that the defendants had sexual intercourse with each other just before the finding of the indictment, this is sufficient proof of adultery or fornication, and if, in addition to this one act, they believe, beyond a reasonable doubt, from the evidence, that the minds of the parties agreed or consented that they would repeat the act, opportunity permitting and offering, then the parties are guilty of living in adultery and fornication, though held proper in *Bodiford* v. *State,* 86 Ala. 67, 11 Am. St. Rep. 20, is now believed to be incorrect and erroneous, though the question is not decided.

INDICTMENT against Nathan Hall, a married man, and Betsy Skipper, an unmarried woman, for living together in a state of adultery and fornication. The opinion and *syllabus, supra,* state the facts.

W. D. Roberts, for the appellants.

William L. Martin, attorney-general, for the state.

McCLELLAN, J. That part of the general charge to which an exception was reserved should not have been given. It is abstract, in a sense, and misleading, in that it assumes as a fact that the defendant Hall had no legitimate business at the house of the defendant Skipper, when the evidence on this point was wholly negative in its character, and did not exclude a contrary inference. The charge, moreover, was upon the effect of this negative testimony, and directed the jury to consider the fact of Hall's having no legitimate business at Skipper's house as tending to show adulterous intercourse, when, in view of the character of the testimony on that point, they might have inferred the non-existence of the fact itself. The right to draw this inference was, in substance, denied to the jury, and for this error the judgment must be reversed: *Burney* v. *State,* 87 Ala. 80. The charge, in other words, assumes a fact as proved, when the evidence only tends to establish it, and is an invasion of the province of the jury: *Jones* v. *Fort,* 36 Ala. 444.

The charge given at the instance of the solicitor appears to be in the language of an instruction held to be proper in the case of *Bodiford* v. *State,* 86 Ala. 67; 11 Am. St. Rep. 20. We are all now inclined to the opinion that it is not a correct exposition of the law; but as the present case must be reversed on the other point adverted to, we deem it unnecessary to decide this question.

The judgment of the circuit court is reversed, and the cause remanded.

———   •

LIVING IN ADULTERY. — As to what constitutes the crime of "living together" in adultery, see *Bird* v. *State,* 27 Tex. App. 635; 11 Am. St. Rep. 214, and note; *Smith* v. *State,* 86 Ala. 57; 11 Am. St. Rep. 17; *Bodiford* v. *State,* 86 Ala. 67; 11 Am. St. Rep. 20, and note; *State* v. *Carroll,* 30 S. C. 85; 14 Am. St. Rep. 883.

PROPER SUBJECTS OF INSTRUCTIONS TO JURIES, and to what extent the court may comment upon the evidence: Note to *State* v. *Whit,* 72 Am. Deo 538–549.

———————

PARKER *v.* PARKER.

[88 ALABAMA, 362.]

EQUITY — REFORMATION OF DEED CONVEYING HOMESTEAD. — Equity will correct a misdescription in a deed made by mutual mistake, and executed by husband and wife, conveying land held by them as tenants in common, and constituting part of their homestead, when it appears that the purchaser paid full value and the conveyance was sufficient to pass the wife's interest, though she was ignorant of the fact that she was a part owner of the land conveyed.

L. L. Dean, and Smith and Lowe, for the appellants.

Weaver and Selheimer, for the appellee.

McCLELLAN, J. The misdescription in the deed of Martin and Elizabeth Parker to John D. Parker, to correct which this bill is filed, is substantially admitted, and, moreover, clearly proved. The land which was intended to be conveyed, and which the deed as corrected by the decree below does convey, was held as tenants in common by the grantors, who were husband and wife, and constituted a part of their homestead. The resistance to the reformation prayed for is predicated chiefly, if not entirely, on the homestead character and common ownership of the property, in connection with the fact that, at the time of the execution of the deed, none of the parties knew that Elizabeth Parker owned an undivided one-half interest in the land. So far as the contention of the appellants proceeds upon the idea that a reformation in matter of description of the wife's conveyance of the homestead will not be decreed, it is wholly untenable. The point, upon exhaustive consideration, has been otherwise determined by this court; and the same principles which underlie the conclusion then reached, with respect to the homestead, force a like conclusion in regard to the correction of the misdescription in a conveyance by husband and wife of the latter's statutory separate estate. We entertain no doubt of the jurisdiction of equity to reform an instrument of the class last mentioned, so as to make it speak the true intention of the parties in the identification of the property: *Gardner* v. *Moore*, 75 Ala. 394; 51 Am. Rep. 454.

The deed involved here was executed with all the formalities essential to a valid conveyance of the homestead, and of any individual interest which the wife may have held in the land as her statutory separate estate. The purpose of it, as the proof, aside from the instrument itself, clearly shows, was to pass the entire fee to the grantee. The consideration paid was commensurate with the value of the whole estate. We know of no rule of law, nor can we conceive any logic of facts, which would support the distinction which is urged upon us, between the effect to be given to a conveyance by the wife of separate estate, made in ignorance of her property rights, and a conveyance by one *sui juris* under the same circumstances. A grantor, whether of the one class or the other, would, we have no doubt, be conclusively held to a knowledge of the true state of the title under which he or she held, and to have conveyed with reference to that title. But were this otherwise, the result of this case would not be affected thereby. It is immaterial here whether the wife's ignorance of her separate statutory interest in the land intended to be conveyed would operate to defeat the deed to the extent of that interest.

The office of the remedy invoked in this case is, not to establish and effectuate rights, — not to have the effect of the deed adjudged, — but rather to declare the *status* which the parties intended to create, and upon which such rights as they would have acquired under a correct instrument may be asserted and defended. The real question is, not what the deed was intended to mean, or how it was intended to operate, but what it was intended to be: Kerr on Fraud and Mistake, 428; 3 Pomeroy's Eq. Jur., sec. 1375; *Connor* v. *Armstrong*, 86 Ala. 265. And while equity will not decree a vain and useless thing, and consequently will not a reform a deed which when corrected will be wholly inoperative, yet the relief will be granted with respect to misdescription of property, upon clear proof of mutual mistake, whenever the reformed instrument will operate to pass any estate in the land intended to be conveyed, though, by reason of facts not apparent on the face of the paper, such estate is less in quantity, or a different kind, than that which would otherwise have passed. It is therefore immaterial whether Elizabeth Parker's undivided half-interest in the land will pass by the deed as corrected. In any view, the conveyance is efficient to vest the interest of Martin Parker in the grantee, and he is entitled to relief, when he comes into equity and asks that his deed be so corrected, in consonance with the intent of all parties, as that he may protect his rights in and to that interest.

It is very clear, from this record, that no injury resulted to the appellants from the failure of the court to allow them further time to answer the amendments of the bill, made on the day of the final decree; and if this failure, in the absence of a motion or request for further time, was erroneous, — and we do not decide that it was, — it will not authorize a reversal.

The decree of the city court is affirmed.

REFORMATION OF DEEDS. — Deeds may be reformed in equity for mistakes made in reducing to writing the true agreement entered into by and between the parties: *Finlayson* v. *Finlayson*, 17 Or. 347; 11 Am. St. Rep. 836, and note 844, 845. But evidence to reform a deed for mistake must be clear, positive, and convincing: *Turner* v. *Shaw*, 96 Mo. 22; 9 Am. St. Rep. 319, and note. In *Parker* v. *Parker*, 88 Ala. 365, the reformation of a conveyance, executed by a husband and wife, was decreed, upon the authority of the principal case, because of a mistake in the description of the realty sought to be conveyed.

ALEXANDER *v.* HILL.

[88 ALABAMA, 487.]

MORTGAGES — PURCHASE BY MORGAGEE UNDER POWER — LIMITATIONS AS AGAINST INFANT HEIRS. — A purchase by a mortgagee at his own sale, under a power in the mortgage not authorizing him to purchase, gives the mortgagor an option in ordinary cases, if expressed in two years from the time of sale, of affirming or disaffirming it, and on disaffirming, to redeem. This limitation is judicial, and will be extended to infant heirs of the mortgagor, he being dead when the sale was made, so as to allow them two years after attaining majority to disaffirm the sale, provided the period is not extended beyond twenty years from the date thereof.

MORTGAGES — PURCHASE BY MORTGAGEE UNDER POWER — RIGHT TO COMPEL ELECTION. — A mortgagee who purchases at his own sale, under a power in the mortgage not authorizing him to purchase, gives the mortgagor an option to affirm or disaffirm the sale within two years thereafter, and if he disaffirms, to redeem; but the mortgagee may, by bill filed against the person having such option, whether he is *sui juris* or not, compel an election and foreclosure, if the sale is disaffirmed.

MORTGAGES — PURCHASE BY MORTGAGEE AT HIS OWN SALE UNDER POWER — RIGHT TO REDEEM. — A purchase by a mortgagee at his own sale, under a power in the mortgage not authorizing him to purchase, gives the mortgagor an option to affirm or disaffirm the sale within two years thereafter, and if he disaffirms, to redeem. This is a judicial limitation, and will not be extended in favor of infants, who succeed to the right of one who, at the time of the sale, is free from disability, and entitled to affirm or disaffirm.

BILL by the infant heirs of a mortgagor to cancel a purchase made by the mortgagee at his own sale, under a power in the mortgage not authorizing him to purchase. The bill alleges that the mortgagor was dead at the time such sale was made, and prays that it be vacated and redemption allowed.

W. D. Bulger, for the appellants.

Hewitt, Walker, and Porter, for the appellee.

McCLELLAN, J. The purchase by a mortgagee at his own sale, under a power which did not authorize him to become the purchaser, "arms the mortgagor with the option, if expressed in a reasonable time, of affirming or disaffirming the sale"; and if he elects to disaffirm, he is entitled to redeem the land so sold from the mortgagee: *Garland* v. *Watson*, 74 Ala. 324; *Harris* v. *Miller*, 71 Ala. 26; *Ezzell* v. *Watson*, 83 Ala. 120; *Knox* v. *Armistead*, 87 Ala. 511; 13 Am. St. Rep. 65.

What is a reasonable time within which to thus disaffirm such sale must ordinarily be availed of has, by analogy to the statute giving that period to redeem after a valid foreclosure,

been held to be two years from the date of sale: *Comer v.
Sheehan*, 74 Ala. 452; *Ezzell* v. *Watson*, 83 Ala. 120.

Whether the fact that the party upon whom the right to
disaffirm has devolved is an infant should extend the time
within which the sale may be avoided, — that is, would make
such an extraordinary case as would not fall within the rule
limiting the exercise of the option to two years, — has never
been decided by this court.   The second head-note in the case
of *Mewburn's Heirs* v. *Bass*, 82 Ala. 622, stating that the exception in favor of infants, contained in the statute of limitations, did not apply to such a case, is not supported by the
opinion; and moreover, the question was not involved in that
case.   Neither the statute of limitations, nor any exceptions
provided for therein, have any bearing on the question.   The
limitation of two years within which sales of the class under
consideration must ordinarily be disaffirmed is not a statutory, but a judicial, limitation; it is not the result of legislative mandate, but of judicial opinion, that such period is
usually a reasonable time for the exercise of the option of
affirmance or disaffirmance with which a purchase by the
mortgagee at his own sale arms the mortgagor.   The basis of
the doctrine is laches, and not staleness of demand.   The sale
cuts off the equity of redemption, as long as it is permitted to
stand, but leaves in the mortgagor and those claiming under
him the right to disaffirm it, and the consequent right to redeem upon such disaffirmance.   But the law requires diligence of the mortgagor in the assertion of this right, and, in
the absence of special circumstances, holds him to have
waived the right, and to have affirmed the sale, unless he
elects to the contrary within two years.   The whole theory of
the limitation, therefore, rests on the presumption of ratification after the lapse of two years "in ordinary cases."   In
extraordinary cases, cases involving peculiar circumstances,
which rebut the presumption, it will not be indulged.

Instances may be readily imagined in which, for a want of
knowledge on the part of the mortgagor, that the mortgagee
was the purchaser at his own sale, he could not be held to a
ratification within two years; for it would be anomalous to a
degree to hold him estopped by his non-action with respect to
a state of facts, of the existence of which he was, without fault,
wholly ignorant.   And so, too, in cases in which the peculiar
exigency is the legal capacity of the mortgagor, or those standing in his right, not only to know the facts, but also to act

upon them if known, it is manifest the presumption of ratification cannot be indulged. This class of cases embraces all persons not *sui juris*; as infants, idiots, lunatics. Should an infant or an idiot or a lunatic be held to know that a mortgagee of his lands has purchased at a sale under a power which did not authorize him to purchase, and be chargeable with laches, if he fails for two years to repudiate the transaction? Can a person not *sui juris*, wholly incapable of making or ratifying any contract, with certain exceptions based on principles having no application to contracts of this character, be held to be a binding and legal affirmance of a voidable act of his mortgagee, and this solely on the ground that he, although legally incapable of exercising the option to affirm, has failed for two years to disaffirm the sale? We do not think so. We can conceive no state of facts which would authorize the presumption from mere lapse of time, short of twenty years, that a person not *sui juris* had ratified and affirmed a sale made under the circumstances shown in the present bill. Before such presumption can be admitted, before the "ordinary case," referred to in our adjudications, is made out, it must appear that the person who has the option to affirm or disaffirm must for two years have been cognizant of the facts from which the option springs, and for a like period legally competent to make a binding election. This doctrine would allow infants two years after they attained full age to disaffirm such a sale, provided always that the period was not extended beyond twenty years from the date of sale.

This rule may work a hardship on mortgagees; but, after all, the hardship results from their own unauthorized acts, and not from the law. Moreover, we entertain no doubt of the right of the mortgagee, who has thus purchased at his own sale, to come into a court of equity at any time, by bill filed against the persons having the option of affirmance or disaffirmance, whether *sui juris* or not, and compelling an election and foreclosure of his mortgage if the sale is disaffirmed. In such cases the chancery court, by proper decree, is competent to make an election for infants, which will bind them and give repose to title, just as the decree of that court in the present case, should complainants be held, on final hearing, entitled to relief, would bind them to an election which they could not otherwise have made: *Goodman* v. *Winter*, 64 Ala. 410; 38 Am. Rep. 13; *Robinson* v. *Robinson*, 19 Beav. 494; *In re Chisholm*, 31 Ch. Div. 466–472; *Starring* v. *Borren*,

55 Barb. 595; 1 Pomeroy's Eq. Jur., sec. 509; 3 Pomeroy's Eq. Jur., sec. 1176.

We need hardly say, that if, at the time of such sale, the person entitled to make the election is free from disability, the time in which the option is to be expressed will not be extended in favor of infants, who subsequently succeed to his right.

This bill is filed by infant heirs of a mortgagor. Its purpose is to have a sale of the premises under the mortgage vacated, and redemption allowed, on the ground that the mortgagee purchased at the sale. Demurrers were filed, which set up laches, and the long delay of complainants in making their election to disaffirm. The city court sustained these demurrers, and its decree in that behalf is alone assigned as error. It follows, from the views we have expressed, that the decree in a question must be reversed, and the cause remanded.

PURCHASE BY MORTGAGEE AT SALE UNDER POWER. — A mortgagee who buys at a sale made under a power to sell contained in the mortgage thereby gives to the mortgagor an option to affirm or disaffirm the sale within a reasonable time, provided the mortgagee was not authorized to become a purchaser by the terms of the mortgage: *Knox* v. *Armistead,* 87 Ala. 511; 13 Am. St. Rep. 65. Purchase of land by a mortgagee thereof at a sale under a power is voidable at the option of the mortgagor: *Gibson* v. *Barbour,* 100 N. C. 192; *Martin* v. *McNeely,* 101 N. C. 634.

MOSES BROTHERS *v.* JOHNSON.

[88 ALABAMA, 517.]

VENDOR AND VENDEE. — RIGHT OF ELECTION UNDER EXECUTORY CONTRACT FOR SALE OF LAND, the title remaining in the vendor with the right, on default of the payment of an installment of the purchase-money, to annul the contract and retake possession, and to retain out of moneys paid under the contract a certain sum as rent, is a right reserved for the vendor's benefit, and he alone can exercise it.

VENDOR AND VENDEE. — RELATIONS BETWEEN a vendor and vendee of land under an executory contract of purchase are, in legal effect, the same as those existing between a mortgagor and mortgagee as to mutual, legal, and equitable rights and remedies.

VENDOR AND VENDEE — RIGHT OF VENDOR TO PRESERVE HIS SECURITY. — A vendor under an executory contract for the sale of land, who retains the title as security for the purchase-money, sustains the same relation to the vendee, on the question of security, as does a mortgagee to a mortgagor.

VENDOR AND VENDEE — RIGHT OF VENDOR TO RESTRAIN WASTE UNDER AN
EXECUTORY CONTRACT TO PURCHASE LAND. — A vendee in possession,
under an executory contract for the sale of land in which the vendor retains the title, may be enjoined from committing waste by cutting timber in the absence of a condition permitting it, when the vendor shows
that he has no security but the land, and that the value thereof is thereby
impaired.

John Gindrat Winter, for the appellants.

E. P. Morrissett, for the appellee.

STONE, C. J.   The appellants, who were the complainants,
sold 160 acres of land to the defendant, at the agreed price of
$1,440, — nine dollars per acre.   Only five dollars of the pur-
chase-money was paid.   The balance, including interest, was
agreed to be paid in annual installments, running through
about five years from the date of the purchase, January 5,
1889.   Complainants retained the title, giving to Johnson, the
purchaser, their obligation to make him title on payment by
him of the purchase-money and accruing taxes.   The agreement stipulated further that if Johnson failed "to pay any of
said installments when due," then Moses Brothers "have the
right to annul this agreement, and take possession of the
premises, and to retain out of the moneys paid under this
agreement [by Johnson] sixty dollars per annum as rent of
the premises, said amount being hereby agreed and declared
by said parties to be the annual rental value of the premises,
returning the surplus, if any, to" Johnson.

What we have copied contains every stipulation in the
agreement which sheds any light on Johnson's rights acquired under the purchase.   Nothing is said about felling
timber or clearing lands, or of Johnson's right to take and
hold possession, further than is implied in the language copied
above.   Johnson did take possession immediately after the
agreement was executed, and was in possession when this bill
was filed, August 26, 1889.   No part of the debt for the purchase-money had then matured, and there then remained unpaid about fourteen hundred dollars.

Under our interpretation of the agreement, Johnson had the
clear right to enter into possession of land, and to remain
in possession until he made default in the payment of some
installment of the purchase-money.   On such default, Moses
Brothers had the option, secured by the contract, to put an
end to the agreement, so far as it evidenced a sale, to convert
Johnson's holding into a tenancy *ab initio*, and to retake pos-

session of the land. This is a right of election reserved for their benefit, and they alone can exercise it: *Collins* v. *Whigham*, 58 Ala. 438; *Wilkinson* v. *Roper*, 74 Ala. 140.

When a vendor of real estate enters into an executory agreement to convey title on the payment of the purchase-money, he sustains, in substance, the same relation to the vendee as a mortgagee does to a mortgagor. Each has a legal title, which, in the absence of stipulations for possession, will maintain an action of ejectment. Each can retain his legal title against the other party until the purchase-money or mortgage debt is paid, unless he permits the other to remain in undisturbed possession for twenty years. And yet each is at last but a trustee of the legal title for the mortgagee or vendee, if the purchase-money or mortgage debt, as the case may be, is paid or seasonably tendered. The same mutual rights and remedies, legal and equitable, and the same limitation to the right of recovery, obtain in the one relation and in the other: *Relfe* v. *Relfe*, 34 Ala. 500; 73 Am. Rep. 467; *Bizzell* v. *Nix*, 60 Ala. 281; 31 Am. Rep. 38; *Chapman* v. *Lee*, 64 Ala. 483; *Sweeney* v. *Bixler*, 69 Ala. 539.

We have found but a single case precisely like the present one in its facts. In *Scott* v. *Wharton*, 2 Hen. & M. 25, a sale of land had been made on a credit, and title retained by the vendor. The vendee went into possession, and a bill was filed by the vendor charging him with committing waste, by cutting timber, and praying for an injunction. The court treated the case precisely as if it had been a bill by mortgagee against mortgagor to restrain him from lessening the security by felling and removing the timber: *Fairbank* v. *Cudworth*, 33 Wis. 358.

We feel safe in holding that a vendor who sells on credit, retaining the title as security for the purchase-money, sustains the same relation to the vendee, so far as the question of security is concerned, as does the mortgagee to the mortgagor.

In *King* v. *Smith*, 2 Hare, 239, it was said to be an established rule, "that if the security of the mortgagee is insufficient, and the court is satisfied of that fact, the mortgagor will not be allowed to do that which would directly impair the security,—cut timber upon the mortgaged premises. . . . . The cases decide that a mortgagee out of possession is not, of course, entitled to an injunction to restrain the mortgagor from cutting timber on the mortgaged property. If the security is sufficient, the court will not grant an injunction merely because the mortgagor cuts, or threatens to cut, timber. There must be a special case made out before the court will interfere. The difficulty is in determining what is meant by a 'sufficient security.' Suppose the mortgage debt, with all the expenses, to be one thousand pounds, and the property to be worth one thousand pounds, that is, in one sense, a sufficient security; but no mortgagee who is well advised would lend his money unless the mortgaged property was worth one third more than the amount lent at the time of the mortgage." This was considered the rule, and the only safe rule, under English values. In that country, land values were, in a measure, stationary. In this, they are fluctuating. To be a "sufficient security" with us, there should be a much broader margin between the amount of the debt and the estimated value of the property mortgaged for its security than is considered sufficient in that older country.

This court is fully committed to the same doctrine. In *Coker* v. *Whitlock*, 54 Ala. 180, this court ruled, that when the mortgagor is committing waste which impairs the security or renders it insufficient, chancery, at the suit of the mortgagee, will restrain him by injunction: *Coleman* v. *Smith*, 55 Ala. 368; *Hammond* v. *Winchester*, 82 Ala. 470; *Sullivan* v. *Rabb*, 86 Ala. 433; also 2 Daniell's Chancery Practice, *1629, note 3; *Usborne* v. *Usborne*, 1 Dick. 75; *Brady* v. *Waldron*, 2 Johns. Ch. 148; *Robinson* v. *Preswick*, 3 Edw. Ch. 246; *Murdock's Case*, 2 Bland, 461; 22 Am. Dec. 381; *Downing* v. *Palmeteer*, 1 Mon. 64.

The bill charges, and the answer admits, that the land, which is the subject of this suit, is in value not exceeding the sum of the purchase-money that remains unpaid. The bill also charges that the defendant is insolvent. To this charge the answer interposes a general denial, but accompanies it with a statement as follows: "This defendant denies that he is insolvent, and avers that he is solvent; that, except the debt he owes for this land, his liabilities are small, and that he owns real estate in his own name, not subject to exemption as a homestead, in Montgomery County, Alabama, that is worth much more than any liabilities or debts he owes, excepting his debt for this land." We understand this language to mean that defendant's other property will pay his other debts; but we cannot interpret it as affirming that it will pay any certain sum above his other debts. This leaves the land in controversy as the sole security for its promised purchase-money. The bill also charges that the land lies near the city of Montgomery, where fire-wood is in demand, and commands ready sale; and that to denude the land of its timber would greatly diminish its value as a security. The answer admits the truth of each of these averments, except the last, which it denies. It sets up that the land is fertile, and would be made more valuable if cleared of its timber and brought under cultivation. This last averment must be treated as affirmative, defensive matter, the proof of which rests with defendant. Such averment, until proved, furnishes no ground for dissolving the injunction: 1 Brickell's Digest, p. 678, secs. 567, 568.

It may be, as contended, that the right to clear the land, sell the timber, and put the land in cultivation, were inducements — controlling inducements — to enter into the purchase. They were not expressed as terms of the contract, and defendant failed to stipulate for any such privilege. Considering the proximity of the land to a market for the fire-wood, — an averment not denied, but admitted, — we feel forced to presume, as charged in the bill, that the land is more valuable with the timber on it than if cleared and put in cultivation. Hence we hold that the averment to the effect that the value of the land would be enhanced by clearing it is affirmative matter, the burden of proving which is on the defendant. We may state here that injunction is the only relief prayed, and is the only proper relief in a case like the present one.

However it may be made to appear by proof, the pleadings do not make a case for a dissolution of the injunction; and the decretal order dissolving the injunction must be reversed, and the injunction reinstated.

Reversed and rendered.

————

WASTE. — A lessee is answerable for waste to the lessor, no matter by whom committed: *Powell* v. *Dayton etc. R. R. Co.*, 16 Or. 33; 8 Am. St. Rep. 251.

VENDOR AND VENDEE. — A vendor's position, when he has not conveyed the title to the land sold, is similar to that of a mortgagee: *Salmon* v. *Hoffman*, 2 Cal. 138; 56 Am. Dec. 322, and note 326.

SMITH *v.* GEORGIA PACIFIC RAILWAY COMPANY.

[88 ALABAMA, 538.]

RAILROADS — DUTY TO PASSENGERS AT STATION OF DESTINATION. — A railroad company is under duty to its passengers not to expose them to unnecessary danger, and not to intentionally or negligently mislead them by causing them to reasonably suppose that their point of destination has been reached, and that they may safely alight, when the train is in an improper place; but the mere announcement of the name of the station is not an invitation to alight; still, when followed by a full stoppage of the train soon thereafter, it is ordinarily notification that it has arrived at the usual place of landing passengers, and whether the stoppage of the train, after such announcement, and before arriving at the platform, is negligence, depends upon the attending circumstances.

RAILROADS — DUTY TO PASSENGERS AT STATION OF DESTINATION. — Neither the announcement of the station, nor stopping the train before it arrives at the platform, if required by law or usage to avoid collisions or accidents, is negligence *per se* in a railroad company toward a passenger injured while attempting to alight.

RAILROADS — DUTY TO PASSENGERS AT STATION OF DESTINATION. — When the name of a station is called, and soon thereafter the train is brought to a stand-still, a passenger may reasonably conclude that it has stopped at the station, and endeavor to alight, and may recover if injured in his attempt to do so, unless the circumstances and indications are such as to render it manifest that the train has not reached the usual and proper landing-place.

RAILROADS — WHEN NEGLIGENCE OF PASSENGER AT STATION OF DESTINATION A QUESTION OF LAW. — When the station is announced, and the train stopped soon thereafter, in the daytime, to take a side-track, at a spot where there is no depot or platform, and all the surroundings indicate that it is not a proper place for landing, a passenger who attempts to alight, and is injured in so doing, cannot recover, in the absence of circumstances caused by the railroad company inducing him to reasonably suppose that he was attempting to alight at the proper place. In such case, his injury is accidental, if not the result of his own negligence, and the jury should be so instructed, and of his inability to recover.

Kelly and Smith, for the appellant.

Knox and Bowie, for the appellee.

CLOPTON, J.   Appellant's injuries, for which he sues, were received while alighting from a train at Heflin, a regular station on defendant's road.   His right of recovery is founded on the allegation that his injury was caused by the negligence of defendant's servants.   The specific negligence complained of is alleged to consist in calling out the name of the station, bringing the train to a stand-still immediately thereafter, thereby inducing plaintiff to believe, and to act upon the belief, that the train had reached the usual place for landing passengers, and suddenly starting it without giving him notice.

Plaintiff's act in leaving the train being voluntary, it is incumbent on him, in order to entitle him to a recovery, or before the opinion of a jury is required to be taken as to the question of negligence, to produce evidence from which the inference may be reasonably drawn that his injury was caused by the negligence of the defendant. We shall therefore direct our consideration to the question, whether, on the facts clearly proved, and having regard to the liberty to draw inferences therefrom, the court would have been justified in taking the question of negligence from the jury; for if on the facts which admit of no dispute, and allowing all adverse inferences, it would have been the duty of the court to set aside the verdict, had one been rendered in favor of plaintiff, and the affirmative charge in favor of defendant was authorized, we need not consider the various rulings of the court: *Bentley* v. *Georgia Pac. R'y Co.*, 86 Ala. 484.

A railroad company, being a carrier of passengers, is under obligation to use reasonable care to transport them safely. This general duty includes the specific duty not to expose them to unnecessary danger, and not intentionally or negligently mislead them by causing them to reasonably suppose that their point of destination has been reached, and that they may safely alight, when the train is in an improper place. Calling out the name of the station is customary and proper, so that passengers may be informed that the train is approaching the station of their destination, and prepare to get off when it arrives at the platform. The mere announcement of the name of the station is not an invitation to alight; but when followed by a full stoppage of the train soon thereafter, is ordinarily notification that it has arrived at the usual place of landing passengers. Whether the stoppage of the train after such announcement, and before it arrives at the platform, is negligence, depends upon the attendant circumstances. The rule is aptly expressed in *Bridges* v. *Railway Co.*, L. R. 6 Q. B. 877, by Willes, J.: "It is an announcement by the railway officers that the train is approaching, or has arrived at the platform, and that the passengers may get out when the train stops at the platform, or under circumstances induced and caused by the company, in which the man may reasonably suppose he is getting out at the place where the company intended him to alight. To that extent, calling out is an invitation."

A reference to a few leading cases will aid in the solution

of the question, whether, on the facts hereafter stated, plaintiff should or could have supposed that the train had reached the usual place for the discharge of passengers. In *Bridges* v. *Railway Co., supra*, the executrix and wife sued for injuries suffered by her husband, which resulted in his death. The train on which he was a passenger had to pass through a tunnel before reaching the main platform. There was within the tunnel a platform, similar to but narrower than the main platform. The train went partially up to the main platform and stopped, the last two carriages remaining in the tunnel; the last but one opposite the small platform, and the last, in which the deceased was riding, opposite a heap of rubbish lying near the track. A passenger, who had alighted on the platform from the carriage next to the last, found the deceased lying on the heap of rubbish, fatally injured. There was no light in the tunnel, and it was filled with steam. The name of the station had been called in the usual way. It was ruled, on appeal from the exchequer chamber to the house of lords, that it might be reasonably inferred that the deceased, having heard the name of the station called, and finding that the train had stopped, got out of the carriage, supposing that he would alight on the platform, and that the evidence furnished matter on which it was necessary to take the opinion of a jury: L. R. 7 H. L. 213.

In *Central R. R. Co.* v. *Van Horn*, 38 N. J. L. 133, the name of the station which was plaintiff's destination was announced while the train was in motion, and soon thereafter it was brought to a full stop, some distance from the station. The plaintiff went out on the platform of the car for the purpose of alighting, and, while standing thereon, the train was suddenly put in motion towards the depot, whereby she was thrown off and injured. This was at night. It is said: "The court would not be warranted in saying that it is not negligence to give notice of the approach to a station, and then stop the train short of such station in the night-time. Such a course would naturally tend to jeopardize passengers; for it would induce them to believe that they had arrived at the station designated, and they would, in the ordinary course, go to the car platform. At night, this must be the inevitable result."

In *Taber* v. *Delaware etc. R. R. Co.*, 71 N. Y. 489, Andrews, J., says: "The plaintiff was justified, under the circumstances, in supposing that she had reached her destination, and that

the train was at the place where passengers were to alight; at
least, the jury might have come to the conclusion that she
was free from negligence.   The defendant was bound to take
notice of the circumstances, viz., that the station had been
announced; that passengers for Williards would naturally
assume that the train, when it stopped, was at the station,
and at the place where they were to alight; that, by reason
of the darkness of the night, and the absence of a depot, or
other external indication of a station, passengers, especially
those not familiar with surrounding objects, would not, by
observation, know that the train had run beyond the highway
crossing; that passengers, in the absence of notice, would,
according to the usual custom, start to leave the train as soon
as it came to a stand-still."   In that case, the night was dark,
and there was no depot or station light, nor anything to indicate the stopping-place, which was a highway crossing, to a
person not familiar with it.   It was held that whether notice
should have been given to the passengers, as a reasonable precaution, that the train was to back, and whether the omission
to do so was negligence, was a question for the jury.

On the other hand, in *Mitchell* v. *Chicago etc. R'y Co.*, 51
Mich. 236, 38 Am. Rep. 566, 18 Am. & Eng. R. R. Cas. 176,
the plaintiff intended to take another train at the crossing of
two railways.   Before arriving at the junction, the name of
the station was called out, and the train came to a full stop,
as required by law, before reaching the crossing.   Plaintiff
hurried to leave the car, went down the steps where there was
no platform or other convenience for landing, and as she was
stepping off, the cars were suddenly started to go forward to
the depot, when she fell and was injured.   This was in daylight, and it does not appear that any person employed on
the train observed her.   It was held that the injury was
purely accidental, unless plaintiff was herself negligent, and
that the company was not liable.   Campbell, J., said: "The
only cause of the mischief, leaving defendant's carelessness or
negligence out of view, was her mistaken supposition that the
cars had stopped at the station, and that she therefore should
get out.   There was nothing at the spot to indicate a landing-
place, and there was at the proper place, a short distance
farther on, a building and platform used for that purpose.
The stoppage of the cars was required by statute, as well as
by usage, as a precaution against collisions.   The calling of
the station was not shown to have been out of the usual

course, and, from the distance mentioned, we can hardly see how it could have been delayed. No one representing the company, whether conductor or brakeman, is shown to have known or suspected that plaintiff had put herself in peril, or left her place. Nothing is shown which put them in fault for not knowing this."

We have specially referred to the cases cited, because they distinguish between the instances in which the negligence of the defendant is and is not a question for the jury, and have made the foregoing extracts, because they clearly declare the principles on which the distinction rests. They all concur that neither the announcement of the station, nor stopping the train before it arrives at the platform, if required by law or usage for the purpose of avoiding collisions or other accidents, is negligence *per se.* In *Bridges* v. *Railway Co., supra,* Baron Pollock observes, in reference to the conduct of the passenger who was injured: "Had he known that the rubbish was there instead of the platform, to jump out onto it with such a fall as would break his leg, and occasion mortal internal injuries, would indeed have been negligent and rash in the extreme. But it was two hours after sunset, there was no light in the tunnel, and the deceased was near-sighted; and he might well have supposed that he would step on the platform, as did the passenger in the next carriage, with impunity." It will be observed that in each of the cases in which it was ruled there was evidence of negligence sufficient to be submitted to the jury, there existed the element that, by reason of the want of light or other things, the passenger may have been deceived into supposing the train had arrived at the platform, or place where it was intended he should alight. Comparing all the cases, we deduce that when the name of the station is called, and soon thereafter the train is brought to a stand-still, a passenger may reasonably conclude that it has stopped at the station, and endeavor to get off, unless the circumstances and indications are such as to render manifest that the train has not reached the proper and usual landing-place.

The undisputed facts are: Heflin was the point at which the regular passenger trains met and passed each other. It was customary for the east-bound train, on which plaintiff was a passenger, to take the side-track, leaving the main track unobstructed for the passage of the train going westwardly. This was necessary to avoid collision. Heflin was plaintiff's point of destination. As the train was approaching, the name of the station was called as usual, and the train was stopped very soon thereafter, the object being to take the side-track. On its stopping, plaintiff went out of the rear door of the car, and was descending with one foot on the first step of the car, and the other about touching the ground, when the train moved forward to go to the depot, which caused him to fall. It was drawn to the usual place for the discharge of passengers, and again stopped. The rear of the car from which plaintiff was getting off was about two hundred yards from the depot-building, the proper place for the discharge of passengers. The train was first stopped in a cut about 360 feet long, and from 5 to 11 feet deep. This was in daylight, about one o'clock, P. M. Plaintiff had been in Heflin once before, but, as he states, arrived and departed in the night-time, and was not about the depot in daytime. Nevertheless, he knew, or ought to have known, that there was a depot at which passengers got off and on the trains, and that it was not in such a cut. All the surroundings indicated that the spot at which plaintiff attempted to leave the train was not the proper place for landing. From the description of the place given by witnesses, and shown by the diagram in evidence, it is unreasonable to conclude or infer that any person possessing the ordinary sense of sight, and using it, could have supposed that the train had arrived at the place where the company intended passengers to get off. It does not appear that any of those in charge of or employed on the train noticed the plaintiff when leaving it, or had cause to suspect his intention to get off. There were no circumstances or surroundings caused by the company which should have induced plaintiff to reasonably suppose he was getting out at the place where the company intended him to alight. The evidence clearly establishes that his injury was accidental, if not produced by his own negligence. On the undisputed facts, the court would have been justified in giving the affirmative charge in favor of defendant.

Affirmed.

CARRIERS OF PASSENGERS — DUTY TO PASSENGERS AT POINT OF DESTINATION. — Railway company must announce the name of the station upon arriving thereat, and give passengers opportunity to alight in safety: *Dorrah v. Illinois Cent. R. R. Co.*, 65 Miss. 14; 7 Am. St. Rep. 629, and note; compare *New York etc. R'y Co. v. Doane*, 115 Ind. 435; 7 Am. St. Rep. 451; *McDonald v. Long Island R. R. Co.*, 116 N. Y. 546; 15 Am. St. Rep. 437, and note.

CONTRIBUTORY NEGLIGENCE is ordinarily a question for the jury to determine: *Kansas City etc. R. R. Co.* v. *Kier*, 41 Kan. 661; 13 Am. St. Rep. 311, and note; but it may be a question of law for the court, where the facts are ascertained, and there is no conflict in the evidence with respect thereto: *Connolly* v. *Knickerbocker Ice Co.*, 114 N. Y. 104; 11 Am. St. Rep. 617.

MEMPHIS AND CHARLESTON R. R. CO. *v.* GRAYSON.

[88 ALABAMA, 572.]

RAILROADS — LEASE ULTRA VIRES. — A lease by a railroad company of its road, rolling stock, and franchise to another railroad for twenty years or longer is *ultra vires* and void, in the absence of express power granted it in its charter or by statute.

CORPORATIONS — STOCKHOLDERS — ESTOPPEL. — A share-holder who has participated, ratified, or acquiesced in the acts of the corporation is estopped, as against it, while it remains bound by its acts, from attacking the validity thereof. Third persons cannot claim such estoppel, either against the corporation, or against the share-holder suing for and in behalf of the corporation for the avoidance of its contract as *ultra vires*.

RES JUDICATA — JUDGMENT IN ACTION COMMENCED PENDENTE LITE. — A judgment of a court of one state having jurisdiction of the parties and of the subject-matter is, in the absence of fraud, binding upon the courts of another state, in a suit involving the same parties and subject-matter, though the suit in the latter state was instituted first.

D. H. Poston, and Milton Humes, for the appellants.

F. P. Ward, L. W. Day, and D. D. Shelby, for the appellee.

McCLELLAN, J. In June, 1877, the Memphis and Charleston Railroad Company leased its road and equipment to the East Tennessee, Virginia, and Georgia Railroad Company for a term of twenty years, to commence in July thereafter. In December, 1879, the lessee in the mean time being in possession of the property, a modification of the original lease was agreed upon by and between the two companies. Both the original and amended leases were duly authorized and ratified by the stockholders of the Memphis and Charleston company. The complainant was owner of stock in the lessor corporation at the time of these transactions, and his shares were represented at the meetings which consummated the lease and ratified the modification of it above referred to, and were voted, with his knowledge and consent, for the lease and amended lease, respectively. In November, 1881, the stockholders of the Memphis and Charleston company adopted a resolution instructing their president and directors to treat the lease to the East Tennessee, Virginia, and Georgia company as invalid, and to proceed to take possession and control of the road. These instructions were not acted on. In August, 1882, the stockholders of the Memphis and Charleston company passed a resolution authorizing the issuance of five millions of dollars of additional stock, and directed the same to be sold at eight cents on the dollar, and the proceeds thereof (four hundred thousand dollars) to be paid to the East Tennessee, Virginia, and Georgia company in consideration of a surrender of said lease. The complainant was present at this meeting, and voted his stock, and protested against the adoption of this resolution; and immediately afterwards filed the present bill against the lessor and lessee corporations, alleging that the lease was *ultra vires* of the lessor corporation, and void; that the East Tennessee, Virginia, and Georgia company was largely indebted to the Memphis and Charleston company by reason of its possession, operation, and use of the road and other property of the latter; and that the directors of the Memphis and Charleston company were about to issue and sell said additional stock, and pay the proceeds thereof to the East Tennessee, Virginia, and Georgia company, in consideration of a surrender and cancellation of said pretended lease.

The bill prays for an injunction against the Memphis and Charleston company, restraining it from the issuance of said additional stock, and the payment of the proceeds thereof for a surrender of the lease, and against the East Tennessee, Virginia, and Georgia company, restraining it from further control, use, etc., of the Memphis and Charleston road; for a receiver to take possession of the road-bed, equipment, etc., of the Memphis and Charleston company, and operate the same for the benefit of the company's stockholders; that upon final hearing said lease and amended lease be decreed to be void, and ordered canceled, and an account be taken between the defendant companies; and that the East Tennessee, Virginia, and Georgia company be adjudged to pay the Memphis and Charleston company whatever amount should be found due thereon for its use and occupation of the latter's road, or on account of inequitable division of traffic receipts between the two roads. No injunction was ever ordered pending the litigation until the final decree, which perpetually restrains the Memphis and Charleston company from issuing the additional stock contemplated by the resolution of August, 1882, and from paying the proceeds thereof for a surrender of the lease.

No receiver was appointed. The final decree declares the lease null and void; but no accounting is decreed, because it was made to appear by the record of a proceeding in a chancery court of the state of Tennessee between the Memphis and Charleston company and the East Tennessee, Virginia, and Georgia company, for the cancellation of the lease, an account, etc., that the parties had already accounted between themselves.

The correctness of the decree of the chancery court of Madison, in so far as it holds abstractly that the lease (original and as amended) was *ultra vires* and void, is not controverted on this appeal. On this point, therefore, we content ourselves with a reference to some of the authorities which sustain the conclusion reached by the court below, — the Memphis and Charleston Railroad Company having no special power under its charter, or under the general laws of the state, to lease its road to the East Tennessee, Virginia, and Georgia Railroad Company: *Pennsylvania R. R. Co.* v. *St. Louis etc. R. R. Co.*, 118 U. S. 294; *Thomas* v. *West Jersey R. R. Co.*, 101 U. S. 71.

The decree is attacked here on two grounds only: 1. That complainant was estopped to question the validity of the lease and the modified lease, by the fact that he was represented at the meetings of the stockholders which authorized or ratified them, and his stock was voted by his proxy, and with his knowledge, for both the original and the amendment thereof; and 2. That the decree of the Tennessee chancery court declaring the lease void, etc., was a merger of complainant's cause of action, and therefore a bar to the further prosecution of his bill in the Alabama court.

It is not seriously denied that the complainant was at one time estopped by his conduct to prosecute this suit against the Memphis and Charleston Railroad Company. The relation existing between him and that company was that of *cestui que trust* and trustee. Acts of the corporation, participated, ratified, or acquiesced in by him as a share-holder, he has no right to call in question in any proceeding in form or effect adversary in its character with respect to his trustee, who in that regard is considered as executing his will. It would be manifestly inequitable to the corporate entity, and to other stockholders, to allow him, so long as the course in which he has set the company continues to be the corporate policy, to appeal to the courts to have that policy reversed, and the

company coerced into a different line of conduct. The shares
owned by complainant having been voted by his representative, and, according to the weight of evidence, with his knowledge and consent, for the lease of July, 1877, and for the
modification thereof resolved upon in December, 1879, he
could not be permitted, while his trustee continued to be committed to the leases, to attack their validity: 1 Morawetz on
Corporations, secs. 630 et seq.; Cook on Stockholders, secs.
683 et seq.

But the operation of this estoppel is between the trustee and
the *cestui que trust*, the corporation and its share-holder. The
latter cannot proceed against the former for doing that which
he has directed to be done; but the company itself is not
estopped to proceed against a third person, or other corporation, for the avoidance of an executory *ultra vires* contract;
and it would be the duty of the company to so proceed: Bigelow on Estoppel, 466–468. This well-settled proposition
demonstrates that the estoppel does not obtain in favor of
third parties, natural or artificial, and that they cannot rely
upon it, either against the corporation *eo nomine*, or against a
stockholder suing for and in behalf of the corporation; for
clearly it would be wholly immaterial to them, whether the
assault on the *ultra vires* contract proceeded from corporate
volition, so to speak, or from the volition of a stockholder, exercising his right to act for the corporation. The Memphis
and Charleston company having, as we have seen, before the
filing of this bill, repudiated the leases of its property to the
East Tennessee, Virginia, and Georgia company, and instructed
its directors to take possession of its road and equipment, the
estoppel resting on complainant was thereby relieved.

As to the effect of the decree of the chancery court in Tennessee, a somewhat more difficult question arises. The bill
in Alabama was first filed; the decree in Tennessee was first
rendered. The suit in Alabama, while proceeding in the
name of a stockholder in behalf of himself and all other stockholders who should come in and make themselves parties,
and nominally against the Memphis and Charleston company,
as well as the East Tennessee, Virginia, and Georgia company,
was, in legal contemplation and effect, for and in behalf of the
Memphis and Charleston company, capable of resulting in no
other relief than such as the latter company was entitled to
have decreed against the East Tennessee, Virginia, and
Georgia company, and hence, for all practicable purposes

incident to the present *status* of the case, is to be considered
as a suit of one corporation against the other: 1 Morawetz on
Corporations, secs. 256, 257, 271.   The suit in Tennessee proceeded in the name of the corporation itself, and its main
objects were the same as those sought to be attained in the
Alabama suit, — the cancellation of the leases of July, 1877,
and December, 1879, and an accounting between the companies.   The only relief insisted on in the domestic action,
which was not prayed for in the foreign suit, was, that the
Memphis and Charleston company be enjoined from the issuance and sale of the five million dollars of additional stock,
authorized by a meeting of stockholders held in 1882.   Even
this relief, while it could not be specially prayed in the Tennessee suit, was necessarily involved and effectuated in that
case, since this stock was to be issued and disposed of only
for the specific purpose of providing a fund with which to pay
the East Tennessee, Virginia, and Georgia company a bonus
for a surrender of the leases; and the leases having been.
decreed void, and ordered canceled, there was no longer any
authorization for the issuance of the additional stock, and no
such action threatened.   The parties and the issues, we therefore conclude, were substantially the same in the two cases;
and it only remains to be considered, on this branch of the
appeal, whether the Tennessee court had jurisdiction to render the decree which was set up as a bar to the further prosecution of this cause in the Madison chancery court.   It is of
course well settled with respect to courts acting within one
and the same territorial jurisdiction, and administering the
laws of the same sovereignty, that the first to take cognizance of a controversy, or the control and custody of the property, cannot be defeated of its right to proceed to a final
determination of the dispute, or to a complete administration
of the property by the subsequent interposition of another
tribunal; but, on the contrary, the pendency of the first action, properly pleaded, will abate the second.   It may be conceded that jurisdiction taken by the court of one state to hear
and determine a controversy, accompanied by the assumption
of custody of the subject-matter in litigation, may be pleaded
in bar of a subsequent proceeding, not merely ancillary in its
character, in a court of another state, or of the United States.
But in each of the cases put, we apprehend the pendency of
the former suit must be pleaded; and if not pleaded, and the
court in which the later proceeding is instituted goes on to

judgment, that judgment will bar the further prosecution of
the older suit.

On the other hand, while there has been some diversity of
adjudications on the point, it may now be considered as settled
in principle, and by the weight of authority, that the pendency
of an action in the courts of one state cannot, except possibly in
the case conceded above, be set up to defeat a subsequent action in a court of another state: Wells on Res Adjudicata,
sec. 530; Story on Conflict of Laws, sec. 609, p. 832, note *c;*
Hatch v. *Spofford*, 22 Conn. 493; 58 Am. Dec. 433; *Percival* v.
Hickey, 18 Johns. 257; 9 Am. Dec. 210; *Drake* v. *Brander*, 8
Tex. 352; *Brown* v. *Jay*, 9 Johns. 221; *Stanton* v. *Embry*, 93
U. S. 554.

Assuming, what is not questioned, that the Tennessee court
had jurisdiction, otherwise than as affected by the pendency
of this case, of the parties to and subject-matter involved in
the bill of the Memphis and Charleston company against the
East Tennessee, Virginia, and Georgia company, it would be
an anomaly to hold that it could not render a final decree
between those parties because of the pendency of a case in
Alabama between the same parties, and involving the same
controversy, when the fact was never pleaded, and would have
availed nothing if it had been pleaded, or to deny to its decree
when rendered, pending the Alabama case, a tithe of the force
and effect it would have had in the absence of the other suit.
This decree is not attacked as fraudulent or collusive. If it
had been fraudulent, or the result of collusion between the two
corporations, it would, of course, exert no influence upon the
litigation pending in the Madison chancery court. Its sole
alleged infirmity, however, results from the fact that it was
rendered on a bill filed after the bill in this case was exhibited.
The objection is untenable. "The first judgment rendered
controls, whether the action in which it is reached be instituted before the other or not; and the rule applies where the
first judgment is rendered in another state": Wells on Res
Adjudicata, sec. 292; *Childs* v. *Powder Works*, 45 N. H. 547;
Duff v. *Little*, 5 Watts, 130; *Casebeer* v. *Mowry*, 55 Pa. St. 422;
93 Am. Dec. 766; *McGilvray* v. *Avery*, 30 Vt. 538; *Wood* v.
Gamble, 11 Cush. 8; 59 Am. Dec. 135; *Rodgers* v. *Odell*, 39
N. H. 452; *Stout* v. *Lye*, 103 U. S. 70, 71. And the same rule
prevails as to decrees: *Lowe* v. *Mussey*, 41 Vt. 392; *Peak* v.
Ligon, 10 Yerg. 468.

The *gravamen* of the bill in each case was the existence of the void leases of the Memphis and Charleston company to the East Tennessee, Virginia, and Georgia company, possession and use by the latter of the former's property under these leases, and the indebtedness of the lessee to the lessor on account of such possession and use. The Tennessee decree determined each and all of these matters. It cancels the leases, it enforces a surrender of the property, and it settles the accounts between the parties. After that decree, there was no lease in existence to be upheld or annulled by our court; no property of one party, in the wrongful possession and enjoyment of the other, to be restored to its rightful control and use; nothing due from the East Tennessee, Virginia, and Georgia company to the Memphis and Charleston company, to be decreed to be paid by the former to the latter. Complainant's cause of action had been destroyed by being merged into the decree of a competent court, and there was nothing left for the chancery court of Madison to act upon: Wells on Res Adjudicata, sec. 530; *Barnes* v. *Gibbs*, 31 N. J. Eq. 317; 86 Am. Dec. 210; Freeman on Judgments, secs. 215–221; *North Bank* v. *Brown*, 50 Me. 214; 79 Am. Dec. 609; *Jones* v. *Jamison*, 12 La. Ann. 35.

Our opinion therefore is, that the court below erred in decreeing cancellation of the lease and amended lease, in adjudging or finding that the parties had accounted between themselves, and in enjoining the Memphis and Charleston company from the issuance of the stock authorized in 1882. All of these matters had been expressly or necessarily settled by the Tennessee decree.

Unquestionably, however, the complainant, Grayson, had a good cause of action when he filed his bill. The answer which set up the foreign decree is therefore to be treated as a plea of *puis darrien continuance;* and the final disposition of this case, as to complainant's costs and reasonable expenses in the prosecution of his suit in behalf of the Memphis and Charleston corporation, should be had accordingly.

Reversed and remanded.

RAILROADS — LEASES BY. — A railroad cannot lease its road to another company unless specially authorized by charter or aided by legislative authority: *State* v. *Atchison etc. R. R. Co.*, 24 Neb. 143; 8 Am. St. Rep. 164. A railroad company cannot lease its road so as to absolve itself from its duties to the public without authority from the legislature: *International etc. R. R. Co.* v. *Eckford*, 71 Tex. 274; *Railway* v. *Morris*, 68 Id. 59; compare *East Line etc. R'y Co.* v. *Culberson*, 72 Id. 375; 13 Am. St. Rep. 805, and note.

Estoppel to Deny Corporate Existence by contracting with the corporation: *Schloss* v. *Montgomery Tr. Co.*, 87 Ala ill: '3 Am. St. Rep. 51, and note; compare *Karns* v. *Olney*, 80 Cal. 90; 13 Am. St. Rep. 101, and note.

Foreign Judgments. — As to the effect and conclusiveness of foreign judgments: Note to *Messier* v. *Amery*, 1 Am. Dec 324-326; note to *Lazier* v. *Westcott*, 82 Am. Dec. 413, 414; *McLaren* v. *Kehler*, 23 La. Ann. 80; 8 Am. Rep. 591; *Brinkley* v. *Brinkley*, 50 N. Y. 184; 10 Am. Rep. 460; *Gunn* v. *Peakes*, 36 Minn. 177; 1 Am. St. Rep. 661, and note. A judgment duly entered in the circuit court of Illinois, and duly transcripted to another state, is valid as a cause of action against a general demurrer: *Nicholas* v. *Farwell*, 24 Neb. 180.

Goodbar, White, and Company *v.* Daniel.
[88 Alabama, 583.]

Executions — Remedy of Purchaser at Sheriff's Sale as against Fraudulent Conveyance. — A purchaser of the legal title to land at sheriff's sale has a plain and adequate remedy at law in ejectment, although the land has been fraudulently conveyed by the judgment debtor prior to sale, and he is not entitled to equitable relief; but when he acquires no title to the land at the sale, his only remedy, if he has any, is in equity.

Executions. — Purchaser at Sheriff's Sale Buys at his Own Risk, and will not be relieved from the effect of his bid upon proof that the execution defendant had no title to the property sold. His bid is an irrevocable satisfaction of the judgment to the extent of the sum bid at the sale.

Husband and Wife — Notice to Husband as Agent of Wife. — Notice of fraudulent facts avoiding a deed, acquired by a husband while acting as agent and trustee for his wife, in investing the proceeds of her separate estate, is constructive notice to her of such facts.

Bill in equity by plaintiffs and appellants, as partners and judgment creditors of J. B. Mackey, against J. M. Daniel and Myra J. Daniel, his wife, to set aside as fraudulent a conveyance of land to Mrs. Daniel by Mackey and wife; to have an account of the money invested by Mackey in the purchase of such land, and the amount thereof declared a lien on the land for the satisfaction of their judgment; to set aside a credit of $250 on their judgment, bid by them at sheriff's sale under their execution, on the ground that such bid was made under mistake and misapprehension of their rights. A demurrer was filed to the bill, on the ground that, — " 3. It shows that complainants had an adequate remedy at law by ejectment." Another demurrer was filed, on the grounds, — "2. Because it does not aver any collusion or knowledge of any wrong or fraud on the part of Mrs. Myra J. Daniel"; "3. Because the levy and sale of the land was a satisfaction *pro tanto* of the complainants' judgment and execution, which a court of equity cannot vacate"; " 7. The complainants having purchased at their own sale, the doctrine of *caveat emptor* applies, and they cannot set aside their sale and purchase on the ground of mistake." Demurrer sustained, decree accordingly, and error is assigned thereon. The other facts are stated in the opinion.

Matthews and Daniel, for the appellants.

Walden and Son, for the appellees.

SOMERVILLE, J.   The court, in sustaining the third ground of the first demurrer, ruled that the complainants, under the facts stated in the bill, had a plain and adequate remedy at law by the action of ejectment.   This view can be supported only on the theory that when the complainants purchased the land in controversy at the sheriff's sale under the execution issued against J. B. Mackey on their judgment, they bought the legal title.   We have many times held that a purchaser of the legal title to land sold under execution at a sheriff's sale has a plain and adequate remedy at law by ejectment, although the land had been fraudulently conveyed by the judgment debtor prior to such sale: *Smith* v. *Cockrell,* 66 Ala. 64; *Teague* v. *Martin,* 87 Ala. 500; 13 Am. St. Rep. 63.   In this case, however, assuming the allegations of the bill to be true, as we must do on demurrer, Mackey never acquired the legal title to the land, but an equity only.   One Pullen formerly owned the land, and conveyed it to Mrs. Mackey, the wife of said J. B. Mackey, the judgment debtor, her husband being alleged to have paid most of the purchase-money out of his own effects.   Mackey and wife afterwards conveyed to Mrs. Myra J. Daniel, one of the defendants in the bill. One of the questions which arose in *Smith* v. *Cockrell,* 66 Ala. 64, was, whether precisely such an interest was subject to levy and sale under execution as a " perfect equity," within the meaning of section 3207 of the Code of 1876, which is now section 2892 of the present Code of 1886.   We held that it was not subject to sale, and consequently, that the purchaser at such execution sale acquired no title of any kind, legal or equitable.

On the authority of that case, the complainants, under the facts stated in their bill, acquired no interest of any kind in

the land, and certainly not the legal title. They had no remedy, therefore, at law, by ejectment, or otherwise. The third
ground of the first demurrer was erroneously sustained.

The complainants are shown to have bid at the sheriff's
sale for the land the sum of two hundred and fifty dollars
($250), and they credited this sum on their judgment against
Mackey, which was for something more than $1,250. The
chancellor properly ruled, in sustaining the third and seventh
grounds of the second demurrer, that this credit was *pro tanto*
a satisfaction of the complainants' judgment, which a court
of equity would not vacate on the ground that the defendant
in execution had no title, and the. complainants acquired
nothing by their purchase at the sheriff's sale. The question
whether a purchaser at sheriff's sale will be relieved from the
effect of his bid, on its being made to appear that the defendant in execution had no title whatever to the thing supposed
to be sold, or whether his bid is an irrevocable satisfaction of
the judgment to the extent of the sum bid at the sale, is one
on which the authorities are about equally divided: Freeman
on Judgments, 3d ed., sec. 478; 2 Freeman on Executions,
2d ed., sec. 54.

The question was settled in this state as far back as the
year 1854. In the case of *McCartney* v. *King*, 25 Ala. 681, it
was held that the amount bid by a judgment creditor for
certain slaves sold at sheriff's sale, to which the judgment
debtor had no title, was properly credited upon the execution,
and was a satisfaction of it, against which a court of chancery
would give no relief by vacating the sale. The principle was
thus stated by Judge Goldthwaite: "The true doctrine, we
think, is this: The purchaser, where the sheriff is not indemnified, buys at his own risk, and if it should turn out that the
defendant in execution has no title to the property, he is notwithstanding liable for the amount of his bid. This is on the
ground of contract. The officer sells and the purchaser buys,
not the thing itself, but the real or supposed right which the
defendant in execution has to it; and the purchase operates
precisely the same as if he had bargained for and obtained a
quitclaim." It appeared in that case that the purchase was
made with notice of the defect of title. That, in our opinion,
can make no difference, in the absence of fraud. The basis
of the whole doctrine is the rule of *caveat emptor*, which is the
established and well-understood rule of sheriff's.sales. This
rule puts every holder upon inquiry as to the defendant's title.

It proclaims to the purchaser that there is no warranty of title, and if he buys, he must do so at his own risk. It warns him to go and inquire before purchasing; so that, if he makes a poor bargain, by parting with his money without getting anything in return for it, he must enter no complaint, — no more than if he had bargained for and obtained a mere quit-claim deed: *Smith* v. *Painter*, 5 Serg. & R. 225; 9 Am. Dec. 344. In the language of Chief Justice Gibson, in *Freeman* v. *Caldwell*, 10 Watts, 9: "The plaintiff's case may be a hard one, but it is not more so than would be the case of a stranger; and to say that every sheriff's vendee who is deprived of the property by title paramount shall have his money again would destroy all confidence in the stability of judicial sales." And again, as observed in another case: "If this was not the law, an execution, which is the end of the law, would only be the commencement of a new controversy." The doctrine of these cases has long been supposed to be the law of Alabama, and we adhere to them as sound: *Jones* v. *Burr*, 53 Am. Dec. 699, and note 701–705; 2 Freeman on Executions, 2d ed., sec. 54, and cases cited.

The bill shows that the defendant, J. M. Daniel, acted as the agent of his wife, Mrs. Myra J. Daniel, in making the purchase of the land, in taking the deed of conveyance for it, and in paying the purchase-money over to the vendor. He thus acted for her in the whole transaction of purchase, as her authorized agent. This was in January, 1882, when the statutes of this state made the husband the trustee of the wife's statutory separate estate, with power to control and manage the same, and charged him with the duty of reinvesting the proceeds of its sale in other property, which also became the separate estate of the wife: Code 1876, secs. 2706, 2709. As husband, therefore, Daniel was the agent of his wife for the purpose of making this investment, independently of his appointment by her to such agency. The bill does not allege positively that the purchase-money used was Mrs. Daniel's statutory separate estate; but, taking its averments most strongly against the pleader, the inference is, that the money and notes invested by her alleged agent were hers, and if hers, presumptively the property was her statutory separate estate: *Steed* v. *Knowles*, 79 Ala. 446.

The alleged fraudulent deed from Pullen to Mrs. Mackey, and the one from Mackey and wife to Mrs. Daniel, are stated to have been executed on the same day, — January 28, 1882.

The averment, then, that J. M. Daniel had knowledge of the fraudulent character of the deed taken from Pullen to Mrs. Mackey, by necessary implication, charges that this knowledge was acquired during the time of his agency, and within the scope of his duty and power as trustee of his wife's separate estate. There are cases which hold to the doctrine, that knowledge of a material fact, acquired by an agent in a former transaction, comparatively recent in point of time, such as he is bound to communicate, if present in his mind and memory while engaged in a second transaction, shall operate as constructive notice to his principal in the second transaction: 2 Pomeroy's Eq. Jur., sec. 672. But there is a long line of decisions in this state which adopt the rule, that notice to an agent, to bind his principal, must have been acquired by the agent during his employment, i. e., while he is actually engaged in the prosecution of his duties as agent, and not at a time antecedent to the period of his agency: *Wheeler* v. *McGuire*, 86 Ala. 398; *McCormick* v. *Joseph*, 83 Ala. 401; *Reid* v. *Bank of Mobile*, 70 Ala. 199; *Pepper* v. *George*, 51 Ala. 190; *Terrell* v. *Br. Bank*, 12 Ala. 502; *Mundin* v. *Pitts*, 14 Ala. 84; *Lucas* v. *Bank of Georgia*, 2 Stew. 321.

This principle is one based on expediency and sound policy. A different rule, as long ago suggested by Lord Hardwick, "would make purchasers' and mortgagees' titles depend altogether on the memory of their counselors and agents, and oblige them to apply to persons of less eminence as counsel, as not being so likely to have notice of former transactions." In other words, a contrary rule would render it hazardous for persons to employ efficient agents of broad knowledge and wide experience, and force selections to be confined to men of ignorance in affairs, and with narrow or no experience: 2 Pomeroy's Eq. Jur., secs. 670, 671. Moreover, a designing agent would be armed with the power of bringing financial ruin on his innocent principal, by the intentional, or even fraudulent, refusal to communicate to him his previous acquired knowledge of a secret equity in property, or other latent defect of title, the concealment of which was dictated by the agent's greed in earning his commission, or other equally selfish end.

In this case, the knowledge of the husband as to the alleged fraud must be constructively imputed to the wife as her knowledge: *White* v. *King*, 53 Ala. 162; *Dunklin* v. *Harvey*, 56 Ala. 177; Wade on Notice, sec. 679.

Under these principles, the court erred in sustaining the second assignment of the second demurrer.

The decree of the chancellor is reversed, and the cause is remanded, that a decree may be rendered on the demurrers in conformity to the principles announced in this opinion.

Reversed and remanded.

JUDICIAL SALES — CAVEAT EMPTOR. — The rule of *caveat emptor* applies to purchasers at judicial sales: *Williams* v. *Glenn*, 87 Ky. 87; 12 Am. St. Rep. 461, and note.

FRAUDULENT CONVEYANCE — ADEQUATE REMEDY AT LAW. — Purchaser of land at a sheriff's sale, under execution against a debtor who has fraudulently conveyed the land to his vendee, has a plain remedy at law by an action of ejectment, and cannot, while out of possession, maintain a bill in equity to cancel the fraudulent conveyance: *Teague* v. *Martin*, 87 Ala. 500; 13 Am. St. Rep. 63, and note.

AGENCY — NOTICE. — Notice to an agent is ordinarily notice to the principal: *City Nat. Bank* v. *Martin*, 70 Tex. 643; 8 Am. St. Rep. 632, and note; *Fitzpatrick* v. *Hartford Life etc. Ins. Co.*, 56 Conn. 116; 7 Am. St. Rep. 288, and note.

MEMPHIS AND CHARLESTON R. R. CO. *v.* WOODS.

[88 ALABAMA, 630.]

CORPORATIONS — POWERS AND DUTIES OF DIRECTORS. — The directors of a private pecuniary corporation are under the same restraints and disabilities as trustees. They have no right to use their official positions for their own benefit or the benefit of any one but the corporation; and if they act as directors for different companies, they cannot represent both in transactions in which their interests are opposed, or detrimental to a minority of the stockholders, no matter if such acts are beneficial to a majority of stockholders in each company, and have received their approval.

CORPORATIONS MAY BE ENJOINED FROM VOTING MAJORITY OF STOCK AT SUIT OF MINORITY OF STOCKHOLDERS. — Where a corporation has acquired the majority of the stock of another corporation, it, its officers, directors, or others acting in its interest, may be enjoined from exercising the voting power that the majority of the stock confers, so as to govern and control the management of such corporation, when the two corporations have the same field of action and operation, and the profits of one may be advanced by lessening those of the other, and where their interests are conflicting as to expenditures and division of earnings.

CORPORATIONS. — MINORITY OF STOCKHOLDERS MAY MAINTAIN SUIT IN THEIR OWN NAMES under an averment that before filing the bill they requested the corporation to sue to prevent illegal action by a majority of the stockholders, and that it failed and neglected so to do.

R. C. Brickell, for the East Tennessee, Virginia, and Georgia Railroad Company, and *Humes, Walker, Sheffey, and Gordon,* for the Memphis and Charleston Railroad Company, appellants.

John W. Weed and John M. McKleroy, for the appellees.

STONE, C. J. This suit was commenced October 27, 1887, and is prosecuted by stockholders of the Memphis and Charleston Railroad Company, representing a minority of the stock.

The case was submitted in the court below on a demurrer to the bill, and on a motion to dismiss it for want of equity. From the chancellor's decree overruling the demurrer, and refusing to dismiss the bill or to dissolve the injunction, the present appeal is prosecuted. Coming before us in this form, we must treat as true all the averments of the bill which are well pleaded, and in the further progress of this opinion they will be stated as facts.

The Memphis and Charleston railroad was constructed under charters obtained from the states of Tennessee and Alabama, and extends from Memphis, in Tennessee, to Stevenson, in Alabama, running partly through Mississippi. One hundred and fifty miles of the track are in Alabama. The entire length of the road is not shown. The capital stock is $5,312,725, divided into 212,509 shares, of $25 each. Of these shares, 106,261—being a majority of the whole number—stand on the books in the name of the East Tennessee, Virginia, and Georgia Railway Company, another corporation, which does not connect with or touch the Memphis and Charleston railroad at any point. The complainants hold eight thousand eight hundred of the shares, representing two hundred and twenty thousand dollars of the capital stock, and they sue in their names, and in the names of such other of the stockholders as may join in the suit.

The Memphis and Charleston railroad has been in operation for a third of a century. The profits of the corportion, if any, prior to the time of its passing under the control of the East Tennessee, Virginia, and Georgia Railroad Company, hereafter shown, we have no certain means of ascertaining, further than that from June, 1858, two years after the completion of the road, to June, 1861, the net earnings were never less than ten, and once as high as sixteen, per cent. We have no account of any earnings during the civil war,—from 1861 to 1865,—and suppose not only that there were no net profits, but that the cessation of hostilities left the road very much out of repair. Extraordinary expenditures became necessary to repair and equip the road, and up to June 30, 1867, the expenditures exceeded the receipts. During the years ending

June, 1868, to June, 1874, surplus profits, amounts not shown, were owned by the road each year, except the two years 1871 and 1872. The sum of the deficiency for these two years was about one hundred and fifty thousand dollars.

The East Tennessee, Virginia, and Georgia Railroad Company obtained its charters from the states of Tennessee and Alabama, and had been many years in operation. It extended easterly far beyond Knoxville, Tennessee; and having absorbed or otherwise obtained control of the Selma, Rome, and Dalton railroad, an Alabama corporation, extended in a southwestern direction 150 miles or more into Alabama, terminating at Selma, in this state. It also operated a line which touched at Chattanooga, in the state of Tennessee, eastward from Stevenson, and distant from it twenty-five or more miles. There was, however, a connecting line between the respective termini, but it belonged to another railroad corporation. The East Tennessee, Virginia, and Georgia Railroad Company had probably many other extensions and connections, not necessary to be noticed here. The extent, distances, and connections of the East Tennessee, Virginia, and Georgia Railroad Company are stated partly on general knowledge.

About 1874, one Wilson was elected president of the Memphis and Charleston Railroad Company, and was continued in the office until 1881. His election was procured through the instrumentality of the East Tennessee, Virginia, and Georgia Railroad Company, and although not exactly coterminous, the two railroads have been operated substantially under one management ever since. In the first instance, the Memphis and Charleston railroad was let by lease to the East Tennessee, Virginia, and Georgia company, the rent agreed on being the net income of the former road above expenses. In a suit instituted for the purpose of testing the legality of that lease, it was set aside as being *ultra vires*. Another suit between the Knoxville and Ohio Railroad Company and the East Tennessee, Virginia, and Georgia company, to which the Memphis and Charleston company was not a party, resulted in the acquisition by the East Tennessee, Virginia, and Georgia company of a large volume, nearly one half, of the shares of stock in the Memphis and Charleston Railroad Company. Later acquisitions placed a majority—a bare majority—of the entire stock of the latter company in the name and asserted ownership of the East Tennessee, Virginia, and Georgia company.

The bill insinuates that each of the two suits named above was collusive, at least in part, and facts averred point in that direction. It is also averred that certain shares of the stock, which were held by the Memphis and Charleston company in its own right, were transferred by the common president of the two companies to the East Tennessee, Virginia, and Georgia company without any authority therefor. Marked bias and partiality in favor of the latter company are charged to have prevailed in these transactions, and it is also charged that the East Tennessee, Virginia, and Georgia company was without the power to acquire and own stock in another railroad company. It is expressly charged that the intent and purpose of the said purchase of stock was to give to the East Tennessee, Virginia, and Georgia company a controlling vote in the management of the Memphis and Charleston company; and the exhibit taken from the record of the suit with the Knoxville and Ohio Railroad Company, if correctly set forth, proves this charge to be true. The bill further charges that, after the agreement of lease noted above, which was in 1877, the two railroads have been operated under one and the same president, and under one and the same management. Inequality and fraud are charged in the combined management of the two roads, greatly to the profit of the East Tennesseee, Virginia, and Georgia company, and to the equal detriment of the Memphis and Charleston company.

The bill makes specific charges of partiality and maladministration, as follows: 1. When the East Tennessee, Virginia, and Georgia company acquired controlling power over the Memphis and Charleston railroad, the repair-shops of the latter had been partially destroyed, but could have been rebuilt at a small expenditure. They were not rebuilt. The rolling stock of the Memphis and Charleston company was carried to the shops of the East Tennessee, Virginia, and Georgia company, at Knoxville, Tennessee, "where the repairing was done at extravagant prices, and mileage was charged for all the distance the rolling stock was carried over the road of the East Tennessee, Virginia, and Georgia Railroad Company." "2. The rolling stock (of the Memphis and Charleston company) was unnecessarily increased at exorbitant cost,"—five hundred thousand dollars at one time,—"and was used by the East Tennessee, Virginia, and Georgia Railroad Company upon its own road, without any compensation" to the Memphis and Charleston Railroad Company for such use. 3. "The Memphis

and Charleston railroad was renewed with steel rails, iron
bridges, and ballast, in advance of the needs of the railroad, to
keep down the apparent net earnings."   4. "Less than the *pro
rata* mileage share of through passenger and freight receipts
from passengers and goods passing over both roads was allowed
to the Memphis and Charleston Railroad Company." The bill
then proceeds to show, by tabulated statement and otherwise,
that the percentage of net earnings, compared with the gross
income of the Memphis and Charleston company, was much
less than that of the East Tennessee, Virginia, and Georgia
company, while the former was more favorably circumstanced
for cheap operation than the latter.

The bill charges that, at the election of officers of the Memphis and Charleston company, held in November, 1886, the
East Tennessee, Virginia, and Georgia company succeeded in
electing seven of, its own directors to be directors of the Memphis and Charleston company, — seven being a majority of the
board.   The directors then elected Thomas to be president of
their board, he being at the same time president of the board
of directors of the East Tennessee, Virginia, and Georgia company.   The two railroads were thus placed substantially under
one and the same government.

As we have said, the bill in this case was filed on the
twenty-seventh day of October, 1887, and it charges that another election of directors would be held on the seventeenth
day of November then next ensuing, — twenty-one days after
the filing of the bill.   It charges further that "if said East
Tennessee, Virginia, and Georgia company, its directors, or
any person on its behalf, shall be permitted to participate or
take any part in said election, or any meeting of the stockholders of the Memphis and Charleston Railroad Company,
the baneful control of the East Tennessee, Virginia, and
Georgia company over its affairs will be continued for another
year, and its legitimate earnings will be diverted from its
stockholders, and under various devices absorbed by the East
Tennessee, Virginia, and Georgia company." The prayer for
injunction is twofold: 1. That the East Tennessee, Virginia,
and Georgia company be enjoined from voting the stock
standing in its name, either in the election of directors of the
Memphis and Charleston company, or in any other meeting
of the stockholders; and 2. That it be enjoined from disposing of its stock, except with the knowledge and approval of
the chancery court.

The reason urged in favor of the second of the above prayers is, that without such restraining order the stock might, and probably would, be transferred to some other name, and still held, and its voting power exercised, in the interest of the East Tennessee, Virginia, and Georgia company.   Under some reorganization, the present corporate name of the latter company is the East Tennessee, Virginia, and Georgia Railway Company.

Under the statutes of this state, a general power is conferred to consolidate two or more railroads, which, when completed, "may admit the passage of burden or passenger cars over any two or more of such roads continuously without break or interruption": Code, sec. 1583.   A railroad corporation "may, at any time, by means of subscription to the capital stock of any other corporation or company, or otherwise, aid such corporation or company in the construction of its railroad for the purpose of forming a connection with the road owned by such corporation or company furnishing aid; or any railroad corporation organized in pursuance of law may lease or purchase any part or all of any railroad constructed by any other corporation or company, if the lines of such roads are continuous or connected ": Code, sec. 1586.   "A corporation now existing, or which may hereafter be organized, for the building, constructing, and operating a railroad, has authority, for the purpose of extending its line or forming a connection, to acquire, hold, and operate a railroad without the state; or within the state, may extend its road, or may build, construct, and operate branch roads from any point or points on its line ": Code, sec. 1587.

It is not contended that any of these sections, or all of them combined, confer in terms the powers which the bill alleges that the East Tennessee, Virginia, and Georgia company claims and exercises in the management and control of the Memphis and Charleston company.   The conduct charged and complained of was not the consolidation of two or more roads; for consolidation was neither effected nor attempted.   Nor were any of the steps taken which the statute prescribes as conditions precedent to lawful consolidation.   Nor was it the connecting of two roads, over which cars could pass "continuously without break or interruption."   It was not giving aid by one corporation to another, "in the construction of its railroad, for the purpose of forming a connection with" it.   Neither the aid nor the purpose existed in this case, if the aver-

ments of the bill be true. It was not a lease or purchase of
the Memphis and Charleston railroad, or any part of it; and
if such lease or purchase or other arrangement had been attempted, the lines of the two roads are not connected. And
the averments of the bill negative the idea that any of these
arrangements, connected operation, or consolidation, if claimed
to be such, were agreed to or consummated by the corporations acting as such. Nor was there any agreement or attempted arrangement, either express or implied, that the
one railroad should acquire, hold, and operate the other; nor
is the Memphis and Charleston railroad in any sense a branch
road from any point on the line of the East Tennessee, Virginia, and Georgia company. It is not a branch road according to the averments of the bill.

We repeat, the sections of the code we have been commenting on do not expressly confer the powers which the complainants complain of as abuses, nor does the East Tennessee,
Virginia, and Georgia company contend that they do. It
could not so contend. Its precise contention is, that those
statutes "evidence a settled policy of the state to encourage
consolidations or combinations of connecting lines."

It is manifestly true that long connecting lines of railroad
are a benefaction. They economize time and labor, and
thereby lessen expense. Common observation, and the simplest processes of reasoning, show this to be too clear to require
argument in support of it. But does the conduct complained
of in this case encourage or promote the consolidation of connecting lines? Is it a legitimate means of accomplishing that
end?

Private corporations can exercise only such powers as are
conferred upon them, and such as are necessary and proper
to carry the granted powers into effect. In this, however, is
included the inherent, incidental power of doing and performing such acts as are necessarily implied in the line of trade
or business of the corporation, as shown by the charter, or law
of its creation: *Wilks* v. *Georgia Pac. R'y Co.*, 79 Ala. 180; 3
Brickell's Digest, 159. Based on this principle, it is contended
for appellee that the East Tennessee, Virginia, and Georgia
company had no power to acquire and hold shares of stock in
the Memphis and Charleston company; that its purchase of
the stock was *ultra vires* and void, and that, as a consequence,
it should not be allowed to exercise the powers, which rightful ownership alone confers; in other words, that to authorize

the exercise of the privileges of a stockholder, the stock must have been lawfully acquired. On this ground it is contended that the ruling of the chancellor in continuing the injunction is free from error. May it not be answered to this contention: 1. That conceding the purchase of the stock by the East Tennessee, Virginia, and Georgia company to have been *ultra vires*, are the complainants in this suit in any position to raise that question? They are not stockholders in the East Tennessee, Virginia, and Georgia company; and can they be heard to complain that a corporation to which they are strangers has misapplied its funds? 2. Does not the bill show on its face that the East Tennessee, Virginia, and Georgia company purchased the stock, not as an investment of its funds, but in the collection of a debt due to it from another railroad corporation? The power of a corporation to acquire property, real and personal, as a means of collecting a debt otherwise doubtful, stands on a very different principle from that which determines its power to purchase such property, as an investment of its funds or capital: *First Nat. Bank* v. *National Exch. Bank,* 92 U. S. 122; 1 Morawetz on Corporations, sec. 431.

We come, then, to the naked inquiry, Can one corporation acquire a majority of the stock of another corporation, and by the exercise of the voting power the majority of stock confers, govern and control the management of such corporation? This question, in its naked form, has rarely been presented to the courts, although it is generally known that such transactions are not infrequent.

In 1 Morawetz on Corporations, section 431, it is said: "The right of a corporation to invest in the shares of another company cannot be implied merely because both companies are engaged in a similar kind of business. A corporation must carry on its business by its own agents, and not through the agency of another corporation." And this doctrine is stated, without dissent, in 4 Am. & Eng. Ency. of Law, 249, note 2. In *Central R. R. Co.* v. *Collins,* 40 Ga. 582, will be found a very full and somewhat pioneer discussion of the power and right of a railroad company to acquire and hold a majority of the stock of another railroad corporation, with a view of controlling its management. It is an able discussion, and although not presented precisely in the form in which the present bill raises it, it enunciates principles which bear on the question in hand. Among many other wise and conservative prin-

ciples declared in that opinion, we transcribe and approve the
following: —

"I am strongly impressed with the conviction, that much
of their [the railroads'] success in developing the resources of
a country is due to the very jealousy which has ever held
them strictly to their charters, and has constantly been careful to prevent any undue accumulation of interest under one
management. The certainty that each stockholder has that
his funds will be applied to known and declared purposes
has made them favorite investments for prudent men; whilst
the rivalry which opposing interests engender begets an energy, economy, skill, and enterprise that have had much to
do with the remarkable progress which such enterprises have
made. A colossal enterprise, assured of handsome dividends
by the possession of a monopoly, may well rest upon its position, knowing that however the country may suffer from its
exactions, its own profits are secure. It is the rivalry of opposing interests, the struggle for success, — nay, even for life, —
with dangerous opposition, that gives life, enterprise, and success to railroads, as to other human undertakings. It has
been the conflict with thirty states' lines, each with its opposing interests, and with numerous seaboard cities, each
seeking to attract the rich outpourings from the great interior,
that has begotten the mighty network of iron which inter-
laces our extensive territory; and I am convinced that there
is no public policy more striking than that which, whilst it
fosters every undertaking, is yet careful ever to keep in view
the danger of a monopoly, and the good effects of rivalry and
conflict between different companies. The Central Railroad is,
and has long been, the pride of Georgia. The skill, energy,
and prudence with which its affairs have been managed re-
flect great credit upon the men who have had these affairs in
their control, and the state may well be grateful for the success that has followed. Yet, we cannot but think it would be
a measure fraught with great public evil to give to that company permission to control and manage its great rival, the
Atlantic and Gulf road."

In the case of *Hazelhurst* v. *Savannah etc. R. R. Co.*, 43 Ga.
13, the principles of the foregoing case are reaffirmed.

The case of *Milbank* v. *New York etc. R. R. Co.*, 64 How. Pr.
20, was like the present one in most of its bearings. In that
case, as in this, one railroad corporation had purchased a majority of the capital stock of another, and proposed to vote the

stock so purchased in the election of directors. Certain stockholders in the latter company, owning a small minority of its
capital stock, filed a bill to enjoin the purchasing company
from voting the stock it had acquired, being a majority of the
shares. The court, in delivering its opinion, said: "In the
case under consideration, the New York, Lake Erie, and Western company have acquired by purchase the majority of all
the stock issued by the Buffalo, New York, and Erie railroad.
If its officers are permitted to vote thereon, they can elect a
board of directors of their own choosing. It would then be
for the interest of the New York, Lake Erie, and Western
Railroad Company to have the Buffalo, New York, and Erie
company managed and controlled in the interest of the former
company. This would be liable to result in injury to these
plaintiffs and their fellow-stockholders, and if so, they have a
right to complain. My conclusions, therefore, are, that while
the New York, Lake Erie, and Western Railroad Company is
the owner of the stock in question, and has the right, while it
remains the owner, to collect and receive the dividends thereon,
and has the right to sell and dispose of the same, it has not
the right to vote thereon; and that the stockholders of the
Buffalo, New York, and Erie Railroad Company have the right
to have it enjoined from so voting, in case it threatened to do
so. Judgment should be ordered for the plaintiffs, in accordance with the views herein expressed, with costs."

It is true that this was not a decision by the court of last
resort. It was by the supreme court, — an intermediate court in
that state. It appears to have been acquiesced in; for no appeal is shown to have been taken: See also *Franklin Co. v.
Lewiston*, 68 Me. 43; 28 Am. Rep. 9; *Sumner v. Marcy*, 3 Wood.
& M. 105; *Mechanics' etc. Mut. Sav. Bank v. Meriden Agency Co.*,
24 Conn. 159.

Corporations aggregate are governed, and must be governed
and made efficient, through the instrumentality of agents.
These agents, in cases of pecuniary corporations, are called
directors, who are elected at stated intervals by the stockholders, for such term as the charter or regulations may prescribe. They may not be trustees in the technical sense, but
their functions are largely and essentially fiduciary: *Hoyle v.
Plattsburg etc. R. R. Co.*, 54 N. Y. 328; 13 Am. Rep. 595.
Says Mr. Morawetz (1 Corporations, sec. 517), the directors
"impliedly undertake to give the company the benefit of their
best care and judgment, and to use the powers conferred upon

them solely in the interest of the corporation. They have no right, under any circumstances, to use their official positions for their own benefit, or the benefit of any one except the corporation itself. It is for this reason that the directors have no authority to represent the corporation in any transaction in which they are personally interested, in obtaining an advantage at the expense of the company.. The corporation would not have the benefit of their disinterested judgment under these circumstances, as self-interest would prompt them to prefer their own advantage to that of the company." A director "falls within the great rule by which equity requires that confidence shall not be abused by the party in whom it is reposed, and which it enforces by imposing a disability, either partial or complete, upon the party intrusted, to deal on his own behalf in respect to any matter involved in such confidence": *Hoyle* v. *Plattsburg etc. R. R. Co., supra,* and authorities cited.

So in 1 Morawetz on Corporations, section 528, is this language: "A person who is agent for two parties cannot, in the absence of express authority from each, represent them both in a transaction in which they have contrary interests. . . . . It follows, therefore, that the directors, or other agents of a corporation, have no implied authority to bind the company by making a contract with another corporation which they also represent." Section 529: "It is well settled that if the same persons are appointed to act as directors of different companies, they have no authority to represent both companies in transactions in which their interests are opposed. It matters not that the acts of the directors are in the interest of a majority of the share-holders in each company, and have received their approval. Nothing can be more unjustifiable and dishonorable than an attempt on the part of those holding a majority of the shares in a corporation to place their nominees in control of a company, and then to use their control for the purpose of obtaining advantage to themselves at the expense of the minority; it would be a conspiracy to commit a breach of trust. The directors of a corporation are bound to administer its affairs with strict impartiality, in the interest of all the share-holders alike; and the inability of the minority to protect themselves against unauthorized acts performed with the connivance of the majority renders their right to the protection of the courts the clearer": *State* v. *Concord R. R. Co.,* 13 Am. & Eng. R. R. Cas. 94; *Pearson* v. *Concord*

etc. R. R. Co., 13 Am. & Eng. R. R. Cas. 94; 102 Wall. 178; 1
Morawetz on Corporations, sec. 530, and note 3; Cook on Stock
and Stockholders, secs. 615, 618.

Although, as we have said, directors of a pecuniary corporation may not be trustees in the technical sense of that term,
they are under the same restraints, and labor under the same
disabilities, which rest on trustees proper, so far as questions
raised by the present bill are concerned. When personal interest antagonizes the disinterestedness and impartiality which ·
the law, as well as morality, exacts in the exercise of fiduciary
trusts, this is, *per se*, a disqualification, not by reason of any
abuse committed, but in fear that weak human nature will
yield to temptation. Justice Field, speaking of the conflict
between duty and interest, says: "Constituted as humanity
is, in the majority of cases duty would be overborne in the
struggle": *Marsh* v. *Whitmore*, 21 Wall. 178; *Nathan* v. *Tompkins*, 82 Ala. 437; *Gr. Luxemburg R'y Co.* v. *Magnay*, 25 Beav.
586.

The averments of the bill in this case show great wrongs
done to the Memphis and Charleston company by reason of
the control exercised in its management by the East Tennessee, Virginia, and Georgia company. It also charges that it
is the intention of the latter company to so vote its stock as to
maintain its control of the Memphis and Charleston railroad.
Whether the charges of past abuses be true or false, they bring
prominently to the notice of the court the character and extent
of wrong and oppression which one corporation may inflict on
another when circumstanced as these are.

It is scarcely necessary that we should specify in what
manner the oppression may be inflicted. The board of directors elected by and for the East Tennessee, Virginia, and Georgia company, we must suppose, owe their election to all the
stockholders, representing all the stock in that company. The
duties of fidelity and impartiality in administering the affairs
of that company, implied in the relation they sustain to it, we
have stated above. They require severe disinterestedness as
between the several share-holders, and unbiased fidelity to the
prosperity and success of the corporation. Now, when the
directors of the Memphis and Charleston company, or a controlling majority of them, owe their election to the East Tennessee, Virginia, and Georgia company, and to that company
alone, it is manifest that questions may and will arise on
which there will be a conflict of interest between the two com-

panies. It is but human nature that, in such conflict, directors thus chosen will give their votes and influence in favor of the company they represent in full, and in whose entire income and emoluments they participate, rather than to the company they represent only to the extent of a trifle above a moiety of its stock,—an integer against a fraction. Both law and reason force the implication that in the governing body of a corporation duty and interest shall not point in opposite directions.

We hold that it is equally against public policy, and against that sound rule which disables trustees, or *quasi* trustees, to act when their duty and interest conflict, that the East Tennessee, Virginia, and Georgia company should be allowed to vote its majority stock, in matters pertaining to the management and control of the Memphis and Charleston company.

We confine our ruling, however, for the present, to cases like this one, where a conflict of interest may arise, in the matter of expenditures and their apportionment, in the division of patronage or of earnings, and to rivalships between different companies having substantially the same field of operation, or where the profits of one enterprise will naturally be enhanced by the diminution of those of the other. There may be other cases to which the rule will apply, but we decline to consider them now.

This case has been very ably argued, and we are not unmindful of the grave consequences that may, and probably will, ensue from our decision, not alone to the East Tennessee, Virginia, and Georgia company, but to many other corporations similarly circumstanced. We have not declared that the law does not authorize that company to acquire and hold stock or shares of stock in another railroad corporation. Its charter not being before us, we have no means of ascertaining what its corporate powers are, further than the implications which naturally arise from its name and its lines of business inform us. We have not declared that if the East Tennessee, Virginia, and Georgia company is without power to acquire and hold shares of stock in another railroad corporation, the complainants in this suit have shown any right to controvert the question of its rightful ownership. Hence, we have not decided that the Knoxville and Ohio Railroad Company was not the rightful, lawful owner of the stock which the East Tennessee, Virginia, and Georgia company acquired from it, nor that the latter company did not acquire a good

title by its purchase. We have not attempted to set aside, or
to declare invalid, either of these sales. We do not controvert the general inherent right, resulting from the ownership
of stock in a corporation, to exercise the elective power such
ownership confers, and to exercise it wisely or unwisely, alone,
or pursuant to an agreement with other stockholders; and
that no one, save the former owner, can question the right to
vote such stock, even when obtained by fraud, or other illegal
means: *Moses* v. *Scott*, 84 Ala. 608. This, we repeat, is the
general rule; and less than this, in an ordinary case, would
be an unauthorized abridgment of the stockholder's property
rights.

Enjoyment and the right of disposition are general attributes of property ownership. Property rights, however, cannot be classed as absolutely independent of social and municipal regulation. "So use your own as not to invade the
equal rights of others," is a maxim as sound in law as it is in
the circle of social intercourse. Its observation and preservation are the end and aim of much wise legislation, of much
judicial administration. But men must be dealt with, not as
faultless, but as frail, and subject to temptation, too strong
for their powers of resistance. Civil liberty is but natural
liberty shorn of its power to transgress the boundary which
separates *meum* and *tuum*, in its comprehensive sense. Hence
it is that the law, with inflexible purpose, has placed restraints
on transactions in which duty and interest conflict. Hence it
is that, when any relation of trust or confidence subsists, the
law scrutinizes with earnest if not severe vigilance any pecuniary transaction that may be had between parties thus
circumstanced. Hence it is that, when one man stands in a
fiduciary relation to another, any contract or bargain and
sale had with the beneficiary is invalid at the mere option of
the latter, if seasonably expressed. The danger of abuse in
such conditions dominates the power of disposition, and the
power to make binding contracts, which we have classed as
among the general attributes of property ownership, must submit to reasonable restraints: *Thompson* v. *Lee*, 31 Ala. 292;
Moses v. *Micou*, 79 Ala. 564; *Huguenin* v. *Basely*, 14 Ves. 273.

It is contended for appellants, that if a majority of the
capital stock of the Memphis and Charleston company had
belonged to an individual, or to a combination of individuals,
instead of being the property of the East Tennessee, Virginia,
and Georgia company, the same power of control could have

been exerted as is complained of in this cause. It is possible that there might be an exceptional extreme case, in which it would advance the interest of the owner or owners of a majority of the stock in a corporation to diminish its income, that the emoluments of another enterprise, in which he or they are more largely interested, may be thereby enhanced. Such case, however, is extremely improbable; and if found to exist, it might possibly present a case of wrong for which injunction could furnish no preventive relief. This is a question we need not decide. As a rule, stockholders, in voting, as in other acts they are called to perform, attempt to promote the welfare of the corporation; for on its success depend their profits. Whether they act wisely or not, no one can be heard to complain of their conduct; for the success of the enterprise and their individual interests are presumed to be identical. In ordinary elections by stockholders, the presumption is, that men will act as their interests prompt them to act, and that their aim is to benefit the corporation in which they are stockholders. Should a case arise in which there is bad faith in the management, and consequent loss to the stockholders, there would seem to be no doubt that redress could be obtained from the faithless governing body.

The case in which the votes are cast by individual stockholders and the one in hand are, presumptively at least, essentially different. In that, duty and interest are in complete accord; in this, if the averments of the bill be true, they are in palpable antagonism. In the one, the presumption is, that the vote will be cast solely in the interest of the corporation holding the election; in the other, that the greater opposing interest will prevail over the lesser, as it is so apt to do in all human conduct. We think it is no answer to the relief prayed in this case, that in another possible supposable case, a wrong very like the one here complained of might be inflicted, and yet the same measure of redress could not be accorded.

It is contended that, if relief be granted in this case, it will greatly embarrass railroad corporations, in the matter of maintaining continuous, connecting lines, so conducive to public convenience, and to economy in transportation.

It cannot be denied that steam has, in many respects, revolutionized the world, and that railroads are among the more potent instrumentalities which have effected that revolution. The nations of the earth have been brought into closer neighborhood and better acquaintance, while Christian civilization has been much more speedily and widely diffused. So commerce and the industrial enterprises have received a new impetus and expansion theretofore unknown in the world's history. An instrumentality possessing such vast capabilities should be cherished and protected in the enjoyment and exercise of all its rights and privileges. The groveling or agrarian spirit which would hinder or embarrass this mighty agency in the full enjoyment of its rightful powers should receive no encouragement or countenance from right-thinking people. On the other hand, the tremendous power that may be wielded by aggregated or incorporated wealth should be kept within due bounds, and restricted to legitimate methods. The pernicious ends to which concentrated wealth may be perverted need not be mentioned here. The virtuous and patriotic utterances of many of the courts of supreme jurisdiction, re-echoed from the highest officials in the federal government, show all too plainly that the public is awakened to the wrongs inflicted through the instrumentality of combined capital. Let us accord to corporations all their rights, and restrain them in the abuse of their powers, should such be attempted.

The principle we have declared in a former part of this opinion will apply with equal force to all employees, agents, and all other persons or corporations who may be acting in the interest or for the benefit of the East Tennessee, Virginia, and Georgia company. Nothing less than an absolute sale of the stock to some person or persons authorized to vote it will relieve it of the infirmity of its present ownership, or authorize the present or any pretended owner to be heard in the government of the Memphis and Charleston company.

The bill does not charge that the East Tennessee, Virginia, and Georgia company contemplates a sale, or pretended sale, of the stock, and does not charge that the company, by any indirect means, will attempt to have its stock voted in its interest. The charge is, that "if said East Tennessee, Virginia, and Georgia company is permitted to transfer said stock, it will conceal its interest in the same under the name of some other party, and through such party reacquire the control it now has with said stock standing in its own name." If such attempt be made, without an actual sale of the stock, it will be a violation of the order made in this case, and can be punished as such. Moreover, an election of directors thus procured would be a fraud perpetrated in defiance of the order of the court, and such election would be annulled on proper application. We hold, however, that in the present stage of this case, and under the averments of the bill, all of which that is pertinent we have copied, there is not enough shown to authorize an injunction against a sale of the stock. That question can be properly raised when an attempt is made, should it ever be made, to violate or evade the principles of the injunction granted in this cause: 1 Brickell's Digest, p. 704, sec. 930; 3 Brickell's Digest, p. 377, secs. 154, 155, 158.

The bill in this case avers that, before filing the bill, the complainants "requested the Memphis and Charleston Railroad Company, by a request addressed to its officers, to take appropriate legal proceedings to prevent the stock standing in the name of the East Tennessee, Virginia, and Georgia Railway Company from being voted upon," etc., "but said corporation has neglected to comply with said request." This averment is sufficient to authorize the stockholders to sue in their own names, if any previous request was necessary to give them that right. Circumstanced as this case is charged to have been, it would seem any previous request would obviously have been denied, and therefore it was not necessary to prefer it: *Tuskaloosa Mfg. Co.* v. *Cox*, 68 Ala. 71; *Nathan* v. *Tompkins*, 82 Ala. 437; *Merchant and Planters' Line* v. *Waganer*, 71 Ala. 581; Green's Brice's Ultra Vires, 673, note *a; Dodge* v. *Woolsey*, 18 How. 331; *Hawes* v. *Oakland*, 104 U. S. 450.

We have stated above that the complainants' bill makes a case for an injunction restraining the East Tennessee, Virginia, and Georgia Railway Company, its agents, directors, and all other persons representing it and its interest, from voting the shares of stock held by that company. We have forborne to state one imperfection in the bill until this time. Many of the essential averments of the bill are stated in this form: Complainants are "informed and believe," or are "advised and believe," without any allegation or charge that the information or advice is true. This form of allegation has always been held in this court to be insufficient. It is not an averment that the information or advice is true, but that the pleader believes it to be true. A full denial of such averment would be, either that complainants had not received such information or advice, or if they received it, they did not believe it. This would not present the issue sought to be raised: 1 Brickell's Digest, p. 702, secs. 907, 908. We will not, however, dissolve the injunction for this imperfection in pleading. Should it not be remedied within a reasonable time, it will become the duty of the chancellor to act upon the bill as if the imperfect averments pointed out had not been made.

The decree of the chancellor is modified, and the cause remanded. Let the appellees pay the cost of appeal.

Modified and remanded.

CORPORATIONS. —Promoters of a corporation, who upon its formation become officers thereof, must be treated as its agents and trustees, and held accountable for any profits realized by them from contracts made for the corporation: *Pittsburg Min. Co.* v. *Spooner*, 74 Wis. 307; see *post*, and note, as to the power of directors to contract with the corporation. Director of a corporation stands in a fiduciary relation to the corporation, and is under the disability of a trustee: *Pearson* v. *Concord R. R. Corp.*, 62 N. H. 537; 13 Am. St. Rep. 590, and note.

CORPORATIONS. — Directors of two corporations cannot act for either when the interests of the two corporations are conflicting: Note to *Pearson* v. *Concord R. R. Corp.*, 13 Am. St. Rep. 607.

CORPORATIONS, SUITS AGAINST, BY STOCKHOLDERS: *Rothwell* v. *Robinson*, 39 Minn. 1; 12 Am. St. Rep. 608, and note 609, 610; *Alexander* v. *Searcy*, 81 Ga. 536; 12 Am. St. Rep. 337.

CORPORATIONS CANNOT PURCHASE, deal in, or hold stock in other corporations, unless so authorized by law: *Franklin Co.* v. *Lewiston Inst. for Savings*, 68 Me. 43; 28 Am, Rep. 9, and note 15. 16.

CASES

IN THE

SUPREME COURT

OF

CALIFORNIA.

CARTER v. MULREIN.

[82 CALIFORNIA, 167.]

SURETIES ON INJUNCTION BOND EXECUTED AFTER ISSUANCE OF WRIT NOT LIABLE. — The sureties on statutory bonds have a right to stand upon the precise terms of their contract. When, therefore, a bond is given in pursuance of an order that an injunction issue on the filing of a bond, the sureties are not liable for damages resulting to the defendant from his obeying a writ of injunction issued and served several days prior to the execution of the bond, no writ having been issued after the filing of the bond.

ACTION on an injunction bond. The opinion states the case.

Langhorne and Miller, for the appellants.

William T. Baggett, for the respondent.

McFARLAND, J. This is an action on an injunction bond alleged to have been executed by the defendant Mulrein as principal, and the other defendants as sureties, in a certain action in the superior court in which the said Mulrein was plaintiff, and I. S. Kalloch and Carter (the plaintiff herein) and others were defendants. Judgment (in the case at bar) went for plaintiff, and the defendants Alpers and Westphal, two of the sureties on the bond, appeal from the judgment, and from an order denying a new trial.

The first point made by appellants is, that the complaint does not state a cause of action, — that point having been made, also, in the court below on an objection by defendants to the admission of any evidence on the part of plaintiff. And we see no escape from holding that the point is well taken.

It fully appears, from the complaint, and is admitted on the argument, that, in the said case of *Mulrein* v. *Kalloch et al.*, an order was signed by the judge of the court on March 3, 1881, and filed March 4, 1881, that an injunction issue "on the filing by plaintiff of a joint and several undertaking to the defendants in the sum of seven thousand five hundred dollars, with two sufficient sureties"; that on said March 4th a writ of injunction was issued and served; that said writ was the only writ of injunction ever issued in said action; that all the alleged damage to plaintiff was caused by his obedience to that writ, and that the bond sued on in the case at bar was not executed until March 12, 1881, eight days after the issuance and service of said writ. The bond recites that "whereas the above-entitled court has made an order that, upon the filing by the above-named plaintiff of an undertaking in the sum of seven thousand five hundred dollars, with two sufficient sureties, a writ of injunction issue. . . . . Now, therefore, in consideration of the premises, and that said writ of injunction may issue, we" undertake, etc. No writ issued after the filing of the undertaking.

It is well settled that sureties on statutory bonds, having no personal interest in the litigation, can stand upon the express terms of their undertaking, and cannot have their liability forced beyond those terms. "A surety has a right to stand on the precise terms of his contract. He can be held to no other or different contract": *People* v. *Buster*, 11 Cal. 220. "His liability arises under his contract merely, and is limited by its terms and conditions": *McDonald* v. *Fett*, 49 Cal. 355. "If there is any principle of law well settled, it is that the liability of sureties is not to be extended beyond the terms of their contract. To the extent and in the manner and under the circumstances pointed out in their obligation, they are bound, and no further; they are entitled to stand on its precise terms": *Pierce* v. *Whiting*, 63 Cal. 543. In the bond sued on in this case, there is no undertaking by the sureties to protect against the injunction which had been issued on March 4th. It referred entirely to a writ of injunction which might issue by virtue of the undertaking upon or after its filing; and no such writ ever issued. No doubt the defendant in that case (plaintiff in this) relied upon that undertaking; but we cannot wrest settled principles of law from their foundations in order to condone the carelessness of parties who fail to look after their rights at the proper time. If the defendants in the injunction suit had paid the slightest attention to their interests when the bond sued on was filed, they would have discovered that it afforded no protection against the writ, which had for several days been issued and served, and that said writ was invalid, unless, indeed, we must presume that some other bond had been filed before the writ issued.

Whether the real facts are different from those averred, and whether plaintiff could better his case by amending his complaint, are matters of which we have no knowledge.

Judgment and order reversed.

SURETYSHIP. — The contract of suretyship is construed strictly in favor of the surety: *Anderson* v. *Bellenger*, 87 Ala. 334; 13 Am. St. Rep. 46.

RICHARDSON v. BUTLER.

[82 CALIFORNIA, 174.]

JURISDICTION OF PROBATE COURT OVER SALE OF LANDS BELONGING TO ESTATE OF DECEASED PERSON does not come from its general jurisdiction over the administration of the estate, but from the petition for the sale, and the petition must comply with the provisions of the statute. A literal compliance with the requirements of the statute is not, however, necessary. A substantial compliance therewith is sufficient.

JURISDICTION OF PROBATE COURT DEPENDS UPON AVERMENTS OF PETITION FOR SALE of lands belonging to the estate of a deceased person, and not upon the truth or falsity of such averments.

DESCRIPTION OF PROPERTY OF DECEDENT BY REFERENCE TO INVENTORY. — A petition for the sale of lands belonging to the estate of a decedent may properly refer to the schedules of the inventory of such estate for a particular description of such lands. And the fact that the inventory refers to a map or diagram on file, which cannot be found at the time of the trial of a cause involving the validity of the sale, seventeen years afterward, will not affect the jurisdiction, if the inventory, taken in connection with the averments of the petition, sufficiently shows what was the interest of the decedent in the lands at the time of his death, contains a full description of the real property of the estate at the time the sale was asked, and gives the court all the information upon the subject required by the statute.

DESIGNATION OF CITY LOT AS "UNIMPROVED" IS SUFFICIENT DESCRIPTION OF ITS CONDITION, in a petition for a probate sale, to give the probate court jurisdiction.

STATEMENT IN PETITION AS TO DEBTS AND EXPENSES OF ADMINISTRATION, WHEN SUFFICIENT. — The statement in a petition for a probate sale that there are no debts, or expenses of administration accrued and unpaid, is

sufficient to vest jurisdiction in the court, so far as that point is concerned, if the prior accounts have been settled, and the petition seeks a
sale, not to pay debts and past expenses, but to provide for a family allowance and future expenses of administration.

ORDER OF SALE IN PROBATE PROCEEDING IS NOT VOID because it provides
that the sale shall cease when a certain sum of money required to be
raised has been obtained, when the lands to be sold consist of several lots
or parcels.

FINDING AS TO NOTICE OF PROBATE SALE CONCLUSIVE WHEN. — The finding
of the court in the order confirming a probate sale that the notice of sale
was posted in three public places is conclusive as against a collateral
attack.

VERIFICATION OF PETITION FOR PROBATE SALE, WHEN SUFFICIENT. — The
verification of a petition for a probate sale is not invalid because the certificate of verification is placed before the schedules which are attached
to it. The schedules are a part of the petition, and are as fully included
in the verification as are the parts that precede the certificate.

MERE TECHNICAL OBJECTIONS WILL NOT BE PERMITTED TO OVERTHROW TITLE
TO LANDS honestly acquired under a probate sale, where there is no pretense that the sale was in fact fraudulent, or without adequate consideration, or in any way unfair.

ACTION to quiet title. The opinion states the case.

Jarboe, Harrison, and Goodfellow, for the appellants.

J. C. Bates, for the respondents.

McFARLAND, J. Action to quiet title. Judgment for plaintiffs, from which, and from an order denying a new trial, the
defendants Kate Dunne and Alice Dunne appeal.

Plaintiffs claim title to the disputed premises as heirs at
law of their deceased father, John Sproul. Defendants claim
title under a probate sale made to their grantors in the course
of the administration of the estate of said Sproul, deceased,
upon the petition of his administratrix, Mary Ann Sproul.
The court below ruled said sale to be void; and, practically,
the only question in the case is, whether or not that ruling
was correct.

The court below merely found, generally, that "said sale
was void in law, and passed no title to said Moxley and King-
well (plaintiffs' grantors), or either of them"; and does not
find any specific facts upon which that conclusion was based.
But the brief of respondents' counsel — waiving for the present appellants' objections to the findings for insufficiency —
discloses the grounds of the finding; and the main one is,
that the petition for the sale did not contain a description of
the real property of the estate and a statement of its condition
and value, as required by section 1537 of the Code of Civil
Procedure.

It is no doubt the settled rule here that the application of an administrator for the sale of lands belonging to the estate is an independent proceeding; that the jurisdiction of the probate court over it does not come from its general jurisdiction over the administration of the estate, but from the petition for the sale; and that the petition must comply with the requirements of the code: *Pryor* v. *Downey,* 50 Cal. 398; 19 Am. Rep. 656, and cases there cited. And we apprehend that this rule is not changed by the provisions of the present constitution, which gives jurisdiction of probate business to a court of general jurisdiction, or by the fact that the code no longer requires a deficiency of personal property to be shown before there can be any valid sale of real property. But as was said in *Stuart* v. *Allen,* 16 Cal. 501, 76 Am. Dec. 551, "in order to the exercise of jurisdiction it is not necessary that there should be a literal compliance with the directions of the statute. A substantial compliance is enough." A court, keeping in view the interests of both heirs and purchasers in good faith for value (as in this case), ought not to consider the provisions of the ccde as presenting an intricate verbal puzzle which must be worked out minutely, and with extreme exactness, in the petition. Such a view would make grave rights of property dependent upon the doing of mere trifling tricks. Looking at the purpose of the code provisions on the subject, — gathered, of course, from their language, — a petition should be considered sufficient if it fully and fairly answers those purposes. And the main purpose, clearly, is to inform the court about the condition of the estate, so that it may pass upon the necessity and propriety of the sale. And with these views, we think that the petition involved in this case was sufficient.

John Sproul died in January, 1869, and the petition was not filed until November, 1874, — nearly five years afterward. It is quite lengthy, and covers sixteen pages of the printed transcript. With respect to the real property as it stood when the deceased died, the petition states that on March 28, 1870, she returned to the court "a true inventory and appraisement of all the estate of said deceased which came to her possession or knowledge, which inventory and appraisement is hereby referred to and made a part hereof." It then states that "the only property which came into the possession of your petitioner, as appears by said inventory and appraisement, was [after mentioning personal property] an undivided

one-half interest in and to the tract of land described in said
inventory, and known as the Sharp and Sproul tract, and
owned in common by said deceased and George F. Sharp, appraised as of the value of thirty-five thousand dollars." This
tract is further described in the petition as "situate in said
city and county of San Francisco, and known as 'outside
lands.'" The petition further states that, under certain acts
and ordinances of Congress, the state of California, and the
city and county of San Francisco, all of said land was reserved and appropriated by said city and county for the purposes of a public park, the owners being compensated, "except
that portion thereof hereinafter described in schedule B, and
another portion thereof assigned to George F. Sharp under the
decree of partition hereinafter referred to." It is then stated
that, after the administration had commenced, the said Sharp
brought an action against petitioner and the heirs of said deceased for partition of all of said remaining land, except that
part described in the second subdivision of said schedule B;
and that on April 21, 1874, by a decree in that action, the
lands described in the first subdivision of said schedule B
were set apart in severalty to the estate of said Sproul, deceased. Said schedule B contains,— 1. Descriptions of all
the various blocks, lots, and parcels of the land thus set off to
the estate, and there is no pretense that such descriptions are
not full and sufficient; and 2. Descriptions of the lots and
parcels in which the estate and said Sharp were still co-tenants, and these descriptions are also sufficient. And the
petition alleges "that the only real property to which said
estate is entitled, or which your petitioner, as administratrix
of said estate, is in or entitled to the possession, is that described in schedule B, and that the condition and value of
said real property are set forth in said schedule."

It is clear, therefore, that the petition set forth full and
clear descriptions of all the real property of the estate at the
time the petition was filed; and as it gave the court complete
information on that subject, it certainly complied with the
main purpose of the code in that regard. But it is urged by
respondents that the sale, and all proceedings of the probate
court with respect to it, should be held absolutely void on this
collateral attack, because, as they contend, there is no sufficient description in the petition of the land of the estate as it
was when Sproul died; that is, "the real property of which
the decedent died seised." The petition, with the inventory

which is a part of it, describes the land first, generally, as the undivided one half of the Sharp and Sproul tract, situated in San Francisco, and then gives a description by metes and bounds, excepting certain parcels heretofore conveyed, which are delineated and marked with certain specific names on a map or diagram on "file herein,"—that is, on file with the inventory; but at the time of the trial—about seventeen years afterward—such map or diagram could not be found on file, or among the papers of the estate, and it is argued that without this map the description is so defective as to upset the jurisdiction. The land, however, down to the decree of partition, was always described as the half of the Sharp and Sproul tract. Now, the averments of the petition are (and the jurisdiction depends on the averments, not upon their truth or falsity) that all of the said land not mentioned in the second subdivision of schedule B was divided by the partition decree; and the parcels set off in severalty to the estate by that decree are fully described in the first part of said schedule. And the second part of said schedule fully describes all the lots and parcels of said tract in which the estate and Sharp were still joint owners. It seems to us, therefore, that the averments of the petition sufficiently showed to the court what the interest of the deceased in the Sharp and Sproul tract was at the time of his death, and contained a full description of all the real property of the estate at the time the sale was asked, and gave to the court all the information upon that subject contemplated by the code, and that the sale was not void for want of sufficient description of real property in the petition: *Stuart* v. *Allen*, 16 Cal. 501; 76 Am. Dec. 551; *Fitch* v. *Miller*, 20 Cal. 352.

The other objections made by the respondents are untenable. The designation of a city lot as "unimproved" is, we think, a sufficient description of its "condition," at least, to give jurisdiction to the probate court.

The statement that there were no debts, or expenses of administration accrued and unpaid, was, we think, sufficient to vest jurisdiction, so far as that point is concerned, where, as in this case, the prior accounts of the administratrix had been settled, and the petition sought a sale, not to pay debts and past expenses, but to provide for family allowance and future expenses of administration.

It appears that the amount necessary to be raised was between ten thousand and eleven thousand dollars; and the property consisting of several separate lots and parcels, the order of sale provided that "such sale shall cease when an amount not less than ten thousand dollars and not exceeding eleven thousand dollars has been obtained"; and respondent contends that the part of the order just quoted makes the whole void. We are unable to see any good reason for that contention.

The probate court, in its order confirming the sale, declared that the notice of sale was posted in three public places. Respondent introduced evidence against the objection of appellants, with intent to show that one of the places was not a "public" place within the meaning of the code. But surely the court, having jurisdiction of the proceeding, could, within that jurisdiction, find the fact that the place was a public place; and such finding cannot be attacked collaterally.

The position of respondent that the petition was not properly verified, because the certificate of verification is placed before the schedules which were attached to it, is not tenable. The schedules were a part of the petition, and were as fully included in the verification as were the parts which preceded the certificate.

We see no other attacks upon the jurisdiction of the probate court to order the sale which require special notice. It may be remarked that there is no pretense that the sale under which appellants claim was in fact fraudulent, or without adequate consideration, or in any way unfair. To the objections made to it, may well be applied that often abused word "technical"; and we do not think that they are sufficient to overturn, for want of jurisdiction, the solemn judgment of a court, or to destroy a title to realty honestly acquired.

Appellants plead, as a defense to the action, section 1573 of the Code of Civil Procedure, which provides that "no action for the recovery of any estate sold by an executor or administrator, under the provisions of this chapter, can be maintained by any heir or other person claiming under the decedent, unless it be commenced within three years next after the settlement of the final account of the executor or administrator." Counsel on both sides, in discussing the issue made by this defense, deal mainly with the question whether this section applies to actions to quiet title, and whether, to make the defense good, it must not appear that the purchasers were in the actual adverse possession for three years.

We are inclined to hold (although we do not here undertake to definitely settle the question) that section 1573 intended to have settled within the time mentioned all questions about the validity of probate sales, and that the words "recovery of any estate" were intended to and do include all actions which involve an "estate" in the land sold, and therefore include an action to quiet title.   But in the case at bar we are not able to see from the transcript that the action was not brought within three years after plaintiffs attained their majority (see section 1574), nor does the record show the date of "the settlement of the final account" of the administratrix. The point, therefore, cannot be raised on the record which is before us.

These views lead us to the conclusion that the findings of the court below, — "that the proceedings on said administratrix's sale of said estate of said John Sproul, deceased, were irregular, invalid in law, and no title passed under said sales"; that "the claims of said defendants, and each of them, are without any legal right," etc.; that "the plaintiffs are the owners in their own right, as their separate property, of the parcels of land described in the amended complaint herein"; and "that defendants have not, nor have either of them, any right, title, estate, or interest" therein, — are erroneous.   This being so, it is unnecessary to inquire if the findings are sufficiently full.   But the case is not one where judgment can be ordered for appellants on the findings.   All we can do is to order a new trial.

Judgment and order reversed, and cause remanded for a new trial.

Hearing in Bank denied.

––––––

IN *Silverman* v. *Gundelfinger*, 82 Cal. 548, in which the principal case was cited, it was held that a substantial compliance with the requirements of the law relating to probate sales is sufficient as against a collateral attack; that such a sale cannot be objected to as void for want of jurisdiction, in ejectment by an heir of the decedent against the purchaser, upon the ground that the petition for the sale failed to state the value of the property sought to be sold, when it stated that a full description of all the real estate of which the decedent died seised, etc., and the condition and value thereof, were set forth in a certain schedule annexed to the petition, which gave a full description of the property in contest, and showed its condition and appraised value; and that, in the absence of a special demurrer for uncertainty, the averment in the body of the petition may be taken as an averment that the amount named in the schedule was the present value of the property at the date of the petition.

PROBATE COURTS. — The jurisdiction of a probate court to order the sale of lands of a decedent is statutory and limited, and must appear from the record; but such jurisdiction attaches when a petition is filed by the proper party, setting forth any of the statutory grounds for a sale: *Goodwin* v. *Sims,* 86 Ala. 102; 11 Am. St. Rep. 21.

PROBATE COURTS. — Proceedings in probate for the sale of a decedent's estate are *in rem*, and cannot be collaterally attacked: *Satcher* v. *Satcher*, 41 Ala. 26; 91 Am. Dec. 498; *Goodwin* v. *Sims*, 86 Ala. 102; 11 Am. St. Rep. 21, and note 27, 28; *Johnson* v. *Beazley*, 65 Mo. 250; 27 Am. Rep. 276.

[IN BANK.]

LUBBOCK *v.* MCMANN.

[82 CALIFORNIA, 226.]

HOMESTEAD IS NOT VITIATED BY SUBSEQUENT ERECTION OF ADDITIONAL DWELLING ON SAME LOT. — Where a house and lot are duly selected and declared a homestead, the subsequent erection of an additional dwelling-house upon the lot does not vitiate such homestead, nor render any part of it subject to seizure and sale under execution, unless the value of the homestead has increased beyond the statutory limit; and in that case a levy can only be made for the purpose of inaugurating proceedings for the admeasurement of the excess in value.

HOMESTEAD ONCE DULY DEDICATED CANNOT BE DEFEATED OR VITIATED except by conveyance, encumbrance, or abandonment executed in the manner provided by the statute.

SUIT for an injunction. The facts are stated in the opinion, and in the opinion of the Department, a synopsis of which is given in the note.

A. A. Sargent and Frank M. Stone, for the appellants.

George D. Collins, and Sawyer and Burnett, for the respondent.

Fox, J. Judgment was rendered in this case in Department One of this court September 9, 1889, affirming the orders appealed from. Reference is made to the opinion filed at that time for a statement of the case, and for the rulings then made upon the points considered, which rulings are still adhered to. The parties have since, by stipulation, waived all controversy upon the points then discussed, but an orderly and intelligible disposition of the case requires that rulings should be had upon those points, and after a careful reconsideration of the case in Bank, we see no reason to change the decision then made, so far as it goes.

Upon the express stipulation, and at the request of counsel on both sides, the case was resubmitted in Bank, for the purpose of having a direct opinion of the court upon the single question of whether or not the second house mentioned in the former opinion—the house built on the rear of the lot since the filing of the homestead declaration—was and is exempt from execution; whether it was and is impressed with the character of homestead to the extent of being exempt from execution on that account. And to avoid future litigation between the parties, it is stipulated that the orders of the court below, from which the appeal was taken, shall be affirmed or reversed, according as we shall now decide this question in the affirmative or negative.

There can be and is no question but that this entire lot was fully impressed with the character of homestead before and at the time this second house was built upon it. The building of the second house did not increase the value of the entire property, including both houses, to an amount which is in excess of that which is by law, and as incident to homestead, made exempt from execution as such. No part of the tract has ever been abandoned, or the homestead claim thereon released, in the manner provided by law. How then, if at all, is it made subject to sale on execution? The strict language of the question submitted confines it to the house: is the house exempt? It certainly is if the land upon which it stands is exempt; for it has become a part of the realty, and can only be separated from the land with the consent of the owner. But we do not understand the intent to be to limit the question to the house alone, as distinguished from the land upon which it stands.

The constitutional provision is, that "the legislature shall protect by law from forced sale a certain portion of the homestead and other property of all heads of families": Art. 17, sec. 1. Here there is no limit to the value of the property thus to be protected. It is left to the legislature to determine what portion, to what limit, and by what means it shall be protected. Exemption is a constitutional right, incident to homestead: *Ham* v. *Santa Rosa Bank*, 62 Cal. 138; 45 Am. Rep. 654; but the extent of such exemption, and the means by which it shall be secured, are made by the constitution the subject of legislative enactment.

Legislating for the purpose of giving effect to this constitutional provision, it has been in the codes provided that "the homestead consists of the dwelling-house in which the claimant resides and the land on which the same is situated, selected as in this title provided": Civ. Code, sec. 1237. Following

this, and in the same title, which extends to and including
section 1269, will be found the provisions as to the mode and
manner of selection in order to avail of the exemption; the
limitation of such exemption; the mode and manner of abandonment or release; the exceptions to the rule of exemption;
and the course to be pursued when the homestead exceeds in
value the limit of the exemption.

Actual occupation as a place of residence at the time of
filing the declaration is necessary in order to impress upon the
premises the character of homestead: Civ. Code, sec. 1263;
Prescott v. *Prescott*, 45 Cal. 58; *Babcock* v. *Gibbs*, 52 Cal. 629;
Dorn v. *Howe*, 52 Cal. 630; *Aucker* v. *McCoy*, 56 Cal. 524. Use
at the time of selection, and selection by the making and recording of the proper declaration, are both essential elements
in the creation of the homestead character. Neither is sufficient for that purpose without the other: *Laughlin* v. *Wright*,
63 Cal. 113; *Maloney* v. *Hefer*, 75 Cal. 424; 7 Am. St. Rep. 180;
In re Allen, 78 Cal. 294.

If, at the time of filing the declaration for record, the two
houses now standing upon this lot had been standing as they
now do, and occupied as they now are, only the one occupied
as the dwelling of the plaintiff, with that portion of the lot
used in connection therewith, would have been impressed with
the homestead character; as to the other house and the land
used in connection with it, the attempt to dedicate it as a
homestead would have been inoperative: *Tiernan* v. *His Creditors*, 62 Cal. 286; *Maloney* v. *Hefer*, 75 Cal. 424; 7 Am. St.
Rep. 180; *In re Allen*, 78 Cal. 294. But it has never been
held, under our statute, that the subsequent erection of a
second house, for whatever purpose such second house was
used, operated to relieve the property *pro tanto*, or any separate part of it, of the homestead character which had already
attached, so as to make it liable to seizure and sale under execution. On the contrary, the statute expressly provides that
the homestead can only be conveyed or encumbered as provided in section 1242, and only be abandoned as provided in
section 1243 of the Civil Code. Also, that it is subject to execution only in the cases provided in section 1241, of which
this is not one. Even a removal from the homestead, followed
by long-continued residence and the acquirement of citizen-
ship in another state, has been held not to operate as an
abandonment of a homestead: *Porter* v. *Chapman*, 65 Cal. 367.
See also *Tipton* v. *Martin*, 71 Cal. 325.

The whole lot being adapted to use as a homestead, and actually used as such at the time of dedication, it then became as an entirety affected with the homestead character. And this is so, without regard to the value of the lot, either at the time of its dedication or at any subsequent period. There is no statutory limit as to the value of the property which may be selected, and upon which the character may be impressed. When the attributes of residence and selection according to law exist so as to express its essence, the homestead becomes an estate in the premises selected, exempted by law from forced sale. They may be of greater or less value than the interest in them exempted by law. The excess, if there be one, in value, though it may be homestead in fact, is subject to the *jus disponendi* of the owner and the claims of his creditors: *Ham* v. *Santa Rosa Bank*, 62 Cal. 139; 45 Am. Rep. 654. But it does not follow that the excess in value is subject to seizure and sale at the instance of an execution creditor. If the property so impressed with the character of homestead is worth more than the homestead exemption, and the creditor desires to avail himself of that excess, the proceedings provided by the code (Civ. Code, secs. 1245–1259) must be taken for the admeasurement and application of such excess: *Waggle* v. *Worthy*, 74 Cal. 268; 5 Am. St. Rep. 440. A judgment creates no lien upon property thus affected, and a levy gives no right, except to inaugurate the proceedings for the admeasurement of such excess: *Barrett* v. *Simms*, 62 Cal. 440. It follows that a sale, unless made under order of court, and for purposes of segregation of the excess as provided in the sections referred to, would convey no title. But though the sale of a homestead under execution conveys no title, it may create a cloud, and involve the homestead claimant in litigation, and will therefore be enjoined: *Culver* v. *Rogers*, 28 Cal. 520; *Eby* v. *Foster*, 61 Cal. 287.

So far as we have been able to discover, no case has before arisen, under our statutes, where the precise question now submitted has been presented. In every case where it has been held that a second tenement used for purposes other than the residence of the family has operated to prevent the homestead character from attaching to such second tenement, and the land used in connection therewith, such second tenement existed at the time of the attempted homestead selection, and was not one constructed after the homestead character had attached to the land. Here the homestead

character had attached before the second building was constructed, and reasoning from the analogy of the statutes and
of the cases cited, the construction of such building was not
an act which relieved it of such homestead character, and
rendered the land subject to direct seizure and sale under
execution.

If the construction of this second building had increased.
the value of the tract claimed as a homestead to an amount
in excess of the homestead exemption, or if for any other
cause it had become or was of greater value than the amount
of such exemption, the plaintiff would have been entitled to
make the levy, as he has done in this case, not for the purpose
of proceeding to sale under the execution, but as a basis of
application to the proper court for proceedings under the statute for the admeasurement of such excess in value, and then
for partition or sale, under the order of the court, as in the
statute provided.   But no provision for such a proceeding has
been made, unless there is such an excess in value.   And
while it is true that, under the rule of law heretofore established, this second house, with the land upon which it stands,
would not have taken on the homestead character if it had
been there at the time of homestead selection, but that the
homestead would then, by reason thereof, have been so limited
in extent as to exclude this house and its grounds, it may
very well be that the legislature did not intend that the homestead should thereafter be limited in extent by reason of future
improvements, even if such improvements were used for purposes of revenue rather than residence, so long as they did
not increase the value beyond the limit of exemption.   Whether
this be so or not, we are compelled to hold that, under the
facts of this case, the statutes, and the authorities cited, this
whole lot is so affected with the homestead character as to be
exempt from sale under execution, and there is no authority
in this proceeding, or in the case in which the execution was
issued, to segregate any part of the lot, and relieve it from
such exemption.   Whether there is such authority anywhere,
we are not now called upon to decide; but without further
legislative action, it would seem to be exceedingly doubtful.

The judgment and order appealed from must be affirmed,
and it is so ordered.

———

PATERSON, J., dissented, and delivered an opinion, of which the following
is a synopsis: It is immaterial whether the second house was placed on the
land before or after the filing of the declaration of homestead.   The stipula-

tion of counsel reduces the question before the court to the simple inquiry, whether or not the house built on the rear of the lot is exempt from execution. It is plain, from the constitutional and statutory provisions on the subject, that property selected and improved as a homestead may retain its homestead character for certain purposes, and yet a portion of it be not exempt from execution: Const. Cal., art. 17, sec. 1; Civ. Code, secs. 1237, 1240. This court has decided that the homestead represents the dwelling-house in which the family resides, with the usual and customary appurtenances, including out-buildings necessary for family use; that the only tests are use and the value, and that the use of the property is an important element to be considered: *Gregg* v. *Bostwick*, 33 Cal. 228; 91 Am. Dec. 637; *Laughlin* v. *Wright*, 63 Cal. 116; Thompson on Homesteads and Exemptions, sec. 130. It has been uniformly held that, in order to be exempt from execution, the property claimed as a homestead must be actually occupied as a residence by the family of the owner, temporary absences excepted, and that any portion of his real estate not so used is not exempt from execution, whatever be its extent or value; and that where houses and lots are rented for money rent to tenants who are not servants or employees of the owner, the latter cannot claim them as a part of his own home and residence, although they may adjoin the same: *Ashton* v. *Ingle*, 20 Kan. 670; *Austin* v. *Stanley*, 46 N. H. 51; *Kunz* v. *Brusch*, 13 Iowa, 371; 81 Am. Dec. 435; *Casselman* v. *Packard*, 16 Wis. 114; 82 Am. Dec. 710. As all other questions are waived, the rear house and the land upon which it stands should be subjected to the satisfaction of the judgment.

In the opinion of Department One, referred to in the prevailing opinion, Fox, J., stated the facts of the case as follows: In 1872, plaintiff and her husband were residing upon a certain lot of land in the city and county of San Francisco, having twenty-five feet front, and extending back eighty feet to an alley. The lot, with the small dwelling-house on the front thereof, was the community property of plaintiff and her said husband. On the 2d of December of that year, she recorded the same as a homestead. The regularity of this dedication and recording of the homestead is conceded. At some period after the property had been so dedicated and recorded as a homestead, the Lubbocks built another small house on the rear of the lot, wholly disconnected from the one in which they lived, and fronting on the alley, which they rented out. Afterward, one Sobey recovered a judgment in a justice's court against the husband of plaintiff, upon which he took out execution, and placed it in the hands of defendant McMann, then sheriff, who, under the direction of the judgment creditor, levied upon the whole lot so recorded as a homestead, and advertised the same for sale. Plaintiff, after notifying the sheriff of the homestead character of the property, and demanding a release from said levy, filed her complaint in this action, setting up the material facts hereinbefore recited, showing the homestead character of the property, alleging that at the time of recording the said homestead claim, the property was not, and is not now, of a greater value than five thousand dollars, and praying for an injunction to restrain the defendant from making such sale. An order was issued to show cause why an injunction should not be granted as prayed, and restraining the sale in the mean time. Upon the return day of the order to show cause, the case was heard upon the complaint of plaintiff, the answer of the defendants admitting all the material allegations of the complaint, and setting up, in addition, the fact of the erection of the second tenement, above referred to, after the recording of the homestead, and the fact that the same was not occupied by the homestead claimants as a place of residence, but was rented out, they residing in the original dwelling-house on the lot; and on demurrer to said answer, that the same did not show facts sufficient to constitute a ground of defense to said action. Counsel concede that it was understood that judgment final should follow the result of the submission of the case on those pleadings and demurrer. The court sustained the demurrer, and judgment went for plaintiff, perpetually enjoining the sale. From this judgment the appeal was taken. The learned judge then stated that there was no error in the order of the court sustaining the demurrer to the answer, and added: "It is admitted that the homestead was regularly created. There is no pretense that it had ever been abandoned, or even that it had been enchanced in value beyond the homestead exemption. The claim is simply that it became 'vitiated' *quoad* the rear of the lot, upon which the new tenement had been erected. But there is no provision of the statute defining by what means or under what circumstances a homestead may become 'vitiated,' nor is any particular part of the homestead tract levied upon as being the part relieved from the homestead lien by this new process of vitiation. The levy is upon the whole tract, an unknown part of which, it is admitted, is still subject to a valid homestead claim. Judgment and order appealed from affirmed." Works, J., concurred. Paterson, J., also delivered a concurring opinion, in which he concurred in the judgment. He contended that the remedy of the execution creditor was against the portion of the premises included within the homestead declaration which had ceased to be part of the homestead. The remainder of his opinion is substantially the same as his dissenting opinion, the substance of which is given above.

HOMESTEADS. — While one holds property exempt from execution as a homestead, he may sell his interest therein: *Kendall* v. *Powers*, 96 Mo. 142; 9 Am. St. Rep. 326, and note; compare *Alt* v. *Banholzer*, 39 Minn. 511, 12 Am. St. Rep. 681, and extended note. A homestead may be mortgaged, when the mortgage follows strictly the statutory provisions: *Jones* v. *Roper*, 86 Ala. 210.

[IN BANK.]

HAYNE *v.* JUSTICE'S COURT.

[82 CALIFORNIA, 284.]

PROHIBITION OF COURT EXCEEDING ITS JURISDICTION. — A court that proceeds in the trial of a cause against an express prohibition of a statute is exceeding its jurisdiction, and may be prevented by prohibition from the supreme court. Where, therefore, a justice's court refuses to stay proceedings in a case not within the exceptions of the Insolvent Act, a writ of prohibition will be issued to restrain it from further proceedings, notwithstanding an order of the superior court in which the insolvency proceedings are pending, assuming to permit such justice's court to proceed with the cause.

PETITION for a writ of prohibition. The opinion states the case.

Geil and Morehouse, for the petitioner.

N. A. Dorn and W. M. R. Parker, for the respondent.

WORKS, J. This is an application for a writ of prohibition to prevent the respondent proceeding to trial and judgment in a cause pending before it.

An action was brought against the petitioner in the justice's court on a promissory note, and an attachment was issued and levied on his property. The petitioner filed his petition in insolvency, and the property attached was released. He filed his answer in the justice's court, setting up the insolvency proceedings, but the plaintiff applied to the superior court in which the insolvency proceedings were pending, and procured an order from that court, permitting the justice's court to proceed with the cause. The petitioner moved the justice's court to desist from further proceedings, but his motion was denied, and the court being about to proceed to judgment, this writ was applied for.

Section 45 of the Insolvency Act (Deering's Code of Civil Procedure, page 686) provides: "And no creditor whose debt is provable under this act shall be allowed, after the commencement of proceedings in insolvency, to prosecute to final judgment any action therefor against the debtor, until the question of the debtor's discharge shall have been determined, and any such suit or proceeding shall, upon the application of the debtor or any creditor, or of the assignee, be stayed to await the examination of the court in insolvency on the question of discharge."

There are certain provisions in the section authorizing the continuation of proceedings in certain cases, but this case is not within any of them.

This is a plain and direct prohibition against any further proceedings in the justice's court, and the petitioner, having brought himself within the statute, is entitled to the writ prayed for.

The respondent does not contend that it has the right to proceed, but claims that in doing so it would not exceed its jurisdiction, but would only commit an error that could be reached by appeal. We cannot agree to this proposition. A court that proceeds in the trial of a cause against an express prohibition of a statute is exceeding its jurisdiction, and may be prevented by prohibition from this court.

The case of *Bandy* v. *Ransom*, 54 Cal. 87, is not in point. At the time it was decided, the Insolvency Act in force contained no prohibition against proceedings in other courts after the commencement of insolvency proceedings. The provision of the statute referred to is a salutary one, calculated to prevent the swallowing up of insolvent estates in unnecessary litigation, and should be enforced. Conceding that an appeal might have been taken, it was not an adequate remedy. It would only add to the costs of litigation, the very thing that the statute was intended to prevent.

Let the writ issue as prayed for.

Rehearing denied.

————

WRIT ON PROHIBITION issues only to restrain the action of courts in excess of jurisdiction, and does not lie to restrain any action which can be reviewed by any of the ordinary methods: *People* v. *Wayne Circuit Court*, 11 Mich. 393; 83 Am. Dec. 754, and note; compare extended note to *State* v. *Commissioners*, 12 Am. Dec. 607, 608. A writ of prohibition lies from the supreme court to prevent an inferior court from exercising jurisdiction, which it has not: *State* v. *St. Louis Court of Appeals*, 97 Mo. 276; *State* v. *Judges of the Court of Appeals*, 40 La. Ann. 771.

————————

[IN BANK.]

Spring Valley Water Works *v.* City and County of San Francisco.

[82 CALIFORNIA, 286.]

WATER RATES, POWER OF COURTS TO INTERFERE WITH ACTION OF SUPERVISORS IN FIXING. — The use of water for sale is a public use, and the price at which it shall be sold is a matter within the power of the board of supervisors to determine; and the constitution of California does not, in terms, confer upon the courts of the state any power or jurisdiction to control, supervise, or set aside any action of the board in respect to such rates. If the board has fairly investigated and exercised its discretion in fixing the rates, the courts have no right to interfere on the sole ground that, in the judgment of the court, the rates fixed are not reasonable; to justify interference by the courts, there must be actual fraud in fixing the rates, or they must be so palpably and grossly unreasonable and unjust as to amount to the same thing. But the power to regulate water rates conferred by the constitution upon boards of supervisors is not a power to confiscate nor to take the property of a water company without just compensation; and whether such power be judicial, legislative, or administrative, it is not above the control of the courts, if it is arbitrarily exercised without a fair investigation, and the rates are so fixed as to render it impossible to furnish the water without loss, so that their action would amount to a palpable fraud, and almost certainly work injustice.

REASONABLE AND JUST WATER RATES, WHAT ARE, WITHIN MEANING OF CONSTITUTION. — When the constitution provides for the fixing of rates or compensation for the use of water, it means reasonable rates and just compensation, and for a board of supervisors to fix rates not reasonable, or compensation not just, is a plain violation of its duty. It has no

right to fix rates arbitrarily and without investigation, or without exercising its judgment or discretion to determine what is a fair and reasonable compensation.

POWER OF COURTS OVER PROCEEDINGS OF MUNICIPAL CORPORATIONS. — A
subordinate municipal body, although clothed to some extent with legislative and even political powers, is nevertheless, in the exercise of all its
powers, just as subject to the authority and control of courts of justice
as any other body or person, natural or artificial.

MAYOR NEED NOT BE MADE PARTY TO ACTION brought by a water company
against a city and county and its board of supervisors, to obtain a judgment setting aside and declaring void an ordinance of said board, and
compelling it to pass a new ordinance, as required by the constitution.

NOTICE OF INTENTION TO FIX WATER RATES NEED NOT BE GIVEN TO
WATER COMPANY. — The constitution does not require a board of supervisors to give notice to a water company of its intention to fix water
rates; but it is, nevertheless, its plain duty to use all proper means to
obtain the information necessary to enable it to act intelligently and
fairly in fixing the rates, and a failure to perform this duty may defeat
its action.

WATER-METERS, ORDINANCE FIXING RATES MAY REQUIRE. — An ordinance
of a board of supervisors fixing water rates may require the water company to furnish a water-meter to each householder at his option, and to
collect only for the water furnished at meter rates, which are different
from the house rates. A regulation requiring the party furnishing water
to furnish the means necessary for its measurement, so that the quantity
furnished and to be paid for may be known, is not unreasonable. The
expense of furnishing such meters cannot be imposed upon the consumer.

ACTION brought to set aside and declare void an ordinance
of the board of supervisors of the city and county of San
Francisco. The opinion states the case.

George Flournoy, Flournoy and Mhoon, and W. W. Foote, for
the appellants.

George W. Chamberlain, amicus curiæ.

William F. Herrin, and Garber, Boalt, and Bishop, for the
respondent.

WORKS, J.   This action is brought to set aside and declare
void an ordinance of the board of supervisors of the city and
county of San Francisco, fixing water rates to be charged for
water to be furnished to said city and its inhabitants for the
year commencing July 1, 1889.

The complaint, after alleging the plaintiff's corporate existence, and its object and purpose, viz., to furnish water to
said city and county, and other preliminary and technical
matters, avers that it has, for the purpose mentioned, "constructed aqueducts, and pumping and other works, and laid

many miles of water-pipe for distributing water to its con-
sumers; and that its aforesaid lands, water rights, works,
buildings, and improvements necessary to enable it to fulfill
the said purposes of its incorporation, are of very great value,
to wit, of a value exceeding twenty-five million dollars"; that
it has projected and has now in course of construction large
additions to its works, necessary to meet the demands of said
city and its inhabitants, and in order to meet the wants of
said city and its inhabitants, and "to meet the expenses and
pay the cost of the said additions to its works and improvements, it will be necessary for the plaintiff to lay out and ex-
pend, during the year ending June 30, 1890, very large sums
of money, amounting in the aggregate to more than one million five hundred thousand dollars"; that for these purposes
it has borrowed large sums of money, amounting in the
aggregate to more than nine million six hundred thousand
dollars, and has an aggregate interest-bearing indebtedness,
secured by mortgage on its property, of nine million dollars;
that the interest which will accrue and have to be paid during the year ending June 30, 1890, will amount in the aggregate to four hundred and ninety-eight thousand dollars; that
the operating expenses of the plaintiff's business for said year
will amount to three hundred and ninety thousand dollars,
and the taxes to be paid by it will amount to seventy thousand six hundred dollars; that its capital stock is ten million
dollars, is divided into one hundred thousand shares, and
held by more than eleven hundred share-holders, and that
the holders of said stock are reasonably entitled to receive in
dividends upon their said stock not less than seven per cent
per annum upon the par value of said stock; that the plaintiff is entitled to receive a reasonable and just compensation
for the services rendered, "and that if so fixed, its aggregate
annual income from such rates would be sufficient to pay the
interest on its indebtedness, the taxes upon its property, and
its operating and other fixed expenses, and to pay dividends
to its stockholders, amounting to at least seven per cent upon
the par value of their stock, and that to this end it was and
is entitled to have its rates for the year commencing July 1,
1889, and ending June 30, 1890, so fixed and established that
its gross income for said year will amount to at least one million six hundred and seventy thousand dollars"; that, as
required by law, the plaintiff furnished said board of supervisors, and filed with the clerk thereof, "a detailed statement,

verified by the oath of the president and secretary of the plaintiff, showing the name of each water-rate payer, his or her place of residence, the amount paid by each such water-rate payer during the year preceding the date of such statement, and also showing all revenue derived by said plaintiff from all sources during said year, and an itemized statement of expenditures made by plaintiff for supplying water during said time; that from said statement it appeared, and so the fact is, that the receipts and expenditures made by the plaintiff from furnishing and for supplying water during said time were as follows, viz.: Receipts — From water rates, $1,421,751.39; from other sources, $12,498.25. Total, $1,434,249.64. Disbursements — For operating expenses, $361,653.65; for interest, $443,257.85; for taxes, $70,624.40; for dividends, $600,000. Total, $1,475,535.90. Balance, expenditures over receipts, $41,286.26."

The complaint further alleges "that said board of supervisors did not during said month of February, 1889, so fix and prescribe said rates for said year, and have not at any time lawfully or duly fixed or prescribed any rates whatever for supplying fresh water to said city and county and its inhabitants during said year; that on the twenty-eighth day of February, 1889, the said board of supervisors assumed and pretended to pass a certain pretended ordinance or order, purporting to fix the maximum rates to be charged for furnishing fresh water to said city and county and its inhabitants for the said year commencing July 1, 1889, and ending June 30, 1890, a true and full copy of which said ordinance or order is hereto annexed, marked "Exhibit A," and made a part of its complaint.

"That the said ordinance or order purports to fix the rates to be charged for supplying fresh water to said city and county and its inhabitants for said year; but that the same is in fact null and void, and of no effect, and that the rates pretended thereby to be fixed are wholly illegal and unauthorized; that the said ordinance or order was passed, or pretended to be passed, without any notice or opportunity to be heard against it on the part of the plaintiff or other person interested; that said order was first introduced in said board of supervisors, without any previous notice to plaintiff, or hearing accorded to plaintiff, with reference to the subject-matter thereof, at a meeting of said board of supervisors held on the twenty-first day of February, A. D. 1889, and was thereafter called up for final passage at a meeting of said board of supervisors held on

the twenty-eighth day of February, A. D. 1889; that the first
information which the plaintiff received thereof was through
the public newspapers, and on said twenty-first day of February, and that the first opportunity which the plaintiff had to
object to said order, or to offer to introduce evidence before
said board of supervisors, showing that said order was unreasonable and unjust, was at said meeting of February 28, A. D.
1889; that at said meeting, and at the first opportunity, and
before the passage of said order, the plaintiff offered to produce
and introduce evidence and testimony before said board, showing that said order was unreasonable and unjust, in that it
would not allow the plaintiff to collect sufficient revenue to
pay its necessary operating expenses, interest on its indebtedness, and taxes, but that the said board of supervisors would
not, and did not, allow the plaintiff to introduce, and refused
to hear, evidence offered by the said plaintiff to show that the
said ordinance or order was, and that the rates pretended to
be fixed thereby were, unreasonable, unjust, and oppressive,
and refused to allow, and did not allow, any evidence whatever to be introduced respecting the reasonableness and justice
of the said ordinance or order, and of the rates purported to
be fixed thereby, but immediately passed and adopted said
order, without giving the plaintiff any opportunity to be heard
whatever; that the rates purporting to be fixed by said ordinance or order were fixed arbitrarily, at random, and by mere
guess-work, without any consideration of or regard to the right
of plaintiff to a reasonable compensation for supplying water
to the said city and county and its inhabitants, or to a reasonable income, or any income, upon its investment, and without
any consideration of or regard to the value of the plaintiff's
works and property, or the amount of its interest-bearing indebtedness, and the annual interest charge thereon, or its operating expenses, or the amount of taxes which it would be
required to pay, or the right of the plaintiff's stockholders to
reasonable, or any, dividends upon their stock, and without
any reference to or consideration of the actual cost of supplying said water, but in total disregard of all such matters; and
that in the passage, or pretended passage, of said ordinance or
order, the said board of supervisors acted wholly without jurisdiction, power, or authority, and in excess of their lawful jurisdiction, power, or authority.

"That the said ordinance or order is, and the rates purporting to be prescribed and fixed thereby are, grossly unjust,

unreasonable, and oppressive; that said rates do not permit of nor provide for a just or fair or reasonable compensation for the water to be supplied during said year by this plaintiff to said city and county and the inhabitants thereof; and that if said ordinance or order is enforced, and if the plaintiff is pre-prevented from charging and collecting any other or greater rates than those prescribed, its gross income from the said rates for the year commencing July 1, 1889, and ending June 30, 1890, will not, and cannot possibly, exceed the sum of seven hundred and fifty thousand dollars; and it will be wholly insufficient to pay the interest on the plaintiff's indebtedness, its operating expenses, and taxes; and not only will not and cannot yield any dividend to its stockholders, but will render it necessary to levy heavy assessments upon said stockholdeis to pay said interest, expenses, and taxes."

It is further averred that the defendants are about to enforce said ordinance; that its passage has already impaired the plaintiff's credit and depreciated the value of its property; and if enforced, it will greatly impair, if not entirely destroy, the plaintiff's credit as well as the value of its property and capital stock, and prevent it from constructing and completing the work necessary to supply water to the city and its inhabitants; and that the ordinance operates, and will operate, to take away the plaintiff's property without due process of law, and deprive the plaintiff of the equal protection of the laws, and that the plaintiff has no adequate remedy at law. There are other allegations in the complaint, but they need not be particularly noticed.

The prayer of the complaint is as follows:—

"Wherefore the plaintiff prays the judgment and decree of this court,—

"1. That the said pretended ordinance or order of the board of supervisors of said city and county is utterly null and void, and of no effect in law.

"2. That the plaintiff is entitled to have the rates for supplying fresh water to said city and county and its inhabitants for the year commencing July 1, 1889, and ending June 30, 1890, and for other years, so fixed that they will, in the aggregate, afford a reasonable and just compensation for the service rendered, and will yield a sufficient annual income to pay the interest on its indebtedness, its running expenses and taxes, and to the plaintiff's stockholders a dividend of not less than seven per cent per annum upon the face value of their stock.

"3. That the court issue its mandatory injunction or other peremptory process requiring the said board of supervisors forthwith to fix the rates for supplying water to said city and county and its inhabitants for the year commencing July 1, 1889, and ending June 30, 1890, in accordance with the foregoing principles; to give plaintiff and all other persons interested due notice and an opportunity to be heard before the said board prior to the final adoption of any order fixing such rates, and to allow the plaintiff and others interested to introduce evidence respecting the reasonableness and justice of such proposed order, and to make, by their counsel, such argument upon the subject as they may see fit.

"4. That each and all of said defendants be personally enjoined from any attempt to enforce, or to cause to be enforced, the said pretended ordinance or order, or from bringing, or causing to be brought, any action or suit against the plaintiff in law or in equity, to enforce any forfeiture of the plaintiff's franchise or works, or for any other purpose, for any refusal or failure of the plaintiff to obey the said pretended ordinance or order, or to conform to the rates thereby prescribed, and from any attempt, directly or indirectly, to compel the plaintiff to furnish water at any other rates than those fixed by the board of supervisors in obedience to the decree and mandate of this court.

"5. That the plaintiff's rights in the premises be forever quieted against each and all of the defendants.

"6. That the plaintiff have such other and further relief as to the court may seem meet and conformable to equity and good conscience, together with the costs of this suit."

There was a demurrer to the complaint, which was overruled, and the defendants declining to answer, judgment was rendered in favor of the plaintiff that the rates and compensation "are grossly unreasonable, unjust, and oppressive, and amount to the taking of the property of the plaintiff for public use without just compensation and without due process of law"; that said ordinance "is outside and in excess of the jurisdiction of the board of supervisors as conferred by article 14, section 1, of the constitution of the state of California, and not a compliance with the provisions of said article and section, and is, and ever has been, illegal, unauthorized, and void." It was further decreed that the ordinance be set aside and vacated, that the defendants be enjoined from enforcing the same, and that they be enjoined from bringing any action against the plaintiff to enforce any forfeiture of its franchise and works on account of any past or future refusal to obey said pretended ordinance, or to conform to said rates, or any of them, quieting plaintiff's rights in the premises, and directing that the board of supervisors proceed forthwith to fix said rates and compensation as provided by the constitution.

The appellants, having seen fit to rest their case upon the facts as stated in the complaint, instead of answering and attempting to show that the board of supervisors had endeavored to comply with the provisions of the constitution by an honest and fair effort to ascertain and fix a fair and reasonable rate for water to be furnished, the only question for us to determine is, whether, under the allegations of the complaint, which are by the demurrer admitted to be true, the plaintiff is entitled to any relief. If so, the judgment must be affirmed.

The appellants take the broad ground that the constitution has conferred upon the board of supervisors the absolute and exclusive right to fix water rates, and that, under no circumstances, have the courts any jurisdiction to interfere with or control such authority; while the respondent contends that there is a limitation on the power of the board which compels the board to fix reasonable rates or compensation, and that whether the rates or compensation fixed by such board are reasonable or not, the courts have the power and jurisdiction to determine.

The constitution, article 14, provides:—

"Sec. 1. The use of all water now appropriated, or that may hereafter be appropriated, for sale, rental, or distribution, is hereby declared to be a public use, and subject to the regulation and control of the state in the manner to be prescribed by law; *provided,* that the rates or compensation to be collected by any person, company, or corporation of this state for the use of water supplied to any city and county, or city or town, or the inhabitants thereof, shall be fixed, annually, by the board of supervisors, or city and county, or city or town council, or any governing body of such city and county, or city or town, by ordinance or otherwise, in the manner that other ordinances or legislative acts or resolutions are passed by such body, and shall continue in force for one year, and no longer. Such ordinances or resolutions shall be passed in the month of February of each year, and take effect on the first day of July thereafter. Any board or body failing to pass the necessary ordinances or resolutions fixing water rates, where necessary,

within such time, shall be subject to peremptory process to
compel action at the suit of any party interested, and shall be
liable to such further processes and penalties as the legislature
may prescribe. Any person, company, or corporation collecting water-rates in any city and county, or city or town, in
this state, otherwise than as so established, shall forfeit the
franchises and water works of such person, company, or corporation of the city and county, or city or town, where the
same are collected, for the public use.

"Sec. 2. The right to collect rates or compensation for the
use of water supplied to any county, city and county, or town,
or the inhabitants thereof, is a franchise, and cannot be exercised except by authority of and in the manner prescribed by
law."

The first point made as to the jurisdiction of the court below is, that, conceding the complaint states a cause of action,
no jurisdiction to hear and determine the question raised
thereby is vested in the superior courts by the constitution or
laws of this state. There is no force in this contention. If
any cause of action is stated in the complaint, it is an equitable one, and of such cases superior courts are given jurisdiction in the broadest terms by the constitution of this state:
Const., art. 6, sec. 5.

We pass therefore to the only real question in the case, viz.,
whether there is any power on the part of any court, no matter how broad and comprehensive its grant of jurisdiction
may be, to review, interfere with, or set aside the action of the
board of supervisors, or whether the power and authority of such
board is exclusive and beyond the reach of the courts under
any and all circumstances.

It must be conceded in the outset that the use of water for
sale is a public use, and that the price at which it shall be
sold is a matter within the power of the board of supervisors
to determine: *Munn v. Illinois*, 94 U. S. 113; *Spring Valley
Water Works v. Schottler*, 110 U. S. 347. Indeed, this is not
controverted by the respondent. The constitution does not, in
terms, confer upon the courts of the state any power or jurisdiction to control, supervise, or set aside any action of the
board in respect to such rates. It may also be conceded, for
the purposes of this case, that when the board of supervisors
have fairly investigated and exercised their discretion in fixing the rates, the courts have no right to interfere, on the sole
ground that in the judgment of the court the rates thus fixed

and determined are not reasonable. That such is the case is attested by numerous authorities: *Nesbitt* v. *Greenwich Board of Works*, L. R. 10 Q. B. 10; *Davis* v. *Mayor of New York*, 1 Duer, 451-497; *Munn* v. *Illinois*, 94 U. S. 113; *Spring Valley Water Works* v. *Schottler*, 110 U. S. 347; *Chicago & N. W. R'y Co.* v. *Day*, 35 Fed. Rep. 866.

But it seems to us that this complaint presents an entirely different question from this. The whole gist of the complaint is, that the board of supervisors have not exercised their judgment or discretion in the matter; that they have arbitrarily, without investigation, and without any exercise of judgment or discretion, fixed these rates without any reference to what they should be, without reference either to the expense to the plaintiff necessary to furnish the water, or to what is a fair and reasonable compensation therefor; that the rates are so fixed as to render it impossible to furnish the water without loss, and so low as to amount to a practical confiscation of the plaintiff's property. If this be true, and the demurrer admits it, a party whose property is thus jeopardized should not be without a remedy. If the action of the board of supervisors was taken as the complaint alleges, they have not in any sense complied with the requirements of the constitution, and their pretended action was a palpable fraud which might result injuriously either to the plaintiff or the city and its inhabitants, and would almost certainly work injustice to one or the other. The constitution does not contemplate any such mode of fixing rates. It is not a matter of guess-work or an arbitrary fixing of rates without reference to the rights of the water company or the public. When the constitution provides for the fixing of rates or compensation, it means reasonable rates and just compensation. To fix such rates and compensation is the duty and within the jurisdiction of the board. To fix rates not reasonable or compensation not just is a plain violation of its duty. But the courts cannot, after the board has fully and fairly investigated and acted, by fixing what it believes to be reasonable rates, step in and say its action shall be set aside and nullified because the courts, upon a similar investigation, have come to a different conclusion as to the reasonableness of the rates fixed. There must be actual fraud in fixing the rates, or they must be so palpably and grossly unreasonable and unjust as to amount to the same thing.

The right of the plaintiff to dispose of the water collected in its reservoirs, at reasonable rates, is the only value it has, and

is the only thing that can bring the plaintiff any return for the
money expended for reservoirs for its storage, and pipes for its
distribution. Not only reservoirs, pipes, and other works and
improvements necessary to carry out the objects of its incorporation, but the water itself, is property which cannot be taken
without just compensation.

The fact that the right to store and dispose of the water is a
public use, subject to the control of the state, and that its
regulation is provided for by the constitution of this state,
does not affect the question. Regulation, as provided for in
the constitution, does not mean confiscation, or a taking without just compensation. If it does, then our constitution is
clearly in violation of the constitution of the United States,
which provides that this shall not be done.

The ground taken by the appellant is, that the fixing of
rates is a legislative act; that by the terms of the constitution
the board of supervisors are made a part of the legislative
department of the state government, and exclusive power
given to them which cannot be encroached upon by the courts.
In other words, the board of supervisors, for the purpose of
fixing these water rates, is a part of one of the co-ordinate and
independent departments of the state government, and, as
such, beyond and independent of any control by the judicial
department.

This court has held that the fixing of water rates is a legislative act, at least to the extent that the action of the proper
bodies clothed with such power cannot be controlled by writs
which can issue only for the purpose of controlling judicial
action: *Spring Valley Water Works* v. *Bryant*, 52 Cal. 132;
Spring Valley Water Works v. *City and County of San Francisco*, 52 Cal. 111; *Spring Valley Water Works* v. *Bartlett*, 63
Cal. 245. There are other cases holding the act to be legislative, but whether it is judicial, legislative, or administrative,
is immaterial. Let it be which it may, it is not above the
control of the courts in proper cases. It has also been held
that where a power is vested in an officer of the state involving the exercise of discretion and judgment on his part,
such discretion and judgment cannot be controlled by the
courts by *mandamus*: *Berryman* v. *Perkins*, 55 Cal. 483.

The right and jurisdiction in this respect is fully and accurately stated in *Davis* v. *Mayor etc. of New York*, 1 Duer,
451–497, as follows: "Nothwithstanding these observations,
the question still remains, Has this court, or any court of equity,

the power to interefere with the legislative discretion of the
common council of this city, or of any other municipal corporation? And to this question I at once reply, Certainly not,
if the term 'discretion' be properly limited and understood;
and thus understood, I carry the proposition much further
than the counsel who advanced it. This court has no right
to interfere with and control the exercise, not merely of the
legislative, but of any other discretionary, power, that the law
has vested in the corporation of the city; and hence I deem it
quite immaterial whether the resolution in favor of Jacob
Sharp and his associates be termed a by-law, a grant, or contract, or whether the power exercised in passing it be legislative, judicial, or executive; for if the corporation had the
power of granting at all the extraordinary privileges which the
resolution confers, the propriety of exercising the power, and
perhaps even the form of its exercise, rested entirely in its discretion. Nor is this all. A court of equity has no right to
interfere with and control, in any case, the exercise of a discretionary power, no matter in whom it may be vested,— a
corporate body or individuals, the aldermen of a city, the directors of a bank, a trustee, executor, or guardian; and I add
that the meaning and principle of the rule, and the limitations to which it is subject, are, in all the cases to which it
applies, exactly the same. The meaning and principle of the
rule are, that the court will not substitute its own judgment
for that of the party in whom the discretion is vested, and
thus assume to itself a power which the law had given to another; and the limitations to which it is subject are, that the
discretion must be exercised, within its proper limits, for the
purposes for which it was given, and from the motives by which
alone those who gave the discretion intended that its exercise
should be governed."

We are not inclined to the doctrine asserted by the appellant in this case, that every subordinate body of officers to
whom the legislature delegates what may be regarded as legislative power thereby becomes a part of the legislative branch
of the state government, and beyond judicial control.

In the case of *Davis* v. *Mayor etc. of New York*, 1 Duer, 451–
497, it is further said:—

"It is this discretion, therefore, that I adopt, and for the
purpose of this opinion I shall treat the resolution as an ordinance or by-law, and its reconsideration and adoption as
properly acts of legislation, in the fullest sense in which the

term 'legislation' can be justly applied to the acts of a corporate body.

"Making these concessions, the denial of the jurisdiction of this court amounts to this: that a court of equity of general jurisdiction has no power, in any case or for any purpose, to restrain the legislative action of a municipal corporation, nor in any manner to interfere with or control its legislative discretion, no matter to what subject the action may be directed, nor how manifest and gross the violation of law, even of the provisions of its own charter, that it may involve, and no matter by what motives of fear, partiality, or corruption its discretion may be governed, nor how extensive and irreparable the mischief that, in the particular case, may be certain to result to individuals or the public from its threatened exercise.

"If this be true as a proposition of law, then the injunction order of this court, from the want of jurisdiction manifest on its face, was wholly void. If the proposition be not true, the order was valid, and should have been obeyed.

"In reply to a question put by the court, it was expressly affirmed by one of the counsel that should the common counsel attempt, by an ordinance, and from motives manifestly corrupt, to convey, for a grossly inadequate or merely nominal consideration, all the corporate property of the city, neither this nor any other court would have power to suppress, by an injunction, the meditated fraud, or when consummated, to rescind the grant, or punish its authors, or divest them of its fruits. There could be no remedy, we were told, but from the force of public opinion, and the action of the people at an ensuing election, and all this upon the ground that neither the propriety nor the honesty of the proceedings of a legislative body, nor, while they are pending, even their legality, can ever be made the subject of judicial inquiry.

"This, it must be confessed, is a startling doctrine. We all felt it to be so when announced, and I rejoice that we are now able to say, with an entire conviction, that, applied to a municipal corporation, it is just as groundless in law as it seems to us it is wrong in its principle, and certainly would be pernicious in its effects.

"The doctrine, exactly as stated, may be true when applied to the legislature of the state, which, as a co-ordinate branch of the government representing and exercising in its sphere the sovereignty of the people, is, for political reasons of manifest force, wholly exempt in all its proceedings from any legal process or judicial control; but the doctrine is not, nor is any portion of it, true when applied to a subordinate municipal body, which, although clothed to some extent with legislative and even political powers, is yet, in the exercise of all its powers, just as subject to the authority and control of courts of justice, to legal process, legal restraint, and legal correction as any other body or person, natural or artificial.

"The supposition that there exists an important distinction, or any distinction whatever, between a municipal corporation and any other corporation aggregate, in respect to the powers of courts of justice over its proceedings, is entirely gratuitous, and as it seems to me is as destitute of reason as it certainly is of authority The counsel could refer us to no case, nor have we found any, in which the judgment of the court has proceeded upon such a distinction; nor in our researches, which have not been limited, have we been able to discover that, by any judge or jurist, the existence of such a distinction has ever been asserted or intimated": Pages 494, 495.

This case was affirmed by the court of appeals of New York, in *People* v. *Sturtevant*, 9 N. Y. 263, 59 Am. Dec. 536, and the doctrine announced meets with our approval.

Counsel for appellants rely mainly in support of their position on the decisions of the supreme court of the United States in what are known as the Granger cases, the leading one of which is the case of *Munn* v. *Illinois*, 94 U. S. 113.   But while there may be some language used in the opinion in that case tending to maintain their contention, there was no such question presented as we have here, and the point made in this case was not decided.   The question there presented is clearly stated by the learned chief justice in his opinion: "The question to be determined in this case is, whether the general assembly of Illinois can, under the limitations upon the legislative power of the states imposed by the constitution of the United States, fix by law the maximum of charges of the storage of grain in warehouses at Chicago and other places in the state having not less than one hundred thousand inhabitants, 'in which grain is stored in bulk, and in which the grain of different owners is mixed together, or in which grain is stored in such a manner that the identity of different lots or parcels cannot be accurately preserved'": Page 123; see also, for a statement of the questions passed upon in this case, *Wabash etc. R'y Co.* v. *Illinois*, 118 U. S. 557–568.

It will be observed from this statement that the only question there was, whether the power to regulate prices rested in the legislature of the state of Illinois at all, and not whether, if it did exist, it was exclusive, and beyond judicial inquiry and control.

That there was no intention to decide that the courts have no jurisdiction to interfere in this class of cases, upon a proper showing, is clearly indicated by what is said by the same court in later decisions, and by judges of other federal courts. In the case of *Spring Valley Water Works* v. *Schottler*, 110 U. S. 347, Chief Justice Waite, who delivered the opinion in *Munn* v. *Illinois*, 94 U. S. 113, said: "That it is within the power of the government to regulate the prices at which water shall be sold by one who enjoys a virtual monopoly of the sale, we do not doubt. That question is settled by what was decided on full consideration in *Munn* v. *Illinois*, 94 U. S. 113. As was said in that case, such regulations do not deprive a person of his property without due process of law. What may be done if the municipal authorities do not exercise an honest judgment, or if they fix upon a price which is manifestly unreasonable, need not now be considered, for that proposition is not presented by this record. The objection here is not to any improper prices fixed by the officers, but to their power to fix prices at all. By the constitution and the legislation under it, the municipal authorities have been created a special tribunal to determine what, as between the public and the company, shall be deemed a reasonable price during a certain limited period. Like every other tribunal established by the legislature for such a purpose, their duties are judicial in their nature, and they are bound in morals and in law to exercise an honest judgment as to all matters submitted for their official determination": Page 354. Again, in *Stone* v. *Farmers' Loan and Trust Co.*, 116 U. S. 307–331, Chief Justice Waite said: "From what has thus been said, it is not to be inferred that this power of limitation or regulation is itself without limit. This power to regulate is not a power to destroy, and limitation is not the equivalent of confiscation. Under pretense of regulating fares and freights, the state cannot require a railroad corporation to carry persons or property without reward; neither can it do that which in law amounts to a taking of private property for public use without just compensation, or without due process of law. What would have this effect, we need not now say, because no tariff has yet been fixed by the commission, and the statute of Mississippi expressly provides 'that in all trials of cases brought for a violation of any tariff of charges, as fixed by the commission, it may be shown in defense that such tariff so fixed is unjust'": Page 331; see also *Dow* v. *Beidelman*, 125 U. S. 680.

In the case of *Georgia Banking Co.* v. *Smith*, 128 U. S. 174–· 179, Mr. Justice Field sums up the former decisions of that court as follows: "It has been adjudged by this court in numerous instances that the legislature of a state has the power to prescribe the charges of a railroad company for the carriage of persons and merchandise within its limits, in the absence of any provision in the charter of the company constituting a contract vesting in it authority over these matters, subject to the limitation that the carriage is not required without reward, or upon conditions amounting to the taking of property for public use without just compensation; and that what is done does not amount to a regulation of foreign or interstate commerce": Page 179.

It will be observed that in all the decisions of the supreme court of the United States, while the power of the state to regulate these charges is recognized, the power is so limited as to authorize just what it is contended should be done by the court in this case.

This same limitation, so necessary to the protection of the rights and property of corporations and individuals vested with a public use, is fully recognized by Brewer, J., now one of the justices of the supreme court of the United States, in *Chicago etc. R'y Co.* v. *Day*, 35 Fed. Rep. 866, 877. After reviewing the Granger cases and other cases above cited, he says: "It is obvious from these last quotations that the mere fact that the legislature has pursued the forms of law in prescribing a schedule of rates does not prevent inquiry by the courts; and the question is open, and must be decided in each case, whether the rates prescribed are within the limits of legislative power, or mere proceedings, which, in the end, if not restrained, will work a confiscation of the property of complainant. Of course, some rule must exist, fixed and definite, to control the action of the courts; for it cannot be that a chancellor is at liberty to substitute his discretion as to the reasonableness of rates for that of the legislature. The legislature has the discretion, and the general rule is, that where any officer or board has discretion, its acts within the limits of that discretion are not subject to review by the courts. Counsel for complainant urged that the lowest rates the legislature may establish must be such as will secure to the owners of the railroad property a profit on their investment at least equal to the lowest current rate of interest, say three per cent. Decisions of the supreme court seem to forbid such a limit to the power of the legislature in respect to that which they apparently recognize as a right of the owners of the railroad property to some reward; and the right of judicial interference exists only when the schedule of rates established will fail to secure to the owners of the property some compensation or income from their investment. As to the amount of such compensation, if some compensation or reward is in fact secured, the legislature is the sole judge": Page 878. See further, as supporting this view, *Pensacola etc. R. R. Co. v. State*, 25 Fla. 310.

Counsel on both sides have shown great industry and research in the presentation of this case, and many authorities are cited bearing more or less directly on this question, but we cannot extend this opinion by noticing or even citing them all. We have cited sufficient, we think, to sustain fully our view that the court below had jurisdiction, and that the complaint presented a case sufficient to call for the interposition of the court in the matter. The conclusion we have reached on this question is decisive of the case, but there are other points made and argued in the briefs which it is proper we should notice.

On the part of the appellant it is contended that a part of the allegations of the complaint necessary to make out a cause of action are of mere conclusions of law, and should not be considered. We think, however, that the allegations referred to, or enough of them to entitle the plaintiff to the relief demanded, are well pleaded. There are other objections to the form of the complaint and the manner of alleging the facts, which are equally groundless. It is further claimed that the mayor of the city should have been made a party, but we do not regard this as necessary.

On the part of the respondent it is contended, in support of the decision of the court below, that notice to the plaintiff of an intention to fix the rates was necessary, and that without such notice being given, the action of the board was a taking of its property without due process of law. But the constitution is self-executing, and as it does not require notice, we think no notice was necessary.

It does not follow, however, that because no notice is necessary the board are for that reason excused from applying to corporations or individuals interested to obtain all information necessary to enable it to act intelligibly and fairly in fixing the rates. This is its plain duty, and a failure to make the proper effort to procure all necessary information from whatever source may defeat its action. Both the corporation and the individuals furnishing the water, as well the public, who must pay for its use, are entitled to a careful and honest effort on the part of the board to obtain such information, and to have it act accordingly.

It is objected to the ordinance that it gives every householder an option to require a meter upon his premises, and to pay for the water furnished at meter rates, which are different from the house rate. It is contended that this does not fix the rate as the constitution requires, but leaves it indefinite and uncertain. We do not think the ordinance is defective in this respect. The rates are definitely fixed, and the fact that there may be one price for the consumer who has a meter, and a different price for one who has none, does not render the ordinance uncertain. It is also contended that the requirement that meters shall be furnished by the plaintiff is unreasonable, and cannot be enforced, but we think otherwise. The requirement that the party furnishing water shall provide the means necessary for its measurement, so that the quantity furnished and to be paid for may be known, is not an unreasonable regulation. The expense of the meter could not be imposed on the consumer: *Red Star Steamship Co.* v. *Jersey City*, 45 N. J. L. 246. There are other objections to the ordinance which we need not notice specifically. It is enough to say that, in our opinion, none of them are well taken.

Finally, we are asked by the respondent to lay down some basis upon which the board must proceed in fixing rates. But we do not feel that we should attempt to lay down such a rule in advance. This must be left for the board to determine.

Judgment affirmed.

THORNTON, J., delivered a dissenting opinion, of which the following is a synopsis: The superior court has jurisdiction of the case attempted to be made by the complaint. The questions to be considered relate to the exercise of jurisdiction, and the limits the law prescribes to the exercise of that jurisdiction. The complaint does not state facts sufficient to constitute a cause of action. It is defective in this: that it does not show on its face, by proper averment, that the rates fixed by the defendant board of supervisors are unjust or unreasonable or oppressive, and will not yield to the plaintiff all the revenue to which, under the law, it is entitled. The averments in regard to the fixing of rates are general and indefinite. The paragraph which is most particular and definite, and on which the decision of the case must turn, avers that the ordinance or order is, and the rates purporting to be prescribed and fixed thereby are, grossly unjust, unreasonable, and oppressive, and cannot yield for the year commencing July 1, 1889, and ending June 30, 1890, more than seven hundred and fifty thousand dollars, — a sum wholly insufficient to pay the interest on the plaintiff's indebtedness, its operating expenses, and taxes. (This paragraph is quoted in the prevailing opinion.) The plaintiff must show to the court, by the averments of the complaint, that the rates allowed by the ordinance will not and cannot produce an income, and will not allow the plaintiff to collect a sum which exceeds in amount seven hundred and fifty thousand dollars. General averments of the character set forth in this paragraph are insufficient. The facts must be pleaded from which the court can perceive, and itself make an estimate, and the estimate so made by the court must show a result from which it can perceive that the rates fixed are unjust and unreasonable, and will produce an income less than that to which the plaintiff is by law entitled. The *data* upon which the computation is to be made must appear by distinct allegation on the face of the complaint. The mere statement of the amount of money which the rates will bring to the company cannot be accepted by the court: *Brinham* v. *Mayor etc.*, 24 Cal. 602. These facts, - not being sufficiently pleaded, are not admitted by the demurrer, which admits only such facts as are well pleaded: *Branham* v. *Mayor etc.*, 24 Id. 602; *Johnson* v. *Kirby*, 65 Id. 487; Stephen's Pleading, 143; Gould's Pleading, c. 9, secs. 5, 6, 24, 29. The facts stated in this paragraph of the complaint are conclusions of fact, or conclusions made up of law and fact, and whether conclusions of fact or conclusions of law and fact, they are alike insufficient: *Branham* v. *Mayor etc.*, 24 Cal. 602. The court cannot accept the conclusions drawn by the pleader in this paragraph as well pleaded and admitted by the demurrer. That the allegation, "the said ordinance or order is, and the rates purporting to be prescribed and fixed thereby are, grossly unjust, unreasonable, and oppressive," is a conclusion either of fact or of law and fact, is too plain to admit of doubt. The same is true of the succeeding allegation, "that said rates do not provide for a just or fair or reasonable compensation for the water to be supplied during said year by the plaintiff to said city and county, and to the inhabitants thereof." This allegation states no issuable fact; it states nothing but conclusions. The next allegation is of the same character. The defendant should not be called on to answer such allegations. Under our system of pleading, the defendant is only required to answer facts as contradistinguished from the law, from arguments, from hypothesis, and from the evidence of the facts: *Green* v. *Palmer*, 15 Cal. 412; 76 Am. Dec. 492. The rule that should apply in this case is that which is applied to pleadings in which fraud is charged. Though fraud is not expressly charged, still the charges are of a gross dereliction of duty, and the facts showing such dereliction should be set forth in the complaint. It is not sufficient to aver fraud in general terms; the facts constituting the fraud must be alleged: *Gushee* v. *Leavitt*, 5 Cal. 160; 63 Am. Dec. 116; *Kinder* v. *Macy*, 7 Cal. 207; *Kohner* v. *Ashenauer*, 17 Id. 580; *Meeker* v. *Harris*, 19 Id. 289; 79 Am. Dec. 215; *Castle* v. *Bader*, 23 Cal. 76; *Semple* v. *Hagar*, 27 Id. 163; *Hager* v. *Shindler*, 29 Id. 60; *Kent* v. *Snyder*, 30 Id. 674; *Perkins* v. *Center*, 35 Id. 713; *Stone* v. *Farmers' etc. Co.*, 116 U. S. 307; *Dow* v. *Beidel-*

man, 125 U. S. 680. The case last cited is a strong authority to show that the complaint in this case does not state facts sufficient to constitute a cause of action.

The complaint here does not furnish *data* or state facts from which a court can see that the rates allowed by the ordinance are not just and reasonable, or that the income which will be received by the plaintiff from such rates will not furnish all the revenue the law allows, or that it can claim. One cannot perceive or calculate, from any facts set forth in the complaint, the amount which rate-payers will have to pay under the rates prescribed by the ordinance each month or for the year. Until such facts are set forth so as to make manifest to judicial cognition what such amount must and will be, it cannot be held that the complaint is sufficient. Charges of an intentional dereliction of duty against a public officer should be made specific in statement, so that he may see in advance what he has to admit or deny, and what evidence he will have to produce to disprove the charges made against him. The board of supervisors have important and responsible duties to perform, and when they are charged with a dishonest and intentional failure to discharge their duties, the complaint should aver in what particulars they have so failed. Such charges should be made in distinct and specific language. The complaint should not be argumentative, nor attempt to show, by inference to be drawn from general statements, that public officers have been guilty of intentionally dishonest conduct in the discharge of their official duties. Courts are bound to assume that the supervisors are men of ordinarily respectable standing, who have a right to be protected so far as the law allows from charges of dishonest official conduct couched in general statements. The statements of the complaint in this case are not sufficient to justify the court in coming to the conclusion that the board of supervisors of the city and county of San Francisco, in fixing water rates to be paid by the rate-payers in February, 1889, have failed in discharging their duty honestly and uprightly, and the court below therefore erred in overruling the demurrer to the complaint.

An enlarged discretion is committed to the board of supervisors in the matter of fixing water rates. They cannot so exercise this discretion as to compel the plaintiff to render the service of supplying water without reward. They must so fix the rates that a sufficient amount of money may be derived from their collection to pay the cost of services, and beyond that some reward or compensation. What such reward or compensation shall be is left entirely to the discretion of the board, and with the exercise of this discretion the courts cannot interfere: *Spring Valley Water Works* v. *Schottler,* 110 U. S. 347; *Stone* v. *Farmers' etc. Co.,* 116 Id. 307; *Dow* v. *Beidelman,* 125 Id. 680; *Georgia etc. Co.* v. *Smith,* 128 Id. 174; *Chicago etc. R. R. Co.* v. *Day,* 35 Fed. Rep. 866; *Hume* v. *Becker,* 35 Id. 883; *Peik* v. *Chicago etc. R. R. Co.,* 94 U. S. 178; *Chicago etc. R. R. Co.* v. *Ackley,* 94 Id. 179; *Winona etc. R. R. Co.* v. *Blake,* 94 Id. 180; *Stone* v. *Wisconsin,* 94 Id. 181. This is the result of all the decisions which have been cited and relied on by the plaintiff's counsel.

According to this rule, the rates must be so fixed as to allow money to be raised to pay the fairly necessary operating expenses of the plaintiff in rendering the service required. Taxes on its property invested and used in rendering such service are to be included as part of such operating expenses. In fixing the compensation, regard must be had to the value of the investment of the plaintiff in rendering the service required of it. The board must get at the value of the property of which the investment of the plaintiff consists, and upon such value they will allow such compensation as in their discretion they shall think fair and right. The board is not bound to fix the rates so as to furnish money to the plaintiff to pay the interest on the bonds negotiated by it. If it has invested the money borrowed on the bonds in purchasing property used by it in rendering the service due from it, the value of the property must be taken into consideration in fixing the reward or income it is to receive. When the value of such property has been considered in fixing the compensation, to allow rates so as to raise a sum sufficient to pay the interest on the bonds would be to allow compensation for the property bought with the money raised on the bonds, and for interest on such money in addition. This would be to allow for it twice.

If any of the money borrowed on the bonds was not invested in the property needed and used in rendering the service required of the plaintiff, it would be manifestly unjust to compel the rate-payers to pay interest on money so borrowed. Nor should they be compelled to raise money to pay for too high a rate of interest on such bonds. The rates should be fixed so as to furnish compensation to the plaintiff, based on the amount invested, and not on its bonds or any other debts. Neither is the board bound to fix rates to furnish the money to be used in the further extension or construction of the plaintiff's water-works. It is not just or right that the rate-payers should buy property for the plaintiff, and pay it interest on it. The board is bound to consider the rights of the rate-payers as well as those of the company.

The notice to the plaintiff was sufficient: Cal. Const., art. 14, sec. 1; Act March 7, 1881, sec. 2, Stats. 1881, p. 54; *State Railroad Tax Cases,* 92 U. S. 575; *Davidson* v. *New Orleans,* 96 Id. 97; *Kentucky Railroad Tax Cases,* 115 Id. 331; *Lent* v. *Tillson,* 72 Cal. 413. It does not appear that the plaintiff made any application to the board for a hearing until the last day of the month (February) in which the rates were to be fixed. It might have asked the board for a hearing at any time after the 3d of December. The court has no right to assume that the board would not have complied with such a request if seasonably made. A request made on the last day of the month within which the board was compelled to act under a penalty of removal from office was unseasonable and unreasonable, and in refusing it the board denied to the plaintiff no right.

The right of the plaintiff to introduce evidence before the board must be left to the discretion of the board. The law gives the plaintiff no such right. The legislature has regulated the matter of evidence by the act of March 7, 1881: Stats. 1881, pp. 54, 55, secs. 2, 3. The statement required by section 2 to be furnished in the month of January of each year was not furnished by the plaintiff in the year 1889 until the thirty-first day of January. It does not appear that it ever furnished the statement required by section 3. The general averment of the plaintiff, that it complied with all the requirements of the act of 1881, is insufficient. No rule of pleading permits or justifies it.

The refusal of the board to permit the plaintiff to introduce further evidence in regard to the adjustment of rates was matter wholly within their discretion, and was not a denial of any of its legal rights. Neither was it bound to hear argument on behalf of the plaintiff. The complaint avers that the ordinance in question was not duly or lawfully passed, or that it was not published five successive days. It was published on the 21st, 22d, 23d, 25th, 26th, and 27th of February, 1889. It was not published on the 24th, which fell on Sunday. This was a sufficient publication. If the ordinance was not duly or lawfully passed, it was void. If it is void, it injures no one, and no wrong exists to be redressed.

As the plaintiff does not appear to have ever furnished to the board of supervisors the statement required by section 3 of the act of 1881, it is not entitled to be heard in a court of equity. It has not done equity; for it has failed to comply with the lawful requirements made upon it. This complaint does not show that the plaintiff has been deprived of due process of law, or that any of its property has been or will be taken for public use without just compensation. The complaint shows that some compensation will be allowed. The amount of it may be small, but with the rate of compensation when it is allowed courts have nothing to do. The constitution and the statute leaves this to the discretion of the board of supervisors. And the courts cannot control this discretion.

MUNICIPAL CORPORATIONS — ORDINANCES. — Ordinances passed by the governing body of a city must be reasonable, not inconsistent with the laws of the state, nor repugnant to fundamental rights; they must not be oppressive, partial, or unfair, nor make special or unwarranted discriminations, and must not contravene common right: *Anderson* v. *City of Wellington*, 40 Kan. 173; 10 Am. St. Rep. 175; note to *Robinson* v. *Mayor of Franklin*, 34 Am. Dec. 627–643; note to *Ward* v. *Greeneville*, 35 Am. Rep. 702, 703.

[IN BANK.]

COLTON *v.* STANFORD.

[82 CALIFORNIA, 351.]

FIDUCIARY RELATION BETWEEN BUSINESS ASSOCIATES. — A business relation between certain persons associated together for the purpose of organizing, controlling, and directing railroad and other corporations, and who sustain towards one another relations of peculiar trust and confidence in regard to such enterprises and their conduct and management, although it may not constitute a partnership, is, nevertheless, a fiduciary relation between the associates.

EXISTENCE OF CONFIDENCE IS PRESUMED IN ALL TRUST RELATIONS, and if it appears that any advantage has come to the trustee in dealing with his *cestui que trust*, the burden is upon him to show that the confidence was not in fact abused. But this presumption may be overcome by proof of the fact that confidence has not been abused, and that the beneficiary has acted, not upon any reliance or confidence placed in the trustee, but upon the advice of an independent, professional, disinterested, and competent adviser; and in such case, the transaction is not voidable at the election of the beneficiary, but it devolves upon him, if he would set it aside, to show either actual or constructive fraud. Such fraud may be shown, in some instances, by presumptions.

COMPROMISE OF DOUBTFUL CLAIMS, WHEN WILL NOT BE RESCINDED BECAUSE OF REPRESENTATIONS NOT BELIEVED OR RELIED UPON. — Where, after the death of one of several business associates, his personal representative, relying upon the advice of disinterested experts and professional friends specially selected to investigate and advise in the premises, and who had full access to all sources of information concerning the matters in controversy, compromises doubtful claims against the surviving associates, who acted in good faith and without intentional fraud, and disclosed every fact within their knowledge, such compromise will not be rescinded upon the ground that such surviving associates did not disclose all facts of which they might have acquired knowledge by a more skillful and diligent search, especially when every fact subsequently discovered could have been discovered before the execution of the compromise agreement as well as after it.

TRUSTEE MAY DISSOLVE TRUST RELATION AND DEAL WITH HIS CESTUI QUE TRUST WHEN. — If a transaction is one in which a trustee may lawfully deal with his *cestui que trust* by first dissolving the trust relation, it is not too late for him to do so at any time before the *cestui que trust* is prevented from making a full and fair investigation and consideration of the business in hand, and before he executes the contract.

PRESUMPTION FROM INDEPENDENT INVESTIGATION MADE ON BEHALF OF CESTUI QUE TRUST. — A presumption that everything material was discovered follows from an independent investigation into the sources of information made by the professional advisers of a *cestui que trust*, and this presumption is fortified by the introduction in evidence of memoranda kept by such advisers, showing unmistakable care and painstaking and a minute consideration of the subject on their part.

EFFECT OF MISREPRESENTATION NOT RELIED UPON BY PARTY TO WHOM MADE. — The rule that where a party to a contract, without belief or without information, makes a representation which is not true, he is as responsible as if he had knowledge of its falsity, where the other party has acted upon such representation, relying upon it as correct, does not apply where such party, discarding the representation as unworthy of belief, proceeds to inquire for himself, is given full and fair facilities for informing himself, and finally acts upon his own judgment and that of his advisers.

EQUITABLE ESTOPPELS MUST BE MUTUAL. Where, therefore, a compromise agreement is effected between plaintiff and defendants, in which railroad bonds involved in the compromise are represented to plaintiff to be worth only sixty cents on the dollar, and are so estimated in the settlement, the fact that, a few days after the execution of the compromise agreement, they are used by defendants to pay the indebtedness of one corporation to another at a valuation of ninety cents on the dollar does not amount to a fraud upon the plaintiff, nor constitute an equitable estoppel preventing the defendants from claiming that they were not worth ninety cents at the time of the compromise, it appearing that the defendants practically dealt with themselves in the transaction, and rated the bonds at what they supposed they would become worth in the future, the transaction being merely a temporary mode of settling up a corporate obligation, and the plaintiff not being in any way bound by the transaction.

MISREPRESENTATION, WHEN NOT BASIS FOR RESCISSION OF CONTRACT. — Under the Civil Code of California, a misrepresentation, in order to avoid a contract, though it need not be the sole cause of the contract, must be of such nature, weight, and force that the court can say "without it the contract would not have been made"; and if the court properly finds, from the evidence, that the contract would have been executed by the plaintiff had the truth been known, and the defendant, upon being made aware of the facts, had still insisted upon the same contract, there is no basis for a rescission of the contract.

MISREPRESENTATION, IF UNIMPORTANT, NOT GROUND FOR RESCISSION WHEN. — A mistaken representation made by the defendant, not being an inducing cause of the plaintiff's action in entering into a compromise agreement, but relating to a matter of comparatively small importance, will not be ground for rescinding the contract by the plaintiff, after the defendant has made large expenditures on the faith of the agreement, which have materially enhanced the value of the property involved in the litigation.

UNCONSCIONABLE ADVANTAGE, WHETHER ONE PARTY HAS TAKEN OF ANOTHER, HOW DETERMINED. — In determining whether or not one party to a compromise agreement has taken an unconscionable advantage of the other party, the question must be determined, not in the light of subsequent events, but upon the circumstances existing at the time of the negotiations and the execution of the contract; and if it appears, upon a consideration of those circumstances, that no advantage was taken, and that the contract was fair, just, and equal, it will not be set aside.

DELAY IN SEEKING RESCISSION AND ENHANCEMENT IN VALUE OF PROPERTY, EFFECT OF. —When a compromise agreement has been effected between plaintiff and defendants under adverse circumstances, in view of which defendants desired plaintiff to prosecute the business at their mutual risk, which plaintiff declined to do, the failure on the part of the plaintiff for more than two years to seek a rescission of the agreement, or to become informed of the facts upon which rescission is sought, until the property involved had become greatly enhanced in value, is an important circumstance to be considered by the court.

ACTION for rescission and an accounting. The opinion states the facts.

G. Frank Smith, Stanly, Stoney, and Hayes, and E. W. McKinstry, for the appellant.

Garber and Bishop, L. D. McKissick, and Creed Haymond, for the respondents.

PATERSON, J.　From the fifth day of October, 1874, down to the time of his death, David D. Colton was associated with defendants in the ownership, control, and direction of certain corporations. Prior to that time, defendants and Mark Hopkins had been the principal owners of the stock of the Central Pacific Railroad Company, the Southern Pacific Railroad Company, and of various other subordinate and connected railroad companies, and also of the Contract and Finance Company. They had associated themselves together for the purpose of securing the co-operation and assistance of all in the furtherance of certain railroad enterprises, and of such others as they should from time to time agree upon. In pursuance of the terms of their association and agreement, they had invested respectively large sums of money, and were giving their time and labor to the management and direction of the corporations above named, and to the acquisition and control of other corporations which they desired to operate in furtherance of the general schemes they then had and might thereafter have in view. Being desirous of securing the aid and co-operation of another associate, negotiations were opened with Mr. Colton, whom the defendants had known for several years prior thereto, which ended in an agreement between him and them that he should become associated with them in like manner as they had theretofore been associated with one another. By the terms of this agreement with the defendants and Mark Hopkins, Mr. Colton was to have twenty thousand shares of the capital stock of the Central Pacific Railroad Company and twenty thousand shares of the capital stock of the Southern Pacific Railroad Company, in consideration of the sum of one million dollars, for which sum he gave his promissory note, with interest at six per cent per annum, payable on or before October 5, 1879. All dividends on the stock were to be applied as payments on the note. It was agreed that Colton was to share in the proportion that his stock bore to the stock issued in all responsibilities, damages, penalties, etc., and to share in all the liabilities of the Central Pacific, Southern Pacific, and Contract and Finance companies, the same as if he had been associated and connected with them from the time of their organization. On the 15th of December, 1874, they organized the Western Development Company, the affairs of which cut a most important figure in the controversy. The capital stock of this company was fixed at five million dollars, of which Stanford, Huntington, Crocker, and Hopkins each took two ninths and Colton one ninth. General Colton's interest in all other properties acquired by the associates came to him through this corporation, except that which he held in the Ione Coal and Iron Company, which had a capital stock of four million dollars, divided equally between the associates, and that which he held in the Colorado Steam Navigation Company, and in the Occidental and Oriental Steamship Company. He was also one of the original incorporators of the Southern Pacific Company of Arizona, organized in 1873, and held thirty thousand shares of the capital stock thereof.

In 1876 the parties made and executed a new agreement, which they antedated as of October 5, 1874. This agreement differs in some material respects from the original. A copy of it is annexed to the complaint, and is set out in the statement of facts. By the terms of this modified agreement the stock sold to Mr. Colton was pledged as collateral security for the payment of the one-million-dollar note, and it was agreed that neither party should sell his interest in the contract without the written consent of all parties thereto.

The enterprises entered into and carried on by these associates during the lifetime of Mr. Colton were of stupendous magnitude, involving face values amounting to hundreds of millions of dollars. The success of their schemes depended upon many things. In the midst of their most important operations both Mr. Hopkins and Mr. Colton were taken from the association by death, the former on March 29, 1878, the latter in October following. The bond of friendship which had bound the five associates together was of the strongest kind, and the confidence which one reposed in another had no limit.

Soon after the death of her husband, Mrs. Colton — this plaintiff — began to make inquiries as to the interest of the estate in the various corporations with which Mr. Colton had been connected. In his last will and testament Mr. Colton had recommended that if his wife should desire the assistance of any one in the settlement of his estate, his friend S. M. Wilson, and his secretary, Charles E. Green, should be called in as co-executors. Mrs. Colton, being the universal legatee, and entirely ignorant of her husband's affairs, called upon and secured the services of Mr. Wilson to aid her. Negotiations were entered into between plaintiff and defendants for a settlement. During these negotiations the plaintiff became suspicious of the motives and conduct of the defendants, believed that they had manipulated the books to deceive her, and that they were unworthy of trust or confidence. Nevertheless, after a thorough examination of the books and many interviews with defendants, a compromise agreement was entered into on the twenty-seventh day of August, 1879, by the terms of which certain stocks, including 408 shares of the Rocky Mountain Coal and Iron Company, were assigned to defendants, the one-million-dollar note was canceled, and all the liabilities of the Western Development Company and other corporations were assumed by them, and the estate of Colton was released therefrom.

About two years after the execution of the compromise agreement, plaintiff discovered many errors in the calculations upon which the compromise had been made. She thereupon served a notice of rescission, and demanded a new accounting. A complaint was drawn up charging the defend-

ants with misrepresentation, concealment, etc., and after
several interviews, to wit, on May 24, 1882, plaintiff commenced this action for a rescission of the compromise agreement of August 27, 1879 (referred to as exhibit F), on the
ground that said agreement had been procured through false
and fraudulent representations made by defendants during
the course of the negotiations which resulted in the execution
of the compromise.

The answer denies the charges of fraud, alleges that whatever statements were made by defendants were made by them
in good faith, believing them to be true, and avers that Colton,
during the time that he was connected with the Western Development Company, fraudulently appropriated to his own
use certain large sums of money belonging to said company
and to these defendants.

After a trial lasting nearly two years, before Hon. Jackson
Temple, — who was at that time judge of the superior court
of Sonoma County, and who has recently left this court on
account of illness, — findings and judgment were rendered
in favor of defendants. From this judgment, and an order
denying the motion for a new trial, the plaintiff has appealed.

Although the record herein covers about twelve thousand
pages of printed matter, there is no substantial conflict in the
evidence. The questions involved in this appeal have been
debated by counsel upon the assumption that the facts found
by the learned judge of the court below are unassailable, and
that the decision is correct, except as to the legal deductions
drawn from the specific facts found.

It is not contended by the appellant that the defendants
knowingly made any false statements or intended to deceive
plaintiff in the negotiations, but it is claimed that the facts
found show the existence of a fiduciary relation between plaintiff and defendants; that in dealing with plaintiff it was the
duty of the defendants to make a full and correct disclosure of
the condition of the business in which Colton held an interest,
whether the plaintiff was relying upon their advice or upon
her own investigation and the advice and judgment of Wilson
and other friends; that it is immaterial whether the parties
believed there was in fact any such duty resting upon the defendants, or whether the plaintiff did actually rely upon and
confide in them; that where the negotiations begin in peace
and confidence between trustee and *cestui que trust,* it matters
not that suspicion, distrust, and fears may lead the bene-

ficiary to make independent investigation during the negotiations, and rely upon independent advice, and her own judgment, in finally concluding the compromise; that the trustee can shake off the duty referred to, if at all, only by a clear and unequivocal dissolution of the trust relation before the negotiations commence; that the business relation between Colton and defendants was a partnership, and that the surviving partners were bound to know the condition of the business, and impart full information thereof to plaintiff; that in cases of this kind the surviving partners must show affirmatively that the settlement was fair and the consideration adequate, the contract being *prima facie* void; that the court erred in ignoring this principle, and in holding that it was for plaintiff to prove fraud; that the findings show both actual and constructive fraud and threats, and that the representations made by defendants with respect to the ownership of the 408 shares of Rocky Mountain Coal and Iron Company stock are sufficient of themselves to call for a reversal of the judgment; that the judgment should be reversed, and a judgment entered in favor of the plaintiff on account of undue influence, concealment, and fraudulent misrepresentations, although it be conceded that the parties making the contract herein sought to be rescinded dealt as strangers, and that the findings do not cover the material issues; and that the court erred in its conclusions of law, and as to the effect of certain evidence.

Many of the topics discussed by counsel are involved in the question whether there existed such a fiduciary relation as called for a full, fair, and accurate statement by defendants of the conditions of the affairs of the several corporations in which Mr. Colton, in his lifetime, had been interested; counsel for appellant contending all the time that such relation did exist, and that by virtue of their superior knowledge and means of information, the duty of making a full disclosure and truthful statement by defendants became imperative and absolutely essential to the validity of any compromise based upon negotiations between the parties. The respondents have claimed at all stages of the litigation that the business relation of the several associates was not that of partners, and that upon the death of Mr. Colton the defendants owed plaintiff no duty other than that which arises from the relation of stockholders in a corporation.

In this branch of the controversy the learned judge of the

court below sided with the respondents, and upon this subject
he expressed his opinion in the following language: "At no
time were the defendants, Leland Stanford, C. P. Huntington,
Charles Crocker, and Mark Hopkins, copartners, or associated
in any business or enterprise as copartners. Nor did they at
any time carry on any business as copartners," etc. "At the
death of Colton the association between him and the defendants and Mark Hopkins entirely ended and ceased. There
was no property belonging to the associates, as such. After
his death, the plaintiff was merely a stockholder in the various
corporations. . . . . After the death of Colton, the individual
defendants had no other power over the affairs of the plaintiff,
and occupied toward her no other relationship, than as controlling the corporations in which she was a stockholder, and
as creditor and pledgees. . . . . . But if a trust relation of this
character existed between these associates, what was the relation of the survivors, upon the death of Colton, to his representative? At his death, the association was entirely ended.
It was a case where confidence was given for confidence, service for service. There was no property belonging to the associates, as such. No power over the affairs of Mrs. Colton or
the estate of D. D. Colton survived his death. His position
was one of great power over many things, through this mutual
confidence. She was merely a stockholder in various corporations. It is true, they continued to be virtual directors of these
corporations, as they and Colton had previously been. But
this no longer depended upon any confidential relations with
the holders of Colton's stock. . . . . The previous relations
with Colton did not affect the question. They and Colton had
no vested interests in any new projects not yet begun. . . . .
There was not, then, after Colton's death, any further active
duties, as trustees, due from defendants to the estate of Colton": 8 W. C. Rep., Supplement, 31.

It must be admitted, however, that the arguments of the
appellant upon this question are most persuasive, and make
the business relation which existed between the associates look
like a partnership for the purpose of organizing, controlling,
and operating railroad and other corporations; but in view of
the manner in which the compromise was effected, and of all
the circumstances surrounding the settlement of the dispute,
we deem it unnecessary to determine this particular question.
There is no doubt that the associates occupied toward one
another relations of the greatest confidence and trust. This

relation of trust and confidence, indeed, was one of extraordinary character, greater than ever existed in any partnership with which we have been acquainted. The power and authority possessed by each associate over the business, property, and standing of others interested with him never was possessed, perhaps, by a member of any other concern or association. That there was a relation of mutual trust and confidence of high character between the associates, and that such relation was recognized by Judge Temple, is apparent from the following extracts taken from his findings and opinion: "Some of their transactions in the payment and disbursement of money were private and confidential between said associates, the character and reason of such disbursements being known only to and by said associates, and not recorded or entered in any books or writings kept by them, or any of said corporations, and said five associates until the death of said Hopkins, and said four associates thereafter until the death of said Colton, had and assumed and sustained relations of intimate and peculiar trust and confidence, each toward and with the others, in regard to their said enterprises, and their management and conduct; and they acquired, obtained, and had confidential information and control each concerning and over the affairs of the property and business connected with, growing out of, and accumulated by and through the enterprises in which said Stanford, Huntington, Hopkins, Crocker, and Colton were associated together. As each new scheme was determined upon, each had his part in the work, though each party then decided for himself whether he would go into each scheme or not, and there was no power in the majority to commit any one to any new enterprise until he approved of it." "Fiduciary relations may exist between stockholders of various corporations who have associated themselves to control such corporations and make them work in harmony; but they would not be partners. And so I conclude, although the corporations managed by these associates cannot be regarded as partnerships, nor as mere instrumentalities of a partnership, the relation between the parties was nevertheless of a fiduciary character. I think it already appears that the parties to the agreement, exhibit A, intended something more than to procure situations for each other as employees in various corporations. They had designs not stated in that paper, which were the real purposes of that association. The fiduciary relation must have existed under our code as to these projected enterprises, and the management of the system of roads they had built and acquired. . . . . Each had invested his money and expended his labor in reliance upon this fidelity of the others ": Page 30, Supplement.

It is a nice question whether the trust relation which had existed between the associates continued to exist after the death of Colton, and impose any active duties upon the survivors as trustees of his estate; but if any such duties were cast upon the defendants by reason of the death of Mr. Colton, they were waived by the plaintiff herself, and the relation of trustee and *cestui que trust* was so entirely discarded and dissolved during the negotiations that they were not bound by any fiduciary relation to counsel, advise, and protect the plaintiff, or to perform any other duty than to deal fairly by her, and in good faith to disclose all facts within their knowledge material for her to know in conducting the negotiations fairly, and to enable her to make a full and unhampered investigation into the matters in controversy.

We have been unable to find a case in which a lump agreement of compromise, entered into by surviving partners and the representative of a deceased partner, or by a trustee and *cestui que trust*, — the latter acting by the advice of experts and able counsel, and renouncing all confidence in the trustees, — after full, fair, and honest investigation, has been rescinded because of actual and unintentional inaccuracies discovered subsequent to the execution of the agreement; nor do we know of any universal rule of equity, or any provision of our code, tending to establish the proposition that from the mere fact of a prior existing fiduciary relationship everything, in the absence of proof, must be presumed against the trustee who has entered into a contract with his *cestui que trust*, regardless of the question whether confidence has in fact been reposed and abused. Of course, in all trust relations the existence of confidence will be presumed, and if it appear that any advantage has come to the trustee in dealing with his *cestui que trust*, the burden will be thrown upon him to show that confidence was not in fact abused. But it has always been held, as we understand it, that this presumption might be overcome by proof of the fact that confidence had not been abused, and that the beneficiary acted, not upon any reliance or confidence placed in the trustee, but upon the advice of an independent, professional, disinterested, and competent adviser. There is a distinction to be made between transactions

occurring directly between the trustee and his beneficiary, and
those transactions in which the trustee deals with himself or
another party. Thus if a trustee, in the execution of his trust,
sells property to himself, the transaction may be set aside by
the *cestui que trust* as void, without giving any reason, or alleging any fraud, or any disadvantage, or inadequacy of price.
In such case there are no two parties to the contract, the trustee dealing with himself alone; but where the trustee deals
directly with the *cestui que trust*, the latter having for himself
an independent adviser, and the trustee making no pretense
of advising him, the transaction is not voidable at the election
of the beneficiary, but it will devolve upon the latter, if he
would set it aside, to show some reason therefor. He must
show either actual or constructive fraud. Of course, the fraud
may be shown in some instances by presumptions.

Section 2219 of the Civil Code provides: "Every one who
voluntarily assumes a relation of personal confidence with
another is deemed a trustee, within the meaning of this chapter, not only as to the person who reposes such confidence,
but also as to all persons of whose affairs he thus acquires information which was given to such person in the like confidence, or over whose affairs he, by such confidence, obtains
any control." Section 2228 is as follows: "In all matters
connected with his trust, a trustee is bound to act in the
highest good faith toward his beneficiary, and may not obtain
any advantage therein over the latter by the slightest misrepresentation, concealment, threat, or adverse pressure of
any kind." Section 2229 is as follows: "A trustee may not
use or deal with the trust property for his own profit, or for
any other purpose unconnected with the trust, in any manner." Section 2235 is as follows: "All transactions between
a trustee and his beneficiary during the existence of the trust,
or while the influence acquired by the trustee remains, by
which he obtains any advantage from his beneficiary, are presumed to be entered into by the latter without sufficient consideration and under undue influence."

That these provisions are consistent with the rules of equity,
as we have construed them, is apparent, we think, when read
in connection with the following provision: "The person
whose confidence creates a trust is called the trustor; the person in whom confidence is reposed is called the trustee; and
the person for whose benefit the trust is created is called the
beneficiary": Civ. Code, sec. 2218. These provisions show that

the fundamental principle of the relation of trustee and *cestui que trust* is that of confidence.

In the case at bar, Mrs. Colton not only did not rest any confidence or reliance upon anything said, done, or omitted to be said and done, by the defendants, or any of them, but she called in and secured the aid of four or five disinterested and competent advisers; among these was Mr. S. M. Wilson, one of the leaders of the bar of this state, a man of irreproachable character, in the prime of life, for twenty-five years the warm personal friend of her husband, and the man whom he had recommended on his death-bed, and she was fully informed by him as to her legal rights. She also obtained the services of Mr. Lloyd Tevis, a skillful and successful financier, to assist Mr. Wilson in his investigations as to the business of the corporations. The investigations made by these gentlemen and the plaintiff lasted for over six months, and were most thorough, careful, and diligent. It is found, as a matter of fact, that they had sources of information other than those possessed by the defendants, and that they were in fact more thoroughly acquainted with, and better qualified to form an accurate judgment as to the condition of, the affairs of the company than any of the defendants. Mrs. Colton had also the advice of Mr. Steinberger, an old friend of her husband, and the advice and assistance of Mr. Green, his secretary for many years, and of Mr. Douty, who was a cousin and intimate friend of General Colton, and a business man of great capacity and experience, and a skillful and expert accountant. All the claims preferred by the defendants on their own behalf were fully discussed, considered, and investigated. The subject-matters of the negotiations were of the most complicated nature, consisting in part of accounts running through many years, and recorded in many volumes of books and thousands of vouchers and papers relating in part to the transactions, some of which had gone out of the memory of the parties thereto.

The court found as a fact, and it seems practically undisputed, that during the negotiations defendants were ready and willing to answer, and did truthfully answer, all questions asked them, and submitted freely all the books and accounts in their possession, or under their control, to the inspection and investigation of the plaintiff and her agents. The plaintiff and her agents knew, partly from discoveries they made themselves, and partly from information given by the defendants before the compromise agreement was executed, that there were many inaccuracies in some of the statements furnished to the plaintiff. Among other important matters in dispute between the parties, and which were compromised, was the right to Western Development Company dividends, amounting, according to plaintiff's valuation, to over half a million dollars. At the time the negotiations were in progress, the plaintiff saw no justice whatever in the transaction; her heart rebelled against the whole matter. She believed that the defendants were unworthy of any credit or confidence, and were endeavoring by all the means in their power to cheat and defraud her. She suspected that the defendants had made some of the charges against her husband, knowing them to be false, and that they had manipulated their books to sustain those charges. No source of information was withheld from them; no means of ascertaining intelligently the true state of the accounts were covered up before they acted upon and compromised the matters upon which. the controversy arose; every fact which has since been discovered could have been discovered before the execution of the compromise agreement, as well as thereafter; the witnesses who could throw any light upon the matters in controversy were within their reach. Mrs. Colton was most anxious to make the settlement. The defendants "insisted that they were not bound to discount the future of their securities for her, thus giving her the benefit of their contemplated enterprises and the expenditure of more millions. She was not entitled to the profits when she would not share the risks." The property in controversy was of immense value,—chiefly speculative value. Mr. Tevis "was known as a bold, enterprising, and successful speculator. He was intimately acquainted with the railroads, and was a man of great wealth, abundantly able to pick up the burden where Colton had dropped it, and carry it along without asking any favors from the defendants," all of which was known to the plaintiff at the time she acted upon his advice and accepted the terms of the compromise: Findings 18, 55, 57; Supplement, p. 67.

The findings show that the defendants in good faith disclosed every fact within their knowledge. There is nothing in the findings to show that plaintiff or her agents were misled as to any matter except the statement in regard to the number of shares of the Rocky Mountain Coal and Iron Company stock, which they claimed to own, though held by Mr. Colton. Of this matter we shall speak hereafter.

Here, therefore, we have a case in which — assuming the existence of a fiduciary relation, and that the presumptions as to confidence and the burden as to proof are as claimed by appellant — the undisputed facts show that there was absolutely no confidence reposed by the beneficiary, but that she acted exclusively upon the advice of several disinterested experts and professional friends, specially selected to investigate and counsel her, because of their ability and familiarity with the affairs of the trustees with whom she was dealing, and who acted toward her in the highest good faith.

To hold that, under such circumstances, a contract entered into by the parties compromising and settling disputes of the most doubtful character and value cannot stand if it subsequently appear that the trustee did not impart to the *cestui que trust*, not only all the knowledge of the transactions of which he was possessed, but all that he might have acquired by diligent and skillful search, would be to place an absolute embargo upon all settlements of disputed questions between parties holding trust relations, although equity favors the amicable adjustment of claims which, like those involved in this settlement, bid fair to become a fruitful source of litigation. Under such a rule it would be difficult to find men fit to be trustees who would accept such a trust; there would be no inducement to compromise doubtful matters, however advantageous the settlement might seem to be to the *cestui que trust*, and no trustee, or his sureties, who had settled with his *cestui que trust*, would feel secure in his position until either time or circumstances had dispelled every possible chance of a successful contest based upon new evidence or a rise in values. Such a construction of the provisions of our code would not only place them in antagonism to all the authorities which have explained and applied the rules of equity governing such contracts between trustee and *cestui que trust*, — and the code provisions are but a digest of these rules, — but would convert a rule intended to prevent ·fraud into one creating an incentive to and a cover of fraud; because it would afford a convenient method for a party who had repudiated any reliance upon or trust in his trustee, and who had acted upon the advice of independent, skilled, and disinterested champions and his own investigations, to turn around when subsequent facts showed that the bargain was to his disadvantage, and say in effect: "It is true, I did not place any confidence in your statements, and told you that I should not, but should

rely on my trusted agents. It is true, I acted only in my own
interest, being sole legatee. It is true, you laid before me all
the means of information, and I and my agents assumed to
act upon them. We had the means of information, and might
have discovered the truth, but were not fully informed. It is
sufficient to say that you did not correctly represent the condition of the business. It was your duty to do so. I admit
that you acted honestly and fairly; that you did not intend
to misrepresent any fact, or any value, and I admit that my
means of information were as good as yours were. It matters
not that I gave you notice in advance, I should not trust you
in anything you said or did, but should rely upon the investigations and advice of my friends, because your representations
were not correct. It was your duty to make them full, fair,
and accurate. I claim a rescission upon the representations
you made, although I did not believe them." If there is a
case in which a court of equity has decreed a rescission under
such circumstances, it has not been called to our attention.
Whatever may have been said as to the presumptions arising
out of proof of a fiduciary relation, the fundamental principle
upon which rescission is granted is always, and under all circumstances, the claim and consideration that confidence has
been reposed and that confidence has been abused. No such
claim can in reason be made where the party seeking the rescission — being of competent age and understanding, and
acting only in his own interest — has undertaken to investigate for himself, called in experts, been given free and fair
means of ascertaining the truth, acted upon his own judgment
and the advice of friends, and repudiated any confidence in or
reliance upon the parties with whom he was dealing. It matters not what the relations of the parties have been prior to or
are at the time of the negotiations for a settlement and compromise of their disputes, the principle is one of universal application, and it is a principle of common sense and of good policy.

It is unnecessary for us to review the authorities on this
subject. They will be found, we think, to fully support the
views we have expressed, and in order to make as brief as
possible this opinion, which, perhaps, is already unnecessarily
extended on this question, we simply cite some of the cases,
without commenting upon the peculiar features of any of them.
We have examined the cases cited by appellant, and find
nothing in them which conflicts with what is said herein:
Kimball v. *Lincoln,* 99 Ill. 578; *Gage* v. *Parmelee,* 87 Ill. 330;

Casey v. *Casey*, 14 Ill. 113; *Farnam* v. *Brooks*, 9 Pick. 213; *Knight* v. *Majoribanks* 11 Beav. 324; *Morse* v. *Royal*, 12 Ves. 355; *Hunter* v. *Atkyns*, 3 Mylne & K.; *Hagar* v. *Thompson*, 1 Black, 80; *Cartright* v. *Burnes*, 2 McCrary, 532; *Geddes's Appeal*, 80 Pa. St. 460; *White* v. *Walker*, 5 Fla. 478; *Hall* v. *Johnson*, 41 Mich. 289; *Bowman* v. *Carithers*, 40 Ind. 90; *Turner* v. *Otis*, 30 Kan. 1; *Murray* v. *Elston*, 24 N. J. Eq. 310; *Korn* v. *Becker*, 40 N. J. Eq. 408; *De Montmorency* v. *Devereaux*, 7 Clark & F. 188; *Hough* v. *Richardson*, 3 Story, 690; *Loesser* v. *Loesser*, 81 Ky. 139; *Motley* v. *Motley*, 45 Ala. 558; *Kisling* v. *Shaw*, 33 Cal. 425; 91 Am. Dec. 644.

It is claimed, however, that the trustee cannot, after negotiations are begun between himself and his *cestui que trust,* dissolve the trust relation, "and place the parties at arm's-length," and that "the rights of these parties and the rules by which they are to be investigated should be determined by the relation of the parties when their negotiations commenced." We see no reason for such distinction. Sugden's definition of the rule applicable in such cases is expressed in the following language: "It must not be understood that a trustee cannot buy from his *cestui que trust* where he is *sui generis;* the rule is, that he cannot buy from himself. If the *cestui que trust* clearly discharges the trustee from the trust, and considers him as an indifferent person, he may purchase; but it must clearly appear that the purchaser, at the time of the purchase, had shaken off his confidential character by the consent of the *cestui que trust,* freely given after full information and bargaining for the right to purchase": 2 Sugden on Vendors, 417, bottom paging 693. There is nothing in this text, or any decision we have seen, requiring a contract preceding the contract to purchase, or compromise, giving the trustee permission to purchase, as a basis for a second contract in which the terms of the sale, or compromise, may be lawfully agreed to. If at the time of the purchase, or compromise, the trustee has shaken off his fiduciary character, and the confidence which is presumed to result therefrom, it matters not what has occurred immediately preceding or long prior to the final transaction. In other words, if the transaction is one in which the trustee may lawfully deal with his *cestui que trust* by first dissolving the trust relation, it is not too late for him to do so at any time before the *cestui que trust* is prevented from making a full and fair investigation and consideration of the business in hand, and before he executes the contract.

Other points discussed at the bar are involved in the question whether plaintiff was induced by fraud, actual or constructive, to enter into the compromise agreement; whether there were false representations, concealments, threats, or any unconscionable advantages gained by defendants through their superior opportunities and power.

Upon every material issue of fact the court below found in favor of defendants, except as to a part of the 408 shares of Rocky Mountain Coal and Iron Company stock; and its finding of fact upon that issue was, in the opinion of the court, insufficient, in view of other findings, to support a decree of rescission.

Since it is claimed, however, that the specific facts found do show fraud, concealments, and undue advantage, notwithstanding the general findings of the court, which negative the charges thereof, it becomes necessary to look into the circumstances under which the compromise was effected.

So far as the exhibits of the condition of the Western Development Company (exhibits D and E) are concerned, the facts found show that there was no fraudulent representation by defendants as to anything contained therein, and that plaintiff did not rely upon them. She relied upon her own judgment and the advice of those who were assisting her, and entered into the compromise agreement after a careful and thorough examination of all the books and vouchers. The court finds that she was not ignorant of any fact or circumstance material to her rights; that there were no misrepresentations or concealments by defendants, but, on the contrary, they answered truthfully all questions relating to the affairs of the company, repeatedly went over the subjects under investigation with Mr. Wilson, and gave him free access to all the books, and secured for him all the assistance and information in their power. The defendants did not pretend to know anything of the condition of the affairs of the Western Development Company outside of what was shown in its records. Mr. Wilson knew this. They told him so. They gave him every facility in their power of ascertaining the true state of the accounts. They instructed their employees to aid him as best they could. With their consent and approval, he had the books carefully and thoroughly examined by experts,— men who had been trusted friends of General Colton,—one of them his cousin, another his secretary. In no part of his testimony does Mr. Wilson indicate that he or the plaintiff

placed any reliance upon the statements contained in exhibits
D or E, or upon any information furnished by the defendants
with regard to the affairs of the Western Development Company. Mr. Wilson was active, alert, self-reliant, and zealous
in the cause of his client,—the widow to whom he had been
recommended by his friend Colton as the one man worthy of
entire confidence and trust in case of trouble. Spurred on by
a keen sense of the trust which had been reposed in him, he
devoted his entire time and energy for a period of about six
months, laboring with clerks and book-keepers, until, as he
says, he had exhausted and tired himself out, sacrificed his
own interests, and had "abused these people to the extremity
almost of fighting personally." In connection with his deposition in this case, there was introduced in evidence his memoranda, taken during the investigations which he and others
were making into the affairs of the Western Development
Company, which showed the most unmistakable care and a
painstaking and minute consideration of the subject. Upon
this showing, no doubt, it was that Judge Temple was induced
to believe and find that plaintiff and her advisers were ignorant of no material fact or circumstance of which she ought
to have been informed. The presumption would follow from
the fact of investigation that everything material was discovered; but the presumption is fortified by the introduction of
these memoranda, and by proof of the fact that many others
had been made which, at the time of the trial, were lost.

Under such circumstances, is plaintiff entitled to a rescission of the contract thus deliberately entered into? We think
she is not. Her counsel claim that there was actual and constructive fraud, and cite sections 1571 and 1572 of the Civil
Code; they say that defendants furnished a list of the assets
of the Western Development Company; that this was equivalent to a positive assertion that the list contained all the assets,—an assertion not true, not warranted by the information
of the parties making it, and therefore fraudulent, although
they believed it to be true; that where a party, acting without
belief or without information, makes a representation which is
not true, the law imputes to him a knowledge of its falsity, and
makes him as fully responsible as if he had such a knowledge.
This is true as a general proposition, where the other party
has acted upon the representation, relying upon it as correct;
but the rule as stated is not upon authority or principle applicable where such party, discarding the representation as

unworthy of belief, proceeds to inquire for himself, is given full and fair facilities of informing himself, takes independent counsel, and finally acts upon his own judgment and that of his advisers. Misrepresentations cannot be predicated upon such a state of facts: 2 Parsons on Contracts, 770; *Percival* v. *Hargar*, 40 Iowa, 289; *Matthews* v. *Bliss*, 22 Pick. 53; *Von Trott* v. *Weise*, 36 Wis. 439; *Hall* v. *Johnson*, 41 Mich. 289; *Light* v. *Light*, 21 Pa. St. 413; *Smith* v. *Kay*, 7 H. L. Cas. 775; *Southern Development Co.* v. *Silva*, 125 U. S. 258; Bigelow on Fraud, 7, 8.

We do not find anything in the authorities cited by the appellant which is in conflict with the views we have expressed. Excerpts from a few of them will show this to be the case. Thus in *Taylor* v. *Fleet*, 1 Barb. 475, the court said: "If the purchaser has acted upon his own judgment, and has not been influenced by the misrepresentations, however untrue they may have been, he has no right to be released from his bargain. But I cannot concur with the counsel for the vendor in his position that the purchaser examined the land with a view to test the accuracy of the representations made by Fleet. On the contrary, all the witnesses agree that no personal examination of the land would enable any person not previously acquainted with its capabilities to determine whether the statements made· by Fleet were true or not. The only means of knowledge within his reach was information to be obtained from those whose experience enabled them to speak from actual observation with respect to the material question which constituted the object for which the purchase was made."

In *Rawlins* v. *Wickham*, 3 De Gex & J. 310, the books showed so plainly the fraud that any man of ordinary capacity could have detected the fraud. The court there says: "During the negotiations for the partnership a paper was produced, which has been kept by Mr. Rawlins from that time, giving an account of the assets of the concern. The amount due to the customers of the bank was there stated to be eleven thousand pounds and a fraction. Upon examination of the books it appears that the real amount exceeded this by many thousands, a fact which an examination of the books by any person of the most ordinary competency would have shown. . . . . Was there any excuse for such a misrepresentation? As regards Mr. Bailey, there was none. He was a professional man, taking an active part in the affairs of the bank, and it was his duty to know them, whether he did or not. Mr. Wickham was an

inactive partner, knowing but little of its affairs, attending
only occasionally at the bank, not meddling with the books, and
probably knowing little or nothing of what they contained.
. . . . He joined with Mr. Bailey in producing the statement
of accounts which I have mentioned, and in ascribing accuracy
to it.   Now, he ought not to have asserted what he did not
know to be true.   He ought to have said, 'It may be true; I
have a good opinion of Mr. Bailey and Mr. Gattrill, but I am
not acquainted with the books, and, as far as I am concerned,
you must look at them for yourself.'   He did not do so, but
joined in a representation which was not true, and, for every
purpose of pecuniary liability, the case is the same as if he
had known that it was not true. . . . . Mr. Rawlins might
have inspected the books. . . . . He, however, did not examine them, and, improbable as it may appear, I must hold that
Mr. Rawlins entered into the partnership in complete ignorance of the contents of the books, and continued so for four
years. . . . . He was entitled to believe their representations
to be accurate without looking at the books.   He was entitled
to continue in that belief until ground for suspicion arose, or
information was given him by one of the partners.   No such
information was given.   They did not complain that he did
not look at the books, and there is reason to believe that they
would not have liked him to examine them."   The difference
between this case and the case at bar is too apparent for comment.

In *Higgins* v. *Samels*, 2 Johns. & H. 467, the language of
the court shows the distinction between the case and the one
at bar.   It is there said: " It is not necessary to show that the
defendants knew the facts to be untrue, if they stated a fact
which was untrue for a fraudulent purpose, they at the same
time not believing that fact to be true.   In that case it would
be both illegal and immoral fraud. . . . . What weighs upon
my mind is the circumstance that the quality of the lime was
not a mere subject of speculation, but a fact which the plaintiff, without any special familiarity with the business, could
have made himself acquainted with."

In *Carpmael* v. *Powis*, 10 Beav. 44, the court uses this language: "Mr. Powis offered to procure the information.   He
did procure it, and communicate it to the plaintiff, who relied
upon it, and entered into the agreement on the credit of it.   It
turned out to be erroneous; but before the agreement, and
until long after the agreement, Mr. Powis appears to have

had no reason whatever to suspect that there was any error. He adopted it implicitly on the authority of Mr. Cuthbert, and very innocently produced it to the plaintiff as a true statement of that upon which the amount of the annuity was to be calculated. If the plaintiff was guilty of any error or laches, it was in giving too much credit to the statement which had been adopted and communicated to him by the defendant's agent as true."

In *Miller* v. *Craig*, 6 Beav. 437, it appears that the plaintiffs, who lived in Scotland, never had an opportunity of examining the accounts. The court said that there was no proof whatever that the plaintiffs relied on Miller as their agent in the treaty with the other executors. On the contrary, they employed their own solicitor, or law agent, in Scotland. The release was signed in confidence, in the belief that the accounts had been truly stated.

In *Reynell* v. *Sprye*, 1 De Gex, M. & G. 709, the court says: "It was said during the whole of the negotiations Captain Sprye not only left Sir Thomas Reynell at perfect liberty to consult his friends and professional advisers, but even on several occasions recommended him to do so. To a great extent this certainly was the case; and if the relief sought in this suit had rested on mere mistake, if Captain Sprye had not, by misrepresentations of fact, which I cannot treat as unintentional, led Sir Thomas to believe that his rights were different from what in truth they were, it may be that the argument to which I am now adverting would have prevailed. In such a case, perhaps, this court might have considered that it was the folly of Sir Thomas Reynell to have acted without advice, and might have refused to assist any person who was so singularly little alive to his own rights. . . . . But no such question can arise in a case like the present, where one contracting party has intentionally misled the other by describing rights as different from what he knew them really to be."

In *Doggett* v. *Emerson*, 3 Story, 732, it appeared to the court that the purchase of the plaintiff was made upon an entire credit given to the representation of Williams as to the quantity and quality of the timber. The plaintiff resided in Boston, and confessedly had no knowledge of timber lands, and had never seen the township in which they were situated. He must therefore have placed implicit reliance upon the statements of Williams. It appeared, also, that Emerson not only knew the contents of the certificates upon which the plaintiff relied, but corroborated the statements therein contained.

In Lewin on Trusts, cited by appellants, the author says: "Before any dealing with the *cestui que trust*, the relation between the trustee and *cestui que trust* must be actually or virtually dissolved. . . . . The parties must be put at such arm's-length that they agree to stand in the adverse situations of vendor and purchaser, the *cestui que trust* distinctly and fully understanding that he is selling to the trustee, and consenting to waive all objections upon that ground, and the trustee fairly and honestly disclosing all the necessary particulars of the estate, and not attempting a furtive advantage to himself by means of any private information. . . . . Where the *cestui que trust* took the whole management of the sale, himself chose, or at least approved, the auctioneer, made surveys, settled the plan of sale, fixed the price, and so had a perfect knowledge of the value of the property, ... Lord Eldon said that if, in any instance, the rule was to be relaxed by consent of the parties, this was the case. . . . . Again, a *cestui que trust* had urged the purchase upon the trustee, who at first expressed an unwillingness, but afterward agreed to the terms, and the sale was supported. So where the trustee had endeavored in vain to dispose of the estate, and then purchased himself of the *cestui que trust* at a fair and adequate price, and there was no imputation of fraud or concealment, Lord Northington said: 'He did not like the circumstance of a trustee dealing with his *cestui que trust*, but upon the whole he did not see any principle upon which he could set the transaction aside. . . . . If it be absolutely necessary that the property should be sold, and the trustee is ready to give more than any one else, he may file a bill in chancery, and apply by motion to be allowed to purchase, and the court will then examine into the circumstances, ask who had the conduct of the transaction, whether there is reason to suppose the premises could be sold better, and upon the result of that inquiry will let another person prepare the particular sale, and allow the trustee to bid'": Sec. 463.

In *Boyd* v. *Hawkins*, 2 Dev. Eq. 208, we find this language: "The prohibition of the trustee to purchase from the *cestui que trust* himself is not found to be so absolute. . . . . Bargains between them are viewed with anxious jealousy. It must appear that the relation has ceased, at least that all necessity for activity in the trust has terminated, so that the

trustee and *cestui que trust* are two persons, each at liberty,
without the concurrence of the other, to consult his own interest, and capable of vindicating it; or that there was a contract
definitively made, the terms and effect of which were clearly
understood, and that there was no fraud or misapprehension,
and no advantage taken by the trustee of the distresses or ignorance of the other party. The purchase must also be fair
and reasonable."

Mr. Pomeroy, in his work on equity jurisprudence, at section 855, uses this language: "When parties have entered
into a contract or arrangement based upon uncertain or contingent events, purposely as a compromise of doubtful claims
arising from them, and where parties have knowingly entered
into a speculative contract or transaction,—one in which they
intentionally speculated as to the result,—and there is in
either case an absence of bad faith, violation of confidence,
misrepresentation, concealment, and other inequitable conduct
mentioned in a former paragraph,—if the facts upon which
such agreement or transaction was founded, or the event of
the agreement itself, turn out very different from what was
expected or anticipated, this error, miscalculation, or disappointment, although relating to matters of fact, and not of
law, is not such a mistake, within the meaning of the equitable doctrine, as entitles the disappointed party to any relief,
either by way of canceling the contract and rescinding the
transaction, or of defense to a suit brought for its enforcement.
In such classes of agreements and transactions the parties are
supposed to calculate the chances, and they certainly assume
the risks, where there is no element of bad faith, breach of
confidence, misrepresentation, culpable concealment, or other
like conduct amounting to actual or constructive fraud."

In *Badger* v. *Badger*, 2 Wall. 87, it appears that Brooks took
advantage of his position as partner, agent, and brother-in-law
of Martin intentionally to conceal from the latter the prosperous condition of the concern, and purchased his interest for a
price totally disproportioned to its real value.

So, also, in *Addington* v. *Allen*, 11 Wend. 383, there appeared
an actual intent to mislead and defraud the plaintiff.

In *Safford* v. *Grout*, 120 Mass. 26, the character of the representations was not disclosed by the record. No objection
was made that they were mere expressions of opinion, judgment, or estimate, or that they were intended to be understood
as expressions of belief only. The court said: "We must pre-

sume that they were legally sufficient to support the action; that is to say, that they were statements of facts susceptible of knowledge, as distinct from matters of mere opinion or belief; and that they were calculated to have, and did have, material influence in deceiving the plaintiff as to the maker's means and ability to pay in inducing them to part with their property."

All that is decided in *Redgrave* v. *Hurd*, L. R. 20 Ch. Div. 24, is, "that where a false representation has been made, it lies upon the party who makes it, if he wishes to escape its effect in avoiding the contract, to show that, although he made the false representation, the defendant, the other party, did not rely upon it. The *onus probandi* is on him to show that the other party waived it, and relied on his own knowledge. Nothing of that kind appears here."

In *Wells* v. *Millett*, 23 Wis. 67, the court assume that if the defendant had been careless or indifferent to ordinary and accessible means of information as to the truth or falsehood of the representation which has been made, he would have had no right to rely upon that.

In *Rohrschneider* v. *Knickerbocker L. Ins. Co.*, 76 N. Y. 218, 32 Am. Rep. 290, the court said that "the fraud was really undisputed. The managers of the defendant had made the false representations, and they knew them to be false, as the dividends of the company never had paid the notes thus given for the one half of the annual premiums. But on the contrary, such dividends had always fallen far short of making such payments; and they must have known that they generally, if not always, would fall short. There was, in fact, no foundation or excuse whatever for making the untrue representations. . . . . It is said on behalf of the defendant that the plaintiff did not rely upon these representations, and was not induced by them to take the policy. But there was sufficient evidence from which the jury could have found that she did thus rely, and was thus induced."

In *Baker* v. *Spencer*, 47 N. Y. 564, the court said that the appellant's claim that the settlement of the action by the giving of a three-hundred-dollar note operated as a compromise of the alleged fraud, and was a bar to the action, might have been well taken if it had appeared, from the pleadings or the findings, that at the time of the settlement the defendant had knowledge of the facts constituting the fraud alleged; but that such claim was not well founded, being based entirely upon the statement that, after giving the note, the plaintiff began to suspect that the defendant had not the right to sell and transfer the agency. The court said: "It does not appear, from the complaint or findings, that the plaintiff had any grounds for his suspicion, or any information on the subject, nor what defense was interposed on the trial before the justice in the action on the five-hundred-dollar note."

The court then proceeds to distinguish the case before it from the case of *Adams* v. *Sage*, 28 N. Y. 103. In the latter case, the court held that "where a party to whom representations were made has the means at hand of determining their truth or falsehood, and resorts to such means, and after investigation, avows his belief that the statements are false, and acts upon such belief by bringing an action to recover money obtained from him by means of the fraudulent representations, he is not entitled to credit when he alleges that upon reiteration of the truth of the same statements by the same party he was induced to enter into an agreement to settle the suit, and was thereby defrauded. Such investigation and ascertainment of facts, and belief in the falsity of the representations made, exclude the idea that any reliance could have been placed upon the repetition of the falsehood, and the verdict of a jury or finding of a referee to the contrary should be set aside as unsustained by the evidence. Indeed, upon such evidence, it would be error to submit to a jury the question whether reliance was or was not placed upon the reiterated false representations. Under the circumstances assumed, the law presumes that the party relied in making the agreement upon his own investigation, and not upon the representations of the party with whom he is dealing. This conduct in acting in opposition to the knowledge acquired by inquiry from one who knows the facts is attributable, and is set down by the law, to his own indiscretion and recklessness, and not to any fraud or surprise of which, under the circumstances, he has any right to complain. . . . . In 2 Parsons on Contracts, 270, the rule is laid down, in relation to defenses to actions on the ground of false representations, that it must appear that the injured party not only did in fact rely upon the fraudulent statement, but had a right to rely upon it in the full belief of its truth, for otherwise it was his own fault or folly, and he cannot ask of the law to relieve him. Many of the cases cited by the author to sustain this rule hold that if the truth or falsehood of the representation might have been tested by ordinary vigilance and attention, it is the party's own folly if he neglect to do so, and he is remediless."

In *Perkins* v. *Gay*, 3 Serg. & R. 331, 8 Am. Dec. 653, the court said: "It is a principle of equity that the parties to an agreement must be acquainted with the extent of their rights, and the nature of the information they can call for respecting them, else they will not be bound. The reason is, that they proceed under an idea that the fact which is the inducement to the agreement is in a particular way, and give their assent, not absolutely, but on conditions that are falsified by the event. [Citing cases.] But where the parties treat upon the basis that the fact which is the subject of the agreement is doubtful, and the consequent risk each is to encounter is taken into consideration in the stipulations assented to, the contract will be valid notwithstanding any mistake of one of the parties, provided there be no concealment or unfair dealing by the opposite party that would affect any other contract. . . . . Every compromise of a doubtful right depends on this principle. . . . . There is an express mutual abandonment of their former rights upon an agreement, that, whether they be good or whether they be bad, neither is to recur to them on any pretense whatever, or claim anything that he does not derive from the terms of the agreement. Each takes his chance of obtaining an equivalent for everything he relinquishes, and if the event turn out contrary to his expectations, so much the worse for him. If there be no intention of fraud, no unfair dealing, and neither party has more knowledge of the fact misconceived than the other had, the contract will bind."

In *Peek* v. *Derry*, L. R. 37 Ch. Div. 577, while the court did not attribute to the defendants any intention to commit a fraud, it found that they had made a statement which was incorrect, to induce the plaintiff to act upon it, without any sufficient reason for making that statement, or any sufficient reason for believing it to be true.

Kerr on Fraud and Mistake thus states the proposition: "If a man to whom a representation has been made knows at the time, or discovers before entering into a transaction, that the representation is false, or resorts to other means of knowledge open to him, and chooses to judge for himself in the matter, he cannot avail himself of the fact that there has been misrepresentation, ... or say that he has acted on the faith of the representation. . . . . If the party to whom the representations were made himself resorted to the proper means of veri-

fication before entering into the contract, it may appear that
he relied on the results of his own investigation and inquiry,
and not upon the representations made to him by the other
party. . . . . If the subject is in its nature uncertain, if all
that is known is matter of inference, or something else, and if
the parties making and receiving representations on the subject have equal knowledge and means of acquiring knowledge,
it is not easy to presume that the representations made by the
one could have much or any influence upon the other": Pages
75–78. Speaking of fiduciary relation, the author says: "A
transaction between them [trustee and *cestui que trust*] will
be supported if it can be shown to the satisfaction of the court
that the parties were, notwithstanding the relation, substantially at arm's-length, and on equal footing, and that nothing
has happened which might not have happened had no such
relation existed. The burden of proof lies in all cases upon
the party who fills the position of active confidence to show
that the transaction has been fair. If it can be shown to the
satisfaction of the court that the other party had competent
and disinterested or independent advice, or that he performed
the act, or entered into the transaction voluntarily, deliberately,
and advisedly, knowing its nature and effect, and that his consent was not obtained by reason of the power of influence to
which the relation gave rise, the transaction will be supported."

In *Shaw* v. *Stine*, 8 Bosw. 159, it is held that the true test
in cases of false representations may be found in the inquiry
whether the plaintiff would have entered into the contract if
the false representations had not been made. If he would,
then the false representations did not contribute to the sale.

In *Matthews* v. *Bliss*, 22 Pick. 53, it is held that, where one
of the parties has an advantageous knowledge, if he exercise
a studied effort to prevent the other from coming to the knowledge of the truth, or if there be any, though slight, false and
fraudulent suggestion or representation, then the transaction
is tainted with turpitude, and alike contrary to the rules of
morality and of law.

In *Gilbert* v. *Endean*, L. R. 9 Ch. Div. 268, there was a material fact intentionally concealed, namely, that the son was
without means, because the father was still alive, and was still
refusing to assist him.

Some of these cases, it will be observed, involve transactions
between trustee and *cestui que trust*, and are applicable to the
first proposition discussed herein.

After the execution of the compromise agreement, the Western Development Company paid an indebtedness of over three million dollars, with interest, to the Central Pacific with Southern Pacific bonds at ninety cents on the dollar. These bonds were represented to plaintiff to be worth sixty cents on the dollar. It is now claimed that the transfer to the Central Pacific, a few days after the compromise, at ninety cents on the dollar is conclusive evidence that they were worth ninety cents on the dollar at the time they were represented to be worth sixty cents, and that this was a fraud on the plaintiff, — at least, that there is an equitable estoppel preventing defendants from claiming that they were not worth ninety cents at the time of the compromise. The transaction seems to have been one in which the defendants practically dealt with themselves. They paid off the debt of the Western Development Company to the Central Pacific company with bonds of the Southern Pacific company, and themselves fixed the value of the bonds at what they supposed they would be worth when they should be called on to pay the Central Pacific bonds. Equitable estoppels must be mutual. If the defendants in attempting to pay off some debt similar to that of the Western Development Company, about the time the compromise was effected, had rated the Southern Pacific bonds at twenty-five cents on the dollar, would their act fix irrevocably the market value of the bonds so that Mrs. Colton would have been bound by their · act, and forever thereafter estopped from proving that in fact they were worth more? The transaction was but a temporary mode of settling up a corporate obligation. The court weighed it as evidence, and as the intrinsic value of the property did not enter into the questions involved in the compromise, we do not perceive any ground upon which plaintiff can complain: *Fitz* v. *Bynum*, 55 Cal. 461; 2 Sutherland on Damages, 374; *Kountz* v. *Kirkpatrick*, 72 Pa. St. 389; 13 Am. Rep. 687. Furthermore, the values set opposite to the names of the stocks mentioned the court finds were not relied upon, and in fact the controversy was chiefly over this very matter, Mr. Wilson insisting all the time that they were too low, and the defendants contending that they could not afford to allow more for them.

The charge that Mrs. Colton was induced by threats to enter into the contract is unequivocally denied by Mr. Wilson in the following testimony: —

"Q. Now, in the course of these negotiations, did the de-

fendants, or any of them, make any threat in reference to
aspersing the memory of General Colton, unless a settlement
was made, or anything of that kind? A. No, sir; nothing of
the kind." ·

Counsel for appellant rely with much confidence for a reversal of the judgment upon the twentieth finding of the court,
which is as follows: —

"That the individual defendants, prior to the execution of
the contract, exhibit F, and during the negotiations which
preceded and led to that contract, stated and represented to
the plaintiff that D. D. Colton had in his hands, and standing
in his name on the books of said company, 408 shares of the
capital stock of the Rocky Mountain Coal and Iron Company,
which were in truth and in fact the property of and belonged
to Stanford, Huntington, Crocker, and the estate of Mark
Hopkins, in equal proportions, and which were held by said
Colton in trust for them and said estate of Mark Hopkins, and
that upon paying the plaintiff, as successor of said D. D. Colton, the cost price of said 408 shares of stock, which they
represented to be $6,625.92, they were entitled to have said
408 shares assigned, transferred, and delivered to them; that
the plaintiff relied upon said statement and representation,
and accordingly did assign and transfer said shares of stock
by and in said agreement and contract sought to be rescinded
by this action; that said representation was not true, and was
made by said defendants without due circumspection, and
was unwarranted by the facts within their knowledge; that in
truth and in fact said Colton did have in his possession, and
there were standing in his name on the books of the company,
only 240 shares of stock, which he held as trustee of said defendants and the estate of Mark Hopkins, and to the extent
of 168 shares said representation was a false representation;
that said representation, however, was not made with any
actual fraudulent intent, but through inadvertence and lack
of due circumspection; and that said contract would have
been executed by the plaintiff had she known the truth in
regard to said stock, if the defendants, upon being made
aware of the facts, had still insisted upon it; that during the
negotiations which resulted in the making of the compromise
expressed in exhibit F, Mr. S. M. Wilson knew precisely what
the claim of defendants was as to the aforesaid 408 shares of
said Rocky Mountain Coal and Iron Company stock; had the
books of last-mentioned corporation before him, including the

dividend-book; knew that Colton had collected dividends for several years on said 408 shares of stock; knew that the claim of defendants to said 408 shares of Rocky Mountain Coal and Iron Company's stock was supported by no written evidence.

' "Defendants also claimed from the estate of Colton the dividends on the stock of the Rocky Mountain Coal and Iron Company, which they asserted he held in trust for them."

It is contended that this finding conclusively establishes the fact that plaintiff was induced to enter into the contract by a false representation as to a material fact; that it is immaterial whether the representation was the result of an innocent mistake, it having been made without due circumspection, which is the equivalent of a positive assertion of a fact without knowing it to be true, or being warranted by the information of the person making it; that it is not necessary the false representation should have been the sole or controlling inducement to the making of the contract, it being sufficient to defeat the contract if it appear that it was one of the inducements and a motive of her action; that the court could not say as a matter of fact or matter of law if she had known the truth in regard to the stock she would have executed the contract, provided the defendants, upon being made aware of the facts, had still insisted upon it.

There are cases in which it could not be said, in view of the evidence, that the party would have entered into the contract if the false representation had not been made, and there are many cases reported in which the courts have said that it was error to apply the rule referred to. But where it clearly appears, from the evidence, that the contract would have been made if the truth had been known, we see no reason why the court may not find the fact and act upon it. If, as a matter of fact, the contract would have been made without regard to the character or force of the representation relied upon for a rescission, the plaintiff cannot complain. As said by Judge Temple: "The power to cancel a contract is a most extraordinary power. It is one which should be exercised with great caution,—nay, I may say, with great reluctance,—unless in a clear case. A too free use of this power would render all business uncertain, and, as has been said, make the length of a chancellor's foot the measure of individual rights. The greatest liberty of making contracts is essential to the business interests of the country. In general, the parties must look out for themselves."

Our code provides that a contract may be rescinded "if the consent of the party rescinding . . . . was given by mistake, or obtained through duress, menace, fraud, or undue influence": Civ. Code, sec. 1689. Section 1565 of the Civil Code says: "The consent of the parties to a contract must be,—1. Free; 2. Mutual; and 3. Communicated by each to the other."

Sections 1566, 1567, and 1568 of the Civil Code read as follows:—

"Sec. 1566. A consent which is not free is nevertheless not absolutely void, but may be rescinded by the parties, in the manner prescribed by the chapter on rescission.

"Sec. 1567. An apparrent consent is not real or free when obtained through,—1. Duress; 2. Menace; 3. Fraud; 4. Undue influence; or 5. Mistake.

"Sec. 1568. Consent is deemed to have been obtained through one of the causes mentioned in the last section only when it would not have been given had such cause not existed."

The most that can be said in support of appellant's contention is, that there is a conflict in the decisions on the subject; but the sections of the Civil Code above quoted are clear and unambiguous in language, and they seem to establish the rule beyond all controversy, that the contract cannot be rescinded when it appears that consent would have been given and the contract entered into notwithstanding the duress, menace, fraud, undue influence, or mistake relied upon. A misrepresentation as the basis of rescission must be material; but it can be material only when it is of such a character that if it had not been made, the contract would not have been entered into. The misrepresentation, it is true, need not be the sole cause of the contract, but it must be of such nature, weight, and force that the court can say "without it, the contract would not have been made."

That the code commissioners recognized the fact of a conflict of authority upon this subject, and desired to settle it in accordance with what seems to us to be the plain meaning of the language used in section 1568, Civil Code, is apparent, we think, from the authorities quoted by them in a note to that section. Thus in *Flight* v. *Booth*, 1 Bing. N. C. 376, the court said: "It is extremely difficult to lay down from the decided cases any certain, definite rule which shall determine what misstatement or misdescription in the particulars shall justify a rescinding of the contract, and what shall be ground of

compensation only. All the cases concur in this, that where
the misstatement is willful or designed, it amounts to fraud;
and such fraud, upon general principles of law, avoids the
contract altogether; but with respect to misstatements which
stand clear of fraud, it is impossible to reconcile all the cases;
some of them laying it down that no misstatements which
originate in carelessness, however gross, shall avoid the contract, but shall form the subject of compensation only; . . . .
whilst other cases lay down the rule that a misdescription in
a material point, although occasioned by negligence only, not
by fraud, will vitiate the contract of sale. In this state of
discrepancy between the decided cases, we think it is, at all
events, a safe rule to adopt, that where the misdescription,
although not proceeding from fraud, is, in a material and
substantial point, so far affecting the subject-matter of the
contract that it may reasonably be supposed that but for such
misdescription the purchaser might never have entered into
the contract at all, in such case the contract is avoided altogether, and the purchaser is not bound to resort to the clause
of compensation." In *Shaw* v. *Stine*, 8 Bosw. 159, a case also
cited by the code commissioners, the court said: "The true
test in such cases may be found in the inquiry whether the
plaintiff would have sold the goods if the false representations
had not been made. If he would, then the false representations did not contribute to the sale, for he would have made
the sale without them." They also cite section 1819 of the
Civil Code of Louisiana, which reads as follows: "The error
in the cause of a contract, to have the effect of invalidating it,
must be on the principal cause when there are several; this
principal cause is called the motive, and means that consideration without which the contract would not have been made."
See also the cases cited by appellant, and reviewed herein on
another topic.

Here the court found that plaintiff never intended after the
death of her husband to go on with the enterprises in which
he and the defendants had been interested; that she did not
intend to take any further risks in the business ventures;
that the transaction was a lumping settlement, all parties understanding it to be such, and that no accurate adjustment
of the accounts could be had; that the representation as to
this stock was made without any actual fraudulent intent, but
through inadvertence, and the plaintiff would have executed
the contract sought to be rescinded had she known the truth in

regard to the matter if defendants had insisted on it; that
Wilson knew exactly what defendants' claim as to the stock
was, had the books of the company, including the dividend-
book, examined them, knew that Mr. Colton had collected
dividends, and that defendants' claim was not supported by
any written evidence; that Wilson made a thorough investigation into the affairs of the Rocky Mountain Coal and Iron
Company, and had many sources of information other than
those possessed by the defendants; and was more thoroughly
acquainted with and better qualified to form an accurate judgment as to the condition of the affairs of that company than
were the defendants, or either of them; that Mr. Douty, cousin
and friend of Mr. Colton, and book-keeper of said company,
Mr. Green, secretary of General Colton in his lifetime, and
Mr. Steinberger, an old friend, frequently consulted with
plaintiff and Wilson in regard to the business in hand; that
plaintiff placed no reliance upon the defendants, and had no
confidence in them; and that before consummating the agreement, she had discovered many inaccuracies in the statements
they had presented. At that time there was one error in the
account of the Western Development Company, which would,
if known, have shown the liabilities of that company to be
one million dollars greater than they were represented.

In a transaction involving such vast properties and values
as we find here, the amount involved in this particular transaction is comparatively a small item,—only about ten thousand dollars. But if the defendants had relied upon their
strict rights in regard to this stock, they would have been entitled to receive back the dividends on the 240 shares wrongfully appropriated, with interest on each one from the time it
was so taken, and plaintiff would have been entitled to receive
the purchase price of the 240 shares, and interest upon it from
the time it was paid. So that if the truth had been stated,
and the controversy as to this particular stock had been settled upon a fair accounting, plaintiff would not have been
more than one thousand or two thousand dollars better off
than the settlement left her. From all the circumstances of
the case Judge Temple concluded that this representation as
to the 168 shares had no material influence. It is true, the
judge states "that the plaintiff relied upon said statement
and representation, and accordingly did assign and transfer
said shares of stock by and in said agreement and contract
sought to be recinded in this action." Plaintiff believed—at

least assumed—the statement of defendants as to this stock to
be true, and therefore assigned it.   This is entirely consistent
with the finding that she would have executed the compromise agreement had she known the truth in regard to the
stock.   From all the circumstances, especially the testimony
of Mr. Wilson, it is made very clear that this representation
was not an inducing cause of plaintiff's action.   Speaking
upon this subject, the court, in its opinion, said that "Wilson
concluded it would do no good unless he could satisfactorily
explain away charges of appropriating one hundred and eighty-
one thousand dollars.   In comparison with these figures, the
sum involved in this unwarranted assertion is small.   But I
think, on general principles, in a matter of such magnitude as
this, such a mistake or misrepresentation would not justify
setting aside the agreement, especially where, as here, expenditures have been made by the defendants on the faith of the
agreement, which have materially enhanced the value of the
property involved in the litigation."   In these observations of
the learned judge we fully concur.

It remains only to consider whether there was any unconscionable advantage taken of plaintiff.   This question must
be determined, not in the light of subsequent events, but upon
the circumstances existing at the time of the negotiations and
the execution of the contract.   The court found that defendants did not obtain great advantage, or any advantage, over
plaintiff, and that the agreement was fair, just, and equal.

The question whether there has been an undue advantage
— an unconscionable exercise of a superior power — depends
largely upon the situation of the parties at the time of the negotiations.

The immediate cause of the trouble between the parties
arose from the fact that after the death of General Colton,
who had been president and treasurer of the Rocky Mountain
Coal and Iron Company from January 1, 1871, until the time
of his death, the books and papers of that corporation showed
that he had used large sums of money belonging to that
company, for which he had never accounted.   He had also
taken large amounts which he designated as salary, in contravention of the terms of his agreement with Mr. Crocker,
and with the other associates.   There were also some serious
irregularities in his account with the Western Development
Company, of which he had been manager from its organization in December, 1874.   The latter company was heavily in

debt. It owed at that time to Stanford, Crocker, and the estate of Hopkins over ten million dollars. Its assets consisted chiefly of railroad stocks and bonds which had no market value. Mrs. Colton concluded before the commencement of the negotiations that she could not go on with the enterprise in which her husband had been interested. (These facts are found by the court.)

In one of the preliminary interviews with Mr. Crocker, when asked whether she wished to pay for the stock purchased by Mr. Colton, and continue along in the execution of the corporate schemes which her husband had helped to advance, she replied that "she was in no condition or state to build railroads"; and her chief adviser, Mr. Wilson, said in his testimony: "Very early in the conversations that I had with Mrs. Colton it was agreed and understood between us that she was to sell out her interest there, and not to remain in the railroad. That was our leading proposition from the beginning of my relation with the business, and we never swerved, or never wavered on that. . . . . We had made up our minds that she should not go ahead. . . . . We had already determined that she should not go ahead, and would get out if she should get a certain sum of money." It must be remembered that the plaintiff herself first sought a settlement, — a fact which deserves attention. As was said in *Morse* v. *Royal*, 12 Ves. 275, by Lord Eldon: "This is not a trustee looking around him and fixing his eye upon this property, as increasing in value. It is in evidence that Morse determined to sell it, and if he could not get what he wanted, that he would put it up at Garaway's; that he frequently teased Vanheylin to purchase it, who was reluctant, but at last said he would go the length of giving five thousand pounds." So in the case at bar, Mr. Huntington, in his deposition, says that he was teased into making the settlement. In many cases we have examined, the fact that the party endeavoring to rescind the compromise agreement made the first proposal, and persuaded the other party to enter into the agreement, has been adverted to and considered by the court as an important factor in determining the rights of the plaintiff to a rescission of the contract: *Harrison* v. *Guest*, 6 De Gex, M. & G. 433; *Montesquieu* v. *Sanoys*, 18 Ves. 311.

The evidence before us shows, without conflict, that the defendants did not want to make the settlement with plaintiff which was made, or any settlement at that time. The circumstances were so unfavorable for the prosecution of the plans which had been laid out, that the surviving associates believed they required more help, financial and executive, rather than more property in the hands of and to be managed by the survivors. Mr. Wilson, in his deposition, referring to this matter, says: "Several times during our later negotiations they had stated that they did not care about buying her out; they would do it at certain prices, and at this rate; but they would prefer she should go on and meet her obligations, and be enabled to meet her advances for the needs of the building of the railroads, if they would be called for from time to time; that they would prefer that she should stay in; they wanted money; they had not any money to pay out, and they wanted money. They preferred to get money in rather than to pay it out." The court also found that the defendants, at the time they requested plaintiff to continue along with them in the corporation, offered to manage her interests for her as well as they could their own, and promised that she should receive the full benefit of their knowledge and experience, and that they would get every dollar they could, and "share with her to the last cent."

The Southern Pacific railroad was finished to the Colorado River, at Yuma, in September, 1877. Mr. Hopkins had always been opposed to building the road east of the Colorado, and for that reason the work of construction stopped at that point. After the death of Mr. Hopkins, which occurred on March 29, 1878, Mrs. Hopkins was very unwilling—in fact, was probably unable before the distribution of the estate, which was in process of administration—to furnish any money, and for that reason opposed the Western Development Company engaging in any new schemes. As stated before, that company was, at the time, heavily indebted to various parties, and its assets consisted of unmarketable stocks and bonds. After the death of Mr. Hopkins the surviving associates concluded that they would build the road east. The organization of a new construction company had been agreed upon during General Colton's lifetime, and but a short time before his death the Southern Pacific of Arizona was incorporated, and he became a member thereof, with thirty thousand shares of the capital stock in his name. The associates had lost the aid and encouragement of both Mr. Hopkins and General Colton, in whose executive ability and good judgment they had unlimited confidence. On May 5, 1879, the supreme court of the United States affirmed the validity of the Thurman act, which took from the defendants twenty-five per cent of the net earnings of the Central Pacific to secure the government. At that time the Central Pacific was apparently the source of all income and credit to the defendants. The debt of the Central Pacific was over one hundred million dollars. The affirmance of the validity of this act threw the associates, especially Mr. Colton, into great despondency. He declared that the construction plant should be sold, and that no more road should be built until they had money laid up in bank. He declaimed bitterly against the communistic tendency of the times. It was a year of remarkable political excitement. There was a general business depression all over the country, and in fact the whole commercial world, for a year or more preceding the time of these negotiations. In the midst of these negotiations, there was in session in this state a constitutional convention, which formulated and promulgated the constitution ratified in May, 1879. Into this constitution there were incorporated many new and novel features, especially those relating to the taxation of railroad property and the fixing of freights and fares. The outlook for the parties was very dark. Of course, it is easy to say, in the light of subsequent circumstances, that their fears as to the evil effects of the provisions of the new constitution were largely groundless, but there was a real panic in railroad affairs at that time. True, confidence was soon restored, and their fears have not been realized. It certainly is not the fault of these defendants that they became despondent during that period, or that the transactions, unfortunately for this plaintiff, were consummated during such gloomy times. It was impossible for them to discontinue their operations without utter disaster to all their enterprises. Their road was built several hundred miles into a desert. To make it useful at all, it was necessary to connect it with the eastern systems of railroads. There was actual danger of active competition. To make the road a success, this competition had to be headed off. The value of the assets of the Western Development Company depended almost entirely upon the completion of the road which had been projected.

It is important, we think, that these facts should be remembered in determining the fairness of the transaction between the parties. It is the misfortune of the plaintiff that she had not the means or disposition to accept and act upon the proposition made by the defendants to continue on with them in their operations. It is an important fact to remember, too, that the demand for the rescission of the compromise agreement came from the plaintiff over two years after the execution of the contract, and at a time when the gloom and depression had given way to an active "boom" in railroad business,—a time when there was a most unprecedented demand for railroad securities, owing to which the defendants found themselves in a most prosperous condition. The court below evidently considered the matter of delay in bringing this action an important factor, especially as the plaintiff had successfully forced a settlement upon the defendants,—at a time when many of their securities had no market value, when they were all subject to great fluctuation, and when the question of the solvency or insolvency of their concerns depended solely upon the market value of such securities,—and had deliberately entered into the settlement with full means of information, and upon full advice of many competent friends. The failure of plaintiff to inform herself as to the facts upon which she relied, and to proceed to rescind the contract until the property had, under fortuitous circumstances, become immensely enhanced in value, is an important circumstance to be considered: *Nicholson* v. *Janeway*, 16 N. J. Eq. 285; *Murray* v. *Elston*, 24 N. J. Eq. 310; *Twin Lick Oil Co.* v. *Marbury*, 91 U. S. 587; *Kitchen* v. *St. Louis etc. R'y Co.*, 69 Mo. 224.

Mrs. Colton was determined to get out of the enterprises without waiting and taking her chances on creating a market. Her one ninth of the indebtedness due from the Western Development Company to Stanford, Huntington, Crocker, and the estate of Hopkins amounted to over eight hundred thousand dollars. If defendants had desired to take any advantage of plaintiff, their opportunities were unbounded. If they had simply refused to pay her any money, what would have become of her? They had a perfect right to refuse to buy her out or furnish her with money with which to meet her outside obligations. The estate was indebted to defendants to the extent of three quarters of a million of dollars, and was pressed with claims amounting to over one hundred and seventy-five thousand dollars. These claims could not have been met if defendants had not supplied plaintiff with money to pay them. They paid a note of Colton to Michael Reese, which alone amounted to over seventy-five thousand dollars. From October, 1878, to the time of the settlement, plaintiff had been allowed to draw about one hundred and seventy-five thousand

dollars for her own use, and to pay off the debts of the estate.
The situation of the plaintiff at that time is best expressed in
her own language. In a letter to Mr. Hunt, dated May 8,
1879, she says: —

"Now, I have managed wonderfully well. The railroad
people agreed to let me draw for my household expenses.
. . . . I have paid a note, bearing interest at eight per cent,
of twenty-five thousand dollars. I have paid a note on call
(no interest), in Europe, of nine thousand dollars. I have
paid eighteen thousand dollars on a call note bearing eight
per cent; a note of twenty-five thousand dollars, held by the
National Gold Bank, of whom David was a director. I held
one hundred shares of this bank stock, and I sold it for eighty-
five cents to the bank, so I still owe them seven thousand
dollars, which I am paying them interest on. They have
treated me very nicely, but I wish to pay them as soon as
possible. Then there were about three thousand dollars of
bills coming in, owing on our country place for labor and lumber for improvements, other immediate obligations of a sacred
nature of about three thousand dollars. Now, we have cut
down at every turn and corner. . . . . They have once or
twice asked if I was making investments, and the last time
they drew they declined to allow me any more until we had
made a settlement. This settlement I am anxious to make,
and am waiting their moves. Now, you will see that I am
not idle. I have had a hard struggle. I have lain awake
nights wondering how I was going to pay a note coming due.
I do not believe the railroad people will settle squarely with
me. I am afraid I shall have trouble. I talk business with
no one except my lawyer. I have had a sale of thorough-bred
stock from the farm. I have sold the carriages and horses,
except just such as we positively needed; I will send you a
catalogue. While I have no business experience, I am learning that I have good judgment in many things, and when I
depend upon myself I do far better than when I depend on
others."

As stated before, the defendants were under no obligations
to purchase from the plaintiff. All parties were in great distress. Plaintiff was in need of money; so were the defendants. If defendants had desired to take an unfair advantage
of Mrs. Colton, all that was necessary to accomplish their
aim was the enforcement of their claims against the estate.
No purchaser other than defendants for the securities in which

the estate was interested could be found. Defendants were
not to blame for that circumstance. If plaintiff had been put
to a forced sale, and defendants had seen fit to take advantage
of their position, and had purchased the interest of the estate
at even nominal figures, could plaintiff have complained, except from a moral standpoint? Mr. Tevis was a man of great
wealth, familiar with railroad matters, and the affairs of the
companies in which the parties were interested. Defendants'
statements as to values were mere matters of opinion, and
they were so understood by everybody concerned. Mr. Wilson and Mr. Tevis were as competent to judge as to the value
of the securities as were the defendants. The defendants did
not deny that the stocks would be worth more in the future;
they expressly so declared. They had confidence in their
own ability and the eventual success of their enterprises; but
plaintiff had no confidence in them or their schemes. It is
the misfortune of the plaintiff — not the fault of defendants —
that the prospect of success was so poor. We must be careful
not to judge a transaction of this kind in the light of subsequent events. There is a natural inclination to do so.

It must be remembered, too, that Mrs. Colton was not destitute of coercive power. Mr. Tevis told defendants they could
not afford to have litigation with plaintiff, — the widow of
their old associate; that it would be prejudicial to themselves
as individuals and to all their enterprises; that she would
have the sympathies of the public, etc. Staggering as they
were under heavy burdens, litigation meant disaster. Their
securities would be injured, and the expense of a protracted
trial, such as would follow a full investigation into the affairs
of the company, would seriously cripple them. Concessions
had to be made on both sides, or ruin would fall upon both.
Concessions were made, and they were honestly and fairly
made. All parties acted upon their best information as to the
amount and character of the property in controversy, and according to their best judgment as to the value thereof. Mr.
Colton had undertaken to carry a burden which was beyond
his strength, and for Mrs. Colton to attempt to carry it was a
proposition which was entirely discarded as an impossibility
before the negotiations began. The inability of plaintiff to go
on was as embarrassing to defendants as it was to her. By
the terms of the compromise plaintiff was released from corporate liabilities amounting to millions of dollars.

How can unfairness or inadequacy be predicated upon such

conduct and such facts? The statement of the circumstances is sufficient, we think, to demonstrate the truth and justice of the finding of the court that defendants were guilty of neither threats, concealments, nor undue exercise of a superior position and power, but that the negotiations which culminated in the contract, exhibit F, were fair, just, and equal.

Other points are made by appellant which we do not deem necessary to consider at length. It is said that the findings do not cover the issues; that the court adopted an erroneous theory as to the relation of the parties,—tried the case on one theory and decided it on another; drew erroneous conclusions of law from the facts found, proved, and admitted; found conclusions of law where facts should have been stated; that the evidence is insufficient to justify the findings of the court in certain particulars,—the most important of which are, the evidence shows, that Mr. Wilson was not an independent adviser; that Mr. Tevis was not possessed of information in regard to the affairs of the corporations to enable him to give reliable advice; that plaintiff would not have entered into the contract had she known the truth as to the stock; that many of the items set forth in that portion of exhibit D after the heading therein, "General D. D. Colton in account with the Western Development Company," were true or correct, and that Mr. Wilson was not informed how the account had been made up, or that the defendants had no personal knowledge of the correctness thereof.

Many of these points were not referred to on the argument, and most of them are apparently abandoned by at least a majority of appellant's counsel in this court. Nevertheless we have given careful attention to each and all of the points made in all the briefs. Some of those last referred to are involved in the questions we have considered at length in this opinion; the others, we think, are without merit.

The ·judgment and the order denying a new trial are affirmed.

FRAUD. — Where parties understand the facts, mistakes of law are not a cause for rescinding a contract, unless one party has a superior means of knowledge, or the parties are in some fiduciary relation toward each other, wherefrom undue influence can be presumed: *Champion* v. *Woods*, 79 Cal. 17; 12 Am. St. Rep. 126, and particularly note. Compare *Fisher* v. *Bishop*, 108 N. Y. 25; 2 Am. St. Rep. 357, and note.

FALSE REPRESENTATIONS SUFFICIENT TO AVOID A CONTRACT: See note to
Lawrence v. *Gayetty*, 12 Am. St. Rep. 36, 37. Compare note to *Brown* v.
Mitchell, 11 Am. St. Rep. 757-759.

ESTOPPELS, TO BE BINDING, must be mutual: *Furgeson* v. *Jones*, 17 Or. 204;
11 Am. St. Rep. 808, and note.

LACHES. — AS TO WHAT CONSTITUTES LACHES, and valid excuses there
for, see note to *Bell* v. *Hudson*, 2 Am. St. Rep. 795-807. Compare *Woodstock
Iron Co.* v. *Fullenwider*, 87 Ala. 584; 13 Am. St. Rep. 73, and note.

[IN BANK.]

HYMAN *v.* COLEMAN.

[82 CALIFORNIA, 650.]

JURISDICTION OF SUPERIOR COURT WHERE JUDGMENT DEMANDED FOR LESS
THAN THREE HUNDRED DOLLARS. — The superior court has no jurisdiction of an action to enforce the liability of the stockholders of a corporation as to stockholders against whom a judgment for less than three
hundred dollars is demanded, although the aggregate corporate indebtedness sued upon exceeds that amount.

EACH STOCKHOLDER OF CORPORATION IS LIABLE AS PRINCIPAL DEBTOR, and
not as a surety, for his proportion of the corporate debts contracted while
he was a stockholder, and this liability commences and a right of action
accrues against the corporation and the stockholders at the same time.
A suspension of the remedy against the corporation does not suspend the
remedy against or affect the liability of the stockholders.

ACTION TO ENFORCE LIABILITY OF STOCKHOLDERS OF CORPORATION MUST BE
BROUGHT WITHIN THREE YEARS after the cause of action accrues, and
the renewal of a note by the corporation does not extend the time prescribed by statute for suing a stockholder, if it does not appear that such
stockholder was a member of the corporation when the new note was
given, and that a new liability was created thereby.

ACTION to enforce liability of stockholders of a corporation.
The opinion states the case.

Severance and Travers, for the appellant.

T. M. Osmont and C. P. Robinson, for the respondents.

BELCHER, C. C. This is an action to recover from the
defendants, as stockholders of a corporation, their several
proportions of an indebtedness due plaintiff from the corporation.

The complaint contains two counts. In the first it is alleged that plaintiff advanced and loaned to the corporation,
on the seventh day of October, 1879, the sum of two thousand
dollars, for which the corporation then and there executed to
plaintiff its promissory note, payable in one year after date,

with interest, and that "said promissory note was renewed by
said corporation each year by the surrender of all former notes
given by said corporation to plaintiff, and the execution and
delivery of new notes to plaintiff for the amounts found due
upon the said indebtedness." It further alleges that the capital stock of the corporation was divided into one thousand
shares, and states the number of shares owned by each defendant on the 7th of October, 1879.

The second count alleges another loan by plaintiff to the
corporation of one thousand dollars, on the sixteenth day of
December, 1879, and the execution of its promissory note for
that sum, payable one year after its date, with interest, and a
like surrender and yearly renewal of same by the corporation.
It further states the number of shares of the capital stock
of the corporation owned by each defendant on the last-named
date.

The complaint then alleges that on the eighth day of September, 1883, an accounting as to the amount of the aforesaid
unpaid indebtedness was had between the corporation and
plaintiff, and that plaintiff then surrendered the notes which
he held, and the corporation executed to him for such indebtedness four new notes, dated December 16, 1883, and payable
one year after date, with interest.

This action was commenced in April, 1885, and is based
upon three of the last-named notes, one of the four having
been paid. The defendants demurred to the complaint, upon
the ground that it did not state facts sufficient to constitute a
cause of action, and that the cause of action was barred by the
statute of limitations.

The court sustained the demurrer, and rendered judgment
for defendants, and the plaintiff appealed.

1. The plaintiff demanded a several judgment against five
of the seven defendants, who appeared, for less than three
hundred dollars. The superior court had therefore no jurisdiction of the action against these five, and as to them the
judgment must be affirmed for that reason: *Derby* v. *Stevens*,
64 Cal. 287.

2. It is not claimed that the renewals of its notes by the
corporation created any new debt or liability against the defendants. And it is clear that if the renewals had had the
effect to extinguish the old debt and create a new one, then
the complaint stated no cause of action, for the reason that
it did not allege that the defendants were stockholders of

the corporation when any of the renewals were made. The only question then is, Did the renewals operate to extend the time of payment of the original indebtedness, and thereby prevent the statute of limitations from begining to run in favor of those who were stockholders when that indebtedness accrued until the last notes matured, on the 16th of December, 1884?

It is settled law in this state that, under our constitution and statutes, each stockholder of a corporation is liable for his proportion of the corporate debts contracted while he was a stockholder, as a principal debtor, and not as a surety: *Mokelumne Hill Canal Co.* v. *Woodbury*, 14 Cal. 265; 73 Am. Dec. 658; *Neilson* v. *Crawford*, 52 Cal. 248; *Sonoma Valley Bank* v. *Hill*, 59 Cal. 107; *Morrow* v. *Superior Court*, 64 Cal. 383.

The liability commences and a right of action accrues against the corporation and stockholders at the same time: *Davidson* v. *Rankin*, 34 Cal. 503; *Mitchell* v. *Beckman*, 64 Cal. 117.

Suspension of the remedy against the corporation does not suspend the remedy against or affect the liability of the stockholders: *Young* v. *Rosenbaum*, 39 Cal. 646.

A judgment against the corporation does not create a new liability, nor extend the time prescribed by the statute of limitations for bringing suit against the stockholders: *Larrabee* v. *Baldwin*, 35 Cal. 168; *Stilphen* v. *Ware*, 45 Cal. 110.

The liability of stockholders is created by statute, and an action to enforce that liability must be brought within three years after the cause of action accrues: Code Civ. Proc., secs. 338, subd. 1, and 359; *Green* v. *Beckman*, 59 Cal. 545; *Moore* v. *Boyd*, 74 Cal. 167.

In New York it has been held that the renewal of a note by a corporation does not extend the time prescribed by statute for suing a stockholder. In *Parrott* v. *Colby*, 6 Hun, 55, the court said: "We think the liability of stockholders in such cases cannot be revived or extended by any renewal or extension of the indebtedness which the creditors may make with the corporation." This decision was affirmed on appeal in 71 N. Y. 597; and in *Jagger Iron Co.* v. *Walker*, 76 N. Y. 521, *Parrott* v. *Colby* is cited, and substantialy the same doctrine announced.

In view of the foregoing authorities, our conclusion is, that the plaintiff's right of action against the defendants comnenced when his first notes matured, and was barred in three years thereafter. We therefore advise that the judgment be affirmed.

HAYNE, C., and FOOTE, C., concurred.

The COURT. — For the reasons given in the foregoing opinion, the judgment is affirmed.

Rehearing denied.   ____

CORPORATIONS. — LIABILITY OF STOCKHOLDERS to creditors of corporations for corporate debts: See extended note to *Thompson v. Reno Savings Bank,* 3 Am. St. Rep. 806 et seq.

STATUTE OF LIMITATIONS IN ACTIONS TO ENFORCE STOCKHOLDER'S STATUTORY LIABILITY: See note to *Thompson v. Reno Savings Bank,* 3 Am. St. Rep. 872. Statute of limitations does not run against creditors' claims for unpaid subscriptions until a call is made or the corporation ceases to be a going concern: Note to *Thompson v. Reno Savings Bank,* 3 Am. St. Rep. 827–829.

CASES

IN THE

SUPREME COURT

OF

COLORADO.

PEOPLE *v.* GRAND RIVER BRIDGE COMPANY.

[13 COLORADO, 11.]

QUO WARRANTO — WHO MAY MAINTAIN. — To enable a private person to maintain *quo warranto* to dissolve a corporation, upon the neglect or refusal of the district attorney to bring such action, he must allege and show some injury peculiarly affecting him, and some interest in the result of the action beyond that common to every citizen of the state.

QUO WARRANTO — CLAIM FOR DAMAGES WILL NOT SUPPORT. — A right to sue for damages arising from the appropriation of land, without compensation, by a corporation, does not give the owner of the land an interest so different from that common to all citizens as to enable him to maintain *quo warranto* to dissolve the corporation.

QUO WARRANTO instituted to dissolve a corporation under section 315, Civil Code (General Statutes of Colorado 1883), in the name of the people upon the relation of Frank S. Byers. The above section of the code is as follows: "An action may be brought by the district attorney, in the name of the people of this state, upon his own information or upon the relation or complaint of a private party, against any person who usurps, intrudes into, or unlawfully holds or exercises any public office, civil or military, or any franchise within his district, in the state; and it shall be the duty of the district attorney to bring the action whenever he has reason to believe that any such office or franchise has been usurped, intruded into, or unlawfully held or exercised by any person, or when he is directed to do so by the governor; and in case such district attorney shall neglect or refuse to bring such action upon the

complaint of a private party, such action may be brought by
such private party, upon his own relation, in the name of the
people of the state." Demurrer to the complaint sustained.
Judgment for defendant, and plaintiff appeals.

W. T. Hughes, for the appellant.

R. H. Gilmore and C. C. Post, for the appellees.

HAYT, J. It is averred in the complaint that the district
attorney of the proper district refused to bring the suit upon
application, and therefore plaintiff claims the right to maintain the action as relator by virtue of the provisions of section
315 of the Civil Code, although it does not appear that he has
any other or different interest in the result than such as he
may have in common with all other citizens of the state. If
the defendant corporation has violated the law, either by doing
some forbidden act, or by neglecting to do some act enjoined
upon it, it is not every person who may call it to account for
such violation. As a general rule, prosecutions for wrongs
done to the public must be instituted by the state through its
properly authorized agents, while the individual can only sue
for injuries peculiarly affecting him; and the provision of the
code permitting an action in the nature of a *quo warranto* to
be brought by a purely private party, upon the neglect or refusal of the district attorney to bring such action, must be
construed with reference to this general rule. In considering
the nature of the interest necessary to entitle a private party
to become a relator, in a case coming before the court while
Mansfield was lord chief justice, it was said: " There is no individual among those who apply to the court at present who
says, 'My franchise is hurt.'—'Who are you? What concern
have you with the corporation?'—'Only one of the king's subjects; I have no concern.'—'What do you come for?'—'To
dissolve the corporation and to disturb its peace.'—'Then what
is to be taken advantage of here?'—'A mere blunder.' There
are many circumstances in this case why the court should not
interfere by granting an information ": *King* v. *Stacey*, 1 Term
Rep. 3.

The language quoted was used in reference to the statute of
9 Anne, chapter 20, relating to informations in the nature of a
quo warranto, under which it was expressly provided that the
information might be exhibited by the proper officer " at the
relation of any person or persons desiring to sue or prosecute

the same": See appendix to High on Extraordinary Legal
Remedies, 585. The same view is taken in Pennsylvania
under a statute containing a similar provision in reference to
the relator as that quoted from the English statute. In *Commonwealth* v. *Philadelphia etc. R'y Co.*, 20 Pa. St. 518, the court
said: "A stranger who has no interest in a corporation except
that which is common to every citizen cannot demand a judgment of ouster in a writ of *quo warranto*. . . . . No mere
stranger should be permitted to demand the forfeiture of a
charter granted by the commonwealth where the state herself
does not demand it. She has a right to waive the forfeiture;
and it is her interest, in many cases, to do so."

It will be noted that the provision in reference to the person who may act as relator is as broad in the English statute
as in our own. In fact, the statute of this and other states
relating to actions for the usurpation of an office or franchise
are generally modifications of this statute of Anne; and the
universal rule of decisions in all cases in which the action
has been brought for the purpose of dissolving a corporation
has been, that the relator, to maintain the action, must have
some interest beyond that common to every citizen; and
further than this we are not concerned in this case: High on
Extraordinary Legal Remedies, sec. 654; *Murphy* v. *Farmers'
Bank*, 20 Pa. St. 415; *State* v. *Smith*, 32 Ind. 213; *State* v. *Stein*,
13 Neb. 530.

It was said in the oral argument that Frank S. Byers, the
relator, is the owner of one of the banks upon which the bridge
rests, and that the defendant had appropriated the same without compensating him therefor, and that this ownership entitles the said Byers to prosecute the action as relator. There
are two conclusive answers to this argument: 1. It does not
sufficiently appear from the complaint that he is such owner;
2. If it did so appear, and also that the defendants took possession of said bank unlawfully, they would, under such circumstances, be trespassers, and liable in damages for the
injury. The public, however, would be in no way concerned
with the controversy; and, as we have seen, this is a sufficient
reason for denying the extraordinary remedy by *quo warranto:
People* v. *Hillside etc. Turnp. Co.*, 2 Johns. 190.

The complaint failing to show any interest in the controversy in Frank S. Byers, the relator, other than such as pertains to every citizen, the trial court properly sustained the
demurrer, and the judgment is accordingly affirmed.

QUO WARRANTO. — PROCEEDINGS, WHEN, HOW, AND BY WHOM INSTITUTED to declare a forfeiture of the franchise of a corporation: See note to *State* v. *Atchison etc. R'y Co.*, 8 Am. St. Rep. 179-202.

QUO WARRANTO. — A petition for an information in the nature of a *quo warranto*, calling upon the defendants to show by what right they exercised the franchise of using a public bridge as their private property, and erecting gates and charging tolls for crossing, stated a good case when it alleged that the court of ordinary of the county had established a public road running from a church to the bridge in question, and had, on the same day, established another public road from the opposite side of the bridge to the county site, and that these roads had been opened, worked, and traveled ever since as public roads; and that the relators, together with other citizens, had built the bridge by private subscription, and it had been used as a public bridge until the defendants put up their gates and charged tolls; and that defendants had no chartered rights thereto, but were usurpers of the rights, privileges, and franchises of owners of public bridges: *Whelchel* v. *State ex rel. Wiley*, 76 Ga. 644.

OMAHA AND GRANT SMELTING AND REFINING COMPANY *v.* TABOR.

[13 COLORADO, 41.]

WITNESS MAY BE IMPEACHED, UPON CROSS-EXAMINATION, by showing that his acts or declarations on previous occasions were at variance with his testimony as given at the trial.

AGENCY OF WITNESS CANNOT BE ESTABLISHED by his own declarations.

TRESPASS — EVIDENCE OF TITLE IN THIRD PERSON NOT ADMISSIBLE. — In trespass for the conversion of ore from a mine, defendant, not pleading justification, cannot defend by showing title in a third person.

MINES — LICENSE TO ONE IS NOT LICENSE TO OTHERS. — Where a party knowing that persons have, under an order of court, entered on a mining claim conflicting with his, and are taking his ore, his consent that another shall join them is not a license to the others to take the ore.

PARTY CALLING WITNESS IS NOT PRECLUDED FROM SHOWING THE TRUTH of any particular fact by any other competent testimony.

CO-TENANCY. — AUTHORITY OF TENANT IN COMMON IN MINE cannot be extended to cover acts of others that he cannot legally do himself; and his consent or license to others to enter and extract ore can only extend to the interest owned by him in the common property.

DEEDS. — PAROL EVIDENCE IS INADMISSIBLE TO SHOW an agreement that possession under a deed is to be retained by the vendor until the purchase price is paid, under Colorado General Statutes, chapter 18, section 9, providing that conveyances of real estate duly executed and delivered carry with them the right to immediate possession, unless a future day for possession is therein specified.

MINES AND MINING — SALE BY GOVERNMENT OF MINERAL LANDS REVOKES FORMER LICENSE. — Subsequent sale of mineral land by the government, and the issue by it of a receiver's receipt for the purchase price, revokes a mere license from the government under which a party had formerly entered, and such licensee cannot set up his former possession as adverse to the grantee.

PURCHASER FROM TRESPASSER, WHEN GUILTY OF CONVERSION. — The purchaser of ore taken from a mine by a trespasser is equally guilty with
the l tter of conversion, whether ignorant or informed of the true ownership.

MEASURE OF DAMAGES FOR CONVERSION OF ORE by a purchaser from a trespasser is the value of the ore sold, together with a sum equal to legal
interest thereon from the time of conversion, less the reasonable and
proper cost of raising it from the mine after it was broken, and hauling
from the mine to the purchaser's place of business.

TROVER by Tabor, Moffatt, Du Bois, Blaine, and Chaffee
against the Omaha and Grant Smelting and Refining Company. Plaintiffs alleged the ownership and possession of a
mine known as the Maid of Erin lode, and as survey lot No.
568, and mineral entry No. 384, from January 1, 1882, to
October 11, 1883; that between July 3 and August 31, 1883,
one Ovens, one Wight, and others, wrongfully entered upon
such property, and took out a large amount of valuable ore,
and sold it to defendants, who converted it to their own use.
Defendants, answering, deny all the allegations of the complaint, except that they have not paid plaintiffs for the ore,
which they admit; and for further defense they allege that, at
the time of the alleged wrongful entry and taking of such ore,
several persons, named Wight, Joslin, Bullock, Park, and
Rucker, were the owners and in possession of the Vanderbilt
mine, which conflicted with and embraced part of the Maid
of Erin mine; that, at the time mentioned in the complaint,
undetermined litigation was in progress concerning the conflicting territory and between the parties; that the owners of
the Vanderbilt mine were taking ore therefrom, and from the
part in conflict with the Maid of Erin mine; that these facts
being unknown to defendants, they purchased the ore as ore
from the Vanderbilt mine, in the regular course of business,
and that, long after such purchase, they were informed that
the ore was taken from the ground in dispute. Plaintiffs,
replying, denied that Wight and others were the owners of
any part of the Vanderbilt mine in conflict with the Maid of
Erin mine, or that any part of the former conflicted with the
latter; and alleged that, prior to the date mentioned as that of
the conversion, the government had sold to plaintiffs the Maid
of Erin mine, and had given a receiver's receipt for the purchase-money; that Wight and others unlawfully went into a
portion of the premises while plaintiffs were in possession,
and mined and carried away the ore mentioned in defendants'
answer; that the entry of Wight and others was through a

shaft on the Big Chief mine, not owned by either party to this suit or to the controversy; and that from such shaft they worked over the boundary and into plaintiffs' mine; and denied that the defendants did not know that Wight and others were taking the ore purchased from plaintiffs' mine. Verdict and judgment for plaintiffs. Defendants assign various errors to the admission and rejection of evidence, to the ruling of the court in giving and refusing instructions asked, and to a refusal to grant a new trial.

Patterson and Thomas, for the appellants.

Wolcott and Vaile, J. B. Bissell, and L. C. Rockwell, for the appellees.

REED, C. The first fifteen and the eighteenth errors assigned are to the ruling of the court on the cross-examination of plaintiffs' witness O. H. Harker.

Counsel, in their argument for appellants, say: " The defendants sought to show, by cross-examination of the plaintiffs' witnesses, that, at the time of the commission of the trespasses complained of, the Maid of Erin mine was owned by the Henriett Mining and Smelting Company and J. B. Du Bois, and that the original trespassers were enjoined, at the suit of these parties, by proper proceedings instituted for that purpose, but they were not permitted to do so." It appears that counsel for appellants (defendants below), upon the trial, attempted, on cross-examination of the witness, to show that the plaintiff Du Bois owned one half of the Maid of Erin property, and the Henriett company the other half, and that the other plaintiffs were not the owners, by showing that the witness had so stated, in a legal document signed and verified by him as manager and agent, in some former proceeding concerning the property, in which case an injunction was issued to restrain a trespass upon the Maid of Erin claim upon the complaint so signed and verified; but the court would not permit it to be done. An examination of the questions asked the witness, which the court did not permit him to answer, will show that none of the testimony sought went to any issue in the case, was not directed to anything in his direct testimony, and was not legitimate cross-examination. Many of the questions were in regard to facts that could only have been proved by production of records or documents. Some of the questions were in regard to suits at law, and proceedings where there is nothing in the record to show he in any way participated, or of which he had any knowledge; and all the testimony sought, in our view of the case, was immaterial, except in so far as it tended to discredit him, or weaken his testimony, by showing that his acts or declarations on previous occasions were at variance and inconsistent with his testimony at that time. This counsel had a right to do by introducing the records or documents, and asking him in regard to oral statements. It appears that in the course of the trial the papers executed by the witness, to which his attention was called, were admitted in evidence for the purpose of impeachment, — the only legitimate purpose they could serve.

It is clear that the title of the Henriett company to one half of the Maid of Erin claim could not have been established by parol statements or the acts of an agent in verifying papers where the facts were so stated. Counsel say this was one purpose for which the evidence was sought to be elicited on cross-examination. Had it been proper cross-examination, and directed to an issue, it was incompetent for the declared purposes for which it was sought. The agency of the witness had not been established by any testimony but his own. He stated under oath, at the time suit was brought, that he was the manager and agent of the Henriett company. This was insufficient. An agency cannot be established by his own declarations: *Harker* v. *Dement*, 9 Gill, 16; 52 Am. Dec. 670; *James* v. *Stookey*, 1 Wash. C. C. 330. If an agency had been proved, it was that at the time of verifying the papers he was the manager and agent of the Henriett company; and his sworn statement that he was such agent, and that his principal owned one half of defendants' claim, could not be binding upon or in any way affect the plaintiffs in this action. And although he was the agent of plaintiffs, in charge of their work in the Maid of Erin, no statement, no matter how solemnly made by him as the agent of the Henriett company, in favor of such company or against the title of plaintiffs, could affect either, much less conclude and estop the plaintiffs, from asserting the contrary, as is urged by counsel. There was no plea of property in the Henriett company, and of entry and justification under such a title. The defendant in this case cannot set up a title of a third person in defense, unless he in some manner connects himself with it: *Duncan* v. *Spear*, 11 Wend. 54; *Weymouth* v. *Chicago etc. R. R. Co.*, 17 Wis. 567; 84 Am. Dec. 763; *Harker* v. *Dement*, 9 Gill, 7; 52 Am. Dec. 670.

It follows that the court did not err in limiting the testimony on the cross-examination to the attempted discrediting of the witness, and in refusing to admit records except for purposes of impeachment.

It is assigned for error that the court allowed plaintiff Tabor to testify to a conversation with McComb after the latter had been called and had given his version of it. Counsel put it upon the ground that a party cannot be allowed to contradict or impeach his own witness. It does not appear that Tabor was called for any such purpose, or that his testimony had that effect. He was called to give his version of what occurred at that interview with McComb. A careful comparison of the testimony of both shows that of Tabor more corroborative of than contradictory to that of McComb,—at least as to the result of such conversation,—although there is some discrepancy in regard to the language used. "The party calling a witness is not precluded from proving the truth of any particular fact by any other competent testimony": 1 Greenl. Ev., sec. 443.

Appellants' counsel rely upon the conversation of Tabor with McComb as a license or consent on the part of Tabor to the entry and taking of the ores from the Maid of Erin ground, and contend that his license or consent as a co-owner to the extent of one sixteenth of the Maid of Erin ground was conclusive upon himself and also upon his co-owners of the other fifteen sixteenths, and was equivalent to a license or consent from all, to the extent of covering the entire property. A license or consent cannot be extended by inference as a consent to enter property not spoken of or referred to in the conversation, and we can find nothing in the testimony of either McComb or Tabor in regard to entering and taking ore from the Maid of Erin ground. It was not attempted to be shown that Ovens, Wight, and Rucker entered under license or consent from Tabor. At the conversation both testify that Tabor was informed the parties had entered under an order from the court, against which he was powerless for the time. It further appears that those parties were in at the time McComb and Tabor had the conversation, and McComb only asked consent to join them. It cannot be contended that such a consent was a license to Ovens, Wight, and Rucker to enter. The testimony went to the jury, and in the eighth and ninth instructions given on prayer of plaintiffs they were instructed, in effect, that they could not limit or reduce the amount to be recovered by reason of the supposed license or consent of Tabor, unless they should find that there was a consent on his part that they should enter through the Big Chief shaft, and take the ore from the Maid of Erin claim; and the same proposition is submitted in the instruction given on behalf of defendants in place of No. 7, refused. These instructions on that point, we think, were correct, and fairly submitted to the jury the question of license or consent. And it is evident from the verdict that the jury found against any such license or consent; and the jury having so found, it would seem unnecessary to determine whether the instructions were correct or otherwise in regard to the extent such consent, if found, should affect or modify the amount; or in other words, whether it should cover the whole taking of ore, or be confined to the one sixteenth owned by Tabor. The jury having found no consent or license on the part of Tabor, defendants could not be prejudiced by the instructions of the court in regard to its effect if it were found.

The question is quite different from what it would be if it related to a transaction in the ordinary course of business relative to the joint property of tenants in common. Here it is attempted to justify a tort, and the injury to the entire property, by the supposed license of one joint owner. If the entry had been made by Tabor in person, and the wrongs attempted to be justified under permission from had been done by him, his co-tenants could have had against him the same actions at law for injuries to their interests that all are attempting to enforce against parties having no interest. It is held "an action on the case sounding in tort may be maintained by one tenant in common against his co-tenant for a misuse of the common property, though not amounting to a total destruction of it": *McLellan* v. *Jenness,* 43 Vt. 183; 5 Am. Rep. 270; *Agnew* v. *Johnson,* 17 Pa. St. 373; 55 Am. Dec. 565; *Lowe* v. *Miller,* 3 Gratt. 205; 46 Am. Dec. 188. "And if one tenant in common assume to own and sell the thing held in common, the other may maintain an action of trover against him": *Burbank* v. *Crooker,* 7 Gray, 159; 66 Am. Dec. 470; *Wheeler* v. *Wheeler,* 33 Me. 347; *Coursin's Appeal,* 79 Pa. St. 220; *White* v. *Osborn,* 21 Wend. 72; *Smyth* v. *Tankersley,* 20 Ala. 212; 56 Am. Dec. 193. The authority of the tenant in common could not be extended to cover acts of others that he could not legally have done himself. Hence the court was correct in holding and instructing the jury that the consent or license of Tabor, if such were found, could only extend to the interest owned by him in the common property.

Appellants further assign for error the ruling of the court in admitting the testimony of Tabor when called by the plaintiffs to show that, by a parol agreement made at the time of the conveyance of the different interests by Tabor, Moffat, and Chaffee in the Henriett company, possession of the property conveyed was to remain in the grantors until the purchase price was paid; that it never was paid, and possession under the conveyance never delivered. A part of such testimony — that which went to show that possession was to be retained — was inadmissible. "All conveyances of real estate, and of any interest therein duly executed and delivered, shall be held to carry with them the right to immediate possession of the premises or interest conveyed, unless a future day for the possession is therein specified": Gen. Stats., c. 18, sec. 9; *Drake* v. *Root*, 2 Col. 685. Under the statute, it is certainly required that the intention to postpone the operation of a deed shall be declared in the instrument, and it cannot be proved by parol.

It follows that the instructions of the court on this point were in part erroneous; that part of the testimony going to . prove that possession of the property was never delivered, and remained in the grantors, was clearly competent and proper; and the instructions of the court were proper on that point.

The admission in evidence of the deeds of reconveyance by the Henriett Mining Company and the assignment of Rider of his cause of action was not erroneous, and should be sustained, — the former investing plaintiffs with full title before the commencement of suit; and of the validity of the latter, so as to enable Moffatt, assignee, to succeed to all the rights of his assignor, there can be no question under our statute.

Had defendants, by proper and competent testimony, attempted to prove the ownership of one half of the Maid of Erin claim in the Henriett company, it would have been inadmissible. There was no attempted justification of entry of Wight and others under the Henriett title of one half.

"Under a plea that the close upon which the alleged trespass was committed was not at that time the close of the plaintiff, the defendant may show lawful right to the possession of the close in a third person, under whom he claims to have acted": *Jones* v. *Chapman*, 2 Ex. 803. "But a bare tort-feasor cannot set up in defense the title of a third person between whom and himself there is no privity of connection ": *Branch* v. *Doane*, 18 Conn. 233. "In justifying under a third person, the defendant must show both the title and the possession of that person": *Chambers* v. *Donaldson*, 11 East, 65; *Merrill* v. *Burbank*, 23 Me. 538; *Reed* v. *Price*, 30 Mo. 442; and that the acts were done by that person's authority: *Dunlap* v. *Glidden*, 31 Me. 510. "A defendant can only justify upon the ground of a better right or title than the plaintiffs have. And it has been held that mere naked possession, however acquired, is good as against a person having no right to the possession ": *Knapp* v. *Winchester*, 11 Vt. 351; *Haslem* v. *Lockwood*, 37 Conn. 500; 9 Am. Rep. 350; *Cook* v. *Patterson*, 35 Ala. 102.

It will be apparent that in the judgment of this court the effort of defendants to set up title to half of the property in the Maid of Erin claim in the Henriett company, without a plea to that effect, and attempting to show privity, or attempting to justify under it, was unwarranted in law, and that no testimony should have been taken in support of any such attempted defense.

Another defense interposed, which seems incompatible with the former, was, that certain parties named in the answer were the owners of the Vanderbilt claim, and that such claim conflicted with and comprised a part of the Maid of Erin claim, and that the claim was in the possession of the owners named under claim and color of title; and that the ground from which the ore was taken was in conflict between the owners of the claim, and that divers suits in regard to the same were pending and undetermined; that Wight and others, while engaged in mining the Vanderbilt claim, took the ores from the ground in controversy, which defendants bought as Vanderbilt ore; and that the same was taken by the owners of such claim while the *locus* was in their possession under color of title.

It was shown in evidence that there were two entries on the property in controversy, — the first by Wight, one of the owners of the Big Chief, in 1882, after the Maid of Erin had a receiver's receipt from the United States land-office, when a drift was run from the Big Chief shaft for the Maid of Erin, and was run over the line twenty or twenty-eight feet into the Maid of Erin ground. The second entry was by the same party and others in the same way and upon the same ground. Neither entry was made by extending the work of

the Vanderbilt claim to its exterior limits, and thus entering
the Maid of Erin property. The party entering and participating in the proceeds of the ores mined were not the owners of
the Vanderbilt, but seems to have been one made up for the
occasion, — part of the owners of the Vanderbilt, some of the
owners of the Big Chief, and perhaps parties owning in neither.

The plaintiffs pleaded title to the Maid of Erin claim from
the government of the United States, and put in evidence a
receiver's receipt for the purchase of the property, of date
November 23, 1881, and a patent from the United States government dated March 17, 1884.

It has been frequently held that a patent for land emanating
from the government of the United States is the highest evidence of title, and in courts of law is evidence of the true performance of every prerequisite to its issuance, and cannot be
questioned either in courts of law or equity, except upon ground
or fraud or mistake, and if not assailed for fraud or mistake,
is conclusive evidence of title. On the 23d of November, 1881,
the government parted with its title to the Maid of Erin property, sold it to Tabor and Du Bois, and gave a receipt. The
government could thereafter no more dispose of the land than
if a patent had been issued. "The final certificate obtained
on the payment of the money is as binding on the government
as the patent. . . . . When the patent issues, it relates back
to the entry": *Astrom* v. *Hammond*, 3 McLean, 107; *Blachley*
v. *Coles*, 6 Col. 350; *Poire* v. *Wells*, 6 Col. 406; *Steel* v. *St. Louis
etc. Smelting Co.*, 106 U. S. 447; *Heydenfeldt* v. *Daney etc. Mining Co.*, 93 U. S. 634.

The patent does not invest the purchaser with any additional property in the land. It only gives him better legal
evidence of the title which he first acquired by the certificate:
Cavender v. *Smith*, 5 Iowa, 189; *Cavender* v. *Smith*, 3 G. Greene,
349; 56 Am. Dec. 541; *Arnold* v. *Grimes*, 2 Iowa, 1; *Carroll* v.
Safford, 3 How. 460; *Bagnell* v. *Broderick*, 13 Pet. 450; *Carman*
v. *Johnson*, 29 Mo. 84; *Hutchings* v. *Low*, 15 Wall. 88. A patent
title cannot be attacked collaterally. "Individuals can resist the conclusiveness of the patent only by showing that it
conflicts with prior rights vested in them": *Boggs* v. *Merced
Mining Co.*, 14 Cal. 362; *Leese* v. *Clark*, 18 Cal. 535; *Jackson*
v. *Lawton*, 10 Johns. 24; 6 Am. Dec. 311.

An "adverse possession" is defined to be the enjoyment of
land or such estate as lies in grant, under such circumstances
as indicate that such enjoyment has been commenced and

continued under assertion or color of right on the part of the possessor: *Wallace* v. *Duffield*, 2 Serg. & R.. 527; 7 Am. Dec. 660; *French* v. *Pearce*, 8 Conn. 440; 21 Am. Dec. 680; *Smith* v. *Burtis*, 9 Johns. 174.

The entry of a stranger, and the taking of rents or profits by him, is not an adverse possession. When two parties are in possession, the law adjudges it to be the possession of the party who has the right: *Reading* v. *Rawsterne*, 2 Ld. Raym. 829; *Barr* v. *Gratz*, 4 Wheat. 213; *Smith* v. *Burtis*, 6 Johns. 197; 5 Am. Dec. 218; *Stevens* v. *Hollister*, 18 Vt. 294; 46 Am. Dec. 154; *Brimmer* v. *Long Wharf*, 5 Pick. 131.

Possession, to be supported by the law, must be under a claim of right, and adverse possession must be strictly proved: *Grube* v. *Wells*, 34 Iowa, 150. The color must arise out of some conveyance purporting to convey title to a tract of land: 3 Washburn on Real Property, 155; *Shackleford* v. *Bailey*, 35 Ill. 391.

The title of the Maid of Erin claim was in the government of the United States until divested by its own act. There could be no adverse possession against the government. The claimants of the Vanderbilt claim entered under license only from the government. Admitting, for the purposes of this case, that the entry under the license was legal, that they had complied with the laws of Congress and the state, and that their possession extended to and was protected to their exterior lines while the fee remained in the government, when the fee passed from the government to the other party conveying the *locus*, before that time in controversy, the supposed license was revoked, and all acts and declarations of the parties themselves, whether by record or otherwise, as establishing a possessory right, were void as against the grantees of the government, and there could be no entry under color of title, except by some right by conveyance, either from the government or its grantees.

The fact of the actual possession and occupancy of the Maid of Erin by plaintiffs was not seriously disputed, and the testimony was ample to warrant the jury in finding the fact. The government had granted the land previous to the entry of Wight and others, and that such possession under a legal title was co-extensive with its bounds is so well settled that authorities in its support are unnecessary.

We do not think the court erred in refusing to admit the testimony offered in support of possessory title of the Vanderbilt in the land from which the ore was taken, nor in refusing the testimony in reference to litigation and suits pending between the parties. Neither the title nor right of possession of plaintiffs could be attacked collaterally as attempted, and the testimony offered under the law as shown above was incompetent and inadmissible to prove either adverse possession or color of title.

From our view of the law controlling the case, as stated above, it follows that the court did not err in refusing the instructions asked on this point by the defendants, or in giving those which were given. They were substantially correct.

The sale of ore by Wight and others, and purchase by the defendants, was a conversion. A "conversion" is defined to be any act of the defendant inconsistent with the plaintiff's right of possession, or subversive of his right of property: *Harris* v. *Saunders*, 2 Strob. Eq. 370, note; *Webber* v. *Davis*, 44 Me. 147; 69 Am. Dec. 87; *Gilman* v. *Hill*, 36 N. H. 311; *Clark* v. *Whitaker*, 19 Conn. 319; 48 Am. Dec. 160.

The defendants, by purchasing the ore, acquired no title, and are consequently equally liable for its conversion as the parties who sold it: *Clark* v. *Wells*, 45 Vt. 4; 12 Am. Rep. 187; *Clark* v. *Rideout*, 39 N. H. 238; *Carter* v. *Kingman*, 103 Mass. 517. And it was a matter of no importance, so far as the legal liability of defendants was concerned, whether they were ignorant or informed of the true ownership: *Morrill* v. *Moulton*, 40 Vt. 242; *Johnson* v. *Powers*, 40 Vt. 611; *West Jersey R. R. Co.* v. *Trenton Car Works Co.*, 32 N. J. L. 517; *Dixon* v. *Caldwell*, 15 Ohio St. 412; 86 Am. Dec. 487; *Hoffman* v. *Carow*, 22 Wend. 285. The principle *caveat emptor* applies.

A person purchasing property of the party in possession, without ascertaining where the true title is, does so at his peril, and although honestly mistaken, will be liable to the owner for a conversion: *Taylor* v. *Pope*, 5 Cold. 413; *Gilmore* v. *Newton*, 9 Allen, 171; 85 Am. Dec. 749; *Spraights* v. *Hawley*, 39 N. Y. 441; 100 Am. Dec. 452.

The question of the proper measure of damages is one of much greater difficulty. We can find no conclusive adjudication in our own court. The decisions of the different states are conflicting and irreconcilable. Athough under our code different forms of action are abolished, the principles controlling the different actions remain the same as before its adoption. Consequently the law applicable and to be admin-

istered in each case depends as much as formerly upon the
nature of the case,—the allegations and the distinctive form
the case assumes. In many states, the courts have attempted
in this action to make the rule of damage correspond to that
in the action of trespass, and make it, in that respect, as full
and complete a remedy. In the state of New York, it was
long held, and perhaps still is, that the increased value of the
property added by the labor and acts of defendant belongs to
the rightful owner of the property, and the value of the property in its new and improved state thus becomes the measure
of damages; but the doctrine has been questioned and severely
criticised in the same state: *Brown* v. *Sax*, 7 Cow. 95. In
trespass, damage for the whole injury, including diminution
in the value of the land by the entry and removal, as well as
of the value of the property removed, may be recovered; and
the character of the entry, whether willful and malicious, or
in good faith, through inadvertence or mistake, is an important element,—an element that cannot enter into the action
of trover. In trover, the specific articles cannot be recovered
as in replevin. Consequently the same rule as to increased
value cannot be applied as in that action, where the specific
property can be followed, and, when identified, taken without
regard to the form it has assumed. It seems, on principle,
therefore (and this is in harmony with the English authorities and those of many of the states), that where a party
makes his election, and adopts trover, the rule of damage
is and should be proper compensation for the property taken
and converted, regardless of the manner of entry and taking,
and, where the chattel was severed from the realty, regardless
of the diminished value of the realty by reason of the taking.
In other words, the true rule should be the value of the chattel as such when and where first severed from the realty and
becoming a chattel. An examination of the authorities will
show that the rule of damages, to some extent, depends upon
the form of action,—whether the action is for an injury to the
land itself or for the conversion of a chattel which had been
severed from the land. This distinction seems well founded
in principle and reason. This view of the law is supported by
Martin v. *Porter*, 5 Mees. & W. 352; *Wild* v. *Holt*, 9 Mees. &
W. 672; *Morgan* v. *Powell*, 3 Q. B. 278; *Hilton* v. *Woods*, L. R.
4 Eq. 432; *Maye* v. *Yappen*, 23 Cal. 306; *Goller* v. *Fett*, 30
Cal. 481; *Coleman's Appeal*, 62 Pa. St. 252; *Cushing* v. *Long-
fellow*, 26 Me. 306; *Forsyth* v. *Wells*, 41 Pa. St. 291; 80 Am.

Dec. 617; *Kier* v. *Peterson,* 41 Pa. St. 357; *Moody* v. *Whitney,* 38 Me. 174; ˙61 Am. Dec. 239.

We are therefore of the opinion that the rule of damages adopted, and the instructions of the court as to the measure of damage, were erroneous, and that it should have been the value of the ore sold, as shown, less the reasonable and proper cost of raising it from the mine after it was broken, and hauling from the mine to the defendants' place of business. We do not find it necessary to decide whether or not plaintiffs' counsel, by stating in the complaint that the ore taken and converted was of a certain value "over and above the cost of mining, digging, and extracting the same from the ground, raising the same to the surface, hauling the same to the defendants' reduction works, and the cost of treating the same," and defendants taking issue upon it precluded them from proving and taking greater damage upon the trial; but if it were necessary, for the purpose of determining this case, we should be inclined to so hold. In this action, value is a material averment, and the plaintiffs have deliberately asserted one rule, and, issue having been taken upon it, should not be permitted to change base, and adopt, upon trial, another more disadvantageous to the defendants.

In this case, it could not have been said the evidence was in support of the allegation or directed to an issue. The testimony should have been directed to the issue, or the pleadings amended.

Counsel for appellees, after obtaining leave from this court, assigned for cross-error the refusal of the court to allow interest on the amount found due from the time of the conversion, and the instruction of the court on that point. It is true, as stated by the learned judge, "that interest, in this state, is a creature of statute, and regulated thereby; that it is only recoverable, in the absence of contract, in cases enumerated in the statute, and that damages to property arising from a wrong or negligence of the defendants is not one of the enumerated cases." This could not come under the last clause of the instruction. It is not for damage to property. It is for the wrongful detention of money belonging to plaintiffs. It is clearly distinguishable from *Denver etc. R. R. Co.* v. *Conway,* 8 Col. 1, 54 Am. Rep. 537, and *Hawley* v. *Barker,* 5 Col. 118. There does not appear to have been any decision in this state directly on the question presented. The same statute has been construed in Illinois (from which state it was taken) as allowing interest

in this class of cases from the time of the conversion, and there
has been an unbroken line of decisions in that state from
Bradley v. *Geiselman*, 22 Ill. 494, to *Illinois Cent. R. R. Co.* v.
Cobb, 72 Ill. 148, in which it is said, reviewing the decisions:
"The doctrine established by these authorities is, where property has been wrongfully taken or converted into money, and
an action of trespass or trover may be maintained, interest
may properly be recovered. And this is based upon the statute which authorizes interest when there has been an unreasonable and vexatious delay of payment. There can be no
difference between the delay of payment of a money demand
and one where property has been wrongfully taken, or taken
and converted into money or its equivalent. The two rest
upon the same principle." The rule is, that when the statute
of another state is adopted, the construction of the statute in
that state is also adopted, and remains the true construction
until authoritatively construed by the courts of the state adopt-
ing it. The general rule in trover is, that the damages should
embrace the value of the property at the time of the conversion, with interest up to the time of judgment; and this rule
has been followed in almost if not all the states, and seems
right on principle. But our statute does not seem to have
received the same construction here as in the state of Illinois.
While in that state it has been put plainly and squarely as
interest under the statute, in our state, damage for the detention of the money equal to the legal interest upon the value of
the chattels converted from the time of the conversion has
been allowed, not as interest, but as damage: *Machette* v
Wanless, 2 Col. 170; *Hanauer* v. *Bartels*, 2 Col. 514; *Tucker* v
Parks, 7 Col. 62.

We think the court erred in its instructions to the jury on
this point. They should have been instructed to add to the
amount found as the value of the ore, as further damage, a
sum equal to legal interest on the same from the time of the
conversion. For the errors in assessing the damage, the case
should be reversed, and remanded for a new trial, in accordance with the views herein expressed.

RICHMOND, C., and PATTISON, C., concurred.

By COURT. For the reasons stated in the foregoing opinion,
the judgment is reversed.

_____

WITNESSES — IMPEACHMENT OF. — As to the impeachment of witnesses by
prior contradictory statements, see note to *Allen* v. *State*, 73 Am. Dec. 762–
770; *Allen* v. *Harrison*, 30 Vt. 219; 73 Am. Dec. 302, and note. The proper

foundation having been laid, a witness may be impeached by prior contra-dictory statements: *State* v. *Barrett*, 40 Minn. 66; *Stayner* v. *Joyce*, 120 Ind. 99. But a party cannot impeach his own witness by prior contradictory statements made by him, unless such witness is one whom the law obliges him to call: *Hildreth* v. *Aldrich*, 15 R. I. 163; nor can a witness be impeached by prior statements made by him, which statements are not inconsistent with his testimony on the trial: *Cotton* v. *State*, 87 Ala. 75. So for the pur-pose of discrediting a witness. it is improper to ask him, on cross-examina-tion, whether he had not taken the "iron-clad oath" for the purpose of holding office in reconstruction times, and if he had not, during the rebellion, voluntarily entered the confederacy, and had not, as a minister of the Gospel, prayed for the success of the confederacy: *Moore* v. *Moore*, 73 Tex. 382.

AGENCY — DECLARATIONS OF AGENT. — An agent's authority cannot be shown by his own declarations: *Baltimore etc. Ass'n* v. *Post*, 122 Pa. St. 579; 9 Am. St. Rep. 147, and note; *Mitchum* v. *Dunlap*, 98 Mo. 418. But an agent may testify as to the extent of his authority: *Phœnix Ins. Co.* v. *Cope-land*, 86 Ala. 551.

TROVER — PLAINTIFF'S TITLE. — Plaintiff's right to recover in an action of trover is not affected by defendant's plea averring title in a third person with whom he has no privity: *Harker* v. *Dement*, 9 Gill, 7; 52 Am. Dec. 670, and note; *Capt* v. *Stubbs*, 68 Tex. 222. One in actual occupation of land may maintain trespass against any one except the real owner, or one having the right of possession: *Nickerson* v. *Thacher*, 146 Mass. 609. In trespass to try title, a joint owner may recover against a stranger, though in his complaint he alleges exclusive ownership of the realty; and defendant cannot show that plaintiff owns the property in common with others, where defendant is not one of the joint owners, and does not claim title from any of them: *Gaither* v. *Hanrick*, 69 Tex. 92. In trespass, trover, or replevin for trees severed or coal mined from unoccupied lands by a trespasser, or by one not claiming title in good faith, the plaintiff may show his title to the land, and defend-ant may offer evidence tending to prove title in a stranger, the object of such evidence being, not to determine the legal title, but who is entitled to possession of the personalty: *Busch* v. *Nester*, 70 Mich. 525.

CONVERSION. — Purchasing personalty from one who has no right to sell, or who has himself previously converted such property to his use, is conver-sion for which trover will lie: *Velsian* v. *Lewis*, 15 Or. 539; 3 Am. St. Rep. 184, and note.

CONVERSION — MEASURE OF DAMAGES. — In an action against a sheriff for personalty wrongfully seised and sold, the measure of damages is the actual value of the personalty, with interest: *Russell* v. *Huiskamp*, 77 Iowa, 728.

CONVERSION — MEASURE OF DAMAGES. — In an action for the value of timber cut and carried away from plaintiff's land, if defendant was not a willful trespasser, the measure of damages is the value of the timber at the time when taken, that is, while it was still standing uncut upon the land: *King* v. *Merriman*, 38 Minn. 47; *Hoxsie* v. *Empire L. Co.*, 41 Id. 548; *Whitney* v. *Huntington*, 37 Id. 197. But one who willfully goes upon another's land, and cuts grass and makes hay, converting it to his own use, is a trespasser, even up to the conversion of the hay; and the measure of damages, in an action of trover for the value of the hay converted, is the value of the hay at the time of its conversion, not the value of the grass while it was standing: *Acrea* v. *Brayton*, 75 Iowa, 719.

DEEDS — PAROL EVIDENCE TO VARY: See note to *Finlayson* v. *Finlayson*, 11 Am. St. Rep. 844, 845.

WALTON v. FIRST NATIONAL BANK.

[13 COLORADO, 265.]

FRAUDULENT CONVEYANCE. — CONFESSION OF JUDGMENT by a failing debtor
in favor of a creditor, with the agreement that the judgment is not to be
made public by being recorded until that is necessary to protect the
interests of such creditor, is fraudulent and void as to the remaining
creditors of the debtor, and will be set aside on their application.

EVIDENCE — DECLARATIONS OF CONFEDERATES IN FRAUD ADMISSIBLE AGAINST
EACH OTHER. — Where a confession of judgment is signed by a failing
debtor in favor of a creditor, under an agreement that such judgment
shall not be recorded unless necessary to protect the creditor, thus
enabling the debtor to obtain a fictitious credit, any declarations or
representations made afterwards by such debtor in obtaining credit are
admissible as against the judgment creditor for the purpose of setting
aside the judgment as fraudulent towards other creditors.

APPEAL from a judgment declaring void, as to other creditors, a judgment by confession, by a debtor in failing circumstances, in favor of a certain creditor.

Hudson and Slaymaker, for the appellants.

Charles E. Gast, for the appellee.

RICHMOND, C. Assignments of error are to the admitting
of evidence, over the objections of defendant, of John H. Werkheiser, to conversations had by him with defendant Howard
P. Walton, to the effect that the indebtedness due his brother
was only six thousand dollars on book-account, for which his
brother held no security, and would not press him, and that
the judgment of the court is at variance with the evidence in
the case and contrary to law.

The basis of the objections to the testimony of Werkheiser
is, that there was no privity existing between Howard P.
Walton and E. T. Walton, as agent, personally or otherwise.

By the complaint and answer the representations of Howard
P. Walton were directly put in issue. In the complaint it is
averred that he stated that E. T. Walton's claim against him
amounted to six thousand dollars, but that he had no security
for the same, and would not press it. E. T. Walton, in his
answer, denies that the plaintiff was misled or deceived by
any act or word of his, or of said Howard P. Walton, with
respect to the said confession of judgment. This, it appears,
makes an issue as to what representations were made by Howard P. Walton concerning the then existing security, to wit,
the confession of judgment of June 19, 1883. It appears that
the relations existing between Howard P. Walton and E. T.

Walton were not only that of debtor and creditor, but Howard
P. Walton was intrusted by his brother to represent him, so-
far as the indebtedness was concerned, and his future actions
relative to the security which it was agreed should be given.
He was left the sole judge of the necessities that might arise
between his brother and his other creditors, and if he personally believed himself able to stem the current of financial
disaster, this confession of judgment was not to be made public by being placed upon the record.   Indeed, he was the sole
judge of the time when the confession of judgment should be
filed and execution issued.   E. T. Walton admits that he
agreed with his brother to hold the confession of judgment
until such time as it would be necessary to enter it to protect
his interests.   Howard P. Walton was to keep the attorney
advised, from time to time, as to the condition of his affairs.
The attorney had no authority or instructions to investigate,
but any insight he obtained of the business condition of Howard P. Walton was through his voluntary admissions or statements; and I am inclined to think that, so far as the question
of securing the indebtedness from Howard P. Walton to E. T.
Walton is concerned, E. T. Walton made his brother, Howard
P. Walton, his representative to that extent, and for the purpose of carrying out the agreement of June 1, 1883.   He had
made and executed a confession of judgment, passed it to the
attorney, who had instructions to keep the same from the public, and only use it in case of absolute emergency.   Therefore,
by the specific denial above referred to, and the circumstances
as they appear in the testimony, I am clearly of the opinion
that the evidence of Werkheiser was admissible as tending to
establish the collusion in the fraud averred by the plaintiff,
to wit, the undue preference, the secrecy of the security, and
the fraudulent prejudice of other creditors.

It is said by Mr. Justice Washington, in delivering the opinion of the court in *American Fur Co.* v. *United States*, 2 Pet.
365, that, "where two or more persons are associated together
for the same illegal purpose, any act or declaration of one of
the parties, in reference to the common object, and forming a
part of the *res gestæ*, may be given in evidence against the
others."

The effect of the arrangement between the Waltons was to
place Howard P. Walton in such a condition that he could
obtain credit and standing with other individuals, and that
E. T. Walton could at any time, by filing his confession of

judgment, protect himself to the prejudice of those who by his own conduct had been induced to give credit to his brother Howard. In other words, he was in a position at any moment, when other creditors were pressing for payment of their claims, to absorb the entire assets, and thus deprive other creditors of any part whereby they could obtain satisfation of any judgment they might secure. Should his brother's affairs turn so as to necessitate prompt action, he would be in a position to enforce his securities for all moneys advanced, and for which he had become liable. The effect of the combination was, that no other creditor, however diligent he might be, however honest or old his claim might be, could have access to any of the property of Howard P. Walton, to the detriment of E. T. Walton, and, the evidence showing the existence of the confession of judgment, the agreement to keep it from the public was, in my opinion, sufficient to establish a confederation between the two which would admit the acts and declarations of one against the other: *Cuyler* v. *McCartney*, 40 N. Y. 221.

Now, as to the findings of the court in regard to the alleged insolvency of Howard P. Walton. By insolvency is meant an inability to fulfill one's obligations according to his undertaking, and general inability to answer in court for all of one's liabilities existing and capable of being enforced; not an absolute inability to pay at some future time, upon a settlement and ending up of a trade, but as not being in condition to pay one's debts in the ordinary course, as persons carrying on trade usually do. If, upon taking a reasonable view of the situation, as appears from the evidence in this case, it could fairly be seen that Howard P. Walton was able, not only to ultimately pay his debts, but to at once recover from the temporary embarrassments and arrangements of his business by a proper application of his means, and could carry on his business and meet his engagements in the ordinary course, and as persons in the same business usually do, he would properly be called solvent. But the testimoncy does not warrant this conclusion. If his inability to pay had been the result of a crisis or peculiar stringency in the monetary affairs of the country, by which he was cut off temporarily from resources upon which he was accustomed to rely, and upon which traders in like circumstances were accustomed to rely, the effect would be the same on the general question of insolvency. It is extremely difficult, if not impracticable, to give a definition of

insolvency that shall be found applicable to all classes of
persons. It is not, indeed, the business of practical jurisprudence to give definitions or lay down abstract propositions, but
to give the rule applicable to the facts proved, even if the abstract rule for the class be the same. The kind and degree
of evidence to establish insolvency would be very different in
the case of a merchant from that requisite in the case of a
farmer. The evidence which would satisfy a jury or a court
of the insolvency of the former might wholly fail to convince
them of that of the latter. It was necessary, in this particular case, for the court to determine the question of insolvency,
and from the evidence the court concluded that he was insolvent at the time referred to; and I am of the opinion that this
finding of the court should not be disturbed, according to the
rule laid down in *Dickson* v. *Moffat*, 5 Col. 117.

The statements of E. T. Walton in his deposition warranted
the conclusion that the confession of judgment of March 25,
1884, was a renewal of the confession of judgment of June 19,
1883. This is what he says: "I afterwards loaned Howard P.
Walton an additional sum of fifteen hundred dollars; and as
this additional loan rendered the confession of judgment which
I had inaccurate as to amount, I let him have it with the
distinct understanding that he should keep Slaymaker advised of his affairs, so that such steps for securing the protection of my interests should be taken as might be required."

The main point, however, in this case is, Was the judgment
of March 25, 1884, void as to creditors? It is argued by appellee, and undoubtedly it was the conclusion of the court,
that this confession of judgment was but the continuation of
the agreement made in June, 1883, to wit, that the moneys
advanced by E. T. Walton should be ultimately embraced in
a confession of judgment, and that the judgment should not
be used or made public unless the situation, financially, of
Howard P. Walton became such as to necessitate prompt and
decisive action; in effect, that E. T. Walton should get control by the first execution of the assets of Howard P. Walton,
and but for the additional loan, or we might say the inac-
curacy of the amount, the first confession of judgment would
never have been changed, the second never given. If the case
had been tried to a jury, and the court had distinctly instructed the jury of the necessity of finding that this judgment was a part of the original transaction and agreement,
and the jury had so found from the evidence, I would be loath

to disturb the verdict; and as this court has determined that a trial by the court upon oral testimony before the judge is controlled by the same principles as a trial by jury, and that they will not disturb the verdict unless manifestly against the weight of the evidence, the findings of the court should not be disturbed in this case. The findings being correct, the judgment was justified. The theory, undoubtedly, of the court below was, and I think it correct, that this entire transaction between E. T. Walton and Howard P. Walton came within the lines of constructive fraud; that is, it was such an act or contract as, although not originating in any actual design or connivance to perpetrate a positive fraud or injury upon other persons, yet, by its tendency to deceive or mislead persons, it was equally reprehensible with positive fraud, and therefore prohibited by law as being equivalent to acts or contracts done *malo animo.*

It is an undoubted fact that had the bank, through its agent, been advised, or in a position to learn, that Howard P. Walton had given a confession of judgment to his brother, to be used when circumstances, in the opinion of himself or the attorney, were such as to necessitate prompt action for his protection, the bank would not have extended the loan evidenced by the note sued on, but on the contrary, good business sense would have suggested the propriety of at once securing the existing indebtedness to the bank; and had it done so, it would then have been confronted by the confession of judgment of June 19, 1883, in the hands of the attorney, ready to be filed at the first warning. The evidence certainly justifies the conclusion that by means of the suppression, or rather by means of the secrecy concerning the security, the facts that it was known only to three individuals, was not known to the bank, nor could it be learned by inquiry, enabled Howard P. Walton to obtain a credit and standing to which he was not entitled.

Counsel for appellant rely on the case of *Smith* v. *Craft*, 17 Fed. Rep. 705. In that case there was an oral promise by a party borrowing from a bank "that he would protect the bank if anything ever occurred by which he was not able to pay his debts; that if he met with losses, he would secure the bank if the bank would loan him money from time to time." There was no security given at the time he obtained the loan, or promise to keep the same secret; and, as the court remarked, "such promise, especially when made in the general terms employed in this instance, has no legal force." Besides, at the time the credit was given, it appears that "the debtor was doing an apparently prosperous business, though largely on credit, and advances were made to him without a belief, or imperative reason for the belief, that he was, or was likely to become, insolvent." But in that case the court was careful to say: "I do not doubt that a promise to secure or to prefer a creditor, made at the time the credit is given, may be fraudulent, but it must be when a fraud is intended, or when the circumstances within the knowledge of the creditor are such that he must know that injury to others will probably result."

It will readily be observed how widely different were the circumstances in the case of *Smith* v. *Craft, supra,* from those presented by this appeal. The circumstances of this case, as they appear in evidence under the pleadings, justify the belief that this agreement to prefer was with the distinct knowledge that Howard P. Walton's circumstances were such as ultimately would necessitate action upon the confession of judgment. He went into business on borrowed capital furnished by his brother, and from first to last was continually appealing to his brother for indorsements or assistance. He even solicited his brother's indorsement of the note given to the bank for four thousand dollars. The solicitude manifest from E. T. Walton's deposition and letters; his continued appeals to his brother that he should protect him; that he should have the first opportunity of proceeding against the assets, and no positive time of payment agreed upon, — is conclusive to the mind that he was personally familiar with the insolvent condition of his brother, and knew of his indebtedness to other parties.

It is not to be understood from this opinion that, in the absence of statutory restriction, a debtor may not, under ordinary circumstances, lawfully give preference to one creditor over others; nor that it is a badge of fraud for a creditor to secure such preference. The transaction between the Waltons in this case is deemed fraudulent, not merely on the ground that E. T. Walton continued to give credit and make advances to his brother when he knew him to be insolvent; for he had a right to trust his brother to any extent, in the ordinary course of business, without imperiling his legal right to secure his debt. Neither is the transaction to be deemed fraudulent merely on the ground that he took a confession of judgment for his debt; for he had a right, in the ordinary course of business, to receive a confession of judgment on account of a lawful debt at any time. But the fraudulent character of the transaction consisted in appellant's taking the security he did under an agreement that it should be kept from the public,— that is, not entered of record so long as the collection of appellant's debt was not thereby imperiled; thus deliberately giving his brother a fictitious financial standing, in his known failing circumstances, and placing him in a position to perpetrate fraud by obtaining credit, as in case of appellee, which would otherwise be withheld, while appellant held the confession of judgment with which to protect himself when others had trusted his brother, and were helpless. Howard Walton, relying upon his brother's agreement not to make the confession of judgment public, could with great assurance make the fraudulent representations to the cashier of the bank that his brother had no security, and was not pressing him. Without such agreement he would feel that judgment was likely to be entered against him at any time, and this would have a tendency to restrain him in his dealings with others. Confessions of judgment are intended to be entered of record in the court. Without such entry, a confession of judgment is only an acknowledgment of a debt, and while the withholding of a confession from the record for a considerable length of time may not be necessarily fraudulent, an agreement between the party giving and the party receiving such an instrument that it shall be kept from the public, or that it shall not be entered of record for an unreasonable or indefinite time, is one of the strongest badges of fraud.

It is proper to be observed that the procedure for entering judgment by confession has been repealed since the time of the transactions referred to in this opinion. It follows, from the above conclusions, that the judgment should be affirmed.

By COURT. For the reasons stated in the foregoing opinion the judgment is affirmed. ____

DEBTOR AND CREDITORS. — Secret securities given and secret preferences made by an insolvent debtor to one of his creditors are ordinarily void as to the other creditors: *Blasdel* v. *Fowle*, 120 Mass. 447; 21 Am. Rep. 533; *Bank of Commerce* v. *Hoeber*, 88 Mo. 37; 57 Am. Rep. 359, and note 363–374; *O'Shea* v. *Collier etc. Co.*, 42 Mo. 397; 97 Am. Dec. 332.

DECLARATIONS OF CONSPIRATORS. — Declarations of a co-conspirator made in furtherance of the common design are admissible against his co-conspirators: *Spies* v. *People*, 122 Ill. 1; 3 Am. St. Rep. 320, and note 487–489; *State* v. *Glidden*, 55 Conn. 46; 3 Am. St. Rep. 23, and note.

JACKSON v. KIEL.

[13 COLORADO, 378.]

NUISANCE — OBSTRUCTING STREET — MEASURE OF DAMAGES. — An unauthorized and complete obstruction of a street or highway by a railway company, in such manner as to prevent ingress and egress by a landowner to and from his premises by means of vehicles, if long continued, is a public nuisance, for which the land-owner may recover damages for the special and peculiar injury not suffered in common with the general public, to the extent of the difference in rental value occasioned by the nuisance, and, under some circumstances, the recovery may take a wider scope.

ACTION by Kiel against Jackson, as receiver of the Denver and Rio Grande Railway Company, to recover damages for the obstruction of a street. A general demurrer to the complaint was overruled. Verdict and judgment for plaintiff, and defendant appeals.

Wolcott and Vaile, for the appellant.

Browne and Putnam, for the appellee.

HELM, C. J.　We shall decline to follow counsel into a discussion of the question whether plaintiff has, and has sufficiently pleaded, a right to recover for injuries to his property occasioned by the construction and operation of the railway mentioned through the intersection of Tenth and Wyncoop streets. The complaint is not artificially worded, but it appears to have been framed upon the theory of an unlawful obstruction or abatable public nuisance, whereby plaintiff suffered a special and peculiar private injury; and we think enough facts are averred in support of this cause of action to justify the court in overruling the general demurrer interposed by defendant.

Both the pleading and evidence show clearly that the ingress and egress to and from plaintiff's property by vehicles was had solely by means of the intersection of Wyncoop Street with Tenth, — the street upon which his lot fronts. In no different way, circuitous or otherwise, could his premises be thus reached. The right to a free use of this space of street intersection for purposes of ingress and egress was therefore as closely identified with his lot, and interference therewith was as peculiar and personal an injury, as if the obstruction had prevented access from his lot to the street immediately adjacent thereto. A complete blockade of Tenth Street at this point would produce damage to his property hardly less direct and serious than would the vacation and closing up of this street in front of his lot.

It appears beyond question that defendant kept a large number of railway cars on Wyncoop Street, across the space of its intersection with Tenth; that, during the entire period covered by the complaint, the obstruction thus created rendered it absolutely impossible for vehicles of any kind to reach plaintiff's premises. The completeness of the obstruction is clearly shown by the testimony of defendant's own witness, the general yard-master of the railway company, who says, among other things: "We have never kept Tenth open, or recognized it as a street." It also, in like manner, appears that, in consequence of this obstruction, plaintiff was seriously damaged by the depreciation of the rents received for his premises.

Tenth Street was a public highway, and an unauthorized obstruction thereof, especially if long continued, would constitute a public nuisance. If we assume that the right of way along Wyncoop Street at this point was lawfully obtained, in the first instance, for the purpose of constructing and operating the railway, such right did not authorize the complete blockade of the crossing. Defendant could not absolutely destroy, for a considerable period, the usefulness of this part of Tenth Street for the usual street purposes, under any license or authority appearing in the record before us. He was bound to so use the right of way obtained as not to permanently prevent the passage of vehicles, and the employment of the street in other ordinary uses. Plaintiff, of course, could not recover for any general inconvenience thus occasioned which he may have suffered in common with the general public; but for the special and peculiar injury shown in this case he was doubtless entitled to compensation.

Appellant has no cause to complain of the measure of damages recognized in the charge to the jury. The difference in rental value occasioned by the nuisance or obstruction is the rule usually adopted in such cases, though, under proper circumstances, the recovery may take a wider scope. The right to recover, if established, includes "the depreciation of rental value, by the difference, in other words, between the rental value free from the effects of the nuisance and subject to it"; 3 Sutherland on Damages, 414, and cases.

The ruling of the court below, from which the first appeal

was prosecuted, and its final judgment, from which the second appeal was taken, are both affirmed.

NUISANCE — OBSTRUCTING STREET OR HIGHWAY. — Railway companies have no right to unnecessarily obstruct streets by letting their cars stand across them; nor in any manner interfere with streets by doing an unauthorized act with respect thereto: Note to *Callahan* v. *Gilman*, 1 Am. St. Rep. 843; *Cleveland etc. R'y Co.* v. *Wynant*, 114 Ind. 525; 5 Am. St. Rep. 644; *Palatka etc. R. R. Co.* v. *State*, 23 Fla. 546; 11 Am. St. Rep. 395; *County of Stearns* v. *St. Cloud etc. R. R. Co.*, 36 Minn. 425. The obstruction of streets by railroad cars is not excused by the fact that it was necessary for the carrying on of the company's business, although the obstruction is only occasional: *State* v. *Chicago etc. R'y Co.*, 77 Iowa, 442. Though the legislature may authorize a railroad company to lay its tracks in a public street, still, in the absence of such legislative grant to the company, it has no right to appropriate and use a street for the purpose of laying the tracks of its trunk line, switches, side-tracks, or branches: *Pennsylvania R. R. Co.'s Appeal*, 115 Pa. St. 514. But a railroad company, authorized to construct and operate its line upon a public highway, is not guilty of a nuisance, so long as it does not interfere with and obstruct the free and comfortable use of the highway by the general public: *People* v. *Park etc. R. R. Co.*, 76 Cal. 156.

OBSTRUCTION OF STREET OR HIGHWAY. — Keeping or storing a wagon in the public street perpetually or habitually is a nuisance: *Cohen* v. *New York*, 113 N. Y. 532; 10 Am. St. Rep. 506. Any obstruction materially interfering with the free use of a street or sidewalk in a thickly populated city is a nuisance: *State* v. *Berdetta*, 73 Ind. 185; 38 Am. Rep. 117, and note. But a tradesman may temporarily obstruct a street, when it becomes necessary in his business operations; yet his temporary obstruction of the street must be reasonable with reference to the rights of the general public: *Callahan* v. *Gilman*, 107 N. Y. 360; 1 Am. St. Rep. 843, and note. Where a public road has been laid across certain lands by proper authority, and has been accepted and traveled by the public for more than ten years, the owner of the fee will be guilty of a nuisance if he obstructs or fences up the road: *Langdon* v. *State*, 23 Neb. 509.

ACTION BY PRIVATE PERSON FOR OBSTRUCTION OF HIGHWAY. — A nuisance which actually obstructs public travel may be abated by any one who is specially injured thereby: *Ely* v. *Parsons*, 55 Conn. 83; *Milarkey* v. *Foster*, 6 Or. 378; 25 Am. Rep. 531, and note; *Trustees etc. Canal* v. *Spears*, 16 Ind. 441; 79 Am. Dec. 444; *Wood* v. *Mears*, 12 Ind. 515; 74 Am. Dec. 222. But in an action by a private person, because of an obstruction in a public highway claimed to be injurious to his property, the character of the injury must be specifically averred in the complaint: *Thelan* v. *Farmer*, 36 Minn. 225. The obstruction of a highway, however, is not a ground of an action by a private person when he has sustained no special damage peculiar to himself, not suffered by the community generally: *Houck* v. *Wachter*, 34 Md. 265; 6 Am. Rep. 332; *Dawson* v. *St. Paul F. Ins. Co.*, 15 Minn. 136; 2 Am. Rep. 109.

NUISANCE — MEASURE OF DAMAGES. — Where a nuisance is not necessarily a permanent one, but may be abated at any time by defendants, the measure of damages is the depreciation in the rental value of the property while the nuisance existed: *Shively* v. *Cedar Rapids etc. R'y Co.*, 74 Iowa, 169; 7 Am. St. Rep. 471, and note.

JENNINGS *v.* FIRST NATIONAL BANK.

[13 COLORADO, 417.]

NEGOTIABLE INSTRUMENTS. — A promissory note containing a condition stating that the consideration therein is "part payment of rent of certain pasture fields," and that the note shall not be paid unless the maker has the use of the premises, is neither negotiable at common law nor under the Colorado statute.

NEGOTIABLE INSTRUMENTS. — PROOF BY ASSIGNEE OF NON-NEGOTIABLE NOTE NECESSARY TO ENABLE HIM TO RECOVER. — The assignee of a non-negotiable note payable on a contingency to recover thereon must prove his ownership of the note, that it is supported by a consideration, and that the contingency has happened.

ERROR IN OVERRULING MOTION FOR NONSUIT IS WAIVED by evidence offered by defendant in his own behalf which supplies the defect existing in plaintiff's proofs.

PLEADING AND PRACTICE. — QUESTION AS TO ILLEGALITY OF CONSIDERATION of a note sued upon cannot be raised for the first time on appeal.

Campbell and McIntyre, and Cage and Hobson, for the appellants.

J. L. Williams and H. B. O'Reilly, for the appellee.

PATTISON, C. This action was begun before a justice of the peace. November 19, 1885, judgment was recovered by appellee, from which an appeal was taken to the county court January 25, 1886, the cause was tried by the court without a jury, and judgment rendered in favor of appellee for the sum of $170, with costs. From that judgment this appeal was taken.

Upon the trial, appellee introduced in evidence a written instrument, of which the following is a copy: —

$200.   COLORADO SPRINGS, COLORADO, May 21, 1885.

On October 1st, after date, I promise to pay to the order of Obediah P. Hopkins two hundred dollars, at the El Paso County Bank, Colorado Springs, Colorado, for value received. Negotiable and payable without defalcation or discount, with interest from June 1, 1885, at the rate of ten per cent per annum until paid. This note is given for part payment of rent of certain pasture fields, and is not to be paid unless I have the use of said premises, in accordance with a certain lease and agreement executed by said Hopkins and myself, of even date herewith.

[Signed]   "JOHN JENNINGS.

"MARY A. JENNINGS."

Indorsed: "OBEDIAH HOPKINS."

After the introduction of this instrument, appellee rested its case, and thereupon the defendants moved for a judgment of nonsuit. The motion was overruled. The ruling of the court upon this motion is the first error assigned.

The grounds upon which the motion for nonsuit was based are not disclosed by the record. It appears, however, from the record, that the motion was overruled after "argument by the counsel for the respective parties." Assuming that the reasons urged in support of the motion here were assigned by counsel in the court below, when the motion was made, the first question presented for consideration is, whether the court erred in overruling the motion. The propositions discussed by appellants' counsel are: 1. That the instrument was not negotiable at common law, nor assignable by indorsement, under the provisions of the statute of this state; and 2. That the instrument being non-negotiable, it was incumbent upon the plaintiff to prove its ownership of the instrument, and that there was a consideration to sustain it. In other words, the position of appellants' counsel is, that appellee should have proven that it was the equitable assignee of the instrument in question, and also that the amount named therein was actually due, because appellants had had the use of the premises as provided by the lease therein mentioned.

The first question, therefore, to be considered is, whether the instrument above set forth is negotiable at common law or under the statute of this state. The instrument is in form a promissory note with a condition added. By the terms of the condition the consideration of the note is declared to be "part payment of rent of certain pasture fields," and that it shall not be paid unless the makers have the use of the premises. This condition must be taken as a part of the note. The nature of the promise to pay must be determined by the construction of the instrument as a whole. Considered as an entirety, it is clear that appellants' liability was dependent upon a contingency. The promise was therefore conditional. It could not be enforced unless it affirmatively appeared that the condition had been performed. The contingency was uncertain, and might never happen. At the time the instrument was made, therefore, no promise or agreement was entered into by the makers that they would pay the sum of two hundred dollars unconditionally and in any event. That an instrument of this nature is not negotiable at common law is well settled: 1

Randolph on Commercial Paper, sec. 7; 1 Daniel on Negotiable Instruments, sec. 41.

Was this instrtment negotiable under the statute of this state? Section 3 of that statute (Gen. Stats., c. 9) provides that "all promissory notes, bonds, due-bills, and other instruments in writing, made by any person, whereby such person promises or agrees to pay any sum of money . . . . to any other person or persons, shall be taken to be due and payable to the person or persons to whom the said note, bond, bill, or other instrument in writing is made." Section 4 provides that "any such note, bill, bond, or other instrument in writing, made payable to any person or persons, shall be assignable by indorsement thereon, ... in the same manner as bills of exchange."

These sections of the statute have been construed by this court. In *Carnahan* v. *Pell*, 4 Col. 190, it is held that "if an instrument, whether it calls for money or property, be not payable unconditionally, and at all events, it is not negotiable under the statute": *Eldred* v. *Malloy*, 2 Col. 320; 20 Am. Rep. 752. The case of *Kiskadden* v. *Allen*, 7 Col. 206, cited by appellee's counsel, does not conflict with this doctrine. The promise contained in the note sued upon in that case was not conditional. The money was to become due and payable in any event.

The statute cited is a substantial transcript of that of the state of Illinois relating to the same subject. The question presented by this case has been discussed and passed upon in numerous cases in that state. In the case of *Kingsbury* v. *Wall*, 68 Ill. 311, it is held that "it is indispensable that all bills of exchange or promissory notes, to be assignable under our statute or at common law, must be certainly payable, and not dependant on any contingency, either as to the event, or the fund out of which payment is to be made, or the parties by or to whom payment is to be made." In the case of *Baird* v. *Underwood*, 74 Ill. 176, the following instrument was held not to be negotiable:—

"ST. CHARLES, November 22, 1871.

"Six months after date I promise to pay to the order of Louis Klink the sum of $120, for value received, on condition said amount is not provided for as agreed by J. Updike.

"C. H. UNDERWOOD."

In the case of *White* v. *Smith*, 77 Ill. 351, 20 Am. Rep. 251, it is held that "to constitute a valid promissory note, it must be payable at some time or other, though it may be uncertain when that time will come. When payable on a contingency, it makes no difference that the contingency does in fact happen afterwards, on which the payment is to become absolute; for its character as a promissory note cannot depend upon future events, but solely upon its character when executed": *Husband* v. *Epling*, 81 Ill. 172; 25 Am. Rep. 273.

In the light of these authorities, it is clear that this instrument was not negotiable. It was therefore not assignable by indorsement. It follows that appellee should have proven that it was the owner of the claim of which the instrument constituted the evidence, and that it was supported by a consideration. The lease, therefore, should have been introduced in evidence by the appellee, and should have been supplemented by proof of appellants' possession under it, and their use of the premises in accordance with its provisions. In the absence of such proof, appellants were entitled to judgment of nonsuit. The overruling of the motion, therefore, was error, for which the judgment should be reversed, if defendants' counsel had elected to stand by his motion.

When the motion for nonsuit had been overruled, appellants sought to establish an affirmative defense, by the introduction of evidence to show that they had not had the use of the premises in accordance with the terms of the lease, and that the note, on that account, was not due. The agreement of lease referred to in the note was introduced by them, and testimony given tending to prove that certain promises and agreements had not been performed by the lessor. It appeared, however, that they entered into possession of the premises under the lease, and that they were in possession at the time the trial was had. When they rested, the plaintiff introduced evidence which tended to establish all the facts essential to recovery. No objection was made by appellants' counsel. It was shown that the instrument sued upon had been bought for a valuable consideration by appellee. The evidence also tended to prove that the covenants and agreements contained in the lease had been substantially performed. Upon this issue, it cannot be said that the judgment was either contrary to the evidence or to the law. It has been held by this court that error in overruling a defendant's motion for a nonsuit is obviated by evidence, offered in his own behalf, which supplies the defect existing in plaintiff's proofs: *Denver etc. R'y Co.* v. *Henderson*, 10 Col. 1. It has also been held that "where a motion for a nonsuit was improperly denied, but the defendant then introduced testimony enabling the plaintiff to supply the defect in his case, that defendant thereby waived the objection": *Smith* v. *Compton*, 6 Cal. 24

In the case at bar, the omission of plaintiff to prove the execution of the lease, and possession under it, was supplied by appellants, who introduced the instrument as the foundation of their affirmative defense. It is true that the parol testimony offered by appellants tended to prove that the condition had not been performed. Nevertheless, when they rested, appellee was permitted, without objection, to introduce evidence in rebuttal, and to supply defects in its case by showing the performance of the contract, and that the money claimed was therefore due and payable. It is clear that, under the authorities cited, the error in overruling the motion for a nonsuit was waived, and cannot now be urged in this court.

It is argued by counsel for appellants that the judgment should be reversed for the reason that the consideration of the note sued upon was illegal, because the lease in question was a violation of the act of Congress of February 25, 1885, entitled "An act to prevent unlawful occupancy of public lands": 23 U. S. Stats. 321.

This question seems to be presented for the first time in this court. The lease claimed to be illegal was introduced by appellants themselves. Its illegality was not urged in the court below, and is not assigned for error in this court. It follows that the question is not before the court, and cannot be considered.

The judgment should be affirmed.

REED, C., and RICHMOND, C., concurred.

By COURT.—For the reasons stated in the foregoing opinion, the judgment is affirmed.

———

NEGOTIABLE INSTRUMENTS. — Commercial paper, to be negotiable, must be certain, unconditional, and not contingent: *Citizens' Nat. Bank* v. *Piollet,* 126 Pa. St. 194; 12 Am. St. Rep. 860, and note; *Chandler* v. *Carey,* 64 Mich. 237; 8 Am. St. Rep. 814, and note.

NOTE PAYABLE UPON A CERTAIN CONTINGENCY cannot be recovered upon without proof of the happening of such contingency: *Chandler* v. *Carey,* 64 Mich. 237; 8 Am. St. Rep. 814.

PROMISSORY NOTES. — An agreement to pay a certain sum of money on a certain date, with interest at seven per cent from date, and eight per cent after maturity, and five per cent attorney's fees, without relief from homestead valuation or appraisement laws, to which is added a waiver by the makers and indorsers of presentment, protest, and notice of protest and non-payment, with the right to extend time of payment, is not a negotiable promissory note: *Second Nat. Bank* v. *Wheeler*, 75 Mich. 546. Where one takes the assignment of a promissory note, agreeing to pay a certain sum therefor if he can use it, the subsequent use of the note renders him liable for the stipulated consideration, even though it does not appear that he received any money upon it: *Mitchell* v. *Hartlep*, 115 Ind. 374. A condition written upon the back of an instrument purporting to be a promissory note, which condition is referred to in the terms of the instrument, forms a part of the contract between the parties, and may cause the construction of the whole instrument to be other than a promissory note: *Ellett* v. *Eberts*, 74 Iowa, 597. An order to "pay four hundred dollars out of funds that may be due me as per our contract" is not absolute, but conditional; and the acceptor's liability depends upon the contingency that, according to the terms of the contract referred to, anything may be due the drawer thereon: *Gerow* v. *Riffe*, 29 W. Va. 462.

BOARD OF ALDERMEN OF DENVER *v.* DARROW.

[13 COLORADO, 460.]

OFFICE AND OFFICER — REMEDY OF OFFICER DISTURBED IN ENJOYMENT OF OFFICE. — Where a person in possession of the office of city alderman seeks to review proceedings taken by the board of aldermen which disturb him in the enjoyment of his office, his only remedy is by *certiorari*.

OFFICE AND OFFICERS — POWER OF COURTS TO REVIEW JUDICIAL ACTION OF CITY OFFICERS. — Though a board of aldermen is made by statute the sole judges of the election and qualifications of its members, still its action in ousting a member is judicial in its nature, and exercised in subordination and subject to the correctional supervision of the courts on review.

OFFICE AND OFFICERS — ALDERMAN CANNOT BE SUMMARILY REMOVED BY RESOLUTION. — Where a board of aldermen is by statute made the sole judges of the election and qualifications of its members, it cannot summarily remove from office by resolution, upon a charge of disqualification, and without notice, hearing, or investigation, one who has been duly elected, qualified, and inducted into office as an alderman.

CERTIORARI to review the action of the board of aldermen of the city of Denver in removing by resolution, and without notice or investigation, the appellee from the position of alderman and president of the board of aldermen of the city of Denver.

Isham White, for the appellants.

Decker and Yonley, for the appellee.

RICHMOND, C. The only question presented for our consideration by either party is: 1. The jurisdiction of the court; and 2. The legality of the action in ousting appellee out of his position as president of the board of aldermen, and amoving him from the office of alderman.

It is contended by appellant that appellee has mistaken his remedy in the prosecution of the writ of *certiorari;* that he should have proceeded by *quo warranto* against his successor in office. If title of one in possession of an office was to be tried, it is conceded *quo warranto* would be the appropriate remedy. But the relator in this case, being in possession of the office, seeks only a review of the proceedings taken by the board of aldermen which disturb him in the enjoyment of it. This can only be done by *certiorari: Bradshaw* v. *City Council of Camden,* 39 N. J. L. 416.

The further contention of appellant is, that, by statute, the board of aldermen are made the sole judges of the qualifications of its members, and that any action they may take in this particular is not a subject of review by the court. In other words, that they can proceed at any time to make or unmake aldermen, without their action being subject to review. "The unquestionable weight of authority in this country is, if an appeal be not given, or some specific mode of review provided, that the superior common-law courts will, on *certiorari,* examine the proceedings of municipal corporations, even although there be no statute giving this remedy; and if it be found that they have exceeded their chartered powers, or have not pursued those powers, or have not conformed to the requirements of the charter or law under which they have undertaken to act, such proceedings will be reversed and annulled. An aggrieved party is, in such case, entitled to a *certiorari ex debito justitiæ:* 2 Dillon on Municipal Corporations, sec. 926, and authorities cited.

Section 323 of the code (Gen. Stats. 1883) provides that "the writ may be granted, on application, by any court of this state, except a justice's, county, or mayor's court. The writ shall be granted in all cases where an inferior tribunal, board, or officer, exercising judicial functions, has exceeded the jurisdiction of such tribunal, board, or officer, and there is no appeal, nor, in the judgment of the court, any plain, speedy, and adequate remedy."

It is not disputed that the controversy between the board of aldermen and appellee was judicial in its nature; and it is conceded that the powers of the board were sufficient for the determination of all questions involved in the controversy. As these were judicial questions, we must regard the board itself as exercising judicial functions, and as exercising such functions in subordination and.subject to the supervision of the courts. It would be very unfortunate if an arbitrary, wanton, and illegal exercise of the powers conferred upon such body were beyond the remedial interposition of the courts.

In Illinois it is held that the common-law writ of *certiorari* may issue from the circuit court to all inferior tribunals and jurisdictions, in cases where they exceed their jurisdiction, or where they proceed illegally, and there is no appeal or other mode of directly reviewing their proceedings: *Miller* v. *Trustees of Schools*, 88 Ill. 27; *Commissioners* v. *Supervisors*, 27 Ill. 141; *Commissioners* v. *Harper*, 38 Ill. 105; *State* v. *Dowling*, 50 Mo. 136.

This disposes of the preliminary question, and the next inquiry is, To what extent can the court go in reviewing the proceedings?

Section 329 of the code (Gen. Stats. 1883) provides that "the review upon the writ shall not be extended further than to determine whether the inferior tribunal, board, or officer has regularly pursued the authority of such tribunal, board, or officer."

It is clear that the courts are confined to the question of jurisdiction, and the regularity of its exercise. To this extent, however, the review will be extended, notwithstanding the provision of section 3, article 2, of the charter of the city of Denver provides that "each board shall be the sole judge of the qualifications, election, and returns of its own members ": *St. Paul* v. *Marvin*, 16 Minn. 102; *Whitney* v. *Board of Delegates*, 14 Cal. 480; *Central Pac. R. R. Co.* v. *Placer Co.*, 43 Cal. 366; *Kendall* v. *Camden*, 47 N. J. L. 66; 54 Am. Rep. 117.

While power is vested in the courts by *certiorari* to review the proceedings of all inferior jurisdictions, to correct jurisdictional errors, they will not rejudge their judgments on the merits. The correctional power extends no further than to keep them within the limits of their jurisdiction, and to compel them to exercise it with regularity: *Chase* v. *Miller*, 41 Pa. St. 410; *Gibbons* v. *Sheppard*, Brightly's Election Cases, 539. In the case at bar, the superior court was not called upon, nor did it assume, to judge of the merits of the controversy between the board of aldermen and appellee, but merely to review the regularity of the proceedings of the board.

It is not necessary to look beyond the record in this case, and this brings us to the question of the legality of the action

of the board in setting aside and annulling the election of appellee on the 7th of April, 1885.

In support of the position assumed by appellant, our attention is called to the case of *Darrow* v. *People*, 8 Col. 417. It
is claimed by appellants' attorney that this opinion warranted
the proceedings taken by the board of aldermen, and that
their conduct in passing the resolution, and ousting appellee
from office, was in fact directed by the court; that the court,
having determined that they were the sole judges of the qualifications of the members of the board, practically determined
that their action was not the subject of review by any court;
that the manner and form of removing a person from the office
of alderman was absolutely and exclusively within the jurisdiction of the board of aldermen, without the power of review
by the courts; that the manner and form of their action could
not be reviewed. We do not so understand the opinion of
this court in that case. On the contrary, we think a careful
review of the opinion will sustain atogether a different position; for the court say, on page 423: "It often happens that
the particular fact which renders a party ineligible to hold a
given position is unknown to the public until long after his
election and induction into office. It is even true that sometimes such disability is not discovered by the candidate himself until he has for a considerable period been performing his
official duties. An obligation rests upon the council, when
the question is properly presented, to investigate the alleged
disability, and if it be proven, to oust the incumbent, though
his term of office be about to expire. There is a marked difference between canvassing the vote, and declaring the result
of such canvass, and investigating a charge of prior disqualification which may afterwards be presented. While the present counsel cannot perform the former duty, they are certainly
in a position to discharge the latter. If any rules or regulations are essential to a proper investigation of alleged dis-
qualifications of aldermen, the same may be supplied." This
language clearly implies that an investigation upon a charge
of prior disqualification was contemplated. It cannot be
claimed that the court intended, or even intimated, that one
who had been duly elected, duly qualified, duly inducted into
office as an alderman, could be summarily removed by resolution upon a charge of disqualification without notice, without hearing or investigation of any kind. The contrary is the
strict letter and spirit of the opinion, and in our judgment, is

in keeping with the majority of authorities upon this question.

It is admitted by the demurrer, and the record discloses the fact to be, that the introduction of this resolution, and its passage, was without any notice to appellee, and in opposition to his direct protest. That he was present when the resolution was passed argues nothing in support of the action of the board. He was present as a member of the board, and when so present, urged a postponement of any action, and asked an opportunity to be heard in opposition to the charges. It is merely recited in the resolution that he has confessed his disqualification for the office. How, when, where, to whom, does not appear. The mere recital does not prove the truth of the allegation. "Much is not proven because much has been said." Can it be said that the *ipse dixit* of one or more individuals to the effect that appellee had confessed that he was not a tax-payer within a year prior to his election to office is sufficient of itself to warrant his summary removal from office?

Not a single authority is produced on the part of appellants in support of this action by the board, and we are confident that not one can be produced. 1 Dillon on Municipal Corporations, secs. 245, 250, 253, 254, lays down these rules: "When the terms under which the power of amotion is to be exercised are prescribed, they must be pursued with strictness. Whether, if the power to expel or remove be given for certain causes, this excludes the right to exercise the power in any other case, will depend upon the intent of the legislature, to be gathered from a consideration of the whole charter or statute."

" Where an officer is appointed during pleasure, or where the power of removal is discretionary, the power to remove may be exercised without notice or hearing. But where the appointment is during good behavior, or where the removal can only be for certain specified causes, the power of removal cannot be exercised, unless there be a charge against the officer, notice to him of the accusation, and a hearing of the evidence in support of the charges, and an opportunity given to the party of making a defense. . . . . The proceeding, in all cases where the amotion is for cause, is adversary or judicial in its character; and if the organic law of the corporation is silent as to the mode of procedure, the substantial principles of the common law as to proceedings affecting private rights must be observed."

"1. The officer is entitled to a personal notice of the proceeding against him, and of the time when the trial body will meet. . . . . But it should contain the substantial fact that a proceeding to amove is intended. . . . . There must be a charge or charges against him specifically, stated with substantial certainty, and reasonable time and opportunity must be given to answer the charges and to produce his testimony; and he is also entitled to be heard and defended by counsel, and to cross-examine the witnesses, and to except to the proofs against him. If the charge be not denied, still it must, if not admitted, be examined and proved": *Mead* v. *Treasurer*, 36 Mich. 419; *Murdock* v. *Trustees*, 12 Pick. 244; *Page* v. *Hardin*, 8 B. Mon. 668; 2 Waterman on Corporations, p. 557, sec. 312; Angell and Ames on Corporations, sec. 429; *Field* v. *Commonwealth*, 32 Pa. St. 484; *Dullam* v. *Willson*, 53 Mich. 392; 51 Am. Rep. 128.

The line of authority is not by any means exhausted, but enough have been cited to show that the action of the board in this case cannot be upheld as a legal and proper exercise of the power conferred. The judgment should be affirmed.

Pattison, C., and Reed, C., concurred.

By Court. For the reasons stated in the foregoing opinion, the judgment is affirmed. ____

Jurisdiction of Law Courts to Review Proceedings of Bodies having Power to Judge of the Election and Qualifications of their Members. — A constitutional provision that each house of a legislature shall be the judges of the elections, returns, and qualifications of its own members is an exclusive grant of power, and constitutes each house the sole and ultimate tribunal to pass upon the qualifications of its own members: *People* v. *Mahaney*, 13 Mich. 481; *State* v. *Kempf*, 69 Wis. 470; 2 Am. St. Rep. 753; *State* v. *Gilmore*, 20 Kan. 551; 27 Am. Rep. 189-192. In the case last cited, the court said: "The constitution declares that 'each house shall be the judge of the elections, returns, and qualifications of its own members.' This is a grant of power, and constitutes each house the ultimate tribunal as to the qualifications of its own members. The two houses, acting conjointly, do not decide. Each house acts by itself and for itself, and from its decision there is no appeal, not even to the two houses; and this power is not exhausted when once it has been exercised, and a member admitted to his seat. It is a continuous power, and runs through the entire term. At any time and at all times during the term of office each house is empowered to pass upon the present qualifications of its own members. If it ousts a member, no court or other tribunal can reinstate him. If it refuses to oust a member, his seat is beyond judicial challenge. This grant of power is in its very nature exclusive, and it is necessary to preserve the entire independence of the two houses. Being a power exclusively vested in it, it cannot be granted away or transferred to any other tribunal or officer. It may appoint a committee to examine and report, but the decision must be by the house itself.

It, and it alone, can remove.   Perhaps, also, it might delegate to a judge or other officer, outside its own body, power to examine and report upon the qualifications of one of its members, but neither it nor the two houses together can abridge the power vested in each house separately of a final decision as to the qualifications of one of its members, or transfer that power to any other tribunal or officer."   "It is apparent that there is a wide difference in the occasions of the use of these phrases, in conferring power upon the highest legislative bodies, and upon the councils of municipalities, or other inferior tribunals.   As to the legislatures, they are used when the people — the sovereignty — has come together by its delegates to organize a government, and to parcel out the three great powers thereof — the legislative, the executive, and the judicial — among the three co-ordinate and principal depositaries to which they are committed.   Though the constitution confers upon specified courts general judicial power, there are certain powers of a judicial nature which, by the express terms of the same instrument, are given to the legislative body, and among them this which we are considering.   All powers are, then, in the hold of the people.   They are about to distribute these powers among the bodies which they at the same time create.   When it is said on such an occasion to either house of the legislature, 'You are to be the judge of the election of the members of your own body,' there is a specific conferment of this particular power; and when it is said at the same time to the judicial body, 'You are to have general jurisdiction in law and equity,' though the conferment of power is general, there is, by the force of the concurrent action, excepted from the general grant the specific authority definitely bestowed with the same breath upon another body.   In such case it may well be that a form of words in the instrument that clearly makes a gift of judicial power to one co-ordinate body should be construed as reserving the particular power thus bestowed from the general conferment of judicial power by the same instrument, at the same time, upon another co-ordinate body.   The power thus given to the houses of the legislature is a judicial power, and each house acts in a judicial capacity when it exerts it.   The express vesting of the judicial power in a particular case so closely and vitally affecting the body to whom that power is given takes it out of the general judicial power, which is at the same time, in pursuance of a general plan that has regard in each part for every other part, bestowed upon another body; both bodies being contemporaneous in origin, and equal in dignity, degree, and proposed duration.   None of these things apply to the council of a city.   It is the creature of the legislature.   It has not the inherent powers of one of the constitutional depositaries of authority.   It is from the outstart a body inferior to the judiciary, and, as a general rule, is answerable unto it.   It is not unsafe for it, nor is it inconvenient, that a power to determine of the membership of it should be given to the courts.   It is not to be feared that it will be destroyed, or its existence be endangered, by the judicial exercise of that power.   It is made by temporary and changeable statute, instead of by fundamental and permanent law.   The authority that created it, the legislature, remains, and may interpose to ward it from harm, or may bring it back to life if harmed fatally ": *People* v. *Hall,* 80 N. Y. 122.

The charters of municipal corporations frequently contain clauses to the effect that the common council or governing body shall judge of the election and qualification of its own members, or of the other officers of the corporation; and the question arises, What effect do such provisions have on the jurisdiction of the courts of law to review the proceedings of the council or board while acting in a judicial capacity?   The better rule is, that the jurisdiction of such court remains, unless it appears manifest with unequivocal certainty that the legislature intended to take it away. Language like the above will not ordinarily have that effect, but will be interpreted as creating a cumulative or primary tribunal only, not an exclusive one. The form of remedy is usually provided by statute, *quo warranto* being most generally employed to review the proceedings of the inferior tribunal. *Mandamus* is, however, sometimes the proper remedy, while *certiorari* may be used when no form of review or appeal is provided by statute, or where the latter writ is especially designated for use on such occasions: *People* v. *Hall,* 80 N. Y. 122; *McVeany* v. *Mayor,* 80 Id. 185; 59 How. Pr. 106; 1 Hun, 35; 36 Am. Rep. 600; *State* v. *McKinnon,* 8 Or. 493; *State* v. *Wilmington City Council,* 3 Harr. (Del.) 294; *Ex parte Heath,* 3 Hill, 42; *Commonwealth* v. *McCloskey,* 2 Rawle, 369; *Ex parte Strahl,* 16 Iowa, 369; *State* v. *Funck,* 17 Id. 365; *Kane* v. *People,* 4 Neb. 509; *Wammack* v. *Holloway,* 2 Ala. 31; *Gass* v. *State,* 34 Ind. 425; *People* v. *Board of Delegates,* 14 Cal. 525; *Kendall* v. *City Council of Camden,* 47 N. J. L. 64; 54 Am. Rep. 117; *McGregor* v. *Board of Supervisors,* 37 Mich. 388.

In *State* v. *Gates,* 35 Minn. 385, there was an application for a writ of *quo warranto* to determine whether the relator or the respondent was elected to the office of alderman, under a charter providing that the city council should be the judges of the election and qualifications of its own members, and the court said: "We are agreed that such a provision without the use of the word 'sole' or 'exclusive,' or some similar form of expression, to indicate an intention to shut out the jurisdiction of the courts, does not affect such jurisdiction." In an exactly similar case in Wisconsin, it was argued that such a provision excluded the jurisdiction of the courts to adjudicate between contestants for the office of alderman, and vested that power solely in the common council. The court determining the question said: "It must be conceded that there are some decisions of courts of high authority which seem to approve this doctrine. But the great weight of authority, and we think the better reason, is opposed to such doctrine. We think the rule is satisfactorily established, that, unless the statute conferring the jurisdiction upon the common council to judge of the election and qualification of its members unequivocally excludes, by express provision or necessary implication, the jurisdiction of the courts in that behalf, such jurisdiction remains in the courts, and that conferred upon the council is only concurrent or temporary": *State* v. *Kempf,* 69 Wis. 470; 2 Am. St. Rep. 753. The same question was presented in *Commonwealth* v. *Allen,* 70 Pa. St. 465–469, where the court said: "We cannot doubt the jurisdiction of the court in this case. There is no true analogy between the state legislature and the council of a city. Their essential relations are wholly different. The council is in no proper sense a legislature. They do not make laws, but ordinances; nor are the members legislators, with the constitutional privileges and immunities of legislators. The council owes its existence, its rules of action, its privileges, and its immunities solely to the law which stands behind and above it; and its ordinances have their binding force, not as laws, but as municipal regulations, only by virtue of the law which infuses them with vigor. Hence all those decisions which evince the unwillingness of courts to interfere with the members of the legislature have no place in the argument. The legislature and the courts, deriving their existence from the constitution itself, are co-ordinate, independent branches of the government, standing upon an equality in the exercise of those powers which the constitution imparts to each in its own sphere. It would ill become a court of justice to attempt to displace a member of the legislature. Its desertion of its appointed orbit would be followed by such a display of incompetency to effect its purpose as would be its most signal rebuke. . . . . If the councils of a city, no matter how large, may defy the law under which they exist, and exercise all their powers, so may the councils of the most humble borough, and thus the law of the land be violated with impunity, unless the courts of justice have power to curb their deviations and correct their misdeeds. The right of this court to issue the writ of *quo warranto* to determine questions of usurpations and forfeitures of office in a public corporation cannot be questioned."

This case, in effect, overruled *Commonwealth* v. *Leech*, 44 Pa. St. 332, and *Commonwealth* v. *Meeser*, Id. 341, maintaining the doctrine that the courts of law have no jurisdiction to review the proceedings determining a contested election as to a membership of a city council, but that duty belongs exclusively to the council in which the seat is claimed. In *Ex parte Heath, supra,* Cowan, J., in speaking of a clause in the New York statute similar to the one we are considering, said: "Admitting the clause, however, to mean that each board shall be judges whether its members have been duly elected, it would still be difficult to show that the enactment amounts to anything more than the bestowment of a power concurrent with our own. The word 'solely' might, by a liberal interpretation, imply an intent to take away the power. So might a statute declaring the decision of an inferior court conclusive or final be construed to take from this court the power to review the decision by *certiorari.* But it has often been held that those or like words shall not be construed to divest the superior court of its supervisory power; and that, to give a statute such an effect, the legislature must say, in so many words, that they intend to take the power away." This language is approved and followed in *State* v. *Fitzgerald*, 44 Mo. 425.

On the other hand, quite a respectable number of authorities of the courts of last resort in various states maintain the rule, that where a charter grants to the members of a body of officers the power to judge of the election and qualification of its members, its decision is final and conclusive, and the superior courts of law are ousted of jurisdiction to review it in any manner: *Mayor* v. *Morgan*, 7 Martin, N. S., 1; 18 Am. Dec. 232; *State* v. *Marlow*, 15 Ohio St. 114; *Seay* v. *Hunt*, 55 Tex. 545. Thus under a provision in a city charter similar to that heretofore considered, the court, in *Linegar* v. *Rittenhouse*, 94 Ill. 208–211, said: "It may be urged that, because the legislature has not particularly specified the manner in which the council shall proceed, therefore no other provision has been made for the contest for this office. We think that the objection has no weight. It has made provision, as we have seen, that it shall be determined by the city council. Suppose the section had in specific terms provided that such contests shall be heard and determined by the city council, would any one have doubted that ample provision had been made for such contests? And yet we do not see that, in substance and effect, these provisions are not equally broad and comprehensive. To our minds, there is no doubt that the city council has full power and complete jurisdiction to decide this contest, and the county court has no such jurisdiction." The same rule is maintained in *People* v. *Metzker*, 47 Cal. 524, where the court said, in effect, that, under such a clause in a city charter, the council possesses exclusive authority to pass upon the subject, and the courts have no jurisdiction to inquire into the qualifications, elections, or returns of members of the council. The same doctrine is maintained in Michigan under the simple clause in city charters that the common council thereof shall be the judge of the election and qualification of its own members: *People* v. *Harshaw*, 60 Mich. 200; *Naumann* v. *Board of City Canvassers*, 73 Id. 252; *Alter* v. *Simpson*, 46 Id. 138; *People* v. *Fitzgerald*, 41 Id. 2; *Doran De Long*, 48 Id. 552. The same rule is followed in *Peabody* v. *School Committee*, 115 Mas. 383.

In re Allison.

[13 Colorado, 525.]

HABEAS CORPUS. — UNLESS THE TRIAL COURT LEGALLY EXISTS and is lawfully constituted, a trial, conviction, and judgment therein are void, and the prisoner must be discharged on *habeas corpus*.

COURT — DEFINITION OF. — PLACE OF MEETING is an important element in the definition that a court consists of persons officially assembled under authority of law, at the appropriate time and place, for the administration of justice.

JUDGMENT OF COURT DE JURE — COLLATERAL ATTACK ON, BY HABEAS CORPUS. — Though a county seat may have been originally unlawfully removed, still long acquiescence in such removal will make the proceedings of a court *de jure* sitting at the place of removal valid, and forbid attacking collaterally, by *habeas corpus*, the regularity of the removal.

DEFENSE OF FORMER JEOPARDY must be raised by special plea in the trial court.

JURY — DISCHARGE OF, UPON DISAGREEMENT, WITHIN DISCRETION OF COURT. — Where the constitution provides that "if the jury disagree, the accused shall not be deemed to have been in jeopardy," it is within the discretion of the court to determine when a disagreement sufficient to justify a discharge of the jury exists. No specific period for deliberation can be designated, nor any absolute rule laid down, to control this discretion; and unless it has been grossly abused, the objection of former jeopardy is not ground for reversal upon error, much less for discharge upon *habeas corpus*.

CRIMINAL LAW — SEVERAL PROSECUTIONS FOR SAME CRIMINAL TRANSACTION. — Under indictments charging the prisoner with robbing three different individual passengers upon the same stage, at the same time, an acquittal or conviction under one indictment is not a bar to a prosecution under the others, as the different robberies are distinct offenses.

JURORS — FAILURE TO UNDERSTAND ENGLISH LANGUAGE DOES NOT DISQUALIFY. — That some of the grand and petit jurors who found the indictment and convicted the prisoner were Mexican electors, and did not understand the English language, does not affect the validity of the trial and conviction.

H. B. O'Reilly, for the petitioner.

Samuel W. Jones, attorney-general, and *H. Riddell*, for the people.

HELM, C. J. The most serious question presented in the case at bar rests upon a challenge to the legal existence of the trial court itself. If there was no lawful court, the pretended

trial and judgment were absolutely void, and it would be idle
to argue that a conviction under such circumstances could
not be inquired into upon *habeas corpus*. Moreover, our *habeas
corpus* statute implies clearly that the court itself must be
lawfully constituted. And were there doubt concerning the
right to inquire, by this proceeding, under the law and decisions elsewhere, into the legal existence of the court passing
sentence, such doubt would be dispelled by the statute. Besides, the jurisdiction mentioned has already been entertained
by this court: *Ex parte Stout*, 5 Col. 509. The foregoing observations must not be understood, however, as applying to
the case of *de facto* judges or other court officers.

The district court is created by the constitution, and its
jurisdiction is therein defined. The office of district judge is
in like manner established, and the title of the incumbent
who tried the case at bar is not questioned. The statute organizing the sixth judicial district, in which Conejos County
is situate, and providing for the terms of court therein, has
never been challenged as unconstitutional, imperfect, or in-
effective.

Relator contends that because his trial was had at the town
of Conejos, three fourths of a mile distant from the town of
Guadaloupe, the court was no court, and the conviction and
judgment are absolute nullities.

The constitution is silent as to the place within the county
where the district court is to perform its appointed work. The
statute ordains that it shall be held at the county seat; but
the county seat, accurately speaking, is something separate
and apart from the place where it is located; for both the
constitution and statute provide for its removal from one
place to another. And the term, as in common parlance applied to a particular town or city, simply designates the town
or city where the county seat is for the time being established.

There may be a removal of the county seat in fact, though
not in accordance with law. And it might be plausibly argued
that, when such a removal takes places, the statute is satisfied
if the court be held where the county offices are, and where
the public business of the county is transacted. This is perhaps true according to the strict letter of the law; for the town
to which the county seat is illegally removed becomes, temporarily at least, the place of its actual location; and the statute specifies no particular town by name, nor does it, in words,
require the court to be held at the place where the county seat

has been regularly and legally established. But this construction of the law is open to serious objection, and might lead to embarrassing results. We prefer to rest our decision upon broader and to us more satisfactory grounds.

No issue is made with the definition usually given, that a court consists of "persons officially assembled, under authority of law, at the appropriate time and place, for the administration of justice"; nor is it denied that the place of meeting is an important element in the definition. We shall maintain the proposition that, under the admitted facts before us, there was a *de facto* location of the county seat at the town of Conejos, and that therefore the judgment under consideration is not vulnerable in the present proceeding.

For more than twelve years Conejos has been regarded as the lawful county seat. During this period, unquestionably, it has been the county seat in fact; that is, the county buildings, offices, and records have, without exception, been at that place, and the county business, including that of the district and county courts, has all been transacted there. The people of the state and the different departments of the state government have recognized Conejos as the place where the county seat was lawfully established. No direct judicial proceeding has ever been instituted for the purpose of determining the legality of such location in fact, or for the purpose of restoring the county seat to Guadaloupe. On the contrary, the inhabitants of the county, so far as we are advised, have universally acquiesced in this disposition of the county seat. During these twelve years property has been bought and sold, and public moneys have been expended in permanent improvements at the town of Conejos, upon the strength of its being the county seat. Estates of deceased persons have been there administered upon, and the interests of minor heirs have been there adjudicated. At that place property rights of all kinds have been litigated and determined, and criminals have been tried, convicted, sentenced, and executed or sent to the penitentiary.

In this state, the power to locate and remove the county seat is lodged by the constitution exclusively with the inhabitants of the county. They may, by a popular vote, establish or change the county seat at will, save that removals cannot be made oftener than once in four years. Their absolute power over the subject is restricted only by the limitation mentioned and the statutory regulations prescribing the manner of calling and conducting the election. The knowledge of the inhabitants of Conejos County that the county seat had in fact been removed from Guadaloupe and established at the town of Conejos cannot be questioned; nor can we presume that, while acquiescing during twelve years in the change, they have been ignorant of the manner in which it took place; and since the entire control of the subject has always been in their hands, we are inclined to the view that their conduct in the premises should be treated as such a confirmation of the unauthorized transfer, or at least such a waiver of objection thereto, as justifies an application of the *de facto* doctrine, so far as judicial proceedings that have taken place under all the forms of law at the town of Conejos are concerned. This conclusion is re-enforced by the facts above narrated, showing a universal outside recognition of Conejos as the *de jure* county seat during the long period mentioned. We are aware of no principle of law that compels us to hold all such proceedings void, and thus entail the appalling consequences that would inevitably follow.

We do not hold that there may be a *de facto* court, although this view has been vigorously and ably maintained: *Burt* v. *Winona etc. R. R. Co.*, 31 Minn. 472, and note. When a court or office is created by statute, and when the statute creating it is unconstitutional, there is no *de jure* court or office, as the case may be: *Ex parte Stout*, 5 Col. 509; and under such circumstances, we have the highest authority for the view that there can be no *de facto* court or office: *Norton* v. *Shelby Co.*, 118 U. S. 425.

But we are here dealing with a court unquestionably *de jure* so far as its establishment and organization are concerned,—a court presided over by a judge, the legality of whose title and office are not challenged; and our position is, simply, that though a county seat may have been originally unlawfully removed, yet subsequent circumstances may supervene which authorize the view that the proceedings of such a tribunal at the place of relocation are valid, and forbid litigating collaterally, by *habeas corpus*, the regularity of the removal.

The foregoing views do not conflict with those expressed in *Coulter* v. *Board etc. of Routt Co.*, 9 Col. 258. A general law exists, as already suggested, providing that the district court shall be held at the county seats of the various counties. The special act considered in the Coulter case applied to the county of Routt alone. It provided for holding the terms of the district court at the town of Yampa, which was not and never had been the county seat. This court held that the act conflicted, in this respect, with the constitutional provision inhibiting special legislation "regulating county and township affairs." Thus it will be seen that the decision is not in conflict with the view that when the county seat itself is removed, though the removal be *de facto* merely, the place of holding the court may, under circumstances like those here presented, also be changed.

We turn, now, to the remaining questions argued by counsel for relator in the present case. It is extremely doubtful if any of these questions are proper for consideration upon *habeas corpus;* but in view of the gravity of relator's situation, and the earnestness with which they are argued, the more serious of them will be briefly noticed.

It is asserted that relator's trial under indictment numbered 70 was absolutely void, for the reason that he had once before been in jeopardy. As to this objection, we observe: 1. That properly it should have been raised by special plea in the court below; 2. That it is not well taken on the merits.

Relator's conviction took place upon his second trial. The record advises us that the jury in the first trial retired on a certain day for deliberation; that they were brought into court the next morning, asked if they had agreed upon a verdict, and answered that they had not. It then recites that since they were not likely to agree, they were discharged by the court. Thus it appears that the jury had deliberated from one day until the next; that they were interrogated upon the probability of agreement by the court; and that, before discharging them, the court satisfied himself that agreement was impossible. Our constitution expressly provides that "if the jury disagree, ... the accused shall not be deemed to have been in jeopardy." Unquestionably the court should employ all legal and reasonable measures to secure a verdict after trial of a cause. On the other hand, however, the law inhibits the coercion of verdicts by improper punishment or influence. Discord exists upon the subject in hand among the adjudicated cases; but, under the foregoing constitutional provision, there can be no doubt as to the view we should favor. It is expressly declared that the jury, upon failure to agree, may be discharged without prejudice to another trial. It is obvious that the court must determine when a disagreement sufficient to justify this discharge of the jury exists. The length of time during which they must deliberate, and the exact circumstances warranting the conclusion that they have failed to agree in a given case, are, of necessity, matters resting largely in the sound discretion of the court. No specific period can be designated, nor can any absolute rule be laid down, to control this discretion, and unless it appears to have been grossly abused, the objection would not be ground for reversal upon error, much less for a discharge upon *habeas corpus:* See, on this subject, Wharton's Criminal Pleading and Practice, 9th ed., secs. 504–506; *United States* v. *Perez*, 9 Wheat. 579.

It is further argued, that three of the indictments upon which relator was sentenced were for one offense, and that for this reason two of the convictions, at least, were wholly illegal. The indictments are not before us, but there is sufficient in the record to convey the requisite information. Relator was not tried for robbing the stage; each of the indictments charged him with robbing a different individual passenger upon the stage. And no doubt can be entertained but that these various robberies were distinct offenses, although committed at the same place and in rapid succession. They constituted separate acts; but even if regarded as a single act, they affected separate objects. And "where one unlawful act operates on several objects, there may be several offenses committed, and so several prosecutions for the same criminal transaction, and an acquittal or conviction for one such offense will not bar a prosecution for the other": *Fox* v. *State*, 50 Ark. 528; Wharton's Criminal Pleading and Practice, 9th ed., secs. 468 et seq. The case at bar is to be distinguished from the case where an act operates upon a single object, and the different alleged offenses are simply degrees or ingredients of one crime. The present objection, like the former, would not even be ground for reversal upon error.

Finally we are told that since some of the grand and petit jurors who found the indictments against relator and tried his cases were Mexicans, and did not understand the English language, there was not due process of law, wherefore his conviction is a nullity, and he should be discharged.

This question is *stare decisis* here: *Trinidad* v. *Simpson*, 5 Col. 65. The reasoning in that case is clear and satisfactory; nothing would be gained by repeating it. The employment of an interpreter renders court proceedings more tedious and expensive. This necessity is therefore to be deplored. But a

Mexican elector, unable to speak or understand any other language than the Spanish, may nevertheless possess all the qualifications for jury duty required by the constitution and statute; and with the aid of an interpreter, he may perform the duties of juror better than many English-speaking citizens. In certain counties of the state, where the great bulk of the population originally were, and a very large proportion thereof still are, Mexicans, it would for many years have been practically impossible to have administered justice under our system of jurisprudence, without their aid in this capacity.

Since the decision above mentioned was rendered, the legislature has expressly declared that neither the county commissioners, the courts, nor the judges shall "discriminate against, reject, or challenge any person, otherwise qualified, on account of such person speaking the Spanish or Mexican language, and not being able to understand the English language": Sess. Laws 1885, p. 263. This statute might not be operative in the present case, for the reason that relator was tried before it took effect; but it is useful as indicating the view upon the subject of the law-making branch of the government. We know of no reason why it should be held void, and therefore, even were it proper to consider objections like the present upon *habeas corpus*, we would now be constrained, in an appropriate case, by legislative command, as well as by precedent, to deny their validity.

The writ is dismissed, and the prisoner remanded to the custody of the warden of the penitentiary.

COURTS — WHAT ARE. — A court is a place where justice is judicially administered. To constitute a court, there must be a place designated by law, and a person who, at that place, is authorized by law to administer justice: *Dunn* v. *State*, 2 Ark. 229; 35 Am. Dec. 54.

HABEAS CORPUS. — The jurisdiction of a court may be inquired into upon a writ of *habeas corpus: State* v. *Neel*, 48 Ark. 283; *In re Morris*, 39 Kan. 28; 7 Am. St. Rep. 512; note to *Commonwealth* v. *Lecky*, 26 Am. Dec. 41–47. But judgments of courts possessing general jurisdiction in criminal cases cannot be reviewed on *habeas corpus: Ex parte Shaw*, 7 Ohio St. 81; 70 Am. Dec. 55; *Platt* v. *Harrison*, 6 Iowa, 79; 71 Am. Dec. 389; *Williamson's Case*, 26 Pa. St. 9; 67 Am. Dec. 374, and note.

FORMER JEOPARDY. — Plea of former conviction must be special, and for its support it is necessary to show the legal conviction of defendant in a court of competent jurisdiction, and also the identity of the person convicted, and of the offense of which he was convicted: *Daniels* v. *State*, 78 Ga. 98; 6 Am. St. Rep. 238. In California, the plea of former jeopardy must be made and entered upon the minutes substantially as prescribed by the provisions of the Penal Code, and if not entered in such form and manner, the jury need not find upon it: *People* v. *O'Leary*, 77 Cal. 30.

FORMER ACQUITTAL OR FORMER CONVICTION AS A DEFENSE: See note to *People* v. *Bentley*, 11 Am. St. Rep. 228, 229.

JURORS — DISQUALIFICATION. — As to whether a juror's inability to under-stand the English language will disqualify him from serving upon the jury: *McCampbell* v. *State*, 9 Tex. App. 124; 35 Am. Rep. 726, and particularly note.

FALLON v. WORTHINGTON.   FALLON v. O'DONNELL.

[13 COLORADO, 559.]

JUDICIAL SALE — VENDOR'S EQUITABLE LIEN NOT SUBJECT TO SALE UNDER EXECUTION. — A vendor who by contract subsequently releases his trust deed for the payment of installments of the purchase price, and reserves merely an equitable lien, possesses only a chose in action, and no inter-est which can be subjected to sale under execution.

JUDICIAL SALE — ESTOPPEL FROM DENYING VALIDITY OF VOID EXECUTION SALE. — Where a vendor and the purchaser of his interest in land at a void execution sale are fully aware of their legal rights, and the vendor knew that the levy had been made, what was intended to be sold, was present at the sale, and consented to the application of the proceeds to the satisfaction of the judgment without protest, received the surplus, and demanded other collateral security pledged for the payment of the judgment debt, he is precluded from denying the validity of the sale, and the sale will constitute an equitable assignment of the vendor's interest in the land to the execution purchaser.

L. C. Rockwell and Luke Palmer, for the plaintiff in error.

T. J. O'Donnell, Hugh Butler, and C. S. Wilson, for the de-fendant in error and appellee.

PATTISON, C.   The questions presented in the above-entitled cases are practically indentical.   They were consolidated, argued, and submitted together, and may be considered and decided as one case.   The issue between the parties is clearly and well defined.   Although many questions are suggested, only so much of the history of the litigation will be given as may be necessary to an understanding of the legal propositions upon which the rights of the parties depend.

December 10, 1880, Dennis Fallon sold and conveyed to R. Harry Worthington the Muscovite lode mining claim, situate in Cascade mining district, Clear Creek County, Colo-rado.   The consideration of the sale and conveyance was the sum of thirty thousand dollars, of which five thousand dollars was paid.   For the balance of the purchase price eighty-four notes were given, eighty-three of which were for three hundred dollars each, and one for one hundred dollars.   These notes were payable monthly.   To secure their payment, a trust

deed was given upon the premises conveyed. By the terms of
the notes and trust deed, payment was to be made from the
proceeds of the property, no personal liability being assumed
by Worthington. Under the conveyance, Worthington entered into possession of and began working the property, and
from the proceeds paid two of the notes. Afterwards, and
prior to May 11, 1881, the parties entered into the agreement
out of which this controversy arose. The trust deed, which
has been mentioned, was released and discharged, and the
agreement substituted therefor.

As the rights of the parties are dependent in some measure,
if not wholly, upon the construction and legal effect of this instrument, it is here recited: "This agreement, made and entered into this eleventh day of May, A. D. 1881, by and between
R. Harry Worthington, of the county of Arapahoe and state of
Colorado, party of the first part, and Dennis Fallon, of the
county of Clear Creek, in said state, party of the second part,
witnesseth: That whereas the said Dennis Fallon has a claim
against and upon the Muscovite lode mine or mining claim,
situate in Cascade mining district, county and state last aforesaid, owned by R. Harry Worthington aforesaid, said claim
amounting to the sum of twenty-five thousand dollars, therefore, in consideration of the premises, and of one dollar to him
in hand paid, the said R. Harry Worthington, for himself and
his heirs and assigns, does covenant and agree to and with
the said Dennis Fallon to proceed to the organization of a
mining company, and to convey to said mining company, so
to be organized by him, upon its organization, the said Muscovite lode, upon condition that the said company, so to be organized as aforesaid, shall proceed to work and develop said
Muscovite lode, and from the proceeds thereof, except as hereinafter provided, pay, or cause to be paid, to the said Dennis
Fallon, or to his use, the said sum of twenty-five thousand
dollars, with interest thereon at the rate of five per cent per
annum; it being herein and hereby understood that the expenses of organizing said company, so to be organized as aforesaid, shall not be charged against said mine or its proceeds,
but that the same shall be wholly borne and satisfied by said
Worthington or said company. And the said R. Harry
Worthington agrees to prosecute immediately the work mentioned in a certain contract, made by him with said Dennis
Fallon, bearing even date herewith, and to furnish the money
to pay for the same, without reference to the organization of

said proposed company, and whether the same shall be organized or not, and to devote all the net proceeds thereof to the payment of said indebtedness to said Fallon until the same shall have been wholly paid and satisfied.

"And the said Dennis Fallon, in consideration of the covenants and agreements aforesaid, to be kept and performed by the party of the first part, and of one dollar to him in hand paid, does herein and hereby covenant and agree for himself, his heirs and assigns, that the said R. Harry Worthington, his heirs and assigns, may work all of said Muscovite lode or mine east of a point one hundred feet, surface measurement, below the lower drift, as at present established, and below an imaginary line running or drawn upon said lode or vein, and the length thereof from said point one hundred feet below the lower drift, as aforesaid, — the same to be worked by said Worthington, or his assigns, at his or their sole expense, and not at the expense of any profits that may arise from the working of the remainder of said lode, being above said point; and all profit that may be derived from said work, so to be carried on at the sole expense of the party of the first part, and from the portion of the lode or vein first aforesaid, shall belong solely to and be the property of said party of the first part, or his assigns, and shall not be liable to be applied to the payment of the indebtedness due said Fallon as aforesaid.

"And the said R. Harry Worthington does covenant and agree that he will cause said Dennis Fallon to be engaged as superintendent of such work as shall be carried on by the company herein proposed to be organized, after the expiration and completion of the contract hereinbefore referred to as of even date herewith, upon that portion of said lode or vein herein made liable for the indebtedness aforesaid, at a monthly salary at the rate of one thousand dollars per annum; the said Fallon agreeing, upon his part, faithfully and well to perform the duties of such superintendent for the best interests of said proposed company.

"And it is herein and hereby mutually agreed that for the payment of the money herein provided to be paid, as herein in manner and form provided for, the said Dennis Fallon shall have, and is hereby given, a lien upon said mine; he, the said Dennis Fallon, herein and hereby expressly waiving and releasing the said R. Harry Worthington and his assigns from all claim and demand therefor, or by reason of anything contained herein, except to the extent of the property of the party of the first part or his assigns in said lode or mine."

To this instrument an addition was made upon the following day, called an *addendum*, which is as follows: "After the completion of said contract, the prosecution of the work on said mine, and the method thereof, under the superintendence of said Fallon, shall depend upon the will and pleasure of said Worthington, being reasonably exercised; provided the same does not operate in defeating said Fallon in obtaining the amount of his lien against said mine in a reasonable time and under reasonable circumstances. The said Worthington or the said company not being able to furnish the money to prosecute the work will be sufficient reason for not prosecuting the same on said mine."

The contract and the *addendum* were each duly signed, sealed, acknowledged, and recorded.

The contract referred to in this instrument provided for the driving of a drift or tunnel upon the property, upon certain terms therein stated. As nothing was done under this contract, it need not be further considered.

The suit was begun September 11, 1882. Very little had been done under the contract by either Worthington or Fallon. The drift had been driven under a contract with a third party, but whether mineral was found or proceeds realized does not appear. Worthington did not organize the mining company, and did not employ Fallon as superintendent, as required by the contract. These omissions and other things were alleged as violations of the agreement, and the relief asked was that Fallon be adjudged to have a lien upon the property for the sum of twenty-five thousand dollars, with interest, as provided by the contract; that Worthington be ordered to pay said sum within a reasonable time; and that, in default of payment, the property be sold, etc.

The only defense interposed which requires consideration arose out of the following transactions: In September, 1881, Charles R. Fish recovered a judgment against the appellant for about nineteen hundred dollars, and caused an execution to be issued and delivered to the sheriff of Clear Creek County. The sheriff levied the execution upon all the right, title, and interest of Fallon in the Muscovite lode, either in law or in equity, and also "upon all the right, title, or interest, either in law or in equity, of said Dennis Fallon in and to the Muscovite lode mining claim that he now has or claims by virtue of certain agreements made and entered into by and between R. Harry Worthington and said Dennis Fallon, on the eleventh day of May, A. D. 1881, and recorded," etc.

Under this levy the property was advertised and sold to O'Donnell for the sum of $2,140, which sum was duly paid by him to the sheriff on the day of the sale.

It appears that appellant was advised of the levy and of the sale to be had under it; that his attorney was present at the sale; that neither Fallon nor his attorney made any objection or protest, either before or at the time the sale was made; that the money paid by O'Donnell was applied in satisfaction of the judgment and costs, leaving a small surplus of about fifteen dollars; that some time after the sale, Fallon, either in person or by attorney, demanded and received from Fish, or his attorney, certain notes and a trust deed which had been deposited with Fish as a collateral to secure payment of the note upon which the judgment was recovered; that his attorney afterwards applied to the sheriff for the surplus of fifteen dollars; that that sum was applied in payment of a sheriff's bill then outstanding against Fallon, with the consent of the attorney and the subsequent acquiescence of Fallon; that Fallon never redeemed, nor offered to redeem, from the sale, and deeds in due form were executed and delivered to O'Donnell after the equity of redemption had expired. Under these deeds, O'Donnell claimed to be the owner of the interest of Fallon, not only in the property itself, but in the contract entered into between Fallon and Worthington. This was the situation of the parties at the time the bill was filed.

O'Donnell was made a defendant to the bill, on account of the interest claimed by him under the conveyance made by the sheriff, and set up as a defense the transactions which have been recited.

Worthington alleged, among other things, that Fallon was without interest in the contract or in the property, having been divested of all interest by the sale under execution. This was the only issue tried by the court. The court found the facts as to the recovery of the judgment by Fish, the issuance of execution, the sale of the property, and the conduct of Fallon and his attorney, as above stated. Upon these findings the decree was predicated. It was adjudged that by virtue of the sale O'Donnell became the owner of all the right, title, and interest of Fallon in the property, whether existing by virtue of the contract or otherwise; that O'Donnell was entitled to

be substituted for Fallon to all his right, interest, and estate
under the said agreement; and that the plaintiff had no cause
of action against the said Worthington," etc.

Can this decree be sustained? This question presents two
propositions: 1. Was Fallon vested with an interest in the
property subject to seizure and sale under execution? 2. If
he was not seised of such an interest, then did his conduct
prior to, at the time of, and subsequent to the sale work an
estoppel, or *quasi* estoppel, by acquiescence, election, or otherwise?

Section 1835 of the General Statutes declares that "all and
singular the goods and chattels, lands, tenements, and real
estate of every person against whom any judgment shall be
obtained in a court of record . . . . shall be liable to be sold
on execution"; and that "the term 'real estate,' in this section,
shall be construed to include all interest of the defendant, or
any person to his use, held or claimed by virtue of any deed,
bond, covenant, or otherwise, for a conveyance, or as mortgagor of lands in fee, for life or for years." Under this provision it is clear that if appellant was vested with any interest in
the property, either legal or equitable, then such interest was
liable to seizure and sale under the execution. It must appear, however, that the interest was a vested interest, which
attached to the body of the land itself, and was held by him
under a legal or equitable title, within the meaning of the law.
Such an interest can only be predicated upon the provisions
of the contract upon which this suit was brought.

It appears that in December, 1880, Fallon conveyed the
property in question. The deed is not contained in the record,
but it may be assumed that it was in the usual form, and
that upon its delivery Worthington was vested with the title
to the premises in fee. That conveyance was in full force at
the time the contract was made. If Worthington conveyed or
Fallon acquired any title, interest, or estate in the property,
either legal or equitable, it was by force of the contract. It is
first necessary, therefore, to consider and determine the legal
effect of this instrument.

The contract first expressly recognizes Fallon's claim upon
the mine to the amount of twenty-five thousand dollars, and
Worthington's ownership of the property. The intent of the
parties is clear and unmistakable. The object sought to be
attained by Fallon was security for the amount of his claim,
and its final payment out of the proceeds of the property.

Worthington desired to accomplish this object without incurring personal liability. The agreement obligated him, or the
company which he might organize, to devote the net proceeds
realized from a certain part of the property to the payment of
Fallon's claim. Fallon's claim was made a charge upon the
property. The agreement to employ Fallon as superintendent, and to provide money for a drift, were independent personal covenants. The real purpose and chief object of the
instrument was to secure application of the net proceeds to
the payment of Fallon's claim. To secure such application,
it was "mutually agreed that for the payment of the money
herein provided to be paid, as herein in manner and form provided for, the said Dennis Fallon shall have, and is hereby
given, a lien upon said mine."

Extraordinary and unusual as are its terms, it seems clear
that, under the contract, it was the duty of Worthington,
either by himself or through corporate organization, to develop and work the property with reasonable diligence, and
if proceeds were realized, to devote the same to the payment
of Fallon's claim. If the property was barren, Fallon would
have no right of action. If proceeds were realized which Fallon might properly claim, and such proceeds were appropriated by Worthington, or by the company organized by him,
then Fallon would have a right of action for breach of contract, in the enforcement of which he might resort to the lien
created by the agreement. The contract, therefore, must be
construed to be a personal contract, providing for a specific
lien upon the property for its enforcement. The entire legal
title was in Worthington. He was in possession of the property. Fallon reserved no interest or estate in the land whatsoever. There was no defeasance provided for by forfeiture or
otherwise. Fallon's right, under the contract, was a chose in
action, to enforce which he had a right to a lien.

No extended discussion of the nature of the lien is necessary. It was defined by the parties themselves. It was a
lien by contract,—an equitable lien. "An equitable lien
arises either from a written contract, which shows an intention to charge some particular property with a debt or obligation, or is declared by a court of equity, out of general
considerations of right and justice, as applied to the relations
of the parties and the circumstances of their dealings": 1
Jones on Liens, sec. 27. A lien necessarily excludes any idea
of ownership by the party claiming it. "A lien, whether

implied or by contract, confers no right of property upon the holder. It is neither *jus ad rem* nor *jus in re.* It is neither a right of property in the thing nor a right of action for the thing. It is simply a right of detainer. 'Liens are not founded on property,' says Mr. Justice Buller [*Lickbarrow* v. *Mason*, 6 East, 21, 24], 'but they necessarily suppose the property to be in some other person, and not in him who sets up the right.' Consequently the interest of the lien-holder is not attachable, either as personal property or as a chose in action": 1 Jones on Liens, sec. 10.

The same author, at section 28, says: "Equitable liens do not depend upon possession, as do liens at law. Possession by the creditor is not essential to his acquiring and enforcing a lien. But the other incidents of a lien at common law must exist to constitute an equitable lien. In courts of equity, the term 'lien' is used as synonymous with a 'charge' or 'encumbrance' upon a thing, where there is neither *jus in re* nor *ad rem*, nor possession of the thing. The term is applied as well to charges arising by express engagement of the owner of property, and to a duty or intention implied on his part to make the property answerable for a specific debt or engagement."

Under the contract, the only interest which Fallon retained in the property was the right to a lien to enforce its provisions. It necessarily follows that he had no interest in the property itself, and that no right, title, or interest was vested in him, either under the contract or otherwise, which was subject to execution. Nothing, therefore, was seized under the writ of execution, and in law nothing passed to O'Donnell by the sale. "It is always indispensable that the property sold should be subject to the license, decree, or writ under which the sale is made. . . . . If property of the defendant is sold, it must be subject to the execution levied upon it, or the proceeding will be entirely inoperative upon his title": Freeman on Void Judicial Sales, sec. 35. "If property is not subject to execution, a levy thereon and a sale thereof based on such levy are utterly void": Freeman on Executions, sec. 109. In the light of these principles, the conclusion is irresistible that the sale under which O'Donnell claims to be entitled to the rights of appellant under the contract was utterly void.

The question which remains to be considered is, whether the conduct of appellant, prior to, at the time of, and subsequent to the sale, was such as to make it inequitable for him to take advantage of this void proceeding.

It is a well-settled elementary principle that a void judicial sale is an exception to the rule that "a confirmation or ratification cannot strengthen a void estate": Freeman on Void Judicial Sales, sec. 50, and cases cited. This exception, however, has ordinarily been applied to cases in which the sale was void because of some irregularity in the proceeding or in the judgment under which it was made, rather than to cases in which the property attempted to be sold was not subject to execution. No case has been found in which the facts are either parallel or analogous with the facts in this case. It would seem, however, that this rule might well be applied to all void judicial sales, without reference to the reasons or principles upon which their invalidity is predicated. The rule is based upon the beneficent principles of equitable estoppel. May it not be applied to this case if the right of Fallon, under the contract, is assignable, either by his own act or by operation of law. As has already been stated, the right secured to him was in the nature of a chose in action, upon which suit might be maintained by him whenever Worthington or his assigns should realize proceeds from the property properly applicable to his claim, and refuse to deliver them to him. Having neither title to the property nor its proceeds, a legal or equitable action would be his only remedy.

That a chose in action, whether dependent upon a contingent or an absolute covenant or promise, is assignable cannot be controverted. The question, then, is, whether, under the circumstances of this case, the sale, in connection with the conduct of the parties, did not constitute an equitable assignment or transfer to O'Donnell of Fallon's interest under his agreement with Worthington.

It is true that the ordinary elements of an estoppel *in pais* are not present in this transaction. These elements are clearly defined in *Griffith* v. *Wright*, 6 Col. 248. There was neither misrepresentation nor concealment of material facts upon which O'Donnell was induced to act. On the contrary, O'Donnell had full knowledge of all the facts, for it appears that he prepared the contract between the parties. It further appears that Fallon's attorney participated in the negotiations which led up to the agreement, and was fully advised of its contents. The parties, therefore, must be deemed to have acted with full knowledge of their rights in the premises.

This being the case, in view of the fact that Fallon and his
attorney knew that the levy had been made, knew what was
intended to be sold, were present at the sale, consented to the
application of the proceeds to the satisfaction of the judgment,
received the surplus, and demanded other collateral which
had been pledged for the payment of the debt, it cannot be
doubted that Fallon acquiesced in the sale. During all the
interval between the levy and the sale he had full opportunity
to protest against it. Had he done so, and had O'Donnell, in
spite of his protest, and against his objection, paid the money
to satisfy the judgment, then he would have been a mere volunteer, and the proceeding would have been held to be without
force or effect.

The case is one, therefore, in which a party has changed his
position through the failure of another to exercise a right
which he might have exercised. The principles of estoppel
by acquiescence or election are clearly applicable. "Wherever
the right of other parties have intervened, or the rights of the
party alleging the estoppel have been otherwise affected by
reason of a man's conduct, or acquiescence in a state of things
about which he had an election, and his conduct or acquiescence, or even laches, was based on a knowledge of the facts
and of his rights, he will be deemed to have made an effectual
election, and he will not be permitted to disturb the state of
things, whatever may have been his rights at first": Bigelow
on Estoppel, 4th ed., 651. "In like manner, if one, without
actually inducing another to act in a particular way, assent
to the thing done, and seek to derive benefit from it, he cannot, in case of disappointment, deny the validity of the act
assented to": Bigelow on Estoppel, 4th ed., 661. The correctness of these principles has been recognized by this court in
Yates v. *Hurd*, 8 Col. 349. Freeman on Void Judicial Sales,
at section 50, says, among other things: "These sales may be
ratified, either directly, or by a course of conduct which estops
the party from denying their validity. Thus if the defendant
in execution, after a void sale of his property has been made,
claims and receives the surplus proceeds of the sale with a
full knowledge of his rights, his act must thereafter be treated
as an irrevocable confirmation of the sale." Again, in the
same section, he says: "Perhaps it is not essential that the
defendant in execution should have directly received any part
of the proceeds of the sale. If he knows of the sale, makes no
objections thereto, and permits the proceeds to be applied to

the payment of his debts, he will, at least in Pennsylvania, be precluded from denying its validity." In *Smith* v. *Warden*, 19 Pa. St. 425, it is held that "equitable estoppels . . . . have place, as well where the proceeds arise from sale by authority of law as where they spring from the act of the party. . . . . The application of this principle does not depend upon any supposed distinction between a void and voidable sale." The same proposition is clearly decided in *Deford* v. *Mercer*, 24 Iowa, 118; *Maple* v. *Kussart*, 53 Pa. St. 349; *McConnell* v. *People*, 71 Ill. 481. These principles are clearly applicable to this case.

As the findings of the court were abundantly sustained by the evidence, it follows that the decree based thereon was correct, and should be affirmed.

REED, C., and RICHMOND, C., concurred.

By COURT. — For the reasons stated in the foregoing opinion, the judgments are affirmed.

EXECUTIONS. — The interest of a vendor, who has made a contract of sale, and received part of the purchase-money, is not subject to execution, even though he retains the legal title: *Burke* v. *Johnson*, 37 Kan. 337; 1 Am. St. Rep. 252. But a vendor's interest in lands contracted to be sold is bound by the lien of a judgment recovered against him while the contract is unexecuted, to the extent to which it is unexecuted: *Kinports* v. *Boynton*, 120 Pa. St. 306; 6 Am. St. Rep. 706, and note.

JUDICIAL SALES — ESTOPPEL. — Persons enjoying the benefits of a judicial sale may thereby be estopped to deny the validity of such sale: *Woodstock Iron Co.* v. *Fullenwider*, 87 Ala. 584; 13 Am. St. Rep. 73. Compare *Moody* v. *Moeller*, 72 Tex. 635; 13 Am. St. Rep. 839.

CASES

IN THE

SUPREME COURT

OF

ILLINOIS.

ILLINOIS CENTRAL RAILROAD COMPANY *v.* SLATER.

[129 ILLINOIS, 91.]

EVIDENCE. — WHEN AN ACCIDENT HAS OCCURRED, AND AN ACTION is on trial to recover damages for injuries sustained thereby, and the accident is alleged to have been the result of negligence, proof of any facts and circumstances attending the accident is competent and proper.

EVIDENCE OF THE SPEED OF A RAILWAY TRAIN IS COMPETENT AND MATERIAL in an action to recover damages for injuries to one run over by such train from the alleged negligence of the person in charge thereof.

EVIDENCE OF THE WEALTH OF A FATHER who, as the administrator of his deceased son, sues to recover for the death of the latter, resulting from defendant's alleged negligence, is not admissible for the purpose of showing that the father could have employed others to perform the services in which his child was engaged at the time of his death, and thereby have saved him from exposure to the dangers incident to that service. A wealthy father is under no obligation to raise his son in idleness lest he should be exposed to danger in the performance of labor.

CONSTITUTIONAL LAW. — THOUGH THE CHARTER OF A RAILWAY CORPORATION DEFINES its duty as to the giving of signals at public highway crossings, a statute subsequently enacted imposing the duty of giving other and different signals is not unconstitutional. The right to impose this and like duties upon railway corporations arises out of the police power which may be exercised by the legislature at its discretion as the public safety may require.

EVIDENCE. — THE FACT THAT A BELL WAS NOT RUNG NOR WHISTLE SOUNDED at a distance of at least eighty rods from the railway crossing may be proved by other than positive or direct testimony. Therefore it is not error to instruct a jury that "it is not necessary, in order to enable plaintiff to recover, that any witness should swear positively that no bell was rung nor whistle sounded upon the train in question at a distance of at least eighty rods from the railway crossing. It is sufficient upon that question that the jury believe, from the evidence in the case, that no bell was rung nor whistle sounded."

CONTRIBUTORY NEGLIGENCE. — THE CARE EXERCISED BY A CHILD SHOULD BE MEASURED by the degree of capacity he is found to possess. Hence it is proper to instruct a jury "that the rule of law as to negligence in children is, that they are required to exercise only that degree of care and caution which persons of like capacity and experience might be reasonably expected to naturally or ordinarily use in the same situation and under like circumstances, provided that the person or persons having control of such children have not been guilty of want of ordinary care in allowing them to be placed in such situations."

DAMAGES, MEASURE OF, FOR DEATH OF MINOR. — In an action by a father, as administrator of his deceased minor son, to recover damages for causing the death of his son, the jury may allow damages for the loss of the services of such son during his minority, though the father would have been entitled to such services had the child lived.

ACTION by an administrator, who was also the father of Arthur B. Slater, for negligently causing the death of the latter while a minor. Judgment was given in favor of the plaintiff both in the trial and the appellate courts.

W. and W. D. Barge, for the appellant.

James H. Cartwright and James W. Allaben, for the appellee.

WILKIN, J. This case originated in the circuit court of Ogle County, and is an action on the case, by appellee, against appellant, for negligently causing the death of Arthur B. Slater, his son. The deceased was about nine years old. When killed he was in a farm-wagon, drawn by two horses, with an elder brother, thirteen years of age. The two boys were in charge of the team, and in attempting to cross the track of appellant, on the public highway, using due care, as is alleged in the declaration, the wagon was struck by a passing locomotive, and both boys killed. The negligence charged in the declaration against the employees of appellant is, the omission to give the statutory signals, keep a proper lookout, running at a dangerous rate of speed, and failing to use reasonable diligence to stop the train in time to avoid the injury. Appellee recovered a judgment in the circuit court for one thousand dollars, which was, by the appellate court, on appeal, affirmed, and appellant again appeals.

The case is submitted in this court on the part of appellant on the same brief and argument filed in the appellate court. That court, by its judgment of affirmance, having settled all controverted facts adversely to appellant, we need give no attention to the lengthy review of the evidence contained in the argument, unless it is found necessary to do so in passing upon questions of law submitted for our decision.

On the trial, appellee was permitted, over objection, to prove the speed at which the train was running at the time deceased was killed, and this, appellant says, was error. One of the acts of negligence charged in the declaration is, that the train was running at a high and dangerous rate of speed at the time of the accident. Surely the plaintiff had a right to prove that averment if he could. But, independent of the allegation, it was proper to prove the rate of speed at which the train was running, as tending to show whether or not deceased, under all the circumstances, exercised due care, and whether other alleged acts or omissions on the part of appellant's servants caused the injury. In other words, any proof of facts and circumstances immediately attending the accident was competent and proper: *Chicago etc. R. R. Co.* v. *Lee*, 87 Ill. 454; *Indianapolis etc. R. R. Co.* v. *Stables*, 62 Ill. 313; *Rockford etc. R. R. Co.* v. *Hillmer*, 72 Ill. 235.

Appellant offered to prove that appellee was a man of wealth at and before the time of the accident; but, on objection, the court refused to allow it to do so. It seems that the purpose for which the evidence was offered was to show that the father was able to employ others to perform the service deceased was engaged in at the time of his death, and thereby have saved him from exposure to danger incident to that service, and it is insisted that such evidence was competent, under the ruling of this court in *Chicago etc. R. R. Co.* v. *Gregory*, 58 Ill. 226, and other cases cited, where, in passing on the question of negligence of parents in the care of their children, it is said the same rule should not be applied to persons dependent for support upon their labor, and those whose resources enable a parent to give constant personal attention to the care of their children, or employ persons for that purpose. It is not pretended that deceased, on account of tender years or want of mental capacity, was incapable of taking care of himself, and therefore the ability of the father to watch over him, or employ others to do so, was wholly immaterial; and to say, as a matter of law, that because a parent may be able to raise his child in idleness, therefore he must do so, lest the child be exposed to danger in the performance of labor, would be monstrous. We find no error in admitting or excluding evidence.

The first, second, third, and fourth instructions given on behalf of appellee are criticised by counsel for appellant, and a reversal insisted upon because they were given. We will notice them briefly in the order named.

The first and second define the duty of railroad companies in this state as to giving signals at public highway crossings in the language of section 68, chapter 104, of our statute, and instruct the jury, that if, by reason of a failure of appellant's servants to perform that duty, deceased was killed, he being free from negligence, appellant would be liable. The principal objection urged to these is, that inasmuch as appellant's charter defines its duty as to the giving of such signals differently from the statute, it was error in the court below to require of appellant's servants a compliance with the statute. The question here sought to be raised is not an open one in this court. The right to impose these and other like duties upon railroad corporations, by statute, grows out of the police power, which may be exercised by the legislature, at its discretion, as the public safety requires: *Galena etc. R. R. Co.* v. *Loomis,* 13 Ill. 548; 56 Am. Dec. 471; *Ohio etc. R. R. Co.* v. *McClelland,* 25 Ill. 123; *Galena etc. R. R. Co.* v. *Appleby,* 28 Ill. 283; see also 2 Redfield on Railways, 428. It is of the first importance that these duties, in the running and management of railroad trains, should be regulated by general statute, and that railroad employees be required to conform thereto, thus avoiding the confusion and increased danger to life and property which would result from the application of different rules to the many different railroads throughout the state.

Objections are urged to the phraseology of these instructions, but we think they are unimportant.

The third instruction, which is, "it is not necessary, in order to enable the plaintiff to recover, that any witness should swear positively that no bell was rung or whistle sounded upon the train in question at the distance of at least eighty rods from the highway crossing. It is sufficient, upon that question, if the jury believe, from all the evidence in the case, that no bell was rung or whistle sounded at a distance of at least eighty rods from the crossing,"—is not open to the criticism made upon it, in view of the evidence in the case. It simply informed the jury that the fact in question might be proved by other than positive and direct testimony.

The fourth is as follows: "The jury are instructed that the rule of law as to negligence in children is, that they are required to exercise only that degree of care and caution which persons of like age, capacity, and experience might be reasonably expected to naturally or ordinarily use in the same situation and under the like circumstances, provided that the parents or persons having the control of such children have not been guilty of want of ordinary care in allowing them to be placed in such circumstances." The giving of this instruction is urged as error, and is said to be directly contrary to the law in this class of cases. We find, however, in *Weick* v. *Lander*, 75 Ill. 93, which was an action by a father, as administrator, for the wrongful killing of his son, twelve years of age, it was said: "It is not to be expected that a boy twelve years old will use the same degree of caution and care as a person of mature years; nor does the law require it. It was proper for the jury, in passing upon the negligence of the deceased, to take into consideration his age and experience." In *Chicago etc. R. R. Co.* v. *Becker*, 76 Ill. 25 (a similar action), the deceased son being only six or seven years of age, it was again said: "The age, the capacity, and discretion of the deceased to observe and avoid danger were questions of fact to be determined by the jury, and his responsibility was to be measured by the degree of capacity he was found to possess." See also *Chicago etc. R. R. Co.* v. *Becker*, 84 Ill. 483. So in *City of Chicago* v. *Keefe*, 114 Ill. 222, 55 Am. Rep. 860, the deceased being a lad between ten and eleven years of age, an instruction, given at the request of the plaintiff, limited the degree of care required of the deceased to such as, "from his age and intelligence, under the circumstances in evidence, was required." The phraseology was condemned, but it was held that, inasmuch as it was in effect the same as if it had been limited to "such care as might be expected of a person of his age and discretion," there was no substantial error in giving it. And it was further said: "The circumstances in evidence are always to be taken into consideration in such cases, and if the intestate exercised such care as, under the circumstances, might be expected from one of his age and intelligence, it was sufficient." These decisions are in harmony with those of other states on the same subject, and but recognize the rule laid down by approved text-writers on negligence: Shearman and Redfield on Negligence, sec. 49; Wharton on Negligence, sec. 309.

The instruction was proper, nor does it, as insisted, conflict with the twenty-fourth, given on behalf of appellant, to the effect that if said sons, or either of them, possessed the knowledge or the ability of adults, the law would exact the same degree of care and prudence of them as from older persons. The first announces the general rule as to negligence in children; the latter, that such general rule would not apply to the deceased and his brother, if the jury should believe, from the evidence, they possessed the capacity of adults.

It is to be borne in mind that this is not, as counsel for appellant assume in argument, a suit by a parent for injury to his child, nor is it a case in which the deceased is shown to have been an infant, incapable of negligence or exercising any decree of care, in which case the contributory negligence, if any, is that of the parent, and not of the child. Hence the authorities cited in support of the position that this fourth instruction is inapplicable to the case are not in point.

Defendant asked, but the court refused, to instruct the jury, that "the father is entitled to the earnings and services of his minor son until such son is twenty-one years of age, and the jury has no right to allow any damages in this case for any loss of services or earnings of Arthur B. Slater during the period of his minority." It is argued, with earnestness, that this instruction contained a correct rule of law applicable to cases of this kind in the admeasurement of damages. To the contrary are the cases of *City of Chicago* v. *Scholten*, 75 Ill. 470; *Rockford etc. R. R. Co.* v. *Delaney*, 82 Ill. 198; 25 Am. Rep. 308; and *City of Chicago* v. *Keefe*, 114 Ill. 222; 55 Am. Rep. 860.

It is suggested, but not seriously urged, that other instructions asked by appellant were improperly refused. Having examined them, and also those given, we are satisfied that no error was committed by the trial court, to the prejudice of appellant in refusing instructions. Thirty-four were asked by appellant, many of them quite voluminous. Twenty-five were given. The issues in the case are few and simple. The trial court might, with great propriety, have refused many more than it did. Certainly appellant has no substantial ground for complaint that the jury was not fully and fairly instructed as to the law, on its behalf.

The judgment of the appellate court is affirmed.

RAILROAD COMPANIES — The ordinance of a city limiting the speed of trains within the city limits to a certain number of miles per hour is competent evidence for the jury in passing upon the question of negligence: *Union Pacific R'y Co.* v. *Rassmussen*, 25 Neb. 810; 13 Am. St. Rep. 527, and note.

RAILROAD COMPANIES. — SIGNALS AT CROSSINGS: See note to *Louisville etc. R. R. Co.* v. *Hall*, 13 Am. St. Rep. 93, 94. In the absence of statutory regulations limiting the speed of railway trains at crossings, such speed must be consistent with the degree of care required of railroads, and if such crossing is dangerous, the company must give warning of the approach of trains by blowing a whistle or ringing a bell, or by some other means: *Guggenheim* v. *Lake Shore etc. R'y Co.*, 66 Mich. 150. It is the duty of the men in charge of a train, moving or about to move, to give timely warning of the train's approach to a crossing or other place where the public have a right to go: *Shelby* v. *Cincinnati etc. R. R. Co.*, 85 Ky. 224.

NEGLIGENCE — CHILDREN. — Children are not expected to use the same degree of care and caution as adults would use under the same circumstances: *Western etc. R. R. Co.* v. *Young*, 81 Ga. 397; 12 Am. St. Rep. 320, and note. Compare extended note to *Westbrook* v. *Mobile etc. R. R. Co.*, 14 Am. St. Rep. 590–596.

MEASURE OF DAMAGES FOR INJURIES TO CHILD. — The extent of recovery in an action for negligence resulting in the death of complainant's child must be limited to compensation for loss of services during the minority of such child: *Cooper* v. *Lake Shore etc. R'y Co.*, 66 Mich. 261; 11 Am. St. Rep. 482. While on the other hand, in an action for damages for personal injuries to a minor, brought by his next friend, the damages for injuries which diminish his capacity to earn a living must be limited to the period after his majority: *Houston etc. R'y Co.* v. *Boozer*, 70 Tex. 530; 8 Am. St. Rep. 615. Where a mother, who was the only living person entitled to damages, sued a railway company for damages for negligently causing her son's death, she properly joined in the suit claims for damages for loss of services during minority, and also for statutory damages: *Gulf etc. R'y Co.* v. *Compton*, 75 Tex. 667. As a basis for damages to a parent for the death of an adult son, the reasonable expectation of benefit the parent would have received had the son lived must be shown; and in absence of legal right of the parent to the services of the deceased, this would depend upon his ability and inclination to confer the benefit upon the parent: *Winnt* v. *International etc. R. R. Co.*, 74 Id. 32.

VILLAGE OF CARTERVILLE *v.* COOK.

[129 ILLINOIS, 152.]

NEGLIGENCE. — WHERE THE CONCURRENT NEGLIGENCE of two or more persons results in the injury of a third person, each is answerable therefor. Hence one who, without any negligence on his part, is pushed or jostled off of a sidewalk which is more than six feet above the ground, and is not protected by any railing or guard, may recover from the village whose duty it was to have kept such sidewalk properly guarded.

J. M. Washburn and W. W. Barr, for the appellant.

B. W. Pope and George W. Young, for the appellee.

SCHOLFIELD, J. The evidence given upon the trial tended to prove that the plaintiff, a boy of some fifteen years of age, while, in the observance of ordinary care for his own safety, passing along a much-used public sidewalk of the defendant, was, by reason of the inadvertent or negligent shoving by one boy of another boy against him, jostled or pushed from the sidewalk, at a point where it was elevated some six feet above

the ground, and was unprotected by railing or other guard,
and thereby seriously injured in one of his limbs.

The objection urged against the ruling in refusing and modi-
fying instructions presents the question whether, conceding
the negligence of the defendant in omitting to reasonably
guard the sidewalk at the point where plaintiff was injured,
by railing or otherwise, the concurring negligence of a third
party, over whom it had no control in producing the injury,
releases it from liability. The supreme court of Massachusetts
have held in *Rowell* v. *City of Lowell*, 7 Gray, 103, 66 Am.
Dec. 464, *Kidder* v. *Dunstable*, 7 Gray, 104, and *Shephard* v.
Inhabitants of Chelsea, 4 Allen, 113, that it does. These cases,
however, seem to rest to some extent upon the phraseology of
the Massachusetts statute, which is less comprehensive in this
class of cases than is the ruling in this court: *Chicago* v. *Keefe*,
113 Ill. 222; 55 Am. Rep. 860. At all events, we are committed to a different line of ruling upon this question. In
Joliet v. *Verley*, 35 Ill. 58, 85 Am. Dec. 342, *Bloomington* v.
Bay, 42 Ill. 503, and *City of Lacon* v. *Page*, 48 Ill. 500, we held
that if a person, while observing due care for his personal
safety, be injured by the combined result of an accident and
the negligence of a city or village, and the injury would not
have been sustained but for such negligence, yet although the
accident be the primary cause of the injury, if it was one
which common prudence and sagacity could not have foreseen and provided against, the negligent city or village will
be liable for the injury.

It is not perceived how, upon principle, the intervention of
the negligent act of a third person, over whom neither the
plaintiff nor the defendant has any control, can be different in
its effect or consequence, in such case, from the intervention
therein of an accident having a like effect. The fo·mer no
more than the latter breaks the casual connection of the negligence of the city or village with the injury. The injured
party can no more anticipate and guard against the one than
the other, and the elements which constitute the negligence
of the city or village must be precisely the same in each case;
and we have accordingly held that where a party is injured
by the concurring negligence of two different parties, each and
both are liable, and they may be sued jointly or separately:
Wabash etc. R'y Co. v. *Shacklet*, 105 Ill. 364; 44 Am. Rep. 791;
Union R'y etc. Co. v. *Shacklet*, 119 Ill. 232. And this is abundantly sustained by decided cases elsewhere: *North Pennsyl-*

vania R. R. Co. v. *Mahoney,* 57 Pa. St. 187; *Cleveland etc. R. R. Co.* v. *Terry,* 8 Ohio St. 570; *Smith* v. *New York etc. R. R. Co.,* 46 N. J. L. 7; *Webster* v. *Hudson River R. R. Co.,* 38 N. Y. 260; Patterson on Railway Accident Law, secs. 39, 95, and cases cited in notes appended to each section. See also Shearman and Redfield on Negligence, 2d ed., secs. 10, 27, 46, 401. And we have applied the same rule in a suit for negligence against a municipal corporation: *Peoria* v. *Simpson,* 110 Ill. 301.

The Massachusetts rule seems to be applied also in Maine: *Moulton* v. *Sanford,* 51 Me. 127; *Wellcome* v. *Leeds,* 51 Me. 313; but it seems to have been elsewhere repudiated when the question has been considered: See *Hunt* v. *Pownal,* 9 Vt. 411, and authorities cited *supra.*

The instructions as given fairly presented the law of the case to the jury; and concurring, as we do, fully with the views expressed in the opinion of the appellate court by Mr. Justice Green (*Village of Carterville* v. *Cook,* 29 Ill. App. 495), we deem it unnecessary to comment further upon the rulings below.

The judgment is affirmed.

NEGLIGENCE OF TWO OR MORE PERSONS RESULTING IN INJURY TO A THIRD. — A person may be injured through the negligence of two or more persons, acting either separately or jointly, and, in either event, he may generally seek and obtain judgment in an action against them jointly or in separate actions against each. When the negligence is that of two or more acting jointly as partners, or, though not partners, in pursuit of some common object, there is little or no difficulty in maintaining that they are jointly and severally answerable to any one who is thereby injured in his person or property. In the case of a partnership, if either of the partners is negligent while engaged in the firm business, though the others are not present, or if one of their servants or agents, while acting within the scope of his duties, is guilty of negligence, whereby a third person is injured, a recovery may be had therefor against the partnership, or perhaps against one or more of its members without joining the others: *Moreton* v. *Harden,* 6 Dowl. & R. 275; 4 Barn. & C. 223; *McMahon* v. *Davidson,* 12 Minn. 358; *Roberts* v. *Johnson,* 58 N. Y. 613. So if two or more hire a chaise, and while jointly in its possession, by their negligence, or by the negligence of either, a third person is injured, a recovery may be had against both: *Davey* v. *Chamberlain,* 4 Esp. 229. If two or more persons, or corporation, are operating a railway, and an injury results to an employee from their neglect to furnish proper machinery, they are jointly and severally liable to him therefor: *Kain* v. *Smith,* 80 N. Y. 468.

It is not essential to the maintenance of an action against two persons for negligence that they should be partners, or engaged in a common enterprise, or even co-owners of the same piece of property: *Andrews* v. *Boedecker,* 126 Ill. 605; 9 Am. St. Rep. 649. Thus, while the owners of a party-wall are not partners, nor ordinarily co-tenants, yet if they owe a common duty to keep it in repair, a recovery may be had against them by any one injured by their non-performance of this duty. *Klauder* v. *McGrath*, 35 Pa. St. 128, 78 Am. Dec. 329, was an action to recover damages for personal injuries sustained by plaintiff by reason of the falling of a party-wall erected on the dividing line between lands owned by the defendants in severalty, and it was claimed that a judgment against them could not be sustained, because they were not jointly liable. The court, however, disposed of this defense by saying: "The maintenance of an insecure party-wall was a tort in which they both participated. The act was single, and it was the occasion of the injury to plaintiff, and it is difficult, therefore, to say why both were not liable, and liable jointly. The case is not to be confounded with actions of trespass brought for separate trespasses done by two or more defendants. Then, if there has been no concert and no common intent, there is no joint liability. If the keeping of the wall safe was a common duty, the failure to do so was a common negligence."

The only portion of the law upon this subject about which there seems now to be any difficulty or doubt relates to the cases in which a person has been injured by distinct negligent acts or omissions of which two or more persons were guilty, but who were not partners nor co-owners, nor engaged in any common design or enterprise. It is well settled that, in many instances, one may be held answerable for injuries resulting from his negligence, though another cause combined with it in producing such injuries, and without this latter cause the injury could not have been inflicted. Thus injuries may have resulted from the negligence of the defendant and an accident happening either to him or the plaintiff, and but for the accident the injuries would have been avoided. In such instances, while the negligence is not the sole, it is deemed to be the proximate, cause, and the liability of the defendant to respond in damages is not less than though it were the sole cause: *Clark* v. *Barrington*, 41 N. H. 44; *Seigel* v. *Eisen*, 41 Cal. 109; *Powell* v. *Deveney*, 3 Cush. 300; *Atchinson* v. *King*, 9 Kan. 550; *Titcomb* v. *Fitchburg R. R. Co.*, 12 Allen, 254; *Palmer* v. *Andover*, 2 Cush. 600; *Austin* v. *N. J. S. Co.*, 43 N. Y. 75; 3 Am. Rep. 663.

When one act of negligence unites with another and like act, or with any other cause, in inflicting injury upon the person or property of another, whose negligence has not also contributed to his injury, and there exists no means of determining the extent to which the injury resulted from either negligent act, it is obvious that each person guilty of negligence must either be held entirely exonerated, or as answerable for the whole damages inflicted in part by his negligence. In all instances in which his negligence can be regarded as the proximate cause, or as one of the proximate causes, of an injury, he is answerable for the whole thereof, either separately or jointly and severally with any other person whose negligence or other wrongful act may also have been one of the proximate causes of such injury. If either person who contributed to an injury was one for whose negligence the party injured could maintain no action, this does not impair his right to recover against the party the consequences of whose negligence he was not obliged to suffer. Therefore, if a servant is injured by the concurrent negligence of his master and of a fellow-servant, he may recover compensation of his master, though if the negligence of the fellow-servant had been the sole cause, no recovery whatever could have been had: *Grand Trunk R. R. Co.* v. *Cummings*, 106 U. S. 700.

If, through the mutual negligence of the officers or employees of two steamboats, or two lines of railways, a collision occurs, the proprietors of the respective boats or lines are severally and jointly liable to the persons injured thereby: *Mills* v. *Armstrong*, L. R. 13 App. Cas. 1; 57 L. J. P. D. 65; 58 L. T. 423; 36 Week. Rep. 870; *Lockhart* v. *Lichtenthaler*, 46 Pa. St. 151; *Colegrove* v. *N. H. etc. R. R. Co.*, 20 N. Y. 492; *Barrett* v. *Third Ave. R. R. Co.*, 45 Id. 628; *Flaherty* v. *Minneapolis etc. R. R. Co.*, 39 Minn. 328; 12 Am. St Rep. 655.

Mr. Thompson, at page 1089 of the first edition of his work upon negligence, attempts to state an exception or limitation to the general rule that two or more persons are jointly and severally answerable when their negligence concurs in injuring a third person. He says: "If A is guilty of negligence which would not have produced the catastrophe but for the subsequent intervening negligence of B, such negligence of B's not being a result which A might reasonably anticipate, nor one against which it was his duty to guard, A will not be responsible for the resulting damages." He adds, however, as a limitation of his limitation: "But an intervening act of an independent voluntary agent does not arrest causation, nor relieve the person doing the first wrong from the consequence of his wrongful act, if such intervening act was one which would ordinarily be expected to flow from the act of the first wrong-doer." In support of this second limitation, Mr. Thompson gives several illustrations from the adjudged cases, most, if not all, of which, in our judgment, while they support his limitation of his limitation, tend to overthrow the original limitation itself. There is and can be no exception to the general rule other than that which attends every liability for negligence, viz., that the negligent act complained of must have been a proximate cause of the injury suffered. Thus if powder is sold to a boy, who takes it home, and it is put away, but his mother and aunt give him part of it, which he fires off, and at a still later date, the mother or aunt gives him some more, in firing off which he is injured, or if a druggist sells an article, harmless in itself, mistaking it for another article, also harmless in itself, and afterwards another person intermixes the article so sold with another article, making thereby a dangerous explosive, from which injury is suffered, there can be no recovery in the one case against the merchant, nor in the other against the druggist, because the original sale was not, in either case, the proximate cause of the accident: *Davidson* v. *Nichols*, 11 Allen, 514; *Carter* v. *Towne*, 103 Mass. 507.

From the rule that persons whose concurring negligence is a proximate cause of injury to another are jointly and severally answerable therefor, it follows, as a matter of course, that neither, when an action is brought against him, can successfully resist it, nor even mitigate the damages recoverable therein by establishing that the negligence of a party not sued contributed to the injury complained of: *Webster* v. *Hudson River R. R. Co.*, 38 N. Y. 260; *Slater* v. *Mersereau*, 64 Id. 138; *Learned* v. *Castle*, 78 Cal. 454.

If a contractor, and a subcontractor under him, are guilty of separate acts of negligence, as where the negligence of the former lets in water from the street, and the negligence of the latter leaves the roof without any proper means for an escape of water, and the two streams, the one from the roof and the other from the street, finally unite and damage plaintiff in such a way that it is impossible to ascertain what portion resulted from the negligence of the contractor, or what from the negligence of the subcontractor, each is answerable for the whole: *Slater* v. *Mersereau*, 64 N. Y. 138. In this case, it will be observed that the negligent acts were entirely distinct from each other, and related to separate parts of the premises, and that the one who was negligent in the street could not foresee that the consequence of his negligence might be augmented by the negligence of the other upon the roof. In

an action against a carrier of passengers for injuries occurring to one of its
patrons, partly by its negligence and partly by the negligence of another
carrier, or of any other person or corporation, the fact that the injury did not
wholly result from the negligence of the defendant constitutes no defense:
Eaton v. *B. & L. R. R. Co.*, 11 Allen, 500; 87 Am. Dec. 730. If a boy who is
riding in a railway car is by its conductor compelled to leave his seat and
to stand upon the platform, where another passenger, in attempting to get
off, carelessly runs against the boy and knocks him off of the platform,
whereby he is injured, the railroad company is answerable. In the action
wherein this was decided, the court said: "It does not alter this liability
that the wrong of a third party concurred with their own in producing
the injury. It may well be that the young gentleman was not justified
in rushing through the crowd, and in aiding in throwing the deceased
from the train, but this does not relieve the defendants' wrong. If they
had not removed the deceased from his seat, and compelled him to stand
upon the platform, he would not have been affected by the illegal act of the
young man. It was his violence concurring with the defendants' illegal conduct in overcrowding their car and in placing the deceased upon the platform
that produced disastrous results. It is no justification for the defendants
that another party, a stranger, was also in the wrong": *Sheridan* v. *Brooklyn
etc. R. R. Co.*, 36 N. Y. 39; 93 Am. Dec. 490. If a dangerous piece of machinery is by its owner placed in a public alley of a city, where it is permitted
to remain until it occasions injury to a third party lawfully using such alley,
both the city and the owner of the machinery must be adjudged guilty of
negligence in permitting it to remain in a public way, where it is liable to
inflict injuries, and an action may be sustained against them jointly by the
person injured: *Osage City* v. *Larkin*, 40 Kan. 206; 10 Am. St. Rep. 186.

If either of the persons whose negligence injures a third is the representative or agent of the latter, or under his control, he cannot recover therefor,
because the negligence of the representative or agent is in law the negligence of his principal, and the principal, if injured, has no cause of action,
for the reason that, being chargeable with the negligence of his agent, he is
deemed guilty of contributory negligence. At one time, the tendency of the
decisions was to impute to one riding upon a car or any vehicle of another
the negligence of the manager of such car, or of the driver of such vehicle:
Carlisle v. *Sheldon*, 38 Vt. 440; *Houfe* v. *Fulton*, 29 Wis. 296; 9 Am. Rep. 568;
Payne v. *Chicago etc. R. R. Co.*, 39 Iowa, 523; *Yahn* v. *Ottumwa*, 60 Id. 429;
Slater v. *Burlington etc. R'y Co.*, 71 Id. 209; *Prideaux* v. *City of Mineral Point*,
43 Wis. 513; 28 Am. Rep. 558. The leading case affirming this rule was
Thorogood v. *Bryan*, 8 Com. B. 115. It was followed until a comparatively
recent period in England: *Armstrong* v. *Lancashire etc. R. R. Co.*, L. R. 10 Ex.
47; but is now overruled even in that country: *The Bernina*, L. R. 12 P. D. 58;
note to 57 Am. Rep. 494. There is at the present time an almost unanimous
concurrence in the rule that one who is riding in a vehicle or car, the manager or driver of which is not his agent or servant, nor under his control,
and who is injured by the negligence of a third person and of such manager
or driver, may recover of the third person for the injuries inflicted through
such concurring negligence: *Noyes* v. *Boscawen*, 64 N. H. 361; 10 Am. St.
Rep. 410; *State* v. *Boston R. R. Co.*, 80 Me. 430; *Nesbit* v. *Town of Garner*, 75
Iowa, 314; 9 Am. St. Rep. 486; *Wabash etc. R'y Co.* v. *Shacklet*, 105 Ill. 364; 44
Am. Rep. 791; *Louisville etc. R. R. Co.* v. *Case*, 9 Bush, 728; *Tompkins* v. *Clay
St. R'y*, 66 Cal. 163; *Town of Albion* v. *Hetrick*, 90 Ind. 546; 46 Am. Rep. 230;
Matthews v. *London Street Tramway Co.*, 58 L. J. Q. B. Div. 12; *Transfer Co.*

v. *Kelly*, 36 Ohio St. 86; 38 Am. Rep. 558; *Bennett* v. *New Jersey R. & T. Co.*, 36 N. J. L. 225; 13 Am. Rep. 435; *New York etc. R. R.* v. *Steinbrenner*, 47 N. J. L. 161; 54 Am. Rep. 126; *Little* v. *Hackett*, 116 U. S. 366; *Philadelphia etc. R. R. Co.* v. *Hoyeland*, 66 Md. 149; 59 Am. Rep. 159; *Robinson* v. *New York etc. R. R. Co.*, 66 N. Y. 11; 23 Am. Rep. 1; *St. Clair St. R'y Co.* v. *Eadie*, 43 Ohio St. 91; *Borough of Carlisle* v. *Brisbane*, 113 Pa. St. 544; 57 Am. Rep. 483, and note; *Town of Kingstown* v. *Musgrove*, 116 Ind. 121; 9 Am. St. Rep. 827; *Brannen* v. *Kokomo etc. Gravel Road Co.*, 115 Ind. 115; 7 Am. St. Rep. 411; *Dean* v. *Pennsylvania R. R. Co.*, 129 Pa. St. 514; 14 Am. St. Rep. 733; *Follman* v. *Milwaukee*, 35 Minn. 522; 59 Am. Rep. 340; *Cuddy* v. *Horn*, 46 Mich. 596; 41 Am. Rep. 178. Hence, where a wife is riding with her husband in a vehicle driven by him, and is injured by his negligence and that of a third person, she may recover against the latter: *Hoag* v. *W. C. & H. R. R. Co.*, 111 N. Y. 199. If, however, one person riding with another, who is driving, sees, or by the exercise of reasonable care must have seen, approaching or impending danger, he must, as in other cases, use reasonable care and diligence to avoid such danger, and if he does not, his contributory negligence will preclude his recovery: *Township of Crescent* v. *Anderson*, 114 Pa. St. 643; 60 Am. Rep. 367; *Dean* v. *Pennsylvania R. R. Co.*, 129 Pa. St. 514; 15 Am. St. Rep. 733; *Brickell* v. *New York etc. R. R. Co.*, 120 N. Y. 290; 17 Am. St. Rep.

In a recent action against a druggist to recover for injuries resulting from his negligence in selling a poisonous drug as quinine, it was held that defendant could not relieve himself from liability by urging that the person whom plaintiff sent to purchase the quinine had also been guilty of negligence in not examining the label upon the vial containing the medicine: *Bruswig* v. *White*, 70 Tex. 504.

The action when an injury has resulted from the negligence of two or more persons may be against both, or separate actions may be brought against each: *Creed* v. *Hartman*, 29 N. Y. 591; 86 Am. Dec. 341. If, however, a judgment rendered in either action is satisfied, such satisfaction operates to release the defendant in the other action, or any other person who is jointly answerable for the negligence: *Lord* v. *Tiffany*, 98 N. Y. 421; Freeman on Judgments, sec. 236.

When one of several persons answerable for a negligent act or omission has satisfied the liability resting upon him, the next question likely to present itself for consideration is, Under what circumstances and to what extent may he enforce indemnity or contribution from the others who were in law jointly and severally liable with him? The general rule is often stated to be, that one of several joint tort-feasors cannot enforce contribution from the others: *Minnis* v. *Johnson*, 1 Duvall, 171; *Rhea* v. *White*, 3 Head, 121; *Becker* v. *Farwell*, 25 Ill. App. 432; *Anderson* v. *Saylors*, 3 Head, 551; *Nichols* v. *Nowling*, 82 Ind. 488; *Merryweather* v. *Nixam*, 8 Term Rep. 186; *Boyer* v. *Bolender*, 129 Pa. St. 324; 14 Am. St. Rep. 723. Even in the case of active torts this rule is applicable only against the one who was himself in fault. But if the act for which recovery has been had was not ordinarily nor necessarily unlawful, and the person seeking contribution or indemnity did not in fact intend any wrong, and the act and the circumstances are not such that he must be presumed to have intended a wrong, then he may recover: *Ackerson* v. *Miller*, 2 Ohio St. 203; *Adamson* v. *Jarvis*, 4 Bing. 66; *Betts* v. *Gibbons*, 2 Ad. & E. 57; *Thweatt's Adm'r* v. *Jones*, 1 Rand. 328; *Farwell* v. *Becker*, 129 Ill. 261, *post*, p. 267. Thus, if an agent, acting under orders from his principal, which he believes the latter has a right to give, commits a trespass for which he is pursued at law and made to respond in damages, he may compel his principal to fully indemnify him if he merely in good faith carried out the latter's orders: *Moore* v. *Appleton*, 26 Ala. 633; *Adamson* v. *Jarvis*, 4 Bing. 66; *Lowell* v. *B. & L. R. R.*, 23 Pick. 24; 34 Am. Dec. 33; and on the other hand, if a servant wrongfully exposes his principal to liability for a tort committed without the latter's authority, no doubt the principal is entitled to indemnity. In each of these cases the party seeking indemnity has been guilty of no personal wrong, actual or presumed, and no principle of public policy forbids the enforcement of indemnity in his favor.

The instances are very numerous in which persons are made to respond in damages for negligence for which they are not personally in fault, as where the negligent act or omission was that of a servant or agent, or consisted in the non-performance by another person of his duty, which, had it been performed, would have prevented the happening of the injury in question. In such cases, if the party who was not culpable is nevertheless compelled to pay damages, he has a cause of action to enforce indemnity from the one who was really culpable. Therefore, if a street or other public highway is obstructed or otherwise placed or left in a dangerous condition, by one who had no right to make the obstruction, or whose duty it was to keep the street in repair, and a person is injured and recovers from the city or town in which such street or highway is, the latter is entitled to indemnity from him who unlawfully placed such obstruction in the street, or neglected to perform his duty to keep it in repair: *Woburn* v. *B. & L. R. R.*, 109 Mass. 283; *Swansey* v. *Chace*, 16 Gray, 303; *Milford* v. *Holbrook*, 9 Allen, 17; 85 Am. Dec. 735; *Minneapolis M. Co.* v. *Wheeler*, 31 Minn. 121. So an occupant of a building, who is compelled to pay damages for injuries suffered by another falling into a hatchway on the premises negligently left open and unguarded by a third person, may compel the wrong-doer to indemnify him: *Churchill* v. *Holt*, 127 Mass. 165; 34 Am. Rep. 355. If a gas company affixes a wire to the chimney of a building, which renders such chimney unsafe, and ultimately causes it to fall upon a passer-by, the owner of the building, though he did not know or assent to the fixing of the wire, is answerable in damages, but after paying such damages, he may maintain an action against the gas company for indemnity. In determining this question the court said: "It is undoubtedly true that when a stranger does a negligent or unlawful act on the land or building of another, and in doing that act occasions injury to a third party, the owner of the land or building is not liable. Such a case would have been presented if the injury had been caused by the fall of the chimney, while the defendant, without the knowledge or permission of the plaintiff, was putting the wire upon the chimney. The injury so resulting would have arisen, not from the unsafe condition of the chimney as a part of the building, but from the negligent act committed without permission and not under the authority of the owner. But the facts show a very different state of things. The wrongful act of the defendant caused the chimney, which was adjacent to the highway, to become unsafe and liable to fall by reason of the strain of the wire, and this condition was continued for a considerable period, and existed at the time of the injury. The owner of a building under his control and in his occupation is bound, as between himself and the public, to keep it in such proper and safe condition that travelers on the highway shall not suffer injury. It is the duty of the owners to guard against the danger to which the public is thus exposed, and he is liable for consequences of having neglected to do so, whether the unsafe condition was caused by himself or another. Nor can the owner protect himself from liability because he did not in fact know that the building was unsafe; he is bound to exercise the proper care required under the circumstances of the case. The liability of the plaintiff, therefore, to Brown and Chick did not depend upon and was not based upon the particular act of the defendant, but upon the determination of the question whether the chimney was unsafe and dangerous to travelers under such circumstances that the owner was responsible for the injury suffered. When two parties act together, committing an illegal or wrongful act, the party who is held responsible in damages for the act cannot have indemnity or contribution from the other, because both are equally culpable or *particeps criminis*, and the damage results from their joint offense. This rule does not apply when one does the act or creates the nuisance, and the other does not join therein, but is thereby exposed to liability and suffers damages. He may recover from the party whose wrongful act has exposed him. In such case the parties are not *in pari delicto* as to each other, though as to third persons either may be held liable. The numerous cases in our own reports are analogous where towns have been held liable for unsafe conditions of the highways, and have recovered from the persons whose acts caused the unsafe condition ": *Gray* v. *Boston Gas Light Co.,* 114 Mass. 149; 19 Am. Rep. 324. A railroad company against which a judgment has been recovered by one who has sustained personal injuries through the obstruction by mail-bags of a sidewalk at its station is entitled to indemnity against a mail-carrier who negligently caused such obstruction. The company and the mail-carrier are not in such circumstances, as to each other, *in pari delicto: Old Colony R. R.* v. *Slavens,* 148 Mass. 368; 12 Am. St. Rep. 558.

If a contractor, who has agreed to erect a building for the owner of a city lot and to make a cellar extending under the sidewalk, negligently leaves open an excavation made by him, and a third person falls into it, and recovers of the owner for the negligence in leaving it open and unguarded, the latter may in turn recover of the contractor: *Pfau* v. *Williamson,* 63 Ill. 16. If a servant to whom goods is intrusted is negligent, whereby they are injured, his master may settle for the damages, and then recover the amount thereof of the negligent servant: *Smith* v. *Foran,* 43 Conn. 244; 21 Am. Rep. 647; *Grand Trunk R'y Co.* v. *Latham,* 63 Me. 177.

In the class of cases last considered, the parties seeking indemnity were without fault, and those of whom it was sought were the ones who, in equity, ought to be held solely answerable. We now approach the consideration of a class of cases in which both the plaintiff and the defendant were in fault, or if neither was in fault, both were equally blameless, and in these cases it is not complete indemnity which is sought, but only proportional contribution. If neither party to the action was personally at fault, but one of them has been compelled to respond in damages, as where one of the servants or agents of a partnership has been guilty of negligence, which the plaintiff, as one of the partners, has been obliged to pay, there is no doubt that he may compel contribution from the other partners: *Horback's Adm'r* v. *Elder,* 18 Pa. St. 33; *Bailey* v. *Bussing,* 28 Conn. 455; *Wooley* v. *Batte,* 2 Car. & P. 499; *Pearson* v. *Shelton,* 1 Mees. & W. 504. In *Churchill* v. *Holt,* 131 Mass. 67, 41 Am. Rep. 191, it was adjudged that if the owner of premises had left them in an unsafe condition, so that injury to a traveler might have happened, and another person had afterwards interfered with them so that they became still more dangerous, and a traveler fell into them, and, being injured, recovered against the owner, that the latter could not compel indemnity nor contribution from the intermeddler, because the acts of both were unlawful; that as both were wrong-doers, and *in pari delicto*, neither could recover indemnity from the other. While the decisions upon the subject are as yet infrequent and meager, we think we may safely say that they maintain that where two or more persons are jointly and equally answerable for negligence, and one of them has been compelled to discharge the whole liability, he is entitled to contribution from the others, provided the circumstances are not such that he must be presumed to have intended to do an unlawful act or an intentional wrong. Where the negligent acts have been separate and distinct, and committed by persons not partners, nor jointly acting nor interested in a common purpose, it may be that the rule is inapplicable; but we have met with no cases either affirming or denying the applicability. But where the neglect is joint, as where it consists of the omission of a duty which each of the parties was equally bound, both in law and in good conscience, to discharge, then each is entitled to contribution from the other. Thus if the owners of a party-wall have permitted it to become in a dilapidated and dangerous condition, or if two counties equally bound to keep a bridge in repair have neglected their duty in this regard, and either has been compelled to pay the damages resulting from such negligence, contribution from the other may be enforced: *Armstrong County* v. *Clarion County*, 66 Pa. St. 218; 5 Am. Rep. 368; *Ankeny* v. *Moffitt*, 37 Minn. 109. Where the officers of a corporation neglected to file certain certificates as required by statute, and thereby all became liable to a creditor of the corporation for the amount of a debt due him from the corporation, it was held that either against whom this liability had been enforced was entitled to contribution from the others: *Nickerson* v. *Wheeler*, 118 Mass. 295.

HEGELER v. FIRST NATIONAL BANK OF PERU.

[129 ILLINOIS, 157.]

CREDITOR'S FAILURE TO DISCLOSE HIS CLAIM. — THE FACT THAT A CREDITOR DOES NOT DISCLOSE THE EXISTENCE OF HIS CLAIM nor have judgment entered thereon when he holds a power of attorney from his debtor authorizing him to enter such judgment, is not a fraud upon those who subsequently become creditors of the same debtor in ignorance of his previous indebtedness, unless there was an agreement between the debtor and the creditor that the existence of the debt should be canceled.

Brewer and Strawn, for the appellant.

G. S. Eldridge, for the appellee.

WILKIN, J. The sole ground upon which a reversal was asked in the appellate court was stated by counsel for appellant in the following language: "The theory upon which complainant seeks a reversal of the decree below will appear from the following extracts from his bill of complaint, viz.: 'That although the notes upon which said judgments were confessed in favor of the Peru bank were dated anterior to the time when the indebtedness for which said judgments were confessed was contracted, still said notes were kept by said bank in its custody, and concealed from the knowledge of complainant, and the judgments thereon were confessed after said glass company became indebted to complainant; that it is inequitable and unjust for said bank to assert a lien upon said premises, under said judgments, as against complainant. Your orator would further represent that, although said judgments in favor of the First National Bank of Peru were not entered up until December 22, 1882, yet said notes both became due in January, 1882, and were each accompanied by power of attorney to confess judgment at any time; that prior to January 10, 1882, the date of the execution of each of said powers of attorney, the De Steiger Glass Company was unable to meet its obligations, and was insolvent, which was then and prior thereto known by said First National Bank of Peru; that said bank had cause for so believing; that just prior thereto said glass company offered to mortgage its property to said bank, but said bank refused, because it would injure the credit of the glass company, and prevent it from obtaining elsewhere further credits and loans; that thereupon said bank took from said glass company said notes, and powers of attorney attached thereto, and agreed to conceal the same, and to allow said glass company to retain the full control of the property, free from any recorded or known lien; that in pursuance of such agreement said First National Bank of Peru, with the intention of allowing said glass company to obtain new and future credit elsewhere, and to defraud its creditors, did keep concealed in its possession for over eleven months, and until December 22, 1882, said judgment notes, when it entered judgments thereon, and took out executions and made levies as aforesaid, with the express purpose of defeating the just claims of your orator and other creditors of said glass company incurred during the period of said concealment, and concealed the amount of indebtedness from the glass company to it until December 22, 1882; that your orator advanced ten thousand dollars September 21, 1882, and four thousand five hundred dollars November 20, 1882, on the false and fraudulent statements of the De Steiger Glass Company as to its financial condition, and upon the delusive and fictitious credit given it by said First National Bank of Peru in allowing it to retain all its property apparently free from encumbrance, and that had your orator known or suspected the existence of said judgment notes he would have given no credits or loans whatever to said glass company; that such concealment enabled the glass company, under the semblance of being the owner of a large amount of unencumbered real estate and personal property, to deceive and mislead your orator and other persons to give it credit that would otherwise have been withheld, by reason of which said glass company did contract the aforesaid debts to your orator, now remaining wholly unpaid; wherefore your orator avers it is inequitable and unjust for said First National Bank of Peru to be allowed to enforce its said pretended liens to the injury of your orator, and until your orator has been paid in full his aforesaid judgment.' "

The briefs and arguments filed in the appellate court are refiled here as the principal arguments in this court.

It must be admitted that if the averment that appellee "agreed to conceal the same, and to allow said glass company to retain the full control of the property, free from any record or known lien, and that in pursuance of such agreement it did conceal," etc., was stricken out of the bill, it would be demurrable for want of equity appearing on its face: *Field* v. *Ridgely*, 116 Ill. 424. There is not a particle of evidence in the record to support that averment, nor is it relied upon in the argument as being essential to complainant's cause. On the contrary, the argument proceeds throughout upon the proposition that the bank took its notes, and held them under circumstances that made its conduct operate as a fraud upon others. There is no pretense that there was any agreement to conceal its claim against the glass company, much less that any such agreement was made for the purpose of enabling the company to obtain credit from others. No evidence can be found in the record proving, or tending to prove, acts or declarations on the part of appellee calculated to induce appellant to give credit to the glass company. There is nothing in the bill, and certainly nothing in the evidence, to show that, at the time appellee took its notes, and refused to take mortgage security, it did not honestly believe that, notwithstanding the insolvency of the glass company, it would, if its credit could be maintained, successfully recover from its embarrassment, continue business, and pay all its debts.

The authorities cited in the brief of appellant lay down correct rules and principles of law, but in our view of this case they are wholly inapplicable. We think the bill was properly dismissed.

In the additional brief and argument filed in this court, it is insisted that the circuit court erred in ordering the property in controversy to be turned over to appellee, and in granting it leave to amend its answer after the cause had been submitted. Neither of these points was presented to the appellate court for decision. The first is not even raised by the assignment of errors. We do not think the order was erroneous. The leave to amend the answer was clearly within the discretionary power of the chancellor.

We find no error in this record, and the judgment of the appellate court will be affirmed.

DEBTOR AND CREDITOR. — Every compositon tainted by preferences is void; and every security given under such circumstances is void: Note to *Bank of Commerce v. Hoeber*, 57 Am. Rep. 363-374. But a creditor may lawfully take from his debtor a conveyance with the honest purpose of securing his own debt, even though he knows that it was intended to hinder and delay other creditors: *Shelley v. Boothe*, 73 Mo. 74; 39 Am. Rep. 481.

FRAUD — CONCEALMENT. — *Suppressio veri* may constitute fraud as well as *suggestio falsi: Beard v. Campbell*, 2 A. K. Marsh. 125; 12 Am. Dec. 362; *Peebles v. Stephens*, 3 Bibb, 324; 6 Am. Dec. 660; note to *Thurston v. Blanchard*, 33 Am. Dec. 710. But a concealment of facts which a party is not bound to disclose does not constitute fraud: *Mills v. Lee*, 6 T. B. Mon. 91; 17 Am. Dec. 118; *Robinson v. Justice*, 2 Penr. & W. 19; 21 Am. Dec. 407; because *suppressio veri*, to constitute fraud, must be a suppression of facts which one party is under legal or equitable obligation to communicate to another: *Juzan v. Toulmin*, 9 Ala. 662; 44 Am. Dec. 448, and note; *Mitchell v. Deeds*, 49 Ill. 416; 95 Am. Dec. 621; *Pickering v. Day*, 3 Houst. 474; 95 Am. Dec. 291.

JUDGMENTS CONFESSED BY AN ASSIGNOR, to be used only in event that an assignment made by him is not sustained, are themselves void if the assignment was made to hinder, delay, or defraud creditors: *Mackie v. Cairns*, 5 Cow. 547; 15 Am. Dec. 477.

GAGE *v.* DAVIS.

[129 ILLINOIS, 236.]

TAX SALES. — THE NOTICE WHICH A PURCHASER AT TAX SALES IS REQUIRED TO GIVE before he becomes entitled to a deed must conform to the statute, and if it fails to inform the owner whether his property was sold for a tax or for a special assessment, or if the date which it specifies as that on which the right to redeem will expire is Sunday, the notice is invalid, and any deed based thereon is void.

TAX SALES — EXPIRATION OF TIME FOR REDEMPTION. — If the day of the month on which the right to redeem from a tax sale falls on a Sunday, it should not be computed, and the owner should be allowed all of the following Monday in which to redeem.

TAX SALES. — IF THE NOTICE OF THE TIME WHEN THE RIGHT TO REDEEM EXPIRES specifies wrong day, it is void, and no valid deed can issue thereon.

John P. Wilson and Franklin P. Simons, for the appellee.

Augustus N. Gage, for the appellant.

By COURT. This is a bill filed by appellee to set aside two tax deeds. The court below rendered a decree in accordance with the prayer of the bill, and from such decree appellant appeals to this court.

The first deed was properly set aside, because of the insufficiency of the following notice: —

"To ——, or whom it may concern: —

"This is to notify you that on the thirteenth day of September, 1873, Henry H. Gage purchased, and afterwards assigned the certificate of purchase to the undersigned, at a sale of lots and lands for taxes and special assessments, authorized by the laws of the state of Illinois, the following described real estate, taxed in the name of William Betts, to wit (except street), sublot 4, all of sublots 5 and 6 of lots 13, 15, 16, and 17, in block 2, west part of Samuel Ellis's Addition to Chicago; said taxes and assessments were levied for the year 1872; and that the time of redemption thereof from said 'sale will expire on the thirteenth day of September, 1875. ASAHEL GAGE."

Section 216 of the revenue act requires the purchaser at a tax sale, or his assignee, to serve, or cause to be served, a notice, which shall state when such purchaser "purchased the land or lot, in whose name taxed, the description of the land or lot he has purchased, for what year taxed or specially assessed, and when the time of redemption will expire."

The notice above quoted fails to state whether the lots were taxed or specially assessed. It does not inform the owner whether his lots were sold for a tax or special assessment. It merely tells him that his lots were sold at a general sale of lots and lands for taxes and special assessments levied for the year 1872. The words "said taxes and assessments were levied for the year 1872" refer back to and define the sale at which the lots in question were sold, but such words cannot be construed to mean that the lots were sold on September 13, 1872, for both taxes and special assessments. For these reasons, the notice was insufficient under our rulings in *Gage* v. *Waterman*, 121 Ill. 115, and *Stillwell* v. *Brammell*, 124 Ill. 338.

The second tax deed was issued to appellant on July 16, 1879, in pursuance of a tax sale on November 3, 1876, for the fourth installment of the South Park assessment. No objec-

tion is made to any of the proceedings prior to the sale. But
it is said that the notice served on the occupant of the premises, in which he was notified that the right to redeem would
expire on the third day of November, 1878, was insufficient,
for the reason that the third day of November, 1878, was
Sunday, and hence that day should have been excluded in
computing the time the owner was entitled to redeem. This
position is predicated on two provisions of the Revised Statutes of 1874, as follows: —

Section 6, chapter 100: "In computing the time for which
any notice is to be given, whether required by law, order of
the court, or contract, the first day shall be excluded and the
last included, unless the last day is Sunday, and then it also
shall be excluded."

Section 1, clause 11, chapter 131: "The time within which
any act provided by law is to be done shall be computed by
excluding the first day and including the last, unless the last
day is Sunday, and then it also shall be excluded."

Section 5, article 9, of the constitution, provides that the
right of redemption from tax sales of real estate shall exist in
favor of the owner for a period of not less than two years from
the date of such sales. Section 210, chapter 120, of the Revised Statutes, provides that lands sold for taxes may be redeemed at any time before the expiration of two years from
the date of sale. The redemption of lands from a sale for
taxes is an act authorized to be done by law,—an act that
seems to fall directly within the terms of the statute. If we
are correct in this, then, as November 3, 1878, was Sunday,
the time provided for redeeming the lands sold on November
3, 1876, did not expire until November 4, 1878. The provision
of the statute requiring the purchaser at the tax sale, or his
assignee, to notify the person in possession of the lands when
the time of redemption will expire is imperative, and a notice
which specifies a wrong date cannot be regarded as any notice
whatever, within the meaning of the statute: *Wisner* v. *Chamberlin*, 117 Ill. 568. From what has been said, it follows that
the deed issued on the sale of 1876 was illegal, and passed no
title.

It is insisted in the argument of appellee that the amount
the court required the complainant to pay as a condition
precedent to vacating the deeds was too large. The appellee,
however, has assigned no cross-errors, and that question does
not arise on the record. If he was dissatisfied with the decis-

ion of the court, he could only call the decision in question by the assignment of cross-errors, which has not been done.

The decree of the superior court will be affirmed.

IN THE CASE OF *Brickey* v. *English*, 129 Ill. 646, the affidavit of the service of the notice of tax sale and of the expiration of the time to redeem stated "that the affiant served, or caused to be served, written or printed, or partly written and partly printed, notice of purchase at said tax sale, upon Thomas, Patrick, and William Hayden, and William English, the only person in actual possession or occupancy of said piece or parcel of land or lot; and also a partly written and partly printed notice was given to D. M. Hardy and William T. Demint, the owners or parties in said piece or parcel of land." The court held that the affidavit was fatally defective on account of its uncertainty in failing to state who served the notice, and how and when it was served.

TAX SALES ARE NOT VALID, unless every substantial requirement of the statute has been strictly complied with: *Alexander* v. *Walter*, 8 Gill, 239; 50 Am. Dec. 688; *Brown* v. *Wright*, 17 Vt. 97; 42 Am. Dec. 481; *Dikeman* v. *Parrish*, 6 Pa. St. 210; 47 Am. Dec. 455; *Lyon* v. *Hunt*, 11 Ala. 295; 46 Am. Dec. 216; *Scales* v. *Alvis*, 12 Ala. 617; 46 Am. Dec. 269.

CLAFLIN *v.* DUNNE.

[129 ILLINOIS, 241.]

JUDGMENT AGAINST A DECEASED PERSON over whom the court had obtained jurisdiction in his lifetime, though irregular, is not void.

JUDGMENT AGAINST A DECEASED PERSON over whom the court had obtained jurisdiction in his lifetime may be reversed on error if his death appears from the record. Otherwise it may be vacated on motion in the court where it was entered. Under the practice act of Illinois, the motion may be made at any time within five years after the rendition of the judgment.

JUDGMENT AGAINST SEVERAL DEFENDANTS, ONE OF WHOM IS DEAD at the time it is rendered, is a unit as to all the defendants, and hence, on a proper motion being made therefor, must be vacated as to all.

PRACTICE — RECORD ON APPEAL. — The supreme court of Illinois will not consider as a part of the record anything which was not before the appellate court when the case was decided there. If the record is amended in the trial court, such amendment will not be considered in the supreme court if it was not made a part of the record of the appellate court.

MOTION by John Claflin, executor of the estate of Horace B. Claflin, to vacate a judgment, entered on the twentieth day of January, 1887, against Horace B. Claflin and others, on the ground that Horace B. Claflin died on the fourteenth day of November, 1885. The action was commenced March 1, 1884, and on the thirteenth day of the same month, all of the de-

fendants appeared in the action, and filed their separate pleas
therein.

Kraus, Mayer, and Stein, for the appellants.

John Maynard Harlan, and Smith and Pence, for the appellee.

CRAIG, J. The first inquiry presented by the record for
determination is, whether the judgment rendered against
Horace B. Claflin is void, or is it voidable only. It will be
observed that this is not a case, in its facts, where the action
was instituted against a dead person, and a judgment followed. In such a case, it may be conceded that the judgment would be void, on the ground that the court never
acquired jurisdiction of the person of the defendant; but this
case stands upon a different basis, and must be decided upon
different grounds. Here the action was commenced while
Claflin was alive. He appeared in court and pleaded to the
action. The court thus had jurisdiction of the subject-matter
and of the person, and the question arises, whether, after the
filing of the plea, the death of Claflin, without notice of the
death being brought to the attention of the court, deprived
the court of jurisdiction to render a judgment in the cause.
The question is one not free from difficulty, and one, too, upon
which the authorities are not harmonious. Freeman on Judgments, section 140, says: "If jurisdiction be obtained over the
defendant in his lifetime, a judgment rendered against him
subsequently to his death is not void." In section 153, the
author says: "Judgments for or against deceased persons are
not generally regarded as void on that account, ... and
while the court ought to cease to exercise its jurisdiction over
a party when he dies, its failure to do so is an error to be corrected on appeal if the fact of the death appears upon the
record, or by writ of error *coram nobis* if the fact must be
shown *aliunde.*" The same doctrine has been announced by
the supreme court of Pennsylvania: *Warder* v. *Tainter,* 4
Watts, 278; *Yaple* v. *Titus,* 41 Pa. St. 203; 80 Am. Dec. 604.
In the last case, it is said: "Now it would seem to be well established that, in civil proceedings against a person, his death
does not so completely take away the jurisdiction of a court
which has once attached as to render void a judgment subsequently given against him. The judgment is reversible on
error if the fact and time of death appear in the record, or in
coram nobis if the fact must be shown *aliunde;* but it is not

void." See also *Coleman* v. *McAnulty*, 16 Mo. 173; 57 Am. Dec.
229; *Spalding* v. *Wathen*, 7 Bush, 662; *Reid* v. *Holmes*, 127
Mass. 326; *Swasey* v. *Antram*, 24 Ohio St. 87.

Whether a judgment rendered against a deceased person
after he had pleaded to the action, like the one in question,
is void or voidable, is a question which has never been directly
presented to this court. Similar questions have, however, been
passed upon by this court. In *Camden* v. *Robertson*, 2 Scam.
508, an action of debt was brought in the name of two plaintiffs. On the trial of the cause, the circuit court allowed the
defendant to prove that one of the plaintiffs was dead before
the action was brought. On appeal, it was held that the
evidence was inadmissible. It is there said: "If one of the
plaintiffs had died before the commencement of the suit, that
fact was no bar to the action, and could only be available to
the defendant by pleading in abatement."

In *Stoetzell* v. *Fullerton*, 44 Ill. 108, where one of the plaintiffs had died pending an action of *assumpsit*, it was claimed
that the judgment, execution issued thereon, and sale under
the execution, were void, and might be attacked in a collateral
proceeding; but the court held otherwise. It is there said:
"The death of Church pending the suit was a fact which might
have been pleaded in abatement, but the defendant chose
rather to try the cause on its merits. It is very clear that
under this plea he could not give in evidence the death of one
of the plaintiffs. If this be so, then surely he ought not to be
allowed to give the fact in evidence in another action, and by
that proof nullify the judgment. . . . . The error, if it be one,
was an error of fact, which could only be corrected by a writ
of error *coram nobis*."

In *Danforth* v. *Danforth*, 111 Ill. 236, where the defendant
died after the cause had been taken under advisement, and a
judgment reversing the judgment of the appellate court was
subsequently entered, on application, the judgment was allowed
to be entered as of the date when the cause was submitted.
The judgment of reversal, the defendant being dead, was held
to be irregular, but not void. It is there said: "Where the
sole defendant is dead when the suit . . . . is brought, it may
be true that a judgment against the deceased defendant is a
nullity, for the reason that the court never acquired jurisdiction of the cause. . . . . But that is not the case here. Here
the court, before taking any steps, was clothed by the act
of the parties and the law with full jurisdiction and rightful

authority to render the judgment it did. Did the death of appellee, not brought to the notice of the court by plea, suggestion, or otherwise, deprive it of such jurisdiction lawfully acquired? We think not."

While these cases do not, in terms, decide the question here involved, yet the plain inference to be drawn from all of them is, that a judgment like the one in question, rendered against a deceased person, is not void. Reference has, however, been made to *Life Association of America* v. *Fassett*, 102 Ill. 315, as a case holding that a judgment against a deceased person is void. It is said in that case, in plain language, that a judgment rendered against a deceased person is void; but upon an examination of the facts there involved, it will be found that no such question was presented in that record. Whether a judgment against a deceased person was void or voidable did not arise in that case, and whatever may have been said upon that branch of the case is *obiter dictum*, and binding upon no one. As said before, there are authorities holding that a judgment rendered against a deceased person is void, but we think the weight of authority and the reason of the rule is, that such a judgment is not void, but voidable. But while a judgment of this character cannot be attacked collaterally, it may be reversed on error, if the fact of the defendant's death appears from the record. If not, the judgment may be vacated by motion in the court where the judgment was rendered. It is an error of fact, which may now be reached by motion, but which was formerly reached by writ of error *coram nobis*. Section 67 of the practice act authorizes the motion to be made at any time within five years after rendition of final judgment. When the motion is made under the statute, the question does not arise collaterally, as is supposed, but the motion to vacate, like a writ of error in a proper case, is a direct proceeding, and calls in question the legality of the judgment.

We think the judgment was erroneous as to Horace B. Claflin, and the superior court erred in not vacating it on motion entered for that purpose.

But it is claimed that although the judgment may be vacated against Horace B. Claflin, it should be sustained as to the other defendants. We do not concur in this view. The judgment is a unit as to all the defendants, and if erroneous as to one, it is erroneous as to all: *Cruikshank* v. *Gardner*, 2 Hill, 333; *Sheldon* v. *Quinlen*, 5 Hill, 441; *Williams* v. *Chal-*

fant, 82 Ill. 218; *Jansen* v. *Varnum*, 89 Ill. 100; *Earp* v. *Lee*, 71 Ill. 194; *Goit* v. *Joyce*, 61 Ill. 489; *Tedlie* v. *Dill*, 3 Ga. 104. The last case cited was an action of *assumpsit* against several defendants, including one who was dead at the time of the rendition of judgment. It is there said: "A judgment, as being an entire thing, cannot be reversed in part and stand good as to the other part, or be reversed as to one party and remain good against the rest."

An amended record has been filed in this court, showing that a motion was made to vacate the judgment on a prior day, and overruled, from which no appeal was taken or writ of error sued out. That record was not before the appellate court, and cannot be considered here. If the record was defective, it ought to have been amended in the appellate court. This court acts upon the record which was before the appellate court, and that alone.

We think the superior court erred in refusing to vacate the judgment, and the judgment of the superior and appellate courts will be reversed, and the cause remanded.

JUDGMENTS AGAINST DECEASED PERSONS. — Judgments rendered against deceased persons are not absolutely void, but merely voidable: *Mitchell* v. *Schoonover*, 16 Or. 211; 8 Am. St. Rep. 282, and note. Compare extended note to *Evans* v. *Spurgin*, 52 Am. Dec. 107-110, for a discussion upon the validity of judgments rendered against deceased persons.

FARWELL v. BECKER.

[129 ILLINOIS, 261.]

JURISDICTION — AMOUNT INVOLVED WHEN THERE ARE TWO OR MORE DEFENDANTS. — Where the amount against each defendant is separate and distinct, the two amounts cannot be united so as to confer jurisdiction, but each must be treated as a separate suit; and if the amount involved as to either one is not large enough to confer jurisdiction, the appeal must fall as to that one.

CONTRIBUTION BETWEEN WRONG-DOERS will be enforced in equity when the person seeking redress is presumed not to have known that he was doing an unlawful act.

CONTRIBUTIONS BETWEEN PERSONS WHO HAVE MADE AN UNLAWFUL LEVY. — If several persons levy upon goods under separate writs of attachment, and the goods are sold by a receiver appointed for that purpose, and the proceeds applied towards the satisfaction of such writs, and an action is subsequently brought by a claimant of the goods against the plaintiffs in the writs, and a judgment recovered for the value thereof, which one of the parties satisfies, he may maintain a suit in equity to enforce contributions from the others in proportion to the respective amounts collected by him and by them by means of such writs.

BILL in equity by John V. Farwell & Co. against Gerhard
Becker and Elbert W. Shirk for contribution. In December,
1881, the plaintiffs and the defendants brought separate actions against the firm of Olquist Brothers, in Jones County
and in Linn County, Iowa, and attached under their separate
writs a stock of goods which Olquist Brothers had sold and
delivered to N. A. Sunberg, and also another stock of goods
sold by Olquist Brothers to N. A. Sunberg and one F. B.
Olquist. The several suits by attachment were prosecuted to
judgment, and a receiver was appointed, who took charge of
the goods, and sold them, and realized from the goods attached
in Jones County $4,080.14. W. A. Sunberg and Sunberg and
Olquist, claiming under the sales hereinbefore mentioned, commenced separate actions against the sheriffs of Linn and
Jones counties, and the complainants and defendants in this
action were substituted as defendants in place of the sheriffs
of those counties. Those actions resulted in judgments in
favor of the plaintiffs therein, and against the plaintiffs and
defendants in the present action; and the complainants in this
action, being pressed for the immediate payment of those judgments, and threatened with a levy upon their property, gave
checks for the full amounts thereof, and took an assignment
thereof in favor of one of their attorneys for the avowed purpose of keeping the judgments alive, and enforcing contribution from their co-defendants. The trial court found that the
defendants, Becker and Shirk, the latter being a member of
the firm of Sherer, Shirk, & Co., were each liable to contribute
in proportion to the respective amounts collected by means of
the attachment writs, and it was decreed that said Shirk pay
complainant $554.75, and that the defendant Becker should
pay $5,047.75.

Tenney, Bashford, and Tenney, for the appellants.

Beck and Charlton, John Gibbons, and Frederick Ullman, for
the appellee.

CRAIG, J. The appellee, Elbert W. Shirk, has entered a motion to dismiss the appeal, so far as he is concerned, on the
ground that the amount involved is less than one thousand
dollars, and the judgment of the appellate court is final.

The bill in this case was brought against two defendants, —
Becker and Shirk. The facts set out in the bill, briefly stated,
are, that Farwell & Co., Becker, Shirk's firm (Sherer, Shirk, &
Co.), and Eisen & Co. were creditors of Olquist Brothers, a firm

doing business at Monticello and Center Point, Iowa. The firm became insolvent, and made transfers of their stock, which the creditors claimed were fraudulent, and thereupon brought attachment suits through the same attorneys. The goods were sold under the attachment proceedings, and enough was realized to pay the claims of Farwell, Becker, and Shirk in full. Trespass suits were brought by the parties who purchased the goods from Olquist Brothers, against the sheriffs who made the levies, for the value of the goods, and after considerable litigation in Iowa, judgments were recovered by the plaintiffs in both of the suits, which judgments were paid by Farwell & Co. They also paid the costs and expenses of defending the suits, and brought this bill to compel Becker and Shirk to contribute *pro rata* to the payment of the amount they had paid out. The circuit court entered a money decree, requiring Becker to pay complainants $5,047.75, and requiring Shirk to pay $554.74. To reverse the decree, each defendant took a separate appeal to the appellate court. The appellate court reversed the decree as to both defendants, and remanded the cause, with directions to dismiss the bill. To reverse that judgment, complainants appeal to this court.

We think it is plain that this court has no jurisdiction, so far as the defendant Shirk is concerned. Although two parties (Becker and Shirk) were made defendants to the bill, the action is against each defendant to enforce a separate and distinct liability. The claim relied upon was separate as to each defendant, and so was the recovery. Shirk was in no manner connected with Becker as to the claim against him, nor was Becker in any manner liable as respects the claim against Shirk. Where the amount against each defendant is separate and distinct, as is the case here, the two amounts cannot be united so as to confer jurisdiction, but each must be treated as a separate suit; and if the amount involved as to either one is not large enough to confer jurisdiction, the appeal must fall: See *Ballard Paving Co.* v. *Mulford*, 100 U. S. 147.

The appeal, as to appellee Shirk, will be dismissed.

Several questions have been discussed by counsel, in the argument, but there is but one question of any importance presented by the record, and that is, whether complainants in the original bill (appellants here) have the right to require Gerhard Becker to contribute to the payment of the judgments rendered in the district courts of Jones and Linn counties, Iowa, and costs, which the complainants had paid, in consequence of the levy on the goods as the property of Olquist Brothers.

It is insisted by appellee that in the attachment and sale of the goods in Iowa, the complainants and Gerhard Becker, the defendant, were all wrong-doers, and that no right of contribution exists between wrong-doers. There are cases which hold that no right of contribution exists between wrong-doers. *Merryweather* v. *Nixon*, 8 Term Rep. 186, may be regarded as a leading case on the subject. *Nichols* v. *Nowling*, 82 Ind. 488, *Peck* v. *Ellis*, 2 Johns. Ch. 131, *Cumpston* v. *Lambert*, 18 Ohio, 81, 51 Am. Dec. 442, and *Spalding* v. *Oakes*, 42 Vt. 343, hold the same doctrine. There are other cases where the same rule has been declared, but we do not think the weight of authority sustains the doctrine that no right of contribution exists between wrong-doers as it is broadly stated in *Merryweather* v. *Nixon*, *supra*. Indeed, the later English cases do not, in our opinion, sustain the doctrine as it is laid down in that case. The question arose in *Adamson* v. *Bidgood*, 4 Bing. 66, and in passing upon the question, among other things, Bert, C. J., said: "It was certainly decided in *Merryweather* v. *Nixon* that one wrong-doer could not sue another for contribution. Lord Kenyon, however, said that the decision would not affect cases of indemnity, where one man employed another to do acts, not unlawful in themselves, for the purpose of asserting a right. This is the only decided case on the subject that is intelligible. The case of *Phillips* v. *Biggs*, Hardr. 164, was never decided, but the court of chancery seemed to consider the case of two sheriffs of Middlesex, where one had paid the damages in an action for an escape, and sued the other for contribution, as like the case of two joint obligors. From the inclination of the court in the last case, and from the concluding part of Lord Kenyon's judgment in *Merryweather* v. *Nixon*, and from reason, justice, and sound policy, the rule that wrong-doers cannot have redress or contribution against each other is confined to cases where the person seeking redress must be presumed to have known that he was doing an unlawful act." What was said in the case cited was approved in a later case,—*Betts* v. *Gibbons*, 2 Ad. & E. 57; see also *Nooley* v. *Batte*, 2 Car. & P. 417.

Story on Partnership, section 220, after stating what is regarded as the general rule,—that no right of contribution is allowed, by the common law, between joint wrong-doers,—says: "But the rule is to be understood according to its true

sense and meaning, which is, where the tort is a known, meditated wrong, and not where the party is acting under the supposition of the entire innocence and propriety of the act, and
the tort is merely one of construction or inference of law."

Armstrong Co. v. *Clarion Co.*, 66 Pa. St. 218, 5 Am. Rep. 386,
sanctions the rule announced in Story, and after reviewing
the authorities on the question, holds that where the tort is a
known, meditated wrong, contribution cannot be had, but
where the party is acting under the supposition of the entire innocence and propriety of the act, contribution may be
awarded.

In *Bailey* v. *Bussing*, 28 Conn. 455,—a leading case on the
subject,—it was held: "The rule that there can be no contribution among wrong-doers has so many exceptions that it can
hardly, with propriety, be called a general rule. It applies
properly only to cases where there has been an intentional
violation of the law, or where the wrong-doer is presumed to
have known that the act was unlawful."

In *Jacobs* v. *Pollard*, 10 Cush. 287, 57 Am. Dec. 105, the supreme court of Massachusetts state the law as follows: "No
one can be permitted to relieve himself from the consequences
of having intentionally committed an unlawful act by seeking an indemnity or contribution from those with whom or
by whose authority such unlawful act was committed. But
justice and sound policy, upon which this salutary rule is
founded, alike require that it should not be extended to cases
where parties have acted in good faith, without any unlawful
design, or for the purpose of asserting a right in themselves
or others, although they may have thereby infringed upon
the legal rights of third persons. It is only where a person
knows, or must be presumed to know, that his acts were unlawful, that the law will refuse to aid him in seeking an
indemnity or contribution. It is the unlawful intention to
violate another's rights, or a willful ignorance and disregard
of those rights, which deprives a party of his legal remedy in
such cases."

Acheson v. *Miller*, 2 Ohio St. 203, 59 Am. Dec. 663, is a case
in its facts quite similar to the present case. In the discussion on the right of contribution, the supreme court of Ohio
said: "The rule that no contribution lies between trespassers,
we apprehend, is one not of universal application. We suppose it only applies to cases where the persons have engaged
together in doing, wantonly or knowingly, a wrong. The case

may happen that persons may join in performing an act which to them appears to be right and lawful, but which may turn out to be an injury to the rights of some third party, who may have a right to an action of tort against them. In such case, if one of the parties who has done the act has been compelled to pay the amount of the damages, is it not reasonable that those who were engaged with him in doing the injury should pay their proportion?" After reviewing the authorities, the court holds that the legal rule is, that when parties think they are doing a legal and proper act, contribution will be had, but when the parties are conscious of doing a wrong, courts will not interfere. See also *Coventry* v. *Barton*, 17 Johns. 141; 8 Am. Dec. 376.

Under the authorities, we think it is clear that if the attaching creditors, at the time they sued out their attachments and seized the goods, acted in good faith, exercising such prudence and caution as an ordinarily prudent person would exercise, with no intention of committing a trespass or injuring any one, but with the honest belief that the transfers made by Olquist Brothers were fraudulent as to creditors, the right of contribution exists, although it ultimately turned out that the seizure of the goods was unlawful and unwarranted. The facts surrounding the transaction at the time the levy was made were such, in our opinion, as to lead any prudent person to believe that the goods were liable to be attached by creditors, as was done. Olquist Brothers were, at the time of the pretended sale, largely indebted to various parties. A day or two before the attachments issued, they claimed to have sold the Monticello store to N. A. Sunberg, and the other stock to N. A. Sunberg and F. B. Olquist, another brother. No effort was made to adjust or pay their liabilities. They retained no other property liable to levy or sale. These and other kindred facts were brought to the attention of the attaching creditors before they proceeded to seize the goods. If the sales were fraudulent, although the possession of the goods was turned over to the purchasers, the creditors had the right to levy. Were not the facts surrounding the transaction such that a reasonably prudent person might well believe that an attempt had been made to defraud creditors? If so, it cannot be said that the attaching creditors, in making the levy, intentionally violated the law. Nor were they presumed to have known that the levy was unlawful. The fact that the goods, when attached, were in the possession of Sunberg, is not a controlling fact. The surrounding circumstances indicated that the pretended sale was fraudulent, and if fraudulent, as it appeared to be, the creditors had a right to attach the goods, although in possession of a pretended purchaser, and a seizure, under such circumstances, cannot be regarded as tortious.

As to the equities of the case, they are with the complainants. The defendant, as well as complainants, sued out attachments, which were levied on the goods. He assisted in defending the actions brought by the claimant of the goods. His debt was fully paid from money arising out of a sale of the goods under the attachment, and as the complainants have been compelled to refund the value of the goods, equity and fair dealing unite in requiring the defendant to contribute his just proportion of the burden which has been cast upon the complainants on account of the seizure and sale of the goods. We think the decree of the circuit court holding Becker liable to contribute was correct.

One other fact remains to be noticed. It appears, from the evidence, that the complainants, when they paid the two judgments rendered against them for taking the goods, did not have the judgments receipted and canceled, but they were assigned to Parkhurst, who was an attorney of complainants. The decree treats the judgments as belonging to complainants, which is the fact; but as they were assigned to Parkhurst, we think the decree should be modified, requiring complainants to procure an assignment of the judgments from Parkhurst, and file the same with the decree, as a condition precedent to the issuing of an execution to collect the amount found due by the decree. In this respect the decree of the circuit court will be modified. In all other respects it will be affirmed.

The judgment of the appellate court as to defendant Becker will be reversed. ———

CONTRIBUTION AMONG WRONG-DOERS: See note to *Kirkwood* v. *Miller*, 73 Am. Dec. 147-149; *Boyer* v. *Bolender*, 129 Pa. St. 324; 15 Am. St. Rep. 723, and note; note to *Village of Carterville* v. *Cook*, *ante*, pp. 250-257.

SEXTON *v.* CHICAGO STORAGE COMPANY.

[129 ILLINOIS, 318.]

ASSIGNMENT OF LEASE, WHAT IS. — IF THE LESSEE ASSIGNS HIS WHOLE ESTATE without reserving to himself any reversion therein, a privity of estate is at once created between the assignee and the original lessor, and the latter then has a right of action directly against the assignee on the covenants running with the land; but if the lessee sublets the premises, reserving any reversion, however small, privity of estate between the assignee and the landlord is not established, and the latter has no right of action against the former.

ASSIGNMENT OF LEASE, WHAT IS. — IF ALL THE LESSEE'S ESTATE IS TRANSFERRED, the instrument of transfer operates as an assignment of the lease, notwithstanding words of demise instead of assignment are used, and the reservation of rent to the grantor or assignor, and of a right of re-entry on the non-payment of rent, or the non-fulfillment of the other covenants in such instrument.

THE RELATIONS OF LANDLORD AND ASSIGNEE OF THE TERM DO NOT RESULT FROM CONTRACT, BUT FROM PRIVITY OF ESTATE, and therefore, when the original lessee has divested himself of his entire term, and thus ceased to be in privity of estate with the original landlord, the person to whom he transmits that entire term must necessarily be in privity of estate with the original landlord, and hence liable as assignee of the term.

SUBLEASING, WHAT IS NOT. — IF A LESSEE TRANSFERS ALL HIS ESTATE TO ANOTHER, such transfer is not converted into a sublease by the fact that the lessee reserved a new and different rent, or the right to declare the transfer void for non-performance of its covenants, and to re-enter for such breach, or at the end of the term, and the instrument of transfer also contained a covenant on the part of the transferee to surrender at the end of the term, or upon the forfeiture of the term for a breach of covenant.

RIGHT TO ENTER FOR BREACH OF CONDITION SUBSEQUENT cannot be alienated. It is not a reversion or estate in land, but a mere chose in action, and when enforced, the grantor is in by the forfeiture of the condition, and not by a reverter; but this rule of law is not abrogated nor modified by a statutory provision declaring that "the grantees of any demised lands, tenements, rents, or other hereditaments, or of the reversion thereof, the assignee of the lessor of any demise, and the heirs and personal representatives of the lessor, grantee, or assignee, shall have the same remedies, by entry, action, or otherwise, for the non-performance of any agreement in the lease, or for the recovery of any rent, or for the doing of any waste, or other cause of forfeiture, as their grantor or lessor might have had if such reversion had remained in such lessor or grantor."

ASSIGNMENT OF LEASE, RIGHT TO OBJECT TO. — A clause in a lease that no assignment thereof shall be valid without the assent in writing of the lessor is for the benefit of the latter, and cannot be urged by the assignee of the lease against the landlord, who has not objected to the assignment.

LANDLORD IS NOT ESTOPPED FROM INSISTING THAT A TRANSFER MADE BY HIS LESSEE was an assignment instead of a subletting by the fact that he refused to release the original lessee and accept the assignee alone, and refused to accept the amount of rent which the assignee had agreed to pay, as a full satisfaction of the lessee's liability, and sued the lessee for rent, and garnished the assignee; for, notwithstanding the assignment, the original lessee remained answerable upon the lease for the payment of the rent which he had therein expressly agreed to pay.

Alexander S. Bradley, John N. Jewett, and Jewett Brothers, for the appellant.

Kenneth R. Smoot, and Monk and Elliott, for the appellees.

SCHOLFIELD, J.   The evidence sufficiently proves that the Chicago Storage Company has "ceased doing business." This is not contested by counsel for appellees, though they seek to avoid its effect by the circumstance, which they claim to be proved, that such failure is solely because of the seizure and appropriation of its property for the payment of rent due from Frank F. Cole alone to appellant. It is therefore manifest that in determining whether the corporation has left debts unpaid, so as to bring the case within section 25, chapter 66, of the Revised Statutes of 1874, as amended by the act of May 22, 1877, in relation to corporations (Laws 1877, p. 66), the first and most important question is, whether the storage company is an assignee of the term of Frank F. Cole, or only a sublessee under him; for if it is an assignee of the term of Frank F. Cole, it stands in his shoes as respects his covenant to pay rent, and its property is liable to be seized and appropriated to the payment of the rent, by distress, as was done. If, however, it is but a sublessee under Frank F. Cole, it is liable only on its covenants to him.

The leases to Frank F. Cole are "for and during" the terms named, "and until the first day of May, 1888." The lease executed by Frank F. Cole to the Chicago Storage Company is of precisely the same premises included by the leases to him, and it is in the identical language of those leases, "for and during" the term named, "and until the first day of May, 1888," so that the terms all end at the same instant of time. No space of time, however minute, therefore, can by any possibility remain after the term of the storage company has ended, before the expiration of the terms of Cole, in which he could enter upon or accept a surrender of the premises.

The general principle, as held by all the authorities, is, that where the lessee assigns his whole estate, without reserving to himself a reversion therein, a privity of estate is at once cre-

ated between his assignee and the original lessor, and the
latter then has a right of action directly against the assignee
on the covenants running with the land, one of which is, that
to pay rent; but if the lessee sublets the premises, reserving
or retaining any reversion, however small, the privity of estate
between the sublessee and the original landlord is not established, and the latter has no right of action against the former,
there being neither privity of contract nor privity of estate
between them. The chief difficulty has been in determining
what constitutes such reservation of a reversion. The more
recent English decisions, and all of the text-books treating of
the question which have been accessible to us, hold that where
all of the lessee's estate is transferred, the instrument will
operate as an assignment, notwithstanding that words of demise instead of assignment are used, and notwithstanding the
reservation of a rent to the grantor, and a right of re-entry on
the non-payment of rent or the non-performance of the other
covenants contained in it: 1 Platt on Leases, 1–9, 102; Wood-
fall on Landlord and Tenant, 7th ed., 211; Wood on Landlord
and Tenant, p. 131, sec. 93; Taylor on Landlord and Tenant,
8th ed., 16, note; 5 Bac. Abr., tit. Leases, sec. 3; 2 Preston on
Covenants, 124, 125; *Boardman* v. *Wilson*, L. R. 4 Com. P. 57;
Doe v. *Bateman*, 2 Barn. & Ald. 168; *Wollaston* v. *Hakewill*, 3
Scott N. R. 616. Undoubtedly many cases may be found
wherein the lessee has granted to another party his entire
term, retaining no reversionary interest in himself, and it has
been held the relation, as between the parties, was that of
landlord and tenant,—or perhaps more correctly, lessee and
sublessee,—because such was clearly the intention of the parties; but this was the result of contract only, and not conclusive upon the original landlord, since he was not a party to it.
The relations of landlord and assignee of a term, however, it
has been seen, do not result from contract, but from privity of
estate, and therefore, when the original lessee has divested
himself of his entire term, and thus ceased to be in privity of
estate with the original landlord, the person to whom he has
transferred that entire term must necessarily be in privity of
estate with his original landlord, and hence liable as assignee
of the term: See Wood on Landlord and Tenant, 132, and authorities cited in note 1; *Van Renseller* v. *Hays*, 19 N. Y. 68;
75 Am. Dec. 278; *Pluck* v. *Diggs*, 5 Bligh, N. S., 31; *Thorn* v.
Woolcome, 3 Barn. & Ald. 586; *Indianapolis etc. Union* v.
Cleveland etc. R'y Co., 45 Ind. 281; *Smiley* v. *Van Winkle*, 6

Cal. 605; *Blumenberg* v. *Myres*, 32 Cal. 93; 91 Am. Dec. 560;. *Schilling* v. *Holmes*, 23 Cal. 230.

Counsel for appellees contend, and the courts below ruled accordingly, that the reservation of a new and different rent, or the reservation to the lessor of the right to declare the lease void for the non-performance of its covenants, and to re-enter for such breach, or at the end of the term, coupled with the covenant of the lessee to surrender at the end of the term, or upon forfeiture of the term for breach of covenant, make the letting by the lessee a subletting, and not an assignment of the term, notwithstanding the lessee has retained in himself no part of the term,—and they rely upon *Collins* v. *Hasbrouck*, 56 N. Y. 157, 15 Am. Rep. 407, *Ganson* v. *Tift*, 71 N. Y. 48, *McNeil* v. *Kendall*, 128 Mass. 245, 35 Am. Rep. 373, and *Dunlap* v. *Bullard*, 131 Mass. 161, as sustaining this contention.

There is general language in *Collins* v. *Hasbrouck*, *supra*, quite as broad as claimed. But no question therein presented called for its use, and its meaning ought to be limited by the facts to which it was applied. There, the first original lease was for the term of ten years from the 1st of April, 1864; the second was for the term of nine years from the 1st of April, 1865. Thus both expired April 1, 1874. The sublease was for the term of two years and seven months from the 1st of September, 1867,—that is to say, until the first of April, 1870, —with the privilege, however, to the lessee to extend the term four years, or until April 1, 1874, by giving two months' notice, etc. The plaintiffs claimed that the leases were forfeited by the subletting, and the court so held. No distinction was taken, in the opinion of the court, between an absolute demise until the end of the term and a mere privilege to have the demise extended four years, which was until the end of the term. We have held that a similar clause in a lease is not a present demise, but a mere covenant, which may be specifically enforced in chancery, or upon which an action at law may be maintained for a breach of covenant: *Hunter* v. *Silvers*, 15 Ill. 174; *Sutherland* v. *Goodnow*, 108 Ill. 528; 48 Am. Rep. 560. And it would seem quite evident that in no view could the reversion have passed until after the grantee elected to have the term for four years longer, and so, when the lease was executed, there was still a reversionary interest in the sublessor, of four years, subject, though it may have been, to be thereafter divested by the election of the sublessee.

In *Ganson* v. *Tift*, *supra*, the sublease provided that at the expiration of the term, or other sooner determination of the demise, the lessee should surrender the demised premises to the lessor, and the court said: "This constitutes a sublease of the premises, and not an assignment of the term."

In *Stewart* v. *Long Island R. R. Co.*, 102 N. Y. 601, 55 Am. Rep. 844, there was a demise by the lessee to the Long Island Railroad Company for a term longer than that held by the lessee. There was also a different rent to be paid than that provided to be paid by the original lease, and there was a reservation of the right to re-enter for non-payment of rent, etc. It was held that, as to the original landlord, this amounted to an assignment of the lease, and that its character was not destroyed by the reservation therein of a new rent to the assignor, with a power of re-entering for non-payment of rent, or by its assumption of the character of a sublease. The court, after laying down the rule substantially as we have heretofore stated it to be recognized by the text-books and recent English decisions, said: "The effect, therefore, of a demise, by a lessee, for a period equal to or exceeding his whole term, is to divest him of any reversionary right, and render his lessee liable, as assignee, to the original lessor; but, at the same time, the relation of landlord and tenant is created between the parties to the second demise, it they so intended,"—citing Taylor on Landlord and Tenant, 7th ed., 109, note *s*, 16, note 5; 1 Washburn on Real Estate, 4th ed., 515, note 6; *Adams* v. *Beach*, 1 Phila. 99; *Indianapolis etc. Union* v. *Cleveland etc. R. R. Co.*, 45 Ind. 281; *Lee* v. *Payne*, 4 Mich. 106; *Lloyd* v. *Cosens*, 1 Ashm. 138; Wood on Landlord and Tenant, Banks's ed., 347, —and then adding: "These rules are fully recognized in this state: *Prescott* v. *Deforest*, 16 Johns. 159; *Bedford* v. *Terhune*, 30 N. Y. 457; 86 Am. Dec. 394; *Davis* v. *Morris*, 36 N. Y. 569; *Woodhull* v. *Rosenthal*, 61 N. Y. 382, 391, 392."

In speaking of the ruling in *Collins* v. *Hasbrouck*, 56 N. Y. 157, 15 Am. Rep. 407, after stating the facts, the court said: "In the opinion, the question is discussed whether the sublease amounted to an assignment of the term of the original lease, or a mere subletting or reletting of part of the demised premises. This question, in view of the result reached on the question of waiver, ceased to be controlling; but in discussing it, the learned judge delivering the opinion made some remarks touching the effect of reserving a new rent in the sublease, and of reserving to the original lessee a right of re-entry for a breach of condition by his lessee, which have given rise to some confusion. The features of the instrument which are above referred to would be proper subjects of consideration for the purpose of determining whether the relation of landlord and tenant was created between the original lessee and his lessor, and bore upon the question then before the court, viz., whether the second lease was a subletting or reletting of part of the demised premises which constituted a breach of the covenant not to sublet or relet. But the question of privity of estate between the original lessor and the lessee of his lessee was not in the case. The determination of the question depends upon whether the whole of the term of the original lessee became vested in his lessee; and the circumstances that the second lease reserves a different rent or a right to entry for breach of condition are immaterial." And after quoting many authorities to sustain that position, the opinion proceeds: "The cases which hold that where a lessee subleases the demised premises for the whole of his term, but his lessee covenants to surrender to him at the end of the term, the sublease does not operate as an assignment, proceed upon the theory that, by reason of this covenant to surrender, some fragment of the term remains in the original lessor [lessee]. In most of the cases, and in the earlier cases in which this doctrine was broached, the language of the covenant was, that the sublessee would surrender the demised premises on the last day of the term."

It is true that in this case, as has been before stated, the lessee demised for a number of years beyond the term for which he held; but it is impossible that, upon principle, there can be any difference between a demise of an entire term; which can leave no possible space of time remaining in the lessor, and a demise for any additional time beyond the term, for since no one can demise what he does not have, all that can pass by the demise, in the latter instance, is the entire term of the lessor. If, here, the demise of Frank F. Cole vests his entire interest in the property, as it professes to do, "for and during" the remainder of his term, "and until the first day of May, 1888," it cannot be that any portion, however short in duration, of the term granted him by the leases of appellant, remained in him, because they are limited by the same words precisely,—namely, "for and during" the term, "and until the first day of May, 1888."

In *McNeil* v. *Kendall*, 128 Mass. 245, 35 Am. Rep. 373, there were easements reserved from the effect of the lease. In *Dun-*

lap v. *Bullard, supra,* however, the facts are analogous in principle to those here involved, and it was held that the demise
of the entire term of the lessee was a sublease, and not an
assignment, because of the right reserved in the lease for
the lessor to re-enter and resume possession for a breach of the
covenants.   But this is held upon the ground that under the
decisions of that court the right to re-enter and forfeit the lease
is a contingent reversionary estate in the property, the court
having previously held, in *Austin* v. *Cambridgeport Parish,* 21
Pick. 215, and *Brattle Square Church* v. *Grant,* 3 Gray, 142, that
where an estate is conveyed, to be held by the grantee upon a
condition subsequent, there is left in the grantor a contingent
reversionary interest, which is an estate capable of devise.   It
has been suggested that these decisions are predicated upon a
local statute: See Tiedeman on Real Property, note 1 to sec.
277, and note 1, on page 904; 6 Am. & Eng. Ency. of Law;
but whether this be true or not, the decisions are plainly contrary to the principles of the common law.

The right to enter for breach of condition subsequent could
not be alienated, as it could have been had it been an estate,
and Coke says: "The reason hereof is for avoiding of maintenance, suppression of right, and stirring up of suits, and
therefore nothing in action entrie or re-entrie can be granted
over."   See also 1 Com. Dig., tit. Assignment, c. 2, p. 688; 3
Com. Dig., tit. Condition, O, 1, p. 129; 4 Kent's Com., 8th ed.,
126, *123; 1 Preston on Estates, 20, *21; Shepherd's Touch-
stone, 117, *121.

It is said in 1 Washburn on Real Property, second edition,
474, *451: "Such a right [i. e., to enter for breach of condition
subsequent] is not a reversion, nor is it an estate in land.   It
is a mere chose in action, and when enforced, the grantor is in
by the forfeiture of the condition, and not by the reverter."
To like effect is also Tiedeman on Real Property, sec. 277; 6
Am. & Eng. Ency. of Law, 903; Taylor on Landlord and
Tenant, 8th ed., sec. 293; *Southard* v. *Central R. R. Co.,* 26
N. J. L. 21; *Webster* v. *Cooper,* 14 How. 501; *Schulenberg* v.
Harriman, 21 Wall. 63; *Nicoll* v. *New York etc. R. R. Co.,* 12
N. Y. 121.

It is true that by section 14 of our statute in relation to
landlord and tenant (R. S. 1874, p. 659), "the grantees of any
demised lands, tenements, rents, or other hereditaments, or of
the reversion thereof, the assignee of the lessor of any demise,
and the heirs and personal representatives of the lessor, gran-

tee, or assignee, shall have the same remedies, by entry, action, or otherwise, for the non-performance of any agreement in the lease, or for the recovery of any rent, or for the doing of any waste, or other cause of forfeiture, as their grantor or lessor might have had if such reversion had remained in such lessor or grantor." But this does not make what was before but a chose in action an estate. The right to enter for breach of covenant is still but a remedy for enforcing performance of a contract, which may be defeated by tender: Taylor on Landlord and Tenant, 8th ed., 302. As is said by the court in *De Peyster* v. *Michael*, 6 N. Y. 507, 57 Am. Dec. 570, in speaking of the effect of a like statute of New York: "The statute only authorized the transfer of the right, and did not convert it into a reversionery interest, nor into any other estate." See also *Nicoll* v. *New York etc. R. R. Co.*, 12 N. Y. 139.

It follows that, in our opinion, the rule assumed to be followed in *Collins* v.·*Hasbrouck, Ganson* v. *Tifft*, and *Dunlap* v. *Bullard, supra*, is not in conformity with the common law, and that it cannot therefore be applied here.

The objection that the written assent of appellant was not obtained to the assignment cannot be urged by appellees. The clause in the leases in that respect is for the benefit of and can be set up by appellant alone. He may waive it if he will, and if he does not choose to set it up, no one else can: *Webster* v. *Nichols*, 104 Ill. 160; *Willoughby* v. *Lawrence*, 116 Ill. 11; 56 Am. Rep. 758; *Arnsby* v. *Woodward*, 6 Barn. & C. 519; *Rale* v. *Farrar*, 6 Maule & S. 121.

But counsel insist that appellant is estopped by his conduct to now allege that the instrument executed by Frank F. Cole is an assignment. We have carefully considered the evidence bearing upon this question, and we are unable to concur in this view. Appellant did refuse to acquiesce in the construction placed by appellees upon the lease of Frank F. Cole, and to settle with them upon that basis. He refused to release Frank F. Cole, and accept the storage company alone, and he refused to accept the amount of rent which the storage company obligated itself to pay Frank F. Cole as a satisfaction of Frank F. Cole's covenant to pay rent to him, but he was all the time willing that the storage company should remain in possession, provided the rent due him by his lease to Frank F. Cole was paid to him. He knew the terms of the lease of Frank F. Cole to the storage company, and he afterwards received rent from it, and permitted it to remain in possession.

The lessee continues, notwithstanding the assignment, liable upon his express covenant to pay rent, and the assignee becomes liable upon the same covenant by reason of his privity of estate, because that covenant runs with the land: Taylor on Landlord and Tenant, 8th ed., sec. 438; 2 Platt on Leases, 356; *Walton* v. *Cronly*, 14 Wend. 63; *Bailey* v. *Wells*, 8 Wis. 141; 76 Am. Dec. 233.

Since appellant might sue Cole on his express covenant to pay rent, and he, having fled the state, take out an attachment in aid thereof, we perceive no reason why he might not, at the same time, take garnishee process against the storage company, and recover any debt which it owed him. There is certainly nothing in this inconsistent with his ultimately enforcing his liability against that company as assignee of Cole's term. It is not shown that the storage company has been, by anything done or said by appellant, induced to do, to its prejudice, anything that it would not otherwise have done. No judgment has been recovered against it, as garnishee of Frank F. Cole, for rent due from it to Frank F. Cole; nor does it appear otherwise to have been compelled to pay money or incur liability by reason of any act or word of appellant proceeding upon the recognition of its being liable to Frank F. Cole, as sublessee, only.

For the reasons given, the decree of the superior court and the judgment of the appellate court are reversed, and the cause is remanded to the superior court for further proceedings consistent with this opinion. ____

ASSIGNMENT OF LEASES, and the respective rights and liabilities of the lessor, assignee, and assignor thereafter: See extended note to *Washington etc. Co.* v. *Johnson*, 10 Am. St. Rep. 557–565.

ASSIGNMENT OF LEASE AND SUBLETTING, distinction between: See note to *Post* v. *Kearney*, 51 Am. Dec. 306, 307; compare *Hessel* v. *Johnson*, 129 Pa. St. 173; 15 Am. St. Rep. 716, and note; *Coburn* v. *Goodall*, 72 Cal. 498; 1 Am. St. Rep. 75, and note.

FARRIS v. PEOPLE.

[129 ILLINOIS, 521.]

CRIMINAL LAW. — THAT EVIDENCE OF A DISTINCT AND SUBSTANTIVE OFFENSE CANNOT BE ADMITTED in support of another offense is a general rule, as laid down by all the authorities. This rule excludes all evidence of collateral facts, or those which are incapable of affording any reasonable presumption or inference as to the principal fact or matter in dispute; and the reason is, that such evidence tends to draw away the minds of the jurors from the point at issue, and to excite prejudice, and mislead them, and moreover, the adverse party, having had no notice of such a course of evidence, is not prepared to rebut it.

CRIMINAL LAW — EVIDENCE OF OTHER OFFENSES. — The mere fact that evidence may tend to prove the commission of other crimes, or to establish collateral facts, does not necessarily render it incompetent, provided it is pertinent to the point in issue, and tends to prove the crime charged; but to make one criminal act evidence of another, a connection between them must have existed in the mind of the actor linking them together for some purpose he intended to accomplish; or it must be necessary to identify the person of the actor by some connection which shows that he who committed the one must have done the other. If the evidence be so dubious that the judge does not clearly perceive the connection, the benefit of the doubt should be given to the prisoner.

CRIMINAL LAW — EVIDENCE OF ANOTHER OFFENSE. — Where one is on trial for murder, and evidence has been received of the killing by him of the deceased in the presence of the latter's wife, it is error to permit her to testify that the prisoner committed a rape upon her soon after the killing, on the same day, and while still on the premises of the deceased. Such evidence is not admissible to prove the motive of the prisoner, where the fact of the killing is not denied, and there is no substantial proof that the prisoner acted in self-defense. The admission of the evidence is prejudicial, because it is calculated to inflame the minds of the jurors against the defendant, rather than to prove him guilty of murder; and though, from the other testimony, it is clear and undoubted that he committed the crime of murder as charged, still the admission of the testimony will be regarded as a prejudicial error, if the jury had the right, by their verdict, to spare the prisoner's life. The admission of proof of the other distinct and revolting crime may have prevented the jury from exercising their discretion in favor of the prisoner to the extent of sparing his life.

H. W. Masters, M. C. Quinn, and Arthur Keithley, for the plaintiff in error.

George Hunt, attorney-general, and Kinsey Thomas, state's attorney, for the people.

WILKIN J. At the August term, 1888, of the Fulton circuit court, plaintiff in error was indicted for the murder of one Stephen McGehee. On his petition, the venue was changed to Peoria County, and at the December term, 1888, of the circuit court of that county he was found guilty of murder, and

sentenced to be executed. He sues out this writ of error, and
urges a reversal of the judgment below, principally on the
ground that the trial court erred in admitting improper evidence on behalf of the people, to his prejudice.

Mrs. Debbie McGehee, wife of the deceased, was the principal witness in the case. She had been married to the defendant, Farris, but had obtained a divorce from him, and on
February 28, 1888, married the deceased. She had not lived
with the defendant since May 9, 1884. She testifies that
about noon, on the 18th of April, 1888, while she, her husband, and the children were eating dinner, defendant came to
the east door of the room in which they were sitting, with a
revolver in his right hand. Her husband spoke to him, saying, "How do you do?" He replied, "How are you?" and
immediately said, "You damned son of a bitch, I have come
to kill you, and I am going to do it"; that McGehee started
to get up, when the defendant fired upon him, and was about
firing the second shot, when deceased, still being in the act of
rising, exclaimed, "Oh, don't!" The second shot was fired,
and McGehee fell. There is no dispute as to the fact that, by
one or both of these shots, McGehee was instantly killed.
Immediately the defendant threatened to kill Mrs. McGehee,
but she and her little boy succeeded in forcing him out of the
house, and overcame him. He then begged them to let him
up, and upon his promising that he would not kill her, they
did so. Thereupon he proposed to go in the house and get
some coffee, but she told him that none had been prepared
for dinner, and as he and the children went in the house, she
ran in the direction of one of the neighbors. She had gone
but a short distance when she discovered that he was pursuing her, and calling upon her to stop. He came up to where
she was, and again threatened to shoot her. She sat down on
the ground, and he and the children also sat down near her,
and she says they then had some conversation, in which he
inquired why she married McGehee, and said that her mother
had told him to kill McGehee. They remained there a short
time, when she asked him to hitch up the team for her, so
that she might go to her parents, and he promised to do so.
They went to the barn, he going in, but she remaining at first
outside. He commanded her to come on in. At this point
an objection was made by counsel for defendant as to any
evidence of what took place there, upon the ground "that it
was no part of the *res gestæ*"; and in ruling upon that objec-

tion, the court held and stated that the prosecution "might prove that the defendant committed the crime of rape upon Mrs. McGehee within a reasonable time after the killing, upon the theory that such evidence tended to prove the motive or intent with which the homicide was committed." She then proceeded to testify that she went in the barn upon his demanding that she should, and sat down, and that they there had some further conversation, but not about McGehee. He finally refused to hitch up the team, and they left the barn and "started to town." He made some inquiry as to what was kept in an old house near by, and proposed to go in and see. He went in, and told her to come in, but she refused until he again told her to do so, when, through fear, she obeyed. Before they went in, he gave the revolver to the little boy, and sent the children to the barn. He then made an indecent proposal to her, which she refused. Thereupon he struck her, and pushed her against the side of the house, she resisting, and attempting to push him away. Counsel for the people then ased her, "What did he do?" Answer: "He mistreated me." Question: "What then occurred? You need not have any hesitancy about telling what was done there. The jury want to know all the facts." And counsel proceeded, by direct questions, to prove by her that the defendant then and there committed a rape upon her. This occurred, as she testifies, about a half hour after the shooting.

As to the circumstances connected with the shooting, Mrs. McGehee is fully corroborated by Eddie Farris, a son of defendant and herself, about eleven years old. The evidence shows that defendant was intoxicated to some extent, and had been drinking for several days; but Mrs. McGehee swears that he knew what he was doing, and there is no reason to doubt her evidence as to that fact. After the evidence of Mrs. McGehee, it was also shown by the state that defendant recently, prior to the killing, made threats against deceased. The only attempt at justification was, that the shooting was done in self-defense, and it is not now claimed that there was any substantial proof in the case upon which to base it.

The foregoing statement will be found sufficiently full for a satisfactory consideration of the question whether or not it was competent for the prosecution to prove the crime of rape, as allowed by the court below, that being the only question which we deem it important to notice.

The general rule that evidence of a distinct, substantive

offense cannot be admitted in support of another offense is laid down by all the authorities. It is in fact but the reiteration of the still more general rule, that in all cases, civil or criminal, the evidence must be confined to the point in issue; it being said, however, by authors on the criminal law, that in criminal cases the necessity is even stronger than in civil cases of strictly enforcing the rule, for where a prisoner is charged with an offense, it is of the utmost importance to him that the facts laid before the jury should consist exclusively of the transaction which forms the subject of the indictment and matters relating thereto, which, alone, he can be expected to come prepared to answer: 3 Russell on Crimes, 5th ed., 368; 1 Roscoe on Criminal Evidence, 8th ed., 92.

"No fact which, on principles of sound logic, does not sustain or impeach a pertinent hypothesis, is relevant, and no such fact, therefore, unless otherwise provided by some positive prescription of law, should be admitted as evidence on a trial. The reason of this rule is obvious. To admit evidence of such collateral facts would be to oppress the party implicated, by trying him on a case for preparing which he has no notice, and sometimes by prejudicing the jury against him. . . . . To sustain the introduction of such facts, they must be in some way capable, as will presently be seen more fully, of being brought into a common system with that under trial": Wharton on Criminal Evidence, sec. 29. "In criminal cases there are peculiar reasons why the test before us should be applied to proof of collateral crimes": Wharton on Criminal Evidence, sec. 30.

"This rule," says Greenleaf (volume 1, section 52), (not confining it to criminal cases), "excludes all evidence of collateral facts, or those which are incapable of affording any reasonable presumption or inference as to the principal fact or matter in dispute; and the reason is, that such evidence tends to draw away the minds of the jurors from the point in issue, and to excite prejudice, and mislead them; and moreover, the adverse party, having had no notice of such a course of evidence, is not prepared to rebut it."

In *Sutton* v. *Johnson*, 62 Ill. 209, which was a civil suit, for an assault and battery, and assault with intent to commit a rape, a witness on behalf of the plaintiff was allowed to testify that the defendant had told him "that he and his wife had not been getting along well together, and he had to be too intimate with the hired woman, or was forced to be too inti-

mate with the hired woman," not stating who the woman was,
and for that error alone a judgment in favor of the plaintiff
was reversed, Mr. Justice Sheldon saying, in the opinion rendered: "This evidence did not tend to prove the assault, ...
and did tend to prejudice the jury against the defendant.
There should not have been brought into the trial of the simple issue in this case anything which might be regarded as
slanderous matter, or other improper conduct of the defendant, to make against him, and by its consideration be likely to
influence the verdict of the jury."

It is conceded that the mere fact that testimony may tend
to prove the commission of other crimes, or to establish collateral facts, does not necessarily render it incompetent, provided it is pertinent to the point in issue, and tends to prove
the crime charged; but the general rule is against receiving
evidence of another offense, and no authority can be found to
justify its admission, unless it clearly appears that such evidence tends, in some way, to prove the accused guilty of the
crime for which he is on trial. Says Agnew, J., in *Shaffner* v.
Commonwealth, 72 Pa. St. 65, 13 Am. Rep. 649: "To make one
criminal act evidence of another, a connection between them
must have existed in the mind of the actor, linking them together for some purpose he intended to accomplish; or it must
be necessary to identify the person of the actor by connection
which shows that he who committed the one must have done
the other." And he adds: "If the evidence be so dubious
that the judge does not clearly perceive the connection, the
benefit of the doubt should be given to the prisoner, instead of
suffering the minds of the jurors to be prejudiced by an independent fact, carrying with it no proper evidence of the
particular guilt."

In *Lapage* v. *State,* 57 N. H. 245, 24 Am. Rep. 69, Cushing,
C. J., after citing many cases in which such proof was held
competent, and showing that in each of them some logical
connection existed between the independent crime proved and
that charged, says: "It should also be remembered that this
being a matter of judgment, it is quite likely that courts
would not always agree, and that some courts might see a
logical connection when others could not. But however extreme the case may be, I think it will be found that the courts
have always professed to put the admission of the testimony
on the ground that there was some logical connection between
the crime proposed to be proved, other than the tendency to

commit one crime, as manifested by the tendency to commit the other."

In *Commonwealth* v. *Ferrigan*, 44 Pa. St. 386, Thompson, J., says: "The rule on this subject may, in substance, be stated to be, that when facts and circumstances amount to proof of another crime than that charged, and there is ground to believe that the crime charged grew out of it, or was in any way caused by it, such facts and circumstances may be proved, to show the *quo animo* of the accused."

Again, in *Commonwealth* v. *Merriam*, 14 Pick. 518, 25 Am. Dec. 420, Putnam, J., said: "Evidence should be excluded which tends only to the proof of collateral facts. It should be admitted if it has a natural tendency to establish the fact in controversy. If the evidence is irrelevant, it should be rejected, for two reasons: 1. It would have a tendency to mislead the jury from the true subject of the inquiry; and 2. No man is to be expected to go to trial prepared to prove things which are unconnected with the issue."

Our conclusion, from all the authorities, is, that whatever be the object of the testimony, — whether to prove guilty knowledge, as in prosecutions for passing forged notes or counterfeit money, where proof of other offenses of the same kind is competent; to prove that the act was not accidental, or done by mistake, as in case of poisoning or embezzlement; to prove motive, as on trial of a husband for the murder of his wife, in which case, in the absence of direct evidence, proof of adultery by the prisoner with another woman was held competent; or in cases where the prisoner says he did not do the act, and supports his denial with the assertion that no motive existed within him for the commission of such a crime, or to refute some anticipated defense, — proof of a distinct, substantive crime is never admissible, unless there is some logical connection between the two, from which it can be said the one tends to establish the other. In this case, it must be borne in mind that there is no evidence whatever connecting the two acts, or tending to show wherein the commission of the rape had any bearing upon or tendency to explain the commission of the homicide, and therefore, if it be held that evidence of the one tended to prove the other, it must be upon the ground that there is some natural or obvious connection between the two acts. Did the proof of rape in this case tend to prove defendant guilty of murder? What element in the crime of murder was wanting when this evidence was admitted, or what fact in evidence necessary to make out the crime of murder did it tend to strengthen or corroborate? It seems clear to us that these are questions which puzzle the legal mind, and can only be answered so as to sustain the admissibility of the evidence in question, if at all, by drawing exceedingly fine distinctions.

To the other question,—Was it not evidence calculated to inflame the minds of the jury, and prejudice them against the defendant, rather than prove him guilty of murder?—the answer is obvious. It is insisted that the object was to show a motive, and for that purpose the learned judge held it competent. In the first place, under the facts proved, it was not necessary to prove a motive. In cases of doubt as to whether the party charged did the criminal act, proof of motive is important, and often decisive; but in this case, the state having shown the deliberate shooting, under circumstances showing both express and implied malice, proof of motive was not necessary to a conviction; and while the prosecution doubtless had the right to add that proof by competent evidence, it may well be doubted whether testimony so strongly calculated to prejudice the jury against the defendant should have been admitted, even though it tended to prove a motive, such proof not being necessary to the case. But no theory has been suggested upon which it can be said that the commission of the crime of rape tended to show a motive for the homicide, and after a most careful examination of all the evidence, and a consideration of it in all its phases, we can discover no rational connection between the two acts, whereby it can be inferred that desire, purpose, or intent to commit the crime upon Mrs. McGehee could have influenced the mind of defendant to take the life of deceased. To so hold seems to us not only illogical, but unnatural and unreasonable.

It is contended by counsel for the people that the prosecution had a right to show all that the defendant did from the time he came to the place of the killing until he left it, as parts of one and the same transaction. Here, again, we must deal with the question, When is it competent to prove a crime distinct from the one for which the accused is on trial? We have already seen, the general rule of evidence excludes such proof. An exception to that rule allows it when the acts form one transaction: 1 Wharton's Crim. Law, sec. 649. As in Heath's case, where it was held competent to show, under the circumstances of the case, that the prisoner, shortly before the killing, shot a third person, notwithstanding the evidence tended to prove a distinct felony, such shooting and the killing of the deceased appearing to be connected as parts of one transaction: 1 Rob. (Va.) 735. Or where on trial for breaking into a booking-office, evidence was admitted that the prisoner had on the same night broken into three other booking-offices belonging to three other stations on the same railway, the four cases being all mixed up together: *Rex* v. *Cobden*, 3 Fost. & F. 76. The same principle obtains when it is sought to prove some distinct act as part of the *res gestæ*, in which case "the principal points of attention are, whether the circumstances and declarations offered in proof were contemporaneous with the main fact under consideration, and whether they were so connected with it as to illustrate its character": 1 Greenl. Ev., sec. 108. Here, as we have said, there is no proof to connect the two acts, nor is there any such obvious relation between them that it may be inferred that the one in any way characterized the other. We are convinced that there is no theory upon which the competency of this testimony can be sustained, without breaking down firmly established rules of evidence.

It is suggested, and pressed by way of argument, that although the trial court may have erred in allowing this proof, yet the case being so clearly made out by other evidence, and the defense so utterly futile, the error should be held harmless. If the only punishment for the crime of murder in this state was death, the point would be entitled to weight. If it was within the province of the court to assume that the jury would have inflicted the death penalty because the proof of guilt justified it, or if our decision was to affect this case alone, we might hesitate to order a reversal on this theory. The legislature has seen fit to clothe juries with a wide discretion in fixing the punishment to be inflicted upon one convicted of murder. Every defendant on trial for that crime is entitled to the full benefit of the statute. When all else has failed him, he has a right to stand before a jury unprejudiced by incompetent, irrelevant evidence, and appeal to them to spare his life. It is impossible for us to know what the jury in this case would have done but for the introduction of this incompetent evidence, much less is it our province to say what they should have done, and no opinion is expressed on that subject. We can only judge of the influence of such testimony upon the minds of the jury by experience and observation common to us all. Here was proof of a distinct felony,—the disgusting and abhorrent facts attendant upon the commission of that most brutal and infamous crime given in detail. No one need be told that from that moment, if the evidence was believed, all feeling of commiseration and mercy toward the defendant must have fled the minds of the jury. There was left for him no possible escape from the death penalty. But aside from all these considerations, we are required to settle a rule of evidence in criminal trials, not merely with reference to this case, but in consideration of future consequences and other rights, and we cannot, from that consideration alone, hesitate to hold that there was such manifest and prejudicial error in the admission of evidence by the trial court in this case as must work a reversal of its judgment.

The judgment will be reversed.

OTHER CRIMES, EVIDENCE OF.—As to when evidence of other crimes is admissible against the defendant in a criminal prosecution, see extended note to *Strong* v. *State*, 44 Am. Rep. 299-308. Evidence of a prior crime can have no legitimate place in the investigation of the commission of a subsequent crime by the same person: *People* v. *Sharp*, 107 N. Y. 427; 1 Am. St. Rep. 851. And evidence of a crime different from the one charged is never admissible, except to show motive, intent, or guilty knowledge: *People* v. *Greenwall*, 108 N. Y. 296; 2 Am. St. Rep. 415, and note; *People* v. *Meyer*, 73 Cal. 548. But under the statute of Massachusetts, the conviction of a felony or a misdemeanor may be shown, to affect the credibility of a witness: *Commonwealth* v. *Ford*, 146 Mass. 131. Where boycotters proclaim intention to do as in a former boycott, evidence of what was done in the former boycott is admissible: *State* v. *Glidden*, 55 Conn. 46; 3 Am. St. Rep. 23. Though generally the commission of another crime cannot be proved to raise the inference of guilt of the crime charged, yet where, upon a charge of rape, the prosecuting witness voluntarily testifies, without objection from defendant, to prior intercourse with her without her consent, she may testify that on such prior occasion she was overcome by fear, and did not therefore inform her mother of the facts: *People* v. *Lenon*, 79 Cal. 626.

GINDELE *v.* CORRIGAN.

[129 ILLINOIS, 582.]

WHERE ADMIRALTY JURISDICTION OF THE UNITED STATES COURT ATTACHES, IT UNDOUBTEDLY EXCLUDES the jurisdictions of the state courts, and a state cannot confer jurisdiction upon its courts in such cases; but it is essential to a suit *in rem* in admiralty against a vessel that an actual seizure be made of the vessel, and it be subjected primarily to the satisfaction of the judgment.

LIENS AGAINST VESSELS MAY BE ENFORCED IN THE STATE COURTS, where the proceeding to enforce them does not amount to an admiralty proceeding *in rem*, or otherwise conflict with the constitution of the United States.

ADMIRALTY — ATTACHMENT OF VESSELS. — THERE IS NO MORE VALID OBJECTION TO ATTACHMENT PROCEEDINGS TO enforce a lien in a suit *in personam*, by holding a vessel by mesne process to be subjected to execution on a personal judgment when recovered, than there is in subjecting her to seizure on the execution. Both are incidents of a common-law remedy, which a court of common law is competent to give.

CONSTITUTIONAL LAW — PROCEEDINGS AGAINST VESSELS. — Where, under the statute of Illinois, a proceeding is commenced against a vessel whose owners are alleged to be unknown, to recover damages resulting from its collision with another vessel, and a writ of attachment is issued, under which the vessel is attached, and thereafter the persons claiming to be her owners give bonds for the release of the attachment as provided by statute, and the vessel is thereupon discharged and released, and after due trial judgment is rendered against the principal and sureties on the bond, the proceeding becomes *in personam*, and has no similitude to admiralty proceedings *in rem*, and the state courts have jurisdiction to enter judgment.

PROCEEDING by John Corrigan against the steam canal-boat Nunnemacher, under chapter 12 of the Revised Statutes of Illinois, known as the water-craft act. The petition stated a cause of action arising from collision of the Nunnemacher with the canal-boat Midnight, belonging to the plaintiff, both vessels being at the time of collision domestic vessels, engaged in commerce wholly within the state of Illinois, and having their home port within the state, and being there enrolled and licensed pursuant to law. Corrigan sued out of the circuit court a writ of attachment, under the provisions of the statute, against the Nunnemacher, alleging in his petition that her owners were unknown. After the writ had been issued, and the Nunnemacher seized thereunder, John Gindele claimed an interest as part owner, and bonded and released the boat from seizure pursuant to the statute. He thereafter entered his appearance in the action, and filed his answer. The answer was afterwards withdrawn by leave of the court, and a motion was made to dismiss the proceedings for want of jurisdiction. Corrigan then amended the petition, after which the motion to dismiss for want of jurisdiction was again interposed. The motion was overruled, and a trial was had before a jury, terminating in a verdict in favor of Corrigan.

C. E. Kremer and C. W. Brown, for the appellants.

Duncan, O'Connor, and Gilbert, and Haley and O'Donnell, for the appellee.

SHOPE, C. J. This was a proceeding by attachment, under chapter 12 of the Revised Statutes of this state, by John Corrigan, against the steam canal-boat Nunnemacher, for an injury to the canal-boat Midnight, upon the waters of the Illinois and Michigan canal, through the alleged gross negligence of those in charge of the defendant boat.

It is first urged that the circuit court of Will County had no jurisdiction of the subject-matter. It is contended that the collision, if produced by negligence, as alleged, was a maritime tort, and therefore within the exclusive jurisdiction of the courts of admiralty, by virtue of the act of Congress of 1789. Where the admiralty jurisdiction of the United States court attaches, it undoubtedly does so to the exclusion of the jurisdiction of the state court: Cohen's Admiralty Law, 1; and a state cannot confer jurisdiction upon its courts in such cases: Id.; *Stewart* v. *Potomac Ferry Co.*, 12 Fed. Rep. 296; *The Hine* v. *Trevor*, 4 Wall. 555. It is, however, essential to a suit *in rem*, in admiralty, against the vessel, that an actual seizure be made of the vessel, and it be subjected primarily to the satisfaction of the judgment. Without such seizure, the court acquires no jurisdiction of the vessel: Cohen's Admiralty Law, 22, 23; *Brennan* v. *Steam-tug Anna P. Darr*, 4 Fed. Rep. 459; *Miller* v. *United States*, 11 Wall. 294.

In *Loy* v. *Steamboat Aubury*, 28 Ill. 412, 81 Am. Dec. 292, which was trespass, for assault and battery by the mate upon the plaintiff while a passenger, brought under the act of the legislature of this state, of February 16, 1857, this court held that the action would lie; citing *Steamboat Champion* v. *Jantzen*, 16 Ohio, 91, and *Canal-boat Huron* v. *Simmons*, 11 Ohio, 458. In *Schooner Norway* v. *Jensen*, 52 Ill. 373, it was held that the act of 1857, giving a summary remedy in certain cases against steamboats and other water-craft, was not confined in its operation to vessels navigating the rivers within or bordering upon this state, but embraced those employed upon any of the navigable waters of the state, and that a sailor

injured on board a vessel through the negligence of the owner
might proceed, under that act, by attachment and seizure of
the vessel. The second section of the act authorized suits
against the owner or owners or master of the craft, or against
the craft itself, and section 4 provided for the seizure of the
craft. In *Tugboat E. P. Dorr* v. *Waldron*, 62 Ill. 221, 14 Am.
Rep. 86, which was an attachment for supplies, this court held
that the proceeding had no resemblance to a libel in a court
of admiralty, but was of the same character as an ordinary
attachment, requiring notice to be given of the pendency of
the suit, and that by it no prior liens were interfered with;
citing *Germain* v. *Steam-tug Indiana*, 11 Ill. 535.

The action in this case was for a tort, which, in the language
of the appellate court, may be defined "to be an injury or
wrong committed, with or without force, to the person or property of another, and such injury may arise by either the non-
feasance, malfeasance, or misfeasance of the wrong-doer."
The common law affords a remedy for torts, although they
may be committed upon a navigable stream; but in such case
the remedy is not exclusively *in rem*, or such as pertains to a
court of admiralty. The common-law remedy is by an action
in personam,—that is, against the wrong-doer in person,—and
not primarily or solely against his property. The state may,
by statute, authorize the attachment of the property of the
debtor or tort-feasor as a security for the satisfaction of the
judgment to be recovered, and in such case the proceeding is
in personam, and not *in rem*. The object of the attachment,
in such case, is to secure a lien upon the property seized for
the payment of the judgment, and not for the condemnation
of the property attached.

In the case of *The Moses Taylor*, 4 Wall. 411, the court say:
"The case before us is not within the saving clause of the
ninth section of the act of 1789. That clause saves only to
suitors 'the right of a common-law remedy where the common
law is competent to give it.' It is not a remedy in the common-law courts which is saved, but a common-law remedy. A
proceeding *in rem*, as used in the admiralty court, is not a
remedy afforded by the common law. It is a proceeding under the civil law. Where used in the common-law courts, it
is given by the statute."

In *The Hine* v. *Trevor*, 4 Wall. 555, the same court say: "If
the facts of the case before us, in this case, constitute a case of
admiralty cognizance, then the remedy, by a direct proceeding

against the vessel, belonged to the federal courts alone, and
was excluded from the state tribunals. . . . . It is said that
the statute of Iowa may be fairly construed as coming within
the clause of the ninth section of the act of 1789, which saves to
suitors, in all cases, the right of a common-law remedy, where
the common law is competent to give it.   But the remedy
pursued in the Iowa courts, in the case before us, is in no sense
a common-law remedy.   It is a remedy partaking of all essential features of an admiralty proceeding *in rem.* . . . . While
the proceeding differs thus from the common-law remedy, it is
also essentially different from what are in the West called
suits by attachment, and in some of the older states foreign
attachments.   In these cases there is a suit against the person of defendant by name, and because of inability to serve
process on him, on account of non-residence, or for some
other reason mentioned in the various statutes allowing attachments to issue, the suit is commenced by a writ directing
the proper officer to attach sufficient property of the defendant
to answer any judgment which may be rendered against him.
This proceeding may be had against an owner or part owner
of a vessel, and his interest thus subjected to sale in a common-law court of the state.   Such action may be also maintained in the common-law courts by such remedy as the
common law gives."   See also *The Belfast,* 7 Wall. 624, and
The Lottawana, 21 Wall. 558.

In *Johnson* v. *Chicago and Pacific Elevator Co.,* 119 U. S.
388, that court again says: "Liens under state statutes, in
suits *in personam,* are of every-day occurrence, and may extend to the lien on vessels, where the proceedings to enforce
them do not amount to admiralty proceedings *in rem,* or otherwise conflict with the constitution of the United States.   There
is no more valid objection to the attachment proceedings to
enforce the lien in a suit *in personam,* by holding the vessel
by mesne process to be subjected to execution on the personal
judgment when recovered, than there is in subjecting her to
seizure on the execution.   Both are incidents of a common-
law remedy, which a court of common law is competent to
give."

Such has been the uniform construction placed upon the act
of Congress referred to.   In the case at bar, after the seizure
of the boat, the personal bond of appellants, as part owners
and sureties, was substituted, and the vessel was thereby released and discharged from the seizure, and thereafter the

case proceeded to final judgment as a proceeding in *personam.* The suit was originally entitled *John Corrigan* v. *The Propeller Nunnemacher*, and the unknown owner or owners of said propeller Nunnemacher. After the trial, the plaintiff, by leave of the court, amended the title of the case so as to make the bondsmen, George A. Gindele, George T. Adams, and John Andrus, the defendants, and thereupon judgment was rendered *in personam* against said bondsmen, as it is provided shall be done by section 21 of chapter 12 of the Revised Statutes of this state, known as the water-craft act.

In *Langdon* v. *Wilcox*, 107 Ill. 606, this court said: "A proceeding under the water-craft act is essentially, in many of its features, like a proceeding *in rem* in admiralty, though differing from the latter, it is believed, sufficiently to avoid any conflict with the constitution of the United States, which gives to the federal court exclusive jurisdiction in admiralty." By section 15 of said act, where the vessel has been seized under the attachment provided for in the act, the owner, or other person interested, may release the same, and have a return of the property attached, upon entering into bond, "conditioned that the obligors will pay all money adjudged to be due such [the] claimants, with costs of suit." Section 21 of the act provides that when the vessel is seized on mesne process, and is released upon bond given by the owner or the persons interested therein, and filed in the court in which the proceeding is pending, the bond shall stand in the place of the vessel, and judgment or decree shall be rendered against the principal and sureties of the bond, providing that in no case shall the judgment exceed the penalty of the bond, and expressly providing that "the subsequent proceedings, after the bond is filed, shall be the same as now provided by law in personal actions in the courts of record in this state." It is manifest that appellants have voluntarily submitted themselves to the jurisdiction of the state court; and it is clear that after having done so, by filing the bond provided by the statute for the release of the vessel, the proceeding was no longer *in rem*, but necessarily *in personam*, and no other than a personal judgment could have been rendered. This being so, the proceedings here have no similitude to an admiralty proceeding *in rem*, and we are of opinion that the circuit court had jurisdiction to render the judgment, and also that the motion to dismiss the suit, entered after the filing of such bond, was properly overruled.

The point is also made that there was no proof that the plaintiff was the owner of the canal-boat injured by the collision. This is a question of fact, which is settled by the verdict of the jury and judgment of the appellate court, and cannot be considered here.

Finding no error in the record, the judgment of the appellate court is affirmed.

JURISDICTION OF ADMIRALTY COURTS IS EXCLUSIVE. — Jurisdiction conferred upon federal courts in civil cases of admiralty is exclusive: *Walters* v. *Steamboat*, 24 Iowa, 192; 95 Am. Dec. 722; *Thoms* v. *Southard*, 2 Dana, 475; 26 Am. Dec. 467; *Phegley* v. *The David Tatum*, 33 Mo. 461; 84 Am. Dec. 57; but it is jurisdiction over admiralty causes, not jurisdiction over all causes affecting foreign vessels, or over liens on such: *Randall* v. *Roche*, 30 N. J. L. 220; 82 Am. Dec. 233. Nor is the jurisdiction of federal courts exclusive as to admiralty actions arising upon lakes, but concurrent with the state courts: *Thorsen* v. *The J. B. Martin*, 26 Wis. 488; 7 Am. Rep. 91.

A proceeding against a vessel by an action *in rem* for damages from a tort can be pursued only by the federal courts: *Young* v. *Ship Princess Royal*, 22 La. Ann. 388; 2 Am. Rep. 731. Compare note to *Johnson* v. *Dalton*, 13 Am. Dec. 566-568, for a discussion of the jurisdiction of torts committed upon the high seas. Jurisdiction *in personam* as well as *in rem* is vested in the maritime courts of the United States: *Case* v. *Woolley*, 6 Dana, 17; 32 Am. Dec. 54.

And it may be said that the test of admiralty jurisdiction is the nature of the claim upon which the action is founded, and not the form of remedy pursued: *Steamer Petrel* v. *Dumont*, 28 Ohio St. 602; 22 Am. Rep. 397. So that when an action falls within the admiralty jurisdiction of the federal courts, such jurisdiction being exclusive, the state courts cannot take it away: *Walters* v. *Steamboat*, 24 Iowa, 192; 95 Am. Dec. 722. Consequently, state courts have no jurisdiction of an action against a vessel by name; for this falls within the exclusive jurisdiction of the federal admiralty courts: *Griswold* v. *Steamboat Otter*, 12 Minn. 465; 93 Am. Dec. 239. Proceedings in rem against vessels cannot be resorted to in state courts: *Steamer Petrel* v. *Dumont*, 28 Ohio St. 602; 22 Am. Rep. 397.

CASES

IN THE

SUPREME COURT

OF

INDIANA.

CRAVENS v. EAGLE COTTON MILLS COMPANY.

[120 INDIANA, 6.]

CONTRACTS — CONSTRUCTION OF. — Where the words of a contract are clear in themselves, it must be construed accordingly; but where they admit of more than one construction, that will be adopted which will give it effect, and in cases of doubt, the practical construction given by the parties will be of controlling influence.

CORPORATIONS. — STOCK SUBSCRIPTIONS IN A CORPORATION are unaffected by collateral pending negotiations between that corporation and another, relative to the purchase of property with which to carry on the former.

CORPORATIONS — CONSTRUCTION OF CONTRACT TO SUBSCRIBE FOR STOCK. — Where a subscriber for stock in a corporation seeks to avoid his subscription on the ground that a collateral contract between his corporation and another has been changed or varied, it is competent to show that no contract had in fact been consummated between the corporations at the time that the contract of subscription was made, in order to aid the construction of the latter contract.

CORPORATIONS — SUBSCRIPTIONS FOR STOCK. — A stipulation in a contract of subscription for stock, by which the amounts subscribed are not to become payable until a collateral contract for the purchase of certain property has been ratified by the corporation, is not a condition precedent to the payment of stock subscriptions, but is an independent covenant to the effect that no contract for such purchase should be finally made without the consent of a majority of the stockholders.

CORPORATIONS. — SUBSCRIBER FOR STOCK IN A CORPORATION cannot defeat an action to collect such subscription by showing that the corporation or its directors have done corporate acts beyond the corporate powers, or have managed the corporate affairs in a negligent, fraudulent, or reckless manner.

CORPORATIONS. — SUBSCRIPTIONS FOR STOCK in a corporation upon condition that a specified amount of subscriptions shall be obtained is a continuing offer to take and pay for the amount subscribed upon the terms proposed; and whenever the specified amount of solvent subscriptions is obtained

within a reasonable time, that is an acceptance of the offer by the corporation. The contract of each subscriber then becomes absolute and unconditional, and payable upon call of the directors.

CORPORATIONS. — SUBSCRIBER FOR STOCK in a corporation cannot withdraw
his subscription, even though it is conditional, unless unreasonable delay
occurs in performing the condition.

CORPORATIONS — EXISTENCE — ESTOPPEL. — Where both the corporation and
the subscriber, in entering into a contract of subscription for stock, assume the existence of the corporation, both are estopped from denying
it, in a suit to compel payment of the subscription.

C. E. Walker, A. D. Vanosdol, and *H. Francisco,* for the appellant.

C. A. Korbly and *W. O. Ford,* for the appellee.

MITCHELL, J.   This action was brought by the Eagle Cotton Mills Company, of. Madison, Indiana, a manufacuring
corporation organized under the general law of this state, to
collect four thousand dollars alleged to be due from Charles
L. Cravens upon a subscription made by the latter to the capital stock of the plaintiff. The facts are set out at great
length, and in minute detail, in a special finding made by the
court. Those material to present the questions for decision
are the following: In November, 1883, a communication was
presented to the Merchants' and Manufacturers' Club, a voluntary association of the city of Madison, in which it was stated
that the Eagle Cotton Mills Company, a corporation owning
and operating two large cotton-mills in the vicinity of Pittsburgh, Pennsylvania, with a view of transferring its business
to this state, would sell all its machinery, including the good-
will of its business, to an Indiana corporation, if one were
legally organized. The price proposed was one hundred thousand dollars, of which amount forty thousand dollars would
be required to be paid in cash, and sixty thousand dollars in
the capital stock of the new corporation. The scheme was
regarded favorably by the club, and by the citizens of Madison, and the Eagle Cotton Mills Company, of Madison, Indiana, was duly organized and incorporated on the thirteenth
day of November, 1883, the object of its formation being to
acquire and own a cotton-mill, and to engage in the manufacture of raw cotton into textile fabrics. The proposition theretofore made to the Merchants' and Manufacturers' Club was
under consideration when the Eagle Cotton Mills Company
was organized, and while its stock was being subscribed for.
The capital stock was fixed at two hundred and fifty thousand
dollars, and was divided into shares of twenty-five dollars

each. The defendant was one of the incorporators of the company, an active promoter of the organization, and solicited subscriptions to its stock, and subscribed for 160 shares in his own name. It was stipulated in the contract of subscription that the several subscribers should pay for the number of shares set opposite their respective names upon the call of the board of directors, provided solvent subscriptions to the amount of one hundred and twenty-five thousand dollars, including sixty thousand dollars promised to be subscribed by the Eagle Cotton Mills Company, of Pittsburgh, should first be obtained; and provided further, that the amount subscribed was not to be payable until the contract with the last-named company, for the purchase of its mills, had been ratified by the votes of those holding a majority of the stock subscribed outside the city of Pittsburgh. It is found that solvent subscriptions for the required amount had been secured, and that on the third day of April, 1884, after considering various propositions from the Pittsburgh corporation and others, a contract for the purchase of substantially the entire plant, including the good-will of the latter corporation, had been executed. The Madison corporation agreed to pay the other twenty thousand dollars in cash, and to transfer ninety-five thousand dollars of its paid-up capital stock as a consideration for the property, which was to be transferred and delivered to it at Madison, Indiana. It was also stipulated in the contract that the president of the Eagle Cotton Mills Company, of Pittsburgh, should be elected a director and president of the Madison corporation, and that a Mr. Townsend should act as secretary for the last-named company, at a stipulated salary. This agreement was ratified on the day on which it was executed, by the votes of those holding a majority of the shares of stock, at a stockholders' meeting regularly called. A location was obtained, mills erected, and put in successful operation at Madison, Indiana. It is found that the defendant's subscription was accepted by the corporation, and that after the contract between the two corporations had been executed, but before it was ratified, the defendant gave notice to the plaintiff's board of directors that he withdrew his name from the subscription as a stockholder. The defendant refused to pay any part of his subscription. The facts found, and the conclusions of law thereon stated by the court, formed the basis of a judgment in favor of the plaintiff for the full amount of the subscription, with interest.

On the appellant's behalf it is contended that the contract of subscription was subject to two conditions precedent, viz.: " 1. That one hundred and twenty-five thousand dollars of solvent subscriptions, including sixty thousand dollars promised by the Eagle Cotton Mills Company, of Pittsburgh, Pennsylvania, should be obtained; and 2. That the contract with the above-named company for the purchase of its mills should be ratified by the votes of those holding a majority of the capital stock."

Conceding that the first condition had been fully performed, the appellant's position, as we understand it, is, that the second condition had not been performed, because the contract entered into with the Pittsburgh corporation, and ratified by the vote of the stockholders of the plaintiff corporation, was not the one made or contemplated by the parties, and referred to in the contract of subscription, and that the defendant had, therefore, the right to withdraw his name as a subscriber. Moreover, it is said that the contract between the two corporations was, for various reasons, *ultra vires,* and void.

The court found that the contract which the stockholders of the Madison corporation ratified was not made until after the stock was all subscribed; that an arrangement of some kind was under contemplation at the time, but had not been definitely agreed upon, and that there was in fact no contract between the two corporations when the subscription was made.

The appellant assumes that the written contract of subscription shows that a definite contract existed for the purchase of the Pittsburgh company's mills at the time the subscriptions were made; that he subscribed for stock with reference to that contract, and that the finding of the court that there was no contract rests upon a violation of the rule which declares that parol evidence will not be heard to explain, modify, or contradict a written contract. This assumption is not warranted by the terms of the writing. While it is quite apparent that an arrangement of some kind was under contemplation at the time the subscriptions for stock were made, whereby the Eagle Cotton Mills Company of Pittsburgh might subscribe for sixty thousand dollars stock in the Madison corporation, and sell its mills to the latter, the plain inference is, that the final contract to that end had not yet been consummated. If a contract for the purchase of the mills had actually been executed, it would have been worse than idle to stipulate that no subscriptions to the stock should be collect-

ible until after the contract had been ratified by a majority of
the stockholders. It can hardly be conceived as possible that
a contract was first made whereby the new corporation became
bound to purchase the mills of the old, and that subscriptions
for stock were afterwards taken subject to the condition that
if the stockholders refused to ratify the contract, the subscriptions were to become uncollectible. The rule that a formal
written contract, which appears upon its face to be complete,
cannot be enlarged, modified, or contradicted by proof of prior
or contemporaneous parol negotiations or agreements, is abundantly settled, and receives the fullest recognition in the decisions of this court: *Singer Mfg. Co.* v. *Forsyth*, 108 Ind. 334;
Carr v. *Hays*, 110 Ind. 408; *Tucker* v. *Tucker*, 113 Ind. 272.

It is equally well settled, however, that the first duty of the
court in interpreting a contract is to discover the intention of
the parties, and while that must be done solely by considering
the meaning of the language employed in the instrument, yet
when the terms employed are susceptible of more than one
meaning, it is the duty of the court, not only to regard the
nature of the instrument, but also to inform itself of the circumstances which surrounded the parties at the time, so as to
interpret the language employed from the standpoint which
the parties occupied when they executed the contract: *Daugh-
erty* v. *Rogers*, 119 Ind. 254, and cases cited; *Heath* v. *West*, 68
Ind. 548; *Ketcham* v. *Brazil etc. Co.*, 88 Ind. 515; *Nash* v.
Towne, 5 Wall. 689; *Scott* v. *United States*, 12 Wall. 443; *Chesapeake etc. Canal Co.* v. *Hill*, 15 Wall. 94; *Reed* v. *Merchants'
Mut. Ins. Co.*, 95 U. S. 23; *Reynolds* v. *Commerce Fire Ins. Co.*,
47 N. Y. 597.

If the words of the instrument are clear in themselves, it
must be construed accordingly, but if they are susceptible of
more meanings than one, the court must avail itself of the
light enjoyed by the parties when the contract was executed,
so as to arrive at the meaning of the words, and give them
a correct application to the persons and things described:
Springsteen v. *Samson*, 32 N. Y. 703. Where the language
employed admits of more than one construction, one of which
renders the contract insensible, that construction will be
adopted which will give effect to the contract; and in cases
of doubt, the practical construction which the parties themselves have given it will be of great, if not controlling, influence: *Reissner* v. *Oxley*, 80 Ind. 580; *Lyles* v. *Lescher*, 108 Ind.
382, and cases cited; *Chicago* v. *Sheldon*, 9 Wall. 50.

The relations existing between the Pittsburgh corporation and the plaintiff at the time the appellant subscribed for stock were matters collateral to the contract of subscription, and in no manner affected or entered into the contract of the latter with the plaintiff: *Singer Mfg. Co.* v. *Forsyth*, 108 Ind. 334; *Eighmie* v. *Taylor*, 98 N. Y. 288.

It was essential, however, in order that the contract of subscription might be intelligently applied to the collateral matters therein referred to, that the court should be informed of the relations existing between the two corporations at the time the subscription was made. It was therefore competent for the plaintiff, when the appellant claimed exoneration from his subscription on the ground that the contract between the two companies, in respect to the amount of stock which the Pittsburgh company had agreed to subscribe, or the terms upon which it had agreed to sell its mills, had been changed, or that the agreement had been varied in any other respect, to show that no contract had in fact been consummated, and that the situation of the parties was such as to make it apparent that the contract referred to was one that might possibly be made in the future. This in no way tended to alter or modify the contract of subscription, but to give it intelligent application to the collateral matters to which it referred.

It is contended that one corporation cannot sell its property and good-will to another, and that the agreement that the president of the one should be elected a director and president of the other was invalid, and that the whole contract was therefore *ultra vires*. We do not deem it necessary to enter upon an examination of these questions. In the view we take, the stipulation in the contract of subscription by which the amounts subscribed were not to become payable until the contract for the purchase of the mills had been ratified was, in no sense, a condition precedent to the liability of the subscribers for stock. As we have seen, that stipulation had reference to a matter wholly aside from and collateral to the contract of subscription. It was essentially an independent covenant, by which it was, in effect, agreed that no contract should be finally made for the purchase of the Pittsburgh company's mills without the consent of the majority of the stockholders. The Madison corporation in no way bound itself to purchase the cotton-mills owned by the Pittsburgh company, nor was its absolute right to collect its stock subscriptions in any way conditioned upon the future purchase of those mills. If the Pittsburgh mills had never been purchased, or if, after the contract of purchase was negotiated, it had been rejected by the stockholders, it would hardly be maintainable that the Madison corporation would have thereby lost its right to enforce payment of its stock subscriptions in order to carry out the purpose for which the corporation was organized. To give the contract the construction contended for would enable the subscribers to withdraw all their subscriptions, and deprive the corporation of its capital to such an extent as to disable it from conducting its business: *Pittsburgh etc. R. R. Co.* v. *Biggar*, 34 Pa. St. 455; *Boyd* v. *Peach Bottom R'y Co.*, 90 Pa. St. 169; Morawetz on Corporations, secs. 92, 93.

Since it was not made a condition precedent to the appellant's liability that a contract with the Pittsburgh corporation of a specified character should first be made, he cannot now defeat the collection of his subscription by assailing the contract that actually was made. He was content that the board of directors should exercise their best judgment in obtaining and agreeing upon terms of purchase, with the stipulation that his subscription should not become payable until the contract of purchase, if one was agreed upon, was ratified by a majority of the stockholders. This the court finds has been fairly done, and it is now too late to assail the contract in an action to collect the subscription price of stock. Thus it has been said: "A subscriber for stock in a corporation cannot defeat an action to collect such subscription by the defense that the directors or the corporation itself have done corporate acts which are beyond the corporate powers. There are other remedies open to the subscriber. He may either impair such *ultra vires* acts, or may have them set aside if already accomplished. . . . . Thus it has been held that a subscriber cannot defeat an action to collect his subscription by showing that the corporation has, without authority of law, and in excess of its powers, executed a lease or sale of the road; or illegally issued its bonds; or purchased shares of its own stock, or of another corporation; or changed the location or route of the road. The last instance, especially, has been a frequent defense, but has been uniformly discountenanced by the courts whenever the change is made, not by an amendment to the charter, but by the arbitrary, unauthorized act of the corporate authorities. . . . . A stockholder cannot defeat an action

to collect his subscription by the defense that the corporate
affairs have been managed fraudulently or recklessly or negligently. The stockholder's remedy for such evils is of a different nature. For fraud, he may bring the guilty parties to
an accounting. For mismanagement, his only remedy is the
corporate elections. In no case bas he been allowed to escape
liability on his subscription by reason thereof. Thus it is no
defense that the corporate authorities fraudulently placed an
over-valuation on property purchased by them for the corporation; nor that they made a fraudulent contract with a construction company ": Cook on Stock and Stockholders, secs.
187, 188; 1 Wood on Railway Law, secs. 43, 45.

These subscriptions are made to take stock in an existing
or proposed corporation, upon a condition precedent, as, for
example, upon condition that a specified amount of subscriptions should thereafter be obtained. The contract of the several subscribers is twofold in character. It is, in a sense, a
contract between the several subscribers, which cannot be
withdrawn or revoked as to any one without the acquiescence
of all. It is also a continuing offer or proposition to the corporation to take and pay for the amount of stock subscribed,
upon the terms proposed, whenever the specified amount of
subscriptions shall have been obtained. The obtaining of the
amount specified within a reasonable time is an acceptance of
the proposition or offer by the corporation, and the contract of
each subscriber then becomes absolute and unconditional:
Minneapolis etc. Co. v. *Davis,* 40 Minn. 110; 12 Am. St. Rep.
701; Morawetz on Corporations, sec. 47. A subscriber cannot
withdraw his subscription, even though it be conditional,
unless unreasonable delay occurs in performing the condition:
Johnson v. *Wabash etc. Plank Road Co.,* 16 Ind. 389; *Lake
Ontario etc. R. R. Co.* v. *Mason,* 16 N. Y. 451; *McClure* v.
People's etc. R'y Co., 90 Pa. St. 269.

When the plaintiff obtained solvent subscriptions for the
amount specified, that became an effectual acceptance of the
offer of all those who had previously subscribed. Their subscriptions were no longer conditional, but they then became
absolute, and were thereafter payable according to the terms
of the contract on the call of the board of directors: *New Albany etc. R. R. Co.* v. *Pickens,* 5 Ind. 247; *Estell* v. *Knightstown
etc. Co.,* 41 Ind. 174; *Beckner* v. *Riverside etc. Co.,* 65 Ind. 468;
Phœnix etc. Co. v. *Badger,* 67 N. Y. 294, 300. The subscribers
thereupon became entitled to all the rights and privileges of

stockholders, and they came under the correlative obligations
and duties of holders of stock in a corporation: *Butler University* v. *Scoonover*, 114 Ind. 381; 5 Am. St. Rep. 627.

Questions of minor importance, involving the right of the
plaintiff corporation to prosecute the suit in its own name, its
power to make by-laws, and whether or not it was fully organized when the subscription in question was made, are
presented in the briefs. It is sufficient to say, while these
questions in no way affect the merits, we have considered
them, and find no error in the record. Both parties having,
by entering into the contract sued on, assumed the existence
of the corporation, both are now estopped from denying it:
Whitney v. *Wyman*, 101 U. S. 392.

The judgment is therefore affirmed, with costs.

CONSTRUCTION OF CONTRACTS. — In construing a written contract, every
word should, if possible, be given its appropriate and proper force: *Chrisman*
v. *State Ins. Co.*, 16 Or. 284; *Winfield* v. *Winfield Gas Co.*, 37 Kan. 24. Yet
a contract should be so construed as to give effect to the intention of the
parties: *Mathews* v. *Phelps*, 61 Mich. 327; 1 Am. St. Rep. 581; and when it
is uncertain whether words are used in an enlarged or restricted sense, they
should be construed most favorably to the covenantee: *Paul* v. *Travelers Ins.
Co.*, 112 N. Y. 472; 8 Am. St. Rep. 758. Still courts will follow the construction which the parties themselves, by their acts, put upon their own
contracts: *Louisville etc. R'y Co.* v. *Reynolds*, 118 Ind. 170. When words
which, by custom, have acquired a specific meaning are used in a contract,
the court will give them such interpretation, even though some of the parties were ignorant of the customary meaning of such words: *Long* v. *Davidson*, 101 N. C. 170. And when a certain use is plainly and exclusively
within the language of a grant, the purpose, as expressed, will be effectuated
without looking to any extrinsic circumstances to ascertain the intention of
the parties; for the court will not make a contract, but will find one made
by the parties, and must do this on the words employed by the parties themselves, unless such words are of uncertain meaning, in which case the words
must be taken in the sense intended by the parties: *Wilczinski* v. *Louisville
etc. R'y Co.*, 66 Miss. 595. But the construction of a contract must always
be reasonable; the intent of the parties must be ascertained from a fair interpretation of all the terms of the contract, while if any particular phrase or
clause is repugnant to or inconsistent with the plain intention of the parties,
it should be rejected: *Coleman* v. *Commins*, 77 Cal. 548. When a contract
is evidenced merely by the written correspondence of the parties, the court
must construe the writings, and instruct the jury as to their meaning and
legal effect: *Beck* v. *West*, 87 Ala. 213.

ESTOPPEL TO DENY CORPORATE EXISTENCE by contracting with the corporation as such: See *Schloss* v. *Montgomery Trade Co.*, 87 Ala. 411; 13 Am.
St. Rep. 51, and note. When a person, by his deed, declares the grantee
therein to be a corporation, he thereby estops himself to deny the corporate
existence of the grantee: *Ragan* v. *McElroy*, 98 Mo. 349. As to the estoppel
of stockholders from attacking the validity of corporate existence, see note
to *Thompson* v. *Reno Sav. Bank*, 3 Am. St. Rep. 827.

CORPORATIONS. — AS TO CONDITIONS LIMITING OR RELIEVING THE LIA-
BILITY OF SUBSCRIBERS for unpaid subscriptions, see note to *Thompson* v.
Reno Sav. Bank, 3 Am. St. Rep. 823, 824.

SUBSCRIPTION BY ONE TO STOCK IN A PROPOSED CORPORATION is a contract binding and irrevocable from the date of the subscription: *Minneapolis
T. Machine Co.* v. *Davis*, 40 Minn. 110; 12 Am. St. Rep. 701; and to the same
effect, substantially, is *Minneapolis T. Machine Co.* v. *Crevier*, 39 Minn. 417.

HOLLAND *v.* BARTCH.

[120 INDIANA, 46.]

PLEADING NEGLIGENCE. — COMPLAINT CHARGING NEGLIGENCE against a
bicycle-rider must state the particular acts constituting the negligence
in the riding of the bicycle, that defendant may know with what particular acts of negligence he is charged.

BICYCLES ARE VEHICLES, AND ENTITLED TO THE RIGHTS OF THE ROAD; but
have no lawful right to the use of the sidewalk, and the rider of a bicycle
is placed upon an equality with and governed by the same rules as
persons riding or driving any other vehicle.

HIGHWAYS — RIGHT OF BICYCLE-RIDER. — Riding a bicycle in the center of
a highway at the rate of fifteen miles an hour, to and within twenty-five
feet of the heads of horses attached to a carriage, is not actionable negligence. To make it such, it must be charged and shown to have been
done at a time or in a manner or under circumstances evidencing a disregard for the rights of others.

C. C. Binkley, for the appellant.

T. J. Study, for the appellee.

OLDS, J. This is an action for damages. The first paragraph of the complaint alleges that "the plaintiff, on the sixteenth day of August, 1885, was seated in a two-seated carriage,
to which two gentle and well-broken horses, both properly
harnessed with good and sufficient harness, were properly and
securely attached and hitched in the usual way, which said
horses were then and there carefully and properly driven by
a careful and competent driver seated in said carriage, and
was then and there driving said team and carriage, in which
plaintiff was seated as aforesaid, on the public road and highway leading from Cambridge City, Indiana, to Jacksonburg;
and when about two miles east of said Cambridge City, and
in said county of Wayne, and driving carefully along and
upon said highway, and in the part thereof usually driven
upon by such teams and carriages, they were met at the
place in said highway last above named by said defendant,
seated upon and riding a large bicycle, the wheel of which

bicycle was sixty inches in diameter, who then and there negligently and carelessly rode said bicycle at a rapid rate of
speed, to wit, fifteen miles per hour, and negligently and carelessly ran the same along and in the center of said highway,
at said rapid rate of speed, towards and into the faces of said
horses, and in this way approached to within twenty-five feet
of the faces of said horses, when and whereby said horses
became and were greatly frightened, and became and were
wholly unmanageable, and ran away, and in their fright ran
along said road at a great speed, and upset said carriage,
whereby the plaintiff was thrown violently to the ground," and
sustained severe injuries, etc.

The averments of the defendant's acts of negligence are the
same in the second and third paragraphs of the complaint as
in the first paragraph. There is a variance as to some other
averments, it being averred in the second that the strap by
which one of the horses was fastened to the end of the pole of
the carriage broke, and after the horses became frightened, the
defendant dismounted and took hold of the bridle of one of the
horses and endeavored to hold them, but let go of the horse
before the driver dismounted.

The infancy of the defendant was suggested, and Reuben
Bartch was appointed as his guardian *ad litem*. The defendant moved the court to require the plaintiff to make her complaint more specific as to how and in what manner the
defendant rode and 'used said bicycle negligently and carelessly, and in what the alleged carelessness and negligence of
the defendant consisted in the use of the said bicycle, and
what acts and conduct of the defendant in riding and using
said bicycle were negligently and carelessly done and performed by him, by reason of which said horses were frightened
and caused to run away, causing said injuries to the plaintiff
alleged in the complaint; which motion to make each paragraph of said complaint more specific was sustained by the
court, and exceptions reserved. The plaintiff refused to amend
said paragraphs and make them more specific, and assigns
the ruling of the court on the motion as error.

The allegations of the defendant's negligence in these paragraphs of complaint, in brief, charge that the plaintiff and
defendant were traveling towards each other upon the highway, the plaintiff in her carriage, and the defendant upon his
bicycle, and that the defendant then and there negligently
and carelessly rode his bicycle, at the rate of speed of fifteen

miles per hour, up to and within twenty-five feet of the faces of the horses drawing the carriage in which the plaintiff was seated, whereby the horses became and were greatly frightened, and became and were wholly unmanageable.

The allegations of negligence are general, and the theory we take of these paragraphs of complaint is, that the negligence sought to be charged consists in the manner in which the defendant rode the bicycle, and not in the fact that he rode it at the rate of fifteen miles per hour, or along the center of the road to and within twenty-five feet of the faces of the plaintiff's horses.

Taking the theory we do of these paragraphs of the complaint, the defendant had the right to have the court require the plaintiff to make her complaint more specific by stating the particular acts constituting the negligence in the riding of the bicycle, that he might know with what particular acts of negligence he was charged: *Cincinnati etc. R. R. Co.* v. *Chester*, 57 Ind. 297; *Hawley* v. *Williams*, 90 Ind. 160; *Cleveland etc. R'y Co.* v. *Wynant*, 100 Ind. 160.

The third paragraph differs somewhat from the first and second in the language used, but the acts charged are the same as in the other paragraphs, and we think the ruling of the court in sustaining the motion to make each paragraph of the complaint more specific was correct.

The next errors assigned are the sustaining the demurrers to the fourth and fifth paragraphs of the complaint.

The fourth paragraph is substantially the same as the first, except in the allegations of the negligence of the defendant, which are as follows: " Plaintiff was met at said place in said highway and public road by said defendant, who was then and there seated upon and riding a large bicycle, whose wheel was sixty inches in diameter, which said bicycle, with a rider seated upon it, as was well known to said defendant, was an unusual vehicle with which to travel upon such highway, and as he well knew was a frightful object for ordinary horses to meet, and was well calculated to and did frighten horses unaccustomed to meeting such vehicles with a rider mounted thereon; and well knowing these things, said defendant rode such bicycle at a very rapid rate of speed, to wit, at the rate of fifteen miles per hour, towards and into the faces of said horses, along and upon the middle of said highway, coming towards said horses until he approached to within twenty-five feet of the faces of said horses, which said act of riding said bicycle at such rapid rate of speed, and on and upon the center of said highway, until he approached within said twenty-five feet of the faces of said horses, knowing, as he well did, the effect of the same upon horses being driven on such highway, was negligent and careless; and by such act of so negligently and carelessly riding said bicycle so up in front of and in the faces of said horses, said horses then and there and thereby became and were greatly frightened, and became and were wholly unmanageable," and in their fright ran away, etc.

The fifth paragraph only differs from the fourth in that it alleges that when the horses became frightened they jumped back, and one of the straps fastened to the end of the buggy-pole broke, and defendant dismounted and seized the bridle-rein of one of the horses, and undertook to hold said horse until the driver could alight and hold the other horse, and the driver jumped from the carriage, and before he could get to and seize and hold the other horse, the defendant carelessly and negligently released his hold upon the horse so held by him, and the horses ran away and injured the plaintiff.

It is manifest that the defendant is not liable under this paragraph of the complaint, unless he is liable for causing the original fright of the horses.

The liability of the defendant sought to be charged in this paragraph, as in the other, is in causing the horses to become frightened. The injury is the primary result of the fright to the horses.

In determining the sufficiency of these paragraphs of complaint, it is proper to consider the rights of the parties. The acts of negligence charged in each of these paragraphs of complaint is the riding of the bicycle upon and along the center of the highway, at the rate of fifteen miles per hour, up to and within twenty-five feet of the faces of the horses.

In the case of *Mercer* v. *Corbin*, 117 Ind. 450, 10 Am. St. Rep. 76, it is held that a bicycle is a vehicle, and entitled to the rights of the road, and has no lawful right to the use of the sidewalk.

In the case of *State* v. *Collins*, decided by the supreme court of Rhode Island (Dec. 21, 1888), the court says: "The question raised by the exceptions is, whether a bicycle is a carriage or vehicle, within the meaning of the Public Statutes of Rhode Island, chapter 66, section 1, which enacts that 'every person traveling with any carriage or other vehicle, who shall meet any other person so traveling on any highway or bridge, shall seasonably drive his carriage or vehicle to the right of the center of the traveled part of the road, so as to enable such person to pass with his carriage or vehicle without interference or interruption.' We are of the opinion that it is a carriage or vehicle which carries a person mounted upon it, and which is propelled and driven by him. The word 'vehicle' is certainly broad enough to include any machine which is used and driven on the traveled part of the highway for the purpose of conveyance upon the highway. The purpose of the section is to prevent accident or collision, and such accident or collision may happen from a bicycle and other carriage meeting, unless the rule laid down in the section is observed."

In the case of *Taylor* v. *Goodwin*, L. R. 4 Q. B. Div. 228, 27 Week. Rep. 489, a bicycle was held to be a carriage.

Although but few courts have passed upon and defined the rights of persons riding upon and propelling or driving bicycles, yet such as have, unanimously place them upon an equality and governed by the same rule as persons riding or driving any other vehicle or carriage, and we think this the proper rule to adopt. Although the use of the bicycle, for the purpose of locomotion and travel, is quite modern, yet it is a vehicle of great convenience, and its use is becoming quite common; while traveling upon the highways by means of horses has been in vogue much longer, and is more universal at present than by means of bicycles, yet persons traveling by means of horses have no superior rights to those traveling upon the highway by improved methods of travel which are adapted to and consistent with the proper use of the highway.

In the case of *Wabash etc. R'y Co.* v. *Farver*, 111 Ind. 195, 60 Am. Rep. 696, speaking of the use of a portable engine, the court says: "It would not do to say that the operation of a portable engine near a public highway necessarily resulted in creating a nuisance, when it is, according to daily experience, during certain seasons of the year, to see steam thrashing-machines in operation on every hand, and often necessarily close to public highways. Road-engines propelled by steam, and portable engines operated by steam, have become familiar in every agricultural community. To declare that their use near or their passage over a public highway constituted a nuisance would be practically to prohibit their use in the manner in which they are customarily employed and moved from place to place. It must be supposed that horses of ordinary gentleness have become so familiar with these objects as to be safe when under careful guidance." The same may be said of bicycles; to declare their use upon the public highways a nuisance would prohibit their use in the manner in which they are intended, and it must be supposed that horses of ordinary gentleness have become so familiar with them as not to scare at them, and as to be safe when under careful guidance.

In the case of *Macomber* v. *Nichols,* 34 Mich. 212, 22 Am. Rep. 522, the court says: " Injury alone will never support an action on the case; there must be a concurrence of injury and wrong. If a man does an act that is not unlawful in itself he cannot be held responsible for any resulting injury, unless he does it at a time or in a manner or under circumstances which render him chargeable with a want of proper regard for the rights of others. In such a case, the negligence imputable to him constitutes the wrong, and he is accountable to persons injured, not because damage has resulted from his doing the act, but because its being done negligently or without due care has resulted in injury. If the act was not wrongful in itself, the wrong must necessarily be sought for in the time or manner or circumstances under which it was performed, and injury does not prove the wrong, but only makes out the case for redress after the wrong is established."

In this case, the acts complained of in each paragraph of the complaint are the riding of the bicycle in the center of the highway, at the rate of fifteen miles per hour, to and within twenty-five feet of the faces of the plaintiff's horses. It is these acts which are charged as negligence and as a wrong, but, as we have held, they are not unlawful acts, and are not a wrong; hence they constitute no cause of action. To make a person liable for the doing of such acts, they must be charged to have been done at a time or in a manner or under circumstances which render him chargeable with a want of proper regard for the rights of others, which is not done in either paragraph of the complaint. While the use of the locomotive is of infinitely more benefit than the bicycle in affording means of travel, so the danger arising from its use is also infinitely greater, yet the horse, the locomotive, and the bicycle are all used as affording a means of travel, and more or less danger attaches to each.

In discussing the liability of horses to become frightened at the locomotive, the learned Judge Cooley, in delivering the opinion in *Macomber* v. *Nichols, supra,* says: "Horses may be, and often are, frightened by locomotives in both town and country, but it would be as reasonable to treat the horse as a public nuisance from his tendency to shy and be frightened by unaccustomed objects, as to regard the locomotive as a public nuisance from its tendency to frighten the horse. The use of the one may impose upon the manager of the other the obligation of additional care and vigilance beyond what would otherwise be essential." Further on in the opinion he says: "If one in making use of his own means of locomotion is injured by the act or omission of the other, the question is not one of superior privilege, but it is a question whether, under all the circumstances, there is negligence imputable to some one, and if so, who should be accountable for it."

The complaint in this case proceeds, and it can only be held good, on the theory that the plaintiff, riding in her carriage, had rights superior to the defendant, who was riding upon his bicycle, and such is not the law. They met upon the highway, each possessing equal rights to the use of it, for riding and driving their respective vehicles.

The fourth and fifth paragraphs of the complaint were each insufficient, and the court properly sustained the demurrers thereto.

There is no error in the ruling of the court.

Judgment affirmed, with costs.

NEGLIGENCE, HOW PLEADED. — An allegation of negligence, as applied to the conduct of a party, is not a mere conclusion of law, but a fact properly pleadable: *Rolseth* v. *Smith,* 38 Minn. 14; 8 Am. St. Rep. 637, and note; yet a failure to state, in detail, the facts constituting negligence may not render a complaint bad on demurrer: *Louisville etc. R'y Co.* v. *Cauley,* 119 Ind. 142; *Lawrenceburgh F. Co.* v. *Hinke,* 119 Ind. 47; compare *Louisville etc. R'y Co.* v. *Crunk,* 119 Id. 542, 12 Am. St. Rep. 443, as to motions to make more specific complaints alleging negligence. But, as a general rule, complaints averring negligence on the part of defendant must allege the particular acts the doing of which or the neglect to do which constitute defendant's negligence: *Kohn* v. *Hinshaw,* 17 Or. 308. On special exception to the allegations in a petition, it is not sufficient to allege that the servants of defendant were grossly negligent in operating the train, in failing to give proper signals, etc.; that the train was under control of defendant's agents, — there being no allegation showing any willful act, omission, or gross neglect on the part of the agents representing defendant, nor any ratification of such acts on the part of the defendant: *Winnt* v. *International etc. R. R. Co.,* 74 Tex. 32. But a complaint for the negligent killing of plaintiff's husband, which states the circumstances attending the killing, alleging that deceased was run over and killed by a certain train of defendant, that death was occasioned through the negligence of defendant's servants who were operating the train, is sufficient, against demurrer on the ground that it states no specific act of negligence: *Sullivan* v. *Missouri P. R'y Co.*, 97 Mo. 113. In an action against a railroad company for injuring cattle, a complaint stating that the animals were injured by defendant's train is, under the Arkansas statute, a sufficient allegation of negligence on the part of the defendant: *St. Louis etc. R'y Co.* v. *Brown*, 49 Ark. 253. So in an action to recover for the negligent killing of a cow, a complaint alleging that the train was so negligently operated by defendant's agents that plaintiff's cow was killed, and that the cow was killed on account of such negligence, is sufficiently definite: *Western R'y Co.* v. *Lazarus*, 88 Ala. 453. Yet it is not incumbent upon a complainant suing for damages occasioned by negligence, after proving an accident which raises the inference of negligence, to go further, and show the particular acts constituting such negligence, when, from the circumstances of the case, it is not within his power to do so: *Gulf etc. R'y Co.* v. *Smith*, 74 Tex. 276.

BICYCLES. — Bicycles must be regarded in law as a sort of vehicle: *Mercer* v. *Corbin*, 117 Ind. 450; 10 Am. St. Rep. 76; *State* v. *Yopp*, 97 N. C. 477; 2 Am. St. Rep. 305. The leading case holding that a bicycle is a vehicle is the English case, *Taylor* v. *Goodwin*, L. R. 4 Q. B. Div. 228, cited in *Mercer* v. *Corbin, supra*. Since sidewalks are intended for the use of foot-travelers, not for the use of vehicles, and a bicycle is a vehicle within the meaning of the law, a person has no right to ride or drive his bicycle upon a sidewalk: *Mercer* v. *Corbin, supra*. So under a statute making it unlawful for any one to ride or drive upon a town or village sidewalk, a rider of a bicycle riding along a town sidewalk upon his bicycle may be responsible for any injuries occasioned by him, even though no injury was intended: *Id.* In the case of *State* v. *Yopp, supra*, it was decided that a statute forbidding the use of a bicycle, tricycle, or other non-horse vehicle upon a highway, without express permission of the road superintendent, was constitutional. The holding in that case was based upon the theory that particular vehicles, such as bicycles, from their peculiar appearance and their unusual manner of use, frighten horses, and thereby imperil passengers traveling in horse vehicles over the highway, and that the legislature has power always to provide reasonable regulations with respect to highways, to insure safety and comfort to passengers going over them in the usual modes of conveyance. But this decision seems contrary to the rule laid down in the principal case, in which it is said that "persons traveling by means of horses have no superior rights to those traveling upon the highway by improved methods of travel which are adapted to and consistent with the proper use of the highway," and to declare the use of bicycles upon the highway "a nuisance would prohibit their use in the manner in which they are intended, and it must be supposed that horses of ordinary gentleness have become so familiar with them as not to scare at them."

ADAMS EXPRESS COMPANY *v.* HARRIS.

[120 INDIANA, 73.]

COMMON CARRIERS — CONNECTING CARRIER. — A contract of carriage not providing that its stipulations shall inure to the benefit of any other carrier than the one with whom it was made, and not designating any other carrier along the line, cannot be invoked to aid an intermediate carrrier who undertakes to carry the goods.

PLEADING EXISTENCE OF PARTNERSHIP OR CORPORATION. — WHERE PLAINTIFFS' NAMES ARE GIVEN IN FULL in the title of the case, it is unnecessary to repeat them in alleging that they are partners; or if the name of defendant imports that it is a corporation, that fact need not be specially averred.

COMMON CARRIER WAIVES HIS RIGHT TO DETAIN GOODS FOR FREIGHT, when he puts his refusal to deliver upon the ground that they are not in his possession at the place where the demand is duly made.

COMMON CARRIERS — WHEN BOUND BY ACT OF AGENT. — Agent of carrier invested with general authority to adjust claims against it binds it by his declarations made while endeavoring to secure the adjustment of such a claim.

COMMON CARRIER — CONTRACT LIMITING DAMAGES recoverable of a common carrier will not control, where negligence is shown, and there is no proof that a lower rate of freight was given on account of the limitation placed upon the value of the property.

J. H. Jordan and O. Matthews, for the appellant.

G. A. Adams and J. S. Newby, for the appellees.

ELLIOTT, C. J. The material facts pleaded by the appellees as their cause of action are these: On and prior to the seventeenth day of January, 1885, they were partners, engaged in business as nurserymen; on that day a lot of fruit-trees was delivered to the United States Express Company at Champaign, Illinois; the trees were owned by the plaintiffs, and were directed to them at Mooresville, Indiana; the United States Express Company undertook to carry the trees to Indianapolis, and there deliver them to some other carrier, to be transported to their destination; a written contract was made between the United States Express Company and the plaintiffs, which contained, among others, these provisions: That the person or corporation to whom the trees shall be delivered for transportation from the end of that company's line to their destination shall not be deemed the agent of the company, but shall be deemed the agent of the plaintiff; that the company shall not be liable for injury to the goods, unless it "be proved to have occurred from the fraud or gross negligence of the company or its servants, nor shall any demand be made upon the company for more than fifty dollars, at which sum said property is hereby valued." There is no provision in the contract for the benefit of any carrier except the United States Express Company, nor is any other carrier named. The trees were delivered to the defendant in good condition, at Indianapolis, and it carried them to Mooresville; after they had reached there, the plaintiffs went to the office of the defendant prepared to pay the charges and receive the trees, and although they were then in the possession of the defendant's agent, he denied that they had been received; on a subsequent day the plaintiffs went again to the defendant's office, received the trees and paid the freight on them. The trees were so injured, through the negligence of the defendant, as to be utterly valueless. The plaintiffs had sold the trees to divers persons, and had agreed to deliver them on the nineteenth day of October, 1885, and the refusal of the defendant to deliver the trees when first demanded caused the plaintiffs to lose the profits of the sales made by them, for the reason that the delay prevented them from delivering the trees to the purchasers in accordance with their contract.

The contention of the appellant is, that the contract between the United States Express Company and the plaintiffs bound both them and the appellant; that the latter, when it accepted the goods for transportation, became bound to comply with the provisions of the contract, and secured a right to all its stipulations in favor of the first carrier; and that the contract continued in force for the benefit of all the parties until the goods were delivered at their destination. The opposing contention is, that the contract between the United States Express Company and the plaintiffs did not inure to the benefit of the appellant, and that when it accepted the goods for transportation it received them under the law, and became bound by the ordinary rules which prevail in cases where there is no special contract.

If the appellant had been designated in the contract with the first carrier as one of the intermediate carriers, or if the contract had provided that its stipulations should inure to the benefit of all the carriers, then the contention of the appellant would find strong support from the authorities: *United States Express Co.* v. *Harris,* 51 Ind. 127; *St. Louis etc. R'y Co.* v. *Weakly,* 50 Ark. 397; 7 Am. St. Rep. 104; *Halliday* v. *St. Louis etc. R'y Co.,* 74 Mo. 159; 41 Am. Rep. 309; *Evansville etc. R. R. Co.* v. *Androscoggin Mills,* 22 Wall. 594; *Maghee* v.

Camden etc. R. R. Co., 45 N. Y. 514; 6 Am. Rep. 124; *Lamb*
v. *Camden etc. R. R. Co.*, 46 N. Y. 271; 7 Am. Rep. 327.

But the contract does not provide that its stipulations shall
inure to the benefit of any other carrier than the one with
whom it was made, nor does it designate any other carrier
along the line. Its provisions apply only to the carrier with
whom the contract was directly made, and they leave it to
that carrier to select the carrier from the termination of its
line to the end of the route. The authorities are substantially
agreed that in such a case the intermediate carrier cannot
successfully claim the benefit of the provisions of the original
contract: *Martin* v. *American Express Co.*, 19 Wis. 356; *Bancroft* v. *Merchants' etc. Co.*, 47 Iowa, 262; 29 Am. Rep. 482;
Merchants' etc. Co. v. *Bolles*, 80 Ill. 473; *Camden etc. R. R. Co.*
v. *Forsyth*, 61 Pa. St. 81; *Ætna Ins. Co.* v. *Wheeler*, 49 N. Y.
616.

The rule declared by the decisions we have referred to is
the only one that can be defended on principle; for where the
contract designates only one carrier, there is no privity between the owners and the undesignated carriers. But where
the contract is a through one, by designated carriers, there is
a privity of contract; for it is justly inferable that the contract
was intended for the benefit of all who perform services under
it. So, too, where the contract declares that it is for the benefit of intermediate carriers, it may be enforced, since it is a
contract for the benefit of a third person; and as it is beneficial to him, it is natural to presume that its terms were
assented to, and formed the contract under which the goods
were transported. Where, however, the contract is solely for
the benefit of the original parties, it is not possible to apply
this rule to it.

Where, as here, the names of the plaintiffs are given in full
in the title of the cause, it is unnecessary to repeat them in
alleging that the plaintiffs were partners. It is sufficient to
allege that the plaintiffs were partners, without again giving
their names. The name of the defendant imports that it is a
corporation, and it was therefore not necessary to specifically
aver that it was a corporation: *Adams Express Co.* v. *Hill*, 43
Ind. 157; *Indianapolis Sun Co.* v. *Horrell*, 53 Ind. 527; *Sayers*
v. *First Nat. Bank*, 89 Ind. 230.

The defendant's denial of the possession of the goods at
Mooresville excused the plaintiffs from making a tender of
the carrier's charges. A common carrier waives his right to

detain goods for the freight, if he puts his refusal to deliver them to the owner upon the ground that they are not in his possession at the place where a demand is duly made: *Vinton* v. *Baldwin*, 95 Ind. 433, and cases cited; *Mathis* v. *Thomas*, 101 Ind. 119; *Platter* v. *Board etc.*, 103 Ind. 360; *House* v. *Alexander*, 105 Ind. 109; 55 Am. Rep. 189.

Where a corporation invests an agent with general authority to adjust claims against it, the declarations of that agent, made while endeavoring to secure an adjustment of the claim, are competent evidence against his principal. This general rule has often been applied in insurance cases, and must necessarily apply in such cases as this; for otherwise the corporation would be entirely without a representative.

In deciding, as we have, that the provisions of the contract with the United States Express Company cannot be taken advantage of by the appellant, we have disposed of the point that the damages are limited to fifty dollars; but if we were wrong in this, still the limitation will not control, since there is evidence of negligence, and no evidence that a lower rate of freight was given on account of the limitation placed upon the value of the property: *Rosenfeld* v. *Peoria etc. R'y Co.*, 103 Ind. 121; 53 Am. Rep. 500; *Bartlett* v. *Pittsburgh etc. R'y Co.*, 94 Ind. 281; *United States Ex. Co.* v. *Backman*, 28 Ohio St. 144.

As there was evidence of negligence, and no evidence that there was any special consideration inducing the owners to places a less value on their property than its actual worth, the limitation, even conceding it to be available to the appellant as a part of the contract, is nullified.

The instructions of the court are quite as favorable to the appellant as the law warrants, and the evidence fully supports the verdict.

Judgment affirmed. ———

PLEADING EXISTENCE OF CORPORATION. — Where a corporation is plaintiff in an action, it need not be alleged in the complaint that plaintiff is a corporation: *Central Bank* v. *Knowlton*, 12 Wis. 624; 78 Am. Dec. 769, and note.

PARTNERSHIP MAY BE SUED in the individual name of its members, as well as in the partnership name: *Markham* v. *Buckingham*, 21 Iowa, 494; 89 Am. Dec. 590.

PRESUMPTION FROM A COMPANY'S NAME AS TO WHETHER IT IS A CORPORATION. — The name "Wetumpka Lumber Company" does not import that the company is a corporation, rather than a partnership or an unincorporated association; nor does the presumption of incorporation arise from the fact that its business is transacted by and through a president and secretary: *Clark* v. *Jones*, 87 Ala. 475.

CARRIERS OF FREIGHT — CONTRACT LIMITING CARRIER'S LIABILITY. — A carrier cannot absolve itself from or limit its liability for its own negligence: *Missouri Pacific R'y Co.* v. *Ivy*, 71 Tex. 409; 10 Am. St. Rep. 758, and particularly note; *St. Louis etc. R'y Co.* v. *Weakly*, 50 Ark. 397; 7 Am. St. Rep. 104, and note; *Southern Pac. R'y Co.* v. *Maddox*, 75 Tex. 301. But if a bill of lading limits a carrier's liability to the invoice value of goods in the event of loss through his fault, damages in such case must be computed in the usual way up to that value, irrespective of the market value of the goods as damaged at the point of destination: *Brown* v. *Cunard S. S. Co.*, 147 Mass. 58. A carrier may stipulate that it shall not be liable for money lost by its default, unless claim is made therefor by a written demand at its office within thirty days after its delivery to the company: *Glenn* v. *Southern Exp. Co.*, 86 Tenn. 594. And a carrier may limit its liability by contract so that it shall not be held liable as a common carrier beyond its own line: *Gulf etc. R'y Co.* v. *Baird*, 75 Tex. 256. As to a carrier's power to limit its liability by contract, see note to *Bissell* v. *New York etc. R. R. Co.*, 82 Am. Dec. 379, 380.

CARRIER'S LIEN FOR FREIGHT CHARGES is lost, if the goods are delivered to consignee by the carrier: *Hale* v. *Barrett*, 26 Ill. 195; 79 Am. Dec. 367; but the lien is not lost where goods are taken from the possession of the owner *in invitum* or by operation of law: *Newhall* v. *Vargas*, 15 Me. 314; 33 Am. Dec. 617. Yet delivery of a part of goods shipped under one bill of lading does not defeat the carrier's lien on the remainder for the whole amount of unpaid freight: *Fotheringham* v. *Jenkins*, 1 Cal. 42; 52 Am. Dec. 286. Compare *Everett* v. *Coffin*, 6 Wend. 603; 22 Am. Dec. 551.

AGENCY. — DECLARATIONS OF AGENT, when admissible against his principal: *Sidney Sch. F. Co.* v. *Warsaw Sch. District*, 122 Pa. St. 494; 9 Am. St. Rep. 124, and note.

CONNECTING CARRIERS. — A connecting carrier, by receiving freight from another carrier, under a contract between the consignor and the latter, becomes the agent of such other carrier to complete his contract, to the extent of shipping the freight over so much of his route as forms a part of the route over which the shipment was to be made, and is entitled to the benefit of all valid limitations of the carrier's liability contained in the contract: *St. Louis etc. R'y Co.* v. *Weakly*, 50 Ark. 397; 7 Am. St. Rep. 104; *Gulf etc. R'y Co.* v. *Baird*, 75 Tex. 256. But see *Bancroft* v. *Merchants' Despatch Tr. Co.*, 47 Iowa, 262; 29 Am. Rep. 482; note to *Wells* v. *Thomas*, 72 Am. Dec. 240-242.

PURVIANCE *v.* JONES.

[120 INDIANA, 162.]

NEGOTIABLE INSTRUMENTS. — DELIVERY, ACTUAL OR CONSTRUCTIVE, of a note is as essential to its validity as the signature of the maker.

NEGOTIABLE INSTRUMENTS — DELIVERY — WHAT SUFFICIENT. — While actual or manual delivery is not indispensable to the validity of a note, still it must appear that the maker, in some way, evinced an intention to make it an enforceable obligation against himself, according to its terms, by surrendering control over it, and intentionally placing it under the control of the payee, or of some third person for his use.

NEGOTIABLE INSTRUMENTS — DELIVERY, WHEN INSUFFICIENT. — Where there is nothing to indicate that the maker ever surrendered control of his note, or that it was ever within the power or control of the payee, or of any person for his use or benefit, there is no delivery, and the note is a nullity.

NEGOTIABLE INSTRUMENTS — COMPELLING DELIVERY — STATUTE OF LIMITATIONS. — Party who has advanced money on the faith that a note has been delivered to a third person for his benefit may compel the delivery to be perfected, or if he has been induced to abstain from enforcing his claim until it is barred by the statute of limitations on the faith of such assurance, he may compel the delivery of the note, or require it to be treated, in an equitable suit, as having been delivered as represented after the death of the maker, with the note still in his possesssion.

L. P. Milligan and O. W. Whitelock, for the appellant.

J. C. Branyan, M. L. Spencer, W. A. Branyan, and O. E. Barrett, for the appellee.

MITCHELL, J. The only question presented on this appeal is, whether or not the facts found support the conclusion that a certain note filed by John D. Jones against the estate of Joseph W. Purviance, deceased, had been duly executed by the intestate in his lifetime. It appears that the intestate received $1,525.98 in August, 1873, as the proceeds of the sale of a quantity of wheat sold by him, belonging to Jones, who was his son-in-law. Purviance requested permission to use the money for a short time. Jones consented.

The court found as a fact that, about the year 1880, or perhaps prior thereto, Jones requested that a mortgage be given him to secure the money which had been thus received and used, but that his father-in-law declined, assigning as a reason for his refusal that he had signed a note for the amount and left it in the bank for his son-in-law's benefit, so that the latter would lose nothing in case of his, the intestate's, death. The latter had, in fact, filled out and signed a note for the amount received for the wheat, making it payable to John D. Jones, due in one day, and bearing date August 26, 1873. Across the back of the paper there was written the following: "This note is explained in a statement signed by me and filed." The intestate was president of the First National Bank of Huntington at the time, and continued to occupy that position until a short time prior to his death, which occurred in November, 1885. Jones never called at the bank for the note, which was found with the intestate's private papers after his death.

The foregoing constitutes a summary of the facts upon which the court stated, as a conclusion of law, that the note had been duly delivered.

It will be observed that, beyond the declaration of the intestate that he had signed a note and left it in the bank for the plaintiff's benefit, it does not appear that it ever had been so left, or that it had ever been out of the possession of the intestate, or under the control of the plaintiff, or of any one else for his use.

That an instrument is not complete and effectual until it has been delivered, or until that has been done which is legally equivalent to a delivery, is elementary. An actual or constructive delivery, being the final act in the execution of a note, is as essential to impart validity to the paper as is the signature of the maker. Until that is done, it is a nullity: *Scobey* v. *Walker*, 114 Ind. 254; 1 Daniel on Negotiable Instruments, secs. 63 et seq. The transaction is simple enough where there has been an actual delivery, but it is not always easy to determine what acts constitute a delivery by construction of law.

While it is not indispensable that there should have been an actual manual transfer of the instrument from the maker to the payee, yet, to constitute a delivery, it must appear that the maker, in some way, evinced an intention to make it an enforceable obligation against himself, according to its terms, by surrendering control over it, and intentionally placing it under the power of the payee, or of some third person for his use. The acts which consummate the delivery of a promissory note are not essentially different from those required to complete the execution of a deed. Act and intention are the two elements essential to the delivery of a deed, which is ordinarily effected by the simple manual transfer of possession from the grantor to the grantee, with the intention of passing the title and relinquishing all power and control over the instrument itself. The final test is, Did the maker do such acts in reference to the deed or other instrument as evince an unmistakable intention to give it effect and operation, according to its terms, and to relinquish all power and control over it in favor of the grantee or obligee? *Weber* v. *Christen*, 121 Ill. 91; 2 Am. St. Rep. 68; *Stone* v. *French*, 37 Kan. 145; 1 Am. St. Rep. 237.

All that appears in the special finding in the present case is a recital of a merely evidentiary character, to the effect that the intestate refused, when requested, to execute a mortgage to secure the debt, and assigned as a reason that he had signed a note and left it in the bank for the plaintiff's benefit. There is no finding that the note had in fact been left with

the bank for the plaintiff's benefit, or that the latter in any
way changed his position or purpose because of the declaration made to him; and the fact that the note was found
among the intestate's private papers, with a memorandum
upon it, indicates that it never was out of his possession.
The only facts found by the court are, that the note was
signed by the intestate, and that it was found among his private papers after his death. The declarations made by the
intestate, and set out in the special finding, are nothing but
evidence. If it had been found as a fact that the note had
actually been left with the bank for the plaintiff's benefit,
even though the intestate subsequently withdrew it, the legal
conclusion might have been warranted that the paper had
been constructively delivered. As we have seen, there is no
finding of that character.

There is nothing in the facts found to indicate that the intestate ever surrendered control of the note, or that it ever
was within the power or control of the plaintiff, or of any person for his use or benfit. It is impossible, therefore, by any
facts within the finding, to support the legal conclusion that
the note was delivered: *Woodford* v. *Dorwin*, 3 Vt. 82; 21 Am.
Dec. 573; 1 Parsons on Notes and Bills, 49.

It may be that the evidence was such as to have justified a
finding that the note had been delivered to the bank for the
plaintiff's benefit; but the fact was not so found. The intestate, having received the plaintiff's money, may have induced
him to forego any effort to enforce collection, upon the assurance that a note had been left with the bank for the amount
of the debt for his benefit. If the plaintiff rested upon that
assurance until the statute of limitations had barred the debt,
the estate may now be estopped to say that the note was not
delivered, as against one who relied upon the statement, and
who would now suffer actual pecuniary loss if the note, actually signed, was not treated as having been delivered according to the representation made and relied upon.

Where money has been advanced on the faith that a note
has been delivered to a third person, the promisee would be
entitled to compel the delivery to be perfected. So if the
plaintiff was induced to forego his purpose to secure his
money before the statute had barred his claim, by the assurance that a note had been delivered to the bank for his benefit, he may be entitled to compel the delivery of the note, or
to require it to be treated, in an equitable suit, as having been

delivered to the bank as represented.   The facts found, however, do not make such a case.

The judgment must therefore be reversed, with costs, and, to the end that complete justice may be done, a new trial is ordered.

———

DELIVERY OF NEGOTIABLE INSTRUMENTS. — The delivery of a note is essential to its validity: *Foy* v. *Blackstone*, 31 Ill. 538; 83 Am. Dec. 246; *Woodford* v. *Dorwin*, 3 Vt. 82; 21 Am. Dec. 573; for a note has no legal inception until it is delivered to some person as evidence of a subsisting debt: *Catlin* v. *Gunter*, 11 N. Y. 368; 62 Am. Dec. 113, and note 118.

The maker of a note, which he never delivered, cannot be held liable thereon, even when it is in the hands of a *bona fide* holder: *Burson* v. *Huntington*, 21 Mich. 415; 4 Am. Rep. 497; *Cline* v. *Guthrie*, 42 Ind. 227; 13 Am. Rep. 357; *Chipman* v. *Tucker*, 38 Wis. 43; 20 Am. Rep. 1; but see *contra*, *Kinyon* v. *Wohlford*, 17 Minn. 239; 10 Am. Rep. 165.

It is not indispensable to the delivery of a promissory note that it should pass into the personal possession of the payee.   If delivery is made to a person for the benefit of the payee unconditionally, such delivery is sufficient: *Gordon* v. *Adams*, 127 Ill. 223.   Yet the delivery of a note may be conditional: *Brown* v. *St. Charles*, 66 Mich. 71; in which case it was decided that the payee of a note, given on the delivery by the payee of a deed to realty to the maker of the note upon condition that if the maker failed to sell the property in the deed conveyed to third parties, the title of payee should be defeated, and the same returned to the maker, held merely a conditional title to the note subject to be defeated by a failure of the maker to sell the land, and would be liable in trover for the value of the note, if he disposed of the note, and the land was not sold.

———

Lucas *v.* Pennsylvania Company.

[120 INDIANA, 205.]

RAILROAD COMPANIES — DUTY TO KEEP JOINTLY USED PLATFORM IN REPAIR. — A platform used by railroad companies in common as a connection between their stations, and upon which a passenger going from one station to the other would probably walk, must be kept in safe repair; and such passenger not in fault, injured through this neglect of duty, may recover of each or both of the companies.

E. D. Crumpacker, P. Crumpacker, and H. A. Gillett, for the appellant.

J. Brackenridge, for the appellee.

ELLIOTT, C. J.   The special verdict rendered in this case is set forth in the opinion delivered in the case of *Louisville etc. R'y Co.* v. *Lucas,* 119 Ind. 583, and the only question presented by this appeal is, whether the facts stated entitled the appellant to a judgment against the appellee.

We have no brief or argument from the appellee, and we are unable to discover any ground upon which the judgment can be sustained; for the facts stated very satisfactorily show that both of the defendants were guilty of a breach of duty. The appellant had alighted from the train of one of the defendants, and was making her way to the proper place to take passage on the train of the other. She was not an intruder as to either, but she was entitled to protection from both. Neither had a right to permit a platform which it was natural that a reasonable and prudent person would traverse in passing from one station to the other to become and remain unsafe. The situation of the platforms and the surroundings were such as to make it natural for a person alighting, as the appellant did, from a train of the one defendant, intending to take passage on the train of the other defendant, to pursue the course she took in her attempt to pass from the one station to the other.

The defendants were bound to know that passengers who intended to pass from the one station to the other might be misled by the situation and construction of the platform, and it was the duty of both to provide against injury to passengers by making safe the platform used by them in common, and upon which one going from one station to the other would probably walk: *Longmore* v. *Great Western R'y Co.*, 19 Com. B., N. S., 183; *McKone* v. *Michigan Central R. R. Co.*, 51 Mich. 601; 47 Am. Rep. 596; *Louisville etc. R. R. Co.* v. *Wolfe*, 80 Ky. 82; *Knight* v. *Portland etc. R. R. Co.*, 56 Me. 234; 96 Am. Dec. 449; *Hulbert* v. *New York Central R. R. Co.*, 40 N. Y. 145.

In the appeal of the Louisville, New Albany, and Chicago Company, we stated the rule of law which governs railroad companies in cases like this, and that is perhaps all that we need do; but the rule is so well stated in a very recent work that we quote it: "The depot and connected grounds, visited by coming and going passengers, should be fitted up with a careful regard to their comfort and safety. The approaches, the tracks around, the platforms and places for entering and leaving the cars, the passages to the cars, every spot likely to be visited by passengers seeking the depot, waiting at it for trains, or departing, should be made safe and kept so, and at reasonable times should be lighted. And passengers not in fault, injured through a neglect of this duty, may have compensation": Bishop's Non-Contract Law, sec. 1086. Many decisions are adduced in support of the text.

The fact that the negligence of the Louisville, New Albany, and Chicago Company concurred with that of the appellee does not relieve the latter from liability: *Louisville etc. R'y Co. v. Lucas, supra*, and authorities cited; *Town of Knightstown v. Musgrove*, 116 Ind. 121; 9 Am. St. Rep. 827; *Colegrove v. New York etc. R. R. Co.*, 20 N. Y. 492; 75 Am. Dec. 418; *Cuddy v. Horn*, 46 Mich. 596; 41 Am. Rep. 178; *Kain v. Smith*, 80 N. Y. 458; *Wabash etc. R'y Co. v. Shacklet*, 105 Ill. 364; 44 Am. Rep. 791.

Judgment reversed, with instructions to render judgment on the special verdict against both of the defendants in the action.

RAILROAD COMPANIES — DUTY AS TO STATION-GROUNDS. — Railroad companies as carriers of passengers must provide reasonably safe stational accommodations and safeguards where they usually take on and put off passengers: *Moses v. Louisville etc. R. R. Co.*, 39 La. Ann. 649; 4 Am. St. Rep. 231, and note; *Little Rock etc. R'y Co. v. Cavaness*, 48 Ark. 106; *Fordyce v. Merrill*, 49 Ark. 277; *Missouri Pac. R'y Co. v. Neiswanger*, 41 Kan. 621; 13 Am. St. Rep. 304, and note; *Louisville etc. R'y Co. v. Lucas*, 119 Ind. 583; *New York etc. R'y Co. v. Doane*, 115 Ind. 435; *Palmer v. Pennsylvania Co.*, 111 N. Y. 488.

BOARD OF COMMISSIONERS OF WABASH COUNTY *v.* PEARSON.

[120 INDIANA, 426.]

COUNTY, LIABILITY OF, FOR SAFETY OF PUBLIC BRIDGES. — A county is not an insurer of the safety of public bridges; and if ordinary care is exercised in constructing and maintaining them, no liability can exist against the county.

COUNTY, LIABILITY OF, FOR SAFETY OF PUBLIC BRIDGE. — A traveler injured by a falling bridge cannot recover against the county, unless he shows that it was guilty of actionable negligence.

NEGLIGENCE — PLEADING. — FACT THAT BRIDGE HAS BEEN USED SAFELY for thirteen years will not overcome a direct averment of negligence in its construction.

STATUTE OF LIMITATIONS DOES NOT BEGIN TO RUN AGAINST A CAUSE OF ACTION for injury through defendant's negligence until the injury is received, although the negligence was committed thirteen years prior thereto.

PLEADING — NEGLIGENCE. — Where the pleadings show that plaintiff's injury was the proximate result of defendant's negligence, this is sufficient without direct averment to that effect.

WHERE NEGLIGENCE AGAINST COUNTY IN CONSTRUCTING BRIDGE causing an injury is alleged, it is unnecessary to state that the county had notice of its unsafe condition at the time of the injury.

COUNTY, LIABILITY OF, FOR SAFETY OF BRIDGE. — Where a county undertakes to repair a bridge which is in an unsafe condition, it must use ordinary care and skill in so doing.

COUNTY — LIALILITY FOR SAFETY OF BRIDGE. — A county undertaking to repair a bridge must use ordinary care in selecting the means and persons
to do the work; but if such care is exercised, and the bridge remains
unsafe, the county is not liable for injury.

EVIDENCE — HEARSAY — SURGEON WHO ATTENDED AN INJURED PARTY may
give in evidence such party's statements as to the nature and location of
the pain from which he was suffering.

VENIRE DE NOVO. — WHERE VERDICT IS PERFECT ON ITS FACE, and so fully
finds the facts as to enable the court to pronounce judgment upon it, a
motion for a *venire de novo* will be denied, although the verdict may not
find upon all the issues.

W. G. Sayre, H. C. Shively, J. B. Kenner, and J. I. Dille,
for the appellant.

J. T. Hutchens, for the appellee.

ELLIOTT, C. J.   The appellee's complaint is in three paragraphs, and charges the appellant with having negligently
failed to keep a public bridge safe for travel.

Our decisions settle the question of the liability of counties
for a negligent breach of duty respecting public bridges; but
they do not hold, by any means, that a county is to be regarded
as an insurer of the safety of those structures.   If ordinary
care is exercised in constructing and maintaining the bridges,
there can be no liability: *State* v. *Demaree*, 80 Ind. 519,
and cases cited; *Patton* v. *Board etc.*, 96 Ind. 131; *Board etc.*
v. *Legg*, 110 Ind. 479.   The fact that a bridge gives way, and
a traveler is injured, is not of itself sufficient to charge the
county; for it must appear that the county authorities were
guilty of actionable negligence: *Board etc.* v. *Dombke*, 94 Ind.
72.   The question, therefore, which is presented by the ruling
on the demurrer to the several paragraphs of the complaint,
is, Does each of them sufficiently show that there was a negligent breach of duty?

The objection urged against the first paragraph of the complaint is, that the fact that the bridge was safely used for thirteen years overcomes the statement that it was negligently
constructed of unsafe and unsuitable materials, but in our
judgment this objection cannot prevail.   The direct statements of the pleading overcome the inference which the appellant draws from the mere isolated evidentiary fact which
is found among others in the complaint.

The appellee's cause of action did not accrue until he was

injured, and although the defendant's negligence runs back
to 1871, the action is not barred by the statute of limitations.
The two elements of the appellee's cause of action are the legal
injury and the resulting damages: *City of North Vernon* v.
Voegler, 103 Ind. 314. The statute did not begin to run until
the right of action accrued, and this did not accrue until the
two elements came into existence. There is therefore no force
in the argument that the acts of negligence were committed
in 1871, and that the statute then commenced to run, notwithstanding the fact that the appellee was not injured until 1884.

The facts pleaded show that the appellee's injury was the
proximate result of the appellant's wrong, and this is sufficient
without a direct averment: *Louisville etc. R'y Co.* v. *Thompson*,
107 Ind. 442; 57 Am. Rep. 120; *Louisville etc. R'y Co.* v. *Wood*,
113 Ind. 544.

In the second paragraph of the complaint it is averred that
the appellant negligently constructed the bridge of unsafe and
unsuitable material, and it thus appears that the appellant
itself was the wrong-doer, so that the case does not fall within
the rule that a public corporation cannot be liable for suffering a bridge or highway to become unsafe, unless it has notice
of the defect. If the original wrong is that of the corporation
itself, and is of such a nature that it endangers the safety of
travelers, it is not necessary to allege that it had notice of the
unsafe condition of the bridge or highway. If the negligence
is in the construction of the highway or bridge, then it is not
necessary to aver notice: *Board etc.* v. *Bacon*, 96 Ind. 31. It
must, of course, be appropriately shown that ordinary care
was not exercised; and where negligence is averred, this is
shown.

The allegation in the second paragraph that the bridge had
not been inspected by a qualified inspector may be conceded
to be without force and still the paragraph upheld; for if this
allegation be entirely rejected, there will remain facts sufficient to constitute a cause of action. It is unnecessary, therefore, to consider the effect of this allegation, although we are
inclined to the opinion that it adds nothing to the complaint.

The attack on the third paragraph of the complaint cannot
be maintained. If a public corporation knows that a bridge
or highway is unsafe because of the need of repairs, and it
undertakes to repair, it must exercise ordinary care and skill.
If, as is here charged, the corporation knew when it employed
persons to make the repairs that they were incompetent, it did

not exercise ordinary care. A corporation charged with the duty of keeping a bridge in repair must select the proper means and persons to do the work, if by the exercise of ordinary care such a selection can be made. If, however, ordinary care is used in selecting suitable persons, and in requiring the persons selected to exercise their skill with reasonable prudence and diligence, the bridge still remains unsafe, there will be no liability: *City of North Vernon* v. *Voegler*, 103 Ind. 314. But here the averments are, that the corporation knew that the persons selected were incompetent, and knew that their work was so unskillfully and negligently done as to leave the bridge in an unsafe condition, and there is therefore a liability for the injury which resulted from this negligent breach of duty.

There was no error in permitting the surgeon who attended the appellee to give in evidence the statements of the appellee as to the nature and location of the pain from which he was suffering. This question has long been settled in this court: *Board etc.* v. *Leggett*, 115 Ind. 544, and authorities cited; *Louisville etc. R'y Co.* v. *Wood*, 113 Ind. 544; *Louisville etc. R'y Co.* v. *Falvey*, 104 Ind. 409; *Cleveland etc. R. R. Co.* v. *Newell*, 104 Ind. 264; 54 Am. Rep. 312.

The motion for a *venire de novo* was properly overruled. There is no imperfection in the verdict, for sufficient facts are stated to enable the court to pronounce judgment, and under the rule which prevails in this state, the failure to find upon all the issues does not entitle a party to a *venire de novo: Wilson* v. *Hamilton*, 75 Ind. 71; *Jones* v. *Baird*, 76 Ind. 164; *Glantz* v. *City of South Bend*, 106 Ind. 305; 1 Works on Practice, sec. 971, and cases cited in note. This has been the rule since the decision in *Graham* v. *State*, 66 Ind. 386, although the earlier cases declared a different rule: *Quill* v. *Gallivan*, 108 Ind. 235, and cases cited; *Bartley* v. *Phillips*, 114 Ind. 189; *Indiana etc. R'y Co.* v. *Finnell*, 116 Ind. 414. In the case of *Glantz* v. *City of South Bend, supra*, the court referred to *Bosseker* v. *Cramer*, 18 Ind. 44, and some other cases, and after showing that the doctrine of those cases had been denied in *Graham* v. *State, supra*, and that the later cases approved the doctrine of that case, declared, in effect, that the rule as stated in *Graham* v. *State, supra*, must be considered as established. The effect of the decisions has been to overrule *Bosseker* v. *Cramer, supra*, although the express statement that it was overruled has probably not been made. We feel bound to adhere to what has so long been the rule, and to hold, as has been so often held in recent cases, that where the verdict is perfect on its face, and so fully finds the facts as to enable the court to pronounce judgment upon it, a motion for a *venire de novo* will be denied, although the verdict may not find upon all of the issues. .

Judgment affirmed. ——

IN THE ABSENCE OF STATUTE, counties are not liable for damages occasioned by a failure to repair public bridges: Note to *Lehigh County* v. *Hoffort,* 2 Am. St. Rep. 591.

COUNTY BRIDGES. — The proper meaning of the Iowa code, section 527, is, that it fixes absolutely the liability of counties for public bridges, over streams crossing the public highways, which exceed forty feet in length, and that their liability for constructing and maintaining bridges forty feet or less is not affected by said section, but depends upon the necessity and importance of each bridge to the public, its cost and character, and the financial ability of the road district to maintain and construct it: *Casey* v. *Tama County*, 75 Iowa, 655. Prior to 1887, in counties under township organization, the respective towns, not the county, were vested with the power of building and repairing bridges: *Whitcomb* v. *Reed*, 24 Neb. 50. County commissioners cannot be controlled in the exercise of their discretion in building county bridges: *Delaware County's Appeal*, 119 Pa. St. 159; *State* v. *Commissioners*, 119 Ind. 444. Where it is imperative upon the county commissioners to keep in repair a county bridge, for which the county has appropriated money, a writ of *mandamus* will issue to enforce their obligation: *State* v. *Commissioners*, 39 Kan. 700; but they cannot be compelled to rebuild a bridge which is not necessary for the use of the highway, the rebuilding of which would be an injudicious expenditure of public funds: *Commissioners* v. *State*, 113 Ind. 179. Where a bridge company sold its bridge to the township commissioners, the bridge became a free public bridge, which was under the control of the village authorities, in whose limits it was located, and such village had the right to control, improve, and repair the bridge to the exclusion of the township commissioners, even though the latter assumed control of the bridge: *Marseilles* v. *Howland*, 124 Ill. 547. In Wisconsin, the duty of repairing bridges is imposed by statute upon the township in which they are located: *Town of Saukville* v. *State*, 69 Wis. 178. But in the absence of statute, the fact that a bridge is a long one, and expensive to maintain, will not compel the county to maintain or even assist in maintaining it: *Shawnee County* v. *Topeka*, 39 Kan. 197; nor does the fact that a city and county concurred in the purchase of a bridge, and for some time exercised joint control thereof, and contributed jointly to its maintenance, render such county liable for its maintenance in the future: Id.

EVIDENCE — DECLARATIONS OF AN INJURED PARTY. — Declarations of an injured person, made just after receiving the injury, as to how he was injured, etc., are admissible as part of the *res gestæ;* but his mere narrative declarations of past events are inadmissible, even though made to his attending physician: Note to *Leahey* v. *Cass Ave. etc. R'y Co.*, 10 Am. St. Rep. 306; *Dundas* v. *City of Lansing*, 75 Mich. 499; 13 Am. St. Rep. 457. Exclamations of pain, and declarations made by a sick person, when the nature of the illness is in issue, made to the attending physician during the pain or sickness relative to the nature and symptoms thereof, are admissible: Note to *Peple* v. *Vernon*, 95 Am. Dec. 66–68.

WESTHAFER *v.* PATTERSON.

[120 INDIANA, 459.]

VENDOR AND VENDEE. — VENDOR CANNOT SET ASIDE AND RESCIND HIS CON-
VEYANCE of land on the ground that his grantor's title to land in another
state, deeded to him in consideration of his conveyance, is defective for
want of conformity to the law of that state, when the defect complained
of is not fatal to the validity of the deed, and when he makes no offer to
reconvey.

DEEDS. — ACKNOWLEDGMENT IS NOT GENERALLY ESSENTIAL to the validity
of a deed as between the parties, but is only necessary in order to the
effectual admission of the deed to record.

DEEDS. — FORMAL DEFECTS IN ACKNOWLEDGMENTS of deeds, or the omission
of words of identification, can generally only be taken advantage of by
subsequent purchasers for value.

OFFICERS TAKING ACKNOWLEDGMENTS TO DEEDS have the right and may be
compelled at any time to correct mistakes in their certificates.

VENDOR CANNOT RESCIND HIS CONTRACT OF CONVEYANCE so as to reclaim
what he has parted with, and at the same time hold on to what he has
received in the transaction.

T. J. Brooks and *S. M. Reeve*, for the appellant.

E. Moser and *H. Q. Houghton*, for the appellee.

MITCHELL, J. The propriety of the ruling of the circuit
court in sustaining a demurrer to the complaint is the only
question involved in this appeal. Westhafer charged in his
complaint that he had conveyed certain real estate, in the
state of Indiana, of which he was the owner, to the defendant,
Patterson, and that, by agreement, he received, as a consideration for the conveyance made by him, a deed of conveyance
from one John M. Nickless, which purported to convey to the
plaintiff certain real estate in the state of Tennessee, which
the defendant, Patterson, had purchased from Nickless, but
which the latter had never conveyed. It is alleged that John
M. Nickless, the plaintiff's grantor, derived his title to the
Tennessee land through a deed executed by William Nickless
and wife, which latter deed the plaintiff avers was not executed and acknowledged in conformity with the statutes of
the state of Tennessee, certain sections of which are set out in
the complaint. These statutes require the officer before whom
a deed is acknowledged to state in his certificate that he is
personally acquainted with the grantor, and also to annex to
any deed in which a husband and wife join a certificate to
the effect that the wife appeared before him privately, and
apart from her husband, and acknowledged the deed freely,
voluntarily, etc. It is alleged that the requirements of the

foregoing statutes were not observed in the respects above mentioned, in the acknowledgment, or the certificate indorsed upon or annexed to the conveyance from William Nickless and wife to the plaintiff's grantor, John M. Nickless. Without alleging any other infirmity in the deed or defect in the title, the plaintiff demanded judgment setting aside his conveyance to the defendant, Patterson, and for general relief.

It does not appear that the plaintiff offered to reconvey the Tennessee land before the commencement of the action, nor does he offer in his complaint to do so, under the direction of the court. There is nothing to show that any request was ever made to have the acknowledgment of the deed or the defective certificate corrected by the grantors therein, nor is it averred that the grantors in that deed are asserting any adverse claim to the land, or that the plaintiff was not in the complete and quiet possession and occupancy of it at the time the suit was commenced.

There are, therefore, at least two grounds upon which the ruling of the court in sustaining the demurrer to the complaint can be sustained: 1. It does not appear that there is any substantial defect in the plaintiff's title to the Tennessee land. Notwithstanding the defect in the certificate of the officer before whom the deed was acknowledged, the conveyance may have transferred a perfect title as between the parties to it. As a general rule, a deed may be valid and binding on the parties who execute it, so as to pass the title to the grantee without any certificate of acknowledgment: *Fryer* v. *Rockefeller*, 63 N. Y. 268. Generally, the necessity for an acknowledgment arises out of registry acts, which require certain formal proof of the execution of the deed before it can be recorded, in such a way as that the record shall furnish constructive notice of its contents, so as to affect subsequent purchasers. An acknowledgment is, therefore, not, as a general rule, essential to the validity of a deed as between the parties to it, but it is only necessary in order to the effectual admission of the deed to record: *Hubble* v. *Wright*, 23 Ind. 322; *Mays* v. *Hedges*, 79 Ind. 288; *Behler* v. *Weyburn*, 59 Ind. 143; *Doe* v. *Naylor*, 2 Blackf. 32; 5 Am. & Eng. Ency. of Law, 443.

Ordinarily, only subsequent purchasers for value can take advantage of the omission of words of identification or other formal defects in the certificate of acknowledgment: *Mastin* v. *Halley*, 61 Mo. 196; *Chouteau* v. *Burlando*, 20 Mo. 482; 1 Am. & Eng. Ency. of Law, 154, 158.

At common law a married woman had no power to make a valid conveyance of her separate real estate. Her power in that respect is conferred and regulated by statute in the several states. Hence, where the certificate of acknowledgment is made an essential feature of the conveyance of the separate estate of a married woman, the form prescribed must be observed, or the deed will be invalid: *Jordan* v. *Corey*, 2 Ind. 385; 52 Am. Dec. 516; *Woods* v. *Polhemus*, 8 Ind. 60.

It does not appear that the conveyance in question involved the separate estate of a married woman, and if it did, we are not advised that the statutes of the state of Tennessee prescribe any particular form of certificate as essential to the validity of the conveyance between the parties to it. So far as appears, the statutes set out with the complaint relate entirely to the requisites of a certificate of acknowledgment as prescribed by the recording acts. Moreover, officers have the right, and it is a duty which they may be compelled at any time to perform, to correct mistakes in their certificates. *Jordan* v. *Corey*, 2 Ind. 385; 52 Am. Dec. 516; 1 Am. & Eng. Ency. of Law, 149.

Assuming that the officer before whom the deed was acknowledged did his duty, and examined the wife separate and apart from her husband, it would follow that the informality in the certificate was the result of a mere clerical omission which might be corrected on proper application: *Fleming* v. *Potter*, 14 Ind. 486.

2. Even though the title was defective on account of the omission in the certificate, the conveyance was not void, and, as has been seen, it does not appear that the plaintiff offers, or has offered, to reconvey. It is familiar law that a party will not be permitted to rescind a contract so as to reclaim what he has parted with, and at the same time hold on to what he has received in the transaction. *Higham* v. *Harris*, 108 Ind. 246, and cases cited; *Patten* v. *Stewart*, 24 Ind. 332; *Home Ins. Co.* v. *Howard*, 111 Ind. 544; *Thompson* v. *Peck*, 115 Ind. 512. So long as the plaintiff manifests a disposition to hold on to the land conveyed to him, he can acquire no standing in a court of equity to rescind the contract. There was no error.

The judgment is therefore affirmed, with costs.

ACKNOWLEDGMENTS TO DEEDS. — Acknowledgment of a deed is an essential part thereof, without which the deed is not entitled to be recorded: *Wolf* v. *Fogarty*, 6 Cal. 224; 65 Am. Dec. 509; *Jordan* v. *Corey*, 2 Ind. 385; 52 Am. Dec. 516.

FOR THE LAW APPLICABLE TO ACKNOWLEDGMENTS OF INSTRUMENTS GEN-
ERALLY, see extended note to *Livingston* v. *Kittelle*, 41 Am. Dec. 168–184.

MISTAKES IN ACKNOWLDGMENTS. — An acknowledgment must be sustained if possible: *Touchard* v. *Crow*, 20 Cal. 150; 81 Am. Dec. 108; and
mistakes therein may be corrected at any time by the acknowledging officer:
Jordan v. *Corey*, 2 Ind. 385; 52 Am. Dec. 516, and note to the same, pages
519–525, upon the question of amending and perfecting acknowledgments.
Where a foreign notary, in taking an acknowledgment to a deed, fails to sign
his christian name, but merely gives his initials, and in the copy of his commission and in the certificate attached thereto, his full christian name is given,
the discrepancy is insufficient to warrant a rejection of the deed in evidence:
Denny v. *Ashley*, 12 Col. 165.   An acknowledgment signed by the county
clerk as such, and with the seal of the county attached, is sufficiently authen-
ticated: *Southwick* v. *Davis*, 78 Cal. 504.   An acknowledgment which states
that the person acknowledging it was known to the notary "to be the person
who makes the foregoing declaration," is sufficient without the use of the
words, "whose name is subscribed to the within instrument": Id.   The application of the curative acts of 1883, in Arkansas, is not limited to the
obvious omission of words from acknowledgments, but extends to every case
in which the acknowledgment of a deed is insufficient to give full legal effect to
its terms: *Johnson* v. *Parker*, 51 Ark. 419.

ACKNOWLEDGMENTS OF DEEDS. — Any instrument expressing an obligation
by its maker to transfer land to another, duly acknowledged, may be recorded, no matter what its form may be: *Chamberlin* v. *Boon*, 74 Tex. 659.
Where the execution of a deed is proved, it is immaterial whether the deed
was acknowledged or not; and such unacknowledged deed passes title equally
with one duly acknowledged: *Missouri P. R'y Co.* v. *Houseman*, 41 Kan. 300;
and where there are no witnesses to a deed, and no acknowledgment, the
maker of the deed may testify to its execution: *Bohn* v. *Davis*, 75 Tex. 24.
No authority exists in the judge of a court of record, in another state, to take
an acknowledgment of a deed to land in Texas: *Talbert* v. *Dull*, 70 Id. 675.
Where it is claimed by a wife that her acknowledgment to the joint deed of
herself and husband was not what it purports to be, the burden is upon
her to show such fact by a most convincing proof: *Ford* v. *Osborne*, 45
Ohio St. 1.   And where a lost or destroyed deed is satisfactorily shown to
have had attached to it a certificate of acknowledgment by the grantor and
wife, by an officer authorized to take such acknowledgments, that fact of itself,
after the lapse of twenty-eight years, is sufficient to overcome the wife's denial that she ever released her dower by deed or otherwise: *Berdel* v. *Egan*,
125 Ill. 298.   An officer who took an acknowledgment is a competent witness to support or to impeach it: *Mays* v. *Pryce*, 95 Mo. 603.

VENDOR AND VENDEE. — Abatement in purchase-price on account of a
defect of title or quantity of land sold: See *Heavner* v. *Morgan*, 30 W. Va. 335;
8 Am. St. Rep. 55.

RESCISSION OF A CONTRACT FOR THE PURCHASE OF REALTY: See *Wright* v.
Dickinson, 67 Mich. 580; 11 Am. St. Rep. 602, and particularly note 611.   A
failure of a vendor to return money received by him of his vendee, who obtained possession of the property by fraudulent representations, cannot be
urged as a defense by a third person, whom such vendor sues to obtain possession of such property: *Benesch* v. *Waggner*, 12 Col. 534; 13 Am. St. Rep.
254.

AS TO WHAT A PARTY IS BOUND TO DO, who seeks to recind a contract, see
extended note to *Johnson* v. *Evans*, 50 Am. Dec. 672–681.

CINCINNATI, INDIANAPOLIS, ST. LOUIS, AND CHICAGO RAILROAD COMPANY *v.* COOPER.

[120 INDIANA, 469.]

RAILROADS — NEGLIGENCE — DUTY TO INJURED PASSENGER ON TRACK. — Where a passenger is thrown upon the track through the negligence of a railroad company, and is there left in a dazed and partially unconscious condition from the fall, where he is run down and killed by another train belonging to the company, having knowledge of his fall and condition of mind, the company is liable for the injury. In such case, the passenger is not a trespasser, and the negligence of the company is the proximate cause of death.

COMMON CARRIER — DUTY TO INJURED PASSENGER ON TRACK. — A common carrier is bound to know that trains are running upon its own road, and it is under duty to a passenger negligently thrown upon its track, and left in a dazed condition, to take steps to prevent injury to him from danger which it knew he was likely to incur from its trains, and it does not matter that the injury incurred was not foreseen, if it was such as might naturally result.

COMMON CARRIER IS NOT BOUND TO PROTECT DRUNKARDS from the consequences which result from their own wrongs or follies. Still it owes them some duties, and cannot negligently suffer harm to come to them while they are passengers.

COMMON CARRIER IS ANSWERABLE FOR INJURY TO DRUNKEN PASSENGER, where the injury results, not from the drunken condition of the passenger, but from the carrier's breach of duty.

COMMON CARRIER — NEGLIGENCE. — Recklessness in a common carrier, reaching in degree to an utter disregard of consequences, may supply the place of a specific intent to inflict an injury.

JURY TRIAL. — INSTRUCTIONS given need not be repeated.

S. Stansifer, for the appellant.

G. W. Cooper and C. S. Baker, for the appellee.

ELLIOTT, C. J. The material facts, stated in the second paragraph of the appellee's complaint, are these: On the eighteenth day of April, 1885, Uriah Holland, the appellee's intestate, entered a train of the appellants, which carried both passengers and freight, at the city of Columbus, and paid his passage to the town of Hope, a regular station on the line of appellant's road. When the train on which the intestate was a passenger reached the station at Lambert, a point between the city of Columbus and the town of Hope, the appellant's employees failed and neglected to announce the name of the station, but some one in the car called out "Hope," as if naming the station. After the train had stopped at Lambert, the intestate, believing it to be the station for which he had taken passage, endeavored to alight from the train in the usual manner, and the employees of the appellant, without giving any warning or notice, carelessly and negligently caused the train to be suddenly started, and the intestate, without any fault on his part, was thrown violently from the platform of the car, on which he was standing, to the track. The fall rendered him unconscious, and of this the appellant had knowledge, as well as of its cause. Soon after the occurrence, and while the intestate was upon the appellant's track in a dazed and partially unconscious condition, at a point seventy rods distant from Lambert, the appellant's employees in charge of a passenger train, and having knowledge of the fact of his fall from the train and his condition in time to have avoided injury to him by the exercise of ordinary care, negligently, and without giving any signal or warning of the approach of the train, or taking any precaution to avoid injuring him, caused the passenger train to run upon him, thus causing his death, without any fault or negligence on his part.

If the intestate had been on the track through no fault of the appellant, and without knowledge on its part of his condition, no action could be maintained; but he was on the track through the fault of the appellant, and it did know of his condition. The rule applicable to cases where persons trespass on the company's track cannot govern in such a case as this. Even if it should be conceded that there was no breach of duty on the part of the appellant in failing to announce the station, still there was negligence in starting the train with a sudden jerk: *Louisville etc. R. R. Co.* v. *Crunk*, 119 Ind. 542; 12 Am. St. Rep. 443; *Indianapolis etc. R. R. Co.* v. *Horst*, 93 U. S. 291; *Doss* v. *Missouri etc. R. R. Co.*, 59 Mo. 27; 21 Am. Rep. 371; *Andrist* v. *Union Pacific R'y Co.*, 30 Fed. Rep. 345. But we might go further, and concede that there was no negligence in starting the train, and still we should be required to hold that a cause of action is stated, inasmuch as the fact that the intestate was known to have been thrown to the track, in an effort to alight from the train, and rendered unconscious, made it the duty of the appellant to use care to prevent injury to him from its own trains. A railway carrier of passengers has no right, where care and diligence can prevent it, to leave a helpless passenger, who has fallen from one of its trains, in a situation of known danger. If a passenger, without fault on his part or that of the carrier, but as the result of a pure accident, should be thrown from a train upon the

track and rendered helpless, it would be the duty of the railway carrier, if the facts were known to it, to use proper care
and diligence to prevent injury from passing trains.

The appellant was bound to know that trains were running
upon its own road, and it was under a duty to the passenger
who was thrown upon its track to take steps to prevent injury to him from the danger which it knew he was likely to
incur from its trains. It does not matter that the injury
which actually occurred was not foreseen; it is enough that
it was such as might naturally result: *Billman* v. *Indianapolis
etc. R. R. Co.*, 76 Ind. 165; 40 Am. Rep. 230; *Dunlap* v. *Wagner*, 85 Ind. 529; 44 Am. Rep. 42; *Louisville etc. R'y Co.* v.
Wood, 113 Ind. 544 (566), and cases cited; *Hill* v. *Winsor*, 118
Mass. 251; *Lane* v. *Atlantic Works*, 111 Mass. 136. "It is not
necessary," said the court in *Hill* v. *Winsor*, 118 Mass. 251,
"that injury in the precise form in which it in fact resulted
should have been foreseen." It needs no argument to demonstrate the truth of the proposition that danger must be presumed from passing trains if one in a state of bewilderment
is left upon the track. A long line of cases affirm that one
who goes upon a track even with mental and physical faculties undiminished is in fault, because he enters a place of
danger, and the one who wrongfully puts another in such a
place does a wrong, and is precluded from averring that the
injured person was where he had no right to be. Here the
carrier knowingly left its passenger upon the track, knowing,
also, that injury from a fall from its train had impaired his
mental faculties, and it cannot be held blameless, and its
passenger declared a trespasser.

The wrong of the carrier in leaving its injured passenger
on the track exposed to great and known peril, without mind
enough to care for himself, was the proximate cause of his
death. The case is stronger, not weaker, in the fact that those
in charge of the train which ran upon him were informed as
to his misfortune and his injury; for the two acts of negligence combined in one efficient cause, and the effect which
might naturally have been expected did in fact result. The
concurring wrongs blended in one strong unity, producing a
legal tort for which the wrong-doer must make compensation:
Evansville etc. R. R. Co. v. *Crist*, 116 Ind. 446; 9 Am. St. Rep.
865; *Indianapolis etc. R'y Co.* v. *Pitzer*, 109 Ind. 179; 58 Am.
Rep. 387.

If, as counsel tacitly assume, it were true that Holland's

misfortune was due solely to his own wrong in voluntarily becoming intoxicated, we should have a very different case. We should, if such were the case, hold the paragraph of the complaint, in which appears the statement that he was intoxicated, to be insufficient. This we should do, for the reason that we are satisfied that a carrier is not bound to protect a drunken man from the consequences which result from his own folly or wrong: *Welty* v. *Indianapolis etc. R. R. Co.*, 105 Ind. 55; *McClelland* v. *Louisville etc. R'y Co.*, 94 Ind. 276; *Louisville etc. R. R. Co.* v. *Sullivan*, 81 Ky. 624; 50 Am. Rep. 186. But a drunken man is not an outcast, and the railway carrier cannot negligently suffer harm to come to him while he is a passenger. It owes him some duty, which, at its peril, it must not omit. It is not to answer for his folly, but for its own breach of duty: *Atchison etc. R. R. Co.* v. *Weber*, 33 Kan. 543; 52 Am. Rep. 543; *Railway Co.* v. *Vallclcy*, 32 Ohio St. 345; 30 Am. Rep. 601. Here, the drunken condition of the deceased was not the cause of his injury, for, as the complaint avers and the demurrer admits, the cause of his injury was the carrier's breach of duty, and for that breach of duty the carrier is answerable.

It is a just and beneficent principle, running through all the cases, that a railway company must do what humanity requires, where it acts with knowledge of another's helpless condition: *Atchison etc. R. R. Co.* v. *Weber, supra; Railway Co.* v. *Valleley, supra; Weymire* v. *Wolfe*, 52 Iowa, 533; *Northern Central R'y Co.* v. *State*, 29 Md. 420; 96 Am. Dec. 445; *Walker* v. *Great Western R'y Co.*, L. R. 2 Ex. 228; *Swazey* v. *Union Mfg. Co.*, 42 Conn. 556; *Atlantic etc. R. R. Co.* v. *Reisner*, 18 Kan. 458; *Marquette etc. R. R. Co.* v. *Taft*, 28 Mich. 289 (opinion by Cooley, J.); *Terre Haute etc. R. R. Co.* v. *McMurray*, 98 Ind. 358; 49 Am. Rep. 752; *Louisville etc. R'y Co.* v. *Phillips*, 112 Ind. 59; 2 Am. St. Rep. 155.

If, let it be supposed for illustration, a man should be seen bound to the track in time to avoid running upon him, it would certainly be an actionable wrong to run a train upon him; and the case made by the complaint differs from the supposed one only in degree, for if the man on the track is so helpless, from mental incapacity, as not to be conscious of his acts, and this is known to the railway company, it is its duty to use reasonable care to prevent injury to him. In such a case, the presumption that the man will leave the track cannot apply, although it would apply if his condition were un-

known to the employees of the company, or had not been
caused by them.   In this instance, the man was a passenger,
and his presence on the track, as well as his incapacity to
avoid danger, was the result of the carrier's negligence.   In
no sense was he a mere trespasser, for by the wrong of the
railroad company he was thrown upon the track, and there
left in no condition to care for himself.

Among the instructions given by the court is this: "To
establish the charge of willfulness, as set out in the fourth
paragraph of the complaint, I instruct you that an actual intent to do the particulary injury alleged need not be shown;
but if you find, from all the evidence, that the misconduct of
the defendant's servants was such as to evince an utter disregard of consequences, so as to inflict the injury complained of,
this may of itself tend to establish willfulness."

In our judgment, this instruction expresses correctly an abstract rule of law.   Recklessness, reaching in degree to an
utter disregard of consequences, may supply the place of a
specific intent: *Palmer* v. *Chicago etc. R. R. Co.*, 112 Ind. 250;
Brannen v. *Kokomo etc. G. R. Co.*, 115 Ind. 115; 7 Am. St. Rep.
411; *Indiana etc. R'y Co.* v. *Wheeler*, 115 Ind. 253.

The appellant's theory that the occurrence at Lambert's
station must be excluded from consideration is embodied in
several instructions asked, but refused.   In refusing these instructions there was no error.   The occurrence at that place,
as is evident from what has been said, exerted an important
influence upon the case, even if appellant's general theory
were correct; for from it there was reason for inferring that
the wrong which brought the intestate upon the track and into
danger was that of the appellant, and it also supplies ground
for the inference that the appellant's employees in charge of
the passenger train which killed Holland knew his condition,
knew what caused it, and knew that he was exposed to danger.   It warranted, at least, the inference that he was not a
mere trespasser.   But more than this, that occurrence may
well be regarded as the cause of the unfortunate consequences
which culminated in Holland's death.   It is not, of course,
proper to affirm in the instructions, as matter of law, that it
should be so regarded, but it was proper that, as matter of
fact, it should receive consideration by the jury.   On the other
hand, it would have been error to assert, as matter of law, that
what occurred at Lambert was not the proximate cause of the
injury.   If, as the jury might well have inferred, the negli-

gent conduct at Lambert was the cause of Holland's death, then the conduct of those in charge of the train which killed him cannot be assigned controlling force. If the intestate's death was the probable result of the wrong at Lambert, the right of action was complete, and the defendant liable for the legal consequences of that wrong. If death was the result, then, for causing death, the appellant is responsible.

As strongly as it could well be done the court directed the jury that if Holland's presence on the track, and his injury, were owing to his drunken condition there could be no recovery, and the fact that this direction was not repeated does not give appellant just reason to complain.

It is a general rule that instructions need not be repeated, and this rule disposes of many of the questions argued by counsel: *Union M. L. Ins. Co.* v. *Buchanan*, 100 Ind. 63.

We do not hold, nor mean to hold, that if the appellant had been free from fault at Lambert, the notice of Holland's condition would have required it to run its trains so slowly as to avoid the possibility of injuring him. On the contrary, we held that the wrong which produced his mental incapacity, and caused him to wander along the tracks in a dazed condition, is the one which constitutes the chief element of the right of recovery. The instructions of the trial court do not place the right of recovery upon the acts of those in charge of the train which ran over Holland, but they do clearly assert that if his condition was caused by the negligence of the defendant at Lambert, and that his presence at the place of danger was the result of that condition, the appellee is entitled to recover. If there is any criticism at all to be made upon the instructions, it is that they are too favorable to the appellant, for they place too much stress upon the conduct of the persons in charge of the train which killed Holland.

We have considered all the questions argued by counsel, but we do not deem it necessary to discuss them in detail, for the questions we have discussed are those which arise in the case and control its decision.

Judgment affirmed.

CARRIERS OF PASSENGERS. — Expulsion of passengers by the carrier, when, where, and how may be exercised: See extended note to *Chicago etc. R. R. Co.* v. *Parks*, 68 Am. Dec. 570–573. As to the liability of carriers for injuries to passengers, generally, see extended note to *Ingalls* v. *Bills*, 43 Am. Dec. 355–367. In the case of *Louisville etc. R. R. Co.* v. *Sullivan*, 81 Ky. 624, 50 Am. Rep. 186, a carrier was held responsible for expelling a drunken pas-

senger from a car for refusing to pay fare, the conductor knowing his condition, and putting him off, not at a station, but in the snow, where he was
frozen. But in the case of *Railway Co.* v. *Valleley*, 32 Ohio St. 345, 30 Am
Rep. 601, where the conductor, who had the right to expel an unruly and
drunken passenger, and exercised every reasonable degree of prudence, considering the time, place, and circumstances, is well as the condition of the
drunken man himself, expelled such a passenger, who was subsequently run
over by another train not in fault, the expulsion was held not to have been
the proximate cause of the death so as to make the railway company responsible for the same. For persons may be expelled from vehicles of common
carriage on account of intoxication, offensive conduct, or boisterous demon-
strations: *Vinton* v. *Middlesex R. R. Co.*, 11 Allen, 304; 87 Am. Dec. 714, and
particularly note 716, 717; *Sullivan* v. *Old Colony R. R. Co.*, 148 Mass 119;
Peavy v. *Georgia Pac. R'y & Bkg. Co.*, 81 Ga. 485; 12 Am. St. Rep. 334.
Carrier having the right to eject one who is not a trespasser must eject him
at a regular station; but a trespasser may be ejected at a place other than the
station, provided he is not wantonly exposed to the peril of serious personal
danger: *Hardenbergh* v. *St. Paul etc. R'y Co.*, 39 Minn. 3; 12 Am. St. Rep.
610, and note.

ROLLET *v.* HEIMAN.

[120 INDIANA, 511.]

DEED — AVOIDANCE OF, FOR INSANITY. — A judgment creditor cannot set
    aside as fraudulent a deed because of the insanity of the grantor; such
    deed can only be avoided by the grantor or his privies in blood or es-
    tate.

PLEADING AND PRACTICE.— COMPLAINT TO SET ASIDE A FRAUDULENT DEED,
    alleging that it was accepted by the grantee with knowledge of its fraud-
    ulent purpose, and as a mere volunteer who has paid no consideration,
    states a good cause of action.

J. E. Williamson, for the appellants.

D. B. Kumler, V. Bisch, and G. F. Denby, for the appellee.

ELLIOTT, C. J. Heiman, the appellee, is the judgment creditor of Joseph Rollet, one of the appellants. The facts, stated
in the second paragraph of his complaint, are, in substance,
these: The plaintiff recovered judgment against Rollet for
$347; the judgment is unsatisfied, and the debtor has no other
property subject to execution. At the time of the execution of
the promissory note upon which the judgment is founded,
Rollet owned real estate of the value of five thousand five hundred dollars, and he also owned personal property of the value
of eight hundred dollars. He was the owner of this property
on the twenty-seventh day of October, 1883, the note was executed on the twenty-eighth day of April, 1883, and the judgment on it was recovered on the fourth day of Feb..ry,

1884. Rollet, by reason of the excessive use of intoxicating liquors, was incapaciated from engaging in ordinary business pursuits. Nurrenbarn is the brother-in-law of Rollet, and on the twenty-seventh day of October, 1883, induced the latter to convey to him all of his property. The deed was executed by Rollet and wife, conveying to Nurrenbarn the real estate then owned by Rollet. The consideration for the conveyance was the promised payment of three thousand nine hundred dollars, and the assumption by the grantee of two mortgages on the property. The property was worth at least three thousand dollars more than the price fixed. The consideration expressed in the deed was not paid by the grantee. The alleged payment of three thousand nine hundred dollars was in fact not made, but was pretended to be made by the release of debts due from Rollet to Nurrenbarn, which debts were mere fictions, having no existence. Immediately after the execution of the deed, Nurrenbarn made a gift of a great part of the personal property to Sophia Rollet, the wife of the judgment debtor. The conveyance was made with the intent to cheat, hinder, and delay the creditors of Rollet, and it was accepted by the grantee with full knowledge of all the facts.

The complaint is not well drawn. It contains much that is mere matter of evidence, and such matter obscures and weakens a pleading. We attach no importance whatever to the argument of the counsel that the complaint describes many badges of fraud, and is therefore good; for badges of fraud are simply matters of evidence, and in pleading it is the facts, and not the evidence, that must be alleged. The complaint contains matters which are not proper in a complaint by a judgment creditor to set aside a fraudulent conveyance, and these matters so confuse the pleading as to make it somewhat difficult to determine its character.

If the complaint sought simply to set aside the conveyance because of the mental incapacity of Rollet, we should be strongly inclined to hold that no cause of action was shown to exist in the judgment creditor. We believe the law to be against the right of a judgment creditor to set aside such a conveyance as fraudulent, for we think that the deed of an insane person can only be avoided by the grantor or his privies in blood or estate: *Price* v. *Jennings*, 62 Ind. 111; *Shrock* v. *Crowl*, 83 Ind. 243; *Campbell* v. *Kuhn*, 45 Mich. 513; 40 Am. Rep. 479; *Breckenridge* v. *Ormsby*, 1 J. J. Marsh. 236; 19 Am. Dec. 71.

A pleading, as we have often held, is to be judged from its general scope and tenor, and so this complaint must be judged. Judging it by this established rule, we cannot allow the isolated averment of Rollet's mental incapacity to control the general frame and tenor of the pleading. This averment, like those of matters of evidence, must be treated as mere surplusage, and surplusage will not vitiate a pleading. Our judgment is, that the complaint is to be regarded as one to set aside a fraudulent conveyance accepted by the grantee with knowledge of the fraudulent purpose, and as a mere volunteer who has paid no consideration.

Judgment affirmed.

INSANE PERSONS, DEEDS OF. — Deeds executed by insane persons as grantors are not void, but merely voidable: *Pearson* v. *Cox*, 71 Tex. 246; 10 Am. St. Rep. 740, and particularly note 744; note to *Allis* v. *Billings*, 39 Am. Dec. 749. Privies in blood and in representation can avoid the deed of an insane person, but privies in estate cannot: *Breckenridge* v. *Ormsby*, 1 J. J. Marsh. 236; 19 Am. Dec. 71.

WASSON *v.* LAMB.

[120 INDIANA, 514.]

BANKS AND BANKING — ACCOUNT BETWEEN BANK AND DEPOSITOR. — As money is paid in and drawn out of a bank, or other debts and credits are entered by the consent of both parties in the general banking account of the depositor, a balance is considered as struck at the date of each payment or entry on either side of the account.

BANKS AND BANKING. — ENTRY OF AMOUNT AND DATE OF DEPOSIT in the pass-book of the depositor, made by the proper officer, binds the bank as an admission, and is generally conclusive upon it as an account stated, when the pass-book is balanced.

BANKS AND BANKING. — CHECKS, DRAFTS, OR OTHER EVIDENCES OF DEBT received by a bank in good faith as deposits, and credited as so much money, transfers their title to the bank, and it becomes legally liable to the depositor as for so much money deposited as of the date of the credit.

BANKS AND BANKING. — DEPOSIT OF TAX RECEIPTS, treated by mutual consent of the bank and depositor as so much cash deposited to the credit of the latter, will be regarded in legal effect as a deposit of money, and the transaction will be treated as if the bank had paid the taxes, and then received the money on deposit, in the absence of evidence of fraud.

BANKS AND BANKING. — DEPOSITOR OF TAX RECEIPTS who has received credit on the books of the bank as for so much cash deposited, and has afterwards checked out a sum of money, including the amount of the tax receipts, cannot claim that the taxes were not paid, and, after letting the transaction stand until by an assignment by the bank the rights of other creditors have intervened, he cannot recover the money on the

ground of false representations of the solvency of the bank at the time
of the deposit, especially when he has not been injured by such representations.

J. S. Duncan, C. W. Smith, and J. R. Wilson, for the appellant.

R. Hill, for the appellee.

MITCHELL, J. This is an appeal from a judgment and
decree of the Marion circuit court, by which Wasson, as
treasurer of Marion County, was perpetually enjoined from
asserting or enforcing an alleged lien for taxes against certain
real estate which had been transferred to Robert M. Lamb,
as the assignee of Alfred and John C. S. Harrison. The question for decision arises upon the following facts: In April,
1884, Wasson was the treasurer of Marion County, and for
some months prior thereto kept an account in Harrison's
bank, a private banking-house owned and conducted by Alfred and John C. S. Harrison in the city of Indianapolis.
With a view of inspiring confidence in the solvency of the
firm, and to induce the appellant to believe that their bank was
a safe place for the deposit of money, one of the partners, at
divers time prior to the twenty-third day of April, 1884, falsely
represented to him that the firm was solvent. These representations, although relied on by the appellant, were known to be
false by the member of the firm who made them. On the date
above mentioned, the appellant, as county treasurer, delivered
to the partner above referred to receipts for taxes due from
himself and the firm and others, to the amount of $2,086.65,
that amount being at the same time entered as a credit on the
pass-book, or bank-book, in which the appellant kept the account of his deposits and checks with the bank. At the time
the receipts were delivered and the credit entered as above, the
appellant marked the taxes as having been paid on the tax
duplicate, and charged himself with the several amounts.
This credit included the amount assessed and due as the
taxes, the collection of which was enjoined by the decree from
for which this appeal is prosecuted. It appears that the credit
the amount of the receipts was not entered on the books of the
bank until the twenty-eighth day of April, 1884, five days after
it was credited by a member of the firm on the appellant's pass-
book, at which time the balance to his credit was $49,764.67.
The appellant's bank-book was balanced on the tenth day of
May, 1884. The balance included the amount of the tax

receipts. After that date the appellant made deposits and drew checks against his balance until in July, 1884, when the bank, being insolvent, suspended payment and made an assignment, with a balance standing to the credit of the appellant amounting to $9,233.72. If the amount of the tax receipts is considered as having been deposited in the bank as of the date the credit was entered on the appellant's pass-book, then he has drawn out more than he deposited since that date, including the $2,086.65. If, however, it is not to be considered as deposited until it was entered on the books of the bank, no part of it has been since drawn out. The learned court below was of the opinion that the deposit should be considered as made when the appellant was credited with the amount on his pass-book, and that, having since that time checked out more than he has since deposited, including the amount credited for taxes, he was in no way injured by the misrepresentations concerning the solvency of the bank.

This conclusion is unquestionably correct. The general rule which governs in keeping the account between a bank and a depositor is, that as money is paid in and drawn out or other debts and credits are entered by the consent of both parties, in the general banking account of the customer, a balance may be considered as struck at the date of each payment or entry on either side of the account: *Nat. Mahaiwe Bank* v. *Peck*, 127 Mass. 298; 34 Am. Rep. 368; *Lamb* v. *Morris*, 118 Ind. 179.

Ordinarily, whenever a deposit is made, the amount and date thereof are entered by the cashier or teller in the bank-book or pass-book of the depositor, and such entries, when made by the proper officer, bind the bank as admissions. In some cases it has been held that they become conclusive upon the bank like an account stated, when the bank-book is balanced: Morse on Banks and Banking, 3d ed., sec. 291. The settled rule is, where checks, drafts, or other evidences of debt are received in good faith as deposits, if the bank credits them as so much money, the title to the checks or drafts is immediately transferred to the bank, and it becomes legally liable to the depositor as for so much money deposited: *Cragie* v. *Hadley*, 99 N. Y. 131; 52 Am. Rep. 9; *Metropolitan Nat. Bank* v. *Loyd*, 90 N. Y. 530. So where a bank credits a depositor with the amount of a check drawn upon it by another customer, and there is no want of good faith on the part of the depositor, the act of crediting is equivalent to a payment in money. "Nor can the bank recall or repudiate the payment because, upon an examination of the accounts of the drawer, it is ascertained that he was without funds to meet the check, though when the payment was made the officer making it labored under the mistake that there were funds sufficient": *City Nat. Bank etc.* v. *Burns*, 68 Ala. 267; 44 Am. Rep. 138; *Bolton* v. *Richard*, 6 Term Rep. 139; *Oddie* v. *Nat. Bank*, 45 N. Y. 735; 6 Am. Rep. 160.

Where, therefore, the holder of a check, or other genuine instrument representing a fixed sum, delivers it to a bank, and receives an unqualified credit as for a definite sum of money, the transaction is equivalent to an actual deposit of so much cash as of the date of the credit: *First Nat. Bank* v. *Burkhardt*, 100 U. S. 686. Thus in *Titus* v. *Mechanics' Nat. Bank*, 35 N. J. L. 588, a dispute having arisen concerning the title to certain checks, the court said: "They were received and credited in a cash account as cash. . . . . By such crediting, the bank became the owners of these bills, as they do of legal-tender notes or bank-bills so deposited. And had the defendants failed the next day, the plaintiffs could not have demanded these identical checks as their property, left for collection, against a receiver or an assignee in bankruptcy; the plaintiff had received the price of these checks by having it credited on their overdrafts, and by drawing for it": *Hoffman* v. *First Nat. Bank*, 46 N. J. L. 604; Morse on Banks and Banking, secs. 569, 570.

In like manner, according to the opinion of Lord Eldon, if bills are deposited and entered in the customer's account as cash, with his knowledge and consent, so that he becomes entitled to draw against the amount, he will thereby be precluded from claiming the bills: *Ex parte Sargeant*, 1 Rose, 153; *Ayres* v. *Farmers' etc. Bank*, 79 Mo. 421; 49 Am. Rep. 235; Story on Agency, sec. 228, note.

Upon principle, there can be no reason why, if parties choose to treat a deposit of paper, or other securities, as cash, so that it is available to the depositor as cash, the transaction should not be regarded as equivalent to a deposit of money. Thus, as was said by Wallace, J., in *St. Louis etc. R'y Co.* v. *Johnston*, 27 Fed. Rep. 243: "When a sight-bill is deposited with a bank by a customer at the same time with money or currency, and a credit is given him by the bank for the paper just as a like credit is given for the rest of the deposit, the act evinces unequivocally the intention of the bank to treat the bill and the money or currency, without discrimination, as a deposit of cash, and to assume towards the depositor the relation of a debtor instead of a bailee of the paper. If the customer assents to such action on the part of the bank by drawing checks against the credit, or in any other way, he manifests with equal clearness his intention to be treated as a depositor of money." If by mutual consent the bank and the appellant chose to treat the tax receipts as so much cash deposited to the credit of the latter, the transaction must be regarded according to the intention of the parties at the time.

The conclusion which follows from what has preceded is, that when the appellant transferred the tax receipts to the bank, and received credit for the amount thereof, the transaction was, in legal effect, the same as if he had deposited the amount in cash. He had the right to draw his check against it the next moment after the credit was entered, precisely as if he had made the deposit in money. Moreover, the court finds that he did check against it, so as to actually draw the amount out of the bank. This being so, the result is, assuming that there was no fraud in the transaction, when the tax receipts were delivered, and the taxes marked paid on the duplicate, and the appellant was credited on his bank-book with $2,086 65, as cash, he, in legal effect, received the amount of the taxes in cash, and the transaction was consummated and closed precisely as if the bank had paid the taxes, and then received the money on deposit from the appellant on the twenty-third day of April, 1884: *National Bank* v. *Burkhardt,* 100 U. S. 686.

We need not inquire whether or not the facts found present such a case as would have entitled the appellant to set the transaction aside on the ground of fraud, and obtain a preference over other creditors of the bank. It is enough to say that, having received credit as for so much cash deposited, and having checked out a sum of money after the credit was given him, which included the amount of the tax receipts, for which he obtained credit, he is not in a situation to say that the taxes, which he claims the right to collect, were not in fact paid. He must stand precisely as any other depositor whose money was obtained by the false representations of the officers of the bank, since he has been content to let the transaction stand until, by the assignment, the rights of other creditors, who may be in like situation with him, have intervened. There was no error.

The judgment is affirmed, with costs.

BANK DEPOSITS — CHECKS. — Where a bank receives as a deposit a genuine check drawn upon itself from the payee thereof, it becomes immediately the debtor of the depositor for that amount; and a subsequent return of the check to the depositor will not relieve the bank from liability, even though the check was an overdrawing upon the account of the drawer of the check: *Oddie* v. *National City Bank*, 45 N. Y. 735; 6 Am. Rep. 160; to the same effect is *City National Bank* v. *Burns*, 68 Ala. 267; 44 Am. Rep. 138; but a contrary rule is laid down in *National Gold Bank and Trust Co.* v. *McDonald*, 51 Cal. 64; 21 Am. Rep. 697. A bank receiving from a customer a check on another bank, indorsed "for deposit," and procuring it to be certified by the drawee, becomes immediately liable to the depositor for the amount as money had and received: *National Commercial Bank* v. *Miller*, 77 Ala. 168; 54 Am. Rep. 50. A bank receiving bank-bills from a depositor must account for them at par, even though they were depreciated in value both at the time received and afterwards: *Marine Bank* v. *Chandler*, 27 Ill. 525; 81 Am. Dec. 249.

CONCLUSIVENESS OF ENTRIES IN BANK-BOOKS. — If a depositor's bank-book accompanied the deposit, and an entry was then made by a clerk authorized to make it, it is an original entry, and, in the absence of fraud, conclusive on the bank: *Hepburn* v. *Citizens' Bank*, 2 La. Ann. 1007; 46 Am. Dec. 564; *First National Bank* v. *Mason*, 95 Pa. St. 113; 40 Am. Rep. 632. Credits in a depositor's book are as binding upon the bank as a formal receipt: *Union Bank* v. *Knapp*, 3 Pick. 96; 15 Am. Dec. 181. Yet in *Watson* v. *Phœnix Bank*, 8 Met. 217, 41 Am. Dec. 500, it was questioned whether the ledger of a bank, produced by a bank president, was *prima facie* evidence of the credits contained therein.

AS TO DEPOSITS IN BANKS, GENERALLY, see note to *In the Matter of the Franklin Bank*, 19 Am. Dec. 418-431.

LEONARD *v.* BROUGHTON.

[120 INDIANA, 536.]

JUDGMENT ENTERED NUNC PRO TUNC IS BINDING to the same extent as though entered at the proper time, except as to parties who in the mean time have in good faith acquired rights without notice of any judgment.

JUDGMENT ENTERED NUNC PRO TUNC on an official bond takes effect as of the date for which it is entered, as against creditors of the judgment defendant who have in the mean time obtained judgment liens for pre-existing obligations, when it does not appear that they have been misled or have parted with value, or acquired rights during the interval elapsing between the date of the judgment and the time of the making of the *nunc pro tunc* entry.

GENERAL LIEN OF JUDGMENT CREDITOR upon lands of his debtor is subject to all equities existing against such lands in favor of third persons at the time of the recovery of the judgment.

JUDGMENTS — NUNC PRO TUNC ENTRY — LIEN. — Judgments on bonds payable to the state bind the real estate of the debtor from the date of the commencement of the action, and if such judgment is not binding, but the action is pending until it is correctly entered *nunc pro tunc*, the judgment lien takes effect from the commencement of the action.

CONSTITUTIONAL LAW — ISSUANCE OF EXECUTION. — A statute providing that
    after the expiration of ten years from the entry of a judgment execution
    can only issue on leave of court relates only to the remedy, and applies
    to issuing execution on all judgments, whether rendered before or after
    its enactment, and is clearly within legislative authority.

ISSUE OF EXECUTION AND SALE without objection from the judgment debtor
    makes a valid sale which cannot be questioned by other judgment credi-
    tors who have since obtained liens for pre-existing debts.

JUDGMENT CREDITOR LOSES NO RIGHTS BY MERE FAILURE TO ENFORCE
    COLLECTION of his judgment, when rights of third parties have not in-
    tervened, and he has no notice or knowledge of their claims.

T. R. Marshall, W. F. McNagney, and H. C. Zimmerman, for
the appellants.

A. A. Chapin and R. P. Barr, for the appellees.

OLDS, J. This is an action to quiet title. There was a
demurrer sustained to the complaint, and exceptions taken,
and judgment on demurrer for defendants. Error is assigned
as to the ruling of the court on the demurrer to the complaint.

The plaintiffs in this action are Willington Y. Leonard,
Henry W. Franks, and Merritt C. Skinner, and the defendants
are Samuel Broughton, Jacob C. Zimmerman, Charles M.
Clapp, as administrator of the estate of Milton M. Clapp,
deceased, and Peter Sunday. The complaint is very lengthy,
and sets out the facts in detail and with particularity, showing that the plaintiffs became the purchasers at a valid sheriff's
sale of the real estate described in the complaint, on executions
duly issued upon three valid judgments rendered in the Noble
circuit court, at various dates from the sixth day of November,
1879, and the dates of the issuing of the executions thereon,
one of the judgments on which executions issued, and being
·the senior judgment on which said executions issued, was a
judgment in favor of the plaintiff Franks, rendered November
6, 1879, for $136.41, and costs; one a judgment rendered
in favor of Uriah Franks against said Mendenhall and plain-
Leonard, January 21, 1880, for $235.50, and costs, on which
Leonard was surety; and the other a judgment in favor of said
Uriah Franks against said Mendenhall and plaintiff Skinner,
rendered January 21, 1880, for $577.79, and costs, on which
Skinner was surety, — which two last judgments, for which they
were respectively liable, said Leonard and Skinner had paid
before the issuing of said executions, and said executions were
respectively issued for their use, and the executions were all
duly issued and levied upon the real estate described in the

complaint as the property of the principal judgment debtor, Isaac Mendenhall; that said real estate was duly advertised and sold by the sheriff of said Noble County to satisfy said executions and judgments, on the twenty-second day of December, 1883, and the plaintiffs became the purchasers of the same for the sum of seven hundred dollars, and a certificate of purchase was duly issued; that said real estate was not redeemed from said sale, and after the expiration of one year, on May 25, 1885, on surrender of the sheriff's certificate, a deed was duly issued to said purchasers; and that said seven hundred dollars purchase-money at said sheriff's sale was applied, first to the liquidation of the executions in favor of plaintiff Franks in full, and the balance applied *pro rata* to the payment of the executions in favor of said Leonard and Skinner. The complaint further alleges and sets out in detail the fact that Mendenhall made a fraudulent sale and conveyance of said real estate to one White, on the thirty-first day of December, 1878, and White to Chapman, and the prosecution of an action to set aside such sale and conveyance, and that notice of such proceedings was filed in the *lis pendens* record of said county, and a recovery had in said cause, and a decree entered setting aside such sale and conveyance, and an order for White and Chapman to convey the real estate, which they did, conveying the same to the plaintiffs; that by reason of such facts alleged in the complaint, the plaintiffs are the owners in fee-simple of the said real estate described in the complaint.

It is then averred in the complaint that the defendants Broughton, Zimmerman, and Clapp as administrator, claim title to the same real estate in the manner following: That at the March term of said Noble circuit court, 1875, a certain action was therein pending, wherein the state of Indiana, on the relation of James C. Stewart, auditor of Noble County, was plaintiff, and the defendants herein, Samuel Broughton and Jacob Zimmerman, and the defendant Clapp's intestate, William M. Clapp, together with Nelson Prentiss, Ephraim Cramer, Cornelius Grim, and Isaac Mendenhall, and Isaac Mendenhall as the administrator of the estate of John Mendenhall, deceased, were defendants; that said action was brought upon the bond of the said Isaac Mendenhall, theretofore late county treasurer of said county, and the said other defendants as sureties thereon, for the recovery of the sum of $1,360, for an alleged defalcation by said Isaac Mendenhall as such county treasurer, and which sum it was alleged he had failed to account for and pay over to his successor in going out of office; that in said cause in said court, upon appearance having been by said defendants therein first entered, and upon answers filed to the complaint on said bond, and after issue joined therein, a trial was had and a finding made for the plaintiff therein, and judgment rendered by the court thereon on the tenth day of March, 1875, for $1,360, and entered up in order-book No. 7, page 53, of said court, against said Isaac Mendenhall alone; although said day's proceedings of said circuit court for said tenth day of March, 1875, including said judgment last aforesaid, were, by said clerk of said court, entered and written up in said order-book of said circuit court, yet the plaintiffs say that neither said day's proceedings nor the entry of said judgment were then, or at any other time, ever signed by the judge rendering said judgment, or before whom said proceedings were had; nor has said judgment entry and day's proceedings of said court for said day, or either of them, ever been signed by any judge of said court, or of any court, or by any judge whatever; but on the contrary, said day's proceedings, and said order-book entry of judgment, each and both remain wholly unsigned by any judge of any court, or by any judge whatever.

Plaintiffs further say that, on the eighth day of January, 1878, the attorney for the plaintiff in the judgment last named filed with the clerk of said court a written *precipe* for an execution on said judgment against said Mendenhall, so rendered on said tenth day of March, 1875, as aforesaid; that, on the nineteenth day of January, 1878, pursuant to said order, said clerk issued an execution on said last-named judgment, directed to the sheriff of Noble County, for service, which said writ came to the hands of the sheriff on the last-named day aforesaid; and plaintiffs say that afterwards, on the seventh day of March, 1878, the then county commissioners of said county indorsed upon said execution, in writing, by them severally signed as such county commissioners, an order and direction to said sheriff to hold said writ, and not to execute the same until further orders from said county commissioners, which order is as follows: "The sheriff will await further orders before enforcing collection on the within writ. March 7, 1878." Signed by William Broughton, John P. McWilliams, and William Imes, county commissioners. And said plaintiffs say that said order and directions never having been canceled, recalled, or modified, the said execution was

by said sheriff held until the expiration thereof, when, on the
eleventh day of September, 1878, the said sheriff made return
thereof to the clerk of said court, indorsed thereon, as follows: —

"By within order of the county commissioners, this writ
was held, and the full time having expired, it is now by their
order returned unsatisfied this eleventh day of September,
1878.   NATHANIEL P. ENGLES, Sheriff."

It is further averred that afterwards, on the twenty-second
day of September, 1881, the then county auditor of said Noble
County, by his attorney, filed in the office of the clerk of said
court a motion to correct said judgment; that said motion was
entitled as follows: "The State of Indiana, on relation of
James A. Stewart, auditor of Noble County, versus Isaac Mendenhall, Samuel Broughton, Jacob C. Zimmerman, William
M. Clapp, Charles M. Clapp, administrator of the estate of
William M. Clapp, deceased, Nelson Prentiss, Ephraim Cramer, Cornelius L. Grim, and Isaac Mendenhall, as administrator of the estate of John Mendenhall, deceased"; that it
was alleged in said motion that at the March term, 1875, of
said court, the action was pending upon the bond as aforesaid,
and that the defendants in said action appeared thereto; issues
were joined, and the cause submitted to the court for hearing
and trial on an agreed statement of facts, and the court found
for the plaintiff in said action, against all of the defendants, in
the sum of $1,438.38, and that said court thereupon rendered
judgment against all of said defendants in accordance with
said finding, and that, notwithstanding the finding so made
and judgment so rendered and pronounced by the court, the
clerk of said court, by inadvertence, mistake, and misprision,
entered up said judgment in the order-book of said court for
the sum of $1,360, instead of $1,438.38, and against the defendant Isaac Mendenhall alone, instead of against him and
all of the other defendants, as the same was given and pronounced, and should have been rendered, and said motion
further recited the said agreement upon which said judgment
was rendered, and a copy of the entry and minutes made by
the judge on the judge's docket, and said motion asked for
the correction of said judgment as to the amount, changing the
said amount from $1,360 to $1.438.38, and by making the
same a judgment against all of said defendants instead of a
judgment against said Isaac Mendenhall alone, and upon the
making of such corrections, that the order-book entry be ·

signed, and that such correction be made now as of said
March 10, 1875; that the defendants named in said motion,
except said Cornelius Grim and Ephraim Cramer, appeared
to said motion, and filed their answers therein; that upon
issue being joined in said cause or proceeding on said motion
and answers, the same was submitted to the court for hearing
and trial, whereupon, on the tenth day of January, 1883,
the court found ·for the relator, and made an order directing
said judgment to be entered up against all'of said defendants,
nunc pro tunc, for the sum of $1,360, which order and judg-
ment was thereupon, by the clerk of said court, entered up in
the order-book of said court, and signed by the judge, but
that the original order-book entry was not, nor has it ever
been, signed by any judge. And it is further averred, that,
long before the filing of said motion and the making of said
nunc pro tunc entry, the term of office of said Stewart had expired, and said Keiser had been elected and was serving as
his successor; that afterwards, on the second day of April,
1883, and without having first applied and obtained leave of
court therefor to issue an execution on said alleged judgment
of March 10, 1875, a *precipe* was filed, and an execution was
issued on the judgment so ordered, on the tenth day of January, 1883, to be entered up, *nunc pro tunc*, and delivered to
the sheriff of said county, and he levied the same upon the
real estate in controversy, described in the complaint, and
said sheriff duly advertised and sold the same on the nineteenth day of May, 1883, to defendants, appellees herein,
Broughton, Zimmerman, and Clapp, and issued to them a certificate of purchase for the same, and at the expiration of one
year from such sale, a deed was duly issued to said defendants for the same, and defendants now claim title to said
premises by virtue of said sale and sheriff's deed, and not
otherwise; that before said last-named sale to defendants, the
said defendants had full knowledge and notice of all the rights
and claims, legal and equitable, in and to said real estate of
said plaintiffs; that at the time of the rendition of said judgment of March 10, 1875, against said Isaac Mendenhall, the
said Mendenhall then was, and thereafter continued to be,
until the thirty-first day of December, 1878, the owner, and in
the open and notorious possession, of a large amount of personal property subject to execution, in said county, of the
value of $2,000; that from March 10, 1875, to December 31,
1878, said judgment against Mendenhall for $1,360, with in-

terest and costs, could have been collected of said Mendenhall, and made out of the personal property aforesaid, had the
said plaintiff and the said plaintiff's relator, his agents and
attorneys in said last-named judgment, or either of them, exercised due and reasonable diligence in that behalf, but that
they took no steps toward the collection of the same; that, on
the contrary, plaintiffs had used all possible diligence for the
collection of their judgments.

It is further averred that the defendants herein permitted
said lands to become delinquent for the non-payment of taxes,
and permitted the same to be sold on the ninth day of February, 1885, by the treasurer of Noble County, for taxes then due
and accrued thereon, in the sum of $116.48, and defendants
became the purchasers for said sum at said tax sale, and paid
said sum, and took a certificate of purchase for the same, and
still hold and retain said certificate of purchase; that said
claim of title to said real estate by said defendants, in virtue of
and by reason of the matters and facts in the premises alleged,
is adverse to the plaintiffs thereto, and that said defendants'
claim of title by reason of the facts alleged is without right,
unlawful, and unfounded, and casts a cloud upon the plaintiffs'
title: Prayer for quieting plaintiffs' title.

We have stated in brief the material allegations in the complaint.

By the averments in the complaint, it appears that the execution sale, at which the appellants herein became purchasers
of the real estate, was made to satisfy three executions, one
issued on a judgment rendered in favor of appellant Franks
against Isaac Mendenhall, one issued on a judgment rendered
in favor of Uriah Franks against Isaac Mendenhall and appellant Leonard, Leonard being surety, and having paid the
judgment and execution issued for his use, and the other issued on a judgment rendered in favor of Uriah Franks against
Isaac Mendenhall and appellant Skinner, Skinner being surety,
and having paid the judgment execution issued for his use;
the two latter judgments were rendered on the same date, and
subsequent to the former, and the proceeds of the sale were
applied, first to the payment of the senior judgment in favor of
appellant Franks, and the balance applied *pro rata* on the two
junior judgments, and they stand in the position of judgment
creditors holding judgments rendered on pre-existing debts,
and no averments as to having been parted with anything of

of value, or extending credit to the judgment debtor on the faith of his real estate being unencumbered.

It is important, first, to consider the effect of the *nunc pro tunc* entry of the judgment. The court, on the tenth day of January, 1883, entered up a judgment as of the date of March, 10, 1875, for $1,360. This judgment was entered of record in the order-book and signed by the judge.

The effect of this record was to enter a judgment as of the former date; and when entered, it stood as a judgment of that date, and had the same effect as if it had been properly entered of record and signed by the judge on March 10, 1875.

Freeman, in his work on judgments, states the law in regard to *nunc pro tunc* entry of judgments thus: "The entry of judgments or decrees *nunc pro tunc* is intended to be in furtherance of justice. It will not be ordered so as to affect third persons who have acquired rights without notice of the rendition of any judgment. Generally, such conditions will be imposed as may seem necessary to save the interests of third parties who have acted *bona fide*, and without notice; but if such conditions are not expressed in the order of the court, they are, nevertheless, to be considered as made a part of it by force of the law": Freeman on Judgments, 3d ed., sec. 66.

And in section 67 he says: "With the exception pointed out in the above section, a judgment entered *nunc pro tunc* must be everywhere received and enforced in the same manner and to the same extent as though entered at the proper time. Though an execution may have issued, and proceedings under it culminated by the sale of property, when there was nothing on the record to support it, yet the omission was one of evidence, and not of fact, and the evidence being supplied in a proper manner, full force and effect will be given to the fact as if the evidence had existed from the beginning."

This we regard as a correct statement of the law, and if the appellants are not within the exception, and have not in good faith acquired rights without notice of the rendition of any judgment, they are bound by the judgment as if correctly rendered and entered as of the former date. It is therefore important to inquire into the transaction, and determine whether or not the appellants acquired any *bona fide* rights between the date of the judgment of March 10, 1875, and the date of the correction in January, 1883, for the plaintiffs herein are bound by the judgment, and their rights are to be determined the same as if said judgment had been properly entered and signed on March 10, 1875, unless they have some superior or intervening equities in their behalf. The facts alleged show, and the court has adjudicated, that the plaintiff in the case of *State ex rel. Stewart* v. *Mendenhall et al.*, was entitled to a judgment for the amount for which it was rendered on March 10, 1875, which was prior to the rendition of any of the judgments in favor of plaintiffs. Under the facts alleged, and in equity, these appellees were entitled to a prior judgment lien to the appellants, but by an omission in the entering and signing of the judgment it is contended they did not acquire a valid lien, and the court, on proper showing, restored their rights, and entered their judgment of the proper date.

It appears, from the facts averred, that the judgments in favor of the appellants were rendered upon pre-existing obligations; their rights were fixed prior to the rendition of the judgments, and it does not appear that they were misled, or that they parted with anything of value, or acquired any rights during the interval which elapsed between the date the judgment should have been properly entered and the making of the *nunc pro tunc* entry, except that they acquired a judgment lien; and the rule is, that the general lien of a judgment creditor upon lands of his debtor is subject to all equities existing against the lands of the judgment debtor in favor of third persons at the time of the recovery of the judgment. Parol trusts may be established, showing the apparent owner had no interest in the lands subject to the lien of a judgment, and a satisfaction of a judgment may be set aside against junior judgment lien-holders; and the facts alleged show that the sale was to the appellees before the sale to the appellants of the real estate in question in this case: *Lapping* v. *Duffy*, 65 Ind. 229; *Wainwright* v. *Flanders*, 64 Ind. 306; *Travelers Ins. Co.* v. *Chappelow*, 83 Ind. 429; *Peck* v. *Williams*, 113 Ind. 256.

We do not think a judgment creditor can be said to have acquired any rights: *Herbert* v. *Mechanics'* etc. *Ass'n*, 90 Am. Dec. 601; *Thompson* v. *Rose*, 41 Am. Dec. 121.

And the appellants have no superior or intervening equities which prevent the *nunc pro tunc* entry of the judgment from operating against them, and their rights are to be measured and determined as if the judgment had been properly entered and signed as of the orignal date. The correction of the judgment placed the parties in the same attitude they would have been if the omission to enter up the record had not occurred.

But if this theory is incorrect, the conclusion is manifestly correct, for other reasons.

Judgments on bonds payable to the state bind the real estate of the debtor from the date of the commencement of the action, and the action upon the bond must be considered to have been commenced prior to March 10, 1875; and if the first judgment is illegal, or amounted to no judgment at all, of which appellants were bound to take notice, and the action was pending until judgment was rendered upon the motion in January, 1883, the lien would antedate the other judgment liens: *Fleenor* v. *Taggart*, 116 Ind. 189; *Deming* v. *State*, 23 Ind. 416.

Taking the view we have in regard to the *nunc pro tunc* entry, it is unnecessary to consider the force and effect of the judgment as entered prior to the correction, and this, in effect, disposes of the case; for, as the complaint shows, the appellees had a judgment lien, and the appellants were not entitled to a judgment against them quieting their title to the real estate; but as the question is presented as to the right to have execution issue on the judgment after the expiration of five years from the rendition thereof, we will pass upon it. The execution issued in 1883; section 674, Revised Statutes of 1881, was in force at that time, and it provides that "writs of execution as now used for the enforcement of judgments are modified in conformity to this act; and any party in whose favor judgment has been heretofore or shall hereafter be rendered may, at any time within ten years after the entry of judgment, proceed to enforce the same as provided in this act."

Section 675 provides that after the expiration of ten years execution can only issue on leave of court. This statute relates wholly to the remedy, and applies to the issuing of execution on all judgments, whether rendered before or after its enactment, and is clearly within legislative authority: *Flinn* v. *Parsons*, 60 Ind. 573; *Henderson* v. *State*, 58 Ind. 244; *Pierce* v. *Mills*, 21 Ind. 27.

Even if it had been necessary to have had leave of court to issue the execution, the execution having issued and sale made upon it without objection from the judgment debtor, it cannot afterwards be questioned, and the sale made upon it would be valid, and cannot be questioned by other judgment creditors: *Jones* v. *Carnahan*, 63 Ind. 229; *Mavity* v. *East-*

ridge, 67 Ind. 211; *Johnson* v. *Murray,* 112 Ind. 154; 2 Am.
St. Rep. 174; *Rose* v. *Ingram,* 98 Ind. 276; *Richey* v. *Merritt,*
108 Ind. 347; *Hollcraft* v. *Douglass,* 115 Ind. 139.

There is no force in the allegations in the complaint that
the judgment defendant, Mendenhall, had personal property
out of which the judgment might have been collected prior
to December 31, 1878.   During that time there were no other
judgments against Mendenhall, and no allegations even in
the complaint that the relator, or plaintiff, in the action upon
the bond, had any knowledge of the appellants' claim, and a
judgment creditor loses no rights by the mere failure to enforce the collection of his judgment.   There is no error in the
record.

Judgme..t affirmed, with costs.

JUDGMENTS — NUNC PRO TUNC ENTRY OF. — This is the subject of an extended note to *Ninde* v. *Clark,* 4 Am. St. Rep. 828–834.

JUDGMENT LIENS. — As to what the general lien of a judgment may attach,
see *Doyle* v. *Wade,* 23 Fla. 90; 11 Am. St. Rep. 334, and note; *McClellan* v.
Solomon, 23 Fla. 437; 11 Am. St. Rep. 381, and note; *Parks* v. *People's Bank,*
97 Mo. 130; 10 Am. St. Rep. 295, and note; *Jackson* v. *Holbrook,* 36 Minn.
494; 1 Am. St. Rep. 683, and note.   The lien of a judgment is always subject to the equities of third persons: Note to *Filley* v. *Duncan,* 93 Am. Dec.
346, 347.

JUDICIAL SALES. — Irregularities in judicial sales can be questioned only
by the judgment debtor in a direct proceeding, not by his creditors: *Lawson*
v. *Jordan,* 19 Ark. 297; 70 Am. Dec. 596; and regularity of process cannot
be questioned collaterally by a stranger to a sale under execution: *Durham*
v. *Heaton,* 28 Ill. 264; 81 Am. Dec. 275.

ZIGLER *v.* MENGES.

[121 INDIANA, 99.]

RECLAMATION OF WET LANDS AND DRAINING OF MARSHES AND PONDS is
of public utility, and is conducive to public welfare, health, and convenience.

DUTY OF LOCAL TRIBUNALS AS TO PARTICULAR DITCH. — The legislature
having declared that the drainage of wet lands is a matter of public
benefit, nothing is left to the local tribunals beyond the duty of determining whether a particular ditch will be of public utility, or will
be conducive to the public health, welfare, and convenience.   If the particular ditch will drain any considerable body of wet lands, it is of public utility and benefit.

POLICE POWER, AUTHORITY TO DIRECT DRAINAGE OF WET LANDS IS VALID
EXERCISE OF, WHEN. — Where the drainage of wet lands will promote
the health, comfort, and convenience of the public, the authority to

direct it is exercised by virtue of the police power; and the drainage act
is a constitutional and valid exercise of that power.

ASSESSMENTS MAY BE LEVIED TO PAY EXPENSE OF DRAINAGE OF WET LANDS
wherever such drainage will promote the public health; and from the very
fact that it will accomplish this result, assessments may be authorized
without proving what particular citizens will be beneficially affected; it
is, however, necessary to show that the land-owner will receive a special
benefit, in order to authorize the levying of an assessment.

EXPEDIENCY OF CONSTRUCTION OF DITCH, BY WHOM TO BE DETERMINED. -
Whether it is practicable or expedient to construct a ditch upon the
route proposed is a matter to be determined by the officers to whom
the authority to locate ditches is intrusted, and their decision is not
subject to review or control by the courts.

CIRCUIT COURT MAY REMAND DRAINAGE CASE TO BOARD OF COMMISSIONERS
for further proceedings in a proper case.

COSTS IN DRAINAGE CASE. — The court does not err in refusing to include
costs made by the remonstrant in a drainage case in the cost of constructing the ditch, nor in denying his motion to tax all the costs of appeal against the petitioners who have succeeded on many of the issues.

DESCRIPTION OF LAND INSUFFICIENT TO AUTHORIZE ASSESSMENT WHEN. —
A finding that six acres of remonstrant's land will be benefited, without stating what six acres will be benefited, is not a sufficient description to authorize an assessment.

PETITION for construction of a ditch. The opinion states
the case.

J. H. Baker, J. H. Defrees, Jr., and H. C. Dodge, for the appellant.

H. D. Wilson and W. J. Davis, for the appellees.

ELLIOTT, C. J.   The appellee petitioned for the construction
of a ditch, and the appellant remonstrated against it.   A
special verdict was returned, of which this is the substance:
The lands along the entire line of the proposed ditch, except
for a distance of three hundred feet at the lower end, are wet
and marshy.   The natural trend of the land through which
the ditch will run is such as to cause the surface water, when
unobstructed, to flow from a southeast direction north and
west in the general direction of the ditch.   Before the Lake
Shore and Michigan railroad was built, which was about the
year 1852, the surface water from the lands along the line of
the ditch, as well as the lands farther south and east, flowed
to a point near the terminus of the ditch, and there accumulated.   The subsoil at that point is of such a nature that the
water sinks away in two weeks' time.   In building the railroad, the earth was thrown up on either side, and an embankment was constructed on which the track was laid; on either

side of this embankment an excavation was dug, and these excavations are from two to four feet lower than the adjoining land. After the construction of the railroad, the surface water from the lands of the petitioners and of the remonstrant, as well as from other lands, continued to flow in the direction and along and near the south line of the proposed ditch, and accumulated in the ditches or excavations along the railroad embankment, where it sank away in the ground. For many years before the petition for the ditch was filed, an old ditch existed along nearly the extire line of the proposed ditch, and into this old ditch the water from the surrounding lands flowed, and was conducted to the excavations along the railroad embankment. The line of the proposed ditch is the only natural or artificial practical waterway for the flow of the water from adjoining lands, and there is no other practical outlet for such water except the excavations along the side of the embankment constructed by the railroad company. The proposed ditch will be of public utility, it will be conducive to the public health, convenience, and welfare, and the proposed route is practicable. It has not a sufficient outlet in the case of a freshet. Six acres of appellant's land will be benefited to the amount of twenty-four dollars. The benefit to the lands consists in making them dryer, and better adapted to cultivation. The land of appellant lying north of the railroad will be damaged in the sum of one hundred dollars. The verdict also states that the lands of other persons named will be benefited; but we think it unnecessary to give names and details.

We are satisfied that facts are found which enable the court to adjudge that the proposed ditch will be conducive to the public health, convenience, and welfare, and that it will be of public utility. Laying out of consideration the general statements of the jury, we think facts appear which justify the conclusion the verdict declares. The reclamation of wet lands and the draining of marshes and ponds is of public utility, and is conducive to public welfare, health, and convenience: *Anderson* v. *Kerns Draining Co.,* 14 Ind. 199; 77 Am. Dec. 63; *O'Reiley* v. *Kankakee etc. Co.,* 32 Ind. 169; *Seely* v. *Sebastian,* 4 Or. 25; *Coster* v. *Tide Water Co.,* 18 N. J. Eq. 54, 66; *Springfield* v. *Gay,* 12 Allen, 612; *Wright* v. *Boston,* 9 Cush. 233; *Hagar* v. *Reclamation District,* 111 U. S. 701. As said in *Ross* v. *Davis,* 97 Ind. 79: "It is not necessary, in order that the use may be regarded as public, that the whole community, or any large portion of it, may participate in it.

If the drain be of public benefit, the fact that some individuals may be specially benefited above others affected by it will not deprive it of its public character." The community is benefited by anything that makes considerable bodies of land arable, and adds to their taxable value, and so it is by anything that lessens disease. The legislature has declared that the drainage of wet lands is a matter of public benefit, and it has left to the local tribunals nothing more than the duty of determining whether a particular ditch will be of public utility, or will be conducive to the public health, welfare, and convenience. If the particular ditch will drain any considerable body of wet lands, it is of public utility and benefit: *Coster* v. *Tide Water Co., supra; O'Reiley* v. *Kankakee etc. Co., supra.* Judge Cooley says: "Where any considerable tract of land, owned by different persons, is in a condition precluding cultivation, by reason of excessive moisture, which drains would relieve, it may well be said that the public have such an interest in the improvement, and the consequent advancement of the general interest of the locality, as will justify the levy of assessments upon the owners for drainage purposes. Such a case would seem to stand upon the same solid ground with assessments for levee purposes, which have for their object to protect lands from falling into a like condition of uselessness": Cooley on Taxation, 2d ed., 617.

Our own cases, already cited, refer the authority to direct the drainage of wet lands to the police power of the state, and in so far as the drainage does promote the health, comfort, and convenience of the public, it is by virtue of this great power that the authority is exercised. The police power, it has been said, is "that inherent and plenary power in the state which enables it to prohibit all things hurtful to the comfort, safety, and welfare of society": *Lake View* v. *Rose Hill Cemetery Co.,* 70 Ill. 191; 22 Am. Rep. 71. "All laws," says another court, "for the protection of the lives, limbs, health, and quiet of persons, and the security of all property within the state, fall within this general power of the government": *State* v. *Noyes,* 47 Me. 189. By our own and many other courts this doctrine has been affirmed: *Hockett* v. *State,* 105 Ind. 250; 55 Am. Rep. 201; *Eastman* v. *State,* 109 Ind. 278; 58 Am. Rep. 400; *Wilkins* v. *State,* 113 Ind. 514; *Slaughter House Cases,* 16 Wall. 36; *Civil Rights Cases,* 109 U. S. 3; *Smith* v. *Alabama,* 124 U. S. 465; *Nashville etc. R'y Co.* v. *Alabama,* 128 U. S. 96. The removal of causes that produce disease and serious dis-

comfort does promote the health and welfare of the public,
and in enacting a law providing for the removal of such causes
no provision of the constitution is violated in compelling private persons who receive a special benefit to bear the expense;
on the contrary, in enacting such laws a high constitutional
duty is discharged, and no private rights are invaded where
special benefits accrue, although the expense is imposed upon
the property of the citizens. In speaking of the police power,
Judge Cooley says: "Laws imposing on the owners the duty
of draining large tracts of land which in their natural condition are unproductive, and are a source of danger to health,
may be enacted under the same power, though in general the
taxing power is employed for the purpose; and sometimes
land is appropriated under the eminent domain": Cooley's
Constitutional Limitations, 5th ed., 734. A clear and vigo-
rous statement of the law upon this subject is found in the
case of *Donnelly* v. *Decker*, 58 Wis. 461; 46 Am. Rep. 637. "It
would seem to be most reasonable," said the court in that case,
"that the owner of the lands drained and reclaimed should
be assessed to the full extent, at least, of his special benefits,
for he has received an exact equivalent and a full pecuniary
consideration therefor, and for that which is in excess of such
benefits, should be paid on the ground that it was his duty to
remove such an obvious cause of malarial disease and prevent
a public nuisance. The duty of one owner of such lands is
the duty of all, and in order to effectually enter upon and
carry out any feasible system of drainage through the infected
district, all such owners may be properly grouped together to
bear the general assessment for the entire cost proportionably.
Assessment in similar cases is not taxation." Mr. Tiedeman,
in speaking of legislation compelling private property to bear
the expense of drainage, says: "The constitutionality of such
legislation has, as a reasonable exercise of the police power of
the state, been generally sustained, on the general ground that
the state may impose upon the owner the duty of draining his
low lands, in consideration of the consequent increase in the
value of his lands": Tiedeman's Limitation of Police Power,
445.

As the drainage act is constitutional, because a valid exercise of the police power, and as the exercise of that power in
itself implies that the purpose for which an assessment is
directed is for the public good, the purpose is necessarily a
public one. As the purpose is necessarily public in all cases

where health, comfort, and convenience are promoted, there
can remain in such cases no other questions than such as relate to the procedure and the amount of the benefits or damages assessed: *Ford* v. *Ford*, 110 Ind. 89 (93). Wherever the
reclamation or drainage of wet lands will promote health, there
is a constitutional warrant for levying assessments to pay the
expense of the drainage of such lands, and, from the very fact
that it will accomplish this result, assessments may be authorized without proving what particular citizens will be beneficially affected. It is, in other words, not necessary to
supplement proof of the fact that the drainage of a marsh or
pond will conduce to public health or welfare by evidence
of the number of persons who will be benefited. It is necessary, however, in order to authorize the levying of an assessment, to show that the land-owner will receive a special benefit:
Lipes v. *Hand*, 104 Ind. 503. But it is one thing to be compelled to prove special benefits in order to justify special
assessments, and quite another thing to be compelled to show
who or what numbers will be benefited in health or comfort
by a system of drainage.

We neither hold nor mean to hold that benefit to the property of an individual will warrant an assessment; for if the
benefit is solely to private property, irrespective of general
or public considerations, no compulsory assessment would be
valid, since one citizen cannot be compelled to contribute to
the improvement of another's property. If, however, it can
be justly concluded, from the nature of the system of drainage adopted, that there will be a material element of public
good in the result, then the purpose is a public one, and property may be assessed. Nor would it change the conclusion if
a pond or marsh was wholly on the land of one of the citizens; for although he might be compelled to bear the greater
part of the expense, or indeed the entire cost, it would be
for the reason that his property received the principal benefit,
and not because it was his duty to drain the pond or marsh.
Of course, if the property of such an owner received the whole
of the special benefit, and no public purpose is subserved, it
must bear the entire expense; but it is difficult to conceive a
case in which this could happen, for the removal of a cause of
disease or discomfort must necessarily benefit, in some degree,
property in the vicinity. Where the element of public good
exists, there is authority to levy an assessment; but it is
otherwise where there is no such element in the case. If the

property owner was bound to remove from his land causes of disease placed there by nature, it might well be held that he must bear the entire burden; but he owes no such duty to the community, nor is he liable to any one for injury arising from such a cause. An owner of land is responsible for injuries resulting from the construction of artificial swamps or ponds; but, independently of statutory regulation, he is under no duty, at his own expense (although he may be compelled to pay the entire benefit which accrues to his property), to drain natural ponds or marshes: *Reeves* v. *Treasurer*, 8 Ohio St. 333.

In view of the findings of the jury, we cannot hold that the construction of the ditch will not be conducive to public health, comfort, and convenience: *Blizzard* v. *Riley*, 83 Ind. 300; *Kyle* v. *Miller*, 108 Ind. 90; *Meranda* v. *Spurlin*, 100 Ind. 380; *Ford* v. *Ford*, 110 Ind. 89. We must take the judgment of the jury upon the facts, and the only question which we are required to decide upon this branch of the case is, whether the facts are sufficient to entitle the appellee to a judgment declaring the work to be conducive to the public health and welfare. We are not at liberty to draw inferences of an evidentiary character; for the facts found in the verdict are, as said in *Locke* v. *Merchants' Nat. Bank*, 66 Ind. 353, "the inferential facts." The conclusions of the jury are conclusions of fact, drawn from evidentiary facts, and these conclusions of fact, and not the evidence, are the proper elements of a verdict: *Blizzard* v. *Riley, supra; Hagaman* v. *Moore*, 84 Ind. 496; *Bennett* v. *Meehan*, 83 Ind. 566; 43 Am. Rep. 78.

The facts which appear in the verdict bring the case within the rule declared in *Heick* v. *Voight*, 110 Ind. 279, where it was said: "That the work will either promote the public health, or improve a public highway, or be of public utility, is to be regarded as a legislative declaration that it is of such a public character as to justify the exercise of the power of eminent domain to the extent required in its accomplishment." It was also said that: "It follows, necessarily, that if the finding be such as to affirm either of the propositions above stated, the construction of the drain is to be deemed a work of such a public character as to warrant its prosecution in the manner provided by law."

Whether it is practicable or expedient to construct a ditch upon the route proposed, is a matter to be determined by the officers to whom the authority to locate ditches is intrusted. In *Heick* v. *Voight, supra*, it was said: "Whether the project was more comprehensive, or whether it embraced and affected more lands, than was necessary in order to accomplish the drainage of the petitioner's lands, in the cheapest and best manner, was a subject for the exclusive judgment of the commissioners of drainage. Their determination of that subject was not reviewable by the court." "In this regard," said the court in *Anderson* v. *Baker*, 98 Ind. 587, "the decision of the commissioners of drainage is analogous to the decision of the common councils of cities upon the question of benefits from the construction of sewers; it is final in each particular proceeding, in the absence of fraud." The same doctrine was explicitly asserted in *Meranda* v. *Spurlin, supra*, and in *Markley* v. *Rudy*, 115 Ind. 533. The rule declared in these cases is no more than the proper application of the general principle, asserted in a great number of cases, that where a discretion is conferred upon local authorities it cannot be reviewed or controlled by the courts: *Weaver* v. *Templin*, 113 Ind. 299, and cases cited; *Kirkpatrick* v. *Taylor*, 118 Ind. 329. In *Ford* v. *Ford, supra*, it was said: "We find in the record of the trial in the circuit court the following admission: 'The ditch in controversy, proposed to be constructed, will be conducive to public health, convenience, and welfare. The route of said ditch as proposed, ... if constructed, would be the best route for a ditch to drain the lands of said Callender Ford, and would thoroughly drain and dry the same.' With this admission in the record, there remained no controverted question of fact for trial, except whether the assessment made against Callender Ford's land was in proportion to the benefits to be derived therefrom." So it is here, the ditch, as the record shows, will be conducive to the public health, convenience, and welfare, and therefore there is, as we have said, but one question for trial. We have looked into the cases in other courts, and find many sustaining the rulings in our own: *Hunter* v. *Mayor etc.*, 5 R. I. 325; *East Saginaw etc. R. R. Co.* v. *Benham*, 28 Mich. 459; *Dingley* v. *City of Boston*, 100 Mass. 544; *Aken* v. *Parfrey*, 35 Wis. 249. In the case last cited it is held that a verdict need not refer to matters which the statute does not require the jury to decide, but if it does, the finding on such a point will be treated as surplusage, and will not vitiate the verdict. Where, however, the verdict does find upon matters which it is made the duty of the jury to pass upon, the finding cannot be disregarded by the court: *Wilmington etc. Co.* v. *Dominguez*, 50 Cal. 505.

The jury did decide all the questions presented by the remonstrance and properly before them, and the court did right in following the verdict in its judgment upon the points which we have discussed. The appellant brings before us questions which affect only his rights, and we can consider no others. If the proceedings are effectual against the attacking or objecting party, they will be upheld. We cannot, therefore, consider what other parties, if any, are affected by the proceedings.

The circuit court may, in the proper case, remand a drainage case to the board of commissioners for further proceedings, and this is such a case: *Sunier* v. *Miller*, 105 Ind. 393; *Bryan* v. *Moore*, 81 Ind. 9.

We cannot hold that the court erred in refusing to include costs made by the remonstrant in the cost of constructing the ditch: *Board etc.* v. *Fullen*, 118 Ind. 158. Nor do we think that the court erred in denying the appellant's motion to tax all costs of appeal against the appellees, for they succeeded on many of the issues.

In the absence of the evidence, we cannot say that there was any error in assessing benefits and damages. The verdict shows that there was a benefit, and this controls; for we cannot, on the face of the verdict, adjudge that there was no benefit, and we have no *data* to guide us except such as the verdict supplies.

It was not necessary for the jury to specifically describe the tract of land which the ditch would drain. The assessment is laid upon the land benefited, and not merely upon the land actually drained; for the benefit may extend beyond the specific parcel which is reclaimed: *Baker* v. *Clem*, 102 Ind. 109. The land on which the assessment is levied should be described with reasonable certainty, but this is all that is required: *Boatman* v. *Macy*, 82 Ind. 490. There is, however, no such description of the appellant's land as will authorize an assessment, and for this reason the verdict cannot be sustained. The finding is, that six acres of appellant's land will be benefited, but what six acres will be benefited is not stated.

Judgment reversed. ____

WHAT PURPOSES JUSTIFY IMPOSITION OF TAXES OR ASSESSMENTS. — No principle of law is more firmly established than that the legislature can neither impose nor authorize subordinate agencies of government to impose taxes or assessments for other than public purposes: Cooley on Taxation, 2d ed., 115; *Loan Association* v. *Topeka*, 20 Wall. 655; *Davis* v.

Gaines, 48 Ark. 370; *Anderson* v. *Kerns Draining Co.*, 14 Ind. 199; 77 Am.
Dec. 63; *National Bank* v. *City of Iola*, 9 Kan. 689; *Cypress Pond Draining
Co.* v. *Hooper*, 2 Met. (Ky.) 342; *Opinion of Judges*, 58 Me. 591; *Allen* v.
Inhabitants of Jay, 60 Id. 124; *Jenkins* v. *Andover*, 103 Mass. 94; *Lowell* v.
City of Boston, 111 Id. 454; 15 Am. Rep. 39; *People* v. *Township Board of
Salem*, 20 Mich. 452; 4 Am. Rep. 400; *State* v. *Foley*, 30 Minn. 350; *Coates*
v. *Campbell*, 37 Id. 498; *Weismer* v. *Village of Douglas*, 64 N. Y. 91; 21 Am.
Rep. 586; *Reeves* v. *Treasurer of Wood Co.*, 8 Ohio St. 333; *Sharpless* v. *Mayor
of Philadelphia*, 21 Pa. St. 147; 59 Am. Dec. 759; *Grim* v. *Weissenberg School
District*, 57 Pa. St. 433; 98 Am. Dec. 237; *Philadelphia Association* v. *Wood*,
39 Pa. St. 73; *Soens* v. *City of Racine*, 10 Wis. 271; *Brodhead* v. *Milwaukee*,
19 Wis. 624; 88 Am. Dec. 711; *Curtis* v. *Whipple*, 24 Wis. 350; 1 Am. Rep.
187; *Whiting* v. *Sheboygan etc. R. R. Co.*, 25 Wis. 167; 3 Am. Rep. 30; *Commercial Bank of Cleveland* v. *City of Iola*, 2 Dill. 353. Dixon, C. J., in delivering the opinion of the court in *Curtis* v. *Whipple*, *supra*, said: "If we
turn to the cases where taxation has been sustained as in pursuance of the
power, we shall find in every one of them that there was some direct advantage accruing to the public from the outlay, either by its being the owner
or part owner of the property or thing to be created or obtained with the
money, or the party immediately interested in and benefited by the work to
be performed, the same being matters of public concern; or because the proceeds of the tax were to be expended in defraying the legitimate expenses of
government, and in promoting the peace, good order, and welfare of society.
Any direct public benefit or interest of this nature, no matter how slight, as
distinguished from those public benefits or interests incidentally arising from
the employment or business of private individuals or corporations, will undoubtedly sustain a tax." Black, C. J., in delivering the opinion of the
court in *Sharpless* v. *Mayor of Philadelphia*, *supra*, said: "Neither has the
legislature any constitutional right to create a public debt, or to lay a tax,
or to authorize any municipal corporation to do it, in order to raise funds for
a mere private purpose. No such authority passed to the assembly by the
general grant of legislative power. This would not be legislation. Taxation
is a mode of raising revenue for public purposes. When it is prostituted to
objects in no way connected with the public interests or welfare, it ceases to
be taxation, and becomes plunder." And Mr. Justice Miller, in delivering the
opinion of the supreme court of the United States in the case of *Loan Association* v. *Topeka*, 20 Wall. 664, said: "We have established, we think, beyond cavil, that there can be no lawful tax which is not laid for a public
purpose. It may not be easy to draw the line in all cases so as to decide
what is a public purpose in this sense and what is not. It is undoubtedly
the duty of the legislature which imposes or authorizes municipalities to
impose a tax to see that it is not used for purposes of private interest instead
of a public use, and the courts can only be justified in interposing when a
violation of this principle is clear, and the reason for interference cogent.
And in deciding whether, in the given case, the object for which the taxes
are assessed falls upon the one side or the other of this line, they must be
governed mainly by the course and usage of the government, the objects for
which taxes have been customarily and by long course of legislation levied,
what objects or purposes have been considered necessary to the support and
for the proper use of the government, whether state or municipal. Whatever
lawfully pertains to this, and is sanctioned by time and the acquiescence of
the people, may well be held to belong to the public use, and proper for the
maintenance of good government, though this may not be the only criterion

of rightful taxation." And in the case of *Cole* v. *City of La Grange*, 19 Fed. Rep. 871, it was said that "an attempt, through the guise of the taxing power, to take one man's property for the private benefit of another is void, an act of spoliation, and not a lawful use of legislative or municipal functions."

It is in many cases exceedingly difficult to determine whether a purpose or object is public or private. On this subject Judge Cooley says: "There is no such thing as drawing a clear and definite line of distinction between purposes of a public and those of a private nature. Public and private interests are so commingled in many cases that it is difficult to determine which predominates; and the question whether the public interest is so distinct and clear as to justify taxation is often embarrassing to the legislature, and not less so to the judiciary. All attempts to lay down general rules whereby the difficulties may be solved have seemed, when new and peculiar cases arose, only to add to the embarrassment, instead of furnishing the means of extrication from it." See also *Anderson* v. *Kerns Draining Co.*, 14 Ind. 199; 77 Am. Dec. 63; *Weismer* v. *Village of Douglas*, 64 N. Y. 91; 21 Am. Rep. 586.

In determining whether or not a purpose or object is public, no pinched or meager sense should be put upon the words, and if it be so near the border-line as to make it doubtful on which side it is domiciled, the courts should not set their judgment against that of the law-makers: *Weismer* v. *Village of Douglas, supra.* It is not necessary, in order that a use may be regarded as public, that it should be for the use and benefit of the whole community, or any large portion of it. It may be for the inhabitants of a small or restricted locality; but the use and benefit must be in common, not to particular individuals or estates: *Ross* v. *Davis*, 97 Ind. 83; *Coster* v. *Tide Water Co.*, 18 N. J. Eq. 68; *Soens* v. *City of Racine*, 10 Wis. 271. In *Seely* v. *Sebastian*, 4 Or. 29, Boise, J., in delivering the opinion of the court, said: "By public use is meant for the use of many, or where the public is interested."

It is for the legislature to determine for itself in every case whether a particular purpose is or is not one which so far concerns the public as to render taxation admissible: Cooley on Taxation, 2d ed., 103; *Booth* v. *Town of Woodbury*, 32 Conn. 118; *Harris* v. *Dubuclet*, 30 La. Ann. 662; *Thomas* v. *Leland*, 24 Wend. 65; *Sharpless* v. *Mayor of Philadelphia*, 21 Pa. St. 147; 59 Am. Dec. 759; *Town of Bennington* v. *Park*, 50 Vt. 178; *Brodhead* v. *Milwaukee*, 19 Wis. 624; 88 Am. Dec. 711. But the courts must ultimately determine whether a use is a public use or not: *Coster* v. *Tide Water Co.*, 18 N. J. Eq. 54.

In the note to *Beekman* v. *Saratoga etc. R. R. Co.*, 22 Am. Dec. 686–707, the question as to what is a public use for which property may be taken in the exercise of the right of eminent domain is very fully discussed. But a more liberal construction of public purposes is admissible in the law of eminent domain, where an error in the direction of too great liberality cannot be so seriously detrimental, than in the law of taxation, where a like error may result in injustice more seriously harmful: Cooley on Taxation, 2d ed., 113.

It is apparent from what has been said that it is impracticable to lay down any rigid rules by which to determine what purposes justify the imposition of taxes or assessments. The most that can be done is to ascertain what purposes have and what have not been held by the authorities to authorize the imposition of taxes and assessments. It would be a waste of time to enumerate all the purposes for which taxes or assessments may be properly levied and collected, because it is universally admitted that they may be levied and collected to meet the long list of ordinary governmental expenses.

It is not intended, therefore, to attempt to state all the purposes for which taxes or assessments may be imposed, but only to name those that approach more or less nearly to the line which divides a public from a merely private use.

Public Charities are generally recognized as public uses, for which the taxing power may be properly exercised: Cooley on Taxation, 2d ed., 124; *Shepherd's Fold* v. *Mayor etc. of New York*, 96 N. Y. 137. In this case it was held that the legislature of New York might authorize the city of New York to pay a gross sum annually to a private corporation organized for the purpose of caring for and educating orphan and friendless children.

Educational Institutions. — It is now well recognized that it is not only the right but the duty of government to make proper provision for the education of the children of the people; and the supplying of the means for public education is a purpose for which it is eminently proper that the power of taxation shall be exercised. Not only may the taxing power be properly exercised in providing means for the general support of education, but the legislature may authorize municipal corporations to tax themselves for the erection of state educational institutions to be built within them: *County of Livingston* v. *Darlington*, 101 U. S. 407; *Burr* v. *City of Carbondale*, 76 Ill. 455; *Hensley Township* v. *People*, 84 Id. 544; *Marks* v. *Trustees of Purdue University*, 37 Ind. 155; *Merrick* v. *Inhabitants of Amherst*, 12 Allen, 500.

Preservation of Public Health. — Taxes may be imposed for the purpose of preserving the public health. Money may be raised by taxation for the purpose of preventing the spread of small-pox: *Solomon* v. *Tarver*, 52 Ga. 405. And also for the purpose of draining marshes and ponds for the purpose of maintaining and preserving the public health: Cooley on Taxation, 2d ed., 137; *Anderson* v. *Kerns Draining Co.*, 14 Ind. 199; 77 Am. Dec. 63; *O'Reilly Kankakee V. D. Co.*, 32 Ind. 169; *Ross* v. *Davis*, 97 Id. 79; *Ford* v. *Ford*, 110 Id. 89; *New Orleans Draining Co., Praying, etc.*, 11 La. Ann. 338; *Coster* v. *Tide Water Co.*, 18 N. J. Eq. 54; *Woodruff* v. *Fisher*, 17 Barb. 224; *Hartwell* v. *Armstrong*, 19 Id. 166; *Sessions* v. *Crunkilton*, 20 Ohio St. 349; *Seely* v. *Sebastian*, 4 Or. 25; *Donnelly* v. *Decker*, 58 Wis. 461; 46 Am. Rep. 637. In delivering the opinion of the court in *Sessions* v. *Crunkilton*, 20 Ohio St. 356, McIlvaine, J., said: "The question is made, whether the uses and purposes named in the statute are within the meaning of 'public welfare,' as used in the constitution. We have no doubt that both public health and convenience are embraced in 'public welfare.' That this statute may be used (and probably is sometimes) for the purpose of promoting private interests, in the name of 'public health and convenience,' we need not stop to deny. It is enough for us to know that the principal object intended and authorized by the legislature was the public welfare; and that whenever private interests are promoted by the making of ditches, etc., they are merely incidental, when the statute is properly executed." And the legislature may authorize a tax for the straightening, widening, and deepening of natural streams for the purposes of drainage: *Lipes* v. *Hand*, 104 Ind. 503.

Construction of Levees. — The construction of levees to prevent the waters of a stream from overflowing its banks is a public use, for which the legislature may impose taxes: *State* v. *Cage*, 34 La. Ann. 506; *Daily* v. *Swope*, 47 Miss. 367; *Egyptian Levee Co.* v. *Hardin*, 27 Mo. 495; 72 Am. Dec. 276.

Public Highways. — Ordinary public highways and canals are universally recognized as public uses, within the meaning of the law of taxation. So railroads are very generally regarded as public uses, as is shown in the note to *Sharpless* v. *Mayor of Philadelphia*, 59 Am. Dec. 782–785.

Public Parks. — The acquisition, maintenance, and improvement of public parks are public uses, for which the power of taxation may be properly exercised: Cooley on Taxation, 2d ed., 129; *People* v. *Salomon*, 51 Ill. 37; *People* v. *Brislin*, 80 Id. 423; *Dunham* v. *People*, 96 Id. 331; *Attorney-General* v. *Burrell*, 31 Mich. 25; *State* v. *Leffingwell*, 54 Mo. 458; *County Court of St. Louis Co.* v. *Griswold*, 58 Id. 175; *Matter of Commissioners of Central Park*, 50 N. Y. 493.

Public Buildings. — A tax may be imposed for the erection of public buildings, such as school-houses, court-houses, and state-houses: *Harris* v. *Dubuclet*, 30 La. Ann. 662; *Williams* v. *School District*, 33 Vt. 271.

Municipal Gas and Water Works. — The furnishing of means and appliances for lighting the streets of cities and towns, and the supplying of their inhabitants with water for domestic use and for the extinguishment of fires, are public purposes everywhere recognized as authorizing the exercise of the taxing power: Cooley on Taxation, 2d ed., 134; *Mayor etc. of Rome* v. *Cabot*, 28 Ga. 50; *Wells* v. *Mayor etc. of Atlanta*, 43 Id. 67; *Nelson* v. *City of La Porte*, 33 Ind. 258; *Western S. F. Society* v. *City of Philadelphia*, 31 Pa. St. 175; *Attorney-General* v. *City of Eau Claire*, 37 Wis. 400.

Bounties. — The payment of bounties to volunteers to fill quotas and avoid drafts has been held to be a public purpose, which authorizes state and municipal taxation: Cooley on Taxation, 2d ed., 136; *Waldo* v. *Town of Portland*, 33 Conn. 363; *Coffman* v. *Keightley*, 24 Ind. 509; *Board of Commissioners of Miami Co.* v. *Bearss*, 25 Id. 110; *City of Lowell* v. *Oliver*, 8 Allen, 247; *Kunkle* v. *Town of Franklin*, 13 Minn. 127; 97 Am. Dec. 226; *Comer* v. *Folsom*, 13 Minn. 219; *Wilson* v. *Buckman*, 13 Id. 441; *Crowell* v. *Hopkinton*, 45 N. H. 9; *Shackford* v. *Town of Newington*, 46 Id. 415; *Cass Township* v. *Dillon*, 16 Ohio St. 38; *Speer* v. *School Directors*, 50 Pa. St. 150; *Weister* v. *Hade*, 52 Id. 474; *Washington Co.* v. *Berwick*, 56 Id. 466; *Grim* v. *Weissenberg School District*, 57 Id. 433; 98 Am. Dec. 237; *Brodhead* v. *Milwaukee*, 19 Wis. 524; 88 Am. Dec. 711. And municipalities may impose a tax to pay sums of money advanced by persons to relieve the municipalities from drafts, on an understanding, based on informal corporate action, that such sums should be refunded: Cooley on Taxation, 2d ed., 137; *State* v. *Sullivan*, 43 Ill. 412; *Johnson* v. *Campbell*, 49 Id. 316; *State* v. *Trustees of Richland Township*, 20 Ohio St. 362; *Weister* v. *Hade*, 52 Pa. St. 474. And also to compensate persons who have subscribed for the payment of bounties: *Hilbish* v. *Catherman*, 64 Id. 154. The legislature may authorize a town to levy a tax to raise money to pay for substitutes for drafted men: *Booth* v. *Town of Woodbury*, 32 Conn. 118; but not to refund to individuals sums of money paid by them for substitutes: *Freeland* v. *Hastings*, 10 Allen, 570. And the power of taxation may be exercised for the purpose of raising money to support the wives and children of soldiers absent in the war: *Inhabitants of Veazie* v. *Inhabitants of China*, 50 Me. 518.

Discharge of Moral or Equitable Obligation. — It is competent for the legislature to impose a tax, or to authorize the imposition of a tax, for the purpose of raising means to discharge a moral or equitable obligation, such as a just man should recognize in his own affairs, whether required to do so by law or not: Cooley on Taxation, 2d ed., 128; *People* v. *Burr*, 13 Cal. 343; *Beals* v. *Amador Co.*, 35 Id. 624; *Wilkinson* v. *Cheatham*, 43 Ga. 258; *Baker* v. *Inhabitants of Windham*, 13 Me. 74; *Friend* v. *Gilbert*, 108 Mass. 408; *Pike* v. *Middleton*, 12 N. H. 278; *Gilbert* v. *Supervisors of Chenango Co.*, 13 N. Y. 143; *Trustees of Fireman's Fund* v. *Roome*, 93 Id. 313; *Board of Education* v. *McLandsborough*, 36 Ohio St. 227; 38 Am. Rep. 582; *Lycoming* v. *Union*, 15 Pa. St. 166; *Sherman* v. *Carr*, 8 R. I. 431; *Briggs* v. *Whipple*, 6 Vt. 95; *New*

Orleans v. *Clark*, 95 U. S. 644. Thus in *Friend* v. *Gilbert*, 108 Mass. 408, it was decided that a town might raise a tax to pay extra compensation to a contractor for building a town-house, though the town was not legally bound to pay it. In *Board of Education* v. *McLansborough*, 36 Ohio St. 227, 38 Am. Rep. 582, it was held that the legislature might authorize the imposition of a tax to raise money to replace money that had been stolen from a public officer without fault on his part. And in *Wilkinson* v. *Cheatham*, 43 Ga. 258, it was held that an act which authorized the levy and collection of a tax to compensate certain lot-owners in a town, for damages sustained by them by reason of the removal therefrom of the county seat, was valid.

Grist-mill. — In *Township of Burlington* v. *Beasley*, 94 U. S. 310, it was decided that, under a statute declaring all grist-mills public institutions, a tax may be laid to aid in the construction and equipment of such mills.

Library for Supreme Court. — In *Swann* v. *Kidd*, 79 Ala. 431, it was held to be a legitimate exercise of the taxing power for the legislature to impose a tax-fee of six dollars for the benefit of the supreme court library, in each case decided by that court. The court in that case said: "The maintenance of a library to aid the judiciary department in the proper administration of the law is a public benefit, — one to which taxes in the treasury have long been appropriated."

PURPOSES FOR WHICH TAXATION CANNOT BE IMPOSED. — *Private Business Enterprises.* — It is well settled that taxation cannot be imposed for the purpose of establishing, aiding, or maintaining private business enterprises whose sole object is the private emolument of the proprietors, no matter how beneficial to the community such enterprises may be: Cooley on Taxation, 2d ed., 126; *Loan Ass'n* v. *Topeka*, 20 Wall. 655; *Commercial Nat. Bank* v. *City of Iola*, 2 Dill. 353; *Cole* v. *City of La Grange*, 19 Fed. Rep. 871; *Mc-Connell* v. *Hamm*, 16 Kan. 228; *C. B. U. P. R. R. Co.* v. *Smith*, 23 Id. 745; *Opinion of Judges*, 58 Me. 590; *Allen* v. *Inhabitants of Jay*, 60 Id. 124; 11 Am. Rep. 185; *Weismer* v. *Village of Douglas*, 64 N. Y. 91; 21 Am. Rep. 586.

Private Drains. — The legislature cannot impose or authorize a tax for the purpose of draining private lands for the emolument of the owners of such lands: *Anderson* v. *Kerns Draining Co.*, 14 Ind. 199; 77 Am. Dec. 63; *Butler* v. *Supervisors of Saginaw Co.*, 26 Mich. 22; *State* v. *Driggs Drainage Co.*, 45 N. J. L. 91.

Public Defense. — In Massachusetts it has been held that towns have no authority to tax their inhabitants to raise money in time of war to pay militia, or for other purposes of defense, because this duty is not a duty of the corporation, but of the government: *Stetson* v. *Kempton*, 13 Mass. 272; 7 Am. Dec. 145.

Private Schools. — The legislature cannot authorize a tax to be raised for the benefit of a private educational institution, whether incorporated or not: *Curtis* v. *Whipple*, 24 Wis. 350; 1 Am. Rep. 187. Nor to support a school as a public school which is founded by a charitable bequest that gives the superintendence to trustees, a majority of whom are to be elected by the inhabitants of the town, yet limited to be members of certain religious societies: *Jenkins* v. *Inhabitants of Andover*, 103 Mass. 94.

Private Dam. — A tax cannot be imposed for the purpose of constructing a dam to improve a private waterway; nor to enable private persons to lease water from a town: *Coates* v. *Campbell*, 37 Minn. 498; *Attorney-General* v. *City of Eau Claire*, 37 Wis. 400.

Private Loans. — The legislature cannot authorize a city to raise money by taxation to loan to private owners of lots, the buildings upon which have been burned down, in order to assist them to rebuild: *Lowell* v. *City of Boston*, 111 Mass. 454; 15 Am. Rep. 39.

Public Celebrations. — A town or city cannot, unless authorized by the legislature, raise money by taxation for the purpose of celebrating the national holiday, or other great historical events: *City of New London* v. *Brainard*, 22 Conn. 552; *Hodges* v. *City of Buffalo*, 2 Denio, 110; *Tash* v. *Adams*, 10 Cush. 252; Cooley on Taxation, 2d ed., 129.

Lobbying. — In *Inhabitants of Frankfort* v. *Inhabitants of Winterport*, 54 Me. 250, it was held that the taxing power cannot be exercised for the purpose of raising money to pay for sending lobbyists to the legislature. But in *Frost* v. *Inhabitants of Belmont*, 6 Allen, 152, it was decided that a town may appropriate money to pay the expenses incurred by individuals, prior to its incorporation, in procuring the passage of its charter. And in *Bachelder* v. *Epping*, 28 N. H. 354, it was decided that a town may pay the expenses of a person who goes to the legislature to induce it to pass a law requiring a court to be held at that town.

LOCAL ASSESSMENTS. — The legislature may levy assessments for many of the purposes for which it may impose taxes. But "to warrant the levy of local assessments, there must not only exist in the case the ordinary elements of taxation, but the object must also be one productive of special local benefits ": Cooley on Taxation, 2d ed., 622. It is impracticable, if not impossible, to enumerate all the purposes for which local assessments are admissible. But some of them may be named, with some of the cases in which the assessments were sustained. To pay for the cost of land required for opening streets: *Nichols* v. *Bridgeport*, 23 Conn. 189; *Goodrich* v. *Winchester & D. T. Co.*, 26 Ind. 119; *Dorgan* v. *Boston*, 12 Allen, 223; *Power's Appeal*, 29 Mich. 504; *Matter of Twenty-sixth Street*, 12 Wend. 203; *Litchfield* v. *Vernon*, 41 N. Y. 123; *Hammett* v. *Philadelphia*, 65 Pa. St. 146. To grade, pave, plank, and otherwise improve streets, and also to repave, replank, and regrade them: *Willard* v. *Presbury*, 14 Wall. 676; *Chambers* v. *Satterlee*, 40 Cal. 497; *People* v. *Austin*, 47 Id. 353; *Gurnee* v. *City of Chicago*, 40 Ill. 165; *City of Indianapolis* v. *Mansur*, 15 Ind. 112; *City of Lafayette* v. *Fowler*, 34 Id. 140; *Bradley* v. *McAtee*, 7 Bush, 667; *Broadway Baptist Church* v. *McAtee*, 8 Id. 508; *Jones* v. *Aldermen etc. of Boston*, 104 Mass. 461; *Williams* v. *Mayor etc. of Detroit*, 2 Mich. 560; *Wilkins* v. *City of Detroit*, 46 Id. 120; *Macon* v. *Patty*, 57 Miss. 378; *McCormack* v. *Patchin*, 53 Mo. 33; *People* v. *Mayor of Brooklyn*, 4 N. Y. 419; *In re Dugro*, 50 Id. 513; *Petition of Brady*, 85 Id. 268; *In re Smith*, 99 Id. 424. To provide and keep in repair sidewalks: *Palmer* v. *Way*, 6 Col. 106; *White* v. *People*, 94 Ill. 604; *Hydes* v. *Joyes*, 4 Bush, 464; *O'Leary* v. *Sloo*, 7 La. Ann. 25; *Lowell* v. *Hadley*, 8 Met. 180; *Macon* v. *Patty*, 57 Miss. 378; *Woodbridge* v. *City of Detroit*, 8 Mich. 274; *Hudler* v. *Golden*, 36 N. Y. 446; *Buffalo City Cemetery Co.* v. *Buffalo*, 46 Id. 503; *Deblois* v. *Barker*, 4 R. I. 445; *Washington* v. *Mayor etc. of Nashville*, 1 Swan, 177; *Mayor of Franklin* v. *Maberry*, 6 Humph. 368. For the construction of levees: *Excelsior P. & M. Co.* v. *Green*, 39 La. Ann. 455. To drain swamps: *Reeves* v. *Treasurer of Wood Co.*, 8 Ohio St. 333. For dredging a river that is a public highway: *Johnson* v. *Milwaukee*, 40 Wis. 315. Among other purposes for which special assessments may be levied may be mentioned parks, drains, sewers, water, gas, and public buildings.

TAYLOR *v.* EVANSVILLE AND TERRE HAUTE RAIL-ROAD COMPANY.

[121 INDIANA, 124.]

FELLOW-SERVANT, WHO IS NOT. — A master mechanic of a railroad company, who has entire control of its shop, men, machinery, and work, with full authority to employ and discharge workmen and to select and change the machinery, is not the fellow-servant of a machinist in the company's employ, to whom he gives a specific order for the execution of certain work, which order the machinist is bound to obey, but the representative of the master, and if, through the negligence of such master mechanic the machinist is injured while performing the work, the company will be liable.

VICE-PRINCIPAL, WHO IS. — An employee invested with the sole charge of a branch or department of the employer's business, and whose duties are not those of a mere workman, but those of one whose duty it is to manage a distinct department, and to give orders to other employees as to the duties they should perform, is not a fellow-servant of such other employees, but a vice-principal, while he is engaged in giving orders or directing their execution.

EMPLOYEE IN ENTERING SERVICE DOES NOT ASSUME RISK created by the negligent act of the master's representative in making unsafe work which he specifically orders the employee to perform.

ACTION for personal injuries. The opinion states the case.

J. Brownlee and W. H. Gudgel, for the appellant.

J. E. Iglehart and E. Taylor, for the appellee.

ELLIOTT, C. J. The appellant was a machinist, in the service of the appellee, engaged in work at its shop in the city of Evansville, under the control of its master mechanic, John Torrence. The master mechanic had the entire control of the shop, of all the employees therein, and of all work; he had full authority to employ and discharge the machinists and workmen, and he had authority to select and to change machinery. On the twenty-first day of April, 1884, the appellee desired to inspect the head of the equalizer on one of its locomotives, for the purpose of ascertaining whether the key could be changed, and its master mechanic ordered the appellant to disconnect the equalizer, and remove it from its place, in order to enable the master mechanic to examine it. While the appellant was engaged in the work of removing the key of the equalizer, under the master mechanic's direction, the equalizer was negligently pulled out of its place by the master mechanic, and it fell upon the appellant, and very severely injured him. The equalizer was a piece of iron weighing two hundred pounds, and it was caused to fall upon the appellant by the negligence of the master mechanic, and without any fault on the appellant's part.

It is established law in this jurisdiction that the common master is not responsible to an employee for an injury caused by the negligence of a co-employee. From this rule, so long settled, we cannot depart: *Indiana etc. R'y Co.* v. *Dailey*, 110 Ind. 75; *Capper* v. *Louisville etc. R'y Co.*, 103 Ind. 305; *Indiana Car Co.* v. *Parker*, 100 Ind. 181; *Bogard* v. *Louisville etc. R'y Co.*, 100 Ind. 491; *Atlas Engine Works* v. *Randall*, 100 Ind. 293; 50 Am. Rep. 798.

It is also settled that the fact that the one employee is the superior of the other makes no difference, for the question is not one of rank; the question is, Were they fellow-servants? If they were, there can be no recovery against the master for injuries caused by the negligence of the co-employee: *Drinkout* v. *Eagle Machine Works*, 90 Ind. 423; *Brazil etc. Co.* v. *Cain*, 98 Ind. 282; *Indiana Car Co.* v. *Parker*, 100 Ind. 181; *Pittsburgh etc. R'y Co.* v. *Adams*, 105 Ind. 151; *McCosker* v. *Long Island etc. R. R. Co.*, 84 N. Y. 77; *Crispin* v. *Babbitt*, 81 N. Y. 516; 37 Am. Rep. 521; *Moore* v. *Wabash etc. R. R. Co.*, 21 Am. & Eng. R. R. Cas. 509.

If Torrence was acting in the capacity of a co-employee at the time his negligence caused the appellant's injury, the action cannot be maintained, although he was the appellant's superior, and had the right to retain or discharge him. An agent of high rank may be, at the time an act is done, a fellow-servant of an employee occupying a subordinate position: *Hussey* v. *Coger*, 112 N. Y. 614; 8 Am. St. Rep. 787. If, for instance, the general superintendent should take hold of one end of an iron rail to assist an employee of the company in loading it on the car, he would be, as to that single act, a fellow-employee, although as to other acts he might be the representative of the master.

Where, however, the agent whose negligence caused the injury is at the time in the master's place, then he is not a co-employee, but a representative of the employer. His breach of duty is then the employer's wrong, for in such cases the act of the representative is the act of the principal. By whatever name the position which the agent occupies may be called, he is the representative of the master if his duties are those of the master; but if his duties are not those of the master, then he is no more than a fellow-employee with those engaged in the common service, no matter what may be his nominal rank:

Indiana Car Co. v. *Parker,* 100 Ind. 181; *Pennsylvania Co.* v. *Whitcomb,* 111 Ind. 212; *Krueger* v. *Louisville etc. R'y Co.,* 111 Ind. 51; *Indianapolis etc. R'y Co.* v. *Watson,* 114 Ind. 20; 5 Am. St. Rep. 578; *Louisville etc. R'y Co.* v. *Sandford,* 117 Ind. 265; *Cincinnati etc. R'y Co.* v. *Lang,* 118 Ind. 579; *Franklin* v. *Winona etc. R. R. Co.,* 37 Minn. 409; 5 Am. St. Rep. 856; *Anderson* v. *Bennett,* 16 Or. 515; 8 Am. St. Rep. 311; *Atchison etc. R. R. Co.* v. *McKee,* 37 Kan. 592; *Gunter* v. *Graniteville etc. Co.,* 18 S. C. 262; 44 Am. Rep. 573.

Our judgment is, that, at the time the appellant was injured, Torrence, the master mechanic, was performing the master's duty, and not merely the duty of a fellow-servant. He was in control of the shop where the appellant was working; he was the only representative of the master at that place; men, machinery, and work were under his control. He gave the orders which it was the duty of those under him to obey, and he alone could give orders as the master's representative. He gave the specific order under which the appellant acted. He did not join the appellant as a fellow-servant in doing the work, but he commanded it to be done. He was in the position of one exercising authority, and not in that of one engaged in common with another in the same line of service.

The obligation to make safe the working-place and the materials with which the work is done rests on the master, and he cannot escape it by delegating his authority to an agent. It is also the master's duty to do no negligent act that will augment the dangers of the service. In this instance, Torrence was doing what the master usually and properly does when present in person, for he was commanding and directing the execution of what he had commanded. By his own act he made it unsafe to do what he had commanded should be done. Acts of the master were, therefore, done by one having authority to perform them, and the breach of duty was that of one who stood in the master's place. It is not easy to conceive how it can be justly asserted that one who commands an act to be done, and who possesses the authority to command and enforce obedience from all servants employed in a distinct department by virtue of the power delegated to him by the master, is no more than a fellow-servant, for, in the absence of the master, the command, if entitled to obedience, must be that of the master conveyed through the medium of an agent. Nor can it be held, without infringing the principle of natural justice, that if he who is authorized to give the command makes its

execution unsafe, the employee, whose duty it is to obey, has
no remedy for an injury received while doing what he was
commanded to do. Nor do the better reasoned authorities
justify such a conclusion. The decisions are conflicting, it is
true, but the decided weight of authority is, that where the act
is such as the master should perform, he is liable, no matter
by whom the duty is performed. "As to such acts," said the
court in *Flike* v. *Boston etc. R. R. Co.*, 53 N. Y. 549, 553, 13
Am. Rep. 545, "the agent occupies the place of the corporation, and the latter should be deemed present, and consequently liable for the manner in which they are performed."
In this instance, Torrence was not a fellow-servant while engaged in commanding work to be done and directing the
execution of the command, although if it had appeared that
he was engaged with the appellant in doing the work, within
the line of the latter's service, it might, perhaps, be otherwise.
"The true test," said the court in *Gunter* v. *Graniteville etc.
Co., supra*, "is whether the person in question is employed to
do any of the duties of the master; if so, he then cannot
be regarded as a fellow-servant, or co-laborer with the opera-
tives, but is a representative of the master, and any negligence
on his part in the performance of the duty of the master thus
delegated must be regarded as the negligence of the master."
The rule thus stated goes further than we are required to do
in this instance, for we need go no further than to hold that
while engaged in ordering the work to be done, and in super-
vising its performance, the master mechanic represented his
principal; if, however, it had appeared that the master mechanic was not the person in charge of the men, and the shop
and its equipments, but was, although a superior agent, engaged in doing the same general work as that for which the
appellant was employed, it would be different. As the facts
appear in the record, the master had invested the master mechanic with full authority over the appellant and all others
employed in the shop under his control, thus bringing the case
within the decision in the case of *Atlas Engine Works* v. *Randall, supra*, where it was said: "If the agent or servant to whom
the power to command is given exercises that power, and
fails to discharge the obligation, to the hurt of the servant
who is without fault, the failure is that of the master, and he
must respond." In the case now at our bar, the agent who
had the power to command, and who exercised it, himself
violated the duty which rested upon him as the representa-

tive of his principal, and by his own act of negligence brought injury upon the employee engaged in doing the work he was ordered to do. Although the case of *Hawkins* v. *Johnson*, 105 Ind. 29, 55 Am. Rep. 169, belongs to a somewhat different class from the one to which this case belongs, still what is there said as to the right of an employee to obey the directions of a superior is applicable here, and strongly tends to support our conclusion. What we have said of *Hawkins* v. *Johnson, supra*, applies also to the case of *Rogers* v. *Overton,* 87 Ind. 410. Many of the cases go much further than we do here; for they assert that an employee is justified in obeying the orders of one who has a right to command, unless the danger of obedience is so apparent that a reasonably prudent man would not assume the risk: *Stephens* v. *Hannibal etc. R. R. Co.*, 96 Mo. 207; 9 Am. St. Rep. 336; *Huhn* v. *Missouri Pac. R'y Co.*, 92 Mo. 440; *Keegan* v. *Kavanaugh*, 62 Mo. 230. Whether these decisions go beyond the true line or not we neither inquire nor decide; but we do affirm that the reasoning, in so far as it covers and is limited to a case such as this, is unanswerable; for here the master mechanic had the right to command, and he was the only person in the shop who could rightfully command, the employees serving under him.

The duty of the master mechanic, as it appears from the complaint, was to order what should be done, and this, it has been well decided, is intrinsically the master's act, and not that of a mere fellow-servant: *Theleman* v. *Moeller*, 73 Iowa, 108; 5 Am. St. Rep. 663; *Brann* v. *Chicago etc. R. R. Co.*, 53 Iowa, 595; 36 Am. Rep. 243.

We do not affirm that an employee, with authority to command, may not be a fellow-servant; on the contrary, we hold that one having authority to command may still be a fellow-servant, but we hold, also, that where the position is such as to invest the employee with sole charge of a branch or department of the employer's business, the employee, as to that branch or department, may be deemed a vice-principal while engaged in giving orders or directing their execution: *Chicago etc. R. R. Co.* v. *Hoyt*, 122 Ill. 369; *Wabash etc. R'y Co.* v. *Hawk*, 121 Ill. 259; 2 Am. St. Rep. 82. "Where," it is said in a well-considered case, "a master places the entire charge of his business, or a distinct department of it, in the hands of an agent, exercising no discretion and no oversight of his own, it is manifest that the neglect of the agent of ordinary care in supplying and maintaining suitable instrumentalities for the work required to be done is a breach of duty for which the master should be held liable": *Cooper* v. *Pittsburgh etc. R'y Co.*, 24 W. Va. 37. Substantially the same statement of the rule is made in *Mullan* v. *Philadelphia etc. Co.*, 78 Pa. St. 25; 21 Am. Rep. 2. This rule applies to the case made by the complaint before us, and it is that case, and that alone, to which our discussion is directed, and to which our conclusions apply. If it appeared that the master mechanic worked with the machinists in the shop, as a foreman or a like agent ordinarily does, we should have a different case; this, however, does not appear; for, on the contrary, it does appear that the master mechanic was invested with sole control of the shop, and that his duties were not those of a mere workman, but those of one whose duty it was to manage a distinct department, and to give orders to the machinists and other employees as to the duties they should perform. We cannot further comment upon the decisions on this branch of the case which we have examined, but refer, without comment, to some of them: *Hough* v. *Texas etc. R. R. Co.*, 100 U. S. 213; *Ford* v. *Fitchburg R. R. Co.*, 110 Mass. 240; 14 Am. Rep. 598; *Wilson* v. *Willimantic Co.*, 50 Conn. 433; 47 Am. Rep. 653; *Mayhew* v. *Sullivan etc. Co.*, 76 Me. 100; *Atchison etc. R. R. Co.* v. *McKee, supra; Missouri Pac. R'y Co.* v. *Peregoy*, 36 Kan. 424; *Central Trust Co.* v. *Texas etc. R. R. Co.*, 32 Fed. Rep. 448.

It is important to bear in mind that the appellant was performing a special duty enjoined upon him by a superior whom it was his duty to obey. Although the work was within the general scope of his service, nevertheless he was performing it under a special order. It was, therefore, a wrong on the part of the agent having the right to order him to do the specific work to increase the peril of the service by his own negligence. The employee acting under the specific order had a right to assume, in the absence of warning or notice, that his superior who gave the order would not, by his own negligence, make the work unsafe: *Cincinnati etc. R. R. Co.* v. *Lang, supra; Coombs* v. *New Bedford etc. Co.*, 102 Mass. 572; 3 Am. Rep. 506; *Haley* v. *Case*, 142 Mass. 316; *Goodfellow* v. *Boston etc. R. R. Co.*, 106 Mass. 461; *Crowley* v. *Burlington etc. R'y Co.*, 65 Iowa, 658; *Abel* v. *President etc.*, 103 N. Y. 581; 57 Am. Rep. 773; *Reagan* v. *St. Louis etc. R'y Co.*, 93 Mo. 348; 3 Am. St. Rep. 542; *Lewis* v. *Seifert*, 116 Pa. St. 628; 2 Am.

St. Rep. 631. We adhere firmly to the rule declared in such cases as *Indianapolis etc. R'y Co.* v. *Watson, supra,* and *Louisville etc. R'y Co.* v. *Sandford, supra,* that the employee assumes all the risks incident to the service he enters; but we assert that the rule does not apply where a superior agent, representing the master, orders the employee to do a designated act, and while the employee is engaged in doing what he was specially ordered to do, that superior, by an act of negligence, causes the employee to receive an injury. The employee, in entering the service, does not assume a risk created by the negligent act of the master's representative in making unsafe work which he specifically orders the employee to perform. If the master mechanic had been no more than a co-employee working with the appellant, or if the appellant had entered the service knowing that the master mechanic was to work with him, then he would be held to have assumed the risk arising from the master mechanic's negligence while working or acting merely in the capacity of a fellow-servant.

We hold that the facts stated in the complaint are sufficient to compel the appellee to answer.

Judgment reversed. ────

FELLOW-SERVANTS, WHO ARE NOT. — For instances where persons are not fellow-servants, see note to *Fisk* v. *Central P. R. R. Co.,* 1 Am. St. Rep. 32, 33; *Lewis* v. *Seifert,* 116 Pa. St. 628; 2 Am. St. Rep. 631; *Wabash etc. R'y Co.* v. *Hawk,* 121 Ill. 259; 2 Am. St. Rep. 82; *Smith* v. *Wabash etc. R'y Co.,* 92 Mo. 359; 1 Am. St. Rep. 729; *Darrigan* v. *New York etc. R. R. Co.,* 52 Conn. 285; 52 Am. Rep. 590; *Krogg* v. *Atlanta etc. R. R.,* 77 Ga. 202; 4 Am. St. Rep. 79, and note; *Louisville etc. R. R. Co.* v. *Brooks,* 83 Ky. 129; 4 Am. St. Rep. 135; *Theleman* v. *Moeller,* 73 Iowa, 108; 5 Am. St. Rep. 663; *East Tennessee etc. R. R. Co.* v. *De Armond,* 86 Tenn. 73; 6 Am. St. Rep. 816; *Cincinnati etc. R. R. Co.* v. *McMullen,* 117 Ind. 439; 10 Am. St. Rep. 67; *Stephens* v. *Hannibal etc. R. R. Co.,* 96 Mo. 207; 9 Am. St. Rep. 336, and note; *Denver etc. R. R. Co.* v. *Driscoll,* 12 Col. 520; 13 Am. St. Rep. 243.

MASTER AND SERVANT. — A master is responsible for injuries to his servant occasioned by the negligence of a co-servant, when the negligent co-servant exercises supervision or control over the injured employee: *Anderson* v. *Bennett,* 16 Or. 515; 8 Am. St. Rep. 311; *Jones* v. *Old Dominion etc. Co.,* 82 Va. 140; 3 Am. St. Rep. 92; *Louisville etc. R'y Co.* v. *Lahr,* 86 Tenn. 335; *Faren* v. *Sellers,* 39 La. Ann. 1011; 4 Am. St. Rep. 256, and note. And a servant cannot be said to have assumed the risk of negligence of a fellow-servant who is his superior, standing in the place of the master: *East Tennessee etc. R. R. Co.* v. *De Armond,* 86 Tenn. 73; 6 Am. St. Rep. 816, and note.

VICE-PRINCIPAL, WHO IS: *Wabash etc. R'y Co.* v. *Hawk,* 121 Ill. 259; 2 Am. St. Rep. 82.

JONES *v.* VERT.

[121 INDIANA, 140.]

JUDGMENT IN FORECLOSURE DOES NOT CONCLUDE STRANGERS TO CONTRO-
. VERSY IN WHICH IT WAS RENDERED. The rule that a judgment in a
foreclosure suit, or in a suit to quiet title, is conclusive of any claim or
title adverse to the plaintiff in the case, as against all who were made
parties, applies only between parties and others in privity with them,
and does not preclude those who were strangers to the controversy in
which the judgment was rendered from again bringing the same matter
into contest. And therefore, an answer in a suit to foreclose a vendor's
lien for unpaid purchase-money, which sets up a judgment in a former
suit in which both the plaintiff and the defendant in the present suit
were made defendants, the plaintiff appearing and setting up his vendor's lien, quieting the title of the defendant in that suit as against all
the parties thereto, except a mortgagee whose mortgage was, on his
cross-complaint, foreclosed, does not show a good defense of former adjudication as against the holder of such vendor's lien.

DOCTRINE OF FORMER ADJUDICATION IS LIMITED, IN ACTIONS IN PERSO-
NAM, TO PARTIES and privies, and the party who invokes it must be one
who tendered to the other an issue to which the latter could have demurred or pleaded.

QUESTION BETWEEN CO-DEFENDANTS NOT DETERMINED BY JUDGMENT BE-
TWEEN PLAINTIFF AND ONE OF THEM. — Where one of two defendants
makes an issue with the plaintiff, a judgment settling the issue so made
in favor of the defendant does not determine the question between the
co-defendants.

ACTION to foreclose vendor's lien. The opinion states the
case.

W. Garver, F. B. Pfaff, R. R. Stephenson, and W. R. Fertig,
for the appellant.

J. I. Little and D. W. McKee, for the appellees.

MITCHELL, J.   This was an action by Sally D. Jones against
John Vert and others, heirs of William Vert, deceased, to enforce and foreclose a vendor's lien on real estate for unpaid
purchase-money due the plaintiff from the estate of William
Vert.

The defense was predicated upon the following facts, which
were set up by way of answer: In 1885, Sophia Sterne commenced a suit in the Hamilton circuit court to foreclose a
mortgage theretofore executed by William Vert and wife, covering the real estate against which the plaintiff was seeking
to enforce a vendor's lien. The plaintiff, as well as the defendants in the present action, was made a party defendant to
the foreclosure suit. The plaintiff appeared to the action and
answered, setting up the lien which she is now seeking to

enforce. It is alleged that the court gave judgment against Sophia Sterne in the foreclosure suit, and also entered a decree quieting the title of the defendants to the real estate described in the complaint, against all the parties to the suit except John W. Hannah, who held a mortgage on the land, which, upon his cross-complaint, was foreclosed. The foregoing facts were held to constitute a good defense of former adjudication as against the appellant, Mrs. Jones.

The facts pleaded fall far short of making a good defense.

It is undoubtedly true that a judgment in a foreclosure suit, or in a suit to quiet title, is conclusive of any claim or title adverse to the plaintiff in that case, as against all who were made parties; and this is so whether the adverse interests, or titles, of the defendants are specially set up or not: *Adair* v. *Mergentheim*, 114 Ind. 303; *Barton* v. *Anderson*, 104 Ind. 578.

But this rule applies cnly between parties and others in privity with them, and does not preclude those who were strangers to the controversy in which the judgment was rendered from again bringing the same matter in contest. "It is generally put in the books that the plaintiff must be not only the same person, but he must be suing in the same right": *McBurnie* v. *Seaton*, 111 Ind. 56.

In actions *in personam*, the doctrine of former adjudication is limited to parties and privies; and by parties will be understood parties to the issue on which the judgment was pronounced. The party who invokes the doctrine of former adjudication must be one who tendered to the other an issue to which the latter could have demurred or pleaded: *Harvey* v. *Osborn*, 55 Ind. 535.

Where one of two defendants makes an issue with the plaintiff, a judgment settling the issue so made in favor of the defendant does not determine the question between co-defendants: *Leaman* v. *Sample*, 91 Ind. 236; *Gipson* v. *Ogden*, 100 Ind. 20.

"The thing demanded must be the same, the demand must be founded upon the same cause of action, the demand must be between the same parties, and found by them against each other in the same quality": Wells on Res Adjudicata, sec. 14.

Ordinarily, four things must concur before the principles of *res adjudicata* can be invoked: 1. A suit; 2. A final judgment; 3. Identity of subject-matter; 4. Identity of parties. The facts pleaded show that all these elements were absent, except the judgment: *State* v. *Page*, 63 Ind. 209.

There was no suit between the present plaintiffs and defendants, no cross-bill having been filed: *Quick* v. *Brenner*, 120 Ind. 364. The subject-matter in litigation was different, and the parties were not the same. The defendants in the foreclosure suit might possibly have put the validity of the vendor's lien in issue by filing a cross-complaint: *Woolery* v. *Grayson*, 110 Ind. 149. This does not appear to have been done, and we cannot presume that it was. There does not seem to have been any issue tendered or made between the defendants. In short, there does not appear to have been any suit pending between them. Any judgment, therefore, that the court may have pronounced, which purported to settle any title or claims between the defendants, was *coram non judice* and void: *McFadden* v. *Ross*, 108 Ind. 512; *Griffin* v. *Wallace*, 66 Ind. 410.

The judgment is reversed, with costs.

The death of the appellant having been suggested, it is hereby ordered that the judgment be reversed as of the date of the submission of this cause.

———

JUDGMENT IN FORECLOSURE DOES NOT CONCLUDE AN INTERESTED PARTY who was not made a party to the foreclosure proceedings: *Love* v. *Francis*, 63 Mich. 181; 6 Am. St. Rep. 290; *Boutwell* v. *Steiner*, 84 Ala. 307; 5 Am. St. Rep. 375; *Berlack* v. *Halle*, 22 Fla. 236; 1 Am. St. Rep. 185; *Bates* v. *Ruddick*, 2 Iowa, 423; 65 Am. Dec. 774; *San Francisco* v. *Lawton*, 18 Cal. 465; 79 Am. Dec. 187.

FORMER ADJUDICATION, UPON WHOM BINDING: See note to *Sauls* v. *Freeman*, 12 Am. St. Rep. 199, 200.

RES ADJUDICATA, INSTANCES OF: See note to *Hawk* v. *Evans*, 14 Am. St. Rep. 250–252; *Gould* v. *Sternburg*, 128 Ill. 510; 15 Am. St. Rep. 138, and note.

———

SHIRK v. THOMAS.

[121 INDIANA, 147.]

REGISTRATION OF DEED ADDS NOTHING TO ITS EFFECTIVENESS as a conveyance; all that it accomplishes is to impart notice.

PURCHASER OF LAND AT SHERIFF'S SALE DOES NOT OBTAIN TITLE BY SALE, for the title does not pass until the year for redemption expires, and a deed is executed by the sheriff.

LIEN OF JUDGMENT OR ATTACHMENT DOES NOT EXTEND BEYOND INTEREST of the debtor in the land. It does not displace prior equities or rights.

RIGHT OF PARTY FOUNDED SOLELY ON LIEN OF JUDGMENT OR ATTACHMENT IS SUBORDINATE to that of a purchaser in good faith.

CREDITOR HOLDING CLAIM FOR PRE-EXISTING DEBT IS NOT BONA FIDE PURCHASER within the meaning of the registry law of Indiana. No lien has been released, nor any money advanced by the creditor, on the faith that his debtor continued to be the owner of the land. It is only those who stand in that position that the registry law protects against unrecorded deeds.

JUDGMENT CREDITOR IS NOT BONA FIDE PUCHASER, within the meaning of the registry law, where the sole foundation of his right is his own judgment; and he cannot prevail against a purchaser in good faith holding under an unrecorded deed.

JUDGMENT CREDITOR PURCHASING AT HIS OWN SALE ACQUIRES ONLY INTEREST WHICH JUDGMENT DEBTOR HAD in the property at the time when the judgment was entered.

L. M. Lauer, for the appellants.

M. A. Packard, O. M. Packard, and C. P. Drummond, for the appellees.

ELLIOTT, C. J.   The facts pleaded by the appellants as their cause of action, shortly stated, are these: The ancestor of the appellants acquired title to the land in controversy by warranty deed from James H. Tyner, executed on the sixth day of December, 1884, and recorded on the eighteenth day of February, 1885, and James H. Tyner acquired title from Albert H. Tyner, then the owner of the land, by a warranty deed, executed on the first day of August, 1884, but not recorded until May of the following year.   On the twenty-eighth day of October, 1884, William S. Thomas caused a writ of attachment to issue against Albert H. Tyner, alleging as a cause for the issuing of the writ that he was not a resident of this state.   On the eighth day of January, 1885, judgment was rendered in favor of Thomas in the attachment proceedings, but neither the appellants nor their ancestor's grantor were parties to the proceedings, nor did they have any notice of them.˙ On the seventh day of July, 1886, an order of sale was issued, and on the thirty-first day of the same month, the land was sold under the order to Thomas.   James H. Tyner paid a valuable consideration for the land, and purchased it in good faith.   The appellants went into possession under their deed, and were in possession at the time of the sale.

The deed executed by Albert H. Tyner to James H. Tyner, on the first day of August, 1884, was effectual to vest title in the grantee without recording.   The registry of a deed adds nothing to its effectiveness as a conveyance; all that it accomplishes is to impart notice: *Way v. Lyon,* 3 Blackf. 76 (79).   The law upon this subject is thus stated in *Kirkpatrick v. Caldwell,* 32 Ind. 299: "It is only subsequent purchasers and encumbrancers in good faith and for value who are protected against an unrecorded mortgage. As against all the world besides, the registry imparts no virtue or force whatever to the instrument. As against the mortgagor and the estate while it remains in his hands, the lien is as perfect without registry as it is with it. It is so, also, against his general creditors while he lives, and after his death."

The appellee Thomas did not obtain title to the land by the sale, for title does not pass until the year for redemption expires and a deed is executed by the sheriff: *Felton* v. *Smith*, 84 Ind. 485; *Brown* v. *Cody*, 115 Ind. 484 (486); *Bodine* v. *Moore*, 18 N. Y. 347. But if it were conceded that he acquired title at the time of the sale it would not aid him, for at that time the deed from Albert H. Tyner to James H. Tyner was of record, and the appellee was bound to take notice of it: *Brower* v. *Witmeyer*, 121 Ind. 83, and cases cited.

Thomas did not have at any time before this action was begun anything more than a statutory lien. His rights are such, and such only, as the lien created by statute gives him. He has no title to the land, but only such a right as the statute creates; the extent and effect of that right is measured and limited by the statute: *Gimbel* v. *Stolte*, 59 Ind. 446; *Houston* v. *Houston*, 67 Ind. 276; *Duke* v. *Beeson*, 79 Ind. 24; *Davis* v. *Rupe*, 114 Ind. 588 (595); *Hervey* v. *Krost*, 116 Ind. 268 (273); *Watson* v. *New York etc. R. R. Co.*, 47 N. Y. 157.

The lien of a judgment or attachment does not extend beyond the interest of the debtor in the land. It does not displace prior equities or rights. In strictness, neither a judgment nor an attachment is a lien upon land; both are simply charges against land existing by virtue of statute. "'Lien upon a judgment,'" said an eminent English judge, "is a vague and inaccurate expression": *Brundson* v. *Allard*, 2 El. & E. 17; *Peck* v. *Juness*, 7 How. 611; *Waller* v. *Best*, 3 How. 111; *Dames* v. *Fales*, 5 N. H. 70. In speaking of an attachment, Judge Story said, in *Ex parte Foster*, 2 Story, 131: "Now, an attachment does not come up to the exact definition or meaning of a lien, either in the general sense of the common law, or in that of the maritime law, or in that of equity jurisprudence." But usage has, perhaps, justified the employment of the term "lien" as denoting a charge upon property created by statute, yet it is not to be supposed that such a charge is equal in dignity or force to that of a mort-

gage or of a lien created by equity; on the contrary, it is
intrinsically nothing more than such a general charge as the
statute creates: *Sherwood* v. *City of Lafayette*, 109 Ind. 411
(413); 58 Am. Rep. 414; *Elston* v. *Castor*, 101 Ind. 426 (440);
51 Am. Rep. 754. The source of the appellee's right is the statutory charge, and no claim can be successfully urged by him
which rises higher than the source of all the right he has, so
that it is quite clear that if his right is founded solely on the
lien of the judgment or of the attachment, it is subordinate
to that of a purchaser in good faith. This conclusion is inevitable if the line of principle is traveled, and there is no
reason sufficient to even constitute an apology for wandering
from the true line. Our decisions have, for the most part,
kept to the true course. Pursuing this course, it has been
often held that a deed or mortgage may be reformed as against
a judgment creditor: *White* v. *Wilson*, 6 Blackf. 448; 39 Am.
Dec. 437; *Sample* v. *Rowe*, 24 Ind. 208; *Busenbarke* v. *Ramey*,
53 Ind. 499 (501); *Figart* v. *Halderman*, 75 Ind. 564 (568);
Boyd v. *Anderson*, 102 Ind. 217. In direct point is the reasoning of the court in the case last cited. "It is settled law in
this state," said the court, "that judgment creditors are in
no sense purchasers; that their judgments are simply general
liens upon whatever interest the judgment defendants may
have had in the land."

If the interest which Thomas acquired under the sale made
on the judgment obtained by him had been perfected by the
execution and delivery of a deed, he could not defeat the appellants. If he had changed position, and parted with value
without notice, and on the faith that the title to the land remained in Albert H. Tyner, it would, perhaps, be different;
but he did not change position; he was throughout simply a
creditor, endeavoring to enforce collection of an antecedent
debt. The law is well established in this state, and so it is
generally held elsewhere, that a creditor holding a claim for a
pre-existing debt is not a *bona fide* purchaser within the meaning of our registry law: *Brower* v. *Witmeyer, supra; Petry* v.
Ambrosher, 100 Ind. 510 (514); *Wert* v. *Naylor*, 93 Ind. 431;
Busenbarke v. *Ramey, supra*. No lien was released, nor any
money advanced by the creditor, on the faith that his debtor
continued to be the owner of the land, so that he cannot be
considered as occupying the position of a *bona fide* purchaser:
Fitzpatrick v. *Papa*, 89 Ind. 17. It is only those who stand in
that position that our registry law protects against unrecorded

deeds: *Runyan* v. *McClellan*, 24 Ind. 165. The provision of the statute is, that deeds not recorded within forty-five days after their execution "shall be fraudulent and void as against any subsequent purchaser, lessee, or mortgagee in good faith and for a valuable consideration": R. S. 1881, sec. 2931. Registry is the creature of statute. If there were no statute requiring a registry, all persons would be bound, at their peril, to take notice of a conveyance under which possession was taken, and a deed not recorded is good as against all persons not protected by the statute. A judgment creditor is not within the provisions of our statute, for he is not a mortgagee nor a lessee, nor is he a purchaser in good faith. Where, as here, the sole foundation of the claimant's right is his own judgment, he is not a *bona fide* purchaser, and he cannot prevail against a good-faith purchaser holding under an unrecorded deed.

We are aware that in some of the decisions of this court there was a departure from the true rule, and that it was declared in those cases that a judgment creditor who purchases at his own sale is a *bona fide* purchaser: *Rooker* v. *Rooker*, 75 Ind. 571; *Gifford* v. *Bennett*, 75 Ind. 528; *Vitito* v. *Hamilton*, 86 Ind. 137.

These decisions cannot be sustained, for they are opposed to principle, and to our earlier decisions, and they are denied by all of our later cases. They have, indeed, been overruled, and must be regarded as without force. They are opposed in principle by the early case of *White* v. *Wilson*, *supra*, and they are in direct and irreconcilable conflict with the well-reasoned case of *Glidewell* v. *Spaugh*, 26 Ind. 319, wherein the court quoted, with approval, Chancellor Walworth's statement of the law in the case of *Keirsted* v. *Avery*, 4 Paige, 9. "It is now settled," said the chancellor, "that a judgment, being merely a general lien on the land of the debtor, the lien is subject to every equity which existed against the land in the hands of the judgment debtor at the time of the docketing of the judgment. And the court of chancery will protect the equitable rights of third persons against the legal lien, and will limit that lien to the actual interest which the judgment debtor has in the estate." *Glidewell* v. *Spaugh*, *supra*, has been approved and followed again and again: *Watkins* v. *Jones*, 28 Ind. 12; *Troost* v. *Davis*, 31 Ind. 34; *Hampson* v. *Fall*, 64 Ind. 382; *Monticello etc. Co.* v. *Loughry*, 72 Ind. 562; *Jones* v. *Rhoads*,

74 Ind. 510 (513); *Sharpe* v. *Davis*, 76 Ind. 17; *Boyd* v. *Anderson*, *supra; Heberd* v. *Wines*, 105 Ind. 237; *Blair* v. *Smith*, 114 Ind. 114; 5 Am. St. Rep. 593. The rule laid down in *Glidewell* v. *Spaugh, supra,* has been adopted and enforced in many other cases. *Miller* v. *Noble*, 86 Ind. 527; *Hays* v. *Reger*, 102 Ind. 524; *Foltz* v. *Wert*, 103 Ind. 404; *Wright* v. *Tichenor*, 104 Ind. 185; *Wright* v. *Jones*, 105 Ind. 17; *Taylor* v. *Duesterberg*, 109 Ind. 165.

In *Taylor* v. *Duesterberg, supra,* the court, in speaking of judgment creditors, said: "Their right is to be confined to the actual interest which their debtor had in the property." It was said by the court in *Foltz* v. *Wert, supra,* that "courts of chancery will so control the legal lien of the judgment as to restrict it to the actual interest of the judgment debtor in the property," and in support of this doctrine the cases of *Armstrong* v. *Fearnaw*, 67 Ind. 429; *Wharton* v. *Wilson*, 60 Ind. 591; *Huffman* v. *Copeland*, 86 Ind. 224; *Jones* v. *Rhoads, supra,* and other cases were cited. Still stronger is the statement in *Heberd* v. *Wines, supra,* for it was there said: "It is settled in this state, that judgments are simply general liens upon whatever interest the judgment debtor may have in lands, and no more."

The great weight of authority, evidenced by our own well-considered cases, as well as by the decisions of other courts than our own, is that a judgment creditor who buys at his own sale obtains only the interest which the judgment debtor had in the property at the time the judgment was entered: *Mansfield* v. *Gregory*, 8 Neb. 432; *Galway* v. *Malchow*, 7 Neb. 285; *Metz* v. *State Bank*, 7 Neb. 165; *Carney* v. *Emmons*, 9 Wis. 109; *O'Neal* v. *Wilson*, 21 Ala. 288; *Stevens* v. *King*, 21 Ala. 429; *Rutherford* v. *Green*, 2 Ired. Eq. 121; *National Bank etc.* v. *King*, 110 Ill. 254; *Treptow* v. *Buse*, 10 Kan. 170; *Emerson* v. *Sansome*, 41 Cal. 552; *Taylor* v. *Eckford*, 11 Smedes & M. 21. In *Harral* v. *Gray*, 10 Neb. 186, the rule was applied against a purchaser at a sheriff's sale in favor of a party claiming under an unrecorded deed, and it was said: "This brings the case quite within the holding of this court in *Mansfield* v. *Gregory*, 8 Neb. 432. Under that decision it may be considered settled—if, indeed, the courts of the country had not long since settled it—that a prior unrecorded deed, made and delivered in good faith for a valuable consideration, so as to pass title in law, will take precedence of an attachment or judgment, provided such first-mentioned deed be recorded before any deed to the premises be recorded, which is based upon such attachment or judgment."

Counsel for the appellees argue the case as if the cross-complaint had not been withdrawn, and in this they are in error, for the record shows that the answers and cross-complaint were withdrawn, and that the demurrers to the complaint were reargued and sustained. There is, therefore, nothing before us except the ruling upon the demurrers to the complaint, and that ruling was clearly wrong.

The judgment is reversed, with instructions to overrule the demurrers to the complaint, and to proceed in accordance with this opinion.

REGISTRATION OF A DEED IS CONSTRUCTIVE NOTICE only to subsequent purchasers and encumbrancers: *Karns* v. *Olney*, 80 Cal. 90; 13 Am. St. Rep. 101; and compare *Fresno Canal Co.* v. *Rowell*, 80 Cal. 114; 13 Am. St. Rep. 112. For the necessity and effect of the registration of deeds and conveyances, see cases collected in note to *Hockenhull* v. *Oliver*, 12 Am. St. Rep. 238; note to *Hibbard* v. *Zenor*, 9 Am. St. Rep. 503, 504. A purchaser is not charged with notice of the record of a deed made by a vendee of the same vendor, if such vendee's deed is not of record so as to complete the chain of title; and one not chargeable with notice of the registration of a deed cannot be affected by any facts set forth in the recitals found in such deed: *Lumpkin* v. *Adams*, 74 Tex. 97. But ordinarily, the record of an older deed is notice to the grantees in a subsequent deed of the same premises: *King* v. *Haley*, 75 Id. 163. A purchaser who has made, without avail, due inquiries with respect to an unrecorded deed is protected in purchasing the title which appears upon the records: *Tabor* v. *Sullivan*, 12 Col. 137.

JUDICIAL SALES. — The rule of *caveat emptor* is applicable to purchasers at judicial sales: *Williams* v. *Glenn*, 87 Ky. 87; 12 Am. St. Rep. 461, and particularly note; *Jones* v. *Blumenstein*, 77 Iowa, 362. A purchaser at judicial sales takes only the interest in the land owned by the defendant in execution: *King* v. *Haley*, 75 Tex. 163; for a sale under execution transmits only the debtor's estate in the same condition and subject to all equities under which he held it: *Threadgill* v. *Redwine*, 97 N. C. 241.

JUDICIAL SALES — BONA FIDE PURCHASERS. — A judgment creditor who purchases at a sale under execution, in the absence of notice of an outstanding equity, is an innocent purchaser for value, and entitled to protection as such: *Ettenheimer* v. *Northgraves*, 75 Iowa, 28. The purchase of a stranger in good faith at an execution sale will be protected against secret infirmities: *Carden* v. *Lane*, 48 Ark. 216; 3 Am. St. Rep. 228. But the general rule is, that judgment creditors, purchasing at their own sale, are not *bona fide* purchasers without notice: *Ayres* v. *Duprey*, 27 Tex. 593; 86 Am. Dec. 657, and especially cases cited in note 669.

JUDGMENT LIENS, NATURE OF, AND TO WHAT ATTACH: See *Slattery* v. *Jones*, 96 Mo. 216; 9 Am. St. Rep. 344, and notes. A judgment is a lien upon the equitable estate of a defendant at the time of its rendition or subsequently acquired: *Rand* v. *Garner*, 75 Iowa, 311. Unless the abstract of the judgment is indexed in the manner pointed out by statute, no lien can exist: *Nye* v. *Moody*, 70 Tex. 434; *Nye* v. *Gribble*, 70 Id. 458. Where a *bona fide* purchaser of land pays the price, obtains a title-bond and possession from his grantor prior to the filing an abstract of judgment rendered against the grantor, the judgment is not a lien upon the property: *Elwell* v. *Hitchcock,* 41 Kan. 130. But a judgment has been decided to be a lien upon land which has been previously conveyed by an unrecorded deed, of which the judgment creditor did not have actual notice at the time the judgment was entered: *Doyle* v. *Wade,* 23 Fla. 90; 11 Am. St. Rep. 334; but a creditor, by obtaining judgment merely, does not thereby acquire any estate in his debtor's land, and a deed made before such judgment, and recorded before a sale thereunder, is notice to a purchaser thereat, and will defeat his title: *Parks* v. *People's Bank,* 97 Mo. 130; 10 Am. St. Rep. 295, and note. A purchaser of land, bound by a judgment lien of which he had knowledge at the time of purchasing, is not entitled to be considered a *bona fide* purchaser under the occupying-claimant act, as against a purchaser at a judicial sale under proceedings to enforce such lien: *Rounsaville* v. *Hazen,* 39 Kan. 610. A judgment lien, which is created during the pendency of another suit with respect to the same property, may be extinguished by the determination of such suit against defendant: *Harrington* v. *Latta,* 23 Neb. 84. It may happen that a court of equity, having acquired jurisdiction of certain equities arising between parties, can enforce the lien of a judgment by judicial sale: *Currie* v. *Clark,* 101 N. C. 321.

Every Interest of a Debtor in Land, whether legal or equitable, is bound by the lien of a judgment rendered in the same county: *Eneberg* v. *Carter,* 98 Mo. 647; 14 Am. St. Rep. 664.

Judicial Sales — Sheriff's Deed. — No title passes at a sheriff's sale of real property until the delivery of the sheriff's deed: *Blodgett* v. *Perry,* 97 Mo. 263; 10 Am. St. Rep. 307, and note.

Judicial Sales. — Purchasers at execution sales, before the expiration of the period of redemption, have an interest in the property purchased in the nature of a lien thereon: *Swain* v. *Stockton Sav. Bank,* 78 Cal. 600; 12 Am. St. Rep. 118. But a purchaser at an execution sale does not acquire title before the expiration of the statutory time within which redemption may be made: *Bowman* v. *People,* 82 Ill. 246; 25 Am. Rep. 316.

Rushville Gas Company *v.* City of Rushville.

[121 Indiana, 206.]

Vote of Majority of Quorum is Sufficient to Adopt Measure. — If a quorum of a municipal council is present, and a majority of such quorum vote in favor of a measure, it will prevail, although an equal number refrain from voting. Where, therefore, three of the six members composing a common council of a municipal corporation vote in favor of a 'resolution, the other three members, though present, declining to vote, the resolution is legally adopted.

Common Council of City has Power to Contract for Lighting the city or to furnish light from works of which it is or may become the owner, both under the general act of incorporation and under the provisions of the act entitled "An Act in relation to the lighting of cities and towns, and furnishing the inhabitants thereof with the electric light and other forms of light, and providing for the right of way and the assessment of damages, and declaring an emergency": Elliott's Supp., sec. 794. And this act is constitutional, and complies with the requirements of the constitution as to subject and title.

MUNICIPAL CORPORATION HAS POWER TO ISSUE BONDS IN PAYMENT FOR PROPERTY which it has authority to purchase, unless there is some statutory or constitutional prohibition.

Suit for an injunction.   The opinion states the case.

B. L. Smith, C. Cambern, T. J. Newkirk, and U. D. Cole, for the appellant.

A. B. Irvin, G. H. Puntenny, W. A. Cullen, and J. D. Megee, for the appellees.

ELLIOT, J.   The mayor of the city of Rushville appointed a committee, composed of the members of the common council, to investigate and report upon the question of the expediency of buying an electric-light plant and machinery. The committee, in due time, reported to the common council in favor of making the purchase. On the third day of April, 1889, action was taken on the report at a regular meeting, at which all of the members of the common council were present, and the following resolution was introduced: "Resolved, that the report of the special committee, relating to lighting the city, be adopted, and that the officers therein named be instructed to sign the contract named therein."

Three of the six members composing the common council voted in favor of the resolution, but the other three members, although present, declined to vote, and the mayor declared that it was adopted. By virtue of this resolution, the city is about to enter into a contract with the companies named in the report for the purchase of an electric-light plant and the power to run it, for which the city is to pay the sum of $10,150. Acting under the resolution, the Edison Manufacturing Company has put up poles, strung wires on them, and placed in operation a system of electric lights, and the city will buy the plant and machinery, unless enjoined. The city has contracted with the Buckeye Engine Company for a steam-engine and appliances to be used in operating the machinery of the Edison company plant at a cost of $2,200. Unless enjoined, the city will issue bonds to pay for the plant, machinery, engine, and appliances.

The meeting at which the resolution was adopted was a regular one, attended by all the members of the common council, and all who voted at all voted in favor of the resolu-

tion. The question, therefore, is: Does the fact that three of
the members present declined to vote authorize the conclusion
that the resolution was not legally adopted? In our judgment
it does not.

The rule is, that if there is a quorum present, and a majority
of the quorum vote in favor of a measure, it will prevail, although an equal number should refrain from voting. It is not
the majority of the whole number of members present that is
required; all that is requisite is a majority of the number of
members required to constitute a quorum. If there had been
four members of the common council present, and three had
voted for the resolution and one had voted against it, or had
not voted at all, no one would hesitate to affirm that the resolution was duly passed, and it can make no difference whether
four or six members are present, since it is always the vote of
the majority of the quorum that is effective. The mere presence of inactive members does not impair the right of the majority of the quorum to proceed with the business of the body.
If members present desire to defeat a measure they must vote
against it, for inaction will not accomplish their purpose.
Their silence is acquiescence rather than opposition. Their
refusal to vote is, in effect, a declaration that they consent
that the majority of the quorum may act for the body of which
they are members.

The rule we have asserted is a very old one. The doctrine
is thus stated by one of the earliest writers on municipal corporations: "After an election has been properly proposed, whoever has a majority of those who vote, the assembly being
sufficient, is elected, although a majority of the entire assembly altogether abstain from voting; because their presence
suffices to constitute the elective body, and if they neglect to
vote, it is their own fault, and shall not invalidate the act of
the others, but be construed an assent to the determination of
the majority of those who do vote": Willcock on Municipal
Corporations, sec. 546. In a recent American work it is
said: "Those who are present, and who help to make up the
quorum, are expected to vote on every question, and their
presence alone is enough to make the vote decisive and binding, whether they actually vote or not. The objects of legislation cannot be defeated by the refusal of any one to vote
when present. If eighteen are present, and nine vote, all in
the affirmative, the measure is carried. the refusal of the
other nine to vote being construed as a vote in the affirma-

tive, so far as any construction is necessary": Horr and Bemis on Municipal Police Ordinances, 42. The principle involved is asserted in many cases: *State* v. *Green*, 37 Ohio St. 227; *Launtz* v. *People*, 113 Ill. 137; *County of Cass* v. *Johnston*, 95 U. S. 360, 369; *St. Joseph Tp.* v. *Rogers*, 16 Wall. 644; *State* v. *Mayor*, 37 Mo. 270; *Everett* v. *Smith*, 22 Minn. 53; *Oldknow* v. *Wainwright*, 2 Burr. 1017; *King* v. *Bellringer*, 4 Term Rep. 810; *Inhabitants* v. *Stearns*, 21 Pick. 148.

We cannot agree with appellant's counsel in the construction which they place upon the words of Judge Dillon found in section 279 of his work on municipal corporations; for, as we read what the author says, it is directly against the appellant. What is said by Judge Dillon is this: "So if a board of village trustees consists of five members, and all or four are present, two can do no valid act, even though the others are disqualified by interest from voting, and therefore omit or decline to vote; their assenting to the measure voted for by the two will not make it valid. If three only were present, they would constitute a quorum; then the votes of two, being a majority of the quorum, would be valid, certainly so where the three are all competent to act." In the first sentence, Judge Dillon refers to cases where there is not a quorum present, because there is not the requisite number of qualified members in attendance. He is speaking of the effect of the presence of disqualified persons in that sentence, not of the effect of a vote of the majority of a quorum composed of qualified members of the body. In the last sentence, he speaks of a case where there is a qualified quorum present, and he instances such a case as we have here; for here four would be a quorum, and, according to his rule, three of the four could adopt a measure, if there were no opposing votes. The case referred to by the author in support of the proposition embodied in the first sentence quoted is that of *Coles* v. *Trustees*, 10 Wend. 659. In that case, three of five town trustees were disqualified from voting, and there was, of course, no quorum of competent members, and consequ ntly no capacity to act. The court said: "The act requires tnree out of five, or a majority, to make a quorum. If there were but three present, then the votes of two, being a majority, would be valid. Here were five trustees, three of whom were incompetent to vote by the act; and being so, it seems to me, so far as the vote was concerned, they were not trustees for any purpose." It is obvious, therefore, that no such case was before the court as that now before us; for here all the members were present, and the measure was adopted by a majority vote of the quorum. One of the cases cited in support of the proposition contained in the second sentence of the section quoted by us is that of *Warnock* v. *City of Lafayette,* 4 La. Ann. 419, wherein it was held that a statute requiring a two-thirds vote to pass a measure meant two thirds of the quorum present, and not two thirds of the entire membership of the city council. Another case cited is *Buell* v. *Buckingham,* 16 Iowa, 284, in which the opinion was written by Judge Dillon himself, and where it was held that a majority of a bare quorum may bind the corporation. The opinion quotes with approval, from the opinion of Lord Mansfield in *Rex* v. *Monday,* Cowp. 538, this language: "When the assembly are duly met, I take it to be clear law that the corporate act may be done by the majority of those who have once regularly constituted the meeting." The opinion also approves Chancellor Kent's statement that "a majority of the quorum may decide."

The decision in the case of *State* v. *Porter,* 113 Ind. 79, lends no support to the appellant's argument, and the reasoning of the court is strongly against it. The point actually decided was, that no act could be lawfully done unless a quorum was present; but it was said: "The general rule is, that when a council or collective body, consisting of a given number of members, is authorized by a statute to do an act, or to transact business, authority is thereby given to that body to act upon the subject committed to it, or to transact the business which it is authorized to conduct, whenever a majority of the members thereof are lawfully present: Cushing's Parliamentary Law, sec. 247. The body cannot act without the presence of a quorum, and the act of the quorum is the act of the body: *State* v. *Wilkesville Township,* 20 Ohio St. 288; *McFarland* v. *Crary,* 6 Wend. 298." The logical sequence from the premises thus laid down is, that the vote of the majority of the quorum present is effective. In *Hamilton* v. *State,* 3 Ind. 452, this court quoted, with approval, the statement of the court in *Downing* v. *Ruger,* 21 Wend. 182, 34 Am. Dec. 223, that "where the authority is public, and the number is such as to admit of a majority, that will bind the minority, after all have duly met and conferred," but denied its application, because the statute required all the members of the body to be present at its meetings, and all were not present. The doctrine of *Hamilton* v. *State, supra,* is therefore not opposed to the later cases, but on the contrary, is in harmony with them; for it recognizes the general rule that where the statute does not otherwise provide, a majority of the quorum may, when a quorum is present, lawfully transact business. The case of *State* v. *Edwards,* 114 Ind. 581, is not in point; for what was there decided is, that a county auditor has no right to vote upon a resolution, although he has a right to vote in case an effort to elect a county superintendent results in a tie.

It would not benefit the appellant if we should hold that the councilmen present, and not voting, did in effect oppose the resolution, and certainly, the utmost that can, with the faintest tinge of plausibility, be claimed is, that their votes must be counted as against the resolution. It is inconceivable that their silence should be allotted greater force than their active opposition would have been entitled to have assigned it had it been manifested. If we should assume that their votes are to be counted against the resolution, then the mayor had the casting vote, and by declaring the resolution adopted he gave it in favor of the measure. This is so expressly decided in *Small* v. *Orne,* 79 Me. 78. But we think that the law is as stated by Willcock, and that the members present and not voting assented to the adoption of the resolution.

We have no doubt that the common council had power to contract for lighting the city, or to furnish light from works of which it is or may become the owner. The power exists under the general act of incorporation. But we need not rest our decision upon that act, for the authority is conferred by an act entitled "An act in relation to the lighting of cities and towns, and furnishing the inhabitants thereof with the electric light and other forms of light, and providing for the right of way and the assessment of damages, and declaring an emergency": Elliott's Supp., sec. 794. The object of this act is single, and it embraces but one subject. The subject is that of light, and the object that of enabling the citizens to obtain electric or other lights. The act is similar in its general scope and effect to acts providing for furnishing towns and cities with water, natural gas, and artificial gas, and it is not obnoxious to any constitutional objection. Whatever was germane to the subject of the act—that is, the subject of light —it was proper to embody in the bill. We have no doubt of its constitutionality.

The first section of the act provides that the common council of any city shall "have power to light the streets, alleys, or other public places with the electric light, or other form of light, and to contract with any individual or corporation for lighting such alleys, streets, and other public places with the electric light or other form of light," and this provision, taken in itself, is broad enough to authorize the common council to buy and operate the necessary plant and machinery. But statutes are not to be considered as isolated fragments of law, but as parts of one great system: *Bradley* v. *Thixton*, 117 Ind. 255; *Morrison* v. *Jacoby*, 114 Ind. 84; *Chicago etc. R'y Co.* v. *Summers*, 113 Ind. 10; 3 Am. St. Rep. 616; *Robinson* v. *Rippey*, 111 Ind. 112; *Humphries* v. *Davis*, 100 Ind. 274; 50 Am. Rep. 788. If there were any doubt as to the meaning of the act, it would be removed by considering it, as it is our duty to do, in connection with the general act for the incorporation of cities, for that act confers very comprehensive powers upon municipal corporations as respects streets and public works, and contains many broad general clauses akin to those which Judge Dillon designates as "general welfare clauses." Our own decisions fully recognize the doctrine that municipal corporations do possess, under the general act, authority as broad as that here exercised, and the operation of that act is certainly not limited or restricted by the act of 1883: *Wood* v. *Mears*, 12 Ind. 515; 74 Am. Dec. 222; *City of Richmond* v. *McGirr*, 78 Ind. 192; *City of Anderson* v. *O'Conner*, 98 Ind. 168; *Leeds* v. *City of Richmond*, 102 Ind. 372.

Where a municipal corporation has authority to purchase property, it may issue its bonds in payment unless there is some statutory or constitutional prohibition: *Miller* v. *Board etc.*, 66 Ind. 162; *Second Nat. Bank etc.* v. *Danville*, 60 Ind. 504; *Daily* v. *City of Columbus*, 49 Ind. 169; *Board etc.* v. *Day*, 19 Ind. 450; *City of Lafayette* v. *Cox*, 5 Ind. 38. In the case of *City of Richmond* v. *McGirr*, *supra*, it was said: "As to the kind and form of the evidences and obligations to be executed, the council, in the exercise of a sound discretion, must determine, and their determination, in the absence of fraud, is final." Many authorities are cited in support of this ruling, and it is undoubtedly correct as applied to municipal corporations of such a class as cities and counties, but not as applied to school corporations and like corporations, with very limited powers. The decision in the case of *City of Aurora* v. *West*, 22 Ind. 88, 85 Am. Dec. 413, has no relevancy to the question here under discussion, for there the question was as

to the power of the city to incur a debt in aid of a railroad
company, while here the question is as to the authority of the
city to issue bonds in payment for property it had power to
purchase.   The case of *State* v. *Hauser*, 63 Ind. 155, does
not decide that a city may not issue bonds to pay for water-
works purchased; what it decides is, that a city may not
issue and sell bonds in order to obtain money to construct
water-works.   The difference between that case and this is
very broad and very plain; here bonds are to be issued to pay
for property purchased; there they were issued to be placed
on the market for sale.   Issuing bonds to pay for property
purchased is a very different thing from issuing bonds to
obtain money.

Judgment affirmed.

MUNICIPAL CORPORATIONS. — The acts of the majority of councilmen present at a town meeting bind not only the minority who are present, but all
who are absent: *Chamberlain* v. *Dover*, 13 Me. 466; 29 Am. Dec. 517.   And
in the absence of express regulation to the contrary, a proposition is carried
at a meeting of a board of city aldermen by a majority of the votes cast,
when from the journal it appears that a quorum was present: *Attorney-General*
v. *Shepard*, 62 N. H. 383; 13 Am. St. Rep. 576.   Where upon the passage of
an ordinance by a town council the record shows that the mayor and five
trustees voted in favor of the ordinance, and it did not appear that any other
members of the council were present, it was not necessary, under the statute
requiring the calling of the yeas and nays, to call for the yeas and nays:
Town of Bayard v. *Baker*, 76 Iowa, 220.

MUNICIPAL CORPORATIONS — CONTRACT FOR LIGHTING STREETS. — A city
authorized to contract generally, and to provide for lighting its streets, contracted with an incorporated gas company for lighting its streets for thirty
years, granting to said company the exclusive privilege of supplying the city
with gas for that period.   Although the charter of the city forbade its
incurring an indebtedness exceeding five per cent on the valuation of its taxable property, and the contract, if carried out, would have exceeded that
amount, nevertheless the contract was valid, so far at least as it was executed
on the part of the gas company: *City of East St. Louis* v. *East St. Louis etc.
Co.*, 98 Ill. 415; 38 Am. Rep. 97.

MUNICIPAL CORPORATIONS, POWER TO ISSUE BONDS. — As to the power of
a municipal corporation to issue bonds, see note to *De Voss* v. *Richmond*, 98
Am. Dec. 664 et seq.; note to *City of Galena* v. *Corwith*, 95 Am. Dec. 559.
When a city has lawfully incurred an indebtedness, it has the power, unless
prohibited by its charter or by statute, to issue bonds therefor: *City of Wil-
liamsport* v. *Commonwealth*, 84 Pa. St. 487; 24 Am. Rep. 208; *State* v. *Benton*,
25 Neb. 756; *State* v. *Babcock*, 25 Id. 709; 25 Id. 278; 22 Id. 614.

HANCOCK *v.* YADEN.

[121 INDIANA, 366.]

PLEA OF ACCORD AND SATISFACTION MUST AVER DELIVERY AND ACCEPT-
ANCE. — A plea of accord and satisfaction which does not aver a delivery
and an acceptance of the goods in satisfaction of the debt is bad.

PLEA OF PAYMENT IS BAD IF IT DOES NOT STATE FACTS IN BAR of the
action.

PAYMENT CANNOT BE MADE IN GOODS where there is no agreement to receive them in payment.

ANTECEDENT CONTRACT ASSUMING TO WAIVE RIGHT TO RECEIVE WAGES
FOR MINING COAL IN MONEY IS VOID. — An antecedent contract between the owner of a coal mine and his employee, whereby the latter
agrees to waive his right to be paid his wages in lawful money of the
United States, is entirely void, so far as it assumes to waive his right to
receive his wages in money, being in violation of the statute, sections
1599 and 1610, Elliott's Supplement.

POWER OF LEGISLATURE TO PROHIBIT CONTRACTS WAIVING RIGHT TO RE-
CEIVE WAGES IN MONEY. — The legislature has power to enact a statute
forbidding the execution in advance of contracts waiving the right of
employees to the payment of their wages in money.

ACTION to recover wages. The opinion states the case.

J. T. Beasley, A. B. Williams, and G. A. Knight, for the appellants.

E. S. Holliday and G. A. Byrd, for the appellee.

ELLIOTT, J. It is alleged in the complaint that the appellee was employed by the appellants to render service for them
as a miner in a coal mine of which they were the owners;
that, under this employment, he did render service for them
in mining coal; that his services were reasonably worth five
dollars per day; that he demanded payment for his services
in lawful money of the United States, and that payment was
refused. The appellants answered the complaint in two
paragraphs, but as the only difference between the paragraphs
is that one pleads a verbal contract and the other a written
one, it is only necessary to give a summary of one, as the
questions which arise are substantially the same as to both
of the paragraphs. The answer admits the employment, and
admits, also, the allegation that the appellee rendered the
services for which he sues, but it sets forth a written contract,
alleges that the services were performed under the contract,
and avers that the appellants sold and delivered to the plaintiff in payment of his claim, and to the full amount of the
wages earned by him, divers articles of goods, wares, and merchandise. The provisions of the contract, in so far as they

are material to the questions argued, are these: "The said
William P. Yaden further agrees to accept his pay, or any
part thereof, at the option of said Hancock and Conkle, in
goods and merchandise at their store, near their said coal
mine, and the said William P. Yaden hereby expressly waives
his right to demand and receive his wages and pay for mining coal every two weeks in lawful money of the United States,
as now provided by law he shall be paid." The court sustained a demurrer to the answer, the appellants stood by their
answer, and judgment was rendered against them.

To clear the case from embarrassments, and make the way
plain to a consideration of the controlling question, we preface
our discussion by remarking that the answer is not a plea of
accord and satisfaction, nor a plea of set-off, but a plea of payment, and the ultimate conclusion to be reached depends upon
the answer to the question whether it is sufficient as such a
plea. That it is not a plea of accord and satisfaction is clear,
but if it were to be so regarded, it would be bad, because it
does not aver a delivery and an acceptance of the goods in
satisfaction of the debt. Another prefatory matter deserves
passing thought, and that is this: The plea is a plea of payment, founded on a contract made before the performance of
the services and professing to bar the action; if, therefore,
the plea does not state facts in bar of the action, it is bad.
Whether it does state facts in bar of the action depends upon
the validity of the antecedent contract which is the principal
support of the plea, and as that contract is indivisible, if part
is illegal the whole must fall. The sufficiency of the answer
must, it is clear, depend entirely upon the validity of the contract on which it is founded, since if that contract is invalid
there is no agreement to accept payment in goods or merchandise, and where there is no such agreement payment cannot be made in property. Another thing may be added by
way of preface, and that is this: We are not here concerned
with the question of what parties may do after services have
been performed, for here the question is, What contract may
they make before the relation of employer and employee
begins?

It is sufficiently evident from what we have said that the
only question which we can properly consider or decide is,
whether the antecedent contract was valid in so far as it assumes to waive the right of the appellee to be paid his wages
in lawful money of the United States; and to this question

we confine our discussion, and give judgment upon it, and no other. Our judgment is that the antecedent contract is entirely void in so far as it assumes to waive the appellee's right to receive his wages in money. If there were no valid statute prohibiting such a contract, it would be competent for the parties to make it, so that the ultimate judgment of the court hinges upon the question whether there is a valid statute prohibiting such contracts. There is a statute which, in terms, prohibits such contracts, and if it does not violate some provision of the constitution it totally destroys the contract upon which the defense is founded: Elliott's Supp., secs. 1599, 1610. Our judgment is, that the provision of the statute forbidding the execution of contracts waiving a right to payment in money is one that the legislature had power to enact.

It is a fundamental principle that every member of society surrenders something of his absolute and natural rights in all organized states. Without some yielding of absolute rights, civil government would be impossible. "But every man," says Blackstone, "when he enters into society gives up a part of his natural liberty." "Property and law," as Bentham says, "are born and must die together." The right to dispose of property or labor is a right not wholly surrendered by the citizen, nor yet entirely beyond control by the legislature of the state. The right to contract is an incident of this *jus disponendi*. But the right to contract is not, and never has been, in any country where, as in ours, the common law prevails, and constitutes the source of all civil law, entirely beyond legislative control. The statute of frauds enables contracting parties to avoid contracts not in writing. The law declares that payment in part of an ascertained debt shall not extinguish it, although the parties agree that it shall do so: *Ogborn* v. *Hoffman*, 52 Ind. 439; *Smith* v. *Tyler*, 51 Ind. 512; *Markel* v. *Spitler*, 28 Ind. 488. A party will not be allowed to contract to waive the benefit of homestead or exemption laws: *Maloney* v. *Newton*, 85 Ind. 565; 44 Am. Rep. 46; *Kneettle* v. *Newcomb*, 22 N. Y. 249; 78 Am. Dec. 186; *Curtis* v. *O'Brien*, 20 Iowa, 376; 89 Am. Dec. 543; *Moxley* v. *Ragan*, 10 Bush, 156; 19 Am. Rep. 61. A debtor cannot waive stay of execution by contract: *McLane* v. *Elmer*, 4 Ind. 239; *Develin* v. *Wood*, 2 Ind. 102. By the English law, a seaman cannot, by contract, waive his right to wages: Kay on Shipmaster and Seamen, 626. Parties cannot, by contract, bind themselves in advance not to resort to the courts for the redress of wrongs: *Bauer* v. *Sam-*

son Lodge, 102 Ind. 262; *Dugan* v. *Thomas*, 79 Me. 221. A contract providing that a party shall not remove a cause to the federal court is void: *Home Ins. Co.* v. *Morse*, 20 Wall. 445; *Doyle* v. *Continental Ins. Co.*, 94 U. S. 535. A party will not be allowed to contract, without limitation, that he will not engage in a particular business: *Taylor* v. *Saurman*, 110 Pa. St. 3. A statute may require parties to insert in a promissory note the words "given for a patent": *Herdic* v. *Roessler*, 109 N. Y. 127; *New* v. *Walker*, 108 Ind. 365. Priority in the allowance and payment of claims may be regulated by legislation: *United States* v. *Fisher*, 2 Cranch, 358. A lien for miner's wages may be made superior to the royalty due to the owners of mine from the lessees or operators: *Warren* v. *Sohn*, 112 Ind. 213. Much beyond the doctrine declared in the cases to which we have referred is the ruling in *Churchman* v. *Martin*, 54 Ind. 380, wherein it was held that a statute prohibiting parties from contracting to pay attorney's fees is constitutional. The truth is, that without law as one of its factors, there is really no such thing as a contract. The law is a silent but a ruling factor in every contract: *Long* v. *Straus*, 107 Ind. 94; 57 Am. Rep. 87; *Hudson Canal Co.* v. *Pennsylvania Co.*, 8 Wall. 276, 288. The case before us affords an example, for where a man, upon request, performs services for another, the law implies that he shall be paid for them, and paid in money. It needs no positive agreement to pay in money to entitle a creditor to demand money, for the law decrees that the payment shall be in money. The statutory provision under discussion does no more than enforce this legal right, by commanding that men shall not make a contract dispensing with the lawful mode and medium of payment.

The authorities to which we have referred, and to which it would be no great task to add others, prove that the law-making power of the state does not have authority over the right to contract. That this legislative authority is limited no one doubts; but it is limited only by the constitution. In that instrument are found the only limitations upon the law-making power of the state: *Hedderich* v. *State*, 101 Ind. 564; 51 Am. Rep. 768; *McComas* v. *Krug*, 81 Ind. 327; 42 Am. Rep. 135; *Beauchamp* v. *State*, 6 Blackf. 299. But no limitation in that instrument so operates as to prevent the law-making power from prohibiting classes of citizens from contracting in advance that the wages of miners shall not be paid in lawful money of the United States. It would be not only unnecessary, but improper, to enter upon the work of ascertaining to what extent the constitution restrains the legislature from regulating or restricting the right to contract; for all that can with propriety be here decided is, that it does not restrain the legislature from enacting laws which operate to maintain or protect the medium of payment established by the sovereign power of the nation.

It cannot be denied, without repudiating all authority, that the legislature does possess some power over the right to contract, and if it does, then nothing can be clearer than that this power extends far enough to uphold a statute providing that payment of wages shall be made in money, where there is no agreement to the contrary made after the services have been rendered. Whether the legislature may absolutely declare that nothing shall be payment but money, we need not inquire; for all that is important here is to decide that it may prohibit a contract from being made in advance, waiving the right to payment in what the law says shall be the medium of payment.

We cannot conceive a case in which the assertion of the legislative power to regulate contracts has a sounder foundation than it has in this instance; for here the regulation consists in prohibiting men from contracting in advance to accept payment in something other than the lawful money of the country for the wages they may earn in the future. It is of the deepest and gravest importance to the government that it should unyieldingly maintain the right to protect the money which it makes the standard of value throughout the country. The surrender of this right might put in peril the existence of the nation itself. Suppose that in the years of the war, when gold was worth such an extraordinary premium, the owners of supplies required by the government had, by concerted action, refused to accept anything in payment but coin, would the nation have been powerless to protect what it had decreed should be money? Or again, suppose that the persons holding the needed supplies had refused to take anything but property in exchange, and that it was impossible to procure the species of property demanded, would the government have been helplessly at their mercy? The protection from such evils is in the right to establish and maintain, by coercive measures if need be, what by the law is made money of the nation. We do not use these illustrations for more than their worth; we employ them simply to show the imperious necessity that exists for the retention, in its unbroken integrity, of the power to establish and maintain a standard of value. What is necessary to national or state life the government possesses, and it is for the legislature to judge what measures are essential to the complete and effective exercise of a power which it possesses.

It is not simply the government, as a government, that is interested in the power to establish and maintain a standard of value; for to every citizen engaged in any business of life it is of vital importance that there should be a fixed and unchanging standard. Without it, business, except of the most meager kind, would be at an end, and commerce would be practically annihilated.

The decisions of the highest tribunal of the country go very far to sustain our conclusions. It is the law, as that court has declared it in able opinions, that the government has a right to provide a currency for the whole country, and to drive out all other circulating mediums by taxation or otherwise: *Veazie Bank* v. *Fenno*, 8 ·Wall. 533. This was asserted by Chief Justice Chase, speaking for the majority of the court, although he and the majority of the court, as it was then constituted, did not go so far upon other phases of the case as the court did go in the subsequent case which now stands as declarative of the law of the land: *Legal Tender Cases*, 12 Wall. 457. In *Hepburn* v. *Griswold*, 8 Wall. 603, a different view was taken upon some phases of the general question from that declared in the *Legal Tender Cases*, *supra*, but not upon the proposition we have stated. The power to establish necessarily implies the power to maintain: *United States* v. *Fisher*, 2 Cranch, 358; *McCulloch* v. *Maryland*, 4 Wheat. 316; *United States* v. *Marigold*, 9 How. 560. It is for the legislature to judge what means are necessary and appropriate to accomplish an end which the constitution makes legitimate. It is therefore competent for the legislative branch of the government to devise and establish such rules as in its judgment will best protect the standard of value which its laws have fixed. The rule to which we have referred is a familiar one, but it has been so admirably stated by Mr. Justice Bradley that we may be pardoned for quoting his language. Replying to an objection pressed by counsel, he said: "The answer is, the legislative department, being the nation itself, speaking by its representatives, has a choice of methods, and is master of its own discretion ": *Legal Tender Cases, supra, vide* p. 561.

The power exercised by the legislative department in fixing the standard of value closely resembles that by which the standard of weights and measures is established and maintained. In truth, there is no difference in the inherent nature of the powers; the difference is in the subject-matter to which they are applied, rather than in the powers themselves. The power of the state extends so far as to enable it to declare and enforce penalties against persons who violate the law regulating the standard of weights and measures or the standard of values. It is upon the theory that matters connected with the regulation of the standard of values are within the legislative power that statutes defining and punishing usury are sustained. It is true, we know, that the federal Congress is the proper authority to regulate the standard of values, but it does not follow from this that a state may not do what it can to prevent the debasement of the standard fixed by Congress. It can, of course, neither lower that standard nor pass laws hostile to those enacted by Congress, but it may support the efforts of the national legislature as far, at least, as it is within the power of a state to do so. The principle which rules this phase of the subject is closely analogous to that established by the decisions affirming the right of the state to proscribe as a felon one who counterfeits the national money: *Dashing* v. *State*, 78 Ind. 357; *Snoddy* v. *Howard*, 51 Ind. 411; *Chess* v. *State*, 1 Blackf. 198; *Fox* v. *State*, 5 How. 410; *United States* v. *Field*, 16 Fed. Rep. 778.

The provision of the statute to which our decision is directed operates upon all members of the classes it enumerates. It neither confers special privileges nor makes unjust discrimination. All who are members of the classes named are entitled to its benefits or subjected to its burdens. It is open to every citizen to become a member of any of the classes designated, and the privileges conferred belong on equal terms to all: *Johns* v. *State*, 78 Ind. 332; *McAunich* v. *Mississippi etc. R. R. Co.*, 20 Iowa, 338. It denies no privilege to any one, for it leaves it free to every citizen to become a member of the classes specified, and it operates alike upon all who enter those classes.

The statute operates upon both the employer and the employee. It may, it is true, in its practical operation, especially benefit the wage-earner, but that is no fault; at all events, the fault is not such a grievous one as to compel the courts to strike it down. It fixes no price upon any man's labor; it leaves the parties to do that, but it does require them to refrain from contracting, before the relation of employer and employee begins, for payment in anything except the lawful money of the United States. It does not preclude parties from making an accord and satisfaction after wages have been earned and services rendered, although it does command that the antecedent contract shall not provide that payment may be made in something other than lawful money of the nation.

Judgment affirmed.

<hr>

ACCORD AND SATISFACTION. — A plea of accord and satisfaction must allege not only a clear accord, but that it was executed, and that the amount tendered was accepted: *Hearn* v. *Kiehl*, 38 Pa. St. 147; 80 Am. Dec. 472; *Russel* v. *Lytle*, 6 Wend. 390; 22 Am. Dec. 537; *Brooklyn Bank* v. *De Grauw*, 23 Wend. 342; 35 Am. Dec. 569; *Kromer* v. *Heim*, 75 N. Y. 574; 31 Am. Rep. 491; *Diller* v. *Brubaker*, 52 Pa. St. 498; 91 Am. Dec. 177.

PAYMENT IN PROPERTY: See note to *Jones* v. *Perkins*, 64 Am. Dec. 142, 143.

CONTRACTS. — As to the validity of contracts whose considerations are other contracts based upon violations of law, see note to *De Leon* v. *Trevino*, 30 Am. Rep. 106–112.

CONSTITUTIONAL LAW. — The term "liberty" means right of man to be free in the enjoyment of his faculties, subject only to such restraints as are necessary to the common welfare, and the term cannot be narrowed to mean merely freedom from physical restraint: *People* v. *Gillson*, 109 N. Y. 389; 4 Am. St. Rep. 465.

<hr>

HINCHCLIFFE v. KOONTZ.

[121 INDIANA, 422.]

RES GESTÆ, EVIDENCE ADMISSIBLE AS PART OF. — Declarations made contemporaneously with or immediately preparatory to a particular litigated act, which tend to illustrate and give character to the act in question, are admissible as part of the *res gestæ*. Where, therefore, in an action to recover for an alleged breach of a contract of hiring, the disputed question is whether the hiring was for a year or for an indefinite period, a letter written by the defendants to the plaintiff on the day before the hiring, containing a declaration that the writers desired to see the plaintiff the next day, with a view of securing his services for the coming year as foreman, though not received by the plaintiff till the day after the contract was completed, is admissible in evidence as corroborative of the plaintiff's version of the contract.

EXTENT TO WHICH CROSS-EXAMINATION MAY BE CARRIED IN ORDER TO SHOW BIAS, prejudice, or interest on the part of the witness, is a matter resting in the sound discretion of the court.

INTOXICATION OF EMPLOYEE, EVIDENCE OF NOT ADMISSIBLE WHEN. — In an action by an employee to recover for his wrongful discharge, evidence that after his discharge he was frequently seen on the streets in an intoxicated condition, is inadmissible, in the absence of any offer to show that his intoxication had become so habitual as to affect his capacity to perform such services as he had engaged to perform, or that he had actually lost an opportunity to obtain employment on account of intoxication.

EMPLOYEE WRONGFULLY DISCHARGED NEED NOT TENDER HIS SERVICES, nor keep himself in readiness to re-enter his employer's service. He is only bound to use reasonable diligence to obtain other employment of the same kind, and it lies upon the defendant to show that he did not use diligence, or that other similar employment was offered and declined. He is not bound to accept employment of a substantially different character or grade.

AMOUNT OF DAMAGES TO WHICH EMPLOYEE WRONGFULLY DISCHARGED IS ENTITLED is, *prima facie,* the amount stipulated to be paid; but this amount may be reduced by the defendant's making it appear that the plaintiff either did procure, or could by reasonable effort have procured, other employment, or that he occupied his time at his own or other remunerative business.

ACTION for breach of contract. The opinion states the case.

A. D. Bartholomew and *H. A. Gillett,* for the appellants.

W. Johnston and *E. D. Crumpacker,* for the appellee.

MITCHELL, C. J. This was an action by John Koontz against William E. and George Hinchcliffe, to recover damages for the alleged breach of a contract, whereby the former was hired to serve the latter as foreman of their brick-yard for the period of one year at an agreed salary. It is charged that after the plaintiff entered upon the performance of his contract the defendants wrongfully dismissed him, without any fault on his part, and that although he had made diligent effort, he had been unable to obtain any other work that he could perform.

There was a verdict and judgment for the plaintiff below. A number of questions are presented on this appeal under an assignment that the court erred in overruling the motion for a new trial.

It was a subject of dispute at the trial whether the appellee was, as he claimed, hired for one year, or whether he had been employed, as the defendants asserted the fact to be, for an indefinite period.

As tending to support the appellee's claim, the court admitted a letter in evidence, written by the defendants the day before the contract of hiring was made, in which it was stated that one of the latter desired to see him the next day, at a place appointed, with reference to securing his services " as foreman for the coming year." It appeared that this letter, although written the day before, was not received by the plaintiff until the day after the contract of hiring was completed, and it is now urged that it was for that reason error to admit it in evidence. This objection is without merit. The letter was admissible upon the ground that it was in effect a declaration made contemporaneously with and explanatory of the act of hiring: *Durham* v. *Shannon*, 116 Ind. 403; 9 Am. St. Rep. 860.

Declarations made contemporaneously with or immediately preparatory to a particular litigated act, which tend to illustrate and give character to the act in question, are admissible as part of the *res gestæ: People* v. *Vernon*, 35 Cal. 49; 95 Am. Dec. 49, and note; *Louisville etc. R'y Co.* v. *Buck*, 116 Ind. 566; 9 Am. St. Rep. 883.

The character and purpose of an act are frequently indicated by what is said by the person at the time, or while in the immediate preparation to do the act. This letter falls within the principle above stated. It was written in immediate preparation of the act of hiring, and contained a declaration that the writers desired to see the plaintiff the next day, with a view of securing his services for the coming year as foreman. It illustrates, throws light upon, the act of which it was the immediate forerunner.

The letter was not of itself evidence of the fact that the hiring was for the period of one year, but, like any other admission of an adverse party, it was proper to be considered as corroborative of the plaintiff's version of the contract; *Milne* v. *Leisler*, 7 Hurl. & N. 786; *Eastman* v. *Bennett*, 6 Wis. 232.

It is next urged that error was committed by the refusal of the court to allow certain questions to be put to witnesses which it is claimed tended to show feeling, interest, and bias on the part of the witnesses. While it is undoubtedly true that a witness may be required to explain anything that would tend to show such bias, prejudice, or interest as would incapacitate him from testifying impartially and accurately, yet the extent to which a cross-examination may be carried in the direction indicated by the questions rejected is a matter resting in the sound discretion of the court: *Bessette* v. *State*, 101 Ind. 85. That discretion was not abused in the present case.

The appellants proposed to prove that the plaintiff was frequently seen on the streets in an intoxicated condition

after ˏhe was discharged. This evidence was properly excluded. It is quite true that an employee wrongfully discharged must not voluntarily render himself incapable of performing other service substantially similar to that which he
had engaged to perform, but the appellants made no offer to
show such a degree of intoxication as in any wise affected his
capacity for service. The burden was on the appellants to
show that the plaintiff might have had other similar employment; and, in the absence of any offer to show that his intoxication had become so habitual as to affect his capacity to
perform such services as he had engaged to perform, or that
he had actually lost an opportunity to obtain employment on
account of intoxication, the evidence was not admissible.

It is not necessary for an employee, wrongfully discharged
from service, thereafter to tender his services, or keep himself
in readiness to re-enter the employer's service. His duty is to
use reasonable care and diligence in obtaining other employment of the same kind, and it lies upon the defendant to
show that he did not use diligence, or that other similar employment was offered and declined. *Howard* v. *Daly*, 61 N.
Y. 362; 19 Am. Rep. 285; *Chamberlin* v. *Morgan*, 68 Pa. St.
168; *King* v. *Steiren*, 44 Pa. St. 99; 84 Am. Dec. 419.

And it may be remarked, as applicable to one of the instructions of which complaint is made, that while a servant
wrongfully discharged is obliged to use reasonable diligence
in obtaining other employment, he is not bound to accept
employment of a substantially different character or grade.

Many other questions relating to rulings of the court in admitting and excluding evidence are made on the briefs. The
questions are not substantially different in character from
those already remarked upon. We have carefully examined
the several points made, and it is sufficient to say, without
setting out each in detail, that they are not sustained.

The charge of the court comprises a series of thirteen separate propositions, in which the law covering every feature of
the case is expounded to the jury with admirable precision
and clearness.

In a case like the present the amount of damages to which
the plaintiff in entitled, in case the dismissal was wrongful, is
prima facie the amount stipulated to be paid. This may be
reduced in the event the defendant makes it appear that the
plaintiff either did procure, or could by reasonable effort have
procured, other employment, or that he did occupy his time at

his own or other remunerative business: *Howard* v. *Daly, supra; Perry* v. *Simpson etc. Co.*, 37 Conn. 520, 540; 8 South. L. Rev. 432, 449.

Without entering upon the task of stating each of the numerous objections urged against the instructions, it is enough to say we have subjected them to a critical examination, and have çarefully considered the plausible argument in support of the objections, and find no error of which the appellants have any cause for complaint. Within the often repeated rule, we cannot reverse the judgment on the evidence.

The judgment is affirmed, with costs.

———

RES GESTÆ, WHAT CONSTITUTES. — As to what declarations are admissible as part of the *res gestæ,* see *Tetherow* v. *St. Joseph etc. R'y Co.*, 98 Mo. 74; 14 Am. St. Rep. 617; *Cook* v. *Pinkerton*, 81 Ga. 89; 12 Am. St. Rep. 297, and note; *Durham* v. *Shannon*, 116 Ind. 403; 9 Am. St. Rep. 860; *Hemmingway* v. *Chicago etc. R'y Co.*, 72 Wis. 42; 7 Am. St. Rep. 823; *Bush* v. *Roberts*, 111 N. Y. 478; 7 Am. St. Rep. 741, and note; *St. Louis etc. R'y Co.* v. *Weakly*, 50 Ark. 397; 7 Am. St. Rep. 104; *New York etc. Co.* v. *Rogers*, 11 Col. 6; 7 Am. St. Rep. 198, and note. In a suit by a mother for the death of her son, a fireman, who was killed in a collision, where a witness heard a conversation between the operator and the fireman, in which the former informed the latter that the passenger train would meet his train at the next station, such conversation was competent as part of the *res gestæ:* *Gulf etc. R'y Co.* v. *Compton*, 75 Tex. 667. It is also competent to show that about a half-hour before an accident upon a railroad, caused by the spreading of rails upon the track, a track-walker reported to the section-boss the condition of the track: *Texas etc. R'y Co.* v. *Lester*, 75 Id. 56. In an action by the widow and children of a railway employee whose death was caused by a switch-engine running upon him, it is competent to show that another man at the same time, under the same circumstances, was killed or injured by the backing of the switch-engine: *Missouri P. R'y Co.* v. *Lehmberg*, 75 Id. 61. Where a plaintiff remained in his wagon upon a falling bridge until it fell, in suing for injuries sustained by him in the fall, he was properly permitted to testify as to his thoughts at the time, that the railing would stop the wagon, as reason for not leaving the wagon before it fell from the bridge: *Baldridge etc. Bridge Co.* v. *Cartrett*, 75 Id. 628. The declarations and conversations held by a presiding officer of an election with others when votes were challenged as illegal are competent as *res gestæ,* where the fairness of the election is in issue: *Little* v. *State*, 75 Id. 617. Bills of sale of personalty, purchased by one for another, and delivered when the price was paid, and receipts for payments thereon, each reciting the name of such other person as the purchaser, and signed by the vendor, are competent as part of the *res gestæ* to show for whom the purchase was made: *Brooks* v. *Duggan*, 149 Mass. 304. In a suit for the value of mules killed in a railroad collision, it is competent for plaintiff to show how the mules were killed, and that the engineer was drunk: *Southern P. R'y Co.* v. *Maddox*, 75 Tex. 300.

As to what declarations are not admissible as a part of the *res gestæ,* see *Savannah etc. R'y Co.* v. *Holland*, 82 Ga. 257; 14 Am. St. Rep. 158; *Fordyce* v. *McCants*, 51 Ark. 509; 14 Am. St. Rep. 69; *Dundas* v. *City of Lansing*, 75 Mich. 499; 13 Am. St. Rep. 457, and note; *Erie etc. R. R. Co.* v. *Smith*, 125

Pa. St. 259; 11 Am. St. Rep. 895, and note. Declarations on the part of the engineer after the train had been stopped, showing ill-will and a threatening nature toward the injured person, are not admissible as part of the *res gestæ: Gulf etc. R'y Co.* v. *York,* 74 Tex. 364. Declarations made by a testator to his executor just prior to his death, and more than five years after the date of the will, as to what was intended by the will, and who wrote it, constitute no part of the *res gestæ: In re Gilmore,* 81 Cal. 240. Evidence inadmissible as part of the *res gestæ,* but admissible upon other grounds, cannot, after its admission, be considered as *res gestæ: Kuhns* v. *Wisconsin etc. R'y Co.,* 76 Iowa, 67.

CROSS-EXAMINATION. — The court may confine counsel within reasonable limits in cross-examination of witnesses; and the exercise of the court's discretion in doing so, if not abused, is not reviewable on appeal: *Birmingham etc. Fire Ins. Co.* v. *Pulver,* 126 Ill. 329; 9 Am. St. Rep. 599.

MASTER AND SERVANT — WRONGFUL DISCHARGE. — A wrongfully discharged servant must use reasonable efforts to obtain service elsewhere; but the burden of proving that a discharged servant could have obtained employment elsewhere is upon defendant: *Emery* v. *Steckel,* 126 Pa. St. 171; 12 Am. St. Rep. 857, and note. Where a servant has been discharged wrongfully before the expiration of his term of employment, he is *prima facie* entitled to recover to the extent of his wages for the whole term: Id.

PLAKE v. STATE.

[121 INDIANA, 433.]

INDICTMENT CHARGING ACCUSED WITH HAVING DISCHARGED CONTENTS OF PISTOL INTO PERSON of another, with the intent to purposely, unlawfully, and with premeditated malice, kill and murder such person, is sufficient.

REASONABLE DOUBT AS TO SANITY OF ACCUSED, EFFECT OF. — If the evidence is of such a character as to create a reasonable doubt as to whether or not the accused was of unsound mind at the time the crime was committed, he is entitled to a verdict of acquittal.

PERSON MAY NOT BE CRIMINALLY RESPONSIBLE, THOUGH HAVING SUFFICIENT MENTAL CAPACITY TO KNOW RIGHT FROM WRONG, if his will-power is so impaired that he cannot resist an impulse to commit a crime, for in that case he is not of sound mind. But if the will is simply overborne by ungoverned passion, there may be criminal responsibility.

INSANITY IS QUESTION OF FACT FOR JURY. — Whether insanity exists or not, and what is its character and extent, is a question of fact to be determined by the jury from the evidence, and it is not the province of the court to instruct the jury, as a matter of law, that insanity is a physical disease.

INDICTMENT for murder. The opinion states the case.

C. Kellison, for the appellant.

C. P. Drummond, prosecuting attorney, for the state.

ELLIOTT, J. The indictment charges that the appellant did unlawfully and feloniously touch and wound Frank L. Johnson by discharging into his person the contents of a pistol, loaded with powder and ball, " with the intent then and thereby him, the said Frank L. Johnson, feloniously, purposely, and with premeditated malice, to kill and murder."

Counsel asserts that the indictment is bad, because it does not allege that the touching and wounding were done purposely and maliciously, but we regard this contention as entirely destitute of merit. Where an indictment charges that the contents of a pistol were discharged by the accused into the person of another, with the intent to purposely, unlawfully, and with premeditated malice kill and murder such person, it is sufficient: *Keeling* v. *State*, 107 Ind. 563; *Williams* v. *State*, 47 Ind. 568; *Cronkhite* v. *State*, 11 Ind. 307.

There was evidence upon the question of the appellant's mental incapacity, which required the court to instruct the jury upon the question of criminal responsibility, and the court did give several instructions upon this subject. The entire series of instructions proceed upon a radically erroneous view of the law of criminal responsibility, and we do not deem it necessary to notice them in detail. We state a few settled principles, and adjudge the instructions to be erroneous because they are inconsistent with these principles.

If the evidence is of such a character as to create a reasonable doubt whether the accused was of unsound mind at the time the crime was committed, he is entitled to a verdict of acquittal: *Polk* v. *State*, 19 Ind. 170; 81 Am. Dec. 382; *Bradley* v. *State*, 31 Ind. 492; *McDougal* v. *State*, 88 Ind. 24.

A person may have sufficient mental capacity to know right from wrong, and to be able to comprehend the nature and consequences of his act, and yet be not criminally responsible for his acts; for if the will power is so impaired that he cannot resist an impulse to commit a crime, he is not of sound mind: *Goodwin* v. *State*, 96 Ind. 550, and cases cited; *Conway* v. *State*, 118 Ind. 482. If the lack of will power is the result of a diseased state of the mind, there is mental unsoundness within the meaning of the law; but if the will is simply overborne by ungoverned passion, there may be criminal responsibility: *Goodwin* v. *State*, *supra*, and authorities cited.

It is not the province of the court to instruct the jury that insanity is a physical disease. It is a question of fact, to be determined from the evidence, whether insanity exists, and what its character and extent is; and not one to be determined as a matter of law by the court: *Grubb* v. *State*, 117 Ind. 277. The province of the court is to state the general rules of law to the jury, and it has no right to charge, as matter of law, that insanity is a physical disease of any particular organ of the body. It is not safe to take from works upon medical jurisprudence definitions of insanity, for they are, in many instances, merely speculative opinions, and they are also opinions upon a subject on which it is impossible to reconcile the discordant views of theoretical writers. It must, in each particular case, be a question of fact to be determined from the evidence whether there was insanity, and what was its cause and character.

We do not deem it necessary to discuss other questions argued, for it is not probable that they will arise on another trial.

Judgment reversed. ____

CRIMINAL LAW — REASONABLE DOUBT. — It is error in a criminal prosecution for the trial court to refuse to instruct the jury as to the burden being upon the prosecution to prove beyond a reasonable doubt every element of the crime of which the defendant may be convicted: *People* v. *Cohn*, 76 Cal. 386; and it is only necessary that a defendant produce sufficient proof of circumstances of mitigation or excuse, to raise a reasonable doubt as to the guilt of the crime charged, or as to the existence of the mitigating circumstances: *People* v. *Elliot*, 80 Id. 297. In *Perry* v. *State*, 87 Ala. 30, a charge asserting that "the probability of reasonably accounting for the death of the deceased by accident, or by other means than the lawful act of defendant, must be excluded by the circumstances proved; and it is only when no other hypotheses will explain all the conditions of the case, and account for all the facts, that it can be safely and justly concluded that it was caused by him,"— was held to have been properly refused. And in *Munkers* v. *State*, 87 Id. 95, a charge asserting the right to an acquittal, if the jury "have reason to believe" certain facts hypothetically stated, was properly refused. In *Shubert* v. *State*, 66 Miss. 446, it was held error to instruct the jury that if there was any fact in evidence, which if true would cause the jury to reasonably doubt the guilt of the accused, and if the jury were uncertain whether such fact was true, they should acquit; for such an instruction invokes a doubt upon a doubt. In *Johnson* v. *State*, 27 Tex. App. 163, where the court charged: "It is not sufficient, to secure a conviction, for the state to make out a *prima facie* case, but the guilt of the defendant must be shown beyond a reasonable doubt; and the failure or inability of the defendant to show his innocence does not lend any additional probative force to the incriminative facts, if any, shown by the state, or raise any presumption of guilt against the defendant,"—it was decided that the charge, though abstractly correct, was calculated to lead the jury to believe that in the opinion of the court the defense had failed to show innocence. A reasonable doubt of the guilt of an accused, independent of exculpatory proof, entitles an accused to an acquittal: *Zwicker* v. *State*, 27 Id. 539; *Johnson* v. *State*, 27 Id. 163.

ASSAULT WITH INTENT TO KILL — INDICTMENT. — An indictment under the statute for willful and malicious shooting and wounding, with intent to kill, need not charge that the act was done feloniously; for every act essential to constitute the crime is set out in the statute, and an indictment which follows the language of the statute is good: *Cundiff* v. *Commonwealth*, 86 Ky. 196; and to the same effect is *People* v. *Savercool*, 81 Cal. 650; *People* v. *Forney*, 81 Id. 118. An indictment for assault with intent to commit murder, charging that G. J. "did then and there unlawfully, in a rude, insolent, and angry manner, touch C. W., with intent then and there him, the said C. W., feloniously, purposely, and with premeditated malice, to kill and murder, contrary," etc., is good: *State* v. *Jenkins*, 120 Ind. 268. An indictment for assault with a deadly weapon, alleging that the assault was committed "upon the person of one John Caffey," sufficiently shows that a human being was the subject of the assault: *People* v. *Forney*, 81 Cal. 118; to the same effect is *State* v. *Knadler*, 40 Kan. 359. As to the necessity of describing in the indictment the weapon used in making the felonious assault: *State* v. *Henn*, 39 Minn. 476; *People* v. *Savercool*, 81 Cal. 650.

INSANITY AS A DEFENSE TO CRIME: See note to *Parsons* v. *State*, 60 Am. Rep. 212–225; note to *State* v. *Marler*, 36 Am. Dec. 402–411. Charges as to insanity as a defense in criminal cases are properly refused, even though abstractly correct, when there is no evidence in the case showing any form of mania or mental incapacity, to a degree which confers irresponsibility for crime: *Perry* v. *State*, 87 Ala. 30.

STATE EX REL. LAW *v.* BLEND.

[121 INDIANA, 514.]

REPEALING CLAUSE IN UNCONSTITUTIONAL ACT FALLS WITH REST OF ACT, WHEN. — Where it is not clear that the legislature, by a repealing clause attached to an unconstitutional act, intended to repeal the former statute upon the same subject, except upon the supposition that the new act would take the place of the former one, the repealing clause falls with the act to which it is attached.

ACT IN PART UNCONSTITUTIONAL MAY BE VALID AS TO PART NOT UNCONSTITUTIONAL, WHEN. — When a part of an act is unconstitutional, if, by striking from it all that part which is void, that which is left is complete in itself, sensible, capable of being executed, and wholly independent of that which is rejected, the courts will reject that which is unconstitutional, and enforce the remainder.

VALIDITY OF INDIANA ACT OF MARCH, 1883. — The Indiana act of March, 1883, creating a board of metropolitan police in all cities having a population of twenty-nine thousand or more inhabitants, is constitutional and capable of being enforced, except in so far as it makes a residence of three years in the city in which he is appointed next preceding his appointment a condition of a police commissioner's eligibility, and in so far as it provides for the appointment of officers equally from the two leading political parties.

INFORMATION. The opinion states the case.

A. Gilchrist, C. A. De Bruler, and D. B. Kumler, for the appellants.

J. S. Buchanan, J. Brownlee, and P. W. Fry, for the appellees.

COFFEY, J. The information in this cause charges that the relators, Edward E. Law, Alexander H. Foster, and Adolph Goeke, constitute the board of metropolitan police of the city of Evansville; that each of said relators was duly appointed a commissioner of police of said city by the governor, secretary of state, auditor of state, and treasurer of state of the state of Indiana, pursuant to the provisions of the act providing for a metropolitan police in all cities of twenty-nine thousand or more inhabitants, etc., the same being chapter 74 of the acts of the legislature of the state of Indiana for the year 1883, viz.: Said Edward E. Law was so appointed such commissioner on the first day of January, 1887; said Foster on the first day of January, 1888, and said Goeke on the first day of January, 1889; that at the time of their respective appointments, said relators were each of them more than twenty-one years of age, and were each of them duly qualified electors in the city of Evansville, county of Vanderburgh, and state of Indiana; that each of said relators was, at such times, a citizen of the state of Indiana, and of the United States; that each of said relators, at the time of his appointment as such commissioner of police, had resided in the city of Evansville for threee years and more prior to his appointment, and that the relators were, at the time of their several appointments, and are now, one of them of opposite politics to the other two, viz.: Said Edward E. Law is, and was at the time of such appointment, a Democrat, and the other relators are, and were at the time of their appointment, Republicans; that each of the relators, at the time of his appointment, was, and now is, eligible to said office of commissioner of police, and each of them had and has all the qualifications required by said act for such office; that each of the relators was appointed to such office for the full term of three years, and each of them accepted such office and took the oath and gave the bond required by said act, and did all other acts necessary to entitle him to hold said office; that said commissioners were duly organized as a board of metropolitan police for said city, and by virtue of their offices they were, on the tenth day of April, 1889, and for a long time prior thereto had been, discharging their duties as such com-

missioners of police, and were in charge and control of the
police force of said city; and it was their right and duty at
said time, and is now as such board of metropolitan police, to
control and manage the police force of said city in the manner
provided in said act; that on the tenth day of April, 1889, the
defendants, claiming to act under the provisions of an unconstitutional and void act of the legislature of this state for the
year 1889, providing for a board of metropolitan police and
fire department in certain cities of this state, the same being
chapter 112 of the acts of said legislature for the year 1889,
wrongfully and unlawfully intruded themselves into said office
of police commissioners for the city of Evansville, and although the supreme court of this state has held said pretended act to be altogether null and void, the defendants,
Fred Blend, Charles Kehr, and James Nugent, continue wrongfully and unlawfully to hold said office, under a pretended
authority from the common council of the city of Evansville,
and refuse to surrender said offices, and they refuse to turn
over to the relators the control of the police force of said city,
although often requested so to do; that by said wrongful and
unlawful acts of the defendants the relators are kept out of
the offices and franchises to which they are legally entitled as
above stated; that they have sustained damages in the sum
of three thousand dollars. Wherefore the relators pray for a
decree declaring and establishing their right to said office, and
that they have judgment, etc.

The court sustained a demurrer to this information, and the
appellant excepted. Judgment for appellees for costs.

The assignment of error calls in question the correctness of
the ruling of the Vanderburgh superior court in sustaining
the demurrer to the above information.

An act of the legislature passed on the fifth day of March,
1883 (section 705, Elliott's Supp.), creates a board of metropolitan police in all cities in this state having a population of
twenty-nine thousand or more inhabitants, as shown by the
United States census of 1880. The act provides that such
board shall be appointed by the governor, secretary, auditor,
and treasurer of the state. This act also defines and specifically sets forth the duties of such board of metropolitan
police.

By an act of the legislature passed on the seventh day of
March, 1889, the legislature attempted to abolish the board
of metropolitan police created by the act of March 5, 1883, and

to create a board of metropolitan police and fire department.
This act provides for the election of the members of the first
board by the general assembly, and confers on the mayor of
such cities the power to appoint the members of all future
boards.

The act provides that all laws and parts of laws coming in
conflict with it, and especially the act providing for a metropolitan police in cities of twenty-nine thousand inhabitants,
are by this act repealed: Elliott's Supp., sec. 721.

In the case of *City of Evansville* v. *State*, 118 Ind. 426, and
the case of *State* v. *Denny*, 118 Ind. 449, the act of March 7,
1889, was held to be in conflict with the constitution of the
state, and therefore void.

It is contended by the appellees in this case that, although
the body of the act referred to is void, still the repealing clause
is valid, and that it repeals the act of March 5, 1883, and
leaves the control of the police power of the cities therein
named to the common council of such cities. It is earnestly
maintained by the appellants, on the other hand, that when
the act to which the repealing clause is attached fell, the repealing clause fell with it; and that, as a consequence, the act
of March 5, 1883, still remains in force.

In the case of *Meshmeier* v. *State*, 11 Ind. 482, it was held
that a repealing clause attached to an unconstitutional act of
the legislature might repeal a former valid statute upon the
same subject. The general principle announced in that case
is undoubtedly correct, for it must be conceded that the legislature may use such language in the repealing clause attached
to an unconstitutional law as to leave no doubt as to its intention to repeal a former law, in any event. In such case the
law intended to be repealed would cease to exist, even though
the law to which the repealing clause was attached should
fail by reason of being in conflict with the constitution.

Where, however, it is not clear that the legislature, by a
repealing clause attached to an unconstitutional act, intended
to repeal the former statute upon the same subject, except
upon the supposition that the new act would take the place of
the former one, the repealing clause falls with the act to which
it is attached: Bishop's Written Laws, sec. 34; *Tims* v. *State*,
26 Ala. 165; *Sullivan* v. *Adams*, 3 Gray, 476; *Childs* v. *Shower*,
18 Iowa, 261; *Shephardson* v. *Milwaukee etc. R. R. Co.*, 6 Wis.
578; *State* v. *Burton*, 11 Wis. 50; *Devoy* v. *Mayor*, 35 Barb.
264; *People* v. *Tiphaine*, 3 Park. Cr. 241; *Devoy* v. *City of New*

York, 36 N. Y. 449; *State* v. *Hallock*, 14 Nev. 202; 33 Am.
Rep. 559.

In the case of *Meshmeier* v. *State*, 11 Ind. 482, the learned
judge who wrote the opinion admits that the authorities are
against the conclusion there reached; but says that he is unable to bring his mind to agree with the authorities upon the
subject then under consideration.

It is believed that the conclusion reached in that case has
never been followed either by this or any other court in the
Union.

Mr. Bishop, in commenting on this case in his valuable
work on the written laws, section 34, says: "But not only
the reason just suggested shows that this doctrine cannot be
sound in principle; it is also unsound, and it has been so adjudged, because, as observed in the Alabama court, if the new
law is void, the provisions of the former law cannot with propriety be said to be in conflict, or contravention of it."

The supreme court of Iowa, in considering this case in the
case of *Childs* v. *Shower*, 18 Iowa, 261, said: "In that case,
the repealing clause in an unconstitutional statute was, 'that
all acts and parts of acts inconsistent with the provisions of
this act are hereby repealed'; and the court held (Hanna, J.,
dissenting) that the prior law was repealed. The reasoning
of the majority seems to be refined and technical. They
admit that an unconstitutional law cannot repeal a prior law
by implication. But here they say is 'an express repeal.'
This, as it seems to us, is where the error lies. There was no
positive and unconditional repeal, a repeal only so far as the
two should be legally inconsistent."

As a consequence of this reasoning, the Iowa court refused
to follow the case of *Meshmeier* v. *State*, 11 Ind. 482. Indeed,
it is in conflict with all the authorities above cited, and we
know of no case to be found which in the remotest degree is
supposed to give it any support.

It is contended, however, by the appellee, that it is manifest
from the language used that the legislature intended to repeal
the act of 1883 in any event. But we are unable to agree
with counsel in this construction. We must accord to the
legislature the belief that the act of 1889 was constitutional,
and the intention that the provisions of that act would take
the place of the act of 1883. The manner of selecting police-
officers under the act of 1889 is not materially different from
the mode prescribed by the act of 1883. The mode of select-

ing police commissioners was changed, but the intention of the legislature to keep up the old system of selecting police-officers is perfectly plain.

We cannot say that the legislature would have passed the repealing clause in question had it not intended that the act of 1889 should take the place of the act which it attempts to repeal. Under such circumstances, according to all the authorities except *Meshmeier* v. *State*, 11 Ind. 482, the repealing clause must fall with the act to which it is attached.

We are of the opinion that the repealing clause in question is void, and that it does not repeal the act of March 5, 1883.

In so far as the case of *Meshmeier* v. *State*, 11 Ind. 482, is in conflict with this opinion the same is hereby modified.

It is not seriously contended that the act of March 5, 1883, is unconstitutional; indeed, there would seem to be no room for such a contention. It was recognized as a valid act in the case of *City of Indianapolis* v. *Huegele*, 115 Ind. 581.

It has been so often decided that the state has the right to prescribe the manner of selecting the constabulary, including the police force of a city, that it seems not to be now an open question: *People* v. *Draper*, 15 N. Y. 532; *People* v. *Shepard*, 36 N. Y. 285; *People* v. *Mahaney*, 13 Mich. 481; *State* v. *Covington*, 29 Ohio St. 102; *Police Commissioners* v. *City of Louisville*, 3 Bush, 597; *State* v. *Hunter*, 38 Kan. 578; *Mayor etc.* v. *State*, 15 Md. 376; 74 Am. Dec. 572; *State* v. *Seavey*, 22 Neb. 454.

This right is fully recognized in the case of *City of Evansville* v. *State*, *supra*, and *State* v. *Denny*, *supra*.

The act of 1883, now under consideration, is easily distinguished from the act of 1889, where the state undertook to control the selection of officers in no wise connected with the constabulary, and whose duties were of a local character, affecting local interests and local government. But while it is admitted that the law we are now considering is within the power of the legislature, and that it is not, in its general scope, in conflict with any provision of the state constitution, it is earnestly insisted that certain provisions therein are unconstitutional, and that such provisions are so interwoven with the other provisions of the law as that the whole must fall.

It is quite well settled that where a part of a statute is unconstitutional, if such part is so connected with the other parts as that they mutually depend upon each other as conditions, considerations, or compensations for each other, so as to warrant the belief that the legislature intended them as a whole, and if they could not be carried into effect the legislature would not have passed the residue independently of that which is void, then the whole act must fall: Cooley on Constitutional Limitations, 5th ed., 213; *Meshmeier* v. *State, supra; State* v. *Denny, supra; Griffin* v. *State,* 119 Ind. 520. On the other hand, it is equally well settled, that when a part of a statute is unconstitutional, if, by striking from the act all that part which is void, that which is left is complete in itself, sensible, capable of being executed, and wholly independent of that which is rejected, the courts will reject that which is unconstitutional and enforce the remainder: Cooley on Constitutional Limitations, 5th ed., 178; *Clark* v. *Ellis,* 2 Blackf. 8; *Maize* v. *State,* 4 Ind. 342; *State* v. *Newton,* 59 Ind. 173; *Ingerman* v. *Noblesville Tp.,* 90 Ind. 393.

The question in this case is, therefore, whether we can eliminate from the act of March, 1883, that which is in conflict with the constitution of the state, and enforce the remainder of the law; or, in other words, are the unconstitutional provisions in that act so connected with its other provisions as that they must all stand or fall together?

Under section 1 of the act under consideration, a person to be eligible to the office of police commissioner must be a resident of the city for which he is appointed, for a period of at least three years next before his appointment.

Section 2 provides that the metropolitan police board shall have power to appoint a superintendent of police, captains, sergeants, detectives, and such other officers and patrolmen as they may deem advisable, said captains, sergeants, detectives, and such other officers and patrolmen to be appointed equally between the two leading political parties of said city.

In the case of *Evansville* v. *State,* and *State* v. *Denny, supra,* it was held that provisions similar to those found in this act were in conflict with our state constitution. It was not so held because the legislature had not the power to provide that such officers as police force should be made non-partisan, but it was so held because the act of 1889 was so drawn as to disfranchise all persons who did not belong to one or the other of the two leading political parties. There can be but little doubt as to the power of the legislature to make the constabulary of the state non-partisan, but in doing so it must not disfranchise any considerable body of the electors, as all are, under our form of government, eligible to the elective offices within the gift of the people. That it was the intention of the legislature by the act of March 5, 1883, to remove the selection of the police force of the state from local political influence, and to make it as far as possible non-partisan, there can be no doubt.

Striking out the objectionable features of this law, the remainder is capable of being enforced in such a manner as to fully carry out the objects sought to be attained. By the first section of the act, the commissioners are required to take an oath to the effect that they will not appoint or remove any person on account of his political opinions. If such oath is observed, the police power of the cities, covered by the act, will conform to police power sought to be created by the legislature.

In our opinion, the act of March, 1883, except in so far as herein indicated, is in force, and governs the manner of selecting and controlling the police power of the cities therein named. It follows that the superior court of Vanderburgh County erred in sustaining the demurrer to the imformation in this cause.

Judgment reversed, with instructions to overrule the demurrer to the information, and for further proceedings not inconsistent with this opinion.

————

STATUTES PARTLY VALID AND PARTLY VOID: See note to *State* v. *Deal,* 12 Am. St. Rep. 218, 219. An entire act will not be declared invalid merely because some single section is in conflict with the constitution; but a clause of a statute which, as enacted, is unconstitutional, cannot be changed in meaning so as to give it some operation, when it cannot operate as the legislature intended: *People* v. *Perry,* 79 Cal. 106.

CONSTITUTIONAL LAW. — Section 10 of the metropolitan police act of 1883, of Indiana, is constitutional: *City of Indianapolis* v. *Huegele,* 115 Ind. 581.

CASES

SUPREME COURT

OF

IOWA.

BULL *v.* FULLER.

[78 IOWA, 20.]

EXECUTORS AND ADMINISTRATORS — ADMINISTRATORS IN TWO STATES — PAYMENT TO ONE DISCHARGE AS TO OTHER. — The voluntary payment by the debtor of a debt due a deceased person to his legally authorized administrator in the state of his domicile is a valid discharge as against another administrator of the deceased afterwards appointed in another state, where a note which is the evidence of the debt paid was merely deposited for safe-keeping.

ACTION to recover the amount of a promissory note. Plaintiff, a resident of New York, was named as the executor of Mrs. Hurlbut in her will, made during a temporary residence in that state. The only property she had there was the note in suit, which was deposited with a resident of that state for safe-keeping. She afterwards died at her home in Vermont, and an administrator of her estate was appointed there, while plaintiff was appointed her executor in New York. Defendant, the maker of the note in suit, resided in Iowa, and knew nothing of the will, the New York executor, or that the note was deposited there, and paid the amount of the note to the Vermont administrator, who did not then have, nor has he ever had, possession of the note. Judgment for defendant, and plaintiff appeals.

R. G. Phelps, for the appellant.

Phelps and Temple, for the appellee.

GRANGER, J. Under the foregoing statement, it will be observed that administration is being had on the estate of Mrs.

Hurlbut both in New York and Vermont, and that both administrations are claimed as original, with disputed rights as to the proceeds of the note in suit. The arguments in the case would lead us to determine the dispute as between the respective representatives; not that the administrator in Vermont is a party here, but the argument proceeds upon the theory that there is but one rightful recipient of the proceeds of the note, and if payment is made to another, it is no discharge of the debt. We are not disposed to consider the question of the validity of the appointment of the plaintiff as executor in New York; for we think the case may be disposed of consistently with the validity of both appointments, and we are by no means prepared to say that original administration may not be granted in two states upon the same estate. It is true that Mrs. Hurlbut died in Vermont; and we do not understand appellant to contend but that, as to property other than the note in suit, the administrator in Vermont is the rightful custodian; and as to this note, the claim for administration in New York is based upon the fact that, at the time of Mrs. Hurlbut's death, the note was there. It is a question of some doubt if the mere presence of a note in a state other than the residence of the deceased owner would justify administration there. It is nearer in harmony with the authorities that the residence of the debtor is the property *situs* to justify such proceedings: *Wyman* v. *Halstead*, 109 U. S. 654. This point, however, we do not decide, as cases might arise in which notes, as property, would authorize administration. Our reference to the question here is to avoid any undue inference from the particular facts of this case. With the fact established that administration in Vermont was authorized, and defendant paid the note there before administrative proceedings were adopted in New York, we think the question is clearly settled upon authority. In the case of *Wilkins* v. *Ellett*, 108 U. S. 256, the *syllabus* was prepared by the judge who wrote the opinion, and is as follows: "When a debt due to a deceased person is voluntarily paid by the debtor at his own domicile, in a state in which no administration has been taken out, and in which no creditors or next of kin reside, to an administrator appointed in another state, and the sum paid is inventoried and accounted for by him in that state, the payment is good as against an administrator afterwards appointed in the state in which the payment is made, although this is the state of the domicile of the deceased."

That case is stronger against appellant than the case at bar, as, in that case, the debtor went from the domicile of the deceased and paid the debt, while in this he went to the domicile and made the payment. The court, in the opinion, uses this language: "If a debtor, residing in another state, comes into the state in which the administrator has been appointed, and there pays him, the payment is a valid discharge everywhere." The significance of this language is much aided by the fact that the case is one between administrators of the same estate, deriving their authority from appointments in different states, which, for practical purposes, is the *status* of this case.

This case involves no rights as to third parties. It is purely a question of locality of administration. A payment has been made to an unquestioned administrator, with no other administration at the time pending, and with the note merely deposited in another state for safe-keeping. To allow an estate, under such circumstances, to profit by a double payment of the debt, or to compel a second payment, and require the debtor to seek repayment from the administrator in Vermont, when the money is already in the hands of a representative of the estate, merely in the interest of a double administration, would indeed be a burlesque upon the administration of justice. The money is already in the estate. No citizen in New York claims any interest in this particular property. It is merely a question as to which of two representatives of the estate shall receive it. As to the defendant, that is a matter of no concern. The estate owned the note. It has the money. The defendant should not be required to answer further. We think the defendant's plea of payment is established.

Affirmed.

_____

PAYMENT TO A FOREIGN ADMINISTRATOR is a legal payment of a deposit which, by the by-laws of the bank, was payable to the personal representative of the depositor in the event of his decease: *Schluter* v. *Bowery Savings Bank*, 117 N. Y. 125; 15 Am. St. Rep. 494.

LAW OF THE SITUS PREVAILS OVER THE LAW OF THE DOMICILE as to the order of payment of debts of a decedent, in case his estate is insolvent: *Deringer* v. *Deringer*, 5 Houst. 416; 1 Am. St. Rep. 150.

WIMER v. ALLBAUGH.

[78 IOWA, 79.]

SLANDER — EVIDENCE OF MEANING OF WORDS USED. — Where a petition in slander charges that defendant said of and concerning plaintiff that "she is ornrier than two hells," meaning to charge her with being a whore, the word "ornrier" being of doubtful and uncertain meaning, the intent and meaning of its use as understood by those who heard it may be established by proof, but the testimony of witnesses who did not hear that word used, but heard other words not slanderous in character, is inadmissible to prove their understanding of the word charged.

PLEADING — WAIVER OF INSUFFICIENCY OF. — When an objection to the sufficiency of a petition can be taken by motion or demurrer but is not, and the party answers and proceeds to trial, this constitutes a waiver of the objection, and it cannot be afterwards raised by an instruction to the jury.

IN SLANDER THE AWARDING OF PUNITORY DAMAGES is entirely within the sound discretion of the jury.

IN SLANDER A MALICIOUS ACT MAY BE DEFINED as one done with an evil intent; if a more specific instruction is desired, it must be asked.

JURY TRIAL. — WHEN MORE SPECIFIC INSTRUCTIONS ARE DESIRED than those given, the party must so request, and when this is not done, the court will not, except in cases of manifest prejudice, interfere with the verdict.

Newman and Blake, and R. Caldwell, for the appellant.

Arthur Springer, D. N. Sprague, and E. W. Tatlock, for the appellee.

GRANGER, J.   The petition charges, in substance, that the defendant said of and concerning the plaintiff, "She is a whore"; and "She is ornrier than two hells, and I can prove it," — meaning to charge her with being a whore.

1. On the trial the following testimony was given on behalf of plaintiff by her sister Sadie: "On January 1, 1887, defendant said to my sister Rosa, that she was ornrier than two hells. I was present, and heard it at the time. Question: I will ask you to state, Sadie, what you understood him to charge by that. Answer: I understood by the language used that he meant them words against our character; that we was unchaste. I understood him to mean by that that Rosa was an unchaste woman." Substantially the same testimony was given by plaintiff and Amanda Grant, against the objections of the defendant, and the rulings are assigned as error. It is charged in the petition that in using the expression defendant meant to charge plaintiff with being a whore. The words themselves do not signify that. Without explanation, we regard them of very uncertain meaning. Consider-

able is said in argument as to the word "ornery." It has not such a place in the English language that any lexicographer has ventured to define it, or give it authoritative recognition. It has much of the impress of a provincialism. Its use seems to be peculiar to certain localities of people. People generally have heard the word used, and know something of its import. While it is a word used to express kind or quality, it is not alone applicable to persons. It is doubtless never used to express good qualities. Its use is generally to express the opposite. It does not, in some of its uses, differ from the word "common" or "mean." Substitute either of these words in the expression charged, and the legal *status* would not be materially different; and in such a case there could be no question as to the right of the party to prove what the understanding of the hearers was. In such cases the expressions are ambiguous. They may have one meaning or another, and the intent and understanding must be established by proof: *McLaughlin* v. *Bascom*, 38 Iowa, 660, and cases there cited.

2. The defendant's wife and one Ellen Mulhern were sworn for the defendant, and defendant asked of each, in substance, if they understood any language used by Mr. Allbaugh to import a want of chastity. The question was objected to as leading and incompetent, and the objection was sustained. The argument of appellant is, that if the understanding of plaintiff's witnesses was material, that of the defendant's would be. The reasoning is certainly good, if the circumstances are the same. The witnesses for the plaintiff testified that they heard the speaking of the words charged, and of their understanding of them. The witnesses for the defendant each say they did not hear the words, but heard other words, which would in no sense constitute a cause of action. They could not, of course, testify as to their understanding of the words charged, for they did not hear them. It is not competent to prove an understanding as to other words.

3. The defendant asked the court to give to the jury the following instruction, which was refused: "The court instructs the jury that to say of a woman or girl that 'she is ornrier than two hells,' will not warrant the innuendo, meaning, or construction that she is a prostitute, although you may find, from the evidence, that the defendant did speak of and concerning the plaintiff the above words. Then, upon that branch of the case, you are instructed that the plaintiff cannot recover, and you will find for the defendant." Of this refusal the defend-

ant complains. The instruction merely presents a question as to the sufficiency of the pleading. The point urged was as manifest on the face of the petition before answer as after the taking of the testimony. If the objection could have been taken by motion, or demurrer to the petition, and was not, and the party answered and proceeded to trial, it was a waiver of the objection, and cannot afterwards be raised by an instruction to the jury: Code, sec. 2650; *Great Western Printing Co.* v. *Tucker*, 73 Iowa, 755; *McIntire* v. *McIntire*, 48 Iowa, 511.

4. Complaint is made of the following instruction given by the court: "Damages in cases of this sort are of two classes, —compensatory and punitory. The former are such as are awarded to compensate the injured party for the injury caused by the wrong, and must be only such as make just and fair compensation, and are due when the wrong is established, whether it was committed maliciously — that is, with an evil intention—or not. Punitory damages are such as may be awarded only when the wrong is shown to be malicious, and are to be assessed by the jury in their sound discretion, without bias or feeling, according to the malignity shown, and in such reasonable sum as will tend to prevent future evils of like kind and degree."

Several criticisms are urged against the instructions, as follows: 1. "It does not tell the jury that they shall or shall not consider the question of exemplary damages." It had no right to so tell the jury. It was with the jury a discretionary matter. 2. It is urged that the word "malicious" was not defined by the court. The instruction seems to define a malicious act as one done with evil intent. If more was desired, it should have been asked. The term is not a technical one, but a word of frequent and general use, and commonly understood. 3. Complaint is made as to the court's failure to more specifically instruct as to the measure of actual damage. There is an instruction as to the measure of such damage, and, so far as it goes, it is not erroneous. It would be better if more specific. Generally, where the court instructs upon a question, and a party desires it more specific, he should ask it, that the court may know of his wishes before verdict, and grant or refuse his request. Where this is not done, the court will not, except in cases of manifest prejudice, interfere. We have noticed the errors assigned and argued, and see no reason why we should disturb the judgment below.

Affirmed.

SLANDER — EXEMPLARY DAMAGES. — Where actual malice is shown in an action of slander, the jury may always give exemplary damages: *Newman* v. *Stein,* 75 Mich. 402; 13 Am. St. Rep. 447, and note. As to when exemplary or punitive damages may be awarded in actions for slander, see cases cited in note to *Reeves* v. *Winn,* 2 Am. St. Rep. 289; note to *Terwilliger* v. *Wands,* 72 Am. Dec. 426 et seq.

SLANDER — EVIDENCE. — In an action for slander, the whole conversation is admissible, so long as it constituted one transaction, and led up to the words charged as slanderous in the declaration: *Newman* v. *Stein,* 75 Mich. 402; 13 Am. St. Rep. 447. As to how far the testimony of witnesses is admissible regarding their impressions relative to the meaning and application of the words used, see note to *Van Vechten* v. *Hopkins,* 4 Am. Dec. 352–354. Words having a covert, ambiguous, or uncertain meaning may be alleged and proved to have been used with intent to defame, and to have been understood in a particular sense by those to whom they were published or spoken: *Maynard* v. *Fireman's F. Ins. Co.,* 34 Cal. 48; 91 Am. Dec. 672, and note 681; citing *Chamberlin* v. *Vance,* 51 Cal. 84, and *Nidever* v. *Hall,* 67 Cal. 83.

SLANDER AND LIBEL — "MALICE" DEFINED. — Malice means a want of legal excuse: Note to *Terwilliger* v. *Wands,* 72 Am. Dec. 429, 430; *Maynard* v. *Fireman's F. Ins. Co.,* 34 Cal. 48; 91 Am. Dec. 672, and note.

LIBEL AND SLANDER. — Where words amount to a libelous charge against some person, but it is left uncertain as to whether or not plaintiff is the person libeled, such application may be shown by proof of extrinsic facts, and such extrinsic facts need not be alleged in the complaint: *Petsch* v. *Dispatch etc. Co.,* 40 Minn. 291. So where libelous or slanderous words, written or spoken about one, are read or heard by persons conversant with the facts, it is competent to show by their testimony who, in their opinion, was referred to by the language used: *Prosser* v. *Callis,* 117 Ind. 105. But where, in an action for slandering a plaintiff, the words averred to be slanderous are ambiguous, it must be left to the jury to determine under the circumstances what meaning was intended by defendant in using the alleged slanderous words: *Reeves* v. *Bowden,* 97 N. C. 29.

WAIVER OF OBJECTION TO PETITION. — An objection available by way of demurrer or answer is deemed waived, unless so taken advantage of in apt time: *Silver Valley Mining Co.* v. *Baltimore etc. Co.,* 99 N. C. 445.

ELLSWORTH *v.* RANDALL.

[78 IOWA, 141.]

VENDOR AND VENDEE — RESCISSION OF CONTRACT TO CONVEY — FRAUDULENT REPRESENTATIONS. — Where a contract for the sale of land is made by a vendor, through the agents of the vendee, and upon their false representations that the vendee is another than the true purchaser, the vendor may, upon discovering the falsity of the representations, rescind the contract upon repayment or tender of the purchase-money received.

TAX SALE — RECOVERY OF AMOUNT PAID. — Mere volunteer who redeems land sold for delinquent taxes is not entitled to recover the amount paid.

ACTION for the specific performance of an agreement for the sale and conveyance of lands. Judgment for defendant. Plaintiff appeals.

W. S. Palmer, for the appellant.

Pitts and Kessey, for the appellee.

ROBINSON, J. 1. Appellant claims that he entered into a valid agreement for the purchase of a quarter-section of land described in the petition, by virtue of certain correspondence had with defendant, White B. Randall, carried on in behalf of plaintiff by his agents, Lewis and Dodge. Defendant denies that a valid agreement of sale was entered into, and alleges that said agents represented that they were seeking to obtain the conveyance in controversy for certain persons who held a tax title to the land; that any agreement on his part was made with the understanding that such representations were true; and that they were in fact false. On the sixth day of October, 1885, Lewis and Dodge wrote defendant that they had an offer of one hundred and fifty dollars for his title to the land, and asked if they should prepare and send him papers. On the nineteenth day of the same month defendant wrote the agents, that "if they will give me one hundred and fifty dollars, besides your cost, I will give them the Randall claims on the land." He also wrote them to send the necessary papers, including a blank deed, to him to be executed by the heirs of a former owner of the land. The deeds were sent as requested, with a form of an affidavit as to the insanity and death of the former owner, and directions as to the execution of the papers. A draft for twenty-five dollars, "to show the good faith of the party," was also inclosed. November 2, 1885, defendant acknowledged receipt of the letter, with its inclosures, and suggested a change in the affidavit, and that, if it could be made, he thought the parties could agree. He also stated that he would deposit the draft in bank until the matter was arranged, and if the agreement was not made he would return the money. November 6, 1885, Lewis and Dodge wrote defendant, waiving that part of the affidavit to which objection had been made, and inclosing a new form. December 5, 1885, defendant wrote Lewis and Dodge as follows: "You may begin to think that I am rather slow about getting that matter settled; but I have not been able to get around to all of the heirs yet, but will soon. Everything is favorable, though. I will be able to get the papers to you by the 1st of January, I think, without any doubt. So if you will be a little patient, all right." In answer to that letter the agents wrote: "If you get the papers around by January 1st, as proposed, it will not inconvenience us." That is the portion of the correspondence upon which plaintiff relies as constituting the agreement of which he asks a specific performance. Whether, if considered alone, it would constitute an agreement which could be enforced, we need not determine.

It is shown that on the twenty-second day of June, 1885, defendant wrote to Lewis and Dodge, asking for information in regard to the land in question; that on the tenth day of August, 1885, they wrote to one Harden, as attorney for Moser Brothers, who held the tax title, to ascertain what they would give for the Randall title; that considerable correspondence between Lewis and Dodge and Harden followed, but without resulting in an offer to purchase on the part of the Mosers. The last letter of that correspondence appears to have been written by Harden on the twenty-third day of October, 1885. It informed Lewis and Dodge, in effect, that when it was shown that the Randall claim was a cloud on the tax title, parties interested in that title would be ready to negotiate. It appears that Lewis and Dodge were authorized to act as agents for plaintiff; but the extent of their agency is not clearly shown. It does not appear when, if ever, plaintiff authorized them to purchase the Randall title for him; but he testifies that all their acts in his behalf in the matter in controversy, performed after October 6, 1885, are approved. Lewis and Dodge had been instrumental in selling to Moser Brothers the tax title under which they claim. August 3, 1885, they wrote defendant that they had written the attorney of the tax-title owner in regard to the Randall title. September 2, 1885, they wrote to defendant that they had heard from the attorney. After making some suggestions as to the title, they state: "We sold the land to the present owner, and have an interest in getting it fixed up." September 14, 1885, they wrote defendant as follows: "Your favor of eighth inst. at hand, and noted. Requested him to wire me if he wanted the claim, so I could wire you before the nineteenth, at your request. I think, probably, he will take it, although I am not certain. Will let you know as soon as heard from." We do not find the letter to which that was an answer, but from the dates conclude that the Harden correspondence was referred to.

It appears that when the correspondence with defendant was commenced, Lewis and Dodge expected to induce Moser Brothers to purchase the Randall title, and, in substance, so informed him; but when they refused to make an offer, Lewis and Dodge submitted a proposition to purchase, but without disclosing the fact that it was not made on behalf of the owners of the tax title. When the deeds were sent to defendant for execution he supposed the grantee named was the tax-title owner. When he discovered that plaintiff was not the person for whom the agents represented that they were acting, he had the right to refuse to complete the contract, if one had been made, and his reason for so doing is not material. It is urged by appellant that an agreement has been clearly established; that in making the sale, defendant only desired to get the largest sum possible for his interest; that he was in fact indifferent as to the grantee, and that his interests were not prejudiced by the change. But it was the right of defendant to select his grantee: *Knight* v. *Cooley*, 34 Iowa, 221. He gave to Lewis and Dodge no general authority to sell, but, at most, accepted an offer which he had been induced to believe was made by the tax-title owner, and was under no obligation to convey to another.

2. Complaint is made of the action of the district court in not allowing a recovery for the twenty-five dollars paid to defendant by Lewis and Dodge. A member of that firm visited defendant at his home in Michigan, and there tendered him one hundred and twenty-five dollars, and demanded for plaintiff a conveyance of the land in controversy. Defendant refused the tender, and offered to return the twenty-five dollars, but the agent declined to receive it. This action was, in fact, commenced two days before the aforesaid tender and demand on the part of the plaintiff were made. The petition alleges the payment of the twenty-five dollars, and demands general equitable relief; but there was no controversy over the fact that payment had been made as charged. Appellee expresses a willingness to refund the money; but in view of the circumstances of this case, it would be inequitable to allow appellant costs on account of it. He will, therefore, be allowed to take judgment for twenty-five dollars, without costs.

3. Plaintiff has redeemed the land in controversy from a sale made for the delinquent taxes of 1876, and complains of the refusal of the district court to allow him the amount of money paid to redeem. But plaintiff has failed to show such an interest in or claim to the land as authorized him to redeem. In making redemption he acted as a mere volunteer, and is not entitled to recover for the amount paid.

4. Other questions discussed by counsel are not material to

a determination of this cause, and therefore need not be decided. With the modification specified, the judgment of the district court is affirmed.

RESCISSION OF CONTRACT — FRAUDULENT REPRESENTATIONS. — A grantor cannot avoid a transfer on account of a fraudulent purpose on the part of the grantee, if he had notice of the facts and circumstances from which such purpose is inferred: *Arnold* v. *Hagerman*, 45 N. J. Eq. 186; 14 Am. St. Rep. 712, and note as to the right of rescinding a contract. For false representations for which a contract may be rescinded, see note to *Lawrence* v. *Gayetty*, 12 Am. St. Rep. 36, 37; note to *Williams* v. *McFadden*, 11 Id. 350, 351.

MONEY PAID FOR THE REDEMPTION OF LANDS sold for illegal taxes, to prevent the issuance of a deed to a purchaser, cannot be recovered back: Note to *Baltimore* v. *Lefferman*, 45 Am. Dec. 165, 166; note to *Peters* v. *R. R. Co.*, 51 Am. Rep. 823, 824. Money voluntarily paid, not in ignorance of facts, cannot be recovered back: *Gould* v. *McFall*, 118 Pa. St. 455; 4 Am. St. Rep. 606, and particularly note. Compare *Cox* v. *Welcher*, 68 Mich. 263; 13 Am. St. Rep. 339, and note.

McCANDLESS v. BELLE PLAINE CANNING CO.

[78 Iowa, 161.]

NEGOTIABLE INSTRUMENTS — PROMISSORY NOTE — EVIDENCE TO SHOW CAPACITY IN WHICH PERSONS SIGN. — A promissory note in the ordinary form, reading "we promise to pay," and signed "Belle Plaine Canning Co., A. J. Hartman, President, H. Wessel, Secretary," in the absence of a clause showing the capacity in which the parties signed, binds all the persons signing, including the corporation, and extrinsic evidence is inadmissible to show the intention of the parties who signed the note.

George C. Scrimgeour, and Gilchrist and Whipple, for the appellants.

J. J. Mosnat and J. D. Nichols, for the appellee.

ROTHROCK, J. The note upon which the action was founded is in these words:—

"$1,500.   BELLE PLAINE, Iowa, July 21, 1884.

"One year after date, we promise to pay to Eliza J. McCandless, or order, at the law office of J. J. Mosnat, in Belle Plaine, Iowa, the sum of fifteen hundred dollars, for value received, with interest thereon at the rate of seven per cent per annum, payable annually. Should any of the interest not be paid when due, it shall become a part of the principal, and bear interest at the rate of ten per cent per annum. If this note is not paid when due, and suit is brought hereon, the holder shall be entitled to recover reasonable attorney's fees

therefor; and all indorsers and guarantors of this note hereby
severally waive demand and notice of non-payment.

"Belle Plaine Canning Co.

"A. J. Hartman, President.

"H. Wessel, Secretary."

The Belle Plaine Canning Company, defendant, is a corporation. No defense was made in its behalf, and judgment was
rendered against it by default. The defendants Wessel and
Hartman claimed that they were not liable upon the note, because they signed the same, not as individuals, but for and in
behalf of the Belle Plaine Canning Company. A number of
witnesses were introduced upon the trial, and their testimony
was taken as to what occurred when the note was given, in
the way of explanation of the signatures of said Wessel and
Hartman, and which testimony tended to show that said
defendants signed the note in their official capacity, and not
otherwise. And there was evidence tending to show that the
plaintiff believed, when she received the note, that said defendants were makers thereof as individuals. The plaintiff testified that, before the note was executed, she asked Wessel
what security he would give, and he replied that he would
give his own name and Hartman's name on the note. After
the evidence was all introduced, the court, on motion of the
plaintiff, directed the jury to return a verdict against the defendants for the amount of the note.

The question to be determined on this appeal is, whether the
court erred in directing the verdict. In the case of *Heffner*
v. *Brownell*, 70 Iowa, 591, the promissory note upon which
the suit was brought was in substantially the same form
as the note in the suit at bar. It was a note purporting to be
signed by a corporation, and by " B. I. Brownell, President,"
and " D. B. Sanford, Secretary." It was held that the note
on its face purported to bind all the persons who executed it,
including the corporation. The judgment was reversed, and
the cause remanded for a new trial. The defendant Brownell
thereupon filed an answer, in which he alleged that the note
sued on was the note of the corporation alone, and that it was
given for an indebtedness of the corporation alone; that said
defendant was president and D. B. Sanford was secretary of
the corporation, and it was their duty, under its by-laws,
to execute in its name all contracts entered into by it; that, in
pursuance of that authority, they signed the note, intending
to bind the company only, which facts were well known to

plaintiff at the time, and that he accepted it with the understanding that the company alone was to be bound. There was a demurrer to this answer, which was overruled, and the cause was again appealed to this court, and we held that the demurrer should have been sustained upon the ground that extrinsic evidence was not admissible to show the intention of the parties who signed the note: *McCormick H. M. Co.* v. *Gates,* 75 Iowa, 343. We discover no good reason for not following the opinions in that case; and, as the question here presented is the same, the judgment in this case must be affirmed.

PRINCIPAL AND AGENT. — A note signed "S. G. D., Agent," must be treated as the note of S. G. D., and parol evidence is inadmissible to show that it is the note of another person: *Tarver* v. *Garlington,* 27 S. C. 107; 13 Am. St. Rep. 628, and particularly note 631, 632. But whether the true relation of the parties to a note is that of principal or surety may be shown by parol evidence: *Chapeze* v. *Young,* 87 Ky. 476; *First N. Bank* v. *Gaines,* 87 Ky. 597.

MILLER *v.* MILLER.
[78 IOWA, 177.]

HUSBAND AND WIFE — CONTRACT BETWEEN RELATING TO MARITAL RELATIONS, WHEN VOID. — A contract between husband and wife, by which the wife agrees to faithfully observe and perform the duties imposed upon her by her marital relations, and by which the husband agrees to provide the necessary expenses of the family, and to pay the wife for her individual use a certain sum annually in monthly payments, so long as she faithfully keeps the terms and conditions of the contract, is against public policy and void.

Cole, McVey, and Clark, for the appellant.

C. P. Holmes, for the appellee.

ADAMS, C. J. The contract sued upon is in these words: "This agreement, made this fifth day of August, 1885, between the undersigned, husband and wife, in the interests of peace, and for the best interests of each other and of their family, is signed in good faith by each party, with the promise, each to the other, and to their children, that they will each honestly promise to help each other to observe and keep the same, which is as follows, to wit: All past causes and subjects of dispute, disagreement, and complaint, of whatever character or kind, shall be absolutely ignored and buried, and no allusion thereto by word or talk to each other or any one else shall ever be made. Each party agrees to refrain from scolding, fault-finding, and anger, in so far as relates to the future, and to use every means within their power to promote peace and harmony, and that each shall behave respectfully, and fairly treat each other; that Mrs. Miller shall keep her home and family in a comfortable and reasonably good condition, and Mr. Miller shall provide for the necessary expenses of the family, and shall, in addition thereto, pay Mrs. Miller, for her individual use, two hundred dollars per year, payable sixteen and two thirds dollars per month, in advance, so long as Mrs. Miller shall faithfully observe the terms and conditions of their contract. They agree to live together as husband and wife, and observe faithfully the marriage relation, and each to live virtuously with the other."

The petition demurred to is quite long. We cannot set it out. The defendant demurred upon the ground that it showed the contract to be without consideration and against public policy. His position is that the plaintiff merely agreed to do what by law she was bound to do. The majority think that the defendant's position must be sustained. The writer of this opinion is not able to concur in that view. The petition sets out several reasons and inducements for making the contract. Among other things, it avers, in substance, that the defendant, while improperly spending money upon other women, refused to furnish the plaintiff with necessary clothing, and she had been compelled to furnish it herself by her personal earnings. This the demurrer admits. It appears to the writer, then, that the plaintiff had the right to separate from the defendant, and go where she could best provide for her wants. This right she waived in consideration of the defendant's contract sued upon. The waiver of the right, it seems to the writer, constituted a consideration for the contract; but as the majority think otherwise, the judgment must be affirmed.

ON REHEARING.

GRANGER, J. Since the former hearing of this case, a majority of the members of this court have retired and others are substituted, and of those retired are Adams, J., and Seevers, J., who did not concur in the former holding. The former opinion, prepared by Chief Justice Adams, states in general terms the conclusion of the majority, and very briefly expresses some reasons for the dissent. One reason for granting the rehearing is that the views of the court may be expressed in support of its conclusions, whatever they may be.

The action is by a wife against her husband, to recover on a contract, which is in the following words: "This agreement, made this fifth day of August, 1885, between the undersigned, husband and wife, in the interest of peace, and for the best interests of each other and of their family, is signed in good faith by each party, with the promise, each to the other, and to their children, that they will each honestly promise to help each other to observe and keep the same, which is as follows, to wit: All past subjects and causes of dispute, disagreement, and complaint, of whatever character or kind, shall be absolutely ignored and buried, and no allusion thereto by word or talk to each other or any one else shall ever be made. Each party agrees to refrain from scolding, fault-finding, and anger, in so far as relates to the future, and to use every means within their power to promote peace and harmony; that each shall behave respectfully, and fairly treat the other; that Mrs. Miller shall keep her home and family in a comfortable and reasonably good condition, and Mr. Miller shall provide for the necessary expenses of the family, and shall, in addition thereto, pay Mrs. Miller, for her individual use, two hundred dollars per year, payable sixteen and two thirds dollars per month, in advance, so long as Mrs. Miller shall faithfully observe the terms and conditions of this agreement. They agree to live together as husband and wife, and observe faithfully the marriage relations, and each to live virtuously with the other." The petition recites the contract, avers a breach of its conditions for payment of the monthly installments, and asks for judgment.

The petition is assailed by demurrer on two grounds: 1. That the contract for the payment of the money is void as against public policy; and 2. That it is not supported by a consideration. The district court sustained the demurrer, and the plaintiff, relying upon her petition, appeals from a judgment against her.

1. The theory upon which appellant seeks to escape the force of the claim that this contract is against public policy is, that the agreement to pay the yearly or monthly amounts is but a post-nuptial settlement of such amount in favor of the wife, and therefore sanctioned by law. We must consider the averments of the petition in the light of the contract, which is the basis of recovery, and statements of the petition

not in harmony with a right of recovery on the contract are not well pleaded, and are not admitted by the demurrer.

We think it important to first settle the question, For what is the plaintiff entitled to recover, if at all? The contract is decisive of this question, and, for the purposes of the demurrer, will override any opposing statements of the petition. The contract recites that "Mr. Miller shall provide for the necessary expenses of the family, and shall, in addition thereto, pay Mrs. Miller, for her individual use, two hundred dollars per year, payable sixteen and two thirds dollars per month, in advance, so long as Mrs. Miller shall faithfully observe the terms and conditions of their contract." Whatever may have induced the making of the contract, one thing is certain, — the ground of recovery from time to time is a faithful observance of the contract. If payment of the amounts is enforced, this observance must be pleaded, and if denied, it must become a matter of judicial inquiry. Now, looking to the contract, we find that the plaintiff has agreed to do just what is demanded by her marital relations and is essential to domestic felicity. If she does this, under the letter of her contract, she may recover; if she does not, she cannot recover. Conceding, for the purpose of this branch of the case, that the contract is supported by a consideration independent of her promise therein, and looking exclusively to the question, Is its enforcement against public policy? we may properly ask, does it not contain all the objectionable features of a contract, confessedly with no other consideration than a promise to observe marital duties, or in other words, to do what, without the contract, the law required her to do? Now, if a husband and wife, without any domestic discord to serve as an inducement to such a contract, should make an agreement that the husband should pay to the wife, monthly, a stated sum, merely because of her observance of an agreement not to scold, find fault, or get angry, and to use every means in her power to promote peace and harmony, and behave respectfully towards her husband, would the court, upon a refusal by the husband, compel a payment? We think not, nor do we think counsel would seriously contend, in such a case, that it should; for the reason that judicial inquiry into matters of that character, between husband and wife, would be fraught with irreparable mischief, and forbidden by sound considerations of public policy.

It is of the genius of our laws, as well as of our civilization, that matters pertaining so directly and exclusively to the home, and its value as such, and which are so generally susceptible of regulation and control by those influences which surround it, are not to become matters of public concern or inquiry. This thought has vindication throughout our system of jurisprudence. The marital obligations of husband and wife in the interest of homes, both happy and useful, have a higher and stronger inducement than mere money consideration, and they are generally of a character that the judgments or processes of the courts cannot materially aid, and are clearly so in the case we have supposed. We are not referred to, nor do we find, a case wherein a recovery has been justified on a contract of this character. It is to be kept in mind that public policy is not against the payment of money, if it is done voluntarily; but the evil which the law anticipates arises from the enforcement of such a contract, which, if legal, should of course be enforceable. Now, the inquiry is, keeping in view the question of public policy, how does the case at bar differ from the supposed case? It is said in argument that in this case the husband had been guilty of such conduct as to justify the wife in leaving him, and would have been entitled to a separate support, and it was because of this contract that she consented to live with defendant, and that the amount was settled upon the wife in pursuance of the agreement. Stripped of the conditions upon which payment is to be made, such a contract might not be questioned.

The enforcement of this contract as to payments involves an inquiry into just the facts which we have been urging as against public policy. The payments are to be made " so long as Mrs. Miller shall faithfully observe the terms and conditions of their contract." If, then, she seeks to compel payment, she must do so by averring her compliance in general terms, and the husband may answer, putting in issue the facts; and then follows the inquiry if at some time she did not scold or find fault. Was she not at some time angry? Has she kept the family in a comfortable condition? Now, as before stated, the enforcement of this contract is just as dependent upon the inquiry into such facts as would be the supposed case, and exactly the same evil consequences flow therefrom. It needs no argument to show that such inquiries in public would strike at the very foundations of domestic life and happiness. Public policy dictates that the door of such inquiries shall be closed; that parties shall not contract in such a manner as to make such inquiries essential to their enforcement. What element could be introduced into a family that would tend more directly to breed discord than this contract? A failure to pay from any cause not her fault renders the husband liable to judgment, and this from month to month, or from year to year. No misfortune frees him from this obligation, save that of the loss or misconduct of his wife. In the very nature of things, a demand for such a payment would engender ill feelings and provoke complaints as to conduct that would otherwise pass unnoticed, or at least without attention. An effort at compulsory payment would almost certainly bring before the courts allegations of misconduct, based upon incidents of little moment, to be magnified or belittled in the interest of success in court.

Mr. Bishop, in his work on contracts, speaking of the enforcement of contracts for services by the wife to the husband, treats, in part only, of what might be expected on the trial of issues of fact in the case at bar, when he says: "If the wife spends an afternoon in visiting her mother instead of making jellies, shall the husband bring her into court, to determine the abatement to be made from the sum he had promised her for work in keeping his boarding-house? Shall there be a lawsuit to settle the allowance for tending the baby, which is partly his and partly hers? If her washing is sent to a laundress, and her clothes had been soiled in part in doing his work, and in part in doing her own, and in part in tending the baby of both, shall the judge of a court be employed in instructing the jury how to adjust the account between them?" Sec. 948. When we think of the thousand occurrences of life to provoke an unpleasant word, to stimulate anger or a word of fault-finding, and think of the circumstances in domestic life from which they may arise, we can best understand the character of the inquiries likely to arise in the enforcement of the contract in the case at bar. That which should be a sealed book of family history must be opened for public inspection and inquiry. The law, except in cases of necessity will not justify it.

The cases to which we are referred by appellant are unlike this as to their facts. The case of *Adams* v. *Adams*, 91 N. Y. 381, 43 Am. Rep. 675, is where a suit for divorce was pending, and the suit was settled and dismissed by the plaintiff, she condoning his offense of adultery, and returning to live with him, he giving his note in settlement. The note was held valid. We have not held in this case, that if the plaintiff was seeking to recover on an absolute promise to pay because of any consideration, the contract would not be good, nor do we hold that it would. We only say now, that, with the conditions of this contract as to payments, its enforcement is against public policy.

2. The other question presented by the demurrer is as to the contract having for its support a consideration. With our holding on the other branch of the case, it is not necessary for us to determine this, and we do not. In our treatment of the case we have assumed, for the purpose of argument, that there was a consideration to support it. That assumption was only for argument, and is not to be taken as our judgment upon the question.

Affirmed.

HUSBAND AND WIFE. — What contracts are and what are not valid when between a husband and wife, see note to *Kantrowitz* v. *Prather*, 99 Am. Dec. 599, 600; note to *Turner* v. *Shaw*, 9 Am. St. Rep. 323–326.

CONTRACTS BY A WIFE TO SUPPORT HER HUSBAND, based upon the consideration of conveyances to her of real estate, are void: *Corcoran* v. *Corcoran*, 119 Ind. 138; 12 Am. St. Rep. 390. For the law requires that the husband shall provide a reasonable support to his wife according to her station in life; and such support includes not merely food and clothing, but such comforts and surroundings as are necessary and reasonable for home enjoyment in the society in which she lives: *Thill* v. *Pohlman*, 76 Iowa, 638; and at common law, a wife's earnings and services belong to her husband so long as they live together as man and wife: Note to *Bailey* v. *Gardner*, 13 Am. St. Rep. 859; *Ulrich* v. *Arnold*, 120 Pa. St. 170; *Bangs* v. *Edwards*, 88 Ala. 382.

FOSTER *v.* REID AND GARDNER.

[78 IOWA, 205.]

LANDLORD AND TENANT—SUBTENANT BOUND BY TERMS OF HIS LESSOR'S LEASE. — A subtenant, with knowledge that his lessor is a tenant, is chargeable with notice of and is bound by the terms of the lease by which he held. Therefore, where the tenant's lease gives the landlord a lien upon crops grown upon the leased premises for unpaid rent, such lien extends to crops grown by the subtenant.

LANDLORD AND TENANT—ENFORCEMENT OF LANDLORD'S LIEN—INTERVENTION OF SUBTENANT—BURDEN OF PROOF. — In an action by a landlord to enforce his lien for unpaid rent, a plea of intervention by the subtenant, alleging that no rent is due, and that the action is collusive and fraudulent as between the landlord and the tenant, places the burden of proof upon the subtenant to prove his allegations.

ACTION by M. L. Foster to enforce a landlord's lien for unpaid rent against his tenant, G. W. Criner. Reid and Gardner, the subtenants of Criner, filed a petition in intervention,
claiming part of the crops levied upon. Judgment for plaintiff, and the intervenors appeal.

James McCabe, for the appellants.

C. S. Keenan, for the appellee.

ROBINSON, J. Appellants were subtenants of Criner as to a
portion of the premises leased to him for the year 1887. They
knew that he held the premises under a lease from plaintiff,
but claim to have been ignorant of its terms. That lease was
for the term of four years from the first day of March, 1885,
and provided that Criner should pay a rental of two hundred
dollars on the first day of March of each year. It also provided that the premises leased should not be sublet, neither
in whole nor in part, without the written consent of lessor, and
that she should have a "lien for rent at any time remaining
unpaid" upon certain personal property of Criner, and upon
all "crops to be grown."

1. Appellants claim that the proof does not show that plaintiff is entitled to the corn in controversy. The lease from
plaintiff to Criner was proven, and admitted in evidence.
The judgment against Criner was *prima facie* evidence of the
amount due thereon, and was not in any manner attacked.
Intervenors, having knowledge that their lessor was a tenant
of plaintiff, were chargeable with knowledge of the terms by
which he held, and are bound by them. Criner's lease gave
to plaintiff a lien upon crops grown upon the leased premises
"for rent at any time remaining unpaid": *Fejavary* v. *Broesch,*
52 Iowa, 88; 35 Am. Rep. 261.

2. The petition of intervention alleges that nothing was due
to plaintiff from Criner; that any indebtedness which had existed had been paid; and that the action against Criner was
prosecuted through collusion between him and plaintiff to defraud his creditors, and to wrongfully appropriate the property
of intervenor. The burden of proof as to these allegations was
upon intervenors, but they fail to sustain them by evidence
sufficient to authorize the court to submit the issues they tendered to the jury. The corn in controversy was raised upon
the leased premises, and by the terms of the lease to Criner,
is subject to a lien for the unpaid rent. Intervenors failed to

introduce evidence which even tended to show that it was exempt from such lien, and the action of the court in directing a
verdict for the plaintiff was correct. Its judgment is therefore
affirmed.

———

LANDLORD AND TENANT. — ASSIGNMENT OF LEASES, and the respective rights
and liabilities of the parties thereafter: See extended note to *Washington Nat.
G. Co.* v. *Johnson*, 10 Am. St. Rep. 557–565.

LANDLORD AND TENANT. — Distinction between assignment of lease and
subletting: See note to *Post* v. *Kearney*, 51 Am. Dec. 306, 307.

LANDLORD AND TENANT. — As to the remedies of a lessor against a sublessee, see note to *Fulton* v. *Stuart*, 15 Am. Dec. 544, 545.

BURDEN OF PROOF ORDINARILY IS CAST UPON THE PARTY who substantially asserts the burden of the issue: Note to *Oldham* v. *Kerchner*, 28 Am.
Rep. 308, 309; *Elkinton* v. *Brick*, 44 N. J. Eq. 154; *Bullock* v. *Rouse*, 81 Cal.
591; *Sedgwick* v. *Taylor*, 84 Va. 820; *Brown* v. *Scott*, 87 Ala. 453; or, as the
rule has been otherwise stated, "the burden of proof in the whole action lies
upon the party who would be defeated if no evidence were given on either
side ": *Royal Ins. Co.* v. *Schwing*, 87 Ky. 410.

Thus, where a plaintiff seeks to have a deed canceled for fraudulent representations, it devolves upon him to prove that he was induced by such
fraudulent representations to execute the deed: *Severance* v. *Ash*, 81 Me. 278.
And where the bonds of a city are issued since the present constitution of
Illinois took effect, in payment of a subscription in aid of a railroad company,
under a vote of the people had before that time, the burden rests upon those
affirming the validity of the bonds to show that they were lawfully issued:
Eddy v. *People*, 127 Ill. 428. So where in a suit for a failure to perform a
contract wherein defendant had agreed to sink a shaft five hundred feet "on
the vein of ore cropping out on said claim," it is shown that the shaft was
stopped within the stipulated five hundred feet, the burden of proof rests
upon defendant to show that the vein of ore, along which the shaft was to
proceed, had terminated: *Woodworth* v. *McLean*, 97 Mo. 325. And when, in
a proceeding under the statute for the trial of the right of property to goods,
the return of the sheriff does not disclose the fact of who had possession of
the property when found by a writ of attachment, the burden of proving
that the goods were in possession of the defendant in attachment is upon the
plaintiff: *Bonz* v. *Schneider*, 69 Tex. 128. The burden is upon a mining claimant, who claims a quartz ledge under a location made within the limits of a
town site after the date of the town-site patent, to prove that the ledge was
known to be valuable for mining purposes within the boundaries of the town
lot in controversy at the date of the patent, or before its improvement for
residence under the town-site title: *Richards* v. *Dower*, 81 Cal. 45. In an
action by an indorsee upon a promissory note which was obtained from the
maker by fraud, the burden is upon the plaintiff to show that he is a *bona
fide* holder of the note: *Giberson* v. *Jolley*, 120 Ind. 301; and to the same effect
is *Lincoln Nat. Bank* v. *Davis*, 25 Neb. 376. Where a city, being sued for injury from its defective sidewalk, relies upon the defense of contributory negligence, the burden of proof lies upon it to prove such contributory negligence:
Gordon v. *Richmond*, 83 Va. 436.

But the burden of proof may sometimes shift. Thus, where it is shown that
undue influence existed in obtaining the execution of a will, and the mind of

one was reduced to a state of vassalage to the mind of another, and a gift was made by the former to the latter, then the burden of proof will be shifted. The gift will be presumed to be void, and the burden of upholding its fairness will rest upon the recipient of the gift: *Gay* v. *Gillilan*, 92 Mo. 250. But in *Starratt* v. *Mullen*, 148 Mass. 570, where an action was brought for goods sold and delivered and for money loaned, and the defense was set up that the goods were delivered and the money given as orally agreed by the plaintiff for the use of money already supplied him by defendant, the burden of proof does not shift, but remains upon plaintiff all the while to prove that the goods were sold and the money loaned.

It always becomes immaterial upon whom the burden of proof rests, when all the evidence concerning the transaction inquired into is introduced: *McCormick* v. *Holmes*, 41 Kan. 265.

The party upon whom is cast the burden of proof is always entitled to the concluding argument: *Lieb* v. *Craddock*, 87 Ky. 526; *Olds Wagon Co.* v. *Benedict*, 25 Neb. 372.

McGorrisk v. Dwyer.
[78 Iowa, 279.]

FIXTURES — WHAT WILL PASS AS SUCH UNDER CHATTEL MORTGAGE. — A track-scale erected for use in connection with an elevator built upon leased land will pass as a fixture under a chattel mortgage of the elevator, "with all the machinery therein, and all the fixtures thereto belonging."

REPLEVIN to recover a track-scale claimed to be included in a chattel mortgage of an elevator, "with all the machinery therein, and all the fixtures thereto belonging." Judgment for plaintiff, and defendant appeals.

A. H. Stutsman and N. S. Hammack, for the appellant.

S. L. Glasgow, and R. Ambler and Son, for the appellee.

GRANGER, J. 1. There is a concession in argument by both parties that the elevator covered by the mortgage as well as the scale in controversy are chattel property; that there is no freehold estate to which the term "fixture" can apply. The case presents this question, Is the track-scale a fixture belonging to the elevator building? The question has led counsel in argument to consider the legal significance or application of the word "fixture," and it is urged by appellant that, as a legal term, it depends upon the real estate for its support, and that, as appellee regards and treats the elevator building and the scale as chattel property, its character is fixed, and the scale not being a fixture, it cannot be regarded as included in the mortgage; the term "fixture" therein being the only one that could embrace the scale in question. A discussion of the term "fixture," in the abstract, would be of little avail in the face of the facts with which we are confronted. It is true, the term is used by the parties to the mortgage, and it is equally true that it is used only with reference to the building as chattel property. But is it, because of that, without significance in the transaction? The parties to the mortgage were dealing with reference to property which ordinarily attaches to and is a part of realty, being buildings thereon. Fixtures, to a great extent, are directly connected with buildings, as a part of the realty, and but for the buildings, they could in no sense be considered as real estate. In cases where the buildings are a part of the realty, law-writers and courts are wont to associate the term "fixture" directly with the buildings, and speak of them as fixtures to the mill or store or other buildings. This is because of the relationship of the fixture to the building as distinct from the land, and is by no means a misapplication of the term. As the parties to the mortgage have employed the term "fixture," we know of no rule of construction to warrant us in disregarding it, because technically applicable to real estate, if the purpose of its use is manifest from the record. To us it seems clear that its use in the mortgage in question is not different from what it would be if the elevator building was actually a part of the realty, and the language was used in a real estate mortgage, and specified the building and "fixtures belonging thereto." In such a case, it would only be necessary to inquire if the scale was a fixture belonging to the building, and the finding upon such inquiry would determine its character. If in this case the scale has such a relation to the elevator that, with the elevator a part of the real estate, the scale would be a real estate fixture, then it is so related to the elevator as a chattel, within the purpose of the parties, — that is, a "fixture belonging thereto."

2. It remains to be considered if the scale, in view of the facts of the case, is a fixture belonging to the elevator. In this respect much depends upon the intent and purpose with which the scale was placed, as it was, in connection with the elevator; the intent and use in such cases having much to do with determining its character as a fixture: *Congregational Society* v. *Fleming,* 11 Iowa, 533; 79 Am. Dec. 511. It is plain, from the record, that the land on which the elevator was placed was leased, and the elevator placed in close proximity to the railroad track, because the elevator was to be used in receiving and shipping grain over the line of road, and

that, as to the cars on the track, grain was to be transferred to and from the elevator. The elevator was used for the purpose of shelling corn and cleaning grain for shipment, in which case cars were unloaded into the hopper connected with the scale, and by means of conveyors taken to the building for such purposes as might be required. The entire testimony in the case shows that the scale was bought for use with the elevator, and after being adjusted, it was mainly used for the purpose of carrying on the business of the elevator. It seems to have been as much a part of the elevator, for the purpose of its business, as the machinery in the elevator, and for such purposes as closely connected therewith. The connection of the scale with the elevator by means of the hopper-frame was open, visible, and could easily be known by all.

The point is urged that the scale was not on the land leased of the railroad company for the purpose of erecting the elevator; but we see no particular force in the argument. It is on land adjacent thereto, and so adjusted as to be used in connection with the elevator, and would be as clearly a fixture in one case as in the other, as between these parties. It was placed on the land adjacent by license from the railroad company, and the railroad company makes no question or claim as to the scale.

The doctrine of "trade fixtures" has received some attention in argument, but such doctrine is mainly applicable to right of removal of fixtures by a tenant as against his landlord. No such question is presented in this case, and the rule is of little avail in reaching a conclusion. We have only to deal with the question of the scale as a fixture belonging to the elevator, so as to pass with the latter under the mortgage. We are agreed that it is.

Affirmed.

FIXTURES. — As to what are and what are not fixtures, see *Lavenson* v. *Standard Soap Co.*, 80 Cal. 245; 13 Am. St. Rep. 147, and particularly note 153-155; *Cavis* v. *Beckford*, 62 N. H. 229; 13 Am. St. Rep. 554; *Laird* v. *Railroad*, 62 N. H. 254; 13 Am. St. Rep. 564; *Collamore* v. *Gillis*, 149 Mass. 578; 14 Am. St. Rep. 460, and note.

Esch Brothers *v.* Home Insurance Company.

[78 Iowa, 334.]

Pleading — Changing Action at Law into Suit in Equity by Amendment. — A party, by bringing his action at law to recover upon a policy of insurance, is not estopped from amending his pleadings after answer, and before the case is finally submitted to the court, so as to change it into a suit in equity to reform the policy.

Insurance — Reformation of Policy of Fire Insurance. — Where a mortgagee applies to a general agent of an insurance corporation, and states his wish to obtain insurance upon his interest as mortgagee, and his application and the consideration for the insurance are accepted, whereupon he requests the agent to write the policy so as to effect this purpose, and relies upon him to determine what form is necessary under the law of insurance for that purpose, the agent is bound to write the policy so as to insure the mortgagee's interest in his own name, and if the agent adopts a wrong form, the policy may, after loss, be reformed in equity so as to express the intention of the parties, notwithstanding the rules of the company forbid the issuance of policies to mortgagees.

Insurance — Reformation of Policy. — Where an applicant for insurance correctly states his interests in the property, and distinctly asks for insurance thereon, and the agent of the insurer agrees to comply with his requests, and assumes to decide upon the form of policy to be written for that purpose, but, by mistake of law, adopts the wrong form, equity will reform the policy so as to make it an insurance upon the interests named.

Insurance — Increase in Interest not Breach of Condition. — A mortgagee's interest in property insured by him is increased instead of diminished by foreclosure, and hence the foreclosure is not a breach of the condition in the policy that it is forfeited by a change in title to the property insured.

Insurance — Change in Use of Premises. — A condition in the policy, forfeiting it if the insured property is so changed as to increase the risk, is not broken by a change of the premises from a restaurant to a paint and wagon shop, when the evidence shows that such change diminished the risk.

Action originally commenced at law by Esch Brothers to recover upon a fire insurance policy which purported upon its face to insure Bridget Donegan against loss by fire on certain premises for one year from date, in the sum of four hundred dollars, the insurance, in case of loss, to be first payable to Esch Brothers, as their interest in the premises might appear. The policy was dated April 15, 1884. The plaintiffs were required, on motion of defendant, to state the interests held by them and by said Donegan at the time of the issuance of the policy, and at the time of the loss thereunder. They filed an amended complaint, in which they alleged that on May 8, 1883, they obtained judgment of foreclosure against said Donegan, the absolute owner of the premises, and that afterwards, on July 17, 1884, they received a sheriff's deed to the property; that they alone applied for the insurance, paid the premium, and at the time stated to the agent of the insurance company the nature and extent of their title to the premises insured; that they alone wanted their interest therein insured, and that said Donegan would not redeem; that the agent informed them that, notwithstanding these facts, he would insure them, whereupon he issued the policy in suit; that after they had procured the sheriff's deed, and before the loss, they informed the agent of this fact, and desired to know if the policy should be changed, when he informed them that the policy insured their property. A demurrer was interposed, on the ground that the plaintiffs were not proper parties, and not entitled to maintain the action; that it appeared from the complaint, as amended, that the insured had alienated the property, and was without interest therein at the time of the loss. This demurrer was sustained, and plaintiffs then filed a substituted petition, which was stricken out on motion of defendant; they then filed a second substituted petition, again stating the facts above set out, together with those stated in the opinion in relation to the reformation of the policy, and praying that the policy be so reformed as to insure the interests alone of the plaintiffs in the property, to the extent of four hundred dollars, for one year, and to insert in the policy the names of plaintiffs instead of said Donegan; that plaintiffs have judgment upon the policy as reformed for four hundred dollars, with interest; and that the case be transferred to equity. Defendant answered and plaintiffs replied, and after hearing, plaintiffs' petition was dismissed, and they appealed. The other facts are stated in the opinion.

Utt Brothers, for the appellants.

Cole, McVey, and Clark, for the appellee.

GIVEN, C. J. 1. Following the order pursued in the argument, we first notice appellee's contention, that plaintiffs, having made sworn proofs of loss, and proceeded at law upon the policy, cannot now maintain this action in equity to reform the policy, and are estopped to deny the correctness of the contract as sued upon. Numerous authorities are cited, to the effect that where a party has two inconsistent remedies, he is called upon to elect which he will pursue, and having elected, he cannot, after defeat, pursue the other remedy. Such is not this case. The plaintiffs have but one remedy, and that is for the reformation of the policy. They have no remedy upon the policy as written. Their petition at law alleged the errors in the policy substantially as alleged in their petition in equity. This case seems to be exactly within the ruling in *Barnes* v. *Hekla Fire Ins. Co.*, 75 Iowa, 11; 9 Am. St. Rep. 450. In that case the action was commenced at law, and a recovery sought on the policy. The defendant pleaded that the policy contained a provision against additional insurance, and that defendant had procured additional insurance. The plaintiff amended, alleging that at the time the contract of insurance was entered into it was agreed that the plaintiff should have the right to take out additional insurance; that such an agreement was omitted from the policy by mistake, oversight, or through the fault of the defendant, and asked a reformation of the policy. The defendant denied the allegation of the amended petition, and also pleaded that plaintiff, having knowledge of the matters pleaded, was estopped from setting the same up, because he had elected to prosecute an action at law on the policy, and having made an election of remedies, he was bound thereby. The court says: "Conceding that plaintiff had knowledge of the fact that the defendant asserted it would rely on the defenses it did, still, we think he could bring an action at law on the policy, and ascertain certainly whether the defendant would plead such defense or not, before resorting to equity. He could not know what the defense would be before it was pleaded. Under the statute in relation to amendments, we have no hesitation in holding that the party is not estopped, by bringing an action at law, from amending his pleadings before the case has finally been submitted to the court, so as to change it into an action in equity. We feel confident the universal practice is in accord with this view." We think this case fully answers appellee's first contention, and the further claim, that the "amendment as made by the second substituted petition is a substantial change in the original cause of action, and not authorized by the code of Iowa."

2. The next and most important question is, whether the plaintiffs have shown themselves entitled to have the policy of insurance so reformed as to make it a contract insuring them to the extent of their interest, not exceeding four hundred dollars, instead of Bridget Donegan. It is well established by the admissions in the pleadings and by the proofs that the title to the property insured was as alleged by the plaintiffs,

both at the time the policy was issued and at the time of the
loss; that Bridget Donegan omitted to keep the property insured; that J. R. Stillman was agent of defendant, with power
to contract insurance of property, take risks, collect premiums,
and issue policies; that plaintiffs applied to said agent to have
their interest in said property insured in the defendant company, and explained to him fully what their interest was; that
Stillman, as such agent, agreed to insure the plaintiffs in the
defendant company, on their interest in said property, to the
amount of four hundred dollars for one year, for the consideration of twenty dollars, which was then paid by the plaintiffs;
that it was left with Stillman to write the policy accordingly,
and that the policy was written as set out by Stillman, and
forwarded to and received by the plaintiffs, with the understanding and belief on the part of said Stillman and the
plaintiffs that the policy so written did insure the plaintiffs,
as it was agreed it should.   There is no pretense that Bridget
Donegan ever sought, desired, knew of, or paid for the insurance.   The case is almost identical in its facts with *Bailey* v.
American Cent. Ins. Co., 13 Fed. Rep. 250, and *Williams* v.
Ins. Co., 24 Fed. Rep. 625.   In the former case, McCrary, J.,
held: "Where a mortgagee applies to the agent of an insurance
company, and states plainly he wishes to obtain insurance alone upon his interest as mortgagee, requests the agent
to write the policy so as to effect this purpose, and relies upon
him to determine as to what form is necessary, under the law
of insurance, for that purpose, this court holds that the agent
is bound to write a policy which shall insure the mortgagee's
interest in his own name.   I regard it as well settled by authority, and well supported by reason, that if the applicant
correctly states his interests, and distinctly asks for an insurance thereon, and the agent of the insurer agrees to comply
with his requests, and assumes to decide upon the form of the
policy to be written for that purpose, and by mistake of law
adopts the wrong form, a court of equity will reform the instrument so as to make it insurance upon the interests named.
Such a determination is eminently just and equitable, since
the insurance company always prepares the contracts and in-
serts therein its own terms."   In the latter case, Justice Miller
announced the rule to be that "where an instrument fails to
represent what both parties intended to have it represent, and
one party has drawn up the instrument and the other party
merely accepted it, and the fault was on the part of the

party drawing up the instrument, it can be reformed. It would be a harsh rule if a person applying to an insurance agent, who is supposed to know the legal value of the language used in such policies, which he is drawing up every day, and who is supposed to know exactly what is desired, if that agent fails to do that which was intended,—it would be harsh to say that the instrument shall not be reformed, and that chancery shall not give relief." The right of the plaintiffs to a reformation of the policy upon the facts is fully supported in *Fink* v. *Ins. Co.*, 24 Fed. Rep. 318, and in *Longhurst* v. *Star Ins. Co.*, 19 Iowa, 364, and many other authorities that might be cited. It is urged that the rules of the defendant company forbid the issuing of policies to mortgagees, but require their issue to mortgagors. That the plaintiffs had an insurable interest is not questioned, nor that the company could contract to insure such interest. The agent, Stillman, had general authority to contract insurance, and did contract to insure the plaintiffs' interest, and receive the consideration therefor, which passed to and is still held by his principal. We think the defendant should not be heard to question the authority of its agents under these circumstances. We are of the opinion, from the facts that the contract was to insure the plaintiffs, and not Bridget Donegan, and that by a mistake of law on the part of the defendant's agent the policy was made to insure Bridget Donegan instead of the plaintiffs, and should be so reformed as to run to the plaintiffs as the insured to the extent of their interest at the time the policy was issued, not exceeding four hundred dollars.

3. It remains to be determined whether the policy, as reformed, has been broken by reason of the change in title, resulting from Bridget Donegan's failure to redeem. This was not a diminution of the interests of the assured, but an increase, and hence not a breach of the policy: See *Bailey* v. *American Cent. Ins. Co.*, *supra*, and authorities cited therein.

4. It appears by the testimony that, at the time the policy was issued, the premises were occupied as a restaurant and dwelling, and at the time of the loss it was being occupied as a wagon and paint shop. The policy provides that "in case use or occupation of the above-mentioned premises, at any time during the period for which this policy would otherwise continue in force, shall be so changed as to increase the risk thereon, except as may be hereinafter agreed to by this corporation in writing upon this policy, from thenceforth, so long as

the same shall be so used, this policy shall be of no force or effect." This provision is against changes that "increase the risk." Mr. Stillman, who was entirely familiar with both occupations, and with the classifications of risks, testifies: "The occupation of this building was changed, after the policy was issued, and before the fire, from restaurant to wagon and paint shop. But I did not think the change increased the risk enough to increase the rate. The rate was high in the first place. I did not think the change here did increase the hazard. It was kept as a low dive before. I think the risk was improved. Without regard to moral hazard, a wagon and paint shop is a greater risk; but because of a moral hazard, I did not think the risk was increased."

5. It appears that the loss was total, and that the plaintiffs were damaged thereby to the fullest amount of their insurance, four hundred dollars, which became due and payable to them on the fifth day of April, 1885. The judgment of the district court dismissing the plaintiff's petition is reversed, and decree will be entered in this court reforming the policy of insurance as prayed for, with judgment in favor of the plaintiffs for four hundred dollars, with six per cent interest from the fifth day of April, 1885, and for costs.

Reversed.

———

PLEADING — AMENDMENT. — If, in an action commenced in time upon an insurance policy providing that no action can be maintained thereon which is not commenced within one year after the death of the insured, judgment for plaintiff is reversed because the relief asked for is legal, while that to which he is entitled is equitable, he may then, though more than a year has elapsed since the commencement of the action and the reversal, so amend his original pleadings as to demand the equitable relief to which he is entitled: *Newman* v. *Covenant Mutual Ins. Ass'n*, 76 Iowa, 56; 14 Am. St. Rep. 196.

INSURANCE POLICY — REFORMATION OF. — An insurance policy may be reformed for fraud or mistake: *Barnes* v. *Hekla Ins. Co.*, 75 Iowa, 11; 9 Am. St. Rep. 450, and particularly cases cited in note 453; compare also *Continental Ins. Co.* v. *Ruckman*, 127 Ill. 364; 11 Am. St. Rep. 121; *Spurr* v. *Home Ins. Co.*, 40 Minn. 424. A bill will lie, to protect a mortgagee's interest, to reform an insurance policy for mistake, where the name of the occupant and supposed owner of the premises was inserted as such in the policy, neither party having actual notice or knowledge of an adverse title growing out of an execution sale, to set aside which a suit was then pending by such occupant, but the insurance agent being informed that the title was in dispute: *Balen* v. *Hanover Ins. Co.*, 67 Mich. 179. But in *St. Paul F. & M. Ins. Co.* v. *Shaver*, 76 Iowa, 283, it was decided that an insurance policy could not be corrected or reformed for a mistake which was not mutual.

FIRE INSURANCE. — Where a policy was issued to plaintiff's husband upon property on which she held a mortgage, and the loss was made payable to mortgagees, and she was the only mortgagee, and the husband, after the fire, transferred to her the lot upon which the building stood, in consideration of the amount due on the mortgage, which was thereupon canceled, she had a right of action on the policy as a mortgagee, and was not divested of that right by the purchase of the lot and the cancelation of the mortgage: *Bartlett v. Iowa Ins. Co.*, 77 Iowa, 86.

FIRE INSURANCE — INCREASE OF RISK. — Under a policy providing that it should become void if without consent of the company the insured should cause an increase of risk, where the assured, for a portion of the term included under the policy, used the premises for illegal sales of liquors, but afterwards, and before the loss by fire, obtained a license to sell liquors, in an action on the policy, if the temporary illegal use of the premises caused an increase of risk, the policy may be treated as wholly void: *Kyte v. Commercial Union Ins. Co.*, 149 Mass. 116.

WYMORE *v.* MAHASKA COUNTY.

[78 IOWA, 396.]

NEGLIGENCE OF PARENT NOT IMPUTABLE TO MINOR CHILD. — An administrator may recover for fatal injuries to his intestate, an irresponsible child incapable of committing negligence, when such injuries are caused by the wrongful and negligent acts of the child's parents, or of others having him in charge, even though the negligent parents will inherit the amount recovered.

ACTION by an administrator to recover damages resulting from the death of a minor child, alleged to have been caused by the negligence of defendant. Judgment for defendant, and plaintiff appeals.

Bolton and McCoy, and G. C. Morgan, for the appellant.

John F. Lacey, and Blanchard and Preston, for the appellee.

ROBINSON, J. In August, 1883, Henry Smith, with his family, consisting of his wife, a daughter, and plaintiff's intestate, then about two years of age, attempted to drive over a county bridge of defendant in a wagon drawn by two horses. The bridge fell while the team was on it, and the wagon and its occupants fell to the stream below. The fall resulted in the death of the mother and plaintiff's intestate. The plaintiff claims that at the time in question the bridge was out of repair and in a dangerous condition, and that defendant is chargeable with knowledge of that fact; that it fell in consequence of that condition; and that decedent did not contribute to the injuries of which plaintiff complains.

1. It seems to be conceded, and the record satisfies us, that the jury were instructed to return a verdict for defendant, on

the ground that the father and mother of decedent were not shown to be free from negligence which contributed to his death. It is not claimed that he could have been guilty of contributory negligence, but it is insisted that negligence on the part of his parents would be imputable to him; hence that it was necessary for plaintiff, in order that he might recover, to show that the negligence of the parents did not contribute to the injury in controversy. So far as we are advised, the question now presented to us has never been directly determined by this court, although it seems to have been assumed in some cases that the negligence of the parent might be imputed to the child. Of that kind is the case of *Walters* v. *Chicago etc. R'y Co.*, 41 Iowa, 78; but in that it was held that the negligence of the person in whose charge the parents had placed the child could not be imputed to the parent, and through the parent to the child. In *Slater* v. *Burlington etc. R'y Co.*, 71 Iowa, 209, the point was expressly reserved from decision. The doctrine of imputable negligence was considered in *Nesbit* v. *Town of Garner*, 75 Iowa, 315; 9 Am. St. Rep. 486; but the question now under consideration was not involved in that case. That the negligence of the parent is imputable to the child has been affirmed by numerous courts of high standing: See *Hartfield* v. *Roper*, 21 Wend. 615; 34 Am. Dec. 273; *Morrison* v. *Erie R'y Co.*, 56 N. Y. 302; *Thurber* v. *Harlem etc. R'y Co.*, 60 N. Y. 327; *Lynch* v. *Smith*, 104 Mass. 53; 6 Am. Rep. 188; *Gibbons* v. *Williams*, 135 Mass. 335; *Fitzgerald* v. *St. Paul etc. R'y Co.*, 29 Minn. 336; 43 Am. Rep. 212; *Brown* v. *European etc. R'y Co.*, 58 Me. 384; *Leslie* v. *City of Lewiston*, 62 Me. 468; *Hathaway* v. *Toledo etc. R'y Co.*, 46 Ind. 26; *Toledo etc. R'y Co.* v. *Grable*, 88 Ill. 442; *Atchison etc. R'y Co.* v. *Smith*, 28 Kan. 542; *Meeks* v. *Southern Pac. R'y Co.*, 52 Cal. 603; *Stillson* v. *Hannibal etc. R'y Co.*, 67 Mo. 674. Among the cases holding to the contrary are the following: *Bellefontaine etc. R'y Co.* v. *Snyder*, 18 Ohio St. 408; 98 Am. Dec. 175; *Huff* v. *Ames*, 16 Neb. 139; 49 Am. Rep. 716; *Galveston etc. R'y Co.* v. *Moore*, 59 Tex. 64; 46 Am. Rep. 265; *Erie etc. R'y Co.* v. *Schuster*, 113 Pa. St. 412; 57 Am. Rep. 471; *Robinson* v. *Cone*, 22 Vt. 214; 54 Am. Dec. 67; *Daley* v. *Norwich etc. R. R. Co.*, 26 Conn. 591; 68 Am. Dec. 413; *Norfolk etc. R. R. Co.* v. *Ormsby*, 27 Gratt. 476; *Boland* v. *Missouri R. R. Co.*, 36 Mo. 489; *Whirley* v. *Whiteman*, 1 Head, 619; Beach on Contributory Negligence, secs. 41–43. See *Battishill* v. *Humphreys*, 64 Mich. 514; 1 Shearman and Red-

field on Negligence, secs. 70–83, and notes. It seems to us
that the authorities last cited announce the better rule. The
parent is not in any proper sense the agent of the child. The
former is required to give to the latter care, protection, and
support, and in return may exact service and obedience. But
these duties are imposed by law, and are not the result of any
contract between the parties. In this case, the child was
taken into the wagon, and exposed to the accident which resulted in his death, without volition on his part. He certainly
was free from fault. If his parents, by their negligence, contributed to his death, that does not seem to us to be a sufficient reason for denying his estate relief. Such negligence
would prevent a recovery by the parents in their own right:
Smith v. *Hestonville etc. R'y Co.*, 92 Pa. St. 450; 37 Am. Rep.
705; *Huff* v. *Ames*, 16 Neb. 139; 49 Am. Rep. 716; *Bellefontaine etc. R'y Co.* v. *Snyder*, 24 Ohio St. 670; 1 Shearman and
Redfield on Negligence, sec. 71; *Erie etc. R'y Co.* v. *Schuster*,
113 Pa. St. 412; 57 Am. Rep. 471; *Glassey* v. *Hestonville etc.
R'y Co.*, 57 Pa. St. 172. See also *Albertson* v. *Keokuk etc. R'y
Co.*, 48 Iowa, 294; Beach on Contributory Negligence, sec. 44;
Pratt Coal and Iron Co. v. *Brawley*, 83 Ala. 371; 3 Am. St.
Rep. 751; *Evansville etc. R. R. Co.* v. *Wolf*, 59 Ind. 90. But it
appears to us to be unjust and contrary to reason to hold that
the irresponsible child should be responsible for the wrongful
acts of his parents or others who may have him in charge.
He is incapable by himself of committing any act of negligence, and cannot authorize another to commit one; therefore it seems unreasonable to require him or his estate to suffer
loss because of the neglect or unauthorized acts of his parents
or others. Some authorities seem to make a distinction between cases where the contributory negligence of the parent
occurs while he has the child under his immediate control,
and other cases which occur when the child is away from the
parent; but we are of the opinion that there is no sufficient
ground for the distinction claimed. The authority of the
parent does not depend upon the proximity of the child.

2. It is claimed that appellant ought not to recover, for the
reason that it is not shown that the parents of the child were
free from contributory negligence; and since they inherited his
estate, the rule which would bar a negligent parent from recovering in such a case in his own right ought to apply. But
plaintiff seeks to recover in the right of the child, and not for
the parents. It may be that a recovery in this case will result

in conferring an undeserved benefit upon the father, but that is a matter which we cannot investigate.   If the facts are such that the child could have recovered had his injuries not been fatal, his administrator may recover the full amount of damages which the estate of the child sustained.

3. Other questions are discussed by counsel, but as they are of such a nature as not to be likely to arise on another trial, they need not be further considered.   The judgment of the district court is reversed.   ____

PARENT AND CHILD — IMPUTED NEGLIGENCE. — As to whether or not negligence of a parent can be imputed to a child, see *Westbrook* v. *Mobile etc. R. R. Co.*, 66 Miss. 560; 14 Am. St. Rep. 587, and particularly extended note.

————

SKILLMAN *v.* CHICAGO, MILWAUKEE, AND ST. PAUL RAILWAY COMPANY.

[78 IOWA, 404.]

STATUTE — CONSTRUCTION — CONSTITUTIONAL LAW. — A statute providing that "in any case where the construction of a railway has been commenced by any corporation or person, and work on the same has ceased, and has not, in good faith, been resumed for a period of eight years, the land and the title thereto shall revert to the owner," applies where work was commenced and abandoned prior to the enactment of the statute, and not resumed until three years after its enactment, and more than eight years after the abandonment; nor does such construction make the statute retroactive in effect, since it does not create, but only declares the effect of, a suspension of the work for eight years.

STATUTES — CONSTRUCTION — CONSTITUTIONAL LAW. — A statute providing that "in any case where the construction of a railway has been commenced by any corporation or person, and work on the same has ceased, and has not, in good faith, been resumed for a period of eight years, the land and the title thereto shall revert to the owner," is not unconstitutional, as interfering with vested rights, impairing the obligations of contracts, or depriving the holder of the right of way for a railroad of its property without due process of law, since such right of way is but an easement attached to the use of the land for public purposes, and when such use is abandoned, the right ceases to exist.

AD QUOD DAMNUM proceeding for the value of land appropriated and taken for the construction of a railway.   Judgment for plaintiff, and defendant appeals.

Chambers, McElroy, and Roberts, for the appellant.

Harned and Mohland, and Sampson and Brown, for the appellee.

BECK, J. 1. The *ad quod damnum* proceeding was commenced in 1884. The defendant's answer, filed upon the appeal in the district court, alleges that it was in possession of the land in question at the time the proceeding was commenced, and occupying it with the railroad tracks. It shows that it derives the title and right to the occupancy of the land under certain deeds conveying the right of way to defendant's grantors and finally to defendant; that plaintiff conveyed the right of way in 1867 to the St. Louis and Cedar Rapids Railway Company, which constructed the road-bed upon the land in that year, or soon after. Defendant holds title by certain original and mesne conveyances, transferring to it the title acquired by the St. Louis and Cedar Rapids Railway Company, which need not be more particularly referred to in this connection. The defendant, in its cross-bill, shows that a conveyance of the right of way under which it holds misdescribes a part of the land occupied by its railroad, and asks for a proper correction of the mistake. The plaintiff, in answer to defendant's cross-bill, alleges that in 1871 the construction of the railroad over his lands was abandoned, and was only resumed in 1883 by defendant, and thereby defendant acquired no interest in the lands in suit, and no right to occupy them for purposes connected with its railroad. The question thus raised by the pleadings, involving the abandonment of the right of way, is decisive of the case, and first demands our attention.

2. Code, section 1260, as amended by chapter 15, Acts Eighteenth General Assembly, provides that "in any case where the construction of a railway has been commenced by any corporation or person, and work on the same has ceased, and has not been, in good faith, resumed by any corporation or person for a period of eight years, the land and the title thereto shall revert to the owner of the section, subdivision, tract, or lot from which it was taken." The evidence shows beyond controversy that the work upon the railroad now owned by defendant ceased in 1871, and was in no manner resumed until 1883, when defendant proceeded to build and complete it. A period of about twelve years intervened between the abandonment of the work and its resumption by defendant, which was about three years after the enactment of the statute above quoted. That more than eight years intervened between the cessation of work on the railroad and its resumption is not denied. The language of the statute

plainly applies to the case of railroads which had been commenced and abandoned before the enactment of the statute,
and whereon work was resumed within a period of less than
eight years thereafter. The interpretation that the period of
eight years must have run after the enactment of the statute
is in conflict with the construction demanded by the gram-
matical rules of our language.

3. But counsel for defendant insists that this construction,
if recognized, gives a retrospective effect to the statute, and is
therefore void. Without conceding that the statute is void if,
in some instances, it has a retroactive effect, we express the
opinion that the statute in question has no such effect. It
provides that a suspension of work for eight years operates
as the abandonment of the railway. It applies to all cases
where there has been a suspension for eight years. It does
not create a suspension for the specified period, or any part
thereof. It simply prescribes the effect of such a suspension.
Neither does it provide that an abandonment shall be declared
for a suspension not had. It does not attempt to give effect
to a suspension before it happened.

4. Counsel for defendant insist that the statute in question
interferes with vested rights, impairs the obligations of contracts, and deprives the holder of the right of way in question of its property therein without due process of law, and is
therefore in conflict with familiar constitutional guaranties.
Brief consideration, we think, will show that these objections
to the statute are without foundation. The right of way in
question is an easement, — the right to occupy land for purposes connected with the rights and franchises of a public
carrier. The property right of the holder of a right of way
does not attach to the land independent of and disconnected
from its use for public purposes. Its occupancy and public
use, present or prospective, when the land may be prepared
for such use, must run together. If the public use becomes
impossible, or is abandoned, the right to hold the land ceases.
It cannot be that corporations and individuals may acquire
easements, and never use them, yet hold the land upon which
they are located. When there ceases to be an easement, present or prospective, there ceases to be anything to which the
holder of the easement can hold. Indeed, the very thing
which he acquired has vanished, and of course he ceases to
hold any property, for the subject of the property no longer
exists.

Keeping in view the fact that the prior grantors of defendant had but an easement in the land, and such easement has been abandoned under the provisions of the statute, it requires neither argument nor authority to convince the mind that defendant has no vested rights, by contract, to hold that which it has abandoned, and no property subject to deprivation without due process of law, which are protected by the constitutional guaranties to which we have just referred.

5. We reach the conclusion that defendant held no right to the land upon which the right of way was located, and its possession thereof was without authority. It is therefore liable to the plaintiff, the owner of the land, for the value thereof, which shall be assessed in the *ad quod damnum* proceedings.

The questions in the case attracting much attention, which involve the rights of the parties under the deed misdescribing a part of the land in controversy, and other questions in the case, need not be discussed, as the judgment of the district court, for the reasons we have presented, must be affirmed.

STATUTES SHOULD ALWAYS BE INTERPRETED TO OPERATE PROSPECTIVELY, and not retrospectively, unless their language is so clear as to preclude all question as to the intention of the legislature: *Lane's Appeal,* 57 Conn. 182; 14 Am. St. Rep. 94, and note. But retrospective laws regulating matters of procedure are not necessarily void: Note to *City Council* v. *O'Donnell,* 13 Am. St. Rep. 739.

VESTED RIGHTS. — The rule is, that vested rights cannot be impaired: Note to *Goshen* v. *Stonington,* 10 Am. Dec. 134, 135.

SCHOLLMIER *v.* SCHOENDELEN.

[78 IOWA, 426.]

GIFT — VALIDITY — ASSIGNMENT OF BANK DEPOSIT TO BE PAID AFTER DEATH OF DEPOSITOR. — Where a bank depositor has the bank cashier write at the close of the account in the deposit-book, containing a rule that the deposit can only be drawn upon the production of the book, the following: "May 28, '86· Pay to order of S. and H. all of the within deposit after my decease,"—and thereafter neither deposits nor draws any money from the bank, but immediately delivers the book to the assignees, who hold it during the assignor's life and draw the deposit after the latter's death, these facts show a completed assignment, which creates an irrevocable vested interest in the assignees during the lifetime of the assignor, subject to the happening of a future event before the right to draw the money is perfected, and such assignment is not open to the objection that it is of a testamentary character, and void as not being executed in the manner provided by law.

Heinz and Hirschl, for the appellants.

Cook and Dodge, for the appellee.

ROBINSON, J.   Katharine Schollmier died intestate on the twenty-fifth day of December, 1886.   For about fifteen years before her death she had made her home with the defendants, her daughters, living a part of that time with one of them, and the remainder with the other.   In her lifetime she kept an account with the German Savings Bank, and on the twenty-eighth day of May, 1886, it had to her credit a balance of $1,730.18.   On that day decedent visited the bank with her bank-book, which contained a statement of her account with it, and had the assistant cashier write on the page next after the end of the account the following: "May 28, '86· Pay to order of Elizabeth Schoendelen and Dorothea Hasenmiller all of the within deposit after my decease."   This was signed by decedent.   Two days after her death defendants drew from the bank the balance aforesaid, together with $65.40 accrued interest, making a total so drawn of $1,795.58.   Plaintiff seeks to recover that amount, with interest, as belonging to the estate of decedent.   Defendants claim that decedent made her home with them, as aforesaid, under a verbal agreement, by virtue of which they were to furnish her with the necessaries of life so long as she should live, in consideration of which they were to have all the property which she should own at the time of her death, and that the amount received by them was so received pursuant to said agreement.   They further claim that for many years prior to decedent's death they supported her, and in so doing expended large sums of money at her instance and request, and that the money in question was assigned to them on the twenty-eighth day of May, 1886, in consideration of said support and expenditures. They also claim that decedent, on the date last named, assigned said money to them in apprehension of her death.

1. The defendants, to maintain their defense, rely chiefly upon the assignment written in the bank-book.   They contend that it created and transferred to them an interest when it was executed, and that the postponing of the right to the full enjoyment of such interest until the death of the assignor did not have the effect to defeat it.   Plaintiff insists that the assignment was of a testamentary character, and that not having been executed in the manner provided by law for such instruments, is invalid, and that view seems to have been held

by the court below. In our opinion, the proper effect to be given the assignment must depend upon the intent of the decedent with respect to it. In terms, it is a full assignment of the amount shown by the book to be due at the time it was made, not of the amount which should be due at the death of the assignor. No right to revoke or rescind it is shown to be reserved, and if it was treated by the assignor as a completed transaction, we think it passed a present interest in the bank account, and is not vulnerable to the objection made by plaintiff. The power to create such an interest was recognized in *Burlington University* v. *Barrett*, 22 Iowa, 72; 92 Am. Dec. 376. See also *Craven* v. *Winter*, 38 Iowa, 472. In *Leaver* v. *Gauss*, 62 Iowa, 314, it was held that an instrument somewhat in the form of a deed was of a testamentary character, for the reason that it expressly provided that the grantees should have no interest under it so long as the grantors, or either of them, should live; but there is no such provision in this case. The bank-book in which the assignment was written contains the following rule: " No money deposited in this bank can be drawn out in whole or in part unless the depositor produces his book, or his certificate, if there was one. In case a book or certificate is lost or stolen, the owner should at once give the bank written notice. If notice is not given, and the bank pays the deposit in whole or in part on the presentation of the book or certificate, then the bank is not responsible, and cannot be compelled to pay the second time, though it be ascertained that the party to whom payment was made was not entitled thereto." It is not claimed that a certificate had been issued to decedent. No money was deposited or drawn out by her after the making of the assignment. The bankbook was in the possession of one of the defendants after that date, and before the death of decedent. These circumstances tend to show that the book was delivered to defendants to perfect the assignment and to enable them to obtain the money in controversy, and if that was done by the assignor, we think defendants acquired an interest in the money during her lifetime; and for the purposes of this appeal, it is not necessary to determine whether the interest so acquired was by gift *inter vivos,* or a gift *causa mortis,* or by the execution of the agreement for support claimed by defendants. We are of the opinion that there was sufficient evidence of a completed assignment to require the cause to be submitted to the jury.

2. It is claimed by appellant that the making of the assignment was of itself sufficient to create a vested interest in defendants, and cases are cited in support of that claim: See *Ellis* v. *Secor*, 31 Mich. 185; 18 Am. Rep. 178; *Gerrish* v. *New Bedford Institution*, 128 Mass. 159; 35 Am. Rep. 365; *Davis* v. *Ney*, 125 Mass. 590; 28 Am. Rep. 272; *Martin* v. *Funk*, 75 N. Y. 134; 31 Am. Rep. 446; *Ray* v. *Simmons*, 11 R. I. 266; 23 Am. Rep. 447; *Blasdel* v. *Locke*, 52 N. H. 238; *Harris* v. *Hopkins*, 43 Mich. 272; 38 Am. Rep. 180. We think there should be some evidence in addition to the writing to show that it was regarded by its maker as a completed transaction, and that according to her intent nothing but the lapse of time was required to give to defendants the right to the possession of the money. As already stated, a delivery of the bank-book containing the assignment, in view of the rule of the bank quoted and other facts shown of the record, would be evidence that decedent regarded the transaction as completed on her part.

3. It is contended on the part of appellee that the assignment was so drawn as to be revocable, and the case of *Basket* v. *Hassell*, 107 U. S. 602, is cited as sustaining that position. In that case a certificate of deposit was indorsed by its owner during his last sickness as follows:—

"Pay to Martin Basket, of Henderson, Kentucky, no one else; then not till my death. My life seems to be uncertain. I may live through this spell. Then I will attend to it myself.   ·   H. M. CHANEY."

After making this indorsement, Chaney delivered the certificate to Basket, and died. The court speaks of the transaction as being, "in substance, not an assignment of the fund on deposit, but a check upon the bank against a deposit, which, as is shown by all the authorities, and upon the nature of the case, cannot be valid as a *donatio mortis causa*, even where it is payable *in præsenti*, unless paid or accepted while the donor is alive." But there is a marked difference between the effect of the indorsement in that case and the assignment in this. While in that case the indorsed certificate was delivered, yet the language of the indorsement showed clearly that it was not to take effect in case the indorser recovered. As stated by the court, the donor attached to his indorsement and delivery a condition precedent, which must happen before it became a gift. In this case the conditions related to the time when the interest transferred might be enjoyed, and not to its transfer.

The decision in that case rested in part upon the doctrine that a check against a deposit is not in effect an assignment of it, and does not withdraw it from the control of the depositor: See also *Curry* v. *Powers*, 70 N. Y. 212; 26 Am. Rep. 577. But it is the settled law of this state that a check or order drawn against funds may operate as an equitable assignment of them to the amount of the order, and that notice of the check or order given to the holder of the funds would be sufficient to hold them, even without an acceptance: *Manning* v. *Mathews*, 70 Iowa, 504; *County of Des Moines* v. *Hinkley*, 62 Iowa, 638; *Roberts* v. *Corbin*, 26 Iowa, 316; 96 Am. Dec. 146. In *First Nat. Bank of Canton* v. *Dubuque etc. R'y Co.*, 52 Iowa, 378, 35 Am. Rep. 280, this question was considered, and the authorities to some extent reviewed, and the following among other conclusions announced: "That an order upon the whole of a particular fund, though not accepted, will operate as an equitable assignment of the fund, and bind it in the hands of the drawee after notice; but that such order does not possess the property of negotiability." In this case the entire fund on deposit was assigned, and the bank had due notice of that fact. By the terms of the deposit it could be drawn out only when the book should be produced. The evidence tends to show that the book was delivered to defendants by decedent in her lifetime. •If this was done, or the assignment was in any other manner given effect, the ownership of the money evidenced by the book was vested in defendants, subject to the happening of a future event before the right to withdraw the money from the bank should be perfected.

4. In view of what we have already said, it is unnecessary to refer specially to various questions in regard to the introduction of evidence discussed by counsel. If the bank-book was delivered to defendants by decedent after the assignment was made, for the purpose of carrying it into effect, nothing further need be shown in the present condition of the pleadings to enable defendants to succeed; but should they be unable to show such delivery, it may be material to inquire into such facts as will tend to show the intent of decedent in regard to the assignment. The judgment of the district court is reversed.

GIFTS, VALIDITY OF AND WHAT CONSTITUTE. — To constitute a valid gift, there must be, on the part of the donor, an intent to give and a delivery of the thing given to or for the donee in pursuance of such intent, and also an acceptance of the gift on the part of the donee: *Beaver* v. *Beaver*, 117 N. Y.

421, 15 Am. St. Rep. 531, and cases cited in note. So a deposit of money in
a bank by a father in the name of his daughter, with the intention that such
deposit shall take effect as a gift to her, subject to his right of income while
living and to his wife's right of income therefrom during her life, if she survived him, is a valid gift of such money to the daughter if she assents thereto
upon being informed of the deposit and its purpose, even though the father
retains the deposit-book during his life to enable him to draw the income:
Smith v. *Ossipee etc. Bank,* 64 N. H. 228; 10 Am. St. Rep. 400, and cases cited
in note.

JANNEY *v.* SPRINGER AND WILLARD.

[78 IOWA, 617.]

PARTNERSHIP — PAYMENT OF PARTNER'S INDIVIDUAL DEBT WITH FIRM
PROPERTY VOID AS TO PARTNERSHIP. — A contract between a partner
and his individual creditor, to the effect that the latter is to take partnership property in payment of his debt, is void as against the firm without its consent or ratification, and it is immaterial that the partnership
displayed no firm sign, and that the creditor was ignorant of its existence at the time of making the contract, if it had in fact publicly existed
for three years with no effort at concealment.

ACTION on account. Judgment for plaintiff, and defendants
appeal.

Liston McMillen, for the appellants.

Bolton and McCoy, for the appellee.

ROTHROCK, J. It appears, from the evidence, that at the
time the account accrued, A. A. Paine & Co., a partnership,
were the keepers of a feed-store, and that the individual members of the partnership were A. A. Paine and J. M. Janney,
plaintiff in this action. W. W. Springer and C. F. Willard
were at the same time engaged in the business of importing
and selling high-bred horses from France, under the partnership style of Springer and Willard. A. A. Paine & Co. furnished the ground feed, the value of which is in controversy
in this action, which feed was consumed by the said horses.
Some time after the account accrued, the firm of A. A. Paine
& Co. was dissolved, and at the dissolution of the firm the
ground feed account was assigned to Janney in the settlement
of the partnership. He brought this action against the firm
of Springer and Willard, and against Springer as an individual member of the firm. The defendants claimed that Willard bought the feed of A. A. Paine, and paid him therefor.
The real facts relied upon as a defense were, that A. A. Paine
was indebted to Willard upon a promissory note, and that

Willard bought the feed of Paine under the agreement that the price of the same was to be applied on the note, and in payment thereof. After both parties had introduced their evidence, the plaintiff filed a motion for an order directing the jury to return a verdict for the plaintiff. The motion was sustained, upon the ground that an agreement between Willard and Paine, that Willard should purchase the feed, and pay for the same by the discharge of Paine's individual indebtedness, was void as to Janney, the other member of Paine & Co., unless Janney in some way assented to or ratified the transaction. We do not understand that this proposition is controverted by counsel for appellants.

But it is contended, in behalf of appellants, that the question as to whether there was such a partnership as A. A. Paine & Co. should have been submitted to the jury. We do not think this position can be sustained. The existence of the firm was shown by the testimony of these witnesses, and there was no evidence to the contrary. It is said there was no firm .sign erected at the place of business of the partnership, and that defendants had no knowledge of the existence of the firm. This want of knowledge and omission to use a sign was in no sense conflicting evidence upon the question of a partnership in fact. It having been established beyond question that the feed was partnership property, it was incumbent on the defendants to show that Janney in some way assented to the alleged agreement to pay the individual debt of Paine in partnership property, or that he (Janney) in some way ratified the act after it was done: *Thomas* v. *Stetson*, 62 Iowa, 537; 49 Am. Rep. 148. There was no evidence of such assent or ratification.

The only other question necessary to be noticed in the case is the claim of counsel for appellants, that, as they had no knowledge that Janney was in partnership with Paine, they had the right to deal with Paine as though he were the sole owner of the feed. It may be this position would be sound if there were any evidence that Janney was a dormant or silent partner. But there is no such evidence. The .partnership existed for some three years. Janney was personally and publicly engaged in the business, and his daughter was bookkeeper of the partnership. There was no evidence of any act of concealment of the partnership. It is true that for part of the time there was no partnership sign upon the building. But there was no sign of any kind, and therefore no effort to mislead any one as to the true relation of the parties. We think that, under the facts of the case, the question of knowledge as to the partnership is immaterial. In our opinion, the court rightfully directed a verdict for the plaintiff.

Affirmed.   .   ——

PARTNERSHIP. — One partner cannot appropriate the firm assets, by transferring them in satisfaction of his individual debt, without authority or consent of his copartners: *Cannon* v. *Lindsey*, 85 Ala. 198; 7 Am. St. Rep. 38, and note. Compare *Davies* v. *Atkinson*, 124 Ill. 474; 7 Am. St. Rep. 373, and extended note; note to *Williams* v. *Lewis*, 7 Am. St. Rep. 408, 409. A debt due a firm cannot be garnished by a creditor of one of the partners: *Crescent Ins. Co.* v. *Bear*, 23 Fla, 50; 11 Am. St. Rep. 331.

KAUFMAN BROTHERS AND COMPANY *v.* FARLEY MANUFACTURING COMPANY.

[78 IOWA, 679.]

TRIAL — ASSIGNMENT OF ERROR that "the court erred in sustaining the motion made by plaintiff at the close of defendant's testimony, and directing a verdict for plaintiff," is not open to objection as not being sufficiently specific, or as assuming that the motion asked the court to direct a verdict for plaintiffs.

AGENCY — EVIDENCE OF AGENT'S AUTHORITY TO MAKE CONTRACT, AND OF CUSTOM. — Where the authority of an acknowledged agent to make a contract giving a jobber an exclusive right to sell a certain line of cigars in a certain territory is questioned, the evidence of another jobber of like goods in the same territory that a custom or usage existed for such traveling agents to make similar contracts to the one in suit is admissible, and should be submitted to the jury to aid it in determining whether the agent had authority to make the contract in question.

CONTRACTS — EVIDENCE — SUFFICIENCY OF TO ESTABLISH CONTRACT. — In an action for breach of a contract made by the vendor's agent, whereby the vendee was to have the exclusive right to sell a certain line of goods in a designated territory, in which the evidence shows that the vendee was to have the goods for sale as long as he "pushed them," the question whether the vendee agreed to work up the trade, and to put men into the field to canvass for the goods, should be submitted to the jury.

CONTRACT — CONSTRUCTION — RIGHT TO TERMINATE. — A contract to furnish a vendee with a certain line of goods for sale in a specified district, with a provision that the goods shall be sent him as he orders them, and as long as he has sale for them, is an agreement on the part of the vendor to furnish the goods as ordered by the vendee, and not only to fill orders taken by him; nor can the vendor terminate the contract at pleasure.

STATUTE OF FRAUDS — PART PERFORMANCE OF CONTRACT SUFFICIENT TO AVOID. — Where, under a contract to furnish a vendee with a certain line of goods in a designated district so long as he orders and has sale for them, the delivery and receipt of payment for one lot of goods under an order on the contract is such part performance as to take it out of the operation of the statute of frauds.

CONTRACT NOT VOID FOR INDEFINITENESS. — A contract to furnish a vendee with a certain line of goods for exclusive sale in "Dubuque, and the territory tributary thereto," is not void for indefiniteness in describing the territory embraced in the terms of the contract.

EVIDENCE — ORDER OF PROOF. — The trial court may, in its discretion, exclude evidence offered out of order.

APPEAL — WHAT WILL BE CONSIDERED ON — WHERE EXCEPTIONS ARE TAKEN AND ERRORS ASSIGNED, independent of the motion for a new trial, which was filed too late to be available as a ground upon which to base an assignment of error, the appellate court may review and reverse the action of the court below.

Utt Brothers and Michel, for the appellant.

Powers and Lacy, for the appellees.

GRANGER, J. This action was brought to recover of defendant the value of a quantity of cigars. The claim of plaintiffs is admitted, and the issues are upon the answer and reply. Plaintiffs are manufacturers and wholesale dealers in cigars in the city of New York. The defendant is a corporation doing business in Dubuque, Iowa, as jobbers, and their business includes the sale of cigars in Dubuque and the country tributary thereto. The averments of the cross-petition, in brief, are, that in March, 1885, the plaintiff company agreed to give to the defendant the exclusive right to sell in Dubuque, and country tributary thereto, a certain brand of cigars known as "Our Bob," which brand the plaintiffs had the exclusive right to manufacture; that in consideration of the plaintiffs' agreement, the defendant was to employ men to travel and sell such cigars, and establish a trade therein in said territory; that in pursuance of such agreement, the defendant did employ men so to travel, who expended time and money in building up a trade for said cigars; that for the purpose of such trade plaintiffs were to ship the defendant cigars when ordered, and so long as defendant desired to deal in the cigar, or so long as the trade continued; that the agreement was observed by both parties to the 23d of June, 1885, when the plaintiffs violated the agreement by refusing to furnish cigars to the defendant for such trade. The plaintiffs deny these allegations of the cross-petition. At the trial in the district court the defendant introduced evidence tending to establish the contract, the breach, and damage. At the close of the defendant's testimony, on motion of plaintiffs, the court struck out the evidence introduced on the question of damage, and as to the refusal of plaintiffs to furnish cigars, and directed the jury to return a verdict for plaintiffs for the amount of their claim.

1. Appellees claim that alleged errors in the case cannot be considered, because the assignment is not sufficiently specific. One assignment is, that "the court erred in sustaining the motion made by plaintiff at the close of defendant's testimony, and directing a verdict for the plaintiff." The argument treats this assignment as involving a "misapprehension" of appellees' motion, to the extent of assuming that the motion asked the court to direct a verdict for plaintiffs. It is true, the motion does not ask that, and we think it equally true that the assignment does not convey such a meaning. It merely assigns error in sustaining the motion, whatever it was, and in directing the verdict as the court did. Thus understood, there is no misapprehension, and the assignment calls attention directly to the error complained of, which is the purpose of the assignment. It is true that of the assignments made some are unnecessary, being the same assignment made in different forms. This practice is quite common, and induced by a spirit of caution to avoid failure in having the assignment considered. Other assignments we think are sufficient, and will receive notice.

2. We first notice the error assigned as to ruling on motion to strike the testimony. The testimony is so directly involved in the consideration of this point that we set out a part of it, and will, as it becomes important, refer to other points. J. K. Farley, for defendant, said: "Defendant company is and has been engaged for the past seven years in jobbing teas, coffees, and other like groceries; also cigars and crackers. During all of that time I have been its secretary, treasurer, and business manager. The territory we covered is northern Iowa, southern Dakota, Minnesota as far as Red Wing, and southern Wisconsin, and northern Illinois. For over seven years we have jobbed cigars over this territory, and have kept about five men on the road. We buy our cigars from the manufacturers in the East. The first business transaction we ever had with the plaintiffs was in relation to their 'Our Bob' cigars. Mr. Katz, representing plaintiffs' firm, called on me in fore part of March, 1885. He told me he had a special brand of cigars he would like for us to take hold of, and talked a good deal about their merits, as being the finest thing on the market. It was having a big trade in the East, and he would like to

have us take hold of it. He said it was the finest five-cent cigar made in New York City; that he wanted us to take hold of them, and talk of that character, and he would guarantee us a big sale on them, and that he would give us the exclusive sale of the cigar in Dubuque, and the territory tributary to it; that he wouldn't sell to anybody else in Dubuque; and Mr. Katz said that he would not sell the cigars any nearer than Omaha on the west, St. Louis on the south, Chicago on the east, and St. Paul on the north, so that they wouldn't conflict with us; and insisted in that way on me taking hold of the cigars. I told him that we had a large stock of cigars, and that we could not take hold of them without dropping something out; that it was an injury to us to do so; and he insisted, and at last we gave him an order, with the understanding, as stated, that we were to have the exclusive control of the cigars for Dubuque, and territory tributary, and he would not sell anybody else, as stated; and the cigars came in due time. A lot of advertising matter was also sent us,— street signs and such things. When Mr. Katz made these representations to me, I told him if his house would furnish us with goods, give us the exclusive sale for Dubuque, and the territory tributary, he could ship us a case of goods. He said, 'The house will do so,' and took the order. He said they would furnish us the goods as long as we pushed them. He [Katz] said they would furnish us the goods as long as we had a sale for them, and as we ordered them, and as long as we ordered them. The price was to be twenty-eight dollars per thousand. We were to make a large profit. After this agreement I gave an order to Mr. Katz for ten thousand cigars. Plaintiffs acknowledged the receipt of the order in writing."

If there was a contract, as alleged, it was made by an agent of the plaintiffs, and a ground of the motion is, that it does not appear that such agent had authority to make the contract. It appears that one Katz was the agent of the plaintiffs, and as such was at Dubuque at the time the contract is alleged to have been made, and that he was selling defendant job lots of cigars, and a ten-thousand lot was shipped to defendant, and the receipt for the order speaks of it as being "through our Mr. Katz"; and of the fact of this agency we think there is no dispute,— that the dispute is merely as to the extent of the agency. Such a question is, of course, one of fact. Was there, then, testimony such as to entitle the jury to pass on that question? — the precise question being, did the agent have authority to bind the plaintiffs to a contract as alleged?

Mr. D. D. Meyer was a witness for defendant, and gave testimony as follows: "Live in city of Dubuque. I have been engaged in manufacturing, jobbing, and retailing cigars here and in this territory for twenty years. We procure most of our cigars from manufacturers in New York. We buy from their traveling salesmen who visit us. I know a general usage and custom relating to the authority of these agents, giving exclusive right to sell a certain brand of cigars in a certain territory. This usage extends all over the country. I never did business in any other town, but have done business with men representing houses all over the country. The usage or custom is, the traveling men have the right to make contracts giving the jobbers exclusive right to certain territory. They all do it. Cross-examination: If they did not give the exclusive right, the jobbers would not take hold of it; they would not do it under any circumstances." We then have the case of an agent engaged in introducing a brand of cigars in the West, and dealing with a local jobbing house in the discharge of his duties. Under such circumstances, what authority had the defendant a right to presume the agent possessed? The power and authority usually exercised in like cases. While the point is not so ruled, it is recognized in *Strickland* v. *Council Bluffs Ins. Co.*, 66 Iowa, 466, and is supported by *City of Davenport* v. *Peoria etc. Ins. Co.*, 17 Iowa, 276. In 1 Wait's Actions and Defenses, 221, the rule is stated as follows: "In determining what authority has been given, it may, as a general rule, be assumed that the principal intended to give, and that the authority conferred includes and carries with it, the power to employ all the usual and necessary means of executing it in such manner as to accomplish the objects which the principal had in view in creating the agency." The author cites abundant authorities for its support, and we think the rule is nowhere questioned on authority. With this rule to guide, there should be no question but that, with the testimony of Meyer, the question as to the authority of the agent was one for the jury. If his testimony is true, other agents in like business generally possessed the authority claimed to have been exercised by Katz, and the authority exercised was a necessary means to accomplish the purpose of his agency.

In defense of the ruling on the motion, it is urged that the

contract under which the damage is claimed is too indefinite
and uncertain; and among the reasons specified are these:
" There is no agreement on the part of defendants to work
up the trade, nor to put men into the field to canvass." The
evidence does not, in terms, state such an agreement, but it
does show that defendant bought cigars for sale in that territory, and that defendant was to have the goods for sale as long
as it "pushed them." This is surely evidence of the fact of
such an agreement. Whether sufficient or not was a question
for the jury, and the testimony very plainly shows that the
men were making the canvass, and that expenses were incurred in so doing.

The point is made, that if there was such a contract, plaintiffs were only required to furnish cigars to fill orders taken by
the defendant; but no such agreement is alleged or attempted
to be proved. The disclosures by the record as to the contract
in that respect are, that the cigars were to be furnished as
ordered by defendant, and the shipments made purport to have
been made in pursuance of such orders. The orders spoken of
are the orders of defendant.

It is also said that plaintiffs had the right to terminate the
contract at any time, and that they did so by refusing to furnish more cigars. The record does not sustain the claim. The
averments of the petition are, and also the proofs, that the
cigars were to be furnished as long as defendant wanted or
ordered and had sale for them. In this respect the contract is
not so indefinite as to be void: In defense of the motion to
strike, it is also urged that the contract is within the statute
of frauds, and the proofs offered are not competent, not being
in writing. The code on that subject, referring to contracts to
be evidenced in writing, is section 3664: "Such contracts embrace, — 1. Those in relation to the sale of personal property,
when no part of the property is delivered, and no part of the
price is paid." For the purpose of this question we must consider that the contract was made, as it turns upon the query,
if any part of the property was delivered, or any part of the
price paid. Conceding, for argument, that the contract was
made, we then have the undisputed facts that two lots of cigars
were ordered and delivered, — the lots being ten thousand
cigars each, — and one lot was paid for. We think this clearly
a part performance of the contract. The contract was to deliver or furnish cigars to establish and supply the trade in a
certain section. A part of the goods was furnished and applied

to the purpose, and a part paid for. The spirit of the law as to
the exceptions in proving such contracts would be violated to
hold that each lot was a separate transaction or contract. If
the contract was made, the plaintiffs had no discretion as to
supplying the orders if the trade continued. Each order was not
a new contract, but in fulfillment of the old one. With these
rulings the testimony of Farley and Meyer certainly presented
a question for the jury as to whether there was a contract, and
a breach thereof; and if so, it was error to strike out the testimony tending to show the damage.

3. Again, it is said that the contract is too indefinite to be
valid, because of the uncertainty as to territory embraced in
its terms. The point does not receive elaboration in argument, and we doubt if much reliance is placed upon it. The
contract, as alleged, is: "Dubuque, and the territory tributary
thereto." There is certainly a section of country tributary to
Dubuque for the purpose of such a trade, and it is certainly a
matter not insusceptible of proof; and again, the parties, by
their contract, seem to have eliminated much of the difficulty
anticipated, for it appears in the testimony above quoted that
there was an agreement that the plaintiffs should not sell
nearer than Omaha on the west, St. Louis on the south, Chicago on the east, and St. Paul on the north. While, perhaps,
with this and other testimony it would be very difficult, if not
impossible, to establish definite lines as bounding the territory
intended, the regulations of trade and the experience of tradesmen would enable the court to so find the fact as to meet the
intent of all parties, and enforce the contract with reasonable
certainty. If A should employ B as a traveling salesman in
Dubuque and the territory tributary thereto, we do not think
it would be held that either could avoid the contract merely
because of indefiniteness as to the territory. The law assumes that the parties contracted understandingly upon the
question, and the court will not dismiss them without inquiry
as to the fact, where its ascertainment is a matter of reasonable certainty. The case should not be confounded with the
rule as to contracts being disregarded because of indefiniteness
ness arising from the terms or language used in the contract,
where the intent of the parties cannot be understood.

4. Errors are assigned as to the rulings on the introduction
of testimony. Several questions were asked Mr. Farley bearing on the question of damage, and from appellees' argument
we infer that the rulings excluding the testimony were based

on the order of proofs as to which the court has a discretion; and as the rule as to the proper measure of damage is not before us, we think it unnecessary to consider the assignments.

5. The verdict in the case was returned on the 14th of November, and the motion for a new trial was not filed until the 18th, which was afterwards overruled, and it is urged that no error can be based thereon because not filed within the time provided by law. The position is likely correct as to errors based on the motion; but exceptions were taken and errors assigned independent of the motion for a new trial, and with such a record this court may review and reverse the action of the court below: Code, sec. 3169; *Drefahl* v. *Tuttle*, 42 Iowa, 177; *Brown* v. *Rose*, 55 Iowa, 734. Other cases are to the same effect.

The foregoing disposes of the necessary questions, and the judgment is reversed.

CUSTOM AND USAGE. — Parties to a contract are presumed to have contracted with reference to a uniform and well-established custom pertaining to matters concerning which they make the contract, provided such custom is not in contravention of well-settled rules of law, and is reasonable: *Smythe* v. *Parsons*, 37 Kan. 79; compare *Clark* v. *Baker*, 11 Met. 186; 45 Am. Dec. 199, and note. When there is nothing in a contract to negative the inference that the parties thereto contracted with reference to the usage which prevails in that particular trade or business to which the contract relates, then the usage may be shown in evidence for the purpose of ascertaining with greater certainty what was intended by the terms of the contract: *Dwyer* v. *City of Brenham*, 70 Tex. 30. And when a custom prevails among those who are engaged in a particular science, trade, or calling, persons engaged in such science, trade, or calling are competent to testify as to the existence of such custom: *Long* v. *Davidson*, 101 N. C. 170.

JURY TRIAL — SUFFICIENCY OF EVIDENCE. — It is the right of the jury to judge of the sufficiency of the evidence introduced to establish a fact: *Mynning* v. *Detroit etc. R. R. Co.*, 64 Mich. 93; 8 Am. St. Rep. 804, and note. So the effect of evidence, its credibility and its weight, is for the jury to determine: *Patterson* v. *Hayden*, 17 Or. 238; 11 Am. St. Rep. 822, and note.

JURY TRIAL. — The order of proof is largely a matter of discretion with the trial court: *Hannen* v. *Pence*, 40 Minn. 127; 12 Am. St. Rep. 717; *Village of Ponca* v. *Crawford*, 23 Neb. 662; 8 Am. St. Rep. 144; *Runyan* v. *Price*, 15 Ohio St. 1; 86 Am. Dec. 459.

CONTRACT OF EMPLOYMENT WITH TERM OF SERVICE AT DISCRETION. — When, in a contract of employment, the term of service is left to the discretion of either party, or indefinite, or determinable by either party, then either may put an end to it at will: *East Line etc. R. R. Co.* v. *Scott*, 72 Tex. 70; 13 Am. St. Rep. 758.

PART PERFORMANCE TO TAKE CONTRACT OUT OF STATUTE OF FRAUDS: See extended note to *Christy* v. *Barnhart*, 53 Am. Dec. 539-547. Part performance of a parol contract, which the statute requires to be reduced to writing, has no effect at law to take a case out of the provisions of the statute of frauds: *Henry* v. *Wells,* 48 Ark. 485.   An oral contract not to be performed within a year from its making, and not relating to land, is not taken out of the operation of the statute by part performance, as that equitable doctrine applies only to contracts relating to realty: *Osborne* v. *Kimball,* 41 Kan. 187; *Thorp* v. *Bradley,* 75 Iowa, 50.   But payment of purchase-money and change of possession, under an oral contract for the sale of land, not followed by permanent improvements by vendee, is not such performance as will take the contract out of the statute of frauds: *Bradley* v. *Owsley,* 74 Tex. 69.   Marriage alone is not part performance: *Adams* v. *Adams,* 17 Or. 247.   But with respect to contracts concerning realty, whole or part performance will take the contract out of the operation of the statute of frauds: *Tate* v. *Foshee,* 117 Ind. 322; *Slingerland* v. *Slingerland,* 31 Minn. 198.

CASES

IN THE

SUPREME COURT

OF

KANSAS.

ATCHISON, TOPEKA, AND SANTA FÉ RAILROAD COMPANY v. MORGAN.

[42 KANSAS, 23.]

FIXTURES. — PHYSICAL ANNEXATION TO REALTY is not alone sufficient to change the character of personal property from a chattel to a fixture.

FIXTURES. — WHETHER A CHATTEL BECOMES A FIXTURE depends upon the character of the act by which it is put into its place, the uses to which it is put, the policy of the law connected with its purpose, and the intention of those concerned.

FIXTURES. — PLACING A STRUCTURE ON LAND TO IMPROVE IT and make it more valuable is evidence that such structure has become a fixture; but if it is erected for a use which does not enhance the value of the land, it remains a chattel.

FIXTURES. — BEFORE PERSONAL PROPERTY CAN BECOME A FIXTURE by actual physical annexation to land, the intention of the parties and the uses to which it is put must combine to change its nature from that of a chattel to that of a fixture.

FIXTURES — PROPERTY ANNEXED BY MISTAKE. — Where a railroad company digs a well, puts in a pump and boiler, and erects a boiler-house for the sole use of operating its road, under the belief that it is occupying its own land, and only discovers its mistake after several years of occupation, the structures do not become fixtures, but may be removed by the company without paying the owner of the land therefor.

ACTION to enjoin further trespass, and to recover damages for trespass already committed. The opinion states the facts. Judgment for plaintiff, and defendant appeals.

George R. Peck, A. A. Hurd, and C. N. Sterry, for the plaintiff in error.

William Thomson, for the defendant in error.

HOLT, C. The plaintiff in error, defendant below, complains of two errors in the trial of the action,—one, allowing damages for the boiler, and its removal; the other, in decreeing a perpetual injunction against the removal of the pump. Both of the alleged errors involve the application of the same principles, and require the determination of the same question, namely, whether the several pieces of property retained their character as chattels, or became fixtures. What we may say of one thing in this connection will usually apply to all the others. It will be conceded that before plaintiff could recover for the conversion of the boiler, it must have become a part of his real estate. The boiler originally was the property of defendant, and it could have done with it as it pleased; and the only way it could have become divested of its ownership, under the facts in this case, was in the manner of placing it on plaintiff's land. If it then became a fixture, it was the property of plaintiff.

Hill gives this definition of fixtures: " By the term 'fixtures' are designated those articles which were chattels, but which, by being physically annexed or fixed to the real estate, become a part of and accessory to the freehold." It is frequently a difficult and vexatious question to ascertain the dividing line between real and personal property, and to decide upon which side of the line certain property belongs. When we compare a thing at the extremity of one class with a thing at the extremity of the other, the difference is obvious; but when we approach the question of fixtures, which is the dividing line between real and personal property, there is often great difficulty. The decisions of the courts are apparently as diverse as the peculiarities of the facts in the different cases that are decided; and being largely governed by the particular facts of each case, the citation and examination of decisions often tend to confuse rather than to enlighten the judgment.

In the statement of facts it is agreed that the boiler was placed on the ground upon a cast-iron base, was not set in masonry, and was connected with the pump by a steam-pipe, for the purpose of furnishing steam from the boiler to operate the pump, and thereby carry water to the tank. This of itself does not necessarily show such a physical attachment to the realty as constitutes a fixture: *Hendy* v. *Dinkerhoff*, 57 Cal. 3; 40 Am. Rep. 107; *Towne* v. *Fiske*, 127 Mass. 125; 34 Am. Rep. 353; *Kimball* v. *Grand Lodge etc.*, 131 Mass. 59; *Balliett* v.

Humphreys, 78 Ind. 388; *Hoyle* v. *Plattsburgh etc. R. R. Co.,* 51
Barb. 45.

But attachment to the realty is not alone sufficient to change
the character of personal property; it is only one of several
tests to determine whether property originally a chattel has
become a fixture by being used for a particular purpose; and
however the rule may have been formerly, it is not now deemed
to be the controlling test.   Tyler, on page 101 of his treatise
on Fixtures, says: "The simple criterion of physical annexation is so limited in its range, and so productive of contradiction, that it will not apply with much force, except in respect
to fixtures in dwellings."

In *Meigs's Appeal,* 62 Pa. St. 28, 1 Am. Rep. 372, it is said:
"In determining what is a fixture, the notion of physical attachment is exploded; it is now determined by the character
of the act by which the structure is put into its place, the
policy of the law connected with its purpose, and the intention
of those concerned."

This Pennsylvania case lays down the rule more broadly,
perhaps, than that of some other courts, yet it shows the tendency of modern decisions: See also Ewell on Fixtures, 20,
293.   There is scarcely any kind of machinery, however com-
plex in its character, or no matter how firmly held in its place,
which may not with care be taken from its fastenings and moved
without any serious injury to the structure where it may
have been operated, and to which it may have been attached.
That the simple fact of annexation to the realty is not the sole
and controlling test of whether a certain article is a fixture
or not, is very well illustrated by the fact that trees growing
in a nursery, and kept there for sale are personal property,
while trees no larger, if transplanted to an orchard, become
real estate.   On the other hand, there are very many things,
although not attached to the realty, which become real property by their use, — keys to a house, blinds and shutters to the
windows, fences and fence-rails, etc.

It can readily be seen that one of the tests of whether a
chattel retains its character or becomes a fixture is the uses to
which it is put.   If it be placed on the land for the purpose
of improving it, and to make it more valuable, that is evidence
that it is a fixture.   Applying this criterion to the boiler, we
are led to inquire whether this benefited the land of plaintiff.
The real estate upon which this boiler was placed was a nar-

row strip in the city of Burlingame, and it cannot be contended
that this well, boiler, and the attachments could have greatly
benefited this small tract of land. They were not placed there
for the purpose of enhancing its value; ordinarily it would not
enhance the value of such property in a city, as this small
piece of ground, by digging a well thereon like the one in
question; and the only value added thereto by placing a pump,
boiler, and boiler-house like those in controversy would be
what they were worth as chattels. The test of whether real
estate is benefited by the act of annexation has been repeatedly
applied by the courts to determine whether the chattel annexed became a fixture or not: 11 Alb. L. J. 151; *Ottumwa
W. M. Co.* v. *Hawley*, 44 Iowa, 57; 24 Am. Rep. 719; *Taylor*
v. *Collins*, 51 Wis. 123; *Huebschmann* v. *McHenry*, 29 Wis. 655;
Minnesota Co. v. *St. Paul Co.*, 2 Wall. 645; *Northern Cent. R'y
Co.* v. *Canton Co.*, 30 Md. 347; *Wagner* v. *Cleveland etc. R. R.
Co.*, 22 Ohio St. 563; 10 Am. Rep. 770.

It has been held that before personal property can become
a fixture by actual physical annexation, the intention of the
parties and the uses for which the personal property is to be
put must all combine to change its nature from that of the
chattel to that of the fixture: *Teaff* v. *Hewitt*, 1 Ohio St. 511;
69 Am. Dec. 634; Ewell on Fixtures, 293; *Ottumwa W. M. Co.*
v. *Hawley*, *supra*. In this connection, it is well enough to note,
also, the circumstances under which this boiler was placed upon
the land of plaintiff. It is conceded that the railroad company
was a trespasser, yet it was not a willful one; it dug the well,
put in the pump and boiler, and erected the boiler-house, under
the belief it was occupying its own land, and only discovered
its mistake after some years of occupation. There is nothing
to show that it wished to gain anything by digging the well
where it was located rather than on its own land; in fact, it is
stated that two feet of the well is upon its own land. It can
be safely presumed that the well would have been as good a
one if it had been placed on defendant's side of the division
line instead of plaintiff's. It dug the well, put in the pump
and boiler, for the sole purpose of operating its railroad, and
not to improve the land where the property was placed.

The company began condemnation proceedings to obtain
the land, but did not follow them to a conclusion; if it had, it
would have been compelled to only pay for the land, and not
for its own improvements thereon. This rule is well estab-

lished by authority: *Cohen* v. *St. Louis etc. R'y Co.*, 34 Kan. 158; 55 Am. Rep. 242; *Justice* v. *Nesquehoning V. R. R. Co.*, 87 Pa. St. 28; *Daniels* v. *Chicago etc. R. R. Co.*, 41 Iowa, 52; *Lyon* v. *Green Bay etc. R. R. Co.*, 42 Wis. 538; *Greve* v. *St. Paul etc. R. R. Co.*, 26 Minn. 66; *Wagner* v. *Cleveland etc. R. R. Co.*, *supra*; *Schroeder* v. *De Graff*, 28 Minn. 299.

While it is the general rule, in regard to annexation made by a stranger with his own materials on the soil of another without his consent, that the owner of the materials loses his property, because he is presumed to have parted with it and dedicated it to the owner of the land, yet the peculiar circumstances under which this well was dug would indicate there should be a modification in this instance: *Lowenberg* v. *Bernd*, 47 Mo. 297. If the company had placed it there, even under a mistake, for the purpose of ultimately improving the real estate, the law might, under this state of facts, have held it to be the property of the owner of the real estate; but under the agreed statement it was placed there solely for the purpose of better operating its own railroad. If it had been placed on its own right of way, and that afterward abandoned, then, under a respectable list of authorities, it would have been permitted to take away the pump, boiler, and boiler-house. We can see no reason for a distinction that would have allowed any compensation to plaintiff if condemnation proceedings had been instituted, after occupation and placing improvements upon the land, and prosecuted to a conclusion, and an action brought in the way this one was. In one case, the authorities are an almost unbroken current that the railroad company could not have been compelled to pay for its own property placed upon the land. We also think it should not be required to do so now. We believe, in this action, because the improvements did not and were not intended to benefit the realty, that the pump, boiler, and building should be held to be personal property, and not fixtures. We are well aware that very many authorities hold that the buckets in a well are real property; unquestionably, between vendor and vendee and mortgagor and mortgagee this is the rule; but under the facts in this case, considering the use to which these articles were put, and the relations of the parties, we are constrained to believe that that rule does not apply.

For the reasons given above, we recommend that the judgment awarding damages against the defendant be reversed, and the injunction so granted be modified as to allow the defendant to remove the pump.

By the COURT. It is so ordered.

FIXTURES, WHAT ARE: See *Hopewell Mills* v. *Taunton Sav. Bank,* 150 Mass. 519; 15 Am. St. Rep. 235, and note 239. Compare *McGorrisk* v. *Dwyer,* 78 Iowa, 279; *ante,* p. 440, and note.

BARNEY *v.* DUDLEY.

[42 KANSAS, 212.]

LIFE INSURANCE — CONVERSION OF POLICY — MEASURE OF DAMAGES. — In an action to recover for conversion of a life insurance policy, the measure of damages is the present value of the benefit stated in the policy, less the value of premiums required to procure a similar policy on the same life calculated upon his expectancy of life, when the insured is in good health and his life insurable; but when he is not, this may be shown to reduce his expectancy, and it may also be shown by expert evidence that by reason of ill health a greater rate of premium would be required to reimburse him on account of his shortened expectancy of life, and if, from a computation of the present value of the benefit and the present value of the premiums to be paid during the life, the value of the benefit is greater than the value of the premiums, the difference is the measure of damages for the conversion.

ACTION by plaintiff against defendant and another to recover the value of a life insurance policy in favor of plaintiff's husband and payable to her at his death. She alleges that defendants have unlawfully and wrongfully converted such policy to their own use. Verdict for plaintiff. Defendants moved for a new trial, and their motion was sustained, from which an appeal was taken and the ruling of the lower court affirmed, after which a motion for a rehearing was filed.

G. C. Clemens, for the motion.

W. P. Douthitt, and Overmyer and Safford, against the motion.

CLOGSTON, C. The motion for a rehearing is denied; but, inasmuch as this case goes back for a new trial, it is thought better to establish the rule or measure of damages the plaintiff is entitled to if she should recover. The plaintiff had, before the conversion of this policy, paid in as premiums $803.60. This included fourteen semi-annual premiums of $57.40 each. Now, to establish this sum as the plaintiff's measure of recovery, with interest, would be to allow the insured free insurance during the seven years in which premiums have been paid. This rule would not be a correct one, for the insured would have paid no consideration for the insurance during that period of time. The general rule is, as between the insured and the insurance company, when the company's business is wound up, or a policy is canceled, where an action is brought for damages, that the measure of damages is the difference between the rate of premium paid for the old insurance and what another company of equal credit and standing would charge to issue a new policy on the same life, and the difference in the rates of premium calculated upon his expectancy of life. This is upon the ground that the insured is placed in as good a condition as he was before his policy was canceled. This seems just and equitable: *People* v. *Security Life Ins. Co.*, 78 N. Y. 114; 34 Am. Rep. 522; *Bell's Case*, L. R. 9 Eq. 717; *Universal Life Ins. Co.* v. *Binford*, 76 Va. 103; *Phœnix etc. Ins. Co.* v. *Baker*, 85 Ill. 410. But it is claimed that this rule is not an equitable one as applied to the facts of this case. It is shown here that Barney, by reason of ill health, is now non-insurable. This, then, presents a different question, a question that has been discussed in many courts, and always a conclusion reached with doubts as to its correctness. The rule above stated we think not equitable as applied to this case, for this reason: the insured, at the time of taking the insurance, does it upon the thought and reason that disease and sickness are likely to happen to him. Insurance would be effected upon few lives, we think, if the insured was certain that no such mishap would overtake him, and that only by old age would death come; and insurance companies insure each individual with this in view. The premiums are figured upon a contingency of accident, sickness, and premature death, and now to apply this rule to this case would leave the plaintiff robbed of a part of the contract against accident and premature decay: *Holdich's Case*, L. R. 14 Eq. 79.

Again, to establish a rule that would make the tables of mortality the only evidence of the number of premiums the plaintiff would be compelled to pay, and deduct these premiums from the face of the policy, would practically deprive the plaintiff of the very thing that insurance was taken to guard against, and plaintiff would recover no benefit by reason of the ill health of the insured which prevents reinsurance. This general rule is held to apply to both classes in the case of *People* v. *Security Life Ins. Co.*, 78 N. Y. 114; 34 Am. Rep.

522; but that was a case where the insurance company was going out of business, and was closing up its affairs, and the court established that general rule in that case because of the impossibility and impracticability of ascertaining the state of health of each person holding a policy therein. The defendants in this case stand upon a different footing from the insurance company in that case. Here the insurance company is still carrying the policy, and the defendants will receive the benefit from it. They have elected to appropriate and withhold this policy from the plaintiff, seeking to pay the premiums, and finally to recover at the death of Barney. When they place themselves voluntarily in this position, they cannot complain if the strongest rule is held against them.

It is said in *People* v. *Security Life Ins. Co., supra:* " But the health of the policy-holder may since his insurance have become so impaired that his life is not now reinsurable, and hence in his particular case the value to be arrived at upon this basis [speaking of the general rule] would not be the measure of his damage." So we think as applied to these defendants the rule ought to be such as will give the plaintiff the full value of the policy at the time of its conversion, with interest. How to arrive at this value, as we said before, is a difficult question, — one surrounded with uncertainties, depending upon the opinions of persons or insurance companies; but as before said, the defendants voluntarily assumed the risk, and they cannot complain. We therefore think the general rule above stated applicable to this case, with the modification, that if Barney is not insurable by reason of ill health or accident, that fact may be shown to reduce his expectancy. It may also be shown by experienced and expert insurance men that by reason of the ill health of the insured a greater rate of premium would be required to reinsure him on account of the shortened expectancy of his life. All these things may be given for the purpose of aiding the jury in determining his expectancy, and in this way determining the actual value of the policy at the time of its conversion; for if the insured's expectancy has been reduced in proportion to such reduction the value of his policy has increased.

It was said in *Bell's Case,* L. R. 9 Eq. 717: " As to the lives, it will be assumed, until the contrary is shown, that they are all in a normal state; that no other change has taken place than that which arises from the advance of age. If in addition to that, either from accident or illness, a higher rate of assurance is required, that must be added to the proof.   That is one of the things which the office has assured against, and the chance of life has diminished." See also *Speer* v. *Life Ins. Co.*, 36 Hun, 322. ·

We think the rule is fair and equitable as between the plaintiff and defendants, and therefore recommend that it be adopted.

By the COURT.   It is so ordered.

MEASURE OF DAMAGES IN ACTIONS OF TROVER for the conversion of property: *Woolley* v. *Carter*, 11 Am. Dec. 527, 528; *Hersey* v. *Walsh*, 38 Minn. 521; 8 Am. St. Rep. 689, and note.

KANSAS, NEBRASKA, AND DAKOTA RAILWAY COMPANY *v.* CUYKENDALL.

[42 KANSAS, 234.]

DAMAGES — ABUTTING LOT-OWNER. — In order to justify a recovery for damages by an abutting city lot-owner against a railroad company authorized to construct and operate its road along a street, there must be such a practical obstruction of the street in front of the lots that the owner is denied ingress to and egress from them.

Ware, Biddle, and Cory, for the plaintiff in error.

Kirk, Schoonover, and Bowman, for the defendant in error.

SIMPSON, C.   Cuykendall commenced his action in the district court of Anderson County, alleging that he was the owner in fee-simple of the north half of lots 9, 10, 11, and 12, in block 76, in the city of Garnett; that said lots front 70 feet on Main Street and 180 on Seventh Avenue, are improved by a dwelling-house, fencing, and otherwise, and are occupied by plaintiff and his family as a residence; that the dwelling-house faces on Main Street, and the outlet and inlet to the property is over and upon these two streets; that the railroad company, on or about the first day of March, 1886, constructed, and has ever since operated, its line of road in and upon said Main Street, and made an embankment six feet in height near the east side of said Main Street, and directly up to and fronting against the west side of plaintiff's property; that said embankment and line of railroad are so constructed as to obstruct the street, and are illegally and improperly made and maintained; and he prays for a judgment for damages.   The railroad company pleads a city ordinance granting it the right

of way over and upon said street and others, and that the line
was constructed in accordance with the terms and conditions
of the ordinance. At the trial the following special interroga-
tories were answered by the jury, and a verdict returned in
favor of Cuykendall for $190.

"1. Is the defendant's railway constructed along and upon
Main Street west of plaintiff's property? A. Yes.

"2. What is the distance from plaintiff's lots to the railroad
on Main Street? A. Northwest corner, thirty-three and a half
feet, more or less; southwest corner, twenty-seven feet, more
or less.

"3. How many feet on Main Street is there on the east side
of defendant's railroad and between the railroad and plaintiff's
property that is now open for use? A. Outside of sidewalk,
fifteen feet more or less.

"4. Does the defendant's railroad obstruct the means of
ingress to and egress from plaintiff's premises to and upon
Main Street? A. Yes.

"5. Does the defendant's railroad obstruct the means of
ingress to and egress from plaintiff's premises upon Seventh
Street? A. No.

"6. If the defendant's railroad obstructs the plaintiff's ingress and egress to and from Main Street, state in what such
obstruction consists. A. By defendant's railroad embankment.

"7. If defendant's railroad obstructs the plaintiff's ingress
and egress to and upon Seventh Avenue, state in what such
obstruction consists. A. Nothing."

The question involved in this case has been the subject of
much consideration in this court, and three opinions have
been rendered which mark with some degree of reasonable
certainty the line between the liability and non-liability of
railroad companies whose lines are constructed along public
streets, to abutting owners for damages. These cases are:
Atchison etc. R. R. Co. v. *Garside*, 10 Kan. 552; *Central Branch
etc. R. R. Co.* v. *Andrews*, 30 Kan. 590; *Ottawa etc. R. R. Co.*
v. *Larson*, 40 Kan. 301. The rule to be deduced from these
cases, and from what has been said by the court in the cases
of *Central Branch etc. R. R. Co.* v. *Twine*, 23 Kan. 585, 33
Am. Rep. 203, *Kansas City etc. R. R. Co.* v. *Hicks*, 30 Kan.
288, and *Heller* v. *Atchison etc. R. R. Co.*, 28 Kan. 625, is, that
in order to justify a recovery for damages by the abutting lot-
owner, there must be such a practical obstruction of the street

in front of the lots that the owner is denied ingress to and egress from them. While the title to the streets is in the county, the legislature has given to the city government the power of full control. The abutting lot-owner has no greater right to the use of the public street than a railroad company that has been authorized to construct its line along it. Each must respect the use of the other, but nothing short of a practical obstruction of the use by one will be a cause of action to the other. A railroad is not an unreasonable obstruction to the free use of a street, but rather a new and improved method of using the same, and germane to its principal object as a passage-way, like the electric, steam-moter, and horse-car lines: Mills on Eminent Domain, sec. 199; *Briggs* v. *Lewiston etc. R'y Co.*, 79 Me. 363; 1 Am. St. Rep. 316; *Slatten* v. *Des Moines V. R'y Co.*, 29 Iowa, 149; 4 Am. Rep. 205. So that if the location and construction of the line of railroad are authorized by the city council, and its location in the street is such as to give the lot-owner ingress to and egress from his lots, such use of the street by the railroad company does not interfere with the use of the lot-owner, and consequently he cannot recover for those remote and indirect inconveniences "arising from smoke, noise, offensive vapors, sparks, fires, shaking of the ground," and other annoyances: *Atchison etc. R. R. Co.* v. *Garside*, 10 Kan. 552. But where the location of the track is such that space enough is left in the street in front of the lots of the abutting owner, so that he can pass between the sidewalk and track, and the railroad is operated in a legal and proper manner, the lot-owner cannot recover because the space within which he has heretofore passed from and to his lots is restricted.

There are cases in which a different rule would be applied, as where the city council has not authorized the use of the street by the railroad company, or where the railroad is operated in an illegal or wrongful manner, or where the railroad company has practically obstructed the whole street so that no one can pass and repass; but the facts in this case call for the application of the rule as laid down above. The jury specially find that there is a part of the street immediately in front of the lots owned and occupied by the defendant in error, and outside of the sidewalk fifteen feet in width between the sidewalk and the side of the railroad which is open for use, and this gives him reasonable ingress and egress. There is another reason why the defendant in error cannot recover. His property is situated on the corner of Main Street and Seventh Avenue, fronting on Main Street seventy feet, and fronting on Seventh Avenue one hundred and sixty feet. The jury specially find that the railroad does not obstruct the means of ingress to and egress from plaintiff's premises to and upon Seventh Avenue, the law being that "although one public way to property is closed, if there is another left, the property owner sustains no actionable damage." See the Garside case, and the following authorities cited therein: *Fearing* v. *Irwin*, 55 N. Y. 486; *Castle* v. *Berkshire*, 11 Gray, 26; *Ingram* v. *Chicago etc. R. R. Co.*, 38 Iowa, 669; *Burr* v. *Oskaloosa*, 45 Iowa, 275; *Petition of Concord*, 50 N. H. 530; *Lutterloh* v. *Mayor etc.* 15 Fla. 306.

If the plaintiff in error could recover in this action at all, it would be on the theory that there was such a departure by the railroad company from the terms and conditions of the ordinance of the city authorizing its location and construction, that the railroad track and embankment was a nuisance; that while the city gave the railroad company the use of a part of the street, it did not authorize the use of the particular portion of the street, and that the road was not constructed and operated in a legal manner. If these facts had appeared in the record, what would be the measure of damages? Proof of damages at the trial was confined in the evidence to the difference in market value before and after the construction of the road, and while the instructions of the court approached nearer to the right basis, the true measure was not reached. It is doubtful, under the supposed state of facts, whether the plaintiff below could recover only such damages as had occurred up to the commencement of the action: *Uline* v. *New York Central R. R. Co.*, 101 N. Y. 98; 53 Am. Rep. 123; 54 Am. Rep. 661, and authorities cited in that case. "Where one creates a nuisance, and permits it to remain, so long as it remains it is treated as a continuing wrong, and giving rise over and over again to causes of action": *Kansas Pac. R'y Co.* v. *Mihlman*, 17 Kan. 224.

It is recommended that the judgment of the district court be reversed.

By the COURT. It is so ordered.

———

The case of *Kansas, Nebraska, and Dakota R'y Co.* v. *McAfee*, reported in 42 Kan. 239, argued and submitted in connection with the principal case, was an action for damages by the owner of the south half of the same lots involved in that controversy. The action was commenced against plaintiff in error and the Missouri Pacific Railway Company, alleging complete obstruction to the property by both railroad tracks. For the reasons given in the principal case, the court was of opinion that there could be no recovery against the plaintiff in error. The Missouri Pacific Railway Company had constructed a switch, or "Y," so near the sidewalk adjoining the property as to practically prevent access to the street, and this without authority from the city. The property owned by defendant in error did not front on any other street, and the only access to it was from Main Street. The embankment of this switch, or "Y," was on Main Street in front of the property mentioned, and was four feet five inches high. The distance from the line of the property fronting on Main Street to the east rail of the switch was seven feet two inches, including the sidewalk and eastern slope of the embankment on which the rails are placed, thus practically obstructing the street in front of the lots, and preventing access to or egress from them. Under this state of facts, the court was of opinion that the defendant in error was entitled to recover as against the Missouri Pacific Railway Company in the sum of $333, and the· judgment of the lower court to that effect was affirmed.

STREET RAILROADS. — When land has been lawfully taken for a street, legislative and municipal authority may authorize the construction and operation of a street-railroad upon it, without providing for additional compensation to the land-owner: *Briggs* v. *Lewiston etc. R. R. Co.*, 79 Me. 363; 1 Am. St. Rep. 316, and note. But compare *Theobold* v. *Louisville etc. R'y Co.*, 66 Miss. 279; 14 Am. St. Rep. 564, and note 569, as to the use of streets for railroad purposes, and the rights of abutting lot-owners.

STATE v. REYNOLDS.

[42 KANSAS, 320.]

CRIMINAL LAW — DEATH CAUSED BY PHYSICIAN WHEN NOT A CRIME. — A skillful and competent physician who examines the womb of his patient to ascertain whether she is pregnant, and the condition of the part, with an instrument commonly used for such purpose, and not likely to be used to produce an abortion, and who, without culpable negligence or unlawful intent, while so doing, accidentally inflicts an injury which causes the patient's death, is not guilty of any crime.

J. F. Ward and *J.· G. Waters*, for the appellant.

L. B. Kellogg, attorney-general, for the state.

JOHNSTON, J.   Vernon M. Reynolds was prosecuted in the district court of Wichita County for murder. The information upon which he was tried charges substantially that on the fifteenth day of July, 1888, Dr. Reynolds unlawfully and feloniously, and with malice aforethought, wounded and injured one Samanda Biehn with a certain steel instrument, called a surgeon's sound, thereby inflicting a mortal wound on her womb, which caused her death on the fourteenth day of November, 1888. Upon the trial, which occurred at the June term, 1889, the defendant was convicted of manslaughter in the first degree; and from a judgment upon this conviction he appeals to this court.

It is quite clear that the judgment is unsupported by the testimony, and must be reversed and set aside. Samanda Biehn died on November 14, 1888, and the evidence derived from the *post-mortem* examination tended to show that the immediate cause of her death was peritonitis, which was probably induced by a cut discovered on the womb, about half an inch long and one eighth of an inch deep. The appellant was a practicing physician and surgeon, and Samanda was his patient, who had applied to and received treatment from him for womb disease. She was working in a tailor-shop from February, 1888, and in the early part of July complained of her health, when her employer advised her to consult with Dr. Reynolds, which she did. There is no dispute but that he treated her for some illness, and that an examination was made by him about the 15th of July, 1888, in which an instrument called a surgeon's sound was used. The theory of the prosecution, and the one on which the case was given to the jury, was, that the sound was used by the appellant for the purpose of producing an abortion, and that while engaged in the commission of that act he inflicted the wound which caused her death. In submitting the case, the court instructed the jury that "if Vernon M. Reynolds did, by the use of some instrument, while in the commission of an unlawful act, inflict a wound upon the person of the deceased, and that said wound was the cause of the death of said deceased, and that said wound was inflicted without malice, express or implied, then the offense would be manslaughter in the first degree." And further, that "homicide is excusable when committed by accident or misfortune in doing any lawful act, by lawful means, with usual and ordinary caution, and without unlawful intent."

There is a total failure of proof to show any malice or intent to kill, and none to show that the surgeon's sound was used by the doctor in the commission of an unlawful act. The attorney-general frankly concedes that if the conviction stands it must rest alone on what is termed a dying declaration of the deceased. This declaration was made about three months after the sound had been used by the doctor, and thirty-four days before her death. She continued in her regular employment until the day preceding the one on which the statement was made, and although the physician who attended her is called as a witness, he was not asked and did not state that he ever told her the illness would be fatal, or that she was likely to die.

From all the circumstances surrounding the case, which need not be detailed here, we entertain great doubts of the admissibility of her dying statement in evidence. The conclusion we have reached, however, makes it unnecessary to determine that question. If we assume her declarations to be competent testimony, they still fail to show any criminality on the part of the appellant. She states that the doctor had sexual intercourse with her, after which he used the sound. According to the witness Kammer, to whom the statement is is said to have been made, when asked why the sound was used, she said: " He told me he was afraid she was becoming in a family way; that she had not had her monthly courses at the proper time. It was a week or ten days past the time." She did not state the purpose for which the sound was used,— whether for an abortion, or merely to examine and ascertain her condition; and the proof of the experts who examined the womb is that she had not been pregnant. The testimony offered by the state is to the effect that the sound is a proper instrument for making an examination of the womb, and not one likely to be used to produce an abortion. The testimony of Dr. Reynolds as to the treatment and the purpose of the operation is as follows:—

" Q. Now state, doctor, what operation you performed upon the person of Samanda Biehn on that occasion. A. I suppose you are aware that I had been doctoring her? You just want that question answered. I went there for the purpose of seeing how she was getting along, and she was complaining as she had been before, and I told her I had better make an examination of the parts, and she said, 'All right'; so I took this instrument just in that shape [shows the jury how he did it], and I introduced it just as you see right there, introduced it in that way, and then it is turned up in that shape.

" Q. Explain to the jury what that is. A. That is a speculum.

" Q. State to the jury whether or not that is the same kind of a speculum that you used in that case. A. I would say it is not.

"Q. What is the difference? A. The difference between them is this: this one has three prongs; the one I used was in only two parts.

"Q. Any other difference? A. Yes, sir; some other difference. It is best that this here run down in this way, and these two places here. After I got the instrument inserted in that shape, I turned it so. The mouth of the womb was turned in. While I was doing that, she complained, — she was very tender, — and after I did that I looked there, and the mouth of the womb was in shape so that I could see it. Says I, 'You are unwell.' And she says, 'I don't know.' She had been troubled with ulcers, and I thought it might be caused by these ulcers.

"Q. State to the jury whether you used that kind of an instrument. A. I had an instrument similar to that. And I took my dressing forceps first; I took up a piece of cotton just in that way, and I sponged off the parts, and found that it was ulcers which had made her trouble, and I sponged the places, and found the ulcers were bleeding to some extent. There was too much hemorrhage there for it to come from ulcers. I says, 'You are surely unwell.' Says she, 'It may be that I am.' I says, 'If you are unwell, it is useless for me to make any application.'

"Q. State to the jury what wound, if any, you inflicted upon the person of Samanda Biehn that day. A. I never inflicted any wound at all.

"Q. Did you ever perform any operation on her except that which you have testified to? A. I have performed no operation only that stated.

"Q. State to the jury whether you ever inflicted any wound upon the person of Samanda Biehn. A. I never did.

"Q. State for what purpose that instrument was used upon that Sunday. A. I used the instrument for doctoring the patient the same as I would any other patient.

"Q. What was the matter with the patient? A. She had been troubled with womb troubles.

"Q. I will ask you to state to the jury if this girl was pregnant at that time, — at the time you performed this operation. A. I would say that she was not, because was unwell at the time.

"Q. State to the jury whether or not at any time you have ever performed any operation for the purpose of performing an abortion. A. I never did."

Accepting the statement of the deceased to the fullest extent, there is an absence of evidence to prove that the sound was used for the purpose of procuring an abortion, and, as we have seen, the appellant specifically denies that such was the purpose for which the operation was performed. As a matter of fact, there was no pregnancy, and therefore no occasion for an attempt to produce abortion. It will be conceded that if the doctor was not engaged in an unlawful act, but used the instrument to make an examination with a view of ascertaining her condition, and did so without culpable negligence or unlawful intent, he is not guilty, although while doing so he may have accidentally inflicted the injury which caused her death: *State* v. *Schulz*, 55 Iowa, 628; 39 Am. Rep. 187; *Rice* v. *State*, 8 Mo. 561; *Commonwealth* v. *Thompson*, 6 Mass. 137; 1 Hale P. C. 429; 2 Bishop's Crim. Law, 695; 3 Wharton and Stillé's Medical Jurisprudence, secs. 754 et seq.

The testimony goes no farther, and the conviction cannot stand. The appellant was a physician and surgeon, and there is no attempt to show that he was not competent and skillful in his profession. The instrument used in the examination was suitable and proper, and such as is commonly used for that purpose; and proof requisite to a conviction of recklessness in the use of the instrument, or of evil intent, is entirely wanting. In fact, the record does not fairly establish that the wound found on her womb was even inflicted by the instrument which Dr. Reynolds used in the examination, or that it could have been made at a period so remote as when that operation was performed.

Dr. Smith, a witness for the state, who examined Samanda in October, and attended her in the last illness, was unwilling to give an opinion that an instrument had been used prior to the time he was called to attend her in October. He was then inclined to think that violence had been used in the treatment of the womb, either by herself or some one else, but that the inflammation or peritonitis from which she died might have been caused by a cold, or any rough treatment of the womb. He stated that a well-defined wound, apparently made by some instrument, was found on the womb at the *post-mortem* examination, but that it might have been made by an instrument like the point of a probe or a syringe.

Dr. Knapp, another witness called by the state, who was a practicing physician, and the coroner before whom the *post-*

mortem examination was conducted, gave the following testimony:—

"Q. I will ask you to state if you could tell upon the examination you made, if you are able to state the cause of the death of Samanda Biehn? A. I had an opinion of it at that time.

"Q. What is that opinion? A. That she died from peritonitis.

"Q. What was the condition, if you know, of the womb? A. It was highly inflamed and congested; the cervix was highly congested.

"Q. What was the condition of the mouth of the womb as to its being injured? A. I should think that it had been meddled with.

"Q. State to the jury whether, on that examination which was made, there was anything from which you could ascertain the cause of the death, except the appearance and condition of the womb. A. There was nothing.

"Q. Describe the wound that was on the mouth of the womb at that time. A. I don't know that I can very well.

"Q. State to the jury what was indicated by the condition of the wound that you refer to; how long had it been made? A. From the appearance of it, it would seem that it had been made very recently. Half the neck of the womb presented the appearance of having been handled very roughly.

"Q. What do you mean by the expression 'very recently'? A. Well, within three or four weeks.

"Q. State what your conclusion is in regard to the likelihood of that wound having been inflicted as long previous as July 15th. A. I don't believe it was.

"Q. What kind of an instrument would you say produced that wound? A. Some blunt instrument. It could be inflicted with the nozzle of a syringe, or with a blunt-pointed lead-pencil, with a family catheter, or any blunt instrument of the size of a lead-pencil.

"Q. Doctor, I will ask you to state to the jury whether or not a wound like that which appeared upon this womb, inflicted in July, 1888, would be recognizable in November, 1888. A. In my opinion, it would not be recognizable if it was left alone.

"Q. State to the jury whether or not such a wound as that you have described as being upon this womb might not have been a cut. A. I think it was a cut. It did n't look to me as if it was made by a blunt instrument.

"Q. State to the jury whether or not, in your opinion, that wound was made with a surgeon's sound, or any kind of a sound. A. I don't believe it was.

"Q. State to the jury, doctor, what is the ordinary use of the sound. A. Explorations of the outside of the womb, and, where you can see, to explore the interior of the womb; and it is never used for abortions at all."

This is the evidence of the prosecution, and is corroboration of that given by Dr. Reynolds. It is the testimony of two of the principal witnesses for the state, and tends strongly to show that the wound which caused the peritonitis and death was inflicted long after July, when the sound was used by Dr. Reynolds, and also that it was made by some other instrument than a surgeon's sound. If a wound was made subsequent to July, 1888, as seems to have been the case, it was done by some one other than the defendant; for the undisputed evidence is, that he did not use an instrument nor perform an operation on the patient after the one conceded to have been performed in July.

We are clearly of the opinion that the judgment is unsupported by the testimony and unauthorized by law; and it will therefore be reversed, and the defendant discharged from custody.

———

HOMICIDE CAUSED BY A PHYSICIAN. — If death results from disease, not from an operation performed by a physician, the.physician is not liable for such death, even though the disease resulted from the operation, provided the physician performed the operation with the patient's consent, believing that such an operation was proper to be performed: *State v. Housekeeper*, 70 Md. 162; 14 Am. St. Rep. 340, and note 343, with reference to the skill and care required of physicians.

A physician may, by his negligence in causing the death of his patient, be guilty of manslaughter, or, if the injury falls short of deprivation of life, he may be guilty merely of a misdemeanor: Note to *Howard v. Grover*, 48 Am. Dec. 486, 487. Thus a physician may be found guilty of manslaughter for causing the death of his patient by wrapping him in clothes saturated with kerosene oil: *Commonwealth v. Pierce*, 138 Mass. 165; 52 Am. Rep. 264. But while a physician may be criminally responsible for his gross negligence in causing the death of a patient, he is not liable for a mere mistake in judgment: *State v. Hardister*, 38 Ark. 605; 42 Am. Rep. 5; and a physician honestly and to the best of his ability prescribing for a patient is not criminally answerable for his death from the medicines so prescribed: *State v. Schulz*, 55 Iowa, 698; 39 Am. Rep. 187.

KANE AND COMPANY *v.* BARSTOW.

[42 KANSAS, 465.]

AGENCY — AUTHORITY OF AGENT TO COLLECT. — Authority to an agent to sell goods does not include authority to collect pay for the goods sold.

AGENCY — AGENT'S AUTHORITY. — RULE THAT PRINCIPAL IS BOUND by the acts of his agent within the apparent scope of his authority is applicable only when there have been previous transactions of a similar character, in which the agent exceeded his powers, and which have been ratified by the principal without question, and without knowledge on the part of the third party of a limitation of the agent's authority, and an excess in the particular case, whereby such party is led to believe that the agent has all the powers assumed.

AGENCY — EVIDENCE. — AGENT'S DECLARATIONS OF HIS AGENCY are inadmissible in an action between the principal and a third party, for the purpose of establishing the agency.

M. A. Thompson, for the plaintiffs in error.

Lasley and Borah, for the defendants in error.

SIMPSON, C.   Thomas Kane & Co. commenced their action against the defendants in error, before a justice of the peace in Rice County, to recover the sum of $31.80 for two slate-stone blackboards, furnished the school district of which the defendants in error were the officers.   An appeal was taken to the district court, a trial had by jury, and a verdict and judgment for the defendants in error.   The only controverted question of fact is that of payment.   The blackboards were sold to the school district by one Roberts, whose agency for the purposes of sale is undisputed.   The question is, whether he was authorized to receive payment.   The defendants in error paid Roberts, and defend the payment on the sole ground that, as he was the acknowledged agent for the sale, he was the apparent person to whom to make the payment.   The goods were shipped about the fifth day of October, 1885, from Chicago, to L. S. Barstow, Little River, Kansas.   With the goods was sent a bill with the following heading: " Settlements must be made directly with us; in no case with an agent or salesman, unless he presents our written authority.   We shall hold purchasers responsible for the strict observance of this rule."   The blackboards were to be paid for in thirty days, but the payment was not made to Roberts until about the twenty-second of February, 1886.   On the second day of November, 1885, Kane & Co. sent a bill to Barstow, stating therein that it was payable in Chicago.   On the first day of January, 1886, they sent a bill to Barstow, stating therein that it was payable in

Chicago. The defendants in error denied knowledge of these bills, and denied ever having received any notice not to pay to Roberts. They admitted that they received bills, but denied knowledge of the notice not to pay agents. This was the only transaction between the parties. There had been no previous dealings with Kane & Co. through Roberts or any one else. On this state of facts the trial court was requested by the plaintiffs in error to instruct the jury as follows:—

"1. Since the principal is bound only by such acts of his agent as have been authorized or allowed, proof that an agent has authority to make a sale of goods, or to take orders for them to be filled by the principal, is not sufficient to prove that the agent has the authority to collect the pay for the goods afterward. The defendants must prove that Roberts, the man to whom they paid, was authorized to receive the money, or else fail in their defense.

"2. That the rule that a principal is bound by the acts of his agent, which are within the apparent scope of the agent's authority, has no application to this case; this rule is applicable only where there have been previous transactions of a similar character in which the agent exceeded his powers, but which the principal ratified without question or without information, the opposite party being ignorant of the limitation of the agent's authority, and the excess in the particular instance, thereby leading the opposite party to believe that the agent has all the powers that he assumed to have."

These instructions the court refused to give, but charged the jury as follows: "It is claimed by the plaintiffs in this suit that Roberts had no authority from them to collect payments for these blackboards, and this is a material question in this case; and as to what is the apparent authority of an agent is also a material question for the jury to consider. A principal is bound by the representations of his agent; and is also bound by the contracts which his agent makes within the apparent scope of the agent's authority. If the agent had the authority in this case to collect money, or if the collection of money was within the apparent scope of his authority, and if the defendants made payment to him without any further knowledge of his authority, except what was apparent, then it would be payment to the principal, and if such payment was made, the plaintiffs cannot recover in this case. It is within the apparent scope of an agent's authority, where he has authority to sell, to collect for such sales; for instance, in this case, if Mr. Roberts had the authority to sell blackboards for the plaintiffs, it was apparently within the scope of his authority to collect payment for such sales, and not authorized to collect; in order that the defendants would be held responsible for any payments they might make to Mr. Roberts on such sales, it was the duty of the plaintiffs to notify the defendants of the limit of their agent's authority. There has been introduced in evidence what is claimed by the plaintiffs to be a copy of the bill which was sent with the goods to the defendants at the time they were shipped, upon which it is claimed there was said to be a statement as to the manner in which these goods should be paid for; under that statement there appeared to be a limited authority to their agent,—that is, he is limited to the authority to sell goods, but has no authority to collect pay for the goods. If this knowledge was made known to the defendants, or if it was made known or brought to the knowledge of the defendants before they made a payment to Mr. Roberts, if they made a payment to their agent, Mr. Roberts and Son, then they would not be heard to say in defense they had made a payment to the agent, because in such a case they were notified by the principal that they should not pay their agent, and in that case any payment made to the agent would be made at the defendants' own risk."

We think the first instruction prepared by the plaintiffs in error fairly embodies the law applicable to the state of facts presented. It is laid down in the text-books, and declared in many decisions of courts of last resort, that authority to an agent to sell goods does not include authority to collect pay for goods thus sold: Story on Agency, secs. 98, 99, 181, 191, and cases cited. It is claimed by the attorney for the plaintiffs in error that the following cases are in point on this question. We have examined a few of them, and find that they declare the doctrine: *Higgins* v. *Moore*, 34 N. Y. 417; *Kornemann* v. *Monaghan*, 24 Mich. 36; *Butler* v. *Dorman*, 68 Mo. 298; 30 Am. Rep. 795; *McKindly* v. *Dunham*, 55 Wis. 515; 42 Am. Rep. 740; *Clark* v. *Smith*, 88 Ill. 298; *Greenleaf* v. *Egan*, 30 Minn. 316; *Kohn* v. *Washer*, 64 Tex. 131; 53 Am. Rep. 745; *Crosby* v. *Hill*, 39 Ohio St. 100; *Graham* v. *Duckwall*, 8 Bush, 12; *Seiple* v. *Irwin*, 30 Pa. St. 513.

The instruction of the court, that "it is within the apparent scope of an agent's authority, where he has authority to sell, to collect for such sales; for instance, in this case, if Mr. Roberts had the authority to sell blackboards for the plaintiffs, it was apparently within the scope of his authority to collect payment for such sales," — is squarely in the face of all these authorities as cited above.

The second request of the plaintiffs in error embodies the law on that point, as announced by this court in the case of *Banks* v. *Everest*, 35 Kan. 687, and should have been given. In this action between the principal and third parties who seek to establish the agency of Roberts, his declarations that he was the agent of Kane & Co. never ought to have been permitted to go to the jury as evidence of his agency, under any circumstances.

For these errors occurring at the trial, we recommend that the judgment be reversed, and the cause remanded, with instructions to grant a new trial.

By the COURT.   It is so ordered.

———

AGENCY. — No one can rely upon an agent's own statements concerning his agency: *Baltimore etc. Ass'n* v. *Post*, 122 Pa. St. 579; 9 Am. St. Rep. 147, and note; *Tanner etc. Co.* v. *Hall*, 86 Ala. 305.

PRINCIPAL AND AGENT — AUTHORITY OF AGENT. — The general rule is, that the acts of general agents, within the general scope of their authority, bind the principals, and third persons are not affected by any private instructions to such agent: *Ruggles* v. *American etc. Ins. Co.*, 114 N. Y. 415; 11 Am. St. Rep. 674, and particularly note; unless such third parties have actual notice of the limitation upon the agent's authority: *Phœnix Ins. Co.* v. *Spiers*, 87 Ky. 286. Even a special agent, who acts within his apparent power, will bind his principal by his acts, although he may have received private instructions limiting his special authority: *Howell* v. *Graff*, 25 Neb. 130. Yet where one relies upon an ostensible agency to sustain an unauthorized pledge, he must give evidence of similar transactions in which the acts of the alleged agent were authorized or ratified: *Robinson* v. *Nevada Bank*, 81 Cal. 106. In *Southern P. R'y Co.* v. *Maddox*, 75 Tex. 300, it was held that an agent of a shipper of stock is not, by virtue of such agency, authorized to contract with the carrier fixing the value of the stock. In *Henderson* v. *Beard*, 51 Ark. 483, where an agent was simply authorized to sell land, he was decided to have no authority to sell it on credit without retaining a lien by contract for the security of the purchase-money. The authority of an agent to collect money for his principal does not authorize him to receive anything but money in payment: *Hurley* v. *Watson*, 68 Mich. 531. So in *Wilcox etc. Co.* v. *Lasley*, 40 Kan. 521, where an agent had authority to collect a note, but was not authorized to receive anything in payment but money, it was decided that he could not accept his own note in payment. But in *Knowles* v. *Street*, 87 Ala. 357, it was held that although authority to a clerk to sell goods and collect debts might not empower him to purchase a stock of goods in payment of a debt, yet, where a general agent is left in charge of his principal's business, and is specially instructed to look after a particular debt, and arrange it in some way, it could not be assumed that his authority was limited to the collection of debts in the usual mode upon the sale of goods.

In *Low* v. *Warden*, 77 Cal. 94, it was decided that the president of a bank, authorized to collect a note, with instructions not to let it become outlawed, had no authority to extend the time of payment so as to deprive the owner of his right to sue thereon before the note is outlawed, if it is not paid in fact.

A clerk, with whom a blank mortgage is left to be filled up, and executed to his principal as mortgagee, has no authority to write a letter in his name directing the dismissal of a suit pending in the name of his principal, because the mortage was to be accepted in satisfaction of the claim sued upon: *Cobb* v. *Malone*, 86 Ala. 571.

If an agent has, in a particular case, taken notes for rent, but it is not shown whether they were taken as security or as payment, the taking of the notes, with the knowledge of the principal, does not establish that the agent had authority to accept a note from another tenant in payment of rent: *Scully* v. *Dodge*, 40 Kan. 395; compare *Robinson* v. *Nevada Bank*, 81 Cal. 106, cited above.

But when an agent, in executing a duty to his principal, under the terms of his authority, finds that a liberal compliance with his instructions would injure his principal, he may, in exceptional cases, assume a power not conferred upon him, and, by acting in good faith, bind his principal: *Bergstrom* v. *Franklin*, 74 Tex. 38.

The authority of an agent need not necessarily be proved by an express contract of agency. It may be proved by the habit and course of business of the principal, or inferred from circumstances: *Mitchum* v. *Dunlap*, 98 Mo. 419.

AGENT — AUTHORITY OF AN AGENT, EMPOWERED TO SELL, TO RECEIVE PAYMENT. — An agent to solicit orders for goods has no implied authority to receive payment for them: *McKindly* v. *Dunham*, 55 Wis. 515; 42 Am. Rep. 740; *Kohn* v. *Washer*, 64 Tex. 131; 53 Am. Rep. 745. So one authorized to sell property and take a note in payment of the price in the name of his principal is not impliedly authorized to receive payment thereof: *Draper* v. *Rice*, 56 Iowa, 114; 41 Am. Rep. 88. In *Butler* v. *Dorman*, 68 Mo. 298, 30 Am. Rep. 795, where an agent sold goods only by sample, on a credit of four months, being forbidden to receive payment, and six days thereafter he drew, in his own name, for part of the purchase price, which was paid to him, but not paid by him to his principal, it was held that the payment did not protect the purchaser.

But a traveling agent to sell goods, who has not the possession of the goods, may still receive payment so as to bind his principal, where such is the general and established usage, and as such has been recognized by the principal: *Meyer* v. *Stone*, 46 Ark. 210; 55 Am. Rep. 577; compare *Trainor* v. *Morrison*, 78 Me. 160; 57 Am. Rep. 790.

WYGAL *v.* BIGELOW.

[42 KANSAS, 447.]

CHATTEL MORTGAGE — REMEDY OF MORTGAGOR AFTER FRAUDULENT SALE. — Where a chattel mortgagee, at his own sale, unlawfully, fraudulently, and unfairly buys the mortgaged property of a much greater value than the debt, and converts it to his own use, disposing of a large portion of it so as to be disabled from returning it or of allowing redemption, the mortgagor is entitled to recover from him the excess in value of the property thus converted over the amount of the mortgage debt, without payment or tender of payment thereof.

CHATTEL MORTGAGE — RIGHT OF MORTGAGEE TO PURCHASE AT HIS OWN SALE. — A chattel mortgagee may purchase at his own sale under the mortgage, conducted in fairness and good faith, but if he abuses his power and becomes the purchaser unfairly and dishonestly he will be required to account to the mortgagor therefor.

CHATTEL MORTGAGE — RIGHTS OF MORTGAGEE AFTER FRAUDULENT SALE. — An unfair or fraudulent sale of mortgaged chattels by the mortgagee will not defeat or extinguish the rights of the mortgagor, as the mortgagee has no right by an unfair sale to sacrifice the property and deprive the mortgagor of any surplus over the debt which might arise from a sale fairly and honestly conducted.

CHATTEL MORTGAGE — SALE IN PARCELS. — Where mortgaged chattels, consisting of many different articles, can easily be offered for sale separately or in lots or parcels, a sale of the whole in lump, or two lumps, under a power of sale contained in the mortgage, may be regarded as unfair, especially when it is shown that the property brought much less at the sale than its actual value.

ACTION to foreclose a mortgage on real estate, and to recover the amount due from the mortgagors to the mortgagee. D. Wygal and Son were indebted to Bigelow in the sum of $3,236.19, for which they gave their notes, secured by a chattel mortgage on a blacksmith-shop and wagon-shop, with all the tools and fixtures therewith connected. The first of these notes fell due, and the mortgagee, feeling himself insecure, demanded additional security, whereupon S. Wygal and wife gave him their mortgage on the property mentioned in the opinion as additional security. All the notes remained unpaid, and when they together with interest amounted to four thousand three hundred dollars, the mortgagee gave notice, sold, and became the purchaser of the property mentioned in the chattel mortgage for two thousand six hundred dollars. S. Wygal and wife subsequently conveyed the land mortgaged to one Williams, subject to the Bigelow mortgage thereon, which the mortgagee afterwards sought to foreclose in this action, and after paying a prior mortgage thereon, to apply the proceeds of the foreclosure sale to the payment of his debt.

D. Wygal, S. Wygal and wife, and Williams all answered, alleging that the mortgage on the real property was given for one thousand dollars, and no more; and also alleging that the property named in the chattel mortgage was worth, and was inventoried and invoiced, after allowing a reduction of over ten per cent, at $6,241; that the mortgagee pretended to offer the same for sale at public auction on default, and that he bid in for himself and pretended to buy all such property in lump, or in two separate parcels, for two thousand six hundred dollars, which he converted to his own use, and afterwards disposed of large portions of the property, thus preventing the mortgagors from redeeming. Defendants claim to have been damaged in the sum of three thousand nine hundred dollars, for which they pray judgment. Other facts are stated in the opinion.

W. T. Johnston and *Selwyn Douglas*, for the plaintiffs in error.

Brayman and *Stevens*, for the defendant in error.

HORTON, C. J. Upon the trial of this case in the court below, the burden of the issues, under the pleadings, was upon the defendants. The plaintiff objected to the introduction of any testimony to sustain the answers, and this objection having been sustained, judgment was rendered for $1,009.92, the balance claimed to be due to the plaintiff upon the notes of D. Wygal & Son, and for a foreclosure of the mortgage of Sylvester Wygal and wife on lot 2, in block 30, in Paola, to pay the judgment and costs. All the answers must be treated as if filed before the trial, as the court below so treated and considered them. The principal question in the case is, can the defendants, under the allegations of the answers, recover damages justly proportioned to the injuries alleged by them? or can relief only be granted to them upon payment or tender of payment of the mortgage debt? If it appeared from the pleadings that the plaintiff still held in his possession or under his control the personal property described in the chattel mortgage, then perhaps payment of the debt or tender of payment by defendants ought to precede any claim for damages or any return of the property. But as it is alleged that the personal property was unlawfully, fraudulently, and unfairly converted to the use of the plaintiff, and that he has disposed of large portions of the same, the defendants cannot redeem on account of the conduct of the plaintiff. The chattels cannot be returned, as the plaintiff has disposed of large portions thereof, and the defendants, the mortgagors, are entitled, if the allegations of their answers are true, for judgment against the plaintiff, the mortgagee, for the excess of the value of the personal property over the amount of the notes and interest: *Leach* v. *Kimball*, 34 N. H. 568; *Hungate* v. *Reynolds*, 72 Ill. 425.

Some of the courts hold that relief can be granted only to a mortgagor upon payment or tender of payment of the whole mortgage debt, and then, although the mortgagee has disposed of the property, a court of equity will give relief by decreeing damages. But in this state the distinction between courts of equity and courts of law has been abolished, and it was useless and unnecessary to tender any payment of the mortgage debt, if the plaintiff has unlawfully, fraudulently, and unfairly converted to his own use the personal property of the defendants of a much greater value than the debt, and subsequently to such conversion has disposed of large portions of the property, so as to be disabled from returning the same, or of allowing any redemption thereof.

In *Case* v. *Boughton*, 11 Wend. 106, the court say that, the property being of sufficient value to satisfy the debt, no further act besides taking possession was necessary to constitute payment. In this case, if the property taken by the plaintiff was of sufficient value to satisfy his debt, and if it has been unlawfully, fraudulently, and unfairly purchased by him, no judgment ought to be rendered for any balance claimed upon the notes. The personal property was placed in the mortgagee's hands for the purpose of being appropriated for the satisfaction of the notes, and the mortgagors had the right to have it faithfully and fairly applied for that purpose. If it was not so appropriated, the mortgagee is liable.

In this state, we think that the mortgagee of the chattel may purchase at a sale under the mortgage, but the relation which the mortgagee holds to the debtor imposes on him the observance of fairness and good faith. If he abuses the power which he holds, and becomes the purchaser unfairly and dishonestly, he will be required to account to the mortgagor therefor: Herman on Chattel Mortgages, sec. 219; *Jones* v. *Franks*, 33 Kan. 497.

" If the mortgagee carries out in good faith the terms of the agreement, and makes the very disposition which he has con-

tracted to make, and has broken no contract, he has been guilty
of no bad faith to the mortgagor, and ought to be chargeable with
only the actual proceeds of the property thus disposed of by
him": *Denny* v. *Van Dusen*, 27 Kan. 437.

The unfair or fraudulent sale of mortgaged property by a
mortgagee should not and will not defeat or extinguish the
rights of the mortgagor. The mortgagee has no right by any
unfairness to sacrifice the property and deprive the mortgagor
of the surplus over the debt, which by a fair and honestly
conducted sale might arise. If the property consists of many
different articles which can be easily offered for sale separately,
or in lots or parcels, a sale of the whole in a lump, or in two
lumps, in some cases might be regarded as an unfair mode of
sale, especially if it were shown that the property brought
much less at the sale than its actual value: Jones on Chattel
Mortgages, 3d ed., sec. 797; *Hungate* v. *Reynolds*, 72 Ill. 425.
We cannot say, as a matter of law, upon the allegations in the
answers, that the property was wrongfully and unfairly disposed of; nor can we say that the property was sold fairly and
in good faith according to the terms of the mortgage. These
are matters for a jury under proper instructions from the trial
court. The defendants were entitled to have a fair and *bona
fide* sale. The trial court should have permitted the testimony to go to the jury to determine whether this was done or
not. Upon the issues in the case, it was important to determine whether the sale was made by the mortgagee in a manner
calculated to produce the best price for all the articles sold.
As all the testimony offered in support of the answers was rejected, no opportunity was permitted the defendants to show
that the sale was unlawful, fraudulent, or unfair. In this the
court committed error.

We are referred to *Hamlyn* v. *Boulter*, 15 Kan. 376, that the
defendant's answers were insufficient because they did not
allege the payment of the debt or the tender thereof. In that
case it does not appear that the defendant unlawfully, fraudulently, or unfairly disposed of the mortgaged property. It
does appear, however, from the opinion, that Hamlyn was
surety for Boulter; that he held a chattel mortgage upon property as security, and all the court decided in that case was,
that no action could be maintained by Boulter against him for
the conversion of the mortgaged property until he had been
fully repaid, or indemnified for his liability as surety, — this,
and nothing more.

In accordance with the usual practice of this court, the petition in error is allowed to be amended as requested in the motion on file.

The judgment of the district court will be reversed, and the cause remanded for further proceedings in accordance with the views herein expressed.

RIGHTS AND REMEDIES OF CHATTEL MORTGAGOR WHOSE PROPERTY HAS BEEN WRONGFULLY SOLD. — Under a power contained in the mortgage, the mortgagee may, upon forfeiture, sell the property at a *bona fide* sale, and thus cut off the mortgagor's equity of redemption. To be effective in this particular, the sale must in all respects be fairly and honestly conducted, and not clandestine nor collusive. The mortgagee has no right by any unfairness to sacrifice the property for less than its fair market value: *Bird* v. *Davis*, 14 N. J. Eq. 467; *Walker* v. *Stone*, 20 Md. 195; *Charter* v. *Stevens*, 3 Denio, 33; 45 Am. Dec. 444; *Freeman* v. *Freeman*, 17 N. J. Eq. 44; *Warwick* v. *Hutchinson*, 45 N. J. L. 61. The conduct and fairness of a sale of chattels by the mortgagee, and the rights acquired by and under such sale, are always open to investigation at the instance of the mortgagor. A sale under judicial sanction is therefore safer, and when the amount is large, advisable: *Freeman* v. *Freeman*, 17 N. J. Eq. 44. When the validity of such a sale is in issue, the burden is upon the mortgagee to show that his conduct in selling or in making the purchase was in all things fair and frank, and that he sold or paid for the property what it was reasonably worth: *Jones* v. *Franks*, 33 Kan. 497; *Black* v. *Hair*, 2 Hill Ch. 622. Perhaps it may as well be stated here, as a general rule, that the mortgagee cannot purchase at his own sale under a power in the mortgage, in the absence of an agreement between the parties or of a statutory provision to that effect. A purchase so made invalidates the sale, and does not bar the mortgagor of his equity of redemption. If the mortgagee so purchasing converts the property to his own use, he becomes thereby liable for its value: *Waite* v. *Dennison*, 51 Ill. 319; *Imboden* v. *Hunter*, 23 Ark. 622; 79 Am. Dec. 116; *Phares* v. *Barbour*, 49 Ill. 370; *Korns* v. *Shaffer*, 27 Md. 83; *Cushing* v. *Seymour, Sabin, & Co.*, 30 Minn. 301; *Alger* v. *Farley*, 19 Iowa, 518; *Beard* v. *Westerman*, 32 Ohio St. 29. By such act the mortgagee becomes liable to the mortgagor for the actual value of the property at the time of the sale, without reference to the amount bid: *Webber* v. *Emmerson*, 3 Col. 249. His liability in such case is for the difference between the mortgage debt and the actual value of the property sold, notwithstanding he was himself not guilty of any willful fraud: *Hungate* v. *Reynolds*, 72 Ill. 425.

Collusion between the mortgagee and a third person, by which the latter is to bid off the property for the use of the mortgagee, vitiates the sale: *Pettibone* v. *Perkins*, 6 Wis. 589; *Alger* v. *Farley*, 19 Iowa, 518. If the mortgagee buys the property and then sells to another at a profit, the mortgagor may claim and recover such profit: *Cunningham* v. *Rogers*, 14 Ala. 147; *Griswold* v. *Morse*, 59 N. H. 212. And if he sells to himself at an unfair or inadequate price, the mortgagor may treat him as a wrong-doer, and recover the value of the property at the time of the sale: *Lee* v. *Fox*, 113 Ind. 98. So if the mortgagee sells the property without the knowledge or consent of the mortgagor, and in violation of an agreement or understanding between them, and purchases at a grossly inadequate price, rendering no account of the sale to the mortgagor, the latter may have the sale declared void: *Boyd* v. *Beaudin,* 54 Wis. 193. Of course this rule does not apply when an agreement exists between the parties that the mortgagee may become a purchaser at his own sale. In such case he may purchase at a sale fairly and honestly conducted: *Syfers* v. *Bradley,* 115 Ind. 345; *Emmons* v. *Hawn,* 75 Id. 356; *Lee* v. *Fox,* 113 Id. 98; *Goodell* v. *Dewey,* 100 Ill. 308; *Gear* v. *Schreir,* 57 Iowa, 666. But his relation to the mortgagor is such as to impose upon him the utmost fairness and good faith, and if he abuses his power and becomes the purchaser, he must be regarded as holding the property as security for his debt only, and therefore subject to redemption: *Lyon* v. *Jones,* 6 Humph. 533.

Even when the sale is fairly conducted and the property sold for its actual value, the mortgagee, when he is the purchaser, becomes the trustee of the mortgagor as to the surplus above the mortgage debt which the property brought at the sale, and he must account to the mortgagor therefor after the debt and expenses are paid: *Flanders* v. *Thomas,* 12 Wis. 410; *Vick* v. *Smith,* 83 N. C. 80. The mortgagor is entitled to the aid of a court of equity in obtaining an account of the trust fund: *Korns* v. *Shaffer,* 27 Md. 83. But generally, a resort to equity is not necessary, and perhaps is improper; at least a suit at law may be maintained to recover the surplus. Thus in *Davenport McChesney,* 86 N. Y. 242-245, Andrews, J., said, in a case where the mortgagee himself became the purchaser: "The defendant was properly held to account for the excess of the purchase price of the property sold on the chattel mortgage beyond the legal claims secured thereby. He assumed to sell all the mortgaged property under the power of sale contained in the mortgage, and afterwards took possession of and claimed the property under this title. The mortgagor could elect to treat the entire sale as valid, and to regard the amount for which the property sold beyond the amount applicable to the mortgage debt as unpaid purchase-money in the hands of defendant." To the same effect is *King* v. *Van Vleck,* 109 N. Y. 363. If the mortgagor accepts the surplus arising from such a sale, he cannot assert its invalidity from any cause: *France* v. *Haynes,* 67 Iowa, 139; *McConnell* v. *People,* 71 Ill. 481.

In some of the states the doctrine prevails that the mortgagee may purchase at a fairly conducted public sale under a power contained in the mortgage; and when he becomes the purchaser, may hold the property for his own benefit, free from any equity of redemption. This rule prevails in New York: *Olcott* v. *Tioga R. R. Co.,* 27 N. Y. 546-566; 84 Am. Dec. 298; *Hall* v. *Ditson,* 55 How. Pr. 19; South Carolina: *Mills* v. *Williams,* 16 S. C. 593; Tennessee: *Lyon* v. *Jones,* 6 Humph. 533; California: *Wright* v. *Ross,* 36 Cal. 414; Indiana: *Emmons* v. *Hawn,* 75 Ind. 356; *Syfers* v. *Bradley,* 115 Id. 345; *Lee* v. *Fox,* 113 Id. 98, 105, where it is said: "A mortgagee of personal property does not hold the legal title to the mortgaged property in trust for the mortgagor. He holds it in his own right, and is in no sense a trustee, except as to the surplus which may remain after paying the mortgage debt. The sale is for the purpose of extinguishing the mortgagor's equity, and where the sale is fairly made, at public auction, in pursuance of the power, the mortgagor's equity of redemption is effectually cut off, even though the mortgagee be the purchaser. A mortgagee of personal property is not within the rule which prohibits the trustee from purchasing at his own sale, provided he acts fairly. The most that could be held in case the mortgagee became a purchaser at his own sale, made under a power, would be to cast upon him the burden of showing that the sale was fairly and openly made, in strict compliance with the power, and that the price paid was not so clearly and grossly disproportionate to the value of the property as to

raise a presumption of fraud or bad faith. If it appeared that the price paid
was grossly inadequate, or that the property was sacrificed, the sale ought to
be set aside, at the election of the mortgagor; and if it were shown that the
mortgagee had converted the property after a merely colorable sale, or refused to acknowledge the mortgagor's right to redeem, he should be held to
account for its fair value at the time of the appropriation."

In those states where the rule prevails that the mortgagee may purchase
at his own sale, a purchase so made by him is generally held valid in law, and
voidable in equity for unfairness, only at the instance of the interested parties: *People* v. *Wiltshire,* 9 Brad. App. 374; *Lee* v. *Fox,* 113 Ind. 98; *Olcott* v.
Tioga R. R. Co., 27 N. Y. 546; 84 Am. Dec. 298. Even where such sale is
claimed to be irregular and unfair, the interested parties must take prompt
action to avoid the sale or redeem the property before the rights of innocent third parties have intervened, and the right to question the regularity
of the sale becomes barred by delay: *People* v. *Wiltshire, supra; Wylder* v.
Caane, 53 Ill. 490.

Returning now to the general question of sales under a power contained in
the mortgage, it may be stated that such sales must be fair and *bona fide*
to effect an extinguishment of the equity of redemption. The mortgagee
has no right, by practicing unfairness, to sell the property at price less than
its value, and thus deprive the mortgagor of any surplus above the amount
of the debt, which may remain after a sale properly conducted, or thereby
make him liable for a deficiency. But in case the mortgagee acts wrongfully
and unfairly in thus disposing of the property, the mortgagor has no remedy
at law, but must resort to a bill in equity in the nature of a bill to redeem.
So far as legal rights and obligations are concerned, after forfeiture the
mortgagee may treat the property as his own, and deal with it as he may
choose, without incurring liability at law: *Stoddard* v. *Dennison,* 38 How. Pr.
296; *Pratt* v. *Stiles,* 17 How. Pr. 211; and when the court finds, upon his bill
filed for that purpose, that the mortgagor is entitled to redeem, it will enter
a personal degree against the mortgagee for the excess in value of the property over the amount found due on the mortgage: *Flanders* v. *Chamberlain,*
24 Mich. 305. Or, in other words, in a suit against the mortgagee, for selling the mortgaged chattels unfairly, the measure of damages would be the
difference between the price realized and the actual value of the property, or
the excess of such value above the amount of the mortgage debt: *Warwick*
v. *Hutchinson,* 45 N. J. L. 61; *Bird* v. *Davis,* 14 N. J. Eq. 467; *Denny* v.
Faulkner, 22 Kan. 89. In this connection it may be stated that under a
power of sale the mortgagee has no right to dispose of the property otherwise than for cash: *Edwards* v. *Cottrell,* 43 Iowa, 194.

Where the sale by the mortgagee is fairly and honestly conducted under
the power, he must account to the mortgagor for, and the latter is entitled
to recover, any excess arising from the sale and remaining after the mortgage
debt and necessary costs and expenses are paid: *Ashworth* v. *Dark,* 20 Tex.
826; *Kohn* v. *Lynn,* 34 Mich. 360; *Flanders* v. *Chamberlain,* 24 Id. 305; *Flanders* v. *Thomas,* 12 Wis. 410; *Korns* v. *Shaffer,* 27 Md. 83; *Bryan* v. *Roberts,* 1
Stroh. Eq. 342; *Pratt* v. *Stiles,* 17 How. Pr. 211; *Denny* v. *Faulkner,* 22 Kan.
90. The sale should always stop when sufficient property has been sold to
satisfy the mortgage debt, with interest and necessary costs and expenses.
The mortgagee's title to the remaining property is then extinguished. The
power to sell then becomes *ipso facto* exhausted, and cannot be further exercised. If the mortgagee, after satisfying by sale his secured debt, goes on
and sells the remaining portion of the mortgaged chattels, he becomes in

equity the trustee of the mortgagor as to the remainder of the property sold, and must account to him for its value. The mortgagee's sale of the residue of the property remaining after enough has been sold to satisfy his debt and expenses is a conversion of the property, for which trover will lie in favor of the mortgagor: *Charter* v. *Stephens*, 3 Denio, 33; 45 Am. Dec. 444; *Stromberg* v. *Lindberg*, 25 Minn. 513; *Griswold* v. *Morse*, 59 N. H. 211; *Beckley* v. *Munson*, 22 Conn. 299; *West* v. *Crary*, 47 N. Y. 423; *Bearss* v. *Preston*, 66 Mich. 11. In *Botsford* v. *Murphy*, 47 Mich. 537, the mortgage provided that goods seized under it should be sold a public auction after notice, and that the power of sale should be limited to so much of the property as the sale should show was needed to pay the debt. The mortgagee retailed part of the goods at private sale, and the court said "that, as he did not observe the method agreed upon in selling, the mortgagor could elect to have the amount to be sold ascertained, and in an action on the note secured by the mortgage the jury should have been charged to find the market value of the goods sold at private sale."

Where the mortgaged property consists of many parcels, and the mortgagee offers the whole for sale in a lump instead of offering it in such lots as would suit the convenience of bidders, this is considered an unfair method of sale. A mortgagee thus acting and bidding off the whole for less than his debt does not acquire such title as a court of equity will protect and confirm against the owner of the equity of redemption: *Hannah* v. *Carrington*, 18 Ark. 85. In *Hungate* v. *Reynolds*, 72 Ill. 425, a mortgagee sold ten head of mortgaged horses in one lot to his agent for less than the mortgage debt, when other bidders were present who wished to purchase a part only of the horses, and who suggested that they be offered for sale separately. The mortgagor thereupon filed his bill in equity to have the note and mortgage surrendered and canceled, and that the mortgagee pay him the difference between the amount remaining due on the mortgage debt, after deducting the amount for which the horses sold, and their reasonable value, or what they would have brought if sold separately, and the court granted the relief prayed for. Again, in *Stromberg* v. *Lindberg*, 25 Minn. 513, the rule was laid down that the holder of a chattel mortgage, proceeding under the power of sale, if he can, without prejudice or great inconvenience to himself, satisfy his debt by a sale of a portion of the property, is bound to do so if the interests of the mortgagor require it, and if the mortgagee unfairly sells the whole he is liable to the owner of the equity of redemption for the damages thus caused. "Where the mortgagee forecloses under the power of sale in the mortgage, he stands, with respect to the mortgagor's rights in the property, in the position of a trustee, and is held to the exercise of good faith and proper care and diligence to avoid any sacrifice of those rights, not necessary to the reasonable enforcement of his own. Although the mortgage cover much more property than is necessary to his security, he may, under his mortgage, for his security, take possession of the whole; but where, without prejudice or great inconvenience to himself, he can satisfy his debt by a sale of part, he is, if the interests of the mortgagor require it, bound so to sell. If he unnecessarily sell the whole, and especially if he do so not in good faith to satisfy his debt, but, as the court below in this case has found, in order to secure, by use of the power of sale, some further advantage, to effect some purpose not contemplated by the mortgage, he ought to be, and is, liable to the mortgagor for the damages sustained by him through such oppressive use of the power of sale. The claim of the mortgagor in such a case is not a debt which is the subject of levy ": *Stromberg* v. *Lindberg*, 25 Minn. 513.

Fraud and collusion between the mortgagee and purchaser, by which the property is sold for a grossly inadequate price, is also ground for invalidating the sale. To establish such fraud and collusion, the assignee of the mortgagor in bankruptcy may show by parol evidence that the mortgagor had a valuable interest in the property by proof of the real amount and character of the encumbrance: *Robinson* v. *Bliss,* 121 Mass. 428.

In most of the states the statute requires the mortgagee to give the mortgagor notice of the sale, either by mail, publication, posting, or personally, within a certain time before sale, and if the mortgage is silent in this respect, the statute must be strictly followed or the sale will be void: *Campbell* v. *Wheeler,* 69 Iowa, 588. But when the mortgage provides how and upon what notice the sale may be made, these express provisions preclude all implications on the subject and must be accurately followed: *Flanders* v. *Chamberlain,* 24 Mich. 305; *Whitaker* v. *Sigler,* 44 Iowa, 419. Where the mortgage provides that the property is to be sold in a certain place, notice of the sale must be given to take place in such place unless the parties otherwise agree: *Tootle* v. *Taylor,* 64 Iowa, 629. In case of such agreement the sale may be made at another place: *Darnall* v. *Darlington,* 28 S. C. 255; and the notice of sale need not state whose property is to be sold, the name of the property and its location, if the time and place of sale are properly described and the mortgage is of record: *Manwaring* v. *Jenison,* 61 Mich. 117–143; *McConnell* v. *Scott,* 67 Ill. 274; *Waite* v. *Dennison,* 51 Id. 319.

COULSON *v.* WING.

[42 KANSAS, 507.]

LAND PATENTED TO HEIRS OF DECEDENT — VOID SALE BY ADMINISTRATOR. — Where a patent to land is procured by an administrator on behalf of his intestate, and issued to the heirs of the latter, the land does not become part of the intestate's estate, and a sale of it under order of the probate court to pay the debts of the estate is null and void as against the heirs.

LAND PATENTED TO HEIRS OF DECEDENT — MONEY ADVANCED BY ADMINISTRATOR NO LIEN. — Where an administrator pays the price of land entered upon by his decedent, and the patent thereto is issued to the heirs, the money so advanced is no lien against the land, nor can it be sold under order of court to repay the administrator.

PRACTICE — PARTIES — WAIVER OF DEFECT. — Where a defect of parties is not apparent on the face of the petition, and is not taken advantage of by answer, it is waived.

EJECTMENT BY CO-TENANT — PARTIES. — A tenant in common may bring ejectment against one who has no title, without joining the remaining co-tenants in the action.

Love and Snelling, for the plaintiffs in error.

Shepard, Grove, and Shepard, for the defendants in error.

HOLT, C. In the spring of 1879 Sophia C. H. Martin settled on the west half of the northwest quarter of section 25 and the east half of the northwest quarter of section 26, in

township 33 south, range 6 west, in Harper County, Kansas.
This land was then a part of the Osage trust land, and she
settled upon it to secure it under the pre-emption laws of the
United States. She resided thereon until her death, April 25,
1880. On the 6th of May, 1880, one A. G. Everett was duly
appointed administrator of her estate. Afterward, on October
5th, the said administrator duly entered the land in the name
of and for the benefit of said Sophia C. H. Martin's heirs, and
soon after obtained a patent conveying the said land "unto
the said heirs of Sophia C. H. Martin, deceased, and to their
heirs." Shortly afterward the said administrator applied to
the probate court of Harper County for leave to sell said land
for the payment of the debts of the estate of Sophia C. H.
Martin, and notified all of these plaintiffs, as her heirs, of such
application. The probate court, after hearing testimony, directed this property to be sold to pay the debts of the estate,
and it was accordingly sold to James L. Vickers, who, on the
13th of October, 1881, conveyed it to George H. Coulson, plaintiff in error. The defendants in error filed their petition in
ejectment against him in the Harper district court, on the
twenty-fourth day of January, 1886. They are the children,
and all the children, of Sophia C. H. Martin, deceased. The
defendant filed a general denial, and in addition set forth the
facts as detailed above, by which he acquired possession of
the land. The action was tried in the Harper district court
at the January term, 1887, and a judgment rendered in favor
of the plaintiffs for the possession of the land.

We think the judgment of the court below was correct.
The defendant had no valid title to the land; the proceedings of
the probate court under which this land was sold were absolutely
null and void, and conveyed no title whatever in the land as
against the heirs of Mrs. Martin. This tract was never her
property during her lifetime, nor did it become a part of her
estate after her death; the patent conveyed the land to
her heirs, not to her. Chief Justice Horton, in *Rogers* v.
Clemmans, 26 Kan. 522, speaking for the court in a similar
case, said: "The title to the land was derived by the heirs
at law under the act of Congress directly from the United
States. They did not take it from the decedent, subject to the
debts and costs of administration. They had the right to
convey and give possession as grantees of the United States,
and any attempted sale made by the administrator of the estate of Charles Mayo, deceased, was an absolute nullity, and

no title was communicated thereby to any purchaser. As the land was no part of the estate of the decedent, the probate court had no power to make any order to sell the same for the debts of the estate or for the costs of administration. The proceedings to subject this land so patented by the United States to the heirs of Charles Mayo, deceased, to pay the debts of such deceased, were not only without authority of law, but absolutely null and void, as the probate court had no jurisdiction over the land and property so patented to the minors. While the probate court has, by the constitution and statutes, jurisdiction over the settlement of estates of deceased persons, and upon due proceedings may subject the personal and real property thereof to the payment of the debts of the decedent, and also the costs of administration, it has no authority to reach out and dispose of property belonging to the heirs of a decedent which is in no respect subject to the debts or liabilities of such decedent. While the probate court has jurisdiction to hear and determine all applications made by administrators to sell the real estate of their decedents which is liable to sale, and while this necessarily involves the power of determining whether in any particular case the real estate sought to be sold is liable or not, yet where it appears from all the proceedings that the land is no part of the estate, and no way subject to the debts of the decedent, jurisdiction is not obtained. In this case, the proceedings had before the probate court on January 7, 1863, granting the sale of the lands, show upon their face that the lands were pre-empted after the death of the intestate; therefore the probate court had no authority to treat them as a part of the estate, or to sell or otherwise dispose of them."

In that case the heirs of the deceased were not notified of the proceedings in the probate court; in this case they were; yet we think that is immaterial. The probate court had no jurisdiction whatever over the property in question; it never belonged to Mrs. Martin, nor was it a part of her estate in any way: *Delay* v. *Chapman*, 3 Or. 459.

It is claimed further that the debt of the estate for which this land was sold was incurred by the administrator to obtain the money to pay out this land in controversy; this would not change the rule enunciated above: *Black* v. *Dressell's Heirs*, 20 Kan. 153. He obtained no order from the probate court to borrow the money; in fact, it would not have been in the power of the probate court to make such an order; he had under the law no right to encumber the estate by borrowing money for the purpose of paying out on this land.

The defendant claims, however, that there was a defect of parties. This was not raised by demurrer (it could not have been, to the petition filed in this case), nor by the answer. It was sought, however, on the trial, to prove that Sophia C. H. Martin at the date of her death was a married woman, and therefore that her husband would be one of her heirs, and the failure to join him as a party plaintiff in this action would be such a defect of parties that they could not recover. The defendant alleges that the refusal of the court to allow them to prove that Mrs. Martin was a married woman at the time of her death was error. We think that the question of defect of parties cannot be raised in the introduction of evidence. Our statute provides (Civ. Code, secs. 89, 91) that if a defect of parties plaintiff or defendant does not appear upon the face of the petition, the objection may be taken by answer; and if no objection be taken either by demurrer or by answer, the defendant shall be deemed to have waived the same. There was nothing in the answer to indicate there was a defect of parties: *Kansas Pac. R'y Co.* v. *Nichols*, 9 Kan. 235; 12 Am. Rep. 494; *Parker* v. *Wiggins*, 10 Kan. 420; *Humphreys* v. *Keith*, 11 Kan. 108; *Seip* v. *Tilghman*, 23 Kan. 289; *Jeffers* v. *Forbes*, 28 Kan. 174; *Thomas* v. *Reynolds*, 29 Kan. 304. In any event these parties were tenants in common: *Markoe* v. *Wakeman*, 107 Ill. 251; *Tarrant* v. *Swain*, 15 Kan. 146; Freeman on Cotenancy and Partition, secs. 86, 92. As tenants in common they had the right to bring this action against one who had no title, even though the other tenants in common were not joined in the action: *Robinson* v. *Roberts*, 31 Conn. 145; *Sherin* v. *Larson*, 28 Minn. 523; *Weese* v. *Barker*, 7 Col. 178; *Sharon* v. *Davidson*, 4 Nev. 419; *Perkins* v. *Blood*, 36 Vt. 273; *Hart* v. *Robertson*, 21 Cal. 346; *Treat* v. *Reilly*, 35 Cal. 131.

We recommend that the judgment be affirmed. ·

By the COURT. It is so ordered.

FOR A DISCUSSION OF THE LAW RELATIVE TO LAND PATENTS issued to a deceased person or to the heirs of a decedent, see note to *Cobb* v. *Stewart*, 83 Am. Dec. 467–470. The sale of a decedent's land under an order of the probate court transfers no title when he, at the time of his death, had a mere pre-emption claim to the land, notwithstanding the fact that the land is afterwards entered in the name of his heirs: *Burns* v. *Hamilton*, 33 Ala. 210; 70 Am. Dec. 570. A patent issued by the United States to a deceased person inures to the benefit of his heirs: *McInnis* v. *Pickett,* 65 Miss. 354.

PARTIES. — If a defendant, by his answer or demurrer to plaintiff's petition, does not present to the trial court the legal incapacity of the plaintiff to sue, such defect is waived by him: *Meyer* v. *Lane,* 40 Kan. 491. Defect of parties shown by the petition and not demurred to is waived under the Kentucky code: *Metcalfe* v. *Brand,* 86 Ky. 331; 9 Am. St. Rep. 282.

FRICK COMPANY *v.* KETELS.

[42 KANSAS, 527.]

HOMESTEADS — MORTGAGE ON HOMESTEAD AND OTHER PROPERTY — RIGHT OF MORTGAGOR. — Where a mortgage upon a homestead and other real estate is being foreclosed, the mortgagor has the right, as against the mortgagee, and all other creditors and lien-holders whose rights are not prior or superior to those of the mortgagee, to require that, before the homestead shall be resorted to for the purpose of satisfying the mortgage, all the other property shall be first exhausted.

J. W. Green, for the plaintiff in error.

V. H. Harris, and Rossington, Smith, and Dallas, for the defendants in error.

VALENTINE, J.   The Frick Company, a corporation, holding a mortgage upon all the real estate of Knut Ketels, including his homestead occupied by himself and wife and family, and the company prosecuting an action in the district court of Douglas County to foreclose such mortgage as against all such real estate, attempted, without the consent and against the will of the mortgagors, Ketels and wife, to release the mortgage of record as to that portion of the real estate not included in the homestead, and moved the court to dismiss its foreclosure action as to that portion of the real estate, so that it might proceed in its foreclosure action as against only the homestead, which motion the court overruled, and required the Frick Company to proceed in its foreclosure action as against all the mortgaged property, and rendered a judgment requiring that the Frick Company, in satisfying its foreclosure judgment, should first exhaust all the mortgaged property not included in the homestead before resorting to the homestead, although such a procedure might leave Ketels's other creditors, who were asking for a marshaling of the securities, without any security for their debts. This attempted release and dismissal above mentioned were originated for the purpose that Frick and Company, another corporation, differ-

ent from the Frick Company, might enforce a judgment lien
which it had against the land which the Frick Company desired to release. This judgment lien extended only to the
property not included in the homestead, and was also inferior
and subsequent to the mortgage lien. We do not think that
the court below committed any error in its aforesaid rulings:
Butler v. *Stainback*, 87 N. C. 216, 220; *Wilson* v. *Patton*, 87
N. C. 318, 324; *Dickson* v. *Chorn*, 6 Iowa, 19; 71 Am. Dec.
382; *Foley* v. *Cooper*, 43 Iowa, 376; *Bartholomew* v. *Hook*, 23
Cal. 277; *McLaughlin* v. *Hart*, 46 Cal. 638; *Brown* v. *Cozard*,
68 Ill. 178; *McArthur* v. *Martin*, 23 Minn. 74; *Ray* v. *Adams*,
45 Ala. 168; *Marr* v. *Lewis*, 31 Ark. 203; 25 Am. Rep. 553;
Colby v. *Crocker*, 17 Kan. 527; *La Rue* v. *Gilbert*, 18 Kan. 220.

Mr. Freeman, in his work on executions, uses the following
language: "The more reasonable view is, that the equity of
the homestead claimants to retain their home is at least equal
to that of their creditors to have it sold, and therefore that
chancery will not aid the latter by compelling the judgment
creditor to first resort to the homestead. Perhaps a more
difficult question is, May one who has a lien on homestead
and other property be compelled by the homestead claimants
to first resort to the latter? On the one side, it is insisted
that the right to compel a marshaling of assets never existed
in favor of judgment debtors, but only in behalf of persons
claiming under them, and that the creation of the lien by the
homestead claimants was, in effect, an agreement on their
part that the lien-holder might, at his discretion, sell any of
the property which was subject to such lien, and that such
agreement precludes such claimants from exercising any control over such discretion. But homestead laws should be
liberally construed, and no intention should be presumed;
nor should any interpretation be indulged which is at variance with the natural and obvious purpose of the parties.
The claimants, in the absence of any expression of a contrary
intent, should be presumed to intend no further peril to their
homestead than necessity demands, while he who received a
mortgage from them should be regarded as obtaining a mere
security for his debt, and not the right to employ that security in such a mode as to needlessly imperil the homestead.
Hence a mortgage on a homestead and other property may
fairly be interpreted as a waiver of the homestead right only
so far as may be necessary to secure the debt; or in other
words, as a stipulation that the homestead may be sold, if the

other property proves inadequate to satisfy the mortgagee's demand. Under this interpretation, the homestead claimants are entitled to compel the sale of the other property in preference to the homestead, and need not submit to the sale of the homestead until the other securities have been exhausted, without fully discharging the debt": 2 Freeman on Executions, sec. 440.

It is also said in the case of *Wilson* v. *Patton*, 87 N. C. 318, among other things, as follows: "Lest it may be supposed we have overlooked the point raised in the argument before us with regard to marshaling the fund, we take occasion to say that, in our opinion, that rule of equity has no application to a case where the homestead is involved. It is a 'consecrated right' granted by the constitution, and is an equity superior to all other equities."   See also the reasoning in the case of *Colby* v. *Crocker*, 17 Kan. 530 et seq.

If anything is said or decided in the case of *Chapman* v. *Lester*, 12 Kan. 592, contrary to the views herein expressed, the same is hereby overruled.   But this decision is not in conflict with that, as the following language, used in the opinion of the court in that case, will show, to wit: "It may also be proper to say that we do not deny that a court of equity may, in a decree of foreclosure of a mortgage upon a homestead and other property, direct that the homestead be the last property offered for sale by the sheriff."

We think no error was committed by the court below. In our opinion, where a mortgage upon the homestead and other real estate is being foreclosed, the mortgagor has the right, as against the mortgagee and all other creditors and lienholders whose rights are not prior or superior to those of the holder of the mortgage, to require that before the homestead shall be resorted to for the purpose of satisfying the mortgage debt, all the other mortgaged property shall first be exhausted.

The judgment of the court below will be affirmed.

———

HOMESTEAD. — Where a mortgage covers a homestead and other property which is subject to a lien of a subsequent judgment, the debtor has no right to have the latter exhausted to satisfy the mortgage in order to preserve his homestead: *White* v. *Polleys*, 20 Wis. 503; 91 Am. Dec. 432.   The statutory provision that other property of a debtor shall be exhausted in satisfaction of debts antecedent to homestead law, before resort is had to the homestead, is directory merely: *Denegre* v. *Haun*, 14 Iowa, 240; 81 Am. Dec. 480, and note.

GREEN *v.* GREEN.

[42 KANSAS, 654.]

VOID JUDGMENT — VACATING — JURISDICTION. — Appearance by attorney, upon motion to contest the service of process upon defendant, is a special and limited appearance, and does not confer jurisdiction upon the court; hence a judgment rendered upon such appearance is void, and must be set aside.

ACTION for divorce by Harriet F. Green, against Oliver Green. She attempted to make service upon him by publication. The defendant did not appear nor answer, and judgment was rendered against him October 1, 1887. On October 3d he filed a motion to set aside such judgment, which motion is sufficiently stated in the opinion. Upon the hearing of the motion the court held it a general appearance on the part of defendant, sustained the motion, set aside the judgment, and gave defendant ten days in which to answer. This he failed to do, and on January 16, 1888, judgment was rendered in favor of plaintiff. On January 17, 1888, defendant filed his motion to set aside this last judgment. The motion was overruled, and defendant appeals.

Welch and Welch, for the plaintiff in error.

John T. Bradley, for the defendant in error.

HORTON, C. J. The first question we are called upon to consider is, whether the motion which was filed by Oliver Green on October 3, 1887, and decided October 12, 1887, was a special or general appearance in the action. If the appearance of a party, though called special, is upon other than jurisdictional grounds, it is a general appearance: *Burdette* v. *Corgan,* 26 Kan. 104. So, if a motion contests the service only, and does not go beyond jurisdictional grounds, it is a special or limited appearance. The motion was presented to set aside the judgment of October 1, 1887, on the ground solely that no proper service had been made upon the defendant. By the motion, the defendant, Oliver Green, made a special appearance only. This motion did not give the court jurisdiction over the person of the defendant, nor authorize the court to require him to answer or plead. When the plaintiff, Harriet F. Green, obtained her judgment on the sixteenth day of January, 1888, there was on file in the district court, among the papers of the cause, the affidavit of C. M. Welch, showing that the firm of Messrs. Welch and Welch had no authority from Oliver Green to appear generally for him, and that their authority in the case was limited to the special motion filed. It is true that the attention of the district court was not called to this affidavit, but that was not the fault of the defendant. Harriet F. Green might have called the court's attention to this affidavit. She took her judgment at her peril, and as the district court had no jurisdiction over the person of the defendant, the judgment is void and must be set aside: *Reynolds* v. *Fleming*, 30 Kan. 106; 46 Am. Rep. 86. In that case it was said: "In this state it is held that a judgment rendered without jurisdiction is void; that a personal judgment rendered without notice to the defendant is rendered without jurisdiction, and is consequently void; that a judgment void for want of notice may be set aside, on a motion made therefor by the defendant; and that this may be done in cases where it requires extrinsic evidence to show the judgment was rendered without notice and without jurisdiction."

As to what constitutes a special appearance, see *Branner* v. *Chapman*, 11 Kan. 118; *Simcock* v. *First Nat. Bank*, 14 Kan. 529; *Bentz* v. *Eubanks*, 32 Kan. 321.

The judgment of the district court will be set aside, and the case remanded for further proceedings.

JUDGMENTS VOID FOR WANT OF JURISDICTION. — The absence of legal service or authorized appearance is jurisdictional, and without jurisdiction no judgment can be entered under which any rights can be lost or acquired: *Great West Mining Co.* v. *Woodmas*, 12 Col. 46; 13 Am. St. Rep. 204, and cases cited in note.

APPEARANCE IN ACTIONS. — Appearance of a party entitled to notice, after judgment, merely to give notice of appeal, is not such an appearance as will dispense with the necessity of notice: *McKinney* v. *Jones*, 7 Tex. 598; 58 Am. Dec. 83, and note; nor is a motion by an attorney, to set aside a judgment taken by default, an appearance for the party: *Chahoon* v. *Hollenback*, 16 Serg. & R. 425; 16 Am. Dec. 587. The appearance of a defendant under protest, at a time to which an adjournment had been improperly had, cannot have the effect of reviving process which had failed from non-appearance at the time named in the writ: *Martin* v. *Fales*, 18 Me. 23; 36 Am. Dec. 693. Special appearance for a special purpose does not waive jurisdiction over the person: *Dailey* v. *Kennedy*, 64 Mich. 208; *Kinkade* v. *Myers*, 17 Or. 470; *Chesapeake etc. R. R. Co.* v. *Heath*, 87 Ky. 651.

PLANT v. THOMPSON.

[42 KANSAS, 664.]

AGENT'S RIGHT TO COMMISSIONS. — An agent employed to sell real estate, who first brings it to the notice of the person who ultimately becomes the purchaser, is entitled to his commissions on the sale, although the latter is effected by the owner of the property, nor can the owner evade his liability to pay the agent his commissions by selling for a sum less than the price given the agent, when the reduction is made of the owner's own accord.

ACTION by Miller and Thompson against Plant and wife to recover commissions on the sale of real estate placed in their hands for sale. The other facts are stated in the opinion. Judgment for plaintiffs, and defendants appeal.

G. N. Elliott, for the plaintiffs in error.

Hazen and Isenhart, for the defendants in error.

HOLT, C. In the petition in error, the overruling of the motion for a new trial is not assigned as an error, but there is no point made upon this plainly and squarely in the briefs of plaintiffs. If the attention of defendants had been called to it, that defect might have been cured in this court; in the manner it is presented in the briefs, we shall disregard it. The defendants claim that there was error in giving and refusing instructions, and that the verdict is contrary to the evidence. There is really but little conflict in the evidence brought before us. Taking even the uncontradicted testimony, we believe the judgment is correct, and without following specifically the objections of defendant, we will give our reasons for affirming it. From the testimony of Mrs. Plant, it appears that her attention was first called to Kellam as a probable purchaser by the plaintiffs. To be sure, they entered into no negotiations with him for a sale, and it was sold for a less price than that given the agents. It was also sold by her without any aid from the plaintiffs, except that her attention was directed to Kellam by them. This view of the case is as favorable to the defendants as the testimony will justify, and yet, under the circumstances, the plaintiffs were entitled to their commission. They introduced the purchaser to the seller, and by that means the sale was made.

In *Lloyd* v. *Matthews*, 51 N. Y. 124, in a case similar to this one, the court says: "It is sufficient to entitle a broker to compensation that the sale is effected through his agency as its procuring cause; and if his communications with the purchaser were the cause or means of bringing him and the owner together, and the sale resulted in consequence thereof, the broker is entitled to recover."

In *Arrington* v. *Cary*, 5 Baxt. 609, it is said: "When a broker or agent is employed to sell real estate, and produces a person who ultimately becomes a purchaser, he is entitled to his commissions, although the trade may be effected by the owner of the property."

Also, from *Carter* v. *Webster*, 79 Ill. 435, we quote a part of the opinion, which explains itself: "Plaintiff engaged Bruner to secure a purchaser for defendant's land, and according to the custom that prevails, Bruner induced Gun, another real estate agent, to interest himself to find a buyer for the land. Gun did mention the fact that this property was for sale, to Mr. Mears, and through the information thus obtained, Mr. Mears, Sen., went directly to defendant, and bought the property of him. The effect of what plaintiff did was to present to defendant a person who made an offer for the property that he was willing to and did accept. This was all plaintiff undertook to do, ... or all he had to do to earn his commissions."

In *Royster* v. *Mageveney*, 9 Lea, 148, it is said: "If a broker is employed to sell property, and he first brings the property to the notice of the purchaser, and upon such notice the sale is effected by the owner, the broker is entitled to commissions."

The court in *Tyler* v. *Parr*, 52 Mo. 249, speaking by Judge Wagner, said: "The law is well established that in a suit by a real estate agent for the amount of his commission, it is immaterial that the owner sold the property and concluded the bargain. If, after the property is placed in the agent's hands, the sale is brought about or procured by his advertisement and exertions, he will be entitled to his commissions." See also *Sussdorff* v. *Schmidt*, 55 N. Y. 319; *Lincoln* v. *McClatchie*, 36 Conn. 136; *Shepherd* v. *Hedden*, 29 N. J. L. 334; *Winans* v. *Jaques*, 10 Daly, 487; *Goffe* v. *Gibson*, 18 Mo. App. 1; *Anderson* v. *Cox*, 16 Neb. 10; *Bell* v. *Kaiser*, 50 Mo. 150; *Williams* v. *Leslie*, 111 Ind. 70; *Doonan* v. *Ives*, 73 Ga. 295; *Dolan* v. *Scanlan*, 57 Cal. 261; *Armstrong* v. *Wann*, 29 Minn. 126; Fitch on Real Estate Agency, 119, 120.

The claim of the plaintiffs for commission is not affected because the defendants saw fit to sell the same land for a price less than they gave it to plaintiffs to sell. In this connection Mrs. Plant testified: "I thought if I could make the sale myself I could sell it cheaper, and would not have to pay commission." The defendants will not be allowed to take advantage of their introduction to the purchaser by plaintiffs, and reap the benefits of the sale made to him in consequence, and then escape all liability of paying them their commission because they sold the land for a sum less than the price given their agents, where the reduction was made of their own accord: *Stewart* v. *Mather*, 32 Wis. 344; *Kock* v. *Emmerling*, 22 How. 69; *Woods* v. *Stephens*, 46 Mo. 555; *Reynolds* v. *Tompkins*, 23 W. Va. 229; *Lincoln* v. *McClatchie, supra;* Wharton on Agency and Agents, sec. 329.

We recommend that the judgment be affirmed.

By the COURT. It is so ordered.

REAL ESTATE AGENTS — COMMISSIONS. — A broker is entitled to his commission when he procures a purchaser with whom his principal is satisfied, and who actually contracts for the property at a price satisfactory to the owner: *Conkling* v. *Krakauer*, 70 Tex. 735. As to when and under what circumstances a broker will be entitled to commissions on the sales of real estate, see *Ward* v. *Cobb*, 148 Mass. 518; 12 Am. St. Rep. 587, and particularly note 589, 590. A real estate agent is entitled to the commission agreed upon for exchanging real estate placed in his hands, if the terms of exchange are accepted by the owner, as the obligation to pay the commission then becomes fixed: *Lockwood* v. *Halsey*, 41 Kan. 166. Where a real estate agent agrees to produce a purchaser, he must act in good faith, and the employer is not bound to accept a purchaser produced by the agent, nor to pay the commission, unless such purchaser stands ready, able, and willing to purchase upon the terms proposed: Id. But when the agent complies with the contract of his employment, and the real estate owner without good reason refuses to fulfill the contract made by his agent with the proposed purchaser, if such purchaser is able, willing, and ready to purchase, then the agent is entitled to his commission or compensation, to be regulated by the terms of the contract, or by established usage if there is no express contract fixing the compensation: *De Cordova* v. *Bahn*, 74 Tex. 643.

ATCHISON, TOPEKA, AND SANTA FÉ RAILROAD COMPANY *v.* LINDLEY.

[42 KANSAS, 714.]

CONTRIBUTORY NEGLIGENCE — DANGEROUS POSITION VOLUNTARILY ASSUMED. — Where a shipper is accompaning his stock on a freight train, and, being ordered or directed by the conductor to "get on top of the cars and signal," voluntarily assumes such position, knowing it to be peculiarly dangerous and perlious, and that it is not necessary for him to be there to care for his stock, or as a passenger, he is guilty of such contributory negligence that he cannot recover for injuries received in falling or being thrown from the train while in such position, in the absence of gross negligence or malice on the part of the employees in charge of the train.

George R. Peck, A. A. Hurd, O. J. Wood, and Robert Dunlap, for the plaintiff in error.   •

Charles Willsie, for the defendant in error.

HORTON, C. J.   This was an action by D. C. Lindley against the Atchison, Topeka, and Santa Fé Railroad Company, for injuries received while traveling on a stock train, and resulted in a verdict against the company for $9,650. McCambridge was the conductor of the train, Allen was the engineer, and Guy the head brakeman. Lindley was a live-stock dealer, fifty years of age, residing in Albion, Harper County, in this state. He had shipped live-stock for thirty-four years. The alleged cause of action occurred on the sixteenth day of July, 1885. Lindley had shipped on the defendant's train one car-load of hogs, and one car-load of cattle, from Perth station, in Sumner County, to be transported to Kansas City, Missouri, and was on top of one of the stock-cars just before his injuries. He arrived at Eudora, a station between Topeka and Argentine, between five and six o'clock in the morning. The train consisted of forty-five cars, loaded with stock. Soon after arriving at Eudora, eight or ten of the cars, with the caboose, broke or separated from the main train.

The petition alleged, among other things, that "the conductor then in charge of the train, totally disregarding the safety of human life, and being grossly careless of the safety of the passengers on the train, and well understanding the culpably negligent manner in which the engineer was handling the train, carelessly and negligently asked, directed, and induced the plaintiff to climb up on the top of the cars, and signal for the front portion of the train to be backed up so as to have the rear and front portions of the train coupled together, and then

signal the cars containing hogs needing water in the hind part
of the train, so that the conductor could water them; that the
front part of the train was then backed up to the hind portion of the train, and while the brakeman was between the
cars, making the coupling, and while plaintiff was on top of
the cars, looking in an opposite direction from the engineer,
the latter, then and there operating the engine of the train,
did then and there, with gross and wanton negligence, and with
utter disregard for human life, without any warning, suddenly
throw open the throttle of the engine and turn on all the steam
power possible, so that the engine started up with the cars with
so much force and power that the life of any human being upon
the top of the train was unsafe; that the train started up so
suddenly and with such a tremendous jerk that it threw the
plaintiff clear off his feet and pitched him head foremost down
upon the railroad track, where he would have been run over and
mashed if he had not been snatched from his perlious condition."

The evidence upon the part of Lindley tended to show that
when the train stopped at Eudora, he got out of the caboose
with McCambridge, the conductor, and T. V. Borland, another shipper having stock upon the train; that they walked
up to the water-tank; that the engine and three car-loads of
hogs had passed the tank; that the plaintiff then asked the
conductor if he would not back up the train, and water the
three cars that had passed the tank; that the conductor said,
"No, the hogs are not yours"; that finally the train was
backed up to water or shower the hogs; that the conductor,
who was standing at the water-tank, looking down at Lindley
and Borland, said: "You fellows stand down there, and when
a car of cattle or horses comes along that you don't want
watered, throw down your hands, and I will turn the water
off, and when you come to a car-load of hogs, throw up your
hands, and I will shower them"; that Lindley and Borland
did as the conductor suggested; that about a dozen or fourteen car-loads of hogs were then watered; that when the last
car-load of those cars was watered, the conductor looked down
again, and said to Lindley and Borland: "You fellows get up
on top and help signal until the last car-load of hogs comes .
up, and we will water them"; that Lindley and Borland got
upon the top of the train as requested; that Lindley got upon
the hind end, but stepped from there to a car near the engine;
that Borland remained on the end car; that the train then

backed down to where the detached portion of it was; that
when the train got down to the detached cars, it stopped quite
a long time; that Lindley had curiosity enough to walk down
to where Borland was; that at this time the train was standing still; that when the plaintiff came near to where Borland
was, the brakeman was in the act of coupling the cars; that
the plaintiff saw Borland looking down at him; that plaintiff walked up toward Borland, and got near the end of the
car; that just at that moment Borland threw up his hands,
and said: "Look out!" that the crash then came; that the
coupling-pin broke, and the cars separated; that Lindley fell
off, and was severely bruised and injured. The court charged
the jury, among other things, as follows: "If you find, from
the evidence, that the plaintiff went upon the top of the train
at the request of the conductor of the train, to assist the train-
men in giving signals to the engineer to back up the train
for the purpose of coupling on to the part which had been
detached, you would be justified in finding that he went upon
the train voluntarily, as the conductor in so doing would be
acting beyond the scope of his employment."

The jury also made the following findings of fact:—

"Who made the coupling at the time of the accident? and
was he the head brakeman? Guy, the head brakeman?

"Was the plaintiff, D. C. Lindley, watching the brakeman
between the cars making the coupling at the time of the accident? Yes.

"Was it a part of the duties of the plaintiff, D. C. Lindley,
in taking care of the two car-loads of stock on the train, to
assist the train-men in managing, running, or coupling the
cars on the train, and in making signals to the engineer?
No."

The plaintiff contends that he was thrown or pitched off
the top of the car by a sudden forward motion of the train,
and in this he is supported by the findings of the jury. The
defendant insists that Lindley fell off the car while the slack
of the train was running out. The important question in the
case is, whether, under the allegations of the petition, the testimony of the plaintiff, the instructions of the court, and the
special findings of the jury, the plaintiff is entitled to recover.
We think not. Lindley knew, according to his own testimony,
the places of danger and safety upon the train. He was under
no obligation to climb upon the top of the train and signal
the conductor or any other employee. "Out of curiosity" he

walked down to the end of the car where the brakeman was coupling the train. At the time of the accident he was watching the brakeman coupling the cars. He assumed a position on the top of the cars which he knew was peculiarly dangerous and perilous. It was not necessary for him to be there to care for his stock, or as a passenger. The order or direction of the conductor to him, " to go on top of the cars and help signal," was entirely without the routine of the conductor's duties; and as it was voluntarily obeyed•by Lindley, it could not fasten any liability on the railroad company. If he acted as an employee or brakeman, it was of his own volition. He occupied merely the position of a passenger who voluntarily assumed a very dangerous position to make signals at the request of the conductor as a matter of accommodation.

In *McCorkle* v. *Chicago etc. R'y Co.*, 61 Iowa, 555, it is said: " Plaintiff got off a cattle train at night to examine his cattle when the train stopped for that purpose, and not hearing the signal to start, attempted to get on a freight-car after the train had started, because he supposed, from the ' lively rate ' the train was moving, he would not be able to get on the caboose at the rear of the train, which had been provided for passengers. At the time he attempted to get on the freight-car, he had a ' prod-pole ' and a lantern in his hand. His foot caught in a hole caused by a defective plank in the bridge over which the train was passing, and he fell from the car and was injured. *Held*, that he was guilty of contributory negligence, and not entitled to recover."

In *Pennsylvania R. R. Co.* v. *Langdon*, 92 Pa. St. 21, 37 Am. Rep. 651, it is said: " On the other hand, should a passenger insist upon riding upon the cow-catcher, in the face of the rule prohibiting it, and as a consequence should be injured, I apprehend it would be a good defense to an action against the company, even though the negligence of the latter's servants was the cause of the collision or other accident by which the injury was occasioned. And if the passenger, thus recklessly exposing his life to possible accidents, were a sane man, more especially if he were a railroad man, it is difficult to see how the knowledge or even the assent of the conductor to his occupying such a position could affect the case. There can be no license to commit suicide. It is true, the conductor has the control of the train, and may assign passengers their seats. But he may not assign a passenger to a seat on the cow-catcher, a position on the platform, or in the baggage-car. This is known to every intelligent man, and appears upon the face of the rule itself. He is expressly required to enforce it, and to prohibit any of the acts referred to, unless it be riding upon the cow-catcher, which is so manifestly dangerous and improper that it has not been deemed necessary to prohibit it. We are unable to see how a conductor, in violation of a known rule of the company, can license a man to occupy a place of danger so as to make the company responsible."

In *Lehigh V. R. R. Co.* v. *Greiner*, 113 Pa. St. 600, it is said: "Where one negligently and without excuse places himself in a position of known danger, and thereby suffers an injury at the hands of another, either wholly or partially by means of his own act, he cannot recover damages for the injury sustained. The contributory negligence which prevents recovery for an injury, however, must be such as co-operates in causing the injury, and without which the injury would not have happened."

In *L. R. & F. S. R'y Co.* v. *Miles*, 13 Am. & Eng. R'y Cas. 10, it is said: "But there are certain portions of every railroad train which are so obviously dangerous for a passenger to occupy, and so plainly not designed for his reception, that his presence there will constitute negligence as a matter of law, and preclude him from claiming damages for injuries received while in such position. A passenger who voluntarily and unnecessarily rides upon the engine or the tender, or upon the pilot or bumper of the locomotive, or upon the top of a car, or upon the platform, cannot be said to be in the exercise of that caution and discretion which the law requires of all persons who are of full age, of sound mind, and ordinary intelligence."

In *Flower* v. *Pennsylvania R. R. Co.*, 69 Pa. St. 210, 8 Am. Rep. 251, an engine with one freight-car had been detached from a train, and was stopped at a water-station. The fireman requested a small boy standing near to put in the hose and turn on the water. While he was climbing on the tender to do this, the other freight-cars belonging to the train came down without a brakeman, and struck the car behind the tender. The boy fell, and was crushed to death. The court held that the company owed no special duty to the boy, saying: "The case turns wholly on the effect of the request of the fireman, who was temporary engineer. Did that request involve the company in the consequences? . . . . The fireman, through his indolence or haste, was the cause of the boy's loss of life.

Unless his act can be legally attributed to the company, it is equally clear the company was not the cause of the injury. The maxim, *Qui facit per alium, facit per se*, can only apply where there is an authority, either general or special. It is not pretended there was a special authority. Was there a general authority which would comprehend the fireman's request to the boy to fill the engine tank with water? This seems to be equally plain without resorting to the evidence given, that engineers are not permitted to receive any one on the engine but the conductor and fireman, or superintendent; that it is the duty of the fireman to supply the engine with water; that he has no power to invite others to do it, and can leave his post only on a necessity."

In *Baltimore etc. R. R. Co.* v. *Jones*, 95 U. S. 439, Jones was one of a party of men employed by a railroad company in constructing and repairing its roadway. They were usually conveyed by the company to and from the place where their services were required, and a box-car was assigned to their use. Mr. Justice Swayne, delivering the opinion of the court, said: "The plaintiff had been warned against riding on the pilot and forbidden to do so. It was next to the cow-catcher, and obviously a place of peril, especially in case of collision. There was room for him in the box-car. He should have taken his place there. He could have got into the box-car in as little if not less time than it took to climb on the pilot. The knowledge, assent, or direction of the company's agent as to what he did is immaterial. If told to get on anywhere, that the train was late, and that he must hurry, there was no justification for taking such a risk. As well might he have obeyed a suggestion to ride on the cow-catcher, or put himself on the track before the advancing wheels of the locomotive. The company, though bound to a high degree of care, did not insure his safety. He was not an infant, nor *non compos*. The liability of the company was conditioned upon the exercise of reasonable and proper care and caution on his part. Without the latter, the former could not arise. He and another who rode beside him were the only persons hurt upon the train. All those in the box-car, where he should have been, were uninjured. He would have escaped also if he had been there. His injury was due to his own folly and recklessness. He was himself the author of his misfortune. This is shown with as near an approach to a demonstration as anything short of mathematics will permit."

In *Georgia Pac. R. R. Co.* v. *Propst*, 83 Ala. 518, it was decided that "a railroad company is liable, as principal, for injuries received by a person who was employed by the conductor of a freight train as brakeman during the trip, while acting under the orders of the conductor, in coupling cars; but not if the person so acting and injured was only a passenger, who was not employed by the conductor, nor under any obligation to obey his orders."

In the opinion, rendered by Chief Justice Stone, it was said that "so far as this count informs us, the plaintiff was a mere passenger on the train; and so far as the right to control or direct the movements of the plaintiff is shown in this count, the conductor would have had as much authority over any other passenger, or even a by-stander, as he had over him. Such order or direction, as averred, is entirely without the routine of the conductor's duties."

In *Georgia Pac. R. R. Co.* v. *Propst*, 85 Ala. 203, the conductor addressed the plaintiff as follows: "Will, come here, and make this coupling for me"; and the plaintiff was injured in conforming to this order or request. The court said: "Such an order or direction could not fasten a liability on the railroad corporation." See also *Gilliam* v. *South etc. R. R. Co.*, 70 Ala. 268; *Howard* v. *Kansas City etc. R. R. Co.*, 41 Kan. 403.

We are referred to *Indianapolis etc. R. R. Co.* v. *Horst*, 93 U. S. 291, as decisive in favor of the recovery of the plaintiff. That case decides that a shipper accompanying his stock on the train is entitled to the rights of a passenger, but in many particulars widely differs from this. In that case the shipper was commanded by the conductor to get out of the caboose and go on top of the train, because the caboose was about to be detached. The shipper had no choice but to obey, or leave his stock to go forward without any one to accompany or take care of them. In this case there was a caboose accompanying the train, where the plaintiff might have ridden in safety. He did not go upon the top of the train to accompany his stock, or to take care of them; he went, as before stated, merely to comply with the order or request of the conductor to assist in signaling the train. The other cases referred to by the plaintiff are not contrary, we think, to the law as before declared.

In answer to one of the questions, the jury stated that the plaintiff was not "guilty of negligence in going on top of the

train at Eudora just prior to the accident." This finding of
the jury, however, is not conclusive. If the plaintiff's evidence, with all the legitimate inferences which a jury might
reasonably draw from it, is insufficient to sustain a verdict in
his favor, so that a verdict for the plaintiff, if one should be
returned, would be set aside, the court may properly direct a
verdict for the defendant without submitting the evidence to
the jury. In *Atchison etc. R. R. Co. v. Plunkett*, 25 Kan. 188,
the jury found that Plunkett, at the time of his injuries, was
in the exercise of reasonable and ordinary care. This finding
was not considered sufficient to authorize the verdict, in view
of the testimony and the other findings. Mr. Justice Valentine in that case said: "If the findings in detail contradict
the general findings, we may order the judgment to be rendered in accordance with the findings in detail, and wholly
ignore the general findings. For instance, where a question
of negligence arises in the case, the jury cannot be allowed to
say conclusively, after finding certain special facts, that these
facts constitute negligence, when in fact and manifestly they
do not constitute negligence."

Finally, it is claimed that although Lindley might have
been guilty of contributory negligence, he is entitled to recover, because the conductor and engineer of the railroad company were guilty of gross negligence. Neither the findings
of the jury nor the testimony introduced in the case establishes that the company or any employee was guilty of such
gross negligence as amounted to wantonness: *Southern Kan. R'y
Co. v. Rice*, 38 Kan. 398; 5 Am. St. Rep. 766; *Kansas Pac.
R'y Co. v. Whipple*, 39 Kan. 531. Allen, the engineer, testified that the fireman signaled him to stop. Bradshaw, the
fireman, testified that Guy, the head brakeman, signaled him.
The jury found that the engineer did not see the plaintiff on
top of the train just prior to the accident; therefore, he was
not actuated either by gross negligence or malice toward him
or any one else. The conductor did not give the engineer the
signal to move forward. The jury, in returning their answers
about the negligence of the employees of the train, found as
follows: —

"Q. Were any of the men who were running or operating
the train guilty of any negligence at the time of the accident?
If yes, in what did it consist? A. Yes; the hurried manner
in which the employees of the train managed the same.

"Q. Did the engineer who was operating the engine at the

time of the accident to the plaintiff and just prior thereto, use ordinary care in handling the engine? A. No."

These answers do not tend to show malice or gross negligence.

The judgment of the district court will be reversed, and the cause remanded for a new trial.

CONTRIBUTORY NEGLIGENCE. — One who takes an exposed position upon a train not designed for the use of passengers assumes the special perils of that position, whether he takes it by license, non-interference, or express permission of the conductor: *Files* v. *Boston etc. R. R. Co.*, 149 Mass. 204; 14 Am. St. Rep. 411, and note. Compare *New York etc. R. R. Co.* v. *Enches*, 127 Pa. St. 316; 14 Am. St. Rep. 848, and note.

CASES

IN THE

SUPREME COURT

OF

MICHIGAN.

TOWNSHIP OF OTSEGO LAKE *v.* KIRSTEN.

[72 MICHIGAN, 1.]

OFFICIAL BONDS — EVIDENCE OF OFFICER'S INDEBTEDNESS. — In a suit on a township treasurer's official bond, his books are proper evidence to show his indebtedness to the township, and a supervisor who has participated in a settlement with him, and has examined his books and vouchers, may also testify as to the amount thus found due.

OFFICIAL BONDS — RELEASE OF TOWNSHIP OFFICER AND SURETIES. — Where, upon a settlement with a township treasurer, the amount found due from him to the township is neither disputed nor doubtful, the township board has no authority to release him or the sureties on his official bond from his and their legal obligation to pay the amount due, in the absence of any well-grounded apprehension as to the legal liability of the bondsmen for the debt.

JURY AND JURORS — RIGHT TO ASCERTAIN FOR WHICH PARTY JUROR WILL DECIDE, IF THE EVIDENCE IS EQUALLY BALANCED. — When selecting a jury, a juror may be asked which side he would be inclined to favor, if at the close of the trial the evidence were equally balanced between the parties, to ascertain his bias, and for the purpose of exercising a peremptory challenge if necessary.

ASSUMPSIT on a town treasurer's bond. Judgment for plaintiff. Defendants bring error.

Main J. Connine and A. A. Crane, for the appellants.

A. D. Marshall, and T. A. E. and J. C. Weadock, for the plaintiff.

CHAMPLIN, J. Adelbert Kirsten was township treasurer of the town of Otsego Lake. To qualify himself to act, he gave to the township a bond, as required by law, with Hyman Joseph and De Witt Wilson as sureties.

At the close of his official term the township board examined and audited his accounts as such treasurer, and found that he was indebted to the township in the sum of $1,037.71. The township board immediately notified the sureties of this fact, and that the township would hold them responsible on the treasurer's bond.

The board commenced their examination on April 15, 1887, and concluded it on the 18th. On the 16th Kirsten secured his sureties by a bill of sale on his stock of goods. The money found due the township not having been paid, this action was brought upon the township treasurer's bond.

The surety, Hyman Joseph, and the principal, Adelbert Kirsten, defend on the ground that, after the amount of the defalcation was ascertained, the township board settled with the sureties, and took their several and respective promissory notes in full of all claims against them. These defendants appeared by separate attorneys, and pleaded separately.

On the trial of the cause, the plaintiff introduced the books of the township treasurer, from which it appeared that he was indebted to the town in the sum stated. There does not appear to have been any conflict in the testimony respecting this fact, and it may be regarded as undisputed. It was proved by the record and by the testimony of the witnesses who examined the accounts.

This testimony was competent, and there was no error in overruling the objections of defendant's counsel to the introduction of the township treasurer's books in evidence, nor in permitting the supervisor, who was a member of the township board, and who took part in the examination of the books and vouchers, to answer the question, "What sum was found to be due from Kirsten to the township?"

The township board and Kirsten met for the purpose of looking over his accounts, and to ascertain how much, if any, was due to the township, and there was no valid obligation to his stating what sum they found to be due.

After the plaintiff rested its case, the counsel for defendants, to maintain the issue on their part, offered in evidence the record of the proceedings of the plaintiff township board, as recorded on pages 102 and 103 of their record, being the proceedings of a meeting of that board held on April 20, 1887, for the purpose of showing that on that day the said township board settled all claims of the township against defendant Adelbert Kirsten, as its treasurer, and against defendants

Hyman Joseph and De Witt Wilson, as sureties on his official
bond, both arising on said bond, and otherwise, and then and
there accepted the promissory notes of said Joseph and said
Wilson, due in one year thereafter, whereby all action on said
bond became suspended until such notes were due, and
whereby all remedy upon said bond became superseded; and
for the purpose of showing that said township has no right of
action against said Joseph and Wilson, arising out of said
suretyship, until said notes became due; to which offer counsel for plaintiff objected as incompetent, irrelevant, and immaterial, which objection was by the court sustained, for the
reason that the township board had no power to make such a
settlement as the one set forth in the minutes of the meeting;
to which ruling counsel for defendants then and there excepted;
the record of which proceedings so offered in evidence, and so
excluded upon objection, is in the words and figures following:—

"APRIL 20, 1887.

"At a meeting of the township board, duly convened and
held.

"Present: Charles W. Bahel, supervisor; A. R. Vanderwoort,
justice of the peace; A. Assal, township clerk. Absent: Frank
Buell, justice of the peace.

"Board called to order by C. W. Bahel in the chair.

"The business of the meeting was stated to be the adjustment of the matter caused by the default of A. Kirsten, the
outgoing treasurer, to account for the balance of $2,485.98
found to be due the township on settlement with said treasurer.

"In adjustment of said matter, it was moved and supported
that we accept the notes of the bondsmen of said treasurer for
the sum of $368.50 each, payable in one year from date, to-
gether with the agreement, to the effect that if there is no error
discovered in the collection of the taxes of 1886, made by said
treasurer, the said treasurer will be released from the payment
of the sum of $300, making the amount of the shortage of
$1,037.71. Motion carried.

"Moved and supported that the supervisor take charge of
the notes given by the bondsmen of A. Kirsten. Carried.

"Moved and supported that we adjourn *sine die.*

"C. W. BAHEL, Supervisor.
"A. ASSAL, Township Clerk."

The insufficiency of the defense under which this proof was
offered is that it nowhere appears that the claim of the town-

ship for the balance of $1,037.71 against Kirsten was either disputed or doubtful. Kirsten had received this amount of money, which he had not accounted for or paid over as required by law, and the township board had no legal authority to release either Kirsten or his sureties on his bond from his and their legal obligation to pay the amount to the township. The action of the board was, in effect, making a gratuity to Kirsten of over three hundred dollars of the township's money, without necessity, right, or authority. Tax-payers might justly complain of such action as an illegal perversion of the township's money. Had it been a disputed claim, or if there had existed any well-grounded apprehension as to the legal liability of the bondsmen for the debt, it might have afforded grounds for a compromise.

No reason appears for the extraordinary action of the board taken on April 20th, but the record shows that on April 22d a full board was duly convened, and by a unanimous vote it was resolved that counsel be employed, and suit brought upon the bond, thus ignoring, as well they might, the action taken on the 20th.

This is a much stronger case than that of *Township of Boardman* v. *Flagg*, 70 Mich. 372, where a settlement had been made, and a balance struck, which the township treasurer paid over to his successor. Afterwards it was ascertained he had collected moneys belonging to the township, which did not appear upon his books from which the settlement was made, and was not included in the settlement, and it was held that the township clearly had the right to recover the money still remaining in the treasurer's hands, and that the township was not estopped by the settlement made by the township board.

Error is also assigned upon a question, which was permitted to be put to a juryman when being selected to try the cause, by the plaintiff's attorney, as follows: "Suppose, at the close of the testimony, it was equally balanced as between the plaintiff and defendants, which side would you be inclined to favor?"

The juryman answered: "Well, I think I should favor the sureties. I won't be certain. I think so."

The counsel afterwards challenged this juror peremptorily, and he was excused.

The point was decided in *Monaghan* v. *Agricultural F. Ins. Co.*, 53 Mich. 238–246.

The judgment of the circuit court must be affirmed.

EVIDENCE — BOOKS OF ACCOUNT AS EVIDENCE: See note to *Merrill v. Ithaca etc. R. R. Co.*, 30 Am. Dec. 142; *Sickles* v. *Mather*, 32 Id. 524, 525; *Miller* v. *Shay*, 145 Mass. 162; 1 Am. St. Rep. 449, and note 451.

ACCOUNTS — EVIDENCE. — Proof of an account should be made by producing the books in which it is entered, or by offering a copy thereof: *McDonald* v. *Clough*, 10 Col. 59. But books of account of a merchant are not evidence in his own favor with respect to payments in them to his customer: *Oberg* v. *Breen*, 50 N. J. L. 145. For books of account are only receivable in evidence when they contain charges by one party against the other, and then only under the circumstances and in the manner provided for by statute: *Pollard* v. *Turner*, 22 Neb. 366. Where on a trial, plaintiff, on cross-examination by defendant, stated that certain erasures in an account-book and a leaf torn therefrom had been done by him in order to correct errors, defendant was properly denied the privilege of introducing such account-book in evidence: *Campbell* v. *Holland*, 22 Neb. 587.

COMPETENCY OF JURORS: Note to *Nelms* v. *State*, 53 Am. Dec. 101; note to *Smith* v. *Eames*, 36 Id. 521–533. As to the rejection of a juror for bias or prejudice, see note to *Commonwealth* v. *Brown*, 9 Am. St. Rep. 744–748.

CARMICHAEL *v.* CARMICHAEL.

[72 MICHIGAN, 76.]

WILLS — AGREEMENT FOR TESTAMENTARY DISPOSITION OF PROPERTY. — A person may make a valid agreement to make a particular disposition of his property by will.

WILLS — AGREEMENT FOR TESTAMENTARY DISPOSITION OF PROPERTY — SPECIFIC PERFORMANCE. — Where husband and wife agree by parol contract to make a certain testamentary disposition of their real estate by last will, and such contract is strictly performed by the husband, and the benefits provided by him in his will accepted by his wife after his death, there is such part performance of the oral contract as to take it out of the statute of frauds, and equity will then prevent the wife from violating her part of such agreement by a conveyance in fraud of the beneficiaries named therein. In an action to set aside such conveyance by her, such beneficiaries are proper parties complainant, and she is a proper party defendant.

BILL for specific performance of an oral agreement for the testamentary disposition of real estate. Bill dismissed, and complainants appeal.

J. V. Rogers and E. L. Koon, for the complainants.

A. St. John and Thomas A. Wilson, for the defendants.

MORSE, J. The complainants are two sons and a daughter of Charles Carmichael, Sen., now deceased, and the defendant Ann Carmichael. The defendants Ira Carmichael and Charles Carmichael are brothers of the complainants. Hattie E. Disbrow is a sister. Charles I. Carmichael, known in the record as Charles Ira, is a son of the defendant Ira Car-michael.

Charles Carmichael, Sen., in 1858, lived in Wheatland, in the county of Hillsdale, and owned 160 acres of land. In that year, the complainant Delos Carmichael was convicted of a state-prison offense. His father was his bail. Delos absconded, with the full consent of all the family. His father settled the bond at an expense of something over one thousand dollars.

About this time the father deeded 120 acres of his land to his son Charles, reserving and keeping the title to forty acres, the homestead, and in his own name. The 120 acres was afterwards deeded back to the father, excepting forty acres, which, at his request, was conveyed by Charles to his mother, the defendant Ann Carmichael.

Soon afterwards, and up to 1866, different conveyances were made by the father to his children, in which his wife joined. By these deeds, Ira received fifty-eight acres; Charles, Jr., thirty-five acres; and John, twenty-two acres. Hattie was given one thousand dollars with which to purchase twenty acres of land. This left sixty acres remaining in the name of the father, and forty acres in the name of the mother, lying together in one tract. The children took possession of the re-spective pieces of land conveyed to them. It does not appear that any provision was made at this time for the complainants Delos and Matilda.

November 9, 1872, the father and mother made wills. The will of the former bequeathed all the personal property to his wife absolutely, and the sixty acres of land to her during her lifetime. At her death, Charles was to have ten acres, and five hundred dollars to be paid out of the real estate; and the remaining fifty acres was to be divided equally between John, Delos, and Matilda. The will stated that Ira and Hattie had received what was intended as their portion of the estate. The wife devised to her husband all her personal property abso-lutely, and the forty acres during his lifetime. At his death, the land was to be divided equally between John, Delos, and Matilda.

It is the theory of the complainants' bill that these convey-ances to Ira, John, and Charles, the payment of the one thou-sand dollars to Hattie, and the two wills, were intended by the father and mother as an equitable division of their property among their children, the whole shares of Delos and Matilda, and a portion of John's, being postponed in delivery until after the death of both parents. The evidence seems to support this theory.

It is also alleged in the bill that this disposition of the property was mutually agreed to by the father and mother, and that the inducement of Charles, Sen., to make his will as he did was because of the promise of the defendant Ann Carmichael that she would make her will as she did; that each will was made and executed in pursuance of a mutual promise and agreement that each should be so made as aforesaid; and that without said promise and agreement by the one to the other, neither of said wills would have been so made. This promise and agreement, if made, was in part an oral one.

Charles, Sen., died June 28, 1884. Up to this time neither of said wills had been revoked or altered, and both were in the possession of one William Mercer, with whom they were deposited soon after their execution. In the mean time no further advancements had been made to any of the children.

A few days after the death of their father, the children made an arrangement with their mother by which the personal property, about three thousand six hundred dollars, was divided equally among them, they giving their obligations to her to pay her interest upon that sum while she lived.

Delos and Matilda resided away from their mother, — Matilda in Allegan County, and Delos out of the state. Hattie and Ira lived near to her.

August 14, 1884, the mother conveyed by warranty deed her forty acres to Hattie and Charles Ira, and on the same day they deeded one third of the same to Ira. These three on the same day gave the mother a life lease of the same premises. These conveyances were all recorded on the day they were executed, but the register was requested not to have the fact of such execution and record published. It was nearly a year before the existence of these conveyances was discovered by the complainants. They then sought to settle the matter, and procure from Ira, Hattie, and Charles Ira a deed of the premises back to their mother, but were unable to do so. They then filed the bill in this cause.

The bill, after averring the facts, alleges that the defendant Ann Carmichael, at the time she deeded the property, was seventy-eight years of age, old, and feeble both physically and mentally, and easily influenced; that the three beneficiaries of these conveyances, knowing her condition, conspired to-

gether to poison and prejudice her mind against the complainants, and to unduly influence her against them, in which
conspiracy they succeeded, and operating fraudulently, and
for the express purpose of cheating complainants out of
their just rights under the said wills, obtained this deed to
Hattie and Charles Ira without any consideration whatever;
that the mind of their mother was so weak and open to undue
influence that she was not competent to execute this conveyance, and was not fiᵥ to do business; that it was obtained by
undue influence, and by false and untruthful statements; that
she did not know at the time she executed the deed that Ira
was to have any interest in the land, and never intended it;
that said conveyance was obtained by fraud practiced upon
said Ann Carmichael by Ira, Hattie, and Charles Ira, and
that it was done to deprive complainants of their title to the
same after the death of the said Ann; that the one-third interest was conveyed to Ira without the knowledge of the said
Ann.

The complainants, therefore, pray that the deeds and the
life lease be set aside, and that injunction issue restraining
said defendants from disposing of, transferring, or in any
manner interfering with said real estate, or any part thereof,
and for such other relief as may be necessary to enforce and
protect their rights in the premises.

The defendants admit receiving the property advanced to
them about the time of the execution of the wills, and admit
the execution of them, and the terms thereof, as set forth in
the bill; but deny that said wills were made under any such
understanding or agreement between their father and mother
as claimed by the bill. They deny the incompetency of Ann
to make the deed to Hattie and Charles Ira, and deny any
fraud or undue influence in the execution of the same. They
allege that Ann was fully competent to dispose of the said
forty acres of land, and that she conveyed the same of her
own free-will and accord, and in consideration of the care and
kindness that said Hattie and Charles Ira had before that
time bestowed upon her, and in further consideration that
they should care for and support her as long as she lived.

The case was heard upon pleadings and proofs before Hon.
Richard A. Watts, judge of the Hillsdale circuit, who found
that the deed of Ann Carmichael to Hattie E. Disbrow and
Charles Ira Carmichael was obtained by fraud and undue
influence practiced upon her by the defendants Ira, Hattie,

and Charles Ira, but felt compelled to deny relief to the complainants, for two reasons: —

1. Because he was not satisfied that the contract claimed to have been made between the father and mother as to their wills was established, and that such contract, if made out, being an oral one, " would be invalid and not enforceable; relating, as it did, largely to real estate, it would be void under the statute of frauds."

2. That the deed cannot be set aside because of undue influence and fraud in this suit, because the complainants have no such interest in the land in question as entitles them to relief; that, in order to vacate and set aside the conveyances complained of, proceedings must be taken in the interest and name of Ann Carmichael, or in the name of a guardian appointed to represent her interest.

He therefore dismissed complainants' bill without prejudice.

We fully agree with the circuit judge that the deed from Ann to Hattie and Charles Ira was procured by fraud and undue influence, and that Ann was not competent at that time to dispose of the land to any one.

We are further satisfied that the claim of complainants as to the contract is correct. We have no doubt from the two wills and their terms, and the oral evidence connecting them, that the father and mother came to a mutual understanding and agreement as claimed by the complainants; that the wills were made for the express purpose of securing to complainants an equal undivided share of ninety acres of land, encumbered with the five-hundred-dollar bequest to Charles, Jr.; that the making of one will was an inducement to the making of the other, and that the contract and inducement of the father has been carried out and performed by his death with his will executed and standing as he promised; that the children all knew of these wills, and the arrangement and purpose under which they were made. They acquiesced in it. They took possession of their share of the real estate, and have ever since held and enjoyed their respective shares, except Hattie, who took her one thousand dollars in lieu of land.

The complainants were put off in the enjoyment of their own until the death of the survivor of their parents. The mother to-day holds the use of sixty acres of land, and had all the personal property of her husband by virtue of her agreement to will the forty acres owned by her to the complainants. The fact that she made an arrangement by which she divided the personal property among all the children, and took back notes for the use of the same during her life, does not alter her condition. She had the property, and disposed of it as she saw fit, and disposed of it equitably. It has passed equally into the hands of the children, where it naturally would have belonged at her death. The will and contract of the father having been performed on his part with her, the children having acquiesced in the contract, and had their full share, can these defendants, Ira, Charles Ira, and Hattie, now, in fraud of the complainants' rights, acquire this forty acres at Ann's death?

We think not. If they can, it must be because some narrow technicality stands in the way of justice. In the first place, the will of Ann stands. When she made the deed to Charles Ira and Hattie she was not mentally competent to destroy that instrument, even if the law would permit her to do so. There is no doubt but it is competent for a person to make a valid agreement binding himself to make a particular disposition of his property by last will and testament: *Faxton* v. *Faxon*, 28 Mich. 159; *Sword* v. *Keith*, 31 Mich. 247; *De Moss* v. *Robinson*, 46 Mich. 62; 41 Am. Rep. 144; *Mundy* v. *Foster*, 31 Mich. 313, and note; *Johnson* v. *Hubbell*, 10 N. J. Eq. 332; 66 Am. Dec. 773; *Van Dyne* v. *Vreeland*, 11 N. J. Eq. 370; 12 N. J. Eq. 142; Williams on Executors, 6th ed., 14, and note, 162, 163.

But the defendants claim that the contract, resting partly in parol, is void under the statute of frauds, so far as it related to real estate.

It is to be remembered, however, that the contract on the part of the father has been fully performed, and that Ann Carmichael, the mother, has received and accepted the benefits of such performance. A court of equity, under these circumstances, will not permit her to rescind this contract. If this were an oral agreement to convey lands, there is performance enough shown on the part of the father, and acceptance by Ann, to authorize a decree for specific performance of such contract. And by the same principle that would govern in such a case, the performance of the contract in the present case upon the part of the father takes the agreement out of the statute of frauds. The non-fulfillment of this contract upon the part of Ann Carmichael would be a fraud which equity will not allow. Therefore it will decree the performance of the agreement upon Ann Carmichael, or take such steps as shall be necessary to prevent her from violating her part of the contract in fraud of the rights of these complainants. The complainants are not proceeding in this suit as heirs at law of Charles Carmichael, Sen., but as parties having a vested interest in this real estate under the contract of their father and mother, which agreement, having been fully performed by the father, will be enforced against the mother. They are therefore proper parties to this suit, and Ann Carmichael is a proper party defendant.

The decree of the court below will be reversed, with costs of both courts, and a decree entered here as prayed by complainants.

_____

THE CASE of *Bird* v. *Pope*, 73 Mich 483, is similar in many respects to the principal case. In that case, the defendant, Pope, in 1885, was a bachelor aged seventy-five years, the owner of forty acres of land, mostly uncleared, and of an old log house which he had reserved upon another parcel of land sold by him. The complainant, Bird, and the defendant entered into an oral contract by which it was agreed that complainant should take possession of such land, move the log house upon it as a place to dwell in, and have the same as his own upon the death of defendant, provided he supported and found a home for him during the remainder of his life. In pursuance of this agreement, Pope executed his will, by which he bequeathed to Bird said land and all personal property owned by him at the time of his death. He and Bird then entered into a written contract, by which it was agreed by Bird that in consideration for such will he would take Pope "into his own family and provide for him in sickness and health, to clothe him, and pay all doctor bills." The will and contract were then placed in the hands of defendant Johnson for safe-keeping. The parties afterwards undertook to move the log house, but found it impracticable to do so on account of its age and rottenness. Bird then expended some three hundred dollars in building a new house upon the land willed to him by Pope, and in 1886 gave the latter a room in such house, which room was carpeted, had a stove, bed, and other furniture. Pope found no fault with the room, except that he wanted a rocking-chair, and continued to live with Bird, the latter supporting him until March, 1887, when he left the house permanently, without cause, although Bird had faithfully kept and performed, and was still willing to keep and perform, his part of the contract. During a portion of this time Pope was quite ill and was nursed by Bird and his wife to his entire satisfaction, and when recovering he went before a notary public and made a deed of the same land to Bird, which deed was also deposited with Johnson, with directions to deliver it to Bird upon Pope's death.

On April, 17, 1887, Pope destroyed this deed and canceled the will, and then executed a deed to Johnson of the same land, in consideration for a mortgage for twelve hundred dollars, and an agreement that Johnson should support him during life. Johnson then gave Bird notice to vacate the premises, and commenced an action of ejectment against him. Bird filed his complaint in this case, substantially setting out the facts as detailed above, and alleging that the conveyances between Pope and Johnson were in fraud of his rights, which Johnson knew at the time of their execution. He prayed that an injunction issue preventing the continuance of the ejectment suit, that they be enjoined from conveying or encumbering the land, and that such deed and mortgage be declared fraudulent and void as against his rights.

Defendant Pope, in his answer, admitted the execution of the will and contract, and his intention that Bird should have the land if he performed his contract; but denied that he ever gave him possession of it, or intended to do so during his lifetime, and claimed that Bird violated his contract in not moving the log house upon the land, by which he lost its value, two hundred dollars; admitted the delivery of the deed from himself to Bird, and its delivery to Johnson, and the execution of the conveyances between himself and Johnson; averred his right to execute them, and denied that they were a fraud upon Bird, and also admitted the ejectment proceedings; denied that Bird properly supported him, and averred that he failed to furnish him with proper support, care, nursing, medicines, and an easy-chair while ill; admitted leaving Bird's house, but alleged that it was because he was not well treated.

The circuit court, after hearing the evidence in the case, found the facts as stated by the complainant to be true, and his theory well supported by the proofs, and thereupon decreed that the deed from Pope to Johnson was fraudulent and void as against the rights of Bird, and that it therefore be annulled; that Pope and Johnson be enjoined from deeding, conveying, or encumbering the premises in dispute in any manner. The appellate court affirmed the decree of the circuit court, and after reviewing the evidence in the case, said: "The court was right in holding, under this agreement as proven, that the conveyances between Johnson and Pope were in fraud of the just rights of the complainant; and the decree might have gone further, in the interest of justice. The defendant Pope could not, by revoking his will, and leaving the house of complainant, alter or disturb the effect of the agreement between them when Bird was not at fault, and was willing to perform his contract to the end. There was no fraud in the procuring of the contract or the execution of the will, and there is no claim of any. The will and the contract were dictated by Pope, independently of Bird; and everything relating to the taking possession of the land, and the improvements made thereon, including the building of the house, was done with the assent, at least, of Pope. The only reasons assigned for attempting to destroy the force and effect of the will, which was made in part performance of the agreement between them, are found to be groundless. Bird, by his performance of the agreement so far, has acquired rights in the land which cannot be taken away from him by any act of Pope; and rights which, if he continues to perform his agreement, or tenders a willingness to do so, which is prevented only by the refusal of Pope to accept such performance, will, at the death of Pope, entitle him to the premises by a specific performance of the contract. This he may lose by his own wrongful acts hereafter, or by a voluntary abandonment of the land; but Pope is powerless to convey the premises away from him, or to drive him off the land, if Bird performs, or is willing to perform, his contract to the end."

The court cited, in support of these views, and of the rule that it is entirely competent for a person to make a valid agreement, binding himself to make a particular disposition of his property by last will and testament, *Leonardson* v. *Hulin*, 64 Mich. 1, and the principal case.

It was contended by counsel for the defendants on the argument in the appellate court that the contract between the parties must stand on the will and written contract, and that parol evidence was not admissible to show the oral agreement as to the working and living upon the land, the improvements made thereon, and the possession of the same. On this point the court said: "This is not so. This is not a case where the whole contract was reduced to writing, thus shutting out any oral talk between the parties. Here the agreement was orally made. In pursuance of the agreement, the will was executed, and also the contract. But these were not all of the arrangements between the parties, as both admit in their pleading and in their testimony. In such case the whole agreement may be put in evidence, and the parties are not confined to the writings which form only a part of it"; citing, in support of this view, *Richards* v. *Fuller,* 37 Mich. 161; *Phelps* v. *Whitaker,* 37 Id. 72; *Trevidick* v. *Mumford,* 31 Id. 470; *Sirrine* v. *Briggs,* 31 Id. 443; *Rowe* v. *Wright,* 12 Id. 291; *Bowker* v. *Johnson,* 17 Id. 42; *Facey* v. *Otis,* 11 Id. 217.

The opinion in this case was delivered by Morse, J., Sherwood, C. J., and Champlin and Campbell, JJ., concurring therein. Long, J., did not sit.

AGREEMENTS TO MAKE PARTICULAR DISPOSITION OF PROPERTY BY WILL, generally: See note to *Johnson* v. *Hubbell,* 66 Am. Dec. 784–790; *Bolman* v. *Overall,* 80 Ala. 451; 60 Am. Rep. 107, and note. A sealed instrument agreeing for a valuable consideration to make a will to the prejudice of the rights of the covenantor's heirs is valid: *Taylor* v. *Mitchell,* 87 Pa. St. 518; 30 Am. Rep. 383; but an oral promise to devise is revocable, and as to real estate is void, and the consideration paid may be recovered if the devise is not made as agreed: *De Moss* v. *Robinson,* 46 Mich. 62; 41 Am. Rep. 144, and foot-note. However, a part performance of a parol agreement to make a particular disposition of property by will takes it out of the statute of frauds: *Johnson* v. *Hubbell,* 10 N. J. Eq. 332; 66 Am. Dec. 773, and note 788, 789. Compare *Manning* v. *Pippen,* 86 Ala. 357, 11 Am. St. Rep. 46, where it is decided that a promise in writing to make a will, in consideration of a deed executed at the time, is supported by a valid consideration, and a binding agreement; but that an oral promise by a wife to make her will in favor of her husband, in consideration of land deeded by him to her, is void as within the statute of frauds.

JOHNSTON HARVESTER COMPANY *v.* MILLER.

[72 MICHIGAN, 265.]

WITNESS — CROSS-EXAMINATION — IMPEACHMENT. — Where defendant denies the execution of a note in suit, and alleges that it is a forgery, and the agent of plaintiff who procured the note testifies in chief that he saw defendant sign it, the latter is entitled, upon cross-examination, to everything that took place on that occasion, and when upon such cross-examination the witness states that he knew nothing about the consideration of the note, he may be asked if he has not made different statements out of court of what occurred at the time of the signing, and if he denies having made such statements, they may be proved by defendant in defense.

WITNESS — CREDIBILITY OF, HOW MAY BE TESTED ON CROSS-EXAMINATION. — Where defendant denies the existence of a note sued on, and claims it to be a forgery, and the agent of plaintiff, who claims to have procured it, also claims, on his examination in chief, that he was present and saw defendant sign it, he may be compelled to testify on cross-examination to the negotiation of another forged note, purporting to have been signed by defendant, when he does not claim his privilege of not answering because it might criminate him. Such evidence is admissible as affecting the credibility of the witness, and also as tending to show that he obtained the note in suit fraudulently.

EXPERT EVIDENCE — COMPARISON TO TEST KNOWLEDGE OF HANDWRITING. — Where expert witnesses have testified entirely from comparison to the genuineness of a disputed signature, they may, on cross-examination, to test the value of their knowledge, be asked to make comparison between two signatures of a witness, one admitted by him to be genuine, and the other claimed by him to have been written by another, but by his authority and direction; and the fact that such witnesses did not know whether the signatures were made by one man or two, but added value to the test.

PRINCIPAL AND AGENT — NOTICE TO AGENT IS NOTICE TO PRINCIPAL. — A principal employing an agent to sell machinery, but agreeing with him that notes given in payment shall be taken in the name of the principal, and guaranteed by the agent, is chargeable, in an action against the maker of a note taken by the agent, with the latter's knowledge that such note was not taken in payment for machinery.

PRINCIPAL AND AGENT. — PRINCIPAL CANNOT RATIFY FRAUD OF HIS AGENT by accepting a note which is the fruit of such fraud, and suing upon it, and claiming at the same time to be a holder of the note in good faith, because the agent did not acquaint him with the circumstances under which he procured it when he sent it to him, but led him to suppose that it had been taken in the ordinary course of his agency.

Sprague and Carey, for the appellant.

Samuel W. Burroughs, for the defendant.

MORSE, J.   The plaintiff sued the defendant in *assumpsit* upon the following promissory note: —

"$100.   INKSTER, MICHIGAN, November 28, 1885.

"On or before the first day of January, 1887, for value received, I, the undersigned, of the township of Taylor, county of Wayne, state of Michigan, promise to pay to the order of the Johnston Harvester Company one hundred dollars ($100), payable at express office, Dearborn, Michigan, with interest at seven per cent per annum from November 1, 1885, until due, and ten per cent after due.   JOSEPH MILLER.

"P. O. Address: Taylor; County, Wayne; State, Michigan."

This note was indorsed as follows: —

"For value received, I hereby guarantee the prompt payment of the within note, and waive protest, demand, and notice of non-payment thereof.   GEORGE REYNOLDS.

"Post-office: Inkster, Michigan. Date, December 17, 1885."

The defendant pleaded the general issue, and gave notice '
that the alleged note was without value and consideration, and
that it was a forgery, and never executed by him. He also
filed an affidavit, denying under oath its execution. Verdict
and judgment in the court below for defendant.

Reynolds was the agent of plaintiff in selling machines, and
acted as such agent under a written contract. One Samuel
Clay, a farmer, was owing him one hundred dollars. Clay
had delivered oats, under the usual Bohemian scheme, to defendant, and held his note for one hundred dollars. Clay
said to Reynolds that if they could get defendant to take up
his note, and give a new one to Reynolds, "it would clear
them both."

Reynolds and Clay were the only witnesses for plaintiff.
They testify that the note from defendant to Clay was written
on an ordinary half sheet of white note-paper, and Reynolds
did not wish to take it, because his company (the plaintiff)
would not receive a note in payment of Reynolds's indebtedness to them, unless it was written upon one of its blanks.
They went together to Miller's house, and proposed the arrangement to him. He at once accepted the proposition, and
executed and delivered the note in suit to Reynolds. The
Clay note was then delivered to defendant, and burned. Reynolds knew nothing of the consideration for the old note until
after the new note was made and delivered to Reynolds. Then
the defendant said that if the Bohemian Oats Company did
what was right with him, he holding the usual bond, he would
pay the new note; but if they did not, he would not pay it.

Reynolds also testified that he never acquainted the plaintiff with this transaction, or the consideration of the note, but
indorsed it a few days after its execution, and forwarded it to
plaintiff in payment of a balance due from him to the company.

Miller testified in his own behalf that, in the fall of 1885,
one Riggs, an agent for a Bohemian Oats Company, contracted
with him for the sale of ten bushels of Bohemian oats, and
gave him a bond, or contract, by which the said company
agreed to purchase twenty bushels of the same kind of oats, to
be raised from the seed so purchased by him; that in pursuance of this contract, he gave the promissory note to Clay,
who delivered the oats contracted for; that the company failed
to fulfill the bond or contract on their part.

He further testified that Reynolds and Clay came to his

house on the twenty-eighth day of November, 1885, and requested him to make a new note for the one hundred dollars, payable to the order of Reynolds; that he did so, conditioned, however, with an oral understanding that unless the Bohemian Oats Company purchased the twenty bushels from him, as agreed in the bond, he would not pay the new note. But he testified further that the note in suit was not the note he then executed, and that he never made or signed any such note at that or any other time; that the note he made and delivered to Reynolds was not written upon a printed blank, but was upon an ordinary sheet of white letter-paper, and did not provide for the payment of any more than seven per cent interest before or after due.

The plaintiff, in opening his case, proved the execution of the note by the testimony of Reynolds. The court, against the objection of plaintiff's counsel, permitted a cross-examination of the witness, not only with reference to the execution of the note, but upon other matters pertinent to the claim of the defense. He was asked if he had not made certain statements to different persons to the effect that he knew the Clay note had been given for Bohemian oats when he received it, and before the exchange of notes was made. Then witnesses were permitted to testify in impeachment of his answers to such questions. It is claimed that by asking these questions the defendant made Reynolds his own witness, and was bound by his answers.

We think there was no error committed in this respect. Reynolds testified in chief that he was present with Clay at the house of Mr. Miller, and saw defendant sign the note, and that he was the agent of the plaintiff. The defendant was entitled, upon cross-examination, to everything that took place at the house on that occasion; and when, upon such cross-examination, the witness stated that he knew nothing about the consideration of the Clay note, or what it was given for, as he did testify, then the defendant was entitled to ask him if he had not made different statements out of court of what occurred there, and if he denied making any such statements, to prove it when he was making his defense.

It is also assigned as error that the counsel for defendant was permitted to interrogate the witness Reynolds, and show by his own testimony that he had before this sold a grinder or pulverizer to the defendant, who paid him the price in cash,—thirty-five dollars; and that afterwards he turned in to a com-

pany at Ann Arbor a thirty-five-dollar note, purporting to be
signed by the defendant, which was not given for the grinder;
and that the grinder was the only implement he ever sold defendant, the price of which was thirty-five dollars. We think
this evidence was admissible as affecting the credibility of the
witness, who did not claim his privilege of not answering it,
because it might tend to criminate him. It was also competent for another reason. It had some tendency to show that
the witness obtained the note in this case fraudulently: See
Stubly v. *Beachboard*, 68 Mich. 422.

Two experts in handwriting, both of whom had never seen
defendant write, were examined, and from a comparison between the signature to the note in suit, and signatures of Miller
in the case admitted to be genuine, gave their opinion that the
defendant signed the note. To test the value of their evidence,
the counsel for the defense asked them to make comparisons
between two signatures of the witness Reynolds in the case, —
one admitted by him to be genuine, and the other claimed by
him to have been written by another than himself, but by his
authority and direction. One saw a very close similarity be-
between the letters " yn " in the two signatures, while the other,
not seeing this, insisted that the " lds " were very much alike.

The object evidently was to show the fallibility and unreli-
able character of the testimony. The plaintiff's counsel insist
that this was error, and invoke the rule that a writing, the
genuineness of which is disputed, cannot be used to test his
accuracy.

We do not think the rule applies in this instance. It was
not claimed that one of these signatures was the genuine signature of Reynolds; but it was used, as not being his signature, in comparison with his admitted signature, for the
express purpose of ascertaining what was the value of the opinions of these experts. We know of no rule prohibiting such a
test, when the writings are properly in the case, as they were
here. The sequel showed that the opinions of the experts were
of but little worth, and we are not disposed to limit or confine
the opportunities for testing and determining the accuracy
and value of expert evidence. These men were testifying entirely from comparison, and it was competent, by the comparison thus made upon cross-examination, to show that they
differed radically in their views of the similarity of letters, and
that one as well as both might be easily mistaken in their as-
sumptions from a comparison of signatures. The fact that the

witnesses did not know whether the signatures were made by one man or two but added to the value of the test.

It was claimed upon the trial that the plaintiff was a good-faith holder of the note, and that it received the same in the usual course of business, in payment of an antecedent debt, from Reynolds. The agreement between the plaintiff and Reynolds, under which the latter acted as agent of the former, confined such agency to the sale of the plaintiff's machines, and the taking of orders for the same, and notes for the payment of those sold and delivered, which notes Reynolds was to guarantee. If the jury found that the note in suit was a forgery, as claimed by the defendant, of course the fact of the plaintiff's being a *bona fide* holder would make no difference.

But it was further contended by the defendant, that in taking the note, Reynolds was the agent of the company, and that the plaintiff was bound by his knowledge that it was given in payment of a Bohemian oat transaction.

The counsel for the plaintiff requested the court to instruct the jury that, "the plaintiff's evidence being uncontradicted, that the plaintiff is an innocent purchaser for a valuable consideration, and is the present owner of the note sued upon, and the note being unpaid, the only question left for" their consideration was whether or not the note was signed by the defendant,—whether it was his genuine note or not; and that they could not consider any evidence relative to the consideration of this note between Miller and Clay, and Miller and Reynolds.

The court refused to so charge the jury, and instructed them, in substance, that if they believed the testimony on behalf of the defendant as to the circumstances attending the execution of the note, and that there was notice to Reynolds that the new note which he received (the note sued upon in this case) was given to take the place of an old note, which was given for Bohemian oats, then the defendant must prevail. In another part of the charge he left it to the jury to say whether or not, under the contract between the plaintiff and Reynolds, and the circumstances attending the procurement of the note, he was the agent of the plaintiff in the taking of it. This is the main controversy in the case.

It seems to us that Reynolds, upon his own testimony, must be considered to have been acting as the agent of the company when he procured this note. It was made payable to the order of the plaintiff, and upon the company blanks. It is evident that they received it as a note taken by their agent, and sent it back to him to collect under their contract with him. He guaranteed it in compliance with the contract. He swears that he sent it to them in payment of his indebtedness to them, but it is plain they did not receive it in settlement with him. The contract under which he was employed stipulated: —

" 10. The second party further agrees to keep a correct account of all machines sold, separate and apart from his other accounts; to make all notes or drafts given for machines payable to the first party or its order; to keep said account-books, notes, or drafts subject to use and inspection of said first party, or its agent, attorney, or assigns; and to comply with the terms of sale above mentioned, unless otherwise authorized or instructed in writing to the contrary, by said party of the first part.

" 11. The second party further agrees to forward to the first party, at Chicago, Illinois, so often as requested during the time of selling said machines, a report of sales showing the number of machines sold, the terms of sale, and the number of machines unsold, and to remit with each report the money and notes received for machines sold up to that time; also to collect said notes free of charge, when returned to him for that purpose, and forward the money by express, or by draft, as directed by said first party."

No one appears on behalf of the plaintiff in this suit, except Reynolds, to testify how this note was received, or what the knowledge of the company was as to the circumstances of its inception. He was authorized to remit either in notes payable to the order of the company, and guaranteed by him, or in money, for his sales. He claims he sent this note in lieu of money. He said nothing to plaintiff about it, however, but remitted it as he would a note taken on sale of a machine, and upon the same blanks. The company, under the contract, received it, then, as their note taken by their agent, and must take it with the same knowledge that the agent had. It is not necessary, therefore, to examine the question argued before us, whether under any circumstances the payee of a note can be considered a good-faith holder for value, as against the maker.

It is plain that Reynolds, in taking the note in suit upon the blanks of the plaintiff, and guaranteeing its payment, as he did notes received upon the sales of machines, acted as the agent of the company. The fact that he sold no machine to defendant does not alter the case. The note, by his act, was made the property of the company at its inception, so that when it was delivered to Reynolds it was delivered to him as the agent of the company. If he was not the agent when he procured it, he received it for the company as their agent. No other officer of the corporation had anything to do with the transaction by which this note became the property of the plaintiff. The company, therefore, must be bound by his acts and his knowledge, if they undertake to recover upon this note. If the taking of this note was not within the scope of Reynolds's agency under the contract, and the making of it upon the blanks of the company and to the order of plaintiff was a fraud upon them, they should, when this fact was ascertained, have repudiated it, and looked to Reynolds for the amount of it.

The plaintiff cannot ratify the fraud of Reynolds upon the defendant by accepting this note and suing upon it, and claim at the same time to be a good-faith holder of the note, because Reynolds did not acquaint the company of the circumstances under which he procured it when he sent it to them, but led them to suppose that it had been taken in the ordinary course of his agency under the contract.

The judgment is affirmed, with costs. .

IMPEACHMENT OF WITNESSES. — As to the rules of practice governing the impeachment of witnesses, see note to *Allen* v. *State*, 73 Am. Dec. 762 et seq.

IMPEACHMENT OF WITNESS UPON CROSS-EXAMINATION. — The extent to which the cross-examination of a witness may be carried for the purpose of impeachment: See note to *Turnpike Road Co.* v. *Loomis*, 88 Am. Dec. 321–324. Where a witness, on cross-examination, is asked regarding a conversation with a view to impeachment, he is entitled to give the whole of the pertinent matter of such conversation in evidence: *Savannah etc. R'y Co.* v. *Holland*, 82 Ga. 257; 14 Am. St. Rep. 158; but a witness cannot be impeached upon matters not relevant to the issue: *Gulf etc. R'y Co.* v. *Coon*, 69 Tex. 730. As to the cross-examination of witnesses generally, see note to *Hitchcock* v. *Moore*, 14 Am. St. Rep. 480, 481; *Birmingham F. Ins. Co.* v. *Pulver*, 126 Ill. 329; 9 Am. St. Rep. 598. Upon cross-examination of a witness, after reading his testimony given upon a former trial as printed in the record used in the supreme court, he may be asked if he did not so testify: *Toohey* v. *Plummer*, 69 Mich. 345. Where a witness is recalled and examined as to particular facts, it is proper to limit the cross-examination to the particular matters testified to by the witness when recalled: *Moellering* v. *Evans*, 121 Ind. 195. A witness cannot be contradicted upon immaterial matters testified to by him on cross-examination: *Alger* v. *Castle*, 61 Vt. 53. A witness may be subjected to a rigid cross-examination to show his bias or prejudice: *Commissioners* v. *Minderlein*, 67 Md. 566.

PRINCIPAL AND AGENT. — Notice to an agent when imputed to his principal: See note to *Fairfield Sav. Bank* v. *Chase,* 39 Am. Rep. 322–331; *City Nat. Bank* v. *Martin,* 70 Tex. 643; 8 Am. St. Rep. 632, and note; *Fitzpatrick* v. *Hartford L. etc. Ins. Co.,* 56 Conn. 116; 7 Am. St. Rep. 288, and note.

PRINCIPAL AND AGENT. — A principal must affirm or repudiate the contract of his agent in its entirety: *Shoninger* v. *Peabody,* 57 Conn. 42; 14 Am St. Rep. 88, and note.

PARK *v.* DETROIT FREE PRESS COMPANY.

[72 MICHIGAN, 560.]

NEWSPAPER LIBEL — CONSTITUTIONAL LAW. — A statute purporting to confine recovery in certain cases of libel against newspapers to what it calls actual damages as defined therein, is unconstitutional and void.

LIBEL — CHARGING CRIME. — When a man is charged in a newspaper with doing what, if done by him, can be nothing else but a crime, it cannot be said not to involve a criminal charge, because other persons might not be so guilty.

LIBEL — WHAT CONSTITUTES. — It is the thing charged on the person libeled, as done by him, and not by some one else, which makes the libel. It must especially injure him, if believed among those who know him personally, and if to them the charge made involves a crime, the degree of which makes it disgraceful, it involves it none the less because the publisher did not so consider it by mistake of law or fact.

LIBEL — PROTECTION TO PRIVATE CHARACTER — CONSTITUTIONAL LAW. — Right of full legal protection to private character from libelous assault can no more be removed by statute than such protection to life, liberty, or property.

LIBEL. — Distinction is always drawn between intentionally false and wicked published assaults on character, and those which are not actually designed to create a false impression, although necessarily tending to injure reputation if false in fact; but both are actionable.

LIBEL — CONSTITUTIONAL LAW. — A statute which attempts to relieve newspaper publishers from responsibility for every injury to character by libel, whether intentionally false or not, is unconstitutional and void.

LIBEL — PROOF OF CIRCULATION. — A plaintiff in an action of libel may show that various persons called his attention to the libelous article.

LIBEL — PROOF OF CIRCULATION. — The mischief of a libel consists in the fact that it is actually seen by third persons, and the circulation of the paper containing it is allowed to be shown, as making it probable that the article has been read by several persons.

LIBEL — PRIVILEGED COMMUNICATIONS. — The parties to an action are privileged from suit for accusations made in their pleadings, because the latter are addressed to courts where the facts can be fairly tried, and to no other readers.

LIBEL — PAPERS AND PLEADINGS IN SUIT NOT PRIVILEGED. — The public has no right to any information on private suits until they come up for public hearing or action in open court, and when any publication is made involving such matters, they possess no privilege, and the publication must rest either on non-libelous character or truth to defend it.

LIBEL — LIABILITY OF PUBLIC PRESS. — The public press occupies no better position than private persons publishing the same libelous matter, and so far as actual circulation is concerned, there can be no question which is the more likely to spread it.

LIBEL — MATTER COLLECTED BY NEWSPAPER REPORTER NOT PRIVILEGED. — Any one, whether reporter or otherwise, who undertakes to give to the public the contents of a document which speaks for itself, and in which he has no personal interest, is bound, if he would release his liability, to use such degree of care as is reasonably sure to prevent mistake, and to publish nothing not so obtained which will inure to the injury of another.

CASE for libel.   Judgment for defendant.   Plaintiff brings error.

James H. Pound, for the appellant.

Black, Moran, Wilkins, and Gray, for the defendant.

CAMPBELL, J.   Plaintiff sued defendant for publishing a libel against him, to the effect that he had been the day before, which was June 23, 1888, arrested and brought before one of the justices in Detroit on a charge of bastardy, and on his plea of not guilty was released on his personal recognizance, to appear on June 29th for his preliminary examination.

To this cause of action the defendant pleaded the general issue, with notice of special defense, to the effect that one of its reporters, who was a prudent and skillful person, obtained the information in good faith from the clerk of the court, and that it was published without malice or negligence, and is claimed to be privileged; that on the next day a correction was published as conspicuously as the libel, to the effect that the plaintiff was the attorney for the prosecution, and not the defendant in the bastardy case, and that the mistake occurred through the justice's clerk, who gave plaintiff's name as the defendant, and that on the file-wrapper plaintiff's name was so placed as to appear as defendant; that everything was done in good faith, and that the falsehood was due to mistake. Defendant claimed that, under the statute, nothing but actual damages, within the limited statutory definition of that term, could be recovered.

Upon the trial, proof was made of the publication of the libel, and of the circulation of the paper, and that plaintiff was, and had been for several years, a married man, and a member of the Detroit bar, and the father of children. On cross-examination, plaintiff testified that he was employed to prosecute Clixby, the defendant in the bastardy case, and was not present in court when he was arrested, but attended the examination subsequently, and after the libel was published. There was some conflict as to what occurred, subsequently to the publication of the libel, in the clerk's office, between Mr. Kinney, the clerk, and Mr. Robison, the reporter, and some conflict whether Robison got his information from the clerk or from examining the file. The justice swore positively that Robison asked him about the case as the Clixby case first, and that he referred him to the clerk, and Robison denied that he saw the justice at all. There was also a conflict whether Robison knew plaintiff.

The apology was published the day after the libel. Above it was an open heading, reading as follows:—

"Record of the Courts.—The Legal Mills are Grinding Chiefly on Matrimonial Misunderstandings. — Correction of an Annoying Error. — Probate Notes. — Miscellany. — Correction of an Annoying Error."

This was published in the same part of the paper with the libel. It is not disputed that, so far as plaintiff is concerned, it was a full retraction.

Several questions are presented concerning the reception and rejection of evidence. The court below instructed the jury at some length, but to the general effect that the liability of the defendant was relieved by the statute of 1887 by the retraction, if there was no bad faith; that the article charged no crime, unless the reporter had reason to believe the plaintiff was married; that the fact that the plaintiff was not living with his family—his wife being insane—was one of the facts to be taken into consideration, as well as his not being known to the reporter; that if the case was within the statute, no actual damages having been shown, there could be no recovery. Further reference will be made to the charge more specifically. The jury under the charge, although not positively, were practically ordered to find and did find for the defendant.

As the statutes of 1885 and 1887 were the decisive element in finding a verdict for the defense without even nominal damages, that question requires first attention.

By act No. 233, Laws of 1885, it was enacted that, in suits brought for the publication of libels in any newspaper, the plaintiff should only recover actual damages if it shall appear that the publication was made in good faith, and did not involve a criminal charge, and its falsity was due to mistake or misapprehension of the facts; and that in the next regular issue of said newspaper after such mistake or misapprehension was brought to the knowledge of the publisher or publishers, whether before or after suit was brought, a correction was published in as conspicuous a manner and place in said newspaper as was the article sued on as libelous. By section 3 of the act of 1885 it was enacted: " The words ' actual damages ' in the foregoing section shall be construed to include all damages the plaintiff may show he has suffered in respect to his property, business, trade, profession, or occupation, and no other damages."

The statute of 1887 merely changed the words "the foregoing section" to "this act": Laws of 1887, p. 153.

This act was held by the court below to exempt defendant because bastardy is not in the strict sense a criminal proceeding, unless the defendant or Robison knew, or should have known, plaintiff to be a married man, so that the charge would be adultery.

If the case depends on that statute, and if that statute is valid, the construction given goes beyond the language, and does not seem to be the proper one. When a man is charged with doing what if done by him can be nothing else than a crime, it cannot be said not to involve a criminal charge, because other persons might not be so guilty. It would lead us into conjecture to seek out any meaning in this statute beyond the language. There seems to have been an idea in the minds of its framers that charges of crime were so much more heinous than other charges as to make it proper to punish them in heavy damages in spite of good faith, when charges of things not crimes are treated as comparatively trivial. But every one knows that there are many technical crimes involving no infamy, and acts not indictable which are utterly disgraceful. We can hardly imagine the legislature meant to disregard the common-sense rule that it is the thing charged on the person libeled as done by him, and not by some one else, which makes the libel. It must especially injure him, if believed, among those who know him personally, and if to them the charge made involves a crime, the degree of which makes it disgraceful, it involves it none the less because the publisher did not so consider it by mistake of fact or law..

But we do not think the statute controls the action, or is within the power of constitutional legislation. This will, in our judgment, appear from a statement of its effect if carried out. It purports to confine recovery in certain cases against newspapers to what it calls "actual damages," and then defines actual damages to cover only direct pecuniary loss in certain specified ways, and none other. In some of these defined cases, the proof of any damages in this sense would be impracticable, and in all, it would be very difficult. They are confined to damages in respect to property, business, trade, profession, or occupation. It is safe to say that such losses cannot be the true damage in a very large share of the worst cases of libel. A woman who is slandered in her chastity is, under this law, usually without any redress whatever. A man who income is from fixed investment or salary or official emolument, or business not depending upon his repute, could lose no money directly unless removed from the title to receive his income by reason of the libel, which could seldom happen. If contradicted soon, there could be practically no risk of this. And the same is true concerning most business losses. The cases must be very rare in which a libel will destroy business profits in such a way that the loss can be directly traced to the mischief. There could never be any loss when employers or customers know or believe the charges unfounded. The statute does not reach cases where a libel has operated to cut off chances of office or employment in the future, or broken up or prevented relationships not capable of an exact money standard, or produced that intangible but fatal influence which suspicion, helped by ill will, spreads beyond recall or reach by apology or retraction. Exploded lies are continually reproduced without the antidote, and no one can measure with any accurate standard the precise amount of evil done or probable.

There is no room for holding, in a constitutional system, that private reputation is any more subject to be removed by statute from full legal protection than life, liberty, or property. It is one of those rights necessary to human society that underlie the whole social scheme of civilization. It is a thing which is more easily injured than restored, and where injury is capable of infinite mischief. And, on the other hand, it is one where the injury is frequently, and perhaps generally, aggravated by malice. The law has, therefore, always drawn distinctions between intentionally false and wicked assaults on character and those which were not actually designed to create a false impression, although necessarily tending to injure reputation if false in fact; but it has made both actionable.

This statute has not, apparently, attempted to relieve any persons but the publishers of newspapers from responsibility for every injury to character by libel, whether intentionally false or not. If a person not a publisher had written in a letter just what this paper published, and had done so under the same impression which Mr. Robison had, the statute would not save him from full responsibility for the damages of all kinds to which the general rules of law have always subjected persons guilty of libel. While the statute is certainly ambiguous, we cannot attribute to the legislature the monstrous wrong of shielding the intended malice of writers who impose on fair-minded publishers from responsibility for newspaper libels because the publishers themselves may be innocent of deceit, or of making the publishers responsible for the full degree of actual malice in the writer who misinforms them. In the present case, the reporter himself admitted that he was not disposed to make as full a retraction as the managers required him to make; but their good faith should not be impugned by his reluctance.

It is not competent for the legislature to give one class of citizens legal exemptions from liability for wrongs not granted to others; and it is not competent to authorize any person, natural or artificial, to do wrong to others without answering fully for the wrong. We do not think this statute has any bearing on the case, and the court erred in making it control.

As the case must go back for a new trial, it is necessary to notice some other questions likely to arise again, and which probably might have been differently decided had the statute been left out of view.

Plaintiff was not allowed to show that various other persons called his attention to the libelous article. We can see no reason why such facts were not pertinent. The mischief of a libel consists in the fact that it is actually seen by third persons. The circulation of a paper is allowed to be shown, as making it probable that the article has been read by several persons. Evidence of actual knowledge cannot be inferior to presumption. In *Steketee* v. *Kimm*, 48 Mich. 322, a claim was made that there could be no presumption, in an American community, that articles in Dutch would be read by any one; but we had no difficulty in finding that Hollanders could and might do so. It would certainly have been proper, in that case, to show that Hollanders actually did read the libel, and there was convincing proof that it affected the plaintiff's business. In many if not most cases, actual pecuniary injury to business could not be shown without incidentally or directly indicating that there must have been individual readers.

There was a good deal of testimony in the case admitted, under objection, from reporters, and perhaps some others, concerning difficulty in getting personal access to files of the justices, and how they usually obtained information as to their contents, and upon what information they acted. The testimony was conflicting on this.

The whole defense in this case rested on the claim that bastardy proceedings are not criminal, but rest on the footing of civil remedies. There is no rule of law which authorizes any but the parties interested to handle the files or publish the contents of their matters in litigation. The parties, and none but the parties, control them. One of the reasons why parties are privileged from suit for accusations made in their pleadings is, that the pleadings are addressed to courts where the facts can be fairly tried, and to no other readers. If pleadings and other documents can be published to the world by any one who gets access to them, no more effectual way of doing malicious mischief with impunity could be devised than filing papers containing false and scurrilous charges, and getting those printed as news. The public have no rights to any information on private suits till they come up for public hearing or action in open court; and when any publication is made involving such matters, they possess no privilege, and the publication must rest on either non-libelous character or truth to defend it. A suit thus brought with scandalous accusations may be discontinued without any attempt to try it, or, on trial, the case may entirely fail of proof or probability. The law has never authorized any such mischief. In *Scripps* v. *Reilly*, 35 Mich. 371, 38 Mich. 10, 24 Am. Rep. 575, this court found it necessary to decline accepting the doctrine of privilege in such cases. It has been uniformly held that the public press occupies no better ground than private persons publishing the same libelous matter, and so far as actual circulation of libels is concerned, there can be no question which is more likely to spread them. It is undoubtedly true that there is a somewhat general taste and curiosity for knowledge about other people's affairs, which has called into existence a class of news-gathering that is designed to gratify that taste without circulating falsehoods, and it is easy enough to see that mistakes may occur without any improper purpose, and in spite of care. But when the mistake does occur, and leads to mischief, the party injured cannot be called upon to suffer for the public amusement or entertainment.

Any one, whether reporter or otherwise, who undertakes to give to the public the contents of a document which speaks for itself, and in which he has no personal concern, is bound, if he would reduce his liability, to use such a degree of care as is reasonably sure to prevent mistake, and to publish nothing not so obtained, which will inure to the injury of another. There can be no different standard applied to reporters than to others, and the rule laid down by the court, that such care as reporters generally use is the standard, is not a correct rule. It may be true that they are usually careful; and in *Tryon* v. *Evening News Ass'n*, 39 Mich. 636, it was held libelous to charge a reporter with violating confidence, as having a direct tendency to injure him in his calling. Any rule which should put the press and its managers on a less honorable footing would lessen public confidence, and help nobody. But their work in such matters is not privileged. The subject of relative responsibility was recently considered in *Bronson* v. *Bruce*, 59 Mich. 467, 60 Am. Rep. 307, and it was held that all persons must be treated as alike responsible.

There was a reference in the opinion below to the plaintiff, as not living with his family, as a consideration to be taken into view in dealing with the reporter's knowledge; and such reference was made to it on the argument in this court as to indicate that stress may have been laid on it improperly, and with a wider bearing. There was nothing to indicate that the reporter's action or acquintance with plaintiff could have been in any way affected by this fact. The only evidence on the subject indicated that plaintiff was unfortunate enough to have an insane wife. How this could be allowed to operate to his prejudice or affect his standing we cannot see.

While there is a good deal more that is open to criticism on the record, it is evident that the view taken of the legislation upon newspapers colored the entire case. The questions presented have been dealt with so often in this court that we cannot suppose the circuit judge meant to disregard our rulings. When it is understood that the case is governed by the rules heretofore applied in similar cases, there is not much more that needs to be suggested. It cannot be claimed that the article was not libelous. Neither can it be claimed, even under the statute, that a retraction removes the liability. The law as to mitigation has been very fully settled already.

The judgment must be reversed, with costs, and a new trial granted. ____

FOR A THOROUGH AND COMPLETE DISCUSSION of the law pertaining to newspaper libel, see *McAllister v. Detriot Free Press Co.*, 76 Mich. 338; 15 Am. St. Rep. 318, and particularly extended note thereto.

CITY PLANING AND SHINGLE MILL COMPANY *v.* MERCHANTS', MANUFACTURERS', AND CITIZENS' MUTUAL FIRE INSURANCE COMPANY.

[72 MICHIGAN, 654.]

INSURANCE — CONSTRUCTION OF CLAUSE AVOIDING POLICY. — The temporary closing of an insured mill for forty-two days without notice to the insurers, when such closing is caused by want of logs to manufacture, such logs being daily expected, but detained by low water, is not such "ceasing to operate" as will avoid a policy of fire insurance providing that it shall become void if "the mill shall cease to be operated" without notice to or consent of the insurers.

INSURANCE — EVIDENCE OF NECESSARY CLOSING OF INSURED MILL. — In an action to recover for the loss of a mill temporarily closed for want of logs to operate, because of low water, and insured under a policy providing that it should be void if "the mill shall cease to be operated" without notice to or consent of the insurer, the insured may show that other mills in the immediate vicinity were closed at the same time from the same cause.

INSURANCE — WAIVER OF CONDITION IN POLICY. — Where after loss the insurer is fully informed of facts which might work a forfeiture under the policy, and he informs the insurer that he does not intend to stand on technicalities contained in the policy, such action is a waiver of a condition in the policy, and it cannot afterwards be insisted upon in defense.

ASSUMPSIT on a policy of fire insurance. Judgment for plaintiff. Defendant brings error.

William E. Grove and W. H. Haggerty, for the appellant.

Wing and Samuels, for the plaintiff.

MORSE, J. The only question of real importance in this case is, whether the mill of plaintiff, at the time it burned, had "ceased to be operated" within the meaning of the policy of insurance sued upon.

The shingle-mill of plaintiff was situated on the bayou of

the Pere Marquette Lake, at Ludington, about 125 feet east of a planing-mill owned and operated by plaintiff, from which it received its motive power by a cable connecting both mills. The stock of logs for the use of the shingle-mill was obtained from the pineries some fifty miles from Ludington, and were run down the Pere Marquette River. These logs were delivered by the Pere Marquette Boom Company, which had charge of the running, driving, sorting, booming, and delivery of logs on this river and its tributaries.

The mill was insured in the defendant company February 4, 1886, for two thousand dollars, by an agent who was on the ground, and filled out the application and made a survey of the premises. Among other things, the policy contained the following clause: —

"If the insured shall make any false representations of the condition, situation, or occupancy of the property hereby insured, or shall conceal any fact material to the risk, or in case of over-valuation, or any misrepresentation whatever by the insured, either in a written application or otherwise, or if the insured shall have, or shall hereafter effect, any other insurance on the property hereby insured, or on any part thereof, without the permission of this company indorsed hereon, or if the risk shall be increased either by the occupancy of the premises in such a manner as to increase the hazard, or by the erection or occupancy of adjacent buildings, or if the premises shall become vacant or unoccupied, or, if a mill or manufactory, it shall cease to be operated (unless shut down for repairs) without a notice to and consent of this company indorsed hereon in each and every case, this policy shall become void; provided, however, that mills or manufactories capable of being operated during certain seasons only shall not be deemed vacant when shut down for the customary period."

The mill was burned September 10, 1886, and totally destroyed. At the time of the fire it was not running, and had not been running since July 29, 1886. On the last-named day, the plaintiff shows (and it was not disputed in the evidence) that the stock of logs in its boom was exhausted, and the operations of the mill temporarily suspended. A new supply of logs was expected soon, and from day to day up to the time of the burning. The plaintiff had logs in the Pere Marquette River in course of transportation by the boom company, and a boom of logs for its use reached the mill on the day of the fire. The planing-mill was kept in operation all the time, and the shingle-mill crew were waiting, expecting to go to work when logs arrived.

It was also shown that the summer of 1886 was a very dry one, and the water being low was the reason of the logs being delayed. The mill was not shut down for good, or for repairs, but temporarily closed waiting for logs. No notice of the stoppage was sent to the insurance company, as the plaintiff claims, because work was intended to be resumed as soon as the logs came, and they were expected daily. It was further shown, against the objection and exception of defendant, that it was a usual and frequent occurrence that other mills in the same locality were shut down or unable to operate this same season and other seasons on account of the low water.

The defendant claimed on the trial that it was not liable, because the mill had ceased to be operated without notice to it, in violation of the clause in the policy heretofore quoted. The court submitted this question to the jury, who found specially that the mill had not ceased to be operated within the meaning of the policy. The plaintiff recovered.

The court did not err in so submitting the question. Indeed, from the undisputed evidence, as a matter of law, it must be held that the clause was not violated. The stoppage of the mill was occasioned solely by the want of logs to manufacture. The logs were expected daily, and their not being received was not the fault of plaintiff. It was a mere temporary suspension, which, in the first place, was supposed would only last a few days, and after that from day to day. This clause cannot mean that a stoppage of this kind for a day, or even a week, for want of running material, an event quite likely to occur once or more in any season, would be considered "ceasing to operate." The policy speaks of premises becoming vacant or unoccupied, "or, if a mill or manufactory, it shall cease to be operated." This must mean something more than a temporary suspension. It must mean a closing with the intention of ceasing operation, not a shutting down for a few days or weeks because of the happening of events incident to the conducting of a mill in that locality, and which might be reasonably expected, such as the want of logs because of low water, which caused the suspension in this case: See *Whitney* v. *Black River Ins. Co.*, 72 N. Y. 120; 28 Am. Rep. 116; *Lebanon Mut. Ins. Co.* v. *Leathers*, Penn., February 23, 1887; *American Fire Ins. Co.* v. *Brighton Cotton Mfg. Co.*, 125 Ill. 131. See also *Stupetski* v. *Trans-Atlantic*

F. Ins. Co., 43 Mich. 373; 38 Am. Rep. 195; *Shackelton* v. *Sun Fire Office*, 55 Mich. 288; 54 Am. Rep. 379; *Poss* v. *Western Assurance Co.*, 7 Lea, 704; 40 Am. Rep. 68.

It was proper to show the location of the planing-mill and its connection with the mill burned, and that it was in operation, as a part of the surroundings of the fire, and as bearing on the main question. So the fact of mills shutting down temporarily for the same reason as this mill was admissible, showing that such stoppages were incident to and to be expected in that locality.

After the mill was burned there was considerable correspondence between the companies, as well as interviews between the members of the plaintiff corporation and the president and secretary of the defendant. The president of the company visited Ludington to ascertain about the loss, in the latter part of September, 1886. On that occasion the plaintiff's evidence shows that he was informed of the exact time, forty-two days, that the mill was idle. He admits he was told the mill was idle, but did not suppose it was over ten days. The defendant company, in answer to an inquiry, was informed by letter, dated January 3, 1887, of the number of days the mill had been shut down. After that the secretary at Grand Rapids called the attention of Mr. Filer, one of the members of the plaintiff company, to the clause in the policy, but said the insurance company did not intend to stand on technicalities. The first intimation given plaintiff that defendant intended to resist payment of the loss was in a letter written March 9, 1887, six months after the fire.

The question whether the defendant, under these circumstances, had not waived the defense here insisted upon, was also submitted to the jury, who found a waiver. We think there was no error in this. We have not set out in this opinion the full facts upon which the waiver was claimed, because we think the plaintiff, under the law, as applied to the undisputed facts, was entitled to a verdict, waiver or no waiver. But the facts claimed, if believed by the jury, were in law sufficient to support their finding that the defense was waived.

We find no error in the case. The judgment is affirmed, with costs.

————

For a Discussion of the Signification of the Terms "Vacant and Unoccupied," and such like expressions in insurance policies, see note to *Moore* v. *Phœnix Ins. Co.*, 10 Am. St. Rep. 390–396.

FIRE INSURANCE — CONDITION IN THE POLICY THAT THE ESTABLISHMENT
SHALL NOT CEASE TO BE OPERATED. — Where an insurance policy contained a
condition that if the manufacturing establishment should cease to be operated
without the consent from the company, the insurance should cease, and there
was indorsed upon the policy at its delivery, "other insurance permitted without notice, and permission granted to set up and operate machinery, and to
make such repairs and alterations as may be necessary to keep the premises in
good order during the time of this policy, without prejudice thereto," it was
decided that a temporary suspension of some parts of the business, others being
carried on, or a temporary suspension of all work for a want of a supply of
materials, was not a breach of the condition: *American Fire Ins. Co.* v. *Cotton
Mfg. Co.*, 125 Ill. 132. To the same effect substantially is *Whitney* v. *Black
River Ins. Co.*, 72 N. Y. 117; 28 Am. Rep. 116. In *Poss* v. *Western Assurance
Co.*, 7 Lea, 704, 40 Am. Rep. 68, it was held that a fire insurance policy
issued on a manufactory, conditioned to be void if the premises became unoccupied, or should cease to be operated, was not avoided by a temporary
cessation occasioned by the prevalence of yellow fever.

SPEIER *v.* OPFER.

[73 MICHIGAN, 35.]

MARRIED WOMAN IS NOT LIABLE ON JOINT CONTRACT WITH HER HUSBAND
for the making of improvements upon real property held by them jointly,
by entireties. Property so held is not such separate property of the
wife as the Michigan statute gives her power to make contracts in
relation to.

ASSUMPSIT. The opinion states the case.

John G. Hawley, for the appellants.

John Ward, for the plaintiffs.

LONG, J. This action was brought in the circuit court for
the county of Wayne to recover for work and labor, and
for material furnished, by plaintiffs in the erection of a building on premises owned jointly by defendants, who are husband
and wife. Plaintiffs had verdict and judgment in the court
below for $297.67. Defendants bring error.

On the trial, plaintiffs gave evidence tending to show that
between October 22 and December 7, 1883, they made a contract with the defendants jointly for furnishing the material
and doing the work in building and repairing a dwelling-house
and saloon upon premises owned jointly by the defendants in
the city of Detroit; that the contract price was $308, and the
extra work done, $12.50. At the time the contract was first
talked over the defendants were together, and agreed to let the

plaintiffs know the next day whether they should go on with the job. The next day Mrs. Opfer called upon the plaintiffs, and said they should go forward with the work. When the work was about half completed, plaintiffs called upon Mrs. Opfer for money, when she told them she had it in the bank, and the next day would pay them one hundred dollars. No part has ever been paid.

The claim on the part of defendants is, that the work was not done in accordance with the terms of the contract, but was so bad as to be practically worthless.

Evidence was then given by plaintiffs that the work was done in accordance with the contract. The defendant John Opfer also testified that the contract was made with himself alone, and that his wife was not a party to it.

It was shown on the trial, and not disputed, that the defendants were husband and wife, and that the premises on which the work was done had been deeded to them jointly, as husband and wife, about three months before the making of the contract, and that they occupied the premises at the time of the making of the contract, and had continued to occupy them ever since. But while the repairs were going on the defendants did not occupy, exclusively, the portion of the building undergoing repairs. The building was a saloon and dwelling-house together.

At the close of the testimony the counsel for defendants requested the court to instruct the jury, — 1. That in this case no verdict can be rendered against Mrs. Opfer; 2. That, under the pleadings and evidence, the plaintiffs cannot recover.

These instructions the court refused to give, but submitted the questions to the jury, upon the claims made by the respective parties under the contract, directing the jury that, if the contract was made with the two defendants, and the work was done in substantial compliance with the contract, their verdict must be for the plaintiffs; if not so done, then the jury should allow what the work was reasonably worth. If, however, the contract was made with John Opfer alone, and not with the two jointly, then the plaintiff could not recover.

Error is assigned upon the refusal of the court to give defendants' requests in charge to the jury, and upon the charge of the court directing the jury that if they found the work was not in substantial compliance with the contract, yet, if they found there had been an acceptance of the work,—that is, if the defendants had the benefit of it, and availed themselves of it,—then the plaintiff should recover what the reasonable value of the work was, irrespective of the contract.

Under this charge, the jury found that the contract was a joint one between the husband and wife, but made some deductions by reason of the work not having been done in accordance with the contract, and undoubtedly undertook to allow what the work was worth.

The real point in controversy here is, however, whether the wife can be held liable upon a joint contract with her husband for improvements made upon real property owned by them jointly. By the rules of the common law, a married woman has no power to bind herself by contract, or to acquire to herself, and for her exclusive benefit, any right by a contract made with her. A married woman could not be sued upon a mere personal contract made during coverture, although joined with her husband, as she had no general power to contract. Whatever power the wife has to contract is conferred by the constitution and statutes. Our statute has not removed all the common-law disabilities of married women. It has not conferred upon her the powers of a *feme sole*, except in certain directions. She has no power to contract except in regard to her separate property: How. Stats., secs. 6295–6297; *Jenne* v. *Marble*, 37 Mich. 319.

In this case, the property to be improved and benefited was held by husband and wife jointly, and not as the separate property of the wife. Only at the death of the husband could the wife claim it as her separate property. During the lives of both, neither has an absolute inheritable interest; neither can be said to hold an undivided half; they take by entireties; and at the death of the wife the whole passes at once to the husband: *Manwaring* v. *Powell*, 40 Mich. 371; *Allen* v. *Allen*, 47 Mich. 74; *Ætna Ins. Co.* v. *Resh*, 40 Mich. 241. Neither has such a separate interest that he or she could sell, encumber, or devise, or which his or her heir could inherit: *Vinton* v. *Beamer*, 55 Mich. 559; *Fisher* v. *Provin*, 25 Mich. 347. It is an entirety in which both take the same and inseparable interest. Neither can affect the other's rights by a separate transfer, and whatever will defeat the interest of one will defeat the other's: *Vinton* v. *Beamer, supra.*

This is not such separate property of the wife as the statute gives her power to make contracts in relation to. She can neither sell, encumber, nor control it while living, nor devise it at her death. It is not like property which she inherits, which she may dispose of at will. These common-law disabilities of a married woman being only partially removed by our statutes, one who relies upon a wife's contract must show that it relates to her separate property. The wife is liable to be sued upon contracts or engagements made by her in cases where her husband is not in law liable.

In *Bassett* v. *Shepardson*, 52 Mich. 3, this court held that the wife could not become a partner in business with her husband. This ruling is followed in *Artman* v. *Ferguson*, 73 Mich. 146; *post*, p. 572.

In *Russel* v. *People's Sav. Bank*, 39 Mich. 671, Mr. Justice Cooley, in speaking of a case in which a married woman had indorsed the note of a corporation, says: "Such a contract is therefore not within the words of the statute. Neither is it within the spirit of the statute, for that had in view the relieving of the wife from disabilities which operated unfairly and oppressively, and which hampered her in the control and dispor tion of her property for the benefit of herself and her family. It was not its purpose to give her a general power to render herself personally responsible upon engagements for any and every consideration which would support a promise at the common law. . . . . The test of competency to make the contract is to be found in this, that it does or does not deal with the woman's individual estate. Possible incidental benefits cannot support it."

There is no conflict of authority upon this question, that the contract of a married woman, to be enforced, must have relation to her separate estate. In the present case, the property being held by husband and wife jointly, by entireties, it cannot be treated as her separate property, so that she becomes liable under the contract, even if one was made as claimed by the plaintiffs. The action cannot be maintained against the defendants jointly. As this must dispose of the case, we need not discuss the other questions raised.

The judgment of the court below must be reversed, with costs, and a new trial ordered.

MARRIED WOMEN. — Contracts of married women are void at common law: *Snell* v. *Snell*, 123 Ill. 403; 5 Am. St. Rep. 526, and note. The contract of a married woman cannot be enforced against her, unless the consideration inures to her or to the benefit of her separate estate: *Bank of New Hanover* v. *Bridgers*, 98 N. C. 67; 2 Am. St. Rep. 317; *Stowell* v. *Grider*, 4S Ark. 220. In *Waterbury* v. *Andrews*, 67 Mich. 281, it was decided that the note of a married woman, given to secure her husband's debt, was void, and would not be enforced even in the hands of a *bona fide* holder, whether negotiable or not.

In *Rines* v. *Mansfield*, 96 Mo. 394, it was decided that while the act of a married woman, in joining her husband in the signing of a note and mortgage against her land, not being a part of her separate estate, is void as to the note, it does not follow that the mortgage was invalid; for a married woman in Missouri can mortgage her land of which she is not seised as her separate estate. So in *Security Company* v. *Arbuckle*, 119 Ind. 69, it was decided that to bring a mortgage executed by a husband and wife upon land owned by them as tenants in entireties, to secure a loan of money made upon their joint application, within the prohibition of the Indiana statute, making the wife's contracts of suretyship void, it must affirmatively appear that the money received did not inure to the benefit of the wife, or to her separate estate, or to the joint estate. But in *Ellis* v. *Baker*, 116 Ind. 408, it is held that under the Indiana statute a mortgage executed by a married woman upon her separate estate, to secure her husband's debt, is void as to her. See *Rogers* v. *Union etc. Ins. Co.*, 111 Ind. 343; 60 Am. Rep. 701.

Frost *v.* Atwood.

[73 Michigan, 67.]

Liens can only be Created by Agreement, or by some Fixed Rule of law, and it is not one of the functions of courts to create them.

Purchaser at Judicial Sale Buys at his Peril, and is bound to satisfy himself of the authority under which the sale is made.

Executor has No Power to Dispose of Lands by Virtue of his Office; and whenever he undertakes to meddle with lands without authority, he cannot bind them any more than a stranger. The owner, whether devisee or otherwise, is in no way affected by his action, which is void for all purposes.

No Lien on Premises Unlawfully Sold at Probate Sale is Created by Use of Money Received. In all probate sales, valid or invalid, the officer making the sale receives the money, and usually appropriates it; but such use creates no lien on the premises sold. What he receives without lawful authority does not concern the estate, and he can no more create a lien by spending that money than by spending any other. If the estate owes him, he must pursue his remedy as the law gives it, and his claim must first be established before he can get any remedy. The use, if made, is not made for the benefit of the particular piece of land that he attempted to sell, but for the whole estate; and if it becomes a claim, it is a claim against the whole estate, and not against a part of it.

Personal Service cannot be Dispensed with except in cases distinctly provided for by statute.

Power to Compel Contribution by Devisees being Wholly Statutory, the statute cannot be supplemented by creating charges which it does not authorize the probate court to make.

Decree for Contribution by Devisees to Pay Debts of Estate is No More than Personal Judgment, to be enforced by execution.

PROPERTY TURNED OVER TO DEVISEES AND LEGATEES DOES NOT CONTINUE TO BE SPECIFICALLY BOUND for any possible future deficiency. Their interests vest at once, and should not be needlessly interfered with by the executor.

EXECUTOR IS ONLY PERSON AUTHORIZED TO ENFORCE CONTRIBUTION from devisees and legatees for the payment of debts, and he has no power to sell or grant this authority to any one else. If he seeks relief in the probate court, he must enforce it by execution.

BILL in equity. The opinion states the case.

Howard and Roos, and A. M. Stearns, for the complainants.

Dallas Boudeman, for the defendant.

CAMPBELL, J. The bill of complaint in this cause was filed to establish a claim under a probate sale which has been twice declared absolutely void by this court, as illegal, and not merely irregular: *Atwood* v. *Frost,* 51 Mich. 360; 59 Mich. 409. Those were ejectment suits, in which Mrs. Atwood, the owner of the land, had been summarily ousted, and was driven to her action to regain possession. After her title was legally vindicated, this bill was filed against her, based entirely on alleged equities claimed to have arisen in favor of the purchaser under the void probate sale. The court below dismissed the bill, and complainants appeal.

Although the facts appeared somewhat in the reports of the former decisions, it will be necessary to refer to them here as far as required to explain the litigation. As in most such controversies, there is some matter in the record of no importance.

Benjamin Atwood, of Wakeshma, in Kalamazoo County, died in 1874, leaving a will, whereby several specific devises of real estate were made to several devisees, and there were also made some money bequests and some general dispositions. To testator's widow and two of his sons, bequests were made of money aggregating twelve hundred dollars; but one thousand dollars of this fell back into the estate. To a daughter Angeline Carney, a strip of land was given, twenty rods wide by one hundred and sixty long. To his daughter Sarah Jane Dibol he gave the forty acres now in controversy. To his daughter Cynthia Atwood he gave a designated tract of about one hundred and twenty acres. He devised for the benefit of a grandson, Clarence Atwood, another parcel, the size of which does not appear in the will. The rest of his real and personal property he ordered his executors to sell to pay debts and legacies, giving any unexpended balance to be equally divided between his son Ephraim and his three daughters. Sylvester Fredenburg was made executor.

The inventory valued the real estate in Kalamazoo County, a part of which was specifically devised, at $6,890, and in Calhoun County at $5,640, and personalty, besides household, at $2,109.18. The debts allowed were $3,792.44, which was less than fifty per cent of the undevised property. The widow elected to take her dower, and it was set off in Kalamazoo County, covering part of the land in dispute. Defendant is the widow, but does not claim title as such.

As the personalty and the land not specifically devised largely exceeded in appraised value the debts and legacies, the devisees were allowed to hold undisturbed possession. The sum of five hundred dollars was used, without objection, for a monument.

Why the executor did not pursue the directions of the will and sell the necessary lands seasonably, under the power of sale therein contained, does not appear. But for some reason, various licenses were obtained, and sales made with no apparently profitable result; for in 1880 the executor's account was settled, showing securities in his hands of $2,120.73, and debts unpaid to the amount of $4,353. In July, 1880, more than six years after probate of the will, the executor filed a petition setting out that all but the lands in Kalamazoo County, which were specifically devised, had been sold, leaving a balance of debts and expenses of over $2,000, and praying that the deficiency be made up by resort to the legatees and devisees. The probate court found a deficiency of $2,232.27, and proceeded to estimate the value at that time of the devises and legacies, as follows: Angeline Carney's land was reckoned at $350, and she was held liable to contribute $110.25; Sarah Jane Dibol's land was estimated at $1,200, and she was charged $378; Cynthia Atwood's land was put at the value of $3,490, and she was charged $1,067.77; Clarence Atwood's land was reckoned at $1,950, and that share was assessed $614.25.

All these parties were ordered to pay their assessed sums in twenty days, and in default each parcel was to be sold under a license which had been granted in 1879 for the sale of the lands belonging to the estate. Sarah J. Dibol resided in Indiana, and was served with notice by mail, if at all, and not personally in the jurisdiction. The bill avers that the notice to all parties was by publication. There is no proof in the printed record.

On November 1, 1880, upon an *ex parte* petition filed on that day, and without notice to any one, the probate judge increased the charges against each devisee, and charged Sarah Jane Dibol with the sum of $431.57. The executor went on and sold her interest to William Frost for $445, on December 14, 1880; and in this way, if the sale had been valid, Mrs. Dibol would have been deprived of her whole estate to pay her share of the deficiency. In the suits before referred to, this court held the sale void. And in both of these cases, without referring to any other objections, it was held that the only way to collect such assessments, if made by the probate court, and valid, was by execution against the debtor, and not by sale of the land.

In order to ascertain the relative titles and claims of the parties to this suit, some further explanation is necessary.

On July 15, 1875, Mrs. Dihol mortgaged her land to Charles C. Peavey, of Battle Creek, for five hundred dollars. In October, 1878, a foreclosure sale was had under this mortgage to Mr. Peavey. On June 2, 1880, Peavey sold the land for eight hundred dollars to defendant Sarah J. Atwood, who went into possession, her deed being recorded December 16, 1881. At the time when the probate court undertook to make the assessments in question, Mrs. Dibol's title had for some time been transferred of record to Peavey, and actually sold by him to Mrs. Atwood, who already had dower set off in a part of it.

The complainant William Frost, when he bid off these lands, had no money to pay for them, and borrowed two thousand dollars of Elihu Kirby, and gave him a mortgage on this and other land. Kirby is dead, and Frost joined his personal representatives in filing this bill to charge the price paid to Mr. Fredenburg on the land, in spite of the illegality of the sale.

The only ground of relief relied on is that the money paid to the executor for the probate title, and used by him for the purposes of the estate, ought to be refunded for failure of consideration, and treated as a lien on the land to which title failed.

It is difficult to understand on what principle such a claim can be set up. No rule is better settled than that liens can only be created by agreement, or by some fixed rule of law. It is not one of the functions of courts to create them: *Bennett* v. *Nichols*, 12 Mich. 22; *Wright* v. *Ellison*, 1 Wall. 16;

Lyster's Appeal, 54 Mich. 325; *Perkins* v. *Perkins*, 16 Mich. 162; *Rowley* v. *Towsley*, 53 Mich. 329.

There is no reason for allowing the complainants to set up a lien in this case which would not apply with equal force to execution sales or other judicial sales under equitable or probate decrees and orders. But such a doctrine would be a novelty. Every one is bound to satisfy himself of the authority under which a judicial sale is made, and buys at his peril. It would be a contradiction in terms to hold a sale void for want of authority to make it, and yet valid enough to create a lien for the purchase-money. Where individuals sell their own lands and receive pay for them, there can be no want of authority, and the question is only one of title. But a sale made by quitclaim deed, without covenants, and without fraud or misrepresentation, does not entitle the purchaser to reclaim his money. This bill is an attempt not only to give to a void probate sale the effect of a warranty deed, but to go further, and bind the land itself, which was sold without right, for its repayment.

An executor has no power to dispose of lands by virtue of his office, and no such power was given by Mr. Atwood's will as to any land specifically devised. Whenever he undertakes to meddle with lands without authority, he cannot bind them any more than any stranger. The owner, whether devisee or otherwise, is in no way affected by his action, which is void for all purposes. Heirs or devisees are only bound by what he does legally.

It is difficult to see how the case can be affected by the use which the executor made of the money. In all probate sales, valid or invalid, the officer making the sale receives the money and usually appropriates it. But it never has been supposed, and it is not legally true, that such use creates any lien on the premises unlawfully sold. What he receives without lawful authority does not concern the estate, and he can no more create a lien by spending that money than by spending any other. If the estate owes him, he must pursue his remedy as the law gives it, and his claim must first be established before he can get any remedy. The use, if made, is not made for the benefit of the particular piece of land that he attempted to sell, but for the whole estate; and if it becomes a claim, it is a claim against the whole estate, and not against a part of it.

It is a very serious question whether the action of the

probate court in apportioning the deficiency was within the jurisdiction of the court in law or in fact. It involves all the elements of a suit at law, or a proceeding in equity for contribution. Leaving out of sight the important consideration that more than six years had elapsed after the probate of the will before any attempt was made to enforce these claims, the record indicates that no attempt was made to bring the parties interested before the court, except by some unexplained form of public notice. So far as this particular piece of land is concerned, it was dealt with as the property of Mrs. Dibol, who had for some years had no interest in it, and who did not live in Michigan. If the land itself was to be charged for contribution, no proceeding could be valid that did not bring the owner before the court; and we have discovered no provision attempting to give such power to the probate court. It was held in *Durfee* v. *Abbott*, 50 Mich. 278, that there is no power to dispense with personal service in any case except in cases provided for distinctly by statute. There is no such statute in this case. The fact that Mrs. Dihol was treated as the proper person to contribute would of itself exclude any purpose of reaching her grantees. But as the whole power to compel contribution is statutory, the statute cannot be supplemented by creating charges which it does not authorize the probate court to make.

In the cases decided by this court heretofore the decisions went entirely on the ground that any apportionment lawfully made by the probate court would be no more than a personal judgment to be enforced by execution. We see no reason for receding from that doctrine.

The statutes relating to this subject do not contemplate that property once turned over to the devisees and legatees shall continue to be specifically bound for any possible future deficiency. It may consist of personalty as well as realty, and of stocks or securities as well as specific chattels. It was held in *Eberstein* v. *Camp*, 37 Mich. 176, that the interest of the legatee vested at once, and should not be needlessly interfered with by the executor. In the present case, the record does not show that if the executor had done his duty the debts would not have been fully paid within the proper statutory period, without any deficiency arising. And when he sees fit to allow all parties to rest on the idea that they can do what they will with their legacies and devises, the statute gives him no power to recall them. By section 5818, Howell's Statutes, provision is made for contribution by parties who have received their property. By section 5819 it is provided that if any person liable to contribute is insolvent, the rest must make up his share, and if dead, the claim must be proved against his estate. This is only consistent with the idea of a personal obligation, and not a claim on specific property. Section 5820 is the only section declaring how the liabilities shall be enforced. The probate court is empowered, by decree for that purpose, to settle the amount of the several liabilities, and how much and in what manner each person shall contribute, "and may issue execution as circumstances may require."

There is no provision declaring a lien, and none providing for its sale or enforcement. There is not even any provision directing that the execution shall bind the specific property.

The only person authorized by law to enforce contribution for the payment of debts is the executor. He has no power to sell or grant this authority to any one else. If he seeks relief in the probate court he must enforce it by execution.

Section 5820 also provides that the claimant may have a remedy in any proper action or complaint in law or equity. A proceeding at law could only be to obtain a personal judgment against some one person at a time. A proceeding in equity could be had to reach all parties bound to contribute in one suit. This section does not provide for proceedings at law or in equity as supplementary to a probate decree, but as elective remedies, which always existed independently, and were left untouched.

Had the statute designed to create specific claims against the land, it would not have been silent as to means of enforcement. And it could not have lawfully omitted to provide for defense by persons who had bought out the property. A devisee whose interest has been disposed of could not represent his or her grantee for the purpose of binding property. It may make no great difference to the devisee what is done with the land in which he has no further interest. The statute contemplates that the devisee shall contribute, because the devisee has received what turns out to be more than his share. But it mentions only devisees and legatees. Probate courts have no general power to affect lands or reach third persons. It is only common law and equitable tribunals that have general jurisdiction over persons and property. If the law, in a matter of this kind, had been intended to do more than fix personal liability, or to litigate the interests of third persons, it would not have been silent as to methods.

But all this has been already settled in the ejectment suits. The action of the executor in attempting to sell under the probate license was entirely beyond any power given him by law, and no rights could arise under it.

There can be no doubt that the second order, which increased the shares to be contributed, was void as entirely *ex parte*. And if the case were open to discussion on the general merits, there has been such delay, both before and since the attempted sale, as to require serious consideration at least.

Some reference was made on the hearing to the case of *Detroit etc. Ins. Co.* v. *Aspinall*, 48 Mich. 238, as bearing on this suit. It is only in point as holding that a mortgage given by a personal representative under license is void, unless in full compliance with law. There is nothing in the case which favors the idea that the advancement of money would create any lien on the land. If so, there would have been no need of a mortgage, and no sense in holding it void. The creditor who advanced the money in that case was allowed to recover because his money was applied specifically upon a valid mortgage against the estate, and he was held entitled to be subrogated to the mortgagees, upon the familiar principle that a trust resulted to him, on the application of his money on the mortgage, to have it stand in his behalf. The subrogation was not, in that case, allowed to secure the lender on any more than was put into that mortgage. The balance was not protected by our decree. In the present case, there was no claim open to subrogation, and no money lent to the executor or to the estate. Frost did not intend to become a creditor of the estate, but attempted to become a purchaser from a vendor who had nothing to sell. We think the decree dismissing the bill was right, and it should be affirmed.

JUDICIAL SALES. — The rule of *caveat emptor* applies to purchasers at judicial sales: *Williams* v. *Glenn*, 87 Ky. 87; 12 Am. St. Rep. 461, and cases cited in note.

LIENS. — A LIEN MAY ORIGINATE either by contract or by the operation of law: *Andrews* v. *Wilkes*, 6 How. 554; 38 Am. Dec. 450; but the law will not create a security by way of a lien, where the party has carved one out for himself: *Clower* v. *Rawlings*, 9 Smedes & M. 122; 47 Am. Dec. 108. For the definition and general nature of a lien, see *Donald* v. *Hewitt*, 33 Ala. 534; 73 Am. Dec. 431. In *Hodges* v. *Roberts*, 74 Tex. 517, it was decided that any person capable of contracting may create a lien upon his own property to secure the debt of another, without subjecting himself to any further obligation than the lien contract imposes. In *Ostertag* v. *Galbraith*, 23 Neb. 730, it was held that even a verbal agreement between a debtor and creditor, by which the former gave a lien upon certain property to the latter, was valid between the parties, although void as to creditors and subsequent purchasers in good faith.

EXECUTOR'S POWER TO SELL OR DISPOSE OF LANDS. — As to when an executor takes a power of sale by implication, see *Lindley* v. *O'Reilly*, 50 N. J. L. 636; 7 Am. St. Rep. 802, and particularly note 817. Generally, an executor cannot sell the land of the decedent, except by order of the probate court: *Fallon* v. *Butler*, 21 Cal. 24; 81 Am. Dec. 140; *Corbett* v. *Rice*, 2 Nev. 332. But he may sell without an order from the probate court, when he has a power of sale expressly conferred upon him by the will: *Russell* v. *Russell*, 36 N. Y. 581; 93 Am. Dec. 540; *Stokes* v. *Stokes*, 66 Miss. 456; *King* v. *Merritt*, 67 Mich. 194; *Potter* v. *Adriance*, 44 N. J. Eq. 14; *Twitty* v. *Lovelace*, 97 N. C. 54; *Giberson* v. *Giberson*, 43 N. J. Eq. 116; or conferred by implication, from the terms of the will: *Rankin* v. *Rankin*, 36 Ill. 293; 87 Am. Dec. 205, and particularly note. But no lands can be sold pending an administration, until the decedent's estate has been properly inventoried and appraised: *Chifflet* v. *Willis*, 74 Tex. 246.

In *Estate of Radovich*, 74 Cal. 536, 5 Am. St. Rep. 466, it was held that an executor could not even sell his testator's personalty without an order from the court; but in *Chandler* v. *Chandler*, 87 Ala. 301, it was decided that, independent of any testamentary provisions, an executor has full legal title to all choses in action belonging to his testator, and may dispose of them absolutely without an order of court; but that he has not such power to dispose of the tangible personalty of his testator, and must not sell it without an order from the court.

EXECUTORS WHO PAY LEGACIES WITHOUT TAKING REFUNDING BONDS, or retaining sufficient money in their hands to pay the debts of the estate, and are compelled to use their own personal funds for that purpose, cannot as of course come into equity and compel the legatees to refund the amount so advanced; although there are often peculiar circumstances which may entitle executors so situated to relief: *Alexander* v. *Fox*, 2 Jones Eq. 106; 62 Am. Dec. 211; *Davis* v. *Newman*, 2 Rob. (La.) 664; 40 Am. Dec. 764. As to the liability of property in the hands of heirs, legatees, devisees, or alienees, for the payment of decedent's debts: See *Ticknor* v. *Harris*, 14 N. H. 272; 40 Am. Dec. 186, and cases cited in note. The exercise of the right of an executor under the Michigan statute to take possession of the real estate of the testator is permissible only when the necessity therefor arises, and until then a devisee, who has entered upon the enjoyment of his estate, cannot be disturbed: *Rough* v. *Womer*, 76 Mich. 375.

PERSONAL SERVICE OF PROCESS. — Personal service of process is not absolutely essential in all cases; for the legislature may, in its discretion, provide for notice by publication, or some other kind of constructive notice where personal notice is for any reason impracticable: Note to *Flint River S. S. Co* v. *Foster*, 48 Am. Dec. 272, 273.

ROSZEL *v.* ROSZEL.

[73 MICHIGAN, 133.]

MARRIAGE TO WHICH ONE OF PARTIES DISSENTS INVALID. — Where one of the parties to an alleged marriage, instead of assenting to the contract, positively dissents, there is no legal or valid marriage, although a ceremony is gone through with by the officiating minister or magistrate.

BILL to annul a marriage. The opinion states the case.

Godwin, Adsit, and Dunham, for the complainant.

C. C. Howell, for the defendant.

CHAMPLIN, J. Complainant, being sixty-eight years of age, and a widower, on January 12, 1884, married the defendant, who was then sixty years of age, and was known by the name of Arvilla Pratt. The bill alleges that many years previously she had been married to one Calvin C. Pratt, but that she represented to complainant that she was free from him, and had a lawful right to marry. These parties lived together very agreeably for a time, but soon disputes and difficulties arose between them, resulting in complainant's filing his bill praying for the annulment of the marriage contract, on the ground that defendant was not legally divorced from Pratt, and had not the right to enter into the marriage contract, and that Pratt was still living. The defendant answered, denying that Pratt was ever lawfully married to her, for the reason that at the time he had a wife, to whom he was legally married, living, and that she was still living. After some proofs had been taken, the complainant, by leave of the court, amended his bill, charging, on information and belief, that in about the year 1841, defendant was also married to one Christian Zenniger, in the township of Bedford, Cuyahoga County, in the state of Ohio, and afterwards lived and cohabited with him as his wife, and that he believes the marriage is still in force.

Aside from some proofs taken by a commissioner in the state of Ohio, the proofs appear to have been taken in open court before the circuit judge, as in a case at law, and both parties were sworn without an order for that purpose, and without objection. It developed from the proofs that Pratt was still alive, but that at the time of his marriage with defendant he was lawfully married to one Jane C. Pratt, and that she was still alive, and the marriage relation between them had never been severed.

The right of the complainant to the relief asked for hinges upon the legality of the marriage of defendant with Christian Zenniger. This marriage is alleged to have occurred in 1841. Defendant was then a girl of eighteen years of age. Zenniger was a farm laborer. There is no written evidence introduced of the marriage, but the complainant relies upon the testimony of a Mrs. Willey, who is a sister of defendant, who testifies that she was present, and saw Zenniger and defendant married by Esquire Allen, a justice of the peace, who resided in the neighborhood. Complainant also introduced in evidence the testimony of two of his daughters to an admission of defendant that she was married to Zenniger.

The defendant claims that there was a marriage ceremony performed by Esquire Allen, but she denies that she was ever married to Zenniger, for the reason that she never assented to such marriage. She testifies that her parents attempted to force her into a marriage to Zenniger when she was but eighteen years of age; that she told the justice that if he tied the knot forty times it would not stay tied, for she did not like him, and should not live with him; that they made her stand up, "and when the man asked me if I would take him to be my husband I said, 'No, I wont'; and on every question he asked me that I ought to have answered, 'Yes,' I said, 'No,' plain, and the next day I ran away."

She testified that she had never slept with Zenniger, or lived with him as his wife; that the night of the marriage she slept with her sister, and fastened herself in the room, and excluded Zenniger, and in this she is corroborated by Mrs. Willey; that the next morning early she ran away to Warrensville, where she staid until her father brought her back, when a further attempt was made to compel her to life with Zenniger by removing some things into an old log house; that she consented to go into the log house on condition that one of her younger sisters would go with her; that she went there with her sister on Friday afternoon, and that night she sat up all night, and also on Saturday night; that on Saturday night Zenniger told her he had wronged her, and asked for forgiveness, and said "that it was her mother's doings; that she told him if he could get me fast it was all right"; that he left that night, and she never saw him afterwards. Eight or nine years after he left she heard that Zenniger was married to another woman. She testifies positively that she never consented to marry Zenniger.

The testimony of complainant's daughters relative to her admissions fully corroborates the testimony of defendant that she never consented to the marriage of herself to Zenniger. No evidence of any license for such marriage can be found in the proper office, and no return appears ever to have been made of such marriage by Esquire Allen.

It is laid down by Mr. Bishop, in his work upon marriage and divorce, that "the ruling principle as to the constitution of marriage is that it is a mutual contract, — a consensual contract, — to the formation of which the consent of both parties must be really, deliberately, definitely, and irrevocably given."

Intention is the essential ingredient, as in every other contract; and when, as the proofs show in this case, one of the parties, instead of assenting to the contract, positively dissents from it, there can be no legal or valid marriage, although a ceremony is gone through with by the officiating minister or magistrate.

"When all the facts are covered by direct proofs, and there is no room to presume others, they will be held to constitute marriage only when they disclose a concurring .consent to it by the two minds at the same instant ": Bishop on Marriage and Divorce, sec. 248.

Here, under the proofs, it cannot be claimed that defendant employed words of consent which Zenniger may have relied upon to also give his concurrence; for the testimony is, that she did not consent, and when asked if she consented to take Zenniger for her husband, said "No." She is not, therefore, estopped, either by words or conduct, from asserting that she never consented to the marriage, and her conduct immediately after and since has been consistent with her claim of non-assent.

A short time after this alleged marriage with Zenniger she was married to Henry Myers, a young man who resided in the neighborhood, and who was fully aware of the Zenniger affair, with whom she lived a number of years, and had three children. Myers afterwards petitioned for a divorce, on the ground of gross neglect of duty towards Myers for three years prior to the filing of the petition, and a divorce for this cause was granted him on December 15, 1856. Afterwards, and before the marriage between the parties to this suit, Myers died.

We do not think the proof makes out a legal marriage between the defendant and Pratt, or between the defendant

and Zenniger; and as these were the only grounds relied on
for relief, we think the decree of the circuit court should be
reversed, and the bill of complaint dismissed, with costs of
both courts, but without prejudice.   An allowance of seventy-
five dollars over taxable costs will be made to defendant for
solicitor's services in defending the suit.

MARRIAGE IS BY THE CIVIL LAW defined by the maxim, *Consensus non
concubitus, facit matrimonium:* Note to *Taylor* v. *Swett,* 22 Am. Dec. 157.
Want of consent invalidates a marriage: *Fornshill* v. *Murray,* 1 Bland, 479;
18 Am. Dec. 344; *Mountholly* v. *Andover,* 11 Vt. 226; 34 Am. Dec. 685; *True*
v. *Ranney,* 21 N. H. 52; 53 Am. Dec. 165.   But mere consent to marry is
not enough under the California Civil Code: *Sharon* v. *Sharon,* 79 Cal. 635.
So in *Clancy* v. *Clancy,* 66 Mich. 202, where complainant and defendant
signed a contract to thenceforth and forever live as man and wife, but each
agreed to retain the right to buy, sell, and transfer his or her property without question from the other, the court held that the contract was merely for
a concubinage between the parties.

MARRIAGE PROCURED BY FRAUD, ABDUCTION, OR TERROR is not void
but voidable, and may be vacated by the person imposed upon: *Tomppert* v.
Tomppert, 13 Bush, 326; 26 Am. Rep. 197; *Ferlat* v. *Gojon,* 1 Hopk. Ch.
478; 14 Am. Dec. 554.

ARTMAN *v.* FERGUSON.

[73 MICHIGAN, 146.]

HUSBAND AND WIFE CANNOT ENTER INTO CONTRACT OF PARTNERSHIP between themselves, and thus render themselves jointly liable for the contracts of the firm thus established.   Under the Michigan statute, a wife
has no power to contract, except in regard to her separate property.

ASSUMPSIT.   The opinion states the case.

Thomas A. Wilson, for the appellants.

Richard Price and Austin Blair, for the defendants.

LONG, J.   This action is brought in the circuit court for the
county of Jackson, on the common counts in *assumpsit,* to
recover for goods sold and delivered to the defendants, doing
business at Jackson as Peter Ferguson & Co.

The defendants are husband and wife, and the plaintiffs
sought to show that after their marriage they formed a copartnership, and carried on the retail carpet business in the
city of Jackson, under the firm name of Peter Ferguson & Co.,
and that during such time the goods involved in this suit were
sold to them; that Margaret W. Ferguson was, at the time of
the formation of such copartnership, possessed of property in

her own right, of the value of twenty thousand dollars, and furnished the entire capital for the business, and provided a place to carry on such business; that Peter Ferguson had no means, and was to and did manage the business; that the copartnership continued until after the last item of goods mentioned in the bill of particulars was sold.

This evidence was objected to by defendants' counsel, on the ground that it was not competent for husband and wife to enter into a copartnership with each other. The circuit court sustained the objection, and directed a verdict for defendants. Plaintiffs bring the case to this court by writ of error.

The only question arising is, whether the husband and wife can enter into a contract of partnership between themselves, and thus render themselves jointly liable for the contracts of the firm thus established.

At the common law, married women were incapable of forming a partnership, since they were disabled, generally, to contract or to engage in trade; and the husband and wife were wholly incapacitated to contract with each other. Whatever rights or powers the husband and wife have to contract with each other, or that the wife may have to enter into a copartnership to carry on trade or business, must be conferred by our constitution and statutes. There was never any impediment to the acquisition of property through purchase by a married woman. The difficulty was that at the common law the ownership passed immediately to the husband by virtue of the marriage relation.

Our statute has not removed all the common-law disabilities of married women. It has not conferred upon her the powers of a *feme sole*, except in certain directions. It has only provided that her real and personal estate acquired before marriage, and all property, real and personal, to which she may afterwards become entitled in any manner, shall be and remain her estate, and shall not be liable for the debts, obligations, and engagements of her husband, and may be contracted, sold, transferred, mortgaged. conveyed, devised, and bequeathed by her as if she were unmarried; and she may sue and be sued in relation to her sole property as if she were unmarried: How. Stats., secs. 6295–6297. In all other respects she is a *feme covert*, and subject to all the restraints and disabilities consequent upon that relation.

A partnership is a contract of two or more competent persons to place their money, effects, labor, and skill, or some or all of them, in lawful commerce or business, and to divide the profit and bear the loss in certain proportions. That a married woman may, when she has separate estate, be a copartner with a person other than her husband, is held in many states, under the married woman's statutes. But where the statute gives her no power, or only a limited power, to become a partner, the rule of the common law prevails, and she cannot enter a firm. It has been held by a great preponderance of authorities, even under the broadest statutes, that a married woman has no capacity to contract a partnership with her husband, or in other words, to become a member of a firm in which her husband is a partner, even in those states in which she may embark in another partnership; and though she holds herself out as such partner, and her means give credit to the firm, she is held not liable for the debts, as she cannot, by acts or declarations, remove her own disabilities: *Lord* v. *Parker*, 3 Allen, 127; *Bowker* v. *Bradford*, 140 Mass. 521; *Haas* v. *Shaw*, 91 Ind. 384; 46 Am. Rep. 607; *Payne* v. *Thompson*, 44 Ohio St. 192; *Kaufman* v. *Schoeffel*, 37 Hun, 140; *Cox* v. *Miller*, 54 Tex. 16; *Mayer* v. *Soyster*, 30 Md. 402.

In this state, a married woman was subject to the common-law disabilities of coverture until the passage of the married woman's act of 1855: How. Stats., secs. 6295–6299. This act does not touch a wife's interests in her husband's property, and these remain under the restrictions of the common law, unless they are removed by some other statute. The wife's common-law disabilities are only partially removed by the act, and one who relies on a wife's contract must show the facts, in order that it may appear whether she had capacity to make it: *Edwards* v. *McEnhill*, 51 Mich. 160. Under our statutes, a wife has no power to contract except in regard to her separate property. The constitution and statutes are clear against her right to make a mere personal obligation unconnected with property, and not charging it, so that she cannot become personally bound jointly with her husband, nor as a surety, by mere personal promise: *De Vries* v. *Conklin*, 22 Mich. 255; *West* v. *Laraway*, 28 Mich. 464; *Emery* v. *Lord*, 26 Mich. 431.

In *Jenne* v. *Marble*, 37 Mich. 326, Mr. Justice Campbell, speaking with reference to a lease, said: "The language of the statute is no broader than the equitable rules concerning separate property, laid down in the same words in most of the old decisions. . . . . The disabilities of testimony are entirely inconsistent with the idea that a husband and wife may deal with each other as third persons can. This is impossible, if they cannot testify concerning their contracts; and when the law recognizes, as it always has done, the peculiar power of substantial coercion possessed by husbands over wives, it would not be proper to infer any legal intent to remove protection against such influence from any vague provisions which no one supposes were ever actually designed to reach such a result, and which can only be made to do it by an extended construction. Any one can readily see the mischiefs of allowing persons thus related to put themselves habitually in business antagonism, and legislation which can be construed as permitting it is so radically opposed to the system which is found embodied in our statutes generally, that it should be plain enough to admit of no other meaning."

It is the purpose of these statutes to secure to a married woman the right to acquire and hold property separate from her husband, and free from his influence and control, and if she might enter into a business partnership with her husband, it would subject her property to his control in a manner wholly inconsistent with the separation which it is the purpose of the statute to secure, and might subject her to an indefinite liability for his engagements. A contract of partnership with her husband is not included within the power granted by our statute to married women. This doctrine was laid down in *Bassett* v. *Shepardson*, 52 Mich. 3, and we see no reason for departing from it. The important and sacred relations between man and wife, which lie at the very foundation of civilized society, are not to be disturbed and destroyed by contentions which may arise from such a community of property, and a joint power of disposal and a mutual liability for the contracts and obligations of each other.

The judgment of the court below must be affirmed, with costs.

———

Married Women. — As to the statutory regulations of Michigan affecting the separate estate and property of a married woman, see note to *Kirkpatrick* v. *Buford*, 76 Am. Dec. 382, 383.

Married Woman cannot, by Reason of her Disability arising from coverture, form a contract of partnership: *De Graum* v. *Jones*, 23 Fla. 83; *Brenner* v. *Jones*, 23 Id. 83; not even for the purpose of only subjecting her separate estate to the obligations of the proposed partnership: *Carey* v. *Burruss*, 20 W. Va. 571; 43 Am. Rep. 790. In Michigan, the common-law rule that a wife, during coverture, is incapable of entering into an executory contract continues in force and effect, except in the cases where the statutes of that state have given to her all the powers of a *feme sole* with reference to her separate property and estate: *Ring* v. *Burt*, 17 Mich. 465; 97 Am. Dec. 200; see also *Speier* v. *Opfer*, 73 Mich. 35, *ante*, p. 556, and note. But where a wife authorizes her husband to contract concerning and for the benefit of her separate estate, and in so doing, to use the name of an ostensible firm composed of herself and husband, she is liable upon an obligation executed by him in that form for such a purpose: *Noel* v. *Kinney*, 106 N. Y. 74; 60 Am. Rep. 423. So when a married woman carries on a business under the assumed name of a partnership, she may be sued in the partnership name, and is estopped from setting up her coverture as a defense against creditors who have dealt with her upon the faith of her assumed partnership name: *Le Grand* v. *Eufaula Nat. Bank*, 81 Ala. 123; 60 Am. Rep. 140.

ALPIN *v.* BOARD OF SUPERVISORS OF GRAND TRAVERSE COUNTY.

[73 MICHIGAN, 182.]

STATE, SUIT OR SET-OFF AGAINST. — A suit or a claim for a set-off cannot be maintained, directly or indirectly, against the state, when it involves a common-law issue. Hence, as against a petition for a *mandamus* to compel a county to levy a tax to pay a sum due the state, the county cannot successfully urge that the state owes it a sum with which it should be credited before making such levy.

Moses Taggart, attorney-general, and R. W. Butterfield, for the relator.

Thomas W. Browne, and Pratt and Davis, for the respondent.

SHERWOOD, C. J. The petition for *mandamus* in this case is to compel respondent to levy a tax to pay the sum of $11,616.60, being the amount petitioner claims the county owed the state on July 1, 1887. Respondent admits the correctness of the amount claimed, except $2,149.18. Respondent claims that there had been an open and continuous account, consisting of debits and credits, between the county and state since 1856, and that the county is entitled to have the last-named sum charged back to the state on a correct accounting, which has never yet been had between the parties. The respondent insists upon its right to have the sum it claims set off against the amount the state demands, and asks that this court shall so adjust the account before it directs that the writ shall issue.

It is not claimed that the amount respondent asks to have set off has ever been submitted to the auditing officers of the state for allowance, or that they have ever passed upon or allowed the same, or that the amount has ever been adjudicated as due to the county from the state by any court or other competent authority.   No question is made but that the state charged lawfully the amount the county now claims, but the claim is, that, by reason of something that has since occurred, the county is entitled to have the money back.

The set-off claimed by the county is in its nature in *assumpsit*, and the right claimed to make the set-off is only an irregular form of action against the state; and a suit cannot be maintained, directly or indirectly, involving a common-law issue only, against the state: *Ambler* v. *Auditor-General*, 38 Mich. 746; *Auditor-General* v. *Supervisors*, 62 Mich. 579; *People* v. *Miles*, 56 Cal. 401; *United States* v. *Robeson*, 9 Pet. 319; *United States* v. *Gilmore*, 7 Wall. 491; *Watkins* v. *United States*, 9 Wall. 765.

Other considerations might be mentioned, making it proper to issue the writ in this case, but the foregoing are sufficient.

The writ must be granted, but without costs.

In *Alpin* v. *Van Tassel, Treasurer of Tuscola County*, 73 Mich. 28, one of the questions involved was similar to that decided in the principal case. The defendant in that case, having received the state taxes, refused to pay them over, on the ground that he had been ordered not to do so by the supervisors of the county, who, on their part, insisted that the state owed the county on some old accounts, in which the county had been charged in excess of its legal obligation to the state.   The court determined, however, as in the principal case, that it would not enter upon the office of settling accounts between the state and county, and that the county treasurer would not be permitted to refuse to pay over money, which he had collected for the state, on the ground that the county claimed to be entitled to moneys due it from the state.   The following language of the court is pertinent to the question determined in the principal case: "What we are asked to do is to consider, in a suit on behalf of the state, which could always sue in its courts to enforce its rights, a counterclaim which, in a suit by individuals, could, at best, be put in as a set-off, which is neither more nor less than a cross-action allowed by statute, and only by statute, to be put in under a plea, instead of by an independent suit.   There is no authority in any officer or agency of the state to subject it to any such proceeding.   There is no form of action in which such a counterclaim as is relied on here is regarded as in the nature of a defense, in the proper sense of the term.   It is attempting to oppose an alleged old claim against the state to its collection of a new one entirely independent, and to make a general balance apply in reduction of a specific demand. That could not be done in any case between individuals, except by statute. Such a claim would not be a valid tender on a debt, and could not be applied as payment except by agreement.   Independent claims can always be disposed of separately, and must be where no statute provides otherwise."

SET-OFF, WHEN NOT AVAILABLE AGAINST STATE. — Immunity from suit possessed by a state as a prerogative of its sovereignty applies to a cross-action by way of a set-off, unless otherwise expressly provided by statute: *Moore* v. *Tate*, 87 Tenn. 725; 10 Am. St. Rep. 712, and note.

PEOPLE *v.* ARMSTRONG.

[73 MICHIGAN, 288.]

MUNICIPAL CORPORATION CAN PASS NO ORDINANCE WHICH CONFLICTS WITH ITS CHARTER, since it derives all its powers from legislative acts.

ORDINANCE PASSED BY MUNICIPAL CORPORATION PURSUANT TO POWER, not in conflict with the constitution, to pass ordinances of a specified and defined character, conferred in terms by the legislature, cannot be impeached as invalid because it would have been regarded as unreasonable if it had been passed under the incidental power of the corporation, or under a grant of power general in its nature. But where the power to legislate on a given subject is conferred, but the mode of its exercise is not prescribed, then the ordinance passed in pursuance thereof must be a reasonable exercise of the power, or it will be pronounced invalid.

UNAUTHORIZED PROVISIONS OF MUNICIPAL ORDINANCE DO NOT INVALIDATE WHOLE ORDINANCE, if they can be separated from the rest of the ordinance without so mutilating it as to render it inoperative.

ORDINANCE OF CITY OF DETROIT PROHIBITING CIRCULATION, DISTRIBUTION, OR GIVING AWAY OF CIRCULARS, handbills, or advertising cards of any description, in or upon any of the public streets and alleys of said city, does not come within any express or implied power given to the city by its charter; and even if the charter could be held to authorize it, this part of the ordinance would not be a reasonable exercise of the power granted.

REASONABLENESS OR UNREASONABLENESS OF CITY ORDINANCE IS NOT DETERMINED BY ENORMITY of some offense which it seeks to prevent and punish, but by its actual operation in all cases that may be brought thereunder.

CITY ORDINANCE, TO BE REASONABLE, MUST TEND IN SOME DEGREE TO ACCOMPLISHMENT OF OBJECT for which the corporation was created and its powers conferred.

SUBJECT IS LEFT ENTIRE MASTER OF HIS OWN CONDUCT, under our constitution and system of government, except in the points wherein the public good requires some direction or restraint.

CERTIORARI. The opinion states the case.

Corliss, Andrus, and Leete, for the petitioner.

John W. McGrath, city counselor, and Fred H. Warren, assistant, for the respondent.

LONG, J. This case comes from the recorder's court of the city of Detroit by writ of *certiorari.* The complaint is made under section 12, chapter 55, Revised Ordinances of the city of Detroit, as amended August 22, 1885, and charges that at the city of Detroit, on June 18, 1888, within the corporate limits of said city, on Woodward Avenue, at the corner of Grand River Avenue, the defendant, John Armstrong, then and there unlawfully and willfully did circulate and distribute and give away circulars, handbills, and advertising cards, to the evil example of all others in like cases offending, and contrary to the ordinances of said city, etc.   The conceded facts proven on the trial are, that defendant was distributing cards on the corners of Woodward and Grand River avenues, in the city of Detroit, on the evening of June 18, 1888; that defendant is one of the invitation committee referred to in the cards; that no cards were to be seen upon the ground or sidewalk at or near the place of distributing the same; that cards were given to those only who expressed or appeared to desire the same, and took the same willingly; that the use of the Young Men's Christian Association privileges offered by the cards was entirely gratuitous; that cards were offered persons unknown to defendant.   The cards were in the following form and size: —

```
THE                          INVITES
INVITATION  CORDIALLY
COMMITTEE                    YOU
             TO SPEND
THIS OR ANY MONDAY NIGHT,
      From 7:45 to 9 o'clock,
AT THE Y. M. C. A. BUILDING.
      ICE WATER AND FANS.
```

The provisions of the charter of the city of Detroit, under which it is claimed the city had power to pass the ordinance under which the complaint is made, reads: That the council shall "have power to provide for cleaning the highways, streets, avenues, lanes, alleys," etc., "of dirt, mud, filth, and other substances"; also "to prohibit and prevent encumbering or obstructing of streets, lanes, alleys, cross-walks, sidewalks, and all public grounds and spaces, with vehicles, animals, boxes, signs, barrels, posts, buildings, dirt, stones, brick, and all other materials or things whatsoever, of every kind and nature"; also "to control, prescribe, and regulate the manner in which the highways, streets, avenues, lanes, alleys, public grounds, and spaces within said city shall be used and enjoyed"; also "to prohibit and prevent the flying of kites, and all practices, amusements, and doings therein having a tendency to frighten teams and horses." The ordinance under which the complaint is made reads: —

"Sec. 12. Hereafter, no person shall himself, or by another, post, attach, place, print, paint, or stamp any placard, circular, show-bills, or advertisements, of any description whatever, except such as may be expressly authorized by law, on any street or sidewalk, or upon any public place or object in the city, or upon any fence, building, or property belonging to the city, or upon any telegraph pole, telephone pole, electric-light pole or tower, or upon any hitching-post, horse-block, or curb-stone, in any public street or alley in the city of Detroit, and no person shall himself, or by another, circulate, distribute, or give away circulars, handbills, or advertising cards of any description in or upon any of the public streets and alleys of said city."

On the trial of the case, defendant's attorney asked for the discharge of the defendant, which the court overruled, and found the defendant guilty, and imposed a fine of three dollars, in default of payment of which fine defendant was ordered to be imprisoned in the Detroit house of correction for a period not exceeding twenty days. The said fine was imposed under authority of section 19, chapter 55, of the ordinance, which reads: —

"Sec. 19. Any violation of the provisions of this ordinance shall be punished by a fine not to exceed one hundred dollars, and the cost of prosecution; and in the imposition of any fine and costs, the court may make a further sentence that the offender be imprisoned in the Wayne County jail or the Detroit house of correction until the payment thereof; provided, however, that the period of such imprisonment shall not exceed the term of six months."

The allegations of error contained in the affidavit for the writ of certiorari are: That the ordinance upon which this complaint is based is invalid, in that the common council had no authority under the charter of the city to adopt the same; that the ordinance is invalid, because unreasonable, oppressive, and in contravention of constitutional rights; that the court had no authority to impose any fine or penalty, because the ordinance under which the penalty is claimed to be imposed is unconstitutional, in that it permits and authorizes the imposition of fines and penalties excessive and unreasonable, and entirely disproportionate to offenses created and specified; that the court had no authority to impose a penalty, and the judgment is void, because the ordinance under which the penalty imposed is claimed to be authorized is illegal, in that it provides for variable and uncertain penalties for offenses charged; that the defendant should have been discharged.

Corporations derive all their power from legislative acts, and they can pass no ordinance which conflicts with the charter. Where the legislature, in terms, confers upon a municipal corporation the power to pass ordinances of a specified and defined character, if the power thus delegated be not in conflict with the constitution, an ordinance passed pursuant thereto cannot be impeached as invalid because it would have been regarded as unreasonable if it had been passed under the incidental power of the corporation, or under a grant of power general in its nature. In other words, what the legislature distinctly says may be done will not be set aside by the courts, unless in conflict with the constitution, because they may deem it unreasonable. But where the power to legislate on a given subject is conferred, but the mode of its exercise is not prescribed, then the ordinance passed in pursuance thereof must be a reasonable exercise of the power, or it will be pronounced invalid: 1 Dillon on Municipal Corporations, sec. 262.

The fact, however, that an ordinance covers matters which the city has no power to control is no reason why it should not be enforced as to those which it may control. The unauthorized provisions do not invalidate the whole ordinance, if they can be separated from the rest of the ordinance without so mutilating it as to render it inoperative: *Kettering* v. *Jacksonville*, 50 Ill. 39.

It is insisted upon the part of the prosecution that the power contained in the charter is sufficient to warrant the passage of the ordinance. There is an express power in the charter to provide for cleaning the highways, streets, avenues, lanes, alleys, public grounds and squares, cross-walks, and sidewalks, in said city, of dirt, mud, filth, and other substance; also to prevent the encumbering or obstructing of streets, lanes, alleys, etc., and to control, prescribe, and regulate the manner in which the highways, streets, etc., shall be used and enjoyed, as well as to prohibit and prevent the flying of kites, and all practices, amusements, and doings therein having a tendency to frighten teams and horses, or dangerous to life or property. This is not an express grant of power to the city

of Detroit to pass a by-law or ordinance to prohibit a person
from circulating, distributing, or giving away circulars, handbills, or advertising cards of any description, in or upon any
of the public streets and alleys of said city, and to punish by
fine and imprisonment in the county jail or the Detroit house
of correction for violation, and there is no such power implied
in these provisions of the charter.

Even if it could be held that the charter authorized it, this
part of the ordinance is not a reasonable exercise of the power
granted.   It is true that the miscellaneous throwing to the
winds of hand-bills, circulars, or advertising cards may be an
act that it would be very desirable to prohibit.   Such a distribution of cards or paper of any kind would not only litter up
the street, and become a nuisance upon and along the streets,
sidewalks, and cross-walks, but naturally would tend to frighten
teams and horses hitched upon or being driven along the streets,
and great danger might be apprehended to life and limb.
Yet the reasonableness or unreasonableness of an ordinance is
not determined by the enormity of some offense it seeks to
prevent and punish, but by its actual operation in all cases
that may be brought thereunder.   It is conceded in the present case that these cards were given to those only who expressed, or appeared to express, a desire for the same, and
that no cards were to be seen upon the ground or sidewalk at
or near the place where the defendant was distributing them;
and it is not pretended that the rights of any person were interfered with by defendant, or that any teams or horses were
frightened.   There was no indiscriminate scattering of the
papers to the winds, and the cards, of the size of one and one
half inches by three inches, contained nothing but what was
legitimate and proper for publication and distribution.   The
card itself was not only harmless, but the words printed thereon
were an invitation to a moral and Christian assembly of people, gathered together for the public good.   If this act can be
classed as an offense punishable by fine and imprisonment,
then the selling or distributing of newspapers upon the streets
of the city would be punishable in the same way.

To render ordinances reasonable, they should tend in some
degree to the accomplishment of the object for which the corporation was created and its powers conferred.   The unreasonableness of this ordinance is made apparent when we
consider the penalty which may be imposed for its violation,
—a fine of one hundred dollars, and costs of prosection, and

in default of payment, imprisonment in the county jail or
Detroit house of correction for a period of six months. If the
conviction could be sustained, then any person upon any
public street or alley, anywhere within the corporate limits of
the city of Detroit, giving away advertising cards, however
remote the street or alley from the business centers, could be
convicted and punished in like manner.

Laws which attempt to regulate and restrain our conduct
in matters of mere indifference, without any good end in view,
are regulations destructive of liberty. Under our constitution and system of government the object and aim is to leave
the subject entire master of his own conduct, except in the
points wherein the public. good requires some direction or restraint. What direction or restraint is required for the public
good in the mere act of giving away an advertising card or
handbill? This part of the ordinance is not aimed at the
littering up of the streets, or to the frightening of horses, but
the offense is made complete in itself by the mere act of distributing or giving away these enumerated articles.

In *Frazee's Case*, 63 Mich. 396, 6 Am. St. Rep. 310, it was
held by this court that a city ordinance providing that "no
person or persons, association, or organizations, shall march,
parade, ride, or drive in or upon or through the public streets
of the city of Grand Rapids, with musical instruments, ban-
ners, flags, torches, flambeaux, or while singing or shouting,
without having first obtained the consent of the mayor or
common council of said city," is unreasonable and invalid,
because it suppresses what is, in general, perfectly lawful, and
leaves the power of permitting or restraining processions to
an unregulated official discretion. In that case Chief Justice
Campbell, speaking for the court, said: "No one in his senses
could regard a penalty of five hundred dollars for such trivial
offenses as most of those covered by this by-law as within any
bound of reason."

Many decisions of the courts of other states are to be found
holding by-laws, much less stringent and arbitrary in their
terms, unreasonable and invalid: 1 Dillon on Municipal Corporations, sec. 253; *Clinton* v. *Phillips*, 58 Ill. 102; 11 Am.
Rep. 52; *Kip* v. *Paterson*, 26 N. J. L. 298; *Commissioners* v.
Northern L. Gas Co., 12 Pa. St. 318; *Commonwealth* v. *Robertson*, 5 Cush. 438.

This ordinance not only does not come within the power

granted by the charter, but it is also unreasonable and unwarranted.

It follows that the conviction must be set aside, the proceedings quashed, and defendant discharged.

MUNICIPAL ORDINANCES. — Municipal corporations can only exercise such powers as are expressly granted, or those necessarily or fairly implied in or incident to the former, and those which are essential and indispensable to the declared objects and purposes of the corporation: *Huesing* v. *City of Rock Island*, 128 Ill. 465; 15 Am. St. Rep. 129. All city charters, laws, and regulations must be construed in conformity to constitutional principles, and in harmony with general laws; for the legislature has no power to subject the people of cities to the uncontrolled and arbitrary will of common city councils: *Matter of Frazee*, 63 Mich. 396; 6 Am. St. Rep. 311; *Mayor* v. *State*, 15 Md. 376; 74 Am. Dec. 572; So the power to enact a city ordinance must be vested in the governing body of the city by the legislature in express terms, or be necessarily or fairly implied in and incident to the powers expressly granted; and any fair, reasonable doubt concerning the existence of the power is to be resolved against the corporation: *Anderson* v. *Wellington*, 40 Kan. 173; 10 Am. St. Rep. 175, and note.

Ordinances passed by the governing body of a city must be reasonable: *Anderson* v. *Wellington*, 40 Kan. 173; 10 Am. St. Rep. 175; and are void if not reasonable: *Western etc. R. R. Co.* v. *Young*, 81 Ga. 397; 12 Am. St. Rep. 320; *Chaddock* v. *Day*, 75 Mich. 527; 13 Am. St. Rep. 468, and note; *Hughes* v. *Recorder's Court of Detroit*, 75 Mich. 574; 13 Am. St. Rep. 475. Yet no ordinance can be held unreasonable which is expressly authorized by the legislature: *A Coal-Float* v. *Jeffersonville*, 112 Ind. 15. So that the power of courts to pass upon the validity of a city ordinance with reference to its reasonableness is confined to cases where the legislature has enacted nothing on the subject-matter of the ordinance, and where the ordinance was passed under a supposed incidental power implied from powers expressly granted: Id.; but courts may inquire into the reasonableness of ordinances passed by a municipality, where the powers granted are expressed in general and indefinite terms: *Haynes* v. *Cape May*, 50 N. J. L. 55.

In *Commonwealth* v. *McCafferty*, 145 Mass. 384, a case somewhat analogous to the principal case, the court held that an ordinance providing that "no person shall carry or cause to be carried or placed upon any sidewalk any show-board, placard, or sign, for the purpose of there displaying the same," was reasonable and valid.

The grant of general power to a municipal corporation must be regarded as subject to the limitation forbidding the passage of ordinances which create nuisances injurious to private rights of property, where such consequence is not a necessary result of the exercise of the power granted: *Edmondson* v. *Moberly*, 98 Mo. 523; but the mere fact alone that an ordinance general in its application injures in a peculiar manner a particular individual will not authorize a presumption that it was enacted for the purpose of annoying him, and render the ordinance unreasonable and void for that reason: *Shinkle* v. *Covington*, 83 Ky. 420.

MUNICIPAL ORDINANCE, LIKE A STATUTE, MAY BE VALID in some of its provisions, and invalid in others: *Ex parte Byrd*, 84 Ala. 17; 5 Am. St. Rep. 328.

BABBITT *v.* BUMPUS.

[73 MICHIGAN, 331.]

ATTORNEY IS COMPETENT TO TESTIFY AS TO VALUE OF HIS SERVICES in an action to recover therefor, and may show by his own testimony his experience and knowledge, and give his judgment as to the value of his services; and he may also testify as to his knowledge of the charges of other attorneys for like services in similar cases.

TESTIMONY SHOWING THAT LESS WAS CHARGED BY OPPOSING ATTORNEYS in the cases in which the plaintiff rendered the services as attorney for which he sues, and that the services rendered by them were as important as, and of as much or even greater value than, were those of the plaintiff, is properly excluded.

TESTIMONY DESCRIPTIVE OF CHARACTER OF SERVICES CHARGED FOR BY ATTORNEY is admissible in an action brought by him to recover for such services.

IT IS COMPETENT TO SHOW AMOUNT INVOLVED IN SUITS for the management and trial of which an attorney brings suit, because the amount involved in the issues has much to do with the value of the services rendered, and the responsibility assumed by the attorney.

LAWYER IS NOT INSURER OF RESULT IN CASE IN WHICH HE IS EMPLOYED, unless he makes a special contract to that effect and for that purpose. When he is employed in a case, there is no implied contract that he will bring to bear learning, skill, or ability beyond the average of his profession; nor can more than ordinary care and diligence be required of him, unless a special contract is made requiring it.

QUESTIONS INVOLVING PROPER SERVICE TO BE RENDERED BY ATTORNEYS should be very carefully considered by courts and jurors, when attorneys employed under the usual implied contract have acted in good faith, and with a fair degree of intelligence in the discharge of their duties. Under such circumstances, the errors they may make must be very gross before the attorneys can be held responsible. They should be such as to render wholly improbable a disagreement among good lawyers as to the character of the services required to be performed, and as to the manner of their performance under all the circumstances in the given case, before such responsibility attaches.

PARTY HAS RIGHT TO HAVE HIS CASE GO TO JURY IN ITS PLAINEST, SIMPLEST FORM, and if it is properly embodied in a request in that form prepared by counsel, and furnished to the court, it ought to be thus given, and the request ought not to be ignored by the court. And if the substance of such request be not as well given by the court in its own language, the omission will be error.

SPECIAL REQUESTS FOR FINDING OF QUESTIONS OF FACT SHOULD BE SUBMITTED to the jury when asked for by a party. It is his privilege to have such questions found specially.

COURT HAS NO RIGHT IN CHARGING JURY TO EXPRESS OPINION that they are not warranted by the testimony in saying that the plaintiff was in any way negligent in the performance of the services as an attorney, for which he sues.

ASSUMPSIT.   The opinion states the case.

Samuel W. Burroughs, for the appellant.

Conely, Maybury, and Lucking, for the plaintiff.

SHERWOOD, C. J. This action is brought by plaintiff to recover of the defendant the value of services rendered for her as attorney and counselor at law in the prosecution of a suit in the circuit court for the county of Washtenaw, in chancery, wherein Isaac N. Bumpus was complainant, and Myron M. Bumpus was defendant, — a partition case, — for the division of eighty acres of land. The plaintiff appeared in the case for defendant and disclaimed, Myron having, before the suit was commenced, quitclaimed his interest in the land to this defendant; and nothing further seems to have been done in the case.

Also for services in a suit in the Wayne circuit court, in chancery, wherein the defendant and Samuel R. Bumpus were complainants, and Isaac N. Bumpus was defendant, for the purpose of obtaining the title to certain lands held by Isaac, who was a son of Mrs. Bumpus. The complainants' bill was dismissed on the hearing, and complainants appealed to this court, and the decree was affirmed; plaintiff being their solicitor therein: See *Bumpus* v. *Bumpus*, 59 Mich. 95.

Also for retainer and services in a suit in the circuit court for the county of Washtenaw, in chancery, wherein Isaac N. Bumpus was complainant, and Mrs. Bumpus and her husband were defendants. This suit was to obtain specific performance of a contract. The defendants were beaten on the hearing, and a decree of eight thousand dollars was rendered against Mrs. Bumpus. From this decree she appealed to this court, and the decree was reversed, and the complainant's bill dismissed: See 53 Mich. 346.

Also for services in a partition case in chancery, in the Washtenaw circuit, wherein Isacc N. Bumpus was complainant, against Mrs. Bumpus and others. This case was subsequently settled.

Also for retainer and services in the case of *People* v. *Myron M. Bumpus*, informed against for the crime of murder.

It is for retainer and services and disbursements in these cases that the plaintiff makes his claim against the defendant, amounting, as he presents his bill, to the sum of $2,165.25, and upon which he credits the defendant with the payment of $1,484.75, and brings his suit for the balance, being $680.50.

Defendant pleaded the general issue, and gave notice that she would show on the trial set-off, under the common counts, to the amount of $1,684.75; and further, that such services, if rendered for the defendant, were so rendered under an agree-

ment, that the plaintiff was to have a retainer in each case
where defendant was a party, of twenty-five dollars, and the
further sum of twenty-five dollars per day for each day that
the plaintiff was actually engaged in court upon the trial and
hearing of said cases, and that the retainers were to be full
pay for all other services, and that she has fully performed her
said agreement with the plaintiff; that the plaintiff failed and
neglected to perform his agreement with her, but negligently
did her business, failed to take and perfect appeals when he
should have done so, and mismanaged her said business, and
so improperly advised her in relation thereto, as to unnecessarily cause her to pay and lay out large sums of money,
which she should recoup against the plaintiff.

Upon the trial of the case, the plaintiff recovered a verdict
for five hundred dollars. The defendant brings error, basing
the same upon the rulings of the court upon receiving the
testimony,—all of which appears in the record,—as well as
upon the charge and refusals to charge.

The plaintiff was sworn in his own behalf as to the value of
his services, and the first and second errors assigned are aimed
at this testimony. He was a competent witness, under our
statute, for that purpose, and, like all other witnesses upon
that subject, was entitled to show his own experience and
knowledge, and give his judgment as to the value of his
services, and upon his own theory of the case, which was to
the effect that there was no special agreement as to the amount
he was to have for his work, but that, when he was inquired
of by his client, or by those who were authorized by her to
engage his services, as to what he charged, he told them his
retainer was twenty-five dollars, and for services such sums as
are stated in his bill; and it was entirely competent for him
to testify as to his knowledge of the charges of other attorneys
for like services in similar cases. He thereby only gave
evidence of his own qualifications to speak of the value of his
own services charged for, and this is always proper. And the
same may be said of the witness Robison's testimony, referred
to in the eighth assignment of error, relating to the same subject. No error was committed in any of these rulings.

Thirteen assignments of error relate to the exclusion of
testimony on the part of the defendant, showing that less was
charged by the attorneys for the other side, in the same causes
when the plaintiff was engaged for her, than was charged by
the plaintiff, and that the services of the former were quite as

important as, and of as much or even greater value than, were those of the plaintiff. The circuit judge did right in rejecting this testimony.

The defendant's counsel might not have charged what their services were worth, or even performed them gratuitously, as is often the case where parties are unable to pay.

The court allowed the plaintiff, in describing the services he performed for defendant, to say that "I had consultations with Mary Ann Bumpus, Samuel R. Bumpus, Myron Bumpus, and a great number of witnesses."

Defendant moved to strike this testimony out, because such service was not specifically stated in the declaration or bill of items. This was not done. There was no error in this ruling. The testimony descriptive of the character of the services charged for was admissible under the pleadings.

It was also competent to ask the plaintiff, when on the stand, what was the amount involved in the five suits, or in any one or more of them; also the total amount charged for his services in either or all of them. The amount involved in the issue has very much to do with the value of the services rendered, and the responsibility assumed by the attorney. The court stated the law correctly in his rulings upon these several subjects. The total amount charged was certainly competent, as the reasonableness of this was one of the questions to be passed upon by the jury, if they did not find a contract relating thereto as claimed by either of the parties.

Six exceptions were taken by defendant's counsel to remarks made by the circuit judge which she deemed prejudicial to her case, and which it is claimed ought not to have been made. We have examined what was said on these several occasions by the circuit judge, as it appears in the record, and we do not think either of these exceptions should be sustained. A lawyer is not an insurer of the result in a case in which he is employed, unless he makes a special contract to that effect and for that purpose. Neither is there any implied contract, when he is employed in a case, or any matter of legal business, that he will bring to bear learning, skill, or ability beyond that of the average of his profession. Nor can more than ordinary care and diligence be required of him, without a special contract is made requiring it. Any other rule would subject his rights to be controlled by the vagaries and imaginations of witnesses and jurors, and not infrequently to the errors committed by courts. This the law never has done; and the fact that the best lawyers in the country find themselves mistaken as to what the law is, and are constantly differing as to the application of the law to a given state of facts, and even the ablest jurists find themselves frequently differing as to both, shows both the fallacy and danger of any other doctrine; and especially is this so as to questions of practice, the construction of statutes, and particularly those arising under our criminal and probate laws. Frequently we find the decisions of courts of last resort in the different states directly opposed to each other upon the same questions, and resting upon the same state of facts. These all admonish courts and jurors that great care and consideration should be given to questions involving the proper service to be rendered by attorneys when they have acted in good faith, and with a fair degree of intelligence, in the discharge of their duties when employed under the usual implied contract. Under such circumstances, the errors which may be made by them must be very gross before the attorney can be held responsible. They should be such as to render wholly improbable a disagreement among good lawyers as to the character of the services required to be performed, and as to the manner of their performance under all the circumstances in the given case, before such responsibility attaches. We find no error under either or any of these exceptions, committed in the rulings of the circuit judge upon this subject.

The next group of exceptions, numbering four, relates to the testimony given by witness Crane. They mostly concerned the value of Babbitt's services, and the manner in which he conducted the defendant's business, and certain transactions and telegrams between counsel. We have examined them all in the record, and find no fault in the judge's rulings concerning them.

The next four assignments presented by defendant and argued, are:—

1. Referring to one of defendant's suits which was discontinued, defendant's counsel asked witness Myron Bumpus, "Did I advise you [meaning Mr. Burroughs] to discontinue it?"

2. "Well, about how much will it cost you to go on with that case?"

3. "Why did your mother, through you [Myron], take Mr. Babbitt's advice, rather than mine?"—meaning Mr. Burroughs.

4. "Was it not because Mr. Babbitt was your attorney of record, and because he had control of the case as such?"

These questions were all put to the witness Myron Bumpus, who, it was claimed, acted for his mother, the defendant, and were all irrelevant, under the view we take of the case, and the court committed no error in excluding the answers.

It appears, when the settlement of one of the suits occurred, Myron, who acted for his mother, requested Mr. Babbitt to so make it that it would be final as to all matters between her and Isaac Bumpus, the plaintiff. This Isaac's counsel would not consent to, and the settlement was made without it, and Isaac brought suit again against the defendant, and about three months thereafter discontinued it. This second suit was brought in the Wayne circuit, and counsel for defendant asked Myron, when on the stand, "What was the damage you sustained by the bringing of the Wayne County suit after the settlement?"

The witness was not allowed to answer, and we think properly so. It did not appear that it was by Babbitt's fault that the defendant was subjected to the claimed expense. This was defendant's thirty-fourth assignment of error.

We see nothing in defendant's tenth, thirty-second, or thirty-third assignments of error needing further notice. None of them can be sustained.

At the close of the trial, the defendant's counsel asked the court to instruct the jury as follows —

"5. Myron Bumpus, without conflict, appears to have had the management of defendant's business in all the litigation referred to in this case for which the plaintiff seeks to recover; and that the bargain, either under plaintiff's or defendant's version, was made by and between plaintiff and Myron; and that if the jury believe, from Myron's testimony, that some time after plaintiff came to Detroit in the interest of Myron in the murder case, and that this was after all the services were performed by plaintiff, and that Myron called at the office of Mr. Babbitt, and there requested the plaintiff to show his books, and make a settlement, and that plaintiff refused so to do, claiming that it was unnecessary, as he (plaintiff) had looked his books over, and found that he was indebted to defendant, having received enough moneys to pay him for all his services, then, and in such case, the plaintiff cannot recover, and the verdict of the jury must be for defendant."

"7. Plaintiff has introduced testimony tending to show the

value of his services, and if he relies upon value rather than upon his express contract as alleged, he must stand by the actual value of his services, and must accept, under the law, such amounts as those services were reasonably worth; and if, from all the testimony in this case, the jury believe the amounts which he has received, and of which he acknowledges credits, were sufficient in amount to compensate him for his services, then, and in such case, he cannot recover, and the verdict of the jury must be for the defendant."

We think these requests state the law applicable to the facts in this case in terse and succinct language, and we can see no reason why they should not have been given; and their substance was really not given in the general charge, or, if it was, it was in a manner that might be easily misunderstood by the jury. A party has the right to have the law of his case go to the jury in its plainest, simplest form; and if it is properly embodied in a request in that form, prepared by counsel, and furnished to the court, it ought to be thus given, and the request should not be ignored by the court. We have had occasion to allude to this subject before, and when the court declines to give such requests, it must appear that the substance of them has been as well given by the court in its own language, or the omission will be error.

The defendant requested the court to submit five special questions in writing to the jury for their special finding, as follows: —

"1. What was the value of plaintiff's services?

"2. Has not defendant paid and caused to have been paid to plaintiff sufficient amounts of money and produce to compensate him in full for his services and expenses?

"3. Has not defendant paid and caused to have been paid to plaintiff the following amounts, to wit: $1,484.85; credited produce admitted, $45.46; note of August 15, 1883, amounting to $150; total, $1,680.31?

"4. At the time plaintiff was discharged, in April or May, 1883, did not plaintiff admit to Myron that he had looked the matter all over, and that he was in defendant's debt at the time?

"5. Was not the bargain between plaintiff and defendant that plaintiff was to have had twenty-five dollars for each retainer, and twenty-five dollars for his services for each day actually engaged in the courts, and expenses, for his services?"

"The Court: I will decline to do that, Mr. Burroughs."

The first, second, and third of these special requests should have been submitted to the jury. They ask for the finding of questions of fact, and it was the privilege of the defendant to have them found specially

We think, when the court said, in speaking of the duty of the plaintiff while in the service of the defendant as her attorney, "Now, an attorney is obliged to do the very best he can. In this case here, it has been done. . . . . I don't think you are warranted by the testimony in saying that Mr. Babbitt was in any way negligent,"—he went too far.

While these statements may not have prejudiced the rights of the defendant before the jury, it is not our privilege to say they did not. They might have done so, and such certainly was their tendency. We think it was error.

For the errors mentioned, the judgment must be reversed, and a new trial granted. ____

SKILL AND FIDELITY REQUIRED OF AN ATTORNEY. — An attorney is bound to the highest honor and integrity, and must exercise the utmost good faith; but he is not bound to use extraordinary diligence, but only reasonable skill and diligence: *Cox* v. *Sullivan*, 7 Ga. 144; 50 Am. Dec. 386. An attorney is liable for gross ignorance or gross negligence in the performance of his professional duties: *Pennington* v. *Yell*, 11 Ark. 212; 52 Am. Dec. 262; but he is not responsible when he acts honestly and in the way he thought best for the interests of his clients: Id.; *Lynch* v. *Commonwealth*, 16 Serg. & R. 368; 16 Am. Dec. 582. He is liable, however, when he disobeys lawful instructions of his client, when such disobedience results in loss to the client: *Gilbert* v. *Williams*, 8 Mass. 51; 5 Am. Dec. 77.

COMPENSATION OF ATTORNEYS. — *Generally.* — The contract of an attorney to carry on or defend a suit is an entire contract: *Eliot* v. *Lawton*, 7 Allen, 274; 83 Am. Dec. 683. When a lawyer is employed professionally to take entire charge of matters, involving at the same time professional services, and also services which are not so strictly special that others than lawyers might not perform them, it is impossible to draw any line, and say the attorney is not employed professionally throughout: *Kelly* v. *Richardson*, 69 Mich. 431. When an attorney performs distinct services for his client without any general employment, he may charge a separate price for each service, proving its separate value; but such a rule is unreasonable under circumstances where there is a general employment: Id. But where an attorney makes twenty writs where only one is necessary, he cannot recover for the writs, nor for fees in the suits thus unnecessarily commenced: *Timberlake* v. *Crosby*, 81 Me..249. Where a railroad company contracted to pay an attorney reasonable fees for assisting in the trials of cases against the company, the right of the attorney to compensation is not limited to services rendered in trials in the narrowest technical meaning of the word; but he may recover for services necessarily rendered in the actions: *Louisville etc. R. R. Co.* v. *Reynolds*, 118 Ind. 170. A contract by a client to convey land to his attorney as compensation for services may be specifically enforced, if the attorney has fully complied with his part of the contract: *King* v. *Gilder-sleeve*, 79 Cal. 504.

Agreements for Contingent Fees. — As to what contracts of attorney for contingent fees are champertous and void: Note to *Bowman* v. *Phillips*, 13 Am. St. Rep. 300; *Ormerod* v. *Dearman*, 100 Pa. St. 561; 45 Am. Rep. 391. As to contracts of attorneys for contingent fees, which are valid and enforceable, see *Brodie* v. *Watkins*, 33 Ark. 545; 34 Am. Rep. 49; *Perry* v. *Dicken*, 105 Pa. St. 83; 51 Am. Rep. 181; *Blaisdell* v. *Ahern*, 144 Mass. 393; 59 Am. Rep. 99. In *Polsley* v. *Anderson*, 7 W. Va. 202, 23 Am. Rep. 613, where an attorney made a special contract to prosecute a suit for a certain fixed fee and a further contingent fee in case of success, and the client afterwards dismissed the case without the attorney's consent, it was held that the attorney was not entitled to recover the whole contingent fee, but could recover, either on special count or *quantum meruit*, reasonable value for his services. So in *Swinnerton* v. *Monterey County*, 76 Cal. 113, where an attorney employed by a county to prosecute an action against a county officer to recover moneys alleged to be illegally retained, under an agreement whereby his compensation was made contingent upon the success of the suit, upon being discharged before the termination of the suit, it was held that he could not recover damages for the breach of the contract of employment, where it appeared that the suit ought not to have resulted in favor of the county had it been prosecuted to judgment.

Value of an Attorney's Services. — To determine the value of services rendered by an attorney, it is proper to receive evidence as to the prices usually charged and paid for similar services by other attorneys in the same neighborhood, practicing in the same court: *Knight* v. *Russ*, 77 Cal. 410; but while opinions of professional witnesses who are familiar with the character and compensation usually paid for legal services are entitled to great weight, such opinions are only to be considered in connection with the other testimony in the case, from all of which the court or jury must determine the value: *Bentley* v. *Brown*, 37 Kan. 14. In an action of *assumpsit* for services by an attorney, the value of the retainer is included in the cause of action, though not specified in the complaint, and may be proved under an issue tendered as to the value of the services: *Knight* v. *Russ*, 77 Cal. 410.

Attorney Employed as Assistant Counsel. — Where an attorney enters into a contract with a client, to prosecute an action to final judgment for a stipulated sum, and such attorney employs another attorney to assist him in the case, the client will not be liable for fees to the second attorney, unless he requests his employment or urges his retention in the case: *Sedgwick* v. *Bliss*, 23 Neb. 617. In *Verner* v. *Sullivan*, 26 S. C. 327, where an attorney was employed as assistant counsel in a case, and argued the case below, and prepared a written argument for the hearing on appeal, and gave it to the principal counsel, it was held that he had not abandoned the case, and was entitled to compensation; for an attorney, not employed by special contract for the entire case, may recover on a *quantum meruit* for services actually rendered, even though he leaves the case, without detriment to his client, before its final determination.

SMITH *v.* SMITH.

[73 MICHIGAN, 445.]

NOTICE CHARGING WIFE WITH DESERTING HER HUSBAND IN HIS SICKNESS contains matter libelous *per se.*

QUALIFIED PRIVILEGE EXISTS IN CASES WHERE SOME COMMUNICATION IS NECESSARY and proper in the protection of a person's interest, but this privilege may be lost if the extent of its publication be excessive.

NOTICE BY HUSBAND NOT TO CREDIT WIFE, WHEN PRIVILEGED AND WHEN NOT. — It is only when a husband has permitted his wife to trade upon his credit that notice to tradesmen is necessary to protect his interests. In such a case a notice to the public not to give her credit upon his account is justifiable, and to that extent privileged; but the insertion in such notice of words defamatory of the wife is not justifiable, and such words are evidence of malice.

RULE THAT IF MATTER CHARGED AS LIBELOUS BE FALSE, AND PUBLICATION MALICIOUS, it is not privileged, applies to communications or publications which are upon proper occasions qualifiedly privileged.

FATHER-IN-LAW, WHO CAUSES TO BE PUBLISHED AND PAYS FOR PUBLICATION OF LIBEL against his son's wife, cannot defend against an action brought by her by showing that her husband indicted the libel, and directed him to publish it.

CASE for libel. The opinion states the facts.

John M. Corbin and Thomas A. Wilson, for the appellant.

H. S. Maynard and Philip T. Van Zile, for the plaintiff.

CHAMPLIN, J. This is an action for libel, alleging that defendant composed and published, or caused to be composed and published, in a certain newspaper, a notice signed by Henry O. Smith, as follows: —

"NOTICE.

"My wife, Mrs. Henry O. Smith, deserted me in my sickness, and has informed me I could get another woman, for she had quit. I forbid all persons from harboring or trusting her on my account.   HENRY O. SMITH.

"EATON RAPIDS, December 27, 1883."

The declaration contains two counts, —one alleging that the defendant composed and published, and the other that he caused to be composed and published, the libel set out. The plea was the general issue.

The first question raised is, whether this notice contains libelous matter *per se.* We think it does. It charges her with deserting her husband in his sickness. If this charge be true, Mrs. Smith was guilty of the basest ingratitude, and of conduct deserving the contempt of all right-minded people. The words which follow show that the charge made was intended to be understood in a sense derogatory to the plaintiff.

The next question to be considered is, Was the publication of the notice privileged? A qualified privilege exists in cases where some communication is necessary and proper in the protection of a persons interest, but this privilege may be lost if the extent of its publication be excessive. The rule is thus stated in Odgers on Slander and Libel, 225: "So with an advertisement inserted in a newspaper defamatory of the plaintiff, if such advertisement be necessary to protect the defendant's interest, or if advertising was the only way of effecting the defendant's object, and such object is a lawful one, then the circumstances excuse the extensive publication. But if it was not necessary to advertise at all, or if the defendant's object could have been equally well effected by an advertisement which did not contain the words defamatory of the plaintiff, then the extent given to the announcement is evidence of malice to go to the jury."

If a wife leave her husband's home without cause or provocation, and he is willing to suitably supply her with necessaries, or with money to purchase them, he cannot be held liable, on the basis of a presumption of authority, or of an implied agency, for goods purchased by her on his credit. Notice to the public would not be necessary in such a case. It is only when he has permitted her to trade upon his credit that notice to tradesmen is necessary to protect the husband's interests. In such case, a notice to the public not to give her credit upon his account would be justifiable, and would be to that extent privileged. But he would not be justified in inserting in such notice words which were defamatory of the wife; and if he does so, such defamatory words are evidence of malice. There is another rule which applies to communications or publications which are upon proper occasions qualifiedly privileged; and that rule is, that if the matter charged as libelous be false, and the publication malicious, it is not privileged. In this case, the facts were submitted to the jury, and they have found that defendant did not have reasonable and probable cause to believe that said notice signed by his son was substantially true, and that in what he did in relation to the publication of the notice he was actuated by malice towards the plaintiff. The court also instructed the jury that the burden of proof was upon the part of the plaintiff to prove by a preponderance of evidence that the defendant caused this notice to be published knowing it to be false. The jury, having returned a general verdict of guilty under this charge, as well as the special verdict above that he was actuated by malice, does away entirely with the defense of privilege.

It is also urged by counsel in behalf of the defendant, that, as the testimony shows the notice was written by the husband of the plaintiff, and sent by him to be published in the paper, the plaintiff is not entitled to recover, for the reason that a married woman could not bring an action of slander or libel against her husband at the common law, and the statutes of this state that give a married woman the same right to sue and be sued in relation to her own property have not gone so far as to allow a married woman to sue her husband in an action of tort for libel; that in a suit brought against her husband she would not be allowed to testify; and that the defendant stands in privity with the husband, who is now deceased; that the husband's defense would be his defense. We are not prepared to decide that a married woman in this state may not maintain an action of libel against her husband. This, however, is not such a case, nor is it any excuse or defense for this defendant to show that his son, who was plaintiff's husband, indicted the libel, and directed defendant to publish it. The testimony is uncontradicted that defendant caused it to be published, and paid for its publication. The special verdict, which was given in response to questions submitted to the jury, appears to have been supported by testimony introduced in the cause, and is consistent with the general verdict rendered, and we discover no error in the record which warrants us in setting it aside.

The judgment is affirmed.

———

NEWSPAPER LIBEL, and the law relating thereto, generally, see *McAllister* v. *Detroit Free Press Co.*, 76 Mich. 338; 15 Am. St. Rep. 318, and particularly extended note.

LIBEL — PRIVILEGED COMMUNICATIONS: See *Bodwell* v. *Osgood*, 3 Pick. 379; 15 Am. Dec. 228, and note 232, 233; *Byam* v. *Collins*, 111 N. Y. 143; 7 Am. St. Rep. 726, and note. Conditionally privileged communications must be shown to be malicious by affirmative evidence, in order to sustain an action for libel thereon: *Kent* v. *Bongartz*, 15 R. I. 72; 2 Am. St. Rep. 870, and note; *Bradstreet Co.* v. *Gill*, 72 Tex. 115; 13 Am. St. Rep. 768; *Chaffin* v. *Lynch*, 84 Va. 884. But if a publication does not contain a libelous charge, then, no matter what the author intended, no action will lie: *Mosier* v. *Stoll*, 119 Ind. 245.

In *Chaffin* v. *Lynch*, 84 Va. 884, it was held that one insult could not be set off against another; but that if a man was attacked by another in a newspaper, he might reply, and his reply would be privileged, provided he did not use unnecessarily defamatory language, and made the reply in good faith as a self-defense. But subsequent publications of libel or other like publications are admissible to show the *animus* of the publisher: *Behee* v. *Missouri P. R'y*, 71 Tex. 424.

LIBEL. — UNCERTAINTY AS TO WHO WAS INTENDED TO BE LIBELED. — Where language in an alleged libelous charge is in itself so vague and uncer-tain that it could not be intended to have been used in reference to any particular person, it is not actionable: *Petsch* v. *Dispatch P. Co.*, 40 Minn. 291.

LIBEL — BURDEN OF PROOF. — Where a defendant to a libel suit pleads justification, he thereby assumes the burden of proof, and is entitled to the opening and closing arguments: *Stith* v. *Fullinwider*, 40 Kan. 73; but defend-ant's evidence need only preponderate, for he is not required to establish his justification beyond a reasonable doubt: *Edwards* v. *Knapp*, 97 Mo. 432.

VANDERLIP *v.* CITY OF GRAND RAPIDS.
[73 MICHIGAN, 522.]

CONSTITUTIONAL LAW — TAKING OF PROPERTY, WHAT IS. — Where a city, in grading a street, raises an embankment upon nearly thirty-five feet of the entire frontage of an abutting lot, thereby burying a portion of the dwelling-house and barn of the owner, this is as much a taking as to that part of the lot covered by the embankment as though the owner had been ejected by any other means, and is plainly within the inhibition of the constitution. And in such a case, the law does not require the owner to wait until his property is completely destroyed, and then turn him over to his action of trespass to recover his damages, but equity, when ap-appealed to, will interfere to restrain the threatened destruction.

BILL for injunction. The opinion states the case.

Earle and Hyde, for the complainant.

J. W. Ransom and M. J. Smiley, for the defendants.

LONG, J. The bill is filed in this cause for an injunction to restrain the city of Grand Rapids and the other two defend-ants, who are contractors, from dumping or piling earth or other materials on the lots of the complainant, and from depos-iting earth or other materials adjacent to her premises, so that the same will slide down thereon; and also from trespassing upon, invading, encroaching upon, or taking said premises, or any part thereof. The cause was heard in the superior court of Grand Rapids, in chancery, on bill and answer; and on November 16, 1888, a final decree was entered as prayed in the bill. Defendants appeal.

The facts, as shown by the bill and answer, are in brief as follows: The complainant is the owner of two lots in the city of

Grand Rapids, lying on the west side of College Avenue, immediately north of the right of way of the Detroit, Grand Haven, and Milwaukee Railway Company. These lots have a frontage of 144 feet on College Avenue, and extend back 170 feet, and for which she paid, in 1878, $900. The answer admits the lots to be worth $800. Here the complainant resides with her husband and children. The avenue has never been graded at this point, and follows the natural surface of the ground, and is sixty-six feet in width. It is now proposed to grade the avenue north, from south of the railroad track across said track, past the lots of the complainant, and so on to the northern limits of the city. At a point some five hundred feet south of the railroad track, up to which the avenue is graded, the natural surface of the ground and the avenue thereon descends quite rapidly, so that in front of complainant's lots it is twenty-six feet below the proposed grade at that point. Then, passing the complainant's lots, the present surface of the avenue rises even more rapidly, and at a greater height, than it does from her lots south, so that her lots lay in a depression about twenty-six feet below the proposed grade of the avenue. The ridge of ground that crosses the avenue some five hundred feet north of complainant's premises is higher than the ridge south of the railroad track, and swings around the north and west sides of the complainant's lots, and immediately at the rear of the lots, until it meets the railroad track; so that, if the city does as it proposes, — raise the grade of College Avenue twenty-six feet above the present level, or twenty-two feet above the sills of complainant's dwelling-house, as the answer admits it is proposed to do, — complainant's lots will be left in a depression, surrounded by the embankment of the avenue on the east, the railroad track and ridge on the south, and the northerly ridge on the north and rear, and entirely cut off from access to the avenue.

The answer denies the allegation in the bill that there is no alley to the rear of the lots, and no possible way to get in or out when the avenue in front is raised, and charges that there is a public alley in the rear of and adjoining said premises leading north to More Street. But complainant claims that while there is an alley laid out on the plat of this part of the city, on the rear of said lots, it only exists on the drawing, and is a fancy sketch, and cannot be actually placed there without great expense, and the removal of a large area of hill.

Upon the complainant's premises are situated her dwelling-house and barn; the house being an ordinary two-story frame dwelling-house, with kitchen extension at rear, and standing gable end to the avenue, the east front or end being only twenty-four feet and nine inches from the west line of the avenue. In this east end of the house windows are placed on both stories looking upon the street.

On May 14, 1888, the city entered into a contract with the defendants, Mathewson and Kloote, to grade and improve College Avenue, on the unimproved part, past complainant's property, according to certain plans and specifications, in carrying out of which it would result, as the answer admits, that College Avenue would be raised in front of complainant's dwelling twenty-two feet above the sills thereof, and some twenty-six feet above the level of the front of complainant's lots; that when so raised the avenue will be of the full width of sixty-six feet on top of the embankment in front of complainant's house, and if the walls of the embankment were to be raised perpendicularly, the face of the wall would be only twenty-four feet and nine inches distant from the east end of the house. But by the said contract and specifications it is not proposed to raise the avenue between retaining walls, so that the embankments at the present surface of the ground will be only sixty-six feet in width, as on the top, but it is proposed to raise it by a fill of earth sixty-six feet wide on top, and slanting out on either side towards the bottom, in conformity to the natural slope of earth when so dumped.

According to the admissions of the answer, when the fill is made as proposed (and the work was to begin at once, by the terms of the contract, and be completed before August 15, 1889), the earth of the embankment will slide back thirty-four feet and nine inches, over upon complainant's lots, across their east front, and ten feet past the side of her house, and will bury the east end of her house in the slope of the fill five feet and nine inches, measured perpendicularly. This will bring the dirt high enough to crush through the front windows of the first story, and flow in and over the floor of her front room, besides taking and occupying for street purposes, without purchasing the same, or taking any proceedings to condemn, a strip of land off of the front of complainant's said lots of nearly thirty-five feet in width, and one hundred and forty-four feet long. The answer admits the fill will also pass the side of complainant's barn, and bury that on the front end three feet and three inches; that the city has not taken or begun any proceedings to condemn said lots, or any part thereof, for street purposes, and has not contemplated taking any such proceeding, nor has offered to buy said lots, or any part thereof, or offered to pay for the same, or to recompense complainant for the taking, damage, or destruction.

The theory of the answer appears to be that the city, under its powers to grade and improve its streets, has the right to raise the grade of College Avenue in front of complainant's lots to the height of the proposed grade, and that if, in doing so, the earth of the fill slides over upon complainant's land, even to the extent stated above, it is an incident to the improvement of the street, and the damages, if any, suffered by the complainant, are consequential, and such that she has no remedy for; that the filling in of the avenue opposite said premises, in the manner proposed, is not a taking of the private property adjoining for public use; and that the city is not required to take proceedings to condemn the same.

The defendants contend that the city of Grand Rapids, by virtue of its charter, has ample authority to make the contemplated improvements. Section 1, title 6, of the charter (Local Acts of 1877, pp. 157, 158), provides: "The common council shall have the care and supervision of the highways, streets, bridges, lanes, alleys, parks, and public grounds in said city, and it shall be their duty to give directions for the repairing, preserving, improving, cleansing, and securing of such highways, bridges, lanes, alleys, parks, and public grounds, and to cause the same to be repaired, cleansed, improved, and secured from time to time, as may be necessary, to regulate the roads, streets, highways, lanes, parks, and alleys already laid out, or which may hereafter be laid out; and to alter such of them as they shall deem inconvenient."

Section 2, title 6, Local Acts of 1877, page 504, provides: "The board of public works of said city shall have power, and are empowered, to grade, gravel, raise, level, repair, amend, pave, or cover with broken or pounded stone, plank, or other material, all streets, alleys, lanes, highways, public grounds, or sidewalks in said city, and such designated portions of any street, alley, lane, or highway in said city as the common council by a majority vote of all the members elect shall by resolution declare to be a necessary public improvement."

It is also provided in section 6 of the act organizing said board of public works (3 Local Acts of 1873, pp. 56, 58): "Said board of public works is hereby empowered to determine and establish the grade lines of all streets, highways, lanes, alleys, sidewalks, and public grounds in said city, and to locate all necessary sewers, drains, culverts, vaults, arches, and bridges, wells, pumps, and reservoirs, in said city; to cause to be graded, graveled, paved, planked, or covered with other materials all such streets, highways, lanes, alleys, sidewalks, and public grounds in said city, and to construct all such main and lateral sewers, drains, culverts, vaults, arches, and bridges, wells, pumps, and reservoirs, in said city, as the common council of the city of Grand Rapids shall by resolution declare to be necessary improvements."

It is contended by counsel for the defendants that the law is settled that, unless the charter or statute authorizing the corporation to proceed with such improvements, expressly provides a remedy for parties who suffer consequential damages, the corporation is not liable to property owners for such consequential damages necessarily resulting from either establishing a grade or changing an established grade on streets, and if the legislature gives or provides a remedy in such cases, that remedy alone can be pursued. In support of this proposition counsel for defendants cite section 990 (783), Dillon on Municipal Corporations. Judge Dillon says: "The courts by numerous decisions in most of the states have settled the doctrine that municipal corporations, acting under authority conferred by the legislature to make and repair, or to grade, level, and improve streets, if they keep within the limits of the streets, and do not trespass upon or invade private property, and exercise reasonable care and skill in the performance of the work resolved upon, are not answerable to the adjoining owner, whose lands are not actually taken, trespassed upon, or invaded, for consequential damages to his premises, unless there is a provision in the charter of the corporation or in some statute creating the liability. There is no such liability, even though in grading and leveling the street a portion of the adjoining lot, in consequence of the removal of its natural support, falls into the highway. And the same principle applies, and the same freedom from implied liability exists, if the street be embanked or raised so as to cut off or render difficult the access to the adjacent property. And this is so although the grade of the street has been before established, and the adjoining property owner had erected buildings or made improvements with reference to such grade."

The leading case in this country upon this subject is that

of *Callender* v. *Marsh*, 1 Pick. 417, 430, decided in 1823. The defendant, acting as highway surveyor for the city of Boston, cut down the street in front of plaintiff's house so as to lay bare its walls, and endanger its falling, to remedy which he was obliged to incur large expense. The court, having determined that the work was authorized by legislative enactment, proceeded to consider whether the plaintiff's property was taken within the meaning of the constitution, and whether he could recover upon any ground. This question they solved in the negative. The court held this provision applied only to property actually taken and appropriated by the government, and not to consequential damages; that when the highway was established, whether by condemnation or otherwise, the public acquired not only the right to pass over the surface in the state it was in when first made a street, but also the right to repair and amend the street in such manner as the public needs might from time to time require; that the liability to damages by such alterations was a proper subject for the inquiry of those who laid out the road, or if the title was acquired by purchase, the proprietor might claim compensation not only for the land taken, but for such damages; and that persons purchasing upon a street after the lay-out were supposed to indemnify themselves against loss by reason of further improvements, or to take the chance of such further improvements. The court also say that the same principle applied as in case of adjoining proprietors. This case has had an important influence in molding the law of this country: Lewis on Eminent Domain, sec. 94.

A few years after the decision in *Callender* v. *Marsh*, *supra*, the same question arose in Tennessee and Kentucky, and was decided in the same way: *Humes* v. *Mayor*, 1 Humph. 403; 34 Am. Dec. 657; *Keasy* v. *City of Louisville*, 4 Dana, 154; 29 Am. Dec. 395. This same question was elaborately considered by the New York court of appeals in *Radcliff* v. *Mayor*, 4 N. Y. 195, 203; 53 Am. Dec. 357, in 1850. The street was cut down in front of plaintiff's premises, so that his soil, shrubbery, fences, etc., fell into the street, and he was put to great expense in restoring his premises, and adapting them to the new grade. The case was said "to fall within the principle that a man may enjoy his land in the way such property is usually enjoyed, without being answerable for the indirect or consequential damages which may be sustained by an adjoining land-owner."

In leveling and grading the street, says the court, they (the defendants) were at work on their own land, doing a lawful act, for a lawful purpose. It was also held that the damages complained of were not a taking, within the constitution, and consequently that the laws authorizing the acts which produced the injuries were valid, and a complete justification.

In conformity with those cases, it has been held in nearly every state in the Union that there can be no recovery for damages to abutting property resulting from a mere change of grade in the street in front of it; there being no physical injury to the property itself, and the change being authorized by law. These conclusions have been made to rest upon one or more of the following grounds:—

1. That when a street or highway has been laid out, compensation is given once for all, not only for the land taken, but for damages which may at any time be occasioned by adapting the surface of the street to the public needs.

2. That the public, as proprietors of the street, stand in the same relation to the abutting lot-owners as an individual would who owned the strip of land constituting the street, and that their rights, duties, and liabilities are determined by the same rules as apply to adjoining proprietors of land.

3. That this species of damages is not a taking, within the meaning of the constitution, and consequently, if the work occasioning the damages is authorized by law, no action will lie: Lewis on Eminent Domain, sec. 97.

Counsel for defendants cite *Pontiac* v. *Carter*, 32 Mich. 164, and insist that the same principles were involved in that case as in the present. In that case, however, the question involved was the liability of a municipal corporation for an injury resulting from exercise of its legislative powers, and it was denied that any liability could arise so long as the corporation confined itself within the limits of its jurisdiction. It was a case of incidental injury to property caused by the grading of a street. The plaintiff's premises were in no way involved, but they were rendered less valuable by the grading. The injury was mainly or wholly owing to the fact that the plaintiff's dwelling had been erected with reference to a grade previously established, and now changed. This court in that case followed the rules laid down in *Callender* v. *Marsh, supra.* This case was followed and approved in *Detroit* v. *Beckman*, 34 Mich. 125, 128; 22 Am. Rep. 507. Cooley, C. J., delivering the opinion of the court, citing several cases, says: " All of which follow the early case of *Callender* v. *Marsh,* 1 Pick. 418, in which it was decided that no recovery could be had for incidential injury to property occasioned by the grading of a street, no question of negligence in the performance of the work being involved. In this state the question which lies at the foundation of this suit is not an open one. In *Larkin* v. *Saginaw Co.,* 11 Mich. 88, it was decided that no action would lie for an injury resulting from an exercise of legislative authority. In *Pontiac* v. *Carter,* 32 Mich. 164, which was a case of injury by a change in the grade of a street to buildings previously erected with reference to an established grade, the point was quite fully discussed, and the liability of the city denied. These cases are decisive of the present."

In *Ashley* v. *Port Huron,* 35 Mich. 296, 24 Am. Rep. 552, *Pontiac* v. *Carter, supra,* and *Detroit* v. *Beckman, supra,* were cited and approved.

These cases, and the other cases cited by counsel for defendants, have been ruled upon the principle that the acts complained of did not amount to a taking of the private property of another. The learned counsel for the defendant, admitting that this principle underlies these cases, yet insist that the acts complained of in the bill in this case no more amount to a taking, within the meaning of the constitution, than the cutting down of the street, and destroying the foundation and lateral support of the soil of the adjacent proprietor, so that it falls into the street; in other words, that a municipal corporation, under the principles laid down in these cases, acting under legislative authority, may elevate the grade of the street, and allow the dirt and other substances of which the street is being constructed to flow down upon and cover a portion or the whole of the . private property of the adjacent proprietor, and such acts would no more amount to a taking, within the constitution, than the act of cutting down the street so that the lateral support of the adjacent proprietor is destroyed, and his soil allowed to fall from his premises into the street, would be a taking; that, the latter act being held by the great weight of authority in this country not to amount to a taking, the same principle must be applied here, and the act declared not a taking within constitutional principles; and that such acts would be *damnum absque injuria.*

We do not agree with the learned counsel in this proposition. Conceding the weight of authority to favor the proposition that no remedy is given to an adjoining proprietor or abutter upon a public street where a municipal corporation, acting under legislative authority, excavates in a street so that in bringing it to a grade as a public improvement the lateral support of the abutting premises is destroyed, and a portion of the premises permitted to fall or cave into the street, yet the facts in the present case clearly take it out of the principles upon which these cases are held. We do not, however, mean to be understood as deciding that the rule referred to is correct in the broad terms in which some of the cases lay it down, or that cities can lawfully do injury where private parties would be liable for it. The real point in question is, whether the acts contemplated by the city and these contractors in grading this street, under the conceded facts in the answer, amount to a taking of private property within the meaning of the constitution.

The constitution of this state provides that "the property of no person shall be taken for public use without just compensation therefor": Art. 18, sec. 14. "The property of no person shall be taken by any corporation for public use without compensation being first made, or secured in such manner as may be prescribed by law": Art. 15, sec. 9. "When private property is taken for the use or benefit of the public, the necessity for using such property, and the just compensation to be made therefor, except when to be made by the state, shall be ascertained by a jury of twelve freeholders"' Art. 18, sec. 2.

Security to private property is also guaranteed by the constitution of the United States, which provides: "Nor shall private property be taken for public use without just compensation": Amends. Const., art. 5.

The legislature is powerless to do that which the constitution prohibits, and whatever power the city of Grand Rapids or its board of public works may possess, under the charter of the city or the board of public works acts, can have no force if the acts contemplated by the city, under its contract, for the improvement of the street, amount to a taking of private property, and comes within the inhibition of these constitutional provisions. The right of exclusion, or the right of complete possession and enjoyment, is one of the essential elements of property in land. Can it be said that, if the acts are done as contemplated by this contract for the improvement of this street, the complainant has that exclusive enjoyment and com-

plete possession which the constitution and the laws guarantee
to her? The plans require the grade to be sixty-six feet in
width at the top, and slanting out on either side towards the
bottom, in conformity to the natural slope of the earth when
so dumped; thus throwing the dirt over upon complainant's
lots something over thirty feet, the entire width of the front of
her lots, a distance of one hundred and forty-four feet, and
burying a portion of her dwelling in this embankment, closing
up the door and the lower windows. This is as much a taking
as to that part covered by this embankment as though the
complainant had been ejected by any other means. It is an
encroachment upon the land itself, and the complainant has
not that full, complete, and absolute control and enjoyment of
it, and property in it, as before the embankment was erected.
The case comes plainly within the inhibition of the constitution. Counsel cite no case where such acts are held not to
amount to a taking, and on principle, no case can be found
which upholds the doctrine for which counsel for defendant
contend. In *Broadwell* v. *City of Kansas*, 75 Mo. 213, 42 Am.
Rep. 406, the defendant raised the grade of a street about even
with the top of plaintiff's house, and the filling encroached
upon his lot to such an extent as to crush and ruin his house.
The court says: "Moreover, section 16, article 1, of the constitution of 1865, provided that 'no private property ought to be
taken or applied to public use without just compensation.' Here
the city and its servant took the property of plaintiff within
the meaning of that section. The taking of property within
that prohibition may be either total or absolute, or a taking
pro tanto. 'Any injury to the property of an individual, which
deprives the owner of the ordinary use of it, is equivalent to a
taking, and entitles him to compensation. So a partial destruction or diminution of value of property, by an act of
government, which directly and not merely incidentally affects
it, is to that extent an appropriation.'"

In *Hendershott* v. *City of Ottumwa*, 46 Iowa, 658, 26 Am.
Rep. 182, it was claimed by the plaintiff that the city could
not legally deposit earth on its streets so that it would roll
down the sides of the embankment, upon his lots, while the
city claimed that it had the right to widen the top of the embankment to the full width of the street, even though the
earth rolled down upon plaintiff's lots. The court says "that
the city had the right to grade the street to the full width, for
the purposes of public travel, but it had no right to deposit

earth on plaintiff's lots. . . . . No one would claim that the
city, in making the embankment, had the right to enter upon
plaintiff's lots and deposit the earth directly thereon. . . . . It
seems to us that the city is equally liable for depositing the
earth in the street in such a manner that, without ceasing its
motion, it passed at once upon the lots. . . . . It is a direct
encroachment upon the soil of the adjacent lots, by depositing
that upon the earth which was not there before. We have
found no case, after diligent search, where it has been held
this may be done. On the contrary, many cases recognize a
different doctrine.'

The court further says: "The authorities cited by counsel
for defendant are all cases where the street was excavated to
the line of the adjacent lots, or cases where it does not appear
that the embankment actually encroached upon the lots. . . . .
Acts of the city were done within the limits of the street, and
in making the excavations or embankments there was no encroachment upon the soil of the adjacent owners."

Mr. Justice Cooley, in his work on constitutional limitations, fifth edition, page 671, says: "Any proper exercise of
the powers of government, which does not directly encroach
upon the property of an individual, or disturb him in its possession or enjoyment, will not entitle him to compensation, or
give him a right of action."

But on page 675 he lays down the principle that "any injury to the property of an individual which deprives the owner
of the ordinary use of it is equivalent to a taking, and entitles
him to compensation."

In *Pumpelly* v. *Green Bay Co.*, 13 Wall. 180, Mr. Justice
Miller says: "We are not unaware of the numerous cases in
the state courts in which the doctrine has been successfully
invoked that for a consequential injury to the property of the
individual arising from the prosecution of the improvements
of roads, streets, rivers, and other highways for the public
good, there is no redress, and we do not deny that the principle is a sound one in its proper application to many injuries to
property so originating. . . . . But we are of opinion that the
decisions referred to have gone to the uttermost limit of sound
judicial construction in favor of this principle, and in some
cases beyond it; and that it remains true that where real estate
is actually invaded by superinduced additions of water, earth,
sand, or other material, or by having any artificial structure
placed on it, so as to effectually destroy or impair its useful-

ness, it is a taking within the meaning of the constitution, and that this proposition is not in conflict with the weight of judicial authority in this country, and certainly not with sound principle."

These views are fully sustained by the following cases: *Northern Transportation Co.* v. *Chicago*, 99 U. S. 635; *Eaton* v. *Boston etc. R. R. Co.*, 51 N. H. 504; 12 Am. Rep. 147; *Ashley* v. *Port Huron*, 35 Mich. 296; 24 Am. Rep. 552; *Grand Rapids Booming Co.* v. *Jarvis*, 30 Mich. 308; *Ryan* v. *Brown*, 18 Mich. 196; 100 Am. Dec. 154; *Gardner* v. *Trustees*, 2 Johns. Ch. 162; *City of Aurora* v. *Reed*, 57 Ill. 29; 11 Am. Rep. 1; *Nevins* v. *Peoria*, 41 Ill. 502; 89 Am. Dec. 392; *Cumberland* v. *Willison*, 50 Md. 138; 33 Am. Rep. 304; *Hay* v. *Cohoes Co.*, 2 N. Y. 159; 51 Am. Dec. 279; *Arimond* v. *Green Bay etc. Canal Co.*, 31 Wis. 316; *Pettigrew* v. *Evansville*, 25 Wis. 223; 3 Am. Rep. 50; *Rowe* v. *Portsmouth*, 56 N. H. 291; 22 Am. Rep. 464; *Hooker* v. *New Haven etc. Co.*, 14 Conn. 146; 36 Am. Dec. 477; *Thurston* v. *St. Joseph*, 51 Mo. 510; 11 Am. Rep. 463; *Goodall* v. *Milwaukee*, 5 Wis. 32; *Rhodes* v. *Cleveland*, 10 Ohio, 160; 36 Am. Dec. 82; *Chicago* v. *Taylor*, 8 Sup. Ct. Rep. 820; *Schneider* v. *Detroit*, 72 Mich. 240.

In *Ashley* v. *Port Huron, supra*, this court say: "The right of an individual to the occupation and enjoyment of his premises is exclusive, and the public authorities have no more liberty to trespass upon it than has a private individual. . . . . A municipal charter never gives, and never could give, authority to appropriate the freehold of a citizen without compensation, whether it be done through an actual taking of it for streets or buildings, or by flooding it, so as to interfere with the owner's possession."

And in *Grand Rapids Booming Co.* v. *Jarvis, supra*, it was said: "That the flowing of lands against the owner's consent, and without compensation, is a taking of his property in violation of that provision of our constitution, ... is a proposition which seems to me so self-evident as hardly to admit of illustration by any example which can be made clearer, and which therefore can hardly need the support of authorities." See also *Davies* v. *City of East Saginaw*, 66 Mich. 37. What it is claimed the city has a right to do here is not a mere temporary use of the lands of complainant, but is a continuing use and occupancy of her premises. And no one can claim that it would not amount to a trespass. It deprives her of its use for all time that such embankment is permitted to remain.

In addition to this, from the situation and surroundings of her premises, with hills upon two sides, and the railroad track upon the third, this embankment, if permitted to be erected and maintained, would effectually cut off all approach to it from any direction, and absolutely destroy its use, and render it without value for residence purposes, and of little value for any purpose whatever.

It is contended, however, by counsel for defendants that, while this may be a subject of an action for trespass, it is not a cause for an injunction; that public works cannot be stopped by injunction, where the facts disclosed and relied upon show an adequate remedy at law; that the complaint is of a threatened trespass upon complainant's premises, and nothing else; and this, not by a direct act of the contractors or of the public authorities, but as an incident to the improvement of the street proposed to be made. The facts disclosed by this record show something more than a mere trespass threatened upon complainant's premises. If the defendants are permitted to go forward, as they claim the legal right to do, it amounts to a destruction of valuable property rights, the invasion without legal right of the home of complainant, and the taking of the property without compensation. This constitutionally they cannot do. The common council of Grand Rapids, or the board of public works, have no power to determine that this property is necessary for public use. The constitution points out the tribunal to determine this question. Under such circumstances, the law does not require a party to wait until his property is completely destroyed, and then turn him over to his action of trespass to recover his damages, but equity, when appealed to, will interfere to restrain the threatened destruction. In *Koopman* v. *Blodgett*, 70 Mich. 610, 14 Am. St. Rep. 527, this court granted an injunction restraining the interference with the natural flow of water in Clam River. Mr. Justice Campbell, in that case, says: "That defendants have given frequent occasion for damage suits is obvious. But it is equally obvious that such a remedy is inadequate. It has always been settled that the owner of realty is entitled to the aid of equity to prevent permanent and continually recurring injuries to the enjoyment of his property. To deprive him of such enjoyment is to deprive him of the property itself, wholly, or to the extent of the mischief. Neither can it be allowed for wrong-doers to rely on their own wrong to change or lessen his means of redress. When they do mischief, it is their own fault if they render a stringent remedy necessary, and they, and not the party, must take the consequences."

The principle is also laid down in *Stone* v. *Roscommon Lumber Co.*, 59 Mich. 24, and an injunction was granted. In *Ryan* v. *Brown*, 18 Mich. 212, 100 Am. Dec. 154, the court said: "Where a trespass is calculated to do permanent damage to the freehold, the jurisdiction has always been exercised, and the circumstances of this case show that injury must be very serious, if permitted."

From the circumstances shown by this record, we are of opinion that the court below properly allowed the injunction to issue.

The decree of the court below must be affirmed, and the injunction made perpetual. Complainant will recover her costs.

———

TAKING OF PROPERTY FOR PUBLIC USE, WHAT IS. — In early times it was held that property could be deemed to be taken, within the meaning of a constitutional provision that private property should not be taken for public purposes without just compensation, only when the owner was wholly deprived of its possession, use, and occupation. But a more just and liberal doctrine has been long since firmly established. An actual physical taking of property is not necessary to entitle its owner to compensation. A man's property may be taken within the meaning of this constitutional provision, although his title and possession remain undisturbed. To deprive him of the ordinary beneficial use and enjoyment of his property is, in law, equivalent to the taking of it, and is as much a taking as though the property itself were actually taken: Lewis on Eminent Domain, sec. 56; Tiedeman on Limitations of Police Power, 397; Cooley on Constitutional Limitations, 6th ed., 670; *Hooker* v. *New Haven & N. Co.*, 14 Conn. 146; 36 Am. Dec. 477; *Rigney* v. *City of Chicago*, 102 Ill. 64; *Boston & Roxbury Mill Corporation* v. *Newman*, 12 Pick. 467; 23 Am. Dec. 622; *Grand Rapids B. Co.* v. *Jarvis*, 30 Mich. 308; *Ashley* v. *Port Huron*, 35 Id. 296; 24 Am. Rep. 552; *West Orange* v. *Field*, 37 N. J. Eq. 600; 45 Am. Rep. 670; *Seifert* v. *City of Brooklyn*, 101 N. Y. 136; 54 Am. Rep. 664; *Arimond* v. *Green Bay etc. Co.*, 31 Wis. 316; *Pumpelly* v. *Green Bay Co.*, 13 Wall. 166.

The flowing of a mill by the erection of a dam is a taking of the mill and mill privilege: *Lee* v. *Pembroke Iron Co.*, 57 Me. 481; 2 Am. Rep. 59. Barrows, J., in delivering the opinion of the court in that case, said: "He who assumes, under color of legislative authority, to overflow an ancient mill, 'takes' that mill and privilege from the owner as directly and effectually as though he entered upon the premises and demolished the building." The taking of an easement, or the encroachment upon it, is the taking of property: *People* v. *Haynes*, 49 N. Y. 587; *Story* v. *New York Elevated R. R. Co.*, 90 N. Y. 122; 43 Am. Rep. 146. In the former case, Allen, J., in delivering the opinion of the court, referring to the occupancy and use of premises for the purpose of constructing and maintaining ditches for draining lands, said: "It was the imposition of a burden upon the lands subjecting them to an easement in behalf of the public derogatory to the rights of the proprietor, and depriving him of the full and free enjoyment of them." And Tracy, J., in delivering the opinion of the court in the latter case, said: "The defendant's railroad, as authorized by the legislature, directly encroaches upon the plaintiff's easement, and appropriates his property to the uses and purposes of the corporation. This constitutes a taking of property for public use." And in *Ward* v. *Peck*, 49 N. J. L. 42, it was held that a law authorizing a road overseer to enter upon private property, and cut and make a drain to draw off the water from a highway, was void because it attempted to take private property without making the just compensation required by the constitution. The taking of a franchise is the taking of property within the meaning of the constitution; and the erection of a free bridge, by legislative authority, near a toll bridge, to take away the whole of the travel, is a taking of the franchise of the toll-bridge company: *Red River Bridge Co.* v. *Mayor etc. of Clarksville*, 1 Sneed, 176; 60 Am. Dec. 143.

The permanent flooding of land by the erection and construction of artificial obstructions in a natural watercourse amounts to the taking of the land, within the meaning of the constitutional provision: *Conniff* v. *City and County of San Francisco*, 67 Cal. 45; *Hooker* v. *New Haven & N. Co.*, 14 Conn. 146; 36 Am. Dec. 477; 15 Conn. 312; *Nevins* v. *City of Peoria*, 41 Ill. 502; 89 Am. Dec. 392; *City of Aurora* v. *Reed*, 57 Ill. 29; 11 Am. Rep. 1; *City of Pekin* v. *Brereton*, 67 Ill. 477; 16 Am. Rep. 629; *Toledo etc. R'y Co.* v. *Morrison*, 71 Ill. 616; *Grand Rapids B. Co.* v. *Jarvis*, 30 Mich. 308; *Ashley* v. *Port Huron*, 35 Id. 296; 24 Am. Rep. 552; *Weaver* v. *Mississippi and Rum River Boom Co.*, 28 Minn. 534; *McKenzie* v. *Mississippi and Rum River Boom Co.*, 29 Id. 288; *Eaton* v. *Boston etc. R. R. Co.*, 51 N. H. 504; 12 Am. Rep. 147; *Trenton Water Power Co.* v. *Raff*, 36 N. J. L. 335; *Gulf etc. R'y Co.* v. *Donahoo*, 59 Tex. 128; *Pettigrew* v. *Evansville*, 25 Wis. 223; 3 Am. Rep. 50; *Arimond* v. *Green Bay etc. Co.*, 31 Wis. 316; *Pumpelly* v. *Green Bay Co.*, 13 Wall. 166. In the case of *Ashley* v. *Port Huron*, *supra*, Cooley, C. J., delivering the opinion of the court, said: "A municipal charter never gives and never could give authority to appropriate the freehold of a citizen without compensation, whether it be done through an actual taking of it for streets or buildings, or by flooding it so as to interfere with the owner's possession. His property right is appropriated in the one case as much as in the other." And Depue, J., in delivering the opinion of the court in *Trenton Water Power Co.* v. *Raff*, 36 N. J. L. 343, said: "The destruction of private property, either total or partial, or the diminution of its value by an act of the government, directly, and not merely incidentally, affecting it, which deprives the owner of the ordinary use of it, is a taking within the meaning of the constitutional provision."

Where a railroad company was given by law the right to deposit stone and earth upon the land of a private owner, outside of the sixty feet appropriated to the road, this was held to be in a sense the taking of such owner's property, for which he was entitled to compensation: *East Pennsylvania R. R. Co.* v. *Schollenberger*, 54 Pa. St. 545. And see also *Eaton* v. *Boston etc. R. R.*, 51 N. H. 504; 12 Am. Rep. 147; *Thompson* v. *Androscoggin R. I. Co.*, 54 N. H. 545. In the case of *Eaton* v. *Boston etc. R. R.*, *supra*, Smith, J., in delivering the opinion of the court, said: "To constitute a 'taking of property,' it seems to have sometimes been held necessary that there should be 'an exclusive appropriation,' 'a total assumption of possession,' 'a complete ouster,' an absolute or total conversion of the entire property, 'a taking the property altogether.' These views seem to us to be founded on a misconception of the meaning of the term 'property,' as used in the various state constitutions. . . . . If property in land consists in certain essential rights, and a physical interference with the land substantially subverts one of those rights, such interference 'takes,' *pro tanto*, the owner's 'property.' . . . . From the very nature of these rights of user and of exclusion, it is evident that they cannot be materially abridged without, *ipso facto*, taking the owner's 'property.' If the right of indefinite user is an essential element of absolute property or complete ownership, whatever physical interference annuls this right takes 'property,' although the owner may still have left to him valuable rights (in the article) of a more limited and circumscribed nature. He has not the same property that he formerly had. Then, he had an unlimited right; now, he has only a limited right. His absolute ownership has been reduced to a qualified ownership."

It may be stated as a general principle, that where the lawful rights of an individual to the possession, use, and enjoyment of his land are in any degree abridged or destroyed by reason of the exercise of the power of eminent domain, his property is, *pro tanto*, taken for public use: Lewis on Eminent Domain, sec. 56; *Glover* v. *Powell*, 10 N. J. Eq. 211.

But if the individual's property is not directly encroached upon, his property is not taken, within the meaning of the constitutional provision, although he may be put to some additional expense in maintaining his exclusive use and occupation of it. An instance of this occurs in a case where a public road is laid out along the line of a proprietor's land without taking any portion of it, so that he is compelled to maintain the whole of the fence which was before a partition fence, the expense of which was shared by his neighbor. In such a case he is not entitled to any compensation: *Kennett's Petition*, 24 N. H. 139; *People* v. *Supervisors of Oneida County*, 19 Wend. 102; Cooley on Constitutional Limitations, 6th ed., 668; *Transportation Co.* v. *Chicago*, 99 U. S. 635. In delivering the opinion of the court in the last case, Mr. Justice Strong said: "Acts done in the proper exercise of governmental powers, and not directly encroaching upon private property, though their consequences may impair its use, are universally held not to be a taking within the meaning of the constitutional provision." In the case of *Green* v. *Swift*, 47 Cal. 536, it was held that if an act is passed authorizing the channel of a river to be turned or straightened where it empties into another river, and the performance of the work causes the current of the river emptying into the other to destroy land on the opposite side of such other river, the damage thus sustained is not taking land for public use. When land is taken by the public for a particular use, it cannot be applied, under such sequestration, to any other use, to the detriment of the land-owner: *Imlay* v. *Union Branch R. R. Co.*, 26 Conn. 249; 68 Am. Dec. 392; *State* v. *Laverack*, 34 N. J. L. 201; *Commissioners* v. *Kempshall*, 26 Wend. 404; *Smith* v. *City of Rochester*, 92 N. Y. 463; 44 Am. Rep. 393.

The appropriation of a country highway to the use of a steam-railroad is undoubtedly the imposition of a new servitude, and amounts to the taking of the property of an abutting owner, to whom additional compensation must be made: Cooley on Constitutional Limitations, 6th ed., 683; *Hastings etc. R. R. Co.* v. *Ingalls*, 15 Neb. 123. And where the fee of the streets of a city is in the abutting owner, the construction of a steam-railroad in such streets is, by the greater weight of authority, regarded as the imposition of a new servitude, for which compensation must be made to the owner: *Southern Pacific R. R. Co.* v. *Reed*, 41 Cal. 256; *Imlay* v. *Union Branch R. R. Co.*, 26 Conn. 249; 68 Am. Dec. 392; *South Carolina R. R. Co.* v. *Steiner*, 44 Ga. 546;

Indianapolis etc. R. R. Co. v. *Hartley*, 67 Ill. 439; 16 Am. Rep. 624; *Cox* v. *Louisville etc. R. R. Co.*, 48 Ind. 179; *Stange* v. *Hill etc. R'y Co.*, 54 Iowa, 669; *Elizabeth etc. R. R. Co.* v. *Combs*, 10 Bush, 382; 19 Am. Rep. 67; *Jeffersonville etc. R. R. Co.* v. *Esterle*, 13 Bush, 667; *Williams* v. *N. Y. Central R. R. Co.*, 16 N. Y. 97; 69 Am. Dec. 651; *Ford* v. *Chicago etc. R. R. Co.*, 14 Wis. 609; 80 Am. Dec. 791; *Hanlin* v. *Chicago etc. R'y Co.*, 61 Wis. 515; *Heiss* v. *Milwaukee etc. R. R. Co.*, 69 Id. 555; *Van Bokelen* v. *Brooklyn City R. R. Co.*, 5 Blatch. 379; Cooley on Constitutional Limitations, 6th ed., 676. But see *New Albany etc. R. R. Co.* v. *O'Daily*, 12 Ind. 551; 13 Id. 353; *Morris etc. R. R. Co.* v. *City of Newark*, 10 N. J. Eq. 352; *Case of Philadelphia etc. R. R. Co.*, 6 Whart. 25; 36 Am. Dec. 202.

Where, however, the fee in the soil of the street is vested in the city, it seems that the legislature may authorize the construction of a railroad in the street without requiring compensation to be made, either to the city or to the abutting owner: Cooley on Constitutional Limitations, 6th ed., 678; *Savannah etc. R. R. Co.* v. *Mayor etc. of Savannah*, 45 Ga. 602; *Moses* v. *Pittsburgh etc. R. R. Co.*, 21 Ill. 516; *Chicago etc. R. R. Co.* v. *Joliet*, 79 Id. 125; *Millburn* v. *Cedar Rapids etc. R. R. Co.*, 12 Iowa, 246; *Franz* v. *Railroad Co.*, 55 Id. 107; *Rinard* v. *Burlington etc. R'y Co.*, 66 Id. 440; *Harrison* v. *New Orleans etc. R'y Co.*, 34 La. Ann. 462; 44 Am. Rep. 438; *Grand Rapids etc. R. R. Co.* v. *Heisel*, 38 Mich. 62; 31 Am Rep. 306; 47 Mich. 393. But see *Crawford* v. *Delaware*, 7 Ohio St. 459; *Street R'y* v. *Cumminsville*, 14 Id. 541; *Railway Co.* v. *Lawrence*, 38 Id. 41; *Railroad Co.* v. *Hambleton*, 40 Id. 496; *Columbus etc. R'y Co.* v. *Witherow*, 82 Ala. 190; *Theobald* v. *Louisville etc. R'y Co.*, 66 Miss. 279; Cooley on Constitutional Limitations, 6th ed., 682, note. The building and operating of a horse-railway in the streets of a city are, by the great weight of authority, regarded merely as an extension of the ordinary uses to which the streets have been dedicated, and not the imposition of any new servitude for which the abutting owner is entitled to additional compensation: *Carson* v. *Central R. R. Co*, 35 Cal. 325; *Market Street R'y Co.* v. *Central R'y Co*, 51 Id. 583; *Elliott* v. *Fair Haven etc. R. R. Co.*, 32 Conn. 579; *Savannah etc. R. R. Co.* v. *Mayor etc. of Savannah*, 45 Ga. 602; *Eichels* v. *Evansville St. R'y Co.*, 78 Ind. 261; *Brown* v. *Duplessis*, 14 La. Ann. 842; *Briggs* v. *Lewiston etc. R. R. Co.*, 79 Me. 363; *Peddicord* v. *Baltimore etc. R'y Co.*, 34 Md. 463; *Hiss* v. *Baltimore etc. R'y Co.*, 52 Id. 242; 36 Am. Rep. 371; *Hodges* v. *Baltimore etc. R'y Co.*, 58 Md. 603; *Attorney-General* v. *Metropolitan R. R. Co.*, 125 Mass. 515; *Hinchman* v. *Paterson etc. R. R. Co.*, 17 N. J. Eq. 75; 86 Am. Dec. 252; *Hogencamp* v. *Paterson etc. R. R. Co.*, 17 N. J. Eq. 83; *Jersey City & B. R. R. Co.* v. *Jersey City & H. R. R. Co.*, 20 Id. 61; *Paterson etc. R. R. Co.* v. *Mayor etc. of Paterson*, 24 Id. 158; *Stoudinger* v. *City of Newark*, 28 Id. 187; *Citizens' Coach Co.* v. *Camden etc. R. R. Co.*, 33 Id. 267; *West Jersey R. R. Co.* v. *Cape May etc. R. R. Co.*, 34 Id. 164; *Mahady* v. *Bushwick R. R. Co.*, 91 N. Y. 148; 43 Am. Rep. 661; *Cincinnati etc. R'y Co.* v. *Cumminsville*, 14 Ohio St. 523; *Texas etc. R'y Co.* v. *Rosedale*, 64 Tex. 80; *Hobart* v. *Milwaukee City R. R. Co.*, 27 Wis. 194; *Van Bokelen* v. *Brooklyn City R. R. Co.*, 5 Blatch. 579. But the construction and operation of a railroad operated by horse-power, on a street, for the purpose of transferring freight-cars from the terminus of one railroad to another, are an imposition of an additional burden, and entitle the abutting lot-owners to compensation: *Carli* v. *Stillwater St. R'y & T. Co.*, 28 Minn. 373. And the construction of an elevated railroad in the streets of a city is, as to the owners of lots abutting on the streets, a taking and appropriation of the easement in the streets, within the meaning of the constitution, where the lots have been conveyed by the city to the owners, with a covenant that the streets shall remain open forever: *Story* v. *New York Elevated R. R. Co.*, 90 N. Y. 122; 43 Am. Rep. 146; *Lahr* v. *Metropolitan Elevated R'y Co.*, 104 N. Y. 268; Cooley on Constitutional Limitations, 6th ed., 681.

Land taken for a street cannot be appropriated as a site for a market-house without making compensation to the abutting owner: *State* v. *Laverack*, 34 N. J. L. 201; nor for a public pound or a jail: *State* v. *Mayor etc. of Mobile*, 5 Port, 279; 30 Am. Dec. 564; *Lutterloh* v. *Mayor etc. of Cedar Keys*, 15 Fla. 306; nor for a house in which to confine tramps: *Winchester* v. *Capron*, 63 N. H. 605. In delivering the opinion of the court in *State* v. *Laverack, supra*, Beasley, C. J., said: "I think it undeniable that the appropriation of this land to the purposes of a market was an additional burden upon it. Clearly, it was not using it as a street. So far from that, what the act authorized to be done was incongruous with such use; for the market was an obstruction to it, considered merely as a highway."

Whenever land is taken or dedicated for a city street, it is undoubtedly appropriated for all the ordinary and usual purposes of such a street. Sewers may be constructed in it, and gas and water pipes may be laid in it for the purpose of supplying the inhabitants with water and gas: *Crooke* v. *Flatbush etc. Co.*, 29 Hun, 245; *State* v. *Laverack*, 34 N. J. L. 201. But the laying of such pipes in an ordinary country road is the imposition of an additional servitude, and compensation must, therefore, be made to the abutting owner: *Bloomfield G. L. Co.* v. *Calkins*, 62 N. Y. 386; *Sterling's Appeal*, 111 Pa. St. 35; 56 Am. Rep. 246.

The erection in suitable places in the streets of cities and towns, of monuments and works of art, is not the imposition of an additional servitude, nor the taking of private property, where they do not interfere with public travel: *Tompkins* v. *Hodgson*, 2 Hun, 146.

The erection of telegraph or telephone poles in a street or highway is held by some authorities to be the imposition of an additional servitude for which compensation must be made to the abutting owner: *Board of Trade Tel. Co.* v. *Barnett*, 107 Ill. 507; 47 Am. Rep. 453; *Broome* v. *New York & N. J. Telephone Co.*, 42 N. J. Eq. 141; *Dusenbury* v. *Mutual Tel. Co.*, 11 Abb. N. C. 440; *Tiffany* v. *United States I. Co.*, 67 How. Pr. 73; *Metropolitan Telephone and Telegraph Co.* v. *Colwell Lead Co.*, 67 Id. 365. While other authorities hold that the erection and maintenance of such poles in a street or highway are a proper use of such street or highway, and that the legislature may authorize their erection without providing for any additional compensation: *Pierce* v. *Drew*, 136 Mass. 75; 49 Am. Rep. 7; *Julia Building Association* v. *Bell Tel. Co.*, 88 Mo. 258; *People* v. *Thompson*, 65 How. Pr. 407. But entering upon a railroad company's right of way, and erecting, constructing, and maintaining thereon a line of telegraph, is a taking of the company's property within the meaning of the constitution: *Southwestern R. R. Co.* v. *Southern and Atlantic Tel. Co.*, 46 Ga. 43; 12 Am. Rep. 585. A town or village may take part of a street for the site of a reservoir in which to store water for sprinkling the streets, without making further compensation: *West* v. *Bancroft*, 32 Vt. 367.

The discontinuance or closing up of a street or highway, causing inconvenience to an owner, is not a taking of his property within the meaning of the constitution: *City of East St. Louis* v. *O'Flynn*, 119 Ill. 200; *Barr* v. *City of Oskaloosa*, 45 Iowa, 275; *Fearing* v. *Irwin*, 55 N. Y. 486; *McGee's Appeal*, 114 Pa. St. 470.

The right of access by an abutting owner to a stream is an incorporeal hereditament appurtenant to his land, and depriving him of it is a taking of his property within the meaning of the constitution: Tiedeman on Limitations of Police Power, 398; *Railway Co.* v. *Renwick,* 102 U. S. 180; *Yates* v. *Milwaukee,* 10 Wall. 497; *Chicago etc. R. R. Co.* v. *Stein,* 75 Ill. 41.

The deprivation of the rights of persons entitled to the use of water in a natural stream or pond is the taking of private property within the meaning of the constitution: *City of Emporia* v. *Soden,* 25 Kan. 588; *Ætna Mills* v. *Inhabitants of Waltham,* 126 Mass. 422; *Ætna Mills* v. *Brookline,* 127 Id. 69; *Cowdery* v. *Inhabitants of Woburn,* 136 Id. 409; *Smith* v. *City of Rochester,* 92 N. Y. 463.

Where a highway is laid out across a railroad, the company is entitled to include in its damages the expense of cattle-guards, fencing, and other outlays to complete the approaches, besides the cost of maintaining them; and a statute which imposes this expense upon the railroad company is in conflict with the constitutional provision forbidding the taking of private property without just compensation: *People* v. *Lake Shore etc. R'y Co.,* 52 Mich. 271; *Chicago etc. R'y Co.* v. *Hough,* 61 Id. 507. Under the Texas statute, the changing of a second-class to a first-class road, or of a third-class one to a second-class one, is a taking of the property of the abutting owner: *Thompson* v. *State,* 22 Tex. App. 328; *Bradley* v. *State,* 22 Id. 330.

In *Protzman* v. *Indianapolis etc. R. R. Co.,* 9 Ind. 467, 68 Am. Dec. 650, it was held that the raising of the grade of a street by a railroad company for the use of its track is not the taking of the property of the abutting owner within the meaning of the constitution. And in *Kehrer* v. *Richmond City,* 81 Va. 745, where a property owner was obliged to remove earth thrown down upon his land in grading a street in a lawful manner, and to erect a barrier four feet high along the front of his lot to prevent the earth from falling and covering up his premises, and to erect steps to secure ingress and egress, it was held that this was not a taking within the meaning of the constitutional provision. In delivering the opinion of the court in that case, Lewis, P., said: "The property of the plaintiff has not been taken, nor have his rights been unlawfully invaded. And if, in consequence of the acts complained of, he has been obliged, as he avers, to erect a barrier for the protection of his property, or steps in order to have ingress and egress to and from his premises, or if his business has been injuriously affected and the value of his property diminished, it is mere incidental injury, caused by the prosecution, in a lawful manner, of a public improvement, for which there is no redress."

The destruction of private property by a fire department of a city in order to stay a conflagration is not a taking of private property within the meaning of the constitution: *Keller* v. *City of Corpus Christi,* 50 Tex. 614; 32 Am. Rep. 613. And an act authorizing a city to subscribe to the capital stock of a railroad company is no taking of private property in any sense, for any purpose or for any use: *Sharpless* v. *Mayor of Philadelphia,* 21 Pa. St. 147; 59 Am. Dec. 759. In most, if not all, of the state constitutions adopted since 1869, provision is made for compensating owners of property "injured" or "damaged," as well as that which is actually taken.

WHETHER REMOVAL OF LATERAL SUPPORT FROM OWNER'S LAND IN GRADING STREET IS A TAKING OF HIS PROPERTY. — This subject is discussed at length in the note to *Fellowes* v. *City of New Haven,* 26 Am. Rep. 457–462.

TREAT v. DUNHAM.

[74 MICHIGAN, 114.]

ATTACHMENT — EFFECT OF RECITALS OF INDEBTEDNESS IN AFFIDAVIT. — When an officer justifies the holding of goods under a writ of attachment valid upon its face, the recital of indebtedness in the affidavit raises a presumption of such indebtedness. If this presumption is rebutted, it then devolves upon the officer to prove the indebtedness by other evidence than the affidavit; but in the absence of such rebutting proof, the attachment papers are a sufficient showing upon the part of the officer to enable him to contest the title of the party seeking to reclaim the goods taken, whether the action is replevin, trespass, or trover.

ATTACHMENT — EFFECT OF APPEAL FROM JUDGMENT. — A judgment against a plaintiff in attachment which is appealed from does not dissolve the attachment, but the lien continues until the final disposition of the case.

ATTACHMENT — JUDGMENT AS EVIDENCE. — A judgment against a plaintiff in attachment is not admissible in evidence for the purpose of showing that there was no indebtedness due, at the time of issuing the writ of attachment, from the defendant to the plaintiff, until four days after the rendition of the verdict upon which the judgment is based.

S. M. Constantine and *W. G. Howard*, for the appellant.

H. O. Bliss and *Dallas Boudeman*, for the plaintiff.

MORSE, J. The plaintiff in this case is a physician, residing in Stewart, Iowa, and sues in trover for the conversion of certain merchandise, which he claims he purchased of his brother, John E. Treat, at Three Rivers, in this state. The goods consisted of a portion of a stock of jewelry, and were, at the time of the purchase, in the store of the said John E. Treat. The plaintiff claims that he bought all of the stock, furniture, and fixtures in his brother's store, paying therefor the sum of five thousand dollars, and taking a bill of sale of the same, dated June 17, 1887.

The defendant justified under a levy upon the goods by virtue of a writ of attachment issued in favor of the Julius King Optical Company and against John E. Treat. The levy was made June 27, 1887, at which time the defendant claimed the goods were the property of said John E. Treat. The circuit judge directed a verdict in favor of the plaintiff for the sum of $936.75. The defendant brings error.

The plaintiff, upon the trial, made his case by showing his bill of sale and purchase for the consideration therein expressed, and that he was in possession of the property when it was taken by the defendant, and the value was over nine hundred dollars.

The defendant offered no evidence of an indebtedness of the defendant in attachment, John E. Treat, to the plaintiffs in attachment, save the recital in the affidavit upon which the writ was based; and this was the reason assigned by the circuit judge for taking the case from the jury; the court holding that, until such indebtedness was shown, the defendant had no standing in court to question the good faith of the plaintiff in his purchase. It was also shown by the plaintiff, against the objection of defendant's counsel, that before the trial, and on February 8, 1888, judgment in the attachment suit was entered against the King Optical Company, and in favor of John E. Treat. It is claimed by plaintiff's counsel that it was necessary for the defendant, the officer justifying under the attachment, to prove the existence of a debt, due at the time the writ was issued, from John E. Treat to the plaintiffs in the attachment suit, and that this could not be proven by the affidavit for the writ. The counsel relies upon the ruling of this court in *Cook* v. *Hopper*, 23 Mich. 516, to support this proposition.

The counsel further argues that even if he be incorrect in this claim, the fact established, that judgment had been entered against the plaintiffs in the attachment suit before the trial of this cause, ended the case of the defendant, as he could not justify his holding of the property under a writ of attachment in a case wherein judgment had passed against the plaintiffs in such writ. He cites, to sustain this position, the following cases: *Rinchey* v. *Stryker*, 28 N. Y. 45; 84 Am. Dec. 324; *Orr* v. *Keyes*, 37 Mich. 385; *Wilson* v. *Martin*, 44 Mich. 509; *Rolfe* v. *Dudley*, 58 Mich. 208.

As these two questions are vital ones, we will discuss them first, and afterwards notice the other errors assigned.

1. We think the circuit judge was in error upon the proof of indebtedness. When a sheriff, or other officer, as in this case, justifies the holding of goods under a writ of attachment valid upon its face, the recital of indebtedness in the affidavit must be taken as *prima facie* evidence of such indebtedness. It may be disputed; and if it is, it then devolves upon the officer to prove the indebtedness to the satisfaction of the court and jury, and by other evidence than the affidavit. But the putting in evidence of the attachment papers, if they are valid upon their face, in the absence of any proof tending to show that no indebtedness exists as a basis for such attachment, is a sufficient showing upon the part of the officer to

enable him to contest the title of the party seeking to reclaim
the goods taken, whether the action be replevin, trespass, or
trover.   The case of *Cook* v. *Hopper, supra*, does not conflict
with this holding.   It was held in that case that the recital in
the affidavit was not conclusive, and'that such recital could be
contradicted: See *Cook* v. *Hopper*, 23 Mich. 511.   In the case
at bar, no evidence was introduced by the plaintiff to dispute
the affidavit of indebtedness, excepting the record of the judgment in the attachment case, which had been rendered three
days before the trial of this case.

2. We will now consider the effect of this judgment upon
the case at bar.   The matter comes before us in a peculiar
way, and the result, if the judgment in the case at bar is
affirmed, will be somewhat complicated, and perhaps end in a
failure of justice.   A writ of error was sued out in both cases.
The attachment case of the *Julius King Optical Co.* v. *John E.
Treat* was first argued before us.   From the record in that
case, it appears that the judgment therein, upon which the
plaintiff in this case seeks to predicate his judgment, was
obtained upon rulings of the court below which we find to be
erroneous, and a new trial has been granted.   There is therefore now no judgment in that case: See *Optical Co.* v. *Treat*,
72 Mich. 599.   It also appears from the record in the attachment suit that the recovery of the plaintiffs therein depends,
not upon the question whether John E. Treat was indebted to
the King Opitcal Company, but whether or not the indebtedness was due at the time the writ was issued, and that the
question to be thus determined is one of fact entirely, and
resting in parol.   It will therefore be seen that if we hold, in
the case at bar, that the existence of this judgment, at the
time of the trial, is conclusive in favor of the plaintiff in
this suit, and entitles him to an affirmance of the judgment
he has recovered, we bar the officer levying the attachment
from any claim upon the goods attached, and he must pay
their value to plaintiff.   The attachment process is nullified,
without regard to the question whether the plaintiff, or his
brother, John E. Treat, the attachment debtor, owned the
goods taken at the time they were seized under the attachment writ; and if, upon another trial of the attachment suit,
it shall be determined, as it may be, that the debt was due at
the time the writ was issued, there will be a failure of justice
as by the affirmance of the judgment in the case at bar the
lien of the King Optical Company upon these goods, and their

right to contest the validity of the sale from John E. Treat to his brother, will be forever lost, when in right such contest ought to be allowed.

We allude to this condition of the record in the two cases, and a result which may be probable, not for the purpose of adapting the law to the peculiar exigencies of this case, but for the purpose of showing the necessity of a careful examination to ascertain what the true rule of law is in cases of this kind, keeping in view the familiar principle that the law is seldom, and never ought to be, made the instrument of a real injustice, or to uphold a wrong.

We are satisfied, upon a careful examination of the subject, that the judgment was not admissible in evidence for the purpose of showing that there was no indebtedness due, at the time of the issuing of the attachment writ, from the defendant in attachment to the plaintiffs in attachment. The attachment was not dissolved immediately upon the entry of this judgment, and such judgment could not bar the right of the defendant in this suit to plead his writ, and contest the ownership of the property. The judgment entered in the attachment suit on the same day the verdict was rendered, and only three days before the verdict in the case at bar, was not, under our practice, competent evidence in this suit to show that there was no debt due from John E. Treat to the Julius King Optical Company at the time the attachment writ was issued. A judgment, under our practice, against the plaintiff in attachment which is appealed from, does not dissolve the attachment, but the lien of the writ continues until the final disposition of the case against him.

It may be said in answer to this that the judgment in this instance had not been appealed from at the time it was offered and received in evidence, and therefore it stood of record as a finality, and was admissible as such. The record does not show whether this is so or not; but, taking it for granted that no steps had yet been taken to take out a writ of error, yet we think the judgment was not in a condition to be introduced in evidence for the purpose of shutting out the defense. It was not usual, in the earlier practice, to enter judgment upon a verdict at once. The practice now very generally prevails of entering the final judgment at once upon the verdict of the jury or finding of the court, subject, however, to be set aside if a motion for new trial or in arrest be made and granted: 1 Green. Pr., 289. The circuit court rules, as they now stand, give two days in which to move for a new trial or in arrest of judgment. If a motion for new trial is made and denied, two days are also allowed after such denial in which to move in arrest: Rules 31, 32. If the judgment is entered upon the verdict before the two days in which these motions are permitted to be made by the rules, such judgment is provisional, and cannot be considered as final until the expiration of that time. It cannot be made the basis for any proceeding upon it as a final judgment before the two days, in any event: *Harvey* v. *McAdams*, 32 Mich. 472. And we think that it cannot be so used until four days after the rendition of the verdict. This is the time allowed by the rules, without reference to further time being granted by the court, for the entry of both motions in case the losing party may see fit to claim the privilege of first entering his motion for a new trial, and then to supplement it, if denied, by his motion in arrest. And four days must elapse under the circuit court rules before a default absolute can be entered, except in those circuits where a shorter time is permitted. And under the common-law practice a judgment entry was regarded as *nisi*, and not absolute until four days after verdict.

The judgment of the court below is reversed, with costs, and a new trial granted. ____

ATTACHMENT — RECITALS IN THE AFFIDAVIT. — Where, on the trial of a replevin case in favor of the vendee of an attachment debtor, the officer seeks to justify under the attachment proceedings, which have not matured into a judgment, the fact of the indebtedness charged in the affidavit for attachment at the time of the purchase must be established, and the affidavit is not conclusive proof of such fact: *Manning* v. *Bresnahan*, 63 Mich. 584.

ATTACHMENT. — Where attached property is ordered discharged upon the petition of a third party claiming it, under the Iowa code, the plaintiff, in order to prevent the operation of the order, must perfect his appeal within two days thereafter: *Ryan* v. *Heenan*, 76 Iowa, 589. After a judgment in the defendant's favor in a justice's court the attachment is discharged and released from the effect of the attachment writ, notwithstanding an appeal is taken from the judgment, and upon appeal judgment is rendered against the defendant, instead of in his favor: *Loveland* v. *Alvord etc. Mining Co.*, 76 Cal. 562.

ATTACHMENT — JUDGMENT AS EVIDENCE. — In an action on a delivery bond given for attached goods, a judgment rendered against the defendant in the attachment suit is admissible in evidence, even though it does not recite that the attachment was confirmed: *New Haven L. Co.* v. *Raymond*, 76 Iowa, 225.

CLIFTON v. JACKSON IRON COMPANY.

[74 MICHIGAN, 183.]

VENDOR AND VENDEE — RESERVATION IN CONTRACT OF SALE ANNULLED BY
DEED.—Where, under a contract for the sale of land, the vendor reserves
the timber thereon, and the right to remove it within a certain time, but
afterward, and within the time specified, conveys the land by warranty
deed, omitting the reservation, the timber passes to the vendee.

VENDOR AND VENDEE — CONTRACT OF SALE CANNOT CONTROL SUBSEQUENT
DEED. — A contract for the sale of land containing a reservation cannot
contradict or control a subsequent warranty deed not containing such
reservation, in the absence of mistake.

E. P. Royce, for the appellant.

F. O. Clark, for the plaintiff.

CAMPBELL, J.   Plaintiff sued defendant for trespass in cutting his timber in the winter of 1885–86.   The defense set up
was, that the timber, though on plaintiff's land, belonged to
defendant.   This claim was based on the fact that, on September 22, 1877, a little more than eight years before the
trespass defendant made a contract to sell the land trespassed
on to plaintiff, but with this reservation: "Reserving to itself,
its assigns and corporate successors, the ownership of pine,
butternut, hemlock, beech, maple, birch, iron-wood, or other
timber suitable for sawing into lumber, or for making into
fire-wood or charcoal, now on said tract of land, and also the
right to cut and remove any or all of said timber, at its option,
at any time within ten years from and after the date of these
presents."

There were some unimportant provisions, also, not now
material.   Plaintiff showed that on November 4, 1885, the
defendant conveyed to him the land in question, by full
warranty deed, and with no exceptions or reservations whatever.   The testimony of defendant's agent, who cut the land,
tended to prove that when the cutting was done the defendant's manager did not dispute plaintiff's title, but gave the
agent to understand that it belonged to plaintiff, but that some
arrangement would be made about it; that plaintiff was then
absent, and there was no conversation with him or his wife
on the subject.   The bill of exceptions certifies that no other
evidence was given concerning the right to cut timber.   Upon
these facts, the court held that the deed conveyed the right in
the timber to plaintiff, and that he owned it.

Had no deed been made, it is agreed that the reservation

would have prevailed. But a previous contract cannot contradict or control the operation of a deed. It was competent for defendant to relinquish any contract reservation, and a deed which grants and warrants without any reservation has that effect. We do not hold that if the deed were so made by some mistake within the cognizance of equity, the mistake might not be corrected. Neither need we consider whether, after such a deed, there might not be such dealings as to render such timber-cutting lawful, by license, express or implied. In this case there was no testimony tending to show that the deed was not supposed and intended to close up all the rights of the parties.

The judgment must be affirmed.

———

MERGER OF CONTRACT OF SALE IN DEED. — The rule is generally recognized, and almost universally applied, that all articles of agreement for the sale of land are merged in and extinguished by a subsequent deed thereof between the parties. Such a deed, when delivered and accepted, is deemed, in the absence of fraud and mistake, to express the final and entire contract between the parties, and any inconsistencies between the original contract of sale and the subsequent deed are, in general, to be explained by the latter: *Jones* v. *Wood,* 16 Pa. St. 25; *Carter* v. *Beck,* 40 Ala. 599; *Davenport* v. *Whisler,* 46 Iowa, 287; *Frederick* v. *Youngblood,* 19 Ala. 680; *Davis* v. *Clark,* 47 N. J. L. 338; *Houghtaling* v. *Davis,* 10 Johns. 297; *Williams* v. *Hathaway,* 19 Pick. 387; *Gibson* v. *Richart,* 83 Ind. 313–315. Mr. Rawle, in the fourth edition of his treatise on covenants for title, at page 566, lays down the rule thus: "But when the contract has been consummated by the execution and delivery of the deed, a different rule comes in. Being thus consummated, any inconsistencies between the terms of the contract and the terms of the deed are, in general, to be governed solely by the latter, into which the former are merged; and the purchaser's only right to relief from defects and encumbrances, whether at law or in equity, depends, in the absence of fraud, solely upon the covenants for title which he has received." Although the learned author, in thus stating the doctrine, speaks only of the purchaser, we apprehend that the rule applies with equal force to the vendor. In accordance with the propositions of law as above laid down, it has been decided that the acceptance by the purchaser of a deed from his vendor is a complete execution of the vendor's antecedent agreement to convey, and annuls it; and an action at law cannot afterwards be maintained upon the agreement on account of the deficiency of the land conveyed by the deed: *Carter* v. *Beck,* 40 Ala. 599. So where the vendor, by articles of agreement, covenanted to convey to his vendee a tract of land at a certain price per acre, and a deed was accordingly subsequently executed, whereupon the purchase-money was paid according to the number of acres expressed in the deed, parol evidence is not admissible to show that there was a mistake in the quantity expressed in the deed, nor will an action for money had and received, to recover the amount paid for the number of acres alleged to be deficient, be maintainable in such case: *Howes* v. *Barker,* 3 Johns. 506. An oral agreement by a vendor, made before the execution of the deed, to procure for the vendee an outstanding title to the land conveyed, is merged in the covenants of the deed: *Coleman*

v. *Hart,* 25 Ind. 256.   In *Bryan* v. *Swain,* 56 Cal. 616, the plaintiff agreed
to execute a good and sufficient deed conveying the title to certain lands, and
he subsequently made a deed which was accepted by the defendant as a full
performance of the contract.   At the time of the acceptance of the deed the
defendant knew that the title to part of the land was in the United States,
and the court determined that his rights depended on the deed, and not on
the prior agreement, the latter being merged and extinguished in the former.
A bond conditioned for the conveyance of a good and indefeasible title to a
certain tract of land, and for the quiet and peaceable enjoyment of the same
until the execution of the deed, is merged in a deed subsequently executed
by the vendor and accepted by the vendee, in pursuance of the agreement
and bond: *Shontz* v. *Brown,* 27 Pa. St. 123.

As between the vendor and the vendee of land, the acceptance of a deed,
and execution and delivery of bonds for the purchase-money, closes the
question upon the prior agreement; merges it in the conveyance, and precludes the parties from afterwards claiming, either, on the one side, an allowance for a deficiency in the quantity of land conveyed, or, on the other side,
payment for a surplus: *Cronister* v. *Cronister,* 1 Watts & S. 442.   Representations of freedom from encumbrance made during negotiations for the sale of
land, and without fraud, are merged in the deed of conveyance, by which
the sale is subsequently consummated: *Fritz* v. *McGill,* 31 Minn. 536.   The
rule as established by this line of authorities and adopted in the principal
case was lately applied in the case of a deed executed subsequently to a
lease made under similar circumstances.   In this case the lease was made for
a long period of years with certain conditions attached, and subsequently,
but before the expiration of such time, a deed of conveyance of the same
land was made by the same parties for a valuable consideration, reciting the
lease, but omitting the conditions, and it was adjudged by the court that
the lease merged in the conveyance, and that the grantees held the property
freed from the conditions in the lease: *St. Philip's Church* v. *Zion Presbyterian
Church,* 23 S. C. 297.

Although the above cases firmly establish the rule, that, in the absence of
fraud or mistake, the subsequent execution of a deed in pursuance of a prior
contract for the sale of land, merges in the former all conditions and covenants contained in the latter, whether recited therein or not, and makes the
presumption final and conclusive that the deed contains the entire contract
between the parties, still some cases may be found which maintain that such
deed is only *prima facie* evidence of the whole contract.   Thus in *Houghtaling* v. *Davis,* 10 Johns. 297, the court decided that the acceptance of a deed
pursuant to articles of agreement is *prima facie* evidence of the execution of
the entire contract, and the rights and remedies under it are determined by
the deed, and the original contract becomes null and void; and in *Seitzinger* v.
Weaver, 1 Rawle, it is said, in effect, that the presumption of law is, that the
acceptance of a deed in pursuance of articles of agreement is in satisfaction of all prior covenants; and although there may be cases where such
acceptance is but part execution of the contract, yet, to rebut the legal
presumption, the intention to the contrary must be clear and manifest.   Our
own view is in keeping with that adopted by the majority of the cases, that
the presumption is to be deemed conclusive, and that, as was said in *Jones* v.
Wood, 16 Pa. St. 25, "by such an acceptance the parties to the transaction are
absolutely precluded from looking behind the conveyance for subjects of
strife suggested by their prior negotiations and contracts; for the last step is
esteemed as undisputably expressive of their final conclusions."   The case of

Cox v. Henry, 32 Pa. St. 18, seems to be opposed to the reason and the rule of all the other cases above cited; for it is determined in that case that where a special covenant to indemnify the vendee against all costs, charges, and damages, on account of any action that may be brought against him by any claimant of the land, is entered into at the time that the contract of sale is made, and retained by the vendee after receiving the conveyance in which there is no similar covenant, such special covenant is not merged in or extinguished by such deed.

LAFFREY v. GRUMMOND.

[74 MICHIGAN, 186.]

COMMON CARRIERS — LIABILITY FOR LOSS OF BAGGAGE. — Where a common carrier by steamer has transported the baggage of a passenger, and placed it in the warehouse of another at the place of destination, such warehousing being within the contemplation of both parties, the carrier is not liable for its accidental loss by fire while so stored awaiting the arrival of the owner.

Edwin F. Conely, for the appellant.

Stewart and Galloway, for the plaintiff.

CAMPBELL, J. Plaintiff sued defendant as owner of a passenger steamer for baggage destroyed by fire on land in a warehouse. The facts, as practically established, were these: Plaintiff lives in Detroit, but was on July 29, 1887, at St. Ignace, in Mackinac County, and desired to return to Detroit, stopping at Alpena by the way. Defendant owned two boats, the Flora and the Atlantic, running from St. Ignace to Detroit, and continuously across lake Erie, — the Flora to Toledo and the Atlantic to Cleveland. Both stopped in due course at Alpena and Detroit. Plaintiff took passage on the Flora. She told the clerk she wanted to stop at Alpena for a short time to get an abstract, and it would require a stay of half an hour. She was told that the boat would stop about two hours, and she could take her ticket straight through to Detroit. The steamer was behind time, and she was advised, before reaching Alpena, to take a stop-over check, and come down on the next steamer, as she could not probably wait long enough. Plaintiff did so, and after finishing her business, found the boat gone. Before landing at Alpena, she asked the porter if she had better remove her baggage, and he told her if it was put off, and she returned in time, it would have to be put on again, and if she did not return, it would be all right, and would be taken care of. Her baggage had been checked through to Detroit. On reaching Detroit, the baggage was put in Ashley and Mitchell's warehouse, they being defendant's Detroit agents, and was burned, without fault, that night. The Atlantic arrived, in due course, four days later. The court below ruled that defendant was liable for the baggage absolutely, and not exempted by the fire.

There is some variance in the authorities concerning the circumstances which terminate a passenger carrier's liability, and they are not entirely harmonious in principle, and they are not uniform on different lines of carriage. The doctrine which holds passenger carriers liable for baggage has not always existed, and has grown up out of changes in methods of carriage. It has always differed somewhat, in regard to conditions of delivery, from the liability attaching to handling freight; and while it is very generally and properly spoken of as a duty arising from the relation of common carriage, it is also treated by various writers as in many respects analogous to the duties of innkeepers. It is certainly quite similar to the duty of innkeepers in the case of passenger steamers on long trips, the main business of which is boarding and lodging passengers, the carriage of whose baggage is purely incidental.

The extent of a carrier's liability concerning a passenger's baggage was discussed by an equally divided court in *McKee* v. *Owen*, 15 Mich. 115. In that case, a steamboat owner was sued for property claimed to have been stolen from a stateroom while the passenger was asleep. The court below gave judgment for defendant. The opinion of two judges for reversal placed the liability on the ground that the defendant was, as to the loss in question, in the position of an innkeeper. The opinion in favor of affirmance held he was not an innkeeper in fact, and that as passenger carrier he was not so broadly liable as an innkeeper, and only liable for articles placed in his custody. The case, therefore, decides nothing beyond the fact that the liability for baggage is not larger than that of an innkeeper, although in some respects analogous.

It was subsequently held by this court that an innkeeper is not liable for loss by accidental fire: *Cutler* v. *Bonney*, 30 Mich. 259; 18 Am. Rep. 127. The acts of Congress do not hold a carrier by water liable for such a fire: *Americau Transportation Co.* v. *Moore*, 5 Mich. 368, affirmed by the supreme court of the United States in 24 How. 1. In order to hold defendant here, it must be held that his liability exceeds that of an innkeeper. It must also be held that a liability that did not exist while the baggage was in transit on board the steamer was created when the transit ceased, and the baggage was put into warehouse. This seems to be unreasonable.

When Mrs. Laffrey arranged, as she did arrange, to have her baggage forwarded, she had a right to expect it would not be neglected, and would be properly cared for; but she was also bound to expect that it would be dealt with in the usual way, and would be left in Detroit, and not kept on board the steamer, which had a further destination. She held the check for it, which prevented delivery to any one else, and she was to come down on another boat some days later. The baggage would necessarily be landed and cared for in a warehouse, which in this instance was not the warehouse of defendant, but was owned by other parties, who acted as local agents, as is usual for steamboats. The baggage was subject to delivery on call and presentation of the check; but plaintiff expected delay, and that it must be some days, at least, before it would be called for, and must be stored meanwhile in some way.

The reasonable view seems to us to be that the warehousing at the termination of the transit was within the contemplation of both parties; and it also seems to us that it would be irrational to create a constructive relation of carriage, after the real carriage terminated, which should involve a larger responsibility than the actual carriage, and to hold defendant for a loss by fire in a warehouse which is not chargeable to a warehouseman as such, and would not have been chargeable to defendant if it happened on board. We can get no particular help from comparing precedents, but we think there is no rule which under our own decisions should create an exceptional liability against defendant.

The judgment should be reversed, with costs, and a new trial granted. ____

LIABILITY OF CARRIERS FOR LOSS OF BAGGAGE: See *Ahlbeck* v. *St. Paul etc. R'y Co.*, 39 Minn. 424; 12 Am. St. Rep. 661, and notes. A carrier is liable for a passenger's baggage delivered to and received by it for transportation, not for storage, although for the convenience of the carrier the passenger may consent to some delay in the transportation: *Shaw* v. *Northern Pac. R. R. Co.*, 40 Minn. 144. As to what properly constitutes baggage, see *Connolly* v. *Warren*, 106 Mass. 146; 8 Am. Rep. 300, and particularly note 302–304.

CARRIERS. — Delivery of goods at the point of destination, in good condition, is necessary to relieve the carrier from liability as such; and if the consignee, after due notice, refuses or neglects to receive them, the carrier may relieve itself from liability by placing them in a warehouse for the assignee: *Scheu* v. *Benedict*, 116 N. Y. 510; 15 Am. St. Rep. 426, and note.

KNOWLES *v.* MULDER.

[74 MICHIGAN, 202.]

VICIOUS ANIMALS — DUTY OF OWNER WITH NOTICE OF VICIOUSNESS OF. — When it appears that a domestic animal is vicious, and has a propensity to do mischief, of which facts the owner or keeper has notice, either express or implied, the law imposes the duty upon him of keeping such animal secure, from which duty a liability arises in favor of any person who, without fault on his part, is injured by it, either in person or property, through the negligence of such owner or keeper.

VICIOUS ANIMALS — NOTICE OF VICIOUSNESS. — The owner of a domestic animal may be chargeable with notice of its viciousness through his negligence to take notice of its vicious habits.

VICIOUS ANIMALS — NOTICE OF VICIOUSNESS. — If a person has a dog in his possession for a considerable length of time, and such dog has all that time been in the habit of rushing into the highway in front of the owner's residence, and of barking at, chasing, worrying, or attacking passing teams in a ferocious manner, a question is presented to the jury to find whether the owner was aware of such habit, or if not, if he was negligent in not knowing it, and the facts may be such that it may well be found that he ought to have known it, and therefrom imply notice to him. The length of time such vicious habit is shown to have existed has an important bearing upon whether notice or knowledge of such habit may be inferred or imputed to the owner.

CONTRIBUTORY NEGLIGENCE — CHARGE RELATING TO, WHEN NEED NOT BE REPEATED. — In a case involving contributory negligence, where the charge on that question as given is clear and unambiguous, it is unnecessary to repeat it when stating the elements which plaintiff must prove to make out his case; and if counsel are apprehensive that the jury has lost sight of the charge as to contributory negligence, the attention of the court should be called to it before the case is finally submitted.

Clink and Jones, for the appellant.

De Long and O'Hara, for the plaintiff.

CHAMPLIN, J.   The parties to this suit are farmers and neighbors, living on adjoining sections of land, one in the township of Ravenna, and the other in the township of Moorland, in Muskegon County.   The defendant is the owner of a dog which had been in his possession upwards of two years. On August 7, 1887, the plaintiff was riding in a buggy drawn by one horse, past defendant's house, in the public highway. His hired man was sitting in the seat with him, and each was leading a colt by the halter behind the buggy.   A third colt was following loose behind them.   The colts were two years old, had been halter-broken, and were gentle.   Plaintiff claims that, as he was driving past defendant's house on a slow trot, defendant's dog came running out into the highway, and barked and attacked the colts, frightening them, and causing them to jump against his buggy; one of them jumping upon him, and throwing him out of and under the buggy, and seriously injuring him.

This suit is brought to recover damages for such injury. Defendant pleaded the general issue, and a trial was had, and the jury returned a verdict for the plaintiff. Objection is made to the sufficiency of the declaration. If the defendant did not deem it sufficient, he should have demurred. It discloses a cause of action, and will be considered sufficient after verdict.

It is also claimed that there was no testimony showing, or tending to show, that defendant knew, or had cause to believe, that his dog was vicious, and in the habit of attacking teams or passers-by in the highway. This objection is taken for the first time in this court. It is inconsistent with defendant's third request to charge, which was as follows: "If the injury of plaintiff was caused by one of defendant's dogs running into the highway, and biting or attacking the plaintiff's colts, or either or any of them, still the plaintiff cannot recover, unless you further find that defendant knew, or should have known, that this same dog was in the habit of so running out into the highway when people were passing, and barking at or attacking them, and had not used proper diligence to restrain him,"—and which was substantially given by the court in the following language: "If the injury to the plaintiff was caused by one of the defendant's dogs running into the highway, and biting or attacking the plaintiff's colts, or either or any of them, still plaintiff cannot recover, unless you further find that the defendant knew, or ought to have known, that this same dog was in the habit of so running out into the highway when people were passing, and barking at or attacking them, and did not use proper diligence in restraining him."

We have looked into the record, and we cannot say that there was no evidence tending to prove knowledge on the part of defendant of the vicious propensity of this dog to run out into the street, and bark at and attack teams of those traveling by. Numerous instances of the kind were testified to by witnesses, and there was testimony from which the jury were warranted in drawing the inference that defendant knew of this vicious habit of the dog. The length of time the defendant had owned the dog, his habit of running out into the street, giving chase to and barking at passers-by in vehicles, before the occurrence complained of, the conversation as testified to by plaintiff which he had with defendant, when he told him his dog was to blame for the injury, and defendant's remark that it must have been the little dog, for the big one did not run out into the street, and the further fact that it was the smaller of the two dogs owned by the defendant which, as is claimed, did the mischief, were all proper to be considered and weighed by the jury, and had, if believed, some tendency to show knowledge of the vicious habit charged against the dog.

The defendant's counsel submitted three questions to the jury, which were answered by them, as follows —

"1. Was the injury that plaintiff claims to have sustained caused by either of defendant's dogs?" to which the jury answered, "Yes."

"2. Were either of defendant's dogs out in the highway at the time plaintiff was injured?" to which the jury answered, "Yes."

"3. Have either of defendant's dogs been out in the highway prior to the time the plaintiff was injured?" The jury answered, "Yes."

And, in addition to a general verdict for the plaintiff, the jury returned therewith special findings of fact: —

1. That defendant's dog was in the habit of going out into the highway when teams were passing.

2. That defendant's dog was in the highway opposite the defendant's house when the accident happened.

3. That the defendant knew, or ought to have known, that his dog was in the habit of going into the highway to bark when teams were passing.

This special finding was consistent, so far as it went, with the general verdict for the plaintiff.

When it appears that a domestic animal is vicious, and has a propensity to do mischief, of which facts the owner or keeper has notice, either express or implied, the law imposes the duty upon such owner or keeper of keeping such animal secure, from which duty a liability arises in favor of any person who without his fault is injured by it, either in person or property. The principle has its foundation in the maxim that society imposes the duty upon every one so to keep and use his own property as not to wrong and injure others. But in case of domestic animals whose dispositions are universally regarded as peaceable, no action can be maintained at common law

without proof of the *scienter*. If the owner or keeper has notice or knowledge of the vicious disposition of the animal, and
does not secure it so as to restrain it from doing injury to
others, he is negligent in the performance of his duty, for
which negligence he is responsible if injury results therefrom
to others. He may be chargeable with notice through his own
negligence to take note of the vicious habits of his domestic
animal. If a person has a dog in his possession for a considerable length of time, and such dog has all that time been in
the habit of rushing into the highway in front of the owner's
residence, and of barking at, chasing, worrying, or attacking
passing teams in a ferocious manner, a question is presented
to the jury to find whether the owner was aware of such habit,
or, if not, whether he was negligent in not knowing it. The
facts may be such that they may well find that he ought to
have known it, and so from such facts imply notice to him.
The length of time such vicious habit is shown to have existed
has an important bearing upon the question whether notice or
knowledge of such habit may be inferred and imputed to the
owner.

The defendant also claims that the plaintiff ought to be
barred from a recovery in this case on account of his own negligence, which contributed to the result. The contention is,
that it was a careless and negligent act for the plaintiff to
attempt to travel along a public highway, riding in a buggy,
driving a horse, and leading two colts behind by the halter, and
permitting another to follow, over which he had no control; that
his situation while leading the colts was such that he would
have no adequate control over them if from accident, or any
cause, they should become suddenly frightened; that, under
the circumstances, that happened which might have been expected to happen in case the colts took fright from any cause.
Based upon this position, the defendant's counsel framed two
requests to the court to instruct the jury, as follows:—

"1. If you find that plaintiff was guilty of negligence in
passing along the highway in front of defendant's residence,
leading two colts, and with another colt following loose, and
that this fact contributed to the injury which plaintiff claims
to have sustained, the plaintiff cannot recover.

"2. If you find that plaintiff was injured by one of the colts
he was leading, and that his colts commenced playing, or
jumped upon plaintiff's buggy, in consequence of the playing
of defendant's colts, which were in a field near the road, and

not on account of the running out or barking of either of defendant's dogs, then plaintiff cannot recover."

The instructions were given by the court in the language of the requests, and it must be presumed that the jury found that the plaintiff was without fault that contributed to the injury. The defendant's counsel criticise the charge of the court, because, when stating to the jury the elements that went to make up the plaintiff's cause of action, the court did not again mention contributory negligence as a fact which would prevent a recovery, and urge that the jury were thereby misled. We cannot reach this conclusion. The charge as to contributory negligence was plain and unambiguous, and it was unnecessary to repeat it when stating the elements which plaintiff was bound to prove to make out a case. If defendant's counsel were apprehensive that the jury had lost sight of the charge as to contributory negligence, they should have called the attention of the court to it before the case was finally committed to their charge.

The judgment of the circuit court will be affirmed.

VICIOUS ANIMALS — DOGS. — The owner of a vicious dog, who, knowing his disposition, keeps him negligently, is responsible for injuries inflicted by him: *Hinckley* v. *Emerson*, 4 Cow. 351; 15 Am. Dec. 383; *Pickering* v. *Orange*, 1 Scam. 492; 32 Am. Dec. 35; *Coggswell* v. *Baldwin*, 15 Vt. 404; 40 Am. Dec. 686; *Marsh* v. *Jones*, 21 Vt. 378; 52 Am. Dec. 67; *Laverone* v. *Mangianti*, 41 Cal. 138; 10 Am. Rep. 269; *Meibus* v. *Dodge*, 38 Wis. 300; 20 Am. Rep. 6; *Moulton* v. *Scarborough*, 71 Me. 267; 36 Am. Rep. 308; *Glidden* v. *Moore*, 14 Neb. 84; 45 Am. Rep. 98. The owner of a vicious dog keeps him at his own risk, and is, without regard to care and negligence, an insurer against any harm that he might reasonably expect to ensue from such dog and his viciousness: *McCaskell* v. *Elliot*, 5 Stroh. 196; 53 Am. Dec. 706; *Woolf* v. *Chalker*, 31 Conn. 121; 81 Am. Dec. 175. As to the liability of the owner of a dog for injuries sustained from him, see *Godeau* v. *Blood*, 52 Vt. 251; 36 Am. Rep. 751, and particularly note 752, 753. For protection against trespassers, one may ordinarily keep defensive animals: *Loomis* v. *Terry*, 17 Wend. 496; 31 Am. Dec. 306; but regard must be had to human life and human safety: Id.; consequently it is no defense to an action for injury that plaintiff was a trespasser when bitten by defendant's dog, where the owner knew the vicious propensities of the dog, and did not keep him restrained: *Sherfey* v. *Bartley*, 4 Sneed, 58; 67 Am. Dec. 597; *Woolf* v. *Chalker*, 31 Conn. 121; 81 Am. Dec. 175.

In *Burnham* v. *Strother*, 66 Mich. 519, it was decided that one who treats a dog as living at his house, and undertakes to control his actions, is that dog's keeper within the meaning of the Michigan statute, and as such keeper becomes responsible for injuries inflicted upon travelers by the dog.

In *Hathaway* v. *Tinkham*, 148 Mass. 85, it was decided that, under the Massachusetts statute, the owner or keeper of a dog is liable for injuries done by it to any person in the exercise of due care, even though the injury is inflicted in play, without any vicious intent on the part of the dog. And in *Brice* v. *Bauer*, 108 N. Y. 428, 2 Am. St. Rep. 455, it was held that one who keeps a dog must hold him under inspection and observation, and is answerable in damages to one who may be injured by the dog on his own premises, where the animal escaped from his keeper's control.

VICIOUS ANIMALS —SCIENTER — NOTICE TO OWNER. — Knowledge of the owner that his animal was vicious must be alleged and proved in suits for injuries by domestic animals, it they were rightfully in the place where the mischief was done: *Van Leuven* v. *Lyke*, 1 N. Y. 515; 49 Am. Dec. 346; *Decker* v. *Gammon*, 44 Me. 322; 69 Am. Dec. 99; *Smith* v. *Donohue*, 49 N. J. L. 548; 60 Am. Rep. 652. And no action will lie at common law for the first mischief committed by a dog without proving a *scienter: Woolf* v. *Chalker*, 31 Conn. 121; 81 Am. Dec. 175. But in actions against owners of domestic animals, wrongfully in the place where they do mischief, it is not necessary to allege and prove any knowledge on the part of the owner that such animal had previously been vicious: *Decker* v. *Gammon, supra; Angus* v. *Radin*, 5 N. J. L. 815; 8 Am. Dec. 626; *Goodman* v. *Gay*, 15 Pa. St. 188; 53 Am. Dec. 589; *Chunot* v. *Larson*, 43 Wis. 536; 28 Am. Rep. 567. In *Newton* v. *Gordon*, 72 Mich. 642, it was held that, under the Michigan statute, to recover damages for injuries sustained from an assault by a vicious dog, plaintiff need not allege knowledge of the owner that such dog was accustomed to do such mischief.

The owner of an animal not naturally vicious is not liable for injury done by it, unless it be affirmatively shown not only that it was vicious, but that the owner had knowledge of the fact, or that he was so negligently handled by the owner as to cause the injury: *Finney* v. *Curtis*, 78 Cal. 498. But the owner of a dangerous animal is liable for any damage caused by the same, after notice of one instance of similar behavior: *Kittridge* v. *Elliott*, 16 N. H. 77; 41 Am. Dec. 717; *Woolf* v. *Chalker, supra*. Yet the man who is bitten by a dog may recover of the owner by proving that the dog was vicious, and that the owner knew it, without showing that it had ever before bitten any one: *Rider* v. *White*, 65 N. Y. 54; 22 Am. Rep. 600; *Godeau* v. *Blood, supra*. So the owner of a large watch-dog, kept chained by day and loosed at night, is liable to one, without further proof of *scienter*, who was bitten while passing the premises on the highway at night: *Montgomery* v. *Koester*, 35 La. Ann. 1091; 48 Am. Rep. 253; *Goode* v. *Martin*, 57 Md. 606; 40 Am. Rep. 448. And one may recover for an injury from a bite of a dog upon showing the owner's knowledge of its propensity to bite, whether in play or anger: *Evans* v. *McDermott*, 49 N. J. L. 163; 60 Am. Rep. 602, and note 605, 606; compare *Hathawag* v. *Tinkham, supra*.

Knowledge of a servant or agent that a dog in his charge is vicious or dangerous is equivalent to knowledge of such fact by the principal: *Brice* v. *Bauer*, 108 N. Y. 428; 2 Am. St. Rep. 454, and note; but a servant's knowledge of the vicious character of a dog accustomed to follow him about in his master's business, but not put in his care and charge by the master, is not imputable to the master: *Twigg* v. *Ryland*, 62 Md. 380; 50 Am. Rep. 226.

Whatever is calculated to establish the dangerous propensity of an animal in a sufficient degree, and tends to show the owner's knowledge of the same, is conformable to precedent and sufficient after verdict: *McCaskell* v. *Elliot*, 5 Stroh. 196; 53 Am. Dec. 706; thus evidence of previous and of subsequent viciousness is competent: *Kennon* v. *Gilmer*, 5 Mont. 257; 51 Am. Rep. 45; or evidence tending to prove that the dog had killed or worried sheep before: *East Kingston* v. *Towle*, 48 N. H. 57; 2 Am. Rep. 174. If a dog is kept as a watch-dog, the very purpose for which he is kept is notice to his master that he is dangerous: *Brice* v. *Bauer*, 108 N. Y. 428; 2 Am. St. Rep. 454.

TEN EYCK v. PONTIAC, OXFORD, AND PORT AUSTIN RAILROAD COMPANY.

[74 MICHIGAN, 226.]

CORPORATIONS — COMPENSATION OF DIRECTOR FOR SERVICES — EVIDENCE.—
In an action by a director to recover compensation for services rendered
the corporation in aiding the construction of a railroad, the corporation
cannot show that an investment company, which is not a party to the
suit, built the road, and is the owner in fact of all the stock, property,
and franchises, and that the corporation exists only in name for the purposes of maintaining the franchises of a corporation for the investment
company's benefit, and that the claim set up is unjust and inequitable as
to such company, and if established would seriously affect its rights and
property.

CORPORATIONS — PROOF OF PROCEEDINGS OF DIRECTORS. — What is resolved
upon at a meeting of a board of directors of a private corporation may be
shown by the record of the proceedings of the board, if one is kept and
the proceedings entered, but if a record is not kept, or the proceedings
are not recorded, parol evidence is admissible to show what was resolved
upon, and by what vote it was carried.

CORPORATIONS — DUTY OF DIRECTORS. — The directors of a corporation are
its agents, with the entire management of the corporate affairs committed
to their charge, upon the trust and confidence that they shall be cared
for and managed within the limits of the powers conferred by law upon
the corporation, for the common benefit of the stockholders.

CORPORATIONS — DUTIES OF DIRECTORS. — The directors of a corporation are
required to act in the utmost good faith, and in accepting the office they
impliedly undertake to give to the enterprise the benefit of their best
care and judgment, and to exercise the power conferred solely in the interest of the corporation. They have no right to represent the corporation in any transaction in which they are personally interested, in
obtaining an advantage at the expense of the corporation.

CORPORATIONS — DIRECTOR MAY CONTRACT WITH CORPORATION. — A director may enter into a valid contract with the corporation of which he
is agent, when the corporation is represented in the transaction by a
majority of the board of directors.

CORPORATIONS — WHEN BOUND BY ACTION OF BOARD OF DIRECTORS. — It
is not necessary to the binding action of a board of directors of a corporation that each member should take part in its deliberations. A
majority of the members of the board constitute a quorum for the transaction of business, and a majority of the quorum has power to bind the
corporation by its vote, and in many cases there is no impropriety in a
member of the board entering into contract relations with the corporation represented by the other directors.

CORPORATIONS — CONTRACTS WITH AGENTS. — Contracts entered into between
agents of a corporation occupying positions of trust and confidence, and
the corporation, will always be scrutinized with jealous care by the courts,
to see that no advantage is taken of the corporation or the rights and interests of the stockholders jeopardized; but such contracts fairly entered
into and honestly executed, where no one is defrauded or overreached,
are valid.

CORPORATIONS — CONTRACT BETWEEN AND DIRECTORS. — Where a corporation has contracted with a director for his services as an attorney, and also in procuring aid notes and rights of way, and working up an interest in the construction of a railroad in the communities through which it is projected, in order to secure aid in its construction by donations and subscriptions, and also in enlisting capitalists in the enterprise, these services are valuable to the corporation, not embraced in the ordinary duties of a director, and are such as to which the corporation has a right to agree as to the compensation to be paid, and if the director's services were engaged for such purposes and performed, there arises an implied agreement to pay for such services what they are reasonably worth, so far as they have not been fixed by resolution of the board of directors.

CORPORATIONS — STOCKHOLDERS WILL NOT BE HEARD TO COMPLAIN of their own acts as directors.

A. C. Baldwin, for the appellant.

Griffin, Warner, Hunt, and Berry, for the plaintiff.

CHAMPLIN, J. The plaintiff is, and for many years past has been, an attorney at law residing in the city of Pontiac, and he brought this action against defendant to recover for expenses paid and services performed, as agent and attorney of the defendant company, in securing the right of way for its road, and for obtaining aid notes, raising money, securing loans, and making contracts for the construction of its road, covering a period from September, 1881, to November, 1883·

The project, originally, was to construct a railroad from Oxford to Port Austin, a distance of eighty-four miles, and a corporation was formed for that purpose on July 23, 1879, with a capital of $672,000, and seven directors. Each director subscribed to 120 shares of $100 each, and plaintiff was one of the directors. Nothing was done under this organization. Two days later the stockholders signed amended articles of association, by which they extended the southern terminus from Oxford to the city of Pontiac, and changed the name of the corporation to the Pontiac, Oxford, and Port Austin Railroad Company. The capital stock was increased to $800,000, and the number of directors to eight. The articles were again amended, on September 24, 1881, by increasing the capital stock to $1,500,000, and changing the terminus so as to extend it from Pontiac to Caseville.

The plaintiff continued a stockholder and director in the corporation until 1884. On December 5, 1881, plaintiff was re-elected attorney for defendant company. Previous to this, and in the same year, he was employed by the board of directors to go to New York to negotiate a loan and obtain a contract for the construction of the road. These services were successfully performed, and a contract was entered into between defendant and an investment company, bearing date November 12, 1881. On December 20, 1881, the following resolution was passed by the board of directors:—

"At a meeting of the board of directors, held at Oxford, in the county of Oakland, state of Michigan, on December 20, A. D. 1881, pursuant to call of the president, the following proceedings were had, a full quorum being present: On motion, J. Ten Eyck was duly appointed to attend to the obtaining of right of way along the whole line, and to collect in the notes given along the line, in aid of the railroad. The meeting then adjourned. JUNIUS TEN EYCK, Secretary."

The plaintiff's counsel was permitted to prove, by oral testimony of the directors, that all of the eight directors were present at the meeting, and voted for the motion, excepting himself. Plaintiff also offered in evidence, from the records kept by the corporation, the following resolution, passed at a meeting of the board of directors on May 29, 1882, viz.: "Resolved, that the sum of five thousand dollars per year be paid J. Ten Eyck for his services as attorney and solicitor of this company for and during the two years last passed."

The record shows a quorum present. The plaintiff was also permitted to show by parol that all of the directors were present at the meeting, and each, excepting himself, voted for the resolution. The claims for expenses paid out in the services of defendant were not seriously disputed or resisted at the trial. Testimony was given, showing that nearly the entire time of plaintiff was consumed in the service of the company, and his practice as a lawyer was almost entirely given up, clients turned away, and that his services for the company were worth five thousand dollars annually. The jury returned a verdict for the plaintiff.

The errors complained of may all be summarized under three heads:—

1. The court erred in excluding from the jury all testimony relative to the investment company, and the rights acquired and now held by them from the railroad company.

2. In permitting parol evidence to be given of the action of the board of directors, in the absence of any record of such action, and in adding to what was shown by the record as to what number of directors were at the meetings of the board, and that they all voted for the motion and resolution, except Ten Eyck, who did not vote.

3. That being a director of the company, he could not be employed and paid for performing services for the company as attorney or otherwise, and especially would such action be illegal when applied to services already performed.

As to the first point, the error is based upon the fact, which defendant desired to show, that the investment company that built the road are the owners in fact of all the stock, property, and franchises of the Pontiac, Oxford, and Port Austin Railroad Company, and the corporation exists only in name for the purpose of maintaining the franchises of a corporation for the investment company's benefit, and that the claim set up is unjust and inequitable as to such investment company, and, if established, would seriously affect their rights and property. We think the court did not err in excluding this testimony. The investment company is not a party to this suit, and the issues sought to be raised cannot be properly tried in this action. If plaintiff's position as a director, and what he has done and represented to the investment company, estop him from asserting any claim against the corporation, such estoppel cannot be set up as a defense in an action at law against the corporation by it or the investment company.

No notice is taken by the brief of the plaintiff of the second point, and merely a passing notice in the brief of defendant, and no authority is cited in support of the proposition. What is resolved upon at a meeting of a board of directors of a private corporation may be proven by the record of the proceedings of the board, if one is kept, and the proceedings entered, but if a record is not kept, or the proceedings are not recorded, parol evidence is admissible to show what was resolved upon, and by what vote it was carried: *Kalamazoo Novelty Works* v. *Macalister*, 40 Mich. 84. The rule is different with respect to municipal corporations, when the law requires records of their official action to be kept: *Stevenson* v. *Bay City*, 26 Mich. 44; *Hall* v. *People*, 21 Mich. 456.

The third point relied upon is one upon which there is an apparent conflict of authority. .The directors of a corporation are its agents. The entire management of corporate affairs is committed to their charge, upon the trust and confidence that they shall be cared for and managed within the limits of the powers conferred by law upon the corporation, and for the common benefit of the stockholders. They are required to act in the utmost good faith, and in accepting the office they impliedly undertake to give to the enterprise the benefit of their best care and judgment, and exercise the powers conferred solely in the interest of the corporation. They have no right to represent the corporation in any transaction in which they are personally interested, in obtaining an advantage at the expense of the company they represent: 1 Morawetz on Private Corporations, sec. 517. But the rule is not an arbitrary one. It is founded on reason, and should not be applied without regard to the circumstances of the case. Although it has been held by some courts that a director cannot enter into a valid contract with the corporation of which he is agent, although the corporation is represented in the transaction by a majority of the board, yet the decided weight of authority and of reason supports the doctrine that such a contract would be valid: 1 Morawetz on Private Corporations, sec. 527, and cases cited in note 3.

It is not necessary to the binding action of a board of directors that each member should take part in its deliberations. The general rule is, that a majority of the members of the board constitute a quorum for the transaction of business, and a majority of the quorum have power to bind the corporation by their vote. It does not necessarily follow that there is impropriety in a member of the board entering into contract relations with the corporation represented by the other members of the board. There may be cases where there may be manifest propriety in doing so. Suppose the line of a railroad is laid across land owned by one of the directors, may he not enter into a contract to sell a right of way to the corporation? Suppose a director is possessed of superior knowledge, skill, or ability to serve the corporation in matters not strictly within the line of his duty as a director, may it not contract with him for his services?

It is true that contracts entered into between agents of the corporation, occupying positions of trust and confidence, and a corporation will always be scrutinized with jealous care by courts, to see that no advantage is taken of the corporation, or the rights and interests of its stockholders jeopardized; but it cannot be said that contracts fairly entered into, and honestly executed, where no one is defrauded or overreached, are invalid. In this case, the circumstances are free from suspicion. The corporation contracted with him for his services as attorney, and also in procuring aid notes, rights of way, and working up an interest in the construction of the road in the communities through which it was projected, in order to ·

secure aid in its construction by donations and subscriptions, and also in enlisting capitalists in the enterprise. These were services which were not embraced in the ordinary duties of a director of the company. They were valuable to the corporation, and were such as to which they had a right to agree upon the compensation to be paid; and if his services were engaged for the above purposes, and they were performed, there arose an implied agreement that they should pay what such services were reasonably worth, and this the plaintiff proved upon the trial.

The principle laid down in the line of authorities cited by the learned counsel for defendant has not been followed in this state; but the contrary doctrine was asserted in *Niles* v. *Muzzy*, 33 Mich. 61, 20 Am. Rep. 670, which is in consonance with the views above expressed. Had the board of directors engaged any other person to perform the services rendered by the plaintiff, no question could have been made about their liability to pay therefor. The services were performed by the plaintiff at the request of the board of directors; and the law implies a promise to pay what they are reasonably worth, so far as they have not been fixed by the resolution of the board: *Detroit* v. *Redfield*, 19 Mich. 383. The plaintiff introduced testimony tending to show that his services were reasonably worth at the rate of five thousand dollars a year for the entire time claimed by him.

There is another consideration which leads to the same conclusion in this case. During the time for which plaintiff claims pay for services, the members of the board of directors were the only stockholders in the corporation. The resolution and motion above referred to as appearing in the records of the corporation had not only the sanction of the board of directors, but of each individual stockholder of the corporation. They could not be heard to complain as stockholders of their own action as directors, and none of them have complained.

We are all of opinion that there is no error in the record, and that the judgment should be affirmed.

CORPORATIONS — DUTIES OF DIRECTORS. — The directors of a corporation are trustees for the corporation, and hold a fiduciary relation to it. They cannot take part in the passage of resolutions by the board when they are personally interested therein: *Pearson* v. *Concord R. R. Corporation*, 62 N. H. 537; 13 Am. St. Rep, 590; *Smith* v. *Los Angeles etc. Ass'n*, 78 Cal. 289; 12 Am. St. Rep. 53, and note; and resolutions passed by the vote of interested directors of a corporation, making allowances in their own favor, are voidable at the election of the corporation, or at the election of a minority of the stockholders, if the corporation refuses to avoid them, no matter whether they were fair and honest or not: *Graves* v. *Mining Co.*, 81 Cal. 304.

CORPORATIONS. — As to the duties and liabilities of the directors of a corporation generally, see extended note to *Hodges* v. *New England Screw Co.*, 53 Am. Dec. 637–651.

The directors of a corporation are not individually liable to its creditors upon the ground of mismanagement, and of having contracted indebtedness in excess of the limit prescribed by the charter, unless they are made liable by provisions to that effect in the articles of incorporation, or by statute: *Frost Mfg. Co.* v. *Foster*, 76 Iowa, 535; but in the case of *National Bank* v. *Texas etc. Co*, 74 Tex. 422, it was decided that where the directors of a corporation, which has purchased the franchises and property of another corporation, misapply the assets of the latter, leaving debts unpaid, they are personally responsible to the creditors to the extent of the assets received and misapplied.

CORPORATIONS — CONTRACTS WITH DIRECTORS. — As to the power of corporations to enter into contracts with their directors, see note to *Garrett* v. *Burlington Plow Co.*, 59 Am. Rep. 466–471, in which section 517 of Morawetz on Private Corporations is cited to the effect that " the directors of a corporation have no power to bind the company to any contract made with themselves personally "; also note to *Beach* v. *Miller*, 130 Ill. 162; 17 Am. St. Rep.

CORPORATION, WHEN BOUND BY THE ACTS OF ITS DIRECTORS. — A corporation is a legal entity, distinct from the persons who compose it, and is not affected by the personal rights, obligations, or transactions of its individual members: *Moore* v. *Towers*, 87 Ala. 206; 13 Am. St. Rep. 23. The directors of a corporation, as such, can act in behalf of the corporation only as a board, their power being joint, not several: *Buttrick* v. *Nashua etc. R. R. Co.*, 62 N. H. 413; 13 Am. St. Rep. 578; and the corporate powers can only be exercised by the board of directors when a majority of them are duly assembled and acting as a board under the provisions of law: *Gashwiler* v. *Willis*, 33 Cal. 11; 91 Am. Dec. 607, and note; *Regents* v. *Williams*, 9 Gill & J. 365; 31 Am. Dec. 72; *Smith* v. *Los Angeles etc. Ass'n*, 78 Cal. 289; 12 Am. St. Rep. 53, and note.

In *Alta Silver Mining Co.* v. *Alta Placer Mining Co.*, 78 Cal. 629, it was held that neither the president, nor the secretary, nor any other person, has authority to execute a mortgage of the corporate property in the absence of a resolution of the board of directors, passed when such board is duly assembled.

COMPENSATION OF DIRECTORS OF A CORPORATION. — Officers of a corporation cannot recover on *quantum meruit* for services rendered to the corporation as such officers, in the absence of an express contract for compensation: *Kilpatrick* v. *Penrose etc. Co.*, 49 Pa. St. 118; 88 Am. Dec. 497, and cases cited in note; *Citizens' Nat. Bank* v. *Elliott*, 55 Iowa, 104; 39 Am. Rep. 167, and cases cited in note. But in *New Orleans etc. Packet Co.* v. *Brown*, 36 La. Ann. 138, 51 Am. Rep. 5, it was decided that, in the absence of a contract, the managing director of a steamboat company, acting as captain of one of the company's boats, was entitled to compensation for laborious and responsible services, according to custom and value, where he had retained such amount from the company's funds, and his acts had been acquiesced in by the directors. And so in *Mayor etc. of Niles* v. *Muzzy*, 33 Mich. 61, 20 Am. Rep. 670, it was held the mayor of a city, who was a lawyer by profession, might recover the value of his legal services, when he had, without collusion or fraud, been employed under a resolution of the common council to appear for and defend the city in certain litigations. And in *Deane* v. *Hodge*, 35 Minn. 146, 59 Am. Rep. 321, where a corporation appropriated and used a certain patent owned by one of its directors and officers, it was held that such director was not precluded from recovering compensation upon an implied contract.

The directors of a corporation may maintain an action against the corporation for the collection of their demands against it, and to subject property mortgaged to secure their demands; and neither the judgment nor the purchase of the property under it will be fraudulent: *McMurtry* v. *Montgomery Masonic Temple Co.*, 86 Ky. 206.

CORPORATIONS — RECORDS MADE BY OFFICERS OF A CORPORATION are presumed to be true: *Chase* v. *Tuttle*, 55 Conn. 455; 3 Am. St. Rep. 64; compare *State* v. *Kupferle*, 44 Mo. 154; 100 Am. Dec. 265, and note; citing *Chouteau Ins. Co.* v. *Holmes*, 68 Mo. 602. In *Baker* v. *Ducker*, 79 Cal. 366, it was decided that where it appeared that the original constitution and by-laws of a certain church were written by the minister of such church in its record-book, and that the people of the church had acted upon them as their by-laws and constitution, the record was admissible, without further proof of their adoption by the people.

PAROL EVIDENCE — CORPORATION RECORDS. — As to the admissibility of parol evidence to contradict or vary the records of a public corporation, see *Everts* v. *District Township of Rose Grove*, 77 Iowa, 37; 14 Am. St. Rep. 264, and notes. As to the conclusiveness of town records generally, see extended note to *Sawyer* v. *Manchester etc. R. R. Co.*, 13 Am. St. Rep. 550-554.

PEOPLE v. ELLIOTT.

[74 MICHIGAN, 264.]

LOTTERY — WHAT IS. — A lottery is a scheme by which a result is reached by some action or means taken, and in which result man's choice or will has no part, nor can human reason, foresight, sagacity, or design enable him to know or determine such result until the same has been accomplished.

LOTTERY — WHAT CONSTITUTES. — It is the selling and disposing of chances for money for a chance of receiving more, and not the drawing of the chances, that constitutes the lottery. It is of little consequence where the drawing takes place. It need not take place within the state to bring the case within the statute.

LOTTERY — WHAT IS — SETTING UP AND PROMOTING. — A person who carries on the business known as "policy," and who sells numbers for money, which are drawn to determine the right to prizes in a Kentucky lottery, is guilty of setting up and promoting a lottery for money, under the Michigan statute.

G. X. M. Collier, for the respondent.

S. V. R. Trowbridge, attorney-general, and George F. Robison, prosecuting attorney, for the people.

SHERWOOD, C. J. The respondent was convicted in the recorder's court in the city of Detroit, upon an information charging him with setting up and promoting a lottery for money. The information against him is filed under section 9331, Howell's Statutes, and is as follows: —

"*The Recorder's Court of the City of Detroit.*

"In the name of the people of the state of Michigan, George F. Robison, prosecuting attorney in and for the said county of Wayne, who prosecutes for and on behalf of the people of said state in said court, comes now here in said court, in the July term thereof, A. D. 1888, and gives the said court here to understand and be informed that William O. Elliott and Frank F. Johannes, late of said city of Detroit, heretofore, to wit, on June 2, A. D. 1888, at the said city of Detroit, in the county aforesaid, unlawfully did set up and promote a lottery for money, contrary to the form of the statute in such case made and provided, and against the peace and dignity of the people of the state of Michigan.

"GEORGE F. ROBISON, Prosecuting Attorney."

Respondent pleaded not guilty. Upon the trial, the people gave evidence tending to show that the respondent kept an office in Detroit on June 2, 1888, where he acted as a policy dealer; that the business he carried on was called "policy," and was conducted by him as follows: "There is in Kentucky a lottery, in which every day there are thirteen numbers drawn by lot out of seventy-eight. These numbers are drawn to determine the right to prizes in the Kentucky lottery, in which the prizes range in value from eighty dollars to four thousand dollars. When the numbers drawn in Kentucky are made public, they are telegraphed to the respondent at Detroit, who uses them as a basis for his dealing. Persons who wish to play "policy," as he calls it, pay the respondent a sum of money, usually from five to fifty cents, and at the same time select two, three, or four numbers, from one to seventy-eight. If the player selects two numbers, it is called a "saddle." If he selects three, it is called a "gig." If he selects four, it is called a "horse." If all the numbers selected by the player came out in the drawing, he won a certain amount from the policy dealer. In the case of a "gig," or three numbers, if the player won, he received ten dollars for five cents; in the case of a "saddle" the odds were proportionately less; in the case of a "horse," proportionately greater.

The respondent requested the court to instruct the jury as follows: —

"1. If the jury find that the facts in this case do not show that the defendant, William Elliott, did any act to promote within this state any lottery or gift enterprise for money, or in any way was concerned in the setting up, managing, or drawing of any such lottery or gift enterprise, or did in any house, shop, or building owned or occupied by him, or under his control, knowingly permit the setting up, managing, or drawing of any such lottery or gift enterprise, or the sale of any lottery ticket, or share of a ticket, or other device purporting or intending to entitle the holder or bearer to any prize or gift, or interest in any prize or gift, to be drawn in any such lottery or gift enterprise, then their verdict must be of not guilty.

"2. If the jury shall find, as a matter of fact, that the defendant, William Elliott, committed no act which tended towards maintaining or promoting the business of a lottery or gift enterprise for money, or disposing of money in the state of Michigan, their verdict must be not guilty.

"3. The evidence in this case shows that William Elliott, the defendant, did maintain and take part in a game called "policy," which consisted in betting that certain numbers drawn out of the lottery wheel in foreign states would be the winning numbers, and that he was in no wise connected with the maintaining or promoting of those lotteries in said foreign states, and that said lottery enterprises or schemes were not maintained or promoted by said defendant, in this state or in any other state; and while he may be guilty of keeping an unlawful place for gambling, he is not guilty of the offense charged in the information in this case, and therefore I charge you to find a verdict of not guilty.

"4. A lottery is a scheme whereby large numbers of persons are enticed into the purchasing of tickets for the distribution of prizes, in money or property, upon some sort of drawing or allotment by chance, and the lotteries generally involve large sums of money, or large prizes of some kind, and circulate their tickets in large numbers, and in all parts of the country; such tickets being written or printed, or some equivalent device, securing shares in a distribution of prizes. Now, the evidence in this case does not show that the defendant, William Elliott, committed any act which tends towards maintaining or promoting business of a lottery or gift enterprise for money, or disposing of money or property, and thereby your verdict must be not guilty."

The court refused to give these instructions, and respondent's counsel excepted; but did charge the jury, if they were satisfied beyond a reasonable doubt of the truth of the testimony given by the prosecution, they would be warranted in finding the respondent guilty. The court was justified in refusing to give the respondent's requests, and we see nothing improper in the instruction given. The testimony, which was very brief, was not controverted, and the facts make out a case under the statute.

A lottery is a scheme by which a result is reached by some action or means taken, and in which result man's choice or will has no part, nor can human reason, foresight, sagacity, or design enable him to know or determine such result until the same has been accomplished. It was the obtaining of money or property by such means that our statute was intended to prevent and punish, and I think the case before us falls clearly within the statute. If the respondent had drawn the thirteen numbers from the seventy-eight, at his place of business in Detroit, there could be no doubt but that the scheme would have been regarded as a lottery, and within the terms of the statute. It is difficult to see why the selecting and selling of three or more of the thirteen numbers would not be equally within the statute, if they were to draw the prizes, if it was not necessary for the drawing to be done within the state to constitute the offense; and this, I think, was unnecessary: How. Stats., sec. 9335. It is not the drawing of the lots, but the disposing and selling of the chances, that brings the case within the statute. It is promoting the lottery for money by paying the money for the chance of receiving more. It is of little consequence where the drawing takes place. These views, to some extent, will be found supported in the following authorities: *Commonwealth* v. *Sullivan*, 146 Mass. 142; *Commonwealth* v. *Wright*, 137 Mass. 250; 50 Am. Rep. 306; *Wilkinson* v. *Gill*, 74 N. Y. 63; 30 Am. Rep. 264; *State* v. *Lovell*, 39 N. J. L. 458; *Commonwealth* v. *Thacher*, 97 Mass. 583; 93 Am. Dec. 125; *State* v. *Clarke*, 33 N. H. 329–335; 66 Am. Dec. 723; *Hull* v. *Ruggles*, 56 N. Y. 424, 427; *Randle* v. *State*, 42 Tex. 580; *Smith* v. *State*, 68 Md. 168.

It is thought by counsel for defendant that this case is ruled by *People* v. *Reilly*, 50 Mich. 384, 45 Am. Rep. 47. That case, however, is different. There the contingency was one upon which the parties interested could exercise their reason and judgment under an agreement upon which the money was paid, and was in its nature executory. In this case, the money was paid when the chance was obtained, and there was no opportunity for exercising the reason or judgment, or any other faculty of the mind, and hence the lottery.

The judgment must be affirmed.

LOTTERIES. — As to what is and what is necessary to constitute a lottery within the meaning of the law, see extended note to *Yellowstone Kit* v. *State*, 88 Ala. 196, *ante*, p. 38.

PEOPLE v. STUART.

[74 MICHIGAN, 411.]

CONSTITUTIONAL LAW — REMOVAL OF OFFICERS BY GOVERNOR. — A law authorizing the governor to remove county officers for specified causes, upon satisfactory evidence submitted to him, is valid, and not unconstitutional on the ground that the governor cannot be authorized to remove without a conviction first had in a court of competent jurisdiction.

OFFICERS — REMOVAL OF PERSONS FROM THEIR OFFICES FOR CAUSE involves the exercise of judical power.

OFFICERS — REMOVAL. — Holding and exercising an office to which a person has been elected during the term for which he has been elected, is a right of which he cannot be deprived without due process of law, after notice, a hearing, and determination, but the power to remove, so exercised, may be vested in the governor.

CONSTITUTIONAL LAW — REMOVAL OF COUNTY OFFICERS. — The power vested by the constitution in the legislature to provide by law for the removal of county officers is in its nature political, and has reference exclusively to the polity of government, which would be inherently defective if no remedy of a summary nature could be had to remove from office a person who, after his election, had been convicted of crime, or who neglected his duty, or who was guilty of malversation in the administration of his office.

CONSTITUTIONAL LAW — REMOVAL OF COUNTY OFFICERS. — The power vested by the constitution in the legislature to provide by law for the removal of county officers is plenary, and commits to the legislature the whole subject of removal. It may prescribe the mode, which includes everything necessary for the accomplishment of the object. The causes, charges, notice, investigation, and determination, by whom conducted, and the removal determined are in the discretion of the legislature, and may be delegated to the governor.

Fred A. Maynard, for the relator.

Stuart, Knappen, and Van Arman, for the respondent.

CHAMPLIN, J. An information in the nature of a *quo warranto* was filed in the circuit court for the county of Kent, by the relator against the respondent, charging that he had usurped, intruded into, and unlawfully held the office of prosecuting attorney of Kent County, to which the relator was entitled by virtue of an election held on November 2, 1886, at which he was elected prosecuting attorney of Kent County, and qualified, and entered upon the duties of the office until the usurpation of Stuart, on May 5, 1888.

The respondent filed an answer, in which he set forth that on February 7, 1888, one Israel C. Smith, a citizen and resident of the city of Grand Rapids, in said county, exhibited to Cyrus G. Luce, the governor of the state, certain charges in writing, setting forth that said Samuel D. Clay had been guilty of official misconduct as such prosecuting attorney, and in his office and administration of said office of prosecuting attorney, which charges and specifications were particularly set out in the answer, and he prayed the governor to make inquiry into the charges, and that said Clay might be removed from the office of prosecuting attorney for such official misconduct; that such charges were accompanied with the certificate of the attorney-general that in his opinion said charges demanded investigation; that the governor directed an investigation to be had, which, upon due notice to said Clay, was had at Grand Rapids, Michigan, in said county, before Hon. Cyrus E. Perkins, judge of probate of said county; that testimony was taken, reviewed, and certified by the judge of probate, as required by law, and returned to the governor, and after due notice and hearing, the said Samuel D. Clay, in his own defense, on, to wit, May 1, 1888, the said governor became satisfied that said Samuel D. Clay, as such prosecuting attorney, had been guilty of such official misconduct in the occupancy and administration of said office, and in due form of law removed said Samuel D. Clay from said office of prosecuting attorney, and declared the said office vacant; that thereafter, and on May 5, 1888, Hon. Robert M. Montgomery, the judge of the circuit court for the county of Kent, duly appointed the respondent, William J. Stuart, to the office of prosecuting attorney of said county of Kent until January 1, 1889, or until his successor in office should be chosen and qualified; that he duly accepted the appointment, and qualified thereunder, and entered upon the duties and privileges of said office; and denied the usurpation and intrusion charged.

To this answer the relator demurred. The cause was heard

in the circuit court, and demurrer overruled, with leave to reply. He refused to do so, and judgment was entered for respondent, and against the relator for costs. The case was brought before us on a case made after judgment.

Article 12, section 7, of the constitution of this state, reads as follows: "The legislature shall provide by law for the removal of any officer elected by a county, township, or school district, in such manner and for such cause as to them shall seem just and proper."

In pursuance of this provision, the legislature enacted a law authorizing the governor to remove all county officers elected in any county when he should be satisfied from sufficient evidence submitted to him, as in said law provided, that such officer is incompetent to execute properly the duties of his office, or has been guilty of official misconduct, or of willful neglect of duty, or of extortion, or habitual drunkenness, or has been convicted of being drunk, or whenever it shall appear, by a certified copy of the judgment of a court of record of this state, that such officer, after his election or appointment, shall have been convicted of a felony. The law further provides that the charges shall be in writing, and verified, and for service thereof upon the officer, and for an opportunity to be heard. The law also provides for the manner of conducting the inquiry, the taking of testimony, and the return thereof to the governor. No question is raised upon this record that the proceedings pointed out by the statute have not been followed, but the authority of the legislature to depute to the governor the power of removal without a conviction first had in a court of competent jurisdiction is challenged.

The argument on behalf of relator is this: While any officer named in the section of the constitution above quoted may be removed from his office for such cause as shall seem just to the legislature, and while the legislature may designate the manner in which such cause shall be determined, the existence of such cause must be determined, before the removal can be made, by some tribunal invested with power to make such determination by the constitution; that the determination whether the specified cause exists is the exercise of judicial functions, and must therefore be exercised by those tribunals which the constitution has designated as the repository of such functions.

There can be no doubt that the removal of a person from his office for cause involves the exercise of judicial power.

Holding and exercising an office to which a person has been elected, during the term for which he has been elected, is a right of which he cannot be deprived without due process of law, and this requires notice to the party, a hearing, and determination.

The. constitution divides the powers of government into three departments, — the legislative, executive, and judicial (art. 3, sec. 1), and then declares that "no person belonging to one department shall exercise the powers properly belonging to another, except in the cases expressly provided in this constitution" (art. 3, sec. 2).

The legislature, acting under section 7, article 12, *supra*, has conferred upon the executive judicial power, so far as it is necessary to carry out the provisions of that section. The inquiry is, Does that section confer authority upon the legislature to vest the determination of the question, whether cause exists for removal in any other department than the judicial? It will be noticed that the power conferred by this section of the constitution is plenary. The legislature is to provide by law for the removal of county officers, etc., in such manner as to them shall seem just and proper. The power conferred is in its nature political, and has reference exclusively to the polity of government, which would be inherently defective if no remedy of a summary nature could be had to remove from office a person who, after his election, had been convicted of crime, or who neglected his duty, or who was guilty of malversation in the administration of his office. Every person elected to a county, township, or school district office holds it subject to removal in the manner provided by law under this section of the constitution, which commits to the legislature the whole subject of removal. They are to prescribe the mode in which it shall be done, and this includes everything necessary for the accomplishment of the object. The causes, the charges, the notice, the investigation, and the determination, and by whom these shall be conducted, and the removal adjudged, are all in the discretion of the legislature. The answer sets out with particularity the several steps required to be taken by the statute, and the demurrer admits the facts stated; and it follows that the judgment of the circuit court must be affirmed, with costs against the relator.

REMOVAL OF OFFICERS BY THE GOVERNOR. — In the absence of express constitutional authority, the legislature cannot confer upon the governor power to remove state or county officers arbitrarily without a hearing:

Dullam v. *Willson,* 53 Mich. 392; 51 Am. Rep. 128. In the absence of
constitutional or legislative prohibition, the power of removing an officer
is incident to the power of appointing him: *Newsom* v. *Cocke,* 44 Miss.
352, where an act was held constitutional which provided that in all
cases in which the governor "shall have the power under this act, by the
terms of the constitution, to appoint to office, he shall also have the power
of removal from office." But in *Dubuc* v. *Voss,* 19 La. Ann. 210, 92 Am. Dec.
526, it was held that the power to remove, being incident to the power to
appoint, does not apply to governors of states, as their power to remove is
usually limited to particular cases provided for by statutory enactment. As
to when the governor may not declare an office vacant without judicial inquiry, see note to *State* v. *Allen,* 83 Am. Dec. 376.

In *People* v. *Freese,* 76 Cal. 633, it was decided that an officer could be
removed only by the power which appointed him; consequently, a member
of the board of pilot commissioners, who was appointed according to the provisions of the Political Code of California, by the governor, with the advice
and consent of the senate, could not be removed by the governor alone.

In *Biggs* v. *McBride,* 17 Or. 640, whether the power to remove an officer
for cause may be conferred upon the governor, or belongs solely to the judicial department of the government, was not decided; but it was determined
that whoever had the power to remove for cause must give notice to the
delinquent of the particular charges against him, and an opportunity to
defend himself.

PEOPLE *v.* CONVERSE.

[74 MICHIGAN, 478.]

CRIMINAL LAW — EMBEZZLEMENT BY ATTORNEY AT LAW. — A plea to an information for embezzlement of money received by defendant in the course
of his employment as agent, that as an attorney at law he was guilty of
embezzlement of the sum charged, less his reasonable fees, as such attorney, for making the collection, is equivalent to a plea of guilty of the
crime charged.

CRIMINAL LAW — EMBEZZLEMENT BY ATTORNEY AT LAW. — When an attorney collects money for his client, he acts as the agent of the client, as
well as his attorney; and in either case, if, after making the collection,
he appropriates the money to his own use, with intent to deprive the
owner of it, he is guilty of embezzlement.

John C. Patterson, for the respondent.

*S. V. R. Trowbridge, attorney-general, and Herbert E. Winsor,
prosecuting attorney,* for the people.

SHERWOOD, C. J.   The respondent was informed against in
the county of Calhoun for the crime of embezzlement. The
information is as follows: —

" *The Circuit Court for the County of Calhoun.*

"Herbert E. Winsor, prosecuting attorney for the county of
Calhoun, aforesaid, for and in behalf of the people of the state
of Michigan, comes into said court in the December term

thereof, A. D. 1887, and gives it here to understand and be informed, that Eugene M. Converse, late of the city of Battle Creek, in the county of Calhoun and state of Michigan, heretofore, to wit, on the twenty-eighth day of July, in the year one thousand eight hundred and eighty-five, at the city of Battle Creek, in said county of Calhoun and state of Michigan, being then and there agent to John E. Dunning and Daniel W. Hall, the executors of the last will and testament of Rice Hall, deceased, and being then and there the agent of them, the said John E. Dunning and Daniel W. Hall, executors of the last will and testament of Rice Hall, deceased, and not being then and there an apprentice, nor other person under the age of sixteen years, did, by virtue of his said employment, then and there, and whilst he was such agent as aforesaid, receive and take into his possession certain moneys to a large amount, to wit, to the amount of four thousand dollars, of the value of four thousand dollars, of the property of the said John E. Dunning and Daniel W. Hall, as such executors, and which said money came to the possession of the said Eugene M. Converse by virtue of said employment, and the said money then and there fraudulently and feloniously did embezzle and convert to his own use, without the consent of the said John E. Dunning and Daniel W. Hall, as such executors as aforesaid, his said employers, and that so the said Eugene M. Converse did then and there, in manner and form aforesaid, the said money, the property of the said John E. Dunning and Daniel W. Hall, as executors as aforesaid, his said employers, from the said John E. Dunning and Daniel W. Hall, as such executors as aforesaid, feloniously did steal, take, and carry away, contrary to the form of the statute in such case made and provided, and against the peace and dignity of the people of the state of Michigan."

On being arraigned, the respondent pleaded to the information as follows: "As an attorney at law, I am guilty of embezzlement of thirty-five hundred ($3,500) dollars, that being the amount collected and received by me, less my reasonable fees as such attorney for collecting the money."

Upon filing the foregoing plea, the circuit judge directed the following entry to be made:—

"THE PEOPLE OF THE STATE OF MICHIGAN *v.* EUGENE M. CONVERSE.

"Eugene M. Converse, the respondent in this cause, having been duly arraigned ·at the bar in open court, and the information being read to him by Herbert E. Winsor, prosecuting attorney, pleaded thereto 'guilty of the embezzlement of money to the amount of three thousand five hundred dollars.'"

And thereupon, after the court had made the usual private examination of the respondent required by statute, after a plea of guilty, Converse was sentenced to five years' imprisonment at hard labor at Jackson. Subsequently, under the direction of this court, the entire plea made by the respondent when arraigned was incorporated in the record at the circuit, and then respondent removed the record into this court for review.

He assigns as error, among others, that, —

"1. There is no sufficient plea in said cause to form a legal basis for the judgment rendered therein.

"2. The judgment is for a felony, and the plea is for a misdemeanor only, and the judgment is broader than the plea, and the penalty imposed is unauthorized by the plea and statute.

"3. The judgment against the defendant is for embezzlement in the capacity of agent, and the defendant never pleaded guilty of such crime, and he has never been convicted of such crime by a jury."

It is strongly urged by counsel that the information charges the respondent with embezzling four thousand dollars while acting in the capacity of agent for the owners, while, in fact, he only confessed himself guilty by his plea of collecting the money as an attorney at law, and of refusing to pay it over to the owners, less his fees for collecting. There is no question but that the information charges the respondent with the crime of embezzlement. It was to this charge, when arraigned, he was called upon to plead. He pleaded guilty of embezzlement. He is a lawyer, and knew the meaning of the word "embezzlement," and I think there can be no doubt but that he understood when he made his plea that he was pleading guilty to the felony charged. That such was the fact seems to have been verified by the private examination required by statute to be made by the circuit judge before sentencing upon a plea of guilty, and which is shown to have been made in this case. To hold otherwise would be an impeachment of the intelligence of both the prisoner and the court. That the respondent collected the money as attorney is of no consequence. If the act of the respondent complained of contained all the elements of embezzlement, he was guilty of the crime, and was properly convicted.

If an attorney collects money for his client, he in so doing acts as the agent of his client as well as his attorney; and in either case, if, after making the collection, he appropriates the money to his own use, with the intention of depriving the owner of the same, he is guilty of the crime of embezzlement. If this were not so, no attorney could be convicted of the embezzlement of his client's money, and this was certainly never the intention of the legislature in passing the statute creating the crime.

I think the conviction in this case was warranted by the plea of the respondent, and that the judgment should be affirmed.

CAMPBELL, J., dissented, on the point that the answer by the respondent to the arraignment was equivalent to a plea of guilty of the crime charged, and contended that no one could be lawfully sentenced unless convicted of the precise crime alleged, after trial or plea of guilty. He explained that embezzlement made punishable by statute as larceny differs from common-law larceny only in the absence of a felonious taking originally, and covers what, if taken without authority, would be the subject of larceny; in other words, money or property which comes into the hands of an agent as belonging specifically to the principal. The statute is not applicable to fraud or breach of trust, where there is no ownership in the principal, or specific funds or property, or where the wrong done consists in withholding what is only a part of a sum collected and due on an accounting. This crime is embezzlement; but as the common law does not punish embezzlement as such, the punishment must be governed by some express provision of statute, and as the statute in question imposes no penalty on the embezzlement, which it denominates a crime, it is only because it is made larceny that any punishment can be inflicted, and this punishment is governed by the value of the theft, either greater or less; and though the amount named in this record makes it a state-prison offense, a smaller amount would have involved a less penalty.

The only statute which covers a failure to pay over money by attorneys applies to collections made in such capacity, and the crime is not complete until after demand made and refused. It is then a misdemeanor, punishable, without reference to the amount, by imprisonment for not more than a year, and a fine of not more than four times the amount retained may be added or substituted. In the absence of this statute, a failure by an attorney to pay over balances would constitute nothing but a breach of trust. Distinctions have always been drawn between such embezzlement as is made larceny, and that involving an accounting on demand, or under some other legal requirement. These statutory provisions have been adopted from time to time, and have attached different consequences to the crimes, though the construction adopted here makes several of them mere repetitions. The construction placed upon these statutory provisions, and similar to the views here expressed, is shown by the cases of *People* v. *Tryon*, 4 Mich. 665; *Bronson* v. *Newberry*, 2 Doug. 38; *Pennock* v. *Fuller*, 41 Mich. 153; *People* v. *McAllister*, 19 Id. 215. In conclusion his honor says: "The legislation of this state, civil and criminal, has kept separate professional misconduct and violations of duty as agents, and there are readily ascertainable reasons for so doing in the differences which may honestly arise on questions of compensation and accounting. It is never safe to let considerations of the hardship or demerit of a single case destroy distinctions which are expressed in the law. It is an easy matter to amend statutes, but it is not the business of courts to change the legislative meaning. The act confessed by respondent was not a felony, and the information was for a felony. The plea was not a plea of guilty under the information, and when the prisoner failed to plead to what he was charged with, he should have been put upon his trial. Our practice does not allow special pleas on the merits. The only special pleas in bar relate to former proceedings. A plea of guilty outside of the record is no plea, and cannot support a conviction. Its peculiar form should have drawn attention to it. The judgment should be reversed, and the prisoner discharged from state prison."

EMBEZZLEMENT BY AN ATTORNEY. — An attorney at law is an agent or servant, and as such may be guilty of embezzlement, if, after collecting his client's money, he appropriates it to his own use without informing the client of the collection: Note to *Calkins* v. *State*, 98 Am. Dec. 145.

TUTTLE *v.* CAMPBELL.

[74 MICHIGAN, 652.]

TENANCY IN COMMON OF CHATTELS, HOW MAY BE CREATED — NECESSITY FOR DELIVERY OF POSSESSION. — The owner of chattels may sell an undivided share or interest in them, designated as so many dollars' worth of the whole, and the relation thus created will be a common ownership, which, by analogy to such relation in real property, is frequently designated as a tenancy in common of the property; and in such case, no actual delivery is required; for the title passes at the time of the sale, if such is the intention of the parties. Both or either may have the actual possession of the property thus owned, and the possession of one makes him the bailee of his co-owner's share.

SALE — CONSIDERATION. — A sale of an interest in personal property must be supported by a sufficient consideration.

TENANCY IN COMMON OF CHATTELS — CONSENT OF TENANT TO SALE OF WHOLE IMPLIED. — A tenant in common of goods cannot convey the title to the whole stock without the consent of the co-tenant; but such consent will be implied when the goods are retailed in the usual course of business, without objection from and with the knowledge of the co-tenant.

SALE OF ENTIRE STOCK OF GOODS BY TENANT IN COMMON, being out of the ordinary course of business, requires the consent of the co-tenant in order to bind or carry his interest therein to the purchaser.

CO-TENANTS CANNOT SELL WHOLE PROPERTY. — Owners in common of property have a right to sell their own undivided share, but such owner cannot sell the whole property, nor any portion thereof, except his own; and if he disposes of any larger interest, his co-owners are not bound thereby.

CO-TENANT CANNOT SELL WHOLE PROPERTY — INNOCENT PURCHASER NOT PROTECTED. — A co-tenant cannot convey any greater title or interest than he has, and it makes no difference that the purchaser has no notice and is ignorant of the existence of other parties in interest, except where the conduct of the co-tenant estops him from asserting title against the innocent purchaser.

CONVERSION BY CO-TENANT. — Where a tenant in common of goods sells the whole, his co-tenant may treat it as a conversion, and bring trover against his co-tenant to recover his share, or he may retain his title in the goods in the hands of the purchaser, and if he converts them he is likewise liable to such co-tenant.

CONVERSION, WHAT IS, AMONG CO-TENANTS. — A total destruction of the chattel, or a conversion of the whole to his own use, by a tenant in common, or something equivalent, as a total denial of his co-owner's interest in the property, coupled with a total exclusion from possession, will render the owner in possession liable to his co-owner in trover.

CO-TENANCY — REFUSAL TO YIELD POSSESSION NOT CONVERSION. — Where property owned in common is not in its nature divisible, a mere refusal of one tenant in common to yield possession of the property or to admit his co-tenant to a joint possession, without denying his interest or ownership, does not constitute a conversion.

SALES — CONVERSION BY PURCHASER. — One who buys property must, at his peril, ascertain the ownership, and if he buys of one having no authority to sell, his taking possession in denial of the owner's right is a conversion for which trover will lie without demand.

ASSUMPSIT — WAIVER OF TORT TO SUE IN. — Before a party can waive a tort for the conversion of personal property and bring *assumpsit*, the property in the hands of a tort-feasor must have been sold and converted into money, upon the theory that the money has been received for the plaintiff's use.

ASSUMPSIT — WAIVER OF TORT TO SUE IN. — Where a contract may exist, and at the same time a duty is superimposed or arises out of the circumstances surrounding the transaction, the violation of which duty would constitute a tort, and the property has been converted, but not sold, the tort may be waived and *assumpsit* maintained, for the reason that the relation of the parties, out of which the duty violated grew, had its inception in contract and relations of trust and confidence.

CO-TENANCY — TENANT IN POSSESSION IS BAILEE. — Where a tenant in common of personalty has exclusive possession he is a bailee of his co-tenant's share. He holds it upon the trust and confidence that he will care for and use it in an ordinarily careful manner, and will not sell or convert his co-tenant's share to his own use, and if he violates his duty by so converting it, his co-tenant may bring trover for the conversion, or waive the tort and sue in *assumpsit* for its value.

CO-TENANCY — WHEN CO-TENANT CANNOT MAINTAIN ASSUMPSIT FOR CONVERSION OF HIS SHARE. — Where husband and wife are co-tenants of a stock of goods, and the husband, being in exclusive possession, sells them to third parties, one of whom has notice of the wife's interest, and the other, upon demand being made by her for her share, refuses to recognize that she has any interest in the goods, she cannot waive the tort for the conversion, and maintain *assumpsit* to recover the value of her share, for the reason that the goods have not been sold and converted into money.

ASSUMPSIT.   Judgment for plaintiff.   Defendants bring error.

Smith and York, for the defendants.

R. A. Montgomery, for the plaintiff.

CHAMPLIN, J. Some time in 1882, William A. Tuttle, who is the plaintiff's husband, engaged in the business of sell-. ing drugs and medicines, at Williamson, Ingham County. He occupied a store which belonged to his wife, Flora B. Tuttle.

In March of 1884, domestic dissensions caused a separation between Tuttle and his wife, and she left him, and determined upon filing a bill of complaint to obtain a divorce from the bonds of matrimony. To save litigation over the question of alimony, he agreed to give her one thousand dollars in full of all claims against him, to be paid when she obtained a decree for divorce, to secure which, he gave her a certificate of deposit on the bank of Daniel L. Crossman, payable to her order when she should obtain a decree for divorce against her husband. The certificate was then left with Crossman for safe-keeping. This arrangement was so entirely satisfactory, that the parties, on the same day or the next, laid aside their differences and went to living together again. The bill was not filed, neither was the certificate of deposit taken up or canceled with her consent. Harmony, however, did not long prevail in the Tuttle family. Dissensions broke out anew, and Mr. Tuttle, without her knowledge, obtained from Mr. Crossman possession of the certificate, and a short time there-after she found it in his cash-drawer, and took and retained possession of it. It appears that the date of the certificate was March 22, 1884, and when it was obtained Mr. Tuttle depos-ited five hundred dollars, and gave his note to Crossman, due in six months, for the other five hundred dollars. This note was not taken up when he became possessed of the certificate after the reconciliation, and there is no direct testimony that he then withdrew the five hundred dollars cash which he had deposited, although there is a strong inference to that effect from Crossman's testimony. At any rate, in August Mrs. Tuttle held the one-thousand-dollar certificate, and Crossman held Mr. Tuttle's note for five hundred dollars. At this time Mr. Tuttle told her that he had got to sell in order to pay Crossman that one thousand dollars, because he had to secure him at the time he got the certificate, and that she might come on Crossman if he did not settle, and so he had got to sell out to pay him. He finally told Mrs. Tuttle that if she would indorse the certificate of deposit to him she could have a thousand dollars' worth of interest in the stock of drugs and medicines, which offer she accepted, and indorsed the certificate, and Tuttle delivered it up to Crossman on August 19, 1884, and Crossman canceled it, and delivered up to Tuttle his note of five hundred dollars. There was some testimony tending to prove that Tuttle had occupied the store of Mrs. Tuttle over two years, without paying any rent to her, and also had collected the rents of tenants occupying other portions of the building, for which he owed her, and that this indebtedness also entered into the consideration for the one thousand dollars' worth of interest in the stock of goods.

After this transaction, Mr. Tuttle continued to carry on the business until April 25, 1885, when he sold the entire stock of goods and fixtures to defendants for $2,750, $500 of which was paid in cash, and the balance in notes. The last one to mature, being for $250, was made conditional upon defendants being able to obtain a lease of the store from Mrs. Tuttle. An inventory made soon after the purchase, at the cost price, showed the value of the stock to have been a little over $3,160. The bargain was closed on Saturday night, and the next day Mr. Tuttle left the place and remained absent nearly two years, without his whereabouts being known to Mrs. Tuttle. The sale was made without her consent. She had heard that the defendant Campbell was endeavoring to purchase, and he had inquired of her whether she would rent to him the store in case he should purchase, and she refused, and also, as she testifies, expressly notified him in that interview that she was the owner of a thousand dollars' interest in the stock of goods. This interview was about four months before the purchase by defendants. The defendant Hanlon had been a school-teacher in the village, and had heard that the domestic relations of Tuttle and his wife were not entirely harmonious. He was invited by Dr. Campbell to join him in making the purchase, and had been told by him that Mrs. Tuttle refused to rent the store to him, but it was not shown that he had express notice of Mrs. Tuttle's one-thousand-dollar interest in the stock of goods when he purchased. A bill of sale was executed to them jointly by Tuttle, conveying the whole stock of goods then in the store. They thereupon went into possession, and continued the sale of drugs at retail, Mr. Hanlon giving his attention to the selling of the goods in the store. About thirty days after the purchase Mrs. Tuttle went into the store and found Mr. Hanlon there in possession, and stated to him that she had a thousand dollars' interest in the stock, and demanded that he turn out to her a thousand dollars' worth of the goods in the stock, or pay her one thousand dollars for such interest. He absolutely refused to do either, and claimed that they had bought the whole stock, and it was theirs. No demand was made upon defendant Campbell. This suit was then brought by plaintiff, alleging the conversion of her interest in the goods, but waiving the tort, and asking a judgment for their value in *assumpsit.* The trial resulted in a verdict and judgment for the plaintiff for the full amount of her claim, with interest from the date of demand.

Three objections were taken to the admission of testimony. We do not think the errors assigned upon them call for a reversal of the judgment upon any of the grounds stated against the admission of such testimony.

The main grounds of error relied on may be considered under the following heads: —

1. Was the transaction between the plaintiff and her husband such a one as created them owners in common of the stock of goods?

2. If they were such owners in common, would a purchaser from the husband of the whole stock, without notice of his co-owner's rights, acquire a title to the whole stock?

3. If not, is the purchase by Dr. Campbell, with notice of plaintiff's ownership, and the refusal to recognize the rights of Mrs. Tuttle by the defendant Hanlon, evidence of a conversion of the goods by both defendants, so as to sustain an action against both jointly?

4. Where a small portion only of the goods are sold, the balance remaining in possession of the co-owners in common, who deny the right of another owner in common to any of the goods, can the dispossessed owner treat it as a conversion of the whole, and waiving the tort, maintain an action of *assumpsit* to recover the value of the goods converted?

1. The owner of chattels may sell an undivided share or interest in them, and the relation thus created will be a common ownership, which, by analogy to such relations in real property, is frequently designated as tenancy in common of the property. In such case no actual delivery is required. The title passes at time of sale, if such is the intent of the parties. Both or either may have the actual possession of property owned in common, and when one owner has the

actual possession, and the other has not, the owner in possession is simply the bailee of his co-owner's share.

When an undivided share or interest in personal property is sold, there is no more objection to a designation of the interest sold by dollars' worth than there is by designating a part as one half, one fifth, or any other fraction of the whole. In either case, the part sold is a fraction of the whole, and extends to every part and parcel thereof. In one case, the unit is the property; in the other, the unit is the value of the property. But the value represents the property, so that the units are in fact the same. The share conveyed measured by dollars' worth will depend, as regards quantity, upon the total value or worth of the whole property. And, in cases where the property is severable and capable of division in kind without sale, such share may be severed or separated from the rest by taking so many dollars' worth, without regard to the quantity that is left, whether it be much or little, for the balance of the unit will be left after taking out the dollars' worth severed. Of course, a division is more readily made when the unit is the thing, and the share is designated by a fraction of the quantity; but if the owners cannot agree upon the division, then the remedy is a sale, as in other cases. Dollars' worth is often used to measure and designate the share or ownership in property. More particularly is this the case in partnership transactions. No difficulty has been experienced in dividing up the property from the use of such standard as a measurement of interest. A sale of an interest in personal property must be supported by a sufficient consideration. In this case, there was evidence of a present consideration passing from Mrs. Tuttle to her husband, which, if believed by the jury, was sufficient to support the contract. We conclude that the transaction between Mr. and Mrs. Tuttle was such as created them owners in common of the stock of goods.

2. This being so, he could not without her consent convey away her title to the goods to the defendant purchasers. So far as he retailed goods out of the store to customers, her consent would be implied by the course of dealing tacitly permitted by her, without objection. But a sale of the entire stock, being out of the ordinary course of business, would require her consent, in order to bind her or carry her interest to the purchaser. She testified that he had expressly agreed that he would not sell out the entire stock without her knowl-

edge and consent, and that this sale was made in violation of that agreement. Owners in common of property have a right to dispose of their own undivided share, but such owner cannot sell the whole property, nor any portion thereof except his own; and if he undertakes to dispose of any larger interest, his co-owners are not bound thereby: *Russell* v. *Allen*, 13 N. Y. 173, 178, per Dean, J.; *White* v. *Brooks*, 43 N. H. 402; *Welch* v. *Sackett*, 12 Wis. 243; *Frans* v. *Young*, 24 Iowa, 375. The principle is well settled that a seller of personal property can convey no greater title than he has, and it makes no difference that the purchaser has no notice and is ignorant of the existence of other parties in interest: *Couse* v. *Tregent*, 11 Mich. 65; *Dunlap* v. *Gleason*, 16 Mich. 158; 93 Am. Dec. 231; *Trudo* v. *Anderson*, 10 Mich. 357; 81 Am. Dec. 795; *Parish* v. *Morey*, 40 Mich. 417; *Pease* v. *Smith*, 61 N. Y. 477; *Bearce* v. *Bowker*, 115 Mass. 129. Exceptions are found where, through the conduct of the party or by his laches, he is estopped from asserting title as against the innocent purchaser; but this case does not come within the exception. The fact that Hanlon had no notice of plaintiff's interest in the goods before he purchased from Mr. Tuttle is of no importance, and the rule laid down by the court, requiring that they should find as matter of fact that he had notice of her interest in order to entitle her to recover, was more favorable to defendants than they were entitled to, and the question raised by defendants' counsel, that there was no testimony to support such finding, is of no consequence. By their purchase the defendants acquired title to that portion of the stock which their vendor had not sold to Mrs. Tuttle, and to that only, and they stood in the same relation to Mrs. Tuttle, respecting the ownership of the goods, as their vendor stood before their purchase, and were owners in common with her of the entire stock.

3. Ordinarily, when an owner in common sells the goods, the other owner in common may treat this act as a conversion, and bring an action of trover against his co-owner, to recover the value of his share; but he is not obliged to do this. He may retain his title in the goods in the hands of the purchaser, and if he converts them he is likewise liable therefor as his co-owner. What constitutes a conversion, short of a sale, is not definitely settled. A total destruction of the chattel, or a conversion of the whole to his own use, or something equivalent, such as a total denial of his co-owner's interest in the property, coupled with a total exclusion from

possession, will render the owner in possession liable to his co-owner. Owing to the right which an owner in common has to the possession of property so owned, if the property is in its nature indivisible, mere refusal to yield possession of the property or admit to a joint possession, without denying the interest or ownership of his co-owner, will not constitute a conversion. I have no doubt that the claim set up of such exclusive ownership by Hanlon when demand was made upon him, and his denial of and his refusal to recognize the rights of plaintiff, constituted a conversion of the plaintiff's interest in the property, so far as he was concerned. No demand was made of defendant Campbell, and none was necessary, if the testimony of Mrs. Tuttle is to be believed, and under the instructions of the court the jury have given credence to it. The law is laid down in Cooley on Torts, at page 528 (*451), that "one who buys property must, at his peril, ascertain the ownership; and if he buys of one having no authority to sell, his taking possession in denial of the owner's right is a conversion."

Dr. Campbell purchased knowing Mrs. Tuttle's right to the property, and in contravention of it purchased from Tuttle the whole property, without recognizing, but ignoring, her rights or title to any of it, and took possession thereof under his bill of sale conveying the whole property with warranty. This was a conversion of her share in the property by him, and a demand before bringing suit was unnecessary. The third question must be answered in the affirmative.

4. The general rule is, that before a party can waive a tort for the conversion of personal property and bring *assumpsit*, the property in the hands of the tort-feasor must have been sold and converted into money, upon the theory that the money has been received for the plaintiff's use. There is, however, another class of cases, where the property has been converted, but not sold, where the tort may be waived and *assumpsit* brought for the value of the goods converted. This class belongs to those relations where a contract may exist, and at the same time a duty is superimposed or arises out of the circumstances surrounding or attending the transaction, the violation of which duty would constitute a tort. In such cases the tort may be waived and *assumpsit* be maintained, for the reason that the relation of the parties, out of which the duty violated grew, had its inception in contract. These relations are usually those of trust and confidence, such as

those of agent and principal, attorney and client, or bailee and bailor. When an owner in common of personalty has the exclusive possession of the property, he is a bailee of his co-owner's share. In such case there is a contract of bailment implied between the parties, the law implying a delivery from the nature of the case, and the peculiar rights which one owner in common has to such property when reduced to his possession. He takes it and holds it upon the trust and confidence that he will care for it and use it, if he uses it, in an ordinarily careful manner, and will not sell or convert his co-owner's share to his own use. If he violates this trust and confidence by converting the property to his own use, his co-owner may bring trover for the conversion, or, waiving the tort, may sue in *assumpsit* to recover its value. This has been the settled law in this state for many years, and was explicitly declared in *Fiquet* v. *Allison*, 12 Mich. 328, 86 Am. Dec. 54, which case is decisive of this. See also *Coe* v. *Wager*, 42 Mich. 49; *McLaughlin* v. *Salley*, 46 Mich. 219; *Evans* v. *Miller*, 58 Miss. 120; 38 Am. Rep. 313. The facts of this case do not bring it within the principle above stated, and the action of *assumpsit* cannot be maintained.

The judgment must be reversed and a new trial granted.

Co-tenancy in Chattels — Sale by One Co-tenant. — One tenant in common of personal property has not the power to sell or dispose of the entire common property as his own: *Hutchinson* v. *Chase*, 39 Me. 508; 63 Am. Dec. 645; *Burbank* v. *Crooker*, 7 Gray, 158; 66 Am. Dec. 470; but if one tenant in common of a chattel does convert it to his own use by a sale thereof, he becomes liable in trover for the conversion: *Delaney* v. *Root*, 99 Mass. 546; 97 Am. Dec. 52; *Redington* v. *Chase*, 44 N. H. 36; 82 Am. Dec. 189; *Lowe* v. *Miller*, 3 Gratt. 205; 46 Am. Dec. 188; *Warren* v. *Aller*, 1 Pinn. 479; 44 Am. Dec. 406; *Nowlen* v. *Colt*, 6 Hill, 461; 41 Am. Dec. 756, and particularly note; *Farr* v. *Smith*, 9 Wend. 338; 24 Am. Dec. 162, and note; *Hyde* v. *Stone*, 9 Cow. 230; 18 Am. Dec. 501, and note; Freeman on Cotenancy and Partition, secs. 308–311.

In *Hall* v. *Page*, 4 Ga. 428, 48 Am. Dec. 235, it is said: "As a general rule, it is not denied anywhere but that trover will not lie in favor of one tenant in common against his co-tenant. . . . . An exception to this rule is found in the case of a sale of the whole property by one tenant."

However, the contrary doctrine has been held in the case of *Sanborn* v. *Morrill*, 15 Vt. 700, 40 Am. Dec. 701, where it was decided that the sale of a chattel by one tenant in common was not such a destruction of the common property as to authorize an action in trover by the other co-tenant; for the remedy of the other co-tenant was either to disaffirm the sale and become co-tenant with the purchaser, or else affirm it, and call upon the seller for an accounting of the proceeds. And to the same effect is *Welch* v. *Clark*, 12 Vt. 681; 36 Am. Dec. 368; and *Tubbs* v. *Richardson*, 6 Vt. 442; 27 Am. Dec. 570.

But all the cases agree upon the rule, that one tenant in common is guilty

of conversion of the common property by destroying it, or making such a
disposition thereof as is tantamount to its destruction: *Tubbs* v. *Richardson*,
6 Vt. 442; 27 Am. Dec. 570; *Welch* v. *Clark*, 12 Vt. 681; 36 Am. Dec. 368;
Sanborn v. *Morrill*, 15 Vt. 700; 40 Am. Dec. 701; *Bell* v. *Laymen*, 1 T. B.
Mon. 39; 15 Am. Dec. 83; *Hyde* v. *Stone*, 7 Wend. 354; 22 Am. Dec. 582;
Lucas v. *Wasson*, 3 Dev. 398; 24 Am. Dec. 266; *Guyther* v. *Pettijohn*, 6 Ired.
388; 45 Am. Dec. 499; *Rooks* v. *Moore*, Busb. 1; 57 Am. Dec. 569, and notes
to these cases. In *Ripley* v. *Davis*, 15 Mich. 75, 90 Am. Dec. 262, it was
held that trover would lie by one co-tenant against another, where the latter, being bound by contract to deliver and divide the joint property at a
certain place, appropriated it to his exclusive use under a claim of exclusive
right, and under circumstances which render a division and delivery in the
manner agreed practically impossible; for the doctrine that there can be no
conversion among co-tenants does not apply to property in such articles as
grain and money, which are susceptible of convenient division: *Fiquet* v.
Allison, 12 Mich. 328; 86 Am. Dec. 54. But in *Ballou* v. *Hale*, 47 N. H. 347,
93 Am. Dec. 438, it was decided that trover could not be maintained by one
tenant against a co-tenant for taking all or any portion of the crops, and
merely withholding them, and refusing to allow the former to participate
in the use of them. While in the case of *Agnew* v. *Johnson*, 17 Pa. St. 373,
55 Am. Dec. 565, it was decided that one tenant in common might maintain
trover for his interest against his fellow, who had misused the joint property
by appropriating it to uses for which it was not designed, and refused to
apply it to the purposes for which it was held by both.

But still, in the case of *Herrin* v. *Eaton*, 13 Me. 193, 29 Am. Dec. 499, the
rule was laid down that an action of trespass lies against a co-tenant by his
fellow, when the former has destroyed or misused the joint property. Compare note to *Porter* v. *Hooper*, 29 Am. Dec. 483–485, as to when and under
what circumstances trespass will lie by one tenant in common against another.

CO-TENANCY IN CHATTELS. — The possession of one co-tenant of a chattel
which constitutes the common property is, in law, the possession of both:
Hall v. *Page*, 4 Ga. 428; 48 Am. Dec. 235.

WAIVING TORT. — As to when and under what circumstances one may
waive a tort and sue in *assumpsit*, see note to *Webster* v. *Drinkwater*, 17 Am.
Dec. 242-247. In *Fiquet* v. *Allison*, 12 Mich. 328, 86 Am. Dec. 54, where
plaintiffs raised a crop of grain on shares upon defendant's land, and the
latter took possession of the entire lot, and refused to fulfill his contract of
giving up a portion of the joint property to plaintiffs, they were allowed to
convert the transaction into a sale, and sue in *assumpsit* for the price of their
part of the grain; and to the same effect substantially is *McLaughlin* v.
Salley, 46 Mich. 219, and *Watson* v. *Stever*, 25 Id. 387, cited in note to *Fiquet*
v. *Allison*, 86 Am. Dec. 57. Compare extended note to *Evans* v. *Miller*, 38
Am. Rep. 315-321.

SALE OF CHATTELS. — The rule of *caveat emptor* applies to sales of chattels: Note to *Scott* v. *Hix*, 62 Am. Dec. 460. Purchaser of a chattel gets no
better title than the seller possesses: *Agnew* v. *Johnson*, 22 Pa. St. 471; 62
Am. Dec. 303; and a purchaser from a seller who has no title whatever gets
no title: *Saltus* v. *Everett*, 20 Wend. 267; 32 Am. Dec. 541. Not even good
faith will be a defense to an action of trover against one who purchased from
one who had no authority or right to sell: *Hills* v. *Snell*, 104 Mass. 173; 6
Am. Rep. 216; for the true owner of a chattel can never be deprived of his

title thereto without his consent: Note to *Velsian* v. *Lewis*, 3 Am. St. Rep. 197.

SALE OF CHATTELS. — Delivery of possession is not necessary to pass title to personal property, provided there is a valid sale: *Scarbrough* v. *Alcorn*, 74 Tex. 359.

CARPENTER *v.* GREENOP.

[74 MICHIGAN, 664.]

PARTNERSHIP — DEALINGS BETWEEN PARTNERS — REMEDY. — There is no legal nor equitable reason why a partner should not have specific dealings with his firm as well as with any other person, and unless these dealings, from their nature, are intended to go into the general accounting, and wait for their adjustment until dissolution, they give a right to have a remedy according to their exigency, and can be dealt with like any other claims, at law or in equity.

PARTNERSHIP — DEALINGS BETWEEN PARTNERS — ACCOUNTING. — Where partners have seen fit to deal with each other without reference to a final accounting, the transaction is not subject to the necessity of the delay of such an accounting.

NEGOTIABLE INSTRUMENTS — NEGOTIABILITY DOES NOT CEASE WHEN PAPER MATURES. — It is only subject to such equities as exist against the paper at the date when negotiated, and the equities which affect the indorsee are only such as attach directly to the note itself, and do not include collateral matters.

PARTNERSHIP — REMEDY OF PARTNER AGAINST FIRM. — A partner has a right to relief against the partnership when he contracts as a creditor or otherwise therewith, and the transaction is such as to be separated from the general partnership accounting, and the fact that an accounting can only be had at the close of the business indicates clearly that either the partner cannot separately contract with his firm or else there must be some means of enforcing it. A contract which cannot be enforced is nugatory.

NEGOTIABLE INSTRUMENTS — PARTNERSHIP NOTE — RIGHTS OF HOLDER. — A holder by indorsement of a partnership note given to a partner for money loaned by him to the firm, and purchased after maturity in good faith while the firm was still in business, may maintain an action thereon against the firm before its dissolution and final accounting, when the partner taking the note was not indebted to the firm at the time the note was indorsed, and no equities existed against him at that time which did not exist when the note was executed.

Glidden and Bates, for the appellant.

M. Brown and Frank Dumon, for the defendants.

CAMPBELL, J. Plaintiff purchased in good faith, but after maturity, a note of John Greenop & Co., payable to the order of Robert A. Lavery, and indorsed by Lavery. Lavery was a member of the firm of John Greenop & Co., and made the note, with Greenop's consent, for money lent by Lavery to the firm. The note was dated January 21, 1883, payable in six months. It was transferred to plaintiff in 1884 while the firm was still in business, and about a year before it ceased doing business. There was no evidence of the state of accounts, or that Lavery was in any way a debtor to the firm when the transfer was made, or that there were any equities existing against him which did not exist when the note was made.

The court below held that plaintiff could not recover. The reason assigned was, that the note could not be transferred after maturity, so as to enable the indorsee to sue upon it, if suit could not have been brought by the assignor, and that Lavery could have brought no suit on it. The decision also seems to have been based partially on the idea that a partner can have no dealings with his firm which are not subject to the final accounting, and that the equities of such an accounting attach to such claims as he may hold against the firm.

I do not think this doctrine is tenable. It certainly has not been directed in this court. The only case that is seriously claimed as bearing in that direction is *Davis* v. *Merrill*, 51 Mich. 480. That case has no resemblance to this. One member of the firm, named Eastwood, received from the firm, in October, 1874, a note due in one month after date. In 1875 the firm was dissolved, and the affairs were put into the hands of George W. Merrill, one of the partners, to wind up. Merrill's credit in the firm accounts was larger than Eastwood's, and Eastwood had been credited on the books with the amount of the note, which had never been presented or demanded during the period after dissolution. In May, 1881, Eastwood, who had lost the note by accidental fire in January of the same year, assigned to the plaintiff in general terms whatever claims he had against the firm, with no reference to the note as such. It is plain enough that there could have been no recovery in such a case. Even had the note been described, the statute does not authorize the assignee of a negotiable note, who is not an indorsee, to sue in his own name on it. But furthermore, there was no attempt to transfer the note as such. The assignment was one which transferred nothing but Eastwood's claims generally against the company, and must therefore be subject to the partnership settlement. There was no firm in existence for nearly six years before the assignment.

In the present case, the note was transferred by regular indorsement a considerable time before the firm went out of business. It was due already as an independent claim against the firm for money lent, and not for money invested in the business. It was not by its terms, or by the nature of the transaction, to be postponed until the future dissolution of the concern, and there is no accounting in advance of dissolution, unless by agreement.

While there is a difficulty in a suit at law in the name of a party against himself, yet if this is the only difficulty, it goes only to the form of the remedy, and not to its existence. There never was any legal or equitable reason why a partner should not have specific dealings with his firm as well as any other person; and unless those dealings, from their nature, are intended to go into the general accounting, and wait for their adjustment till dissolution, they give a right to have a remedy according to their exigency, and can be dealt with like any other claims. The only reason why they must, under the old practice, be prosecuted at equity instead of at law rose from the necessity, at law, of having plaintiffs capable of suing the defendants. In such a case, the failure of a remedy at law justified a resort to equity. But equity could grant relief in such cases, and, under our present rules, there can be no difficulty at law. Where partners have seen fit to deal with each other without reference to the final accounting, the transaction is not subject to the necessity or delay of such an accounting.

This note was, by its terms, negotiable. It is elementary doctrine that negotiability does not cease when paper matures. It is only subject to such equities as exist against the paper at the date when it is negotiated. And the equities which affect the indorsee are only such as attach directly to the note itself, and do not include collateral matters. This is very old doctrine, and is laid down without qualification. Lord Tenterden and his associates, speaking through Mr. Justice Bayley in *Burrough* v. *Moss*, 10 Barn. & C. 558, refer to the subject in this way: "This was an action on a promissory note, made by the defendant, payable to one Fearn, and by him indorsed to the plaintiff after it became due. For the defendant it was insisted that he had a right to set off against the plaintiff's claim a debt due to him from Fearn, who held the note at the time when it became due. On the other hand, it was contended that this right of set-off, which rested on the statute of set-off, did not apply. The impression on my mind was, that the defendant was entitled to the set-off; but on discussion of the matter with my Lord Tenterden and my learned brothers, I agree with them in thinking that the indorsee of an overdue bill or note is liable to such equities only as attach on the bill or note itself, and not to claims arising out of collateral matters. The consequence is, that the rule for reducing the damages in this case must be discharged." See Chitty on Bills, 220; Story on Bills, sec. 220; *Leavitt* v. *Putnam*, 3 N. Y. 494; 53 Am. Dec. 322; *Baxter* v. *Little*, 6 Met. 7; 39 Am. Dec. 707; and cases in note to page 275 of Bigelow's Cases of Bills and Notes, 437; 3 Kent's Com. 91, and notes.

It was not shown, and cannot be claimed on this record, that there was any unfairness, or want of consideration, or payment, or any other matter bearing on the note in this case when it was transferred, and in such case, it can make no difference when it was transferred. It continued to be a valid note, and capable of transfer by indorsement. That a partner himself may have a remedy of some kind, where the transaction is such as to be separated from the general partnership accounting, does not seem to be questioned. Mr. Collyer refers to several illustrations, in book 2, chapter 3, Partnership, second edition. Judge Story, in his work on partnership, sections 222 et seq., indicates very clearly the right of a partner to relief in the case of contracts, as a creditor or otherwise, with his firm; and the fact, which is referred to in all the books, that an accounting can only be had at the close of the business, indicates as clearly as anything can that either a partner can make no separate contract with his firm at all, or else there must be some means of enforcing it. A contract which cannot be enforced is nugatory. Partnerships are often made for long terms of years. Members become managers on salaries which are payable at regular intervals, and they frequently furnish articles for which they are entitled to pay. No one doubts their rights to pay themselves out of moneys in their charge; but all do not have this opportunity, and to hold that a person must, if his copartners will not advance him what is due, wait the whole term of business for payment, is not reasonable or maintainable.

A very thorough discussion of the various questions is found in the early case of *Smith* v. *Lusher*, 5 Cow. 688, where the judges of the supreme court, and the chancellor and other members of the court for the correction of errors, dealt with the subject in a very exhaustive way, with entire unanimity. The cases of *Nevins* v. *Townsend*, 6 Conn. 5, and *Gray* v. *Port-*

land Bank, 3 Mass. 364, 3 Am. Dec. 156, are also somewhat pertinent. I have found no authority which sanctions the doctrine that plaintiff was precluded by the fact that the note was past due from taking the title by indorsement, and none that allows a note to be affected by collateral equities. When this note was indorsed, there could be no accounting, because the firm continued its ordinary business. The debt was for a loan, and not for investments in the capital. It was distinct from the mutual relations among the partners, and stood as a separate contract.

I think there was nothing to bar recovery, and that the judgment to the contrary should be reversed.

PARTNERSHIP — DEALINGS BETWEEN PARTNERS. — As to when and for what grounds one partner may sue another before settlement and accounting, see *Bull* v. *Coe*, 77 Cal. 54; 11 Am. St. Rep. 235, and cases cited in note. Ordinarily one partner cannot maintain an action at law against the other, nor can the administrator of a deceased partner maintain an action at law against the survivor to recover an alleged balance due until there has been a settlement of the partnership accounts, for which an action lies in equity: *Haynes* v. *Short*, 88 Ala. 562. But while at common law one partner could not sue another, the rule has been to some extent changed under the code practice: *Alexander* v. *King*, 87 Ala. 642. And while the ordinary rule is, that one partner cannot maintain *assumpsit* for moneys received by his co-partner, but must resort to equity for an accounting, there is, however, an exception to the rule; for where the partnership was in a single and completed transaction, one partner may maintain an action in *assumpsit* against the other: *Kutz* v. *Dreibelbis*, 126 Pa. St. 335. But it is well settled that money furnished to one partner by another partner, to enable the latter to meet his obligations to the firm, is a personal transaction, and a suit at law may be maintained for the recovery of the money so loaned without a partnership accounting being had: *Bates* v. *Lane*, 62 Mich. 132.

PROMISSORY NOTES — PURCHASE OF, AFTER MATURITY. — An indorsee of a negotiable instrument after its maturity is considered as receiving dishonored paper, and takes it subject to all infirmities, equities, and defenses to which it was liable in the hands of the payee: *Robinson* v. *Lyman*, 11 Conn. 30; 25 Am. Dec. 52; *Johnson* v. *Bloodgood*, 1 Johns. Cas. 51; 1 Am. Dec. 93; *Lansing* v. *Gaine*, 2 Johns. 300; 3 Am. Dec. 422; *Snyder* v. *Riley*, 6 Pa. St. 164; 47 Am. Dec. 452; *Comstock* v. *Draper*, 1 Mich. 481; 53 Am. Dec. 78; *Weathered* v. *Smith*, 9 Tex. 622; 60 Am. Dec. 186; but in *Annan* v. *Houck*, 4 Gill, 325, 45 Am. Dec. 133, it was held that an indorsee of a note overdue when indorsed does not always take it subject to all the equities to which it would be liable in the indorser's hands.

CASES

IN THE

SUPREME COURT

OF

MINNESOTA.

COOPER *v.* SIMPSON.

[41 MINNESOTA, 46.]

PLEDGE — NEGLIGENCE OF PLEDGEE — EFFECT ON DEBT. — When the value of the thing pledged is lost through the negligence of the pledgee, it does not operate *ipso facto* as a satisfaction or extinction of the debt to the extent of the loss.

PLEDGE — CONTRACT REQUIRING PLEDGEE TO SELL. — A contract or pledge may make it the duty of the pledgee to sell within a specified time, and his failure to do so is then such breach of duty as will render him answerable to the pledgor. In the absence of such contract, the pledgor cannot make it the duty of the pledgee to sell by requesting or directing him to do so.

PLEDGE — LIABILITY OF PLEDGEE FOR NEGLIGENCE. — A pledgee may, by his misconduct with respect to the thing pledged, become liable to the pledgor for depreciation or loss in value in consequence of his negligence.

PLEDGE — RELATIONS BETWEEN PLEDGOR AND PLEDGEE. — In the absence of contract, the pledgor is bound to exercise ordinary care only, and is liable to the pledgee only for negligence.

PLEDGE — RELATIONS BETWEEN PLEDGOR AND PLEDGEE. — After a contract of pledging is made, neither party can, by anything he alone may do, vary the duties or powers attaching to the relation.

Gale and Brown, for the appellant.

B. F. Heuston, Jr., for the respondent.

GILFILLAN, C. J. Action for converting a horse. The defense was, that defendant, being indebted to plaintiff upon a promissory note, executed to him a chattel mortgage upon the horse to secure the debt; and that default having been made in the mortgage, defendant, as authorized by the mortgage took the horse and sold it to satisfy the debt. Plaintiff replied that the debt had been paid and satisfied before the taking. The facts on which the claim of satisfaction of the debt was based were, that when the debt had been reduced by payments until there was but $137.20 unpaid, plaintiff delivered to defendant wheat tickets—that is, receipts for wheat deposited in an elevator—to the amount of 193⅓ bushels, as further collateral security for the debt; and plaintiff gave evidence tending to prove that defendant, while he held the tickets, might have sold them for enough, over and above the elevator charges, to satisfy the debt, but that, he not selling, such charges accumulated until they amounted to more than the value of the wheat, so that the tickets were practically of no value; and also evidence from which the jury might have found that there was an agreement between the parties that defendant should sell the tickets within a specified time, or if they found no such agreement, might have found that the plaintiff, after making the pledge, directed him to sell within a specified time, and that if he had sold as so agreed or directed, the tickets would have brought enough to satisfy the debt.

The exceptions argued on this appeal arose on the charge of the court. We state but one, as it presents, as fully as all of them, the propositions of law upon which, so far as relates to the consequences of defendant's failure to sell, the case was submitted to the jury. At the request of plaintiff, the court charged: "If you find that the wheat tickets were delivered and received as collateral security, with contract that Mr. Simpson should sell within two months, or if Cooper afterwards directed Simpson to sell the wheat, his failure to sell as agreed or as directed would operate to discharge the debt it was given to secure, as far as the then market value of the wheat would go." This charge contains three propositions: 1. That if the value of the thing pledged is lost by failure of duty on the part of the pledgee, it operates to the extent of the loss to extinguish the debt; 2. That if the pledge is made with a contract between the pledgor and pledgee that the latter shall sell within a specified time, it is his duty to do so, and his failure will be a breach of duty for which he will be answerable to the pledgor; 3. That in case of a pledge, without any contract varying the duties of pledgor and pledgee imposed by law upon that relation, the former may make it the duty of the latter to sell, by directing or requesting him to do so. As to the second of these propositions, there cannot be any doubt. The parties to a pledging may, by agreement, vary their common-law powers and duties with respect to the pledge: *Gold-smidt* v. *First Methodist Church,* 25 Minn. 202. Upon the other two the court erred. Of course a pledgee may, by his misconduct with respect to the thing pledged, become liable to the pledgor for loss of the value, or depreciation in value, in consequence of such misconduct. And ordinarily, at any rate, the fact and amount of the loss so caused may be set up as a counterclaim to an action for the debt secured by the pledge. But as this is not an action to recover such debt, that is not the question. The proposition is, that loss to the pledgor by misconduct of the pledgee operates *ipso facto* as a satisfaction or extinction of the debt to the extent of the loss. We are referred to several cases in which language is used that suggests the existence of such a rule, but to none in which it was so decided. The only cases we have found in which the point was directly considered are *Taggard* v. *Curtenius,* 15 Wend. 155, and *Hook* v. *White,* 36 Cal. 299, in which it was held that facts analogous to those claimed to exist in this case, while they might be pleaded as a set-off, could not be sustained as a bar to an action for the debt secured. In *Lamberton* v. *Windom,* 12 Minn. 151 (232), 90 Am. Dec. 301, the matter was pleaded as a defense and counterclaim, and as it was enough for the purposes of the case if it could be sustained either as a defense (strictly) or a counterclaim, it was immaterial which it was. And so the court, though it speaks of the matter as a defense, does not consider the question of pleading, nor whether it operated as a satisfaction or extinction of the debt.

Here are two contracts, — one creating the debt of plaintiff to defendant, the other creating the pledge, including, as plaintiff claims, a contract to sell the pledged property within a specified time, and apply the proceeds upon the debt. A right of action may exist on each; one may be a set-off or counterclaim when suit is brought in the other. But, as said in the Taggard case, there is no such thing as setting up one right of action in bar to another right of action. There may exist facts in a case of pledging which will estop the pledgee from denying that he has disposed of the pledged property, and received and applied the proceeds upon the debt. But there are no such facts in this case. The first proposition in the charge is therefore erroneous. The third is equally so. It leaves out of account altogether the question of negligence on the part of the pledgee. There might be such a contract between the pledgor and pledgee as would make it the absolute duty of the latter to sell within a specified time, in which case his liability, by reason of failure to sell within the time, would not depend on negligence. But in the absence of some such contract, there is no liability of the pledgee to the pledgor except for negligence. The exercise of ordinary care in respect to the thing pledged is the duty which the law imposes on a pledgee, and for a breach of that duty only does he become liable. After the contract of pledging is made, neither party can, by anything he alone may do, vary the duties or powers attaching to the relation. Some cases hold that a request to sell may be an element in the proof of negligence. But we express no opinion on the point, nor do we express any whether, in the absence of express contract, it is the duty of the pledgee, at any time, to sell a chattel pledged.

Order reversed. ————

PLEDGOR AND PLEDGEE. — For the duties and liabilities of pledgees, see note to *Lucketts* v. *Townsend*, 49 Am. Dec. 735, 736.

PLEDGOR AND PLEDGEE. — For the law applicable to sales by a pledgee of pledged property, see note to *Lucketts* v. *Townsend*, 49 Am. Dec. 736, 737; *Hill* v. *Finnigan*, 77 Cal. 267; 11 Am. St. Rep. 279; *McDowell* v. *Chicago Steel Works*, 124 Ill. 491; 7 Am. St. Rep. 381; *Jeanes's Appeal*, 116 Pa. St. 573; 2 Am. St. Rep. 624; *Robinson* v. *Hurley*, 79 Am. Dec. 501–504.

The rule at common law was, that a pledgee must give notice to the pledgor to redeem, before he could sell: *National Bank* v. *Baker*, 128 Ill. 534. Ordinarily, when a pledge of property is made to secure the payment of indebtedness, the pledge cannot be sold until the debt has become due, and notice to redeem has been given, and notice of sale published in some appropriate manner. In *Sharpe* v. *Nat. Bank of Birmingham*, 87 Ala. 645, where shares of stock were pledged as collateral security for a debt, and default was made in payment of such debt at maturity, the pledgee was decided to have the option of either filing a bill to foreclose the pledge by a sale under an order from the court, or to exercise the implied power to sell without resorting to judicial proceedings; but even in the latter case, if he should sell privately without notice and become himself the purchaser, he would still be in the relation of pledgee with respect to the pledged property.

PLEDGOR AND PLEDGEE — CONVERSION BY PLEDGEE: See note to *Robinson* v. *Hurley*, 79 Am. Dec. 505, 506; *Loughborough* v. *McNevin*, 74 Cal. 250; 5 Am. St. Rep. 435. If a part owner of stock certificates pledges them, with the consent of his co-owner, as collateral security for his individual debt, and they are converted by the pledgee, the pledgor may recover them, as if they were his sole property, because the pledgee is estopped to deny the pledgor's absolute ownership: *Sharpe* v. *Nat. Bank of Birmingham*, 87 Ala. 645.

PLEDGOR AND PLEDGEE — DISCHARGE OF PROPERTY held as collateral security: *Price* v. *Dime Sav. Bank*, 124 Ill. 317; 7 Am. St. Rep. 367, and note; compare *Loughborough* v. *McNevin*, 74 Cal. 250; 5 Am. St. Rep. 425, and note.

·PATTERSON v. STEWART.

[41 MINNESOTA, 84.]   -

CORPORATIONS — DIRECTOR'S LIABILITY TO CREDITOR, HOW ENFORCED — PARTIES. — A creditor of a corporation organized under chapter 34, section 142, Minnesota General Statutes of 1878, may sue one or more of the directors to enforce their liability for the debt, without joining all the creditors or all the stockholders subject to liability; nor does the fact that the corporation is in the hands of a receiver take away or suspend the right of action, the statute providing that when such corporation becomes insolvent from a violation of its charter, the directors ordering or assenting to such violation shall be jointly and severally liable for all debts contracted after such violation.

CORPORATIONS — DIRECTOR'S LIABILITY TO CREDITOR — JUDGMENT AGAINST CORPORATION UNNECESSARY. — Where the statute gives a creditor a right of action directly against the directors of an insolvent corporation in his own behalf, it is unnecessary for him, before beginning suit, to first establish his claim against the corporation by judgment. He may make it a co-defendant in the action against the directors, and thus establish his claim.

CORPORATIONS — LIABILITY OF DIRECTORS FOR UNAUTHORIZED ACTS. — If, in a series of acts in violation of a statute giving a creditor a right of action against the directors for thus causing the insolvency of a corporation, those committed prior to the date when the debt was contracted contributed, in connection with those committed afterwards, in producing the insolvency, then the debt was one contracted after such violation, within the meaning of the statute.

CORPORATIONS — LIABILITY OF DIRECTORS FOR UNAUTHORIZED ACTS. — An ultra vires act of the directors of a corporation in executing accommodation paper in the name of the corporation, or in loaning its funds, is an act by the corporation, within the meaning of a statute giving a creditor a right of action against the directors for a violation of the charter of the corporation causing its insolvency.

CORPORATIONS — LIABILITY OF DIRECTORS FOR UNAUTHORIZED ACTS — ASSENT, WHAT CONSTITUTES. — To constitute assent of a director of a corporation to an unauthorized act, there must be something more than mere negligence on his part, — something amounting to willful, or at least intentional, violation of legal duty; but if the director knows that a violation of law is being or about to be committed, and makes no objection, when duty requires him to object, and when he has an opportunity of doing so, this will amount to assent.

APPEAL from an order sustaining a demurrer to a complaint · against a corporation, and one of the directors thereof, for acts sufficiently stated in the opinion.

Rogers, Hadley, and Selmes, for the appellant.

Flandrau, Squires, and Cutcheon, for the respondent.

MITCHELL, J.   If any proof were needed of the chaotic condition of our statutes relating to corporations, it could be found in the confused and diverse provisions scattered through chapters 34 and 76, relating to the enforcement of the personal liabilities of stockholders and officers for corporate debts. In *Dodge* v. *Minnesota etc. Roofing Co.*, 16 Minn. 327 (368), it was assumed, and in *Merchants' Nat. Bank* v. *Bailey Mfg. Co.*, 34 Minn. 323, it was expressly held, that a creditor of a corporation organized under title 2 of chapter 34 might sue the corporation for the debt, and join as defendants one or more of the stockholders to enforce their liability, and that in such action it was not necessary to join all the creditors, or all the stockholders subject to liability. This was put upon' the ground that sections 10 and 11 of that chapter clearly contemplated such an action, different from that provided for in chapter 76. In *Allen* v. *Walsh*, 25 Minn. 543, which was an action by a creditor of an insolvent bank against a stockholder to enforce his individual liability under the banking law, it was held that the exclusive remedy was under chapter 76. This was put mainly upon considerations growing out of the character and purpose of the liability, and the inadequacy of any other form of remedy to accomplish the object of the statute. In *Johnson* v. *Fischer*, 30 Minn. 173, which was an action by a creditor of a manufacturing company organized under the act of 1873, to enforce what was assumed to be the personal liability of a stockholder under Laws of 1878, chapter 56 (Gen. Stats. 1878, c. 34, sec. 111), it was held, following *Allen* v. *Walsh*, *supra*, and for similar considerations, that an action under chapter 76 furnished the exclusive remedy. The present case raises the question of the proper procedure to enforce the personal liability of directors of a manufacturing corporation organized under Laws of 1873, chapter 11, imposed by section 23 of that act (Gen. Stats. 1878, c. 34, sec. 142), for ordering or assenting to violations of the act by which the corporation became insolvent. It will be observed that none of our decisions referred to cover the case.

General Statutes of 1878, chapter 34, section 138 (repealed in 1883), provides that if the president or secretary of the corporation intentionally neglects or refuses to comply with the twelfth section of the act (making and filing an annual certificate), the persons so neglecting and refusing "shall jointly and severally be liable to an action founded on this statute for all debts of such corporation contracted during the period of any such neglect or refusal." Section 139 provides that if the capital stock shall be withdrawn and refunded to the stockholders before the payment of all the debts of the corporation for which such stock would have been liable, the stockholders shall be liable to any creditor, in an action founded on this statute, to the amount of the sum refunded to them, respectively; but if any stockholder shall be compelled, by such action, to pay the debts of any creditor, he shall have the right to call upon all the stockholders to whom any part of the stock has been refunded to contribute their proportionate share. Section 140 provides that if the directors pay a dividend when the coporation is insolvent, or any dividend the payment of which would render it insolvent, knowing the fact, the directors assenting thereto shall be jointly and severally liable, in an action founded on this statute, for all debts due from such corporation at the time of such dividend. Section 141 provides that if certain officers intentionally neglect or refuse to comply with the provisions of the act, and to perform the duties therein required of them, such as so neglect or refuse shall be jointly and severally liable, in an action founded on this statute, for all debts of the corporation contracted during the period of such neglect or refusal. Section 142 (which is the one under which this action is brought) provides that if any corporation organized under the authority of the act "shall violate any of its provisions, and shall thereby become insolvent, the directors ordering or assenting to such violation shall be jointly and severally liable, in an action founded on this statute, for all debts contracted after such violation."

We have referred to these various sections, not only because, as we think, the particular language used is itself strongly indicative of the kind of action intended by the legislature, but because the nature, extent, and purpose of the liabilities imposed illustrate what form of remedy would be adequate and appropriate under the circumstances. In every instance the language used is "in an action founded on this statute," not some other. We cannot agree with counsel for the defendant, that this merely creates a right and a liability, but prescribes no remedy. It is true, it does not specify the particular form of the action; but unless it is indicative of the remedy it has no meaning whatever. Indeed, in a jurisdiction where law and equity are administered separately, it has been held that such language in a statute gave a party an adequate remedy in law, and hence that a bill in equity would not lie: *Bassett* v. *St. Albans Hotel Co.,* 47 Vt. 313. Again, it will be observed that in every instance the liability created is directly to the creditors, and not to the corporation. The corporation could not maintain an action to enforce any such liability; neither could its assignee or receiver, in the absence of some express statutory authority. And right here we think counsel for defendant has fallen into a radical error. He argues that, except in extent, the liability is that which at common law would rest upon directors under similar circumstances; that at common law, for such acts of negligence or misconduct, the directors would be liable primarily to the corporation, and secondarily to the creditors; that the statute does not alter the relative rights of these parties; and hence that creditors, in attempting to enforce the liability, must do so in the right of the corporation or its receiver, and if the corporation is placed in the hands of a receiver the right passes primarily to him. The conclusion sought to be drawn from this line of argument is, that an action under chapter 76, by the receiver, is the only remedy. The relation between a corporation and its officers is that of principal and agent, and for negligence or fraud in the performance of their official duties, resulting in damage to the corporation, they would be doubtless liable to the latter at common law. But the extent of the liability would be the amount of resultant loss. Again, the directors of a corporation are not in any contractual relation with its creditors. They are strangers to each other. The creditors have no cause of complaint on account of any unlawful act of corporate officers, provided sufficient assets remain to pay their claims. Of course, as in case of any other persons, strangers to each other, directors would be liable at common law or equity to make just compensation for any wrong done to the legal rights of creditors. For example, if they misappropriate any part of the capital stock (which in America is held to be a trust fund for creditors), they might be held liable as trustees to the extent necessary to pay the debts; and, as in the case of liability to the corporation, the limit of the liability would be the amount of resultant damage. But the liability imposed under this statute has no relation whatever to the amount of actual damage to either the creditors or the corporation. For doing or failing to do certain things the directors or officers are made absolutely liable for certain classes of debts, although such acts or omissions may not in fact have resulted in a dollar's loss to either the corporation or its creditors. In this respect it is highly penal; so much so that it would not, under the law of comity, be enforced in another jurisdiction. The object is twofold: 1. To enforce diligence and fidelity on the part of corporate officers; and 2. To furnish a prompt and efficient remedy to those creditors who were, or might have been, injuriously affected by the acts of misfeasance or non-feasance.

The question as to the proper remedy to enforce the personal liability of stockholders or directors or officers for corporate debts depends so much upon the terms of particular statutes, or the remedial systems of different states, that not much aid can be obtained from the decisions of other courts. But we think it will be found generally true that, unless a particular remedy is prescribed by statute, the form of the remedy, whether by action at law by each creditor against one or more stockholders or officers, or by bill in equity in which all persons in interest or to be affected are made parties, is made to depend upon the character of the liability. If its object is to create a common fund, limited in amount, for the benefit of all creditors or all of a particular class, so that if one were allowed to proceed alone he might exhaust the fund or get more than his share; or if the liability was only for the deficiency of corporate assets, or only for the excess of debts contracted over the amount permitted by the charter, so that an accounting is necessary; or if for any similar reason an action at law would be inadequate to furnish a complete remedy or protect the rights of all persons interested,—the courts have generally held, in the absence of any express statutory provision, that a suit in the nature of a bill in equity, bringing in all interested parties, must be resorted to. *Hornor* v. *Henning*, 93 U. S. 228, is an example of this kind, and these considerations were given much weight in *Allen* v. *Walsh* and *Johnson* v. *Fischer*, *supra*, in determining that the exclusive remedy was under chapter 76. But no such reason obtains here. The liability of each director is unlimited, except by the amount of the corporate debts which fall within the terms of the statute. What one creditor may collect will not reduce the amount which another may recover. No accounting is necessary in order to ascertain the amount of the deficiency of corporate assets, for the creditor is not bound to resort to them first, nor is his recovery limited to the extent of such deficiency. In fact, a direct action by any creditor against any director not only furnishes an adequate remedy, but it interferes with the rights of no one else. The only possible exception to this might be an action under section 139 against stockholders.

In short, reason but adds force to what seems the plain meaning of the language of the statute, viz., that the right of action is directly to the creditors, to whom severally the directors are jointly and severally liable.

The fact (which appears from the complaint) that the affairs of the corporation have been placed in the hands of a receiver neither takes away nor suspends the creditor's right of action against the directors. The affairs of the directors are not in the hands of a receiver, nor will a suit against them at all interfere with the proceedings to wind up the affairs of the corporation. If it be necessary, as counsel argue, for a creditor to establish his claim against the company, and that it cannot be sued without leave of the receiver or the court, it would not alter the case, except that if such consent could not be obtained it might embarrass the creditor in enforcing his remedy. In what has been said we do not wish to be understood as holding that these statutory liabilities might not also be enforced by proceedings under chapter 76. It would seem that its provisions are broad enough to cover such a case. All that we hold is, that a creditor is not bound to resort to it, because the statute gives him a right of action directly against the directors, and in his own behalf alone. Neither is it necessary that, before suing the directors, the creditor should have first established his claim against the corporation by judgment. There is no occasion for this, inasmuch as he is not required first to resort to the corporate assets. Assuming it to be true that he must establish his claim against the corporation, he may, as was done in this case, make it a co-defendant with the directors, and establish the claim in the same action.

The acts charged in this case as constituting the violation of the act, resulting in the insolvency of the corporation, are, that during all the period from December, 1875, down to January 15, 1888, the directors executed in the name of the corporation large amounts of accommodation paper, for which no consideration was received, and loaned corporate money to other persons, for which no return was ever received, thereby diverting funds to purposes not authorized by law. The allegation is, that by reason of this course of conduct in executing the accommodation paper and making unauthorized loans, the corporation became insolvent, so that on January 15, 1888, its affairs were by the court placed in the hands of a receiver. Plaintiff's debt was contracted in April, 1883, and defendant

claims that inasmuch as the acts which caused the insolvency
were not then completed, therefore it does not fall within the
terms of the statute, — a debt " contracted after such violation."
Such a construction would render the section of very little force.
It rarely occurs that a single act alone renders a corporation
insolvent.   This is usually the result of a series of acts or a
continuous course of conduct.   It this case it was the diversion
of corporate capital, begun in 1875 and continued down to 1888,
which, as alleged, produced the insolvency.   If, in a series of
acts or a continued course of conduct, those committed prior
to the date of plaintiff's debt contributed, in connection with
those committed afterwards, in producing the insolvency, then
the debt was one contracted "after such violation," within the
meaning of the statute.

It is also urged that these acts were merely the unauthorized
acts of the directors, and not of the corporation, within the
language of the statute, which is: " If any corporation, etc.,
shall violate." This would render the section wholly nugatory.
A corporation can act only through its directors and officers,
and it is against just such *ultra vires* or unlawful acts on their
part that the statute is aimed.

The language of the complaint is in substance that defendant was during all this time a director of the corporation, and
did not object to these transactions, but, on the contrary, had
full knowledge of the by-laws or resolutions authorizing the
officers of the corporation to execute this accommodation
paper and make such loans, and that he acquiesced in the
same. It is claimed that this does not amount to an "assent"
within the meaning of the statute.   While there may be some
doubt whether the word "same" refers to the execution of the
paper and making the loans, or to the by-laws or resolutions,
yet we think, fairly construed, this language at least means
that he knew of the adoption of the by-laws or resolutions
authorizing and directing the doing of the illegal acts, that
he occupied a position where it was his duty to object to them,
and yet he interposed no opposition or objection.   Plaintiff's
contention is, that it is the duty of a director to know what is
being done in corporate matters; that it is negligence for him
not to know, — and therefore he is conclusively presumed to
have known, — and not objecting, he must be deemed assenting.   Such a construction would impose this severe statutory
liability for at least every act of mere negligence for which
he would be liable at common law; but as the act is highly

penal, we do not think it ought to receive so broad a construction. The language of the various sections all tends to indicate that the legislature intended that something more than
mere negligence should be necessary to subject a person to
those heavy penalties,—something amounting to willful, or at
least intentional, violation of legal duty, either ordering the
act done, participating in doing it, or assenting to its being
done, with knowledge that it was being, or about to be, done.
This assent, however, need not be express. If a director knew
that a violation of law was being or about to be committed,
and made no objection when duty required him to object, and
when he had the opportunity of doing so, this would amount
to "assent." We think the allegations of the complaint
amount to this.

Order reversed. ____

As to the Statutory Liability of Directors for corporate debts,
upon the ground of neglect of duty, see note to *Hodges* v. *New England
Screw Co.*, 53 Am. Dec. 651.

Personal Liability of Directors. — Where the statute incorporating the
company imposes no personal liability upon its directors to pay the debts of the
corporation, the only action which can be maintained against them is an action on the case: *Lexington etc. R. R. Co.* v. *Bridges,* 7 B. Mon. 556; 46 Am.
Dec. 528. The mere election of a director, under the general act incorporating a manufacturing company, does not make him liable for the debts of the
corporation for a failure to comply with the law. To render him liable under
the statute, there must be evidence, express or implied, that the director
elected had actually accepted the office: *Cameron* v. *Seaman,* 69 N. Y. 397;
25 Am. Rep. 212, and note 217, 218.

In *Allison* v. *Coal Co.*, 87 Tenn. 60, where the charter of the corporation
provided that "if the indebtedness of said company shall at any time
exceed the capital stock paid in, the directors assenting thereto shall be individually liable to the creditors for said excess," the directors were held
individually liable for such specific debts only as were contracted with their
assent in excess of the paid-up capital and remained unpaid after the corporation assets were exhausted.

NORTON *v.* BAXTER.

[41 MINNESOTA, 146.]

PLEDGE REMAINS AS SECURITY AFTER DEFAULT. — The general property in a pledge remains in the pledgor after as well as before default, and the pledgee cannot, after default, give it away so as to affect the rights of the pledgor, nor can a pretended and merely colorable sale, without consideration, divest the pledgor of his rights as such, or confer upon the pretended purchaser any greater interest than that held by the pledgee.

PLEDGE — TENDER OF PAYMENT RELEASES LIEN. — An unjustifiable refusal to accept a sufficient tender of payment of the principal debt after maturity discharges the lien against a note and mortgage pledged as collateral security.

PLEDGE — REFUSAL OF TENDER OF PAYMENT RELEASES LIEN. — An unjustifiable refusal to accept a sufficient tender of payment, although such tender is not kept good, discharges the lien on the pledge as against one who, subsequently to the pledging, has *bona fide* acquired rights in the pledged property.

PLEDGE — PRETENDED SALE BY PLEDGEE DOES NOT DIVEST LIEN OF PLEDGE. — A fraudulent sale of pledged property by the pledgee does not invest the purchaser with title, so as to affect the rights of the pledgor.

Noxon and Benton, for the appellants.

Charles J. Bartleson, and Brooks and Hendrix, for the respondent.

DICKINSON, J. This is an action to foreclose a mortgage upon a lot of land, designated as lot 14, executed by the defendants Tousley and wife to the plaintiff, in August, 1887, and to bar or enjoin these appellants, Lucy Baxter and Stephen H. Baxter, from proceeding to enforce an earlier mortgage, executed by one Nye, in 1866, under circumstances to be hereafter referred to. This appeal by the two defendants just named is from a judgment granting that relief. The mortgage last referred to, which the appellants claim the right to enforce as the earlier lien, was executed under these circumstances: September 20, 1886, Tousley and wife conveyed several lots of land, including this lot 14, to one Nye, without consideration, and for the use and benefit of the grantor, Tousley. The same day Nye gave to Tousley her (Nye's) promissory note for two thousand five hundred dollars, for the accommodation only of the payee, and executed to him a mortgage upon the same land, in terms securing the payment of the note. Subsequently, prior to Tousley's mortgage to the plaintiff, Nye reconveyed the property to Tousley. While Tousley held the accommodation note of Nye and the mortgage securing it, in October, 1886, he borrowed seven hundred dollars from the defendant Stephen H. Baxter, and a brother, William Baxter, giving to them his note therefor, payable to the defendant Lucy Baxter. As collateral security, Tousley executed an assignment to Lucy Baxter of the Nye note and mortgage, and delivered it to the Baxter brothers. Lucy Baxter had no interest in this transaction, and knew nothing of it, her name being employed for the benefit of the brothers. An agreement accompanied the assigned note and mortgage, authorizing the sale of the pledge after notice, upon default of Tousley to pay the debt secured thereby. June 22, 1888, W. H. Baxter, assuming to act in behalf of Lucy, after notice to Tousley, offered the pledged note and mortgage for sale at auction. Tousley bid $800 for it, and no other *bona fide* bid was made; but the note and mortgage were struck off to one Prouty, at $817. The securities were then assigned to him, although he paid nothing therefor, and he reassigned the same to Stephen H. Baxter. June 29, 1888, Tousley tendered to the Baxter brothers, who then had possession of the Nye note and mortgage, and to Stephen H. Baxter, the sum of $820 in payment of his own note, which the Nye note and mortgage had been pledged to secure.* This tender was sufficient in amount to pay his debt. The tender was refused.

The pretended sale of the pledged securities to Prouty, and the assignment of the same to him, and by him to Stephen H. Baxter, were not effectual as a sale of the securities so as to extinguish or prejudice the previously existing rights of the pledgor. The general property in the pledge remained in the pledgor after as well as before default. The default of the pledgor to pay his debt at maturity in no way affected the nature of the pledgee's rights concerning the property, except that he then became entitled to proceed to make the securities available, in the manner prescribed by law or by the terms of the contract. It is not the case of a defeasible title becoming absolute at law by default in the performance of the prescribed condition. The property was held as security before default. It was held only as security after default. The pledgee was authorized to sell the securities, and by a sale in good faith the pledgor would have been divested of his property. But the pledgee could not give it away, so as to affect the rights of the pledgor, nor could a pretended and merely colorable sale, without consideration, divest the pledgor of his rights as such, or confer upon the pretended purchaser any greater interest than that held by the pledgee.

The question which the appellants now present is, whether, upon tender of payment of the principal debt, the pledged note and mortgage ceased to be available and enforceable as collateral securities. It is a general principle that tender of payment of a debt, to secure which personal property has been pledged, discharges the lien, terminating the special property rights of the pledgee: *Coggs* v. *Bernard*, 2 Ld. Raym. 909, 917; *Ratcliff* v. *Davies*, Cro. Jac. 244; *Hancock* v. *Franklin Insurance Co.*, 114 Mass. 155; *Hathaway* v. *Fall River Nat. Bank*, 131 Mass. 14; *Ball* v. *Stanley*, 5 Yerg. 199; 26 Am. Dec. 263; *Mitchell* v. *Roberts*, 17 Fed. Rep. 776; *Loughborough* v. *McNevin*, 74 Cal. 250; 5 Am. St. Rep. 435; *Ratcliff* v. *Vance*, 2 Const. S. C. 239; *Kortright* v. *Cady*, 21 N. Y. 343; 78 Am. Dec. 145; *Cass* v. *Higenbotam*, 100 N. Y. 248; *Moynahan* v. *Moore*, 9 Mich. 8; 77 Am. Dec. 468; *Stewart* v. *Brown*, 48 Mich. 383. The appellants concede that while the general rule is that tender of the amount due, at the time it becomes due, discharges the lien of collateral securities, yet contend that such is not the effect of a tender after that time. Such a distinction has been recognized in respect to mortgages, based upon the fact that the legal title has become vested in the mortgagee. No such distinction can be made in the case of bailments of personal property as security. The relations and rights of the parties are unchanged by the occurrence of the default. The pledgee has not even after default the absolute legal title. The character of the bailment is not changed. It is still a pledge, and can be enforced or made available only as such. But the very terms of the contract in this case were, · that if the debt should be paid " before the sale of said property," the property should be returned. ·

The appellants rely, also, upon the fact that, so far as appears, the tender of Tousley was not kept good. There is some conflict in the authorities at the present day as to the necessity for this, in general, in order that the lien of the pledge may be discharged. We deem it unnecessary to determine whether the strict rule of the common law has been modified. It may be conceded, for the purposes of this case, that upon equitable grounds a pledgor, whose tender has been refused, should not be allowed affirmative relief, especially of an equitable nature, unless he has kept good his tender, or at least comes before the court in an attitude of willingness to pay what is due from him: *Tuthill* v. *Morris*, 81 N. Y. 94. The defendants in this case are not entitled to favor upon equitable grounds. The tender made by Tousley, the common debtor of both parties, was sufficient, and, so far as appears, there was nothing to justify the refusal to accept it or to qualify the strict legal effect of the refusal. After an unauthorized, and as it would seem a fraudulent, sale, Baxter, who was a party to it, refusing to accept from Tousley the payment of his debt, asserts in this action the right to hold and enforce the pledged securities, not merely as securities for his debt of seven hundred dollars, but as his own property, the mortgage being an encumbrance of two thousand five hundred dollars, with interest. This plaintiff has not been in default. He owes nothing to the defendants, and is not chargeable with fault because the debtor did not keep his tender good. He also is a creditor of Tousley, having mortgage security junior to that which was pledged to the defendants. Tousley, the common debtor, was bound to pay both. The unjustified refusal of Baxter to accept payment was prejudicial to the plaintiff holding the junior mortgage. The pledged note and mortgage of Nye, if released from the pledge, would not, as to the plaintiff, have been available in Tousley's hands as a senior encumbrance upon the land, having been executed for the accommodation of Tousley. In view of the relations between the plaintiff and Baxter, there appears to be nothing to modify the strict rule of the common law, that a tender of payment of the debt discharges the pledge, so far, at least, as it affects the plaintiff. Of course the debt of Tousley was not thus discharged.

Judgment affirmed.

————

PLEDGOR AND PLEDGEE. — The lien of a pledgee is extinguished by a valid tender to him of the amount due and his refusal to accept it: *Loughborough* v. *McNevin*, 74 Cal. 250; 5 Am. St. Rep. 435, and note.

DOBBIN *v.* CORDINER.

[41 MINNESOTA, 165.]

MARRIED WOMEN — DEEDS OF — ESTOPPEL. — A married woman who, at the request of her husband and with knowledge of the facts, joins him in executing and acknowledging a deed of her real estate, and then delivers it to him for the purpose of completing and delivering it to the purchaser, is estopped, as against the latter, who is innocent and has paid value, to assert the invalidity of the deed, on the ground that when she executed it it was done under her husband's misrepresentations, and was incomplete, not containing the name of the grantee nor a description of the property conveyed, all of which was afterwards inserted without her authority, and the deed delivered to the purchaser.

MARRIED WOMEN — ESTOPPEL AGAINST. — Incident to the enlarged power of married women to deal with others is the capacity to be bound and estopped by their conduct when the enforcement of the principles of estoppel are necessary for the protection of those with whom they deal, although there are limitations upon the application of this doctrine.

MARRIED WOMAN'S DEED IS EFFECTUAL as a conveyance, although there is but one subscribing witness.

Hart and Brewer, for the appellant.

Wilson and Lawrence, for the respondent.

DICKINSON, J.   This action is prosecuted for the purpose of securing the cancellation of a deed of conveyance from the plaintiff and her husband to the defendant.   The plaintiff seeks to avoid the deed, upon the grounds that, as she alleges, the deed, when executed by her, was incomplete, not containing the name of the grantee nor any description of the property conveyed; that, by her husband's misrepresentations, she was induced to sign and acknowledge the instrument in its incomplete form; and that he afterwards, without her authority, inserted the name of the defendant as grantee, and the description of the property, and delivered the deed to the defendant.   By the findings of the court the following facts are established: The land had been purchased by the plaintiff's husband, who paid a part of the purchase price.   The conveyance was made to the plaintiff, who gave a mortgage upon the property for an unpaid part of the purchase price. The plaintiff's husband, having bargained with the defendant for the sale of the land to him, prepared a deed for the conveyance of the property, complete in form, except that it did not contain the name of any grantee.   He requested the plaintiff to execute it; and, without objection, she signed and acknowledged it, the husband also joining in the execution of it. She delivered the deed, after her acknowledgment, to her husband, for the purpose of completing and delivering it to the purchaser. The husband then wrote in the name of the defendant as grantee, delivered it to him, and the latter, receiving the deed, paid the price to plaintiff's husband, in good faith, without notice of any defects or omissions in the making or executing of the deed. He assumed, as part of the consideration, the payment of the outstanding mortgage on the property. The plaintiff's allegations as to the fraudulent procuring of her execution of the deed are not sustained by the findings of the court.

It is conceded, on the part of the appellant, the plaintiff, that, in general, one executing a deed of conveyance may give authority to another, by parol, to insert in the deed, after its execution, the name of a grantee, the grantee not having been before named in the deed; but it is contended that a wife cannot confer such authority upon her husband. We deem it unnecessary to decide whether this distinction can be recognized. Without regard to that question, and however it might be decided, we are of the opinion that by her conduct the plaintiff is precluded, upon the principle of estoppel, from asserting, as against the defendant, the invalidity of this deed. Our statutes have gone far to remove the common-law disabilities of married women. The property held by them at the time of their marriage continues to be their separate property after marriage. They may, during coverture, receive, hold, use, and enjoy property of all kinds, and the rents, issues, and profits thereof, and all avails of their contracts and industry, free from the control of their husbands. They are capable of making contracts, by parol or under seal. They are bound by their contracts, and responsible for their torts, and their property is liable for their debts and torts to the same extent as if they were unmarried. Their power to contract and to convey real estate is, however, so far qualified that they cannot contract with their husbands relative to the real estate of either, or by power of attorney or otherwise authorize their husbands to convey their real estate, or any interest therein; and in general, in all conveyances by married women of their real estate their husbands must join. Married women cannot enjoy these enlarged rights of action and of property and remain irresponsible for the ordinary legal and equitable results of their conduct. Incident to this power of married women to deal with others is the capacity to be bound and to be estopped by their conduct, when the enforcement of the principle of estoppel is necessary for the protection of those with whom they deal, although there are, without doubt, limitations upon the application of this doctrine: *Norton* v. *Nichols*, 35 Mich. 148; *Reed* v. *Morton*, 24 Neb. 760; 8 Am. St. Rep. 247; *Knight* v. *Thayer*, 125 Mass. 25; *Bodine* v. *Killeen*, 53 N. Y. 93; *Powell's Appeal*, 98 Pa. St. 403; *Fryer* v. *Rishell*, 84 Pa. St. 521; *Godfrey* v. *Thornton*, 46 Wis. 677; *Lavassar* v. *Washburne*, 50 Wis. 200; *Baum* v. *Mullen*, 47 N. Y. 577; *Patterson* v. *Lawrence*, 90 Ill. 174; 32 Am. Rep. 22; *Reis* v. *Lawrence*, 63 Cal. 129; 49 Am. Rep. 83; *Sharpe* v. *Foy*, L. R. 4 Ch. 35; *In re Lush's Trusts*, L. R. 4 Ch. 591; 2 Pomeroy's Eq. Jur., sec. 814.

This plaintiff had power to convey her estate by deed in which her husband should join. She executed and acknowledged this deed, knowing that it was a deed of conveyance, and contemplating that it was to be delivered and have effect as such, and that the purchaser would pay a consideration therefor. The deed was delivered, as she intended it should be, to a purchaser, who, in good faith, supposing the conveyance to be in all respects valid and effectual, has paid the consideration therefor. Even if her authority to her husband, implied from the circumstances, to fill in the name of the grantee was ineffectual to legally empower him to do so, she ought not now to be allowed, in a court of equity, to defeat the title of the purchaser upon that ground. A grantor not under disability from coverture would be estopped under such circumstances: *Pence* v. *Arbuckle*, 22 Minn. 417. It is equitable that the same principle be applied here for the protection of the defendant; and to so apply it does not, we think, defeat the purposes of the statute declaring invalid any power of attorney or other authority, as between husband and wife, to convey real estate. It is immaterial, in our view of the case, whether or not there was an express authorization of the husband to fill in the name of the grantee. It is enough that the plaintiff intended the instrument to have effect as a conveyance, and that she allowed her husband to take it, after she had executed it, for the purpose of delivering it to the purchaser as a deed of conveyance executed by her. That the plaintiff supposed that her husband was to deliver this deed to the purchaser is shown by her own testimony. The extent of the proof on the part of the plaintiff, as to the misrepresentation of her husband, was that he said to her, when he asked her to execute the deed, that he would like to sell a lot.

Without considering what might have been the effect of fraudulent misrepresentations of the husband in a case where the wife was not chargeable with negligence in the transaction, we regard this evidence as wholly insufficient to justify the granting of relief as against an innocent purchaser. With regard to the rights of purchasers, it was culpable negligence on the part of the plaintiff to execute the conveyance, unless she is to be bound by it. The language of her husband did not justify her in executing the deed without reading it, or at least without more definite information as to its contents, unless she was willing to allow the deed to have effect, whatever the property conveyed might be. It is therefore unnecessary to pass upon the question of the admissibility of the husband's testimony going to rebut the plaintiff's testimony in this particular, and which, as it seems, the court below did not consider.

The deed was effectual as a conveyance, although there was but one subscribing witness: *Morton* v. *Leland*, 27 Minn. 35; *Johnson* v. *Sandhoff*, 30 Minn. 197; *Conlan* v. *Grace*, 36 Minn. 276. The evidence justified the findings of fact.

Judgment affirmed. ____

MARRIED WOMEN — ESTOPPEL. — The doctrine of estoppel is applicable against married women: *McDanell* v. *Landrum*, 87 Ky. 404; 12 Am. St. Rep. 500, and particularly note 503, 504.

In *Cross* v. *Hedrick*, 66 Miss. 61, where a married woman, with her husband, gave a trust deed upon her property to secure a debt for goods for the benefit of both herself and husband, and where joint accounts were given to her at the time, it was held that she could not, eight years after a sale of the land under such trust deed and a recovery from her of the property under judicial proceedings, impeach the sale by showing an arrangement with her husband by which he was to cultivate her lands for his own benefit, so that only the income therefrom should be liable under the Mississippi code.

In *Long* v. *Crossen*, 119 Ind. 3, where a wife transferred her separate estate to her husband, by conveyances importing a money consideration, for the purpose of enabling him to mortgage it as his own property to secure a loan for his own benefit, she was held to be estopped as against the mortgagee, who did not have knowledge that the conveyances were made by the wife to her husband to evade the statute, which prohibited her from entering into contracts of suretyship.

De Kay *v.* Chicago, Milwaukee, and St. Paul Railway Company.

[41 Minnesota, 178.]

RAILROADS — DUTY OF PASSENGER AT WAY-STATION OR WHILE TRAIN IS SIDE-TRACKED. — When a passenger enters a railway train and pays fare to be transported from one station to another, his contract does not obligate the corporation to furnish him with safe egress or ingress at any intermediate station or while the train is side-tracked, and while the train is stopped at such place the duty and safety of the passenger both concur in telling him to remain in the cars. If, under such circumstances, he leaves the cars with the permission of the corporation, or without objection on its part, he does no illegal act, and has the right to re-enter and resume his journey; but for the time being he surrenders his rights as a passenger, and takes upon himself the responsibility of his own movements, and must exercise great care and caution to avoid injury.

RAILROADS — DUTY OF COMPANY AND OF PASSENGER WHEN TRAIN IS SIDE-TRACKED. — Where a railway company permits a through passenger to leave the train while it is side-tracked, it must give reasonable and seasonable notice to him to return when his train is about to start, if he remains near at hand; but if he goes out of sight or hearing, he takes his chances of being left, and the company is not bound to wait for or send after him.

RAILROADS — DUTY OF COMPANY AND OF PASSENGER WHEN TRAIN IS SIDE-TRACKED. — Where a railway company permits through passengers to leave the train while it is side-tracked at an intermediate point, it is bound to use reasonable diligence not to expose them to unnecessary danger while leaving or re-entering the train, yet it is not bound to make such point as safe and convenient as a station platform. A passenger, under such circumstances, assumes the risks necessarily incident to such practice, and must use a degree of care and caution to avoid injury from passing trains, corresponding to the increased risks, as the company gives him no assurance that while crossing or recrossing the main track no other trains will pass, when he has thus left his train for his own convenience or pleasure.

RAILROADS — NEGLIGENCE OF PASSENGER WHEN TRAIN IS SIDE-TRACKED. — Where a railway company has permitted a passenger to leave his train for purposes of his own while it is side-tracked at an intermediate point, to allow another train to pass, the conductor's call of "All aboard" is not an assurance to such passenger that no other train is approaching, but rather an express warning that one is, and does not justify nor excuse him for doing a dangerous act, and recklessly obeying at the risk of his life, when, at most, it is but a question with him of inconvenience in being left and having to take a later train, and he is not confronted with the dilemma of choosing immediately between two dangers, nor, under such circumstances, is the fact that he heard no signals any excuse for not looking, when he had ample opportunity to do so, and it would not have appreciably delayed his progress.

APPEAL from an order refusing a new trial after verdict for plaintiff for five thousand five hundred dollars. Exhibit A, mentioned in the opinion as showing the place of accident, is as follows: —

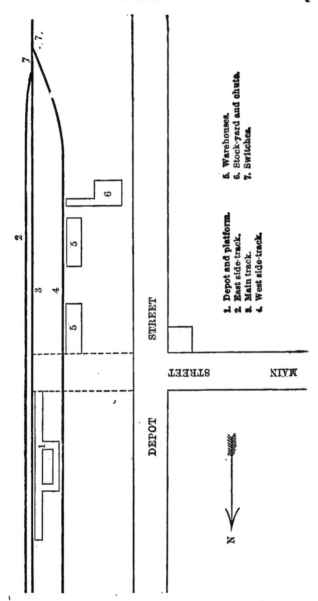

1. Depot and platform.
2. East side-track.
3. Main track.
4. West side-track.

5. Warehouses.
6. Stock-yard and chute.
7. Switches.

H. H. Field, for the appellant.

A. J. Edgerton, George B. Edgerton, W. H. De Kay, Lovely and Morgan, and Walter J. Trask, for the respondent.

MITCHELL, J.   This was an action for damages for personal injuries alleged to have been caused by the negligence of defendant. The defendant denies the alleged negligence on its part, and charges negligence on part of plaintiff. The trial resulted in a verdict for the plaintiff, and the question is, whether this was justified by the evidence.

Plaintiff, at Mitchell, Dakota, entered a mixed train of defendant going south, as a passenger for Sioux City, Iowa. The regular place for this train and a north-bound train (also mixed) to pass each other was at the intermediate station of Parkston, a small prairie village twenty-four miles south of Mitchell. At that station there is a depot and a platform west of and adjoining the main track, the platform extending north and south about one hundred feet each way from the depot. East of and parallel with the main track, and nine feet distant from it, is a side-track, which connects with the main track at a switch some eight hundred feet south of the depot. There is another side-track west of the depot, and about fifty-five feet from the main track, which also connects with it at a switch a little south of the east side-track switch. Both these side-tracks extend about four hundred and fifty feet north of the depot, and there connect with the main track. The village of Parkston is located west of the depot, and consists principally of one street (Main) running east and west down to the depot-grounds. If extended easterly this street would cross the main track at the south end of the depot platform. The crossings at this point are planked, and the ground is level between the tracks. The depot platform is three or four steps above the level of the railway tracks. Adjoining the depot-grounds on the west, and two hundred feet distant from the main track, is what is platted as Depot Street, eighty feet wide and running north and south. On the west of the west side-track, and south of what would be Main Street if extended east, are two warehouses and a small stock-yard and chute. To a person coming eastward from the village to the station, on reaching the west side of Depot Street there would be an unobstructed view of the railroad to the south, which would continue until he came opposite the warehouses and stock-yard referred to, which would obstruct it for a short distance; then, on reaching the west side-track, the view would again be unobstructed, and continue so until the person would reach the main track, — a distance of fifty-five feet in a direct line. The country being level prairie, the railroad would be in plain sight for a long distance. This will all be more fully understood by reference to the map, exhibit A.

On the day in question, the train on which plaintiff was a passenger arrived at Parkston on time, drew up on the main track alongside the depot platform, and stopped a few minutes, doing its work of receiving and discharging freight and passengers. The north-bound train was late this day, and the conductor of plaintiff's train, having received orders to hold for it, after finishing his work at the depot, backed his train (consisting of an engine, four freight-cars, a combination-car, and passenger-coach) up over the north switch, and ran it down on the east side-track, and stopped opposite the depot, with the engine near the street-crossing at the south end of the platform. The object, of course, was to let the north-bound train pass, as it had the right of way on the main track. Before this, however, when plaintiff's train arrived at the station, it seems some of the passengers, including the plaintiff, got out upon the platform, when the conductor stated to some one, in plaintiff's hearing, that the other train was late, and that he would have to wait for it, and that they would have time to go up town. There is a conflict of evidence as to how long the conductor said the train would have to wait, but we must accept as true the evidence most favorable to the plaintiff, viz., "twenty or thirty minutes." In consequence of this statement, the plaintiff left the station, and went up into the village, made one or two small purchases, and started to return, coming down the south side of Main Street; and at or just before he reached the west side-track, as he testifies, he heard the conductor call "All aboard," and the bell ring, and saw the train commence to move. This we also accept as true, although. from other evidence as to subsequent occurrences it would seem not improbable that he underestimates his distance from the depot when he heard the call. We must also accept as true his statement that he had not been absent from the depot over fifteen minutes, and hence that the time the conductor had stated the train would wait had not yet fully elapsed. The cause of the conductor's calling "All aboard," etc., was the approach of the north-bound train. It does not positively appear just where this train was when the conductor made the call, but the general purport of the evidence is, that its head was at or a little inside the south switches. There is much conflict of evidence as to the rate of speed at which this train approached the station, and as to whether it blew a whistle or rang a bell. But here again we must accept as the facts that it approached at an unusual and high rate of speed, and that it gave no signals.

Returning, now, to the plaintiff, when he heard the cry of "All aboard," etc., he started and ran as fast as he could diagonally across the street to the platform, up the steps, and then northerly on the platform some forty feet, and then jumped diagonally, with his face northeasterly, right on to the main track, and was instantly struck by the north-bound train, and received the injuries complained of. Plaintiff knew before he left the depot that this train was expected, and that was what his train had to wait for. He was a young man, in full possession of all his senses, and the day was calm and clear. He never looked to the south, or took any other precaution to ascertain if a train was approaching from the direction, although, for at least the last one hundred feet that he ran, the view to the south was unobstructed, and he could and must have seen the train if he had turned his head in that direction. He testifies that he supposed that this train was so late that his train was not going to wait for it, but he gives no reason for this impression, and none is apparent, unless it is the fact that his train was pulling out a little sooner than the conductor said it would. It is evident that when plaintiff jumped upon the track he did so almost in front of the engine. As one witness expressed it, "the engine was just ready to crawl on to him"; another, "he jumped right in front of the engine"; and still another, "I thought he wanted to kill himself from the way he jumped." The plaintiff testifies: "I heard the cry of 'All aboard' just about the time I jumped." If he meant by this that the conductor called a second time, he is uncorroborated by any other witness. But even if this was so, it is pretty apparent that it had no influence one way or the other on his action, as it is evident, from his hasty and excited manner, that this was already predetermined.

It appears that all who were on the platform, or immediately at the station when the call of "All aboard" was given, who desired to do so, crossed over the main track to their train in safety before the north-bound train reached the depot; also that no one else attempted to cross over as late as the plaintiff, three other passengers, who, like plaintiff, were coming from the village when the signals for starting were given, stopping on the west side of the main track at the street-crossing until the train passed. There is no evidence that the conductor knew where the plaintiff was when he called "All aboard." It is also a fact, not without significance, that of all those who were around the station on that occasion, whether passengers or by-standers, who were examined as witnesses, plaintiff was the only one who did not see the north-bound train before it reached the station.

We think that the evidence justified the jury in finding that the defendant was negligent at least in the matter of running the north-bound train into the station at such a rate of speed without giving any signals of its approach, especially in view of the fact that at the south end of the depot platform there was what was used as a street-crossing. But we are also of opinion that, taking as true every fact favorable to the plaintiff and every one unfavorable to the defendant which there was any evidence reasonably tended to prove, there is no room for any other conclusion than that the plaintiff was grossly negligent in jumping upon the track without taking the least precaution to ascertain whether a train was approaching.

To relieve him from the charge of negligence in this respect, the chief contention of his counsel is, that the act of the conductor, in calling "All aboard," was an assurance to him that he could cross the track in safety; that the rule as to "looking and listening" does not apply to a case like this; that a passenger crossing a track at a station, to leave or get on his train, has a right to assume that the railway corporation will so regulate its trains that it will be safe for him on the track which he is thus invited and required to cross in order to leave the train or to secure his passage. And numerous cases are cited to the proposition that the highway-crossing rule has no application to a case where, by the arrangement of the corporation, it is made necessary for passengers to cross the track in going to or from the depot to the cars.

Properly applied, there is no doubt as to the correctness of this proposition. But we think it will be found, in every case where this rule has been applied, that the cars were standing at the place appointed and designated by the corporation for the exit or entrance of passengers. Such are the cases of *Terry* v. *Jewett*, 78 N. Y. 338; *Brassell* v. *New York Cent. etc. R. R. Co.*, 84 N. Y. 241; and *Klein* v. *Jewett*, 26 N. J. Eq. 474. But here the situation was altogether different, and consequently the rights and duties of the parties were also different. In the first place, plaintiff was not a passenger for this station. Where a passenger enters a railway train and pays the regular fare to be transported from one station to another, his contract does not obligate the corporation to furnish him with safe egress or ingress at any intermediate station. In the next place, this side-track was not the designated or appointed place for the egress or ingress of passengers. The place for that was at the platform on the main track. That was the place where it did such work; it was run in upon the side-track solely for the purpose of letting another train pass. Under such circumstances, as has been well said in one case, the duty and safety of passengers both concur in saying to those not destined for that station that they remain in the cars. That is the place of safety. The uncertainty as to when the other train may pass and as to its rate of speed, and the danger of crossing the track under such circumstances, are all suggestive of risk and of the necessity of great care and caution. But if a passenger, under such circumstances, with the permission of the corporation, or without objection on its part, leaves the cars, he does no illegal act; he has undoubtedly the right to re-enter and resume his journey; but for the time being he surrenders his place as a passenger, and takes upon himself the responsibility of his own movements. If he remains near at hand when his train is about to start, the agents of the railway should give reasonable and seasonable notice for him to return to the car. But if he goes out of sight or hearing, he takes his chances of being left. The company is not bound to wait for him or send after him.

And while, if a railway corporation permits such a practice, it is bound to use reasonable diligence not to expose passengers to any unnecessary dangers while leaving or re-entering the train on the side-track, yet it is not bound to so regulate its business as to make a side-track as safe or convenient a place of ingress or egress as the station platform. The side-track is not made for any such purpose. The passenger is using it for this purpose solely for his own convenience or pleasure, and he must assume the risks necessarily incident to such a practice, and is bound to use a degree of care corresponding to the increased risks. The company gives him no assurance that, while crossing or recrossing the track, no other train will pass. On the contrary, the very purpose for which the train is put upon the side-track, as well as all experience, negatives any such presumption. If a passenger will leave his train under these circumstances, when he attempts to cross the track for the purpose of re-entering it he is bound to exercise reasonable care and caution to avoid injury from passing trains.

This was just the situation of the plaintiff. He had left his
train for purposes of his own. He knew that it was run in
upon the side-track for the express purpose of letting the
other train pass. Common experience should have taught
him that the usual practice is, when a train is delayed for the
passing of another train, for the former to "pull out" as the
other "pulls in." So far from the conductor's call of "All
aboard" being an assurance to him that no other train was
approaching, it amounted, under the circumstances, almost to
an express warning that the delayed train was approaching.
No call of "All aboard" from the conductor could justify him
in recklessly obeying at the risk of his life. He was not confronted with the dilemma of choosing immediately between
two dangers. It was at most a question of inconvenience in
being left and having to take a later train, which was no excuse for doing a positively dangerous act. The fact that he
heard no signals was no excuse for not looking. He had
ample opportunity to look. To do so would not have appreciably delayed his progress. He had but to turn his head to
have seen the train. Indeed, so close to him was it when he
jumped that it is hardly possible to conceive how any person
in possession of his senses could have helped both seeing and
hearing it, even without looking around. It is evident from
the general tone of the testimony of the by-standers who saw
him that his conduct impressed them as unaccountably reckless. His acts cannot be accounted for upon any other theory
except that he had become so excited as to have ceased to be
in full possession of his senses, and so utterly oblivious to
what was going on around him that he rushed recklessly into
a danger patent to everybody else. This was no crime, or
anything that should deprive him of sympathy on account of
his misfortune; but it was such gross negligence as in our
opinion to prevent a recovery in this action.

Order reversed. ——

CARRIERS — DUTY OF PASSENGER. — A through passenger has no right to
leave the cars at a way-station where refreshments are not served, and if he
asks the conductor how long the cars will stop at such station, the latter is
not presumed to know that it is the passenger's desire to alight and consume
the time of the stop in business away from the station; so that the answer of
the conductor neither increases nor diminishes the duty or liability of the carrier to the passenger: *Missouri P. R'y Co.* v. *Foreman*, 73 Tex. 311; 15 Am.
St. Rep. 785, and note as to passengers leaving cars at way-stations.

HANDY v. ST. PAUL GLOBE PUBLISHING COMPANY.

[41 MINNESOTA, 188.]

CONTRACTS — PLEADING ILLEGALITY. — Though it is sometimes necessary to plead the facts upon which the illegality of a contract depends, still it is never necessary to plead the law. When the facts appear either upon the pleadings or proofs, either party may insist upon the law applicable to such proofs.

CONTRACT — MUTUALITY AND ENTIRETY OF CONTRACT ILLEGAL IN PART. — A contract by which it is agreed that a party, upon the payment of certain rates for real estate advertising, is to take entire charge and control of the real estate advertising business in the daily, Sunday, and weekly issues of a newspaper, in consideration of being allowed the difference between the rates paid and those received by him for advertising, the contract to continue for five years, is an entire and indivisible contract, so that any taint of illegality in one part affects the whole of it.

SUNDAY NEWSPAPER ILLEGAL. — The issuing, publishing, and circulating a newspaper on Sunday is not a work of necessity or charity, and was prohibited, and therefore unlawful, under chapter 100, section 20, General Statutes of Minnesota, 1878. Hence a contract concerning advertisements therein was, while such statute remained in force, void.

CONTRACTS — RATIFICATION OF VOID CONTRACT — CHANGE IN LAW. — A contract void because it stipulates for doing what the law prohibits is incapable of being ratified as a whole, even if the law is so changed after the contract was made, and before it is fully performed, as to make it valid after the change went into effect. Every contract must be ratified, if at all, as an entirety.

Flandrau, Squires, and Cutcheon, for the appellant.

H. J. Horn and C. D. O'Brien, for the respondent.

GILFILLAN, C. J. The action is upon a contract pleaded in the complaint, not *in hæc verba,* but according to its supposed effect. The answer denied it; and on the trial, the plaintiff offered in evidence a written contract between the parties, the provisions of which material to this controversy were as follows: The plaintiff, in consideration of being allowed the difference between the rates he might charge for advertising in the various issues of the St. Paul Globe newspaper and the rates thereinafter mentioned, agreed and contracted to take entire charge and control of the real estate advertising business in the daily and Sunday and weekly Globe, and the defendant agreed, in consideration of such services, to put under his full charge and control all real estate advertising business of defendant in the daily and Sunday and weekly Globe. The plaintiff agreed to pay the defendant certain specified rates for said real estate advertising, and the defendant agreed to receive said rates as full payment for all said real estate advertisements which might appear in the daily, weekly, or Sunday

Globe, without regard to the amount plaintiff might charge and receive from advertisers. The contract was to continue for the term of five years, with the option in plaintiff to renew it for another term of five years, or for a shorter time, he to have the right to annul the agreement on giving thirty days' notice of his intention to do so. It was admitted by plaintiff, at the time of making the offer of this contract, that the Sunday Globe referred to in the contract was issued, published, and circulated on Sundays, though set up and printed on Saturdays. The contract was objected to as void upon its face for want of mutuality, and as being against public policy; and it appears to have been argued that it was against public policy because it was an agreement for a violation of the law in regard to Sunday. The court below sustained the objection. The plaintiff, of course, failed in his action, and he appeals from an order denying his motion for a new trial. The same objections are made to the contract here as were made below.

The plaintiff contends that, not having pleaded the illegality of the contract, defendant could not assert it on the trial. It is sometimes necessary to plead the facts upon which the illegality of a contract or transaction depends, but it is never necessary to plead the law. When the facts appear, either upon the pleadings or proofs, either party may insist upon the law applicable to such facts. In this case, the plaintiff had, under the pleadings, to prove the contract upon which he sued. If it be void on its face, he, not the defendant, showed its illegality.

Though the contract appears in some respects a much more favorable one to the plaintiff than to the defendant, it is not wanting in mutuality of promises and engagements, so as to be without mutual considerations. What plaintiff is to do appears by implication rather than by express terms. Fairly construed, the contract created the relation of principal and agent between the defendant, as principal, and the plaintiff, as agent, for the management of defendant's real estate advertising business, — that is, in the charge of procuring advertisements for so much of the space in defendant's paper as it devoted to real estate advertising, — and, in this business, there would arise the duty in the contract. There was, by implication, the promise of plaintiff to manage the business faithfully, and with due regard to the interest of his principal.

The question of the legality of the contract is, therefore, squarely presented; and with a view to that question, and to some propositions that are made in connection with it, it is necessary to say that the contract is entire, so that any taint of illegality in one part affects the whole of it. There is no way of severing it, so we can say that, although its stipulations as to the Sunday Globe may be in violation of law, and therefore void, yet those as to the daily and weekly Globe may be upheld; or so that, although for what was to be done under it prior to January 1, 1886, when the Penal Code went into effect, it was void, it might yet be upheld for all that it provided for after that date. To attempt that would be to attempt making another contract for the parties,—one that the present contract furnishes no reason to suppose they would have made for themselves. All of the provisions of the contract must, therefore, stand or fall together.

The plaintiff insists that the contract was not illegal, for it neither was executed on Sunday nor required plaintiff or defendant to do anything on Sunday. It bound defendant to maintain and issue a weekly, a daily, and Sunday Globe for the time specified in it; and it required plaintiff's services in the preparation and procuring, so far as related to the real estate advertisements, of material for each of those editions of the paper. According to the terms of the contract, the defendant was no more at liberty to discontinue its Sunday edition than to discontinue its daily or weekly edition, or all its editions. The theory of the complaint is, that it was bound to continue them all; so that if to issue, publish, and circulate a newspaper on Sunday was against the law as it existed when this contract was made, then the parties contemplated and stipulated for a violation of the law by each. The law in reference to Sunday in force at the time when the contract was made was section 20, chapter 100, General Statutes of 1878, as follows: "No person shall keep open his shop, warehouse, or work-house, or shall do any manner of labor, business, or work, except only works of necessity and charity, ... on the Lord's day, commonly called Sunday; and every person so offending shall be punished by a fine," etc. A contract which requires or contemplates the doing of an act prohibited by law is absolutely void. No cases of the kind have been more frequently before the courts than contracts which were made on Sunday, or which required or provided that something prohibited by the statute should be done on Sunday; and in no instance has any court failed to declare such a contract void. Unless the issuing and circulating a newspaper on Sunday is, within the meaning of the statute, a work of necessity, it is prohibited by it as much as any other business or work. The newspaper is a necessity of modern life and business; but it does not follow that to issue and circulate it on Sunday is a necessity. There are a great many other kinds of business just as necessary; many, indeed most, kinds of manufactures and mercantile business are indispensable to the present needs of men, but no one would say that, because necessary generally, the prosecution of such business on Sunday is a work of necessity. That carrying on any business on Sunday may be profitable to the persons engaged in it; that it may serve the convenience or the tastes or wishes of the public generally, — is not the test the statute applies. To continue on that day the sale of dry goods or groceries, or the keeping open of markets, saloons, theaters, or places of amusement, might be regarded by many as convenient and desirable, but that would not bring such business within the exception in the statute.

At the time this contract was made, the issuing, publishing, and circulating a newspaper on Sunday was contrary to law; and as the contract provided for that, and as it was indivisible, it was thereby rendered wholly void. The Penal Code went into effect January 1, 1886. Section 229 provides that certain kinds of articles, among them newspapers, may be sold in a quiet and orderly manner on Sunday. Plaintiff contends that the recognition of this contract, and the continuance of business under it for more than a year after the issuance of the Sunday paper became legal by the provisions of the Penal Code, constituted such a ratification of the contract as relieved it of any original taint of illegality. There is a difference in the decisions on the question whether a contract, void merely because it was made on Sunday, may be ratified on a secular day, so as to become valid; but there is no conflict of decisions on the proposition that a contract, void because it stipulates for doing what the law prohibits, is incapable of being ratified. That is this case. The contract contemplated the doing what the law then in force prohibited, and for that reason it was void. It is true, the law was so changed after the contract was made that, from the time of the change, it became, as plaintiff claims, lawful to do those things provided in the contract which were unlawful at the time it was made; and so that, as he claims, a contract like this, made after the change went into effect, would have been valid. But that could not affect the validity of the previous contract, which was void from the beginning. The parties might have made a new contract, to commence on or after January 1, 1886; but, because of the illegality in it, they could not, at any time, ratify this contract from the beginning; and, because it is entire and indivisible, they could do nothing amounting to less than the making of a new contract which could give vitality to it for the time since January 1, 1886. An entire contract must be ratified, if at all, as an entirety.

Order affirmed.

ILLEGAL CONTRACTS — PLEADING. — The illegality of a contract to be available as a defense must be pleaded: *Heffron* v. *Pollard*, 73 Tex. 96, 15 Am. St. Rep. 764.

SUNDAY CONTRACTS. — What are "works of charity or necessity," within the exception of the statute forbidding labor on the sabbath-day, see note to *Hennersdorf* v. *State*, 8 Am. St. Rep. 449. As to the validity of contracts made on Sunday, see note to *Robeson* v. *French*, 45 Am. Dec. 237, 238; *Allen* v. *Duffie*, 43 Mich. 1; 38 Am. Rep. 159, and note 165–167; note to *Coleman* v. *Henderson*, 12 Am. Dec. 292, 293. As to ratification of contracts made on Sunday, see note to *Coleman* v. *Henderson*, 12 Am. Dec. 293, 294. The publication of a sheriff's notice of sale in a Sunday newspaper is invalid: *Shaw* v. *Williams*, 87 Ind. 158; 44 Am. Rep. 756. In *Sheffield* v. *Balmer*, 52 Mo. 474, 14 Am. Rep. 430, where plaintiffs contracted to publish an advertisement in the weekly (Sunday) edition of their paper for a year, which, however, did not appear, it was held that the contract was valid, as it could not be presumed that the contract contemplated any labor to be done on Sunday.

ILLEGAL CONTRACTS. — If any part of a consideration is illegal, the whole contract is void as against public policy, even though the illegal act or promise is coupled with one which is legal: *McNamara* v. *Gargett*, 68 Mich. 454; 13 Am. St. Rep. 355; for illegal contracts cannot be divided and held valid in part and invalid in other parts: *Santa Clara etc. Co.* v. *Hayes*, 76 Cal. 387; 9 Am. St. Rep. 211.

In *Baird* v. *Boehner*, 77 Iowa, 622, where the plaintiff, an unmarried woman, pregnant by defendant, agreed in writing with him to leave and stay away from their place of residence one year, to waive all civil claims against him, and to waive all criminal claims against him, in consideration of certain monthly money payments, and the conveyance to her of certain realty by defendant, the court held that the several elements of the woman's contract were so connected, as constituting the consideration of defendant's promise to pay and convey, that they could not be separated, and the contract was therefore void *in toto*.

ILLEGAL CONTRACTS — RIGHTS OF PARTIES. — As between original parties and all parties *in pari delicto*, the courts will not enforce illegal contracts: *Bowman* v. *Phillips*, 41 Kan. 364; 13 Am. St. Rep. 292; *Leonard* v. *Poole*, 114 N. Y. 371; 11 Am. St. Rep. 667, and note; and there is no liability to a party for failing to perform a *nudum pactum: Metzger* v. *Franklin Bank*, 119 Ind. 359. In *Jones* v. *Hanna*, 81 Cal. 507, the rule was followed that courts will not aid parties in the enforcement of contracts interdicted by law.

GOODSELL *v.* TAYLOR.

[41 MINNESOTA, 207.]

PASSENGER-ELEVATOR — NEGLIGENCE IN CARE OF — PROOF SUFFICIENT TO
ESTABLISH. — In an action for damages sustained from the giving way
of a passenger-elevator in consequence of the breaking of the cable connected therewith, evidence that such cable has been so long in use as to
be seriously worn, weakened, and rendered insecure, and that such
wearing could easily have been seen if properly looked after, is sufficient
to justify the jury in finding negligence in the care and management of
the elevator.

PASSENGER-ELEVATOR — QUESTION OF NECESSITY OF EXAMINATION OF AS
TO ITS SAFETY, FOR JURY. — Whether due care and prudence required
the examination of the cable of a passenger-elevator in order to ascertain its condition as to safety, is not a question of expert evidence, but
is for the jury to determine.

PASSENGER-ELEVATOR. — PRESUMPTION OF SAFETY OF CABLE of a passenger-
elevator does not arise from the fact that it is not obviously dangerous,
and has been used with safety for years, nor will it be presumed that it
will continue safe for use without examination to ascertain its condition,
and if its safety may not have become impaired by wear.

PASSENGER - ELEVATOR — RELATION BETWEEN OWNER AND PASSENGER
THEREIN. — The relations between the owner and manager of a passenger-elevator and those carried in it are similar to those between a
carrier of passengers and those carried by him. Such owner is required to exert the utmost human care and foresight, and is responsible for the slightest degree of negligence; and in case of the giving way
of the elevator, causing injury to a passenger, the burden of proof is on
the owner to show that it occurred through no fault or neglect of his.

TRIAL — PRESUMPTION AS TO CORRECTED INSTRUCTION. — Where the trial
court in its charge corrects a proposition objected to, it will be presumed that the jury accepts the correction as the law of the case.

APPEAL from an order refusing to grant a new trial after
verdict for plaintiff for $1,275.

Clapp ana Woodard, for the appellant.

Mason and Hilton, for the respondent.

GILFILLAN, C. J. Action for damages sustained from the
giving way of an elevator at a hotel, in which the plaintiff
was riding at the time. The objection is made that there was
no evidence of negligence on the part of the owner of the
hotel. The evidence was such as to make that a question for
the jury. The fall of the elevator was in consequence of
the cable breaking. As the evidence suggests no other
cause for its breaking, it must have happened either from
its having been originally insufficient, or from its having
become insecure from wear. It appears to have been in use
three or four years, so far as appears, without accident; and

from that fact, and from direct evidence that it was well constructed, the jury might infer that the break was not from any original defect, but from the consequence of wear. That it had worn, as it would naturally be the case, appears from the testimony. A piece of the cable cut off the broken end was exhibited to the jury, and they could see (as we cannot) whether the wear was such as to seriously weaken the cable, and render it insecure. There was evidence that the wearing could easily have been seen, if properly looked after. From this evidence the jury might find that the break was because the cable had worn till it was unsafe, and that proper care would have discovered it in time to remedy it, and prevent accident. The charge of machinery to the sufficiency of which is intrusted people's lives requires a degree of care which the jury might well find was not observed in this case.

One of defendant's witnesses was asked the question, "whether or not there is anything in the construction of that elevator, and in the appearance of the cable, that would suggest to a prudent man the necessity for having an examination of this cable at the point where it was pointed out to you as where this break occurred." This plaintiff objected to as incompetent, and as calling for an opinion, and it was excluded. The question to what extent the apparent wear impaired the strength of the cable might have been one for an expert, but as held in *Mantel* v. *Chicago etc. R'y Co.*, 33 Minn. 62, whether due care requires this or that to be done is not a question for expert testimony. Whether prudence required an examination of the cable was for the jury to determine, upon the facts and circumstances of the case.

The defendant asked of the court this instruction: "As a general rule, where appliances or machinery have been in use for years, and are not obviously dangerous, and it has uniformly proved safe, it may be presumed to be safe, and its use continued." This request was bad, because it laid out of account that the strength of machinery ordinarily becomes impaired by wear, and that to ascertain if such wear has rendered it unsafe may require some examination. One has no right to assume, because a machine never has given way, that therefore it never will, especially of a machine upon the safety of which the lives of others may depend.

The relation between the owner and manager of an elevator for passengers and those carried in it is similar to that between an ordinary common carrier of passengers and those carried by him. The same reason exists for requiring on the part of the owner the utmost human care and foresight, and for making him responsible for the slightest degree of negligence, and also in case of injury by the breaking or giving way of the elevator, for putting on him the *onus* of proving that it was through no fault or neglect of his. The rule as to care applied by the court below was within this rule.

Exceptions were taken to two propositions in the general charge, and thereupon the court corrected the charge by withdrawing the language excepted to, and instructing the jury that they should disregard the same. The appellant, however, still persists in his exceptions to the propositions as originally given, arguing that they must have made such an impression on the minds of the jury to his prejudice as the correction could not or did not remove. We will not say that there might not be such a case. But it could not have been so in this case. We do not see that the original propositions were incorrect, but however that may be, it must be presumed that whenever the trial court in its charge corrects a proposition, the jury accepts the correction as the law of the case. It is inevitable that the court in its general charge will sometimes inadvertently use language tending to mislead the jury. The purpose of requiring an exception is that the mind of the court may be directed to a proposition stated or language used by it, so that it may have an opportunity to make any correction that it sees fit.

Order affirmed.

———

PASSENGER CARRIERS INSURE THE SAFETY OF THEIR VEHICLES: Note to *Grand Rapids etc. R. R. Co.* v. *Huntley*, 31 Am. Rep. 324–326; note to *Hegeman* v. *Western R. R. Corp.*, 64 Am. Dec. 521–528.

ELEVATORS — THE CARE AND DILIGENCE EXPECTED OF PERSONS using an elevator in their places of business is the same as that resting upon carriers of passengers by coach or railway, and they are held liable for the slightest neglect in regard to the vehicles provided for them, and are bound to use extraordinary diligence and care in their management: *Treadwell* v. *Whittier*, 80 Cal. 575; 13 Am. St. Rep. 175, in which case the law relating to elevators is fully discussed.

DEAN *v.* ST. PAUL UNION DEPOT COMPANY.

[41 MINNESOTA, 360.]

LANDLORD AND TENANT — LIABILITY FOR ASSAULT BY SERVANT OF LAND-LORD'S LESSEE. — A corporation organized for the purpose of furnishing depot and station-house accommodations to different railroads under contract, and which leases a room in its depot to a tenant, who operates and controls a parcel-room therein for hire, is liable to a passenger who, while lawfully upon the premises, is maliciously attacked and beaten by an employee of the lessee of the corporation in charge of the parcel-room, when the corporation knowingly and advisedly permitted its tenant to keep in his employ for more than six years in the depot such employee, of savage and vicious propensities, and who had during such period frequently assaulted and beaten persons lawfully upon such premises.

Davis, Kellogg, and Severance, for the appellant.

Cole, Bramhall, and Morris, I. V. D. Heard, and *John D. O'Brien,* for the respondent.

COLLINS, J.   The plaintiff appeals from an order sustaining defendant's demurrer to the complaint, on the ground that it failed to state facts sufficient to constitute a cause of action. From said complaint, and a stipulation as to certain facts made by the parties, and by agreement considered as if the facts therein stated had been a part of the pleading demurred to, it appears that the defendant is a domestic corporation, organized for and engaged in the business of furnishing and conducting a union depot and station-house in the city of St. Paul, in which several lines of railway deliver and receive passengers by virtue of their contracts with defendant; that on May 17, 1888, plaintiff reached said depot as a passenger upon one of the said roads, and with the intention of pursuing his journey to a point beyond by another road, entered the station-house, approached the parcel-room therein, leased by defendant to a tenant who operated and controlled it, for the purpose of checking his valise, and was there maliciously attacked and beaten by the man in charge, who was in fact the employee of defendant's tenant.   The complaint further alleges that this employee was of vicious temper, of bad character, and had frequently, in a willful and malicious manner, assaulted and beaten people lawfully upon the premises during the six years he had been employed in said parcel-room, all of which was well known to defendant on the day of the attack upon plaintiff.

In support of its demurrer, the defendant corporation contends: 1. That it owed no duty whatever to the plaintiff, because no contractual relation existed between the parties; that therefore he must look to the railway company whose passenger he was or had been, for compensation for his injuries; 2. If it should be held that the duties imposed by railway companies towards their arriving and departing passengers have been assumed by the defendant, it is not responsible in this case, because the alleged assault was not committed by one of its servants or employees, but by the employee of a tenant who was engaged in an independent business, wholly disconnected from that of a common carrier of passengers, and conducted solely for the accommodation and convenience of those who chose to patronize the room, and pay for the privilege of having their parcels temporarily taken care of; finally, if these positions prove untenable, it is argued that the assault of the employee was for purposes of his own, outside of his occupation, in disregard of the object for which he was employed, not committed in execution of it, and therefore in no event can the defendant be held responsible.

It has been announced by this court in *Ahlbeck* v. *St. Paul etc. R'y Co.*, 39 Minn. 424, that in respect to the handling and care of baggage, the relation between the defendant corporation and the carriers who use its depot is that of principal and agent; but, under the allegations of the complaint now before us, it is not essential to determine the precise relations existing between the defendant (organized for the special purpose, and under contract, to furnish to certain railway corporations proper and adequate depot and station-house accommodations for those who are entitled to use the same) and the plaintiff, who, arriving upon the train of one of these carriers, remained its passenger until he had an opportunity, by safe and convenient means, to leave the cars, the railway, and the station-house: *Warren* v. *Fitchburg R. R. Co.*, 8 Allen, 227; 85 Am. Dec. 700. Nor is it necessary to pass upon the contention of the defendant, that, whatever duty it owed the plaintiff as a passenger, it cannot be held liable for the willful act of the servant and employee of one who had leased a room in its depot building for the purpose of carrying on an independent business, not required of the carrier of passengers, and conducted by a tenant solely for the convenience of the traveling public. Nor, as we regard the pleading, need we consider the final position assumed by defendant, that the master is not responsible for the willful acts of his servant, performed outside of his employment, not in execution of it, and for purposes of his own, although the subject has been referred to in *McCord* v. *Western Union Tel. Co.*, 39 Minn. 181, in which is mentioned, approvingly, the case of *Stewart* v. *Brooklyn etc. R. R. Co.*, 90 N. Y. 588, 43 Am. Rep. 185, whereby *Isaacs* v. *Third Ave. R. R. Co.*, 47 N. Y. 122, 7 Am. Rep. 418, relied upon by the respondent, was, in effect, overruled.

This complaint, considered in connection with the stipulation, charges that the defendant knowingly and advisedly permitted its tenant to keep in his employ for more than six years, in its depot building into which it encouraged people to come, and was under contract to admit the plaintiff as an arriving passenger, a man of savage and vicious propensities, and who had, during said period of six years, frequently assaulted and beaten persons lawfully upon said premises, and who, upon the day named, attacked and beat the plaintiff without provocation. Whatever obligation otherwise, by virtue of its contract with the carrier, rested upon the defendant as to the plaintiff, it is manifest that it was bound to use ordinary care and diligence to keep its premises in a safe condition for those who legitimately came there. It had no more right, therefore, to knowingly and advisedly employ or allow to be employed, in its depot building, a dangerous and vicious man, than it would have to keep and harbor a dangerous and savage dog or other animal, or to permit a pitfall or trap into which a passenger might step as he was passing to or from his train.

Order reversed.

———

RAILROAD COMPANIES — STATIONS AND STATION-GROUNDS. —Railroad companies must keep their stations and station-grounds in a condition which will give convenience and safety to their passengers: *Missouri Pac. R'y Co.* v. *Neiswanger*, 41 Kan. 621; 13 Am. St. Rep. 304, and note.

RAILROAD COMPANIES AS CARRIERS OF PASSENGERS must protect their passengers from violence and insult from other passengers, strangers, or their own servants: *Dillingham* v. *Russell*, 73 Tex. 47; 15 Am. St. Rep. 753.

LIABILITY OF MASTER FOR TORTIOUS ACTS OF HIS SERVANT: *Peavy* v. *Georgia R. R. & B. Co.*, 81 Ga. 485; 12 Am. St. Rep. 334, and cases cited in note; *Central R'y Co.* v. *Peacock*, 69 Md. 257; 9 Am. St. Rep. 425, and note; *Williams* v. *Pullman P. Car Co.*, 40 La. Ann. 417; 8 Am. St. Rep. 538, and note.

Rowe v. St. Paul, Minneapolis, and Manitoba Railway Company.

[41 Minnesota, 384.]

Surface Water — Railroad Embankment. — A railroad company is not bound to provide the embankment of its road-bed with sufficient waterways and culverts to allow the usual amount of surface water from surrounding lands to pass under and through the same, when there is no well-defined channel or ravine crossing and closed by the embankment.

Surface Water — Right of Land-owner. — Subject to reasonable restriction, the owner of the lower estate may, in the use and improvement of his land, obstruct or hinder the natural flow of surface water, and turn the same back upon the lands of others, without liability for such obstruction; and though he is not permitted to collect it in a stream or body, and turn it upon the land of others, to their injury, still he is not bound to provide drains to prevent the accumulation of such water on adjacent lands, the natural flow of which is interrupted by changes in the surface of his own lands, caused by improvements thereon. This rule is not modified by the existence of depressions in the land in or over which surface drainage occurs in times of freshet; but if at such times large quantities of surface water are forced into a natural and well-defined channel or ravine, the land-owner must provide a culvert or other means of escape for it.

Appeal from an order refusing to grant a new trial, after dismissal of the action on the ground that the complaint did not state a cause of action.

O. Mosness, for the appellant.

M. D. Grover and W. E. Dodge, for the respondent.

Vanderburgh, J. The defendant's railroad traverses, in a north and south direction, township 142, range 46, which is alleged to be an unusually flat and level prairie, having a gradual and uniform slope of two to four feet to the mile westerly to the Red River. Plaintiff's farm is situate in the same township, about one mile east of the defendant's right of way, which lies consequently two to four feet lower than plaintiff's land. The action is for damages suffered by plaintiff by reason of the obstruction interposed by the defendant's road-bed to the free passage of surface water from the adjacent lands, so as to prevent the drainage thereof through or over defendant's right of way towards the river. Plaintiff owns three quarters of section 10, in the township named, and the complaint alleges that during the year 1882 "said railroad was so improperly, carelessly, negligently, and unskillfully constructed, managed, and maintained, over and across said township 142, range 46, that the road-bed of said railroad

unnecessarily dammed up and impeded, and entirely stopped,
the flow of the usual surface water which naturally gathers
and flows through a large and well-defined *coulée*, or natural
depression in the prairie there, which said *coulée* gathers and
accumulates enormous quantities of said water, and extends
from the east towards the west in an irregular direction, at or
near the center of said section 10, towards and across said railroad of the defendant, and stopped and impeded the usual
surface water which naturally and otherwise would have
passed from the east to the west with the natural slope of the
country across the entire of said section 10, and other lands
thereto adjacent, by reason of wholly inadequate and insufficient water-ways and culverts through the road-bed of said
railroad to allow the usual amount of such surface water to
pass under and through said road-bed, and thereby, in the
spring season of the year aforesaid, the said surface water was
made to accumulate and stand for and during the period of
about three weeks in such enormous quantities that several
miles of country on the east side of said railroad, in said township 142, was overflowed and covered with water; and that
thereby the said land of the plaintiff, for and during the period
of three weeks in the spring of the year 1882, became and was
overflowed and covered with water and then and there and
thereby the crop so growing on said premises, consisting of
about eighty-five acres of grain, of the value of eighteen hundred dollars, became and was greatly damaged, and was wholly
destroyed."

From this it appears that the road-bed stopped and impeded the usual surface water which naturally and otherwise
would have passed from east to west with the natural slope of
the country, and dammed up the "well-defined *coulée* or natural depression in the prairie," extending from near plaintiff's
land, east and west, across the defendant's road, through
which large quantities of water are gathered and accumulated.
It will be observed that the negligence and unskillfulness in
the construction and maintenance of the road complained of
are particularly stated to be the want of adequate and sufficient water-ways and culverts through the road-bed of defendant to allow the usual amount of surface water to pass under
and through the same. The only question in the case, then,
is, whether, upon these facts and the rules of law applicable
thereto, the defendant, as owner of the lower estate, was bound
to provide sufficient drainage through its right of way to pre-

vent the upper or dominant estate from being overflowed by
surface water; it being admitted that adequate water-ways or
culverts have not been provided for such purpose.

In respect to responsibility for the disposition of surface
water, the common-law rule prevails in this state, and, subject to the reasonable restriction, applicable here as in other
cases, that he must so use his own land as not to injure his neighbor, the owner of the lower or inferior estate may, in the use
and improvement of his land, obstruct or hinder the natural
flow of surface water, and turn the same back upon the lands
of others, without liability for injuries arising from such obstruction: *O'Brien* v. *City of St. Paul*, 25 Minn. 331, 336; 33
Am. Rep. 470. He is not permitted to collect it in a stream or
body, and turn it upon the lands of others, to their injury:
Hogenson v. *St. Paul etc. R'y Co.*, 31 Minn. 224; *Township of
Blakely* v. *Devine*, 36 Minn. 53. But he is not bound to provide drains or water-ways to prevent the accumulation of surface water upon adjacent lands, the natural flow of which is
interrupted by changes in the surface of his own lands, caused
by improvements thereon: *Pye* v. *City of Mankato*, 36 Minn.
373; 1 Am. St. Rep. 671; *Alden* v. *City of Minneapolis*, 24
Minn. 254, 262.

In *Hoyt* v. *City of Hudson*, 27 Wis. 656, 9 Am. Rep. 473,
which is cited by the appellant on another point to which we
will refer later in the opinion, the general rule is stated to be,
that the owner has the right to obstruct and hinder the flow
of mere surface water upon his land from the land of another;
that he may even turn the same back onto the land of his
neighbor without incurring liability for injuries caused by
such obstruction; and this we find to be the rule as generally
applied to railway embankments and structures in those states
where the doctrine of the common law prevails: *O'Connor* v.
Fond du Lac etc. R'y Co., 52 Wis. 526; 38 Am. Rep. 753; *Hanlin* v. *Chicago etc. R'y Co.*, 61 Wis. 515, 529; *Kansas City etc.
R. R. Co.* v. *Riley*, 33 Kan. 374; *Abbott* v. *Kansas City etc. R'y
Co.*, 83 Mo. 271, 285; 53 Am. Rep. 581; overruling *Shane* v.
Kansas City etc. R'y Co., 71 Mo. 237; 36 Am. Rep. 480.

The rule is not modified by the existence of depressions or
hollows in the land in or over which mere surface drainage
occurs in times of freshet; but a modification has been suggested in cases where, from the natural formation of the ground,
large quantities of water, from heavy rains or melting snows,
are forced into a channel, and flow in a stream through a nar-

row valley or ravine. In such cases it may frequently be found to be as reasonable and proper to bridge a ravine or provide a way of escape for the waters through an embankment, by a suitable culvert, as in the case of natural streams; and if the channel is well defined and worn by the accustomed flowage of waters therein, it assumes the characteristics of a watercourse, and circumstances may require that similar provision be made for it: *McClure* v. *City of Red Wing*, 28 Minn. 186, 193; *Bowlsby* v. *Speer*, 31 N. J. L. 351; 86 Am. Dec. 216; *Palmer* v. *Waddell*, 22 Kan. 352; *Hoyt* v. *City of Hudson, supra*. And in such cases the effect of the culvert would not be to interfere with the natural flow of the waters beyond the road-bed or bridge, while under other circumstances the resul. might be to gather the surface-waters into streams, to the damage of lands of adjacent owners.

Swett v. *Cutts,* 50 N. H. 439, 9 Am. Rep. 276, also cited by this appellant, recognizes the right of the land-owner to change the diffusion of surface water at his will and pleasure, provided it be done in good faith, and in the enjoyment and for the greater usefulness of his own land. The rule, as stated and adopted by the courts of that state, is, in substance, that the land-owner may disturb the natural drainage to any degree necessary in the reasonable use of his own land; but what is such reasonable use is a question to be determined by the jury, upon the facts and circumstances of each case: See also *Abbott* v. *Kansas City etc. R'y Co., supra.*

Whether, under the circumstances of particular cases as they may arise, any further modification of the rule may not be made by the courts in determining what may be a reasonable use or mode of improving property, is not necessary to discuss here. No such case is made by the complaint. It does not appear that there are any drains, natural or artificial, beyond the road-bed, into which accumulated waters turned through culverts could be carried off or disposed of without trespassing upon the lands of others; and it does not appear that any well-defined channel or ravine of the character above referred to is crossed and closed by the defendant's road-bed. Upon the facts as alleged, we are of the opinion, therefore, that the court was right in dismissing the action. The general averment, that the waters were unnecessarily obstructed by the embankment, only raises the question whether, upon the facts specially stated as the ground of the complaint, the defendant is liable in damages in this action, and raises no issue of fact

in the case.   The general topography of the country, as stated
in the complaint, suggests the necessity, or propriety at least,
both as respects public improvements and private interests, of a
comprehensive system of drainage in that portion of the state.

Order affirmed.

———

SURFACE WATER — RIGHTS OF LOWER PROPRIETOR. — A land-owner may,
in the reasonable use of his own land, lawfully prevent the flow of surface
water onto his premises from the adjacent higher land of another, although
such adjacent land may be injured thereby: *Swett* v. *Cutts*, 50 N. H. 439; 9
Am. Rep. 276, and cases cited in note 284, 285; and to the same effect substantially is *Barkley* v. *Wilcox*, 86 N. Y. 140; 40 Am. Rep. 519.

In *O'Connor* v. *Fond du Lac etc. R'y Co.*, 52 Wis. 526, 38 Am. Rep. 754,
it was decided that a railway company, in the construction of its road, was
not liable for filling up an artificial ditch by which surface-water was drained
from lands of an adjacent owner into a river.   For a railway company, having acquired a right of way, and found it necessary to raise its track above
the natural surface of the land, is not bound to provide culverts or other
means for the passage through the embankment of surface water of the lands
belonging to upper proprietors: *Cairo etc. R. R. Co.* v. *Stevens*, 73 Ind. 278;
38 Am. Rep. 139, and compare cases cited in note to this case.   And in *Gross* v.
City of Lampasas, 74 Tex. 195, the rule is laid down, that a land-owner may
protect his lands from surface water, and to effect this protection, may erect
walls upon his lands to prevent such water from flowing upon it.

But the owner of the lower track cannot throw back surface water naturally
flowing upon his lands from the upper tract: *Nininger* v. *Norwood*, 72 Ala.
277; 47 Am. Rep. 412; *Barrow* v. *Landry*, 15 La. Ann. 681; 77 Am. Dec.
199; *Hooper* v. *Wilkinson*, 15 La. Ann. 497; 77 Am. Dec. 194, and note;
Gibbs v. *Williams*, 25 Kan. 214; 37 Am. Rep. 241, and note 248, 249; *McCormick* v. *Horan*, 81 N. Y. 86; 37 Am. Rep. 479.   For the liability of railway
companies for obstructing the flow of surface water by their embankments, see
Sullens v. *Chicago etc. R'y Co.*, 74 Iowa, 659; 7 Am. St. Rep. 501, and cases
cited in note.   A riparian owner has no right, by erecting an embankment,
to divert the natural course of surface water and turn it upon the lands of
another: *Shane* v. *Kansas City etc. R. R. Co.*, 71 Mo. 237; 36 Am. Rep. 480,
and note 490–492.

A railway company may acquire, by a user of twenty years, the right by
prescription to maintain a culvert so constructed as to cause the lands of an
adjoining upper proprietor to be overflowed: *Emery* v. *Raleigh etc. R. R. Co.*,
102 N. C. 209; 11 Am. St. Rep. 727.   But in *Ogburn* v. *Connor*, 46 Cal. 346,
13 Am. Rep. 213, where defendant, who owned lands below vacant public
lands, built an embankment which obstructed the natural flow of surface
water from the public lands, the court held that he was responsible for damages thereby occasioned to plaintiff, who purchased said public lands after the
construction of such embankment, even though defendant may have maintained such embankment for a period which would ordinarily have given him
a prescriptive right, for no such right could have been acquired as against
the United States, plaintiff's grantor.

SURFACE WATERS — DOMINANT AND SERVIENT HERITAGE. — The owner of
a dominant estate cannot, at common law, direct the waters of a slough, which
is upon his tract, into an artificial channel or a channel wholly different from
that in which they naturally flow: *Dayton* v. *Drainage Commissioners*, 128
Ill. 271.

McDonald *v.* Chicago, St. Paul, Minneapolis, and Omaha Railway Company.

[41 Minnesota, 439.]

Master and Servant — Negligence of Master or Servant, and Assumption of Risk by Employee, Questions for Jury. — In an action by a railroad employee to recover damages for an injury received while engaged, under orders, in turning an engine upon a turn-table, shown by the evidence to have been defective, inadequate, and unsuitable for the use to which it was subjected, and to have been operated, as it was at the time of the accident, by authority of the company, the questions of the company's negligence and of the employee's contributory negligence, as well as whether the latter assumed the risk of such an accident in undertaking and remaining in the employment, should be submitted to the jury.

Master and Servant — Duty of Master to Furnish Safe Machinery. — When a servant is employed on or in connection with machinery, in the use of which danger may arise, it is the duty of the master to use reasonable diligence to guard against accident to his employee, and to make such seasonable repairs or changes as may be necessary to prevent accident or to lessen risk.

Master and Servant. — A Master is under Obligation to Warn his Servant of hazards to which the latter is exposed, and to see that he is not induced to work under the notion that machinery or the instruments upon or with which he is at work, or the place where he is at work, is suitable and safe, when in fact the master knows, or ought to know, that it is not.

Master and Servant — Hazard Assumed by Servant. — It is the duty of the servant to use reasonable care to inform himself in respect to the hazards to which he may be exposed; but unless the risks are patent, he is not under the same obligation to know the nature and extent thereof as is the master, whose duty it is to explain to and warn him of such risks.

Appeal from an order refusing to grant a new trial after verdict of six thousand dollars for plaintiff.

J. H. Howe, C. D. O'Brien, and S. L. Perrin, for the appellant.

I. V. D. Heard and John D. O'Brien, for the respondent.

Vanderburgh, J. The principal questions in this case arise on defendant's exceptions to the ruling of the court in refusing to dismiss the action upon the plaintiff's evidence, and in refusing to direct a verdict upon the whole evidence in the case. The other exceptions which were taken to the admission of testimony in the case do not require any consideration, as we think the legal questions thereby presented are not doubtful or important. The discussion is, therefore, prac-

tically narrowed down to the question whether the decision
of the trial court, affirming that the verdict is supported by
the evidence, is sustained by the record. Plaintiff suffered
the injury complained of while in defendant's employ, in assisting to turn an engine on its turn-table, in East St. Paul,
on the third day of April, 1887. He was one of several employees engaged under the direction of a foreman, whose
duty it was to care for the engines in the round-house, and to
turn the incoming or outgoing engines upon the turn-table
as required. He had been so employed about three months.
The evidence on material points is conflicting; but there is
evidence in the case reasonably tending to prove that the
turn-table, which had been in use for about seven years, was
defective, or inadequate and unsuitable for the use to which
it was subjected; that it was too small for the class of large
engines then in use; that it was raised too high in the center, so that it was not easily kept balanced, but "tipped" or
canted over to one side; that the wheels upon which it turned
in the pit were much worn, and sometimes did not touch the
rails; and that it was ordinarily moved with great difficulty,
by prying or "pinching" with iron bars placed under the
wheels, so that it was a long and laborious task to turn it,
when, if it had been suitable for the purpose, and in good
order, it could have been readily turned with levers in a few
minutes. The evidence also tends to show, that at the time
he commenced work, and while he was there, it was the practice to call to their assistance other engines, as opportunity
might offer, to aid in turning the table. The track ran close
to the table, and a stick about eight feet long and four inches
in diameter, prepared and kept for the purpose, was so adjusted between the engine upon the track and that upon the
table as to enable the former to push the latter along on the
curve a considerable distance, or till beyond reach. This
mode of turning the table sufficiently appears to have been
with the authority and sanction of the foreman, and was frequently resorted to while the plaintiff was there. He testifies
that the foreman ordered it whenever there was a chance to
get an engine for the purpose, and another witness, the engineer upon the switch-engine that assisted in turning the table
when the accident occurred, testifies that the foreman had
asked him to assist in the same way two months before, and
that it was the practice, "off and on," all winter. Notice to
the defendant of the condition of the table would be pre-

sumed after a reasonable time. On the day in question, the switch-engine was passing down the track nearest the table, distant about fourteen inches. Another engine had been backed out upon the turn-table, to be turned around and sent out upon the road. It was a large engine, and the tank extended beyond the table, so that the switch-engine could not pass. Thereupon the "stick" was called for, and the plaintiff and another of the employees procured it and adjusted it between the two engines in the usual way, as plaintiff testifies. Steam was thereupon applied, the turn-table moved a few feet and then "tipped," and the engine thereon ran back upon the curb, the wheels caught, and the stick broke. The two engines were suddenly brought together, and plaintiff's arm crushed between the tenders. Whether the case should have been taken from the jury involved the question of defendant's negligence as well as that of plaintiff's contributory negligence, and whether he assumed the risk of such an accident in undertaking and continuing in the employment.

1. The jury were warranted in finding from the evidence that defendant was fully cognizant of the condition of the turn-table, and the manner in which it was used and operated, and that under the circumstances the use of an engine in assisting to turn it was authorized by it. Undoubtedly the condition of the table induced the particular use, but the jury might also find that such use by the men was under legitimate orders in the course of their employment. In this case the switch-engine that was used was on its way to the coal-house for coal, and the track was obstructed by the other engine on the table, so that it could not pass. Under the evidence in the case, the court did not err in its determination that it was for the jury to consider and find what was the condition of the table, and whether its use and operation was dangerous; whether the accident was occasioned by the alleged defects therein, which caused the engine to be thrown off and stopped; and hence whether, in view of all the facts as they might find them to exist, the defendant had failed in its duty to provide suitable and proper instrumentalities and safe accommodations for their employees in the work and employment they were engaged in. When the servant is employed on or in connection with machinery in the use of which danger may arise, it is the duty of the master to use reasonable diligence to guard against the risk of accident to his employees, and in the exercise thereof to make such seasonable repairs or

changes as may be necessary to prevent or remove it: *Lake Shore etc. R'y Co.* v. *Fitzpatrick*, 31 Ohio St. 479, 485.

2. It is further argued that the evidence conclusively shows that the plaintiff was guilty of contributory negligence, and that the court should have taken the case from the jury for that reason; but we think the suggestions of counsel on this point are such as might more properly be made before the jury, and in our opinion the question was properly left to them. The plaintiff's evidence shows that he had been accustomed to hold the stick in the same way as he did on this occasion, and that it was placed in the usual position. He had not been instructed how to hold it, or warned to do the work differently. He had never known an engine to slip off, or the table to tip in that way. His co-employee, one Alvin, as he says, placed one end of the stick against the draw-bar of the engine on the turn-table, and he placed the other end against the corner of the switch-engine, and the foreman, as he says, then ordered Alvin to come away, but not him; and another witness testifies, without objection, that he regarded Alvin's position dangerous, but not plaintiff's. It appeared to plaintiff to be a proper way to push the table round; and he had no apprehension of danger. If his testimony is true, the mode adopted was not unusual or unauthorized. Whether the stick was negligently placed, and whether the plaintiff's conduct was otherwise negligent under the circumstances, and how much weight should be given to his explanations, were, we think, for the jury.

3. It is also insisted that the danger of accident in the use of the turn-table was among the risks of his employment assumed by plaintiff, and the jury should have been so instructed, and that the verdict should be set aside on that ground. It is the duty of the master to be careful that his servant is not induced to work under the notion that machinery or the instruments upon or with which he is to work, or the place where he is to work, is suitable and safe, when in fact the master knows, or ought to know, that it is not. The plaintiff might assume, unless the danger was patent, that the proper officer understood the nature of the business, and approved the method of operating the table which was adopted, and was in a better position to understand the risks. The situation or circumstances may be such that while the character of machinery and its mode of operation may be sufficiently obvious to the senses, yet the risks attending its use

may not be appreciated or understood by the employee without proper explanation or warning. It is the duty of the servant to use reasonable care to inform himself in respect to the hazards to which he may be exposed, but unless the risks are patent he is not under the same obligation to know the nature and extent thereof as is the master: *Russell* v. *Minneapolis etc. R'y Co.*, 32 Minn. 230; *Wuotilla* v. *Duluth Lumber Co.*, 37 Minn. 153; 5 Am. St. Rep. 832. We are of the opinion that upon the evidence, some of which is referred to above, the court was not warranted in conclusively presuming that the plaintiff knew or was bound to know the hazards of his position, or that any such accident was likely to happen. If the evidence in his behalf is true, it is not probable that the danger of such an accident had ever occurred to him, and, with his limited knowledge of the operation of mechanical forces, it was perhaps not likely to be suggested to him. But whether he did or did not understand and appreciate the danger of working where and in the manner he did, or, in the exercise of reasonable care, ought to have known it, was, under the evidence in this case, a question for the jury: *Lake Shore etc. R'y Co.* v. *Fitzpatrick*, 31 Ohio St. 479, 487. In a late Massachusetts case, the court, in passing upon the same question, say the plaintiff undertook what proved to be a dangerous duty. "The material point of difference between this case and many others is that here it is open for the jury to find that the plaintiff did not know or appreciate the risk of the work upon which he was engaged, and that in the exercise of due care he was not, as a matter of law, bound to know and appreciate the same": *Ferren* v. *Old Colouy R. R. Co.*, 143 Mass. 197.

Order affirmed.

THE CASE of *Hungerford* v. *Chicago etc. R'y Co.*, 41 Minn. 444, was an appeal by defendant from an order refusing to grant a new trial after verdict for one thousand dollars in favor of plaintiff. The cause of action arose out of the following facts as stated by Collins, J.: "In the fall of 1887 plaintiff was employed by defendant for a few days as head-brakeman on one of its freight trains. Prior to this he was wholly without actual experience as a brakeman, although he had obtained some knowledge of the duties by observing others while they were engaged in that kind of work. After a few days' absence from the road he was again employed for the same service, and a few minutes afterwards, while attempting his first coupling, lost the fore-finger of his right hand. This action was brought to recover damages for the loss. The coupling which plaintiff attempted to make was that between the locomotive and the train, which consisted of box-cars, provided with the common coupler or draft-iron, and a caboose, the latter in the rear. The locomotive had previously been fitted up for passenger-train service, with a so-called "goose-neck" draft-iron. This goose-neck is a large casting, bolted upon the rear of the tender in place of the ordinary draft-iron, and its name suggests its form and shape. It projects above, and its face or end service, which is seven by twelve inches, is beyond or further to the rear than is the face or end of the draft-iron usually found upon freight locomotives; so far, in fact, that whenever a locomotive so equipped is brought up with but slight force for coupling to a freight-car, the end of the neck passes over the iron upon the car, and strikes the dead-wood always found just above it, thus inevitably crushing any susceptible object which may be between the end surface of the neck and the wood upon the car. The plaintiff rode upon the tender, evidently in close proximity to the coupling appliance of which he now complains, and in the middle pocket of which he saw a link, through two switches. As the locomotive backed down to the train he took a coupling-pin, walked to the car, closely followed by the locomotive, and when it came back upon him, stood holding the pin above the draft-iron of the car in the usual, proper, and ordinarily safe position for making the connection had a common iron been upon the tender instead of the goose-neck. As it was, his manner turned out to be unsafe and dangerous, for the pin and part of his hand were caught between the end of the neck and the dead-wood, causing the injury for which he claims damages. It seems to be admitted that had an engine of the customary pattern for the freight service been used, plaintiff would not have been injured, for he was attempting the task in the usual way; and it is also admitted that had he been instructed as to the proper manner of coupling under such circumstances, or had he been accustomed to the goose-neck in combination with the freight-car, he would have changed the link from the tender to the car before they came together, or, as the former approached, would have directed the link in the goose-neck into its place in the draft-iron upon the car, completing the coupling, in either case, by dropping the pin from above through an aperture in the neck. This style of draft-iron is of no value whatever upon a freight-engine, is rarely found upon one, and where so used is manifestly much more dangerous than the iron with which such engines are commonly supplied. It was designed expressly for passenger trains, to be used in connection with the Miller coupler and buffer universally found in the passenger service of the present day. A locomotive with such a draft-iron can be readily coupled from the platform of the baggage-car or passenger-coach, and when in place upon the train, the end surface of the neck rests snugly against the buffer of the car. Its office is to take up the slack or play between the locomotive and the car, to prevent jerking, and thus, in connection with the before-mentioned coupler and buffer, to make what is known in railway parlance as a solid train." The rule of law applicable to this state of facts the court stated to be as follows: "That plaintiff when entering into defendant's service as a brakeman on one of its freight trains took upon himself only those risks which were naturally and ordinarily incident to his employment, or which, from the facts before him, it was his duty to infer, and such risks also as might be announced to him as occasion required, and which he thereafter assumed. If defective instrumentalities were furnished for his use, he must not only have known or ought to have known their actual character and condition, but to have understood, or by the exercise of ordinary observation to have realized, the risks to which he was exposed by their use"; citing, as authority decisive of this case, *Russell* v. *Minneapolis etc. R'y Co.*, 32 Minn. 230.

Continuing the discussion of the case, the court said: "The plaintiff testified that he did not see the goose-neck on the locomotive until it was upon him. This testimony is characterized by appellant as incredible, because, as it claims, the casting was large enough, and must have been observed when the plaintiff looked for and discovered the link in a pocket just beneath the neck. We must assume the plaintiff's statement to be the fact, although it may seem strange that the iron escaped his attention. But it must be borne in mind that he was somewhat inexperienced, had worked about one week for defendant, was then laid off for a few days, and had only secured a place the morning of the accident, because another man had failed to report for duty. His mind was upon making a coupling precisely as he had made it before, under like circumstances, and with the same instrumentalities. He had not been informed, nor had he learned by experience, that occasionally a passenger-engine is put upon a freight-train, and therefore may have not been in a condition to either notice or realize the situation that morning. But had he observed the goose-neck, we are not prepared to say that this knowledge would have prevented a recovery in this action. By examining such an appendage when in its place in the train, it will be seen that it passes over the iron of the car, and strikes the buffer above it. On reflection, one who had noticed this, and who knew something of the distance from the end of the iron upon a freight-car and the dead-wood above it, would realize the danger in holding the coupling-pin in the usual way, and by a closer examination of the neck would discover that it is not solid, but has a large vertical aperture through which the pin may be dropped, as before mentioned, although the size of this aperture indicates that it is in part designed to lighten the casting. Even if he did inspect the appliance, it would not conclusively follow that by reason of such inspection, or the examination which he perhaps ought to have given it, that he did or should have understood the risks to which he was exposed in attempting to make the coupling in the usual and prescribed way for brakemen on freight trains. It might not occur to him, although a man of ordinary prudence, that the defendant would expose him without warning to such a risk, or would furnish a locomotive on which was a draft-iron notoriously unsafe when used by inexperienced men in connection with the common box-car; and a person could easily ride upon the tender through the switches, as did plaintiff, without making the discovery that when the car was reached, and its coupling to the tender practicable, the end of the neck would of necessity have passed by and over the iron on the car. Nor would the examination which could be given as the neck approached the brakeman standing at his post, and about to make a coupling, clearly indicate to him that it projected so far as to be dangerous and unsafe. The master well knows, from the measurements, from actual and practical observation, and from knowledge of the purpose for which these various instrumentalities are designed, just when and how they may be used with a reasonable degree of safety to his servants; but he must not expect them to have this same knowledge without some opportunity for acquiring it. Order affirmed."

Master and Servant. — As to the master's duty to furnish safe machinery, and to keep the same in a safe condition, see *Lehigh etc. Coal Co.* v. *Hayes*, 128 Pa. St. 294; 15 Am. St. Rep. 680, and note; *Johnson* v. *Spear*, 76 Mich. 139; 15 Am. St. Rep. 298, and note. As to the master's duty to warn his servant of defects in the machinery, and of unusual risks connected therewith, see *Galveston etc. R'y Co.* v. *Garrett*, 73 Tex. 262; 15 Am. St. Rep. 781, and note. An employee does not assume the risk of the safety of machinery unless he knows the danger, or it is so obvious that he will be presumed to know it; for he takes upon himself the risk of known dangers, and not of others: *Myers* v. *Hudson Iron Co.*, 150 Mass. 125; 15 Am. St. Rep. 176, and note.

HARRISON v. NICOLLET NATIONAL BANK.

[41 MINNESOTA, 488.]

BANKS AND BANKING — BILL OF EXCHANGE, WHAT IS. — A written order on a bank or banker to pay a sum of money at a day subsequent to its date and to the date of its issue is not a check, but is a bill of exchange, and entitled to grace.

BANKS AND BANKING — CHECK, WHAT ESSENTIAL TO CONSTITUTE. — It is requisite to a check that it be drawn on a bank or banker, and that it be payable on demand.

ACTION on the following instrument: —

"45 WASHINGTON AVE., SOUTH,
"HARRISON THE TAILOR.

"$199.92.   MINNEAPOLIS, MINN., March, 27, 1888.

"On April 14th pay to the order of E. Harrison $199.92.

"J. T. HARRISON.

"To Citizens' Bank, Minneapolis, Minnesota.   No. 2884."

— to recover damages on the ground that defendant, on April 14, 1888, and before maturity thereof, did "falsely, wrongfully, and maliciously" cause to be protested the foregoing instrument, indorsed and forwarded to defendant for collection, thereby injuring plaintiff's credit, etc. A demurrer to the complaint was sustained, and plaintiff appeals.

Carman N. Smith, for the appellant.

Woods and Kingman, for the respondent.

MITCHELL, J.   This appeal presents the question whether a written order on a bank or banker to pay a sum of money at a day subsequent to its date, and subsequent to the date of its issue, is a check or a bill of exchange, and hence entitled to grace. The question is one which has given rise to considerable discussion and some conflict of opinion. About all the law there is on it, as well as all the arguments on each side, will be found in Morse on Banking, 3d ed., sec. 331 et seq. The two principal authorities holding such an instrument a check are *In re Brown*, 2 Story, 502, and *Champion v. Gordon*, 70 Pa. St. 474, 10 Am. Rep. 681. Both of these are entitled to great weight, but they stand almost alone; the supreme courts of Rhode Island (*Westminster Bank v. Wheaton*, 4 R. I. 30) and perhaps of Tennessee being, so far we know, the only ones which have adopted the same views. All other courts which have passed upon the question, as well as the text-writers, have almost uniformly laid it down that such an instrument is a bill of exchange, and that an essential characteristic of a check is, that it is payable on demand. This was finally settled, after some conflict of opinion, in New York, — the leading commercial state of the Union, — in the case of *Bowen* v. *Newell* (several times before the courts), 5 Sand. 326, 2 Duer, 584, 8 N. Y. 190, and 13 N. Y. 290, 64 Am. Dec. 550. See also *Morrison* v. *Bailey*, 5 Ohio St. 13; 64 Am. Dec. 632; *Woodruff* v. *Merchants' Bank*, 25 Wend. 673; *Minturn* v. *Fisher*, 4 Cal. 35; *Bradley* v. *Delaplaine*, 5 Harr. (Del.) 305; *Georgia Nat. Bank* v. *Henderson*, 46 Ga. 487; 12 Am. Rep. 590; *Ivory* v. *Bank of State of Missouri*, 36 Mo. 475; 88 Am. Dec. 150; *Work* v. *Tatman*, 2 Houst. 304; *Hawley* v. *Jette*, 10 Or. 31; 45 Am. Rep. 129; 2 Daniel on Negotiable Instruments, secs. 1573–1575; Morse on Banking, 3d ed., secs. 381 et seq.

Nearly every definition of a check given in the books is to the effect not only that it must be drawn on a bank or banker, but that it must be payable on demand: 1 Randolph on Commercial Paper, sec. 8; Byles on Bills, 13; 2 Daniel on Negotiable Instruments, sec. 1566; 1 Edwards on Bills, sec. 19; Bigelow on Bills and Notes, 116; Chalmers's Digest of Bills and Notes, art. 254; Shaw, C. J., in *Bullard* v. *Randall*, 1 Gray, 605; 61 Am. Dec. 433; Bouv. Law Dict.; Burrill's Law Dict. Occasionally the expression is used, "payable on presentation," but evidently — except, perhaps, in Story on Bills — as synonymous with "payable on demand."

As the question is a new one in this state, we would not feel compelled to follow the majority if the better reasons were with the minority. Perhaps the weightiest argument in favor of holding such an instrument a check is the practical one advanced by Sharswood, J., in *Champion* v. *Gordon, supra,* viz., that if held to be a bill of exchange, the holder might immediately present it for acceptance, and if not accepted he could sue the drawer, or if accepted it would tie up the drawer's funds in the hands of the bank, and thus, in either case, frustrate the very object of making it payable at a future day. In answer to this, it may be said that the drawer, if he wished, could very easily avoid such consequences by inserting appropriate provisions in the instrument. On the other hand, if we hold that an instrument not payable on demand may be a check, we are left without any definite or precise rule by which to determine when the paper is a check and when a bill of exchange. The fact that it is drawn on a bank is not alone enough to distinguish a check from a bill of exchange, for noth-

ing is better settled than that a bill of exchange may be drawn
on a banker. Neither will the fact that the maker writes it on
a blank check be any test; for the kind of paper it is written
on cannot control the import and legal effect of its words.
Neither can the question whether it is drawn against a previous deposit of funds by the drawer with the drawee furnish
any criterion; for nothing is clearer than that a bill of exchange, as well as a check, can be drawn against such a deposit,
and that an instrument may be a check, although the drawer
has no funds in the hands of the drawee. Neither will it do
to say that if it is entitled to grace it is a bill, but if not entitled to grace it is a check, because the legal character of the
instrument has first to be determined before it can be known
whether or not it is entitled to grace. In short, if we omit
from the definition of a check the element of its being payable on demand, bankers and business men are left without
any definite rule by which to govern their action in a matter
where simplicity and precision of rule are especially desirable.
It might be expedient to enact, as has been done in New York
and some other states, that all checks, bills of exchange, or
drafts appearing on their face to be drawn on a bank or
banker, whether payable on a specified day, or any number of
days, after date or sight, shall be payable on the day named
in the instrument without grace; or, what might be better
still, to abolish days of grace altogether as a usage which has
already long outlived the condition of things out of which it
had its origin. But this is a matter for legislatures, and not
for courts. We are therefore of opinion that the better rule is
to hold that such an instrument is a bill of exchange, and
hence entitled to grace. We may add that it is always desirable that the decisions of the courts should be in accord with
the business usages and customs of the country. Such usages
are entitled to special weight on a question like this, for the
whole matter of grace on bills and notes had its origin in the
usage of bankers. And so far as we are advised, the general
practice of bankers in this state has been to treat instruments
like this as bills of exchange, and not checks.

Counsel for respondent suggests that, even if we hold that
payment of this paper was demanded and protest made prematurely, yet the action of the court below in sustaining the
demurrer to the complaint should be affirmed on other grounds,
viz., that the act of protesting, etc., was the act of the notary
and not of the bank; that the protest could not have damaged

the financial standing of plaintiff, because the certificate of the notory shows on its face that it was done before maturity; also, that the instrument being of doubtful classification, involving a legal question on which courts differed, the defendant would not be liable for an honest mistake of law. Whatever force there might be in these suggestions, either by way of defense or in mitigation, we think they are unavailing in support of a demurrer to a complaint which alleges that the defendant "falsely, wrongfully, and maliciously caused" the paper to be protested for non-payment, and notices of protest sent out, and which also shows that such notices — which were presumably what, if anything, injured plaintiff's standing and credit—contained nothing indicating that payment was prematurely demanded.

Order reversed.

WHAT IS A BILL OF EXCHANGE. — A bill of exchange is an order in writing directing one person to pay money to a third person: *Rice* v. *Ragland*, 10 Humph. 545; 53 Am. Dec. 737; and its essentials are: 1. That it be payable at all events, and not contingently or out of a particular fund; and 2. That it be for the payment of money only, and not for the performance of any other act or in alternative: *Cook* v. *Satterlee*, 6 Cow. 108; 16 Am. Dec. 432; but a bill payable from a particular fund is good, if the fund is certain, and the mention of it in the bill is only directory to the drawee: *Bank of Kentucky* v. *Sanders*, 3 A. K. Marsh. 184; 13 Am. Dec. 149. Written order, dated and signed, directing one person to pay to another a specified sum, and to charge the amount to the drawer's account, is a bill of exchange, even though it is neither made payable to order or bearer, nor contains words "value received," nor is made payable on a certain day, nor at any particular place: *Kendall* v. *Galvin*, 15 Me. 131; 32 Am. Dec. 141. It may not be essential that the bill be negotiable, but it must be for money certain in amount, and payable absolutely: *Averett* v. *Booker*, 15 Gratt. 163; 76 Am. Dec. 203. Bills of exchange, though not specialties, differ from simple contracts in this, that they are presumed to be for a valuable consideration: *Conine* v. *Junction etc. R. R. Co.*, 3 Houst. 288; 89 Am. Dec. 230.

An order in writing, addressed to an individual, to pay a certain sum of money on a certain day in the future, without grace, to a third party's order, is a bill of exchange, not a check: *Hawley* v. *Jette*, 10 Or. 31; 45 Am. Rep. 129.

WHAT ARE NOT BILLS OF EXCHANGE: See *Van Vacter* v. *Flack*, 1 Smedes & M. 393; 40 Am. Dec. 100; *Woolley* v. *Sergeant*, 8 N. J. L. 262; 14 Am. Dec. 419; *Fairchild* v. *Ogdensburgh R. R. Co.*, 15 N. Y. 337; 69 Am. Dec. 606; *Tevis* v. *Young*, 1 Met. (Ky.) 197; 71 Am. Dec. 474; *Koch* v. *Branch*, 44 Mo. 542; 100 Am. Dec. 324.

FOR THE POINTS OF DIFFERENCE BETWEEN BILLS OF EXCHANGE AND CHECKS, see *Morrison* v. *Bailey*, 5 Ohio St. 13; 64 Am. Dec. 632, and especially note 634.

HULL v. CHICAGO, ST. PAUL, MINNEAPOLIS, AND OMAHA RAILWAY COMPANY.

[41 MINNESOTA, 510.]

COMMON CARRIERS — LIABILITY OF UNDER SPECIAL CONTRACT — BURDEN OF PROOF. — Under a contract limiting the carrier's liability for injury or loss occurring through his negligence, the burden of proof is on him to show, after injury or loss is established, in order to excuse his liability, that such injury or loss was caused by something else than his negligence, and that there was no negligence in fact on his part.

COMMON CARRIERS. — BURDEN OF PROOF IS ON CARRIER to show contract limiting his liability. *Prima facie*, a carrier is liable for goods upon proof of delivery and acceptance for carriage and of loss or damage in carrying, and if any contract exists limiting his liability he must show it, and that the loss came within the exception made by it. The shipper need not establish the non-existence of the contract.

COMMON CARRIERS — LIABILITY OF UNDER SPECIAL CONTRACT. — A common carrier remains such, even though in a particular case he may have, to some extent, limited his liability by contract, and all rules applicable to common carries apply in such case, except in so far as the parties may, by express contract, have varied them. The reasons which require the carrier to excuse his negligence apply with as much force to a case of limited as to a case of full common-law liability.

J. H. Howe, S. L. Perrin, and Weed Munro, for the appellant.

Thomas J. Leftwich, for the respondent.

GILFILLAN, C. J. At Minneapolis plaintiff delivered to defendant, a common carrier, eighteen horses, to be by it transported upon its railroad from Minneapolis to Ashland, Wisconsin. The evidence tends to show they were in good condition when they were so delivered, and that in the course of transportation two died, and several others were injured. The action is to recover damages. On the trial, at the close of the plaintiff's evidence, the court dismissed the action. On plaintiff's motion it afterwards ordered a new trial, and from that order this appeal is taken.

By the written contract for carriage, executed by the parties, it was stipulated that the plaintiff should "load, feed, water, and take care of such stock at his own expense and risk, and will assume all risk of injury or damage that the animals may do to themselves or each other, or which may arise by delay of trains"; and also "that said company shall not be liable for loss by jumping from the cars, delay of trains, or any damage said property may sustain, except such as may result from a collision, or when the cars are thrown from the track in course of transportation." The court below seems to have dismissed the action on the grounds that, under the contract limiting the defendant's liability, the burden of proof upon the matter of defendant's negligence was upon the plaintiff; that he had not introduced evidence of negligence sufficient to make a question for the jury; and that there was contributory negligence on the part of the plaintiff. The only question argued here at any length is, Was it necessary for plaintiff, in order to make out a cause of action, to show that the death of the horses and injury to others was caused by defendant's negligence? or was it enough for him to prove their delivery for carriage in good condition, and the injury to them during the carriage, leaving it then for defendant to excuse itself by showing that the damage was not due to negligence on its part?

But we will say in passing that, wherever the burden of proof lay, the case ought to have gone to the jury, for there was evidence from which the jury might have found that the injury to the horses was caused by the negligent manner in which defendant's train was handled. It appears that with the full train, without detaching any of the cars from the engine, those in charge "bucked snow," as it is called. As a witness described it, "they would take a running jump at a snow-drift." And this appears to have caused so violent shocks that, as a witness testified, one could not stand, and could hardly sit, in the caboose, which seems to have been at or near the rear of the train, while the car in which the horses were was pretty well up in front, where the shocks would be more violent. It ought to have been left for the jury to say whether that was the way in which the train was managed; whether that was a prudent way of managing a train carrying live-stock; and whether the injury to the horses was caused by it. As to contributory negligence on the part of plaintiff, the evidence was not such that the court could properly determine it. The most that can be said of it is, that it ought to have been submitted to the jury.

But, because the court below seems to have granted a new trial for the reason that on the trial it misapprehended the rule as to the burden of proof as to negligence, we will consider that question. The contract, in terms, exempts the defendant from liability for damages, except such as might result from collision or the cars being thrown from the track. This goes further than the law permits a common carrier to go in limiting his liability. Since the *Christenson Case,* —*Christenson* v.

American Express Co., 15 Minn: 208 (270), 2 Am. Rep. 122, —
it has been settled by judicial decision in this state that a
common carrier cannot exonerate himself by contract from
liability for his own negligence, and this rule is now recognized by statute: Laws 1885, c. 188, sec. 26. The most favorable construction for the defendant which could be given to
this contract would hold that it exempts it from liability for
damages from any cause but its own negligence, and collisions,
and the cars being thrown from the track. In *Shriver* v.
Sioux City etc. R. R. Co., 24 Minn. 506, 31 Am. Rep. 353, the
contract attempted to exempt the carrier except for gross negligence. The court held it went further than the law allowed,
and treated it as a contract exempting the carrier except for
negligence of any degree.

The rule as to the burden of proof held in that case is applicable to this; and upon further examination and consideration we are satisfied that the rule is justified by reason and
public policy. The common law excepts from the carrier's
liability loss or damage caused by act of God or the public
enemy. No one would contend but that, where the common-
law liability is not varied by contract, the carrier, to excuse
himself, must show that the loss or damage was within one of
the exceptions to his liability; that it was caused either by
the act of God or of the public enemy. Such proof would
make a *prima facie* case of non-liability. The plaintiff might
then show that but for the carrier's negligence the loss or
damage would not have occurred, though caused apparently
by one of the excepted causes. The reason why proof of loss
by the act of God or the public enemy makes a *prima facie*
case of non-liability is that in the nature of things those causes
of loss arise without fault of the carrier. He can in no case
be responsible for their existence, though he may be for bringing the goods within their operation. Suppose by special contract the parties except one other cause of loss, — say by fire, —
why, in that case, should the owner be required to prove in
the first instance that the loss did not occur from that excepted cause? Inasmuch as such a cause of loss may arise
by negligence of the carrier, it may be doubted (and we do
not in this case decide it) that proof of loss from such a cause,
without evidence that it did not arise through negligence of
the carrier, would make a *prima facie* case of non-liability.
Certainly nothing short of evidence that the loss was from the
excepted cause would excuse him.

It must be borne in mind that the liability is not created by the special contract. The law creates the liability, and merely permits the parties to accept from it certain causes of loss. *Prima facie*, the carrier is liable upon proof of delivery and acceptance for carriage, and of loss or damage in carrying. If there be any contract varying his liability he must show it, and that the loss came within the exception made by it. It is not for the owner to prove there was no such contract. And if such a contract be proved, it would seem illogical to require of him to show that the loss did not occur from the cause excepted by it. If the contract, instead of specifying certain exceptions to the liability, is general in its terms, and excepts from the liability all causes of loss or damage but the carrier's negligence, how does the carrier show that the loss or damage was within the exception but by proof that it occurred from a cause other than his negligence? Some of the courts, to justify putting the burden of proof as to negligence on the plaintiff, consider the carrier, where his liability is varied by contract, as a private or special, and not a common, carrier. This would make the carrier's character, whether common or private, depend, not on the character of the business he is engaged in, or holds himself out to the world to be engaged in, but on whether he has, by contract, varied, even in the slightest particular, the liability which the law, in the absence of contract, imposes on him. We cannot accept such a doctrine. We think the common carrier remains such even though in the particular case he may have, to some extent, limited his liability by contract, and that all the rules of law applicable to common carriers apply to such a case except in so far as the parties may, by express contract, have varied them. The severe rule of liability of the common law was imposed largely from considerations of sound public policy. A common carrier is engaged in a public employment. Ordinarily, one who delivers to him goods parts entirely with his possession and control over them, and knows nothing of what takes place during the carriage, while the carrier has possession and control over them, and is supposed to know, or have the means of knowing, what happens to them, and if they are lost or injured, how it occurred. The common law recognized the danger of collusion, connivance, and fraud between the carrier and his servants or others, which might leave the owner practically at the mercy of the carrier if he was required to prove negligence or fraud. To make such proof he would ordinarily have to call the very men whose recklessness or frailty caused the injury. To prevent this, the law excused the carrier only upon his proving that the loss or damage occurred from the act of God or the public enemy, — causes for which he could not be supposed to be responsible. The reasons which require the carrier to excuse himself for his failure apply with as much force to a case of limited as to a case of full common-law liability.

Order affirmed.   ——

Carriers — Liability Limited by Special Contract. — The rule of the principal case is in accord with the one laid down in *Lindsley* v. *Chicago etc. R'y Co.*, 36 Minn. 539, 1 Am. St. Rep. 692, in which it was decided that, where a carrier's liability is limited by special contract, the burden of proof is upon the carrier to show that any loss *in transitu* was within the exception limiting its general liability. But in *St. Louis etc. R'y Co.* v. *Weakly*, 50 Ark. 397, 7 Am. St. Rep. 104, where live-stock were shipped under a contract limiting the carrier's liability, pursuant to which the shipper took charge of the stock during the transportation, riding for that purpose upon the train with his stock free of additional charge, the court held that the burden of proof was upon the shipper to show that the loss, if any, resulted from the negligence of the carrier. And so in *Platt* v. *Richmond etc. R. R. Co.*, 108 N. Y. 658, where a carrier by contract limited its general liability, so as to exempt itself from loss by fire, unless the same be proved to have occurred from the gross negligence or fraud of the carrier or its employees, it was held that the burden of proof was upon the plaintiff to show that the loss by fire, if any, was caused by the fraud or gross negligence of the carrier or its employees.

Carriers may, by Special Contract, limit their common-law liability, but the terms of such a contract operate merely as exceptions which leave the common-law rule in full force and authority as to all beside: *Atwood* v. *Reliance Trans. Co.*, 9 Watts, 87; 34 Am. Dec. 503. At common law, "the act of God or the public enemy" was not a limit of the exception from liability of a carrier; but ordinarily a carrier was not liable for losses or injuries resulting from the inherent character of the property carried: *Louisville etc. R'y Co.* v. *Bigger*, 66 Miss. 319; *Central etc. R. R. & B. Co.* v. *Smitha*, 85 Ala. 47. But any contract which attempts to relieve a carrier from liability for the full value of property lost by it, during carriage, through the carrier's own negligence, is obnoxious to the objection that it is an attempt to relieve itself from its own negligence: *Southern P. R'y Co.* v. *Maddox*, 75 Tex. 301.

McPherson v. Runyon.

[41 Minnesota, 524.]

Damages for Malicious Prosecution of Civil Action. — An action for damages may be maintained for the malicious prosecution of a civil action without probable cause, to the injury of defendant, although there was no interference with his person or property.

Damages for Malicious Prosecution of Replevin. — An action for additional damages may be maintained for the malicious prosecution of an action of replevin without probable cause, although the defendant in that action recovered therein his damages for the taking and detention of his property.

James H. Foote, for the appellant.

Leon T. Chamberlain, for the respondent.

Dickinson, J. This is an appeal from an order sustaining a general demurrer to the complaint. The cause of action for which a recovery is sought is the malicious prosecution, by this defendant against this plaintiff, of an action in replevin in a justice's court, and the malicious seizure of this plaintiff's property by writ of replevin in that action. It is not claimed that the complaint does not set forth facts showing a right of recovery, if a separate action may be maintained for such cause. The demurrer rests upon the propositions, contended for by the respondent, that the cause of action here asserted was a mere incident of the original action of replevin; that whatever damages this plaintiff might have been entitled to recover for the cause here alleged were recoverable only in that action; and that the judgment therein in favor of this plaintiff is a bar to the recovery now sought. *Sylte* v. *Nelson*, 26 Minn. 105, and *Ward* v. *Anderberg*, 36 Minn. 300, are relied upon in support of this contention. The respondent does not claim that for the prosecution of a civil action, maliciously and without probable cause, a defendant may not in general maintain an action for damages. We have recognized such rights of action in cases where the defendant's property was attached: *Burton* v. *St. Paul, M. & M. R'y Co.*, 33 Minn. 189; and *Cochrane* v. *Quackenbush*, 29 Minn. 376; and if there were peculiar reasons, based upon the fact of the attachment, justifying an action in such cases, it is not perceiv[ ]l why they are not equally applicable where, as in this case, the defendant's property was seized under a writ of replevin. That an action will lie in such a case was held in *Wills* v. *Noyes*, 12 Pick. 324; and this was also recognized in *Magmer* v. *Renk*, 65 Wis. 364.

We do not, however, place our decision upon this limited

ground, but upon the broader proposition that for the prosecution of a civil action maliciously and without probable cause, to the injury of the defendant, he may maintain an action for damages, although there was no interference with his person or property: *Pangburn* v. *Bull*, 1 Wend. 345; *Whipple* v. *Fuller*, 11 Conn. 582; 29 Am. Dec. 330; *Closson* v. *Staples*, 42 Vt. 209; 1 Am. Rep. 316; *Eastin* v. *Bank of Stockton*, 66 Cal. 123; 56 Am. Rep. 77; *Allen* v. *Codman*, 139 Mass. 136; *Marbourg* v. *Smith*, 11 Kan. 554; *Woods* v. *Finnell*, 13 Bush, 628; *Pope* v. *Pollock*, 46 Ohio St. 367; 15 Am. St. Rep. 608; *McCardle* v. *McGinley*, 86 Ind. 538; 44 Am. Rep. 343. The reasons for this conclusion are well set forth in *Whipple* v. *Fuller* and in *Closson* v. *Staples, supra.* See also 21 Am. Law Reg., N. S., 281, 353.

The decision in *Sylte* v. *Nelson*, followed in *Ward* v. *Anderberg*, has not the effect ascribed to it by the respondent. It was there decided that a defendant's assertion in an action of replevin of the right to a return of the property taken from him, and to damages for the taking and detention, did not constitute a counterclaim in such action. It was said also in the opinion that this was not a cause of action in itself upon which the defendant could maintain an action. This decision and the language of the court, relating merely to the ordinary claim of a defendant in replevin to have his property restored to him, with damages for the taking and detention, as an incident in that action, has no bearing upon the question as to whether an action will lie for the malicious prosecution of an action of replevin. For such a cause, indeed, no action could be maintained, or recovery had, until the replevin action should have terminated in favor of the defendant: *O'Brien* v. *Barry*, 106 Mass. 300; and of course the right of recovery for the malicious prosecution could not be asserted as a counterclaim in that same action. It is of course true that but one recovery can be allowed for the same cause; and the damages for the taking and detention, once awarded to the defendant in the original action, cannot be again assessed in an action for malicious prosecution. But the measure of recovery in the latter action is not confined to the injury from the taking or detention of the property. To what particular subjects the proof of damages should be directed or confined, under the allegations of this complaint, no question has been raised, and we do not decide.

Order reversed.

MALICIOUS PROSECUTION OF A CIVIL SUIT IS ACTIONABLE WHEN: See *Pope* v. *Pollock*, 46 Ohio St. 367; 15 Am. St. Rep. 608, and note; *Brand* v. *Hinchman*, 68 Mich. 590; 13 Am. St. Rep. 362, and note; *McCardle* v. *Mc-Ginley*, 86 Ind. 538; 44 Am. Rep. 343, and particularly note 346–348; note to *Williams* v. *Hunter*, 14 Am. Dec. 599–603.

MATTER OF DALPAY.

[41 MINNESOTA, 532.]

FOREIGN ASSIGNMENT — CONFLICT OF LAWS. — An assignment or transfer of property, giving preference to certain creditors, and valid by the laws of another state where made, will not be upheld by the courts of Minnesota when contrary to the policy and laws of that state, as to property situated there.

INSOLVENCY — SITUS OF DEBTS DUE INSOLVENT. — For the purposes of insolvency or other proceedings by creditors, debts or choses in action due the insolvent are treated as having a *situs* at the owner's domicile.

ON petition by H. C. Burbank & Co., and of Kellogg, Johnson, & Co., an order was made by the district court adjudging Joseph Dalpay to be insolvent, and appointing a receiver of his property, from which order he appeals.

Fred. B. Dodge, for the appellant.

Alf. B. Boyesen, and Richardson, Markham, and May, for the respondents.

VANDERBURGH, J. The facts upon which the court made the order appealed from appear in the stipulation of the parties in the record. The appellant's contention is, that no case was made for the appointment of a receiver in these proceedings, on the ground that the property transferred to certain creditors by him, and securing to them a preference, was situated in Dakota Territory, where the assignment thereof was made, and that by the laws of that territory such transfer is recognized as lawful. Among the assigned property, however, was a policy of insurance issued to the appellant by the Syndicate Insurance Company of Minneapolis, in this state, covering property owned by appellant in Dakota, which had previously been destroyed by fire; so that the claim due or to become due under such policy passed to the creditors so preferred, being the firm of Wyman, Mullin, & Co. of Minneapolis. At the time of this alleged transfer, the appellent resided and had his domicile in this state. The insurance company is a local corporation, doing business in the same state; and the debt or claim in question is subject to be reached by judicial proceedings here. The petition in the insolvency proceedings is made by and on behalf of other creditors residing in and doing business in this state, and is rested upon the alleged preference so given to Wyman, Mullin, & Co.; and it is claimed that the transfer was fraudulent under the insolvency act, and that the order appointing a receiver herein was therefore justified.

As between the parties to the assignment, if valid by the *lex loci contractus*, it would be upheld here. It would also be sustained against creditors, if valid where made, and not in contravention of our laws, both as to property situated in the foreign jurisdiction, and property within this state. But the courts of this state cannot be required to give effect to an assignment or transfer of property within it, or of debts due to its citizens, which is found to be contrary to the policy and laws of the state. To uphold the opposite doctrine would be to encourage fraudulent contrivances to defeat the operation of our insolvent or collection laws: *Zipcey* v. *Thompson*, 1 Gray, 243; *Foster* v. *Goulding*, 9 Gray, 50. A different rule, which has no application in this case, is suggested as to citizens of the jurisdiction where the assignment is made, who are seeking a remedy against property in another state: *May* v. *Wannemacher*, 111 Mass. 202, 209. As a general rule, a debt or chose in action, being incorporeal, is deemed to follow the person of the owner, and to be present with him; but for some purposes the courts treat such property or interests as having a *situs* at the place of the owner's domicile. It is so for the purposes of taxation, and for reasons already stated, in insolvency or other proceedings by creditors: *Smith* v. *Chicago & N. W. R'y Co.*, 23 Wis. 267; Wharton on Conflict of Laws, sec. 363. The facts in the case are therefore sufficient to support the order appointing a receiver, which is accordingly affirmed.

In *Ex parte Dickinson*, 29 S. C. 453, 13 Am. St. Rep. 749, it was decided that an assignment for the benefit of creditors, by a citizen of New York, made in that state, and giving a preference to certain creditors, although valid in New York, was void in South Carolina, where the statute forbids the giving of such preferences; and to the same effect are the cases cited in note to that case at page 757. Compare *Woodward* v. *Brooks*, 128 Ill. 222; 15 Am. St. Rep. 104, and note.

DOLE *v.* SHERWOOD.

[41 MINNESOTA, 535.]

AGENCY — AGENT'S RIGHT TO COMMISSION ON SALE OF REAL ESTATE. — Under an exclusive agency to sell real estate on commission, the exclusive right to sell not being given, the owner has a right to make a sale independent of the agent, and in such case will not be liable to the agent for commission unless he sells to a purchaser procured by the agent.

AGENCY — EFFECT OF EXCLUSIVE AGENCY TO SELL LAND. — An exclusive agency to sell land merely prohibits the placing of the property for sale in the hands of any other agent, but not the sale of the property by the owner himself.

ACTION by A. M. Dole, as administrator, to recover five hundred dollars received by defendant for plaintiff's intestate and as his agent.

Woods, Hahn, and Kingman, for the appellant.

Ensign, Cash, and Williams, for the respondent.

MITCHELL, J.   The only question presented by this appeal is, whether the findings of fact support the conclusions of law. The facts are, that on March 14, 1887, plaintiff gave to defendant "the exclusive agency, for thirty days from and after that date, for the sale" of certain real estate on specified terms, and agreed to pay defendant, in case he made a sale, a commission of $640; that defendant accepted the agency, and commenced the expenditure of time and labor in efforts to find a purchaser; that on March 16th plaintiff informed defendant that he himself had sold the land, and requested him to take it off his list, which defendant did, and ceased his efforts to find a purchaser; that plaintiff had not in fact made a sale of the property, but had made a verbal agreement of sale, on which the proposed purchaser had paid some earnest-money, but the purchase was never completed.

It is settled, at least in this state, that where an agency to sell real estate on commission is given, the exclusive right to sell not being given, the owner himself has still the right to make a sale independent of the agent, and in such case will not be liable to the agent for commissions unless he sells to a purchaser procured by the agent: *Armstrong* v. *Wann*, 29 Minn. 126; *Putnam* v. *How*, 39 Minn. 363.   This right on the part of the owner is an implied condition of the agency, subject to which the agent accepts it, and, as his commission is payable only in case of his success in finding a purchaser, the agent takes his chances of the owner himself making a sale. Such a case differs from the present only in the fact that the agency in the latter is exclusive. The court below seems to have treated this as giving the exclusive right to sell. In this we think the learned judge erred. It merely prohibited the placing of the property for sale in the hands of any other agent, but not the sale of the property by the owner himself: *Golden Gate Packing Co.* v. *Farmers' Union,* 55 Cal. 606. This view is entirely consistent with *Fairchild* v. *Rogers,* 32 Minn. 269, for in that case the agent was given the exclusive right to sell, and that, too, for a valuable consideration paid by him to the owner of the property. We have treated the case precisely as if the verbal contract of sale made by the plaintiff had been a binding one, and had been carried out, for that is the view most favorable to the defendant in view of the findings of the court.

Judgment reversed, and cause remanded, with directions to the court below to enter judgment in favor of the plaintiff for the amount claimed in the complaint.

———

REAL ESTATE BROKERS ARE ENTITLED TO THEIR COMMISSIONS WHEN: See *Ward* v. *Cobb,* 148 Mass. 518; 12 Am. St. Rep. 587, and note 589, 590. The broker can never be entitled to a commission when he does not procure a purchaser: *Sloman* v. *Bodwell,* 24 Neb. 790.

CASES

IN THE

COURT OF APPEALS

OF

NEW YORK.

CLARK *v.* FOSDICK.

[118 New York, 7.]

TRUSTEE OF AN EXPRESS TRUST — AN AGREEMENT OF SEPARATION BETWEEN HUSBAND, WIFE, AND A THIRD PERSON, by the terms of which the former is to pay the latter a specified sum towards the support of the wife and her children, constitutes the third person a trustee of an express trust, and authorizes an action to enforce the trust to be brought in his name.

AN AGREEMENT BETWEEN A HUSBAND AND WIFE, WHILE THEY ARE LIVING TOGETHER AS SUCH, FOR THEIR IMMEDIATE SEPARATION, and for a specified allowance for her support, made through the medium of a trustee, is valid; and the trustee may maintain an action thereon to recover any sum due from the husband by the terms of the agreement. Such an agreement, to be valid, must be made in respect to a separation which has occurred, or which is to occur immediately, and not in contemplation of a future possible separation.

DIVORCE. — AGREEMENT OF SEPARATION BETWEEN HUSBAND, WIFE, AND HER TRUSTEE, and for the payment of an allowance to the trustee for her support, is not annulled by the subsequent granting of a divorce at her instance in an action in which no alimony was asked nor granted, and the judgment in which did not refer to nor in any respect purport to deal with such agreement.

DIVORCE. — AGREEMENT OF SEPARATION BETWEEN HUSBAND AND WIFE, though valid, does not prevent either from maintaining against the other an ordinary action for divorce, limited or absolute, according to the ground and the jurisdiction, whether the cause therefor occurred before or after such agreement was entered into.

ACTION to recover an installment due under articles of separation between the defendant, C. P. Fosdick, and his wife, Jennie P. Fosdick. On the 14th of February, 1883, differences having arisen between Fosdick and his wife, they agreed that they would thereafter live separately; and, to carry out such

733

agreement, they entered into articles of separation, to which they, and the plaintiff herein as trustee, were parties, and which articles recited that such differences had arisen, that they, for that reason, thereafter agreed to live separately. As soon as such agreement was executed, they in fact separated, and thereafter continued to live separately. In the agreement of separation, the husband and his father covenanted to pay the trustee named therein a specified sum for the support of the wife and children, and the trustee, on his part, undertook to indemnify the husband against the support of his wife and children, and to pay over to the wife, for her support and that of the children, the sums which should be paid to him by the husband. Afterwards the wife brought an action against the husband for divorce, which was resisted by the latter, but resulted in a decree granting her a divorce, and awarding her the custody of her children. These and other facts being fully set out in the complaint in this action, the defendant demurred thereto, the demurrer was overruled, and judgment entered in favor of the plaintiff, from which the defendant appealed.

H. M. Whitehead, for the appellant.

Horace Russell and Jabish Holmes, Jr., for the respondent.

POTTER, J. The questions to be decided upon this appeal are presented by demurrer to the complaint. The complaint alleges the facts which ordinarily give an action to recover the money promised to be paid the plaintiff, as trustee, under the agreement, but it also alleges a decree of divorcement obtained by the wife after the making of the agreement of separation, and which, the defendant contends, defeats the plaintiff's action. The purpose of thus pleading was to obtain a final judgment upon the rights of these parties in a more speedy and less expensive way.

It will be more orderly to consider, first, the ground of demurrer strictly applicable to the right of the plaintiff, as trustee, to bring the action.

By the express terms of the agreement of separation, the defendant, C. Baldwin Fosdick, agrees to pay to the plaintiff, for and towards the support and maintenance of his wife, the said Jennie P. Fosdick, and their children, the yearly sum of two thousand five hundred dollars, for and during the period of her natural life, unless she remarries, etc., and the plaintiff

and said Jennie agree that said sum so paid shall be in full
satisfaction of the support and maintenance of said Jennie P.
Fosdick and children, and all alimony whatsoever.

This clearly constitutes the plaintiff the trustee of an express trust, and required that an action to enforce or to execute the trust should be brought in his name: Code Civ. Proc.,
sec. 449; *Calkins* v. *Long*, 22 Barb. 97; *Greenfield* v. *Mass. M.
L. Ins. Co.*, 47 N. Y. 430; *Slocum* v. *Barry*, 38 N. Y. 46; *Hughes*
v. *Mercantile Mut. Ins. Co.*, 44 How. Pr. 351.

The next question to be considered is the validity of the
agreement itself. I think it is to be assumed, in the consideration of this appeal, that at the time of executing the instrument which forms the basis of this action, the defendant, C.
Baldwin Fosdick, and Jennie P. Fosdick, were husband and
wife, and were living together as such.

The first inquiry should be to learn whether the courts of
this state have decisively passed upon that question, and if so,
of course we are to follow such holding. It was reluctantly
held by the chancellor, in *Carson* v. *Murray*, 3 Paige, 500, and
then only upon the principle of *stare decisis* as evinced by *Baker* v. *Barney*, 8 Johns. 72, 5 Am. Dec. 326, *Shelthar* v. *Gregory*, 2 Wend. 422, following the English decisions prior to the
Revolution, that "a valid agreement for an immediate separation between husband and wife, and for a separate allowance
for her support, may be made through the medium of a trustee."

The case of *Carson* v. *Murray*, 3 Paige, 483, was upon a bill
in equity by the wife against the executors of her husband,
based upon an agreement of separation, for its enforcement
out of the estate of the deceased husband. The case of *Baker*
v. *Barney*, 8 Johns. 72, was an action to recover of the husband
the price of suitable goods sold to the wife after the separation
of husband and wife, under an agreement making provision for
the support of the wife.

The case of *Shelthar* v. *Gregory*, 2 Wend. 422, was an action
upon the bond and agreement to separate; the defense was,
that after the bond was given, and before the installment or
sum fell due by the terms of the agreement, the wife returned
to and was living with the husband, and was supported by
him. In these cases, the husband and wife were living together when the agreement or articles of separation were executed, and separated immediately thereafter. The ruling of
the court was to the effect that such articles of separation,
considered under these various aspects, were valid. These

holdings were based upon decisions made in the English courts, and I am not aware that the English or our own courts have departed or receded from the principle thus laid down. While husband and wife in *Calkins* v. *Long*, 22 Barb. 98, had actually separated before the agreement of separation was executed, the court, in holding that the agreement was valid, cites numerous decisions, with approval, in England and several of the states of the Union, to the effect that such agreements are valid, and will be enforced, where the separation had taken place before, or takes place immediately after, the execution of the agreement of separation; and this case is said (in a note upon page 110) to have been affirmed by the court of appeals.

Judge Davis, in delivering the opinion of the court in *Walker* v. *Walker*, 9 Wall. 743, while regretting, upon the score of public policy, that the courts of England and of this country had gone so far, was, as was the chancellor in *Calkins* v. *Long, supra,* constrained to hold that "a covenant by the husband for the maintenance of the wife, contained in a deed of separation between them, through the medium of trustees, and where the consideration is apparent, is valid, and will be enforced in equity, if it appears that the deed was not made in contemplation of a future possible separation, but is made in respect to one which was to occur immediately, or for the continuance of one which had already taken place.

The validity of such agreements are recognized and enforced in numerous cases decided by the courts of this and other states: *Carpenter* v. *Osborn*, 102 N. Y. 552; *Pettit* v. *Pettit*, 107 N. Y. 677; *Carson* v. *Murray*, 3 Paige, 483; *Rogers* v. *Rogers*, 4 Paige, 516; 27 Am. Dec. 84; *Allen* v. *Affleck,* 64 How. Pr. 380; *Dupre* v. *Rein*, 7 Abb. N. C. 256.

We come now to consider the question whether the divorce granted upon the application of the wife affected the agreement of separation. Ordinarily that question would be presented by an answer to the complaint by way of defense. That matter is now presented upon behalf of the plaintiff, and as a part of the complaint, and the defendant demurs to it. Of course, the defendant admits the truth of the allegations of the complaint, and just as stated in the complaint. The defendant is confined to that statement, and is not at liberty to resort to any doubtful inferences of fact arising from the circumstances or motives to the making of the agreement, or to any doubtful intendments, from the language or construction of the agreement or the decree of divorce, unfavorable to the plaintiff.

The complaint, after setting forth the agreement of separation, dated February 14, 1883, alleges that on the twenty-third day of September, 1885, the said Jennie Fosdick obtained a decree of absolute divorce from a court of the state of Rhode Island, having power to grant the same, and having jurisdiction of the parties: of the plaintiff by reason of a *bona fide* residence in that state for a year, and of the defendant by reason of his appearance in that court, and the interposition of his defense to the action.

The decree, or a portion of it, is set forth in the complaint in this action, from which it appears "that the bonds of matrimony now existing between the said Jennie P. Fosdick and the said C. Baldwin Fosdick be and the same are hereby dissolved, and that the said Jennie shall have the exclusive custody of her two children, Clark Fosdick and Pauldine Fosdick, until the further order of the court."

The complaint alleges that no alimony was asked or granted in said action, and that the wife relied upon the covenant contained in the agreement of separation in that regard.

It is contended upon behalf of the defendant that this decree estops the plaintiff from maintaining this action. There is nothing in the complaint in this action or in the decree showing the ground upon which such divorce was granted; nor when the ground on which it was granted began, or ceased to exist. And as the estoppel must depend upon the matters set forth in the complaint and the decree, the estoppel cannot prevail unless such decree, upon whatsoever grounds it may have been granted, as matter of law, nullifies the agreement of separation. I say as matter of law, for the reason that there is nothing in express terms that conditions the payment of the money upon her not applying for or obtaining a divorce from her husband. The question is, therefore, whether such decree rendered the article of agreement of separation, or its provision for the payment of the money in suit, of no further effect. It may be here remarked that the agreement in question is to be considered and adjudicated in view of its provisions and the rules applicable to agreements generally. It is to be assumed in the construction of this agreement that it contains all that the parties intended to agree to and that their minds met upon.

By the terms of the agreement under consideration, the

defendant agrees to pay to the plaintiff, for and towards the support and maintenance of his wife, Jennie Fosdick, and their children, the yearly sum of two thousand five hundred dollars for and during the period of her natural life, unless · she remarries, and that in case of the death of the two children, the amount to be paid shall be reduced to two thousand dollars, and that in case of the death of either said husband or wife, the agreement was to be at an end and have no further force or effect.

Thus it will be seen that an application for or the obtaining of a divorce by the wife was not by the agreement made a condition of the payment of the money, or in any manner to affect the defendant's obligation to pay it.

It seems to me very clear, both upon principle and authority, that the defendant's contention is untenable, and that the divorce granted to the wife, Jennie P. Fosdick, is not a bar to this action to recover the money stipulated in the agreement.

As we have seen, the law sanctions agreements in certain circumstances between husbands and wives for separate living, and providing the means for the support and maintenance of the wife and children through the medium of a trustee to receive and disburse the same. Such agreements take the place, as far as they extend, of the duties and obligations of the law in relation to husband and wife and their children. But they do not supersede or render inoperative other duties and obligations imposed by law upon husband and wife toward each other and toward their children. They are still husband and wife, but living apart from each other, and bound to observe all the other marital duties resting upon them as husband and wife and parents, not provided for in the agreement of separation. Neither of them can marry nor commit adultery without incurring the consequences and the penalty prescribed by law to husbands and wives who commit those offenses. Hence we find numerous decisions of the courts in nearly all civilized countries, holding that either husband or wife may, notwithstanding the existence of such agreement between them, maintain against the other the ordinary action for divorce, limited or absolute, according to the ground and the jurisdiction, and whether the ground therefor accrued before or after such agreement was entered into. The following authorities, I think, sustain the proposition: Stewart on Marriage and Divorce, sec. 191; *Grant* v. *Budd*, 30 L. T. 319; *Charlesworth* v. *Holt*, 43 L. J., N. S., pt. 2, Exch. 25; *Wright* v. *Miller*, 1 Sand. Ch.

103; *Carpenter* v. *Osborn,* 102 N. Y. 559; *Pettit* v. *Pettit,* 107 N. Y. 677; *Jee* v. *Thurlow,* 2 Barn. & Cress. 547; *Kremelberg* v. *Kremelberg,* 52 Md. 553.

With these views and authorities, it seems very clear to me that the agreement of separation is valid, and has not been in any wise rendered ineffectual by the decree of absolute divorce granted to the wife.

This case is free from the question often involved in this class of cases, arising from the allowance of a greater or less amount in the decree of divorce than the amount provided in the article of separation. The decree of divorce made no provision for alimony. Nor did the decree change the provision in the article of separation in relation to the custody and control of the children, as I do not apprehend that the omission of the privilege of visiting the children by the father and grandfather, from the decree, changes at all that right as provided in the agreement.

The agreement remains unaffected in that and other respects, capable of enforcement by any of the parties to it by all proper means.

Judgment absolute should be granted, with costs in favor of the respondent. ——

FROM THE JUDGMENT OF THE COURT IN THIS CASE, as well as its judgment in the case of *Galusha* v. *Galusha,* 116 N. Y. 635, 15 Am. St. Rep. 453, Chief Justice Follett dissented, on the ground that the agreement of separation was entered into upon the presumption that the then existing rights and relations of the parties thereto would continue; that the decree of divorce, dissolving their marital relations, cut down the consideration upon which the executory stipulations rested and destroyed the contract; that the defendant was no longer under any obligation to support the woman, because she had ceased to be his wife; and the obligation of the trustee to save the defendant harmless from his obligation to support her was without further foundation or consideration.

AGREEMENT BETWEEN HUSBAND AND WIFE TO SEPARATE. — As to the validity and effect of agreements between husband and wife for separation, see extended note to *Stephenson* v. *Osborne,* 90 Am. Dec. 367–370. The divorce of a husband and wife after they have entered into a valid agreement of separation, or the commission by either of them of an act entitling the other to a divorce, does not avoid or annul such agreement, or entitle either to be released therefrom: *Galusha* v. *Galusha,* 116 N. Y. 635; 15 Am. St. Rep. 453, and note.

TABOR *v.* HOFFMAN.

[118 NEW YORK, 30.]

AN INVENTOR OR AUTHOR HAS, independent of letters patent or of copyright, an exclusive property in his invention or composition, until by publication it becomes the property of the general public.

INJUNCTION. — THE USE OF PATTERNS SURREPTITIOUSLY COPIED from patterns used by an inventor in casting a pump, the patent to which has expired, will be enjoined when such patterns have been copied without the assent of the inventor, and they cannot be duplicated merely by measuring the pump, as where the patterns, owing to the shrinkage in cooling and the expansion in heating the materials used, must vary in size from the corresponding parts of the completed pump.

INJUNCTION. — ONE WHO BY UNFAIR MEANS DISCOVERS THE MODE OF MANUFACTURING AN ARTICLE, or the formula for compounding a medicine, while in the employment of the proprietor, will be enjoined from using it himself, or imparting it to others to the injury to the proprietor.

ACTION to restrain the defendant from using patterns surreptitiously copied from patterns belonging to the plaintiff. The plaintiff was the inventor of the "Tabor Rotary Pump." This pump was patented, and a complete set of patterns were made to be used in its manufacture, and in the making of which much time, labor, and money were spent; the patterns were always kept in plaintiff's possession, and he made various improvements upon the pump, which were incorporated into the patterns. After the patent for the pump had expired, one Walz made for the defendant a duplicate set of patterns from measurements taken from patterns of plaintiff, without his consent or knowledge, and while they were in the possession of Walz to be repaired. The trial court found "that a competent pattern-maker can make a set of patterns from measurements taken from the pump itself without the aid of plaintiff's patterns," but declined to find that this could be done, "with little more expense and trouble than from measurements taken from plaintiff's said patterns." The pump, when finished, was made of brass and iron, which expand unequally in the finished casting, and also contract unequally when cooling during the process of casting. The trial court restrained the defendant from manufacturing any more pumps from the set of patterns made by Walz from measurements taken from the plaintiff's patterns, and from selling, disposing of, or using any of said patterns. The judgment of the trial court having been affirmed at the general term, the defendant appealed.

Brundage and Chipman, for the appellant.

James C. Strong, for the respondent.

VANN, J. It is conceded by the appellant that, independent of copyright or letters patent, an inventor or author has, by the common law, an exclusive property in his invention or composition, until by publication it becomes the property of the general public. This concession seems to be well founded and to be sustained by authority: *Palmer* v. *De Witt*, 47 N. Y. 532; 7 Am. Rep. 480; *Potter* v. *McPherson*, 21 Hun, 559; *Hammer* v. *Barnes*, 26 How. Pr. 174; *Kiernan* v. *Manhattan Q. Tel. Co.*, 50 How. Pr. 194; *Woolsey* v. *Judd*, 4 Duer, 379; *Peabody* v. *Norfolk*, 98 Mass. 452; 96 Am. Dec. 664; *Salomon* v. *Hertz*, 40 N. J. Eq. 400; Phillips on Patents, 333–341; Drone on Copyright, 97–139.

As the plaintiff had placed the perfected pump upon the market without obtaining the protection of the patent laws, he thereby published that invention to the world, and no longer had any exclusive property therein: *Rees* v. *Peltzer*, 75 Ill. 475; *Clemens* v. *Balford*, 14 Fed. Rep. 728; Short's Laws of Literature, 48.

But the completed pump was not his only invention, for he had also discovered means, or machines in the form of patterns, which greatly aided, if they were not indispensable, in the manufacture of the pumps. This discovery he had not intentionally published, but had' kept it secret, unless by disclosing the invention of the pump he had also disclosed the invention of the patterns by which the pump was made. The precise question, therefore, presented by this appeal, as it appears to us, is, whether there is a secret in the patterns that yet remains a secret, although the pump has been given to the world. The pump consists of many different pieces, the most of which are made by running melted brass or iron in a mold. The mold is formed by the use of patterns, which exceed in number the separate parts of the pump, as some of them are divided into several sections. The different pieces out of which the pump is made are not of the same size as the corresponding patterns, owing to the shrinkage of the metal in cooling. In constructing patterns it is necessary to make allowances, not only for the shrinkage, which is greater in brass than in iron, but also for the expansion of the completed casting under different conditions of heat and cold, so that the different parts of the pump will properly fit together and adapt themselves, by nicely balanced expansion and contraction, to pumping either hot or cold liquids. If the patterns were of the same size as the corresponding portions of the pump, the castings made therefrom would neither fit together, nor, if fitted, work properly when pumping fluids varying in temperature. The size of the patterns cannot be discovered by merely using the different sections of the pump, but various changes must be made; and those changes can only be ascertained by a series of experiments, involving the expenditure of both time and money. Are not the size and shape of the patterns, therefore, a secret which the plaintiff has not published, and in which he still has exclusive property? Can it be truthfully said that this secret can be learned from the pump, when experiments must be added to what can be learned from the pump before a pattern of the proper size can be made? As more could be learned by measuring the patterns than could be learned by measuring the component parts of the pump, was there not a secret that belonged to the discoverer, until he abandoned it by publication, or it was fairly discovered by another?

If a valuable medicine, not protected by patent, is put upon the market, any one may, if he can, by chemical analysis and a series of experiments, or by any other use of the medicine itself, aided by his own resources only, discover the ingredients and their proportions. If he thus finds out the secret of the proprietor, he may use it to any extent that he desires without danger of interference by the courts. But, because this discovery may be possible by fair means, it would not justify a discovery by unfair means, such as the bribery of a clerk, who in course of his employment had aided in compounding the medicine, and had thus become familiar with the formula. The courts have frequently restrained persons, who have learned a secret formula for compounding medicines, beverages, and the like while in the employment of the proprietor, from using it themselves or imparting it to others to his injury, thus in effect holding, as was said by the learned general term, "that the sale of the compounded article to the world was not a publication of the formula or device used in its manufacture": *Hammer* v. *Barnes, supra; Morison* v. *Moat,* 21 L. J., N. S., 248; 20 L. J., N. S., 513; *Green* v. *Folgham,* 1 Sim. & St. 398; *Yovatt* v. *Winyard,* 1 Jacob & W. 394; *Peabody* v. *Norfolk, supra; Salomon* v. *Hertz, supra;* Kerr on Injunctions, 181; High on Injunctions, sec. 663.

The fact that one secret can be discovered more easily than another does not affect the principle. Even if resort to the patterns of the plaintiff was more of a convenience than a necessity, still if there was a secret, it belonged to him, and the defendant had no right to obtain it by unfair means, or to use it after it was thus obtained. We think that the patterns were a secret device that was not disclosed by the publication of the pump, and that the plaintiff was entitled to the preventive remedies of the court. While the defendant could lawfully copy the pump, because it had been published to the world, he could not lawfully copy the patterns, because they had not been published, but were still, in every sense, the property of the plaintiff, who owned not only the material substance, but also the discovery which they embodied.

The judgment should be affirmed, with costs.

———

FROM THIS JUDGMENT CHIEF JUSTICE FOLLETT DISSENTED, on the ground that neither the defendant nor the man who made the patterns sustained any relation by contract with the plaintiff. "They were neither the servants nor partners of the plaintiff, and they owed him no duty not owed by the whole world. The act at most was a trespass, and the plaintiff made no case for equitable relief. It is neither asserted nor found that the defendant is unable to respond in damages. The cases cited to sustain the judgment arose out of the relation of master and servant, or between partners, and in all of them the idea had not been disclosed to the public, but had been kept secret by the inventor."

INVENTIONS. — An inventor or discoverer of a secret process of manufacture, whether patentable or not, has property therein which equity will protect against any one who, in violation of a contract and breach of confidence, undertakes to apply it to his own use, or disclose it to third persons, and also against third persons having notice of such relations, although the inventor may not have an exclusive right to it as against the general public, or against those who in good faith acquire knowledge of it: *Peabody* v. *Norfolk*, 98 Mass. 452; 96 Am. Dec. 664, and particularly note 669, 670.

An inventor loses his right to a patent if he suffers the invention to go into public use before he makes application for a patent, even though the articles used are manufactured only by himself or his agents: *Earl* v. *Page*, 6 N. H. 477; 26 Am. Dec. 711. See note to *McCay* v. *Burr*, 47 Am. Dec. 443–451, as to the abandonment of an invention by the inventor. And unless an inventor has patented his medicines, he has no remedy against another who prepares the same kind of medicines, and sells them under the same generic name, provided he does not sell them as the preparations of the inventor: *Thomson* v. *Winchester*, 19 Pick. 214; 31 Am. Dec. 135.

COPYRIGHTS. — AN AUTHOR HAS, PRIOR TO PUBLICATION, a property in his literary productions, capable of being held and transmitted, and in the exclusive enjoyment of which he and his assigns will be protected: *Palmer* v. *De Witt*, 47 N. Y. 532; 7 Am. Rep. 480, and particularly note 488, 489; for an author has a right of property in his books, letters, and other literary productions, unless they have been published with his assent: *Hoyt v. Mc-Kenzie*, 3 Barb. Ch. 320; 49 Am. Dec. 178, and note 180–184, as to property in letters. So in *Aronson* v. *Baker*, 43 N. J. Eq. 365, the court held that every new and innocent product of mental labor is the exclusive property of the author or his transferee so long as it remains unpublished; while in *Keene* v. *Kimball*, 16 Gray, 545, 77 Am. Dec. 426, the representation of a dramatic work of which the author had no copyright, though without his license, was held to be no violation of any right of property, where the author had previously himself caused said work to be represented and exhibited for money; yet in *Tompkins* v. *Halleck*, 133 Mass. 32, 43 Am. Rep. 480, where an unprinted, uncopyrighted play was publicly acted for the pecuniary benefit of the proprietor, and a spectator, who produced a copy of it from memory, and undertook to have it publicly acted for his benefit, the court reversed the decree of the court below refusing to grant the proprietor an injunction against such a reproduction of the play.

For a discussion of literary property in plays and the law of playwrights, see note to *McCrea* v. *Marsh*, 71 Am. Dec. 751–753.

FRANKLIN v. BROWN.

[118 NEW YORK, 110.]

LANDLORD AND TENANT. — THERE IS NO COVENANT IMPLIED IN THE DEMISE OF A FURNISHED HOUSE for immediate use as a residence that it is reasonably fit for habitation. In the absence of an express covenant, unless there has been fraud, deceit, or wrong-doing on the part of the landlord, the tenant is without remedy if the demised premises are unfit for occupation.

LANDLORD AND TENANT. — LEASE OF A FURNISHED HOUSE IS NOT ACCOMPANIED WITH AN IMPLIED COVENANT against external defects, such as nuisances existing on adjacent premises belonging to a stranger, and of the existence of which neither the owner nor the tenant was aware when the lease was entered into.

LESSEE OF REAL PROPERTY MUST RUN THE RISK OF ITS CONDITION, unless he has an express covenant on the part of the lessor regarding that subject.

LANDLORD AND TENANT — IMPLIED COVENANTS. — THE FACT THAT THERE WAS FURNITURE in the house which was leased with it cannot render the landlord answerable to his tenant for a nuisance of which he had no knowledge, and to which he did not contribute, consisting of noxious odors coming from adjacent premises, over which he had no control.

LANDLORD AND TENANT — IMPLIED COVENANTS. — The law will not imply a covenant in a lease, as to conditions not under control of the lessor, and with reference to a nuisance of which both he and the lessee were ignorant, though the lease is of a house and the furniture therein, intended for immediate use and occupation by the lessee.

John G. Agar, for the appellant.

Delos McCurdy, for the respondent.

VANN, J. It is not claimed that any deceit was practiced or false representations made by the plaintiff, as to the condition of the house in question, or its fitness for the purpose for which it was let. The defendant thoroughly examined the premises before she signed the lease, and she neither ceased to occupy nor attempted to rescind until the last quarter of the term. Neither party knew of the existence of the offensive odors when the contract was made. They were not caused by the landlord, and did not originate upon his premises, but came from an adjoining tenement. The lease contained no covenant to repair or to keep in repair, and no express covenant that the house was fit to live in. The defendant, however, contends that, as the demise was of a furnished house for immediate use as a residence, there was an implied covenant that it was reasonably fit for habitation. It is not open to discussion in this state that a lease of real property, only, contains no implied covenant of this character, and that in the absence of an express covenant, unless there has been fraud, deceit, or wrong-doing on the part of the landlord, the tenant is without remedy, even if the demised premises are unfit for occupation: *Witty* v. *Matthews*, 52 N. Y. 512; *Jaffe* v. *Harteau*, 56 N. Y. 398; 15 Am. Rep. 438; *Edwards* v. *New York & H. R. R. Co.*, 98 N. Y. 245; 50 Am. Rep. 659; *Cleves* v. *Willoughby*, 7 Hill, 83; *Mumford* v. *Brown*, 6 Cow. 475; 16 Am. Dec. 440; *Westlake* v. *Degraw*, 25 Wend. 669; Taylor's Landlord and Tenant, 8th ed., sec. 382; Wood's Landlord and Tenant, sec. 379.

But it is urged that the letting of household goods for immediate use raises an implied warranty that they are reasonably fit for the purpose, and that when the letting includes a house furnished with such goods, the warranty extends to the place where they are to be used. This position is supported by the noted English case of *Smith* v. *Marrable*, 11 Mees. & W. 5, which holds that when a furnished house is let for temporary residence at a watering-place, there is an implied condition that it is in a fit state to be habited, and that the tenant is entitled to quit upon discovering that it is greatly infested with bugs. This case has been frequently discussed and occasionally criticised. It was decided in 1843, yet during that year it was distinguished and questioned by two later decisions of the same court: *Sutton* v. *Temple*, 12 Mees. & W. 52; *Hart* v. *Windsor*, 12 Mees. & W. 68. It was approved and followed in 1877 by *Wilson* v. *Hatton*, L. R. 2 Ex. Div. 336, in which, however, there was an important fact that did not appear in the earlier case, as before the lease was signed there was a representation made in behalf of the landlord, that she

believed "the drainage to be in perfect order," whereas, it was
in fact defective, and the contract was promptly rescinded on
this account. The principle that there is an implied condition
or covenant in a lease that the property is reasonably fit for
the purpose for which it was let, as laid down in *Smith* v.
Marrable, has been frequently questioned by the courts of this
country, and has never been adopted as the law of this state:
Edwards v. *New York & H. R. R. Co.*, 98 N. Y. 248; 50 Am.
Rep. 659; *Howard* v. *Doolittle*, 3 Duer, 475; *Carson* v. *Godley*,
26 Pa. St. 117; 67 Am. Dec. 404; *Dutton* v. *Gerrish*, 9 Cush.
89; 55 Am. Dec. 45; *Chadwick* v. *Woodward*, 13 Abb. N. C.
441; *Coulson* v. *Whiting*, 14 Abb. N. C. 60; *Sutphen* v. *See-
bass*, 14 Abb. N. C. 67; *Meeks* v. *Bowerman*, 1 Daly, 99. We
have been referred to no decision of this court involving
the application of that principle to the lease of a ready
furnished house, and it is not necessary to now pass upon
the question because the case under consideration differs
from the English cases above mentioned, in two significant
particulars: 1. It involves a lease for the ordinary period of
one year, instead of a few weeks or months during the fashion-
able season; 2. The cause of complaint did not originate upon
the leased premises, was not under the control of the lessor,
and was not owing to his wrongful act or default. It was
simply a nuisance arising in the neighborhood, but neither
caused nor increased by the house in question. Hence we are
not called upon in this case to decide whether a lease of a furnished dwelling contains an implied covenant against inherent
defects, either in the house or in the furniture therein, but
simply whether the lease under discussion contains an implied
covenant against external defects, which originated upon the
premises of a stranger, and were unknown to the lessor when
he entered into the contract.

It is uniformly held in this state that the lessee of real
property must run the risk of its condition, unless he has an
express agreement on the part of the lessor covering that subject. As was said by the learned general term when deciding
this case: "The tenant hires at his peril, and a rule similar
to that of *caveat emptor* applies, and throws on the lessee the
responsibility of examining as to the existence of defects in
the premises, and of providing against their ill effects."

In *Cleves* v. *Willoughby*, 7 Hill, 83, 86, Mr. Justice Beards-
ley, speaking for the court, said: "The defendant offered to
show that the house was altogether unfit for occupation, and

wholly untenantable. The principle on which this offer was made, however, cannot, I think, be maintained. There is no such implied warranty on the part of the lessor of a dwelling-house as the offer assumes. It is quite unnecessary to look at the common-law doctrine as to implied covenants and warranties, or to its modification by statute: 3 R. S. 594. That doctrine has a very limited application for any purpose to a lease for years, and in every case has reference to the title, and not to the quality or condition, of the property. The maxim *caveat emptor* applies to the transfer of all property, real, personal, and mixed, and the purchaser generally takes the risk of its quality and condition, unless he protects himself by an express agreement on the subject."

In *O'Brien* v. *Capwell*, 59 Barb. 504, the court declared that "as between landlord and tenant, ... where there is no fraud, false representations, or deceit, and in the absence of an express warranty or covenant to repair, there is no implied covenant that the demised premises are suitable or fit for occupation, or for the particular use which the tenant intends to make of them, or that they are in a safe condition for use."

In *Edwards* v. *New* York etc. *R. R. Co.*, 98 N. Y. 249, 50 Am. Rep. 659, it was said in behalf of this court: "If a landlord lets premises, and agrees to keep them in repair, and he fails to do so, in consequence of which any one lawfully upon the premises suffers injury, he is responsible for his own negligence to the party injured. . . . . If he creates a nuisance upon his premises, and then demises them, he remains liable for the consequences of the nuisance as the creator thereof. . . . . But where the landlord has created no nuisance, and is guilty of no willful wrong or fraud, or culpable negligence, no case can be found imposing any liability upon him for any injury suffered by any person occupying or going upon the premises during the term of the demise; and there is no distinction stated in any authority between cases of a demise of dwelling-houses and of buildings to be used for public purposes. The responsibility of the landlord is the same in all cases. If guilty of negligence or other *delictum* which leads directly to the accident and wrong complained of, he is liable; if not so guilty, no liability attaches to him."

These quotations illustrate the strictness with which the courts have refused to imply covenants on the part of the lessor as to conditions under his control. What sound reason, then, is there for claiming that the law will imply a covenant as to conditions not under his control, and with reference to which neither lessor nor lessee can reasonably be supposed to have contracted, as they knew nothing about them? The fact that personal property was in part the subject of the lease can have no bearing upon this question, because neither the furniture nor the place provided for its use was the cause of the unpleasant odors. They were not a part of the leased property, either real or personal, but were independent of it in origin, and accidental in their effect. If smoke from a neighboring manufactory had blown through the windows, or gas had escaped from a leaky main in the street and entered the house, could the lessee have abandoned the premises, or have called upon the lessor to respond in damages? If any nuisance had existed in the vicinity without the landlord's agency or knowledge, but which materially lessened the value of the lease, upon whom would the loss fall? These questions suggest the danger of departing from the established rule as to implied covenants with reference to the condition of leased real property, simply because personal property is included in the lease. The furniture was not the basis of the contract, but a mere incident, and in law the rent is deemed to issue out of the realty: 1 Wood on Landlord and Tenant, 2d ed., 128; *Newman* v. *Anderton*, 2 Bos. & P. N. R. 224; *Emott's Case*, Dyer, 212 b. The difficulty is still more serious when the effort is made to extend the contract of the lessor, by implication only, to causes having only an accidental connection with the property leased, whether real or personal.

We do not think that there was any covenant in the lease in question, implied either by common law or from the acts or relations of the parties, that extended to the grievance of which the defendant complains.

The judgment should therefore be affirmed, with costs.

LANDLORD AND TENANT — IMPLIED COVENANTS IN LEASES AS TO THE FITNESS OF THE PREMISES FOR HABITATION. — On the lease of a house or of land, there is no implied covenant that the premises shall be fit or suitable for the use for which the lessee requires them, whether for habitation, occupation, or cultivation: *Murray* v. *Albertson*, 50 N. J. L. 167; 7 Am. St. Rep. 787; *Davidson* v. *Fischer*, 11 Col. 583; 7 Am. St. Rep. 267, and note; *Cowen* v. *Sutherland*, 145 Mass. 363; 1 Am. St. Rep. 469, and note.

In *Boston Block Co.* v. *Buffington*, 39 Minn. 385, it was decided that, under the Minnesota statute, if a building becomes untenantable during the term of a lease, the lease is terminable at the option of the lessee.

WRIGHT v. MUTUAL BENEFIT LIFE ASSOCIATION.

[118 NEW YORK, 237.]

INSURANCE. — A STIPULATION IN A CERTIFICATE OF LIFE INSURANCE "THAT
No QUESTION AS TO THE VALIDITY of the application or certificate of
membership shall be raised, unless such question be raised within the
first two years after the date of such certificate or membership and during the life of the member therein named," is valid, and excludes the defenses that the decedent and the beneficiary falsely represented that the
decedent was not then suffering, and never had suffered, from certain diseases, which in fact had seriously impaired his health, and that the beneficiary had no insurable interest in the life of the insured.

INSURANCE. — ASSIGNEE OF THE PAYEE OF A CERTIFICATE OF LIFE INSUR-
ANCE has the right to recover the whole amount specified in the certficate,
though the debt owed the payee by the person whose life was insured
was less than the sum insured, or had been paid in the lifetime of the insured, or though a portion of the sum provided by the certificate was designed by the payee in a contingency for the benefit of some person other
than the payee in the policy.

ACTION upon a certificate of life insurance issued by the
defendant on December 6, 1883, upon the life of Charles
Wright, payable to Byron D. Houghton, for the sum of five
thousand dollars. The assured died in June, 1885, and about
six months thereafter Houghton assigned his interest in the
certificate to the wife of the decedent, who is the plaintiff in
this action.

G. H. Crawford, for the appellant.

Francis E. Hamilton, for the respondent.

POTTER, J. This is an action to recover of the defendant
the amount it agreed to pay under a policy or certificate insuring the life of Charles F. Wright.

Upon the trial, after the plaintiff had introduced the necessary proofs to entitle her to a recovery, the defendant offered
to prove, as a defense to the action, that the deceased, Charles
F. Wright, and Byron D. Houghton, the beneficiary named in
the policy, for the purpose of obtaining the policy and defrauding the defendant, falsely represented that Wright, the
insured, was not then suffering, and never had been suffering,
from certain diseases which had seriously impaired his health,
for the purpose of inducing and by means whereof defendant
was induced to issue the policy insuring the life of said
Wright, and that such representations were false, etc.

This evidence was objected to by the plaintiff, that such
proof was inadmissible under the provision of the policy;

"that no question as to the validity of an application or certificate of membership shall be raised, unless such question be raised within the first two years from and after the date of such certificate of membership, and during the life of the member therein named," and the objection was sustained and defendant excepted.

The defendant also offered to show that the beneficiary, Houghton, had no insurable interest in the life of the insured; in short, that it was a speculative and fraudulent scheme, devised and practiced by Houghton, to secure an advantage to himself upon the life of Wright, which must soon terminate from the diseases he was then afflicted with. This was also objected to by the plaintiff and excluded by the court, and defendant excepted, the court holding that the defendant could not show any such thing, unless, during the life of the assured, or during the period of two years from the date of the policy, such question had been raised.

These rulings present the main question upon this appeal, and inasmuch as I have reached the conclusion that the judgment should be affirmed, there is but little, if any, occasion to add anything to the reasons contained in the opinion of the general term affirming the judgment of the trial court in this case: 43 Hun, 61. There does not seem to be room for any doubt in relation to the meaning of the stipulation referred to. The defendant's counsel does not contend that the language of the stipulation or waiver is not plain and comprehensive of everything which can constitute a defense, nor that the stipulation, though indorsed upon the certificate, does not form a part of the contract of insurance. But he argues from certain supposed analogies to stipulations releasing carriers from liability, which have been held not to exempt the carrier from liability for negligence, that it must have been intended between the defendant and the insured to except the defense of fraud from the operation of the stipulation in question: *Mynard* v. *Syracuse etc. R. R. Co.*, 71 N. Y. 180; *Holsapple* v. *Rome etc. R. R. Co.*, 86 N. Y. 275. It does not seem to me that there is any analogy between the two classes of liability, and nothing is more misleading than an assumed analogy.

The liability of a common carrier of persons or property, for injury or loss, was adopted at a very early period, in view of the peculiar exigencies of the carrying trade, as a rule of public policy. The degree and extent of the liability of the carrier for negligence was fixed by law, and not by the terms of a contract between the parties.   There were numerous contingencies incident to the carrying business, other than the negligence of the carrier, which might result in loss or injury to the person or goods carried, and for which the liability of the carrier would depend upon the facts to be established upon a trial.   It might well be held, in construing an agreement of exemption in general terms, that its office and effect was to relieve from those grounds of liability which depended upon the evidence, and not the liability which was fixed by law.   The rules laid down in the cases referred to by the appellant's counsel is merely a rule of the construction of the terms and effect of an agreement.

It by no means holds that liability for negligence may not be stipulated away, for the contrary has been repeatedly held; but the terms of the stipulation in those cases did not provide exemption from liability for negligence.   The case under consideration is an alleged fraud in making a private contract between the parties to it.

The contract contains a great number of material representations in relation to the past and present condition of the insured, and of course they are variable with every applicant for insurance and every person insured.   Such representations, if untrue, constitute a breach of warranty which will avoid the contract of insurance.   If the representations are known by the party making them to be untrue when made, they would also constitute a fraud, and avoid the contract of insurance. The difference between the representations and the proof of them, upon a trial to avoid the contract, would be only the fact whether the party knew the representation was false when he made it.   It is to be presumed that the defendant had some purpose when it offered to the insured a contract containing the stipulation, and that the stipulation itself had some meaning.   The court is asked to hold that the parties to the stipulation understood (for unless the insured so understood the stipulation the defendant was practicing a fraud upon him) that while the stipulation embraced all representations that were untrue, it did not embrace the same representations, if known by the party making them to be untrue.

The practical difference or effect of this would be, that upon a trial to enforce the contract, the proofs of the representation, their materiality and untruth, would have to be made all the same, but the stipulation would come in as a defense to all representations save those the insured knew to be false.   While

I might, perhaps, entertain the idea that the insurer so understood the stipulation, I am very confident that the insured did not so understand it. It seems to me the analogy is based upon an entire misconception of the object and meaning of the stipulation. It is not a stipulation absolute to waive all defenses and to condone fraud. On the contrary, it recognizes fraud and all other defenses, but it provides ample time and opportunity within which they may be, but beyond which they may not be, established. It is in the nature of and serves a similar purpose as statutes of limitations and repose, the wisdom of which is apparent to all reasonable minds. It is exemplified in the statute giving a certain period after the discovery of a fraud in which to apply for redress on account of it, and in the law requiring prompt application after its discovery, if one would be relieved from a contract infected with fraud. The parties to a contract may provide for a shorter limitation thereon than that fixed by law, and such an agreement is in accord with the policy of statutes of that character: *Wilkinson* v. *First Nat. Fire Ins. Co.*, 72 N. Y. 499, 502; 28 Am. Rep. 166.

No doubt the defendant held it out as an inducement to insurance by removing the hesitation in the minds of many prudent men against paying ill-afforded premiums for a series of years, when in the end, and after the payment of premiums, the death of the insured, and the loss of his and the testimony of others, the claimant, instead of receiving the promised insurance, may be met by an expensive lawsuit to determine that the insurance which the deceased has been paying for through many years has not and never had an existence except in name. While fraud is obnoxious and should justly vitiate all contracts, the courts should exercise care that fraud and imposition should not be successful in annulling an agreement, to the effect that if cause be not found and charged within a reasonable and specific time, establishing the invalidity of the contract of insurance, it should thereafter be treated as valid. Hence I fail to perceive any error in the disposition made of this question in the court below.

The right of the plaintiff, as the assignee of the payee specified in the policy, to recover the whole amount provided by the policy, is well settled, even if the debt owing the payee by the person whose life was insured was less than the sum insured, or had been paid in the lifetime of the insured, or if a portion of the sum provided by the policy was designed by the payee in a contingency for the benefit of some other than the payee under the policy: *Olmsted* v. *Keyes*, 85 N. Y. 593, 599.

If there is a legitimate *cestui que trust* (of which there is serious question), the plaintiff is the trustee, and their rights can be adjusted without involving or imperiling the defendant: Code Civ. Proc., sec. 449; *Hutchings* v. *Miner*, 46 N. Y. 456.

I think the judgment should be affirmed, with costs.

LIFE INSURANCE. — A POLICY OF LIFE INSURANCE may contain a valid provision "against its being contested except for fraud": *Kline* v. *National B. Ass'n*, 111 Ind. 462; 60 Am. Rep. 703, and compare note 708, 709, in which it is said that "a stipulation in a life insurance policy, not to question the validity of the policy after the death of the insured is not against public policy, and is valid."

FAIRBANK CANNING COMPANY *v.* METZGER.

[118 NEW YORK, 260.]

A WARRANTY IS AN EXPRESS OR IMPLIED STATEMENT of something which the party undertakes shall be a part of the contract, and, though part of the contract, collateral to the express object of the contract.

A CONTRACT OF SALE WITH A WARRANTY MUST CONTAIN TWO INDEPENDENT STIPULATIONS, VIZ.: 1. An agreement for the transfer of title and possession from the vendor to the vendee; and 2. A further agreement that the subject of the sale has certain qualities or conditions.

WARRANTY. — TO CREATE A WARRANTY IN A SALE, it is not essential that the word "warranty," or any other particular phraseology, be used; but such words as are used must amount to a representation, on which the vendee relies, and which is intended by the parties as an absolute assertion, and not the expression of an opinion.

WARRANTY OF QUALITY. — THE SALE OF A CHATTEL BY A PARTICULAR DESCRIPTION IS A WARRANTY that the article sold is of the kind specified.

WARRANTY. — CONTRACT BY ONE PARTY WITH ANOTHER TO FURNISH BEEF WHICH HAD NOT BEEN HEATED before being killed constitutes a warranty. When beef is subsequently delivered under such contract that has been heated before being killed, the acceptance of such beef, and the sale of a part thereof before the vendee had an opportunity to discover its character and condition, do not preclude him from maintaining an action for damages sustained by breach of the warranty.

WARRANTY. — RIGHT TO RECOVER DAMAGES FOR THE BREACH OF EXPRESS WARRANTY OF QUALITY SURVIVES THE ACCEPTANCE of the goods by vendee, whether the sale be regarded as executory or *in præsenti.* The vendee is under no obligation to return the goods.

ACTION to recover contract price of a load of dressed beef, sold and delivered by the plaintiff to the defendants. The latter interposed a counterclaim for damages, sustained by the fact that the beef furnished had been heated before being killed. The contract between the parties was, that the plaintiff should deliver the beef on board the cars at Chicago to the defendants, which should then and there become their property; and that the beef should not have been heated before killing, should be thoroughly chilled before loading, and should be in first-class condition in every respect, and marketable. The referee found, as a matter of law, that there was no warranty, and directed judgment in favor of the plaintiff, and disallowed the counterclaim.

Gabriel L. Smith, for the appellant.

Henry S. Redfield, for the respondent.

PARKER, J. In the absence of a warranty as to quality and a breach, the defendants' claim for damages could not have survived the use of the property. For in such case, vendees are bound to rescind the contract, and return, or offer to return, the goods. If they omit to do so, they will be conclusively presumed to have acquiesced in their quality: *Coplay Iron Co.* v. *Pope*, 108 N. Y. 232. Therefore, if the referee was right in holding that there was no warranty as to quality collateral to the contract of sale, we need not inquire further, as the judgment must be affirmed. The referee has found the facts, and this court may properly review his legal conclusion as to whether they amounted to a warranty.

"A warranty is an express or implied statement of something which a party undertakes shall be a part of a contract, and, though part of the contract, collateral to the express object of it": 2 Schouler on Personal Property, 327. All contracts of sale with warranty, therefore, must contain two independent stipulations: 1. An agreement for the transfer of title and possession from the vendor to the vendee; 2. A further agreement that the subject of the sale has certain qualities and conditions.

It is not necessary that in the collateral agreement the word "warranty" should be used. No particular phraseology is requisite to constitute a warranty. "It must be a representation which the vendee relies on, and which is understood by the parties as an absolute assertion, and not the expression of an opinion": *Oneida Mfg. Society* v. *Lawrence*, 4 Cow. 440. It is not necessary that the vendor should have intended the representation to constitute a warranty. If the writing contains that which amounts to a warranty, the vendor will not be permitted to say that he did not intend what his language clearly and explicitly declares: *Hawkins* v. *Pemberton*, 51 N. Y. 198; 10 Am. Rep. 595. In that case the defendants purchased at auction an article, relying upon the representation of the auctioneer that it was "blue vitriol." It was in fact "Salzburger vitriol," an article much less valuable. In an action brought against the purchaser, the trial court directed a verdict for the plaintiff. This was held to be error, because the representation at the sale amounted to a warranty.

Judge Earl in delivering the opinion of the court, after collating and discussing the authorities upon the subject of warranty, said: "The more recent cases hold that a positive affirmation, understood and relied upon as such by the vendee, is an express warranty."

In *Kent* v. *Friedman*, 17 Week. Dig. 484, Judge Learned in his opinion says: "There can be no difference between an executory contract to sell and deliver goods of such and such a quality and an executory contract to sell and deliver goods which the vendor warrants to be of such and such a quality. The former is as much a warranty as the latter." The court of appeals subsequently affirmed the judgment of the general term without an opinion: 101 N. Y. 616.

In *White* v. *Miller*, 71 N. Y. 118, 27 Am. Rep. 13, frequently referred to as the "Bristol cabbage-seed case," the court says: "The case of *Hawkins* v. *Pemberton, supra*, adopts as the law in this state the doctrine upon this subject now prevailing elsewhere, that a sale of a chattel by a particular description is a warranty that the article sold is of the kind specified."

So, too, a sale by sample imports a warranty that the quality of the goods shall be equal in every respect to the sample: *Brigg* v. *Hilton*, 99 N. Y. 517, and cases cited.

Now, in the case before us, the defendants undertook to purchase of the plaintiff fresh dressed beef, to be wholesaled in part, and the residue to be retailed to their customers. They endeavored to procure good beef. Not only did they contract for beef that was clean, well-dressed, in first-class condition in every respect, and merchantable, and that was thoroughly chilled before being loaded on the cars, but further, that they should not be given beef that had been heated before being killed.

When, therefore, the plaintiff placed in a suitable car beef well dressed and clean, and of the general description given in defendants' order, it had made a delivery of the merchandise sold, and by the terms of the contract was entitled to be paid as soon as the bill should reach defendants, and before the arrival of the beef made an examination by defendants possible.

But there was another collateral engagement, and yet forming a part of the contract, which the plaintiff had not performed, — an engagement of much consequence to the defendants and their customers, because it affected the quality of the meat. Upon its performance or non-performance depended whether it should be wholesome as an article of food. It was of such a character that defendants were obliged to rely solely upon the representation of the plaintiff in respect thereto. The plaintiff, or its agents, selected from their stock the cattle to be slaughtered. No one else knew or could know whether they were heated and feverish. Inspection immediately after placing the beef in the car would not determine it. That collateral engagement consisted of a representation and agreement that plaintiff would deliver to the defendants beef from cattle that had not been heated before being slaughtered. Such representation and agreement amounted to an express warranty.

The referee found as a fact "that the meat had been heated before being killed"; therefore there was a breach of the warranty, and the defendants are entitled to recover their damages, by way of counterclaim, unless such right must be deemed to have been subsequently waived.

It is not necessary for the disposition of this case to decide, and therefore it is not decided, whether a warranty is implied in all cases of a sale of fresh dressed meat, by the party slaughtering the animals, that they were not heated before being killed, and as some of my associates are averse to any expression whatever upon that question at this time, what is said must be regarded as an individual view rather than that of the court. My attention has not been called to a decision in this state covering that precise question.

It was determined in *Divine* v. *McCormick*, 50 Barb. 116, that in the sale of a heifer for immediate consumption, a warranty that she is not diseased and unfit for food is implied. That decision is well founded in principle, and is in accordance with a sound public policy, which demands that the doctrine of *caveat emptor* shall be still further encroached upon, rather than that the public health shall be endangered.

I see no reason for applying the rule to one who slaughters and sells to his customers for immediate consumption, and denying its application to one who slaughters and sells to another to be retailed by him. In each case it is fresh meat intended for immediate consumption.

The rule is well settled by the courts of last resort in many of the states that a vendor of an article manufactured by him for a particular use impliedly warrants it against all such defects as arise from his unskillfulness, either in selecting the materials or in putting them together and adapting them to the required purpose: See cases cited in 18 Alb. L. J. 324.

One who prepares meat for the wholesale market may be said to come within that rule; because he purchases the cattle, determines whether they are healthy and in proper condition for food, and upon his skill in dressing and preparing the meat for transportation a long distance its quality and condition as an article of diet for the consumer largely depends.

In two of the states, at least, it is held that where perishable goods are sold to be shipped to a distant market, a warranty is implied that they are properly packed and fit for shipment, but not that they will continue sound for any particular or definite period: *Mann* v. *Evertson*, 32 Ind. 355; *Leopold* v. *Van Kirk*, 27 Wis. 152.

The respondent insists that the act of defendants' agent in selling some sixty quarters of the beef, before the car reached Elmira, when the defendants, after making a personal examination, immediately shipped that which remained unsold to the plaintiff, constituted a waiver of their claim for damages. It is undoubtedly the rule that in cases of executory contracts for the sale and delivery of personal property, if the article furnished fails to conform to the agreement, the vendee's right to recover damages does not survive an acceptance of the property, after opportunity to ascertain the defect, unless notice has been given to the vendor, or the vendee offers to return the property: *Reed* v. *Randall*, 29 N. Y. 358; 86 Am. Dec. 305; *Beck* v. *Sheldon*, 48 N. Y. 365; *Coplay Iron Co.* v. *Pope*, 108 N. Y. 232.

But when there is an express warranty, it is unimportant whether the sale be regarded as executory or *in præsenti*, for it is now well settled that the same rights and remedies attach to an express warranty in an executory as in a present sale: *Day* v. *Pool*, 52 N. Y. 416; 11 Am. Rep. 719; *Parks* v.

Morris Ax and Tool Co., 54 N. Y. 586; *Dounce* v. *Dow*, 57 N. Y. 16; *Brigg* v. *Hilton*, 99 N. Y. 517.

In such cases the right to recover damages for the breach of the warranty survives an acceptance, the vendee being under no obligation to return the goods.

Indeed, his right to return them upon discovery of the breach is questioned in *Day* v. *Pool, supra*. And Judge Danforth, in *Brigg* v. *Hilton, supra*, after a careful review of the leading authorities upon the question, states the rule as follows: "Where there is an express warranty, it is, if untrue, at once broken, and the vendor becomes liable in damages, but the purchaser cannot for that reason either refuse to accept the goods or return them."

It follows, from the views expressed, that the judgment should be reversed.

———

WARRANTY — SALES. — Warranties on sales of personalty are of two kinds, express and implied: *Osgood* v. *Lewis*, 2 Har. & G. 495; 18 Am. Dec. 317.

SALES — EXPRESS WARRANTY. — To constitute a warranty, no particular form of words is necessary: *Beeman* v. *Buck*, 3 Vt. 53; 21 Am. Dec. 571; *Chapman* v. *Murch*, 19 Johns. 290; 10 Am. Dec. 227; *Randall* v. *Thornton*, 43 Me. 226; 69 Am. Dec. 56; *Weimer* v. *Clement*, 37 Pa. St. 147; 78 Am. Dec. 411. The case of *McClintock* v. *Emick*, 87 Ky. 160, lays down the rule that no particular form of words is essential to a valid warranty in sales of personalty, and that while a mere expression of opinion is not sufficient to constitute a warranty, any clear, positive affirmation by the vendor made during the negotiation will be construed as an express warranty. And while a warranty is a collateral contract, it must form a part of the transaction involving the sale; and if the seller has possession of the property, no special words are necessary to create the warranty, an affirmation at the time of sale being sufficient, provided the affirmant really intended to warrant, not merely to express an opinion: *Hexter* v. *Bast*, 125 Pa. St. 52; 11 Am. St. Rep. 874, and note; for honest expressions of opinion do not of themselves amount to warranties: *Kinley* v. *Fitzpatrick*, 4 How. (Miss.) 59; 34 Am. Dec. 108; *Schramm* v. *Boston Sugar R. Co.*, 146 Mass. 211; but in *McClintock* v. *Emick*, 87 Ky. 160, it was decided that the intention of an affirmant was immaterial; while in *Hexter* v. *Bast, supra*, it was decided that the affirmant must really intend to warrant. Affirmations by a vendor upon which he intends the vendee to rely, and upon which the vendee does rely, are warranties: *Drew* v. *Edmunds*, 60 Vt. 401; 6 Am. St. Rep. 122, and note. It is a question for the jury to decide whether an affirmation or statement made by a seller in a contract of sale amounts to a warranty, or is merely an expression of opinion: *Jackson* v. *Mott*, 76 Iowa, 264.

SALES — IMPLIED WARRANTY. — An implied warranty of title exists in the sale of personalty: *Hall* v. *Aitken*, 25 Neb. 360; *Paulsen* v. *Hall*, 39 Kan. 365. See note to *Scott* v. *Hix*, 62 Am. Dec. 460–468, as to the implied warranty of title in sales of personalty. The rule of *caveat emptor* ordinarily applies to sales where the seller and purchaser stand upon the same footing, and there is no express warranty: *Eagan* v. *Call,* 34 Pa. St. 236; 75 Am. Dec. 653, and note; *Hight* v. *Bacon,* 126 Mass. 10; 30 Am. Rep. 639, and note 641.

In *Grigsby* v. *Stapleton,* 94 Mo. 423, the court held that the rule of *caveat emptor* did not apply where a vendor sold cattle at a sound price, knowing that their value, by reason of disease, was decreased for the purposes for which they were bought, and he did not disclose to the purchaser the fact that the cattle were so diseased, the purchaser having no experience as to such matters.

For when one sells personal property for a particular purpose, he thereby impliedly warrants the fitness of the property for that purpose: *Blodgett* v. *Detroit Safe Co.,* 76 Mich. 538; *Conant* v. *National Bank,* 121 Ind. 323; compare *Giroux* v. *Stedman,* 145 Mass. 439; 1 Am. St. Rep. 472, and note.

Where one buys the crop of fruit "that may grow or be produced" during a certain season, there is no implied warranty by the seller that the crop shall be of any particular quantity: *Brown* v. *Anderson,* 77 Cal. 236.

As to implied warranties of soundness and quality of goods and chattels sold, see *Blackwood* v. *Cutting Packing Co.,* 76 Cal. 212; 9 Am. St. Rep. 199, and note 206, 207. For implied warranties as to quality of chattels or goods sold by samples, see *Gould* v. *Stein,* 149 Mass. 570; 14 Am. St. Rep. 455, and note; implied warranty of the wholesomeness of bread by a baker: *Sinclair* v. *Hathaway,* 57 Mich. 60; 58 Am. Rep. 327; implied warranty upon articles of food sold: *Howard* v. *Emerson,* 110 Mass. 320; 14 Am. Rep. 608; on sale of seed: *Shisler* v. *Baxter,* 109 Pa. St. 443; 58 Am. Rep. 738; *White* v. *Miller,* 71 N. Y. 118; 27 Am. Rep. 13; *Wolcott* v. *Mount,* 38 N. J. L. 496; 20 Am. Rep. 425, and note; on sale of drugs by a druggist: *Jones* v. *George,* 56 Tex. 149; 42 Am. Rep. 689; on sale of manufactured articles for a particular use: *Harris* v. *Waite,* 51 Vt. 481; 31 Am. Rep. 694; *Gerst* v. *Jones,* 32 Gratt. 518; 34 Am. Rep. 773; *Sweat* v. *Shumway,* 102 Mass. 365; 3 Am. Rep. 471.

REMEDY OF PURCHASER OF GOODS UPON BREACH OF WARRANTY. — A purchaser of goods with warranty is not bound to return them upon discovery of the breach of warranty; he may retain them, and seek his remedy, founded upon the breach of warranty: *Argensinger* v. *Macnaughton,* 114 N. Y. 535; 11 Am. St. Rep. 687, and note 691; *Brigg* v. *Hilton,* 95 N. Y. 517; 52 Am. Rep. 63; *Downing* v. *Dearborn,* 77 Me. 457; *Day* v. *Pool,* 52 N. Y. 416; 11 Am. Rep. 719.

URANSKY *v.* DRY DOCK, EAST BROADWAY, AND BATTERY R. R. CO.

[118 NEW YORK, 304.]

HUSBAND AND WIFE — PLEADING — DAMAGES FOR NEGLIGENCE DIMINISHING THE EARNING CAPACITY OF A MARRIED WOMAN are presumed to belong to her husband, and when she seeks to recover such damages, she must allege that for some reason she is entitled to the fruits of her labor; or if she seeks to recover damages for an injury to her business, she must allege that she was in business on her own account, and by reason of the injury was damaged therein as specifically set forth.

PLEADING. — IN ACTION BY A MARRIED WOMAN FOR DAMAGES SUSTAINED BY REASON OF PERSONAL INJURIES, she should not be permitted to prove that she was injured in business, and had suffered a loss therein by reason of such injuries, unless she had so alleged in her complaint.

John M. Scribner, for the appellant.

Louis Z. Kinstler, for the respondent.

PARKER, J. The recovery had was for damages sustained by the plaintiff, a married woman, by reason of personal injuries received while a passenger on defendant's road.

Presumptively, damages for negligently diminishing the earning capacity of a married woman belong to her husband, and when she seeks to recover such damages, the complaint must contain an allegation that for some reason she is entitled to the fruits of her own labor; or if she seeks to recover damages for an injury to her business, she must allege that she was engaged in business on her own account, and by reason of the injury was injured therein as specifically set forth. No such allegations are contained in the complaint in this action.

Nevertheless the plaintiff was permitted to prove, against the objection of the defendant, that the evidence was irrelevant and immaterial, and called for special damages not alleged in the complaint; that she was engaged in the dressmaking business; sold fancy and dry goods; was accustomed to make from sixteen to twenty dollars per week; and that because of her injuries was prevented from working for two months. This was error: *Gumb* v. *Twenty-third Street R'y Co.*, 114 N. Y. 411; *Saffer* v. *Dry Dock etc. R. R. Co.*, 24 N. Y. 210.

The respondent, in support of the ruling, cited *Hartel* v. *Holland*, 19 Week. Dig. 312, and *Ehrgott* v. *Mayor*, 96 N. Y. 275; 48 Am. Rep. 622.

But the question here presented, involving the right to recover damages, which the law does not presume to be the immediate and natural consequences of the injury in the absence of a special averment of such damages, does not appear to have been raised or passed upon in either case. Therefore they do not support the respondent's contention.

As the exception taken to the ruling of the court referred to calls for a reversal of the judgment, it is unnecessary to consider the other exceptions taken.

The judgment should be reversed.

————

THE RULE HAS BEEN LAID DOWN THAT THE HUSBAND IS THE PROPER PARTY to sue for damages from personal injuries sustained by his wife, and she herself need not even be joined as a party plaintiff: *Western Union Tel. Co.* v. *Cooper*, 71 Tex. 507; 10 Am. St. Rep. 772. But in *Burrell Township* v. *Uncapher*, 117 Pa. St. 353, 2 Am. St. Rep. 664, it is decided that the husband is merely the formal, not the real, party to the record, in an action by husband and wife, in right of the wife, to recover damages for personal injuries sustained by the wife. And in *Lewis* v. *Atlanta,* 77 Ga. 756, 4 Am. St. Rep. 108, where a wife sued, without joining her husband, to recover damages for personal injuries to herself, the court decided that she could not recover the expenses incurred by her in consequence of such injury, unless she showed that she was living separate and apart from her husband; that she was a free trader; that she had separate property; or that she personally undertook to pay, or bound herself to pay, such expenses. Compare *Ballard* v. *Russell,* 33 Me. 196, 54 Am. Dec. 620, note to *Carey* v. *Berkshire etc. R. R. Co.,* 48 Am. Dec. 620, 621, where the rule is laid down that both husband and wife must join in actions for personal injuries to wife, even if he has previously deserted her. However, in *Chicago etc. R. R. Co.* v. *Dunn,* 52 Ill. 260, 4 Am. Rep. 606, *Smith* v. *St. Joseph,* 55 Mo. 456, 17 Am. Rep. 660, *Hunt* v. *Winfield,* 36 Wis. 154, 17 Am. Rep. 482, and *Mewhirter* v. *Hatten,* 42 Iowa, 288, 20 Am. Rep. 618, the rule is, that the husband and wife each have a cause of action separately in such cases; the wife may sue for the injury itself, while the husband may sue for damages occasioned by the loss of his wife's services.

In *Baldwin* v. *Second Street Cable R. R. Co.,* 77 Cal. 390, it was decided that, under the code of California, in actions to recover damages for personal injuries to the wife, she is a necessary party plaintiff, and may sue alone in such an action, if she is living separate and apart from her husband by reason of his desertion of her.

COUDERT *v.* COHN.

[118 NEW YORK, 309.]

LANDLORD AND TENANT. — TENANCY FROM YEAR TO YEAR RESULTS WHEN A LESSEE TAKES POSSESSION OF PREMISES under a lease for a number of years, but which under the statute of frauds is valid for one year only because not in writing, or made by an agent who had no authority in writing to make it.

WHEN A LEASE IS VOID BY THE STATUTE OF FRAUDS BECAUSE FOR A PERIOD GREATER THAN ONE YEAR, and not in writing, and the tenant enters under it, he is treated as a tenant from year to year, computed from the time of its commencement; and if he holds over after the expiration of the first year he becomes a tenant for another year, and cannot terminate such tenancy at an earlier period by giving notice of his intention to quit.

LEASE FOR MORE THAN ONE YEAR, UNLESS MADE IN THE MANNER PROVIDED BY STATUTE, though it cannot vest the term in the lessee, yet in other respects the rights of the parties may be determined by its terms as far as they are consistent with its failure to create any estate or interest in the land, or any duration of term for occupancy for the lessee.

WHERE UNDER A LEASE, VOID BY THE STATUTE OF FRAUDS, THE TIME FOR THE COMMENCEMENT OF THE TERM AND THAT FOR ITS EXPIRATION occur at different parts of the year, the tenancy from year to year which is created by the lease, and the entry of the tenant thereunder, must be computed with reference to the date of the commencement of the term, instead of the date of its termination as designated in such lease.

A. J. Simpson, for the appellants.

George W. Roderick, for the respondent.

BRADLEY, J. The action was brought to recover rent of premises described in a written lease made by the agent of the plaintiffs' intestate to the defendants in January, 1884, for the term of two years and five months, commencing on the first day of March, 1884, and ending on the first day of August, 1886, at the yearly rent of three thousand dollars, payable in equal monthly payments, on the last business day of each month. The authority of the agent to make the lease not being in writing, it was void: 2 R. S., sec. 6, p. 134. The defendants went into possession on the 1st of March, 1884, and continued to occupy and pay rent up to August, 1885, when they left the premises, and sought to surrender the possession up to the plaintiffs' intestate, who declined to accept it. He recovered for the amount of rent, at the rate mentioned in the lease, from the 1st of August to the 1st of March following. While the cases are not entirely in harmony on the subject, the doctrine now in this state is such that the defendants, on going into possession of the premises and paying rent, became, by reason of the invalidity of the demise, tenants from year to year, and in such case the continuance of occupancy into the second year rendered them chargeable with the rent until its close. They could then only terminate their tenancy at the end of the current year: *Reeder* v. *Sayre,* 70 N. Y. 180; 26 Am. Rep. 567; *Laughran* v. *Smith,* 75 N. Y. 205.

The question presented is, When did the rental year arising out of such relation commence and terminate? It is contended by the defendants' counsel that inasmuch as the end of the term designated by the terms of the lease was the 1st of August, 1886, that was the time when the yearly tenancy, in contemplation of law, terminated, and therefore the surrender was properly made on the 1st of August, 1885. It is urged that this view is in harmony with the recognized principle that, although the lease was invalid, the agreement contained in it regulated the terms of the tenancy in all respects, except as to the duration of the term, and *Doe* v. *Bell,* 5 Term Rep. 471, is cited. There a farm was, in January, 1790, let by a parol lease, void by the statute of frauds, for seven years, the lessee to enter upon the land when the former tenant left, on Lady-day, and into the house on the 25th of May following, and was to quit at Candlemas. He entered accordingly, and paid rent. A notice was served upon the tenant, September 22, 1792, to quit on Lady-day. In ejectment brought against him, it was claimed, on the part of the lessee, that his holding was from Candlemas, and therefore the notice was ineffectual to terminate the tenancy. Lord Kenyon, in deciding the case, said and held that "it was agreed that the defendant should quit at Candlemas, and though the agreement is void as to the number of years for which the defendant was to hold, if the lessor choose to determine the tenancy before the expiration of the seven years, he can only put an end to it at Candlemas." That case has, in several instances, been cited by the courts of this state upon the question of the force remaining in the terms of the agreement embraced in a void lease. And in *Schuyler* v. *Leggett*, 2 Cow. 663, it was remarked by Chief Justice Savage, in citing it, that such an agreement "must regulate the terms on which the tenancy subsists in other respects; as the rent, the time of year when the tenant must quit, etc." And the citation was repeated to the same effect by the chief justice in *People* v. *Rickert*, 8 Cow. 230.

The question here did not arise in either of those two cases, nor can they be treated as authority that the time for termination of a tenancy from year to year, in any year other than that of the designated expiration of term, is governed by such designation in a void lease for more than one year rather than by the time of entry. The effect sought to be given in the present case to the case of *Doe* v. *Bell*, *supra*, is not supported by English authority. In *Berrey* v. *Lindley*, 3 Man. & G. 496, the tenant entered into possession of premises under an agreement void by the statute of frauds, by the terms of which he was to hold five years and a half from Michaelmas. Several years after his entry, and after expiration of the period mentioned in the agreement, the lessee gave notice to his landlord to terminate the tenancy at Michaelmas. It was there contended, on the part of the latter, and *Doe* v. *Bell*, *supra*, was cited in support of the proposition that the time designated in the agreement for the termination of the tenancy governed in that respect. But the court decided otherwise, and held that the notice was effectual to terminate the tenancy. The views of the court there were to the effect that, although the tenancy was from year to year, the tenant might, without notice, have quit at the expiration of the period contemplated in the agreement; but having remained in possession, and paid rent sub-

sequently to that time, he must be considered a tenant from
year to year with reference to the time of the original entry.

The same principle in respect to holding over a term was
announced in *Doe* v. *Dobell*, 1 Ad. & E., N. S., 806, where it
was said that " in all cases the current year refers to the time
of entry, unless the parties stipulate to the contrary."

The doctrine of the English cases seems to be that a party
entering under a lease void by the statute of frauds, for a
term, as expressed in it, of more than one year, and paying
rent, is treated as a tenant from year to year from the time of
his entry, subject only to the right to terminate the tenancy
without notice at the end of the specified term. And to that
extent and for that purpose only, the terms of agreement in
such case regulate the time to quit. This right is held to be
reciprocal: *Doe* v. *Stratton*, 4 Bing. 446. That proposition is
not without sensible reason for its support. The lease for more
than one year, unless made in the manner provided by the
statute, cannot be effectual to vest the term in the lessee, yet
in other respects the rights of the parties may be determined by
its terms, so far as they are consistent with its failure to
create any estate or interest in the land, or any duration of
term for occupancy by the lessee. And that principle is
properly applicable to such leases: *Porter* v. *Bleiler*, 17 Barb.
154; *Reeder* v. *Sayre*, 70 N. Y. 184; 26 Am. Rep. 567; *Laughran* v. *Smith*, 75 N. Y. 205, 209.

This view does not aid the defendants. They became tenants from year to year, as from the time of their entry; and
although by virtue of the terms of the agreement, in that
respect, in the lease, they may have been at liberty to quit on
the 1st of August, 1886, if they had remained until then, such
time in that or the year previous could not be treated as the
end of any year of the tenancy. The defendants having entered
upon the second year from the time of the original entry, it
was not within their power to terminate their relation or
liability as tenants until the end of the then current year,
which did not terminate until the 1st of March, was reached.

The conclusion, from these views, necessarily follows that
the judgment should be affirmed.

LANDLORD AND TENANT — VERBAL LEASE FOR MORE THAN ONE YEAR. —
In *Rosenblat* v. *Perkins*, 18 Or. 156, it was decided that a verbal lease of
realty for more than one year was void under the statute of frauds, but if
the lessee entered into possession thereunder, and paid rent to the landlord,
who accepted it, such acts of the parties might create a tenancy from year

to year. But in *McLeran v. Benton*, 73 Cal. 329, 2 Am. St. Rep. 814, it was decided that a lease, purporting to be for years, but which was void by reason of its defective acknowledgment, created merely a tenancy at will, which might be terminated by the lessor at any time. The better opinion is, that such a lease is in itself void, and creates no tenancy whatever; and that if the lessee enters under it, the tenancy is at will, unless from the payment and receipt of rent computed by the year, or from other circumstances, the inference may be legitimately drawn that the parties, notwithstanding the void lease, intend a tenancy from year to year: *Talamo v. Spitzmiller*, 120 N. Y. 37; 17 Am. St. Rep.

The clause in the statute of frauds prohibiting the enforcement of parol leases of land for more than one year has reference to the duration of the term, not to the time of commencement: *McCroy v. Toney*, 66 Miss. 233.

Goshen National Bank v. Bingham.   Bingham v. Goshen National Bank.

[118 New York, 349.]

Purchaser of Certified Negotiable Draft or Check Who Obtains Title without the Indorsement of the Payee holds it subject to all equities and defenses existing between the original parties, though he has paid full consideration therefor, without notice of the existence of such defenses or equities.

Transfer of Certified Negotiable Check, Payable to the Order of the Payee, but without the Latter's Indorsement, vests title thereto in the transferee, subject to all equities and defenses existing in favor of the maker or acceptor against the previous holder, though the payee intended to indorse the check at the time he transferred it.

Relation of Indorsement. — The indorsement of a negotiable draft or check, made after its transfer, in good faith and for full consideration, does not relate back to such transfer so as to give the transferee a title paramount to equities and defenses of which he had notice before such indorsement, but after such transfer to him.

Estoppel. — Certified Negotiable Check or Draft, Transferred without Indorsement to an innocent holder for full consideration, does not estop the bank certifying it from resisting payment on the ground that it had been obtained by fraud and misrepresentation.

Bank Induced to Certify Negotiable Check by the Fraud or Misrepresentation of the Payee, who transfers it to a third person without indorsement, cannot maintain an action against the latter for the possession of such check; neither can he, if he had notice of the fraud before the indorsement, though after such transfer, maintain an action against the bank thereon.

Appeals from judgments in two actions, the first of which was by the bank to recover possession of a certified check, and the second was by the holder of such check to enforce payment thereof from the bank. The check in question was obtained under the following circumstances: B. D. Brown applied to the bank to cash a sight draft for seventeen thousand dollars, drawn by him on William Bingham & Co. of New York, and accompanied by a quantity of bonds of the West Point Manufacturing Company of the face value of seventeen thousand dollars. Brown stated that he had negotiated a sale of these bonds for their face value with Bingham & Co.; that they had instructed him to draw on them at sight for the amount thereof, the draft to be accompanied by the bonds, and that the draft would be paid when presented. All these representations were false. The bonds had no market value; Brown was a bankrupt, and had no funds in the bank. The bank, relying upon these representations, cashed the draft, and placed its proceeds to the credit of Brown, and then gave him a sight draft for twelve thousand dollars, and the certified check, drawn by Brown to his own order, for five thousand dollars, dated November 26, 1884. Two days later, Brown called at the office of Bingham & Co., and represented that he wanted to get some currency. The cashier of Bingham & Co. gave Brown a check on the Corn Exchange Bank for five thousand dollars, which he caused to be cashed. In payment of the check which Brown obtained of Bingham & Co., he delivered to them the certified check hereinbefore referred to, but failed to indorse it. The referee, however, found that both Brown and Bingham & Co. intended that the check should be, and supposed that it was, indorsed, and that if Bingham & Co. had known that it was not indorsed, they would not have paid the consideration thereof. While Bingham & Co. yet held the check, the bank demanded its return, and explained the circumstances under which its certification was obtained. Bingham & Co., however, refused to return it, and some time afterwards obtained an indorsement thereof from Brown, and presented the check for payment. Payment was refused, and the bank brought an action of replevin for possession of the check, and Bingham & Co. commenced an action to recover the amount thereof from the bank certifying it. Judgments were entered in the trial court in favor of the defendant in the action of replevin, and in favor of the plaintiffs in the action to recover the amount of the check.

Henry Bacon, for the appellant.

Joseph F. Mosher, for the respondents.

PARKER, J.   As against Brown, to whose order the check
was payable, the bank had a good defense.   But it could not
defeat a recovery by a *bona fide* holder, to whom the check
had been indorsed for value.   By an oversight on the part of
both Brown and Bingham & Co., the check was accepted and
cashed without the indorsement of the payee.   Before the
authority to indorse the name of the payee upon the check
was procured, and its subsequent indorsement thereon, Bingham & Co. had notice of the fraud which constituted a defense for the bank as against Brown.   Can the recovery had
be sustained?

It is too well settled by authority, both in England and in
this country, to permit of questioning, that the purchaser of a
draft or check, who obtains title without an indorsement by
the payee, holds it subject to all equities and defenses existing between the original parties, even though he has paid full
consideration, without notice of the existence of such equities
and defenses: *Harrop* v. *Fisher*, 30 L. J., C. L., N. S., 283;
Whistler v. *Forster*, 14 Com. B., N. S., 246; *Savage* v. *King*, 17
Me. 301; *Clark* v. *Callison*, 7 Ill. App. 263; *Haskell* v. *Mitchell*,
53 Me. 468; 89 Am. Dec. 711; *Clark* v. *Whitaker*, 50 N. H.
474;- 9 Am. Rep. 286; *Calder* v. *Billington*, 15 Me. 398; *Lancaster Nat. Bank* v. *Taylor*, 100 Mass. 18; 97 Am. Dec. 70;
Gilbert v. *Sharp*, 2 Lans. 412; *Hedges* v. *Sealy*, 9 Barb. 214–
218; *Franklin Bank* v. *Raymond*, 3 Wend. 69; *Raynor* v.
Hoagland, 7 Jones & S. 11; *Muller* v. *Pondir*, 55 N. Y. 325;
14 Am. Rep. 259; *Freund* v. *Importers' and Traders' Bank*, 76
N. Y. 352; *Trust Co.* v. *National Bank*, 101 U. S. 68; *Osgood*
v. *Artt*, 17 Fed. Rep. 575.

The reasoning on which this doctrine is founded may be
briefly stated as follows: The general rule is, that no one can
transfer a better title than he possesses.   An exception arises
out of the rule of the law merchant, as to negotiable instruments.   It is founded on the commercial policy of sustaining
the credit of commercial paper.   Being treated as currency
in commercial transactions, such instruments are subject to
the same rule as money.   If transferred by indorsement, for
value, in good faith and before maturity, they become available in the hands of the holder, notwithstanding the existence of equities and defenses, which would have rendered
them unavailable in the hands of a prior holder.

This rule is only applicable to negotiable instruments which
are negotiated according to the law merchant.

When, as in this case, such an instrument is transferred, but without an indorsement, it is treated as a chose in action assigned to the purchaser. The assignee acquires all the title of the assignor, and may maintain an action thereon in his own name. And like other choses in action, it is subject to all the equities and defenses existing in favor of the maker or acceptor against the previous holder.

Prior to the indorsement of this check, therefore, Bingham & Co. were subject to the defense existing in favor of the bank as against Brown, the payee.

Evidence of an intention on the part of the payee to indorse does not aid the plaintiff. It is the act of indorsement, not the intention, which negotiates the instrument, and it cannot be said that the intent constitutes the act.

The effect of the indorsement made after notice to Bingham & Co. of the bank's defense must now be considered. Did it relate back to the time of the transfer, so as to constitute the plaintiff's holders by indorsement as of that time?

While the referee finds that it was intended both by Brown and the plaintiffs that the check should be indorsed, and it was supposed that he had so indorsed it, he also finds that Brown made no statement to the effect that the check was indorsed; neither did the defendants request Brown to indorse it. There was, therefore, no agreement to indorse. Nothing whatever was said upon the subject. Before Brown did agree to indorse, the plaintiffs had notice of the bank's defense. Indeed, it had commenced an action to recover possession of the check.

It would seem, therefore, that, having taken title by assignment, — for such was the legal effect of the transaction, — by reason of which the defense of the bank against Brown became effectual as a defense against a recovery on the check in the hands of the plaintiffs as well, that Brown and Bingham & Co. could not, by any subsequent agreement or act, so change the legal character of the transfer as to affect the equities and rights which had accrued to the bank; that the subsequent act of indorsement could not relate back so as to destroy the intervening rights and remedies of a third party.

This position is supported by authority: *Harrop* v. *Fisher, Whistler* v. *Forster, Savage* v. *King, Haskell* v. *Mitchell, Clark* v. *Whitaker, Clark* v. *Callison, Lancaster Nat. Bank* v. *Taylor, Gilbert* v. *Sharp,* cited *supra.*

Watkins v. *Maule,* 2 Jacob & W. 243, and *Hughes* v. *Nelson,*

29 N. J. Eq. 547, are cited by the plaintiff in opposition to the view we have expressed.

In *Watkins* v. *Maule* the holder of a note, obtained without indorsement, collected it from the makers. Subsequently the makers complained that the note was only given as a guaranty to the payee, who had become bankrupt. Thereupon the holder refunded the money and took up the note, upon the express agreement that the makers would pay any amount which the holders should fail to make out of the bankrupt payee's property. The makers were held liable for the deficiency: *Hughes* v. *Nelson* did not involve the precise question here presented. The views expressed, however, are in conflict with some of the cases cited, but we regard it in such respect as against the weight of authority: *Freund* v. *Importers' and Traders' Bank, supra,* does not aid the plaintiff. In that case it was held "that the certification by the bank of a check in the hands of a holder who had purchased it for value from the payee, but which had not been indorsed by him, rendered the bank liable to such holder for the amount thereof. By accepting the check the bank took, as it had a right to do, the risk of the title which the holder claimed to have acquired from the payee. In such case the bank enters into contract with the holder by which it accepts the check and promises to pay it to the holder, notwithstanding it lacks the indorsement provided for, and it was accordingly held that it was liable upon such acceptance upon the same principles that control the liabilities of other acceptors of commercial paper": *Lynch* v. *First National Bank of Jersey City,* 107 N. Y. 183; 1 Am. St. Rep. 803. But one question remains.

The learned referee held, and in that respect he was sustained by the general term, that the bank, by its certification, represented to every one that Brown had on deposit with it five thousand dollars; that such amount had been set apart for the satisfaction of the check, and that it should be so applied whenever the check should be presented for payment; and that Bingham & Co., having acted upon the faith of these representations, and having parted with five thousand dollars on the strength thereof, the bank is estopped from asserting its defense.

The referee omitted an important feature of the contract of certification. The bank did certify that it had the money, would retain it, and apply it in payment, provided the check should be indorsed by the payee: *Lynch* v. *First National Bank of Jersey City, supra.*

If the check had been transferred to plaintiffs by indorsement, the defendant would have had no defense, not because of the doctrine of estoppel, but upon principles especially applicable to negotiable instruments: *Mechanics' Bank* v. *New York etc. R. R. Co.,* 13 N. Y. 638.

If the maker or acceptor could ever be held to be estopped by reasons of representations contained in a negotiable instrument, he certainly could not be in the absence of a compliance with the provisions upon which he had represented that his liability should depend.

But it is well settled that the maker or acceptor of a negotiable instrument is not estopped from contesting its validity because of representations contained in the instrument. In such cases, an estoppel can only be founded upon some separate and distinct writing or statement: *Clark* v. *Sisson,* 22 N. Y. 312; *Bush* v. *Lathrop,* 22 N. Y. 535; *Moore* v. *Metropolitan Bank,* 55 N. Y. 41; 14 Am. Rep. 173; *Fairbanks* v. *Sargent,* 104 N. Y. 108; 56 Am. Rep. 490; *Mechanics' Bank* v. *New York etc. R. R. Co., supra.*

The views expressed especially relate to the action of Bingham & Co. against the bank, and call for a reversal of the judgment.

We are of the opinion that the action brought by the bank against Bingham & Co., to recover possession of the check, cannot be maintained, and in that case the judgment should be affirmed.

———

ASSIGNMENT OF A NOTE BEFORE MATURITY, by payee, without indorsement, transfers to the assignee the rights of the payee merely, and though the latter indorses it after maturity, the maker is not thereby divested of the defense of fraud or failure of consideration: *Haskell* v. *Mitchell,* 53 Me. 468; 89 Am. Dec. 711, and note; see also *Lancaster Nat. Bank* v. *Taylor,* 100 Mass. 18; 97 Am. Dec. 70, and note; 1 Am. Rep. 71; *Clark* v. *Whittaker,* 50 N. H. 474; 9 Am. Rep. 286.

NATIONAL CITY BANK OF BROOKLYN *v.* WESCOTT.

[118 NEW YORK, 468.]

PAYMENT BY A BANK ON A RAISED AND ALTERED CHECK, DRAWN BY ONE OF ITS DEPOSITORS, TO A PERSON to whom it has been indorsed for collection, cannot be recovered back of the party to whom it was made, after he has paid over the amount thereof to the person by whom he was intrusted with such collection, and without any notice of the fraudulent character of such check. The person claiming such check cannot be held answerable as an indorser thereof, from the fact that it was paid to his agent, who indorsed his own name thereon without adding the word "agent," or any other word or words to show that his indorsement was other than in his personal capacity.

THE INDORSEMENT OF A CHECK BY ONE APPARENTLY IN HIS PERSONAL CAPACITY CANNOT BE SHOWN to have been the indorsement of his principal, when the latter has not in any way adopted the act.

WHEN A CHECK HAS BEEN INDORSED FOR COLLECTION, THE RIGHT OF THE INDORSEE IS LIMITED to presenting the check and receiving payment thereof, and if he presents it for payment by an agent, the latter has no authority to represent the indorsee in the transaction beyond what is requisite to the performance of the duties of a collection agent, and if he should indorse such check, the indorsement will not enable the bank paying it to recover the amount paid, if it should subsequently be discovered that the check had been fraudulently altered. .The rule is otherwise, when he, by whom or by whose agent the check is presented, apparently receives payment in his own right. Then, with or without indorsement, the person presenting the check warrants its genuineness, and is liable to pay the amount received by him if it is not genuine.

ACTION by a bank to recover $654, an alleged over-payment upon a check drawn by one of its depositors and fraudulently raised. The check, as presented for payment, was dated November 15, 1884, and was in favor of Samuel T. Allen, and was indorsed as follows: "Samuel T. Allen. For collection, New York and Boston Despatch Express Company. A. J. Dunlap, agent." The New York and Boston Despatch Express Company, on November 19, 1884, handed the draft to the Wescott Company for collection. On the last-named day George W. Dixon, agent of the Wescott Company, indorsed his name upon the check, presented it to plaintiff, and received full payment thereof. The moneys received were thereupon delivered to the New York and Boston Despatch Express Company, which, on the 27th of the same month, at Philadelphia, paid the money to the party from whom it had received the check. In the following February the discovery was made that the check had originally been drawn payable to J. W. Smith for the sum of six dollars, and that it had been afterwards feloniously altered by substituting, as payee, Samuel T. Allen, and by increasing the amount from six dollars to six hundred and sixty dollars. The bank, as soon as this discovery was made, demanded of defendant repayment of the amount of the check, which being refused, this action was commenced, resulting in a judgment in the trial court, affirmed at the general term, in favor of the plaintiff.

Edgar Bergen, for the respondent.

Charles A. Da Costa, for the appellant.

BRADLEY, J. The case, as represented by the evidence, was at the trial treated by the counsel for the parties as presenting a question of law only. The request for direction of a verdict for the defendant was refused, and the court directed a verdict for the plaintiff, and exceptions were taken. So that if, in any view which may be taken of it, the evidence is sufficient to support the verdict, the recovery must be sustained: *Dillon* v. *Cockcroft,* 90 N. Y. 649.

In the presentation of the check to the plaintiff for payment, and in paying it, the parties acted in good faith, and upon the assumption that it was in all respects genuine. The drawer of it was one of the plaintiff's depositors, and had been such for considerable time. The signature to the check was his, signed to one drawn by him, and which had been raised in amount from six to six hundred and sixty dollars, and the name of another payee inserted in it. This fraudulent alteration was not discovered until nearly three months after the time the payment was made. In the mean time the money had been paid over to the person who had placed it with the New York and Boston Despatch Express Company for collection.

The payment was made by the plaintiff upon a mistake of fact as to the character of the check; and money paid under such circumstances may be recovered back from the party to whom payment is made. If the Wescott Express Company had been or had assumed to be the apparent owner of the check when it was presented to and paid by the plaintiff, the defendant would have been liable to reimburse the plaintiff: *Canal Bank* v. *Bank of Albany,* 1 Hill, 287; *Bank of Commerce* v. *Union Bank,* 3 N. Y. 230; *Corn Exchange Bank* v. *Nassau Bank,* 91 N. Y. 74; 43 Am. Rep. 655. But in the present case the check was in fact sent to the defendant company for collection, of which the plaintiff was advised by the indorsement upon it to that effect, made by the New York and Boston Despatch Express Company. The defendant, therefore, apparently and in fact represented that company, and in the relation of such agency received the money from the plaintiff: *Montgomery Co. Bank* v. *Albany City Bank,* 7 N. Y. 459. And prior to the time of the discovery of the fraudulent character of the chèck, having handed the money over to the company from which it was so received for collection, the defendant was not liable to the plaintiff as for money paid by mistake: *National Park Bank* v. *Seaboard Bank,* 114 N. Y. 28; 11 Am. St. Rep. 612. It is, however, contended that the defendant was indorser of the check, and became chargeable as such. And to establish the fact that the defendant did indorse it, reference is made to the pleadings. The complaint alleged that the "check so altered, changed, and raised, and properly indorsed, was presented on or about the nineteenth day of November, 1884, by George W. Dixon, as agent of said Wescott Express Company." And the defendant, by the answer, "admits the allegations that the check referred to in said complaint, properly indorsed, was presented to said plaintiff for payment on or about the nineteenth day of November, 1884, by George W. Dixon, as agent of the said Wescott Express Company." This admission, in its import, is no broader than those allegations of the complaint, and they do not charge that the company indorsed the check, and they are entitled to such construction only, in favor of the plaintiff, as the language used fairly requires: *Slocum* v. *Clark,* 2 Hill, 475; *Clark* v. *Dillon,* 97 N. Y. 370. That the check, properly indorsed, was presented to the plaintiff by Dixon, as the agent of the defendant company, does not necessarily furnish the inference of indorsement by the company.

But it is urged that inasmuch as Dixon was the agent of the company, and presented the check as such for payment, his indorsement must or may be that of his principal.

He indorsed his name upon it without anything to indicate that he made it other than individually. It may be that if he had added the word "agent" to his name, it may have been properly shown to have been done by him as such agent, and the indorsement treated as that of his company, upon evidence being given of his authority to make it: *Hicks* v. *Hinde,* 9 Barb. 528; *Babcock* v. *Beman,* 11 N. Y. 200; *Bank of Genesee* v. *Patchin Bank,* 19 N. Y. 312.

Nothing appears in any manner upon the paper characterizing the indorsement of Dixon as made in a representative capacity, or his purpose to so make it, and it would be unduly extending the rule to charge another party in such case as indorser of commercial paper: *Mills* v. *Hunt*, 20 Wend. 431; *Booth* v. *Bierce*, 40 Barb. 114, 136; *Briggs* v. *Partridge*, 64 N. Y. 363; 21 Am. Rep. 617. This view has relation only to the situation produced by the act of making such an indorsement, and without any reference to the effect of an adoption of the act by the principal as against the latter.

The indorsement by the New York and Boston Despatch Express Company appearing by its terms to have been made for the purpose of the collection of the check, the defendant assumed the relation of agency in receiving it and obtaining the money and transmitting it to such indorser.

The restrictive indorsement denied to the defendant the apparent title, and rendered the check non-negotiable, of which the plaintiff was advised by the restriction appearing by the terms of the indorsement. The defendant company took no title to it, and could transfer none. The right of the defendant as the correspondent or agent of the other company, was to present the check to the plaintiff and receive the money. This was the import of the indorsement of that company: *Sigourney* v. *Lloyd*, 8 Barn. & C. 622; *Hook* v. *Pratt*, 78 N. Y. 371; 34 Am. Rep. 539; *White* v. *Miners' Nat. Bank*, 102 U. S. 658. There was, therefore, no implied authority in Dixon, as the agent of the defendant company, to represent it in the transaction beyond what was requisite to the performance of the agency assumed by it, or was legitimately within its purpose. This imposed upon the defendant neither the duty to indorse the check nor to guarantee its genuineness. Nor does it appear that Dixon as such agent had any special authority to do either, or any authority in that respect other than such as arose from his relation of agency. A different case would have been presented if the defendant company, through its agent, had received the money in his own right, or apparently so, from the plaintiff. Then with or without indorsement, the defendant may have been treated as warranting the genuineness of the check, and as liable to the latter for the amount: *White* v. *Continental Nat. Bank*, 64 N. Y. 316, 320; 21 Am. Rep. 612; *Susquehanna Valley Bank* v. *Loomis*, 85 N. Y. 207, 211; 39 Am. Rep. 652.

The cases cited by the plaintiff's counsel, and upon which he relies to support in this respect the recovery, were those in which the implication was permitted that the party presenting paper and receiving payment was the lawful holder having title. The doctrine of guaranty and liability in such case is firmly settled, but for the reasons before suggested it is not applicable to the present case.

No other question seems to require consideration.

The judgment should be reversed and a new trial granted, costs to abide the event.

PAYMENT OF FORGED CHECKS BY BANKS: See note to *National Park Bank* **v.** *Seaboard Bank*, 11 Am. St. Rep. 616.

FOR THE RIGHTS OF AN INDORSEE OF A DRAFT OR CHECK for collection see *Butchers' etc. Bank* **v.** *Hubbell*, 117 N. Y. 384; 15 Am. St. Rep. 515, and note.

BRENNAN *v.* GORDON.
[118 NEW YORK, 489.]

MASTER AND SERVANT — DANGEROUS MACHINERY — THE DUTY DEVOLVES UPON THE MASTER OF A SERVANT, who had previously always acted in the capacity of a common laborer, before putting him in charge of dangerous machinery with which he is not acquainted, to instruct and qualify him for his new duties. If one servant is selected to instruct another in the use of dangerous machinery, their common master is answerable for the servant so selected, and if, by his incompetency or his discontinuance of his duties before the instructions are complete, the servant to be taught is not adequately instructed, and on that account exposes himself to dangers of which he is not aware, and receives personal injuries, the master is liable; and it is no defense that the injuries were caused to the one servant by the negligence of the other, for the latter represents the master, and his negligence is imputed to the master.

ELEVATOR ACCIDENT, LIABILITY FOR. — If one servant is selected to teach another how to run an elevator and to avoid danger in so doing, and the former is guilty of negligence, either in starting the elevator himself or. leaving it in charge of the latter before he is qualified to manage it, or if the machinery is imperfect, and its owners have been negligent in selecting it and putting it in use, and an accident occurs by which the servant being instructed is injured, the master is liable.

MASTER AND SERVANT — DUTY OF MASTER TO SERVANT WHO IS TO BE PLACED IN CHARGE OF AN ELEVATOR, of the management of which he is ignorant, is not fully performed by putting him under the instruction of as competent an instructor as is the master. The duty of the master is to furnish a competent instructor, whether the master himself possesses competency to perform that duty or not; and the master is still answerable, however competent the instructor, if the latter does not continue his instructions for a reasonable length of time, or is guilty of negligence through which the servant to be instructed is injured.

ACTION to recover compensation for injuries suffered by plaintiff through the fall of an elevator. For a long time prior to the month of March, 1881, the plaintiff had been in the employment of the defendant as a porter; but some time in the month of February, in that year, the defendants directed him to perform the duty of running an elevator, which about that time had been placed in their premises, and they selected one H. C. Dillworth to instruct the plaintiff, and qualify him for the new duties which he was asked to assume. The elevator was built and furnished by Reedy & Co., two of whose employees placed it in position and prepared it for use, and it was claimed that these employees instructed the plaintiff, at least in part, in the management of the elevator. On the twenty-eighth day of February, 1881, the elevator, while the plaintiff was in it, was started by somebody, or by some defect in its machinery, and while moving, a beam which was in it came in collision with the roof, and caused a wheel to break and the elevator to fall, by means of which the plaintiff was seriously injured.

Edward C. James, for the appellant.

E. H. Benn, for the respondent.

POTTER, J. This action is brought upon the theory that the plaintiff being inexperienced in the running of an elevator, and that to the knowledge of defendant, and that having been assigned by the defendant to perform this duty, the defendant was bound to qualify him for such service, and that in doing so, if the machinery was found to be defective, or Henry Dillworth, who was assigned as instructor for the plaintiff, was incompetent to perform this duty, or was negligent in his manner of performing it, and that by reason of the premises the plaintiff was injured, the defendants are liable to pay him the damage he had sustained.

The principles of law involved are well defined, and are not seriously controverted by the counsel upon this appeal. Those principles are, that a duty devolved upon the master of a servant hitherto in the capacity of a common laborer, before such laborer should be put in charge of dangerous machinery with which he is not acquainted, to instruct and qualify him for such new duty: *Connolly* v. *Poillon*, 41 Barb. 366, 369; *Ryan* v. *Fowler*, 24 N. Y. 410; 82 Am. Dec. 315; *Noyes* v. *Smith*, 28 Vt. 59; 65 Am. Dec. 222; *Union Pac. R. R. Co.* v. *Fort*, 17 Wall. 553.

That if the master selects a co-servant in his employment to instruct and qualify the servant for the new and more dangerous service, the master must select a competent instructor or be liable for his incompetency or his negligence while performing the duty of instructor, or for discontinuance of his instruction until it is completed, by which the promoted servant is injured, and if such is the case, the master will be liable for the injury, and it will be no defense that the injury was caused by one servant to his co-servant, for the servant whose negligence caused the injury stands for the master, and the latter is liable in such case the same as if the injury was caused by the personal negligence of the master: *Mann* v. *Delaware & H. C. Co.*, 91 N. Y. 500; Wood on Master and Servant, secs. 349, 350, 444; *Brennan* v. *Gordon*, 13 Daly, 208, 210, this case on former appeal; *Loughlin* v. *State of New York*, 105 N. Y. 159, 162, 163; *Union Pac. R. R. Co.* v. *Fort*, 17 Wall. 553.

The questions in dispute in this case, therefore, are, whether the person giving the instructions for the defendants to qualify the plaintiff to run and manage the elevator properly performed that duty, or was himself guilty of negligence in starting the elevator, or leaving it in plaintiff's charge before he was qualified, or whether the machinery was imperfect in any respect, and the defendants were negligent in selecting and putting it in use. If either of these conditions is shown to exist by proper and sufficient evidence to support it, the defendants would be liable to plaintiff for the injuries he.sustained. It does not strike me that it can be reasonably claimed that the machinery was defective in starting up at the time the accident occurred, from inherent defect and without somebody's interference. It was not intended to move and never had been known to move, unless the rope was applied to start it. The testimony in this case is abundant to show that somebody applied the rope to start the elevator up. The difficulty just here is that the evidence is too abundant; so much so, that it is difficult from the superabundance of it to decide who it was that applied the rope to move the elevator up.

The case seems to have been tried upon the true theory to determine whether or not the defendants are liable, and if any mistrial has taken place it is owing to errors in the charge of the learned trial judge, or in receiving or rejecting testimony, or in rulings in conducting the trial.

It is very evident, from a perusal of the case and the exceptions to the rulings upon the evidence, and the requests to charge, and the exceptions thereto, that the trial was very closely contested, and it would be somewhat remarkable if a trial court in the hurry and confusion incident to a trial conducted in this manner, should have avoided the commission of some error. In order to properly dispose of these exceptions, it is necessary to have a just understanding of the questions upon trial. They are, whether Henry Dillworth was designated by the defendants as the instructor of the plaintiff to run and manage the elevator, and if so, whether he properly and sufficiently performed the duty thus devolved upon him by the defendants.

I think there was error in the charge of the court, made at the request of defendant, "if the jury find, as matter of fact, that the plaintiff was put under instruction of a competent instructor, and that the instructor was as well acquainted as defendants with the nature and character of the service which he undertook to perform, he cannot recover." The jury could not otherwise understand this instruction than to mean that the defendants' whole duty to the plaintiff was performed when they assigned as competent an instructor to plaintiff as the defendants were. This was erroneous in two respects. The degree of the instructor's competency was gauged by the competency of the defendants. The plaintiff was entitled to have, and the defendants were bound to provide him with, an instructor competent to teach the art of managing an elevator, regardless of the competency of the defendants in that respect, and of which there was no proof whatever in the case. But the defendants were not only bound to furnish plaintiff with an instructor absolutely competent to manage an elevator, but the defendants were also bound to provide such an instructor for a reasonable length of time to teach the plaintiff how to manage the elevator, and that the instructor should be guilty of no negligence to the injury of the plaintiff while he was being instructed. These relations spring from the fact that during this period the instructor is doing the work, and standing in the place of the defendants, the master.

There are other questions in the case deserving consideration upon this appeal; but I do not deem it necessary or worth the while to discuss them, having reached the conclusion that a new trial must be granted on account of the ruling already considered.

The judgment should be reversed, and a new trial granted, with costs to abide the event.

MASTER AND SERVANT. — A master is not ordinarily liable for damages sustained by a servant from the negligence of a fellow-servant, notwithstanding the latter was higher in authority than the one who was injured: *Wilson v. Dunreath etc. Co.*, 77 Iowa, 429; 14 Am. St. Rep. 304; but an exception to this rule is, that the master is liable when he has negligently selected a servant who is totally incompetent for the work assigned him: Note to *Peterson v. Chicago etc. R'y Co.*, 11 Am. St. Rep. 570; and another exception is, where one of the servants stands in the place of the master to the other: *Louisville etc. R'y Co. v. Lahr*, 86 Tenn. 335; *Denver etc. R. R. Co. v. Driscoll*, 12 Col. 520; 13 Am. St. Rep. 243.

MASTER MUST INFORM HIS SERVANT of increased danger and hazard to which he is about to subject him: *Louisville etc. R'y Co. v. Wright*, 115 Ind. 378; 7 Am. St. Rep. 432.

BEEMAN *v.* BANTA.

[118 NEW YORK, 538.]

DAMAGES FOR BREACH OF WARRANTY TO SO CONSTRUCT A REFRIGERATOR OR FREEZER that chickens could be kept therein in perfect condition, when the warranty was made with the knowledge that the plaintiff relied upon it, and would put chickens in the freezer to be frozen and preserved until the following spring market, may include profits lost by the fact that the chickens which the plaintiff put therein did not keep in perfect condition for sale in such market; and the jury may therefore properly consider evidence tending to show what the chickens which the plaintiff attempted to preserve therein would have been worth had the freezing operated as it was warranted to do.

Rhodes, Coons, and Higgins, and John H. Parsons, for the appellant.

Baldwin and Kennedy, for the respondent.

PARKER, J. The recovery in this action was for damages claimed to have been sustained because of a breach of an express warranty on the part of the defendant to so construct a freezer for the plaintiff as that chickens could be kept therein in perfect condition.

The jury have found the making of the warranty, its breach, and the amount of damages resulting therefrom. The general term have affirmed these findings, and as there is some evidence to support each proposition, we have but to consider the exceptions taken.

The appellant excepted to the charge of the court respecting the measure of damages. Upon the trial he insisted, and still urges, that the proper measure of damages is the cost of so changing the freezer as to obviate the defect, and make it conform to the warranty; and *New York S. Moniter Milk Pan Co.*

v. *Remington*, 109 N. Y. 143, is cited in support of such contention.   That decision was not intended to nor does it modify
the rule as recognized and enforced in *Passinger* v. *Thorburn*,
34 N. Y. 634; 90 Am. Dec. 753; *White* v. *Miller*, 71 N. Y. 133;
27 Am. Rep. 13; *Wakeman* v. *Wheeler and Wilson Mfg. Co.*, 101
N. Y. 205; 54 Am. Rep. 676; *Reed* v. *McConnell*, 101 N. Y.
276; and kindred cases.

In that case, the argument of the court demonstrates:
1. That improper evidence was received; and 2. That the
finding of the referee was without evidence to support it.   No
other proposition was decided.   And the discussion is not applicable to the facts before us.

The plaintiff was largely engaged in preparing poultry for
market, which he had either raised or purchased.   Before
meeting the defendant he had attempted to keep chickens for
the early spring market in a freezer or cooler which he had
constructed for the purpose.   The attempt was unsuccessful,
and resulted in a loss.

The jury have found, in effect, that the defendant, with
knowledge of this intention of the plaintiff to at once make
use of it in the freezing and preservation of chickens for the
May market following, expressly represented and warranted
that for about five hundred dollars he would construct a
freezer which should keep them in perfect condition for such
market; that he failed to keep his contract in such respect,
resulting in a loss to the plaintiff of many hundred pounds of
chickens.

The court charged the jury that if they should find for the
plaintiff, he was entitled to recover, as one of the elements of
damage, the difference between the value of the refrigerator as
constructed, and its value as it would have been if made according to contract.   The correctness of this instruction does
not admit of questioning.   Had the defendant made no use of
the freezer, such rule would have embraced all the damages
recoverable.   But he did make use of it, and such use as was
contemplated by the contract of the parties.   The result was
the total loss of hundreds of pounds of chickens.

The fact that the defendant well knew the use to which the
freezer was to be immediately put, his representation and warranty that it would keep chickens in perfect condition, burdens
him with the damage sustained because of his failure to make
good the warranty.

Upon that question, the court instructed the jury that the

plaintiff was entitled to recover the value of the chickens, less cost of getting them to market, including freight and fees of commission merchant.

The question of value was left to the jury, but they were permitted to consider the evidence tending to show that frozen chickens were worth forty cents a pound in the market during the month of May.

Such instruction we consider authorized. The object of the freezer was to preserve chickens for the May market. The expense of construction and trouble, as well as expense of operation, was incurred and undertaken in order to secure the enhanced prices of the month of May. It was the extra profit which the plaintiff was contracting to secure, and in so far as the profits contemplated by the parties can be proven, they may be considered. Gains prevented, as well as losses sustained, are proper elements of damage: *Wakeman* v. *Wheeler and Wilson Mfg. Co.*, 101 N. Y. 205; 54 Am. Rep. 676.

We have carefully examined the other exceptions to the charge as made, and to the refusals to charge as requested, and also the exceptions taken to the admissibility of testimony, but find no error justifying a reversal.

The insistence of the appellant that the judgment be reversed, because against the weight of evidence, may have been entitled to some consideration by the general term, but it cannot be regarded here.

The judgment should be affirmed.

MEASURE OF DAMAGES upon a breach of warranty, where a thing was sold for a particular purpose, with a special warranty for that purpose: See note to *Passinger* v. *Thorburn*, 90 Am. Dec. 760, 761.

MEASURE OF DAMAGES. — As to when loss of profits may constitute an element of damages, see note to *Sitton* v. *McDonald*, 60 Am. Rep. 488–496; *Griffin* v. *Colver*, 16 N. Y. 489; 69 Am. Dec. 718, and particularly note 724–727.

VAN CLEAF *v.* BURNS.

[118 NEW YORK, 549.]

DECREE OF DIVORCE HAS NO RETROACTIVE EFFECT, except as specially provided by statute. Existing rights already vested are not thereby affected, and can be taken away only by special enactment as a penalty for wrong.

DOWER. — WIFE'S RIGHT TO DOWER WHICH IS VESTED IN HER PRIOR TO A DIVORCE is not divested thereby, unless the statute has so specially declared.

JUDGMENT OF A SISTER STATE CAN HAVE NO GREATER EFFECT HERE than belongs to it in the state where it was rendered.

DOWER. — JUDGMENT OF DIVORCE RENDERED IN ANOTHER STATE DOES NOT DEPRIVE THE WIFE OF HER RIGHT TO DOWER in the lands of which her husband has been previously seised during the marriage, when it is not shown to have that effect in the state where it was rendered, and the cause of divorce is not one recognized by the laws of this state.

CONFLICT OF LAWS. — Statute of New York declaring that a wife shall not be entitled to dower in any real property of her husband if a divorce is granted in an action brought by him is not applicable to a decree of divorce rendered against her in another state, in an action there commenced by her husband, but based upon a cause which could not entitle him to a divorce in New York.

ACTION to recover dower in lands in Brooklyn of which David Van Cleaf, deceased, was seised, while the husband of plaintiff. The defense to the action was, that the plaintiff was precluded from maintaining it by the fact that her husband obtained a decree of divorce against her on the 9th of April, 1881, in the state of Illinois, of which state the decedent was then a resident. The trial court found that such decree had been entered against the plaintiff herein, granting her husband a divorce from her on the ground that she had willfully deserted and absented herself from him without reasonable cause for a space of two years prior to the commencement of the action in Illinois; that the court, in pronouncing judgment, had jurisdiction of the subject-matter of the action and of the parties; that the husband was at that time domiciled in the state of Illinois; that the wife appeared in the action in person, and filed her answer in writing, having first received notice of the action by the service of summons upon her, and that she was at all the times mentioned herein a resident of the city of New York. The trial court dismissed the complaint upon the merits, with costs.

John H. Kemble, for the appellant.

Josiah T. Marean, for the respondent.

VANN, J. Our Revised Statutes provide that "a widow shall be endowed of the third part of all the lands whereof her husband was seised of an estate of inheritance at any time during the marriage": 1 R. S., sec. 1, p. 740; but that "in case of divorce dissolving the marriage contract for the misconduct of the wife, she shall not be endowed": 1 R. S., sec. 8. It is further provided by the Code of Civil Procedure that where final judgment is rendered dissolving the marriage, in an action brought by the wife, her inchoate right of dower in any real property of which her husband then was or was theretofore seised, shall not be affected by the judgment, but that when the action is brought by the husband, the wife shall not be entitled to dower in any of his real property, or to a distributive share in his personal property: Secs. 1759, 1760. These provisions of the code replaced a section of the Revised Statutes which provided that "a wife, being a defendant in a suit for a divorce brought by her husband, and convicted of adultery, shall not be entitled to dower in her husband's real estate, or any part thereof, nor to any distributive share of his personal estate": 2 R. S., sec. 48, p. 146; Repealed Laws 1880, c. 245, sec. 1, subd. 4.

An absolute divorce could be granted only on account of adultery, under either the Revised Statutes or the code: 3 R. S., 6th ed., secs. 38–42, p. 155; Code Civ. Proc., secs. 1756, 1761. According to either, an action could be brought to annul, to dissolve, or to partially suspend the operation of the marriage contract. A marriage may be annulled for causes existing before or at the time it was entered into, and the decree in such cases destroys the conjugal relation *ab initio*, and operates as a sentence of nullity: Code Civ. Proc., secs. 1742, 1754. A marriage contract may be dissolved and an absolute divorce, or a divorce proper, granted for the single cause already mentioned. Such a judgment operates from the date of the decree by relieving the parties from the obligations of the marriage, although the party adjudged to be guilty is forbidden to remarry until the death of the other. It has no retroactive effect, except as expressly provided by statute: *Wait* v. *Wait*, 4 N. Y. 95. An action for a separation, which is sometimes called a limited divorce, neither annuls nor dissolves the marriage contract, but simply separates the parties from bed and board, either permanently or for a limited time: Code Civ. Proc., secs. 1762–1767.

Neither the nature nor effect of the judgment of divorce

granted by the court in Illinois, in favor of David Van Cleaf
against the plaintiff, appears in the record before us, except
that the bond of marriage between them is stated to have been
dissolved upon the ground that she had willfully deserted
and absented herself from her husband without reasonable
cause, for the space of more than two years, prior to the commencement of the action. It does not even appear that the
decree would have the effect upon her right to dower in the
state where it was rendered that is claimed for it here. Apparently, it simply dissolved the marriage relation, and whether
it had any effect by retroaction upon property rights existing
at its date is not disclosed. A judgment of a sister state can
have no greater effect here than belongs to it in the state where
it was rendered: *Suydam* v. *Barber*, 18 N. Y. 468; 75 Am. Dec.
254. There is no presumption that the statutes of the state of
Illinois agree with our own in relation to this subject: *Cutler*
v. *Wright*, 22 N. Y. 472; *McCulloch* v. *Norwood*, 58 N. Y. 562.
If they do, the fact should have been proved, as our courts
will not take judicial notice of the statutes of another state:
Hosford v. *Nichols*, 1 Paige, 220; *Chanoine* v. *Fowler*, 3 Wend.
173; *Sheldon* v. *Hopkins*, 7 Wend. 435; Wharton on Evidence,
secs. 288, 300. Adequate force can be given to the Illinois
judgment by recognizing its effect upon the *status* of the parties
thereto, without giving it the effect contended for by the respondent: *Barrett* v. *Failing*, 111 U. S. 523; *Mansfield* v. *Mc-
Intyre*, 10 Ohio, 27.

The judgment appealed from, therefore, can be affirmed
only upon the ground that a decree dissolving the marriage
tie, rendered in another state for a cause not regarded as
adequate by our law, has the same effect upon dower rights in
this state as if it had been rendered by our own courts, adjudging the party proceeded against guilty of adultery. This would
involve as a result, that the expression "misconduct of the wife,"
as used in the Revised Statutes, means any misconduct, however
trifling, that by the law of any state is a ground for divorce.
Thus it might happen that a wife, who resided in this state
and lived in strict obedience to its laws, might be deprived of
her right to dower in lands in this state, by a foreign judgment
of divorce, based upon an act that was not a violation of any
law of the state of her residence. It is important, therefore,
to determine whether the provision that a wife shall not be endowed, in case of divorce dissolving the marriage contract for
her misconduct, refers only to that act which is misconduct

authorizing a divorce in this state, or to any act which may be termed misconduct, and converted into a cause of divorce by the legislature of any state.

In *Schiffer* v. *Pruden*, 64 N. Y. 47, 49, this court, referring to said provision of the Revised Statutes, said that "the misconduct there spoken of must be her adultery, for there is no other cause for a divorce dissolving the marriage contract." It had before said, in *Pitts* v. *Pitts*, 52 N. Y. 593, that "a wife can only be barred of dower by a conviction of adultery in an action for divorce, and by the judgment of the court in such action." While these remarks were not essential to the decision of the cases then under consideration, they suggest the real meaning and proper application of the word "misconduct," as used in the Revised Statutes, with reference to its effect upon dower.

When the legislature said, in the chapter relating to dower, that a wife should not be endowed when divorced for her own misconduct, and in the chapter relating to divorce, that she would not be entitled to dower when convicted of adultery, the sole ground for a divorce, we think that by misconduct adultery only was meant, or that kind of misconduct which our laws recognize as sufficient to authorize a divorce. The sections relating to dower, and to the effect of divorce upon dower, are *in pari materia* and should be construed together, and when thus construed they lead to the result already indicated: *Beebe* v. *Estabrook*, 79 N. Y. 246, 252. The repeal of section 48, which provided that the wife, if convicted of adultery, should not be entitled to dower, has not changed the result, as sections 1756 and 1760 of the code have been substituted, leaving the law unchanged. They enact, in effect, that when judgment is rendered, at the suit of the husband, dissolving the marriage for the adultery of the wife, she shall not be entitled to dower in any of his real property. There is no change in meaning, and the slight change in language, as the commissioners of revision reported, was to consolidate and harmonize the new statute with the existing system of procedure: Throop's Annotated Code, sec. 1760, note.

The repealed section was pronounced, in *In re Ensign*, 103 N. Y. 284, 57 Am. Rep. 717, "an unnecessary and superfluous provision as respects dower." It was also held in that case that while the relation of husband and wife, both actual and legal, is utterly destroyed by a judgment of divorce, so that no future rights can thereafter arise from it, still, existing rights already vested are not thereby forfeited, and are taken away only by special enactment as a punishment for wrong. It follows that depriving a woman of her right to dower is a punishment for a wrongful act perpetrated by her. Is it probable that the legislature intended to punish as a wrong that which it had not declared to be a wrong? If a divorce granted in another state for willful desertion relates back so as to affect, by way of punishment, property rights previously acquired, must not a divorce for incompatibility of temper, or any other frivolous reason, be attended with the same result? Does the penalty inflicted upon the guilty party to a divorce granted in this state for a single and special reason attach to any judgment for divorce granted in any state for any cause whatever, including, as is said to be the law in one state, the mere discretion of the court?

Our conclusion is, that as nothing except adultery is, in this state, regarded as misconduct with reference to the subject of absolute divorce, no other misconduct is here permitted to deprive a wife of existing dower rights, even if it is the basis of a judgment of divorce lawfully rendered in another state, unless it expressly appears that such judgment has that effect in the jurisdiction where it was rendered, and as to that we express no opinion.

The judgment should be reversed and a new trial granted, with costs to abide the event.

———

Decree of Divorce does not Relate Back, but takes effect only from date of the judgment: *Alt* v. *Banholzer*, 39 Minn. 511; 12 Am. St. Rep. 681; *Wilson* v. *Wilson*, 73 Mich. 620.

Effect of Foreign Divorces: See note to *Tolen* v. *Tolen*, 21 Am. Dec. 747–752.

Judgments of One State cannot be given greater effect, when sought to be enforced elsewhere, than such judgments could have where rendered: *Wood* v. *Watkinson*, 17 Conn. 500; 44 Am. Dec. 562.

SANFORD *v.* STANDARD OIL CO. OF NEW YORK.

[118 NEW YORK, 571.]

FELLOW-SERVANTS, THE SERVANTS OF DIFFERENT MASTERS ARE NOT. — An employee of a firm of stevedores, who are engaged in unloading a vessel, and an employee of the owner of a dock and storehouse, from which the load is to be taken, and who are to furnish a steam-engine and apparatus to be used in the loading, are not fellow-servants, but servants of different masters, and if either is injured by the negligence of the other, the latter's master is answerable therefor.

ACTION to recover for personal injuries. The plaintiff was employed by a firm of stevedores who had undertaken to load a ship with barrels of petroleum, which were in the storehouse and upon the dock of the defendant. The defendant owned a steam-engine and apparatus, which was employed in loading vessels, and they contracted with the firm of stevedores to furnish them the power, and necessary men to run and manage it, required to load the vessel. The plaintiff's injuries, it was claimed, resulted from the fact that the employee of the defendants, without giving any signal, and after work had been stopped for dinner-time, raised a barrel from the dock in such a manner that it knocked against plaintiff, and threw him into the hold of the vessel, causing the injuries of which he complained. The jury returned a verdict for the plaintiff, which the defendant contended was erroneous, basing his contentions on the theory that its servant, whose negligence caused the injury, and the plaintiff were fellow-servants, and that the plaintiff therefore could not recover.

John Brooks Leavitt, for the appellant.

Abel E. Blackmar, for the respondent.

POTTER, J. I entirely agree with the charge of the trial court, that they were servants of different masters; that the man who gave the signal was the servant of the stevedores, Dick and Churchill, and that the man who directed the hoisting and lowering was the servant of the defendant; and that therefore, upon well-settled principles of law, the defendant is liable for the neglect of Gebhard, the man at the drum.

The authorities cited upon the brief of counsel warrant the instruction of the judge to the jury in that regard, and especially the case cited by respondent's counsel, and to be found in *Sullivan v. Tioga R. R. Co.*, 44 Hun, 304, which I consider a clear and able exposition of the law which is to govern the decision of cases of this character. That case was affirmed

by the court of appeals in 112 N. Y. 643; 8 Am. St. Rep.
793.

The judgment should be affirmed, with costs.

———

FELLOW-SERVANTS. — Servants must have a common master to be fellow-servants: *Sullivan* v. *Tioga R'y Co.*, 112 N. Y. 643; 8 Am. St. Rep. 793; *Murray* v. *St. Louis Cable etc. R'y Co.*, 98 Mo. 573; 14 Am. St. Rep. 661; *St. Louis etc. R'y Co.* v. *Rice*, 51 Ark. 469. As to who are and who are not fellow-servants, see note to *Fisk* v. *Central P. R'y Co.*, 1 Am. St. Rep. 31–33.

———

WARREN CHEMICAL AND MANUFACTURING COMPANY *v.* HOLBROOK.

[113 NEW YORK, 586.]

RIGHT TO TERMINATE AGENCY. — WHEN THE COMPENSATION OF AN AGENT IS DEPENDENT UPON THE SUCCESS OF HIS EFFORTS in procuring a contract for his principal and his subsequent performance of the work, the principal will not be permitted to stimulate his efforts with the promise of reward, and then, when the contract is obtained and the compensation assured, terminate the agency for the purpose of securing to himself the agent's profits. Though the principal might have terminated the agency at any time before there was a reasonable assurance that the contract would be obtained, he cannot, after it is obtained, put an end to the agency in bad faith, and as a device to deprive the agent of the fruits of his labor.

STATUTE OF FRAUDS. — CONTRACT FOR THE SALE OF GOODS TO BE SUBSEQUENTLY MANUFACTURED and delivered is not within the statute of frauds. Hence an agreement between a manufacturer of patent roofing and his agent, that the latter should be furnished materials with which to perform certain contracts, is enforceable, though no note or memorandum is made thereof in writing.

STATUTE OF FRAUDS. — THE FACT THAT THE AGREEMENT MAY NOT AND WAS NOT EXPECTED TO BE PERFORMED WITHIN A YEAR does not bring it within the statute of frauds, if it is one which admits of a valid execution within that time.

DAMAGES — LOSS OF PROFITS. — Where plaintiff is seeking to recover for not being permitted to do a certain work which he had contracted to perform, it is proper to receive evidence to show what it would have cost him to do the work, and what compensation he would have become entitled to had he been permitted to do it.

William W. Niles, for the appellant.

William Talcott, for the respondent.

PARKER, J. This action was brought to recover for a quantity of roofing material. The answer admitted the sale, delivery, and balance unpaid to be as set forth in the complaint, and set up by way of counterclaim, in substance, that defendant was the agent of the plaintiff for the district of northern New Jersey for Warren's Anchor Brand National Asphalt Roofing. That by the terms of the agency he solicited contracts for putting on the plaintiff's patent roofing; the contracts to be made with the plaintiff, but the defendant to do the work and pay the plaintiff an agreed price for the material; that within his territory, the plaintiff, aided and assisted by the defendant, procured a contract to put the roofing on some buildings about to be erected, or in process of erection, by the West Shore and Buffalo Railway Company; that it was expressly stated to him by the officers and agents of the plaintiff that he was to do the work. He then proceeded to make the necessary arrangements in order to fulfill the contract, including the purchase of gravel and other materials which the plaintiff did not furnish; that he was only permitted to put on the roof of the round-house, the plaintiff refusing to furnish the materials or suffer him to do the other work; that instead, the plaintiff did the work and retained the moneys paid therefor; that thereby he sustained damages to the amount of $6,756, and demanded judgment therefor, less the amount of plaintiff's claim. He also demanded a further sum, by way of counterclaim, for work done upon another building, but as the verdict of the jury was in favor of the plaintiff as to it, no further reference thereto is required. What may be said hereafter will refer solely to the first counterclaim.

At the close of the testimony the plaintiff moved the court for a dismissal of the counterclaim and for judgment. Several grounds were assigned, but they may properly be grouped into three propositions: 1. There is not sufficient evidence of a contract of agency to authorize a recovery; 2. If there was a contract, then the plaintiff having reserved the right to terminate it, the exercise of such right relieved it from all liability; and 3. In any event the alleged contract was void under the statute of frauds.

The evidence on the part of the plaintiff tended to show that, prior to February, 1872, the Messrs. Morton were acting as agents for the plaintiff in a territory known as northern New Jersey; that at about that time the defendant bought out one of the Mortons, and the new firm was recognized by the plaintiff as its agents. Subsequently the firm was dissolved, and the defendant alone continued the business. The plaintiff was notified of the change and accepted the defendant as its agent; that it was agreed that during the pleasure of

the plaintiff, the defendant should have the exclusive right to
apply the roofing material within the territory of northern
New Jersey.

Under this arrangement the defendant alone, and also in
conjunction with the officers and employees of the plaintiff,
solicited contracts for the putting on of the roofing.   When a
piece of work was obtained, the contract was made by the
plaintiff.   It shipped the patent roofing to the defendant, who
did the work and furnished such other materials as were required to perform the contract, the defendant paying the
plaintiff an agreed price for the patent roofing, and retaining
the balance of the contract price for services rendered in attempting to secure contracts and putting on the roofing.

In the fall of 1881, some of the agents or servants of the
plaintiff called defendant's attention to the amount of roofing
in contemplation by the New York, West Shore, and Buffalo
Railway Company, and requested him to join in an attempt
to secure the job.   This he did, and to that end contributed
both time and money.   The president of the plaintiff requested
that the price be named by the defendant, and asserted that if
the contract should be obtained it would be in the defendant's
territory and would be his job.   It was obtained, and subsequently the defendant was instructed to prepare to perform
the work.   He entered upon its performance, but was only
permitted to roof the round-house.   Whether, by the terms of
the agency, the defendant acquired the exclusive right to use
the plaintiff's roofing materials within the territory in which
the West Shore buildings are situate, was sharply litigated
upon the trial and has been pressed upon our attention here.
Respecting that issue we agree with the learned trial court,
that the establishment of defendant's counterclaim does not
depend upon whether under the original agreement of agency
the defendant was exclusively entitled to put on the roofing
in this territory.   For the evidence at least permitted a finding that not only had he been an agent of the plaintiff for
years, but that such agency was recognized and adopted in
and extended to this particular transaction.

As to the existence of the contract of agency, therefore, a
question was presented for the jury.

It was also urged, in support of the motion for judgment,
that by the terms of the agency the plaintiff was at liberty to
terminate it at any time; that, therefore, the plaintiff did but
exercise a right reserved, of which the defendant cannot be

heard to complain. We cannot assent to that proposition in the breadth contended for it. The right to terminate the agency had only one limitation, it is true, but it had one. The time of its exercise was subject to the ordinary requirements of good faith. When the compensation of an agent is dependent upon the success of his efforts in procuring a contract for his principal, and his subsequent performance of the work, the principal will not be permitted to stimulate his efforts with the promise of reward, and then, when the contract is obtained and the compensation assured after construction, terminate the agency for the sole purpose of securing to himself the agent's profits. At any time before there was a reasonable assurance that the contract would be obtained, the plaintiff might have terminated the agency.

But after it was obtained, and his right to such profits as might accrue became assured, it could not be put at an end in bad faith, and as a more device to deprive the agent of the fruit of his labors.

The defendant's evidence tended to show that the plaintiff's refusal to permit him to complete the work after he had, by his direction, purchased materials and entered upon its performance, was done in bad faith, and for the sole purpose of depriving him of the large profits likely to accrue. On the other hand, the trend of plaintiff's evidence was in the direction of good faith on its part in terminating the agency. Thus was presented a question of fact for the consideration of the jury, and the trial court rightly so held. Assuming that the contract was one for the sale and delivery of patent roofing materials, to be thereafter manufactured and delivered, the most favorable view possible for the plaintiff, it is not within the statute of frauds. True, there was no note or memorandum of the contract. But in this state we regard the established rule to be that a contract for the sale of articles thereafter to be manufactured and delivered does not come within the condemnation of that provision: *Parsons* v. *Loucks*, 48 N. Y. 17; 8 Am. Rep. 517.

While it is true, as insisted by the appellant, that it was not provided by the terms of the contract that it should be performed within one year from its making, neither was it provided that it should not be performed within such period. Nothing whatever was said as to time. Now, the statute does not include an agreement which is simply not likely to be performed, nor yet one which is simply not expected to be performed within the space of a year. Neither does it include an agreement which, fairly and reasonably interpreted, admits of a valid execution within that time, although it may not be probable that it will be: *Kent* v. *Kent,* 62 N. Y. 560; 20 Am. Rep. 502.

The statute, as interpreted by the courts, therefore, does not include this agreement; for there is nothing in its terms inconsistent with complete performance within a year.

It follows that the motion for judgment was properly denied.

The first exception to which our attention is called does not present a question for review. The objectionable evidence constituted the unresponsive portion of an answer to a proper question answered without objection. The plaintiff contented himself with an objection and exception, after answer given, instead of a motion to strike out.

The rejection of the letters marked "G" and "H" for identification appears to have been based, in part, upon the objection that they had no reference to the contract in dispute. As we are prevented from examining them by reason of their exclusion from the printed record, it must be assumed that the trial court rightly determined that they did not relate to the pending controversy.

The evidence offered for the purpose of showing the amount of damages sustained was properly received. It was proved that, by the contract with the railroad company, plaintiff was to receive six and one half cents per square foot. Defendant was permitted to testify that it would have cost him four and one half cents per square foot. The element of damage recoverable in this case consisted of gains prevented. The proper measure, therefore, was the loss of profits, so far as provable: *Wakeman* v. *Wheeler and Wilson Mfg. Co.,* 101 N. Y. 205; 54 Am. Rep. 676.

An examination of each of the many exceptions taken fails to disclose any error justifying a reversal.

Judgment should be affirmed.

———

THE, RULE IS, IF THE PARTY FOR WHOM WORK IS TO BE PERFORMED is justified in preventing the agent or contractor from continuing the work, then such agent or contractor cannot recover compensation for work already done and services performed: *Brent* v. *Parker,* 23 Fla. 200; *Long* v. *Saufley,* 79 Cal. 260; *Beck* v. *West,* 87 Ala. 213; but if the principal is not so justified, the agent or contractor may recover compensation: *Brent* v. *Parker,* 23 Fla. 203; *Cox* v. *McLaughlin,* 76 Cal. 60; and the measure of such compensation is the reasonable worth of the services performed and the expenses incurred: *Codman* v. *Markle*, 76 Mich. 448; *Brent* v. *Parker*, 23 Fla. 200.

In *Durkee* v. *Gunn*, 41 Kan. 496, 13 Am. St. Rep. 300, where an agent had a contract with his principal to sell certain lands, to be disposed of within a time limited, and he was to receive as compensation for his services merely a share in the profits arising out of the sale, and in the performance of such contract he rendered services for several months, expending time and money, and the principal thereupon revoked the agency without excuse, and refused to permit the agent to proceed further in the performance of his agreement, the court held that the agent could recover compensation in damages, the measure of which would be his share in the profits which would have resulted had he been allowed to sell the lands. And to the same effect: *Brent* v. *Parker*, 23 Fla. 200.

STATUTE OF FRAUDS. — Apart from the New York doctrine, the general rule is, that if a contract is for the sale of goods, it is within the statute of frauds, whether the goods are to be manufactured or not: Note to *Crookshank* v. *Burrell*, 9 Am. Dec. 188-190. Compare, also, *Pawelski* v. *Hargreaves*, 47 N. J. L. 334; 54 Am. Rep. 162, and particularly note 164-170.

STATUTE OF FRAUDS. — If a contract be one that may be performed within a year, it is not within the purview of the statute requiring contracts which are not to be performed within a year to be in writing: *Lockwood* v. *Barnes*, 3 Hill, 128; 38 Am. Dec. 620, and note; *Jilson* v. *Gilbert*, 26 Wis. 637; 7 Am. Rep. 100; *Doyle* v. *Dixon*, 97 Mass. 208; 93 Am. Dec. 80, and cases cited in note.

MᴄCREERY v. DAY.

[119 NEW YORK, L]

THE RESCISSION OF A CONTRACT WHILE IN THE COURSE OF PERFORMANCE destroys or annuls any claim which either of the parties might otherwise have in respect of performance, or of what has been paid or received thereon, unless a different intent can be deduced from the agreement of annulment construed in the light of attendant circumstances.

CONTRACT UNDER SEAL COULD NOT AT COMMON LAW BE DISSOLVED by a new parol executory agreement, but the rule is otherwise in equity, and in states where the jurisdiction of law and equity is blended, as in New York, and an equitable defense can be interposed in common-law actions.

CONTRACT UNDER SEAL MAY BE ANNULLED BY A NEW AGREEMENT BY PAROL, followed by actual performance of the substituted agreement, whether made before or after the breach. So a new agreement, although without performance, if based on a good consideration, will be a satisfaction, if accepted as such.

CLAIM FOR INTEREST DOES NOT SURVIVE ACCEPTANCE OF PAYMENT OF THE PRINCIPAL SUM, unless there are special circumstances taking the case out of the general rule.

ACTION to recover sums claimed to be due plaintiffs, under a contract dated March 2, 1882, between plaintiffs, parties of the first part, C. H. Andrews, party of the second part, and

C. K. Garrison, party of the third part. By this contract
plaintiff sold to Garrison a one-fourth interest in a contract
for the construction of a railroad running from Pittsburgh to
Akron, and agreed to turn over to Garrison one fourth part
of all cash, bonds, and stock which should be received from
the Pittsburgh, Youngstown, and Chicago Railroad Company,
which was the corporation owning the railroad to be constructed. Garrison was to pay plaintiffs, for work done and
materials furnished prior to the date of the contract, one hundred and fifty thousand dollars, and was also to pay them,
from time to time, after such date, one fourth of all amounts
expended by them in the further construction of the road. In
the present action the plaintiffs demanded judgment for one
fourth of the moneys expended by them after the date of their
contract with Garrison, and also interest on the one hundred
and fifty thousand dollars, during the time he delayed payment thereon. The answer alleged that on April 13, 1882,
the plaintiffs and Andrews made an agreement with the Pittsburgh and Western Railroad Company to sell the latter a one-
fourth interest in the Pittsburgh, Youngstown, and Chicago
Railroad Company, between Newcastle Junction and Akron,
for one hundred and fifty thousand dollars. The Pittsburgh,
Youngstown, and Chicago Railroad Company was to abandon
the further construction of the projected railroad between
Newcastle Junction and Akron, and another company, known
as the Pittsburgh, Cleveland, and Toledo Railroad Company,
was created to build the railroad, the construction of which
was abandoned, as just stated. On the 6th of November,
1882, Garrison wrote to the plaintiffs and Andrews a letter
admitting the receipt of the papers designed for the completion of the road from Akron to Newcastle Junction by the
Pittsburgh and Western railroad, stating that he would sign
such papers only upon the condition that he was not to pay
any more money than the Humphrey company (the Pittsburgh and Western) paid, as provided in the agreement made
with him on April 13th, "that is, one hundred and fifty thousand dollars, and one fourth of the cost of the road to Newcastle Junction, after that date." Garrison further stated, in
the same letter, that he had given up the agreement of March
2d, and that he no longer desired any interest in the railroad from Newcastle Junction to Pittsburgh. Afterwards,
pursuant to Garrison's letter, the plaintiffs, Andrews and
Garrison, indorsed upon the contract of March 2, 1882, the

following: "It is agreed by the parties hereto, that the within contract is annulled and of no further effect, the same having been superseded by the agreement and arrangement made in lieu thereof, as embodied in the letter of C. K. Garrison, ... dated November 6, 1882, and by a certain agreement made between C. H. Andrews, W. C. Andrews, W. McCreery, James Gallerey, Solomon Humphrey, and C. K. Garrison, all bearing date October 25, 1882." The agreement last referred to was signed by all the parties, and was fully carried out by them. Garrison having afterwards died, the present action was against his executor, Melville C. Day, and others, in whose favor judgment was entered in the trial court.

J. W. Hawes, for the appellants.

William Bronk and Melville C. Day, for the respondents.

ANDREWS, J. The parties, by their agreement indorsed on the contract of March 2, 1882, in terms annulled that contract, and declared that it should be of no further effect. The claim that the annullment of the contract did not discharge Garrison's obligation under the original contract to pay his proportion of expenditures made by the plaintiffs for the construction of the Pittsburgh, Youngstown, and Chicago railroad, between the date of the contract and its annulment, depends on the intention to be deduced from the agreement of annulment, construed in light of the attending circumstances. Where a contract is rescinded while in the course of performance, any claim in respect of performance, or of what has been paid or received thereon, will ordinarily "be referred to the agreement of rescission, and in general no such claim can be made unless expressly or impliedly reserved upon the rescission": Leake on Contracts, 788, and cases cited.

The agreement annulling the original contract recites that the contract had been "superseded by agreements and arrangements made in lieu thereof," embodied in Garrison's letter of November 6, 1882, and the several contracts executed by the parties to that contract, and others, bearing date October 25, 1882. In ascertaining the scope of the agreement annulling the original contract, the letter and the contracts of October 25, 1882, are to be deemed incorporated into the agreement. Construing these several writings together, they plainly show that the parties intended that Garrison should be discharged from all liability under his contract of March 2, 1882, for any

expenditures theretofore made, or thereafter to be made, in
constructing the line between Pittsburgh and Newcastle Junction. The letter was written after Garrison had received the
contracts dated October 25, 1882, for execution, and declares
that he will sign them on the condition and understanding
that he is not to pay anything more than Mr. Humphrey's
company pays, under the plaintiff's agreement with him of
April 13, 1882, "that is, one hundred and fifty thousand dollars, and one fourth of the cost of the road to Newcastle Junction, after that date." The agreement with Mr. Humphrey,
of April 13, 1882, provided for the construction of the part of
the line of the Pittsburgh, Youngstown, and Chicago railroad
between Newcastle Junction and Akron, by a new corporation
to be formed, and that Humphrey should pay the plaintiffs
one hundred and fifty thousand dollars for expenditures incurred and rights acquired on that branch of the road, prior
to the making of the contract, and also one fourth of all expenditures thereafter made in its completion. The letter goes
on to state that the agreement with Mr. Humphrey was made
"after consulting with me, and as it insured my road (Wheel-
ing and Lake Erie railroad) a line to Pittsburgh, I was ready
to assent to it in place of the agreement of the 2d of
March, and you know I have so considered it since, and that
I was owner of one fourth of the new company, all previous
agreements between us being superseded. I do not want any
interest in the road from Newcastle Junction to Pittsburgh.
I will pay whatever Mr. Humphrey's company has paid on
the agreement of the 13th April."

The clear import of the proposition of Mr. Garrison in his
letter is, that he would sign the contracts of October 25, 1882,
provided he should be placed in the same position in respect
to the enterprise as that occupied by the company represented
by Mr. Humphrey, and be relieved from all interest in or
obligation to contribute to the construction of the part of the
Pittsburgh, Youngstown, and Chicago railroad between Pittsburgh and Newcastle Junction. Garrison thereafter executed
the contracts of October 25, 1882, relating to the construction
of the road between Newcastle Junction and Akron, whereby
he assumed other and different obligations from those he had
assumed by his contract with the plaintiffs of March 2, 1882.

The main claim in the action is to recover from Garrison's
estate, under the contract of March 2, 1882, for a share of
expenditures made by the plaintiffs in the construction of the

part of the Pittsburgh, Youngstown, and Chicago railroad between Pittsburgh and Newcastle Junction, after the date of
that contract, and before the execution of the annulment
agreement. The agreement annulling the prior contract is
supported by an adequate consideration. The new obligation
which Garrison assumed under the contracts of October 25,
1882, was alone a sufficient consideration: *City of Memphis* v.
Brown, 20 Wall. 289. There was a consideration also in the
mutual agreement of the parties to the prior contract (which
was still executory, although in the course of performance), to
discharge each other from reciprocal obligations thereunder,
and to substitute a new and different agreement in place
thereof.

The contract of March 2, 1882, is sealed, while the agreement annulling it is unsealed. Upon this fact, the plaintiffs
make a point, founded on the doctrine of the common law,
that a contract under seal cannot be dissolved by a new parol
executory agreement, although supported by a good and valuable consideration, "for every contract or agreement ought to
be dissolved by matter of as high a nature as the first deed":
Countess of Rutland's Case, Coke, pt. v., 25 b. The application
of this rule often produced great inconvenience and injustice,
and the rule itself has been overlaid with distinctions invented
by the judges of the common-law courts to escape or mitigate
its rigor in particular cases. But in equity, the form of the
new agreement is not regarded, and under the recent blending
of the jurisdiction of law and equity, and the right given by
the modern rules of procedure in this country and in England
to interpose equitable defenses in legal actions, the common-
law rule has lost much of its former importance. A recent
English writer, referring to the effect of the common-law procedure acts in England, says: "The ancient technical rule of
the common law, that a contract under seal cannot be varied
or discharged by a parol agreement, is thus practically superseded ": Leake on Contracts, 802. Courts of equity often interfered by injunction to restrain proceedings at law to enforce
judgments, covenants, or obligations equitably discharged by
transactions of which courts of law had no cognizance: 2
Story's Eq. Jur., sec. 1573. It is a necessary consequence of
our changed system of procedure that whatever formerly would
have constituted a good ground in equity for restraining the
enforcement of a covenant, or decreeing its discharge, will now
constitute a good equitable defense to an action on the cove-

nant itself. It was one of the subtile distinctions of the common law as to the discharge of covenants by matter *in pais*, that although a specialty before breach could not be discharged by a parol agreement, although founded on a good consideration, nor even by an accord and satisfaction, yet after breach, the damages, if unliquidated, could be discharged by an executed parol agreement, because, as was said in the latter case, the cause of action is founded, "not merely on the deed, but on the deed and the subsequent wrong": Broom's Legal Maxims, 848, and cases cited. The absurd results to which the common-law doctrine sometimes led is illustrated by the case of *Spence* v. *Healey*, 8 Ex. 668, in which it was held that a plea to an action on covenant for the payment of a sum certain, that before breach defendant satisfied the covenant by the delivery to and acceptance by the plaintiff of goods, machinery, etc., in satisfaction, was bad, Martin, B., saying: "I am sorry I am compelled to agree in holding that the plea is bad. It is difficult to see the correctness of the reason upon which the rule is founded." I suppose there can be no doubt that the facts presented by the plea in the case of *Spence* v. *Healey, supra,* would have constituted a good ground for relief in equity. The technical distinction between a satisfaction before or after breach seems to have been disregarded in this state, and a new agreement by parol, followed by actual performance of the substituted agreement, whether made and executed before or after breach, is treated as a good accord and satisfaction of the covenant: *Fleming* v. *Gilbert*, 3 Johns. 530; *Lattimore* v. *Harsen*, 14 Johns. 330; *Dearborn* v. *Cross*, 7 Cow. 48; *Allen* v. *Jaquish*, 21 Wend. 633. So, also, a new agreement, although without performance, if based on a good consideration, will be a satisfaction, if accepted as such: *Kromer* v. *Heim*, 75 N. Y. 574; 31 Am. Rep. 491, and cases cited.

In the present case it may be justly said that when the agreement annulling the contract of March 2, 1882, was executed, there had been no breach by Garrison of his covenant therein, as he had not been called upon by the plaintiffs to pay his share of the construction account. But it was the plain intention of the parties that the new arrangement then entered into should be a substitute for the liability of Garrison, present and prospective, under the contract of March 2, 1882. The transaction constituted a new agreement in satisfaction of the prior covenant, and was accepted as such. Moreover, it is admitted by the reply that the contracts of

October 25, 1882, were carried out. It is a case, therefore, of an executory parol contract, made in substitution of the prior sealed contract, afterwards fully executed, which clearly, under the authorities in this state, discharged the prior contract.

In respect to the claim to recover interest during the time the payment of the one hundred and fifty thousand dollars was delayed, it is a sufficient answer that the complaint admits that the principal sum was fully paid prior to September 13, 1882. The claim for interest did not survive, there being no special circumstances to take the case out of the general rule: *Cutter* v. *Mayor*, 92 N. Y. 166, and cases cited.

We are of opinion that the facts admitted in the pleadings disclose that there was no right of action, and that the complaint, for this reason, was properly dismissed.

The judgment should therefore be affirmed.

WHERE A CONTRACT IS EXECUTORY, AND BEFORE BREACH thereof, it may be rescinded by mutual agreement of the parties; and so far as it remains executory, an agreement to annul on one side is consideration for such an agreement upon the other side: *Collyer* v. *Moulton*, 9 R. L 90; 98 Am. Dec. 370; *Alden* v. *Thurber*, 149 Mass. 271; and compare note to *Bryant* v. *Isburgh*, 74 Am. Dec. 657, 658. As to whether a contract under seal may be abrogated by a subsequent parol agreement, see *Pratt* v. *Morrow*, 45 Mo. 404; 100 Am. Dec. 381; *Green* v. *Wells*, 2 Cal. 584; *Babcock* v. *Huntingdon*, 9 Ala. 869; *Keating* v. *Price*, 1 Johns. Cas. 22; *Low* v. *Treadwell*, 12 Me. 441; note to *Bryant* v. *Isburgh*, 74 Am. Dec. 658; *Munroe* v. *Perkins*, 9 Pick. 298; 20 Am. Dec. 475.

INTEREST AFTER ACCEPTING PAYMENT OF PRINCIPAL. — In *Robbins* v. *Cheek*, 32 Ind. 328, 2 Am. Rep. 348, it was determined that if a contract provides in express terms for the payment of interest, the acceptance of payment of the whole principal will not debar the creditor from subsequently compelling the payment of the interest. If it is uncertain whether the contract draws interest or not, or if the allowance of interest is discretionary with the jury, then the acceptance of the principal prevents the future recovery of interest: *American Bible Soc'y* v. *Wells*, 68 Me. 572; 28 Am. Rep. 82; *Tuttle* v. *Tuttle*, 12 Met. 551; 46 Am. Dec. 701.

HERMAN *v.* ROBERTS.

[119 NEW YORK, 37.]

GRANTEE OF A RIGHT OF WAY has not only a right to the undisputed passage at all times over the grantor's land, but also to such rights as are necessary or incident to the enjoyment of such right of passage. The grantee may enter upon the land and construct such roadway as he desires, and keep it in repair.

OWNER OF RIGHT OF WAY HAS A RIGHT TO EXCLUDE STRANGERS FROM ITS USE, AND TO RESTRICT SUCH USE OF IT BY THE OWNER OF THE SERVIENT tenement as is inconsistent with the enjoyment of such right of way.

CONSTRUCTION OF A GRANT OF A RIGHT OF WAY CANNOT BE AIDED BY PAROL NEGOTIATIONS; but the language of the grant itself, when uncertain or ambiguous, must be regarded in the light of surrounding circumstances and the situation of the parties.

OWNER OF LAND WHICH IS SUBJECT TO A RIGHT OF WAY has the right to use his land in any way not inconsistent with the easement, and the extent of the easement must be determined by the construction of the grant or reservation by which it was created, aided by circumstances surrounding the estate and the parties, which have a legitimate tendency to establish their intention.

RIGHT OF WAY — OWNER OF SERVIENT LANDS MAY NOT IMPAIR OR OBSTRUCT. — ONE WHO HAS GRANTED ANOTHER A RIGHT OF WAY OF A DEFINITE WIDTH, TO BE USED as a means of access between the latter's country seat or residence and the public highway, has no right, when a road has been constructed over such right of way by the grantee, to enter upon the road and use it for carrying barn-produce and other heavy loads over it, whereby it is cut up and injured, and repairs thereon made necessary, nor has he a right to obstruct any part of the right of way with stone or other materials.

ACTION to restrain the defendant from injuring, by improper use, a carriage road which the plaintiff's testator, Philip Herman, had constructed over lands of the defendant, under a grant of a right of way made by the defendant to said Herman. This grant was dated October 30, 1871, and purported to grant to Herman a right of way "over the lands of the party of the first part, from the north line of the party of the second part to the public highway leading from Lewisburg to the old post-road on a line now staked out, to be forty feet wide between the fences crossing the lands of the party of the first part." Before the grant was made, Herman had a summer residence on his premises, and wished to have a carriage road down a hillside across the defendant's farm to the Lewisburg road. Herman constructed a carriage road at the expense of seven hundred dollars, and maintained it in good condition. The trial court granted an injunction, whereby it enjoined the defendant "from interfering in any way with the use and enjoyment of the roadway, and for using the same for farming or business purposes, in such or in any manner as to damage, or in any wise injure, the roadway or road-bed as now constructed."

Frank B. Lown, for the appellant.

J. Newton Fiero, for the respondent.

RUGER, C. J. The evidence in the case was quite conflicting, and the principal dispute on the trial was whether the defendant had so used the plaintiff's right of way as to injure and impair it, and require the making of repairs thereon to restore its usefulness.

The trial court found, as a matter of fact, "that the defendant has used said roadway for carrying produce and farming utensils upon and along the same, to the injury and annoyance of plaintiff, and threatened to use the same whenever he deems necessary for such purposes, and to use all force necessary for him to pass over such roadway in such manner." The evidence fully supported this finding, and tended to show that the defendant had cut up and injured the road-bed by drawing heavy loads over it, and placing stones thereon, which obstructed the passage.

Under established rules, this court is concluded by this finding, and must assume that the defendant had used the roadway in such manner as to injure it, and threatened a continuance of such use.

This fact clearly entitled the plaintiff to a remedy by injunction to restrain its improper use. The plaintiff obtained this right of way by purchase and grant from the defendant, and it consisted of a piece of land, "as now staked out," across defendant's farm, running from the plaintiff's land to the public highway, a distance of about nine hundred feet, and was plainly intended to facilitate the plaintiff's access to the public road from his residence. This residence was built and used as a gentleman's country-seat, and had no other connection with this public road than the way thus purchased. The land through which the road was constructed was rocky and uneven, and was not adapted to purposes of cultivation or for a carriage road until it had been prepared for that purpose by the plaintiff, which was done at considerable labor and expense. No reservation of a right to use such road by the defendant was incorporated in the deed, and his right to such use depends altogether upon the extent of his interest as the owner of the soil in the servient estate.

No substantial difference exists between the parties as to the rules of law governing the rights of the respective parties in the premises, and the controversy seems to be reduced to the question whether the use proved was materially injurious to the road. Both parties have referred, for the law governing the case, to the rule laid down by Washburn in his work on easements, page 188, stating that "all that the person having the easement can lawfully claim is the use of the surface for passing and repassing, with a right to enter upon and prepare it for that use," and that "the owner of the soil of a way, whether public or private, may make any and all uses to which the land can be applied, and all profits which can be derived from it consistently with the enjoyment of the easement."

The conveyance of the right of way unquestionably gave the grantee not only a right to an unobstructed passage at all times over the defendant's land, but also all such rights as were incident or necessary to the enjoyment of such right of passage: *Bliss* v. *Greeley*, 45 N. Y. 671; 6 Am. Rep. 157; *Maxwell* v. *McAtee*, 9 B. Mon. 21; 48 Am. Dec. 409. The grantee thus acquired the right to enter upon the land, and construct such a road-bed as he desired, and to keep the same in repair. He could break up the soil, level irregularities, fill up depressions, blast rocks, and not only remove impediments, but supply deficiencies, in order to constitute a good road. He had a right to exclude strangers from its use, and to restrict such use of it by the owner of the servient tenement as was inconsistent with the enjoyment of his easement. The owner of the soil was under no obligation to repair the road, as that duty belongs to the party for whose benefit it is constructed: 2 Washburn on Real Property, 311; 2 Hilliard on Real Property, 101.

In considering the extent of the rights of the respective parties in the grant of a right of way, it is not proper to refer to the parol negotiations which preceded its execution, or the colloquium accompanying it: *Bayard* v. *Malcolm*, 1 Johns. 467; *Renard* v. *Sampson*, 12 N. Y. 561; *Long* v. *New York etc. R. R. Co.*, 50 N. Y. 76; but we are to regard the language of the grant, and when that is uncertain or ambiguous, the circumstances surrounding it, and the situation of the parties, with a view of arriving at the true intent of the parties, as was said in *Bakeman* v. *Talbot*, 31 N. Y. 370: "The doctrine that the

facilities for passage, where a private right of way exists, are
to be regulated by the nature of the case and the circumstances of the time and place, is very well settled by authority." In *Burnham* v. *Nevins,* 144 Mass. 92, 59 Am. Rep. 61,
Morton, C. J., says: "These general principles are, that a man
who owns land subject to an easement has the right to use his
land in any way not inconsistent with the easement, and that
the extent of the easement claimed must be determined by the
true construction of the grant or reservation by which it is
created, aided by any circumstances surrounding the estate
and the parties which have a legitimate tendency to show the
intention of the parties." See also *Onthank* v. *Lake Shore etc.
R. R. Co.,* 71 N. Y. 194; 27 Am. Rep. 35.

Under these rules, it is obvious that the rights of the owner
of the easement are paramount to the extent of the grant, and
those of the owner of the soil are subject to the exercise of
such rights. It cannot be assumed, in the absence of any
provisions looking thereto in the grant, that the grantor intended to reserve any use of the land which should limit or
disturb the full and unrestricted enjoyment of the easement
granted. The purpose contemplated by the grant was the
creation of an easement for the plaintiff's use, and not the
reservation to the owner of the use of his land. Every use by
the owner was abandoned except such as might be made in a
mode entirely consistent with the full and undisturbed enjoyment by the grantee of the easement. The idea of a joint use
of the land by both parties, in the sense that a use by the
grantee should at any time give way to a use by the grantor,
is contrary to the plain meaning and intent of the grant. It
cannot be supposed that the grantor, when conveying a right
of way over an impassable tract of land, intended to restrict
his grantee from changing its surface so as to make it passable
and available for the purpose of a road, or that, after the road
had been so constructed, he had the right to enter upon the
land and impair its usefulness, or impose upon the grantee the
duty of keeping such impaired road in repair for the benefit
of the grantor. The full extent of the rights of the grantor in
the soil of the road was to enter thereon and do such acts only
as should not injure or impair the enjoyment of the easement
by the grantee, and when he went beyond such use, he transcended the rights pertaining to his character as the owner of
the soil. The general character of these rights is familiar to
all owners of land, because they are common to all whose

lands abut upon public roads, and they are varied only by the character of the easements enjoyed, and the terms of the grants under which they are possessed. Unless, therefore, something can be found in the terms of the grant which modifies the easement created, that must be held to be the measure of the rights of the parties. No inference can be drawn from the present grant that it was intended that the grantor should enjoy the unrestricted use of the road, with the privilege of so wearing and using it as to subject the grantee to the labor and expense of keeping it in repair. It is apparent, from the character of the property affected and the use to be made thereof, that the plaintiff expected to construct a carriage road for access to and communication with his residence as a gentleman's country-seat. It could not have been contemplated by the parties that such a road was to be used for farming purposes, to draw heavy loads over, and cut it up by the use of the various appliances needed for such purposes. The land over which the road was laid out had never before been so used, and the owner of the soil had theretofore obtained access to his land from the public road by entering upon and traveling over it in other places. The land itself was of small compass and little value, as it was hilly, rocky, sterile, and unadapted to agricultural uses, and it could not, under the circumstances, have been intended that the road was to be built and used to any considerable extent for farming purposes by either the grantor or grantee. The building of fences on both sides of the road showed an intention to preserve it from indiscriminate use, and while the construction of a barway on either side manifested a design that the defendant might thereby have access to his land and cross the road, it was not intended, we think, to give him liberty to so use the road as to impair or destroy its usefulness or character as a carriage road for private use. The right of way granted was to be forty feet wide, and the grantor had a right thereunder, not only to a free passage over the traveled part, but also to a free passage over such portion of the land, inclosed as a way, as he thought proper or necessary to use: *Herrick* v. *Stover*, 5 Wend. 580; *Drake* v. *Rogers*, 3 Hill, 604; Wood on Nuisances, sec. 260. The deposit of stone or other obstructions on such inclosed space in such a way as to interrupt the enjoyment of the easement constituted an obstruction which was inconsistent with the rights possessed by the grantee, and could be properly prevented by injunction. The use of such land for agricultural purposes—the raising of crops, or the deposit of materials thereon, except, perhaps, for temporary purposes—was clearly inconsistent with the rights conveyed by the grant.

It is difficult, if not impossible, to lay down a clear and definite line of use which shall enable the parties always to determine what may be considered a proper and reasonable use as distinguished from an unreasonable and improper one, and such questions must, of necessity, be usually left to the determination of a jury, or the trial court, as a question of fact: *Bakeman* v. *Talbot*, 31 N. Y. 366; 88 Am. Dec. 275; *Huson* v. *Young*, 4 Lans. 64; *Prentice* v. *Geiger*, 74 N. Y. 342.

It is not supposed that it was the intention of the court below to wholly preclude the defendant from the use of the roadway by passing over or across it in such manner as should not materially obstruct passage or injure the road-bed; but it was only intended to prevent an unreasonable use thereof which should sensibly impair its condition or render its use offensive and impracticable to the plaintiff and others having lawful occasion to pass over it.

We think the findings of the trial court are conclusive upon us as to the proper use of the road by the defendant, and that an injunction was properly awarded against him. Some of the members of this court are, however, apprehensive that the order made by the court below is not sufficiently explicit, and may be subject to misunderstanding and misconstruction. We have, therefore, thought best to change its form, so as to express more clearly the rights and duties of the respective parties. The words "willfully or unreasonably" should be inserted after the word "interfering" in the sixth line of the order, in the place of the words "in any way"; and also after the word "as" in the ninth line of said order.

With these modifications the judgment should be affirmed, with costs.

————

AS TO THE RIGHTS OF THE LAND-OWNER AND THE WAY-OWNER in land across which a right of way has been granted, see note to *Welch* v. *Wilcox*, 100 Am. Dec. 118, 119. The grant of an easement implies authority to do anything necessary to secure the enjoyment of it: *Hammond* v. *Woodman*, 41 Me. 177; 66 Am. Dec. 219; but the owner of land subject to an easement has all the rights of an owner, subject only to a reasonable use of the easement: *McTavish* v. *Carroll*, 7 Md. 352; 61 Am. Dec. 353.

WHERE AN EASEMENT EXISTS OVER THE LAND OF ANOTHER, the duty of keeping it in repair rests upon its owner, and he may enter upon the servient estate to make repairs: *Durfee* v. *Garvey*, 78 Cal. 546.

In *Whaley* v. *Jarrett*, 69 Wis. 613, it was decided that a deed of a strip of land, in terms granting "a mere easement of travel and private road purposes, but no other or further estate whatever," etc, did not give to the grantee the right to an open way; but the owner of the servient estate might erect gates at each end thereof in such a manner as not to interfere with the reasonable enjoyment of the way by the grantee, and might require him to close and fasten the gates after passing through.

The owner of a house situated upon a private way, not open to the public, but appurtenant to the lots adjoining it, may compel the removal of obstructions placed therein by adjoining owners: *Stallard* v. *Cushing*, 76 Cal. 472.

LACY v. GETMAN.

[119 NEW YORK, 109.]

CONTRACT OF SERVICE, DISSOLUTION BY DEATH. — DEATH OF MASTER, with whom a servant has contracted to labor for a specified time, dissolves the contract, and the servant cannot recover of the master's estate for services rendered after the latter's death.

Elon R. Brown, for the appellant.

W. A. Nims, for the respondent.

FINCH, J. The relation of master and servant is no longer bounded by its original limits. It has broadened with the advance of civilization, until the law recognizes its existence in new areas of social and business life, and yields in many directions to the influence and necessities of its later surroundings. When, therefore, it is said generally, as the commentators mostly agree in saying, that the contract relations of principal and agent, and of master and servant, are dissolved by the death of either party, it is very certain that the statement must be limited to cases in which the relation may be deemed purely personal, and involves neither property rights nor independent action. Beyond that, a further limitation of the doctrine is asserted, which approaches very near to its utter destruction, and is claimed to be the result of modern adjudication. That limitation is, that the rule applies only to the contract of the servant, and not to that of the master, and not at all, unless the service employed is that of skilled labor peculiar to the capacity and experience of the servant employed, and not the common possession of men in general; and it is proposed to adopt, as a standard or test of the limitation, an inquiry in each case, whether the contract on the side of the master can be performed after his death by his representatives substantially, and in all its terms or requirements, or cannot be so performed without violence to some of its inherent elements.

The agitation of that question has kept the present case passing like a shuttle between the trial and the appellate courts, until it has been tried four times at the circuit, and reviewed four times at general term, and at last has been sent here in the hope of securing a final repose.

The facts are few and undisputed on this appeal. The plaintiff, Lacy, contracted orally with defendant's testator, McMahan, to work for the latter upon his farm, doing its appropriate and ordinary work for a period of one year at a compensation of two hundred dollars. Lacy entered upon the service in March, doing from day to day the work of the farm under the direction of its owner, until about the middle of July, when McMahan died. By his will he made the defendant executrix, but devised and bequeathed to his widow a life estate in the farm, and the use and control of all his personal property whatsoever in the house and on the farm, during the term of her natural life. Lacy knew, in a general way, the terms of the will. He testifies that he knew that it gave to the widow the use of the farm, and that she talked with him about the personal property. It is admitted that the executrix did not hire or employ him, but he continued on to the close of the year, doing the farm work under the direction of the widow until the end of his full year. He sued the executrix upon his contract with the testator, and has recovered the full amount of his year's wages. From that decision the executrix appeals, claiming that the judgment should have been limited to the proportionate amount earned at the death of McMahan, and that the death of the master dissolved the contract.

It is obvious at once that an element has come into the case as now presented which was not there when the general term first held that the contract survived. It now appears that the executrix could not have performed her side of the contract at all after the death of McMahan, by force of her official authority, because she had neither the possession of the farm or personal property upon it, and no right to such possession during the life of the widow. She had no power to put her servant upon the land, or employ him about it, and in her representative character she had not the slightest interest in his service, and could derive no possible benefit from it. The plaintiff's labor, after the death of McMahan, was necessarily on the farm of the widow, by her consent, for her benefit, and under her direction and control, and equitably and justly should be a charge against her alone. The test of power to perform on the part of the personal representative of the deceased fails in the emergency presented by the facts, except possibly upon proof of the consent of the widow.

We have, then, the peculiar case of a contract made to work for McMahan, and under his direction and control, which could not be performed because of his death, transmuted into a contract to work for Mrs. Getman upon a farm which she did not possess, and had no right to enter; and performed by working for the widow, and under her direction and control alone; and this because of the supposed rule that the contract survived the death of the master, and remained binding upon his personal representatives.

It is true that some interest in the personal property on the farm is claimed to have vested in the executrix, notwithstanding the terms of the will, and the inventory filed by her is appealed to, and the necessity of a resort to the personal property with which to pay debts. There is no proof that the testator owed any debts, and the inventory covers nothing as to which Lacy's labor was requisite or necessary, except possibly some corn on the ground, valued at eighteen dollars. All the grain inventoried was in the barn, needing only to be thrashed, and must be assumed to have been there when testator died; and the other property consisted of farm tools and a cow and horse, to the use of which the widow was entitled, and which, if sold to pay possible debts, would have left the servant without means of doing his work, and with nothing to do, unless for the widow. So that the bald question is presented, whether the contract survived the testator's death, and bound his executrix, who was without power or authority of her own to perform, and had no interest in performance.

It seems to be conceded that the death of the servant dissolves the contract: *Wolfe* v. *Howes,* 20 N. Y. 197; 75 Am. Dec. 388; *Spalding* v. *Rosa,* 71 N. Y. 40; 27 Am. Rep. 7; *Devlin* v. *Mayor etc.,* 63 N. Y. 14; *Fahy* v. *North,* 19 Barb. 341; *Clark* v. *Gilbert,* 32 Barb. 576; *Seymour* v. *Cagger,* 13 Hun, 29; *Boast* v. *Firth,* L. R. 4 Com. P. 1. Almost all of these cases were marked by the circumstance that the services belonged to the class of skilled labor. In such instances, the impossibility of a substituted service by the representative of the servant is very apparent. The master has selected the servant by rea-

son of his personal qualifications, and ought not, when he
dies, to abide the choice of another or accept a service which
he does not want. While these cases possess, with a single
exception, that characteristic, I do not think they depend
upon it. *Fahy* v. *North, supra,* was a contract for farm labor,
ended by the sickness of the servant; and quite uniformly the
general rule stated is, that the servant's agreement to render
personal services is dissolved by his death. There happens
a total inability to perform; it is without the servant's fault;
and so further performance is excused, and the contract is
apportioned. If, in this case, Lacy had died on that day in
July, his representative could not have performed his contract.
McMahan, surviving, would have been free to say that he
bargained for Lacy's services, and not for those of another
selected and chosen by strangers, and either the contract
would be broken or else dissolved. I have no doubt that it
must be deemed dissolved, and that the death of the servant,
bound to render personal services under a personal control,
ends the contract, and irrespective of the inquiry whether
those services involve skilled or common labor. For even as
it respects the latter, the servant's character, habits, capacity,
industry, and temper all enter into and affect the contract
which the master makes, and are material and essential where
the service rendered is to be personal, and subject to the daily
direction and choice and control of the master. He was willing to hire Lacy for a year; but Lacy's personal representative, or a laborer tendered by him, he might not want at all,
and at least not for a fixed period, preventing a discharge.
And so it must be conceded that the death of the servant, employed to render personal services under the master's daily
direction, dissolves the contract: *Babcock* v. *Goodrich,* 3 How.
Pr., N. S., 53.

But if that be so, on what principle shall the master be
differently and more closely bound? And why shall not his
death also dissolve the contract? There is no logic and no
justice in a contrary rule. The same reasoning which relieves
the servant's estate relieves also the master's, for the relation
constituted is personal on both sides, and contemplates no
substitution. If the master selects the servant, the servant
chooses the master. It is not every one to whom he will bind
himself for a year, knowing that he must be obedient and
render the services required. Submission to the master's will
is the law of the contract which he meditates making. He

knows that a promise by the servant to obey the lawful and
reasonable orders of his master within the scope of his contract is implied by law; and a breach of this promise in a
material matter justifies the master in discharging him: *King
v. St. John Devizes*, 9 Barn. & C. 896. One does not put himself in such relation for a fixed period without some choice as
to whom he will serve. The master's habits, character, and
temper enter into the consideration of the servant before he
binds himself to the service, just as his own personal characteristics materially affect the choice of the master. The
service, the choice, the contract, are personal upon both sides,
and more or less dependent upon the individuality of the
contracting parties, and the rule applicable to one should be
the rule which governs the other.

If, now, to such a case — that is, to the simple and normal
relation of master and servant, involving daily obedience on
one side and constant direction on the other — we apply the
suggested test of possibility of performance in substantial accord with the contract, the result is not different. It is said
that if the master dies his representatives have only to pay,
and any one may do that. But under the contract, that is by
no means all that remains to be done. They must take the
place of the master in ordering and directing the work of the
farm, and requiring the stipulated obedience. That may
prove to effect a radical change in the situation of the servant,
as it seems to have done in the present case, leading the plaintiff to the verge of refusing to work further for either widow
or executrix, whose views apparently jangled. The new
master cannot perform the employer's side of the contract as
the deceased would have performed it, and may vary so far,
from incapacity or fitful temper or selfish greed, as to make
the situation of the servant materially and seriously different
from that which he contemplated and for which he contracted.

We are therefore of opinion that in the case at bar the
contract of service was dissolved by the death of McMahan,
and his estate was only liable for the services rendered to the
date of his death.

The judgment should be reversed and a new trial granted,
with costs to abide the event.

MASTER AND SERVANT. — Involuntary death of either the master, or the
servant ordinarily terminates the contract of employment: *Griggs* v. *Swift*,
82 Ga. 392; 14 Am. St. Rep. 176, and note. So the death of the principal
usually terminates the relation of principal and agent: *Moyle* v. *Landers*,
78 Cal. 99; 12 Am. St. Rep. 22, and note.

FEITNER *v.* LEWIS.

[119 NEW YORK, 131.]

HUSBAND AND WIFE. — SERVICE OF PROCESS IN CHANCERY UPON WIFE, where the action did not concern her separate estate, might be made upon the husband. Hence it was held that a decree in foreclosure barred the right of dower of a wife who was under age at the time the decree was rendered, though the subpœna was served only upon her husband.

ACTION to recover dower. The plaintiff had joined with her husband in executing a mortgage upon his lands. Afterwards, in the year 1838, a suit of foreclosure was commenced, to which both the husband and wife were parties. A copy of the subpœna was served upon him, and another copy was given to him to deliver to his wife. The wife was an infant at the date of the foreclosure. The trial court held that the failure to serve the wife personally was fatal to the foreclosure proceedings, and that she was, therefore, still entitled to her right of dower.

Thomas J. Rush, for the appellant.

Isaac N. Miller, for the respondent.

GRAY, J. I think the appellants should prevail. The court below fell into the error of supposing that, under the rules and practice in chancery proceedings, a personal service of the writ of subpœna upon the wife was necessary, although the action did not relate to her separate property. The only interest which the plaintiff had was an inchoate right of dower in the mortgaged land. That arose simply from her *status* as wife, and gave her no separate estate.

Chancellor Kent stated the rule, in *Ferguson* v. *Smith*, 2 Johns. Ch. 139, to be "that the service of a subpœna against husband and wife on the husband alone is a good service on both; and the reason is, that the husband and wife are one person in law, and the husband is bound to answer for both. But where the plaintiff is seeking relief out of the separate estate of the wife, it has been deemed necessary in a late case (9 Ves. 488) that the wife should be served." See also *Leavitt* v. *Cruger*, 1 Paige, 422.

This is the exception to the rule, which required personal service upon an infant defendant. The merger of the legal identity of the wife in that of the husband is not affected by the question of her age. The legal unity is not dependent upon the fact of the wife's majority. Therefore, when service was made upon the husband, in accordance with the rule then in force, the court acquired jurisdiction to proceed against both. The theory of the chancery practice was to secure jurisdiction over the person of the infant defendant; and it was effected, in all cases except that of an infant wife, by a personal service of the writ. Thereupon, the infant was bound to appear, and to have a guardian appointed. In case of his neglect to do so, and of no application in his behalf, the court would proceed to make the appointment of itself, or when set in motion by complainant: Hind's Ch. Pr., tit. Appearance; 1 Barb. Ch. Pr. 127. But in the case of an infant wife, and where her separate property was not the subject of the proceeding, no guardian was necessary, for the husband was bound to appear for both through his solicitor, and to put in a joint answer. If she refused to join in the answer, the husband could show the fact of her refusal, and would be permitted to answer separately. Upon this subject, I may refer to the cases of *Foxwist* v. *Tremaine*, 2 Saund. 212, *Chambers* v. *Bull*, 1 Anstr. 269, *Ferguson* v. *Smith*, *supra*, and *Leavitt* v. *Cruger*, *supra*, and to the works on chancery practice. In *Foote* v. *Lathrop*, 53 Barb. 183, a wife sought to avoid a judgment of foreclosure and sale taken against her in 1857, on the ground that she was then confined as insane, and was not personally served with process. Marvin, J., speaking for the general term in the case, in sustaining the order denying her motion, relied solely on the cases of *Ferguson* v. *Smith*, *supra*, *Leavitt* v. *Cruger*, *supra*, and *Eckerson* v. *Vollmer*, 11 How. Pr. 42.

This action was destitute of merits, and lacked support in legal principles, and the complaint should have been dismissed.

The order of the general term denying defendants' motion for a new trial should be reversed, the defendants' exceptions sustained, and a new trial ordered, with costs to abide the event.

———

Wife is a Proper Party to a Bill to Foreclose a Mortgage given by husband and wife, and to subject her dower interest to the payment of the debt, and the chancellor cannot enter a decree against her till she is properly brought in: *Eslava* v. *Lepretre*, 21 Ala. 504; 56 Am. Dec. 266.

LAWTON *v.* STEELE.

[119 NEW YORK, 226.]

THE LEGISLATIVE POWER OF THIS STATE COVERS every subject which, in the distribution of the powers of government between the legislative, executive, and judicial departments, belongs, by practice or usage in England or this country, to the legislative department, except in so far as such power has been withheld or limited by the constitution itself, and subject also to such restrictions as may be found in the constitution of the United States.

LEGISLATIVE POWER TO DECLARE WHAT ACTS SHALL BE DEEMED CRIMINAL, and punished as such, does not extend to declaring that to be a crime which in its nature is and must under all circumstances be innocent, nor can it, in defining crimes or in declaring their punishment, take away or impair any inalienable right secured by the constitution. But it may, acting within these limits, make acts criminal which before were innocent, and ordain punishment in future cases where none before could have been inflicted.

LEGISLATIVE POWER — PUBLIC NUISANCES. — The legislature has power to enlarge the category of public nuisances by declaring places or property used to the detriment of public interests, or to the injury of the health, morals, or welfare of the community, to be nuisances, although not such at common law.

FISHING. — LEGISLATIVE POWER TO REGULATE FISHING IN PUBLIC WATERS has been exercised from the earliest periods of the common law, and it has become a settled principle of law that power resides in the several states to regulate and control the right of fishing in the public waters within their respective jurisdictions.

NUISANCE — FISHING WITH NETS. — The legislature has power to declare that any net found, or any other means or device for taking or capturing fish, set, put, floated, had, found, or maintained in or upon any of the waters of this state, or upon the shores or islands in any waters of this state, in violation of existing or hereafter enacted statutes for the protection of fish, is a public nuisance, and may be abated as such, and summarily destroyed by any person, and to make it the duty of certain specified officers to seize, remove, and destroy the same.

NUISANCES. — THE ABATEMENT OF A NUISANCE WITHOUT FIRST RESORTING TO JUDICIAL PROCEEDINGS may be authorized by statute, because such right of abatement existed at the common law, and was not taken away by the constitutional provision that the owner of property shall not be deprived of it without due process of law.

PUBLIC NUISANCES CAN BE ABATED BY A PRIVATE PERSON ONLY when they obstruct his private right, or interfere at the time with his enjoyment of a right common to many, as the right of passage on a public highway, and he thereby sustains a special injury.

PUBLIC NUISANCES — ABATEMENT OF. — The legislature may, where a public nuisance is physical and tangible, direct its summary abatement by executive officers, without the intervention of judicial proceedings, in cases analogous to those where that remedy existed at the common law.

ABATEMENT OF NUISANCES. — THE REMEDY BY SUMMARY ABATEMENT CANNOT BE EXTENDED BEYOND the purpose implied in the words, and must be confined to doing what is necessary to accomplish it.

LEGISLATIVE POWER — DESTRUCTION OF PROPERTY EMPLOYED AS A PUBLIC
NUISANCE. — The legislature may authorize the removal or abatement of
a public nuisance by executive officers, and such destruction of the property used in maintaining such nuisances as may be requisite for such abatement; but it cannot decree the destruction of property so used as a
punishment of wrong, nor even to prevent the further illegal use of it,
where the property is not a nuisance *per se.* The destruction of fishing
nets, which are by law declared to be public nuisances, may, however, be
authorized on the ground that such destruction is not as a punishment of
wrong, but is a reasonable incident of the power to abate the nuisance.

CONSTITUTIONAL LAW. — IF SOME PROVISIONS OF A STATUTE ARE UNCONSTI-
TUTIONAL, and others not, the general rule requires the courts to sustain
the valid provisions while rejecting the others.

E. C. Emerson, for the appellant.

Elon R. Brown, for the respondent.

ANDREWS, J. The conclusions of the trial judge that Black
River Bay is a part of Lake Ontario, within the meaning of
chapter 146 of the Laws of 1886, and that the nets set therein
were set in violation of the act, chapter 591 of the Laws of
1880, as amended by chapter 317 of the Laws of 1883, were
affirmed by the general term. The trial judge, in his careful
opinion, demonstrated the correctness of these conclusions,
and nothing can be added to reinforce the argument by which
they were sustained.

The point of difference between the trial court and the general term relates to the constitutionality of the second section
of the act of 1880, as amended in 1883. That section is as
follows: "Sec. 2. Any net found, or other means or device for
taking or capturing fish, or whereby they may be taken or
captured, set, put, floated, had, found, or maintained in or
upon any of the waters of this state, or upon the shores
or islands in any waters of this state, in violation of any existing or hereafter enacted statutes or laws for the protection of
fish, is hereby declared to be, and is, a public nuisance, and
may be abated and summarily destroyed by any person, and
it shall be the duty of each and every [game and fish] protector aforesaid, and of every game constable, to seize and remove and destroy the same, ... and no action for damages
shall be maintained against any person for or on account of
any such seizure or destruction." The defendant justified the
seizure and destruction of the nets of plaintiff, as a game protector, under this statute, and established the justification, if
the legislature had the constitutional power to authorize the
summary remedy provided by the section in question. The

trial judge held the act in this respect to be unconstitutional, and ordered judgment in favor of the plaintiffs for the value of the nets. The general term sustained the constitutionality of the statute, and reversed the judgment. We concur with the general term, for reasons which will now be stated.

The legislative power of the state, which by the constitution is vested in the senate and assembly (section 1, article 3), covers every subject which, in the distribution of the powers of government between the legislative, executive, and judicial departments, belongs, by practice or usage in England or in this country, to the legislative department, except in so far as such power has been withheld or limited by the constitution itself, and subject also to such restrictions upon its exercise as may be found in the constitution of the United States. From this grant of legislative power springs the right of the legislature to enact a criminal code, to define what acts shall constitute a criminal offense, what penalty shall be inflicted upon offenders, and generally to enact all laws which the legislature shall deem expedient for the protection of public and private rights, and the prevention and punishment of public wrongs. The legislature may not declare that to be a crime which in its nature is and must be under all circumstances innocent, nor can it in defining crimes, or in declaring their punishment, take away or impair any inalienable right secured by the constitution. But it may, acting within these limits, make acts criminal which before were innocent, and ordain punishment in future cases where before none could have been inflicted. This, in its nature, is a legislative power, which, by the constitution of the state, is committed to the discretion of the legislative body: *Barker* v. *People*, 3 Cow. 686; 15 Am. Dec. 322; *People* v. *West*, 106 N. Y. 293; 60 Am. Rep. 452. The act in question declares that nets set in certain waters are public nuisances, and authorizes their summary destruction. The statute declares and defines a new species of public nuisance, not known to the common law, nor declared to be such by any prior statute. But we know of no limitation of legislative power which precludes the legislature from enlarging the category of public nuisances, or from declaring places or property used to the detriment of public interests, or to the injury of the health, morals, or welfare of the community, public nuisances, although not such at common law. There are, of course, limitations upon the exercise of this power. The legislature cannot use it as a cover for withdrawing property from the protection of the law, or arbitrarily, where no public right or interest is involved, declare property a nuisance for the purpose of devoting it to destruction. If the court can judicially see that the statute is a mere evasion, or was framed for the purpose of individual oppression, it will set it aside as unconstitutional, but not otherwise: *In re Jacobs*, 98 N. Y. 98; 50 Am. Rep. 636; *Mugler* v. *Kansas*, 123 U. S. 661.

There are numerous examples in recent legislation of the exercise of the legislative power to declare property held or used in violation of a particular statute a public nuisance, although such possession and use before the statute was lawful. The prohibitory legislation relative to the manufacture or sale of intoxicating liquors, in various states, has in many cases been accompanied by provisions declaring the place where liquor is unlawfully kept for sale, as well as the liquor itself, a common or public nuisance, and while the validity of prohibitory statutes in their operation upon liquors lawfully acquired or held before their passage, and in respect of the procedure authorized thereby, have been the subject of much contention in the courts, the right of the legislature, by a new statute, to impose upon property held or used in the violation of law, the character of a public nuisance, is generally admitted: *Wynehamer* v. *People*, 13 N. Y. 378; *Fisher* v. *McGirr*, 1 Gray, 1; 61 Am. Dec. 381; *Mugler* v. *Kansas*, 123 U. S. 661.

The legislative power to regulate fishing in public waters has been exercised from the earliest period of the common law. The statute 2 Henry VI., chapter 15, prohibited the use of nets in the Thames, if they obstruct navigation or the passage of fish. Lord Hale, in his treatise (De Jure Maris, p. 23), says that "the fishing which the subject has in this or any other public or private river, or creek, fresh or salt, is subject to the laws for the conservation of fish and fry, which are many." In this state many statutes have been enacted, commencing at an early period, regulating the right of fishing in the waters of the state, prohibiting the use of nets or the taking of fish at certain seasons, and for the protection of certain kinds of fish: 1 R. S. 687 et seq.; 4 Id. 96 et seq. It has become a settled principle of public law that power resides in the several states to regulate and control the right of fishing in the public waters within their respective jurisdictions: *Smith* v. *Maryland*, 18 How. 71; *Hooker* v. *Cummings*, 20 Johns. 100; 11 Am. Dec. 249; *Smith* v. *Levinus*, 8 N. Y. 472; 3 Kent's Com. 415. We think it was competent for the legislature, in exercising the power of regulation of this common and public right, to prohibit the taking of fish with nets in specified waters, and by its declaration, to make the setting of nets for that purpose a public nuisance. The general definition of a nuisance given by Blackstone is, "anything that worketh hurt, inconvenience, or damage." It is generally true, as stated by a recent writer (Wood on Nuisances, sec. 11), that nuisances arise from the violation of the common law and not from the violation of a public statute. But this, we, conceive, is true only where the statute creating a right or imposing an obligation affixes a penalty for its violation, or gives a specific remedy which by the terms of the statute or by construction is exclusive: See *Bulbrook* v. *Goodere*, 3 Burr. 1770. But the principle stated has no application where the statute itself prescribes that a particular act, or the property used for a noxious purpose, shall be deemed a nuisance. The legislature in the act in question, acting upon the theory and upon the fact (for so it must be assumed) that fishing with nets in prohibited waters is a public injury, has applied the doctrine of the common law to a case new in instance, but not in principle, and made the doing of the prohibited act a nuisance. This we think it could lawfully do.

The more difficult question arises upon the provision in the second section of the act of 1883, which authorizes any person, and makes it the duty of the game protector, to abate the nuisance caused by nets set in violation of law, by their summary destruction. It is insisted that the destruction of nets by an individual, or by an executive officer so authorized, without any judicial proceeding, is a deprivation of the owner of the nets of his property without due process of law, in contravention of the constitution. The right of summary abatement of nuisances, without judicial process or proceeding, was an established principle of the common law long before the adoption of our constitution, and it has never been supposed that this common-law principle was abrogated by the provision for the protection of life, liberty, and property in our state constitution, although the exercise of the right might result in the destruction of property. This question was referred to by Sutherland, J., in *Hart* v. *Mayor etc.*, 9 Wend. 590, 24 Am. Dec. 165. He said: "If this is a case in which the corporation or any other person had a right summarily to remove or abate this obstruction, then the objection that the appellants by this course of proceeding may be deprived of their property without due process of law or trial by jury, has no application. Former legal proceedings and trial by jury are not appropriate to and have never been used in such cases." See also opinion of Edmonds, senator, in same case, page 609. In the *License Tax Case*, 5 How. 504, Judge McLean, speaking of this subject, said: "The acknowledged police power of a state often extends to the destruction of property. A nuisance may be abated. Everything prejudicial to the health and morals of a city may be removed." In *Rockwell* v. *Nearing*, 35 N. Y. 308, Porter, J., speaking of the constitutional provision, said "there were many examples of summary proceedings which were recognized as due process of law at the date of the constitution, and to them the prohibition has no application." Quarantine and health laws have been enacted from time to time from the organization of our state government, authorizing the summary destruction of infected cargo, clothing, or other articles by officers designated, and no doubt has been suggested as to their constitutionality. In *Hart* v. *Mayor etc.*, *supra*, a question was raised as to the validity of a city ordinance subjecting a float moored in the Albany basin to summary seizure and sale upon failure of the owner to remove the same after notice. The court held the ordinance to be void, as not within the power conferred upon the city by its charter; but it was held that the common-law right of abatement existed, although the removal of the float in question involved its destruction. *Van Wormer* v. *Mayor etc.*, 15 Wend. 263, sustained the right of a municipal corporation to dig down a lot in the city to abate a nuisance, although in the process of abatement buildings thereon were pulled down. In *Meeker* v. *Van Rensselaer*, 15 Wend. 397, the court justified the act of the defendant as an individual citizen in tearing down a filthy tenement-house, which was a nuisance, to prevent the spread of the Asiatic cholera.

These authorities sufficiently establish the proposition that the constitutional guaranty does not take away the common-law right of abatement of nuisances by summary proceedings, without judicial trial or process. But in the process of abating a nuisance there are limitations, both in respect of the agencies which may be employed, and as to what may be done in execution of the remedy. The general proposition has been asserted in text-books, and repeated in judicial opinions, that any person may abate a public nuisance. But the best considered authorities in this country and England now hold that a public nuisance can only be abated by an individual where it obstructs his private right, or interferes at the time with his enjoyment of a right common to many, as the right of passage upon the public highway, and he thereby sustains a special injury: *Brown* v. *Perkins*, 12 Gray, 89; *Mayor of Colchester* v. *Brooke*, 7 Ad. & E. 339; *Dimes* v. *Petley*, 15 Ad. & E. 276; *Fort Plain Bridge Co.* v. *Smith*, 30 N. Y. 44; *Harrower* v. *Ritson*, 37 Barb. 301.

The public remedy is ordinarily by indictment for the punishment of the offender, wherein, on judgment of conviction, the removal or destruction of the thing constituting the nuisance, if physical and tangible, may be adjudged, or by bill in equity filed in behalf of the people. But the remedy by judicial prosecution, *in rem* or *in personam*, is not, we conceive, exclusive, where the statute in a particular case gives a remedy by summary abatement, and the remedy is appropriate to the object to be accomplished. There are nuisances arising from conduct which can only be abated by the arrest and punishment of the offender, and in such cases it is obvious that the legislature could not directly direct the sheriff or other officer to seize and flog or imprison the culprit. The infliction of punishment for crime is the prerogative of the court, and cannot be usurped by the legislature. The legislature can only define the offense and prescribe the measure of punishment, where guilt shall have been judicially ascertained. But as the legislature may declare nuisances, it may also, where the nuisance is physical and tangible, direct its summary abatement by executive officers, without the intervention of judicial proceedings, in cases analogous to those where the remedy by summary abatement existed at common law. Marvin, J., in his able opinion in *Griffith* v. *McCullum*, 46 Barb. 561, speaking of the remedy for the abatement of nuisances, says: "That which is exclusively a common-law or public nuisance cannot be abated by the private acts of individuals. The remedy is by indictment or criminal prosecution, unless the statute has provided some other remedy." The cases of *Hart* v. *Mayor etc., supra, Van Wormer* v. *Albany, supra,* and *Meeker* v. *Van Rensselaer, supra,* show that the public remedy is not in all cases confined to a judicial prosecution.

But the remedy by summary abatement cannot be extended beyond the purpose implied in the words, and must be confined to doing what is necessary to accomplish it. And here lies, we think, the stress of the question now presented. It

cannot be denied that in many cases a nuisance can only be
abated by the destruction of the property in which it consists.
The cases of infected cargo or clothing, and of impure and un-
wholesome food, are plainly of this description. They are
nuisances *per se*, and their abatement is their destruction. So,
also, there can be but little doubt, as we conceive, that obscene
books or pictures, or implements only capable of an illegal
use, may be destroyed as a part of the process of abating the
nuisance they create, if so directed by statute. The keeping
of a bawdy-house, or a house for the resort of lewd and disso-
lute people, is a nuisance at common law. But the tearing
down of the building so kept would not be justified as the
exercise of the power of summary abatement, and it would
add nothing, we think, to the justification that a statute was
produced authorizing the destruction of the building summarily as a part of the remedy. The nuisance consists, in
the case supposed, in the conduct of the owner or occupants
of the house, is using or allowing it to be used for the immoral
purpose, and the remedy would be to stop the use. This
would be the only mode of abatement in such case known to
the common law, and the destruction of the building for this
purpose would have no sanction in common law or precedent:
See *Babcock* v. *City of Buffalo*, 56 N. Y. 268; *Barclay* v. *Commonwealth*, 25 Pa. St. 503; 64 Am. Dec. 715; *Ely* v. *Board
of Supervisors*, 36 N. Y. 297.

But where a public nuisance consists in the location or use
of tangible personal property, so as to interfere with or obstruct a public right or regulation, as in the case of the float
in the Albany basin (*Hart* v. *Mayor, etc.*, 9 Wend. 571, 24
Am. Dec. 165), or the nets in the present case, the legislature
may, we think, authorize its summary abatement by executive
agencies without resort to judicial proceedings, and any injury
or destruction of the property necessarily incident to the exercise of the summary jurisdiction interferes with no legal right
of the owner. But the legislature cannot go further. It cannot decree the destruction or forfeiture of property used so as
to constitute a nuisance as a punishment of the wrong, nor
even, we think, to prevent a future illegal use of the property,
it not being a nuisance *per se*, and appoint officers to execute
its mandate. The plain reason is, that due process of law requires a hearing and trial before punishment, or before forfeiture of property can be adjudged for the owner's misconduct.
Such legislation would be a plain usurpation by the legislature

of judicial powers, and under guise of exercising the power of summary abatement of nuisances the legislature cannot take into its own hands the enforcement of the criminal or *quasi* criminal law: See opinion of Shaw, C. J., in *Fisher* v. *McGirr, supra,* and in *Brown* v. *Perkins,* 12 Gray, 89.

The inquiry in the present case comes to this: whether the destruction of the nets set in violation of law, authorized and required by the act of 1883, is simply a proper, reasonable, and necessary regulation for the abatement of the nuisance, or transcends that purpose, and is to be regarded as the imposition and infliction of a forfeiture of the owner's right of property in the nets, in the nature of a punishment. We regard the case as very near the border-line, but we think the legislation may be fairly sustained on the ground that the destruction of nets so placed is a reasonable incident of the power to abate the nuisance. The owner of the nets is deprived of his property, but not as the direct object of the law, but as an incident to the abatement of the nuisance. Where a private person is authorized to abate a public nuisance, as in case of a house built in a highway, or a gate across it, which obstructs and prevents his passage thereon, it was long ago held that he was not required to observe particular care in abating the nuisance, and that although the gate might have been opened without cutting it down, yet the cutting down would be lawful: *Lodie* v. *Arnold,* 2 Salk. 458, and cases cited. But the general rule undoubtedly is, that the abatement must be limited by necessity, and no wanton and unnecessary injury must be committed: 3 Bla. Com. 6, note. It is conceivable that nets illegally set could, with the use of care, be removed without destroying them. But in view of their position, the difficulty attending their removal, the liability to injury in the process, their comparatively small value, we think the legislature could adjudge their destruction as a reasonable means of abating the nuisance.

These views lead to an affirmance of the order of the general term. The case of *Weller* v. *Snover,* 42 N. J. L. 341, tends to sustain the conclusion we have reached. The action in that case was trespass for entering the plaintiff's lands, bordering a non-navigable stream in New Jersey, and destroying a fish-basket placed in the waters diverted therefrom, for the catching of fish, contrary to a statute. The court held the statute to be a justification. The case of *Williams* v. *Blackwall,* 2 Hurl. & C. 33, arose under an act of Parliament which author-

ized the summary destruction by fish-wardens of what was
known as salmon-engines, being fish-nets set in violation of
the act.   The case is not an authority upon the power of our
legislature under the limitations of the state constitution, but
the legislation upon which the action was founded shows that
in a country governed by the principles of Magna Charta, such
legislation is not deemed inconsistent with the fundamental
doctrines of civil liberty.

It is insisted that the provision in the act of 1883 authorizes
the destruction of nets found on the land, on shores, or islands
adjacent to waters, where taking of fish by nets is prohibited,
and that this part of the statute is in any view unconstitutional.   Assuming this premise, it is claimed that the whole
section must fall, as the statute, if unconstitutional as to one
provision, is unconstitutional as a whole.   This is not, we
think, the general rule of law, where provisions of a statute
are separable, one of which only is void.   On the contrary, the
general rule requires the court to sustain the valid provisions
while rejecting the others.   Where the void matter is so
blended with the good that they cannot be separated, or where
the court can judicially see that the legislature only intended
the statute to be enforced in its entirety, and that by rejecting
part the general purpose of the statute would be defeated, the
court, if compelled to defeat the main purpose of the statute,
will not strive to save any part: See *Fisher* v. *McGirr, supra.*

The order granting a new trial should be affirmed, and
judgment absolute ordered for the defendant on the stipulation, with costs.

___

LEGISLATURE MAY REGULATE THE COMMON RIGHT OF FISHERY in the
navigable waters of the state, and statutes enacted for that purpose are valid:
Rea v. *Hampton,* 101 N. C. 51; 9 Am. St. Rep. 21, and note.

STATUTES MAY BE VOID IN PART and valid in part: See *State* v. *Deal,*
24 Fla. 293; 12 Am. St. Rep. 204, and note 219.   And the fact that one or
more provisions of an act are unconstitutional does not invalidate so much of
the act as is not open to constitutional objection, when the law remains complete and enforceable after the unconstitutional parts are stricken out: *Gayle*
v. *Owen County Court,* 83 Ky. 61.

MARTIN v. GILBERT.

[119 NEW YORK, 298.]

ESTOPPEL IN ACTION FOR POSSESSION OF PERSONALTY. — When, in an action
to recover possession of personal property, an affidavit is made for the
purpose of obtaining possession of such property, in which it is specifically described, and a requisition is issued and delivered to the coroner
requiring him to take such property from the possession of the defendant, and the defendant, to prevent the delivery of the property to the
plaintiff, gives an undertaking in favor of the plaintiff, reciting that the
coroner has taken all the property described in the affidavit, and that
the defendant requires the return thereof to him, and that the sureties ·
become bound to the plaintiff for the delivery of the property to him, if
delivery thereof should be adjudged, the defendant is estopped, on the
trial, from contending that a part only of the property was in his possession when the action was begun, and was seized by the coroner.

ACTION to recover the possession of property described in
the complaint as 4 overcoats, 223 coats, 224 vests, 243 pairs
of pants, 36 boys' suits, and one pair of boy's pants. The
complaint stated that the plaintiffs had sold and delivered the
above property to one Ruslander, but had been induced to do
so through his false and fraudulent representations, on account
of which the plaintiffs elected to rescind the contract of sale,
and recover the possession of the property; that the defendant,
Gilbert, was the sheriff of Erie County, and as such, unlawfully
detained the property, claiming to hold it under a writ of execution issued against Ruslander; that on the 25th of November, 1886, a writ of replevin was issued in this action to the
coroner of Erie County, requiring him to take said personal
property, under the writ of replevin, from the defendant, who
thereafter executed to the coroner an undertaking, and the
property was thereupon delivered by the coroner back to the
defendant. The undertaking, which was given by the defendant to enable him to obtain a return of the property to him,
was as follows: —

"Whereas, the plaintiffs in this action claim the delivery to
them of certain chattels specified in the affidavit, made on
behalf of the plaintiffs for that purpose, of the alleged value of
$3,622.87, and have caused the same to be taken by the coro-
ner of Erie County, pursuant to the Code of Civil Procedure,
but the same has not yet been delivered to the plaintiffs; and
whereas, the defendant requires a return of the chattels replevied; now, therefore, we, Charles A. Sweet, of the city of
Buffalo, county of Erie, by occupation a banker, and Charles
G. Curtiss, of the same place, by occupation a maltster, do

hereby jointly and severally undertake and become bound to
the plaintiffs, in the sum of $7,245.74, for the delivery of the
said chattels to the plaintiffs, if delivery thereof is adjudged,
or if the action abates in consequence of the defendant's death,
and for the payment to the plaintiffs of any sum which the
judgment awards against the defendant.

"Dated this 27th day of November, 1886.

> "CHARLES A. SWEET.
> "CHARLES G. CURTISS."

Judgment was rendered in favor of plaintiffs for the full
amount claimed by them.

Hadley Jones and Abraham Gruber, for the appellants.

B. Frank Dake, for the respondent.

PECKHAM, J. The defendant claims that neither the affidavit to obtain the requisition, nor the requisition itself, nor
the return of the coroner is in evidence in this case. He says
that not one of them was formally put in evidence, and that,
therefore, the court has no right to regard them or any of
them. We do not think it was necessary to formally put
those papers in evidence in order to have them considered by
the trial court. By section 1717 of the Code of Civil Procedure, all of such papers must be made a part of the judgment
roll in the action, and a copy of each of them must be
furnished to the court or referee upon the trial of the issue of
fact. In looking over the case it would seem to have been tried
upon the assumption that the papers were not only in existence, but were to be regarded by the referee for all legitimate
purposes. Taking them into consideration, we find a statement in the affidavit that "the plaintiffs are the owners of
the following chattels hereinafter particularly described, viz.:
Ready-made clothing as follows: Four overcoats, 223 coats,
224 vests, pants, 243 pairs, 36 boys' suits, one pair of boy's
pants." The requisition is to the coroner of the county of
Erie, and he is required to replevy the chattels described in
the within affidavit. And the coroner certifies and returns
that on the 26th of November, 1886, he executed the requisition indorsed on the affidavit annexed, for the delivery of the
chattels mentioned in the said affidavit, "by taking possession
of all thereof to be found in my county, to wit: Four overcoats, 223 coats, 243 pants, 224 vests, 36 boys' suits, one pair
boy's pants." The return further stated that the defendant

claimed redelivery of said chattels by giving to the coroner an undertaking in due form of law, and that the coroner then redelivered said property to the defendant. In the affidavit a statement is thus found of all the property claimed on the part of the plaintiffs to be in the possession of the defendant, and it is especially described in such affidavit. The requisition requires the coroner to take the property described in the affidavit. The bond given by the defendant, in order to keep the property, recites the fact that the plaintiffs claim delivery to them of certain chattels specified in the affidavit made on behalf of the plaintiffs for that purpose, and that they have caused the same to be taken by the coroner of Erie County, pursuant to the Code of Civil Procedure, but the same not having yet been delivered to the plaintiffs, the defendant requires the return of the chattels replevied, and the condition of the undertaking is, that the sureties undertake and become bound to the plaintiffs in the sum named for the delivery of the said chattels to the plaintiffs, if delivery thereof is adjudged.

Upon the trial the defendant offered to prove that, of the personal property described in the affidavit made by the plaintiffs, the defendant did not have in his possession or under his control, when the demand was made upon him on the part of the plaintiffs and at the time of the commencement of this action, more than one quarter, and that no more than one quarter of such property ever came into his possession, or was in his possession when such property was replevied by the coroner. This evidence was objected to on the part of the plaintiffs as tending to vary or alter the admissions made by the defendant in this action, contained in his undertaking given to the plaintiffs upon the retaking of the goods seized by the coroner, herein described in the affidavit accompanying the requisition. The objection was sustained, and the defendant excepted. The general term of the supreme court has held that this was error, and on account thereof has reversed the judgment and granted a new trial.

We think the referee was right in rejecting the evidence. The affidavit of the plaintiffs described all the property claimed by them, and alleged that it was all in the defendant's possession. The requisition required the coroner to take all that property. He proceeded to the execution of his writ, and in the course of the same he is met by the action of the defendant, which prevents his complying with the terms of the requisition. To prevent such compliance, the defendant offers, as he has a right to do under the statute, an undertaking on his part. That undertaking is provided for by the statute, and in its recital, in order to state for what purpose and under what circumstances it is given, it is set forth in plain language that the plaintiffs claim the chattels specified in the affidavit made on behalf of the plaintiffs, and that they have caused the same to be taken by the coroner of Erie County, pursuant to the Code of Civil Procedure, but the same has not yet been delivered to the plaintiffs, and because the defendant requires the return of the chattels replevied, therefore the sureties agree and undertake, as already mentioned. It was because of this undertaking that the defendant was enabled to retain possession of the property, and that undertaking used by the defendant recites the plain fact of the claim for the property made by the plaintiffs, and that it had been taken by the coroner pursuant to the Code of Civil Procedure. We do not think that under the circumstances the defendant should be allowed to contradict the admissions of fact made in his own bond, by virtue of which he kept the property which had been taken by the coroner, and we think he is properly concluded by the recitals in such bond, upon the question of what property was, as matter of fact, in his possession and taken by the coroner.

We cannot distinguish this case in principle from that of *Diossy* v. *Morgan*, 74 N. Y. 11.

It is true that the facts in the Diossy case differ from those herein. In the former the stone in controversy was on plaintiff's land, and the defendant had placed men at work upon the stone, who were engaged in cutting it and assuming possession and ownership of it. The sheriff took the stone for the plaintiff on the requisition in the replevin action, and the defendant prevented its delivery to plaintiff, and procured its delivery to him by reason of the giving of the bond, which contained an admission that the property was taken from the possession of the defendant by the sheriff. The defendant, upon the trial, sought to show that he did not have possession of the stone when the action was commenced, and this evidence was rejected, and upon appeal to this court it was held that such rejection was proper. It is thus seen that there was no dispute as to the identity of the property, which by virtue of his bond the defendant obtained, with that described in the affidavit, and none that such property was then in defendant's

possession; and the only question was, whether the defendant
should be permitted to show that he did not have possession of
the property when the suit was commenced, although his
bond contained the written admission that he did.   This court
said, per Rapallo, J.: " By means of this undertaking the defendants not merely prevented the delivery of the property by
the sheriff to the plaintiff, but procured the delivery of it to
themselves.   The undertaking contains a plain admission that
it was taken by the sheriff from their possession, and consequently was in their possession at the time of the commencement of the action," etc.   And again: "Our holding is, that
the undertaking contains the admission of a fact, of which the
defendants have availed themselves to obtain possession of
the property, and that therefore they cannot be permitted to
retract it, so as to deprive the plaintiff of his right to a redelivery of the property to him."

Has not this defendant caused a bond to be executed, containing a plain admission of a fact, viz., that the coroner had
taken the property described in the affidavit from his (defendant's) possession? and has not the defendant, by reason of the
bond containing such admission, procured the coroner to re-
deliver to him such property thus taken from him?   Certainly
he has.   If it had not been for the bond the property would
have been delivered to the plaintiff, in which event the defendant could have shown that the property taken was not
described in the affidavit, or was not that of the plaintiff.
Under such circumstances the plaintiffs would have been compelled to prove their whole case, including the fact that the
property actually taken from defendant was the property described in their affidavit and in their requisition to the sheriff.

Instead of this, however, the defendant permits the coroner
to take the property, without a word of denial that it was the
identical property described in the affidavit and requisition,
and in addition thereto he causes the bond to be executed in
order to take back the property, and therein he plainly admits that it is the same property.   But now, upon the trial of
the case, he asks to be permitted to show that not more than
one quarter of the property that was taken was that which was
described in the affidavit.   To allow this is to violate the principle of the Diossy case, which was, that what was solemnly
admitted as a fact by an admission in the bond should not be
contradicted on the trial.   It is also most unjust that it should
be otherwise.   Where property is taken under a requisition,

and the plaintiff sees by the bond which has been executed,
and which by the code is to be delivered to him by the sheriff
(sec. 1708), a plain and distinct admission that the officer has taken the property described in plaintiff's affidavit
and requisition, he has a right to rely on such admission, and
take no further steps towards proving the point as to the possession by the defendant of the very property described in the
requisition. He may also give up any attempt to seek further
for property which the defendant solemnly admits he is himself in possession of. Otherwise, and in just such a case as
this, the defendant having obtained delivery of the property
upon executing the bond, and not having made the least
denial or question at the time of the taking, but that the property taken was the same as the property described in the
requisition, may at once sell or otherwise dispose of it. By so
doing, the plaintiff is precluded from any further examination
of the property, and cannot in that way strengthen his contention that it was identical with that named in the affidavit.
In addition to that, the plaintiff is thrown off his guard by
the defendant's conduct and admission, and naturally would
not on that very account take such steps and secure such proof
as might otherwise be then procured to prove his case on that
point.

Upon the trial, however, the defendant, notwithstanding his
admission in his bond, asks to show that the property is not
identical, and he thus endeavors to reap the advantage which
the admission has given him in causing the plaintiffs to rely
upon the same, and to come unprepared for the trial of such
an issue.

Is it right that he should have such an opportunity at the
plaintiff's expense?

The course of the trial herein shows that the plaintiffs did
rely entirely upon the admission in the bond for the purpose
of proving the identity of the goods taken from defendant's
possession with those described in the affidavit and requisition,
and the bond was received in evidence for that purpose. If
the denial had been made when the property was taken, the
plaintiffs could have looked into the question more fully, and
have satisfied themselves either that the defendant was wrong,
or if right, could have given it up and made further search
regarding the property they claimed. If they concluded to
take it, and the sheriff was satisfied, then they would have
been much more careful as to procuring proof of the identity

of the goods claimed with those taken, and much better prepared to prove such fact upon the trial.   But the course taken
by the defendant wholly disarms them upon that point.   Assuming the truth of the admission, and that there would be
no denial of the fact of identity of goods or possession by
defendant, the plaintiffs might naturally and rightfully rely
upon such admission as to those facts, and simply prepare
themselves to prove the other material facts in the case, viz.,
title to the goods that were taken, assuming them to be the
goods described in the affidavit and admitted in the bond.

It is to prevent such injustice that the Diossy case says
that the fact of the possession of the property by the defendant, which has been admitted in the bond, shall not be contradicted.   In that case, the injustice worked by the other rule
would lie in permitting the defendant to show as a defense
the non-existence of a fact which he had already admitted in
his bond, and by reason of which he had obtained the property, while in this case the injustice would lie in permitting
the defendant to contradict a plain admission in a bond, by
reason of which bond the property taken from him was restored to the defendant, with all the advantages which such
possession could give to him.   The hardship would be with
the plaintiffs to allow such proof.

If the defendant desire to raise the question of identity, he
should raise it, not by admitting it in the bond and subsequently contradicting such admission, but he might sue the
sheriff for the taking, or leave the property in his hands and
try the case, and if successful, the property would be returned,
or its value insured to him.

It is said that the recital in the bond was not necessary, as
the fact is not, by the statute, made necessary to be stated.
I do not see that that makes any difference.   The bond itself
is required by the statute, and in order to make it in any wise
intelligible, it is necessary that some statement should be
made of the purpose for which it is executed, and the recital
in question was made for that purpose, and I cannot see why
it should not be just as conclusive in a case where the defendant wishes to deny the possession of part of the property as
where he wishes to deny the possession of the whole.

The case of *Weber* v. *Manne*, 42 Hun, 557, was reversed in
this court: 105 N. Y. 627.

The same principle has been held in other states.   In *Mead*
v. *Figh*, 4 Ala. 279, 37 Am. Dec. 742, it was held that a bond

for redelivery of a chattel, which recited a levy and contained a promise to produce the chattel, could not be contradicted by showing that there was no such chattel, and that the levy was fictitious. The court said: "The law gives the defendant a right to suspend the collection of the money upon his doing certain acts, and it could not be tolerated that he should be permitted afterwards to say these acts are not binding on him because they assert a falsehood."

In *Lucas* v. *Beebe*, 88 Ill. 427, it was held that a party in a delivery bond, who therein admits the possession of the property, is bound by it; and if in such a bond proceedings before a justice of the peace in a certain entitled action are recited, the maker of the bond cannot contradict the recital by proof that there was no such suit. It is generally supposed, said the court, parties mean to bind themselves when they solemnly and deliberately make such statements in writing, the truth of which is attested by their signatures and seals.

In *Frost* v. *White*, 14 La. Ann. 140, the same holding is maintained. Property was attached, which was bonded by an intervenor, and a motion made to dissolve the attachment on several grounds, one of which was that no property was, in fact, attached. The court said the admission had been judicially made by giving a bond which contained a description of the property attached, and therefore the intervenor was concluded by his admission, and estopped from denying its truth.

In *Shaw* v. *McCullough*, 3 W. Va. 260, the court said that parties voluntarily entering into a forthcoming bond are estopped from all inquiry into the regularity or validity of the levy of the writ of *fieri facias* upon which the bond was taken. The bond recited the fact that the writ had issued, and the property had been levied on under it, and that was conclusive.

In *Schnaider Brewing Co.* v. *Niederweiser*, 28 Mo. App. 233, 236, the defendant offered to show that certain of the property mentioned in the requisition, and recited in the bond as having been taken under it, was, in fact, at the time that the bond was given, and ever since had been, in plaintiff's possession. The evidence was excluded; and the court held such exclusion to be right; because the respondents should not be permitted to contradict by oral testimony their own recitals in the bond given by them.

In *Carpenter* v. *Stearns*, 32 Mo. App. 132, the court said that the defendants, having availed themselves of the benefits of the statute, which allows them to keep the property on giving a bond, are estopped from showing or claiming on the trial that the property described in their delivery bond was never in their possession.

In *Hundley* v. *Filbert*, 73 Mo. 34, the obligors in a delivery bond were estopped by a recital therein from showing that there was no levy upon which the property was taken.

In *State* v. *Williams*, 77 Mo. 463, it was held that a recital in a bond is a solemn admission by the obligor of the truth of the fact recited, and where in an action against him the bond is pleaded *in hæc verba*, the effect is the same as if there were a formal plea of estoppel. The claim was made in the above case that there was no proof that a party named was ever appointed guardian. The consideration of the bond recited that "whereas the above Robert H. Williams is the lawful guardian," etc. The court said, "This recital is a solemn admission by the defendants of Williams's guardianship"; and defendant was held estopped by such admission from questioning the fact.

The case of *Miller* v. *Moses*, 56 Me. 128, contains nothing opposed to these views. There the plaintiff in the replevin suit, in order to get his requisition, gave a bond, and of course it was for all the property which he expected to replevy. He was beaten in the action, and the defendant in that action thereupon sued on the bond to recover damages for taking his property. It was held in the latter action that the recital in the bond as to the purpose for which it issued, and describing all the property claimed, did not estop the defendant in such latter action from showing as a fact that only a part of the property described therein had been subsequently taken by the sheriff. The court said in such case the bond constitutes no estoppel. It is ordinarily given before the goods are replevied. It is based upon the writ, and assumes that what is ordered to be replevied will be. But. if not found, they cannot be, and for those that are found, the bond will be security, and for no more.

This is not our case. Upon the whole, both on principle and authority, we think the evidence was not admissible, and the referee was therefore right in refusing the defendant's offer to show the alleged fact.

We have looked at the other questions arising in this case,

and which the defendant contends were sufficient to procure the reversal of the judgment by the general term. We think there is no merit in any of them.

The general term erred in granting a new trial, and its order should therefore be reversed, and the judgment, upon the report of the referee, affirmed, with costs.

To a subsequent motion for reargument, the court responded by the following opinion:—

PECKHAM, J. Several grounds for this motion are stated. Among them, it is urged that the court overlooked the fact that defendant in his answer denied that he ever had possession of the property mentioned in the plaintiff's complaint or in the affidavit accompanying the requisition, and that it also overlooked the fact that section 1704 of the Code gives a defendant a right to demand a return of the chattels replevied, whether they were mentioned in the affidavit accompanying the requisition or not. Neither fact was overlooked.

The denial in the defendant's answer is of a somewhat ambiguous nature, and whether it could be fairly construed as raising a question as to the identity of the goods taken by the coroner with those described in the requisition, or only a question of title to the chattels, assuming those described in the requisition to have been taken by the coroner, is not clear. But this court assumed it to have been the former. One reason for regarding the proposed evidence as inadmissible was that the defendant, by virtue of his bond, had demanded and received a return of the property, and it being from that time in his possession and under his entire control, he could at once sell or otherwise dispose of the property, and thus effectually prevent any further efforts at identification on the part of the plaintiffs. The service of an answer containing such a denial several weeks after the return of the property to defendant would plainly have no effect, so far as defendant's opportunity to dispose of the property before its service was concerned. This seemed so apparent that it was not thought important to notice that particular fact. It is true, the same thing might be done by a defendant executing the bond without any such recital. In that event, however, the vigilance of the plaintiff would not have been set at rest. He would see that as there was no admission he must rely on his own efforts to prove the fact, and they would probably be at once and vigorously enlisted for that purpose.

The provisions of the Code, section 1704, were also not over-looked. The fact that the defendant has, under that section, the right to a return of the property taken by the sheriff on giving a bond, etc., even though it be not the property de-scribed in the requisition, was noticed and its effect appre-ciated by us. If the property taken be not the property mentioned and described in the requisition, then there is neither necessity nor propriety in reciting in the bond that it is such property. Where such recital is made, it is evidence that the defendant intends to litigate only the question of title, and not the question of the identity of the goods. Under such circumstances there is still greater reason why the plain-tiff should rely on it, and why the defendant should be bound by it. He recovers the possession of the property by reason of the bond, and he therein asserts that it is the same prop-erty mentioned in the requisition. There is nothing in the opinion criticised which shows that the only remedy of the de-fendant in this case was to sue the sheriff or leave the prop-erty in his hands. The counsel has made a most earnest argument in his brief, founded upon the general merits of his claim. We are entirely unconvinced of the error of our de-cision, and we do not share in the fear of the serious calam-ities that may follow our persistence in it. On the contrary, we think gross injustice may follow the adoption of the other rule, as we have attempted to point out.

Two cases have been cited in the brief of the learned counsel which he claims are conclusive upon the question in controversy, and which were not cited on the argument, and upon them he specially bases his application for a reargument of this case. They are *Carpenter* v. *Buller*, 8 Mees. & W. 209, and *Reed* v. *McCourt*, 41 N. Y 435.

The first was an action brought for a trespass alleged to have been committed upon a lot belonging to the plaintiff, and upon a trial before Coleridge, J., the defendant gave in evi-dence a deed made between the defendant and the plaintiff and one William Fanshawe, in which was claimed to be an admission, by way of a recital, that the land in question be-longed to the defendant. The deed was admitted in evidence, but it was contended by plaintiff's counsel that the recital, though so admissible, was not conclusive, and he proposed to show that the admission was made under a misapprehension. The evidence as to the mistake was admitted, and a verdict was found for the plaintiff. The defendant obtained a rule to

show cause why the verdict should not be set aside on the
ground that the recital was conclusive against the plaintiff,
and after argument upon that order the judgment of the
court was delivered by Parke, B., and it was held that the admission was not conclusive, and that the judgement was cor-
recty given for plaintiff. It was held to be not conclusive
because the action in question was not founded on the deed,
but was wholly collateral to it, and therefore the party ought
to be permitted to dispute the facts so admitted.

The case in 41 New York is of the same nature, although
an action of ejectment. The recitals in both cases were,
as stated in each, wholly collateral to the action then on
trial. They had no relation to it whatever, directly or indirectly. It was nothing more than the case of an admission in
a matter in no wise connected with the action in which it was
desired to use it as conclusive evidence. Upon no basis of
common sense could it be done.

But in the case at bar it is entirely different. While technically the action is not upon the undertaking, yet still the
undertaking was executed on the part of the defendant, pursuant to the code, and as one of the steps in the conduct of
this very action, and it was by reason of its execution and
delivery to the plaintiffs that the property which the coroner
had taken was redelivered to the defendant. He thus, in this
action, repossesses himself of the property in dispute, because
of this bond. It is not, therefore, wholly collateral to the action.
It plays a most important part therein, and by reason of its
execution the plaintiffs herein were prevented from themselves obtaining possession of the property.

How can it be said that under such circumstances the instrument is wholly collateral to the action upon trial? So far
from being wholly collateral, it is intimately connected with,
and is part of the steps necessarily and properly taken in the
conduct of, the action itself. The learned counsel for the
respondent admits that if the action had been brought directly
upon the undertaking, the evidence in question would not
have been admissible. It seems to us that it is not necessary
that the action should be distinctly and technically upon the
undertaking itself, in order to rule out the evidence under the
very cases cited. The action must not only be separate and
distinct from one upon the bond, but the bond itself must be
wholly collateral to the action, and, as I have said, it cannot
be contended that the undertaking in this action is wholly

collateral to it, when it is a step in the action itself, taken by
virtue of the law in regard to such cases, and when the defendant has acquired possession of the very property in dispute by reason of the bond.

The action of *Diossy* v. *Morgan*, 74 N. Y. 11, with the decision
in which the counsel finds no fault, was no more brought upon
the undertaking than is this action, and the undertaking is no
more collateral in this action than was the undertaking in
that of Diossy. If the counsel be right in his claim that this
action is not only not brought upon the undertaking, but the
undertaking is wholly collateral to it, then the Diossy case
was, in any event, wrongly decided. But the estoppel, in that
case, was based entirely upon the recital in that undertaking.
The opinion of Judge Rapallo is plain upon that point, and
upon that question the two cases cannot be distinguished.

The other cases cited by the counsel are of the same nature
as those already referred to.

The learned counsel says our decision holds that an unnecessary racital in a written instrument estops the party
making it from denying its truth, not only in actions on the
instrument, but in any case where the instrument may be
invoked as evidence of the facts recited. Also, that a party
to an action, discovering that his opponent inadvertently, and
in the most general terms, has admitted, in writing, a question
in issue, may fold his hands and rely upon the admission as
estopping his opponent from proving the contrary, however
erroneous the admission may be. The decision which we
have made in this case cannot be tortured into holding either
of the two propositions advanced by the counsel. The facts
which we have spoken of so often as almost to be wearisome
are wholly ignored in these statements, and the character of
the action, as related to the instrument containing the recitals,
is mistakenly described.

We see no reason for granting a reargument, and the motion
is therefore denied, with ten dollars costs.

ONE WHO GIVES A FORTHCOMING BOND in an action of claim and delivery
of personalty is estopped to deny that the property was in his possession at
the commencement of the action: *Benesch* v. *Waggner*, 12 Col. 534; 13 Am. St.
Rep. 254; or to show that the sheriff never took possession of part of the
property, and that defendant retained possession thereof: *Hills* v. *Nelms*, 86
Ala. 442. Estoppel by replevy bond, see *Roswald* v. *Hobbie*, 85 Ala. 73; 7
Am. St. Rep. 23.

VOSBURGH *v.* DIEFENDORF.

[119 NEW YORK, 357.]

WHEN NEGOTIABLE PAPER HAS BEEN OBTAINED FROM ITS MAKER BY FRAUD OR DURESS, a subsequent indorsee, to entitle himself to recover upon it, must show that he was a *bona fide* purchaser.

PURCHASER BONA FIDE, WHO IS. — Plaintiff does not establish that he is a *bona fide* purchaser of negotiable paper merely by proving that he paid value therefor before its maturity. He must go further, and show that he had no notice of the fraud with which the instrument was tainted from its origin.

PURCHASER BONA FIDE, PRESUMPTION CONCERNING. — A plaintiff suing upon a negotiable note or bill is presumed, in the first instance, to be a *bona fide* holder, but when the maker has shown that the note was obtained by fraud, the plaintiff will then be required to show under what circumstances and for what value he became the holder.

BURDEN OF PROOF IS UPON THE INDORSEE OF A NEGOTIABLE NOTE, WHICH IS SHOWN TO HAVE BEEN OBTAINED FROM THE MAKER BY FRAUD, to establish that he took it for value in good faith before maturity.

BONA FIDE HOLDER OF A NEGOTIABLE NOTE MAY TRANSFER GOOD TITLE thereto to one who has notice of the fraudulent character of the paper.

Matthew Hale, for the appellant.

Z. S. Westbrook, for the respondent.

O'BRIEN, J. This action was upon an instrument, in form a promissory note, of which the following is a copy: —

"$2,000. GOUVERNEUR, N. Y., December 15, 1886.

"Sixty days after date I promise to pay R. T. Van Valkenburgh, or bearer, two thousand dollars at Spraker's National Bank, Canajoharie, New York, value received, with interest at the rate of six per cent per annum.

"JOHN F. DIEFENDORF."

The defendant is the maker of the note, and at its date was a farmer who lived in the town of Root, about ten miles from Canajoharie, where, by the terms of the instrument, it was payable.

The defenses interposed to the note are: 1. That it was obtained from defendant by fraud and deceit practiced upon him by the payee; 2. That its only consideration was an interest in a patent right for improvements in fire-kindlers, and that it did not comply with the provisions of chapter 65 of the Laws of 1877, requiring the words "given for a patent right" to be written or printed across the face thereof; 3. That the note was void for usury, in that, before it had any legal inception, it was transferred to the plaintiff for one half its face value; 4. That the note was never executed or delivered as a note or valid obligation, and that between the original parties thereto it had been canceled and destroyed, and that the plaintiff was not a *bona fide* holder.

The defendant testified at the trial and gave his version of the transaction, which resulted in his signing the note in question. In brief, it is this: In the month of December, 1886, one Henderson, who falsely represented that he was interested in a firm, composed of himself, the payee of the note, and another person, that was engaged in manufacturing fire-kindlers under a patent, which was a valuable invention, and that the business promised large gains, called upon the defendant at his house and induced him to go to Rochester with him, to the end that he might obtain an interest in the business, or be employed in connection with it. The defendant went to Rochester, and there was introduced to Van Valkenburgh, the payee of the note in question. It does not distinctly appear what took place at Rochester, except that the defendant gave his notes for eight thousand dollars, on the representations, as he claims, that these notes were not to be used or transferred, and were simply memoranda showing his one-third interest in the business of manufacturing and selling fire-kindlers. While defendant was at Rochester, Henderson disappeared, and it seems went to Canajoharie and negotiated the notes thus obtained. In the mean time Van Valkenburgh induced the defendant to go with him to Gouverneur, where they arrived a day or two before the date of the note in question. The defendant supposed he was to aid in some way in the sale of the right to manufacture and sell the fire-kindlers under the patent in which he supposed he had, or was about to have, an interest as an equal partner with Henderson and Van Valkenburgh. On arriving at Gouverneur, they went to a hotel and there met two other persons, who pretended to be anxious to purchase the right covered by the patent for the state of Iowa. These two persons, with the defendant, and the payee of the note in question, went to a room, and there the defendant was induced to sign two notes of two thousand dollars each, of which the note in suit is one. Van Valkenburgh pretended to sell, and the two persons before referred to to buy, two thirds of the right covered by the patent in the state of Iowa for eight thousand dollars, and in the presence of defendant each of them gave, or pretended to give, to Van Valkenburgh his note for four thousand dollars. Defendant was told by Van Valkenburgh that, in order to consummate this sale, it would be necessary for him to go through the form of giving his note for the same amount, that is to say, four thousand dollars, in order to represent the interest that the firm still retained in that state; that after the transaction was completed this note could be returned to him, and that in any event the paper would not be used as a note, or transferred. The defendant assented to this arrangement, and Van Valkenburgh thereupon drew, and procured the defendant to sign and deliver, the two notes of two thousand dollars each. After all the parties had left the room and defendant supposed that the transaction was completed, and that the notes he signed had answered the purpose for which they were intended, he called the attention of Van Valkenburgh to the promise he had made to destroy the notes, whereupon he drew from his pocket two pieces of paper that appeared like the notes defendant had signed, and burnt them in defendant's presence. The defendant and Van Valkenburgh then parted, the defendant returning to his home in Montgomery County, and without seeing either Henderson or Van Valkenburgh afterwards.

The plaintiff claimed to have purchased the note in suit from one Richmond, a few days after its date, and Richmond claimed to have bought it the same day from Henderson. The testimony was, that Richmond, Henderson, and the plaintiff were together at the time of the transaction that resulted in the transfer of the note to the plaintiff; that Henderson delivered to Richmond the two notes of two thousand dollars each, made at Gouverneur, for half their face value; that Richmond kept one of them himself, and delivered the other to the plaintiff, who furnished the money paid Henderson for it, and directed Richmond to purchase it. Richmond testified that he had no knowledge of the fraudulent origin of the paper, or of any fact constituting a defense thereto by the maker. The two persons who were present with the defendant and the payee of the note at Gouverneur when it was made testified in behalf of the plaintiff, and in contradiction of the defendant's version; but neither the plaintiff, Henderson, nor Van Valkenburgh was sworn.

It is plain that the jury could well have found, from the testimony of the defendant and the facts and circumstances surrounding the transaction, that the note in question was procured from the defendant through a gross fraud practiced upon him by the payee. This was the condition of the case when the proofs closed. The trial court thereupon ruled that the plaintiff, as matter of law, was entitled to recover the

amount he had paid for the note, but if anything beyond that
was claimed, then the case was one for the jury. The plaintiff
elected to take a verdict for one half the face of the note, and
interest, and the court, against the defendant's objection and
exception, directed a verdict accordingly, and the judgment
entered thereon has been reversed by the general term.

Apart from the claim that the plaintiff derived title to the
note from one who was a *bona fide* holder, and therefore succeeded to all his rights, which will be noticed hereafter, he
was not entitled to recover as the case stood. For all the purposes of this appeal, it must be assumed that the note was procured by fraud practiced upon the defendant by the payee,
because evidence was given from which such fact could have
been found by the jury. The defendant had a good defense
to the note against the payee, if it had remained in his hands,
and he had attempted to enforce it. The plaintiff was in no
better position, unless, within the law merchant, he was a *bona
fide* holder, and, as against the case made by the defendant on
the trial, the plaintiff did not establish that character for himself by merely producing the note and proving that he paid
one half its face value for it. The learned counsel for the
plaintiff contends that in this case the burden of proving
notice to the plaintiff of the facts connected with the execution
of the note, and of the fraud, if any, was upon the defendant,
and that in the absence of such proof by the defendant the
plaintiff was entitled to recover.

We think that this proposition cannot be maintained.
Doubtless some support may be found for it in ceriain elementary books, and in some of the adjudged cases in other
states. But in this state it must be regarded now as a settled
rule that when the maker of negotiable paper shows that it
has been obtained from him by fraud or duress, a subsequent
transferee must, before entitled to recover on it, show that he
is a *bona fide* purchaser: *First Nat. Bank* v. *Green*, 43 N. Y.
298; *Farmers' etc. Bank* v. *Noxon*, 45 N. Y. 762; *Ocean Nat.
Bank* v. *Carll*, 55 N. Y. 440; *Wilson* v. *Rocke*, 58 N. Y. 642;
Grocers' Bank v. *Penfield*, 69 N. Y. 502; 25 Am. Rep. 231; *Nickerson* v. *Ruger*, 76 N. Y. 279; *Seymour* v. *McKinstry*, 106 N. Y.
240; *Stewart* v. *Lansing*, 104 U. S. 505; *Smith* v. *Livingston*,
111 Mass. 342; *Sullivan* v. *Langley*, 120 Mass. 437.

The plaintiff did not satisfy this rule by showing that he
paid value for the note. It was necessary, in order to entitle
him to recover, to go further, and show that he had no knowl-

edge or notice of the fraud with which the instrument was tainted from its origin. The large discount at which the plaintiff purchased the note, the circumstances attending the purchase, his knowledge of the original parties to the transactions, and especially of Henderson, one of the actors in the scheme which resulted in putting the note in circulation, were all proper subjects for the consideration of the jury, with reference to the plaintiff's innocence and good faith.

In *First Nat. Bank* v. *Green, supra,* Rapallo, J., stated the rule of evidence in such cases in these words: "A plaintiff suing upon a negotiable note or bill is presumed, in the first instance, to be a *bona fide* holder. But when the maker has shown that the note was obtained from him under duress, or that he was defrauded of it, the plaintiff will then be required to show under what circumstances, and for what value, he became the holder: 2 Greenl. Ev., sec. 172; *McClintick* v. *Cummins,* 2 McLean, 98; *Munroe* v. *Cooper,* 5 Pick. 412; *Holme* v. *Karsper,* 5 Binn. 469; *Vallett* v. *Parker,* 6 Wend. 615; 1 Camp. 100; 2 Camp. 574; *Case* v. *Mechanics' B. Ass'n,* 4 N. Y. 166. The reason for this rule, given in the later English cases, is, that 'where there is fraud, the presumption is, that he who is guilty will part with the note for the purpose of enabling some third party to recover upon it, and such presumption operates against the holder, and it devolves upon him to show that he gave value for it': *Bailey* v. *Bidwell,* 13 Mees. & W. 74; *Smith* v. *Braine,* 3 Eng. L. & Eq. 379; and in *Harvey* v. *Towers,* 4 Eng. L. & Eq. 531." The rule established in this case has been adhered to in this court ever since, as will be seen from the cases above cited.

In *Stewart* v. *Lansing, supra,* Waite, C. J., stated the principle thus: "It is an elementary rule that if fraud or illegality in the inception of negotiable paper is shown, an indorsee, before he can recover, must prove that he is a holder for value. The mere possession of the paper, under such circumstances, is not enough: *Smith* v. *Sac Co.,* 11 Wall. 139. Here the actual illegality of the paper was established. It was incumbent, therefore, on the plaintiff to show that he occupied the position of a *bona fide* holder before he could recover."

In *Smith* v. *Livingston, supra,* Morton, J., expressed the rule in the following language: "The indorser of a promissory note, who takes it for value in good faith in the usual course of business, before its maturity, is entitled to recover upon it, though the maker has a good defense against the payee on the ground that it was obtained by fraud. But upon proof that a note is founded in illegality, or was obtained or put in circulation fraudulently, the burden of proof is upon the indorsee to show that he took it for value and in good faith before maturity."

The learned counsel for the plaintiff has called our attention to two cases in this court, which, he insists, sustain the rule contended for by him: *Dalrymple* v. *Hillenbrand*, 62 N. Y. 5; 20 Am. Rep. 438; *Cowing* v. *Altman*, 71 N. Y. 435; 27 Am. Rep. 70.

The first of these cases was an action by the holder against the indorser of a note, given by a firm which had been adjudicated bankrupt under the late act of Congress, to one of its creditors. The payment of the note was resisted by the indorser on the ground that it was illegal or void under the statute prohibiting preferences by bankrupts. It was held that the giving of such a note was not a fraudulent preference under the law, though the makers, when they gave the note, had been adjudged bankrupts, because the advantage thus secured by the creditor was not payable out of the bankrupt's estate, but was due to the fact that the debtors were able and willing to procure the defendant's indorsement. The defense that the note was used by the creditor in violation of a condition upon which the indorsement was given was held untenable because not pleaded. The rule of evidence now under consideration was not involved.

In *Cowing* v. *Altman*, the action was upon a check, payment of which was resisted by the maker, upon the ground that it was given under an agreement to pay an assignee in bankruptcy a compensation greater than that provided by the act, and which was forbidden. It was held that the check was good in the hands of a *bona fide* holder. The check, however, was not transferred until fourteen months after its date, and the controversy in that case turned upon the point whether, when received by the plaintiff, it was not past due and dishonored. But it was shown that the bank from which the plaintiff took the check paid full value for it, and there was no attempt to impeach its right, except upon the ground that the check was past due. The question of actual notice to the bank of the consideration of the check was not raised and was not involved. These cases, when understood, do not decide any principle with respect to the burden of proof in cases where it is shown that the negotiable paper has been procured from the maker by fraud, inconsistent with the rule above stated.

The plaintiff did not meet the requirements of this rule, for he remained silent upon the subject of notice of the circumstances under which the maker gave the note. The most favorable view that could have been taken of the case for the plaintiff would still require the question of his good faith to be passed upon by the jury. It is true that the plaintiff could have recovered if he derived his title to the note from one who was a *bona fide* holder, even though he had notice himself of the fraudulent character of the paper: *Cowing* v. *Altman,* 71 N. Y. 438, 443; 27 Am. Rep. 70; *Cromwell* v. *County of Sac,* 96 U. S. 51; *Commissioners* v. *Clark,* 94 U. S. 278; *Eckhert* v. *Ellis,* 26 Hun, 664; Daniel on Negotiable Instruments, sec. 803, and cases cited; Story on Promissory Notes, sec. 191. And it is contended that Richmond, from whom the plaintiff took the paper, was shown to be innocent of any imperfection in it. But the testimony tended to show that Richmond bought the note from Henderson, as the agent, and by direction of and with funds subsequently furnished by the plaintiff. It is quite clear, we think, that the testimony on this point was of such a character that it could not be held that, absolutely and as a matter of law, Richmond ever had any title to the note, and unless he had, his connection with its purchase, as a mere agent or instrument of the plaintiff, could not confer the character of a *bona fide* holder, or shield the plaintiff from the legal consequences of any notice that he might have had of the fraudulent origin of the paper as between the maker and the payee. The most that can properly be conceded in regard to this branch of the case is, that Richmond's connection with the transfer, and whether as owner or agent of the plaintiff was a question of fact for the jury. The good faith of Richmond was not available to strengthen the plaintiff's case, unless it was found that Richmond was the owner of the note when it was delivered to the plaintiff.

It follows that the general term properly reversed the judgment, and as this conclusion disposes of the case, it is not necessary to consider the other questions raised.

The order appealed from should be affirmed, and judgment absolute ordered for the defendant, with costs.

PRESUMPTIONS IN FAVOR OF A BONA FIDE HOLDER. — The holder of negotiable paper is presumed to be a *bona fide* holder until something is shown in disparagement of his title: *Emanuel* v. *White,* 34 Miss. 56; 69 Am. Dec. 385; *Davis* v. *Bartlett,* 12 Ohio St. 534; 80 Am. Dec. 375.

BONA FIDE INDORSEE TAKES A NEGOTIABLE NOTE unaffected by fraud
in its inception: Extended note to *Bedell* v. *Herring,* 11 Am. St. Rep. 309
et seq.; *Tescher* v. *Merea,* 118 Ind. 586; *Lee* v. *Whitney,* 149 Mass. 448.

BURDEN OF PROOF AS TO BONA FIDE OWNERSHIP. — If the maker, acceptor, or other party bound by the original consideration of negotiable
paper proves that there was fraud in the inception of the instrument, the
general presumption in favor of the holder of the paper is overcome, and
he must show that he acquired the paper for value, before maturity, in the
usual course of business, and under circumstances creating no presumption
that he knew or ought to have known of the fraud: Note to *Bedell* v. *Herring,* 11 Am. St. Rep. 324, 325; *Johnson* v. *Hanover Nat. Bank,* 88 Ala. 271;
Tescher v. *Merea,* 118 Ind. 586.

SOLTAU *v.* GERDAU.

[119 NEW YORK, 380.]

LARCENY. — ONE TO WHOM PERSONAL PROPERTY IS DELIVERED FOR A
SPECIAL PURPOSE, but who intended when he procured such delivery to
appropriate the property to his own use, is guilty of larceny.

FACTORS ACT, CONSTRUCTION OF. — One who obtains possession of property
for the avowed purpose of delivering it to another, to whom he claims to
have sold it as a broker, but who has in fact made no such sale, and intends to appropriate the property or its proceeds to his own use, is a
thief, and can confer no title upon any other person, whether an innocent purchaser from him or not, at the common law, nor under the provision of the New York factors act, which is as follows: "Every factor
or other agent intrusted with the possession of any bill of lading, custom-house permit, or warehouse-keeper's receipt, for the delivery of any
such merchandise, and every such factor or agent, not having the documentary evidence of title, who shall be intrusted with the possession of
any merchandise for the purpose of sale, or as a security for any advance
to be made or obtained thereon, shall be deemed to be the true owner
thereof, so far as to give validity to any contract made by such agent
with any other person, for the sale or disposition of the whole or any
part of such merchandise, for any money advanced, or negotiable instrument or other obligation in writing given, by such other person upon the
faith thereof."

FACTORS ACT, CONSTRUCTION OF. — A DELIVERY ORDER, by which an owner
of personal property directs it to be delivered to a broker with the object of having the broker deliver the property to one to whom he claims to
have sold it for the owner, is not documentary evidence of the title
within the meaning of the factors act; nor is a broker to whom such
order is so delivered one intrusted with the possession of property for the
purpose of sale, within the meaning of those words as used in that act.

ACTION to recover possession of seventy-six baskets of prime
Borneo rubber, F. F. The defendant claimed to be entitled
to the property through one Henry A. Smith, who was a
broker dealing in rubber in New York City. Smith, in December, 1884, approached plaintiff, claiming to be able to sell

ten tons of rubber to the Goodrich Company, of Akron, Ohio, at forty cents per pound; and he also sent to plaintiff the following letter: "Goodrich will take ten tons F. F. Borneo at forty cents, but will probably wait ninety days on half of it, or else have it delivered in two lots. Will arrange that later on. Send your cable to-night." On the next day, Smith, by another letter, wrote plaintiff as follows: "Letter and telegram just found on my return. Closed the Borneo for Goodrich . forty cents, one half commission. Best can do. Will call to-morrow." Plaintiff then cabled for the ten tons of rubber, and Smith, on December 7, 1884, delivered to the plaintiff the following contract: —

"Sold to the B. F. Goodrich Co., Akron, Ohio.

"For account of Robert Soltau, Esq.

H. A. SMITH.

"About twenty-two thousand (22,000 lbs.) of prime Borneo Rubber (mark F. F.), to be delivered during the first half of the month of March, 1885, @ 40c. per lb, half cash sixty days after delivery, and half cash 90 days after delivery.

"H. A. SMITH,

"Broker in India Rubber, 17 William Street.

"Half brokerage, H. A. S.

"No responsibility taken, unless by special agreement."

After the arrival of the rubber, plaintiff, to enable Smith to deliver the rubber to the Goodrich Company, gave him the following order, directed to the transportation company: "Please deliver to bearer F. F. ninety-three baskets of Borneo rubber, ex. Canada, arrived February 22, 1885." Smith never had any contract nor opened any negotiations with the Goodrich Company, and while he represented to plaintiff that he had shipped the rubber to that company, he, as a matter of fact, after obtaining possession of it by means of the delivery order, stored it in the warehouse of Lawson B. Bell, and took a receipt therefor as follows: —

"No. A. 326.   NEW YORK, May 6, 1885.

LAWSON B. BELL.

"Received on storage, in 516–18 Washington Street.

"From Mr. H. A. Smith, and deliverable only upon the return of this receipt, marked ex. S. S. Canada, March 2, '85, F. F. 76 baskets (76) seventy-six baskets rubber. Storage, 4c. per month. Labor in and out, 4c.

"Indorsed: H. A. SMITH."

Smith next stated to plaintiff that the Goodrich company
wished to return seventy-six baskets of the rubber, and plaintiff assented to their return. Smith falsely claimed that the
seventy-six baskets had been returned, and that he had sold
them to the Boston Rubber Shoe Company, and he sent
plaintiff the following pretended contract:—

"Sold to Boston Rubber Shoe Co.

"For account of Robert Soltau, Esq., about five (5)
tons of prime Borneo rubber, to be delivered at any
time during month of July, 1885, at 43c. per ℔. net,
cash 30 days after delivery.

"No responsibility taken, unless by special agreement.
                                        "H. A. SMITH."

H. A. SMITH.

Smith claimed that the seventy-six baskets were stored in
plaintiff's name in the warehouse of E. E. Driggs, and he
procured from plaintiff, June 29, 1885, a delivery order directing Driggs, as warehouseman, to deliver to Smith the seventy-
six baskets of rubber, for the avowed purpose of delivery to
the Boston Rubber Shoe Company. Previous to this time,
and on May 7, 1885, Smith procured a loan of two thousand
dollars from defendant, by delivering to him the warehouse
receipt issued by Bell, and defendant subsequently, pursuant
to an understanding with Smith, sold the rubber, paid the
loan, and turned over to Smith the balance of the proceeds.
The court directed a verdict to be entered for the plaintiff.

Theodore W. Dwight and E. B. Convers, for the appellant.

Mark Cohn, for the respondent.

EARL, J. The trial judge held that the facts of the case
showed that the broker, Smith, obtained the rubber from
the plaintiff by larceny, and upon that ground directed the
verdict. There were no disputed facts, and we think the
evidence so clearly established the larceny that there was
nothing in reference thereto to submit to the jury. It is entirely clear that Smith intended, from the beginning of his
negotiations with the plaintiff in reference to the rubber, to
steal it. No other conclusion or inference, from the evidence,
is justifiable. The plaintiff did not intend to part with the
title of the rubber to Smith, and at most intended that he
should have possession of it for a special purpose. He meant
only to part with the possession of the rubber to Smith, that
he might make delivery of it to the Goodrich company, under

the prior contract of sale, while Smith intended to steal the rubber; and thus the crime of larceny was committed: *Bassett* v. *Spofford*, 45 N. Y. 387; 6 Am. Rep. 101; *Loomis* v. *People*, 67 N. Y. 322; 23 Am. Rep. 123; *Thorne* v. *Turck*, 94 N. Y. 90; 46 Am. Rep. 126; *People* v. *Morse*, 99 N. Y. 662; 2 Bishop's Crim. Law, 7th ed., secs. 799 et seq.

At the time the first delivery order was delivered to Smith, the property was legally in the possession of the plaintiff, and the moment Smith took it he became a trespasser, the theft was complete, and he could at once, without any demand, have been sued for the trespass. The title of the property and the right of possession remained in the plaintiff, and he was deprived of the actual possession thereof wholly by the trespass and theft. In the law, he never consented to part with the possession of the property, and Smith never had possession thereof, rightfully or legally, for one moment. Nothing which subsequently occurred changed the character of Smith's possession. The subsequent delivery order which the plaintiff was induced to give to him, directed to Driggs, in whose warehouse he falsely represented the rubber to be, had no effect whatever. It gave Smith no dominion or control of the rubber, and in no way divested the plaintiff of any control or possession thereof which he then had. It was absolutely nugatory for every purpose. The property had then for nearly two months been stored in the warehouse of Bell in Smith's own name, and the warehouse receipt had for nearly two months been pledged to the defendant. From the time Smith first took possession of the rubber, his possession, so far as he had any, was solely that of a thief, and the actual possession and control of the property was never thereafter restored to the plaintiff. The plaintiff must, therefore, be treated as having been deprived of his property by the common-law crime of larceny, and it follows that the thief could not, independently of the factors act, confer any title or right of any kind, as against the plaintiff, upon any other person. The defendant, therefore, got no right to this rubber, and had no right to deal therewith, or dispose of the proceeds thereof in any way, and the plaintiff's recovery against him is unquestionably right, unless he is protected by the factors act.

It is provided in section 3 of the act, chapter 179 of the Laws of 1830, commonly called the factors act, as follows: "Every factor or other agent intrusted with the possession of any bill of lading, custom-house permit, or warehouse-keeper's receipt, for the delivery of any such merchandise, and every such factor or agent, not having the documentary evidence of title, who shall be intrusted with the possession of any merchandise for the purpose of sale, or as a security for any advances to be made or obtained thereon, shall be deemed to be the true owner thereof, so far as to give validity to any contract made by such agent with any other person, for the sale or disposition of the whole or any part of such merchandise, for any money advanced, or negotiable instrument or other obligation in writing given, by such other person upon the faith thereof." Statutes similar to this have for many years existed in England, and in most if not all the states of the Union, and it has never yet been held, nor, so far as we can discover, claimed, in any reported case, that the factors act can have any operation whatever in the case of goods taken by a common-law larceny from the true owner. If the documents mentioned in the section quoted have been stolen from the owner, then it cannot be said that the thief was intrusted with their possession; and when a factor or agent obtains goods from the true owner by a common-law larceny, it cannot be said that he is intrusted with their possession for the purpose of sale. To bring the case within the section quoted, the factor or other agent must be consciously and voluntarily intrusted with the possession of the documents or merchandise, and the section can have no application whatever to a case where the documents or goods are taken by trespass or theft, and thus the possession of the factor or agent is, from the beginning, tortious, wrongful, and unlawful.

. The first section of the factors act provides as follows: "After this act shall take effect, every person in whose name any merchandise shall be shipped shall be deemed the true owner thereof, so far as to entitle the consignee of such merchandise to a lien thereon," for any money advanced or negotiable security given, etc.; and yet, notwithstanding the broad and explicit language of this section, it was held in *Kinsey v. Leggett*, 71 N. Y. 387, that it has no application to a case where the property has been wrongfully taken from the possession of the owner, and then fraudulently appropriated, and that it applies only to cases where the shipment of the property is made, with the consent of the real owner, in the name of another, thus conferring upon the latter apparent ownership and right of control.

In *Howland* v. *Woodruff*, 60 N. Y. 73, it was held that the factors act was intended for the protection of third parties who, in good faith and in ignorance of any defects of title, advance money or incur obligations upon the faith of merchandise, and the apparent ownership thereof by factors or agents who have been intrusted by the owners with the possession of, or with the documentary evidence of title to, property; that it is the act of the owner in thus conferring upon his factor the apparent ownership and right of disposal, together with the fact that an innocent third person has dealt with the latter in reliance thereon, that estops the former from following his property; but that in order to estop the owner, where the factor has not the documentary evidence of title, actual possession is required. In that case Allen, J., said: "It is the act of the owner in intrusting the factor with the possession of the goods, or the documentary evidence of ownership and right of disposal, in connection with the fact that innocent third persons deal with him on the faith of such apparent ownership, that estops the owner from following his property into the hands of *bona fide* vendees or pledgees, and gives the latter a better title than their vendor or pledgor had." The doctrine of estoppel has never been applied against an owner who has been deprived of his property by larceny. Judge Allen further said, that it was not the interest or the general scope of the act to deprive owners of their property without any fault or act of theirs, and that "the act was intended for the security of those who deal with a factor or agent in the belief that he is the true owner, and that belief must be induced by the act of the owner in intrusting the factor or agent with the apparent ownership." An owner who is deprived of his property by theft is guilty of no act upon which another has the right to rely, and cannot in law be said to intrust the thief with his property.

The case of *Collins* v. *Ralli*, 20 Hun, 246, affirmed in this court, 85 N. Y. 637, upon the opinion delivered in the supreme court, is entirely analogous to this, and is a very precise authority for the conclusion we have reached. There, H. M. Cutler, a cotton broker, called upon the plaintiff, and by falsely and fraudulently representing that he was authorized to purchase cotton for certain mills in Massachusetts, induced the plaintiff to sell certain cotton to the mills and deliver to him a bill of sale thereof to the mills. Upon the representation that he desired to ship the cotton immediately, Cutler procured from the plaintiff a delivery order upon the warehouseman, at whose warehouse Cutler had the cotton weighed and marked and loaded upon a truck. Subsequently Cutler stored the cotton in another warehouse, and took out receipts therefor from the keeper of such warehouse, in his own name first, and afterwards in the name of his brokers. Thereafter the defendants purchased the cotton in good faith, and for value, through their brokers, receiving the warehouse receipts therefor, and subsequently shipped it to Liverpool. Cutler having absconded without paying for the cotton, the plaintiff brought the action against the defendants to recover the value of the cotton received and converted by them; and it was held that Cutler was guilty of larceny in fraudulently obtaining the temporary custody of the cotton, and thereafter converting it to his own use, and that the defendants acquired no title to it by reason of his transfer of it to them; that as the plaintiff had merely intrusted Cutler with the temporary possession of the cotton, to enable him to weigh and cart it for shipment to the pretended purchasers, and had never conferred upon him the apparent title thereto, or any authority to dispose thereof, he was not estopped from reclaiming it from the defendants, though they had purchased it in good faith; that the defendants were not protected by section 6 of chapter 326 of the Laws of 1858, providing that warehouse receipts may be transferred by indorsement, and that any person to whom the same may be transferred shall be deemed and taken to be the true owner of the goods therein specified, so far as to give validity to any pledge, lien, or transfer made or created by such person or persons, as such provision only applies to receipts given for goods stored or deposited by persons having the title thereof, whether real or apparent, or authority so to do from such real or apparent owner. There, as here, the broker, pretending that he had effected a sale of the goods, obtained a delivery order from the plaintiff, and thus having obtained possession of the goods, stored the same in his own name, and thereafter sold them to a *bona fide* purchaser. That case was subsequently followed by *Hentz v. Miller*, 94 N. Y. 64, growing out of the misconduct of the same broker. The learned counsel for the defendant has attempted to distinguish those cases from `this. His attempted distinctions are very ingenious, but we fail to find any distinction in principle between them and this case.

The decision of this case could, we think, be put upon a

nárrower ground than the one upon which we have thus far
placed it. The delivery order given by the plaintiff to Smith,
that he might make delivery of the rubber to the Goodrich
company, was not, within the meaning of the factors act,
documentary evidence of title. It was not a bill of lading,
custom-house permit, or warehouse-keeper's receipt. It was
no evidence whatever of title, and whatever it was, it was not
seen by the defendants, and they did not act on the faith
thereof. Nor was Smith intrusted with the possession of the
rubber "for the purpose of sale." So far as the plaintiff intrusted him with the possession, it was simply that he might
make delivery of the rubber in pursuance of the contract of
sale, which he pretended he had nearly three months previously obtained.

There is, therefore, no aspect of this case, either at common
law or under the factors act, from which it can be said that
the defendant obtained any title whatever to the property of
the plaintiff.

The learned counsel for the appellant, in his argument,
places great reliance upon the case of *Baines* v. *Swainson*, 4 Best
& S. 270. There the plaintiffs, cloth manufacturers, were applied to by one Ernsley, who was a factor and commission
agent, for a sample of their cloths, on the representation that
he could get them a purchaser. The samples having been
sent, Ernsley afterward told the plaintiffs that he had got
them an order for a certain number of ends at a stated price.
The plaintiffs required to know the purchasers, and Sykes and
Son being mentioned, they sent the goods to the warehouse of
Ernsley, who was to pass them on to Sykes and Son, after seeing
the process of perching performed upon them, for which he
was to receive a commission from plaintiffs of one shilling per
end. Ernsley had no authority from Sykes and Son, and he
sold the goods to the defendants, who were cloth merchants,
and bought them *bona fide;* and it was held, per Wightman,
and Crompton, JJ., that Ernsley was an agent "intrusted"
with the cloths within the meaning of the factors act (6 Geo.
IV., c. 94, sec. 4, and 5 & 6 Vict., c. 39, sec. 4), and that consequently the purchase of them from Ernsley by the defendants
was protected; and per Blackburn, J., that Ernsley, being in
possession of the goods, was, according to the statutes (5 &
6 Vict., c. 39, sec. 4), to be taken to be "intrusted" with them
by the owner, unless the contrary was shown, and that was a
question for the jury. Under those statutes, to bring a trans-

action within their provisions, it was not necessary that the goods should be entrusted to an agent for sale, but it was sufficient if there was any mercantile agency; and if the goods were intrusted to a person whose business it was to deal in goods and make sales of them, he was such an agent as was contemplated by the statutes, although they were not intrusted to him for sale. Our factors act is different. In order to bring a case within it, it must appear that the goods were intrusted to an agent for sale, and it is not sufficient that they were intrusted to a mere commercial agent, or to one whose business it was to make sales of goods. Our statute contemplates the act of the owner in voluntarily and specifically intrusting the goods to some factor or agent for sale, and to no other agent and for no other purpose. It is by no means certain that that case would have been decided the same way if the English factors act had been like ours.

That case is further distinguished from this, in that there was no claim made there that the goods had been obtained by Ernsley from the plaintiffs by larceny, and the question of larceny received no consideration. So while that case bears some analogy to this, we do not consider it of controlling weight. The case of *Vickers* v. *Hertz*, L. R. 2 S. & D. App. 113, is also clearly distinguishable from this. There, Vickers ordered eight hundred tons of pig-iron from the Carron Company, and while they held it at his disposal, he employed Campbell Brothers to sell it for him. They wrote to him, "We can now get your price." He agreed, and sent them an order in the following terms: "To the Carron Company. Please deliver to Messrs. Campbell Brothers." Campbell Brothers, instead of employing the document for the purpose of giving delivery to the supposed purchaser, represented the iron as their own, and asked Hertz to make them an advance upon it. Hertz declined until the document should be stamped, and a place of delivery inserted by Vickers. These requirements having been satisfied by Vickers, the Carron Company wrote to Hertz, saying: "We have placed the pig-iron indorsed by Thomas Vickers, Esq., to your credit." Hertz thereupon advanced to Campbell Brothers two thousand four hundred pounds. The act of Campbell Brothers was a gross fraud upon Vickers, who knew nothing of the transfer to Hertz, although he had unsuspectingly facilitated its accomplishment. Campbell Brothers, having become bankrupt, disappeared, and an action was brought by Vickers against Hertz for a delivery of the iron. The defense was, that the iron had been acquired by Hertz legitimately, under an order indorsed by Vickers, and delivered by his factors to Hertz, who afterward sold it for less than he had advanced upon it. Judgment was given in favor of the defendant in that case, which upon appeal was affirmed. There was no question of larceny considered. That case was decided under 5 and 6 Victoria, chapter 39, in the third section of which it is provided that "any agent intrusted with the possession of goods, or of the documents of title to goods, shall be deemed and taken to be the owner of such goods and documents, so far as to give validity to any contract or agreement by way of pledge, lien, or security, *bona fide* made by any person with such agent so intrusted"; and in section 4 of which it is provided "that any order for the delivery of goods, or any other document used in the ordinary course of business as proof of the possession or control of goods, shall be deemed and taken to be a document of title within the meaning of this act"; and it was held there that the delivery order given by the plaintiff to Campbell Brothers was a document of title, within the express and plain meaning of the act, and that therefore the defendant, a purchaser from them, was protected.

It is not very profitable to inquire what would have been the position and rights of these parties if the sales pretended to have been made by Smith had been real, or if the rubber had been, by the delivery orders, placed in his hands for sale on behalf of the plaintiff, an undisclosed principal. The pretended sales, and all the other pretenses of Smith, were mere shams,—devices used by him to accomplish the larceny; and the fact of larceny must dominate this case. The rubber was never in his possession for sale. Six weeks before it arrived in this country he had, as a broker, made the pretended sale to the Goodrich company, and after its arrival he obtained the delivery order, not to make a sale, but to make a delivery of the rubber upon a contract, which, if real, was previously binding upon the parties thereto.

But if the pretended contract of sale to the Goodrich company had been real, and the plaintiff had given to Smith the delivery order to enable him to obtain possession of the rubber for delivery upon the contract, this action would still be undefended. In that case, if he obtained the delivery order with the preconceived design to convert the rubber to his own use, he would have been guilty of larceny, with the effect and disability above mentioned. If he conceived the design to appropriate the rubber to his own use after it came into his possession, he would not have been guilty of larceny, but would still have been unable to confer any title thereto upon the defendant. Then he would have had possession of the rubber for the sole purpose of making delivery thereof upon a real contract, and he would have had the mere possession thereof, and nothing else. He would have been clothed with no *indicia* of title, and with no apparent right to sell.

While mere possession of goods is frequently *prima facie* evidence of title, it is merely *prima facie.* Whoever deals with the possessor does it at his peril, and a purchaser from one having no other apparent title to goods than the possession thereof must see to it that his seller has the title; and if his title fails, and he is obliged to respond to the true owner of the goods, his loss is due to his own misplaced confidence,. and not to that of the owner. Owners of goods for commercial and other purposes must frequently intrust others with the possession of them, and the affairs of men could not be conducted unless they could do so with safety. So long as the possession of the goods is not accompanied with some *indicia* of ownership, or of right to sell, the possessor has no more power to divest the owner of his title, or to affect it, than a mere thief. Here the defendant could have inquired into the title of Smith before he took the rubber in pledge, and his loss is due, not to any wrong, neglect, or misplaced confidence of the plaintiff, but to his own neglect and abused confidence. Smith, having received the goods for delivery to the Goodrich company, could no more pledge them than a common carrier, a depositary, a bailee to do some work upon them, or a mere servant. He had no general agency, but his power was limited to the special purpose for which the rubber was given into his possession. A valid contract of sale having been made binding upon the plaintiff, he was not bound to make delivery through his broker; but he could have delivered the rubber through any other agent; and no one will claim that if the rubber had been put into the possession of a mere agent (not the broker) for delivery, a purchase from such agent would have divested the plaintiff of his title.

A little more may be said to show that Smith obtained no title to the rubber. There is no real evidence that it was intended by him or the plaintiff that he should have the title. He solicited of the plaintiff the right to act as his broker.

He delivered to the plaintiff a bought note showing that the rubber was sold in his name and as his property; and if the transaction had been real, he would, according to the previous custom and his understanding with the plaintiff, have given the purchaser a sold note indicating a sale on account of his principal without writing therein the principal's name. Thus he would have brought the seller and buyer together, and would have made a contract of sale binding upon them, incurring no responsibility himself but that of broker: *Southwell* v. *Bowditch*, L. R. 1 C. P. D. 374. He obtained the delivery order, not to deliver rubber upon his contract, but upon plaintiff's contract. He consulted the plaintiff about taking the rubber back from the Goodrich company, and obtained his consent therefor. He subsequently professed to store it in plaintiff's name, and at all times subsequently professed to the plaintiff to deal with and treat it as his. Clearly, beyond any question, the plaintiff and Smith understood that the title to the rubber was in the plaintiff, and never in Smith; and without the intention of one or both of them, it could not pass from the plaintiff to Smith. The entries upon the plaintiff's books in reference to the rubber were mere matters of book-keeping, having no reference to the title to the rubber, but merely to the proceeds which were expected to reach plaintiff's hands through Smith as his broker.

We have given careful attention to the exhaustive and learned brief of the counsel for the defendant, and while this case is not free from some difficulty, we are constrained to hold that it was properly disposed of below, and that the judgment there should be affirmed, with costs.

Larceny by Bailees. — For a discussion of the law relating to the offense of larceny by bailees, see note to *State* v. *Homes*, 57 Am. Dec. 280–282; *State* v. *Fisher*, 38 Minn. 378. Compare *Crocheron* v. *State*, 86 Ala. 64; 11 Am. St. Rep. 18, and note. In *Morrison* v. *State*, 17 Tex. App. 34, 50 Am. Rep. 120, where one hired a house, and subsequently converted it to his own use, it was held that an indictment for larceny would not lie unless it was shown that the felonious intent existed at the time of the hiring; see also *Krause* v. *Commonwealth*, 93 Pa. St. 418; 39 Am. Rep. 762; *Robinson* v. *State*, 1 Cold. 120; 78 Am. Dec. 487.

YATES COUNTY NATIONAL BANK v. CARPENTER.

[119 NEW YORK, 550.]

EXECUTION. — STATUTES EXEMPTING PROPERTY FROM EXECUTION ARE TO BE LIBERALLY CONSTRUED with a view of promoting the objects of the legislature, and their force and effect are not to be confined to the literal terms of the acts.

EXECUTIONS — EXEMPTION OF PROCEEDS OF PENSIONS. — IF A DWELLING-HOUSE IS PURCHASED BY A PENSIONER, whose only cash payment therefor is made with moneys received by him as collections on his pension certificate, the balance of the purchase price being secured by a mortgage on the property, his interest therein is exempted from execution by the provision of the New York code, declaring that a pension "granted by the United States for military services is also exempt from levy and sale by virtue of an execution, and from seizure for non-payment of taxes, or in any legal proceeding."

Arthur C. Smith, for the appellant.

William T. Morris, for the respondent.

RUGER, C. J. In March, 1882, the Yates County National Bank recovered a judgment in justice's court against Zeno T. Carpenter and others, for about $111, and caused a transcript thereof to be filed in the county clerk's office, July 17, 1884. In June, 1884, the United States government issued and delivered an invalid pension certificate to Zeno T. Carpenter, as a soldier in the United States army, which was deposited by him in the First National Bank of Yates County for collection, in July, 1884. In October, 1884, Carpenter purchased and took a conveyance of a dwelling-house and lot in the village of Penn Yan, his place of residence, from one Hurford, for thirteen hundred dollars, paying the sum of seven hundred dollars cash upon the purchase price, and securing the balance by a mortgage to the grantor upon said lot. The cash payment was made from moneys received by him from the First National Bank, as part of the collection of his pension certificate. Carpenter was a married man, having a wife and five infant children, and the house and lot were purchased for the purpose of securing a home for himself and family. He had no other means or property liable for the payment of debts. In February, 1885, the Yates County National Bank caused an execution upon such judgment to be issued and levied upon said house and lot, and advertised the interest of said Carpenter therein for sale at public auction to satisfy said execution.

Upon proof of these facts, Carpenter moved the county court for an order setting aside the levy, and enjoining the plaintiff from taking any proceedings to enforce said execution by the sale of said real estate, upon the ground that such property was exempt from levy and sale upon execution. That court granted the order asked for; but upon appeal to the general term, this order was reversed, and such motion was denied. The defendant Carpenter appeals to this court from the order of reversal.

At the time of the levy, the only interest Carpenter had in such real estate was an equity of redemption, which we must assume, on the facts in this case, did not exceed in value the sum paid for it, and it therefore represents, to the extent of his interest, the proceeds of his pension. Was this interest liable to levy and sale on execution? The plaintiff insists that it is, and such is the judgment of the court below. The question presented involves the construction of section 1393 of the Code of Civil Procedure, which, so far as the matter here concerned is affected, reads as follows: "A pension heretofore or hereafter granted by the United States . . . . for military . . . . services . . . . is also exempt from levy and sale by virtue of an execution, and from seizure for non-payment of taxes, or in any other legal proceeding." That statutes of this character are to be liberally construed with the view of promoting the objects of the legislation, is established by a uniform course of authority; and that their force and effect are not to be confined to the literal terms of the act, has also been held in numerous cases. In *Hudson* v. *Plets*, 11 Paige, 180, it was held that a creditor's bill would not reach the right of action of a judgment debtor for the conversion of exempt property. In *Andrews* v. *Rowan*, 28 How. Pr. 126, it was held that a receiver of the property of a debtor, appointed in supplementary proceedings, did not take a claim or a judgment thereon, for damages accruing to such debtor from one who had wrongfully taken and sold his exempt property on execution for debt. Justice Grover, writing the opinion of the supreme court in that case, says: "If the judgment rendered for the injury may be acquired by a judgment creditor, by proceedings supplemental to execution, there would be nothing to prevent seizing exempt property, selling it upon execution, and when the debtor had sued and recovered a judgment therefor, compelling the application of such judgment to the payment of the debt for which the property was seized, thus entirely depriving the debtor of the exemption, and enabling the creditor, in this way, to collect his debt from

property that the law has declared not liable for its payment."
The only case in this court bearing upon the subject is that of
Tillotson v. *Wolcott*, 48 N. Y. 188, where it was held that the
exemption of a team, provided for a householder, should also
apply to a judgment recovered by such householder against
one who had tortiously taken and converted it to his own use.
It was said by the court that "the judgment, when recovered
by the debtor for the wrongful invasion of his privilege of the
exemption of his property from levy and sale, represents the
property for the value of which it was recovered." While
the language of the statute did not, in terms, cover a judgment, it was held that it came within its spirit, and could not
be taken by creditors. The opinion of Justice Grover in *Andrews* v. *Rowan*, 28 How. Pr. 126, is referred to and approved
in the opinion of Judge Leonard.

The general exemption laws of the state provide for the
protection of specific articles or classes of property, with a view
of alleviating the condition of the poor by securing to them the
use or consumption of the property exempted; but the present
law has departed from the ordinary form of exemption, and
while seeking to accomplish the same object, provides, in
terms, for the exemption of money or its equivalent. It is
quite obvious that such an exemption can produce no beneficial effect, unless it is extended beyond the letter of the act,
and giving life and force, according to its evident spirit and
meaning. Like other statutes, the section in question must be
construed according to the meaning and intent of the law-
makers, and so as to effectuate their intention, so far as the
language of the act will permit it to be done. Did the legislature intend to limit the force of their exemption to a pension,
so long only as it remained an obligation of the government,
or consisted of cash in the hands of the pensioner? or did they
also intend to protect it after it had been expended in the purchase of articles of property designed to administer to the
comfort and support of such pensioner and his family? If the
latter was not intended, we must ascribe to the law-makers
the absurd intention of granting pensions for the purpose of
satisfying claims against pensioners, and not to provide for the
care and comfort of invalid or aged soldiers. If the soldier is
not protected in the act of exchanging his pension for the necessaries of life, its only effect would be to enable his creditors
to take it in satisfaction of their claims. No benefit is conferred if the protection is not extended beyond the possession

of the money itself; for its only value consists in its purchasing power, and if the soldier is deprived of that, the pension might as well, so far as he is concerned, have remained ungranted.

The plain purpose of the act was to promote the comfort of the soldier; to secure to him the bounty of the government, free from the claims of creditors, and to insure him and his family a safe, although modest, maintenance, so long as their needs required it. In the case of an exemption of specific articles from levy and sale upon execution, it seems to be well settled that it extends not only to the protection of such articles while in use or possession, but also to any claim arising out of their conversion by a wrong-doer, or their destruction by fire, or otherwise, when insured: Freeman on Executions, sec. 235. The rule seems to be just and reasonable, and within the spirit of the exemption. In the case of the exemption of money, or its equivalent, there has been some controversy in the courts with reference to the extent to which the exemption shall be carried. In such case it is somewhat difficult to lay down a rule in precise terms, by which it may be determined, in all cases, what property is liable, and what exempt from levy and seizure upon legal process for the payment of debts; but we entertain no doubt that where the receipts from a pension can be directly traced to the purchase of property, necessary or convenient for the support and maintenance of the pensioner and his family, such property is exempt under the provisions of this statute. Where such moneys can be clearly identified and are used in the purchase of necessary articles, or are loaned or invested for purposes of increase or safety, in such form as to secure their available use for the benefit of the pensioner in time of need, we do not doubt but that they come within the meaning of the statute; but where they have been embarked in trade, commerce, or speculation, and become mingled with other funds so as to be incapable of identification or separation, we do not doubt but that the pensioner loses the benefit of the statutory exemption. These propositions, we think, are fully supported by the cases in this and other states. See Freeman on Executions, sec. 235, tit. Proceeds of Exempt Property.

In *Burgett* v. *Fancher*, 35 Hun, 647, and *Stockwell* v. *Bank of Malone*, 36 Hun, 583, it was held that moneys received from a pension, and deposited in a bank in the name of the pensioner, were not subject to proceedings on the part of creditors to have them applied in payment of debts, although the relations between the depositor and the bank were those of creditor and debtor. The debt represented the pension, and that was exempted by the statute. The case of *Wygant* v. *Smith*, 2 Lans. 185, when limited, as it must be, to the facts appearing in the case, is not an authority for the plaintiff here. In that case the pensioner had embarked his pension in business or trade, and in some transactions had made a profit. It was impossible to identify the fund in the various articles of property in which, through numerous and successive changes, it had become invested, and it was held that the pensioner had lost his right of exemption.

The order of the general term should be reversed, and that of the county court affirmed, with costs to defendant in all courts.

––––

STATUTES ALLOWING EXEMPTIONS must be liberally construed: Note to *Rockwell* v. *Hubbell*, 45 Am. Dec. 252, 253; note to *Alsup* v. *Jordan*, 5 Am. St. Rep. 59.

PENSIONS. — A PENSIONER, UNDER THE UNITED STATES REVISED STATUTES, may use his pension money in any manner he may desire, for his own benefit or for that of his family, free from the attacks of creditors: *Holmes* v. *Tallada*, 125 Pa. St. 133; 11 Am. St. Rep. 880, and note. But in *Foster* v. *Byrne*, 76 Iowa 295, the rule was followed, that the statutes of the United States did not have the effect to exempt from seizure, on execution or attachment, money paid to a pensioner after it came into his hands. And in *Rozelle* v. *Rhodes*, 116 Pa. St. 129, 2 Am. St. Rep. 591, it was decided that pension money was not exempt from execution, after it was received by the pensioner and by him deposited in the hands of a third person for safe-keeping. Compare extended note to *Rozelle* v. *Rhodes*, 2 Am. St. Rep. 596–598, as to when money resulting fronm pensions becomes subject to garnishment.

––––

PEOPLE EX REL. KEMMLER *v.* DURSTON.

[119 NEW YORK, 569.]

CONSTITUTIONAL LAW. — THE CLAUSE OF THE CONSTITUTION PROHIBITING THE INFLICTION OF CRUEL OR UNUSUAL PUNISHMENT confers power upon the courts to declare void legislative acts prescribing punishment for crime, in fact cruel and unusual.

CONSTITUTIONAL LAW. — THE LEGISLATURE HAS POWER TO CHANGE THE MANNER OF INFLICTING THE PENALTY OF DEATH as a punishment for crime.

UNCONSTITUTIONALITY OF STATUTE, HOW MAY BE MADE TO APPEAR. — The testimony of experts and other witnesses is not admissible to show that in carrying out a law, some provision of the constitution may possibly be violated. If it cannot be made to appear that the statute is in conflict with the constitution, by argument deduced from the language of the law itself, or from matters of which the court can take judicial notice, the act must stand.

CONSTITUTIONAL LAW. — WHETHER THE USE OF ELECTRICITY AS AN AGENCY FOR PRODUCING DEATH constitutes a more humane method of executing the judgment of the court in capital cases, was a question for the determination of the legislature, and the determination by the legislature of this question is conclusive upon the courts.

W. Burke Cochran, for the appellant.

Charles F. Tabor, attorney-general, for the respondent.

O'BRIEN, J. The respondent is the agent and warden of the state prison at Auburn, and the relator, being in his custody, applied for a writ of *habeas corpus* to inquire into the cause of detention, which was made returnable by the officer granting it before the county judge of Cayuga County. The relator in his petition for the writ stated that the cause or pretense of the imprisonment complained of was, that after his indictment and trial for the crime of murder in the first degree, and his conviction thereof in the court of oyer and terminer, he was sentenced by that court to undergo a cruel and unusual punishment for that crime, contrary to the constitution of this state and of the United States, and was threatened with deprivation of life without due process of law, by reason of such illegal sentence and judgment of the court. The writ was duly served upon the respondent, who made return thereto that he detained the relator in his custody as agent and warden of the prison by virtue of the judgment of the court of oyer and terminer held in the county of Erie, whereby the relator was duly convicted of the crime of murder in the first degree, and also by virtue of a warraut duly delivered to him under the hand and seal of a justice of the supreme court presiding at the said court of oyer and terminer where the relator was convicted, which recited the indictment, trial, conviction, and sentence of the relator, and directed the respondent to carry the same into effect in these words: " Now, therefore, you are hereby ordered, commanded, and required to execute said sentence upon him, the said William Kemmler, otherwise called John Hort, upon some day within the week commencing on Monday, the twenty-fourth day of June, in the year of our Lord one thousand eight hundred and eighty-nine, and within the walls of Auburn state prison, or within the yard or inclosure adjoining thereto, by then and there causing to pass through the body of him, the said William Kemmler, otherwise called John Hort, a current of electricity of sufficient intensity to cause death, and that the application of such current of elec-

tricity be continued until he, the said William Kemmler, otherwise called John Hort, be dead." This command and direction
to the warden was in accordance with the sentence actually
passed upon the relator after conviction, in these words: " The
sentence of the court is, that within the week commencing
on Monday, the twenty-fourth day of June, in the year of our
Lord one thousand eight hundred and eighty-nine, and within
the walls of Auburn state prison, or within the yard or inclosure adjoining thereto, the defendant suffer the punishment of
death, to be inflicted by the application of electricity, as provided by the Code of Criminal Procedure of the state of New
York, and that in the mean time the defendant be removed to,
and until the infliction of such punishment be kept in solitary
confinement in, said Auburn state prison."

On the return day of the writ the relator and the respondent
appeared by council before the county judge, and by agreement of counsel the production of the relator, pursuant to the
command of the writ, was waived. Counsel for the relator
then offered to prove that the infliction of the penalty named
in the sentence, namely, death by the application of electricity,
is a cruel and unusual punishment within the meaning of the
constitution, and cannot, therefore, be lawfully inflicted. The
attorney-general objected, on the ground that the court had no
authority to take proof in regard to the constitutionality of
the statute. This objection was overruled by the county judge,
and the counsel for the respective parties agreed that a referee
be appointed for the purpose of taking the testimony in pursuance of the offer.

In this way a mass of testimony was given upon both sides,
certified by the referee to the county judge, and embraced in
the extended record before us. The result was, that after a
hearing upon the report of the referee, the county judge dismissed the writ, and remanded the relator to the custody of
-the respondent. When it appeared, from the return of the respondent, that he retained the relator in custody under and
by virtue of the judgment of a court of competent jurisdiction,
wherein the relator was convicted of murder, it was the duty
of the county judge to dismiss the writ, and remand the relator to the custody of the agent and warden of the prison, unless
it could be shown that the court of oyer and terminer was
without jurisdiction to pass the sentence which it did: *People*
v. *Warden*, 100 N. Y. 20; *People* v. *Liscomb*, 60 N. Y. 559; 19
Am. Rep. 211.

It is not denied that the court had such jurisdiction, providing that the legislature had power, under the constitution, to enact chapter 489 of the Laws of 1888, entitled "An act to amend sections 491, 492, 503, 504, 505, 506, 507, 508, 509, of the Code of Criminal Procedure, in relation to the infliction of the death penalty, and to provide means for the infliction of such penalty." Prior to the passage of this statute, the punishment by death in every case was to be inflicted by hanging the convict by the neck until he was dead. This provision of law was changed by the amendments of the code above referred to, and now the section (505) reads as follows: "The punishment by death must, in every case, be inflicted by causing to pass through the body of the convict a current of electricity of sufficient intensity to cause death, and the application of such current must be continued until such convict is dead."

The only question involved in this appeal is, whether this enactment is in conflict with the provision of the state constitution which forbids the infliction of cruel and unusual punishment: Const., art. 1, sec. 5. This provision was borrowed from the English statute, passed in the first year of the reign of William and Mary, being chapter 2 of the statutes of that year, entitled "An act declaring the rights and liberties of the subject, and settling the succession of the crown," usually known as the bill of rights. It enacts, among other things, that "excessive bail ought not to be required, nor excessive fines imposed, nor cruel and unusual punishment inflicted." When this statute was made part of the constitution of the United States, the word "shall" was substituted for the word "ought," and in this form it first appears in the constitution of this state, adopted in 1846. It is not very clear whether the provision as it stands in our constitution was intended as an admonition to the legislature and the judiciary, or as a restraint upon legislation inflicting punishment for criminal offenses. When the statute referred to was enacted in England, it was not intended as a check upon the power of Parliament to prescribe such punishment for crime as it considered proper. Its enactment did not change any law then existing, nor did it mitigate the harshness of criminal punishments in that country, as is shown by the fact that for more than half a century after it appeared on the statute-book, a long catalogue of offenses were punishable by death, many of which were not visited with that extreme penalty before the bill of rights was passed: 2 Bla. Com., c. 33, p. 440.

The history of the times in which this provision assumed the form of a law shows that it was, after all, intended to be little more than a declaration of the rights of the subject. The English people were about to place upon the throne, made vacant by revolution, a foreign prince, whose life had been spent in military pursuits, rather than in the study of constitutional principles, and the limitations of power as then understood in the country he was to govern. This was considered a favorable opportunity to enact, in the solemn form of a statute, a declaration of the principles upon which the people desired the government to be conducted; but whatever the purpose of the statute was in the country where it originated, we think that its presence in the constitution of this state confers power upon the courts to declare void legislative acts prescribing punishments for crime, in fact cruel and unusual. This is the power that is invoked against the amendments to the Code of Criminal Procedure above referred to by the learned counsel for the relator, in an argument addressed to us, interesting on account of its great political and scientific research. We entertain no doubt in regard to the power of the legislature to change the manner of inflicting the penalty of death. The general power of the legislature over crimes, and its power to define and punish the crime of murder, is not, and cannot be, disputed. The amendments prescribed no new punishment for the offense. The punishment now, as before, is death. The only change made is in the mode of carrying out the sentence. The infliction of the death penalty in any manner must necessarily be accompanied with what might be considered, in this age, some degree of cruelty, and it is resorted to only because it is deemed necessary for the protection of society. The act, on its face, does not provide for any other or additional punishment.

In behalf of the relator, this legislation is assailed in no other way than by attempting to show that the new mode of carrying out a death sentence subjects the person convicted to the possible risk of torture and unnecessary pain. This argument would apply with equal force to any untried method of execution, and when carried to its logical results, would prohibit the enforcement of the death penalty at all. Every act of the legislature must be presumed to be in harmony with the fundamental law until the contrary is clearly made

to appear: *Metropolitan Board of Excise* v. *Barrie*, 34 N. Y.
666, 668; *People* v. *Briggs*, 50 N. Y. 553, 558; *People* v. *Home
Ins. Co.*, 92 N. Y. 328, 344; *People* v. *Albertson*, 55 N. Y. 50,
54; *People* v. *Gillson*, 109 N. Y. 389, 397; 4 Am. St. Rep. 465;
People v. *King*, 110 N. Y. 418; 6 Am. St. Rep. 389.

If it cannot be made to appear that a law is in conflict with
the constitution, by argument deduced from the language of
the law itself, or from matters of which a court can take judicial notice, then the act must stand.   The testimony of expert
or other witnesses is not admissible to show that, in carrying
out a law enacted by the legislature, some provision of the
constitution may possibly be violated: *People* v. *Albertson,
supra; People* v. *Draper*, 15 N. Y. 532; *Matter of New York E.
R. R. Co.*, 70 N. Y. 327.

If the act upon its face is not in conflict with the constitution, then extraneous proof cannot be used to condemn it.
The history and origin of the enactment we are now considering may very properly be referred to to test its validity, and
ascertain .its true intent and proper interpretation.   It has
been said that courts will place themselves in the situation of
the legislature, and, by ascertaining the necessity and probable objects of the passage of a law, give effect to it, if possible,
according to the intention of the law-makers, when that can
be done without violating any constitutional provision: *People*
v. *Supervisors*, 43 N. Y. 130.   Chapter 352 of the Laws of
1886, entitled "An act to authorize the appointment of a commission to investigate and report to the legislature the most
humane and approved method of carrying into effect the sentence of .death in capital cases," provided for the appointment
of a commission consisting of three eminent citizens, who were
named therein, and required them to investigate and report
to the legislature, on or before the fourth Tuesday of January,
1887, the most humane and practical method known to modern science of carrying into effect the sentence of death in
capital cases.   To enable this commission to make its investigation most thorough, the legislature extended the time for
it to report for a year longer, by chapter 7 of the Laws of 1887.
This commission, early in the legislative session of 1888, made
its report, accompanied with a proposed bill, which the legislature afterward, and during the same session, enacted, and
this is the statute which is now attacked in behalf of the relator as an unauthorized expression of the legislative will.
The legislature proceeded to change the mode of executing

the sentence of death with care and caution and unusual deliberation. It would be a strange result, indeed, if it could now be held that its efforts to devise a more humane method of carrying out the sentence of death in capital cases have culminated in the enactment of a law in conflict with the provisions of the constitution prohibiting cruel and unusual punishments. Whether the use of electricity as an agency for producing death constituted a more humane method of executing the judgment of the court in capital cases, was a question for the determination of the legislature. It was a question peculiarly within its province, and the means at its command for ascertaining whether such a mode of producing death involved cruelty, within the meaning of the constitutional prohibition, were certainly as satisfactory and reliable as any that are consistent with the limited functions of an appellate court. The determination of the legislature of this question is conclusive upon this court. The amendment to the Code of Criminal Procedure changing the mode of inflicting the death penalty does not, upon its face, nor in its general purpose and intent, violate any provision of the constitution. The testimony taken by the referee, while not available to impeach the validity of the legislation, may, we think, be regarded as a valuable collection of facts and opinions touching the use of electricity as a means of producing death, and for that reason, as part of the argument for the relator, but nothing more. We have examined this testimony, and can find but little in it to warrant the belief that this new mode of execution is cruel within the meaning of the constitution, though it is certainly unusual. On the contrary, we agree with the court below that it removes every reasonable doubt that the application of electricity to the vital parts of the human body, under such conditions, and in the manner contemplated by the statute, must result in instantaneous, and consequently in painless, death.

The order appealed from should be affirmed.

————

CRUEL AND UNUSUAL PUNISHMENTS are prohibited by the constitutions of Alabama: Ala. Const., art. 1, sec. 16; of Arkansas: Ark. Const., art. 2, sec. 9; of California: Cal. Const., art. 1, sec. 6; of Colorado: Col. Const., art. 2, sec. 20; of Delaware: Del. Const., art. 1, sec. 11; of Florida: Fla. Declaration of Rights, 6; of Georgia: Ga. Const., art. 1, sec. 19; of Indiana: Ind. Const., art. 1, sec. 16; of Iowa: Iowa Const., art. 1, sec. 17; of Kansas: Kan. Const., Bill of Rights, 9; of Kentucky: Ky. Const., art. 13, sec. 17; of Maine: Me. Const., art. 1, sec. 9; of Maryland: Md. Declaration of Rights, 16, 25; of Massachusetts: Mass. Const., art. 1, sec. 9; of Michigan: Mich.

Const., art. 3, sec. 31; of Minnesota: Minn. Const., art. 1, sec. 5; of Mississippi: Miss. Const. (1869), art. 1, sec. 8; of Nebraska: Neb. Const., art. 1,
sec. 9; of Nevada: Nev. Const., art. 1, sec. 6; of New Hampshire: N. H.
Const., art. 1, sec. 33; of New Jersey: N. J. Const., art. 1, sec. 15; of New
York: N. Y. Const., art. 1, sec. 5; of North Carolina: N. C. Const., art. 1,
sec. 14; of Ohio: Ohio Const., art. 1, sec. 9; of Oregon: Or. Const., art. 1,
sec. 16; of Pennsylvania: Pa. Const., art. 1, sec. 13; of Rhode Island: R. I.
Const., art. 1, sec. 8; of South Carolina: S. C. Const., art. 1, sec. 38; of
Tennessee: Tenn. Const., art. 1, sec. 16; of Texas: Tex. Const., art. 1, sec.
13; of Virginia: Va. Const., art. 1, sec. 11; of West Virginia: W. Va. Const.,
art. 3, sec. 5; of Wisconsin: Wis. Const., art. 1, sec. 6; of Missouri: Mo.
Const., art. 2, sec. 25; and of Louisiana: La. Const., sec. 9.

CASES

SUPREME COURT

OF

TEXAS.

MISSOURI PACIFIC RAILWAY CO. *v.* WILLIAMS.

[75 TEXAS, 4.]

MASTER AND SERVANT — FELLOW-SERVANTS — MASTER'S LIABILITY FOR NEGLIGENCE OF VICE-PRINCIPAL. — A car-repairer is not a fellow-servant with a foreman of car-repairers, with power to employ and discharge servants under him, and the company is liable for an injury to such car-repairer received through the negligence of such foreman and while engaged in extra hazardous employment under his order and promise of protection.

JURY TRIAL — INSTRUCTIONS. — MODIFICATION OF REQUESTED CHARGE appended thereto in such manner as to show the precise charge asked and the precise modification, and that the whole is intelligible to the jury, so that no injury results to the party making the request, is not error.

JURY TRIAL — INSTRUCTIONS — FAILURE TO REPEAT NOT ERROR. — Where the charge taken as a whole correctly presents the law upon one of the issues, so that the jury could not have been misled by the language used, it is not error to fail to repeat it in presenting every distinct phase of the case made by the testimony upon other issues.

MASTER AND SERVANT — NEGLIGENCE OF MASTER. — When a servant assumes an extra hazardous employment by order of his master and under promise to protect him, the master cannot excuse his failure to keep his promise by proof that the servant also requested others to see that he was not injured.

Whitaker and Bonner, for the appellant.

Gregg and Reeves, for the appellee.

GAINES, A. J. This suit was brought by appellee against appellant to recover damages for a personal injury.

The uncontroverted evidence shows that plaintiff was a car-repairer in the shops of the defendant company at its yard in Palestine. One Monroe was master car-builder, with general supervision of the repair department at that point. One

Holmes was foreman of the car-repairers under him. Plaintiff was ordered by Holmes to go under a car to repair it, which was not upon a repair track, but upon a track used in the transportation department in connection with the main track. Plaintiff obeyed the order of Holmes, and went under the car to repair it, as it was necessary for him to do. While lying under the car it was struck by another car, and the wheel of the car he was repairing driven upon his heel, inflicting a serious injury. The plaintiff testified that before he went under the car Holmes promised him to watch and to see that he was not injured. He also asked two other employees to watch. He relied upon the promises both of Holmes and of another employee of defendant to protect him. He also testified that he was a car-repairer in the employment of the defendant company, and, in connection with others, was under the direct orders and control of Holmes, and that Holmes had the power to employ and discharge the hands under his control. Other witnesses testified to the same facts as to Holmes's power to employ and discharge hands. The defendant introduced testimony tending to show that Holmes did not have this power, but that it was lodged with Monroe, the master car-builder.

The first error assigned by appellant is as follows: "The verdict and judgment are contrary to law and unsupported by the evidence, in that the facts clearly show that Holmes, foreman, etc., did not sustain the relation of vice-principal to appellee, but was only a fellow-servant in respect to the alleged negligence whereby appellee received his injuries. And the facts clearly show that appellee did not rely on the promises of Holmes to protect him, but on the promise of Colby, a volunteer and fellow-servant, and Morris, a switchman and fellow-servant; and that his injuries were not the proximate result of appellant's negligence, but were the result of appellee's own want of due care, or of the negligence of his fellow-servants, for which appellant is not legally liable."

The evidence was sufficient to warrant the finding by the jury that Holmes had the power to employ and discharge hands, and the verdict is conclusive upon that point. The question therefore arises whether he is to be deemed the representative of the company, or a fellow-servant as to the employees under his control. Upon this question the authorities are conflicting. The courts of many of the states hold that it is only when an employee is charged with a duty, which by its implied contract a railroad company has undertaken toward its employee, such as furnishing a safe track and machinery, and the employment of careful and skillful servants, and the injury results to another employee from his neglect to perform that duty, that he is to be deemed the vice-principal of the company, and not the fellow-servant of the injured party. On the other hand, there are numerous cases which hold that the employee who has charge of a special department of a company's business, with power to employ and discharge the servants in his department, is not to be deemed the fellow-servant of those under his control. This rule has been recognized and followed by this court: *Wall v. Railway*, 4 Tex. Law Rev. 37. A servant who has the authority to employ other servants under his immediate supervision exercises an important function of his master, and has as full control over them as the master would have were he present, acting in person. The subordinate in such a case is in fact as much the servant of the agent who employs and controls him as he would be of the master were the latter discharging the functions of his agent. It would seem, therefore, that there is as much reason for holding that a servant assumes the risk of the master's negligence as for holding that he assumes the risk of the negligence of such a superior employee of his master. He may be presumed to exercise an influence over a co-employee who did not employ and has no power to discharge him, calculated to promote care and vigilance on part of the latter, which he cannot or dare not exercise towards one who has the right to terminate his employment. There is reason, therefore, for adhering to the previous ruling of this court, and for holding that if the plaintiff in this case was under the immediate control of Holmes, and Holmes had the power to employ and discharge the servants under him, Holmes is to be treated as the representative of the company, and not the fellow-servant of the plaintiff.

The court was asked by defendant to give the following charge: "If you find that Holmes was not a fellow-servant of plaintiff, but was the representative of the company, but you further find that although Holmes promised to watch for plaintiff, yet he abandoned the watch with plaintiff's knowledge, and then plaintiff continued the work, relying on the promises of Colby and a switchman to keep a lookout and protect him, and Colby and the switchman were fellow-servants of the plaintiff, and plaintiff was hurt by failure of Colby and the switchman not keeping proper watch, then you will find

for defendant." The court refused to give said charge as requested, but of his own motion added, by interlineation, after
the word "knowledge," the following: "And that plaintiff
knew or ought to have known that Holmes would not by himself or others protect him," and then gave the said charge as
so modified. The refusal to give the charge as requested and
the modification are assigned as error. We think the court
did not err in its ruling, for two reasons. In the first place,
while there was evidence showing that Holmes had left the
car under which plaintiff was working, and that plaintiff
knew this, there was none to show that he, plaintiff, knew that
he had abandoned the watch. The plaintiff testified that
when Holmes left the car he went across the track to some
others about fifty feet distant, to rub off some marks upon
them. It was not shown that he could not have watched as
effectually in that position as when he was standing near the
car. Plaintiff testified distinctly that he relied both upon
Holmes and Colby to protect him, and did not at any time
say that he ceased to rely upon Holmes. In the second place,
even if it had appeared that Holmes had abandoned the
watch with plaintiff's knowledge, the jury might reasonably
have concluded that although plaintiff knew it, he still relied
upon him as his superior, who had promised his protection, to
take other steps to secure the object, as effectual as his own
personal attention to the matter.

An objection is made to the mode in which the modification
of the charge was made. In *Southern C. P. Mfg. Co.* v. *Bradley*, 52 Tex. 587, it is said that the judge should give or refuse
a charge asked in the very terms of the request, and that if he
wishes to give it with a qualification, he should rewrite the instruction, embodying the qualification. We think, however,
that when a modification is appended to a requested charge
in such a manner as to show the precise charge asked, and
the precise modification, and the whole is intelligible to the
jury, that no injury results to the party making the request.
The action of the court shows that the charge as requested is
refused, and if the modification be proper there is no good
ground of complaint. It would be different, however, should
the trial judge insert words in a request for instructions without showing in a statement connected therewith the precise
change he had made. Otherwise a charge not requested might
appear in the record as being given at the request of a party
who was prejudiced by the instruction.

The third error assigned is, that "the court erred in charging that 'if plaintiff relied and acted, not on orders and promises of Holmes, but those of other employees of defendant, then he could not recover, such other employees being fellow-servants of his. But if plaintiff received and acted upon Holmes's orders and promises, and was hurt in consequence of Holmes's negligence, without his own negligence contributing to it, he could recover if otherwise entitled, notwithstanding he may have asked and received promises of other employees also,' because said charge was on the weight of evidence, and assumed that Holmes was a vice-principal, and because said charge was misleading, and not warranted by the pleadings or evidence, and in effect authorized the jury to find for appellee, although he may have in fact relied on the promises of Colby or Morris to keep watch; and the court erred in refusing special charge No. 2 asked by appellant."

If that portion of the charge of the court which is copied into the assignment stood alone, it would be manifestly erroneous. But we are of opinion that, taking the charge as a whole, the jury could not have been misled by the language quoted. The entire charge put the plaintiff's case upon the hypothesis that he could not recover unless at the time of the injury he was under the control of Holmes, and acting under his orders, and Holmes had the power to employ and discharge the servants under him. After having so clearly and unmistakably stated this as a proposition of law, the jury could not have been misled by the failure to repeat it in presenting every distinct phase of the case made by the testimony upon other issues.

The special charge No. 2, which is referred to in the assignment, is as follows: "If you believe, from the evidence, that plaintiff, when he went to work under the car, relied on the assurances of protection made by Colby, the yard-master, and a switchman, and Colby was not in a common employment with plaintiff, but promised to look out for plaintiff, at his request, then you will find for defendant."

There was no error in refusing the charge. If Holmes promised to protect plaintiff while at work under the car, and if plaintiff relied upon such promise, and Holmes failed to do this, we think it is no excuse for his failure that plaintiff, in the abundance of his caution, asked others to watch also, and see that he was not injured.

There is no error in the judgment, and it is affirmed.

FELLOW-SERVANTS, WHO ARE, AND WHO ARE NOT: *Murray* v. *St. Louis etc. R'y Co.*, 98 Mo. 573; 14 Am. St. Rep. 661, and note; *Wilson* v. *Dunreath etc. Co.*, 77 Iowa, 429; 14 Am. St. Rep. 304, and note.

MASTER AND SERVANT. — Liability of master for injuries to his servant, occasioned by the negligence or fault of a fellow-servant: *Wilson* v. *Dunreath etc. Co.*, 77 Iowa, 429; 14 Am. St. Rep. 304, and particularly note. Employers are liable to under-servants for the negligence of superintendents and representatives acting within the scope of their employment: *Denver etc. R. R. Co.* v. *Driscoll*, 12 Col. 520; 13 Am. St. Rep. 243.

JURY TRIAL — INSTRUCTIONS. — When a series of instructions upon the same subject are correct as a whole, errors in one or more of such instructions are harmless: *Indianapolis etc. R'y Co.* v. *Watson*, 114 Ind. 20; 5 Am. St. Rep. 578; *Shively* v. *Cedar Rapids etc. R'y Co.*, 74 Iowa, 169; 7 Am. St. Rep. 471; *Hanscom* v. *Drullard*, 79 Cal. 235; *Hamburg etc. Co.* v. *Gotham*, 127 Ill. 599; for an erroneous instruction which has been given may be cured by another instruction correctly stating the law: *People* v. *Clary*, 72 Cal. 59.

ELLIOTT *v.* WESTERN UNION TELEGRAPH CO.

[75 TEXAS 18.]

TELEGRAPH COMPANY, LIABILITY OF. — Where one party writes a dispatch and gives it to another to send, who instead of sending it writes another dispatch, and signs and sends it without notifying the company that it is sent on behalf of the first party, the latter cannot hold the company liable in damages for loss sustained through failure of delivery.

Moore and Hart, for the appellants.

Stemmons and Field, for the appellee.

GAINES, A. J.   This suit was brought by appellants against appellee to recover damages for the failure of the later to deliver a message alleged to have been deposited with the company's agent for transmission to St. Louis.

One of the plaintiffs testified that they were operating a sawmill, and that having broken their saw, he went to the town of Belden and engaged one Stewart, a member of the firm of Galloway and Stewart, merchants, to order them a new saw from St. Louis by telegraph. Stewart testified that he wrote a dispatch on white paper, addressed to the Caruth and Byrnes Hardware Company, St. Louis, Missouri, directing them to ship at once to Galloway and Stewart a saw of the description desired, and signed it in the name of his firm; that one McAllen, the traveling salesman of the St. Louis company, being in town, he handed the dispatch to McAllen, gave him the money to pay the charges, and went with him to the telegraph-office. Upon cross-examination he said that he remained at the door and saw McAllen go to the operator's desk, where he remained some time, but did not see him deliver the telegram. The operator testified that McAllen wrote another dispatch for transmission, signed by himself, ordering the saw to be sent to Galloway and Stewart, and that he did not deliver to him the dispatch about which Stewart testified. The testimony showed that neither dispatch was delivered to the parties addressed.

Upon this evidence the court charged the jury to find for defendant, and in so charging we think there was no error. It appears that in delivering the dispatch written by himself, McAllen was not acting under the authority given him by Stewart, which was to cause to be transmitted the message written by the latter. Being the agent of the company who was addressed, he probably deemed it best to make the order himself. He may have had a personal interest in transmitting it in his own name, since his commissions may have depended upon a sale made through himself. At all events, he was not authorized to send that dispatch for Stewart, and it was not therefore the dispatch of plaintiff, though intended for his benefit. In the case of the *Western Union Tel. Co.* v. *Broesche*, 72 Tex. 654, 13 Am. St. Rep. 843, the person who delivered the message for transmission was authorized to do so by the plaintiff, who was immediately present when it was delivered.

The damages claimed were for the losses accruing by reason of the plaintiffs' mill lying idle for want of the saw. The face of the message did not advise the defendant that it was intended for the benefit of plaintiffs, or that such persons existed, and there was no evidence that defendant's agent knew of the fact that the mill was idle for want of the saw. Therefore plaintiffs could not have recovered damages for the loss resulting from this source. If they had proved that the message written by Stewart was delivered to the agent, they could, under the evidence, have recovered only the money paid for its transmission.

There is no error in the judgment, and it is affirmed.

TELEGRAPHS. — A telegraph company need not be informed that the sender of a telegram is acting as the agent of another, where it is not shown that the company would have acted differently had it known of the agency of the sender: *Western Union Tel. Co.* v. *Broesche*, 72 Tex. 654; 13 Am. St. Rep. 843.

AGENCY. — THE PRINCIPAL MAY SUE upon a contract made by his agent, without giving notice of his interest, although the other party supposed the agent was acting solely for himself: *Foster* v. *Smith*, 2 Cold. 474; 88 Am. Dec. 604.

MORRIS *v.* BALKHAM.

[75 TEXAS, 111.]

EXECUTIONS — VARIANCE BETWEEN EXECUTION AND JUDGMENT. — An execution cannot be amended, after a sale under it, by the substitution of the true christian name of the defendant, as shown by the judgment, instead of another inserted by mistake, so as to validate the sale; and this rule prevails whether notice is given to the execution defendant or his heirs, or not.

ORDER AMENDING AN EXECUTION AFTER DEATH OF JUDGMENT DEFENDANT, without notice to his heirs, is a nullity.

EVIDENCE — ADMISSIBILITY OF, TO PROVE NOTICE. — A party claiming as a homestead property purchased at a sale under execution cannot show, as against such purchaser, that the homestead claimant's attorney gave notice that it was a homestead prior to the sale.

Gammage and Gammage, for the appellants.

Greenwood and Greenwood, for the appellees.

GAINES, A. J. This suit was brought by appellant Adella Morris, joined by her husband, to recover of Hattie A. Balkham, F. C. Bailey, E. M. Fowler, J. A. Reddick, and Sam Berliner a half interest in a lot in the city of Palestine, and for partition. The husband of Hattie A. Balkham was made a party defendant. Fowler, Reddick, and Berliner disclaimed title to the premises in controversy. Bailey appears to have been a tenant of Mrs. Balkham, and in the possession of the lot.

Both parties claim title under a conveyance of the lot in controversy, made February 4, 1881, by C. A. and Hattie Calhoun to H. W. Van Hagen. At that time the appellee Hattie A. Balkham was Van Hagen's wife. He died September 12, 1886, leaving plaintiff Adella Morris, his daughter by a former wife, his sole surviving descendant. On the 9th of December, 1884, Fowler, Reddick, and Berliner recovered a judgment in the district court of Bexar County against Charles Baker and H. W. Van Hagen for the sum of $625.80, and costs. On the twenty-seventh day of March, 1886, a *pluries* execution was issued by the clerk of that court to the sheriff of Anderson County against the property of Charles Baker and William Van Hagen, purporting to be upon a judgment corresponding in all respects with that above mentioned, except that William Van Hagen was named as defendant therein instead of H. W. Van Hagen.

Under this execution, the lot in controversy was levied upon and sold by the sheriff as the property of William Van Hagen, and was bid in for the sum of five hundred ·dollars by the plaintiffs in execution. The sheriff made them a deed purporting to convey all the right, title, and interest of William Van Hagen in the property. H. W. Van Hagen's christian name is shown to have been Hiram Watkins. After the death of Van Hagen, a motion was made by the plaintiffs in the judgment (who were also purchasers at the sheriff's sale), in the district court of Bexar County, to amend the execution under which the lot was sold, so as to make it appear as an execution against the property of H. W. Van Hagen instead of William Van Hagen. The motion contains no prayer for notice to Van Hagen's heirs, and none appears to have been given. Yet, on the seventh day of May, 1887, the court granted the motion, and entered an order amending the execution. On the same day, Fowler, Reddick, and Berliner conveyed the lot to defendant Hattie A. Balkham for the consideration of two hundred dollars.

Such being the evidence, the court gave judgment for the defendants. In this we think there was error. We are aware that many courts have gone very far in allowing amendments of executions, and we have found one decision which holds that an execution may be amended after a sale under it by the substitution of the true christian name of the defendant, as shown by the judgment, instead of another inserted by mistake: *Vogt* v. *Ticknor*, 48 N. H. 242. But in *Battle* v. *Guedry*, 58 Tex. 111, it was held by this court that an execution against P. B. Clements was not supported by a judgment against J. P. Clements, and a sale under such an execution did not pass the title to property owned by the latter. We think it requires no argument to show that the ruling of our court is correct. In the present case the judgment was against H. W. Van Hagen, the execution against the property of William Van Hagen, and the sheriff's deed purports to convey the lot in controversy as the property of William Van Hagen.

The only difference between the case last cited and that now before us is, that in the present case there was an attempt to cure the irregularity by amending the execution after the sale. The order was entered without notice to the heirs of the defendant in execution, who was then dead. It was a nullity. In our judgment, if the proper notice had been given, it would not have been competent for the court to allow the amendment, so as to give validity to the sale. It would be an unjust rule to permit an execution against B, under which his title in a certain parcel of real estate had been sold and conveyed by the sheriff, to be amended so as to make it an execution against A, and to give to the sale the effect of passing the title of the latter in the property. We conclude that the evidence-showed the title of H. W. Van Hagen did not pass by the sheriff's sale, and that the court should have given the plaintiff Adella Morris judgment for one half of the property in controversy, with a decree for partition.

It is also claimed by appellants that the title to the lot in controversy did not pass by the sheriff's sale, because it was the homestead of H. W. Van Hagen and his wife. It had been their homestead, but Mrs. Balkham testified that before the sale was made they had abandoned it as a place of residence, and had moved to San Antonio, with the intention never to return to it. This evidence was uncontradicted, and hence the court did not err in holding that it had ceased to be a homestead.

Neither was there error in refusing to allow plaintiffs to prove that when the lot was sold an attorney representing H. W. Van Hagen and wife gave notice that it was their homestead. Van Hagen and wife could not thus make evidence for themselves, nor can the plaintiff, as the heir of H. W. Van Hagen, avail herself of the declarations of his attorney as evidence in the case.

For the error pointed out, the judgment is reversed and the cause remanded.

———

EXECUTIONS — AMENDMENT. — In some of the states the rule is, that executions may be amended in matters of form, but not in matters of substance: *Hall* v. *Lackmond*, 50 Ark. 113; 7 Am. St. Rep. 84, and particularly note.

EXECUTIONS DEFECTIVE IN PARTICULARS that may affect the title to property sold thereunder cannot be amended after such sale so as to validate it: *McKay* v. *Paris Exch. Bank*, 75 Tex. 181; *post*, p. 884.

———

WILLIS AND BROTHER *v.* HEATH.
[75 TEXAS, 124.]

GARNISHMENT. — MAKER OF NEGOTIABLE PROMISSORY NOTE cannot be charged in garnishment before its maturity, on the ground that he knew when he executed it that it was the purpose of the payee to place the fund beyond the reach of his creditors.

GARNISHMENT — ATTORNEY'S FEE ALLOWED GARNISHEE. — The court may allow the garnishee a reasonable attorney's fee, and, in the absence of proof that the amount fixed by the court was too much, it will be deemed conclusive.

M. L. Morris, for the appellants.

Peteet and Crosby, for the appellee.

GAINES, A. J.   Appellants, being judgment creditors of R. H. Heath and B. D. Wilson, partners composing the firm of Heath and Wilson, sued out a writ of garnishment, and caused it to be served upon appellee.   Appellee answered, denying that he owed the defendants, and that he had any of their effects in his possession.   Appellants contested his answer, alleging in substance that after the accrual of the indebtedness of Heath and Wilson to them, B. D. Wilson sold his interest in the partnership effects to his partner, R. H. Heath, who, in consideration therefor, executed to him four promissory notes for the sum, in the aggregate, of $2,500, with the appellee as his surety; that before the last note fell due, appellee purchased of R. H. Heath the storehouse which had formerly belonged to Heath and Wilson, and the stock of goods belonging to R. H. Heath, and in the transaction assumed the payment of the balance due upon the notes, which amounted to $1,735.35, and that for this sum appellee executed to Mrs. M. F. Wilson, the wife of B. D. Wilson, his promissory note, due two years after date.   This last note was alleged to have been executed on the day before the judgment in favor of appellants, against Heath and Wilson, was rendered. It was also alleged that at the time of its execution R. H. Heath and B. D. Wilson were insolvent, and that it was made for the purpose of hindering, delaying, and defrauding the creditors in the collection of their debts.   The pleading contesting the answer was excepted to, on the ground that the debt sought to be reached was evidenced by a negotiable promissory note, and was therefore not subject to the writ of garnishment, and the exception was sustained, and judgment rendered for the garnishee.

The allegations in appellants' pleading must be taken most strongly against them, and it must therefore be assumed that the note upon which the appellee is sought to be charged was a negotiable instrument.   The appellants' counsel in their brief present the case upon that theory, and concede the general rule that the maker of a negotiable promissory note cannot be subjected to the payment of the same under the writ of garnishment before its maturity.   They claim, however, that the present case is an exception to the rule, because the note in controversy was made negotiable and payable to Mrs.

Wilson for the purpose of defrauding Wilson's creditors. We find no authority for the doctrine for which appellants contend. It is universally held that although ordinarily the garnishee can be held liable under the writ only to the extent of his liability to the debtor of the plaintiff, yet he may be charged with property fraudulently transferred to him by such debtor, although the latter has no cause of action against him.

This is but an application of the familiar doctrine that a fraudulent conveyance is void as to creditors, though good as between the parties. This doctrine is applicable in a case where the garnishee holds the effects of the debtor under a fraudulent assignment or transfer. The maker of a negotiable promissory instrument is not subject to be charged by a writ of garnishment, because if this be done, he is liable to be made to pay the same debt twice over; and we find no authority for holding that the rule is different when he executes the note with the knowledge that it is the purpose of the payee to place the fund beyond the reach of his creditors.

If the maker of a promissory note may be charged in garnishment before its maturity, on the ground that he knew when he executed it that it was the purpose of the payee to place the fund beyond the reach of his creditors, we see no reason why one who pays a debt with a knowledge of a like intent on part of his creditor may not be compelled to pay again at the suit of the creditors of him to whom he has made the payment. The giving of a negotiable promissory note for a debt is a mode of payment.

The case of *Wood* v. *Bodwell*, 12 Pick. 268, is in point, and holds that the maker of negotiable instrument, under such circumstances, is not subject to be charged under the writ of garnishment. In states where the statutes permit the garnishment of a debt evidenced by negotiable instruments, a different rule may prevail. So, also, if after the maturity of a note it be shown that it is in the hands of one who has received it with a knowledge that the payee had transferred with intent to defraud his creditors, the maker may be held chargeable. There a different principle applies. We conclude that appellee was not chargeable in this case.

We have treated the transaction as if the note had been payable to B. D. Wilson instead of his wife.

We find no error in the action of the court in allowing the garnishee an attorney's fee for preparing his answer. In

Johnson v. *Blanks*, 68 Tex. 495, we held that such an allowance in such a case was proper, and that an amount fixed by the court, in the absence of testimony showing that it was too much, would be deemed conclusive.

We find no error in the judgment, and it is affirmed.

GARNISHMENT. — Negotiable paper is not subject to garnishment before maturity: *Hubbard* v. *Williams*, 1 Minn. 54; 55 Am. Dec. 66, and note 68–70; *Davis* v. *Pawlette*, 3 Wis. 300; 62 Am. Dec. 690.

WHEN ATTORNEY'S FEE WILL NOT BE ALLOWED TO GARNISHEE. — After the answer of a garnishee is filed, and an issue is made thereon, he thereafter stands as any other litigant, and cannot be allowed an attorney's fee: *Bernheim* v. *Brogan*, 66 Miss. 184.

MISSOURI PACIFIC RAILWAY COMPANY *v.* JONES.

[75 TEXAS, 15L.]

MASTER AND SERVANT — RAILWAY, LIABILITY OF TO PERSON INJURED IN ITS SERVICE, BUT EMPLOYED BY ANOTHER CORPORATION. — A servant in the general employment and pay of one railway, but engaged in special services for another, through an agreement between the two railways, may recover of the railway for whom such special services are performed for an injury received by reason of its negligence.

RAILROADS — DUTY TO EMPLOYEE. — IT IS NEGLIGENCE in a railway company to leave holes between the cross-ties on its track, after being warned of the danger, and a car-coupler in its employ, who is injured while the track is in such condition, without negligence on his part, may recover, and if the evidence as to his contributory negligence in the matter is conflicting, the question of negligence should be submitted to the jury.

VERDICT FOR SIX THOUSAND DOLLARS for the loss of one hand, caused by the negligence of a railway company toward its employee, is not excessive.

Finch and Thompson, for the appellant.

D. W. Humphreys, for the appellee.

HOBBY, J.   It is urged by the appellant that the petition shows no cause of action against it, and that it does show that plaintiff below was not in its employ, and that the defendant owed him no duty.

The averments, showing appellant's liability, were, that one Phaling, the general yard-master, employed plaintiff, and placed him at work in the yards of the Missouri Pacific Railway Company, to couple and uncouple cars for said company; that this was the result of an agreement between the appellant and the receivers of the Texas Pacific Railway Company, by which the latter were to furnish a crew to make up trains for the Missouri Pacific Railway Company in its yards; that plaintiff and Phaling, the yard-master, received their pay from the receivers, but that plaintiff was at the time working for the appellant, and he was injured without fault on his part, but by the negligence of appellant in failing to keep its yard in repair, and allowing its road-bed and track at the place of injury to become dangerous, by causing its servants to throw out the dirt between the cross-ties, thereby leaving deep and dangerous holes, which plaintiff did not see, and which by stepping into, in attempting to couple the cars of appellant, the injury was done.

These averments were sufficient to establish the relation of master and servant by inference from the service and connection of the companies, and showed the liability of appellant: *Gulf etc. R'y Co.* v. *Dorsey*, 66 Tex. 152.

The second assignment is, that the evidence did not show that plaintiff was in the employ of appellant, nor did it show that the latter owed him any duty as an employee; that if any liability was shown, it was upon the part of the Texas Pacific Railway Company, in whose employ plaintiff was at the time. The substance of appellant's contention under this assignment is, that the case made by appellee showed him to be in the service and pay of one company while recovering damages from another for an accident occurring on its premises, with no proof to sustain the denied averments of a contract by which he was shown to be rightfully there. Nor was there proof that appellant controlled the cars where he was at work.

Upon this branch of the case the facts were that appellee was at the time of, and several months prior to, the injury, at work for appellant in its yards at Fort Worth, Texas. He was employed by Phaling, the yard-master, and received his pay from the Texas Pacific Railway Company. Appellee's duties were to stay in the yard and make up trains. The track on which the injury occurred was kept in repair by appellant. The appellant had control of the yard. It had the track on which appellee was injured dug out between the ties about a day before appellee was hurt; holes were opened out about where he was injured, and there were no ties to put in them. The road-master was informed of the danger, but the track was left in that condition.

The facts show that appellee was the general servant of the Texas Pacific, and the special servant of the appellant. He

performed special services for the latter while the general servant of the former, and while so performing this special service he was the servant of appellant at the time.

There was no proof of an express contract showing the
relation of master and servant between appellant and appellee, but the evidence of the service performed by Jones for the
Missouri Pacific Railway Company, and the connection between the two companies, authorized the inference that this
relation did exist.

In the case of *Railway Co. v. Dorsey*, cited in *Gulf etc. R'y
Co. v. Dorsey*, 66 Tex. 152, the plaintiff was employed to serve
the several companies in their respective yards. It was held
that he was the servant of the one in whose yard he was when
injured.

The proof, we think, shows that by virtue of some arrangement, the precise nature of which could not be ascertained,
between the Texas Pacific and the Missouri Pacific railway
companies, it was the duty of the appellee, who received his
pay from the former company, to switch and couple and uncouple the cars in the yard of the appellant and on its tracks,
over which the appellant had exclusive control, and whose
duty it was to keep said track in repair; and that at the time
of performing these services for the Missouri Pacific he was
injured by reason of its negligence. While engaged in this
service for appellant, with its knowledge and under its agreement that the appellee should perform such service, he was
the servant of the appellant. It was immaterial that he was
not paid directly by appellant. The inference was authorized
that appellant paid the Texas Pacific for his services, which
would be tantamount to a payment to him. The payment we
believe to be immaterial under the facts of this case. He had
for a long time prior to the injury worked for the appellant,
and his labor was accepted up to the time of the injury.
These facts made appellee the servant of appellant in the
transaction in which the damage was sustained, by reason of
the service performed.

The principles announced in *Gulf etc. R'y Co. v. Dorsey*, 66
Tex. 152, fully authorize the recovery in this case against the
Missouri Pacific Railway Company, upon the ground of the
liability of said company to appellee. To the same effect is
the case of *Varny* v. *B. C. R. & M. R. C.*, 42 Iowa, 248.

In the case of *Snow* v. *Housatonic R. R. Co.*, 8 Allen, 441,
85 Am. Dec. 720, which is in many of its features analogous

to the case under consideration, Snow was in the employ and pay of the Western Railway Company and operating its cars, and he was allowed to recover damages from the Housatonic Railroad Company by reason of its negligence in permitting a hole to remain in its road-bed, into which Snow stepped while coupling (as in this case) a moving car of the Western railway which was passing over the road of the Housatonic railroad.

The next assignment is to the effect that the evidence did not show appellant guilty of negligence which ought to render it liable, and that appellee's want of care produced the injury complained of.

The negligence of the appellant is very clearly shown by the evidence to have consisted in leaving the holes between the cross-ties on the track where the injury occurred, and this, too, after being warned of the danger. It is not made to appear that the appellee had any knowledge of this defect in the track, and it was shown by the evidence that he could not have seen these trenches without stooping down at the time, and this could not be done by reason of the moving cars which prevented it. There was testimony that it was the duty of the appellee to remain in between the cars after going in on the track, and try to effect a coupling. Some of the testimony of appellant's witnesses indicate that it was his duty to come out and signal the engineer if the coupling was not at first made. The evidence upon this point being conflicting as to whether appellee was himself negligent in the manner in which he conducted himself while endeavoring to make the coupling, as well as whether appellant's track was in such a condition for the proper discharge of the duties which devolved upon appellee by reason of his employment as he had a right to expect, and as it was appellant's duty to have it, were all questions of fact to be determined by the jury, and we cannot say that the evidence does not fully support their finding upon this point: *Houston etc. R'y Co.* v. *Randall*, 50 Tex. 260.

The fifth assignment is, that the verdict is excessive; it is for six thousand dollars. The injury was such as to deprive appellee of the use of one hand. In the case of *Galveston Oil Mills* v. *Malin*, 60 Tex. 651, the appellee had the flesh torn from his thumb and finger, and a verdict for four thousand dollars was held not to be excessive. In the case of *Union Pacific R'y Co.* v. *Young*, 19 Kan. 493, a verdict for ten thousand dollars was decided not to be excessive for the amputation of a hand. As has been repeatedly said, this is a question peculiarly within the jury's province to determine, and it is only where it is made to appear that they have abused the discretion lodged in them will their action be set aside on this ground.

We think there is no error in the judgment, and that it should be affirmed.

—————

EXCESSIVE VERDICTS: See cases cited in note to *Johnson* **v.** *Missouri Pacific R'y Co.*, 9 Am. St. Rep. 357; note to *Virginia etc. R'y Co.* **v.** *White*, 10 Am. St. Rep. 882. A verdict for two thousand three hundred dollars for an injury to a brakeman, twenty-three years of age, whereby he lost his right thumb, and had his next two fingers permanently injured and his arm weakened, is not excessive: *Whalen* v. *Chicago etc. R'y Co.*, 75 Iowa, 563. But a verdict for four thousand dollars for a slight injury is flagrantly excessive: *South Covington etc. R'y Co.* v. *Ware*, 84 Ky. 267.

TWO RAILWAY COMPANIES USING THE SAME TRACK, respective liability of each: *Killian* v. *Augusta etc. R. R. Co.*, 79 Ga. 234; 11 Am. St. Rep. 410; *Georgia R. R. etc. Co.* v. *Friddell*, 79 Ga. 489; 11 Am. St. Rep. 444.

CONTRIBUTORY NEGLIGENCE IS ORDINARILY A QUESTION OF FACT for the jury to determine: *Kansas City etc. R. R. Co.* v. *Kier*, 41 Kan. 661; 13 Am. St. Rep. 311, and note.

MASTER MUST SUPPLY SAFE APPLIANCES and instrumentalities for the use of his servants: *Fredenburg* v. *Northern etc. R'y Co.*, 114 N. Y. 582; 11 Am. St. Rep. 697, and note; *Southern Kansas R'y Co.* v. *Croker*, 41 Kan. 747; 13 Am. St. Rep. 320. So a railway company is liable to its servants for injuries caused by defects in its track and road-bed: *Snow* v. *Housatonic R. R. Co.*, 8 Allen, 441; 85 Am. Dec. 720, and note; *Meloy* v. *Chicago etc. R'y Co.*, 77 Iowa, 743; 14 Am. St. Rep. 325; or by defects in a railroad switch: *Clapp* v. *Minneapolis etc. R'y Co.*, 36 Minn. 6. A railroad company is not responsible for defects in its track caused by unusual weather or unprecedented floods, against which it could not have guarded by care and skill: *Missouri Pacific R'y Co.* v. *Mitchell*, 72 Tex. 171; *Columbus etc. R'y Co.* v. *Bridges*, 86 Ala. 448; 11 Am. St. Rep. 58, and note. Nor is one railroad company, sending its engineer with one of its engines to haul temporarily for another company the trains of the latter over the latter company's own line, responsible to such engineer for the bad condition of the track, unless it appears that the company knew of the defects in the track, and concealed its information: *Dunlap* v. *Richmond etc. R. R. Co.*, 81 Ga. 136.

McKay v. Paris Exchange Bank.

[75 Texas, 181.]

Judgments and Executions — Amendment. — Judgments or executions, defective in particulars that may affect the title to property sold under them, cannot be amended after such sale so as to validate it.

Judgments and Executions — Amendment. — A judgment or execution, defective in substance, must be amended before a sale is made under it, and such defect cannot be removed by amendment, after the sale, for the benefit of the purchaser. If, however, the defect is one of form only, it may be disregarded, or supplied in any suit involving the question.

Sims and Wright, for the appellants J. M. Ezell and wife, Eugenia Ezell, and A. R. Covington.

H. McKay, T. J. Armistead, and T. J. Brown, for B. H. Epperson, Jr., and Janie Epperson.

H. McKay and T. J. Armistead, for Eugenia Epperson.

H. D. McDonald, and Burdett and Connor, for the appellees.

Henry, A. J. On the twenty-third day of November, 1877, the Paris Exchange Bank recovered a moneyed judgment against J. N. Norris, J. W. Hardison, and B. H. Epperson.

Epperson died in 1878, leaving an independent will, in which R. B. Epperson and J. P. Russell were appointed executors. The will was probated, and the executors qualified.

In 1879, said judgment being unpaid, the bank filed a petition in the district court to revive it against the executors. The judgment was revived accordingly, that part of it directing the issuance of execution being in the following words: "It is therefore ordered, adjudged, and decreed by the court that execution issue upon said judgment against J. P. Russell and R. B. Epperson, as the executors of the estate of B. H. Epperson, deceased, and against John N. Norris and J. W. Hardison."

On the ninth day of February, 1880, execution issued on the revived judgment against " J. P. Russell and R. B. Epperson, executors of the estate of B. H. Epperson," and commanding the sheriff "to cause to be made of the goods and chattels, lands and tenements, of J. P. Russell and R. B. Epperson, executors of the estate of B. H. Epperson," etc. Under this execution, the sheriff sold a number of tracts of land belonging to the estate of B. H. Epperson to W. B. Aikin, one of the appellees.

Subsequently, in May, 1880, an *alias* execution was issued upon the same judgment, commanding the sheriff to levy upon the goods, etc., "of J. P. Russell and R. B. Epperson, as the executors of the estate of B. H. Epperson."

This execution was levied upon a number of tracts of land "as the property of the estate of B. H. Epperson, deceased, J. P. Russell and R. B. Epperson being the executors of the will of B. H. Epperson.":

W. B. Aikin was the purchaser at the sale made under said execution of a part of these tracts. Deeds for the lands sold were made by the sheriff to the purchaser.

The same lands were subsequently sold under other executions against the estate of B. H. Epperson, to other parties.

Before the institution of the proceedings in this case the executors of B. H. Epperson had been removed, and while the administration of his estate was still unclosed, there was no administrator thereof.

The commencement of this cause was by a motion filed in the district court by the Paris Exchange Bank and W. B. Aikin, in the original cause of the bank against Norris, Hardison, and B. H. Epperson, to which the widow and children, and other claimants of the lands purchased by Aikin, were made parties defendant, to correct said judgment and executions. The motion, after describing the judgment and reciting the previous proceedings, charges that in entering the judgment of revival, "through a clerical misprision, said judgment directs such execution to be levied on the property of said executors instead of upon the property of said estate in their hands, and that when the executions were issued, by similar clerical misprisions, the same were made to run against the property of said executors instead of against the estate of said B. H. Epperson in their hands."

The motion concludes with a prayer "for an order amending said revived judgment and the said two executions, so as to make them conform to what they should have been."

All parties, except one, who were made defendants resisted the motion.

The court granted the relief prayed for, ordering that the revived judgment be amended so as to read: "That execution issue upon said judgment against the estate of B. H. Epperson in the hands of J. P. Russell and R. B. Epperson, his executors," etc.; and that both of said executions be so amended "as to run against the estate of B. H. Epperson in the hands of his executors."

From this judgment the defendants prosecute this appeal.

We are of the opinion that the exceptions to the motion should have been sustained, and the proceeding dismissed. If judgments or executions are defective in particulars that may affect the title to property sold under them, it is too late, after sales have been made, to amend either so as to have the effect of affecting such sales.

It is well understood that for a sheriff's deed to convey title to lands it must be supported by a valid judgment and execution. The prudent purchaser will always satisfy himself that they exist. If no judgment is found against the party whose property is being sold, or if the execution under which the sale is made does not direct the sale of such person's property, or if the execution is not supported by the judgment, the probable effect will be to deter bidders, and, by preventing competition, cause a sacrifice of the property sold.

When uncertainty in any of these respects is cast upon the proceedings, and the purchaser may thereby have been enabled to buy the property for a less price than it would have sold for if the proceedings had been proper and regular, we think it would be without warrant of law, and inequitable, to remove the difficulty for his benefit, and at the expense of the party whose property had been sold, and of his other creditors, if he had any.

Where the proceedings are amendable, we deem it to be the better rule to require it to be done before a sale has been made. When the defect is one of substance, it will not be contended that it may properly be removed for the benefit of the purchaser, after the sale, by amendment. If it is one of form only, we see no reason why it may not be disregarded or supplied in any suit in which the question may become involved.

In deciding this appeal, we do not intend to express any opinion as to the sufficiency or insufficiency of any of the proceedings under which the sales were made. Such questions will not be decided unless they shall arise in suits between the different claimants of the property.

The judgment will be reversed, and one rendered here dismissing the motion, at cost of appellees.

Executions, Amendment of. — An execution cannot be amended, after a sale under it, by the substitution of the true christian name of the defendant instead of a name inserted by mistake: *Morris* v. *Balkham*, 75 Tex. 111; *ante*, p. 874, and note. The decisions of the courts of Texas upon the subject of amendments to executions are exceedingly illiberal, and in conflict with the weight of authorities elsewhere: See Freeman on Executions, secs. 63–72.

GULF, COLORADO, AND SANTA FÉ RAILWAY COMPANY *v.* REDEKER.

[75 TEXAS, 310.]

MASTER AND SERVANT — LIABILITY FOR INJURY TO MINOR EMPLOYEE. — Where the master knowingly engages a minor in a dangerous employment, without the father's consent, and the minor is injured in such employment, the master is responsible to the father for the loss of his son's services resulting from such injury.

MASTER AND SERVANT — NECESSITY OF FATHER'S CONSENT TO MINOR'S EMPLOYMENT. — Where the parents live together, the mother's consent, unratified by the father, that their minor son may engage in a dangerous employment, will not justify the employer in making the contract, or in retaining the minor in such employment after knowledge of his minority; and the employer assumes the risk of answering to the father for an injury to the minor, by thus retaining him after notice of the minority.

MASTER AND SERVANT — NECESSITY OF FATHER'S CONSENT TO MINOR'S EMPLOYMENT. — General permission by a father that his minor son may follow railroading for a livelihood does not deprive the father of the right of specifying how and where he shall work; and the father's consent that the minor may be employed in one vocation will not justify the employer in changing the employment of the minor to a more hazardous vocation.

MASTER AND SERVANT — NECESSITY OF FATHER'S CONSENT TO MINOR'S EMPLOYMENT. — Where the employer knows of the minority of his employee, it is his duty to ascertain whether he has a parent, or is an apprentice, and to obtain consent of the parent or master before employing the minor; and it is not the duty of the father to give the employer notice that the employment of the minor is without his permission, in order to enable him to recover for an injury to his son, engaged in a dangerous employment.

NEW TRIAL WILL NOT BE GRANTED ON THE GROUND OF AN EXCESSIVE VERDICT, or because part of the amount was remitted, when the evidence is conclusive that the amount for which judgment was entered was clearly authorized.

Shepard and Miller, for the appellant.

William McLaury, and Ball and McCart, for the appellee.

COLLARD, J. This action was brought by the appellee, Louis Redeker, for loss of services of his minor son J. W. Redeker, expenses, etc., resulting from an injury received while the minor was engaged as an employee of the Gulf, Colorado, and Santa Fé Railway Company on a construction train in the capacity of a brakeman.

On the former appeal of the case, the court, Mr. Justice Gaines delivering the opinion, laid down the following propositions of law. He said: "There can be no question that if the injury was the result of negligence, as alleged in the petition, the father was entitled to a judgment for loss of service and incidental expenses accruing from the injury: *H. & G. N. R'y Co.* v. *Miller*, 49 Tex. 322. We are also of opinion that where one knowingly engages a minor in a dangerous employment without the father's consent, and the minor is injured in such employment, he is responsible to the father for any consequent loss of the son's services to him. This is the rule when the minor is employed by another with the parent's consent, and, without such consent, is put by his employer at a more dangerous business, and thereby receives an injury, the father may recover; and we see no reason why one less stringent should be applied in case the minor is knowingly engaged in a perilous occupation in the first instance against the parent's will": *Gulf etc. R'y Co.* v. *Redeker*, 67 Tex. 191; 60 Am. Rep. 20.

The case was reversed and sent back for another trial, on the ground that it did not appear, from the testimony, that defendant knew that the son was a minor, or that it ought to have been known from his appearance. On the last trial, this evidence was supplied to this extent, that the fact was made known to the conductor before the injury,—the conductor who had employed him, under whom he served, and who had authority to employ and discharge such employees of the company.

On this appeal other questions are at issue. It was shown on the last trial that the father, plaintiff, was only occasionally at home; was employed as engineer on the same road, running between his home, at Fort Worth, and Temple; came in to Fort Worth in the evening, and would go right out again, lying over at Temple; stopped in Fort Worth just about long enough to go home; came in sleepy, and would lie down. Under these circumstances, the father being absent, young Redeker, by his mother's permission, left home to get a position on a railroad (had been idle about six weeks), having been, by his father's consent, previously at work as a fireman on the " T. P." road, both parents having consented that he should follow railroading for a living. He went to Houston, and was employed by defendant's agent as a wiper or watchman, and was, in a few days, put to work as a brakeman on a construction train. While employed as a watchman, he wrote his mother of the fact, but she did not know the character of his work had been changed. His father did not consent to his taking employment with defendant at all.

He says he did not know where he was or what he was doing; but his wife testified that when "he came home and found John had gone to Houston into the railway service, he was not to say angry, but he did n't like it."

The defendant asked the court to charge the jury that if the son went away from home with his mother's consent to enter into railway service, and no notice was given to defendant that he was not permitted to take employment as a brakeman, the plaintiff could not recover. The court refused to give the charge, and in the general charge, informed the jury that the father's consent to the employment was necessary. The court also told the jury that if he entered upon the service of defendant with his mother's consent, and his father was informed of it, and of the character of service he had taken, and then consented to or acquiesced in it, the verdict should be for defendant. The refusal of the court to give the requested charge is assigned as error. Appellant argues that the mother's consent was sufficient authority for defendant to employ the minor. If this is correct, the case must be reversed, because the court made the right to recover depend on the father's consent or acquiescence. We cannot agree to the legal proposition contended for by appellant.

In case the husband abandon the wife, and the necessities of the family demand it, she can act as a *feme sole* in the management and disposition or sale of the community property: *Wright* v. *Hays*, 10 Tex. 135; 60 Am. Dec. 200; *Cheek* v. *Bellows*, 17 Tex. 617; 67 Am. Dec. 683; *Fullerton* v. *Doyle*, 18 Tex. 12; *McAfee* v. *Robertson*, 41 Tex. 358; *Ann Bertha Lodge* v. *Leverton*, 42 Tex. 20; *Heidenhiemer* v. *Thomas*, 63 Tex. 289.

These authorities are cited in support of the doctrine contended for by appellant in this case, but an examination of them will show that two things must concur to give the wife the power to sell the community property: 1. There must be an abandonment by the husband of the wife of a permanent character, or such desertion or protracted absence as leaves to her the necessary responsibility of maintaining the family; 2. The necessity must exist to require the exercise of the power.

Under the facts of this case, it will be seen at once that this principle cannot be invoked to authorize Mrs. Redeker to act independently of her husband, if the question were one of her right to sell or charge community property; however, we do see from these cases that there are circumstances under which the wife may from necessity become the managing head of the family, and may so act without the concurrence of her husband. The husband is by law the managing head of the family, except in extreme cases. At common law he has the right to the custody of the children, except in cases of misconduct, or where the welfare of the child demands that such custody be taken from him and given to the mother, in which case the courts of proper jurisdiction will so direct: Shouler on Domestic Relations, secs. 246–248.

Where the parents live together, the father under our statute is made the natural guardian of the persons of the minor children; where they do not live together their rights are equal: R. S., arts. 2494, 2495.

The *status* of the father in the family is then fixed beyond controversy by our statute. As natural guardian of the children he has the right to their custody and control. We think that his authority and dominion are exclusive, at least to the extent that in general in all matters of such importance that the consent of the parent is required to legalize or justify an act or transaction with or concerning a minor, and the parents are living together, the consent of the father is required, and the consent of the mother will not suffice. There are no facts in this case that should make it an exception to the rule. The parents were living together; the father was necessarily absent from his home the most of his time, following his occupation of engineer, but stopping at home when his business did not call him away. We do not see any fact in the case that would change his ordinary relations with his family or affect his rights and privileges with them. Hence we conclude that Mrs. Redeker's permission to her son, if it had been full and complete, that he could take employment with defendant as a brakeman on a construction train, did not justify defendant in making the contract, or in retaining the minor in such employment after information that he was a minor. When it was ascertained that he was a minor, it was the duty of defendant to obtain the father's consent. Defendant's agent, who employed the minor and had authority to discharge him, knew his father and had been at his house; he took the risk for his company when he retained the son in his employ without the father's consent, after notice of the fact of minority.

By general permission plaintiff had consented that his son could follow railroading for a living, and had consented to his employment on another road as fireman. But it was in proof that firing was not as dangerous as braking, and that braking on a construction train was more dangerous than on a completed road. He had the right to direct his son in taking employment, and to select the kind of employment he should take; he had done so in the instance given. The general permission that he could follow railroading for a living did not deprive the father of the right of specifying how and where he should work.

Had the father actually consented that his son could be employed by defendant as a wiper, a watchman, or a fireman, and without his consent defendant had changed the employment to the more hazardous one of braking on a construction train, the change would have been at the peril of the company.

Plaintiff was not required to give defendant notice that his son was not permitted to serve as a brakeman. It is not shown that plaintiff knew he was in defendant's employ, and if he did, it was not his duty to give the notice. If plaintiff knew of the employment of his son as a brakeman, and acquiesced in it, his acquiescence would be equivalent to consent. The court instructed the jury that this was the law, and that if they should find such acquiescence the plaintiff could not recover. We think this was all that was required. The case did not call for a charge of notice to defendant.

In the opinion on the former appeal of this case the court said: "If the employer knows of the minority, it is his duty to ascertain whether the infant have a parent, or be an apprentice, and if so, to obtain the consent of such parent or the master before making the employment": *Gulf etc. R'y Co.* v. *Redeker*, 67 Tex. 192; 60 Am. Rep. 20. While the plaintiff may consent by acquiescence, no notice to defendant is required if defendant have knowledge of the facts. Defendant must obtain the consent of the parent.

The verdict was "for $3,032 damages and $826 interest." Pending the motion for new trial, plaintiff entered a *remittitur* for all the judgment but $2,100, when the motion for new trial was refused. Defendant claims that the court erred in overruling the motion for a new trial on the ground that the verdict was excessive, and that after plaintiff had remitted he was entitled to a new trial, because he was entitled to a verdict of a jury as to the amount due, and the effect of the court's action in accepting the *remittitur* of the excess was to deprive defendant of a trial by jury.

In support of this assignment of error we are cited to the
case of *Gulf etc. R'y Co.* v. *Coon,* 69 Tex. 730. That was a
suit for damages for injuries to the person, and it required the
intervention of a jury to estimate the damages, which were
left to a great extent to their sound judgment and discretion.
It was held that the law in such cases furnished no measure
by which the court could determine how much of the verdict
was excessive.

In *Thomas* v. *Womack,* 13 Tex. 585, the correct rule is given
as follows: "Where the law recognizes some fixed rules and
principles to regulate the measure of damages by which it
may be determined in how much the verdict is excessive, as
in actions on contracts and for torts done to property the value
of which may be ascertained by evidence, a *remittitur* of the
excess may be received in answer to a motion for a new trial
on the ground of excessive damages."

Where the verdict of a jury is required to fix the amount of
damages, and they fix them at an excessive amount, neither
the court nor counsel can tell how much should be deducted to
make the verdict a proper one, because the jury alone has the
right to fix such uncertain damages. In this case there was
evidence showing a proper account between the parties, the
principles of which are fixed by law. It was proved that the
father lost twenty-two months' wages of his son, and that these
wages were of a certain value, — at least $60 per month, — and
that the father got from his son before he was hurt $40 to $50
per month, — say $40, — which would for twenty-two months
be $880. The trip to Houston cost the parents $29; they paid
out for him at Houston $49; the father was receiving $75 to
$80 per month at the time of the injury, which he lost for six
months while necessarily waiting on his son, — say $75, the
least amount proved; he had to pay out at least $300 for
medicines and medical attention after his son was removed
from the hospital to Fort Worth; his mother nursed him
eighteen months, and it was shown that a nurse would have
cost $2 per day, or $60 per month, — $1,080 for the item of the
mother's nursing, of which if one half only be allowed, the
item would be $540. All of these items of expense, loss of
time, and outlay were necessary, and would not have occurred
but for the injury. So we see that the verdict might have
been for at least $2,248, and that the evidence furnishes the
means of ascertaining the amount at the lowest estimate. The
remittitur was for $148 more than was necessary; plaintiff

remitted more than could have been demanded. We do not see that for that reason the verdict so reduced should not be allowed to stand.

Our conclusion is, the court did not err in refusing a new trial because the verdict was excessive, or because an amount of it was remitted, since the evidence is conclusive that at least the amount for which judgment was entered was clearly authorized by the evidence.

We conclude the judgment of the lower court should be affirmed.

____

MASTER AND SERVANT — PARENT AND CHILD. — To sustain an action by a father for an injury to a minor child employed in a dangerous business without his consent, defendant must be averred and proved to have known. of the minority: *Gulf etc. R'y Co.* v. *Redeker*, 67 Tex. 191; 60 Am. Rep. 20.

EXCESSIVE DAMAGES. — The appellate court will not reverse a judgment because of alleged excessive damages, unless the amount appears to be excessive and outrageous at first blush: *Ohio etc. R. Co.* v. *Judy*, 120 Ind. 397; *Louisville etc. R. R. Co.* v. *Mitchell*, 87 Ky. 327. So a verdict for $1,700 for damages to a farm of 318 acres cannot be called excessive, where some witness testify that the farm was damaged §10 per acre: *Dudley* v. *Minnesota etc. R'y Co.*, 77 Iowa, 408; nor is $6,750 damages for seduction excessive, in the absence of passion or prejudice on the part of the jury: *Baird* v. *Boehner*, 77 Iowa, 623.

____

EQUITABLE LIFE INSURANCE CO. *v.* HAZLEWOOD.

[75 TEXAS, 338.]

LIFE INSURANCE. — WARRANTIES BY APPLICANT for life insurance will be strictly applied, and misstatements therein, made innocently, by mistake, inadvertance, or from false information afforded by others, are fatal to the contract, but such warranties will be strictly applied and limited to the precise undertaking of the party making it.

LIFE INSURANCE — WARRANTIES. — It is only by express agreement that an applicant for life insurance can be held to have warranted that the answers given by him as true were correctly written down and reported.

LIFE INSURANCE — WARRANTIES, CONSTRUCTION OF CONTRACT CONTAINING. — Where the signature of an applicant for life insurance is at the beginning of an examination containing warranties, instead of at its close, this indicates a means of identifying him as the person making the application, rather than as binding him as a party for the truth of the contents of the paper containing answers, partly written by himself and partly by the examiner, and it is therefore error to assume that he "had his answers to said questions put down in writing by the medical examiner," and to direct a verdict for the insurer, if the jury should find the written answers were in "any respect" untrue.

LIFE INSURANCE — WARRANTIES — CONSTRUCTION OF CONTRACT. — An applicant for life insurance who signs an examination containing warranties at the beginning instead of at the close cannot be held as a warrantor for the truth of answers as written by the examiner, unless he knows that they are incorrectly written. In the latter event it becomes his duty to see that the proper corrections are made, and if he fails to do so, although not bound by a warranty, he is estopped from disputing them as written.

LIFE INSURANCE — WARRANTIES. — APPLICANT FOR LIFE INSURANCE, when answering questions of warranty, has the right to rely upon information given him by the agent of the company.

LIFE INSURANCE — WAGERING POLICY — INSURABLE INTEREST. — One not having an insurable interest in the life of another cannot take and hold by an assignment a policy upon the life of such other, and a creditor can only take and hold such policy by assignment to an extent sufficient to secure his debt, and the same rule applies to a beneficiary named in the policy, but who has no insurable interest.

LIFE INSURANCE — INSURABLE INTEREST — DESIGNATION OF BENEFICIARY. — An assignment of a valid policy to one having no insurable interest in the life insured, or the naming of such a one in the policy as beneficiary, does not invalidate it. In such a case the assignee or beneficiary may collect and apply the proceeds to the extinguishment of his debt, if he have one, and such sums as he may have disbursed for the purpose of keeping the policy alive, and the surplus must be paid to the heirs of the insured.

LIFE INSURANCE — INSURABLE INTEREST. — Brothers and sisters have an insurable interest in the lives of each other.

LIFE INSURANCE — INSURABLE INTEREST — LIMITATION OF AMOUNT. — When insurance is obtained by a person on his own life, and made payable, originally or by assignment, to another having no or only a limited insurable interest in his life, the amount for which insurance may be taken out cannot be limited.

LIFE INSURANCE — INSURABLE INTEREST — LIMITATION OF AMOUNT. — When insurance is not contracted for by the person whose life is insured, but by a creditor in his own name, it is immaterial what amount of insurance is contracted for, as no more is collectible than an amount sufficient to pay the debt and disbursements in keeping the policy alive, including interest on both.

Maxey, Lightfoot, and Denton, and Hodges and Lane, for the appellant.

J. A. Templeton, E. B. Perkins, and Edward H. Bennett, for the appellee.

HENRY, A. J.   Upon the application of Henry C. Hazlewood, appellant, in August, 1887, issued its policy upon his life, payable " to Robert R. Hazlewood, if living; if not, then to his brother Henry C. Hazlewood, for the sum of fifteen thousand dollars, payable at the death of the said Henry C."

H. C. Hazlewood was a younger brother of R. R. Hazlewood. He died in March, 1888, aged then about twenty-eight years.

Appellee, beginning with the year 1881, and between that time and the date of the application for the insurance, had advanced to the said Henry C. various sums of money, amounting to about twelve hundred dollars, for which the said Henry acknowledged an indebtedness.

On the back of the application for the insurance, and just above the signatures of both of said Hazlewoods, is a printed agreement in the following words: " It is hereby agreed that all the foregoing statements and answers, as well as those made or to be made to the society's medical examiner, are warranted to be true, and are offered to the society as a consideration of the contract."

In the body of and on the back of the application, and above said signatures, there are a number of questions and answers relating to the risk. Attached to the application is another paper styled "Medical Examiner's Report," at the beginning of which appears the signature of Henry Clay Hazlewood, and at the end of it the name of the medical examiner.

Between the two signatures there appear a great number and variety of questions and answers relating to the history of the said Henry, and of his ancestors and collateral kindred, and to his physique, system, general health, record, habits, and environment. The answers are usually "Yes" or "No," and from the space allowed for them in the form used it is evident that they are required to be monosyllabic.

Some of the answers are evidently made by the medical examiner, and some by the subject of the examination. There is nothing but the nature of the answers to distinguish those of the medical examiner from those of the subject of the examination, and it is not easy to distinguish, in some instances, by which one the answer was really made.

While many of the questions answered by the witness relate to facts necessarily within his knowledge, and to which he evidently ought to have been able to give categorical and truthful answers, there are others seemingly required to be and in fact answered by him, about which he could not, in the nature of things, have had exact and positive knowledge, and about which it is not probable that he could have expressed himself satisfactorily by simply answering " Yes " or " No."

All answers were written down by the medical examiner.

The policy sets out on its face that it is issued "in consideration of the application, and of each statement made therein."

Among the provisions of the policy is one reading: "If any statement made in the application for this policy be in any respect untrue, this policy shall be void."

The application set out on its face: "I certify that I am temperate in my habits, and am, to the best of my knowledge and belief, in sound physical condition, and a satisfactory subject for life assurance." This was signed by the insured and indorsed by the beneficiary.

Under the general health record, the question was asked in the written and printed medical examination, which was sent forward to the company in New York: "13th. Any history of serious illness, injury, or infirmity, etc."; to which the insured answered "No."

"16th. B. When and for what has medical advice been sought within the last three years?" to which the insured answered "Nothing."

The medical examiner of defendant testified that he asked both of the above questions, and the assured answered them as recorded, and made no other statements under those heads. He says: "I wrote the answers; Mr. H. C. Hazlewood was sitting at my left elbow; I asked him each question, and wrote the answer as he gave it; first had him sign at the top, asked him questions, 1 to 18 inclusive, and then wrote the answers. After the examination, he asked me what sort of a risk he was; I told him he could see for himself, and gave him the report, and he read it over for himself. I asked him each question separately, and wrote his answers. He told me he had not sought medical advice in three years. That question is considered material; all are so regarded, as all go to make the report. . . . . Henry Clay Hazlewood gave no history of mental disorder or derangement; applicant ought to have informed me of any mental derangement, — not absent-mindedness, or hallucinations of fear and the like. General belief that some one was after the applicant to kill him, or imagining something to exist that did not, would be a serious question."

In the written examination, the question was asked: "6th. Any history of mental derangement?" to which the applicant answered "No."

In the medical examination is the printed question to the applicant: "8th. A. Ever spat blood, or any history of chronic hoarseness or cough, or of asthma or shortness of breath?" to which the insured answered "No."

The controverted questions as to breaches of warranty raised by the pleadings, referred to in the evidence, and discussed in the brief of appellant's counsel, are thus stated in the brief: "The applicant covenants in writing and warrants that to the best of his knowledge and belief he is in sound physical condition. He warrants that he has not sought medical advice for anything within the last three years. He warrants that there has been no mental derangement. He warrants that there is no application pending for other assurance. He warrants that there has been no severe illness, coughs, or other ailments, etc."

It is contended that the court erred in refusing to give the following charge, at the request of the defendant: "If the jury believe, from the evidence, that Henry Clay Hazlewood, in the application for the policy of assurance, warranted that all the statements in such application, and all the answers and statements made to the society's medical examiner, were true, and that such application was made a part of the policy, and it was therein provided that if any statement in such application was in any respect untrue the said policy should be void, then I charge you that all three of such instruments, taken together, constitute the contract between the parties, and a warranty on the part of the assured that all the statements and answers to the medical examiner were true; and if you further believe, from the evidence, that the said Henry Clay Hazlewood, in his medical examination, in answer to the printed questions propounded by the society, had his answers to said questions put down in writing by the medical examiner opposite said questions, after said Hazlewood had signed said medical examination, and that after said answers were put down he read over and examined the same and assented thereto, and the same was sent forward with the application as the basis of the policy, and the same was issued by the defendant upon the reliance of the truth of such answers, then, if you find from the evidence that said written answers in said medical examination were in any respect untrue, you will find for the defendant." And also "in refusing to grant the defendant's motion for a new trial, in this, that it was clearly proved that the contract was embraced in the application, the answers of the assured to the medical examiner and the policy taken together; and they constitute a warranty that the statements therein made were true, when the facts fully show that they were not true; that at the time of the application the assured was not in sound physical condition, but was in bad health, and misled defendant and its officers by his statements regarding his condition."

The doctrine contended for by appellant, that "a warranty must be strictly complied with," is fully maintained by the authorities quoted in his brief.

Mr. Bliss, in his work on insurance, says: "By introducing them, they stipulate in effect that they are so material that if not strictly complied with the whole contract is rendered void. A misstatement in a warranty is therefore fatal to the contract, although arising from the most innocent mistake, or from false information afforded by others, or from mere inadvertence, and as much so as if made with the must willfully fraudulent intent": Bliss on Insurance, sec. 36, p. 48.

In the case of *Jeffries* v. *Economical Mut. L. Ins. Co.*, 22 Wall. 53, the court says: "The proposition at the foundation of this point is this; that the statements and declarations made in the policy shall be true. This stipulation is not expressed to be made as to important or material statements only, or to those supposed to be material, but as to all statements. The statements need not come up to the degree of warranties. They need not be representations even, if this term conveys an idea of an affirmation having any technical character. 'Statements and declarations' is the expression; what the applicant states and what the applicant declares. Nothing can be more simple. If he makes any statement in the application, it must be true. If he makes any declaration in the application, it must be true. A faithful performance of this agreement is made an express condition to the existence of a liability on the part of the company." Again, on page 56: "Many cases may be found which hold that where false answers are made to inquiries which do not relate to the risk, the policy is not necessarily avoided, unless they influenced the mind of the company, and that whether they are material is for the determination of the jury. But we know of no respectable authroity which so holds, where it is expressly covenanted as a condition of liability that the statements and declarations made in the application are true, and when the truth of such statements forms the basis of the contract."

In the case of *Ætna Life Ins. Co.* v. *France*, 91 U. S. 512, the court adopts the reasoning in the above case, and adds: "It is only necessary to reiterate that all the statements contained in the proposal must be true; that the materiality of such statements is removed from the consideration of the court or jury by the agreement of the parties that such statements are absolutely true, and if untrue in any respect the policy shall be void."

In the case of *New York Life Ins. Co.* v. *Fletcher*, 117 U. S. 519, referred to in the brief of appellant, the insured made certain statements and representations respecting himself, his life, and his past and present health, to which he appended a declaration warranting their truthfulness, and agreeing that they should be the basis of any contract between him and the company, and that if they or any of them were in any respect untrue, the policy which might be issued thereon should be void; and further agreeing that inasmuch as only the officers of the home office had authority to determine whether or not a policy should issue on any application, and as they acted only on the written statements and representations referred to, no statements or representations made or information given to the persons soliciting or taking the application for the policy should be binding on the company, or in any manner affect its rights, unless they were reduced to writing and presented at the home office in the application. The statements and representations, with this declaration accompanying the application, and forming part of it, were forwarded to the home office.

The policy recited that it was issued in consideration and upon the faith of the statements and representations contained in his application, all of which had been warranted by him to be true.

In delivering the opinion of the court, Justice Field says: "It was his duty to read the application he signed. He knew that upon it the policy would be issued, if issued at all. It would introduce great uncertainty in all business transactions if a party, making written proposals for a contract, with representations to induce its execution, should be allowed to show after it had been obtained that he did not know the contents of his proposals, and to enforce it, notwithstanding their falsity as to matters essential to its obligation and validity. Contracts could not be made, or business fairly conducted, if such a rule should prevail. . . . . But here the right is asserted to prove not only that the assured did not make the statements contained in his answers, but that he never read the application, and to recover upon a contract obtained by representations admitted to be false, just as though they were true. If he had read even the printed lines of his application he would have seen that it stipulated that the rights of the company could in no respect be affected by his verbal statements, or by those of its agents, unless the same were reduced to writing, and forwarded, with his application, to the home office."

We think there is a material difference between the undertaking by the insured in that case and in the one before us. In that case he agreed tha the would be bound by the statements as written down, and that no statements not written down should be binding on the company or in any manner affect its rights.

In the case before us the agreement of the insured was, that his answers, made or to be made to the medical examiner, were warranted to be true. He did not warrant that his answers would be written down correctly by the medical examiner, or that the answers given by him would be correctly reported to the company.

While the doctrine of warranty will be strictly applied, it should be as strictly limited to the precise undertaking of the party making it. If, beyond requiring that the insured should warrant the truth of all answers given by him, the company intended, as it had the right to do, that he should also warrant that his answers should be correctly written down and reported, and that he would warrant them not only as given by himself but as written down, the agreement could have been made to so express, and it ought to have been done.

The charge requested by the defendant, as above stated, and refused by the court, reading that if the jury found from the evidence that said " written answers " were " in any respect " untrue they should find for the defendant, extended the warranty of the insured so as to bind him for the truth of the answers as written, instead of their truth as given by him. In view of the fact that plaintiff's contention was that the insured gave true answers to the questions, which were incorrectly written down and reported by the medical examiner, and that the insured did not read the answers, or sign the paper containing them, which there was evidence tending to support, we think the charge was incorrect in this particular.

The signature of the insured, being at the beginning of the examination instead of at its close, seems to us to have been required to be placed there as one means of identifying him as the person who had made the application, rather than for the purpose of binding him, as a party, for the truth of the contents of the paper.

The assumption in the charge that the insured "had his answers to said questions put down in writing by the medical examiner" finds nothing in the evidence to support it.

The direction to find for the defendant if the jury should find the written answers were in "any respect" untrue was, we think, if no other objection to it existed, inapplicable to this case, and tended to mislead the jury. Under it the jury would have been required to consider every answer of the insured, whether any contention existed over it or not, and however difficult it might have proved for them to separate answers really proceeding from the medical examiner himself from those made by the insured; and if they believed any one answer was in any particular untrue, they could have found against plaintiff for that reason.

No charge on the subject ought to have been given that was not confined to such questions and answers as were put in issue by the pleadings and evidence, and the one requested should not have been given, because it was not so limited.

What we have said about the charge is applicable to the assignment of error with regard to overruling defendant's motion for new trial, predicated upon the same ground.

While the insured cannot, as is contended for by appellant, be held bound as a warrantor for the truth of the answers as written, it does not by any means follow that he was under no obligation about their being correctly written down, insomuch as that depended upon him or was properly within his control. He had undertaken to make true answers, and he must be presumed to have known that the object in having them written down was to furnish information to the absent officers of the corporation, of material importance to them in determining whether or not they would execute the contract.

Where there were no circumstances to excite his suspicion to the contrary, we see no reason, however, why he may not have trusted to the medical examiner's correct and honest performance of this duty. We do not think his contract, or the exercise of ordinary prudence, demanded of him to assume that there was any want of capacity, care, or honesty upon the part of the medical examiner, or made it his duty to assume the exercise of a supervisory power over the work of that officer. As a general rule, no doubt, the subjects of insurance will be but little qualified for such a task.

If, however, it did by any means come to the knowledge of the insured that answers given by him had been incorrectly written down, it then became his duty to see that the proper corrections were made, and if he failed to do so, then, although not bound by a warranty, plaintiff ought now to be held estopped from disputing them as written; and if, under such circumstances, incorrectly written answers materially affected the risk, and the issue was properly raised by the pleadings and sustained by the evidence, a recovery ought not to be had.

We deem it sufficient to say that we do not think this character of issue was presented by the pleadings or the charge of the court, and the record before us suggests that the evidence upon it would have been thoroughly conflicting and amply sufficient to support a verdict in favor of plaintiff.

The defendant alleged in its answer that the insurance was taken out by plaintiff as a speculative and wagering policy. It was proved that plaintiff loaned to the insured the money with which he paid the required premium.

The corporation's agent through whom the insurance was effected was permitted to testify to the negotiations preceding the application, tending to show that both the plaintiff and the insured were urged by the agent of the corporation to apply for the insurance; that the premium was paid by the insured, and that he first thought of making the minor children of the plaintiff the beneficiaries in the policy, but finally concluded not to do so, because in the event of his own marriage and desire to change the beneficiary to one more nearly connected with himself, it would be more easily accomplished if his brother was the beneficiary than it would be if his minor children were the beneficiaries.

The application for insurance contains the following questions and answers: "Is any negotiation for other assurance now pending or contemplated?" To which the insured answered in writing, "No." "Has a policy ever been applied for which was not thereafter issued, or which, if issued, was modified in amount, kind, or rates? If yes, for what company, and when?" To which the insured answered in writing, "No."

There was conflicting evidence as to whether the insured had not applied for membership in an order known as the Legion of Honor.

Plaintiff was permitted to prove, by the agent of the corporation by whom the application was secured, that, pending negotiations between him and the insured, and before the insured made answer to said questions, he, the insured, asked him, the agent, " What was meant by that? if it referred to assessment companies or mutual companies?   Witness explained that it did not, and the insured then said he had made application to the Legion of Honor for assurance, whereupon witness told him that the Legion of Honor was a mutual company, and was not regarded as a life insurance company, and he was in-structed by the general agent of defendant not to consider them as assurance companies."

We think the evidence was properly admitted in each in-stance.   On the issue as to whether it was a wagering policy, the statements made by the witness were pertinent, and have no tendency to control any written evidence or the contract. Nor can we see any impropriety in permitting the agent of the corporation to give to the subject of the insurance information about facts proper for him to know.   Lodges that furnish insur-ance to their members may also perform other important func-tions, and a rejection of an applicant by one of them would not necessarily be predicated upon his unfitness for insurance. It may be a rule of the defendant company not to treat such societies as coming within the meaning of the question, and if it is, we are not able to perceive any sufficient reason why the fact that the statement was made may not be proved.

Outside of the evidence objected to, the record fails to show that the insured in fact ever made an application for such membership, or that he was ever rejected.

It is contended that the plaintiff had no insurable interest in his brother's life, wherefore the cause of action sued upon was a wagering contract, and void as against public policy.

The rule is stated generally in Bliss on Life Insurance, sec-tion 7, that "no person can procure a valid insurance upon a life unless he has an interest in such life."

The supreme court of the United States, in the case of *Connecticut Mutual Life Ins. Co.* v. *Schaefer*, 94 U. S. 460, say: " It is generally agreed that mere wager policies — that is, policies in which the assured party has no interest whatever in the matter insured, but only an interest in its loss or de-struction — are void as against public policy.   It is well set-tled that a man has an insurable interest in his own life and in that of his wife and children, a woman in the life of her hus-band, and the creditor in the life of his debtor.   It may be said generally that any reasonable expectation of pecuniary benefit or advantage from the continued life of another creates an insurable interest in such life. And there is no doubt that a man may effect an insurance on his own life for the benefit of a relative or friend.

" The essential thing is, that the policy shall be obtained in good faith, and not for the purpose of speculating upon the hazard of a life in which the assured has no interest."

In the case of *Price* v. *Knights of Honor*, 68 Tex. 366, Chief Justice Willie, speaking for this court, said: "It is almost universally conceded that policies procured by persons having no interest in the life of the insured are void at common law, as against public policy."

In the case of the *Ætna Life Ins. Co.* v. *France*, 94 U. S. 561, it appears that the insurance was applied for by Chew on his own life for the benefit of his sister, Lucetta P. France, who was a married woman, and in no way dependent on her brother for her support. The evidence tended to show that Mrs. France had at different times loaned her brother two thousand four hundred dollars. The insurance was ten thousand dollars.

At the time the policy was issued Chew was unmarried, but was engaged to be married, and was, in fact, married the next day.

The policy was held " sustainable at law on account of the nearness of the relationship between the parties, and especially as Mrs. France, at the time the insurance was effected, was one of Chew's next of kin, prospectively interested in his estate as a distributee."

The doctrine is well settled by the weight of authority, that a person not having an insurable interest in the life of another cannot take and hold, by an assignment, a policy upon the life of such other person, and that a creditor can only take and hold such a policy by assignment to an extent sufficient to secure his debt: *Cammack* v. *Lewis*, 15 Wall. 643; *Warnock* v. *Davis*, 104 U. S. 782; *Price* v. *Knights of Honor*, 68 Tex. 361.

It is contended by appellee that every person has an insurable interest in his own life, and that when he is the actor he may take out an unlimited amount of insurance upon his own life, and make it payable to whoever he may please as beneficiary, without regard to such person having an insurable interest in his life.

In Bishop on Life Insurance it is said: "A person has undoubtedly an insurable interest in his own life, and that interest supports a policy, whether he makes the loss payable to himself, his executors, or his assigns, or to a nominee or appointee named in the policy. Nor is a policy obtained by one on his own life for the benefit of another, which latter advances the premium, necessarily void. The question is, whether the policy was in fact intended to be what it purports to be, or whether the form was adopted as a cover for a mere wager. If the plaintiff and the insured confederate together to procure a policy for the plaintiff's benefit, when he is not and does not expect to be a creditor of the insured, and with a view of having the policy assigned to him without consideration, the policy is void."

The only distinction we can see in any case between the assignment of a policy taken by a person on his own life to one having no insurable interest, and the designating such person without insurable interest in the original transaction as the beneficiary, is that the insurer may not know of the assignment, but would necessarily be aware of the designation in the policy.

So far as the question of public policy is concerned, we can see no substantial distinction between the two proceedings, and if one is invalid, it seems to us the other ought to be held equally so.

An assignment of a valid policy to one having no insurable interest in the life insured does not invalidate the policy. The assignee may collect and apply the proceeds, if he is a creditor, to the extinguishment of his debt, and such sums as he may have disbursed for the purpose of keeping the policy alive, and the surplus may be collected for the benefit of the heirs of the person whose life was insured.

We see no reason why the same rule may not be applied to a person designated in the policy as the beneficiary, treating him, when he has no insurable interest, as an assignee, appointee, or trustee to receive the proceeds for whoever may be lawfully entitled to enjoy them. The insurer will then be required to pay the sum it has promised to pay, and the money cannot be appropriated by anybody not having a legitimate right to it.

The exact degree of relationship that must exist between two persons to give one an insurable interest in the life of the other, on account of the relationship alone, we have not found to be clearly defined. Brothers and sisters seem to be on the dividing line. Whether that degree of relationship can be included has been disputed. The case of *Ætna Life Ins.* v. *France* is an authority in support of the proposition that it may be included, and we are unwilling to hold that it ought to be excluded.

To what extent a creditor may insure the life of his debtor is not announced, when it is decided that he can only appropriate of such insurance an amount sufficient to pay his debt and interest. He must be allowed to provide for a sum sufficient, when collected, to cover his demand, and such disbursements as may be required to keep the policy in force, with accrued interest. The sum required for that purpose may, very many times, exceed the debt. It would be an extreme case, in which a court would be justified in saying that the amount secured was too great.

When the insurance is obtained by a person on his own life, and made payable, originally or by assignment, to another having none, or only a limited insurable interest in his life, as the surplus, after the payment of the charges, will go to the heirs of the party whose life is insured, we see no reason for limiting the amount for which the insurance may be taken out.

When the insurance is not contracted for by the person whose life is insured, but by a creditor in his own name, so that there is no party to the contract except himself and the insurer, it becomes immaterial what amount may be contracted for, as no more will be collectible than will be ultimately sufficient to discharge his debt and disbursements on the policy, including interest upon both.

We find no error in the proceedings, and the judgment is affirmed.

———

VALIDITY OF ASSIGNMENT OF LIFE INSURANCE TO ONE WHO HAS NO INSURABLE INTEREST IN THE LIFE INSURED. — On the question as to whether a person who has taken out a valid policy of insurance on his own life can, during his lifetime, sell or assign the same to one who has no insurable interest in his life, so as to enable the buyer or assignee, upon the death of the assured, to recover the full amount of the policy, provided there is no prohibition in the policy or otherwise against such sale or assignment, the authorities are in hopeless and irreconcilable conflict, and about equally divided.

The better rule, it seems to us, is to hold such a sale or assignment to be a mere wager, and therefore void as against public policy. Most of the cases on this subject have been collected, and either reported in full, extensively quoted from, or cited in the notes to *Currier* v. *Continental Life Ins. Co.*, 52 Am. Rep. 143-145, and *Bursinger* v. *Bank of Watertown*, 58 Am. Rep. 848-858, and it is not our intention to again discuss the cases there collected; but simply to make a brief reference to the leading cases on each side of the subject, and to add the later cases which have been decided since the notes referred to were written.

Among the cases which maintain that the holder of a valid policy of insurance on his own life, payable to himself or to his legal representatives, may assign or sell the same to another, as he may any other chose in action, provided there is nothing in the terms of the policy to prevent such sale or assignment, and that the buyer or assignee thereof is entitled to the proceeds of the same when due, notwithstanding he may have no insurable interest in the life insured, are the following: *Murphy* v. *Red,* 64 Miss. 614; 58 Am. Rep. 855, note; *Bloomington Mut. Life etc. Ass'n* v. *Blue,* 120 Ill. 121; 58 Am. Rep. 852, note; *Mutual Life Ins. Co.* v. *Allen,* 138 Mass. 24; 52 Am. Rep. 245; also 58 Id. 856, note; *Bursinger* v. *Bank of Watertown,* 75 Wis. 75; 58 Am. Rep. 848; *St. John* v. *American Mut. Life Ins. Co.,* 13 N. Y. 31; *Valton* v. *National Fund etc. Ass'n,* 20 Id. 32; *Clark* v. *Allen,* 11 R. L 439; 23 Am. Rep. 496; *Olmstead* v. *Keyes,* 85 N. Y. 593; *Martin* v. *Stubbings,* 126 Ill. 387; 9 Am. St. Rep. 621; *Fitzpatrick* v. *Hartford Life Ins. Co.,* 56 Conn. 116; 7 Am. St. Rep. 288; *Eckel* v. *Renner,* 41 Ohio St. 232; *Succession of Hearing,* 26 La. Ann. 326. On the other hand, there is a line of authority, supported by the better reasoning, which maintains that a person who has no insurable interest in another's life cannot recover upon an insurance policy on such life which is purchased or obtained by assignment during the lifetime of the insured, since a policy so obtained is a mere wager, and void as opposed to public policy: *Franklin Life Ins. Co.* v. *Hazzard,* 41 Ind. 116; 13 Am. Rep. 313; *Missouri Valley Life Ins Co.* v. *Sturges,* 18 Kan. 93; 26 Am. Rep. 761; *Missouri Valley Life Ins. Co.* v. *McCrum,* 36 Kan. 146; *Basye* v. *Adams,* 81 Ky. 368; *Helmetag's Adm'r* v. *Miller,* 76 Ala. 183; 52 Am. Rep. 316; *Alabama Gold Life Ins. Co.* v. *Mobile Life Ins. Co.,* 81 Ala. 329; *Franklin Life Ins. Co.* v. *Sefton,* 53 Ind. 380; *Downey* v. *Hoffer,* 110 Pa. St. 109; *Hoffman* v. *Hoke,* 122 Id. 377; *Seigrist* v. *Schmoltz,* 113 Id. 326; *Commack* v. *Lewis,* 15 Wall. 643; *Warnock* v. *Davis,* 104 U. S. 775. In the case last cited it is said: "But if there be any sound reason for holding a policy invalid when taken out by a party who has no interest in the life of the assured, it is difficult to see why that reason is not as cogent and operative against a person taking an assignment of a policy upon the life of a person in which he has no interest. The same ground which invalidates the one should invalidate the other, so far, at least, as to restrict the right of the assignee to the sums actually advanced by him. In the conflict of decisions on this subject we are free to follow those which seem more fully in accord with the general policy of the law against speculative contracts upon human life."

In *Price* v. *Knights of Honor,* 68 Tex. 361, 368, also referred to in note to *Bursinger* v. *Bank,* 58 Am. Rep. 857, the court, after discussing the opposing cases on this subject, said: "We think those decisions which hold these assignments invalid are based upon the more satisfactory reasoning. When the policy is transferred, it becomes the property of the assignee. He is subject to all the obligations imposed by it, and entitled to all its benefits. He becomes the holder of the policy upon the life of a person whose early death will bring him pecuniary advantage. The temptation to bring about this death presents itself as strongly to him as to a party who originally effects insurance for his own benefit, upon the life of another. Public policy removes the temptation to take human life, and it cannot matter how that temptation is brought about. If by reasons of a contract between two persons the one is tempted by pecuniary interest to destroy the other, the form of the contract is of no importance in testing its validity. The law looks to the substance of the matter, the relation which the parties will bear to each other after the contract is executed; and if its natural effect is to encourage crime, it will be avoided, no matter in what shape it is presented. Those courts holding a contrary view say that a policy of insurance is a chose in action, and the owner of it may dispose of it as he pleases. But when it is asserted that the owner of property may dispose of it at his pleasure, the assertion must be taken with the qualification that he does not violate any provision of law or contravene public policy. It is further said that because a contract is speculative, though human life be the subject of speculation, it is not necessarily invalid; for instance, it is not unlawful to transfer an annuity or an estate in remainder after a life estate. If this reasoning be good, it would validate a policy taken by one having no interest in the life insured, as well as an assignment of a policy to such a person; for it is not unlawful to grant or create an annuity or an estate in remainder after a life estate, any more than it is to transfer one after it is created. Yet wager policies are almost universally held void, while annuities are sustained. Why this should be, it is not necessary to discuss. It is sufficient that no analogy drawn from annuities or life estates can be used to uphold policies procured in violation of public policy, and hence no analogy of this kind can sustain an assignment of the same character." After stating the facts in the case under consideration, the court proceeded to say: "This is not a question between the appellant and the lodge, but between him and the parties who are entitled to the insurance money, if the assignment is void. The assignment did not vitiate the policy, but was of itself of no effect, and left the insurance money payable to the parties originally designated in the certificate. From these views our conclusion is, that the transfer, having been made to one having no interest in the life of the insured, and upon no other consideration than the payment of premiums by the transferee, was void and against public policy, and the insurance money was payable to the original beneficiaries of the certificate."

DAGGETT *v.* WALLACE.

[75 TEXAS, 352.]

BREACH OF PROMISE OF MARRIAGE — PLEADING. — A petition in an action for damages for breach of promise of marriage, averring that by reason of such breach plaintiff has sustained the loss of an advantageous matrimonial connection, the defendant being a man of wealth and social position, and that, in addition, her affections have been disregarded and blighted, her feelings lacerated, and her spirits wounded, resulting in mental distress and humiliation, is sufficient to support a recovery.

BREACH OF PROMISE OF MARRIAGE — SEDUCTION — DAMAGES. — In an action for the breach of a promise of marriage, seduction, if alleged and proved, may be considered in estimating damages.

BREACH OF PROMISE OF MARRIAGE — EVIDENCE OF ENGAGEMENT.— In an action for damages for breach of promise of marriage, plaintiff's evidence as to the time when she became engaged to defendant is not objectionable, on the ground that it states a conclusion, and not a fact.

BREACH OF PROMISE OF MARRIAGE — INSTRUCTIONS.— In an action for breach of promise of marriage, a charge to find for defendant, unless a mutual agreement to marry existed within one year from the commencement of the action, is not erroneous in the absence of a request to charge that the promise must have been made to be performed within one year.

BREACH OF PROMISE OF MARRIAGE — DAMAGES. — Where defendant is a man of wealth and social standing, and has seduced plaintiff under promise of marriage, a verdict of seven thousand five hundred dollars for the breach of his promise of marriage will not be set aside as excessive.

DAMAGES FOR BREACH OF PROMISE OF MARRIAGE rest largely in the discretion of the jury, and are seldom interfered with, unless it is clear that the jury was influenced by prejudice, passion, or corruption.

BREACH OF PROMISE OF MARRIAGE — DAMAGES. — Loss from disappointment of expectation, including the money value of a marriage which would afford a permanent home and an advantageous establishment to plaintiff, wounds and injuries to her affections, and the mortification and anguish resulting from defendant's failure to keep his promise, are to be estimated in computing actual damages for a breach of promise of marriage.

B. P. Ayers, for the appellant.

R. L. Curlock, and Furman and Stedman, for the appellee.

HOBBY, J.   The first assignment, complaining of the court's action in overruling defendant's general demurrer to the petition, we think is without merit; and the statement under it, that the allegations of plaintiff do not show in what respect she was damaged by the alleged breach of defendant's promise of marriage, we do not think is supported by the record.   It is directly averred that by reason of the breach of defendant's promise she has sustained the loss of an advantageous matrimonial connection, he being a man of wealth and social position; and that, in addition thereto, her affections have been disregarded and blighted, her feelings lacerated and her spirits wounded, resulting in mental distress and humiliation. That the plaintiff may recover upon these allegations is well settled: 3 Sutherland on Damages, 316, and cases cited.

We do not think that an inspection of the petition will support the second assignment, to the effect that there was error in overruling defendant's exception to the second count in the petition, wherein damages were sought for plaintiff's seduction by defendant.

The special exception referred to in this assignment assails that part of the petition which seeks to recover exemplary damages, and does not direct the court's attention to plaintiff's allegation with respect to defendant's seduction of her.

There is no attempt in the petition to set up a distinct claim for damages on this ground; and the assignment is not, therefore, well taken.   In so far as this exception may be considered as attacking the averment of seduction because it is not a proper element of actual damage in cases like the present, we think it is also untenable. The policy of the law, it seems, refuses to recognise the right of the female seduced to recover solely for the seduction; and this is upon the principle that she is not entitled to satisfaction from her partner in crime for a supposed injury to which she consents. But while this may not afford a separate and distinct ground of recovery, it is settled by the great majority of cases that in an action for the breach of a promise of marriage, such seduction, if alleged and proved, is proper to be considered in estimating the damages: *Sherman* v. *Rawson*, 102 Mass. 399; 3 Sutherland on Damages, 316. The reason for this is, that it cannot be fairly ascertained to what extent the plaintiff is damaged by the breach of the contract or promise, without considering the condition in which she is left by the defendant's conduct which is complained of: *Kelly* v. *Riley*, 106 Mass. 343; 8 Am. Rep. 336.

The third assignment complains of the admission in evidence of the plaintiff's statement that "about six months after Christmas of 1876, she became engaged to the defendant." This was objected to because the witness should have stated facts, and not conclusions as to conversations, but the conversations. If appellant's position be correct, that this was the statement of a conclusion, and not a fact, which we are not prepared to admit, still it does not appear to us to be a material error in the case. And it is especially unimportant, we think, in view of the evidence, independently of this statement, relative to the actual promise of marriage by defendant. The testimony shows, beyond question, that this promise was repeatedly made by the defendant, subsequent to the time the witness says they became engaged. The last time the promise was made was in the fall of 1885, and the suit was brought in January, 1886.

The remaining assignments, except the last, relate to the court's charge.

The fourth assignment is, that the court erred in charging the jury that "if they believed that within one year prior to the commencement of the suit the plaintiff was induced, by reason of such agreement, to submit to sexual intercourse with defendant, and that he begot her with child, you may consider that fact in estimating the damages." It is not necessary to say more with respect to this assignment than that it has been already disposed of by what has been said with reference to the allegations of seduction being admissible, by way of aggravation, in cases of this character. The charge is, in substance, that that fact, if proved, may be considered. As we have seen, this is in accord with the authorities on this subject.

The fifth and sixth assignments may be considered together. They complain of the following charge: "Unless you believe, from the evidence, that there was a mutual agreement between the plaintiff and defendant to marry each other, and that such agreement existed between them on or after the second day of January, 1885, you shall find for the defendant."

The objection is, that the court should have limited the jury to the consideration of an agreement and promise made, to be performed within one year.

If the jury believed the testimony of the plaintiff, they were fully authorized to find that the promise was made in November, 1885, and was to be performed by Christmas of that year. The petition was filed January, 1886. If the evidence raised any doubt as to whether the promise was to be performed within one year, the defendant should have requested a charge calling the jury's attention to that issue.

The remaining assignment is, that the verdict is excessive. It is for seven thousand five hundred dollars. No reason is assigned by appellant in support of this assignment. It is said that "damages in this character of case rest largely in the discretion of the jury, and this discretion is seldom interfered with, and should be in no case, except where it is manifest that the jury were influenced by prejudice, passion, or corruption": Field on Damages, sec. 534. "The loss from the disappointment of expectation, including the money value of a marriage which would afford a permanent home and an advantageous establishment to the plaintiff, wounds and injuries to the affections, and the mortification and anguish to plaintiff resulting from the defendant's failure to fulfill his promise, are all to be considered in computing actual damages": Field on Damages, sec. 72.

Eliminating from this case the element of seduction, we are not prepared to say that the elements last referred to are not sufficient to support the verdict.

There is nothing in the record which would justify us in the conclusion that the verdict was anything but the honest and candid expression of the jury, based upon the facts before them.

We can perceive no error in the record which, in our opinion, would authorize a reversal of the judgment, and we think it should be affirmed.

BREACH OF PROMISE OF MARRIAGE. — As to actions for breach of promise to marry, see full note to *Burnham* v. *Cornwell,* 63 Am. Dec. 532–548.

BREACH OF PROMISE OF MARRIAGE — SEDUCTION. — Seduction of the plaintiff by the defendant, procured through means of his promise to marry her, is a fact to be considered by way of aggravating the damages: *Sauer* v. *Schulenberg,* 33 Md. 288; 3 Am. Rep. 174; *Thorn* v. *Knapp,* 42 N. Y. 474; 1 Am. Rep. 561; *Kelly* v. *Riley,* 106 Mass. 339; 8 Am. Rep. 336; *Giese* v. *Schultz,* 69 Wis. 521.

BREACH OF PROMISE OF MARRIAGE — CIRCUMSTANCES OF DEFENDANT. — The wealth and pecuniary circumstances of a defendant, in an action for breach of a promise to marry, may be considered in ascertaining the amount of damages sustained by plaintiff: *Lawrence* v. *Cook,* 56 Me. 187; 96 Am. Dec. 443; *Olson* v. *Solveson,* 71 Wis. 663. So the anxiety of mind, caused by defendant's failure to fulfill his promise, is an element of damages: *Tobin* v. *Shaw,* 45 Me. 331; 71 Am. Dec. 547.

EXCESSIVE DAMAGES. — In actions for damages occasioned by a breach of promise to marry, the appellate court will not interfere, on the ground that the damages allowed are excessive, unless it appears the jury were actuated by undue motives when they found their verdict: *Olson* v. *Solveson,* 71 Wis. 663; and substantially to the same effect is *Giese* v. *Schultz,* 69 Wis. 521.

GOULDY *v.* METCALF.

[75 TEXAS, 455]

POWER OF ATTORNEY — ASSIGNMENT FOR BENEFIT OF CREDITORS may be executed by an agent or an attorney in fact especially authorized thereto, but the power must, in express terms, grant the authority.

POWER OF ATTORNEY — CONSTRUCTION. — The authority derived from a general power of attorney is limited to the exercise of the acts authorized by the language employed in granting the special powers.

AUTHORITY CONFERRED BY POWER OF ATTORNEY will be construed strictly, so as to exclude the exercise of any power which is not warranted, either by the actual terms used, or as a necessary means of executing the authority with effect.

J. Jenkins, for the appellant.

W. M. Knight, and Crain and Ramsey, for the appellees.

ACKER, P. J. W. H. Turner, by properly executed power of attorney, granted to H. E. Turner and A. P. Bell authority and powers as follows: "In and about my business to buy, sell, or exchange property; to receive and receipt for money; to sell and dispose of property, to give bills of sale thereto, or to sell and transfer real estate and execute deeds thereto; or to do and perform any lawful act in, or about, or concerning my business, as fully and completely as if I were personally present; and I herein and hereby confirm all their lawful acts

and deeds that they perform in any manner connected with
my business."

Under this instrument the attorneys in fact executed a statutory deed of assignment of Turner's property for the benefit
of his creditors. Appellant Gouldy was named as assignee,
and he took possession of the assigned estate as such.

Appellees Ruder and Pool were creditors of Turner, and
sued out an attachment against him, under which appellee
Metcalf, as sheriff, took from the possession of Gouldy the
stock of merchandise, books and accounts, etc., which he had
received as assignee of Turner.

Gouldy brought this suit as assignee against the sheriff and
plaintiffs in attachment to recover damages for the wrongful
seizure and conversion of the property.

On the trial, plaintiff, having introduced in evidence the
power of attorney, offered the deed of assignment, which was
objected to by defendants upon the ground that "the power of
attorney did not authorize the attorneys in fact to make the
deed." The objection was sustained, and there was no other
evidence offered.

The court, trying the case without a jury, rendered judgment for defendants.

The only question presented is, Did the trial court err in
holding that the power of attorney did not authorize the attorneys in fact to execute the deed of assignment? That a
deed of assignment for the benefit of creditors may be executed by an agent or attorney in fact, specially authorized
thereto, we think has been settled by the decision in *McKee* v.
Coffin, 66 Tex. 307, 308, where it is said: "It is now urged
that the court below erred in admitting in evidence the deed
of assignment, because there is no sufficient evidence that it
was ever executed by S. W. Kniffin. The evidence shows that
he was not present when the deed was executed, but that prior
to its execution he had directed this to be done by those who
did execute it, upon the happening of a then contemplated
contingency."

And again: "What a person under no disability may do
in person, he may ordinarily do through an agent; but it is
claimed that this is not true under the act regulating assignments; that the deed of assignment must be the personal act
of the owner of the property assigned, and, as an evidence of
this, it is urged that the assignor must make oath to the
schedule. It is true that the second section of the act does

require that the inventory and schedule shall be verified by
the oath of the debtor, but this is not essential to the validity
of the assignment, for the tenth section declares that 'no assignment shall be declared fraudulent or void for want of any
inventory or list, as provided herein, but if such list and inventory be not annexed and verified, as provided in this act,
it shall be *prima facie* evidence that the assignor has secreted
and concealed some portion of the property belonging to his
estate from his assignee, unless,' etc. It is said that 'the
processes provided against the assignor, and the penalties
denounced against him, are all personal, and cannot be transferred to and performed by or enforced against an agent.' If
an agent makes a false oath in the course of the business of
his principal, he may be indicted and convicted for false
swearing or perjury, as the case may be, as though the false
oath were taken in his own business."

We think it clear from the foregoing quotations that an
assignment for the benefit of creditors may be made by any
agent or attorney in fact authorized thereto. The instrument
under which the power was exercised in this case does not in
terms grant the authority. The language used in the grant
of general power is certainly very comprehensive, but the
established rule of construction limits the authority derived
by the general grant of power to the acts authorized by the
language employed in granting the special powers.

"When an authority is conferred upon an agent by a formal
instrument, as by a power of attorney, there are two rules of
construction to be carefully attended to: 1. The meaning of
general words in the instrument will be restricted by the con-
text, and construed accordingly; 2. The authority will be
construed strictly, so as to exclude the exercise of any power
which is not warranted, either by the actual terms used, or as
a necessary means of executing the authority with effect":
Ewell's Evans on Agency, 204, 205; *Reese* v. *Medlock*, 27 Tex.
123, 124; 84 Am. Dec. 611.

Applying these rules to this case, and none of the circumstances under which the power was executed being shown, we
are of opinion that the attorneys in fact did not have the
power to make the assignment, and that the court did not err
in so holding.

We are therefore of opinion that the judgment of the court
below should be affirmed.

HECK AND BAKER *v.* MARTIN.

[75 TEXAS, 469.]

JUSTICE'S JUDGMENT — PRESUMPTION IN FAVOR OF. — The justices' courts of Texas are, within their defined limits, tribunals of general jurisdiction, and all reasonable presumptions are indulged in support of the validity of their judgments.

JUSTICE'S JUDGMENT — COLLATERAL ATTACK. — Recitals in justice's judgment, regular in every respect, "that the parties appeared in person and by attorney," cannot be collaterally attacked, and in such proceeding such recitals import absolute verity.

Hunter, Stewart, and Dunklin, for the appellants.

J. A. Holland, for the appellee.

HOBBY, J.   Action of trespass to try title in the usual form, brought by appellee, Martin, against Heck and Baker, appellants, to recover a lot described as lot No. 3, block 32, in Jennings's south addition to the city of Fort Worth. Defendants answered by general demurrer, general denial, and plea of not guilty. There was judgment for the plaintiff (appellee), from which defendants (appellants) appeal.

It was agreed that both parties claim under J. L. Sandidge as a common source of title. On February 20, 1884, Sandidge executed a deed to appellee for the land, which was duly acknowledged and recorded.

The appellants claim title to the lot in question under a deed from the sheriff of Tarrant County, dated the fifth day of January, 1886. On the thirteenth day of November, judgment was rendered in justice court of precinct No. 1, Tarrant County, Texas, in favor of J. G. Reily and against the appellee, J. A. Martin, and one R. M. Bowman, for the sum of $103, with interest at twelve per cent per annum, and cost, including ten per cent attorney fees. On the twenty-fifth day of November, 1886, an execution issued on said judgment against said J. A. Martin and R. M. Bowman, and was on the twenty-eighth day of said month levied on the lot in question as the property of said Martin, and on the fifth day of January, 1886, following, said lot was sold by the sheriff of Tarrant County,

and bought by the appellants, Heck and Baker, who paid
therefor the sum of four hundred dollars. The lot was the
individual property of Martin, and had never been the partnership property of Bowman and Martin.

The judgment of the justice court under which appellants,
Heck and Baker, claim is in due form and regular upon its
face. It recites that citation was issued on the twenty-sixth
day of September, 1885, returnable to the October term of said
court, and that it was returned duly executed on Bowman and
Martin, and Sam Kline, of Freeburg, Kline, & Co. The judgment was rendered on the thirteenth day of November, 1885,
and further recites: "This cause this day coming on to be
heard, the parties appeared in person and by attorney, and
announced ready for trial." After the formal part, the judgment further reads: "It is therefore considered and adjudged
by the court that the plaintiff John G. Reily do have and
recover of defendants J. A. Martin and R. M. Bowman, lately
composing the firm of Bowman and Martin, the sum of one
hundred and three dollars ($103), being principal and inter-
est of the note sued on, together with twelve per cent interest
from date hereof, and all cost in this behalf expended, as well
as the sum of ten dollars attorney fee stipulated in said
note." It was agreed that an execution issued on the judgment the twenty-fifth day of November, 1885; that the same
was in all things regular, and was against J. A. Martin and
R. M. Bowman; that on the twenty-eighth day of November,
1885, it was levied on the lot in controversy, and on the first
Tuesday in January, 1886, the said lot was sold under said
execution, and was bought by Heck and Baker, appellants
herein, who paid the purchase-money therefor, and took the
sheriff's deed to the same.

Appellee, Martin, testified, over appellants' objections, that
he was not served with citation in said case in the justice
court, amd that he did not appear in said case upon the trial
thereof, either in person or by attorney, and that he did not
authorize any one to appear for him, and that he did not
know that said judgment was rendered against him until
after said lot was sold.

L. N. Cooper was also permitted, over objections of appellants, to testify that he was attorney for J. G. Reily in the
case of *Reily* v. *Bowman and Martin*, in the justice court, and
that it had been a long time ago, and he did not remember
distinctly whether J. A. Martin was served with citation or

not, but that it was his impression that he was not;~that Martin was not represented in said cause by any attorney. To all of which evidence of the said Martin and Cooper appellants duly excepted.

The original papers in the suit of *J. G. Reily* v. *Bowman and Martin et al.* were lost.

First assignment: "The court erred in admitting the evidence of Martin and Cooper, to the effect that Martin had not been served with citation in the case of *J. G. Reily* v. *Bowman and Martin et al.*, and did not in fact appear in said case at the trial in the justice court, nor authorize or employ counsel to appear for him in said case, as is recited in the judgment in said case, because the evidence contradicts the judgment in said case, and is wholly inadmissible on the trial of a collateral action, as in this case, and shown by bill of exception herein filed."

Second assignment of error: "The finding and judgment of the court is in no wise supported by the evidence, but is wholly contrary to the evidence, in this: the judgment of the justice of the peace is regular on its face, and recites that the parties to the suit appeared in person and by attorneys, and is rendered against J. A. Martin and R. M. Bowman, lately composing the firm of Bowman and Martin, and is not exclusively a judgment against the firm, if it is at all. The agreement of counsel supplied the execution which was lost. The sheriff's deed is regular, and in all respects good and perfect, and Heck and Baker were outside third parties, who bought relying on the face of the record in that justice court case; and the evidence in all respects established the title in Heck and Baker, and showed that it had been divested out of the plaintiff; and the entire evidence of plaintiff impeaching the justice record was wholly incompetent and inadmissible, so that there is no evidence to support the judgment in this case."

The appellee contends that he was not attempting to attack the judgment of the justice court, collaterally or otherwise, but claims that the judgment was not against him as an individual, but only as a member of the firm of Bowman and Martin; that the execution by virtue of which the lot was sold was issued against J. A. Martin and R. M. Bowman, lately composing the firm of Bowman and Martin, and not against appellee as an individual, but only as a member of the firm.

The rule is well recognized in this state that justice courts, being crèated by the constitution, are within their defined limits tribunals of general jurisdiction, and as such all reasonable presumptions should be indulged in support of the validity of their judgments: *Holmes* v. *Buckner,* 67 Tex. 107; *Williams* v. *Ball,* 52 Tex. 603; 36 Am. Rep. 730. "If the recitals in the record show affirmatively that the court was without jurisdiction as to the person or the subject-matter, no such presumption would obtain, because it would contradict the judgment itself, and destroy the rule inhibiting its impeachment in a collateral proceeding. In determining whether such judgment affirmatively shows that there has been the service of citation authorizing it, the entire decree must be looked to and considered; and if that portion of it relating to the question discloses that there was no service, or service so defective that a judgment by default thereon would be void and not voidable, and the remainder of the record is silent, and there appears no finding of the court from which it may be inferred that there was either service or an appearance, then the absence of jurisdiction would affirmatively appear. . . . . If, however, other parts of the record, and particularly the judgment, which is the final act of the court, entered upon full consideration of all the facts before it, should, as in the present case, show the due service of process or other facts which would give the court jurisdiction of the person, then it would affirmatively appear that such jurisdiction attached, and the rule would apply that in a collateral proceeding the recitals import absolute verity, and cannot be contradicted": *Treadway* v. *Eastburn,* 57 Tex. 209; Freeman on Judgments, sec. 130.

Applying the principles to the judgment in the case before us, there can be no doubt, we think, from its recitals, that it was against J. A. Martin and R. M. Bowman individually. That the service was on both Bowman and Martin, is shown by the language that "the parties appeared in person and by attorney," together with the further recital that the citation was "returned duly executed on Bowman and Martin, and Sam Kline, of Freeburg, Kline, & Co." If it had been served on Bowman only, it is reasonable to suppose that the return would have shown service on "Bowman, of the firm of Bowman and Martin," as in the case of "Sam Kline, of the firm of Freeburg, Kline, & Co." Again, the recital of the recovery in the judgment, the final act of the court, was against "the defendants J. A. Martin and R. M. Bowman, lately composing the firm of Bowman and Martin." This, it is to be presumed under the operation of the rule already stated,"was entered upon full consideration of all the facts before the court" necessary to authorize such act, and with the knowledge that the recovery was authorized by the service of process.

The appellants were purchasers of the lot involved in this suit for a valuable consideration; they were strangers to the original judgment against appellee. They were required to look only to the judgment and execution. There was nothing upon the face of either showing the want of jurisdiction over the person of appellee. Four hundred dollars were paid by the appellants for the land, and there is no tender of any portion of the same by appellee. We do not think that it was competent in this collateral proceeding for the appellee to impeach or contradict the recitals in the judgment referred to. The court erred, we think, in permitting this to be done by the admission of the evidence to which the appellants objected. There was error, also, in not rendering judgment for the appellants.

The judgment should be reversed, and here rendered for appellants.

———

JUSTICES OF THE PEACE. — Ordinarily no presumptions are made in favor of the jurisdiction of justices' courts, being courts of inferior jurisdiction: *McDonald* v. *Prescott*, 2 Nev. 109; 90 Am. Dec. 517, and note. But for the rule in Texas, see *Williams* v. *Ball*, 51 Tex. 603; 36 Am. Rep. 730. And in the case of *Sachse* v. *Clingingsmith*, 97 Mo. 406, where a judgment of a justice of the peace was regular upon its face, and a sheriff's deed recited the issuance of an execution from the circuit court upon a transcript of such judgment, it was held, that in the absence of any showing to the contrary, the validity, issuance, and proceedings under such execution would be presumed regular and proper, and could not be collaterally assailed.

Justices of the peace can only exercise the powers granted them by the constitution and statutes, and their jurisdiction is special, not general: *State* v. *Jones*, 100 N. C. 438.

WESTERN UNION TELEGRAPH COMPANY *v.* ADAMS.

[75 TEXAS, 531.]

TELEGRAPH COMPANIES ARE NOT CHARGED WITH KNOWLEDGE of the importance of delivering cipher dispatches.

TELEGRAPH COMPANY. — DISTINCTION EXISTS BETWEEN cipher dispatches and those intended to convey information by the use of no more words than are necessary when given their accustomed meaning.

TELEGRAPH COMPANY MUST TAKE NOTICE that the utmost brevity of expression is cultivated in correspondence by telegraph, and that that mode of communication is chiefly resorted to in matters of importance, financially and socially, requiring great haste. Hence, when such communications relate to sickness and death, the company must take notice that they are of importance, and that the person addressed has a serious interest in them.

TELEGRAPH COMPANIES ARE NOT RELEASED FROM DILIGENCE when, though the relations of the parties are not disclosed, the nature of the communication is manifest from its terms. If the operator desires information about such relationship he must obtain it from the sender. If not, his principal will be charged with the information that inquiries would have developed.

TELEGRAPH COMPANY — DAMAGES FOR DELAY IN DELIVERING DISPATCH — EVIDENCE OF MENTAL ANGUISH. — In an action for damages against a telegraph company, for delay in delivering a dispatch, evidence of mental anguish felt and exhibited by speech or otherwise, at the time the dispatch was received, is competent and admissible, and at least furnishes no ground for setting aside a verdict that may be sustained without evidence as to the existence or degree of mental pain.

TELEGRAPH COMPANY — DAMAGES FOR DELAY IN DELIVERING MESSAGE — RIGHT OF ACTION. — When a message is sent for the benefit of a married woman, and she is in fact the person damaged by the delay of the company in delivering it, her husband may maintain suit against the company, notwithstanding the fact that the sender of the dispatch had not been previously constituted an agent for that purpose by the party to whom it was sent, and that the former has been reimbursed by the latter for the amount paid in sending the message.

TELEGRAPH COMPANY — RIGHT TO RECOVER FEE PAID FOR TELEGRAM. — Prompt delivery of a telegram is of the essence of the contract, and a failure in this respect is such a breach of it as to authorize a recovery of the consideration paid for it, if the right to do so can be maintained in other respects.

Stemmons and Field, for the appellant.

Richardson and Watkins, for the appellee.

HENRY, A. J. Appellee brought this suit to recover damages for defendant's delay in delivering the following message: —

" WACO, October 12, 1887.

" To F. E. ADAMS, Athens.

" Clara, come quick. Rufe is dying.

[Signed]   " O. M. SIMMONS."

His allegations are, that said message was delivered to appellant's agent at Waco about ten o'clock of said day, and that the message was not delivered to appellee until shortly before noon on the thirteenth day of October, 1887; that appellee was a merchant in Athens, residing there, doing business in the post-office building, within one hundred yards of defendant's office, and on the public square, and that his residence was within one hundred yards of defendant's office; that appellee was well known to the residents of said town; that there were then two trains daily from Athens to Waco, one at ten o'clock and fifty minutes in the evening, the other at seven o'clock and five minutes in the morning, and that on the morning of the 13th of October there was an accommodation train which left Athens for Waco at ten o'clock; that appellee's wife took the first train going to Waco after receiving said message, arriving at Waco on the morning of October 14th; that when she reached Waco her brother was dead, and his body had been sent to a distant part of the state for burial; that they were compelled to take another train to the place of burial; her brother died about six o'clock in the evening of the 13th; that had the message been promptly delivered, appellee's wife could have reached her brother in time to have been with him fourteen hours before his death, and if the message had been delivered before either of the trains on the morning of the 13th, she could have been with him at least six hours before his death; that by reason of appellant's failure to promptly deliver said telegram, and of her being deprived of being with her brother in his last sickness, she suffered great anguish, pain of mind, and was prostrated and broken down in body and mind, and was damaged in the sum of five thousand dollars; that plaintiff repaid Simmons the amount he paid for transmitting the telegram.

To this appellant answered by general demurrer and general denial. The general demurrer was overruled. The trial resulted in a verdict and judgment in favor of appellee for the sum of $2,000.40.

The evidence supported the pleading.

Appellant's proposition under its first three assignments is: "That the message did not disclose that the relation of brother and sister existed between 'Rufe' and 'Clara,' nor do the allegations in the petition disclose that appellant had notice of the relationship existing between them at the time it contracted to transmit said message, and by reason of the want of notice of this fact appellant cannot be held liable for the damages sued for herein."

The rule insisted upon by appellant is too restricted to be safely applied to communications sent by the electric telegraph.

Plaintiff seeks to recover damages on account of mental pain suffered by his wife because of her inability to be with her brother when he was dying. The allegations and the evidence show that her failure to be with him was on account of her failure to receive information of his condition in time to reach him by the means of conveyance that were at her command. It is difficult to conceive of any form of expression that would have more accurately conveyed to her the information intended than would that used in the telegram had it been delivered to her. If any diligence had been used for its delivery when it reached its destination, she would not only have known the condition of her brother that it was intended to communicate, but would have known it in ample time to have reached him while living and conscious.

The mental pain suffered by her on account of being deprived of this privilege is recognized by the law as a ground for the assessment of damages against defendant, if it was induced by its negligence. The contention of defendant, in effect, is, that it can only be held liable for such damages as may be supposed to have been in the contemplation of the parties if the telegram was delayed in its delivery, and that no damage can be held to have been in contemplation of the defendant not suggested by the language of the dispatch, and that all that could be gleaned from this dispatch by its agents was, that some person at Waco wanted some person at Athens, named Clara, to come quickly to Waco, because some person named Rufe was dying.

It seems to be well settled that telegraph companies are not charged with knowledge of the importance of delivering cipher dispatches. As in the nature of things they cannot know the contents of such telegrams, that mode of expression being adopted to keep them from knowing, the rule is a just one that preserves them from the responsibilities that such knowledge would impose on them.

There seems to be an effort to extend this rule beyond the occasion for it, and to practically make all telegrams expressed in abbreviated language cipher dispatches.

We think a distinction in this respect must be made between messages couched in terms intended to conceal their meaning and such as have no such purpose, but are intended to convey information by the use of no more words than are necessary when given their accustomed meaning.

It is well known to the public, and cannot be unknown to telegraph companies, that the utmost brevity of expression is cultivated in correspondence by telegraph. It is as well known that that mode of communication is chiefly resorted to in matters of importance, financially and socially, requiring great dispatch.

When such communications relate to sickness and death there accompanies them a common-sense suggestion that they are of importance, and that the persons addressed have in them a serious interest.

It would be an unreasonable rule, and one not comporting with the uses of the telegraph, to hold that the dispatcher will be released from diligence unless the relations of the parties concerned, as well as the nature of the dispatch, are disclosed.

When the general nature of the communication is plainly disclosed by its terms, instead of requiring the sender to communicate to the unwilling ears of the busy operator the relationship of the parties concerned, a more reasonable rule will be, when the receiver of the dispatch desires information about such matters, for him to obtain it from the sender, and if he does not do so to charge his principal with the information that inquiries would have developed.

A witness was permitted to testify that Mrs. Clara Adams, while waiting for a train to Waco, after the message had been delivered to her, seemed to be in great distress, and said that she would give everything that she possessed to see her brother and talk to him before he died.

As the jury would be instructed that they might, in assessing damages, include her mental anguish in their estimate, it was doubtless thought that evidence of her mental condition, including expressions of it at the time, might be given. As juries may, from their own knowledge and experience of human nature, estimate damage proceeding from that cause without any evidence, it is not important to produce it, and when produced, it ought not, as a general rule, to have a controlling effect; and yet we are not able to see why the fact that mental anguish was felt, and was exhibited by speech or otherwise, may not be proved for what it may be worth. It at least furnishes no ground for setting aside a verdict that might be sustained without any evidence as to the existence or degree of mental pain: 1 Greenl. Ev., sec. 102; Wharton on Evidence, secs. 268, 269.

It is urged that "the court erred in that part of its charge wherein it instructed 'that if such telegram was sent by Simmons for the benefit of Mrs. Clara Adams, and that she has paid back the charges for sending it, then the husband would have a legal right to sue for a breach of the contract,' etc.; because, — 1. Defendant had no notice that the contract was made for Clara Adams; and 2. It had no notice or information that 'Clara,' named in said message, meant 'Clara Adams,' the wife of plaintiff."

If in fact the message was sent for the benefit of Mrs. Adams, and she was the damaged party, we can see no good reason why her husband may not maintain the suit: *Aiken* v. *Western Union Tel. Co.*, 5 S. C. 369; *New York etc. Tel. Co.* v. *Dryburg*, 35 Pa. St. 303; 78 Am. Dec. 338; *Ellis* v. *American Tel. Co.*, 13 Allen, 226; Shearman and Redfield on Negligence, 642.

The party to be in fact accommodated, benefited, or served holds the beneficial interest in the contract. When that one sustains damage from its breach a right of action arises in his favor. We do not attach importance to the reimbursement of the fee for sending the dispatch to the party who paid it. Unless a right of action exists independently of that, it cannot be maintained. If the person sending and paying for the dispatch was not at the time of performing those acts the agent of the sender, he cannot be afterwards made such, so as to give a right of action for large damages, by being refunded the fee paid for the dispatch. At most all that that transaction can amount to, in any case, will be to give to the party that refunds it a cause of action for the amount refunded in a court having jurisdiction of it. If it is paid under such circumstances as to become a debt from the person for whose use the dispatch is sent to the sender, the collection of it will be between themselves, and with that the corporation can have no concern. If it is refunded by the party having otherwise a cause of action against the corporation, it may be included and recovered in the suit brought for the other cause.

We think the question as to who may maintain a suit for damages for the breach of contract does not depend upon the payment of the fee, nor upon the question whether the sender had been previously constituted an agent for that purpose by the party to whom the dispatch is sent, but upon who in fact was to be served, and who is damaged.

If it was intended to serve the receiver, and he accepts the act, we are unable to see why the telegraph company should be excused from the consequences of its neglect to discharge its own duty by reason alone of its ignorance of the relations that may exist between the sender and the receiver of the message.

If the sender, from motives of friendship or any other cause, is willing to confer upon the receiver a benefit, and he is willing to accept it, and out of the transaction there results damage for somebody to receive, and for the corporation to pay, the want of the technical relationship of principal and agent between the other parties ought not to inure to the benefit of the telegraph company to the exclusion of the only party for whose use the other parties intended the transaction.

A charge to the jury that plaintiff could recover the toll paid for transmitting the message is objected to upon the ground that, as defendant performed its contract for transmission and delivery of said message, a delay in its execution does not authorize a recovery of the money paid for the performance of the contract. No authorities are quoted in favor of this proposition, and we know of none. A prompt delivery was of the essence of the contract, and a failure in that respect was such a breach of it as to authorize the recovery back of the consideration paid for it, if a right to do so could be maintained in other respects.

It is contended that "the court erred in not setting aside the verdict because it is excessive in amount; because if the telegram had been promptly delivered, plaintiff's wife could not have reached her brother until after he became unconscious." The facts do not sustain this assignment, and it therefore becomes unnecessary to comment upon it in other aspects.

We find no error in the proceedings for which we think the judgment ought to be reversed, and it is affirmed.

TELEGRAPH COMPANIES — NOTICE OF IMPORTANCE OF MESSAGE. — A telegraph company is liable for such damages as are the direct and natural result of its failure to deliver a message, without regard to the degree of its negligence, where the message discloses upon its face the necessity of its prompt transmission and delivery: *Western Union Tel. Co.* v. *Broesche,* 72 Tex. 654; 13 Am. St. Rep. 843; and notice of the main fact charges the company with any other fact ascertainable by inquiry: *Western Union Tel. Co.* v. *Edsall,* 74 Tex. 329; 15 Am. St. Rep. 835; *Western Union Tel. Co.* v. *Sheffield,* 71 Tex. 570; 10 Am. St. Rep. 790, and note.

GULF, COLORADO, AND SANTA FÉ RAILWAY COMPANY *v.* DWYER.

[75 TEXAS, 572.]

INTERSTATE COMMERCE. — STATE CAN MAKE NO LAW regulating the rate of freight for the carriage of goods between that and another state, although the regulation be construed as applying to so much of the line as lies within its own borders; nor can it make a law which imposes, either directly or indirectly, a burden by way of taxation upon interstate commerce.

INTERSTATE COMMERCE STATES MAY ESTABLISH AND REGULATE WHARVES, BRIDGES, AND FERRIES across streams constituting the boundaries between the states, in the absence of legislation by Congress; provided no burden other than an ordinary charge for their use is imposed upon commerce passing over them.

INTERSTATE COMMERCE. — States may, in the exercise of their police power, enact laws which, though they affect commerce between the states, are not to be considered regulations of that commerce within the meaning of the constitution of the United States.

INTERSTATE COMMERCE — POWER OF STATE — CONSTITUTIONALITY OF STATUTE. — A statute affording a remedy for the breach of a contract of carriage of goods between two states, but which imposes no tax, neither fixes nor regulates rates, makes no discrimination between commerce wholly within the state and that between the state and other states, applies to all carriers and contracts of carriage alike, imposes no new duty on the carrier, and merely provides a penalty for the purpose of enforcing a compliance with an obligation already existing. is a proper exercise of the police power reserved to the state, and therefore valid.

INTERSTATE COMMERCE — POLICE POWER OF STATE. — A statute imposing a penalty on a carrier for refusal to deliver freight upon payment or tender of charges as shown by the bill of lading is a valid exercise of police power, and not unconstitutional as regulating interstate commerce, and applies to freight received within the state by a connecting carrier, though shipped from without the state.

COMMON CARRIERS — CONNECTING CARRIER — CONSTRUCTION OF STATUTE. — A statute requiring a carrier to receive and transport goods without delay, upon tender by a connecting carrier, does not raise the presumption that the carrier receiving freight from another carrier upon a through bill of lading, made without his authority, or express agreement as to the charges, has ratified such bill of lading so as to become a party to the contract. Such presumption only arises when the carrier sought to be charged has either itself executed the bill of lading, authorized another carrier to execute it, or ratified it by some act of its own.

COMMON CARRIERS — WAY-BILL AS EVIDENCE. — In an action against a connecting carrier, under a statute imposing a penalty for refusal to deliver freight upon payment or tender of charges as shown by the bill of lading, the original way-bill showing that defendant, at the time it received the freight, paid accrued charges amounting to as much as the entire charge agreed upon in the bill of lading for transportation for the whole distance, is admissible in evidence as tending to show that it never intended to ratify the contract contained in the bill of lading.

COMMON CARRIERS — NECESSITY OF SHOWING BILL OF LADING UPON DE-
MANDING FREIGHT. — In an action under a statute imposing a penalty
on a carrier for refusal to deliver freight upon payment or tender of
charges as shown by the bill of lading, the exhibition of the latter at the
time of tender and demand is not a condition precedent to recovery in
the absence of a demand for its production.

J. W. Terry, for the appellant.

Bassett, Muse, and Muse, for the appellee.

GAINES, A. J. This case was before this court at a former
term, and was reversed and remanded for a new trial, in accordance with an opinion which is reported in 69 Tex. 707.
The question then presented is not now involved. The action
was brought by appellee against appellant to recover the penalty prescribed by the act of May 6, 1882, for the failure of the
company to deliver to him certain merchandise transported
by it upon his tender of the charges for carriage specified in
the bill of lading. The defendant interposed an exception to
the petition, and now insists that the court erred in overruling it.

The bill of lading was for a certain car-load of nails, received at the city of Pittsburg, in the state of Pennsylvania,
by the Pittsburg, Cincinnati, and St. Louis Railway Company,
and bound that company to transport the merchandise from
that city to the city of Brenham, in the state of Texas, for a
freight charge of $197.50. The statute under which the pro-
ceeding was instituted reads as follows: "That any railroad
company, its officers, agents, or employees, that shall refuse
to deliver to the owner, agent, or consignee, any freight, goods,
wares, and merchandise of any kind or character whatever,
upon the payment, or tender of payment, of the freight
charges shown by the bill of lading, the said railroad company shall be liable in damages to the owner of said freight,
goods, wares, or merchandise to an amount equal to the
amount of the freight charges for every day said freight,
goods, wares, and merchandise is held after payment, or tender of payment, of the charges due, as shown by the bill of
lading, to be recovered in any court of competent jurisdiction": Laws of Called Session of 17th Legislature, 35.

It is urged that the law as applied to the transaction alleged
in the petition is a regulation of commerce between the states,
and is such as only the Congress of the United States has the
power to make. If so, the legislature had no power to make
such a law in reference to bills of lading for the carriage of

goods from another state into this state, and it would be our duty either to construe the act as not applying to such bills of lading, or to hold that as so applied it is in contravention of the constitution of the United States, and therefore void. We would not, however, in construing the act, give it an application that would render any part of it void, unless the intent to so apply it was made manifest by the language of the act itself.

But the question recurs, Is the provision under consideration in contravention of the federal constitution? As to what laws passed by the legislature of a state are to be deemed a regulation of commerce between the states within the meaning of that constitution, there have been numerous decisions in the courts of the United States. Considering the all-pervading influence of the commerce of the country, and that any state law in relation to commercial transactions not confined to those begun and completed within the state would almost necessarily affect in some degree the commerce between the states, the result is not surprising. From the opinions delivered in the case of the *Wabash etc. R'y Co.* v. *Illinois*, 118 U. S. 557, it would seem that the decisions of the supreme court of the United States upon these questions have not been altogether consistent, but it also appears from that and later-cases in the same court that the tendency now is to extend the power of Congress over matters affecting interstate commerce, and correspondingly to restrict that of the states. We think, however, that by the decisions of that court (which are authoritative upon these questions), the following propositions must be deemed to have been settled: —

1. That a state can make no law regulating the rate of freight for the carriage of goods between that and another state, although the regulation be construed as applying only to so much of the line of transit as lies within its own borders: *Wabash etc. R'y Co.* v. *Illinois, supra.*

2. That it can make no law which imposes, either directly or indirectly, a burden by way of taxation upon interstate commerce: *Pickard* v. *Pullman S. Car Co.*, 117 U. S. 34; *State Freight Tax Case*, 15 Wall. 232; *Gloucester Ferry Co.* v. *Pennsylvania*, 114 U. S. 196; *Walling* v. *Michigan*, 116 U. S. 446; *Western Union Tel. Co.* v. *Texas*, 105 U. S. 460; *County of Mobile* v. *Kimball*, 102 U. S. 691; *Robbins* v. *Shelby Taxing District*, 120 U. S. 489; *Leloup* v. *Mobile*, 127 U. S. 640; *Asher* v. *Texas*, 128 U. S. 129.

3. That wharves, and bridges, and ferries across streams constituting the boundaries between the states may be established and regulated by the states, in the absence of legislation on the same subject by Congress, provided no burden other than an ordinary charge for their use be imposed upon the commerce passing over them: *Gilman* v. *Philadelphia*, 3 Wall. 713; *Escanaba etc. Co.* v. *Chicago*, 107 U. S. 678; *Parkersburg Transportation Co.* v. *Parkersburg*, 107 U. S. 691.

4. That in the exercise of their police powers, the states may enact laws which, though they affect commerce between the states, are not to be considered regulations of that commerce within the meaning of the constitution of the United States: *Chicago etc. R. R. Co.* v. *Fuller*, 17 Wall. 560, and cases there cited; *Smith* v. *Alabama*, 124 U. S. 465.

Is the law in question in this suit a proper exercise of the police power of the state? This power relates to such a number and variety of subjects, that it is impossible to define it, except in terms so general that the definition is of but little practical utility in any case difficult of solution. We think, however, the opinions in the cases last cited throw much light upon the question before us.

In *Chicago etc. R. R. Co.* v. *Fuller*, *supra*, the question was as to the validity of a statute of Iowa, which required all railway companies in the state, in September of each year, to fix their rates of fare for passengers and freight, and on the first day of October following to post up at their depots a printed copy of such rates, and to cause a copy to remain posted during the year, and subjected the companies to penalties in case of a failure to comply with its provisions. In the conclusion of their opinion, the court uses this language: "If the requirements of the statute here in question were . . . . regulations of commerce, the question would arise whether, regarded in the light of the authorities referred to, and of reason and principle, they are not regulations of such a character as to be valid until superseded by the paramount power of Congress. But as we are unanimously of the opinion that they are merely police regulations, it is unnecessary to pursue the subject."

In *Smith* v. *Alabama*, *supra*, the court says: "A carrier exercising his calling within a particular state, although engaged in the business of interstate commerce, is answerable, according to the law of the state, for acts of non-feasance or misfeasance committed within its limits. If he fail to deliver goods to the proper consignee at the right time or place, he is liable to

an action for damages, under the laws of the state, in its
courts; or, if by negligence in transportation, he inflicts injury upon the person of a passenger brought from another
state, a right of action for the consequent damage is given by
the local law. In neither case would it be a defense that the
law giving the right to redress was void, as being an unconstitutional regulation of commerce by the state. This, indeed,
was the very point decided in *Sherlock* v. *Alling*, 93 U. S. 99."

The statute we have under consideration, like every other
law which gives a remedy to the shipper against the carrier
for a violation of his contract, does in some remote degree affect
interstate commerce when applied to a contract of carriage
from one state to another. But it imposes no tax; it neither
fixes nor regulates any rates; it makes no discrimination between commerce wholly within the state and that between the
state and other states; it imposes no duty upon any carrier
not already imposed by the common law. It applies to
all railroad companies in the state and to all contracts
of carriage alike, and merely provides a penalty for the purpose of enforcing a compliance with an obligation which already
existed at common law. In respect of the questions before us,
the statute is not distinguishable from any other law affording
a remedy for the breach of a contract of carriage of goods between two states.

We conclude that the statute was a proper exercise of the
police power reserved to the state, and is therefore valid. The
court therefore did not err in overruling the defendant's exception to the petition.

In answer to the petition, the defendant pleaded that the
shipment which gave rise to this controversy was over the
Pittsburg, Cincinnati, and St. Louis Railway to St. Louis, and
thence over the Texas and St. Louis Railway to McGregor,
Texas, where the freight was delivered to its road for transportation to Brenham; that the Pittsburg, Cincinnati, and St. Louis
company had no authority to contract for the carriage of the
nails over its road, and that its agents at McGregor received
the freight for transportation to Brenham at its customary
rates, without having any knowledge of the bill of lading executed by that company; that upon receipt of the freight it paid
the accrued charges as shown by the way-bill to be $197.50,
and that its charges in addition amounted to $35. The entire
charges as shown by the bill of lading were $197.50.

The defendant introduced evidence of the facts alleged in

its answer, and the court charged the jury as follows: "If the court believe from the evidence that the defendant company received the nails at the town of Brenham, this would constitute an affirmance of the original contract of shipment, and the defendant thereby became bound by the terms of the shipment as shown in the bill of lading."

In this we think there was error. Our statutes make it obligatory upon every railroad company in this state to draw over their road, without delay, the passengers, merchandise, and cars of every other railroad company which may enter and connect with their road: R. S., art. 4251; see also arts. 4226, 4227, 4251, 4254. In the absence of a provision of this character it might be proper to hold that a carrier who has received freight from another carrier upon a through-bill of lading, without any express agreement as to the charges, should be presumed to have ratified the bill of lading, though made without its authority, and to have become a party to the contract. But certainly when the carrier is bound by a statute to receive and transport the goods without delay upon tender by the connecting carrier, no such presumption should be indulged. Such a rule would be to force a contract upon a carrier to which he had not given his consent, and compel him to carry at a rate fixed by another company. The result of the construction of the law by the court below is, that a railroad company is not permitted to refuse to receive the goods for transportation, yet if it does receive them, it ratifies by that act a bill of lading made without its authority. This, in our opinion, cannot be tolerated. We so held at the last Tyler term in a case not yet reported. Should a railroad company in Arkansas receive freight to be transported to El Paso, in this state, for a less charge for the whole distance than the customary charge of the Texas road for the transportation over its own line, could the latter be forced to accept the contract? We think not. We do not think the legislature intended that such a construction should be given to the statute under consideration. Our opinion is, that the act only applies when the railroad company that is sought to be charged in damages has either itself executed the bill of lading or authorized another company to execute it, or has ratified it by some voluntary act on its part. Instead of the charge complained of, the court should have given an instruction in substance the same as charge No. 1 requested by defendant.

We think the court should not have excluded the original

way-bill when offered in evidence. In connection with other testimony, it showed that defendant paid at the time it received the nails accrued charges amounting to as much as the entire charge agreed upon in the bill of lading for the transportation of the property for the whole distance, and tended to show that it never intended to ratify that contract.

We infer from the statement appended to the bill of exceptions that the depositions of the witnesses Murray and Dodge were objected to in writing, and were suppressed at a term of the court previous to the trial. If so, the bill of exceptions should have been then taken, and the depositions were properly excluded when offered on the trial.

The plaintiff has filed cross-assignments of error. The goods were first demanded on the 15th of December, 1884, and again on the 27th of January, 1885. On both occasions the charges shown by the bill of lading were tendered. There was a dispute whether or not the bill of lading was presented at the time of the first demand. It was formally exhibited to the company agent when the second tender and demand were made. Under these circumstances, the court charged the jury, in effect, that in order to make the demand, effectual under the statute, the plaintiff must at the time have exhibited his bill of lading; and refused to charge that such presentation of the instrument was not necessary.

We are of opinion that the court erred in these rulings. The statute does not expressly require that the bill of lading shall be shown to the agent of the railroad company when the goods are demanded; nor do we find anything in either the words of the act or the nature of the business from which it ought reasonably to be inferred that the legislature so intended. It is to be presumed, as a matter of law, that a party to a contract knows its contents; and, as a matter of fact, it is not unreasonable to suppose that the agents of a railroad company who receive freight at its destination know the charges which the company is entitled to receive, as shown by the bill of lading. We think, therefore, that it was not intended that the exhibition of the bill of lading, at the time of the tender of the money and demand of the goods, should be a condition precedent to the recovery of the damages. But the statute is strictly penal, and the penalty is severe, and we think a case may arise in which the owner of the goods should not recover if he has refused to exhibit his contract. It is only for a willful disregard of the law that its penalties should be inflicted. Hence, if there should be a mistake, if the agent of the company should not, in fact, know the contents of the bill, and should the owner of the goods, having it in his power, refuse to produce it, he would not be entitled to recover.

In regard to appellee's second assignment of error, it is sufficient to say that it was decided, upon the former appeal, that the defendant had no right to require of plaintiff a receipt for the overcharge, and that if such a right should be insisted upon on another trial, it would be proper to instruct the jury that it did not exist. If no issue should be again made upon the question, we do not see that such an instruction would be either necessary or proper.

For the errors pointed out, the judgment is reversed and the cause remanded. Each party will pay one half of the costs of this appeal. ___

RIGHT OF STATES TO REGULATE COMMERCE IS CONCURRENT WITH THAT OF CONGRESS, provided always, however, that all state regulations inconsistent with those of the federal government must give way: *People v. Coleman,* 4 Cal. 46; 60 Am. Dec. 581.

A STATE LAW MUST ACT DIRECTLY AS A REGULATION OF COMMERCE before it will be pronounced unconstitutional: *Commonwealth v. Erie R'y Co.,* 62 Pa. St. 286; 1 Am. Rep. 399.

A STATE LAW CANNOT BURDEN INTERSTATE COMMERCE by taxation: *Ex parte Rosenblatt,* 19 Nev. 439; 3 Am. St. Rep. 901, and note.

RAILROAD COMMISSION OF ONE STATE CANNOT FIX rates of transportation by carriers between two points within that state over a route extending across an adjoining state: *State v. Chicago etc. R'y Co.,* 40 Minn. 267; 12 Am. St. Rep. 730.

CONTRACT MADE WITHOUT AUTHORITY MAY BE RATIFIED by a connecting carrier, but a ratification will not be presumed from the performance of some duty required by law: *Gulf etc. R'y Co. v. Baird,* 75 Tex. 257.

INDEX TO THE NOTES.

INDEX.

ABANDONMENT.
See Homestead, 3.

ABATEMENT.
See Nuisances, 4–8.

ACCORD AND SATISFACTION.
Plea of Accord and Satisfaction must Aver Delivery and Acceptance. — A plea of accord and satisfaction which does not aver a delivery and an acceptance of the goods in satisfaction of the debt is bad. *Hancock v. Yaden*, 396.

ACCOUNT STATED.
See Banks and Banking, 2.

ACCOUNTING.
See Partnership, 4, 5.

ACKNOWLEDGMENTS.
See Deeds, 4–6.

ADMIRALTY.

1. Where Admiralty Jurisdiction of the United States Court Attaches, It Undoubtedly Excludes the jurisdictions of the state courts, and a state cannot confer jurisdiction upon its courts in such cases; but it is essential to a suit *in rem* in admiralty against a vessel that an actual seizure be made of the vessel, and it be subjected primarily to the satisfaction of the judgment. *Gindele v. Corrigan*, 292.

2. Liens against Vessels may be Enforced in the State Courts, where the proceeding to enforce them does not amount to an admiralty proceeding *in rem*, or otherwise conflict with the constitution of the United States. *Id.*

3. Attachment of Vessels. — There is No More Valid Objection to Attachment Proceedings to enforce a lien in a suit *in personam*, by holding a vessel by mesne process to be subjected to execution on a personal judgment when recovered, than there is in subjecting her to seizure on the execution. Both are incidents of a common-law remedy, which a court of common law is competent to give. *Id.*

4. Proceedings against Vessels. — Where, under the statute of Illinois, a proceeding is commenced against a vessel whose owners are alleged to be unknown, to recover damages resulting from its collision with another vessel, and a writ of attachment is issued, under which the vessel

941

is attached, and thereafter the persons claiming to be her owners give bonds for the release of the attachment as provided by statute, and the vessel is thereupon discharged and released, and after due trial judgment is rendered against the principal and sureties on the bond, the proceeding becomes *in personam*, and has no similitude to admiralty proceedings *in rem*, and the state courts have jurisdiction to enter judgment. *Id.*

ADULTERY.

See CRIMINAL LAW, 14, 15.

AGENCY.

1. AUTHORITY OF AGENT TO COLLECT. — Authority to an agent to sell goods does not include authority to collect pay for the goods sold. *Kane v. Barstow*, 490.

2. AGENT'S AUTHORITY. — Rule that principal is bound by the acts of his agent within the apparent scope of his authority is applicable only when there have been previous transactions of a similar character, in which the agent exceeded his powers, and which have been ratified by the principal without question, and without knowledge on the part of the third party of a limitation of the agent's authority, and an excess in the particular case, whereby such party is led to believe that the agent has all the powers assumed. *Id.*

3. EVIDENCE OF AGENT'S AUTHORITY TO MAKE CONTRACT, AND OF CUSTOM. — Where the authority of an acknowledged agent to make a contract giving a jobber an exclusive right to sell a certain line of cigars in a certain territory is questioned, the evidence of another jobber of like goods in the same territory that a custom or usage existed for such traveling agents to make similar contracts to the one in suit is admissible, and should be submitted to the jury to aid it in determining whether the agent had authority to make the contract in question. *Kaufman v. Farley etc. Co.*, 462.

4. NOTICE TO AGENT IS NOTICE TO PRINCIPAL. — A principal employing an agent to sell machinery, but agreeing with him that notes given in payment shall be taken in the name of the principal, and guaranteed by the agent, is chargeable, in an action against the maker of a note taken by the agent, with the latter's knowledge that such note was not taken in payment for machinery. *Johnston H. Co. v. Miller*, 536.

5. PRINCIPAL CANNOT RATIFY FRAUD OF HIS AGENT by accepting a note which is the fruit of such fraud, and suing upon it, and claiming at the same time to be a holder of the note in good faith, because the agent did not acquaint him with the circumstances under which he procured it when he sent it to him, but led him to suppose that it had been taken in the ordinary course of his agency. *Id.*

6. AGENT'S DECLARATIONS OF HIS AGENCY are inadmissible in an action between the principal and a third party, for the purpose of establishing the agency. *Kane v. Barstow*, 490.

7. AGENCY OF WITNESS CANNOT BE ESTABLISHED by his own declarations. *Omaha etc. Co. v. Tabor*, 185.

8. AGENT'S RIGHT TO COMMISSIONS. — An agent employed to sell real estate, who first brings it to the notice of the person who ultimately becomes the purchaser, is entitled to his commissions on the sale, although the latter is effected by the owner of the property, nor can the owner evade

his liability to pay the agent his commissions by selling for a sum less than the price given the agent, when the reduction is made of the owner's own accord. *Plant* v. *Thompson*, 512.

9. AGENT'S RIGHT TO COMMISSION ON SALE OF REAL ESTATE. — Under an exclusive agency to sell real estate on commission, the exclusive right to sell not being given, the owner has a right to make a sale independent of the agent, and, in such case, will not be liable to the agent for commission unless he sells to a purchaser procured by the agent. *Dole* v. *Sherwood*, 531.

10. EFFECT OF EXCLUSIVE AGENCY TO SELL LAND. — An exclusive agency to sell land merely prohibits the placing of the property for sale in the hands of any other agent, but not the sale of the property by the owner himself. *Id.*

11. RIGHT TO TERMINATE AGENCY. — When the compensation of an agent is dependent upon the success of his efforts in procuring a contract for his principal and his subsequent performance of the work, the principal will not be permitted to stimulate his efforts with the promise of reward, and then, when the contract is obtained and the compensation assured, to terminate the agency for the purpose of securing to himself the agent's profits. Though the principal might have terminated the agency at any time before there was a reasonable assurance that the contract would be obtained, he cannot, after it is obtained, put an end to the agency in bad faith, and as a device to deprive the agent of the fruits of his labor. *Warren etc. Mfg. Co.* v. *Holbrook*, 788.

12. POWER OF ATTORNEY. — Assignment for benefit of creditors may be executed by an agent or an attorney in fact especially authorized thereto, but the power must, in express terms, grant the authority. *Gouldy* v. *Medcalf*, 912.

13. CONSTRUCTION. — The authority derived from a general power of attorney is limited to the exercise of the acts authorized by the language employed in granting the special powers. *Id.*

14. AUTHORITY CONFERRED BY POWER OF ATTORNEY will be construed strictly, so as to exclude the exercise of any power which is not warranted, either by the actual terms used, or as a necessary means of executing the authority with effect. *Id.*

See CARRIERS, 6; CORPORATIONS, 10, 12, 14; DAMAGES, 3; FACTORS; NEGOTIABLE INSTRUMENTS, 22, 23; SALES, 5.

AMENDMENTS.
See JUDGMENTS, 18, 19, 20; PLEADING, 1.

ANIMALS.

1. VICIOUS ANIMALS — DUTY OF OWNER WITH NOTICE OF VICIOUSNESS OF. — When it appears that a domestic animal is vicious, and has a propensity to do mischief, of which facts the owner or keeper has notice, either express or implied, the law imposes the duty upon him of keeping such animal secure, from which duty a liability arises in favor of any person who, without fault on his part, is injured by it, either in person or property, through the negligence of such owner or keeper. *Knowles* v. *Mulder*, 627.

2. VICIOUS ANIMALS — NOTICE OF VICIOUSNESS. — The owner of a domestic animal may be chargeable with notice of its viciousness through his negligence to take notice of its vicious habits. *Id.*

3. VICIOUS ANIMALS — NOTICE OF VICIOUSNESS. — If a person has a dog in his possession for a considerable length of time, and such dog has all that time been in the habit of rushing into the highway in front of the owner's residence, and of barking at, chasing, worrying, or attacking passing teams in a ferocious manner, a question is presented to the jury to find whether the owner was aware of such habit, or if not, if he was negligent in not knowing it, and the facts may be such that it may well be found that he ought to have known it, and therefrom imply notice to him. The length of time such vicious habit is shown to have existed has an important bearing upon whether notice or knowledge of such habit may be inferred or imputed to the owner. *Id.*

APPEAL AND ERROR.

1. ASSIGNMENT OF ERROR that "the court erred in sustaining the motion made by plaintiff at the close of defendant's testimony, and directing a verdict for plaintiff," is not open to objection as not being sufficiently specific, or as assuming that the motion asked the court to direct a verdict for plaintiffs. *Kaufman v. Farley etc. Co.*, 462.

2. WHAT WILL BE CONSIDERED ON. — Where exceptions are taken and errors assigned, independent of the motion for a new trial, which was filed too late to be available as a ground upon which to base an assignment of error, the appellate court may review and reverse the action of the court below. *Id.*

3. RECORD ON APPEAL. — The supreme court of Illinois will not consider as a part of the record anything which was not before the appellate court when the case was decided there. If the record is amended in the trial court, such amendment will not be considered in the supreme court if it was not made a part of the record of the appellate court. *Claflin v. Dunne*, 263.

4. QUESTION AS TO ILLEGALITY OF CONSIDERATION of a note sued upon cannot be raised for the first time on appeal. *Jennings v. First Nat. Bank*, 210.

5. JUDGMENT ON FACTS WITHOUT JURY CONCLUSIVE. — When a jury is waived, a decision of the court upon the facts is, in legal effect, equivalent to a verdict of the jury, and in the absence of statutory power will not be reviewed on appeal, except in cases where such verdict cannot, as matter of law, be supported by any reasonable inferences from the evidence. *Boyd v. State*, 31.

6. ERROR IN OVERRULING MOTION FOR NONSUIT IS WAIVED by evidence offered by defendant in his own behalf which supplies the defect existing in plaintiff's proofs. *Jennings v. First Nat. Bank*, 210.

7. EXCLUSION OF WITNESSES, or of any particular witness, from the court-room during the trial is within the discretion of the trial court, and cannot be reviewed on appeal. *Barnes v. State*, 48.

8. DISCRETION OF COURT. — Refusal of the court to put a witness under the rule, and compel his withdrawal from the court-room during the examination of another witness, is a matter within the discretion of the court, and not subject to review on appeal. *McGuff v. State*, 25.

See ATTACHMENT AND GARNISHMENT, 3; NEW TRIAL; OFFICE AND OFFICERS, 2, 3.

ASSAULT.

See CRIMINAL LAW, 16, 17; LANDLORD AND TENANT, 19.

ASSIGNMENT.

See GIFTS; INSURANCE, 20; LANDLORD AND TENANT, 1-7.

ASSIGNMENTS FOR BENEFIT OF CREDITORS.

FOREIGN ASSIGNMENT — CONFLICT OF LAWS. — An assignment or transfer of property, giving preference to certain creditors, and valid by the laws of another state where made, will not be upheld by the courts of Minnesota when contrary to the policy and laws of that state, as to property situated there. *Matter of Dalpay*, 729.

See AGENCY, 12.

ASSUMPSIT.

1. WAIVER OF TORT TO SUE IN. — Before a party can waive a tort for the conversion of personal property and bring *assumpsit*, the property in the hands of a tort-feasor must have been sold and converted into money, upon the theory that the money has been received for the plaintiff's use. *Tuttle* v. *Campbell*, 652.
2. WAIVER OF TORT TO SUE IN. — Where a contract may exist, and at the same time a duty is superimposed or arises out of the circumstances surrounding the transaction, the violation of which duty would constitute a tort, and the property has been converted, but not sold, the tort may be waived and *assumpsit* maintained, for the reason that the relation of the parties, out of which the duty violated grew, had its inception in contract and relations of trust and confidence. *Id.*

See CO-TENANCY, 9-10.

ATTACHMENT AND GARNISHMENT.

1. EFFECT OF RECITALS OF INDEBTEDNESS IN AFFIDAVIT. — When an officer justifies the holding of goods under a writ of attachment valid upon its face, the recital of indebtedness in the affidavit raises a presumption of such indebtedness. If this presumption is rebutted, it then devolves upon the officer to prove the indebtedness by other evidence than the affidavit; but in the absence of such rebutting proof, the attachment papers are a sufficient showing upon the part of the officer to enable him to contest the title of the party seeking to reclaim the goods taken, whether the action is replevin, trespass, or trover. *Treat* v. *Dunham*, 616.
2. JUDGMENT AS EVIDENCE. — A judgment against a plaintiff in attachment is not admissible in evidence for the purpose of showing that there was no indebtedness due, at the time of issuing the writ of attachment, from the defendant to the plaintiff, until four days after the rendition of the verdict upon which the judgment is based. *Id.*
3. EFFECT OF APPEAL FROM JUDGMENT. — A judgment against a plaintiff in attachment which is appealed from does not dissolve the attachment, but the lien continues until the final disposition of the case. *Id.*
4. RIGHT OF PARTY FOUNDED SOLELY ON LIEN OF JUDGMENT OR ATTACHMENT IS SUBORDINATE to that of a purchaser in good faith. *Shirk* v. *Thomas*, 381.
5. GARNISHMENT. — MAKER OF NEGOTIABLE PROMISSORY NOTE cannot be charged in garnishment before its maturity, on the ground that he knew when he executed it that it was the purpose of the payee to place the fund beyond the reach of his creditors. *Willis* v. *Heath*, 876.

6. Attorney's Fee Allowed Garnishee. — The court may allow the garnishee a reasonable attorney's fee, and in the absence of proof that the amount fixed by the court was too much, it will be deemed conclusive. *Id.*

See ADMIRALTY, 3, 4; EQUITY, 2; JUDGMENTS, 10.

ATTORNEY AND CLIENT.

1. Attorney is Competent to Testify as to Value of his Services in an action to recover therefor, and may show by his own testimony his experience and knowledge, and give his judgment as to the value of his services; and he may also testify as to his knowledge of the charges of other attorneys for like services in similar cases. *Babbitt* v. *Bumpus*, 585.

2. Testimony Showing that Less was Charged by Opposing Attorneys in the cases in which the plaintiff rendered the services as attorney for which he sues, and that the services rendered by them were as important as, and of as much or even greater value than, were those of the plaintiff, is properly excluded. *Id.*

3. Testimony Descriptive of Character of Services Charged for by Attorney is admissible in an action brought by him to recover for such services. *Id.*

4. It is Competent to Show Amount Involved in Suits for the management and trial of which an attorney brings suit, because the amount involved in the issues has much to do with the value of the services rendered, and the responsibility assumed by the attorney. *Id.*

5. Lawyer is not Insurer of Result in Case in Which He is Employed, unless he makes a special contract to that effect and for that purpose. When he is employed in a case, there is no implied contract that he will bring to bear learning, skill, or ability beyond the average of his profession; nor can more than ordinary care and diligence be required of him, unless a special contract is made requiring it. *Id.*

6. Questions Involving Proper Service to be Rendered by Attorneys should be very carefully considered by courts and jurors, when attorneys employed under the usual implied contract have acted in good faith, and with a fair degree of intelligence in the discharge of their duties. Under such circumstances, the errors they may make must be very gross before the attorneys can be held responsible. They should be such as to render wholly improbable a disagreement among good lawyers as to the character of the services required to be performed, and as to the manner of their performance under all the circumstances in the given case, before such responsibility attaches. *Id.*

See ATTACHMENT AND GARNISHMENT, 6; CRIMINAL LAW, 19, 20.

BAGGAGE.
See CARRIERS, 20.

BAILMENT.
See CO-TENANCY, 1, 9.

BANKS AND BANKING.

1. Account between Bank and Depositor. — As money is paid in and drawn out of a bank, or other debts and credits are entered by the consent of both parties in the general banking account of the depositor, a balance is considered as struck at the date of each payment or entry on either side of the account. *Wasson v. Lamb*, 342.

2. ENTRY OF AMOUNT AND DATE OF DEPOSIT in the pass-book of the depositor, made by the proper officer, binds the bank as an admission, and is generally conclusive upon it as an account stated, when the pass-book is balanced. *Id.*

3. CHECKS, DRAFTS, OR OTHER EVIDENCES OF DEBT received by a bank in good faith as deposits, and credited as so much money, transfers their title to the bank, and it becomes legally liable to the depositor as for so much money deposited as of the date of the credit. *Id.*

4. DEPOSIT OF TAX RECEIPTS, treated by mutual consent of the bank and depositor as so much cash deposited to the credit of the latter, will be regarded in legal effect as a deposit of money, and the transaction will be treated as if the bank had paid the taxes, and then received the money on deposit, in the absence of evidence of fraud. *Id.*

5. DEPOSITOR OF TAX RECEIPTS who has received credit on the books of the bank as for so much cash deposited, and has afterwards checked out a sum of money, including the amount of the tax receipts, cannot claim that the taxes were not paid, and, after letting the transaction stand until by an assignment by the bank the rights of other creditors have intervened, he cannot recover the money on the ground of false representations of the solvency of the bank at the time of the deposit, especially when he has not been injured by such representations. *Id.*

6. PAYMENT BY A BANK ON A RAISED AND ALTERED CHECK, DRAWN BY ONE OF ITS DEPOSITORS, TO A PERSON to whom it has been indorsed for collection, cannot be recovered back of a party to whom it was made, after he has paid over the amount thereof to the person by whom he was intrusted with such collection, and without any notice of the fraudulent character of such check. The person claiming such check cannot be held answerable as an indorser thereof, from the fact that it was paid to his agent, who indorsed his own name thereon without adding the word "agent," or any other word or words to show that his indorsement was other than in his personal capacity. *National City Bank of Brooklyn v. Westcott*, 771.

BICYCLES.

See HIGHWAYS, 1, 2; NEGLIGENCE, 9.

BILLS OF EXCHANGE.

See NEGOTIALE INSTRUMENTS, 15.

BILLS OF LADING.

See CARRIERS, 8–10.

BONA FIDE PURCHASERS.

See DEEDS, 2, 3; NEGOTIABLE INSTRUMENTS, 10–14; PLEDGE, 4.

BONDS.

SURETIES ON INJUNCTION BOND EXECUTED AFTER ISSUANCE OF WRIT NOT LIABLE. — The sureties on statutory bonds have a right to stand upon the precise terms of their contract. When, therefore, a bond is given in pursuance of an order that an injunction issue on the filing of a bond, the sureties are not liable for damages resulting to the defendant from his obeying a writ of injunction issued and served several days prior to the execution of the bond, no writ having been issued after the filing of the bond. *Carter* v. *Mulrein*, 99.

See MUNICIPAL CORPORATIONS, 9; OFFICER AND OFFICERS, 9, 10.

BREACH OF PROMISE OF MARRIAGE.
See MARRIAGE AND DIVORCE, 3–9.

BRIDGES.
See COUNTIES, 1–5; INTERSTATE COMMERCE, 2.

BROKERS.
See AGENCY, 8–10.

BURGLARY.
See CRIMINAL LAW, 18.

CARRIERS.

1. CONTRACT LIMITING DAMAGES recoverable of a common carrier will not control, where negligence is shown, and there is no proof that a lower rate of freight was given on account of the limitation placed upon the value of the property. *Adams Ex. Co.* v. *Harris*, 315.

2. LIABILITY OF, UNDER SPECIAL CONTRACT — BURDEN OF PROOF. — Under a contract limiting the carrier's liability for injury or loss occurring through his negligence, the burden of proof is on him to show, after injury or loss is established, in order to excuse his liability, that such injury or loss was caused by something else than his negligence, and that there was no negligence in fact on his part. *Hull* v. *Chicago etc. R'y Co.*, 722.

3. BURDEN OF PROOF IS ON CARRIER to show contract limiting his liability. *Prima facie*, a carrier is liable for goods upon proof of delivery and acceptance for carriage and of loss or damage in carrying, and if any contract exists limiting his liability he must show it, and that the loss came within the exception made by it. The shipper need not establish the non-existence of the contract. *Id.*

4. LIABILITY OF, UNDER SPECIAL CONTRACT. — A common carrier remains such, even though in a particular case he may have, to some extent, limited his liability by contract, and all rules applicable to common carriers apply in such case, except in so far as the parties may, by express contract, have varied them. The reasons which require the carrier to excuse his negligence apply with as much force to a case of limited as to a case of full common-law liability. *Id.*

5. CARRIER WAIVES HIS RIGHT TO DETAIN GOODS FOR FREIGHT, when he puts his refusal to deliver upon the ground that they are not in his possession at the place where the demand is duly made. *Adams Ex. Co.* v. *Harris*, 315.

6. WHEN BOUND BY ACT OF AGENT. — Agent of carrier invested with general authority to adjust claims against it binds it by his declarations made while endeavoring to secure the adjustment of such a claim. *Id.*

7. CONNECTING CARRIER. — A contract of carriage not providing that its stipulations shall inure to the benefit of any other carrier than the one with

whom it was made, and not designating any other carrier along the line, cannot be invoked to aid an intermediate carrier who undertakes to carry the goods. *Id.*

8. CONNECTING CARRIER — CONSTRUCTION OF STATUTE. — A statute requiring a carrier to receive and transport goods without delay, upon tender by a connecting carrier, does not raise the presumption that the carrier receiving freight from another carrier upon a through bill of lading, made without his authority, or express agreement as to the charges, has ratified such bill of lading so as to become a party to the contract. Such presumption only arises when the carrier sought to be charged has either itself executed the bill of lading, authorized another carrier to execute it, or ratified it by some act of its own. *Gulf etc. R'y Co.* v. *Dwyer,* 926.

9. WAY-BILL AS EVIDENCE. — In an action against a connecting carrier, under a statute imposing a penalty for refusal to deliver freight upon payment or tender of charges as shown by the bill of lading, the original way-bill showing that defendant, at the time it received the freight, paid accrued charges amounting to as much as the entire charge agreed upon in the bill of lading for transportation for the whole distance, is admissible in evidence as tending to show that it never intended to ratify the, contract contained in the bill of lading. *Id.*

10. NECESSITY OF SHOWING BILL OF LADING UPON DEMANDING FREIGHT. — In an action under a statute imposing a penalty on a carrier for refusal to deliver freight upon payment or tender of charges as shown by the bill of lading, the exhibition of the latter at the time of tender and demand is not a condition precedent to recovery in the absence of a demand for its production. *Id.*

11. DUTY TO PASSENGERS AT STATION OF DESTINATION. — A railroad company is under duty to its passengers not to expose them to unnecessary danger, and not to intentionally or negligently mislead them by causing them to reasonably suppose that their point of destination has been reached, and that they may safely alight, when the train is in an improper place; but the mere announcement of the name of the station is not an invitation to alight; still, when followed by a full stoppage of the train soon thereafter, it is ordinarily notification that it has arrived at the usual place of landing passengers, and whether the stoppage of the train, after such announcement, and before arriving at the platform, is negligence, depends upon the attending circumstances. *Smith* v. *Georgia P. R'y Co.,* 63.

12. DUTY TO PASSENGERS AT STATION OF DESTINATION. — Neither the announcement of the station, nor stopping the train before it arrives at the platform, if required by law or usage to avoid collisions or accidents, is negligence *per se* in a railroad company toward a passenger injured while attempting to alight. *Id.*

13. DUTY TO PASSENGERS AT STATION OF DESTINATION. — When the name of a station is called, and soon thereafter the train is brought to a standstill, a passenger may reasonably conclude that it has stopped at the station, and endeavor to alight, and may recover if injured in his attempt to do so, unless the circumstances and indications are such as to render it manifest that the train has not reached the usual and proper landing-place. *Id.*

14. WHEN NEGLIGENCE OF PASSENGER AT STATION OF DESTINATION A QUESTION OF LAW. — When the station is announced, and the train stopped soon thereafter, in the daytime, to take a side-track, at a spot

where there is no depot or platform, and all the surroundings indicate that it is not a proper place for landing, a passenger who attempts to alight, and is injured in so doing, cannot recover, in the absence of circumstances caused by the railroad company inducing him to reasonably suppose that he was attempting to alight at the proper place. In such case, his injury is accidental, if not the result of his own negligence, and the jury should be so instructed, and of his inability to recover. *Id.*

15. NEGLIGENCE — DUTY TO INJURED PASSENGER ON TRACK. — Where a passenger is thrown upon the track through the negligence of a railroad company, and is there left in a dazed and partially unconscious condition from the fall, where he is run down and killed by another train belonging to the company, having knowledge of his fall and condition of mind, the company is liable for the injury. In such case, the passenger is not a trespasser, and the negligence of the company is the proximate cause of death. *Cincinnati etc. R. R. Co.* v. *Cooper*, 334.

16. DUTY TO INJURED PASSENGER ON TRACK. — A common carrier is bound to know that trains are running upon its own road, and it is under duty to a passenger negligently thrown upon its track, and left in a dazed condition, to take steps to prevent injury to him from danger which it knew he was likely to incur from its trains, and it does not matter that the injury incurred was not foreseen, if it was such as might naturally result. *Id.*

17. COMMON 'CARRIER IS NOT BOUND TO PROTECT DRUNKARDS from the consequences which result from their own wrongs or follies. Still, it owes them some duties, and cannot negligently suffer harm to come to them while they are passengers. *Id.*

18. COMMON CARRIER IS ANSWERABLE FOR INJURY TO DRUNKEN PASSENGER, where the injury results, not from the drunken condition of the passenger, but from the carrier's breach of duty. *Id.*

19. NEGLIGENCE. — Recklessness in a common carrier, reaching in degree to an utter disregard of consequences, may supply the place of a specific intent to inflict an injury. *Id.*

20. LIABILITY FOR LOSS OF BAGGAGE. — Where a common carrier by steamer has transported the baggage of a passenger, and placed it in the warehouse of another at the place of destination, such warehousing being within the contemplation of both parties, the carrier is not liable for its accidental loss by fire while so stored awaiting the arrival of the owner. *Laffrey* v. *Grummond*, 624.

CARRIERS.

CERTIORARI.

CIVIL RIGHTS.

CHATTEL MORTGAGES.

1. REMEDY OF MORTGAGOR AFTER FRAUDULENT SALE. — Where a chattel mortgagee, at his own sale, unlawfully, fraudulently, and unfairly buys the mortgaged property of a much greater value than the debt, and con-

verts it to his own use, disposing of a large portion of it, so as to be disabled from returning it or of allowing redemption, the mortgagor is entitled to recover from him the excess in value of the property thus converted over the amount of the mortgage debt, without payment or tender of payment thereof. *Wygal v. Bigelow,* 495.

2. RIGHT OF MORTGAGEE TO PURCHASE AT HIS OWN SALE. — A chattel mortgagee may purchase at his own sale under the mortgage, conducted in fairness and good faith; but if he abuses his power, and becomes the purchaser unfairly and dishonestly, he will be required to account to the mortgagor therefor. *Id.*

3. RIGHTS OF MORTGAGEE AFTER FRAUDULENT SALE. — An unfair or fraudulent sale of mortgaged chattels by the mortgagee will not defeat or extinguish the rights of the mortgagor, as the mortgagee has no right by unfair sale to sacrifice the property and deprive the mortgagor of any surplus over the debt which might arise from a sale fairly and honestly conducted. *Id.*

4. SALE IN PARCELS. — Where mortgaged chattels, consisting of many different articles, can easily be offered for sale separately or in lots or parcels, a sale of the whole in lump, or two lumps, under a power of sale contained in the mortgage, may be regarded as unfair, especially when it is shown that the property brought much less at the sale than its actual value. *Id.*

See FIXTURES, 6.

CHECKS.

See BANKS AND BANKING, 3, 6; NEGOTIABLE INSTRUMENTS.

COMMON CARRIERS.

See CARRIERS.

COMPROMISE.

1. UNCONSCIONABLE ADVANTAGE, WHETHER ONE PARTY HAS TAKEN OF ANOTHER, HOW DETERMINED. — In determining whether or not one party to a compromise agreement has taken an unconscionable advantage of the other party, the question must be determined, not in the light of subsequent events, but upon the circumstances existing at the time of the negotiations and the execution of the contract; and if it appears, upon a consideration of those circumstances, that no advantage was taken, and that the contract was fair, just, and equal, it will not be set aside. *Colton v. Stanford,* 137.

2. COMPROMISE OF DOUBTFUL CLAIMS, WHEN WILL NOT BE RESCINDED BECAUSE OF REPRESENTATIONS NOT BELIEVED OR RELIED UPON. — Where, after the death of one of several business associates, his personal representative, relying upon the advice of disinterested experts and professional friends specially selected to investigate and advise in the premises, and who had full access to all sources of information concerning the matters in controversy, compromises doubtful claims against the surviving associates, who acted in good faith and without intentional fraud, and disclosed every fact within their knowledge, such compromise will not be rescinded upon the ground that such surviving associates did not disclose all facts of which they might have acquired knowledge by a more skillful and diligent search, especially when every fact subsequently discovered could have been discovered before the execution of the compromise agreement as well as after it. *Id.*

3. DELAY IN SEEKING RESCISSION AND ENHANCEMENT IN VALUE OF PROPERTY, EFFECT OF. — When a compromise agreement has been effected between plaintiff and defendants under adverse circumstances, in view of which defendants desired plaintiff to prosecute the business at their mutual risk, which plaintiff declined to do, the failure on the part of the plaintiff for more than two years to seek a rescission of the agreement, or to become informed of the facts upon which rescission is sought, until the property involved had become greatly enhanced in value, is an important circumstance to be considered by the court. *Id.*

See ESTOPPEL, 2.

CONCURRENT NEGLIGENCE.

See NEGLIGENCE, 4.

CONFESSIONS.

See CRIMINAL LAW, 5.

CONFLICT OF LAWS.

See ASSIGNMENTS FOR BENEFIT OF CREDITORS; DOWER, 2, 3; JUDGMENTS, 21.

CONSTITUTIONAL LAW.

1. SUBJECT IS LEFT ENTIRE MASTER OF HIS OWN CONDUCT, under our constitution and system of government, except in the points wherein the public good requires some direction or restraint. *People v. Armstrong,* 578.

2. THE CLAUSE OF THE CONSTITUTION PROHIBITING THE INFLICTION OF CRUEL OR UNUSUAL PUNISHMENT confers power upon the courts to declare void legislative acts prescribing punishment for crime in fact cruel and unusual. *People v. Durston,* 859.

3. THE LEGISLATURE HAS POWER TO CHANGE THE MANNER OF INFLICTING THE PENALTY OF DEATH as a punishment for crime. *Id.*

4. UNCONSTITUTIONALITY OF STATUTE, HOW MAY BE MADE TO APPEAR. — The testimony of experts and other witnesses is not admissible to show that in carrying out a law some provision of the constitution may possibly be violated. If it cannot be made to appear that the statute is in conflict with the constitution by argument deduced from the language of the law itself, or from matters of which the court can take judicial notice, the act must stand. *Id.*

5. WHETHER THE USE OF ELECTRICITY AS AN AGENCY FOR PRODUCING DEATH constitutes a more humane method of executing the judgment of the court in capital cases was a question for the determination of the legislature, and the determination by the legislature of this question is conclusive upon the courts. *Id.*

6. THE LEGISLATIVE POWER OF THIS STATE COVERS every subject which, in the distribution of the powers of government between the legislative, executive, and judicial departments, belongs, by practice or usage in England or this country, to the legislative department, except in so far as such power has been withheld or limited by the constitution itself, and subject also to such restrictions as may be found in the constitution of the United States. *Lawton v. Steele,* 813.

CONTRACTS.

of a newspaper, in consideration of being allowed the difference between the rates paid and those received by him for advertising, the contract to continue for five years, is an entire and indivisible contract, so that any taint of illegality in one part affects the whole of it. *Id.*

9. RATIFICATION OF VOID CONTRACT — CHANGE IN LAW. — A contract void because it stipulates for doing what the law prohibits is incapable of being ratified as a whole, even if the law is so changed after the contract was made, and before it is fully performed, as to make it valid after the change went into effect. Every contract must be ratified, if at all, as an entirety. *Id.*

10. THE RESCISSION OF A CONTRACT WHILE IN THE COURSE OF PERFORMANCE destroys or annuls any claim which either of the parties might otherwise have in respect of performance, or of what has been paid or received thereon, unless a different intent can be deduced from the agreement of annulment construed in the light of attendant circumstances. *McCreery v. Day,* 793.

11. MISREPRESENTATION, WHEN NOT BASIS FOR RESCISSION OF CONTRACT. — Under the Civil Code of California, a misrepresentation, in order to avoid a contract, though it need not be the sole cause of the contract, must be of such nature, weight, and force that the court can say "without it the contract would not have been made"; and if the court properly finds, from the evidence, that the contract would have been executed by the plaintiff had the truth been known, and the defendant, upon being made aware of the facts, had still insisted upon the same contract, there is no basis for a rescission of the contract. *Colton v. Stanford,* 137.

12. MISREPRESENTATION, IF UNIMPORTANT, NOT GROUND FOR RESCISSION WHEN. — A mistaken representation made by the defendant, not being an inducing cause of the plaintiff's action in entering into a compromise agreement, but relating to a matter of comparatively small importance, will not be ground for rescinding the contract by the plaintiff, after the defendant has made large expenditures on the faith of the agreement, which have materially enhanced the value of the property involved in the litigation. *Id.*

See COMPROMISE; CORPORATIONS, 10, 11; HUSBAND AND WIFE, 5–9; INSURANCE, 9–12, 14; MARRIAGE AND DIVORCE, 2; MARRIED WOMEN, 1; MASTER AND SERVANT, 1; PARTNERSHIP, 5; SALES.

CONTRACTS OF SALE.
See VENDOR AND VENDEE, 1–9.

CONTRIBUTION.
See DEVISES AND LEGACIES; EQUITY, 1, 2.

CONVERSION.
See ASSUMPSIT, 1, 2; CO-TENANCY, 6–8; INSURANCE, 8; SALES, 12; TRESPASS, 1–3.

CORPORATIONS.

1. JURISDICTION OF SUPERIOR COURT WHERE JUDGMENT DEMANDED FOR LESS THAN THREE HUNDRED DOLLARS. — The superior court has no jurisdiction of an action to enforce the liability of the stockholders of a corporation as to stockholders against whom a judgment for less than

tion in aiding the construction of a railroad, the corporation cannot show that an investment company, which is not a party to the suit, built the road, and is the owner in fact of all the stock, property, and franchises, and that the corporation exists only in name for the purposes of maintaining the franchises of a corporation for the investment company's benefit, and that the claim set up is unjust and inequitable as to such company. and if established would seriously affect its rights and property. *Ten Eyck* v. *Pontiac etc. R. R. Co.*, 633.

10. CONTRACTS WITH AGENTS. — Contracts entered into between agents of a corporation occupying positions of trust and confidence and the corporation will always be scrutinized with jealous care by the courts, to see that no advantage is taken of the corporation or the rights and interests of the stockholders jeopardized; but such contracts fairly entered into and honestly executed, where no one is defrauded or overreached, are valid. *Id.*

11. CONTRACT BETWEEN, AND DIRECTORS. — Where a corporation has contracted with a director for his services as an attorney, and also in procuring aid notes and rights of way, and working up an interest in the construction of a railroad in the communities through which it is projected, in order to secure aid in its construction by donations and subscriptions, and also in enlisting capitalists in the enterprise, these services are valuable to the corporation, not embraced in the ordinary duties of a director, and are such as to which the corporation has a right to agree as to the compensation to be paid, and if the director's services were engaged for such purposes and performed, there arises an implied agreement to pay for such services what they are reasonably worth, so far as they have not been fixed by resolution of the board of directors. *Id.*

12. DUTY OF DIRECTORS. — The directors of a corporation are its agents, with the entire management of the corporate affairs committed to their charge, upon the trust and confidence that they shall be cared for and managed, within the limits of the powers conferred by law upon the corporation, for the common benefit of the stockholders. *Id.*

13. DUTIES OF DIRECTORS. — The directors of a corporation are required to act in the utmost good faith, and in accepting the office they impliedly undertake to give to the enterprise the benefit of their best care and judgment, and to exercise the power conferred solely in the interest of the corporation. They have no right to represent the corporation in any transaction in which they are personally interested, in obtaining an advantage at the expense of the corporation. *Id.*

14. DIRECTOR MAY CONTRACT WITH CORPORATION. — A director may enter into a valid contract with the corporation of which he is agent, when the corporation is represented in the transaction by a majority of the board of directors. *Id.*

15. POWERS AND DUTIES OF DIRECTORS. — The directors of a private pecuniary corporation are under the same restraints and disabilities as trustees. They have no right to use their official positions for their own benefit or the benefit of any one but the corporation; and if they act as directors for different companies, they cannot represent both in transactions in which their interests are opposed, or detrimental to a minority of the stockholders, no matter if such acts are beneficial to a majority of stockholders in each company, and have received their approval. *Memphis etc. R. R. Co.* v. *Woods*, 81.

COUNTIES.

5. LIABILITY FOR SAFETY OF BRIDGE. — A county undertaking to repair a bridge must use ordinary care in selecting the means and persons to do the work; but if such care is exercised, and the bridge remains unsafe, the county is not liable for injury. *Id.*

See NEGLIGENCE, 11; OFFICE AND OFFICERS, 7, 8.

COURTS.

DEFINITION OF. — PLACE OF MEETING is an important element in the definition that a court consists of persons officially assembled under authority of law, at the appropriate time and place, for the administration of justice. *In re Allison,* 224.

See DEVISES AND LEGACIES, 2; JUDICIAL SALES, 7-15; JUDGMENTS, 11, 13.

COVENANTS.

See LANDLORD AND TENANT, 14-18.

CREDITORS' SUITS.

See CORPORATIONS, 4-7.

CRIMINAL LAW.

1. INDICTMENT CHARGING DISJUNCTIVELY OFFENSES OF THE SAME CHARACTER, and subject to the same punishment, will support a general verdict of guilty. *McGuff* v. *State,* 25.

2. PLACE OF IMPRISONMENT. — When, upon conviction, the jury fixes the penalty at "imprisonment for life," without specifying the place of imprisonment, the defendant may properly be sentenced to imprisonment in the state penitentiary for and during his natural life. *Id.*

3. JURORS — FAILURE TO UNDERSTAND ENGLISH LANGUAGE DOES NOT DISQUALIFY. — That some of the grand and petit jurors who found the indictment and convicted the prisoner were Mexican electors, and did not understand the English language, does not affect the validity of the trial and conviction. *In re Allison,* 224.

4. DEFENSE OF FORMER JEOPARDY must be raised by special plea in the trial court. *Id.*

5. CONFESSIONS — WEIGHT OF, FOR JURY. — It is within the exclusive province of the jury to determine the weight of voluntary confessions admitted in evidence without objection. *McGuff* v. *State,* 25.

6. PERSON MAY NOT BE CRIMINALLY RESPONSIBLE, THOUGH HAVING SUFFICIENT MENTAL CAPACITY TO KNOW RIGHT FROM WRONG, if his will power is so impaired that he cannot resist an impulse to commit a crime; for in that case he is not of sound mind. But if the will is simply overborne by ungoverned passion, there may be criminal responsibility. *Plake* v. *State,* 408.

7. REASONABLE DOUBT AS TO SANITY OF ACCUSED, EFFECT OF. — If the evidence is of such a character as to create a reasonable doubt as to whether or not the accused was of unsound mind at the time the crime was committed, he is entitled to a verdict of acquittal. *Id.*

8. INSANITY IS QUESTION OF FACT FOR JURY. — Whether insanity exists or not, and what is its character and extent, is a question of fact to be determined by the jury, from the evidence, and it is not the province of the court to instruct the jury, as a matter of law, that insanity is a physical disease. *Id.*

9. That Evidence of a Distinct and Substantive Offense cannot be Admitted in support of another offense is a general rule, as laid down by all the authorities. This rule excludes all evidence of collateral facts, or those which are incapable of affording any reasonable presumption or inference as to the principal fact or matter in dispute; and the reason is, that such evidence tends to draw away the minds of the jurors from the point at issue, and to excite prejudice, and mislead them, and moreover, the adverse party, having had no notice of such a course of evidence, is not prepared to rebut it. *Farris v. People*, 283.

10. Evidence of Other Offenses. — The mere fact that evidence may tend to prove the commission of other crimes, or to establish collateral facts, does not necessarily render it incompetent, provided it is pertinent to the point in issue, and tends to prove the crime charged; but to make one criminal act evidence of another, a connection between them must have existed in the mind of the actor linking them together for some purpose he intended to accomplish; or it must be necessary to identify the person of the actor by some connection which shows that he who committed the one must have done the other. If the evidence be so dubious that the judge does not clearly perceive the connection, the benefit of the doubt should be given to the prisoner. *Id.*

11. Evidence of Another Offense. — Where one is on trial for murder, and evidence has been received of the killing by him of the deceased in the presence of the latter's wife, it is error to permit her to testify that the prisoner committed a rape upon her soon after the killing, on the same day, and while still on the premises of the deceased. Such evidence is not admissible to prove the motive of the prisoner, where the fact of the killing is not denied, and there is no substantial proof that the prisoner acted in self-defense. The admission of the evidence is prejudicial, because it is calculated to inflame the minds of the jurors against the defendant, rather than to prove him guilty of murder; and though, from the other testimony, it is clear and undoubted that he committed the crime of murder as charged, still the admission of the testimony will be regarded as a prejudicial error, if the jury had the right, by their verdict, to spare the prisoner's life. The admission of proof of the other distinct and revolting crime may have prevented the jury from exercising their discretion in favor of the prisoner to the extent of sparing his life. *Id.*

12. Proof of Character. — A witness who testifies on direct examination that he has never heard anything against defendant may be asked on cross-examination if he has not heard defendant "wore stripes" while working on the streets. *Holmes v. State*, 17.

13. Proof of Character — Witness is incompetent to testify, either affirmatively or negatively, as to character, who knows nothing of the reputation borne by defendant in the neighborhood in which he lived, or where he was known, and who was not in such position, as to defendant's residence or acquaintances, that the fact of his not hearing anything against him would have any tendency to show that nothing had been said, and that therefore his character was good. *Id.*

14. Charge Directing Verdict. — A charge assuming a fact as proved, when the evidence only tends to establish it, invades the province of the jury, and is erroneous. Thus to direct the jury that "the fact that a married man makes frequent visits in the daytime, and sometimes at night, to the house of a woman of known bad reputation for virtue, with-

33. RAPE — EVIDENCE. — Defendant in rape is entitled to prove prior acts of undue intimacy between himself and the prosecutrix to raise the presumption of consent; but he cannot prove jealousy on the part of the husband of the prosecutrix against her and the accused as an incentive for the prosecution. *Id.*

34. RAPE — EVIDENCE. — In a prosecution for rape, a witness cannot testify to the effect that the place, which he supposed or had been informed was the scene of the alleged offense, showed nothing to indicate a struggle, when the place described by him was in no way identified as that at which the crime had been committed. *Id.*

35. RAPE — EVIDENCE. — In prosecutions for rape, the evidence of the husband of the prosecutrix of complaint made by his wife to him regarding the offense, and to the circumstances under which such complaint was made, is admissible. *Id.*

36. SEVERAL PROSECUTIONS FOR SAME CRIMINAL TRANSACTION. — Under indictments charging the prisoner with robbing three different individual passengers upon the same stage, at the same time, an acquittal or conviction under one indictment is not a bar to a prosecution under the others, as the different robberies are distinct offenses. *In re Allison,* 224.

37. EVIDENCE — RES GESTÆ. — Unsworn statements of the person robbed, made to a third person, from one to four hours after the robbery, as to who committed it, are mere hearsay evidence, and inadmissible as part of the *res gestæ. Moses* v. *State,* 21.

38. EVIDENCE OF WITNESS WHO TESTIFIES THAT DEFENDANT CHARGED WITH ROBBERY had made contradictory statements to him as to how certain articles came into his possession, but who cannot recollect and testify wherein such statements differed, should be ruled out as incompetent, and merely an expression of opinion. *Id.*

See CONSTITUTIONAL LAW, 2-5, 7; HABEAS CORPUS; SCHOOLS, 1-4.

CUSTOM AND USAGE.
See AGENCY, 3.

DAMAGES.

1. DAMAGES, MEASURE OF, FOR DEATH OF MINOR. — In an action by a father, as administrator of his deceased minor son, to recover damages for causing the death of his son, the jury may allow damages for the loss of the services of such son during his minority, though the father would have been entitled to such services had the child lived. *Illinois etc. R. R. Co.* v. *Slater,* 243.

2. EVIDENCE OF THE WEALTH OF A FATHER who, as the administrator of his deceased son, sues to recover for the death of the latter, resulting from defendant's alleged negligence, is not admissible for the purpose of showing that the father could have employed others to perform the services in which his child was engaged at the time of his death, and thereby have saved him from exposure to the dangers incident to that service. *Id.*

3. LOSS OF PROFITS. — Where plaintiff is seeking to recover for not being permitted to do a certain work which he had contracted to perform, it is proper to receive evidence to show what it would have cost him to do the work and what compensation he would have become entitled to had he been permitted to do it. *Warren etc. Mfg. Co.* v. *Holbrook,* 788.

DEBTOR AND CREDITOR.

DECEASED PERSONS.

DECREES.

DEEDS.

5. FORMAL DEFECTS IN ACKNOWLEGMENTS of deeds, or the omission of words of identification, can generally only be taken advantage of by subsequent purchasers for value. *Id.*

6. OFFICERS TAKING ACKNOWLEDGMENS TO DEEDS have the right and may be compelled at any time to correct mistakes in their certificates. *Id.*

7. PAROL EVIDENCE IS INADMISSIBLE TO SHOW an agreement that possession under a deed is to be retained by the vendor until the purchase price is paid, under Colorado General Statutes, chapter 18, section 9, providing that conveyances of real estate duly executed and delivered carry with them the right to immediate possession, unless a future day for possession is therein specified. *Omaha etc. Co. v. Tabor*, 185.

8. AVOIDANCE OF, FOR INSANITY. — A judgment creditor cannot set aside as fraudulent a deed because of the insanity of the grantor; such deed can only be avoided by the grantor or his privies in blood or estate. *Rollet v. Heiman*, 340.

9. REFORMATION OF DEED CONVEYING HOMESTEAD. — Equity will correct a misdescription in a deed made by mutual mistake, and executed by husband and wife, conveying land held by them as tenants in common, and constituting part of their homestead, when it appears that the purchaser paid full value and the conveyance was sufficient to pass the wife's interest, though she was ignorant of the fact that she was a part owner of the land conveyed. *Parker v. Parker*, 52.

See FRAUDULENT CONVEYANCES, 1; MARRIED WOMEN, 2–4; VENDOR AND VENDEE, 1, 2.

DEVISES AND LEGACIES.

1. PROPERTY TURNED OVER TO DEVISEES AND LEGATEES DOES NOT CONTINUE TO BE SPECIFICALLY BOUND for any possible future deficiency. Their interests vest at once, and should not be needlessly interfered with by the executor. *Frost v. Atwood*, 560.

2. POWER TO COMPEL CONTRIBUTION BY DEVISEES BEING WHOLLY STATUTORY, the statute cannot be supplemented by creating charges which it does not authorize the probate court to make. *Id.*

3. EXECUTOR IS ONLY PERSON AUTHORIZED TO ENFORCE CONTRIBUTION from devisees and legatees for the payment of debts, and he has no power to sell or grant this authority to any one else. If he seeks relief in the probate court, he must enforce it by execution. *Id.*

4. DECREE FOR CONTRIBUTION BY DEVISEES TO PAY DEBTS OF ESTATE IS No MORE THAN PERSONAL JUDGMENT, to be enforced by execution. *Id.*

DIVORCE.

See MARRIAGE AND DIVORCE.

DOWER.

1. WIFE'S RIGHT TO DOWER WHICH IS VESTED IN HER PRIOR TO A DIVORCE is not divested thereby, unless the statute has so specially declared. *Van Cleaf v. Burns*, 782.

2. CONFLICT OF LAWS. — Statute of New York declaring that a wife shall not be entitled to dower in any real property of her husband if a divorce is granted in an action brought by him, is not applicable to a decree of divorce rendered against her in another state, in an action there commenced

EASEMENTS.

1. **GRANTEE OF A RIGHT OF WAY** has not only a right to the undisputed passage at all times over the grantor's land, but also to such rights as are necessary or incident to the enjoyment of such right of passage. The grantee may enter upon the land and construct such roadway as he desires, and keep it in repair. *Herman* v. *Roberts,* 800.

2. **OWNER OF RIGHT OF WAY** has a right to exclude strangers from its use, and to restrict such use of it by the owner of the servient tenement as is inconsistent with the enjoyment of such right of way. *Id.*

3. **CONSTRUCTION OF A GRANT OF A RIGHT OF WAY** cannot be aided by parol negotiations; but the language of the grant itself, when uncertain or ambiguous, must be regarded in the light of surrounding circumstances and the situation of the parties. *Id.*

4. **OWNER OF LAND WHICH IS SUBJECT TO A RIGHT OF WAY** has the right to use his land in any way not inconsistent with the easement, and the extent of the easement must be determined by the construction of the grant or reservation by which it was created, aided by circumstances surrounding the estate and the parties, which have a legitimate tendency to establish their intention. *Id.*

5. **RIGHT OF WAY — OWNER OF SERVIENT LANDS MAY NOT IMPAIR OR OBSTRUCT.** — One who has granted another a right of way of a definite width, to be used as a means of access between the latter's country seat or residence and the public highway, has no right, when a road has been constructed over such right of way by the grantee, to enter upon the road and use it for carrying barn produce and other heavy loads over it, whereby it is cut up and injured, and repairs thereon made necessary, nor has he a right to obstruct any part of the right of way with stone or other materials. *Id.*

EJECTMENT.

ELECTION.

ELEVATORS.

1. **PASSENGER-ELEVATOR — NEGLIGENCE IN CARE OF — PROOF SUFFICIENT TO ESTABLISH.** — In an action for damages sustained from the giving way of a passenger-elevator in consequence of the breaking of the cable connected therewith, evidence that such cable has been so long in use as to be seriously worn, weakened, and rendered insecure, and that such wearing could easily have been seen if properly looked after, is sufficient to justify the jury in finding negligence in the care and management of the elevator. *Goodsell* v. *Taylor,* 700.

2. **PASSENGER-ELEVATOR — QUESTION OF NECESSITY OF EXAMINATION OF, AS TO ITS SAFETY, FOR JURY.** — Whether due care and prudence required the examination of the cable of a passenger-elevator in order to ascertain its condition as to safety is not a question of expert evidence, but is for the jury to determine. *Id.*

3. **PASSENGER-ELEVATOR.** — Presumption of safety of cable of a passenger-elevator does not arise from the fact that it is not obviously dangerous, and has been used with safety for years, nor will it be presumed that it

will continue safe for use without examination to ascertain its condition, and if its safety may not have become impaired by wear. *Id.*

4. PASSENGER-ELEVATOR — RELATION BETWEEN OWNER AND PASSENGER THEREIN. — The relations between the owner and manager of a passenger-elevator and those carried in it are similar to those between a carrier of passengers and those carried by him. Such owner is required to exert the utmost human care and foresight, and is responsible for the slightest degree of negligence; and in case of the giving way of the elevator, causing injury to a passenger, the burden of proof is on the owner to show that it occurred through no fault or neglect of his. *Id.*

See MASTER AND SERVANT, 10, 11.

EMBEZZLEMENT.

See CRIMINAL LAW, 19, 20.

EMINENT DOMAIN.

TAKING OF PROPERTY, WHAT IS. — Where a city, in grading a street, raises an embankment upon nearly thirty-five feet of the entire frontage of an abutting lot, thereby burying a portion of the dwelling-house and barn of the owner, this is as much a taking as to that part of the lot covered by the embankment as though the owner had been ejected by any other means, and is plainly within the inhibition of the constitution. And in such a case, the law does not require the owner to wait until his property is completely destroyed, and then turn him over to his action of trespass to recover his damages, but equity, when appealed to, will interfere to restrain the threatened destruction. *Vanderlip v. Grand Rapids,* 597.

EQUITY.

1. CONTRIBUTION BETWEEN WRONG-DOERS will be enforced in equity when the person seeking redress is presumed not to have known that he was doing an unlawful act. *Farwell v. Becker,* 267.

2. CONTRIBUTIONS BETWEEN PERSONS WHO HAVE MADE AN UNLAWFUL LEVY. — If several persons levy upon goods under separate writs of attachment, and the goods are sold by a receiver appointed for that purpose, and the proceeds applied towards the satisfaction of such writs, and an action is subsequently brought by a claimant of the goods against the plaintiffs in the writs, and a judgment recovered for the value thereof, which one of the parties satisfies, he may maintain a suit in equity to enforce contributions from the others in proportion to the respective amounts collected by him and by them by means of such writs. *Id.*

See DEEDS, 9; PLEADING, 1.

ERROR.

See APPEAL AND ERROR.

ESTOPPEL.

1. ESTOPPEL IN ACTION FOR POSSESSION OF PERSONALTY. — When, in an action to recover possession of personal property, an affidavit is made for the purpose of obtaining possession of such property, in which it is specifically described, and a requisition is issued and delivered to the coroner requiring him to take such property from the possession of the

EVIDENCE.

EXECUTIONS.

1. REMEDY OF PURCHASER AT SHERIFF'S SALE AS AGAINST FRAUDULENT CONVEYANCE. — A purchaser of the legal title to land at sheriff's sale has a plain and adequate remedy at law in ejectment, although the land has been fraudulently conveyed by the judgment debtor prior to sale, and he is not entitled to equitable relief; but when he acquires no title to the land at the sale, his only remedy, if he has any, is in equity. *Goodbar* v. *Daniel*, 76.

2. PURCHASER AT SHERIFF'S SALE BUYS AT HIS OWN RISK, and will not be relieved from the effect of his bid upon proof that the execution defendant had no title to the property sold. His bid is an irrevocable satisfaction of the judgment to the extent of the sum bid at the sale. *Id.*

3. ISSUANCE OF EXECUTION. — A statute providing that after the expiration of ten years from the entry of a judgment execution can only issue on leave of court relates only to the remedy, and applies to issuing execution on all judgments, whether rendered before or after its enactment, and is clearly within legislative authority. *Leonard* v. *Broughton*, 347.

4. ISSUE OF EXECUTION AND SALE without objection from the judgment debtor makes a valid sale which cannot be questioned by other judgment creditors who have since obtained liens for pre-existing debts. *Id.*

5. STATUTES EXEMPTING PROPERTY FROM EXECUTION ARE TO BE LIBERALLY CONSTRUED with a view of promoting the objects of the legislature, and their force and effect are not to be confined to the literal terms of the acts. *Yates County Nat. Bank* v. *Carpenter*, 855.

6. EXEMPTIONS. — If a dwelling-house is purchased by a pensioner, whose only cash payment therefor is made with moneys received by him as collections on his pension certificate, the balance of the purchase price being secured by a mortgage on the property, his interest thereon is exempted from execution by the provision of the New York code, declaring that a pension "granted by the United States for military services is also exempt from levy and sale by virtue of an execution, and from seizure for non-payment of taxes, or in any legal proceeding." *Id.*

7. ORDER AMENDING AN EXECUTION AFTER THE DEATH OF THE JUDGMENT DEFENDANT, without notice to his heirs, is a nullity. *Morris* v. *Balkham*, 874.

See JUDGMENTS, 18-20; JUDICIAL SALES, 1-6.

EXECUTORS AND ADMINISTRATORS.

1. ADMINISTRATORS IN TWO STATES — PAYMENT TO ONE DISCHARGE AS TO OTHER. — The voluntary payment by the debtor of a debt due a deceased person to his legally authorized administrator in the state of his domicile is a valid discharge as against another administrator of the deceased afterwards appointed in another state, where a note which is the evidence of the debt paid was merely deposited for safe-keeping. *Bull* v. *Fuller*, 419.

2. EXECUTOR HAS NO POWER TO DISPOSE OF LANDS BY VIRTUE OF HIS OFFICE; and whenever he undertakes to meddle with lands without authority, he cannot bind them any more than a stranger. The owner, whether devisee or otherwise, is in no way affected by his action, which is void for all purposes. *Frost* v. *Atwood*, 560.

See DEVISES AND LEGACIES, 1, 3; PUBLIC LANDS, 1, 2.

EXEMPTIONS.
See EXECUTIONS, 5, 6.

EXPERT EVIDENCE.
See WITNESSES, 6.

FACTORS.

1. FACTORS ACT, CONSTRUCTION OF. — One who obtains possession of property for the avowed purpose of delivering it to another, to whom he claims to have sold it as a broker, but who has in fact made no such sale, and intends to appropriate the property or its proceeds to his own use, is a thief, and can confer no title upon any other person, whether an innocent purchaser from him or not, at the common law, nor under the provision of the New York factors act, which is as follows: "Every factor or other agent intrusted with the possession of any bill of lading, custom-house permit, or warehouse-keeper's receipt, for the delivery of any such merchandise, and every such factor or agent, not having the documentary evidence of title, who shall be intrusted with the possession of any merchandise for the purpose of sale, or as a security for any advance to be made or obtained thereon, shall be deemed to be the true owner thereof, so far as to give validity to any contract made by such agent with any other person, for the sale or disposition of the whole or any part of such merchandise, for any money advanced, or negotiable instrument or other obligation in writing given by such other person upon the faith thereof." *Soltau* v. *Gerdau*, 843.

2. FACTORS ACT, CONSTRUCTION OF. — A delivery order by which an owner of personal property directs it to be delivered to a broker with the object of having the broker deliver the property to one to whom he claims to have sold it for the owner, is not documentary evidence of the title, within the meaning of the factors act; nor is a broker to whom such order is so delivered one intrusted with the possession of property for the purpose of sale, within the meaning of those words as used in that act. *Id.*

FERRIES.
See INTERSTATE COMMERCE, 2.

FISHERIES.

LEGISLATIVE POWER TO REGULATE FISHING IN PUBLIC WATERS has been exercised from the earliest periods of the common law, and it has become a settled principle of law that power resides in the several states to regulate and control the right of fishing in the public waters within their respective jurisdictions. *Lawton* v. *Steele*, 813.

See NUISANCES, 2, 4.

FIXTURES.

1. PHYSICAL ANNEXATION TO REALTY is not alone sufficient to change the character of personal property from a chattel to a fixture. *Atchison etc. R'y Co.* v. *Morgan*, 471.

2. Whether a Chattel Becomes a Fixture depends upon the character of the act by which it is put into its place, the uses to which it is put, the policy of the law connected with its purpose, and the intention of those concerned. *Id.*

3. Placing a Structure on Land to Improve It and make it more valuable is evidence that such structure has become a fixture; but if it is erected for a use which does not enhance the value of the land, it remains a chattel. *Id.*

4. Before Personal Property can Become a Fixture by actual physical annexation to land, the intention of the parties and the uses to which it is put must combine to change its nature from that of a chattel to that of a fixture. *Id.*

5. Property Annexed by Mistake. — Where a railroad company digs a well, puts in a pump and boiler, and erects a boiler-house for the sole use of operating its road, under the belief that it is occupying its own land, and only discovers its mistake after several years of occupation, the structures do not become fixtures, but may be removed by the company without paying the owner of the land therefor. *Id.*

6. What will Pass as Such under Chattel Mortgage. — A track-scale erected for use in connection with an elevator built upon leased land will pass as a fixture under a chattel mortgage of the elevator, "with all the machinery therein, and all the fixtures thereto belonging." *McGorrisk v. Dwyer,* 440.

FORGERY.

See Banks and Banking, 6; Witnesses, 2, 3.

FORMER JEOPARDY.

See Criminal Law, 4.

FRAUD.

See Agency, 5; Compromise, 1, 2; Contracts; Debtor and Creditor; Negotiable Instruments, 10, 11, 13, 14, 20, 21; Vendor and Vendee, 7.

FRAUDULENT CONVEYANCES.

1. Complaint to Set Aside a Fraudulent Deed, alleging that it was accepted by the grantee with knowledge of its fraudulent purpose, and as a mere volunteer who has paid no consideration, states a good cause of action. *Rollet v. Heiman,* 340.

2. Confession of Judgment by a failing debtor in favor of a creditor, with the agreement that the judgment is not to be made public by being recorded until that is necessary to protect the interests of such creditor, is fraudulent and void as to the remaining creditors of the debtor, and will be set aside on their application. *Walton v. First Nat. Bank,* 200.

3. Declarations of Confederates in Fraud Admissible against Each Other. — Where a confession of judgment is signed by a failing debtor in favor of a creditor, under an agreement that such judgment shall not be recorded unless necessary to protect the creditor, thus enabling the debtor to obtain a fictitious credit, any declarations or representations made afterwards by such debtor in obtaining credit are admissible as against the judgment creditor for the purpose of setting aside the judgment as fraudulent towards other creditors. *Id.*

See Deeds, 8.

FRAUDULENT SALES.
See CHATTEL MORTGAGES.

GARNISHMENT.
See ATTACHMENT AND GARNISHMENT.

GIFTS.

VALIDITY — ASSIGNMENT OF BANK DEPOSIT TO BE PAID AFTER DEATH OF DEPOSITOR. — Where a bank depositor has the bank cashier write at the close of the account in the deposit-book, containing a rule that the deposit can only be drawn upon the production of the book, the following: "May 28, '86. Pay to the order of S. and H. all of the within deposit after my decease," — and thereafter neither deposits nor draws any money from the bank, but immediately delivers the book to the assignees, who hold it during the assignor's life, and draw the deposit after the latter's death, these facts show a completed assignment, which creates an irrevocable vested interest in the assignees during the lifetime of the assignor, subject to the happening of a future event before the right to draw the money is perfected, and such assignment is not open to the objection that it is of a testamentary character, and void as not being executed in the manner provided by law. *Schollmier* v. *Schondelen*, 455.

GOVERNOR.
See OFFICE AND OFFICERS, 4, 6.

HABEAS CORPUS.

UNLESS THE TRIAL COURT LEGALLY EXISTS, and is lawfully constituted, a trial, conviction, and judgment therein are void, and the prisoner must be discharged on *habeas corpus*. *In re Allison*, 224.
See JUDGMENTS, 13.

HIGHWAYS.

1. BICYCLES ARE VEHICLES, AND ENTITLED TO THE RIGHTS OF THE ROAD; but have no lawful right to the use of the sidewalk, and the rider of a bicycle is placed upon an equality with and governed by the same rules as persons riding or driving any other vehicle. *Holland* v. *Bartch*, 307.

2. RIGHT OF BICYCLE-RIDER. — Riding a bicycle in the center of a highway at the rate of fifteen miles an hour, to and within twenty-five feet of the heads of horses attached to a carriage, is not actionable negligence. To make it such, it must be charged and shown to have been done at a time or in a manner or under circumstances evidencing a disregard for the rights of others. *Id.*
See NUISANCES, 1.

HOMESTEADS.

1. MORTGAGE ON HOMESTEAD AND OTHER PROPERTY — RIGHT OF MORTGAGOR. — Where a mortgage upon a homestead and other real estate is being foreclosed, the mortgagor has the right as against the mortgagee, and all other creditors and lien-holders whose rights are not prior or superior to those of the mortgagee, to require that, before the homestead shall be resorted to for the purpose of satisfying the mortgage, all the other property shall be first exhausted. *Frick* v. *Ketels*, 507.

2. HOMESTEAD IS NOT VITIATED BY SUBSEQUENT ERECTION OF ADDITIONAL DWELLING ON SAME LOT. — Where a house and lot are duly selected and declared a homestead, the subsequent erection of an additional dwelling-house upon the lot does not vitiate such homestead, nor render any part of it subject to seizure and sale under execution, unless the value of the homestead has increased beyond the statutory limit; and in that case a levy can only be made for the purpose of inaugurating proceedings for the admeasurement of the excess in value. *Lubbock* v. *McMann*, 108.

3. HOMESTEAD ONCE DULY DEDICATED CANNOT BE DEFEATED OR VITIATED except by conveyance, encumbrance, or abandonment executed in the manner provided by the statute. *Id.*

See DEEDS, 9; JUDICIAL SALES, 6.

HOMICIDE.

See CRIMINAL LAW, 21-23.

HUSBAND AND WIFE.

1. SERVICE OF PROCESS IN CHANCERY UPON WIFE, where the action did not concern her separate estate, might be made upon the husband. Hence it was held that a decree in foreclosure barred the right of dower of a wife who was under age at the time the decree was rendered, though the subpœna was served only upon her husband. *Feitner* v. *Lewis*, 811.

2. NOTICE TO HUSBAND AS AGENT OF WIFE. — Notice of fraudulent facts avoiding a deed, acquired by a husband while acting as agent and trustee for his wife, in investing the proceeds of her separate estate, is constructive notice to her of such facts. *Goodbar* v. *Daniel*, 76.

3. PLEADING. — DAMAGES FOR NEGLIGENCE DIMINISHING THE EARNING CAPACITY OF A MARRIED WOMAN are presumed to belong to her husband, and when she seeks to recover such damages she must allege that, for some reason, she is entitled to the fruits of her labor; or if she seeks to recover damages for an injury to her business, she must allege that she was in business on her own account, and, by reason of the injury, was damaged therein as specifically set forth. *Uransky* v. *Dry Dock etc. R. R. Co.*, 759.

4. PLEADING. — IN ACTION BY A MARRIED WOMAN FOR DAMAGES SUSTAINED BY REASON OF PERSONAL INJURIES, she should not be permitted to prove that she was injured in business, and had suffered a loss therein by reason of such injuries, unless she had so alleged in her complaint. *Id.*

5. HUSBAND AND WIFE CANNOT ENTER INTO CONTRACT OF PARTNERSHIP between themselves, and thus render themselves jointly liable for the contracts of the firm thus established. Under the Michigan statute, a wife has no power to contract, except in regard to her separate property. *Artman* v. *Ferguson*, 572.

6. TRUSTEE OF AN EXPRESS TRUST. — AN AGREEMENT OF SEPARATION BETWEEN HUSBAND, WIFE, AND A THIRD PERSON, by the terms of which the former is to pay the latter a specified sum towards the support of the wife and her children, constitutes the third person a trustee of an express trust, and authorizes an action to enforce the trust to be brought in his name. *Clark* v. *Fosdick*, 733.

7. AN AGREEMENT BETWEEN A HUSBAND AND WIFE, WHILE THEY ARE LIVING TOGETHER AS SUCH, FOR THEIR IMMEDIATE SEPARATION, and for a specified allowance for her support, made through the medium of a trustee,

is valid; and the trustee may maintain an action thereon to recover any
sum due from the husband by the terms of the agreement. Such an
agreement, to be valid, must be made in respect to a separation which
has occurred, or which is to occur immediately, and not in contemplation
of a future possible separation. *Id.*

8. AGREEMENT OF SEPARATION BETWEEN HUSBAND, WIFE, AND HER TRUS-
TEE, and for the payment of an allowance to the trustee for her support, is not annulled by the subsequent granting of a divorce at her
instance in an action in which no alimony was asked nor granted, and the
judgment in which did not refer to nor in any respect purport to deal
with such agreement. *Id.*

9. AGREEMENT OF SEPARATION BETWEEN HUSBAND AND WIFE, though valid,
does not prevent either from maintaining against the other an ordinary
action for divorce, limited or absolute, according to the ground and the
jurisdiction, whether the cause therefor occurred before or after such
agreement was entered into. *Id.*

See CO-TENANCY, 10; DEEDS, 9; DOWER; LIBEL AND SLANDER, 4-8; MAR-
RIED WOMEN; MARRIAGE AND DIVORCE; WILLS, 2.

IMPUTED NEGLIGENCE.
See NEGLIGENCE, 5.

INDICTMENT.
See CRIMINAL LAW, 1.

INFANTS.
See NEGLIGENCE, 5, 6; MORTGAGES, 1-3; MASTER AND SERVANT, 18-21.

INJUNCTION.
See BONDS; INVENTIONS, 3.

INSANITY.
See CRIMINAL LAW, 6-8; DEEDS, 8.

INSOLVENCY.
SITUS OF DEBTS DUE INSOLVENT. — For the purposes of insolvency or other
proceedings by creditors, debts or choses in action due the insolvent are
treated as having a *situs* at the owner's domicile. *Matter of Dalpay,*
729.

See CORPORATIONS, 4-7.

INSTRUCTIONS.
See TRIAL, 3-11.

INSURANCE.
1. CHANGE IN USE OF PREMISES. — A condition in the policy, forfeiting it
if the insured property is so changed as to increase the risk, is not broken
by a change of the premises from a restaurant to a paint and wagon
shop, when the evidence shows that such change diminished the risk.
Esch v. *Insurance Co.,* 443.

INTEREST.

INTERSTATE COMMERCE.

tion already existing, is a proper exercise of the police power reserved to the state, and therefore valid. *Id.*

5. POLICE POWER OF STATE. — A statute imposing a penalty on a carrier for refusal to deliver freight upon payment or tender of charges as shown by the bill of lading is a valid exercise of police power, and not unconstitutional as regulating interstate commerce, and applies to freight received within the state by a connecting carrier, though shipped from without the state. *Id.*

INTERVENTION.

See LANDLORD AND TENANT, 9.

INVENTIONS.

1. AN INVENTOR OR AUTHOR HAS, independent of letters patent or of copyright, an exclusive property in his invention or composition until, by publication, it becomes the property of the general public. *Tabor v. Hoffman*, 740.

2. INJUNCTION. — THE USE OF PATTERNS SURREPTITIOUSLY COPIED from patterns used by an inventor in casting a pump, the patent to which has expired, will be enjoined when such patterns have been copied without the assent of the inventor, and they cannot be duplicated merely by measuring the pump as were the patterns, owing to the shrinkage in cooling and the expansion in heating, the materials used must vary in size from the corresponding parts of the completed pump. *Id.*

3. INJUNCTION. — ONE WHO, BY UNFAIR MEANS, DISCOVERS THE MODE OF MANUFACTURING AN ARTICLE, or the formula for compounding medicine, while in the employment of the proprietor, will be enjoined from using it himself, or imparting it to others, to the injury to the proprietor. *Id.*

JUDGMENTS.

1. VOID JUDGMENT — VACATING — JURISDICTION. — Appearance by attorney, upon motion to contest the service of process upon defendant, is a special and limited appearance, and does not confer jurisdiction upon the court; hence a judgment rendered upon such appearance is void, and must be set aside. *Green v. Green*, 510.

2. JUDGMENT AGAINST A DECEASED PERSON over whom the court had obtained jurisdiction in his lifetime, though irregular, is not void. *Claflin v. Dunne*, 263.

3. JUDGMENT AGAINST A DECEASED PERSON over whom the court had obtained jurisdiction in his lifetime may be reversed on error, if his death appears from the record; otherwise, it may be vacated on motion in the court where it was entered. Under the practice act of Illinois, the motion may be made at any time within five years after the rendition of the judgment. *Id.*

4. JUDGMENT AGAINST SEVERAL DEFENDANTS, ONE OF WHOM IS DEAD at the time it is rendered, is a unit as to all the defendants, and hence, on a proper motion being made therefor, must be vacated as to all. *Id.*

5. JUDGMENT ENTERED NUNC PRO TUNC IS BINDING to the same extent as though entered at the proper time, except as to parties who in the mean time have in good faith acquired rights without notice of any judgment. *Leonard v. Broughton*, 347.

6. JUDGMENT ENTERED NUNC PRO TUNC on an official bond takes effect as of the date for which it is entered, as against creditors of the judgment

other collateral security pledged for the payment of the judgment debt, he is precluded from denying the validity of the sale, and the sale will constitute an equitable assignment of the vendor's interest in the land to the execution purchaser. *Fallon* v. *Worthington,* 231.

6. EVIDENCE — ADMISSIBILITY OF, TO PROVE NOTICE. — A party claiming as a homestead property purchased at sale under execution cannot show, as against such purchaser, that the homestead claimant's attorney gave notice that it was a homestead prior to the sale. *Morris* v. *Balkham,* 874.

7. JURISDICTION OF PROBATE COURT OVER SALE OF LANDS BELONGING TO ESTATE OF DECEASED PERSON does not come from its general jurisdiction over the administration of the estate, but from the petition for the sale, and the petition must comply with the provisions of the statute. A literal compliance with the requirements of the statute is not, however, necessary. A substantial compliance therewith is sufficient. *Richardson* v. *Butler,* 101.

8. JURISDICTION OF PROBATE COURT DEPENDS UPON AVERMENTS OF PETITION FOR SALE of lands belonging to the estate of a deceased person, and not upon the truth or falsity of such averments. *Id.*

9. DESCRIPTION OF PROPERTY OF DECEDENT BY REFERENCE TO INVENTORY. — A petition for the sale of lands belonging to the estate of a decedent may properly refer to the schedules of the inventory of such estate for a particular description of such lands. And the fact that the inventory refers to a map or diagram on file, which cannot be found at the time of the trial of a cause involving the validity of the sale, seventeen years afterward, will not affect the jurisdiction, if the inventory, taken in connection with the averments of the petition, sufficiently shows what was the interest of the decedent in the lands at the time of his death, contains a full description of the real property of the estate at the time the sale was asked, and gives the court all the information upon the subject required by the statute. *Id.*

10. DESIGNATION OF CITY LOT AS "UNIMPROVED" IS SUFFICIENT DESCRIPTION OF ITS CONDITION, in a petition for a probate sale, to give the probate court jurisdiction. *Id.*

11. STATEMENT IN PETITION AS TO DEBTS AND EXPENSES OF ADMINISTRATION, WHEN SUFFICIENT. — The statement in a petition for a probate sale that there are no debts or expenses of administration accrued and unpaid, is sufficient to vest jurisdiction in the court, so far as that point is concerned, if the prior accounts have been settled, and the petition seeks a sale, not to pay debts and past expenses, but to provide for a family allowance and future expenses of administration. *Id.*

12. ORDER OF SALE IN PROBATE PROCEEDING IS NOT VOID because it provides that the sale shall cease when a certain sum of money required to be raised has been obtained, when the lands to be sold consist of several lots or parcels. *Id.*

13. FINDING AS TO NOTICE OF PROBATE SALE CONCLUSIVE WHEN. — The finding of the court in the order confirming a probate sale that the notice of sale was posted in three public places is conclusive as against a collateral attack. *Id.*

14. VERIFICATION OF PETITION FOR PROBATE SALE, WHEN SUFFICIENT. — The verification of a petition for a probate sale is not invalid because the certificate of verification is placed before the schedules which are attached to it. The schedules are a part of the petition, and are as fully included in the verification as are the parts that precede the certificate. *Id.*

15. MERE TECHNICAL OBJECTIONS WILL NOT BE PERMITTED TO OVERTHROW TITLE TO LANDS honestly acquired under a probate sale, where there is no pretense that the sale was in fact fraudulent, or without adequate consideration, or in any way unfair. *Id.*

16. NO LIEN ON PREMISES UNLAWFULLY SOLD AT PROBATE SALE IS CREATED BY USE OF MONEY RECEIVED. In all probate sales, valid or invalid, the officer making the sale receives the money, and usually appropriates it; but such use creates no lien on the premises sold. What he receives without lawful authority does not concern the estate, and he can no more create a lien by spending that money than by spending any other. If the estate owes him, he must pursue his remedy as the law gives it, and his claim must first be established before he can get any remedy. The use, if made, is not made for the benefit of the particular piece of land that he attempted to sell, but for the whole estate; and if it becomes a claim, it is a claim against the whole estate, and not against a part of it. *Frost* v. *Atwood*, 560.

See DEEDS, 3; EXECUTIONS, 1, 2, 4; PUBLIC LANDS, 1.

JURISDICTION.

AMOUNT INVOLVED WHEN THERE ARE TWO OR MORE DEFENDANTS. — Where the amount against each defendant is separate and distinct, the two amounts cannot be united so as to confer jurisdiction, but each must be treated as a separate suit; and if the amount involved as to either one is not large enough to confer jurisdiction, the appeal must fall as to that one. *Farwell* v. *Becker*, 267.

See ADMIRALTY, 1, 2; CORPORATIONS, 1; HABEAS CORPUS; JUDGMENTS, 1; JUDICIAL SALES, 7, 8, 10.

JURY AND JURORS.

RIGHT TO ASCERTAIN FOR WHICH PARTY JUROR WILL DECIDE, IF THE EVIDENCE IS EQUALLY BALANCED. — When selecting a jury, a juror may be asked which side he would be inclined to favor, if at the close of the trial the evidence were equally balanced between the parties, to ascertain his bias, and for the purpose of exercising a peremptory challenge if necessary. *Township of Otsego Lake* v. *Kirsten*, 524.

See CRIMINAL LAW, 3.

JUSTICES OF THE PEACE.
See JUDGMENTS, 11, 12; PROHIBITION.

LANDLORD AND TENANT.

1. ASSIGNMENT OF LEASE, WHAT IS. — If the lessee assigns his whole estate without reserving to himself any reversion therein, a privity of estate is at once created between the assignee and the original lessor, and the latter then has a right of action directly against the assignee on the covenants running with the land; but if the lessee sublets the premises, reserving any reversion, however small, privity of estate between the assignee and the landlord is not established, and the latter has no right of action against the former. *Sexton* v. *Chicago Storage Co.*, 274.

2. ASSIGNMENT OF LEASE, WHAT IS. — If all the lessee's estate if transferred, the instrument of transfer operates as an assignment of the lease, notwithstanding words of demise instead of assignment are used, and

the reservation of rent to the grantor or assignor, and of a right of re-entry on the non-payment of rent, or the non-fulfillment of the other covenants in such instrument. *Id.*

3. THE RELATIONS OF LANDLORD AND ASSIGNEE OF THE TERM do not result from contract, but from privity of estate, and therefore, when the original lessee has divested himself of his entire term, and thus ceased to be in privity of estate with the original landlord, the person to whom he transmits that entire term must necessarily be in privity of estate with the original landlord, and hence liable as assignee of the term. *Id.*

4. SUBLEASING, WHAT IS NOT. — If a lessee transfers all his estate to another, such transfer is not converted into a sublease by the fact that the lessee reserved a new and different rent, or the right to declare the transfer void for non-performance of its covenants, and to re-enter for such breach, or at the end of the term, and the instrument of transfer also contained a covenant on the part of the transferee to surrender at the end of the term, or upon the forfeiture of the term for a breach of covenant. *Id.*

5. RIGHT TO ENTER FOR BREACH OF CONDITION SUBSEQUENT cannot be alienated. It is not a reversion or estate in land, but a mere chose in action, and when enforced, the grantor is in by the forfeiture of the condition, and not by a reverter; but this rule of law is not abrogated nor modified by a statutory provision declaring that "the grantees of any demised lands, tenements, rents, or other hereditaments, or of the reversion thereof, the assignee of the lessor of any demise, and the heirs and personal representatives of the lessor, grantee, or assignee, shall have the same remedies, by entry, action, or otherwise, for the non-performance of any agreement in the lease, or for the recovery of any rent, or for the doing of any waste, or other cause of forfeiture, as their grantor or lessor might have had if such reversion had remained in such lessor or grantor." *Id.*

6. ASSIGNMENT OF LEASE, RIGHT TO OBJECT TO. — A clause in a lease that no assignment thereof shall be valid without the assent in writing of the lessor is for the benefit of the latter, and cannot be urged by the assignee of the lease against the landlord, who has not objected to the assignment. *Id.*

7. LANDLORD IS NOT ESTOPPED from insisting that a transfer made by his lessee was an assignment instead of a subletting by the fact that he refused to release the original lessee and accept the assignee alone, and refused to accept the amount of rent which the assignee had agreed to pay, as a full satisfaction of the lessee's liability, and sued the lessee for rent, and garnished the assignee; for, notwithstanding the assignment, the original lessee remained answerable upon the lease for the payment of the rent which he had therein expressly agreed to pay. *Id.*

8. SUBTENANT BOUND BY TERMS OF HIS LESSOR'S LEASE. — A subtenant, with knowledge that his lessor is a tenant, is chargeable with notice of and is bound by the terms of the lease by which he held. Therefore, where the tenant's lease gives the landlord a lien upon crops grown upon the leased premises for unpaid rent, such lien extends to crops grown by the subtenant. *Foster* v. *Reid*, 437.

9. ENFORCEMENT OF LANDLORD'S LIEN — INTERVENTION OF SUBTENANT — BURDEN OF PROOF. — In an action by a landlord to enforce his lien for unpaid rent, a plea of intervention by the subtenant, alleging that no

rent is due, and that the action is collusive and fraudulent as between the landlord and the tenant, places the burden of proof upon the subtenant to prove his allegations. *Id.*

10. TENANCY FROM YEAR TO YEAR results when a lessee takes possession of premises under a lease for a number of years, but which under the statute of frauds is valid for one year only because not in writing or made by an agent who had no authority in writing to make it. *Coudert v. Cohn*, 761.

11. WHEN A LEASE IS VOID BY THE STATUTE OF FRAUDS BECAUSE FOR A PERIOD GREATER THAN ONE YEAR, and not in writing, and the tenant enters under it, he is treated as a tenant from year to year, computed from the time of its commencement; and if he holds over after the expiration of the first year he becomes a tenant for another year, and cannot terminate such tenancy at an earlier period by giving notice of his intention to quit. *Id.*

12. LEASE FOR MORE THAN ONE YEAR, UNLESS MADE IN THE MANNER PROVIDED BY STATUTE, though it cannot vest the term in the lessee, yet in other respects the rights of the parties may be determined by its terms as far as they are consistent with its failure to create any estate or interest in the land, or any duration of term for occupancy for the lessee. *Id.*

13. WHERE UNDER A LEASE, VOID BY THE STATUTE OF FRAUDS, THE TIME FOR THE COMMENCEMENT OF THE TERM AND THAT FOR ITS EXPIRATION occur at different parts of the year, the tenancy from year to year which is created by the lease, and the entry of the tenant thereunder, must be computed with reference to the date of the commencement of the term, instead of the date of its termination as designated in such lease. *Id.*

14. THERE IS NO COVENANT IMPLIED IN THE DEMISE OF A FURNISHED HOUSE for immediate use as a residence that it is reasonably fit for habitation. In the absence of an express covenant, unless there has been fraud, deceit, or wrong-doing on the part of the landlord, the tenant is without remedy if the demised premises are unfit for occupation. *Franklin v. Brown*, 744.

15. LEASE OF A FURNISHED HOUSE IS NOT ACCOMPANIED WITH AN IMPLIED COVENANT against external defects, such as nuisances existing on adjacent premises belonging to a stranger, and of the existence of which neither the owner nor the tenant was aware when the lease was entered into. *Id.*

16. LESSEE OF REAL PROPERTY MUST RUN THE RISK OF ITS CONDITION, unless he has an express covenant on the part of the lessor regarding that subject. *Id.*

17. IMPLIED COVENANTS. — THE FACT THAT THERE WAS FURNITURE in the house which was leased with it cannot render the landlord answerable to his tenant for a nuisance of which he had no knowledge, and to which he did not contribute, consisting of noxious odors coming from adjacent premises, over which he had no control. *Id.*

18. IMPLIED COVENANTS. — The law will not imply a covenant in a lease, as to conditions not under control of the lessor, and with reference to a nuisance of which both he and the lessee were ignorant, though the lease is of a house and the furniture therein, intended for immediate use and occupation by the lessee. *Id.*

19. LIABILITY FOR ASSAULT BY SERVANT OF LANDLORD'S LESSEE. — A corporation organized for the purpose of furnishing depot and station-house accommodations to different railroads under contract, and which

leases a room in its depot to a tenant, who operates and controls a par-cel-room therein for hire, is liable to a passenger who, while lawfully upon the premises, is maliciously attacked and beaten by an employee of the leasee of the corporation in charge of the parcel-room, when the corporation knowingly and advisedly permitted its tenant to keep in his employ for more than six years in the depot such employee, of savage and vicious propensities, and who had during such period frequently assaulted and beaten persons lawfully upon such premises. *Dean* v. *St. Paul etc. Co.,* 703.

LARCENY.
See CRIMINAL LAW, 24.

LAW OF THE ROAD.
See HIGHWAYS.

LEASES.
See LANDLORD AND TENANT.

LIBEL AND SLANDER.

1. EVIDENCE OF MEANING OF WORDS USED. — Where a petition in slander charges that defendant said of and concerning plaintiff that "she is ornrier than two hells," meaning to charge her with being a whore, the word "ornrier" being of doubtful and uncertain meaning, the intent and mean-ing of its use as understood by those who heard it may be established by proof, but the testimony of witnesses who did not hear that word used, but heard other words not slanderous in character, is inadmissible to prove their understanding of the word charged. *Wimer* v. *Allbaugh*, 422.

2. IN SLANDER THE AWARDING OF PUNITORY DAMAGES is entirely within the sound discretion of the jury. *Id.*

3. IN SLANDER, A MALICIOUS ACT MAY BE DEFINED as one done with an evil intent; if a more specific instruction is desired, it must be asked. *Id.*

4. NOTICE CHARGING WIFE WITH DESERTING HER HUSBAND IN HIS SICK-NESS contains matter libelous *per se*. *Smith* v. *Smith*, 594.

5. QUALIFIED PRIVILEGE EXISTS IN CASES WHERE SOME COMMUNICATION IS NECESSARY and proper in the protection of a person's interest, but this privilege may be lost if the extent of its publication be excessive. *Id.*

6. NOTICE BY HUSBAND NOT TO CREDIT WIFE, WHEN PRIVILEGED AND WHEN NOT. — It is only when a husband has permitted his wife to trade upon his credit that notice to tradesmen is necessary to protect his interests. In such a case, a notice to the public not to give her credit upon his ac-count is justifiable, and to that extent privileged; but the insertion in such notice of words defamatory of the wife is not justifiable, and such words are evidence of malice. *Id.*

7. RULE THAT IF MATTER CHARGED AS LIBELOUS BE FALSE, AND PUBLICA-TION MALICIOUS, it is not privileged, applies to communications or pub-lications which are upon proper occasions qualifiedly privileged. *Id.*

8. FATHER-IN-LAW, WHO CAUSES TO BE PUBLISHED AND PAYS FOR PUBLI-CATION OF LIBEL against his son's wife, cannot defend against an action brought by her by showing that her husband indicted the libel, and di-rected him to publish it. *Id.*

LICENSES.

LIENS.

LIENS CAN ONLY BE CREATED BY AGREEMENT, OR BY SOME FIXED RULE of law, and it is not one of the functions of courts to create them. *Frost* v. *Atwood*, 560.

See ATTACHMENT AND GARNISHMENT, 3, 4; JUDGMENTS, 7-10, 16; JUDICIAL SALES, 16; LANDLORD AND TENANT, 9; PLEDGE, 2-4; PUBLIC LANDS, 2.

LIFE INSURANCE.

See INSURANCE, 8-20.

LIMITATIONS OF ACTIONS.

STATUTE OF LIMITATIONS DOES NOT BEGIN TO RUN AGAINST A CAUSE OF ACTION for injury through defendant's negligence until the injury is received, although the negligence was committed thirteen years prior thereto. *Wabash County* v. *Pearson*, 325.

See CORPORATIONS, 2, 3; JUDGMENTS, 3; MORTGAGES, 1; NEGOTIABLE INSTRUMENTS, 4.

LIS PENDENS.

See JUDGMENTS, 17.

LOTTERY.

See CRIMINAL LAW, 25, 26-29.

MALICIOUS PROSECUTION.

1. DAMAGES FOR MALICIOUS PROSECUTION OF CIVIL ACTION. — An action for damages may be maintained for the malicious prosecution of a civil action without probable cause, to the injury of defendant, although there was no interference with his person or property. *McPherson* v. *Runyon*, 727.

2. DAMAGES FOR MALICIOUS PROSECUTION OF REPLEVIN. — An action for additional damages may be maintained for the malicious prosecution of an action of replevin without probable cause, although the defendant in that action recovered therein his damages for the taking and detention of his property. *Id.*

MANDAMUS.

See STATE.

MARRIAGE AND DIVORCE.

1. MARRIAGE TO WHICH ONE OF PARTIES DISSENTS INVALID. — Where one of the parties to an alleged marriage, instead of assenting to the contract, positively dissents, there is no legal or valid marriage, although a ceremony is gone through with by the officiating minister or magistrate. *Roszel* v. *Roszel*, 569.

2. CONTRACT BETWEEN, RELATING TO MARITAL RELATIONS, WHEN VOID. — A contract between husband and wife, by which the wife agrees to faithfully observe and perform the duties imposed upon her by her marital relations, and by which the husband agrees to provide the necessary expenses of the family, and to pay the wife, for her individual use, a certain sum annually, in monthly payments, so long as she faithfully keeps

the terms and conditions of the contract, is against public policy, and void. *Miller* v. *Miller*, 431.

3. BREACH OF PROMISE OF MARRIAGE — PLEADING. — A petition in an action for damages for breach of promise of marriage, averring that by reason of such breach plaintiff has sustained the loss of an advantageous matrimonial connection, the defendant being a man of wealth and social position, and that, in addition, her affections have been disregarded and blighted, her feelings lacerated, and her spirits wounded, resulting in mental distress and humiliation, is sufficient to support a recovery. *Daggett* v. *Wallace*, 908.

4. BREACH OF PROMISE OF MARRIAGE — SEDUCTION — DAMAGES. — In an action for the breach of a promise of marriage, seduction, if alleged and proved, may be considered in estimating damages. *Id.*

5. BREACH OF PROMISE OF MARRIAGE — EVIDENCE OF ENGAGEMENT — In an action for damages for breach of promise of marriage, plaintiff's evidence as to the time when she became engaged to defendant is not objectionable, on the ground that it states a conclusion, and not a fact. *Id.*

6. BREACH OF PROMISE OF MARRIAGE — INSTRUCTIONS. — In an action for breach of promise of marriage, a charge to find for defendant, unless a mutual agreement to marry existed within one year from the commencement of the action, is not erroneous, in the absence of a request to charge that the promise must have been made to be performed within one year. *Id.*

7. BREACH OF PROMISE OF MARRIAGE — DAMAGES. — Where defendant is a man of wealth and social standing, and has seduced plaintiff under promise of marriage, a verdict of seven thousand five hundred dollars, for the breach of his promise of marriage, will not be set aside as excessive. *Id.*

8. DAMAGES FOR BREACH OF PROMISE OF MARRIAGE rest largely in the discretion of the jury, and are seldom interfered with, unless it is clear that the jury was influenced by prejudice, passion, or corruption. *Id.*

9. BREACH OF PROMISE OF MARRIAGE — DAMAGES. — Loss from disappointment of expectation, including the money value of a marriage which would afford a permanent home and an advantageous establishment to plaintiff, wounds and injuries to her affections, and the mortification and anguish resulting from defendant's failure to keep his promise, are to be estimated in computing actual damages for a breach of promise of marriage. *Id.*

10. DECREE OF DIVORCE HAS NO RETROACTIVE EFFECT, except as specially provided by statute. Existing rights already vested are not thereby affected, and can be taken away only by special enactment as a penalty for wrong. *Van Cleaf* v. *Burns*, 782.

See DOWER, 1-3; HUSBAND AND WIFE, 6-9.

MARRIED WOMEN.

1. MARRIED WOMAN IS NOT LIABLE ON JOINT CONTRACT WITH HER HUSBAND for the making of improvements upon real property held by them jointly, by entireties. Property so held is not such separate property of the wife as the Michigan statute gives her power to make contracts in relation to. *Speier* v. *Opfer*, 556.

2. DEEDS OF — ESTOPPEL. — A married woman who, at the request of her husband, and with knowledge of the facts, joins him in executing and acknowledging a deed of her real estate, and then delivers it to him for the

purpose of completing and delivering it to the purchaser, is estopped, as against the latter, who is innocent and has paid value, to assert the invalidity of the deed, on the ground that when she executed it it was done under her husband's misrepresentations, and was incomplete, not containing the name of the grantee nor a description of the property conveyed, all of which was afterwards inserted without her authority, and the deed delivered to the purchaser. *Dobbin* v. *Cordiner*, 683.

3. ESTOPPEL AGAINST. — Incident to the enlarged power of married women to deal with others is the capacity to be bound and estopped by their conduct when the enforcement of the principles of estoppel are necessary for the protection of those with whom they deal, although there are limitations upon the application of this doctrine. *Id.*

4. MARRIED WOMAN'S DEED IS EFFECTUAL as a conveyance, although there is but one subscribing witness. *Id.*

See HUSBAND AND WIFE.

MASTER AND SERVANT.

1. DISSOLUTION OF CONTRACT BY DEATH. — Death of a servant, who has contracted to render personal service, ends the contract, whether such service involves skill or only common labor. Death of master, with whom a servant has contracted to labor for a specified time dissolves the contract, and the servant cannot recover of the master's estate for services rendered after the latter's death. *Lacy* v. *Getman*, 806.

2. INTOXICATION OF EMPLOYEE, EVIDENCE OF, NOT ADMISSIBLE WHEN. —In an action by an employee to recover for his wrongful discharge, evidence that after his discharge he was frequently seen on the streets in an intoxicated condition is inadmissible, in the absence of any offer to show that his intoxication had became so habitual as to affect his capacity to perform such services as he had engaged to perform, or that he had actually lost an opportunity to obtain employment on account of intoxication. *Hinchcliffe* v. *Koontz*, 403.

3. EMPLOYEE WRONGFULLY DISCHARGED NEED NOT TENDER HIS SERVICES, nor keep himself in readiness to re-enter his employer's service. He is only bound to use reasonable diligence to obtain other employment of the same kind, and it lies upon the defendant to show that he did not use diligence, or that other similar employment was offered and declined. He is not bound to accept employment of a substantially different character or grade. *Id.*

4. AMOUNT OF DAMAGES TO WHICH EMPLOYEE WRONGFULLY DISCHARGED IS ENTITLED is, *prima facie*, the amount stipulated to be paid; but this amount may be reduced by the defendant's making it appear that the plaintiff either did procure, or could by reasonable effort have procured, other employment, or that he occupied his time at his own or other remunerative business. *Id.*

5. FELLOW-SERVANTS, THE SERVANTS OF DIFFERENT MASTERS ARE NOT. — An employee of a firm of stevedores, who are engaged in unloading a vessel, and an employee of the owner of a dock and storehouse, from which the load is to be taken, and who are to furnish a steam-engine and apparatus to be used in the loading, are not fellow-servants, but servants of different masters, and if either is injured by the negligence of the other, his master is answerable therefor. *Sanford* v. *Standard Oil Co.*, 787.

6. FELLOW-SERVANT, WHO IS NOT. — A master mechanic of a railroad company, who has entire control of its shop, men, machinery, and work,

with full authority to employ and discharge workmen and to select and change the machinery, is not a fellow-servant of a machinist in the company's employ, to whom he gives a specific order for the execution of certain work, which order the machinist is bound to obey, but the representative of the master, and if, through the negligence of such master mechanic the machinist is injured while performing the work, the company will be liable. *Taylor* v. *Evansville etc. R. R. Co,* 372.

7. VICE-PRINCIPAL, WHO IS. — An employee invested with the sole charge of a branch or department of the employer's business, and whose duties are not those of a mere workman, but those of one whose duty it is to manage a distinct department, and to give orders to other employees as to the duties they should perform, is not a fellow-servant of such other employees, but a vice-principal, while he is engaged in giving orders or directing their execution. *Id.*

8. FELLOW-SERVANTS — MASTER'S LIABILITY FOR NEGLIGENCE OF VICE-PRINCIPAL. — A car-repairer is not a fellow-servant with a foreman of car-repairers, with power to employ and discharge servants under him, and the company is liable for an injury to such car-repairer received through the negligence of such foreman and while engaged in extra-hazardous employment under his order and promise of protection. *Missouri P. R'y Co.* v. *Williams,* 867.

9. DANGEROUS MACHINERY. — THE DUTY DEVOLVES UPON THE MASTER OF A SERVANT, who had previously always acted in the capacity of a common laborer, before putting him in charge of dangerous machinery with which he is not acquainted, to instruct and qualify him for his new duties. If one servant is selected to instruct another in the use of dangerous machinery, their common master is answerable for the servant so selected, and if, by his incompetency or his discontinuance of his duties before the instructions are complete, the servant to be taught is not adequately instructed, and on that account exposes himself to dangers of which he is not aware, and receives personal injuries, the master is liable; and it is no defense that the injuries were caused to the one servant by the negligence of the other, for the latter represents the master, and his negligence is imputed to the master. *Brennan* v. *Gordon,* 775.

10. ELEVATOR ACCIDENT, LIABILITY FOR. — If one servant is selected to teach another how to run an elevator and to avoid danger in so doing, and the former is guilty of negligence, either in starting the elevator himself or leaving it in charge of the latter before he is qualified to manage it, or if the machinery is imperfect, and its owners have been negligent in selecting it and putting it in use, and an accident occurs by which the servant being instructed is injured, the master is liable. *Id.*

11. DUTY OF MASTER TO SERVANT WHO IS TO BE PLACED IN CHARGE OF AN ELEVATOR, of the management of which he is ignorant, is not fully performed by putting him under the instruction of as competent an instructor as is the master. The duty of the master is to furnish a competent instructor, whether the master himself possesses competency to perform that duty or not; and the master is still answerable, however competent the instructor, if the latter does not continue his instructions for a reasonable length of time, or is guilty of negligence through which the servant to be instructed is injured. *Id.*

12. DUTY OF MASTER TO FURNISH SAFE MACHINERY. — When a servant is employed on or in connection with machinery, in the use of which dan-

ger may arise, it is the duty of the master to use reasonable diligence to guard against accident to his employee, and to make such seasonable repairs or changes as may be necessary to prevent accident or to lessen risk. *McDonald* v. *Chicago etc. R'y Co.*, 711.

13. A MASTER IS UNDER OBLIGATION TO WARN HIS SERVANT of hazards to which the latter is exposed, and to see that he is not induced to work under the notion that machinery or the instruments upon or with which he is at work, or the place where he is at work, is suitable and safe, when in fact the master knows, or ought to know, that it is not. *Id.*

14. HAZARD ASSUMED BY SERVANT. — It is the duty of the servant to use reasonable care to inform himself in respect to the hazards to which he may be exposed; but unless the risks are patent, he is not under the same obligation to know the nature and extent thereof as is the master, whose duty it is to explain to and warn him of such risks. *Id.*

15. EMPLOYEE IN ENTERING SERVICE DOES NOT ASSUME RISK created by the negligent act of the master's representative in making unsafe work which he specifically orders the employee to perform. *Taylor* v. *Evansville etc. R'y Co.*, 372.

16. NEGLIGENCE OF MASTER. — When a servant assumes an extra-hazardous employment by order of his master, and under promise to protect him, the master cannot excuse his failure to keep his promise by proof that the servant also requested others to see that he was not injured. *Missouri P. R'y Co.* v. *Williams*, 867.

17. NEGLIGENCE OF MASTER OR SERVANT, AND ASSUMPTION OF RISK BY EMPLOYEE, QUESTIONS FOR JURY. — In an action by a railroad employee to recover damages for an injury received while engaged, under orders, in turning an engine upon a turn-table, shown by the evidence to have been defective, inadequate, and unsuitable for the use to which it was subjected, and to have been operated, as it was at the time of the accident, by authority of the company, the questions of the company's negligence and of the employee's contributory negligence, as well as whether the latter assumed the risk of such an accident in undertaking and remaining in the employment, should be submitted to the jury. *McDonald* v. *Chicago etc. R'y Co.*, 711.

18. LIABILITY FOR INJURY TO MINOR EMPLOYEE. — Where the master knowingly engages a minor in a dangerous employment, without the father's consent, and the minor is injured in such employment, the master is responsible to the father for the loss of his son's services resulting from such injury. *Gulf etc. R'y Co.* v. *Redeker*, 887.

19. NECESSITY OF FATHER'S CONSENT TO MINOR'S EMPLOYMENT. — Where the parents live together, the mother's consent, unratified by the father, that their minor son may engage in a dangerous employment, will not justify the employer in making the contract, or in retaining the minor in such employment after knowledge of his minority; and the employer assumes the risk of answering to the father for an injury to the minor, by thus retaining him after notice of the minority. *Id.*

20. NECESSITY OF FATHER'S CONSENT TO MINOR'S EMPLOYMENT. — General permission by a father that his minor son may follow railroading for a livelihood does not deprive the father of the right of specifying how and where he shall work; and the father's consent that the minor may be employed in one vocation will not justify the employer in changing the employment of the minor to a more hazardous vocation. *Id.*

21. NECESSITY OF FATHER'S CONSENT TO MINOR'S EMPLOYMENT. — Where the employer knows of the minority of his employee, it is his duty to ascertain whether he has a parent, or is an apprentice, and to obtain consent of the parent or master before employing the minor; and it is not the duty of the father to give the employer notice that the employment of the minor is without his permission, in order to enable him to recover for an injury to his son, engaged in a dangerous employment. *Id.*

22. RAILWAY, LIABILITY OF, TO PERSON INJURED IN ITS SERVICE, BUT EMPLOYED BY ANOTHER CORPORATION. — A servant in the general employment and pay of one railway, but engaged in special services for another, through an agreement between the two railways, may recover of the railway for whom such special services are performed for an injury received by reason of its negligence. *Missouri etc. R'y Co.* v. *Jones,* 897.

See CONTRACTS, 4, 5; LANDLORD AND TENANT, 19.

MINES AND MINING.

1. SALE BY GOVERNMENT OF MINERAL LANDS REVOKES FORMER LICENSE. — Subsequent sale of mineral land by the government, and the issue by it of a receiver's receipt for the purchase price, revokes a mere license from the government under which a party had formerly entered, and such licensee cannot set up his former possession as adverse to the grantee. *Omaha etc. Co.* v. *Tabor,* 185.

2. LICENSE TO ONE IS NOT LICENSE TO OTHERS. — Where a party knowing that persons have, under an order of court, entered on a mining claim conflicting with his, and are taking his ore, his consent that another shall join them is not a license to the others to take the ore. *Id.*

MISTAKE.

See DEEDS, 9; FIXTURES, 5.

MORTGAGES.

1. PURCHASE BY MORTGAGEE UNDER POWER — LIMITATIONS AS AGAINST INFANT HEIRS. — A purchase by a mortgagee at his own sale, under a power in the mortgage not authorizing him to purchase, gives the mortgagor an option in ordinary cases, if expressed in two years from the time of sale, of affirming or disaffirming it, and on disaffirming, to redeem. This limitation is judicial, and will be extended to infant heirs of the mortgagor, he being dead when the sale was made, so as to allow them two years after attaining majority to disaffirm the sale, provided the period is not extended beyond twenty years from the date thereof. *Alexander* v. *Hill,* 55.

2. PURCHASE BY MORTGAGEE UNDER POWER — RIGHT TO COMPEL ELECTION. — A mortgagee who purchases at his own sale, under a power in the mortgage not authorizing him to purchase, gives the mortgagor an option to affirm or disaffirm the sale within two years thereafter, and if he disaffirms, to redeem; but the mortgagee may, by bill filed against the person having such option, whether he is *sui juris* or not, compel an election and foreclosure, if the sale is disaffirmed. *Id.*

3. PURCHASE BY MORTGAGEE AT HIS OWN SALE UNDER POWER — RIGHT TO REDEEM. — A purchase by a mortgagee at his own sale, under a power in the mortgage not authorizing him to purchase, gives the mortgagor an option to affirm or disaffirm the sale within two years thereafter, and if he disaffirms, to redeem. This is a judicial limitation, and will not be extended in favor of infants, who succeed to the right of one who, at the time of the sale, is free from disability, and entitled to affirm or disaffirm. *Id.*

See CHATTEL MORTGAGES; HOMESTEAD, 1; INSURANCE, 2; JUDGMENTS, 16; VENDOR AND VENDEE, 4, 5.

MUNICIPAL CORPORATIONS.

1. VOTE OF MAJORITY OF QUORUM IS SUFFICIENT TO ADOPT MEASURE. — If a quorum of a municipal council is present, and a majority of such quorum vote in favor of a measure, it will prevail, although an equal number refrain from voting. Where, therefore, three of the six members composing a common council of a municipal corporation vote in favor of a resolution, the other three members, though present, declining to vote, the resolution is legally adopted. *Rushville G. Co. v. Rushville*, 388.

2. MUNICIPAL CORPORATION CAN PASS NO ORDINANCE which conflicts with its charter, since it derives all is powers from legislative acts. *People v. Armstrong*, 578.

3. ORDINANCE PASSED BY MUNICIPAL CORPORATION PURSUANT TO POWER, not in conflict with the constitution, to pass ordinances of a specified and defined character, conferred in terms by the legislature, cannot be impeached as invalid because it would have been regarded as unreasonable if it had been passed under the incidental power of the corporation, or under a grant of power general in its nature. But where the power to legislate on a given subject is conferred, but the mode of its exercise is not prescribed, then the ordinance passed in pursuance thereof must be a reasonable exercise of the power, or it will be pronounced invalid. *Id.*

4. UNAUTHORIZED PROVISIONS OF MUNICIPAL ORDINANCE do not invalidate whole ordinance, if they can be separated from the rest of the ordinance without so mutilating it as to render it inoperative. *Id.*

5. ORDINANCE OF CITY OF DETROIT prohibiting circulation, distribution, or giving away of circulars, handbills, or advertising cards of any description, in or upon any of the public streets and alleys of said city, does not come within any express or implied power given to the city by its charter; and even if the charter could be held to authorize it, this part of the ordinance would not be a reasonable exercise of the power granted. *Id.*

6. REASONABLENESS OR UNREASONABLENESS OF CITY ORDINANCE is not determined by enormity of some offense which it seeks to prevent and punish, but by its actual operation in all cases that may be brought thereunder. *Id.*

7. CITY ORDINANCE, TO BE REASONABLE, must tend in some degree to accomplishment of object for which the corporation was created and its powers conferred. *Id.*

8. COMMON COUNCIL OF CITY HAS POWER to contract for lighting the city or to furnish light from works of which it is or may become the owner, both under the general act of incorporation and under the provisions of the act entitled "An act in relation to the lighting of cities and towns, and furnishing the inhabitants thereof with the electric light and other forms of light, and providing for the right of way and the assessment of damages, and declaring an emergency": Elliott's Supp., sec. 794. And

this act is constitutional, and complies with the requirements of the constitution as to subject and title. *Rushville G. Co.* v. *Rushville,* 388.

9. MUNICIPAL CORPORATION HAS POWER to issue bonds in payment for property which it has authority to purchase, unless there is some statutory or constitutional prohibition. *Id.*

10. WATER RATES, POWER OF COURTS TO INTERFERE WITH ACTION OF SUPERVISORS IN FIXING. — The use of water for sale is a public use, and the price at which it shall be sold is a matter within the power of the board of supervisors to determine; and the constitution of California does not, in terms, confer upon the courts of the state any power or jurisdiction to control, supervise, or set aside any action of the board in respect to such rates. If the board has fairly investigated and exercised its discretion in fixing the rates, the courts have no right to interfere on the sole ground that, in the judgment of the court, the rates fixed are not reasonable; to justify interference by the courts, there must be actual fraud in fixing the rates. or they must be so palpably and grossly unreasonable and unjust as to amount to the same thing. But the power to regulate water rates conferred by the constitution upon boards of supervisors is not a power to confiscate nor to take the property of a water company without just compensation; and whether such power be judicial, legislative, or administrative, it is not above the control of the courts, if it is arbitrarily exercised without a fair investigation, and the rates are so fixed as to render it impossible to furnish the water without loss, so that their action would amount to a palpable fraud, and almost certainly work injustice. *Spring Valley Water Works* v. *San Francisco,* 116.

11. REASONABLE AND JUST WATER RATES, WHAT ARE, WITHIN MEANING OF CONSTITUTION. — When the constitution provides for the fixing of rates or compensation for the use of water, it means reasonable rates and just compensation; and for a board of supervisors to fix rates not reasonable, or compensation not just, is a plain violation of its duty. It has no right to fix rates arbitrarily and without investigation, or without exercising its judgment or discretion to determine what is a fair and reasonable compensation. *Id.*

12. POWER OF COURTS OVER PROCEEDINGS OF MUNICIPAL CORPORATIONS.— A subordinate municipal body, although clothed to some extent with legislative and even political powers, is nevertheless, in the exercise of all its powers, just as subject to the authority and control of courts of justice as any other body or person, natural or artificial. *Id.*

13. MAYOR NEED NOT BE MADE PARTY TO ACTION brought by a water company against a city and county and its board of supervisors to obtain a judgment setting aside and declaring void an ordinance of said board, and compelling it to pass a new ordinance, as required by the constitution. *Id.*

14. NOTICE OF INTENTION TO FIX WATER RATES NEED NOT BE GIVEN TO WATER COMPANY. — The constitution does not require a board of supervisors to give notice to a water company of its intention to fix water rates; but it is, nevertheless, its plain duty to use all proper means to obtain the information necessary to enable it to act intelligently and fairly in fixing the rates; and a failure to perform this duty may defeat its action. *Id.*

15. WATER-METERS, ORDINANCE FIXING RATES MAY REQUIRE. — An ordinance of a board of supervisors fixing water rates may require the water company to furnish a water-meter to each householder at his option, and to collect only for the water furnished at meter rates, which are different from the house rates. A regulation requiring the party furnishing water to furnish the means necessary for its measurement, so that the quantity furnished and to be paid for may be known, is not unreasonable. The expense of furnishing such meters cannot be imposed upon the consumer. *Id.*

16. DAMAGES — ABUTTING LOT-OWNER. — In order to justify a recovery for damages by an abutting city lot-owner against a railroad company authorized to construct and operate its road along a street, there must be such a practical obstruction of the street in front of the lots that the owner is denied ingress to and egress from them. *Kansas etc. R'y Co.* v. *Cuykendall*, 479.

17. THE INDIANA ACT OF MARCH, 1883, CREATING A BOARD OF METROPOLITAN POLICE in all cities having a population of twenty-nine thousand or more inhabitants, is constitutional and capable of being enforced, except in so far as it makes a residence of three years in the city in which he is appointed next preceding his appointment a condition of a police commissioner's eligibility, and in so far as it provides for the appointment of officers equally from the two leading political parties. *State* v. *Blend*, 411.

See EMINENT DOMAIN.

MURDER.

See CRIMINAL LAW, 21-23.

NEGLIGENCE.

1. WHEN AN ACCIDENT HAS OCCURRED, and an action is on trial to recover damages for injuries sustained thereby, and the accident is alleged to have been the result of negligence, proof of any facts and circumstances attending the accident is competent and proper. *Illinois Central R. R. Co.* v. *Slater*, 242.

2. EVIDENCE OF THE SPEED OF A RAILWAY TRAIN IS COMPETENT AND MATERIAL in an action to recover damages for injuries to one run over by such train from the alleged negligence of the person in charge thereof. *Id.*

3. RAILROADS. — It is negligence in a railway company to leave holes between the cross-ties on its track, after being warned of the danger, and a car-coupler in its employ, who is injured while the track is in such condition, without negligence on his part, may recover, and if the evidence as to his contributory negligence in the matter is conflicting, the question of negligence should be submitted to the jury. *Missouri P. R'y Co.* v. *Jones*, 897.

4. WHERE THE CONCURRENT NEGLIGENCE of two or more persons results in the injury of a third person, each is answerable therefor. Hence one who, without any negligence on his part, is pushed or jostled off of a sidewalk which is more than six feet above the ground, and is not protected by any railing or guard, may recover from the village whose duty it was to have kept such sidewalk properly guarded. *Village of Carterville* v. *Cook*, 248.

5. NEGLIGENCE OF PARENT NOT IMPUTABLE TO MINOR CHILD. — An administrator may recover for fatal injuries to his intestate, an irresponsible child incapable of committing negligence, when such injuries are

NEGOTIABLE INSTRUMENTS.

3. DELIVERY, WHEN INSUFFICIENT. — Where there is nothing to indicate that the maker ever surrendered control of his note, or that it was ever within the power or control of the payee, or of any person for his use or benefit, there is no delivery, and the note is a nullity. *Id.*

4. COMPELLING DELIVERY — STATUTE OF LIMITATIONS. — Party who has advanced money on the faith that a note has been delivered to a third person for his benefit may compel the delivery to be perfected, or if he has been induced to abstain from enforcing his claim until it is barred by the statute of limitations on the faith of such assurance, he may compel the delivery of the note, or require it to be treated, in an equitable suit, as having been delivered as represented after the death of the maker, with the note still in his possession. *Id.*

5. A PROMISSORY NOTE containing a condition stating that the consideration therein is "part payment of rent of certain pasture fields," and that the note shall not be paid unless the maker has the use of the premises, is neither negotiable at common law nor under the Colorado statute. *Jennings* v. *First National Bank*, 210.

6. PROOF BY ASSIGNEE OF NON-NEGOTIABLE NOTE NECESSARY TO ENABLE HIM TO RECOVER. — The assignee of a non-negotiable note payable on a contingency to recover thereon must prove his ownership of the note, that it is supported by a consideration, and that the contingency has happened. *Id.*

7. PROMISSORY NOTE — EVIDENCE TO SHOW CAPACITY IN WHICH PERSONS SIGN. — A promissory note in the ordinary form, reading, "we promise to pay," and signed, "Belle Plaine Canning Co., A. J. Hartman, President, H. Wessel, Secretary," in the absence of a clause showing the capacity in which the parties signed, binds all the persons signing, including the corporation, and extrinsic evidence is inadmissible to show the intention of the parties who signed the note. *McCandless* v. *Belle Plaine C. Co.*, 429.

8. NEGOTIABILITY DOES NOT CEASE WHEN PAPER MATURES. — It is only subject to such equities as exist against the paper at the date when negotiated, and the equities which affect the indorsee are only such as attach directly to the note itself, and do not include collateral matters. *Carpenter* v. *Greenop*, 662.

9. PARTNERSHIP NOTE — RIGHTS OF HOLDER. — A holder by indorsement of a partnership note given to a partner for money loaned by him to the firm, and purchased after maturity in good faith while the firm was still in business, may maintain an action thereon against the firm before its dissolution and final accounting, when the partner taking the note was not indebted to the firm at the time the note was indorsed, and no equities existed against him at that time which did not exist when the note was executed. *Id.*

10. WHEN NEGOTIABLE PAPER HAS BEEN OBTAINED FROM ITS MAKER BY FRAUD OR DURESS, a subsequent indorsee, to entitle himself to recover upon it, must show that he was a *bona fide* purchaser. *Vosburgh* v. *Diefendorf*, 836.

11. PURCHASER BONA FIDE, WHO IS. — Plaintiff does not establish that he is a *bona fide* purchaser of negotiable paper merely by proving that he paid value therefor before its maturity. He must go further, and show that he had no notice of the fraud with which the instrument was tainted from its origin. *Id.*

covered that the check had been fraudulently altered. The rule is otherwise when he by whom or by whose agent the check is presented apparently receives payment in his own right. Then, with or without indorsement, the person presenting the check warrants its genuineness, and is liable to pay the amount received by him if it is not genuine. *Id.*

See AGENCY, 4, 5; APPEAL AND ERROR, 4; ATTACHMENT AND GARNISHMENT, 5; BANKS AND BANKING, 4–6; WILLS, 2, 3.

NEWSPAPERS.

See LIBEL AND SLANDER, 9, 18, 20.

NEW TRIAL.

1. VENIRE DE NOVO. — Where verdict is perfect on its face, and so fully finds the facts as to enable the court to pronounce judgment upon it, a motion for a *venire de novo* will be denied, although the verdict may not find upon all the issues. *Wabash Co.* v. *Pearson*, 325.
2. NEW TRIAL WILL NOT BE GRANTED ON THE GROUND OF AN EXCESSIVE VERDICT, or because part of the amount was remitted, when the evidence is conclusive that the amount for which judgment was entered was clearly authorized. *Gulf etc. R'y Co.* v. *Redeker*, 887.

NOTICE.

See DEEDS, 1–3; HUSBAND AND WIFE, 2.

NUISANCES.

1. OBSTRUCTING STREET — MEASURE OF DAMAGES. — An unauthorized and complete obstruction of a street or highway by a railway company, in such manner as to prevent ingress and egress by a land-owner to and from his premises by means of vehicles, if long continued, is a public nuisance, for which the land-owner may recover damages for the special and peculiar injury not suffered in common with the general public, to the extent of the difference in rental value occasioned by the nuisance, and, under some circumstances, the recovery may take a wider scope. *Jackson* v. *Kiel*, 207.
2. NUISANCE — FISHING WITH NETS. — The legislature has power to declare that any net found, or any other means or device for taking or capturing fish, set, put, floated, had, found, or maintained in or upon any of the waters of this state, or upon the shores or islands in any waters of this state, in violation of existing or hereafter enacted statutes for the protection of fish, is a public nuisance, and may be abated as such, and summarily destroyed by any person, and to make it the duty of certain specified officers to seize, remove, and destroy the same. *Lawton* v. *Steele*, 813.
3. LEGISLATIVE POWER — PUBLIC NUISANCES. — The legislature has power to enlarge the category of public nuisances by declaring places or property used to the detriment of public interests, or to the injury of the health, morals, or welfare of the community, to be nuisances, although not such at common law. *Id.*
4. LEGISLATIVE POWER — DESTRUCTION OF PROPERTY EMPLOYED AS A PUBLIC NUISANCE. — The legislature may authorize the removal or abatement of a public nuisance by executive officers, and such destruction of the property used in maintaining such nuisances as may be requisite for such

NUNC PRO TUNC ENTRY.

OFFICE AND OFFICERS.

ORDINANCES.

PARENT AND CHILD.

PARTIES.

PARTNERHIP.

although it may not constitute a partnership, is, nevertheless, a fiduciary relation between the associates. *Colton v. Stanford,* 137.

2. PLEADING EXISTENCE OF PARTNERSHIP OR CORPORATION. — WHERE PLAINTIFFS' NAMES ARE GIVEN IN FULL in the title of the case, it is unnecessary to repeat them in alleging that they are partners; or if the name of defendant imports that it is a corporation, that fact need not be specially averred. *Adams Exp. Co. v. Harris,* 315.

3. DEALINGS BETWEEN PARTNERS — REMEDY. — There is no legal nor equitable reason why a partner should not have specific dealings with his firm as well as with any other person, and unless these dealings, from their nature, are intended to go into the general accounting, and wait for their adjustment until dissolution, they give a right to have a remedy according to their exigency, and can be dealt with like any other claims, at law or in equity. *Carpenter v. Greenop,* 662.

4. DEALINGS BETWEEN PARTNERS — ACCOUNTING. — Where partners have seen fit to deal with each other without reference to a final accounting, the transaction is not subject to the necessity of the delay of such an accounting. *Id.*

5. REMEDY OF PARTNER AGAINST FIRM. — A partner has a right to relief against the partnership when he contracts as a creditor or otherwise therewith, and the transaction is such as to be separated from the general partnership accounting, and the fact that an accounting can only be had at the close of the business indicates clearly that either the partner cannot separately contract with his firm, or else there must be some means of enforcing it. A contract which cannot be enforced is nugatory. *Id.*

6. PAYMENT OF PARTNER'S INDIVIDUAL DEBT WITH FIRM PROPERTY VOID AS TO PARTNESHIP. — A contract between a partner and his individual creditor, to the effect that the latter is to take partnership property in payment of his debt, is void as against the firm without its consent or ratification, and it is immaterial that the partnership displayed no firm sign, and that the creditor was ignorant of its existence at the time of making the contract, if it had in fact publicly existed for three years with no effort at concealment. *Janney v. Springer,* 460.

See HUSBAND AND WIFE, 5; NEGOTIABLE INSTRUMENTS, 9.

PATENTS.
See INVENTIONS.

PAYMENT.

1. PLEA OF PAYMENT IS BAD IF IT DOES NOT STATE FACTS IN BAR of the action. *Hancock v. Yaden,* 396.
2. PAYMENT CANNOT BE MADE IN GOODS where there is no agreement to receive them in payment. *Id.*

See ACCORD AND SATISFACTION; TAXATION, 4.

PENALTY.
See CARRIERS, 9–10; MARRIAGE AND DIVORCE, 10.

PERSONAL EXAMINATION.
See CRIMINAL LAW, 31.

PHYSICIANS AND SURGEONS.
See CRIMINAL LAW, 23.

PLEADING.

1. CHANGING ACTION AT LAW INTO SUIT IN EQUITY BY AMENDMENT. — A party, by bringing his action at law to recover upon a policy of insurance, is not estopped from amending his pleadings after answer, and before the case is finally submitted to the court, so as to change it into a suit in equity to reform the policy. *Esch* v. *Insurance Co.*, 443.

2. PARTIES — WAIVER OF DEFECT. — Where a defect of parties is not apparent on the face of the petition, and is not taken advantage of by answer, it is waived. *Coulson* v. *Wing*, 503.

See CONTRACTS, 7; FRAUDULENT CONVEYANCES, 1; HUSBAND AND WIFE, 3-4; MARRIAGE AND DIVORCE, 1; NEGLIGENCE, 9-11; PARTNERSHIP, 2; TRIAL, 11.

PLEDGE.

1. PLEDGE REMAINS AS SECURITY AFTER DEFAULT. — The general property in a pledge remains in the pledgor after as well as before default, and the pledgee cannot, after default, give it away so as to affect the rights of the pledgor, nor can a pretended and merely colorable sale, without consideration, divest the pledgor of his rights as such, or confer upon the pretended purchaser any greater interest than that held by the pledgee. *Norton* v. *Baxter*, 679.

2. TENDER OF PAYMENT RELEASES LIEN. — An unjustifiable refusal to accept a sufficient tender of payment of the principal debt after maturity discharges the lien against a note and mortgage pledged as collateral security. *Id.*

3. REFUSAL OF TENDER OF PAYMENT RELEASES LIEN. — An unjustifiable refusal to accept a sufficient tender of payment, although such tender is not kept good, discharges the lien on the pledge as against one who, subsequently to the pledging, has *bona fide* acquired rights in the pledged property. *Id.*

4. PRETENDED SALE BY PLEDGEE DOES NOT DIVEST LIEN OF PLEDGE. — A fraudulent sale of pledged property by the pledgee does not invest the purchaser with title, so as to affect the rights of the pledgor. *Id.*

5. NEGLIGENCE OF PLEDGEE — EFFECT ON DEBT. — When the value of the thing pledged is lost through the negligence of the pledgee, it does not operate *ipso facto* as a satisfaction or extinction of the debt to the extent of the loss. *Cooper* v. *Simpson*, 667.

6. CONTRACT REQUIRING PLEDGEE TO SELL. — A contract or pledge may make it the duty of the pledgee to sell within a specified time, and his failure to do so is then such breach of duty as will render him answerable to the pledgor. In the absence of such contract, the pledgor cannot make it the duty of the pledgee to sell by requesting or directing him to do so. *Id.*

7. LIABILITY OF PLEDGEE FOR NEGLIGENCE. — A pledgee may, by his misconduct with respect to the thing pledged, become liable to the pledgor for depreciation or loss in value in consequence of his negligence. *Id.*

8. RELATIONS BETWEEN PLEDGOR AND PLEDGEE. In the absence of contract, the pledgor is bound to exercise ordinary care only, and is liable to the pledgee only for negligence. *Id.*

9. RELATIONS BETWEEN PLEDGOR AND PLEDGEE. — After a contract of pledging is made, either party can, by anything he alone may do, vary the duties or powers attaching to the relation. *Id.*

POLICE POWER.

See CONSTITUTIONAL LAW, 6, 7; DRAINS, 3; FISHERIES; INTERSTATE COMMERCE; NUISANCES, 2-4; RAILROAD COMPANIES, 9.

POWER OF ATTORNEY.

See AGENCY, 12.

PROBATE COURTS.

See JUDICIAL SALES, 7, 15, 16.

PROCESS.

PERSONAL SERVICE CANNOT BE DISPENSED WITH except in cases distinctly provided for by statute. *Frost v. Atwood*, 560.

See HUSBAND AND WIFE, 1.

PROMISSORY NOTES.

See NEGOTIABLE INSTRUMENTS.

PROHIBITION.

PROHIBITION OF COURT EXCEEDING ITS JURISDICTION. — A court that proceeds in the trial of a cause against an express prohibition of a statute is exceeding its jurisdiction, and may be prevented by prohibition from the supreme court. Where, therefore, a justice's court refuses to stay proceedings in a case not within the exceptions of the Insolvent Act, a writ of prohibition will be issued to restrain it from further proceedings, notwithstanding an order of the superior court in which the insolvency proceedings are pending, assuming to permit such justice's court to proceed with the cause. *Hayne v. Justice's Court*, 114.

PUBLIC LANDS.

1. LAND PATENTED TO HEIRS OF DECEDENT — VOID SALE BY ADMINISTRATOR. — Where a patent to land is procured by an administrator on behalf of his intestate, and issued to the heirs of the latter, the land does not become part of the intestate's estate, and a sale of it under order of the probate court, to pay the debts of the estate, is null and void, as against the heirs. *Coulson v. Wing*, 503.

2. LAND PATENTED TO HEIRS OF DECEDENT — MONEY ADVANCED BY ADMINISTRATOR NO LIEN. — Where an administrator pays the price of land entered upon by his decedent, and the patent thereto is issued to the heirs, the money so advanced is no lien against the land, nor can it be sold under order of court to repay the administrator. *Id.*

See MINES AND MINING, 1.

PUNISHMENT.

See CONSTITUTIONAL LAW, 2-5.

QUO WARRANTO.

1. WHO MAY MAINTAIN. — To enable a private person to maintain *quo warranto* to dissolve a corporation, upon the neglect or refusal of the district attorney to bring such action, he must allege and show some injury peculiarly affecting him, and some interest in the result of the action beyond that common to every citizen of the state. *People v. Grand River Bridge Co.*, 182.

2. CLAIM FOR DAMAGES WILL NOT SUPPORT. — A right to sue for damages arising from the appropriation of land, without compensation, by a corporation, does not give the owner of the land an interest so different from that common to all citizens as to enable him to maintain *quo warranto* to dissolve the corporation. *Id.*

RAILROAD COMPANIES.

1. STATUTES — CONSTRUCTION. — A statute providing that "in any case where the construction of a railway has been commenced by any corporation or person, and work on the same has ceased, and has not, in good faith, been resumed for a period of eight years, the land and the title thereto shall revert to the owner," applies where work was commenced and abandoned prior to the enactment of the statute, and not resumed until three years after its enactment, and more than eight years after the abandonment; nor does such construction make the statute retroactive in effect, since it does not create, but only declares the effect of, a suspension of the work for eight years. *Skillman v. Chicago etc. R'y Co.*, 452.

2. STATUTES — CONSTRUCTION. — A statute providing that "in any case where the construction of a railway has been commenced by any corporation or person, and work on the same has ceased, and has not, in good faith, been resumed for a period of eight years, the land and the title thereto shall revert to the owner," is not unconstitutional, as interfering with vested rights, impairing the obligations of contracts, or depriving the holder of the right of way for a railroad of its property without due process of law, since such right of way is but an easement attached to the use of the land for public places, and when such use is abandoned, the right ceases to exist. *Id.*

3. DUTY TO KEEP JOINTLY USED PLATFORM IN REPAIR. — A platform used by railroad companies in common as a connection between their stations, and upon which a passenger going from one station to the other would probably walk, must be kept in safe repair; and such passenger not in fault, injured through this neglect of duty, may recover of each or both of the companies. *Lucas v. Pennsylvania Co.*, 323.

4. DUTY OF PASSENGER AT WAY-STATION OR WHILE TRAIN IS SIDE-TRACKED. — When a passenger enters a railway train, and pays fare to be transported from one station to another, his contract does not obligate the corporation to furnish him with safe egress or ingress at any intermediate station, or while the train is side-tracked, and while the train is stopped at such place, the duty and safety of the passenger both concur in telling him to remain in the cars. If, under such circumstances, he leaves the cars with the permission of the corporation, or without objection on its part, he does no illegal act, and has the right to re-enter and resume his journey; but for the time being he surrenders his rights as a passenger, and takes upon himself the responsibility of his own movements, and must exercise great care and caution to avoid injury. *De Kay v. Chicago etc. R'y Co.*, 687.

5. Duty of Company and of Passenger when Train is Side-tracked. — When a railway company permits a through-passenger to leave the train while it is side-tracked, it must give reasonable and seasonable notice to him to return when his train is about to start, if he remains near at hand; but if he goes out of sight or hearing, he takes his chances of being left, and the company is not bound to wait for or send after him. *Id.*

6. Duty of Company and of Passenger when Train is Side-tracked. — Where a railway company permits through-passengers to leave the train while it is side-tracked at an intermediate point, it is bound to use reasonable diligence not to expose them to unnecessary danger while leaving or re-entering the train, yet it is not bound to make such point as safe and convenient as a station platform. A passenger, under such circumstances, assumes the risks necessarily incident to such practice, and must use a degree of care and caution to avoid injury from passing trains, corresponding to the increased risks, as the company gives him no assurance that while crossing or recrossing the main track no other trains will pass, when he has thus left his train for his own convenience or pleasure. *Id.*

7. Negligence of Passenger when Train is Side-tracked. — Where a railway company has permitted a passenger to leave his train for purposes of his own while it is side-tracked at an intermediate point, to allow another train to pass, the conductor's call of "all aboard" is not an assurance to such passenger that no other train is approaching, but rather an express warning that one is, and does not justify nor excuse him for doing a dangerous act, and recklessly obeying at the risk of his life, when, at most, it is but a question with him of inconvenience in being left and having to take a later train, and he is not confronted with the dilemma of choosing immediately between two dangers, nor, under such circumstances, is the fact that he heard no signals any excuse for not looking, when he had ample opportunity to do so, and it would not have appreciably delayed his progress. *Id.*

8. The Fact that a Bell was not Rung nor Whistle Sounded at a distance of at least eighty rods from the railway crossing may be proved by other than positive or direct testimony. Therefore it is not error to instruct a jury that "it is not necessary, in order to enable plaintiff to recover, that any witness should swear positively that no bell was rung nor whistle sounded upon the train in question at a distance of at least eighty rods from the railway crossing. It is sufficient upon that question that the jury believe, from the evidence in the case, that no bell was rung nor whistle sounded." *Illinois C. R. R. Co.* v. *Slater*, 243.

9. Though the Charter of a Railway Corporation Defines its duty as to the giving of signals at public highway crossings, a statute subsequenty enacted, imposing the duty of giving other and different signals, is not unconstitutional. The right to impose this and like duties upon railway corporations arises out of the police power, which may be exercised by the legislature at its discretion as the public safety may require. *Id.*

See Carriers; Corporations, 20; Master and Servant, 22; Municipal Corporations, 16; Negligence, 1, 2, 3; Nuisances, 1.

RAPE.

See Criminal Law, 16, 30-35.

RATIFICATION.
See CONTRACTS, 9.

REDEMPTION.
See MORTGAGES, 2, 3; TAXATION, 1-3.

REFORMATION.
See DEEDS, 9; INSURANCE, 6, 7.

REGISTRATION.
See DEEDS, 1-3.

REMOVAL OF OFFICERS.
See OFFICE AND OFFICERS, 3-8.

REPLEVIN.
See ESTOPPEL, 1; MALICIOUS PROSECUTION, 2.

RES AJUDICATA.
See JUDGMENTS, 14-17.

RESCISSION.
See COMPROMISE, 2, 3; CONTRACTS, 10-12; VENDOR AND VENDEE, 7-8.

REVERSION.
See RAILROAD COMPANIES, 1, 2.

RIGHT OF WAY.
See EASEMENTS.

ROBBERY.
See CRIMINAL LAW, 36-38.

SALES.

1. CONSIDERATION. — A sale of an interest in personal property must be supported by a sufficient consideration. *Tuttle* v. *Campbell*, 652.
2. CONTRACT NOT VOID FOR INDEFINITENESS. — A contract to furnish a vendee with a certain line of goods for exclusive sale in "Dubuque, and the territory tributory thereto," is not void for indefiniteness in describing the territory embraced in the terms of the contract. *Kaufman* v. *Farley etc. Co.*, 462.
3. EVIDENCE — SUFFICIENCY OF, TO ESTABLISH CONTRACT. — In an action for breach of a contract made by the vendor's agent, whereby the vendee was to have the exclusive right to sell a certain line of goods in a designated territory, in which the evidence shows that the vendee was to have the goods for sale as long as he "pushed them," the question whether the vendee agreed to work up the trade, and to put men into the field to canvass for the goods, should be admitted to the jury. *Id.*
4. STATUTE OF FRAUDS — PART PERFORMANCE OF CONTRACT SUFFICIENT TO AVOID. — Where, under a contract to furnish a vendee with a certain

SCHOOLS.

criminally, if in punishing a pupil he exceeds the exercise of reasonable judgment and discretion, and acts with legal malice, or from wickedness of motive. *Boyd v. State*, 31.

2. SCHOOLMASTERS EXCEED THE LIMIT OF THEIR AUTHORITY to punish pupils when they inflict lasting injury; they act within the limits of it when they inflict temporary pain. *Id.*

3. LIABILITY OF TEACHER FOR PUNISHMENT INFLICTED ON PUPIL. — In determining whether the teacher in correcting a pupil has acted with reasonable judgment, or from malice and wickedness of motive, the nature of the instrument used for correction has a strong bearing and influence on the question of motive or intention. *Id.*

4. TEACHER'S CRIMINAL LIABILITY FOR IMPROPER CHASTISEMENT OF PUPIL. —A schoolmaster is not justified in using a "limb or stick," nor his "clenched fist applied in bruising the pupil's eye," in further correcting a pupil eighteen years of age, after he has been severely chastised, and has apologized. Such implements are not proper instruments of correction to be used on such occasion, and from their use there is ample room to imply legal malice in connection with unreasonable and immoderate correction, which will support a conviction of assault and battery. *Id.*

SEDUCTION.
See MARRIAGE AND DIVORCE, 4.

SET-OFF.
See STATE.

SLANDER.
See LIBEL AND SLANDER.

SPECIALTIES.
See CONTRACTS, 2, 3.

SPECIFIC PERFORMANCE.
See WILLS, 2.

STATE.

STATE, SUIT OR SET-OFF AGAINST. — A suit or a claim for a set-off cannot be maintained, directly or indirectly, against the state, when it involves a common-law issue. Hence, as against a petition for a *mandumus* to compel a county to levy a tax to pay a sum due the state, the county cannot successfully urge that the state owes it a sum with which it should be credited before making such levy. *Alpin v. Supervisors*, 576.

STATUTE OF FRAUDS.

1. CONTRACT FOR THE SALE OF GOODS TO BE SUBSEQUENTLY MANUFACTURED and delivered is not within the statute of frauds. Hence an agreement between a manufacturer of patent roofing and his agent, that the latter should be furnished with materials with which to perform certain contracts, is enforceable, though no note or memorandum is made thereof in writing. *Warren etc. Mfg. Co. v. Holbrook*, 788.

2. THE FACT THAT THE AGREEMENT MAY NOT AND WAS NOT EXECUTED TO BE PERFORMED WITHIN A YEAR does not bring it within the statute of frauds, if it is one which admits of a valid execution within that time. *Id.*

See LANDLORD AND TENANT, 10–13; MARRIAGE AND DIVORCE, 6; SALES, 4; WILLS, 2.

STATUTES.

1. REPEALING CLAUSE IN UNCONSTITUTIONAL ACT FALLS WITH REST OF ACT WHEN. — Where it is not cle.r that the legislature, by a repealing clause attached to an unconstitutional act, intended to repeal the former statute upon the same subject, except upon the supposition that the new act would take the place of the former one, the repealing clause falls with the act to which it is attached. *State v. Blend*, 411.

2. ACT IN PART UNCONSTITUTIONAL MAY BE VALID AS TO PART NOT UN-CONSTITUTIONAL WHEN. — When a part of an act is unconstitutional, if, by striking from it all that part which is void, that which is complete in itself, sensible, capable of being executed, and wholly independent of that which is rejected, the courts will reject that which is unconstitutional, and enforce the remainder. *Id.*

3. IF SOME PROVISIONS OF A STATUTE ARE UNCONSTITUTIONAL, and others not, the general rule requires the courts to sustain the valid provisions while rejecting the others. *Lawton v. Steele*, 814.

See CONSTITUTIONAL LAW; EXECUTIONS, 5; INTERSTATE COMMERCE, 4, 5; FACTORS, 1, 2; MUNICIPAL CORPORATIONS, 17; RAILROAD COMPANIES, 1, 2

STOCKHOLDERS.
See CORPORATIONS, 1–3, 10, 15–17, 21–29.

SUBSCRIPTIONS FOR STOCK.
See CORPORATIONS, 23–29.

SUNDAY.
See CONTRACTS, 6, 8.

SURETYSHIP.
See BONDS; CORPORATIONS, 2; OFFICE AND OFFICERS, 10.

SURFACE WATERS.
See WATERCOURSES, 1, 2.

TAXATION.

1. TAX SALES. — The notice which a purchaser at tax sales is required to give before he becomes entitled to a deed must conform to the statute, and if it fails to inform the owner whether his property was sold for a tax or for a special assessment, or if the date which it specifies as that on which the right to redeem will expire is Sunday, the notice is invalid, and any deed based thereon is void. *Gage v. Davis*, 260.

2. TAX SALES — EXPIRATION OF TIME FOR REDEMPTION. — If the day of the month on which the right to redeem from a tax sale falls on a Sunday, it should not be computed, and the owner should be allowed all of the following Monday in which to redeem. *Id.*

3. TAX SALES. — If the notice of the time when the right to redeem expires specifies wrong day, it is void, and no valid deed can issue thereon. *Id.*

4. TAX SALE — RECOVERY OF AMOUNT PAID. — Mere volunteer who redeems land sold for delinquent taxes is not entitled to recover the amount paid. *Ellsworth* v. *Randall,* 425.

See BANKS AND BANKING, 4, 5; DRAINS.

TELEGRAPH COMPANIES.

1. TELEGRAPH COMPANIES ARE NOT CHARGED WITH KNOWLEDGE of the importance of delivering cipher dispatches. *Western Union Telegraph Co.* v. *Adams,* 920.

2. DISTINCTION EXISTS BETWEEN cipher dispatches and those intended to convey information by the use of no more words than are necessary when given their accustomed meaning. *Id.*

3. COMPANY MUST TAKE NOTICE that the utmost brevity of expression is cultivated in correspondence by telegraph, and that that mode of communication is chiefly resorted to in matters of importance, financially and socially, requiring great haste. Hence, when such communications relate to sickness and death, the company must take notice that they are of importance, and that the person addressed has a serious interest in them. *Id.*

4. COMPANIES ARE NOT RELEASED FROM DILIGENCE when, though the relations of the parties are not disclosed, the nature of the communication is manifest from its terms. If the operator desires information about such relationship, he must obtain it from the sender. If not, his principal will be charged with the information that inquiries would have developed. *Id.*

5. DAMAGES FOR DELAY IN DELIVERING DISPATCH — EVIDENCE OF MENTAL ANGUISH. — In an action for damages against a telegraph company, for delay in delivering a dispatch, evidence of mental anguish felt and exhibited by speech or otherwise, at the time the dispatch was received, is competent and admissible, and at least furnishes no ground for setting aside a verdict that may be sustained without evidence as to the existence or degree of mental pain. *Id.*

6. DAMAGES FOR DELAY IN DELIVERING MESSAGE — RIGHT OF ACTION. — When a message is sent for the benefit of a married woman, and she is in fact the person damaged by the delay of the company in delivering it, her husband may maintain suit against the company, notwithstanding the fact that the sender of the dispatch had not been previously constituted an agent for that purpose by the party to whom it was sent, and that the former has been reimbursed by the latter for the amount paid in sending the message. *Id.*

7. RIGHT TO RECOVER FEE PAID FOR TELEGRAM. — Prompt delivery of a telegram is of the essence of the contract, and a failure in this respect is such a breach of it as to authorize a recovery of the consideration paid for it, if the right to do so can be maintained in other respects. *Id.*

8. TELEGRAPH COMPANY, LIABILITY OF. — Where one party writes a dispatch and gives it to another to send, who, instead of sending it, writes another dispatch, and signs and sends it without notifying the company that it is sent on behalf of the first party, the latter cannot hold the company liable in damages for loss sustained through failure of delivery. *Elliott* v. *Western Union Telegraph Co.,* 872.

TORTS.

See ASSUMPSIT, 1, 2; LANDLORD AND TENANT, 19.

TOWNSHIPS.

See OFFICE AND OFFICERS, 9, 10.

TRESPASS.

1. EVIDENCE OF TITLE IN THIRD PERSON NOT ADMISSIBLE. — In trespass for the conversion of ore from a mine, defendant, not pleading justification, cannot defend by showing title in a third person. *Omaha etc. Co.* v. *Tabor*, 185.

2. PURCHASER FROM TRESPASSER, WHEN GUILTY OF CONVERSION. — The purchaser of ore taken from a mine by a trespasser is equally guilty with the latter of conversion, whether ignorant or informed of the true ownership. *Id.*

3. MEASURE OF DAMAGES FOR CONVERSION OF ORE by a purchaser from a trespasser is the value of the ore sold, together with a sum equal to legal interest thereon from the time of conversion, less the reasonable and proper cost of raising it from the mine after it was broken, and hauling from the mine to the purchaser's place of business. *Id.*

TRIAL.

1. ORDER OF PROOF. — The trial court may, in its discretion, exclude evidence offered out of order. *Kaufman* v. *Farley etc. Co.*, 462.

2. DISCHARGE OF, UPON DISAGREEMENT, WITHIN DISCRETION OF COURT. — Where the constitution provides that "if the jury disagree, the accused shall not be deemed to have been in jeopardy," it is within the discretion of the court to determine when a disagreement sufficient to justify a discharge of the jury exists. No specific period for deliberation can be designated, nor any absolute rule laid down, to control this discretion; and unless it has been grossly abused, the objection of former jeopardy is not ground for reversal upon error, much less for discharge upon *habeas corpus*. *In re Allison*, 224.

3. INSTRUCTIONS given need not be repeated. *Cincinnati etc. R. R. Co.* v. *Cooper*, 334.

4. PARTY HAS RIGHT TO HAVE HIS CASE GO TO JURY IN ITS PLAINEST, SIMPLEST FORM, and if it is properly embodied in a request in that form prepared by counsel, and furnished to the court, it ought to be thus given, and the request ought not to be ignored by the court. And if the substance of such request be not as well given by the court in its own language, the omission will be error. *Babbitt* v. *Bumpus*, 585.

5. SPECIAL REQUESTS FOR FINDING OF QUESTIONS OF FACT SHOULD BE SUBMITTED to the jury when asked for by a party. It is his privilege to have such questions found specially. *Id.*

6. COURT HAS NO RIGHT IN CHARGING JURY TO EXPRESS OPINION that they are not warranted by the testimony in saying that the plaintiff was in any way negligent in the performance of the services as an attorney, for which he sues. *Id.*

7. INSTRUCTIONS. — MODIFICATION OF REQUESTED CHARGE appended thereto in such manner as to show the precise charge asked and the precise modification, and that the whole is intelligible to the jury, so that no

injury results to the party making the request, is not error. *Missouri P. R'y Co.* v. *Williams*, 867.

8. INSTRUCTIONS — FAILURE TO REPEAT NOT ERROR. — Where the charge, taken as a whole, correctly presents the law upon one of the issues, so that the jury could not have been misled by the language used, it is not error to fail to repeat it in presenting every distinct phase of the case made by the testimony upon other issues. *Id.*

9. TRIAL — PRESUMPTION AS TO CORRECTED INSTRUCTION. — Where the trial court in its charge corrects a proposition objected to, it will be presumed that the jury accepts the correction as the law of the case. *Goodsell* v. *Taylor*, 700.

10. WHEN MORE SPECIFIC INSTRUCTIONS ARE DESIRED than those given, the party must so request, and when this is not done, the court will not, except in cases of manifest prejudice, interfere with the verdict. *Wimer* v. *Allbaugh*, 422.

11. WAIVER OF INSUFFICIENCY OF. — When an objection to the sufficiency of a petition can be taken by motion or demurrer, but is not, and the party answers and proceeds to trial, this constitutes a waiver of the objection, and it cannot be afterwards raised by an instruction to the jury. *Id.*

See APPEAL AND ERROR, 1, 3, 5–8; JURY AND JURORS; WITNESSES.

TROVER.

See SALES, 12.

TRUSTS AND TRUSTEES.

1. EXISTENCE OF CONFIDENCE IS PRESUMED IN ALL TRUST RELATIONS, and if it appears that any advantage has come to the trustee in dealing with his *cestui que trust*, the burden is upon him to show that the confidence was not in fact abused. But this presumption may be overcome by proof of the fact that confidence has not been abused, and that the beneficiary has acted, not upon any reliance or confidence placed in the trustee, but upon the advice of an independent, professional, disinterested, and competent adviser; and in such case, the transaction is not voidable at the election of the beneficiary, but it devolves upon him, if he would set it aside, to show either actual or constructive fraud. Such fraud may be shown, in some instances, by presumptions. *Colton* v. *Stanford*, 137.

2. TRUSTEE MAY DISSOLVE TRUST RELATION AND DEAL WITH HIS CESTUI QUE TRUST WHEN. — If a transaction is one in which a trustee may lawfully deal with his *cestui que trust* by first dissolving the trust relation, it is not too late for him to do so at any time before the *cestui que trust* is prevented from making a full and fair investigation and consideration of the business in hand, and before he executes the contract. *Id.*

3. PRESUMPTION FROM INDEPENDENT INVESTIGATION MADE ON BEHALF OF CESTUI QUE TRUST. — A presumption that everything material was discovered follows from an independent investigation into the sources of information made by the professional advisers of a *cestui que trust*, and this presumption is fortified by the introduction in evidence of memoranda kept by such advisers, showing unmistakable care and painstaking and a minute consideration of the subject on their part. *Id.*

See HUSBAND AND WIFE, 6–8; PARTNERSHIP, 1.

VENDOR AND VENDEE.

1. RESERVATION IN CONTRACT OF SALE ANNULLED BY DEED. — Where, under a contract for the sale of land, the vendor reserves the timber thereon, and the right to remove it within a certain time, but afterward, and within the time specified, conveys the land by warranty deed, omitting the reservation, the timber passes to the vendee. *Clifton* v. *Iron Co.*, 621.

2. CONTRACT OF SALE CANNOT CONTROL SUBSEQUENT DEED. — A contract for the sale of land containing a reservation cannot contradict or control a subsequent warranty deed not containing such reservation, in the absence of mistake. *Id.*

3. RIGHT OF ELECTION UNDER EXECUTORY CONTRACT FOR SALE OF LAND, the title remaining in the vendor with the right, on default of the payment of an installment of the purchase-money, to annul the contract and retake possession, and to retain out of moneys paid under the contract a certain sum as rent, is a right reserved for the vendor's benefit, and he alone can exercise it. *Moses Bros.* v. *Johnson*, 58.

4. RELATIONS BETWEEN a vendor and vendee of land under an executory contract of purchase are, in legal effect, the same as those existing between a mortgagor and mortgagee as to mutual, legal, and equitable rights and remedies. *Id.*

5. RIGHT OF VENDOR TO PRESERVE HIS SECURITY. — A vendor under an executory contract for the sale of land, who retains the title as security for the purchase-money, sustains the same relation to the vendee, on the question of security, as does a mortgagee to a mortgagor. *Id.*

6. RIGHT OF VENDOR TO RESTRAIN WASTE UNDER AN EXECUTORY CONTRACT TO PURCHASE LAND. — A vendee in possession, under an executory contract for the sale of land in which the vendor retains the title, may be enjoined from committing waste by cutting timber, in the absence of a condition permitting it, when the vendor shows that he has no security but the land, and that the value thereof is thereby impaired. *Id.*

7. RESCISSION OF CONTRACT TO CONVEY — FRAUDULENT REPRESENTATIONS. — Where a contract for the sale of land is made by a vendor, through the agents of the vendee, and upon their false representations that the vendee is another than the true purchaser, the vendor may, upon discovering the falsity of the representations, rescind the contract upon repayment or tender of the purchase-money received. *Ellsworth* v. *Randall*, 425.

8. VENDOR CANNOT SET ASIDE AND RESCIND HIS CONVEYANCE of land on the ground that his grantor's title to land in another state, deeded to him in consideration of his conveyance, is defective for want of conformity to the law of that state, when the defect complained of is not fatal to the validity of the deed, and when he makes no offer to reconvey. *Westhafer* v. *Patterson*, 330.

9. VENDOR CANNOT RESCIND HIS CONTRACT OF CONVEYANCE so as to reclaim what he has parted with, and at the same time hold on to what he has received in the transaction. *Id.*

See DEEDS, 7; JUDGMENTS, 16; JUDICIAL SALES, 1.

VERDICT.

See NEW TRIAL, 1, 2.

VESSELS.
See ADMIRALTY, 1-4.

WARRANTY.
See DAMAGES, 4; INSURANCE, 9-13; SALES, 6-11.

WASTE.
See VENDOR AND VENDEE, 6.

WATER COMPANIES.
See MUNICIPAL CORPORATIONS, 10-15.

WATERCOURSES.

1. SURFACE WATER — RAILROAD EMBANKMENT. — A railroad company is not bound to provide the embankment of its road-bed with sufficient water-ways and culverts to allow the usual amount of surface water from surrounding lands to pass under and through the same, when there is no well-defined channel or ravine crossing and closed by the embankment. *Rowe* v. *St. Paul etc. R'y Co.*, 706.

2. SURFACE WATER — RIGHT OF LAND-OWNER. — Subject to reasonable restriction, the owner of the lower estate may, in the use and improvement of his land, obstruct or hinder the natural flow of surface water, and turn the same back upon the lands of others, without liability for such obstruction; and though he is not permitted to collect it in a stream or body, and turn it upon the land of others, to their injury, still he is not bound to provide drains to prevent the accumulation of such water on adjacent lands, the natural flow of which is interrupted by changes in the surface of his own lands, caused by improvements thereon. This rule is not modified by the existence of depressions in the land in or over which surface drainage occurs in times of freshet; but if at such times large quantities of surface water are forced into a natural and well-defined channel or ravine, the land-owner must provide a culvert or other means of escape for it. *Id.*

See DRAINS; FISHERIES; NUISANCES, 2, 4.

WHARVES.
See INTERSTATE COMMERCE, 2.

WILLS.

1. AGREEMENT FOR TESTAMENTARY DISPOSITION OF PROPERTY. — A person may make a valid agreement to make a particular disposition of his property by will. *Carmichael* v. *Carmichael*, 528.

2. AGREEMENT FOR TESTAMENTARY DISPOSITION OF PROPERTY — SPECIFIC PERFORMANCE. — Where husband and wife agree by parol contract to make a certain testamentary disposition of their real estate by last will, and such contract is strictly performed by the husband, and the benefits provided by him in his will accepted by his wife after his death, there is such part performance of the oral contract as to take it out of the statute of frauds, and equity will then prevent the wife from violating her part of such agreement by a conveyance in fraud of the beneficiaries

named therein. In an action to set aside such conveyance by her, such beneficiaries are proper parties complainant, and she is a proper party defendant. *Id.*

See DEVISES AND LEGACIES.

WITNESSES.

1. PARTY CALLING WITNESS IS NOT PRECLUDED FROM SHOWING THE TRUTH of any particular fact by any other competent testimony. *Omaha etc. Co.* **v.** *Tabor*, 185.

2. CROSS-EXAMINATION — IMPEACHMENT. — Where defendant denies the execution of a note in suit, and alleges that it is a forgery, and the agent of plaintiff who procured the note testifies in chief that he saw defendant sign it, the latter is entitled, upon cross-examination, to everything that took place on that occasion, and when upon such cross-examination the witness states that he knew nothing about the consideration of the note, he may be asked if he has not made different statements out of court of what occurred at the time of the signing, and if he denies having made such statements, they may be proved by defendant in defense. *Johnston Harvester Co.* **v.** *Miller*, 536.

3. CREDIBILITY OF, HOW MAY BE TESTED ON CROSS-EXAMINATION. — Where defendant denies the existence of a note sued on, and claims it to be a forgery, and the agent of plaintiff, who claims to have procured it, also claims, on his examination in chief, that he was present and saw defendant sign it, he may be compelled to testify on cross-examination to the negotiation of another forged note, purporting to have been signed by defendant, when he does not claim his privilege of not answering because it might criminate him. Such evidence is admissible as affecting the credibility of the witness, and also as tending to show that he obtained the note in suit fraudulently. *Id.*

4. WITNESS MAY BE IMPEACHED, UPON CROSS-EXAMINATION, by showing that his acts or declarations on previous occasions were at variance with his testimony as given at the trial. *Omaha etc. Co.* **v.** *Tabor*, 185.

5. EXTENT TO WHICH CROSS-EXAMINATION MAY BE CARRIED IN ORDER TO SHOW BIAS, prejudice, or interest on the part of the witness, is a matter resting in the sound discretion of the court. *Hinchcliffe* **v.** *Koontz*, 403.

6. COMPARISON TO TEST KNOWLEDGE OF HANDWRITING. — Where expert witnesses have testified entirely from comparison to the genuineness of a disputed signature, they may, on cross-examination, to test the value of their knowledge, be asked to make comparison between two signatures of a witness, one admitted by him to be genuine, and the other claimed by him to have been written by another, but by his authority and direction; and the fact that such witnesses did not know whether the signatures were made by one man or two, but added value to the test. *Johnston Harvester Co.* **v.** *Miller*, 536.

See APPEAL AND ERROR, 7, 8; CONSTITUTIONAL LAW, 5; CRIMINAL LAW, 30.

WRIT OF PROHIBITION.
See PROHIBITION.

Lightning Source UK Ltd.
Milton Keynes UK
UKHW020735160119
335572UK00007B/184/P